The Holy Sacrifice of the Mass;

Dogmatically, Liturgically and Ascetically Explained.

BY

Rev. Dr. Nicholas Gihr.

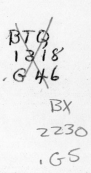

TRANSLATED FROM THE SIXTH GERMAN EDITION.

ST. LOUIS, MO. 1902.

Published by B. HERDER.

17 South Broadway.

NIHIL OBSTAT.

S. LUDOVICI, DIE 17. FEBR. 1902.

F. G. HOLWECK,
Censor theologicus.

IMPRIMATUR.

St. Louis, Mo., Febr. 17th, 1902.

JOHN J. KAIN,
Archbishop of St. Louis.

—BECKTOLD—
PRINTING AND BOOK MFG. CO.
ST. LOUIS, MO.

THE publisher of this work is indebted to the late Archbishop Wm. H. Gross, the late Very Rev. Mark Gross, to Sister Mary Thecla of the Visitation Convent at Baltimore, Md. and Mr. Jacob Gross of St. Louis, Mo., for valuable assistance.

PREFACE TO THE FIRST EDITION.

As the Holy Sacrifice of the Mass is the centre of Catholic worship and life, a more profound knowledge of the Mass is considered essential and most desirable for all the faithful, but especially for the priest. Although literature on this subject is rather abundant, the present volume, which has been drawn from every available source at the Author's command, may not be deemed superfluous.

Its object is, in the main, both practical and ascetical: to appeal not only to the understanding, but also to inflame the heart and to move the will. The selection and the treatment of the matter have necessarily been directed to this object. As it is not our intention to present a purely scientific and exhaustive treatise on the Eucharistic Sacrifice, but to build, upon the foundation of scientific studies and inferences, a work useful and practical for the clergy, certain questions of scientific and historic nature may receive scarcely more than a brief and passing mention. *"In hac conscriptione,"* — says Denis the Carthusian — *"non fuit intentio movere vel tangere nisi ea quae affectum excitare et devotioni possunt proficere, exponendo verba missae devotius quo valebam."* "In this writing it was not my intention in expounding the words of the Mass as devoutly as I could, to raise any question or touch on anything but what might move the heart and excite to devotion." Therefore all polemical, critical quotations and statements open to contradiction have, as much as possible, been avoided. In disputed points we have always seriously and carefully weighed the reasons pro and con ; but in the book itself we have merely stated what appeared to us the most solidly grounded.

As edification and devotion must at all times rest on theological truth and emanate from it, it became necessary to present the Dogma and Rite of the Eucharistic Sacrifice clearly, thoroughly and correctly, according to the spirit and intention of the Church ; thus only do the ascetical considerations and applications find a solid foundation to rest on. *"Est enim,"* says Suarez, *"sine veritate pietas imbecilla, et sine pietate veritas sterilis et jejuna."* "For without truth, piety is feeble ; and without piety, truth is sterile and void." In the explanation of the Rite we have strictly adhered to the words and actions of the liturgical formulae, endeavoring at the same time, in accordance with approved ecclesiastical tradition, to avoid as far as possible all subjectivism and artificiality.

(5)

A correct and clear understanding as well as frequent consideration of the profound and mystical Rite of the Mass, will, in all probability, be the best means to enable the priest to refrain from a thoughtless, habitual mannerism, and lead him to celebrate the adorable mysteries of the Altar with becoming attention, devotion, and reverence. The priest who studies this book will, moreover, find manifold reasoning and argument wherewith to direct the faithful according to their capacity in the proper understanding of the Divine Sacrifice and in their fervent recourse to the Eucharistic fountain of grace. The authorities of the Church have often impressed upon pastors, that this is a chief duty of directors of souls, for the conscientious discharge of which they shall have to render an account before God. Although this volume is principally intended for the use of the clergy, it has been so arranged that the more highly cultured of the laity may also peruse it with profit.

May God grant His blessing and success to this work — especially in our days, when the Church and her faithful children are necessarily more or less constrained to lead a life of sacrifice. May it awaken and foster in many hearts love for the Eucharistic Sacrifice, as well as a cheerful and courageous spirit to undergo willingly the trials and contradictions that self-immolation demands!

ST. PETER'S, FEAST OF THE ASSUMPTION, 1877.

THE AUTHOR.

PREFACE TO THE SIXTH EDITION.

It is now nearly twenty years since this work first appeared in order to proclaim the "unsearchable riches" (Eph. 3, 8.) of the Eucharistic Sacrifice. The divine blessing has been so abundant on it as to warrant us to publish a sixth and larger edition. In preparing it for the press we have made some slight changes, curtailments and additions, thereby rendering it more perfect both in matter and form. We intend soon to publish a work on the "Doctrine of the Sacraments," which will give a more complete explanation and confirmation of the essence of the Eucharistic Sacrifice. The friendly reader is hereby requested to make a memento for

THE AUTHOR.

ST. PETER'S, FEAST OF ST. THOMAS, 1897.

BIBLIOGRAPHY.

Albertus Magnus, Summa de officio Missae. Coloniae, Henr. Quentel. Anno post Jubilaeum tertio.

Amalarius Metensis, De officiis ecclesiasticis libri IV. (Migne, tom. 105, p. 985— 1242).

Arias, Fr., S. J., Thesaurus inexhaustus bonorum, quae in Christo habemus. Monachii 1652.

Arriaga, Roder. de, S. J., Disputationes theologicae in Summam s. Thomae. Antverpiae 1643—1655.

Auber, M. l'abbé, Histoire et Théorie du Symbolisme religieux. 4 tomi Paris 1870.

Bacuez, L., Du divin sacrifice et du prêtre qui le célèbre. Paris 1888.

Badoire, Das heilige Messopfer, dargestellt in dogmatischen, historischen und moralischen Predigten. Schaffhausen 1848.

Baldassari, Ant., d. C. d. G., La sacra Liturgia. Venetia 1715.

Barták, Jos., Versuch, die liturgische Sprache der Kirche vom dogmatischen, historischen und pastorellen Standpunkte zu beleuchten. Königgrätz 1875.

Becanus, Martin. S. J., Summa theologiae scholasticae. Lugduni 1640.

Bechoffen, Ioann., O. S. Aug., Quadruplex Missalis expositio, litteralis scil., allegorica, tropologica et anagogica. Basileae 1512.

Belethus, Ioann., Rationale divinorum Officiorum. (Migne, tom, 202, p. 14—166.)

Bellarminus, Rob., Cardinalis, S. J., De controversiis fidei adversus huius temporis haereticos. Ingolstadii 1601.

Benedictus, XIV., De sacrosancto Missae sacrificio. (Migne, Theolog. cursus complet., tom. 23.)

Berlage, Dr. Ant., Die dogmatische Lehre von den Sacramenten und den fünf letzten Dingen. Münster 1864.

Bernard, M. Th., Cours de Liturgie Romaine. Paris 1884.

Berrisch, Dr. E., Die Stola in ihrer Entstehung, Beschaffenheit, Bedeutung und Anwendung. Köln 1867.

Bertold, Bishop of Chiembse, Tewtsch Rational über das Ambt heiliger mess. 1535.

Bickell, Dr. Gust., Messe und Pascha. Mainz 1872.

Biel, Gabr., Sacri canonis Missae tam mystica quam literalis expositio. Basileae 1515.

Binterim, A. Jos., Die vorzüglichsten Denkwürdigkeiten der katholischen Kirche. Mainz 1828.

Bona, Ioann., Cardinalis, Ord. Cist., Rerum liturgicarum libri duo. Studio et labore Rob. Sala. Augustae Taurinorum 1763.

—— De sacrificio Missae tractatus asceticus. Parisiis 1846.

S. Bonaventura, Opera omnia. Ad Claras Aquas (Quaracchi) 1883—1891.

Bongardt, Fr. A., Die Eucharistie, der Mittelpunkt des Glaubens, Gottesdienstes und Lebens der Kirche. 2. Aufl. Paderborn 1882

Bossuet, Oeuvres complètes. Bar-le-Duc 1870.

Bourbon, A., Introduction aux cérémonies Romaines. Luçon 1864.

Breiteneicher, Mich., Die Sacramente und das heilige Messopfer. Schaffhausen 1869.

Buathier, J. M., Le sacrifice dans le dogme catholique et dans la vie chrétienne. Lyon et Paris 1889.

Businger, L. E., Das unblutige Opfer des Neuen Bundes. Solothurn 1890.

Cavalieri, I. Mich., O. S. Aug., Opera omnia liturgica seu Commentaria in authentica S. R. C. decreta. 5 tomi. Augustae Vindelicorum 1764.

Chaignon, S. J., Der Priester am Altare. 4. Aufl. Mainz 1868.

Cienfuegos, Alb., Cardin., S. J., Vita abscondita seu speciebus eucharisticis velata, per potissimas sensuum operationes de facto a Christo Domino ibidem indesinenter exercita circa obiecta altari et amori vicina. Romae 1728.

Clichtoveus, Iodocus, Elucidatorium ecclesiasticum, ad officium Ecclesiae pertinentia planius exponens et quatuor libros complectens. Parisiis 1548.

Cochem, P. Mart., Erklärung des heiligen Messopfers. Köln 1870.

Condren, S. J., Das Priesterthum und das Opfer Jesu Christi in ihrer Bedeutung. Regensburg 1847.

Coninck, Aegid. de, S. J., De sacramentis ac censuris. Antverpiae 1624.

Contenson, Vinc., O. Praed., Theologiae mentis et cordis. Parisiis 1875.

Corblet, J., Histoire dogmatique, liturgique et archéologique du sacrement de l'Eucharistie. Paris 1885.

Da Sartirana, B. A. M., La Madre Chiesa nelle sue relazioni con Dio e coi suoi figliuoli nella santa Messa. Torino 1873.

De Augustinis, Aemil. M., S. J., De re sacramentaria praelectiones. Libri II priores. Woodstock 1878.

De Herdt, P. I. B., Sacrae Liturgiae praxis. Edit. 7. Lovanii 1883.

De Ponte, Ludov., S. J., De christiani hominis perfectione. 4 tomi. Coloniae Agrippinae 1625.

Diepolder, Dr. Joh. Nep., Das Wesen des eucharistischen Opfers und die vorzüglichsten katholischen Theologen der drei letzten Jahrhunderte. Augsburg 1877.

Dionysius Carthusianus, Opera minora. 2 tomi. Coloniae 1532.

Duchesne, L., Origines du culte chrétien. Paris 1889.

Dufrène, P. Max., S. J., Sacerdos numini eucharistico devotus. Augustae Vindelicorum 1754.

Durandus, Gul., Rationale sive Enchiridion divinorum officiorum. Lugduni 1561.

Durantus, I. Steph., De ritibus Ecclesiae catholicae libri tres. Coloniae Agrippinae 1592.

Du Saussay, Andr., Panoplia sacerdotalis seu de venerando sacerdotum habitu libri 14. Lutetiae Parisiorum 1653.

Eberhard, Dr. Matth., Kanzelvorträge. Trier 1877.

Ebner, Ad., Quellen und Forschungen zur Geschichte und Kunstgeschichte des Missale Romanum im Mittelalter. Iter italicum. Freiburg i. B. 1896.

Einig, P., Tractatus de ss. Eucharistiae mysterio. Treveris 1888.

Eisenring, J. B., Das heilige Messopfer. Einsiedeln 1880.

Fischer, Fr., Lehrbuch der katholischen Liturgik. Wien 1872.

Florus, Diaconus Lugdunensis, Opusculum de expositione Missae. (Migne, tom. 160, pag. 1053—1070.)

Fluck, Dr. Jak., Katholische Liturgik. Regensburg 1853.

Fornici, I., Institutiones liturgicae. Moguntiae 1852.

Franz, Dr. Jos. Theod., Die eucharistische Wandlung und Epiklese der griechischen und orientalischen Liturgien. Würzburg 1880.

Franzelin, Ioann. Bapt., Cardinalis, S. J., Tractatus de ss. Eucharistiae sacramento et sacrificio. Edit. 2. Romae 1873.

Gautier, L., Histoire de la poésie liturgique du moyen âge. Les Tropes. Paris 1886.

Gavanti-Merati, Thesaurus sacrorum rituum. 2 tomi. Augustae Vindelicorum 1763.

Gerbert, M., Abbas O. S. B., Vetus Liturgia Alemannica. Typis San-Blasianis 1776.

S. Germanus, Episc. Paris., Expositio brevis antiquae Liturgiae Gallicanae in duas epistolas digesta. (Migne, tom. 72, pag. 83—98.)

Gobat, Georg, S. J., Alphabetum Sacrificantium. Monachii 1663.

Gotti, V. L., Cardinalis, O. Praed., Theologia scholastico-dogmatica. Venetiis 1750.

Gouda, Guil. de, Ord. s. Franc., Expositio mysteriorum Missae et verus modus rite celebrandi. Coloniae.

Grancolas, M. J., Traité de la Messe et de l'Office divin. Paris 1713.

Guyetus, Carol., S. J., Heortologia sive de festis propriis locorum et ecclesiarum. Venetiis 1726.

Hazé, I. H., De sensu ceremoniarum Missae brevis explicatio. Bruxellis 1869.

Hefele, Dr. Karl Jos., Beiträge zur Kirchengeschichte, Archäologie und Liturgik. 2 Bde. Tübingen 1864.

Henno, Franc., Ord. s. Franc., Theologia dogmatica, moralis et scholastica. Coloniae Agrippinae 1718.

Hergenröther, Dr. Phil., Die Eucharistie als Opfer. Regensburg 1868.

Hildebertus, Vener. Episcopus Turonensis, Liber de expositione Missae; Versus de mysterio Missae. (Migne tom. 171, pag. 1153—1195.)

S. Hildegardis, O. S. B., Scivias sive visionum ac revelationum libri III. (Migne, tom. 197, pag. 383—738.)

Hittorpius, Melch., De divinis catholicae Ecclesiae officiis ac ministeriis varii vetustorum aliquot Ecclesiae Patrum ac Scriptorum libri. Coloniae 1568.

Hnogek, Ant. Adalb., Christkatholische Liturgik. Prag 1837.

Hoffmann, Dr. Jak., Geschichte der Laiencommunion bis zum Tridentinum. Speier 1891.

Holzwarth, Dr. Fr. Jos., Briefe über das heilige Messopfer. Mainz 1873.

Honorius Augustodunensis, Gemma animae sive de divinis officiis et antiquo ritu Missarum etc.: Sacramentarium sive de causis et significatu mystico rituum divini in Ecclesia officii liber. (Migne, tom. 172, pag. 543—806.)

Hoppe, Dr. Ludw. Aug., Die Epiklesis der griechischen und orientalischen Liturgien und der römische Consecrationscanon. Schaffhausen 1864.

Hugo, Cardinalis, O. Praed., Expositio Missae. Nurembergae 1507.

Innocentius III., De sacro altaris mysterio libri IV. (Migne, tom 147, pag. 773 ad 914.)

Ioannes, Episcop. Abrincensis, Liber de Officiis ecclesiasticis. (Migne, tom. 147, pag. 15 sqq.)

Ioannes a via, Iugis Ecclesiae catholicae sacrificii eorumque omnium, quae in eo peraguntur, solida iustaque defensio et assertio. Coloniae 1570.

Jakob, G., Die Kunst im Dienste der Kirche. 4. Aufl. Landshut 1885.

Jarisch, Dr. Ant., Liturgik. Wien 1876.

Jobin, abbé Études sur les lampes du Saint-Sacrement et le luminaire ecclésiastique. Paris 1870.

Katschthaler, Ioann., De ss. Eucharistia. Ratisbonae 1883.

Kenrick, Fr. Patr., Theologia dogmatica. Mechliniae 1858.

Kneip, N., Erklärung des heiligen Messopfers. Regensburg 1876.

Knoll, Sim., Die Ceremonien der heiligen Messe, dem christlichen Volke in Predigten erklärt. Schaffhausen 1863.

Knoll, P. Albert. a Bulsano, Institutiones theologiae theoreticae. Edit. 3. Augustae Taurinorum 1865.

Köppler, W., Priester und Opfergabe. Mainz 1886.

Kössing, Dr. Jos., Liturgische Erklärung der heiligen Messe. 3. Aufl. Regensburg 1869.

Krazer, P. Aug., O. Praed., De apostolicis necnon antiquis Ecclesiae occidentalis Liturgiis liber singularis. Augustae Vindelicorum 1786.

Kreuser, Das heilige Messopfer geschichtlich erklärt. Paderborn 1854.

Krüll, Fr. Hon., Christliche Alterthumskunde. Regensburg 1856.

Lambrecht, H. C. C.; De sanctissimo Missae sacrificio. Lovanii 1875.

Lapini, P. F., La Liturgia studiata nelle sue relazioni colle scienze sacre. Siena 1889.

Laurent, Dr. J. Th., Christologische Predigten. Mainz 1860.

Lebrun, Pierre, Explication littéraire, historique et dogmatique des prières et des cérémonies de la messe. Lyon 1860.

Le Courtier, F. J., Manuel de la Messe ou Explication des prières et des cérémonies du saint sacrifice. 4e édit. Paris 1864.

Lehmkuhl, Aug., S. J., Theologia moralis. Editio quinta. Friburgi 1888.

Lierheimer, Fr. X., Predigten über das heilige Messopfer. Regensburg 1872.

Liguori, St. Alph. de, Der Priester am Altar. Regensburg 1856.

Lohner, Tob., S. J., Instructio practica primo de missae sacrificio. Dilingae 1717.

Lowey, H., Die mystischen Bezeichnungen Jesu Christi als Siloë, Schiloch und Piscis, insbesondere die Bezeichnung der christlichen Opferfeier als Missa. Paderborn 1888.

Lüdtke, Dr. Cl., Erklärung des heiligen Messopfers. Eine Weinachtsgabe für Studirende. Dantzic 1882.

Lüft, Dr· J. B., Liturgik. Mainz 1844—1847.

Lugo, Ioann. de, Cardinalis, S. J., Tractatus de venerabili Eucharistiae sacramento. (Migne, Theol. cursus complet., tom. 23.)

Mabillon, F. I., O. S. B., De Liturgia Gallicana libri III. (Migne, tom 72, pag. 99 sqq.)

—— In Ordinem Romanum Commentarius praevius.—Ordines Romani sexdecim. (Migne, tom. 78, pag. 851 sqq.)

Marzohl and **Schneller,** Liturgia sacra oder die Gebräuche und Alterthümer der katholischen Kirche. Luzerne 1835.

Menne, Xav., Das allerheiligste Sakrament des Altars als Opfer. Paderborn 1876.

Mette, Dr. B., Katholische Populär-Liturgik. Regensburg 1874.

Michael, Bischoff zu Merspurg, Von der heiligen Messe. Siebenzehn christliche Predige auff dem Reichstag im Jar 1548 zu Augspurg gepredigt. Ingolstat 1563. Neue Ausgabe von Hasak unter dem Titel "Ein Vergissmeinnicht." Regensburg 1884.

Micrologus, De ecclesiasticis observationibus. (Migne, tom. 151, pag. 973—1022.)

Mühlbauer, Wolfgang, Geschichte und Bedeutung der (Wachs-) Lichter bei den kirchlichen Functionen. Augsburg 1874.

Müller, Dr. Ern., Theologia moralis. Vindobonae 1876.

Müller, Mich., Cong. S. Red., The Holy Mass: the Sacrifice for the Living and the Dead. New York and Cincinnati 1874.

Müller, H., Missa. Ursprung und Bedeutung der Benennung. Aschaffenburg 1873.

Muratori, De rebus liturgicis dissertatio. (Migne, tom. 74, pag. 847 sqq.)

Noël, Instructions sur la Liturgie. 5 tom. Paris 1861.

Odo, Episcopus Cameracensis, Expositio in Canonem Missae. (Migne, tom. 160, pag. 1053—1070.)

Olier, M., Explication des cérémonies de la grand' Messe de paroisse. Paris 1858.

Olivier, J. H., Solutions théologiques et liturgiques touchant le saint sacrifice de la Messe. Paris 1873.

Orsi, O. Pr., Dissertatio theologica de invocatione Spiritus sancti in Liturgiis Graecorum et Orientalium. Mediolani 1731.

Oswald, Dr. J. H., Die dogmatische Lehre von den Sacramenten. 4. Aufl. Münster 1877.

Pasqualigo, Zach., Cleric. Reg., De sacrificio Novae Legis quaestiones theologicae, morales, juridicae. 2 tomi. Lugduni 1662.

Patroni, Raff., Lezioni di sacra Liturgia ossia Esposizione letterale, mistica, storica e ceremoniale della Messa. Napoli 1881.

Piazza, C. B., L'Iride sacra. Roma 1682.

Platelius, Iac., S. J., Synopsis totius cursus theologici. Coloniae Agrippinae 1688.

Platzweg, Charles, S. J., Betrachtungen über die heilige Messe für Priester und Laien. 2. Aufl. Paderborn 1877.

Pouget, Fr. Am., Institutiones catholicae in modum catecheseos. 2 tomi. Augustae Vindelicorum 1764.

Probst, Dr., Ferd., Verwaltung der Eucharistie als Opfer. 2. Aufl. Tübingen 1857.
—— Liturgie der drei ersten christlichen Jahrhunderte. Tübingen 1870.
—— Verwaltung des hohepriesterlichen Amtes. Breslau 1881.
—— Die ältesten römischen Sacramentarien und Ordines. Münster 1892.
—— Die Liturgie des vierten Jahrhunderts und deren Reform. Münster 1893.
—— Die abendländische Messe vom 5. bis zum 8. Jahrhundert. Münster 1896.

Quadt, M. W., Die Liturgie der Quatembertage. Aachen 1869.

Quarti, P. M., Cleric. regul., Rubricae Missalis Romani commentariis illustratae. Venetiis 1727.

Rabanus Maurus, De clericorum institutione libri III. (Migne, tom. 107, pag. 295—419.)

Raffray, M. X., Beautés du culte catholique. Paris 1858.

Reiners, A., Die Tropen-, Prosen-, und Präfationsgesänge im Mittelaltar. Luxemburg 1884.

Renaudotius, Euseb., Liturgiarum orientalium collectio. 2 tomi. Francofurti ad Moenum 1847.

Rigler, P. P., Pastoralis liturgica seu intelligentia et regula ministerii liturgici. Bulsani 1864.

Romsée, T. I., Opera liturgica. Mechlinae 1838.

Rösen, Dr. K., Der Altar und der Chorraum. Münster 1885.

Rupertus, Abbas Tuitiensis, O. S. B., De divinis officiis libri XII. (Migne, tom. 170, pag. 13—332.)

Sanchez, Gasp., S. J., Spiritualis thesaurus Missae. Ingolstadii 1620.

Sarnelli, P., Lettere ecclesiastiche. Venezia 1716.

Sauter, O. S. B., Das hl. Messopfer. Paderborn 1894.

Schmid, Dr. Andr., Der christliche Altar und sein Schmuck. Regensburg 1871.

Schmid, Fr. X., Liturgik der christkatholischen Religion. Passau 1835.

Scouville, Phil., S. J., Sancta sanctorum sancte tractandi sive religiose sacrificandi methodus. Lucernae 1713.

Ségur, Monsig., de., Die heilige Messe. Mainz 1874.
—— Die Ceremonien der heiligen Messe. Mainz 1876.

Selbst, Dr. Francis Joseph, Der katholische Kirchengesang beim heiligen Messopfer. 2. Aufl. Regensburg 1890.

Sicardus, Episcopus Cremonensis, Mitrale sive de officiis ecclesiasticis Summa. (Migne, tom. 213, pag. 13—434.)

Specht, Dr. Thomas, Die Wirkungen des Eucharistischen Opfers. Augsburg 1876.

Sporer, Patr., Ord. s. Franc., Theologiae moralis sacramentalis Pars II. De sacer-
    dotio, sacrificio et sacramento Eucharistiae. Salisburgi 1688.

Stella, Fr., Institutiones Liturgicae. Romae 1895.

Stentrup, F. Al., S. J., De Verbo incarnato. 4. vol. Oeniponte 1882—1889.

Stephanus de Balgiaco, Episc. Augustod., Tractatus de sacramento altaris. (Migne,
    tom. 172, pag. 1273—1308.)

Stöckl, Dr. Alb., Das Opfer nach seinem Wesen und nach seiner Geschichte.
    Mainz 1861.

Suarez, Franc., S. J., Commentaria ac disputationes in tertiam partem s. Thomae;
    De sacramento Eucharistiae et de Missae sacrificio. Parisiis 1861.

Sylvius, Franc., Commentarius in tertiam partem s. Thomae Aquinatis. Duaci 1622.

Tanner, Ad., S. J., Theologia scholastica. Ingolstadii 1627.

Tapfer, Ant., Analytico-literalis expositio incruenti Missae sacrificii secundum
    ritum Romanum. Curiae 1828.

Thalhofer, Dr. Val., Das Opfer des Alten und Neuen Bundes. Regensburg 1870.
—— Handbuch der katholischen Liturgik. Freiburg 1883—1890.

S. Thomas Aquinas, Summa theologica. Barri-Ducis 1869.

Toletus, Franc., Cardinalis, S. J., In Summam theologiae s. Thomae Aquinatis
    enarratio. Romae.

Tournely, Hon., Cursus theologicus scholastico-dogmaticus et moralis. Coloniae
    Agrippinae 1752.

Triplex Expositio (literalis, mystica et practica) totius Missae. Parisiis 1866.

Ulloa, Joann., de, S. J., Theologia scholastica. Augustae Vindelicorum 1719.

Valentia, Greg. de, S. J., Commentaria theologica. Lutetiae Parisiorum 1609.

Van der Burg, Brevis elucidatio totius Missae. Tornaci 1860.

Vasquez, Gabr., S. J., Commentaria ac disputationes in tertiam partem s. Thomae.
    Lugduni 1631.

Walafridus, Strabo, Liber de exordiis et incrementis quarundam in observationibus
    ecclesiasticis rerum. Ed. Dr. A. Knoepfler. Monachii 1890.

Walter,, Dr. Joseph, Die heilige Messe. Brixen 1881.

Wappler, Dr. Ant., Cultus der katholischen Kirche. 3. Aufl. Vienna 1867.

Weickum, Charles, Das heilige Messopfer. Schaffhausen 1865.

Wersch, Jak. van, Das heilige Messopfer in seiner Wesenheit und in seiner Feier.
    Strassburg 1895.

Wilpert, Jos., Fractio panis. Die älteste Darstellung des eucharistischen Opfers
    in der Cappella Greca. Freiburg 1895.

Wiseman, Cardinal, Abhandlungen über verschiedene Gegenstände (Essays on
    Various Subjects). Regensburg 1854.

Zaccaria, F. A., S. J., Onomasticon rituale selectum. Faventiae 1787.
—— Bibliotheca ritualis. Romae 1776.

Zollner, John Evangelist, Das katholische Christenthum in seinen heiligen Hand-
    lungen, Zeiten und Orten. Regensburg 1869.

CONTENTS.

BOOK I.

Dogmatical and Ascetical Part.

CHAPTER THE FIRST.

SACRIFICE IN GENERAL.

CHAPTER THE SECOND.

THE BLOODY SACRIFICE OF THE CROSS.

(13)

CHAPTER THE THIRD.

THE UNBLOODY SACRIFICE OF THE ALTAR.

ARTICLE THE FIRST.

The Truth and Reality of the Eucharistic Sacrifice.

ARTICLE THE SECOND.

The Essence and Efficacy of the Eucharistic Sacrifice.

ARTICLE THE THIRD.

What Place the Eucharistic Sacrifice holds in the Organization of the Church.

BOOK II.

Liturgical and Ascetical Part.

CHAPTER THE FIRST.

PREPARATION FOR THE HOLY SACRIFICE OF THE MASS.

CHAPTER THE SECOND.

THE RITE OF THE HOLY SACRIFICE OF THE MASS.

FIRST SECTION.

The Preparatory Divine Service.

SECOND SECTION.

The Sacrificial Celebration Proper.

FIRST ARTICLE.

The Offertory.

SECOND ARTICLE.
The Consecration.

THIRD ARTICLE.
The Communion.

BOOK I.

Dogmatical and Ascetical Part

CHAPTER THE FIRST.

Sacrifice in General.

1. On the Virtue of Religion.

Sacrifice is an act and, in fact, the supreme act of religion, for by the offering of sacrifice the Divine Majesty is honored in the worthiest and most perfect manner. The virtue of religion is, so to speak, the very root whence sacrifice springs and develops as a most beautiful blossom and most precious fruit. Therefore we at once perceive that the way for a better understanding of sacrifice can be opened only by previously considering the Christian or supernatural virtue of religion in its principal characteristics. [1]

  1. Religion (*religio*) [2] is a special moral virtue, which enables

_____

[1] We do not intend to treat here of religion as a natural virtue (*virtus acquisita*), which can be acquired, at least in an imperfect degree, by frequent acts, but of religion as a supernatural virtue (*virtus per se infusa*) infused by means of grace into the soul. Religion, as such, is, in the first place, an abiding, persevering disposition inclining us to render unto God the worship due Him. Ease and readiness in the performance of supernatural acts of religion is the fruit of faithful exercise and is obtainable by our own exertions assisted by divine grace. Charity and all the infused moral virtues are inseparably united with sanctifying grace, whilst the two theological virtues of faith and hope (*habitus fidei et spei*) can still exist even after sanctifying grace has been lost.

Cf. Mazzella, S. J., De virtutibus infusis, disput. I. art. 3—12.

[2] The Word *religio* comes principally from *religare* (to bind — namely to God). Diximus nomen *religionis* a vinculo pietatis esse deductum, quod hominem sibi Deus *religaverit* et pietate constrinxerit, quia servire nos ei ut domino et obsequi ut patri necesse est (Lactant. Divin. institut. 1. 4. c. 28). — The thought underlying this explanation is assuredly true; yet the derivation from *religere* (from *relegere*) would grammatically be more correct. In Gellius (4, 9, 1) is found the participle, used adjectively, *religens* = God-fearing. The term religio (from religere = to take carefully into consideration, to ponder over, to weigh conscientiously and reflect upon with due care — especially that which is divine and holy) — would, according to its original signification, be intimately connected with

(17)

and inclines the will to give to God the supernatural honor and adoration due to Him as the Creator and Supreme Ruler, as well as the last end of all things, and particularly of man. The Holy Ghost plants this virtue in the garden of the soul; it is our duty, with the help of grace, so to nourish this noble and precious gift of heaven that it may bear abundant fruit for the honor and glory of God and our own blessing and ultimate salvation.

The virtue of religion makes us courageous and willing to offer to the Divine Majesty due veneration. [1] By means of this virtue we honor the Lord our God inasmuch as we acknowledge and proclaim His greatness, majesty and dominion over us, and at the same time confess our own littleness, lowliness and dependence upon Him. Religion, consequently, includes in itself two requisites: first, lively acknowledgment of His infinite perfection and dignity; and then, an humble subjection to His unlimited power and dominion. This cheerful submission, this humbling of self under the power of God (I Peter, 5—6) is required and commanded by the fundamental relations that exist between us as creatures and God as our Creator. And this relation is one of the most absolute and entire dependence upon God, for He is our first beginning and last end, our Redeemer and Sanctifier. We belong entirely to God and it behooves us to consecrate our being wholly to God; "in God we live and move and are" [2] (Acts 17, 28).

"All my bones shall cry out: Lord, who is like to Thee?" (Ps. 34, 10.) God is a fathomless and shoreless sea of the most perfect being and life: His perfections are inexhaustible and incomparable, surpassing and excelling all things, incomprehensible and unspeakable. God possesses infinite grandeur and dignity. Therefore all rational creatures, being immeasurably below Him,

---

cultus (careful nursing and waiting upon, honor, veneration — from *colere*, cherishing and caring for, esteeming and regarding as holy). *Religiosus*, ait Cicero, *a relegendo* appellatur, qui retractat et tamquam relegit ea quae ad cultum divinum pertineant (S. Isidor. Etymolog. 1. 10. n. 234). — Of this explanation Suarez remarks: Est probabilis deductio, sive vocum similitudinem sive munus ipsum religionis spectemus. (Cfr. De Religione tr. I. 1. I. c. 1).

Cfr. Gutberlet, Lehrbuch der Apologetik. I. 6—7.

[1] Nomine *virtutis* religionis hic non intelligitur habitus aliquis acquisitus et naturalis, sed habitus supernaturalis, per se et quoad substantiam infusus, quo disponimur ad cultum sacrum praestandum in ordine supernaturali et relate ad nostrum finem supernaturalem (Bouquillon, De virtute religionis, 1. I. p. I, c. 2, n. 35).

[2] In officio religionis *quatuor* actus spectari possunt, qui quo perfectiores sunt, eo perfectior est hujus virtutis functio. *Primus* est consideratio infinitae majestatis Dei, et omnia ab ipsa pendere. *Secundus* est consideratio nostri nihili, i. e. nos ex nobis nihil esse, nihil habere, sed quidquid sumus et habemus Dei esse et a Deo assidue pendere. *Tertius*, profunda mentis submissio et inclinatio coram Deo, quo mens haec ipsa interius testetur. *Quartus*, eorundem professio exterior, verbis, gestu corporis vel aliis modis (Lessius, De justitia ceterisque virt. cardin., 1. 2. c. 36, dub. I, n. 6).

owe Him the profoundest respect and veneration. God is not only inconceivably exalted above heaven and earth; but by His creative power He is also the source of all things, for they absolutely depend on Him as to their being, their existence, their activity. Since God is the Creator of all things visible and invisible, He is therefore the sovereign Master and Lord of all that lives and moves in the universe; consequently, He is "the King of kings and the Lord of lords" (1 Tim. 6, 15), to whom all beings owe unconditional and constant service. Since the Almighty God has made all things and since all creatures are the work of His hands, they belong to Him as His property; He has, then, the highest and the most absolute dominion over all creatures, for they exist only for Him, and must act only for Him, and serve Him alone. Most beautifully does the Church express this thought in the Invitatory of the Office of the Dead: *Regem, cui omnia vivunt, venite adoremus* — "Come let us adore the King unto whom all things live."

Holy Scripture frequently delivers these truths in most vivid and striking descriptions. "The Lord is terrible and exceeding great and His power is admirable" (Ecclus 43, 31). "The Lord's ways are in a tempest and a whirlwind and clouds are the dust of His feet" (Nah. 1, 3). God is the Supreme Master and Proprietor of the universe, because it has come forth from His creative hand and is His work; hence the Psalmist joyfully sings: "The earth is the Lord's and the fulness thereof: the world and all they that dwell therein. For He hath founded it upon the seas and He hath prepared it upon the rivers" (Ps. 23, 1—2). "Who hath measured the waters in the hollow of His hand, and weighed the heavens in His palm? Who hath poised with three fingers the bulk of the earth? Behold the gentiles are as a drop of a bucket, and are counted as the smallest grain of a balance: behold the islands are as a little dust. It is He that sitteth upon the globe of the earth; He that stretcheth out the heavens as nothing, and spreadeth them out as a tent to dwell in. Who bringeth out their host by number, and calleth them all by their names; by the greatness of His might and strength and power, not one of them was missing" (Is. 40, 12—26). "And the stars have given light in their watches, and rejoiced. They were called and they said: Here we are; and with cheerfulness they have shined forth to Him that made them" (Bar. 3, 34—35). "O Lord, great art Thou, and glorious in Thy power, and no one can overcome Thee. Let all Thy creatures serve Thee; because Thou hast spoken, and they were made: Thou didst send forth Thy spirit, and they were created, and there is no one that can resist Thy voice. The mountains shall be moved from the foundations, with the waters: the rocks shall melt as wax before Thy face" (Judith 16, 16—18). "He looketh upon the earth, and maketh it tremble: He toucheth the mountains, and they smoke" (Ps. 103, 32).

And what is man in comparison with the Most High, with the Almighty Creator and powerful King, greatly to be feared, who

sitteth upon His throne and is the God of dominion? (Ecclus. I, 8).
"Man's days are as grass, as the flower of the field so shall he
flourish. For the spirit shall pass in him, and he shall not be: and
he shall know his place no more" (Ps. 102, 15—16). Man is earth
and ashes (Ecclus. 17, 31); he is a leaf and a dry straw carried
about by the wind; like a flower he cometh forth and is destroyed
and he fleeth as a shadow (Job 13, 25; 14, 2). Now should not
man — a weak, frail, miserable creature — bow down and humble
himself to the dust, should he not tremble with awe, reverence and
astonishment before the power, grandeur and majesty of God, "whose
throne is the heavens and whose footstool is the earth" (Is. 66, 1).
The pillars of heaven tremble and dread at His beck; the morning
stars praise Him and the sons of God make a joyful melody to Him
(Job 26, 11; 38, 7). The choirs of holy spirits sing in the highest
heavens to the Lord day and night their never-ceasing "Holy, holy,
holy;" the glorified saints prostrate themselves before Him that
sitteth on the throne and adore Him that liveth forever and ever;
they lay down their crowns before the throne, saying: "Thou art
worthy, O Lord our God, to receive glory and honor and power; because Thou hast created all things and for Thy will they were and
have been created" (Apoc. 4, 10—11). In this jubilation of eternal
praise and adoration man also should unite, according to his ability,
in glorifying God, who is justly exalted above all.

2. The virtue of religion, moreover, quickens our zeal and spurs
us on to the performance of acts calculated to render to the Divine
Majesty due honor and glory; and these acts may be divided into
two classes. [1]

a) In the first class are comprised all acts which in themselves
refer to the honor of God and promote it, that is, those which by
their nature are intended and calculated to render to the greatness
of God due acknowledgment and worship. [2] We perform such acts
when, for instance, we pray and offer sacrifice, make and fulfil vows,
adorn churches and decorate altars. [3]

b) The second class includes the acts of all the other virtues —,
figuratively speaking, in so far as they are performed by command
of God, that is, by an inspiration from Him and from a motive of

---

[1] Religio habet *duplices* actus: — quosdam quidem, quos *elicit* per quos homo
ordinatur ad solum Deum, sicut sacrificare, adorare et alia hujusmodi —, alios
autem actus habet, quos producit mediantibus virtutibus, quibus *imperat*, ordinans
eos ad *divinam reverentiam*, quia sc. virtus ad quam pertinet finis, imperat virtutibus, ad quas pertinent ea quae sunt ad finem. — Et secundum hoc actus religionis
per modum imperii ponitur esse, "visitare pupillos et viduas in tribulatione
eorum," quod est actus elicitus a misericordia; "immaculatum autem se custodire
ab hoc saeculo" imperative quidem est religionis, elicitive autem temperantiae vel
alicujus hujusmodi virtutis (S. Thom. 2. 2. q. 81. a. 1. ad 1).

[2] These are according to their distinctive characteristic acts of religion in the
strictest sense — actus *eliciti* religionis.

[3] Ipsius latriae est sacrificium offerre Deo, et hoc sacrificium soli Deo debetur;
et latria dicit cultum soli Deo debitum (S. Bonav. III, dist. 9, a. 2, q. 2).

honoring Him, consequently made with a view and intention of giving glory to God. [1] The virtue of religion can and must direct to the glory of God all the works and exercises of a Christian life, that it may become a perpetual divine service. "Whether you eat or drink, or whatsoever else you do, do all for the glory of God" (1 Cor. 10, 31). [2]

To this effect St. Augustine says: "God is to be honored by faith, hope and charity" (Manuale 1, 3). The acts of faith, hope and charity are in themselves acts, not of the moral virtue of religion, but of the three essentially different theological virtues; yet they may be elicited with the intention of acknowledging the divine truth, fidelity and goodness, and God is thereby greatly honored and glorified. In believing, hoping and loving we give ourselves to God with all the powers of our soul, we lean upon God and rest in God as our last end; in other words, we render to the divine perfections and majesty due homage and submission. — The three divine virtues also condition the development and completion of the Christian life, which is founded on faith, nourished by hope and animated by charity. Faith enlightens the understanding with celestial light, hope endows the soul with supernatural strength, and love inflames the heart with divine fire; thus these three virtues enable us by a new and holy life to announce to men the glorious prerogatives and perfections of God, that they may see our works and glorify our Father who is in heaven (1 Peter 2, 9; Matt. 5, 16). They give rise to the virtue of religion, and excite us to glorify God through works of piety, mercy and penance. [3]

We read in the epistle of St. James (1. 27) these words: "Religion (*religio*) clean and undefiled before God and the Father is this; to visit the fatherless and widows in their tribulation and to keep one's self unspotted from the world." The meaning of the above is — that if we would honor God the Father in a sincere and proper manner, we must be assiduously intent upon assisting the poor, the abandoned and the distressed, upon consoling and comforting them, and, at the same time, endeavor, amid the universal corruption of the world, to serve God alone and to please Him by purity of heart and the righteousness of our ways. Thus the virtue

---

[1] These are acts *imperati* religionis, that is, acts of other virtues, the practice of which is commanded by religion, whereby, without losing their particular character, they become likewise acts of religion.

[2] Ad religionem pertinent non solum oblationes sacrificiorum et alia hujusmodi, quae sunt *religioni propria*, sed etiam actus omnium virtutum, secundum quod referuntur ad Dei servitium et honorem, *efficiuntur actus religionis* (S. Thom. 2, 2, q. 186, a. 1 ad 2).

[3] Dicit S. Augustinus Deum soli fide, spe et caritate, non quod religio *eliciat* actus fidei, spei et caritatis, sed quia vel *eos imperat* vel *ab eis imperatur* (Billuart, De religione dissert. 1, art. 2).

of religion will produce abundant fruits "that in all things and above all things God may be glorified" (ut in omnibus glorificetur Deus). [1]

3. Religion holds the first place among the moral virtues. Although, like all other moral virtues, the virtue of religion is inferior in merit and dignity to the divine virtues of faith, hope and charity, it is, nevertheless, most intimately connected with them, for it regulates the conduct of man toward God. It holds the first rank among the moral virtues, because it approaches nearer to God than the others, in so far as it produces and has for its primary object those acts which refer directly and immediately to the honor of God — that is, whatever acts pertain to the divine service. [2] The sublime virtue of religion ennobles man precisely in this, that it completely subjects him to the will and dominion of God and brings him into the closest communication with the primal Source of all holiness. "For in offering honor and homage to God we submit our mind to Him, and it is in this submission that its perfection consists. An object is perfected by its submitting to its superior. Thus the perfection of the body consists in its being vivified by the soul; and the perfection of the atmosphere in its being thoroughly illumined by the light of the sun." [3] Honoring God fervently renders man truly great and exalted, and imparts to him abundant gain and blessing for his spiritual life.

4. The worship due to the Divine Majesty consists principally in acts of adoration, thanksgiving, petition and propitiation.

As we have seen, God immeasurably excels all creatures, even the highest and the sublimest of the heavenly spirits; He excels them not merely by His infinite dignity and perfection, but also by reason of His boundless power and dominion. Hence at all times and in all places, every creature is dependent upon God. It behooves man as a rational creature consciously and freely and actively to acknowledge his absolute dependence upon God — in a word, to adore God. By adoration (λατρεία, *adoratio latreutica, cultus latreuticus*), we understand that supreme and most perfect homage due, not to any mere creature, but only and solely to God on account of His infinite perfection, majesty and sovereign authority. [4]

---

[1] Omnia secundum quod *in gloriam Dei* fiunt, pertinent ad religiónem, non quasi ad elicientem, sed quasi ad imperantem; illa autem pertinent ad religionem elicientem, quae secundum rationem suae speciei pertinent ad reverentiam Dei (S. Thom. 2, 2, q. 81, a. 4 ad 2).

[2] Religio magis de propinquo accedit ad Deum, quam aliae virtutes morales, in quantum operatur ea, quae *directe* et *immediate* ordinantur in honorem divinum. Et ideo religio praeeminet inter alias virtutes morales (S. Thom. 2, 2, q. 81, a. 6).

[3] S. Thom. 2, 2, q. 81, a. 7.

[4] Cum obsequium diversis possit exhiberi, *speciali* quodam et *supremo modo* Deo debetur, quia in eo est suprema ratio *majestatis et dominii;* et ideo servitium vel obsequium, quod ei debetur, speciali nomine nominatur et dicitur λατρεία (S. Thom. III. dist. 9, q. I. a. 1, sol.1).

God alone is adorable;[1] He alone is the Most High, the Almighty Creator and Ruler of creation. Those rights and perfections which belong exclusively to God, are also to be acknowledged and honored by a special worship, — the worship of adoration. Hence to adore God is at the same time to acknowledge, admire and to praise His majesty and sovereign power; it is profoundly to humble and, in a manner, to annihilate ourselves in the presence of His infinite grandeur and dignity; it is to submit, to consecrate and to resign ourselves unreservedly to Him as our first beginning and our last end. Consequently, adoration is the most excellent and the most precious homage that God can receive from creatures endowed with reason, man included.

Two other religious duties and acts are inseparably connected with adoration — namely, thanksgiving and petition. Because God is adorable, that is, because He possesses infinite perfections, unlimited power, and boundless goodness, He is the inexhaustible fountain whence proceeds every good and perfect gift, in heaven and upon earth.[2] All that we are, that we have and can do, both in the order of nature and in the order of grace, is the outpouring of the overflowing love of God. — Now, with respect to the numberless gifts and graces which we have already received and daily yet receive, we owe heartfelt thanks for them, one and all, to God, our greatest Benefactor; moreover, all the good that we may expect, hope for and implore, can likewise come to us only by the infinitely bounteous hand of God; hence it behooves us to turn to Him in humble supplication.

To adore God, to thank Him and to implore of Him His gifts is therefore a threefold duty incumbent upon man, for the simple reason that man is altogether dependent upon God. But in consequence of his having fallen away from God and become corrupt by sin, there devolves upon him, now laden with iniquity and deserving of punishment, still another obligation, namely, that of appeasing an offended and irritated God, by appropriate propitiation or satisfaction.

5. The acts of religion must above all be interior, that is, be performed with mind and heart; furthermore, they must also reveal

---

[1] To the whole humanity of Christ, as well as to its single parts, for example, the Sacred Heart, the Precious Blood, the Five Wounds, — and also to the Eucharistic Body and Blood of Jesus Christ supreme adoration is due. But, at the same time, it is to be observed that the human nature of Christ in itself (in se), but not on account of itself (propter se) is adorable: the foundation of this absolute adoration of the humanity of Christ lies in the hypostatic union, that is, in this that the Son of God has made this human nature His own and is thereby truly man. Consequently, the one and entire Christ, that is, Christ also as man, or in His human nature, must be adored. — Per gratiam *unionis* Christus dignus est non tantum felicitate gloriae, verum etiam *adoratione latriae*, quae est cultus reverentiae *soli Deo* debitae (S. Bonav. Brevil. P. IV, c. 5).

[2] Deus a quo bona cuncta procedunt — Deus virtutum, cujus est totum, quod est optimum (= bonum). Orat. Eccles.

themselves externally, appear visibly and in a manner become corporeal ; — the virtue of religion, as it must be exercised by man, comprises therefore interior and exterior acts. At the same time it must not be forgotten, that exterior acts of divine worship, to be pleasing to God and conducive to His honor, should always be animated and enlivened by the interior. The exterior acts of religion should proceed from the heart, should express the interior life of the soul, and practically show forth the mind's religious reverence and submission, according to the words of the Royal Prophet: "My heart and my flesh have rejoiced in the living God" (Ps. 83, 3). [1] Why is man commanded to honor God by outward acts?

a) Man is not, as the angels, purely spiritual, but a creature composed of spirit and body. As such he must honor and glorify God in a manner appropriate to his corporeal and rational nature. But man renders the homage of his whole nature only when his body also takes part in his acts of divine worship, so that the interior worship is manifested by outward acts. [2] — Man in his entire being, created by God and dependent upon Him, belongs in body and soul to God ; therefore is man bound to serve and to worship God, his Creator, Preserver and Lord, with the powers of his soul and body, by spiritual and corporal acts. Moreover, the body of a Christian is the temple of the Holy Ghost, for it becomes sanctified by grace, and is to be transfigured by glory. Hence the Church implores God to grant "that we may serve and please Him not only with the soul, but also with the body." [3]

b) The most intimate reciprocity exists between man's interior and exterior acts; they proceed from one another, they mutually assist and complete each other. Those things which stir man's inmost soul — such as joy and sorrow, love and anger, hope and fear —,

---

[1] Deo reverentiam et honorem exhibemus non propter seipsum, quia ex seipso est gloria plenus, cui nihil a creatura adici potest ; sed propter nos, quia videlicet per hoc quod Deum reveremur et honoramus, mens nostra ei subicitur„ et in hoc perfectio consistit: quaelibet enim res perficitur per hoc quod subditur suo superiori, sicut corpus per hoc quod vivificatur ab anima, et aer per hoc quod illuminatur a sole. — Mens autem humana indiget ad hoc quod conjungatur Deo, sensibilium manuductione ... et ideo in divino cultu necesse est aliquibus corporalibus uti, ut eis quasi signis quibusdam mens hominis excitetur ad spirituales actus, quibus Deo conjungitur. Et ideo religio habet quidem *interiores* actus quasi *principales* et per se ad religionem pertinentes ; *exteriores* vero actus quasi *secundarios* et ad interiores actus ordinatos (S. Thom. 2, 2, q. 81, a. 7).

[2] Non est mirum, si haeretici, qui corporis nostri Deum esse auctorem negant, hujusmodi corporalia obsequia Deo fieri reprehendunt. In quo etiam apparet, quod *se homines* esse *non meminerunt*, dum sensibilium sibi repraesentationem necessariam non judicant ad interiorem cognitionem et affectionem ; nam experimento apparet quod per corporales actus anima excitatur ad aliquam cognitionem vel affectionem ; unde manifestum est, convenienter etiam corporalibus quibusdam nos uti ad mentis nostrae elevationem in Deum. (S. Thom. c. gent. l. 3, c. 119).

[3] Ut corpore tibi famulemur et mente — ut corpore tibi placeamus et mente. Orat. Eccles.

involuntarily betray their impression in his exterior: and this is especially the case with regard to the interior acts of religion. And why should not the fervent interior life, the ardent devotion and divine love of a pious soul, be spontaneously manifested in the outward man, and so take possession of his entire being, as to impel him not only "to sing in grace in his heart to God," but furthermore to pour himself out "in psalms and hymns and spiritual canticles" (Coloss. 3, 16), — to join his hands, bend his knees and prostrate his form upon the earth before the face of the Most High ? "My heart hath been glad and my tongue hath rejoiced" (Ps. 15, 9), exclaims therefore the Royal Prophet. "Let my soul be filled with marrow and fatness, and my mouth shall praise Thee with joyful lips" (Ps. 62, 6). — Reversely, the exterior also affects the interior man : outward signs and acts arouse the affections of the spirit, inflame and nourish the fervor of devotion, refresh and invigorate the life of the soul. The interior acts of religion grow in perfection, become durable and constant, when they thus live and exercise their activity in the body, that is, when they, so to speak, assume flesh and blood. When, however, exterior divine worship is neglected, the interior soon languishes and dies.

c) Man is lord and master of irrational creatures, which also must be led to glorify the Creator. But it is principally by exterior worship that man can and must lead the visible creation to serve and praise the Creator. The use in religious service of creatures imparts to external nature a higher consecration and activity. "For the building up and the adornment of the temple, the earth presents its treasures and precious metals ; the ocean, its pearls ; spring, the magnificence of its flowers."

d) Not the individual man alone, but society also, as a religious body, must render to God due homage and submission. Now a common public service (*cultus socialis*) requires external acts. Hence visible, outward worship is necessary as the bond of the religious community, namely the Church.

It behooves us, then, in accordance with our own nature and the express divine commandment, to honor God with our mental and corporal powers, that is, we must not merely by interior but also by outward acts adore Him, thank Him, beseech and propitiate Him.

This fourfold duty is fulfilled principally by *prayer* and *sacrifice*, which are intimately connected with each other, which permeate and complete one another. The interior acts of divine worship manifest themselves outwardly, in the first place, by vocal, that is, by corporal, prayer — then in the offering of sacrifice, which, as the most sublime act of religion, is far more excellent and meritorius than prayer.

6. The virtue of religion is exceedingly precious and rich in blessings. It teaches us humbly to acknowledge our own littleness and misery, and to render to God, of whose goodness there is no end (Ps. 144, 3), due honor in all things, thereby winning for us the

richest blessings. A spirit of reverential homage should, as a heavenly spice and consecration, pervade our whole life, in order to render it daily more and more pleasing and meritorious in the eyes of God. To worship God should be our joy and happiness! "Come let us praise the Lord with joy, let us joyfully sing to God our Saviour. Let us come before His presence with thanksgiving and make a joyful noise to Him with psalms. For the Lord is a great God and a great King above all gods. For in His hands are all the ends of the earth, and the heights of the mountains are His. For the sea is His, and He made it; and His hands formed the dry land. Come let us adore and fall down; and weep before the Lord that made us. For He is the Lord our God, and we are the people of His pasture and the sheep of His hands" (Ps. 94, 1—7). A true knowledge of God and a correct understanding of ourselves furnish the solid basis upon which rest the virtue of religion and the spirit of the most submissive adoration. Ever seeking to know God and ourselves more perfectly is the higher wisdom and the science of the Saints, and after this we should incessantly strive. *Noverim te — Noverim me!* prayed St. Augustine. [1] O God, grant that I may know Thee — *Noverim te!* Give me an intimate knowledge of Thy adorable perfections, which are without measure or number — of Thy infinite grandeur and glory, Thy inconceivable power, wisdom and goodness, Thy unspeakable beauty, sweetness and amiableness; penetrate me with a deep knowledge of "the profound things of Thy divinity, which only the Holy Spirit searcheth" (1 Cor. 2, 10), that is, the works and riches of Thy grace and glory, Thy infinitely just and merciful decrees, the wonderful and inscrutable dispensations of Thy providence! — *Noverim me!* Grant me, moreover, a wholesome knowledge of myself! "O my God, illumine my darkness" (Ps. 17, 29), that Thy light may permit me to look down deeply into the abyss of my nothingness, my misery, my helplessness, my frailty and my sinfulness!

2. Sacrifice in its Proper Sense.

The interior acts and affections of the virtue of religion, that is, of adoration, thanksgiving, petition and satisfaction, manifest themselves in many ways, but find their supreme and most solemn expression in sacrifice. Sacrifice is a special act of divine service, and, as such, differs essentially from all other acts of worship. To form a correct idea of sacrifice, we must inquire what is properly meant by sacrifice, and in what its essence consists. By sacrifice we understand the offering of a visible object, effected through any change, transformation or destruction thereof, in order effectually to acknowledge the absolute Majesty and Sovereignty of God as well as man's total dependence and submission.

---

[1] Soliloq. II, I.

Among the requisites of sacrifice, the gift and its presentation, as well as the object and meaning of the exterior act, chiefly deserve consideration.

1. Sacrifice is the offering of a visible object; hence, in the first place, a visible gift is necessary as an offering to God. This gift ought to correspond to the object in view, and should, therefore, be selected with due regard thereto. Consequently, the offering most appropriate to God is that which is the noblest in the visible creation — human life. Wherefore Christ, in order to present the most perfect sacrifice, offered His precious life on the Cross, according to the will of His Father. In every other case God did not wish that human life should be sacrificed to Him, but rather contented Himself with the interior offering of the heart and its symbolical expression — namely, with the presentation of an irrational creature substituted for human life and offered in its stead. [1] It is at once evident that especially the living and inanimate things which serve directly for the support of man, and thus may represent his life, may be appropriately substituted as offerings for man himself. Before Christ such offerings consisted, for example, of lambs, heifers, doves; bread, wine, oil, salt, incense.

As such gifts were offered to give honor to God, it is self-evident that they had to be as perfect as possible, without blemish or defect. [1] In as far as sacrifice is an external act of worship, its value depends chiefly on the dignity and interior disposition of the person who offers; the value of the gift presented also contributes to make the sacrifice more acceptable to God. Hence when proper sentiments animate the heart, only precious gifts will be selected as offerings for an action so exalted and holy. On the other hand — to make choice of indifferent, trifling or imperfect objects as offerings is a sign that the proper spirit of sacrifice and respect for the Divine Majesty are wanting (cf. Mal. I, 7—8).

2. Not every gift offered to God is a sacrifice. It greatly depends on the way and manner of offering. — Some change or destruction of the gift must take place to constitute a sacrifice. An entire destruction of the gift, or such as is at least morally equivalent,

---

[1] This substitution for man and human life is, as seen in the rite of the Old Testament for the offering of sacrifices, expressed and commanded in the clearest manner (compare the ceremony of laying hands on the head of the animal to be slain, — the sacrifice of the two goats on the great Feast of Atonement). Recall also the sacrifice of Abraham. The patriarch was commanded to sacrifice his only son Isaac: but, in accordance with the will of God, he took a "ram and offered it as a holocaust in place of his son" (Gen. 22, 13). The Fathers teach the same. Cum Patriarchae ... quasi divino spiritu illustrati viderent, magno sibi opus esse obsequio ad suorum humanorum delictorum purgationem, pretium pro salute sua ei, qui vitam atque animam praebuisset, se debere putabant. Sed cum nihil praestantius aut pretiosius anima sua haberent, quod dicarent, pro hac interim brutorum animalium vitam offerebant; pro sua anima *sacrificia suae vitae vicaria* (ἀντίψυχα) offerentes (Euseb. Demonstr. evang. l. I, c. 10).

[1] Omne, quod est optimum, Deo est attribuendum (S. Thom. 1, 2, q. 102, a. 3 ad 4).

pertains essentially to the idea of sacrifice ; hence its outward form. Whatever has not been liturgically transformed, v. g. destroyed, cannot be a real sacrifice (*sacrificium*), but is only a religious gift (*oblatio*), essentially different from sacrifice.[1] Thus we find in all sacrifices mentioned in Holy Writ, that there was ever some mode of destruction or dissolution, appropriate to the nature of the matter of the sacrifice. Thus, the animals were slain and their blood spilled on the altar, incense was consumed by fire, and wine was poured out. The intrinsic and more weighty reason why such a transformation, or destruction, of the gift is requisite for the act of sacrifice, lies in the peculiar meaning and in the special object of sacrifice.

3. Sacrifice, that is, the transformation of the gift offered, is intended to represent symbolically that God possesses absolute authority and dominion over all things — and, consequently, that man is essentially dependent upon God, belongs and is subject to Him and, therefore, that he is bound and is ready to give and dedicate his life entirely to God. God is the Supreme Ruler, infinitely holy, the primal source of all being, and the last end to which all being should return, "that He may be all in all" (I. Cor. 15, 28). And now how could this grandeur and sovereignty of God over all that is and that can be outside of Him, be more appropriately expressed than by the destruction of a visible object, as is done in sacrifice ? How could man's dependence on and obligation to serve God be more suitably made apparent than in sacrifice, wherein a tangible, material object, is destroyed in the place of a human life ?

If the exterior rite of sacrifice is in reality to have the above meaning and be a worship acceptable to God, then it must also be an expression of the interior and spiritual sacrifice, and be animated and vivified by the essential sentiments of sacrifice.[2] — "The visible sacrifice," says St. Augustine, "is a holy sign of the invisible offering."[3]

---

[1] Actus, quo res externas ad Dei cultum consecramus, dividitur in *oblationem et sacrificium;* omnes enim actus, quibus res externas Deo offerimus, sub aliquo ex illis duobus membris constituuntur. Et quamvis oblatio large dicta comprehendat sub se sacrificium ; istud enim quaedam oblatio est, et sub genere oblationis continetur : tamen oblatio specialiter dicta (licet nomen generis retineat) a sacrificio distinguitur. Nam *oblatio* dicitur, quando res integra et immutata offertur ; *sacrificium* vero vocatur, cum res immutatur in ipsa oblatione . . . Res, quae sacrificantur, debent in ipso sacrificio (quod in hoc a simplici oblatione distinguitur) immutari vel mactatione vel combustione vel fractione vel divisione vel alio modo (Salmant. De Incarn. disp. 31, dub. 1, n. 1).

[2] Oblatio sacrificii fit ad aliquid significandum. Significat autem sacrificium, quod offertur *exterius, interius* spirituale sacrificium, quo anima seipsam offert Deo (Ps. 50, 19), quia exteriores actus religionis ad interiores ordinantur. Anima autem se offert Deo in sacrificium sicut principio suae creationis et sicut fini suae beatificationis. Secundum autem veram fidem solus Deus est creator animarum nostrarum ; in solo etiam eo animae nostrae beatitudo consistit. Et ideo sicut soli Deo summo debemus sacrificium *spirituale* offerre, ita etiam soli ei debemus offerre *exteriora* sacrificia (S. Thom. 2, 2, q. 85, a. 2).

[3] Sacrificium visibile invisibilis sacrificii sacramentum, i. e. sacrum signum est (De civit. Dei l. 10, c. 5).

Hence the offering up of sacrifice essentially aims to glorify God as the absolute Lord and supreme Legislator of all creatures, and this is to adore God. This meaning is inseparably connected with sacrifice; it holds the first place, and is ever an act of worship due to God alone, — an act of adoration. [1] — With this main object, thanksgiving and petition are naturally combined, inasmuch as the gift is presented also to honor and acknowledge God as the omnipotent and merciful Dispenser of all good gifts, that is, to show one's self grateful for benefits received, and to supplicate for new graces. — In consequence of the fall of man, sacrifice assumes the additional characteristic of atonement. It is offered to express the need and desire of appeasing the irritated justice of God and of being thereby freed from sin and its punishment. Atonement for sin committed is made by sacrifice, inasmuch as the offended majesty of God is glorified, in order to restore to God the honor of which He had been deprived and to make satisfaction for the injury done to Him. The destruction of the offering is especially suitable to this end. How could sinful man more worthily and more strikingly acknowledge himself deserving of death on account of his fault, and, willing to undergo death in satisfaction for it, than when, by the laying of his hands on the victim, he transfers to it his sins, and slaying it and shedding its blood, offers it to God instead of his own life? [2]

History shows us atonement as always accompanying adoration and holding the rank next to it in the idea of sacrifice. The first and greatest want and desire of fallen man was to appease the anger of an offended God, to obtain mercy and forgiveness for sin; hence it is quite natural that among the guilty, unredeemed generations living before Christ the character of atonement should have been impressed in a marked manner upon their sacrifices. [3] In whatever necessity sinful man presents himself before God, whether to adore, to thank or to petition Him, his first and deepest conviction is that he is a poor sinner, unworthy of being heard and answered by God; hence it is most natural that precisely in the most ardent acts of worship, such as sacrifice, he will always, and at the very start, feel deeply conscious that he is laden with sins and debts to God. How could he, a sinner, more worthily acknowledge the Divine Majesty

---

[1] Illo cultu, qui graece λατρεία dicitur, latine uno verbo dici non potest, cum sit quaedam proprie divinitati debita servitus, nec colimus nec colendum docemus nisi unum Deum. Cum autem ad hunc cultum pertineat oblatio sacrificii, nullo modo tale aliquid offerimus aut offerendum praecipimus vel cuiquam martyri vel cuiquam sanctae animae vel cuiquam angelo (S. Aug. C. Faust. 1, 20 c. 21).

[2] Per occisionem animalium significatur destructio peccatorum, et quod homines erant digni occisione pro peccatis suis, ac si illa animalia loco eorum occiderentur ad significandam expiationem peccatorum (S. Thom. 1, 2, q. 102, a. 3 ad 5).

[3] Aeterne Deus, qui post offendicula lapsus primi hominis instituisti tibi offerri propitiatorii delibamenta libaminis, ut culpa quae praecesserat per superbiam, futuris temporibus expiaretur per munera, quibus honorarentur altaria, honorificarentur et templa (Pontif. Roman. De alt. port. consecrat.)

of the infinitely holy and just God, show his gratitude towards Him in a more appropriate way, and approach Him with greater confidence of being heard?"

It is for this fourfold end that sacrifices are offered: hence there are sacrifices of adoration, of thanksgiving, of petition and of propitiation. [1] These divisions are not made according to the exclusive object of Sacrifice, but only with reference to its predominant end. This means only that in the rite of celebration and in the intention of the person offering, one of these ends is chiefly intended, without, however, excluding the others. Every sacrifice has in itself a fourfold signification: it serves at one and the same time to glorify the Divine Majesty (*sacrificium latreuticum*); to return thanks for benefits received (*sacrificium eucharisticum*); to petition for new benefits (*sacrificium impetratorium*); and finally, to satisfy for sin and its punishment (*sacrificium propitiatorium*).

4. In so far as sacrifice has a symbolical meaning and is a constituent part of public worship, it must positively be instituted by a legitimate authority. [2] The sacrificial service of the Old Law was regulated and ordained by God Himself in its most minute details; in the New Law the essential elements and features of worship proceed directly from Jesus Christ — hence, first of them all, sacrifice, which constitutes the fundamental and central act of divine service. Neither to the Synagogue nor to the Church did God impart the right or the power to institute sacrifices: in His infinite mercy He Himself condescended to prescribe the sacrifices by which He would be honored and propitiated. No mere man, but our Divine Saviour alone could institute so sublime and so excellent a Sacrifice as we possess in the Holy Mass.

5. Sacrifice is an act of worship which can not be performed by anybody but a priest. He alone who has been especially chosen, called and empowered, that is, only the priest can and may perform the office of sacrificer. Sacrifice and priesthood are inseparably connected: no sacrifice can exist without a priesthood, and no priesthood without a sacrifice. A special priesthood is, therefore, required by the very nature of sacrifice, which, as a public, solemn act of worship, must be performed in the name and for the welfare of the religious body by a duly authorized person. — Consequently, it is highly proper that only he who is, at least by his office and dignity, especially separated from sinners and sanctified, should present himself in sacrifice as mediator between an offended God and sinful man. "For every highpriest taken from among men," so writes the Apostle, "is ordained for men in the things that appertain to God, that he may offer up gifts and sacrifices

---

[1] *Maxime* obligatur homo Deo propter ejus majestatem (Sacrifice of Adoration), secundo propter offensam commissam (Sacrifice of Propitiation), tertio propter beneficia jam suscepta (Sacrifice of Thanksgiving), quarto propter beneficia sperata (Sacrifice of Petition) (S. Thom. 1, 2, q. 102, a. 3 ad 10).

[2] Oblatio sacrificii in communi est de lege naturali; sed determinatio sacrificiorum est ex institutione *humana* vel *divina* (S. Thom. 2, 2, q. 85, a. 1 ad 1).

for sins'' (Heb. 5, 1). — It is clear that it belongs to God alone to bestow the honor of the priestly vocation and office, and to determine "who belong to Him, and the holy He will join to Himself ; and they whom He shall choose shall approach to Him" (Num. 16, 5).

6. Nor is it less evident that for the celebration of so holy and solemn an act of worship it is especially becoming to make choice of a sanctified place ; such a place, where sacrifice is offered, is called an altar. Wherever sacrifice and priesthood are found, there also is always an altar.

7. From the above it follows that sacrifice is the most exalted and perfect manner of honoring God, and, therefore, excels all other acts of worship. It also constitutes the principal act, and is the central point of the whole divine service. In this all agree that man by the offering of sacrifice renders to God the highest possible honor and homage. In sacrifice the interior adoration of the Divine Majesty attains its fullest expression. Sacrifice is essentially an act of adoration, and, therefore, always includes the acknowledgment of the divinity of Him to whom it is offered. It is among all acts of worship the prerogative of God, and may be offered only to the one true God.[1] To offer it to a creature, even to the greatest saint or the most exalted of the angels, would be heinous idolatry. — At all times sacrifices have been offered to God,[2] to acknowledge in the most perfect and solemn manner His sovereignty, to express gratitude for favors, to implore fresh blessings from Him and especially to avert the scourges of His avenging justice.

3. Sacrifice in a Figurative Sense.

1. Only such acts of divine worship as contain in themselves all the essential requisites and characteristics of the idea of sacrifice as explained above, are and may be called sacrifices in their proper sense. In the religious, ascetical life virtuous acts, differing essen-

---

[1] Sacrificium certe, nullus hominum est, qui audeat dicere deberi nisi Deo ... quis vero sacrificandum censuit nisi ei, quem Deum aut scivit aut putavit aut finxit? (S. August. De civ. Dei l. 10 c. 4.) — Populus christianus memorias martyrum religiosa solemnitate concelebrat et ad excitandam imitationem et ut meritis eorum consocietur atque orationibus adjuvetur, ita tamen ut nulli martyrum, sed ipsi Deo martyrum, quamvis in.memoriis martyrum, constituamus altaria. Quis enim antistitum in locis sanctorum corporum assistens altari aliquando dixit: Offerimus tibi, Petre aut Paule aut Cypriane, sed quod offertur, offertur Deo, qui martyres coronavit (S. August. C. Faust. 1. 20, c. 21).

[2] Many theologians assert that sacrifice is strictly required and commanded, by the very law of nature, that it is a natural necessity. Others do not grant this, but say that sacrifice is only in an eminent degree in accord with the law of nature, i. e., that it corresponds to the law of nature ; that not only the interior but also the exterior worship of God is assuredly commanded by the natural law, but that this obligation may be fulfilled by performing other acts, for example, by vocal prayer, by the joining of the hands and the bending of the knees. Doubtless, sacrifice is necessary in order to make exterior worship perfect. The Church teaches that human nature calls for a visible sacrifice (hominum natura *exigit* visibile sacrificium — Trid. sess. 22, cap. 1).

ally from sacrifice, are often called by that name. The term sacrifice
applied to such acts is not to be taken in its original and strict
meaning, but is to be understood in a derivative and improper sense:
acts of virtue are and are called sacrifices in a broader sense. — The
word sacrifice, for example, is often used figuratively to designate
good, meritorious actions, inasmuch as they bear a certain resemblance and relationship to true and real sacrifices. [1] This resemblance
and relationship consists chiefly in two points : sacrifice serves to
glorify God — and is accomplished by the destruction of a sensible
object. The various acts of virtue, therefore, resemble sacrifice in so
far as they are performed with the right disposition and intention of
giving glory to God [2], and in so far as they require a certain destruction, that is, the mortification of the perverse and sensual nature of
man [3]. The base, sensual, earthly, material life must be curbed and
overcome, — must die, so that the higher, spiritual, heavenly life of
grace may be vigorously and fully developed in man. Mortification,
however, is painful to man and costs labor and exertion. We are
accustomed to think of this necessary renunciation and self-denial
chiefly when we designate as a sacrifice individual acts of virtue, and
also a life that is wholly Christian and perfect. Some examples [4]
may throw light upon the above and confirm what has been said. [5]

---

[1] Sicut *cultus Dei* multipliciter dicitur, sic et *sacrificium*. Est enim sacrificium *bonae operationis*, et sacrificium *devotae orationis*, et sacrificium *immolationis*.
Primum est *virtutum omnium;* secundum *virtutum theologicarum;* tertium spectat
ad ipsam *latriam*. Ipsius enim latriae est sacrificium offerre Deo, et hoc sacrificium
soli Deo debetur, et *latria* dicit cultum soli Deo debitum. (S. Bonav. III, dist. 9,
a. 2, q. 2).

[2] According to St. Augustine our works are sacrifices only when we perform
them in order to be closely united to God, that is, when we refer them to that
Supreme Good in whom consists our happiness. Unde ipsa misericordia, qua
homini subvenitur, si propter Deum non fit, non est sacrificium. Etsi enim ab
homine fit vel offertur, tamen sacrificium res divina (something divine) est : unde
et hoc quoque vocabulo (sacrificium from sacrum facere) id Latini veteres appella-
verint. (S. Augus., De civit. Dei, 1. 10, c. 6). — Omne opus virtutis dicitur esse
sacrificium, in quantum ordinatur ad Dei *reverentiam*. (S. Thom. 2. 2, q. 81, a. 4 adI).

[3] Mortification (mortificatio) is, as Alvarez de Paz aptly says : mors quaedam
specialis, qua id, quod Deo displicet et homini nocet, corrumpitur, ut mens nostra
jucundiori vita vestiatur, (De exterminat. mali et promot. boni, 1. 2, p. 3, c. 3). —
Bona mors, quae vitam non aufert, sed transfert in melius, bona, qua non corpus
cadit, sed anima sublevatur (S. Bernard., In Cantica serm. 52, n. 4).

[4] In Holy Scripture where the word *sacrifice* is simply used, that is, without
modification or explanation, sacrifice is to be understood in its strict sense ; but
when good works are called sacrifices, that is, when the word is taken in a broader
sense, this is, as a rule, indicated by additional words or at least by the context. —
When sacrifices in the strict sense are enumerated together with such acts of
virtue, or rather placed in contrast with them, they are called simply sacrifices,
e. g., *Misericordiam* volui et *non sacrificium*, et scientiam Dei plus quam holocausta (Os. 6, 6).

[5] Triplex est hominis bonum : — *primum* quidem est bonum animae, quod
Deo offertur interiori *quodam* sacrificio per devotionem et orationem et alios hujusmodi interiores actus ; et hoc est principale sacrificium. — *Secundum* est bonum

2. Acts of charity, works of mercy, whereby the poor and needy are assisted and consoled, are called sacrifices by the Apostle — and this in so far as the Christian intends, in the person of the poor, to give something to God Himself by the alms which he bestows: "Do not forget to do good and to impart; for by such sacrifices God's favor is obtained."[1] The same Apostle called the alms sent to him by the Christians of Philippi, "an odor of sweetness, an acceptable sacrifice, pleasing to God."[2]

To renounce sensual pleasures, to treat the body with rigor and austerity, is still more difficult than to forego worldly goods and possessions; hence St. Paul exhorts the Christians "by the mercy of God that you present your bodies (through mortification) a living sacrifice, holy, pleasing unto God, your reasonable service."[3]

A "sacrifice" which God does not reject, but graciously accepts is "an afflicted spirit," "a contrite and humble heart," that is, a spirit and a heart which, wounded with love and sorrow, penitently bewails and detests the sins and transgressions of its past life.[4]

Prayer stands in intimate relation and connection with sacrifice; for the spirit of prayer and the sentiments of the heart constitute the instrinsic being of sacrifice, the soul of the exterior rite of sacrifice. Hence, as sacrifice is called effective or real prayer (*oratio realis*), on the other hand, prayer is also called sacrifice. Thus the Prophet designated the prayer of praise and thanksgiving as "the sacrifice of the lips" (*vituli labiorum* — Osee 14, 3). Referring to this the Apostle writes: "Let us offer the sacrifice of prayer always to God, that is, the fruit of lips confessing His name."[5] In the Psalms we are invited "to offer to God the sacrifice of praise."[6]

---

corporis, quod Deo quodammodo offertur per martyrium et abstinentiam seu continentiam. — *Tertium* est bonum exteriorum rerum, de quo sacrificium offertur Deo: directe quidem, quando immediate res nostras Deo offerimus, mediate autem, quando eas communicamus proximis propter Deum (S. Thom. 2, 2, q. 85, a. 3 ad 2).

[1] Beneficentiae et communionis nolite oblivisci: *talibus* enim *hostiis* prometuretur Deus (Hebr. 13, 16). The annex *talibus* (such) shows that the word hostia (sacrifice) is here used not in its strict sense.

[2] Odor suavitatis, *hostia accepta*, placens Domino (Phil. 4, 18). — Beatus Apostolus Paulus in necessitate pressurae adjutus a fratribus opera bona quae fiunt, sacrificia Dei dixit esse (Phil. 4, 18) ... Nam quando quis miseretur pauperis, Deum foenerat (lends to God with interest); et qui dat minimis, Deo donat, spiritualiter Deo suavitatis odorem sacrificat (S. Cyprian. De Orat. domin. c. 33).

[3] Ut exhibeatis corpora vestra *hostiam* viventem, sanctam, Deo placentem (Rom. 12, 1). — Exhibet homo Deo corpus suum ut *hostiam* tripliciter: *uno* quidem *modo*, quando aliquis corpus suum exponit passioni et morti propter Deum ... *Secundo* per hoc quod homo corpus suum jejuniis et vigiliis macerat ad serviendum Deo ... *Tertio* per hoc quod homo corpus suum exhibet ad opera justitiae et divini cultus exsequenda (S. Thom. In ep. ad Rom. c. 12, lect. 1).

[4] *Sacrificium* Deo spiritus contribulatus; cor contritum et humiliatum, Deus, non despicies (Ps. 50, 19).

[5] Per ipsum offeramus *hostiam laudis* Deo semper, i. e. *fructum labiorum* confitentium nomini ejus (Hebr. 13, 15).

[6] Immola Deo *sacrificium laudis* (P. 49, 14).

A life that is entirely consumed amid suffering and struggle, in labor and fatigue, for God and His honor, is a holocaust: "As gold in the furnace He hath proved them, and as a victim of a holocaust He hath received them."[1] "The man also who in God's name consecrates himself wholly to God is a sacrifice, in so far as he dies to the world, to live to God."[2]

A sacrifice most perfect and acceptable to the Divine Majesty is pre-eminently the renunciation and consecration of religious persons, who by the threefold perpetual vows of poverty, chastity and obedience, freely and cheerfully renounce the earth and its goods, the world and its pleasures, in order to devote and dedicate themselves in body and soul forever to the service of God.[3]

Sacrifice in a broader sense made up the unspeakably humble and painful life of the poor, virginal and obedient Jesus, whilst His death on the Cross for the redemption of the world is a sacrifice in the strictest sense. The same cannot be said of the bloody death of the martyrs, however precious it was in the sight of the Lord;—their martyrdom had not the character of a real sacrifice. The martyrs indeed (as the Church sings in the divine Office) loved Christ during life and imitated Him in their death, for God's sake they indeed offered their bodies to the torments of death and shed their blood gloriously for the Lord, thereby obtaining unfading crowns; still they were destined neither as sacrificing priests nor as sacrificial victims to consecrate their lives to the adoration and propitiation of the Divine Majesty, but they suffered a violent death only in testimony and in defence of the truth, holiness and divinity of the Catholic faith.[4] Now, "although in the sight of the Lord the death of many saints was precious (Ps. 115, 15), yet none of these innocent victims accomplished the redemption of the world. The just received crowns of victory, but they did not bestow them; from the fortitude of the faithful proceeded models of patience, not gifts of justice."[5]

3. To sacrifice taken in a broad or figurative sense corresponds the figurative or general priesthood of all the faithful. Hence the prince of the Apostles called all Christians "a holy priesthood," chosen and qualified "to offer up spiritual sacrifices acceptable to God by Jesus Christ."[6] The faithful constitute "a holy priest-

---

[1] Tamquam aurum in fornace probavit illos et quasi *holocausti hostiam* accepit illos (Sap. 3, 6).

[2] Ipse homo, Dei nomine consecratus et Deo votus, inquantum mundo moritur ut Deo vivat, sacrificium est (S. August. De civit. Dei. 1. 10, c. 6).

[3] Religionis status est *quoddam holocaustum*, per quod aliquis totaliter se et sua offert Deo (S. Thom. 2. 2, q. 186, a. 7). — Totum Deo dedit, qui seipsum obtulit (S. Hieron. Epist. 53 ad Paulin. n. 11).

[4] It is only in a wider sense that the Church speaks of an *"odoriferum martyrii sacrificium"* (Martyrol. Roman. 18. Febr.). — Etsi fratres pro fratribus moriantur, tamen in fraternorum peccatorum remissionem nullius sanguis martyris funditur, quod fecit ille (Christus) pro nobis: neque in hoc quid imitaremur, sed quid gratularemur contulit nobis (S. Aug. in Joann. tr. 84, n. 2).

[5] St. Leo, 13th Sermon on the Lord's Passion.

[6] *Sacerdotium* sanctum, offerre *spirituales hostias*, acceptabiles Deo per Jesum

hood," in so far as they have by the sacramental character and the sacramental grace of baptism, separated themselves from sinners, being dedicated and sanctified, that by the "spiritual sacrifices" of a new and virtuous life, that is, by prayer, fervor, piety, self-denial, patience, compunction, benevolence and charity for the neighbor they may honor and glorify God.   As often as we perform a good action, with an upright intention directed to God, especially if in the midst of temptation and struggle, we offer a sacrifice to God. [1]

4.   With sacrifice and priesthood the altar is inseparably connected.   The word is also not unfrequently used in a broader sense, that is, figuratively.   Thus St. Augustine writes : "We are the temple of God, because He deigns to dwell in us.   Our heart is His altar, when it is raised toward Him *(cum ad illum sursum est, ejus est altare cor nostrum)*; to Him we immolate bloody sacrifices *(cruentas victimas)*, when we combat unto blood for His truth ; to Him we burn most fragrant incense *(suavissimum adolemus incensum)*, when we are on fire in His presence with devout and holy love ; to Him we present the sacrifice of humility and praise upon the altar of our heart in the fire of inflamed love *(hostiam humilitatis et laudis* **in ara cordis igne fervidae charitatis).**"[2]

4.   The Meaning and Efficacy of the Sacrifices of the Old Law.[3]

1.   By the sin of our first parents, in whom all mankind fell, the original plan of salvation was frustrated.   But God did not wish the unhappy world to perish in an abyss of temporal misery and eternal death ; in the excess of His goodness and love, He determined to raise man from his fall and again to enrich him with gifts of grace and glory.   This restoration was to be effected in the fulness of time, "through the redemption that is in Christ Jesus" (Rom. 3, 24).   Jesus Christ by His sacrifice on the Cross for the redemption of the world, is the salvation of all ages ; from the beginning, there was no name under heaven given to men whereby they were to be saved, other than the name of our Lord and Saviour Jesus Christ (Acts 4, 11).   Already before the Christian era no one could obtain the life of grace and eternal salvation except by adhering to Christ ; this adhesion could then be effected only by supernatural faith in the promised and coming Redeemer.

Christum (1. Petr. 2, 5). Sancti non dicuntur *sacerdotes* ab oblatione corporis Domini, sed sui, quia unusquisque corpus suum offert *hostiam viventem* (Rom. 12, 1). (S. Bonav. IV, dist. 13, a. 1, q. 2 ad 4).

[1] Quisquis igitur omnibus praeceptis coelestibus obtemperavit, hic cultor est verus Dei, cujus *sacrificia* sunt mansuetudo animi et vita innocens et actus boni. Quae omnia qui exhibet, toties *sacrificat*, quoties bonum aliquid ac pium fecerit (Lactant. Divin. instit. 1. 6, c. 24).

[2] S. Augustin., De civit. Dei, 1. 10, c. 3.

[3] Cf. Stöckl, Das Opfer, pp. 65—137 ; 210—334. — Thalhofer, Das Opfer des Alten und Neuen Bundes, pp. 24—142. — Scheeben, Dogmatik, III, 403—418. — Schöpfer, Geschichte des Alten Testamentes, pp. 168 etc.

That this faith, necessary to salvation, as well as the hope and charity springing therefrom, might be within reach of all men, God always imparted His supernatural help and grace. "The mystery of the redemption was at no time inefficacious, not even in the Old Testament. It was not by a new decree nor through a later mercy that God cared for the welfare of man, but from the beginning of the world He opened and designated for all one and the same fountain of salvation. For the grace of God, whereby all the Saints have ever been justified, was merely increased at the birth of Christ, and not then first imparted. This mystery of ineffable love, which at present fills the world, was so powerfully efficacious even in all its figures, that they who believed in the promised redemption did not receive less than they who have received the gift."[1]

2. Among the means of bringing man into supernatural communication with God and the expected Redeemer, sacrifices already before the coming of Christ held a prominent place, yea, the very first place. As Abel even at the threshold of Paradise, so during the patriarchal age, Noah, Melchisedech, Abraham, Jacob, offered sacrifices to God, and God graciously accepted them. Then God Himself through Moses most precisely and minutely regulated and prescribed the entire sacrificial rite of the Old Law. As the Mosaic sacrifices were celebrated by the express will and command of God, thus also were sacrifices in patriarchal times undoubtedly offered up in consequence of a clearer light and by divine inspiration; hence the Apostle writes: "By faith Abel offered to God a sacrifice exceeding that of Cain" (Heb. 11, 4).

In the Ceremonial of the Old Law there were bloody and unbloody sacrifices. The bloody sacrifices were the principal and the most frequent; they again were subdivided into various kinds: a) holocaust (*holocaustum*): in this the animal to be sacrificed was entirely consumed by fire; it was chiefly a sacrifice of praise and worship in acknowledgment of the Divine Majesty;[2] — b) peace-offering (*hostia pacifica*), in which a portion of the flesh was burned, another part was eaten at the sacrificial meal by those who had offered it, and the third part was reserved for the priests; the same had pre-eminently the character of thanksgiving or petition;[3] c) offering of propitiation, called also sin or debt-offering (*hostia*

---

[1] St. Leo, Third Homily for Christmas.

[2] Totum comburebatur, ut, sicut totum animal resolutum in vaporem sursum ascendebat, ita etiam significaretur, totum hominem et omnia quae ipsius sunt, Dei dominio esse subjecta et ei esse offerenda (S. Thom. 1, 2, q. 102, a. 3 ad 8).

[3] Hostia pacifica offerebatur Deo vel pro gratiarum actione, vel pro salute et prosperitate offerentium, ex debito beneficii vel accipiendi vel accepti. Et ista dividebatur in tres partes; nam una pars incendebatur in honorem Dei, alia pars cedebat in usum sacerdotum, tertia vero pars in usum offerentium, ad significandum quod salus hominis procedit a Deo dirigentibus ministris Dei, et cooperantibus ipsis hominibus, qui salvantur (S. Thom. 1. c.).

pro peccato). In this a portion of the flesh was burned and the remainder consumed by the priests;[1] whenever the offering was made
for the sins of the whole people, or in a particular manner for the
sins of the priests, then all was burned. The sacrifice of propitiation
had principally for its object to appease the wrath of God and to obtain the pardon of sin.

3. These sacrifices previous to the Christian era had mainly
the meaning and object essential to every sacrifice: they were acts of
adoration, gratitude, petition and atonement. But in order to be
truly acceptable to God, to possess value and merit in His sight, they
were to be offered with the proper dispositions, that is, the exterior
rite was to be the true expression of the interior act of sacrifice,
of submission, resignation, homage, worship, praise, gratitude, sorrow and compunction.

In consequence of the divine dispensation, the sacrifices of the
Old Law had a still higher meaning, inasmuch as they were typically
to prefigure and represent the approaching sacrifice of Christ on the
Cross.[2] In this consisted their chief object and value.[3] The
typical character of these sacrifices, which rendered them figures
of the sacrifice of Christ, is beyond all doubt most exalted, for
St. Paul fully explains and proves this (Hebr. 8—10). The Old
Law was, indeed, "the bringing in of a better hope, by which
we draw near to God" (Hebr. 7, 19), that is, the preparation
for the New and Eternal Covenant. As St. Augustine teaches,
"in the Old Law the New was hidden, and in the New Law
the Old was unfolded."[4] "In the Old Testament the New was
prefigured; the former was the figure (*figura*), the latter is the
full expression of truth (*expressio veritatis*)."[5]

Now, if the entire Old Testament, and especially its religious
rite, was figurative for the future and preparatory for Christ,
should not also the sacrifices which formed the essential part of
the exterior service have borne the same character and have
served the same end? The Old Law contained "only the shadow
of the good things to come,,"[6] that is, the heavenly gifts of grace

---

[1] Una pars comburebatur, altera vero cedebat in usum sacerdotum, ad significandum, quod expiatio peccatorum fit a Deo per ministerium sacerdotum (S.
Thom. 1. c.).

[2] Per illud singulare sacrificium, in quo Mediator est immolatus, *quod unum
multae in Lege victimae figurabant*, pacificantur coelestia cum terrestribus et ter-
restria cum coelestibus (S. August. Enchirid. c. 16, n. 62).

[3] Patet quare sacrificia placuerunt Deo tempore legis scriptae et spectabant ad
cultum divinum, pro eo quod omnia erant *signa profitentia* et *praefigurantia*
reparationem humanam, quae fuit per oblationem Agni immaculati et effusionem
sanguinis Jesu Christi (S. Bonav. De Myst. Trin. q. 1, a. 2).

[4] In veteri testamento est occultatio novi, in novo testamento est manifestatio
veteris. (S. Aug. De catech. rud. n. 8).

[5] S. Aug. Enarrat. in Ps. 84. n. 4.

[6] "Umbram habens lex futurorum bonorum" (Hebr. 10, 1).

which Christ acquired for us and which He entrusted to the Church;
for this reason the ancient sacrifices were but shadows of the
great atoning sacrifice of Redemption on Golgotha.

4. If we inquire into the efficacy of these sacrifices prior to
the time of Christ, their propitiatory character is most striking.
This is more clearly and forcibly evidenced in the bloody sacrifices, which were also the most frequently offered, since in the
Old Law the consciousness of unpropitiated and punishable guilt
was still predominant. But these bloody sacrifices had not the
power of appeasing an offended and irritated God and of releasing
wretched man from the crushing burden of sin. The Apostle says,
indeed: "It is impossible that with the blood of oxen and goats sins
should be taken away" (Heb. 10, 4), and he therefore calls those
sacrifices "weak and needy elements" (Gal. 4, 9), which could by
no means make the persons who offered them perfect (Heb. 10, 1),
that is, which could neither procure for man the pardon of sin nor
effect interior purification and sanctification.

The carrying out and offering (*ex opere operato*) of the Mosaic
sacrifices imparted only the exterior or legal purification, [1] that is,
they caused the Israelite to be no longer regarded as legally unclean,
and he was, consequently, again permitted to take part in the public
service of God. Thus these sacrifices expressed the necessity of real
atonement and interior purification, and, at the same time, referred
to the future sacrifice of the Cross as the only source of reconciliation,
forgiveness of sin and sanctification. As these imperfect sacrifices
foreshadowed, promised and pledged the perfect redeeming sacrifice
of Christ, they were capable of exciting and fostering true sentiments of sacrifice, that is, they animated the Israelites to faith and
hope, and disposed them to contrition and penance, which are the
necessary conditions of acquiring interior justification (*ex opere
operantis*) [2]. — In the Old Law there was no sacrament which by
its own power and efficacy (*ex opere operato*) could justify and
sanctify the properly disposed recipient; perfect contrition was then
the only means left to adults of obtaining true sanctity and becoming
children of God. Only by a believing hope and contrite love could
men (*ex opere operantis*) draw remission of sin and justification beforehand from the fountain of grace which was to be opened at the
foot of the Cross.

Thus "the old sacrifices were varied and manifold figures of the
real sacrifice of Christ, inasmuch as this *one* sacrifice was prefigured

---

[1] The Apostle calls the same emundatio carnis (Hebr. 9, 13); the theologians
style it expiatio et sanctitas *legalis*.

[2] Poterat mens fidelium tempore legis per fidem *conjungi Christo incarnato
et passo*, et ita ex fide Christi justificabantur, cujus fidei quaedam protestatio erat
hujusmodi caerimoniarum (sc. sacrificiorum) observatio, in quantum erant figura
Christi. Et ideo pro peccatis offerebantur sacrificia quaedam in veteri lege, non
quia ipsa sacrificia a peccato emundarent, sed quia erant quaedam protestationes
fidei, quae a peccato mundabat . . . Peccatum dimittebatur *non vi sacrificiorum*,
sed ex *fide* et *devotione offerentium* (S. Thom. 1. 2, q. 103, a. 2).

by many, just as when *one* idea is expressed in many ways, in order to make a deeper impression [1]. — In this manner the eye of faith was directed to the future, the coming Sacrifice of the Redeemer was confidently and eagerly grasped by the Jews and thus the fruit of the Sacrifice of the Cross was won beforehand. For this the presentiment, the obscure knowledge of the higher meaning concealed in the sacrificial rite was sufficient ; such an understanding of what these sacrifices prefigured could not have been unknown even to the mass of the people, still less could it have been wanting to the specially favored, to whom higher lights concerning the work of redemption were imparted. [2]

CHAPTER THE SECOND.

The Bloody Sacrifice of the Cross.

5. Jesus Christ — the Representative Head of the Human Race.

1. In the sacrifices of the Old Law irrational creatures — objects of possession and enjoyment belonging to the animal or vegetable kingdom — were substituted for man and offered to God in place of human life. Such a substitution was imperfect, inefficacious and, consequently, inadequate. The blood of animals could not atone for sin or relieve man of its debt; but rather kept up "the remembrance of unatoned sin continually alive in those who offered these sacrifices" (Heb. 10. 3, 4), thus awakening the desire of the promised Sacrifice which would, in an incomparably more exalted way, take man's place with God and offer a perfect atonement for the guilt of all sin. This vicarious sacrifice the God-Man, Jesus Christ, offered, inasmuch as He, the Head of the human race, gave His life by a bloody death to present to God not merely a strictly equivalent or fully sufficient, but even a superabundant and overflowing satisfaction for the sins of all mankind.

2. Jesus Christ answered for us and represented us before God, that is, He performed all that God demanded in order to grant us pardon and restore us to grace, — and He indeed performed it for us, that is, in our stead. Hence that which we were obliged to do and yet unable to accomplish, Jesus Christ, as our substitute, performed for us ; — He appeased the Divine Justice and Majesty. The fruits of His sacrifice were to redound to our benefit ; His satisfaction and merits He wished to make over to us, to present them to us that we, being released from sin and its punishment, should also be enriched with the gifts of grace.

It was in order to become, in the most perfect manner imaginable, our substitute or Representative, and to satisfy and merit for

---

[1] S. August De civit. Dei., 1. 10, c. 20. — Cf. S. August. Enarrat. in Ps. 39, n. 12.

[2] Quamvis non omnes sciant explicite virtutem sacrificiorum, sciunt tamen implicite, sicut et habent fidem implicitam (S. Thom. 2. 2, q. 85, a. 4. ad 2).

us, that the Son of God assumed human nature by being born of our race. According to the flesh He was truly, though indeed in a supernatural manner, of our race ; He was *one* of us, He was our Brother. As Christ "gave Himself a redemption for all" (1 Tim. 2, 6), He did not give Himself for strangers, but for His own, for His brethren. "O wonderful exchange," exclaims the Church ; "the Creator of mankind takes a body animated by a soul, and deigns to be born of the Virgin ; and proceeding as man, super-naturally conceived, He imparts to us His divine being !" — From this it follows that Jesus is the spiritual, supernatural Head of man-kind ; this constitutes the mystical body, for which Christ, the Head, offered satisfaction and gained merit. Christ is the second Adam ; as such He superabundantly repaired what the first Adam had destroyed and corrupted. "Therefore as by the offence of one, unto all men to condemnation ; so also by the justice of one, to all men unto justification of life" (Rom. V. 18), that is, as the sin of Adam has come by inheritance upon all his posterity, because God estab-lished him the head of the human family, so, in like manner, the merits and satisfaction of Christ are beneficial to all, because in the order of grace God placed Him at the head of the human race.

3. This consoling truth of the vicarious sacrifice of Christ is frequently alluded to in the writings of the Old and New Testaments ; it is one of the fundamental doctrines of the Christian religion.

How clearly does the Prophet behold and announce (Is. 53, 1—11) the vicarious sacrifice of the sufferings and life of the coming Redeemer ! He calls Christ "the man of sorrows," and says of Him that "He hath borne our infirmities and carried our sorrows," and that "He was wounded for our iniquities, He was bruised for our sins," and this because "the Lord hath laid on Him the iniquity of us all".[1] Our Lord voluntarily and with generous love subjected Himself to these torments and to death, in order to make satisfaction for us ; hence the prophet adds : "He was offered because it was His own will." The fruit of Christ's propitiatory sufferings consists in this, that "by His bruises we are healed."

The Prince of the Apostles had these prophetic words in view when he exhorted the Christians to endure even unjustly inflicted sufferings in silence and with cheerful resignation, looking up to Christ who suffered not only innocently and patiently, but, more-over, in our stead, that is, on account of our sins. "Christ," thus he writes, "who His ownself bore our sins in His body upon the tree (of the Cross), that we, being dead to sin, should live to justice" (1 Peter 2. 24). Christ — the Apostle would say — perfectly in-nocent and sinless, laid the burden of our sins upon Himself and effaced them, inasmuch as He, by the sacrifice of His death on the Cross, atoned and satisfied for them. This expiatory and healing power of the blood of Christ should urge and strengthen us to live hereafter entirely unto justice and holiness of life.

---

[1] Hic *peccata nostra portavit* et pro *nobis dolet* (Resp. eccl.).

"Christ hath redeemed us from the curse of the law, being made a curse for us (ὑπὲρ ἡμῶν)" (Gal. 3, 13), that is, the innocent Lamb of God took upon Himself the burden and punishment of sin in order to free us from it. "But God commendeth His charity toward us, because when as yet we were sinners Christ died for us" (Rom. 5, 8). "In this we have known the charity of God, because He hath laid down His life for us" (1 John 3, 16). "Christ died for all; that they also who live may not now live to themselves, but unto Him who died for them" (2 Cor. 5, 15). The excess of divine love is truly shown in this, that the eternal, the only-begotten Son of God, the King of glory, died the most painful death of the Cross, in order to rescue us poor sinners from the abyss of misery and eternal damnation.

4. This is that "great mystery of godliness, which was manifested in the flesh, was justified in the spirit, appeared unto angels, hath been preached unto the gentiles, is taken up to glory" (1 Tim. 3, 16). O adorable mystery! what unmerited, incomprehensible favor and mercy of God radiates towards us in this marvellous decree and work of the redemption! God's justice required a perfect, an infinite satisfaction — and His mercy gave us the God-Man, Jesus Christ, who as our Mediator offered this satisfaction for us. "God who spared not even His own Son, but delivered Him up for us all, how hath He not also, with Him, given us all things?" (Rom. 8. 32.) Thus hath "God, whose mercies are without number and whose goodness is an inexhaustible treasure," Himself bestowed on us this great atoning sacrifice, which in return He deigned to accept from us[1]. Let us, then, gratefully acknowledge this with the Beloved Disciple : "In this is charity, not as though we had loved God, but because He hath first loved us, and sent His Son to be a propitiation for our sins" (1 John 4, 10). — Still more powerfully should we be penetrated with the desire to return love for love and with most joyful thanksgiving, when we, with full right, apply personally to ourselves what has been done for all; when we so consider the great benefit of redemption as if it had been conferred on ourselves only, as the Apostle so simply and so touchingly expresses it : "And I live, now not I; but Christ liveth in me. And that I now live in the flesh; I live in the faith of the Son of God, who loved me and delivered Himself for me" (Gal. 2, 20)[2]. Thus every one may and should exclaim : Christ has loved me, and for the love of me, has

---

[1] Quid misericordius intelligi valet, quam cum peccatori damnato aeternis tormentis et unde se redimat non habenti, Deus Pater dicit: Accipe Unigenitum meum et da pro te; et ipse Filius: Tolle me et redde pro te? (S. Anselm. Lib. "Cur Deus homo," cap. 9).

[2] Licet ego *in carne vivam*, non tamen secundum carnis inclinationes vivo, sed spiritualiter vivo in fide Christi, Filii Dei et veri Dei qui *dilexit me et tradidit semet ipsum* in mortem *pro me*. Dilexit me amore immenso et aeterno, et in tempore obtulit se in sacrificium pro me, et licet omnes dilexerit sitque pro omnibus mortuus, dico tamen, ipsum *me* dilexisse et *pro me* esse mortuum, qui adeo me dilexit, tantumque ei debeo, quantum si me *solum* dilexisset et pro me solo passus esset (Arias, Thesaur. inexhaust. 1, tr. 4. cap. 18).

sacrificed His blood and life for me, for my sins; for our Saviour in the Garden of Olives and on the Cross had each one of us present to His mind and in His heart, for each one of us He suffered and died, as though each one of us had been alone in the world. This thought should inflame and inspire our heart to make every sacrifice in the service of God. *Quaerens me sedisti lassus — redemisti crucem passus — tantus labor non sit cassus* (Dies irae).

6. The Highpriesthood of Jesus Christ.

As the Representative of the whole human race, Jesus Christ rendered to the offended majesty of God a satisfaction equalling and far exceeding the guilt, in order to take away the sin which was the cause of the separation and enmity existing between heaven and earth. Hence, as mediator between God and man (1 Tim. 2, 5), He established peace, consummated the work of reconciliation, and that too, by the Cross, that is, by the bloody death of the Cross, inasmuch as He offered Himself and His life as a propitiatory sacrifice. Christ's death on the Cross is, therefore, a sacrifice in the strictest sense of the word — truly a death offered in sacrifice and truly a victim. It follows from this that, as Christ during His mortal life on earth exercised the priestly office, i. e., as He really and truly offered sacrifice, He must also be really and truly a priest; for only a priest can and may offer sacrifice. — A closer consideration of the priesthood of Christ will prepare the way to a clearer understanding of the Sacrifice of the Cross.

1. Jesus Christ is "the great Highpriest" (ἀρχιερεὺς μέγας — Hebr. 4, 14) for the whole human race. The truth and dignity of the priesthood of Christ is circumstantially and diversely set forth by the Apostle in his Epistle to the Hebrews (Chap. 4—10). In what do the essence of the priestly office, the vocation and the mission of the priest consist? "For every highpriest taken from among men is ordained for men in the things that appertain to God, that he may offer up gifts and sacrifices for sins" (Heb. 5. 1). Accordingly, the priest is destined and qualified to be a mediator between God and the people; — consequently, to render to the Divine Majesty by sacrifice and prayer due honor and suitable atonement for sin, and to purify and sanctify men by dispensing grace and heavenly blessings.[1] — The proper and essential office of the priest is the offering of sacrifice; the position, rank and prerogatives of the priesthood are

---

[1] All these qualifications are indicated in the name *sacerdos* (= *sacrum vel sacra dans*). Therefore by a priest is meant a consecrated person (*persona sacra*), who by virtue of his ordination is empowered and called to impart that which is holy (*sacra dare* as *dispensator mysteriorum Dei* — 1 Cor. 4, 1). In the next place the priest is *sacra dans* = offerens Deo, in so far as he performs the acts of divine worship (sacrifice and psalmody); — then he is also *sacra dans* = ministrans vel distribuens hominibus, in so far as he imparts grace to men by administering the sacraments and sacramentals. — *Sacerdos . . .* quasi *sacrum dans*: sicut enim rex a regendo, ita sacerdos *a sanctificando* vocatus est; consecrat enim et sanctificat (S. Isid. Hispal. Etymolog. 1. 8, c. 12, n. 17). — Cf. S. August. Enarrat. in Ps. 44, n. 17.

measured and judged by the nature of the sacrifice. Now, since Christ offered an infinitely precious sacrifice of adoration, propitiation, thanksgiving and petition, whereby He procured to God all honor and glory, and to man grace and salvation, He is "the great Highpriest" of the whole human race. Therefore, Christ is not a priest of the same order as those, who before His coming were invested with the priestly office, or who after Him exercise the same: He is, indeed, the most exalted and the most perfect priest; His priestly power is so extensive and so complete, that it cannot be imparted to a mere creature. His divine-human priesthood is the fountain of all the priestly powers and all the divine graces that ever were or may hereafter be imparted to a mere mortal; He is the eternal Highpriest who at all times saves all those who by Him approach to God. He is the Highpriest for all men and for all times. "There were of course priests before Him and there are priests after Him. But the former were destined only to prefigure, by the sacrifices they offered, the one great Sacrifice of Jesus Christ, in order thereby to preserve in mankind faith in the promised Redeemer. The priests of the New Law do not approach the altar in their own name and person, but in the name and in the person of Jesus Christ; and it is He who by them and in them exercises the priestly office, continually representing His great Sacrifice to the Father. Thus, He is in truth, the **ONE** Highpriest for the whole human race"[1].

2. It is God Himself who imparts His powers to the priest. No one can and no one may venture to exercise the priestly office, if he has not been chosen and invested therewith by God. "Neither doth any man take the honor (of priesthood) to himself, but he that is called by God, as Aaron was" (Heb. 5, 4). It is self-evident that Christ is a priest, not according to His divine, but according to His human nature; for it is only by acts of His sacred humanity that He can perform the part of mediator and priest. "So Christ also did not glorify Himself that He might be made a highpriest" (Heb. 5, 5), but God has constituted Him a highpriest forever, and that with a solemn oath: "The Lord hath sworn, and He will not repent: Thou art a priest forever according to the order of Melchisedech" (Ps. 109, 4).

The vocation and selection of Christ for the dignity of highpriest was already contained in the eternal decree of God that His divine Son should redeem the world by means of the Sacrifice of the Cross. — His installation into the office of highpriest took place at the first moment of the Incarnation. Namely, as soon as the human nature was created and hypostatically (personally) united to the Eternal Word, the God-Man undertook, in cheerful obedience to the will and decree of His Heavenly Father, the task and mission of offering His precious life on the Cross as a sacrifice for the world, whereby the ancient sacrifices were not only replaced but far surpassed. This is touchingly expressed by St. Paul quoting and explaining the words of the Prophet (Ps. 39, 7—9. Heb. 10, 5—7).

---

[1] Kleutgen, Predigten, 1. Abth., p. 81—82.

After depicting the impotency and the inadequateness of the priest-hood of the Old Law and of its sacrifices, the apostle continues: "Wherefore when Christ cometh into the world (that is, at the first moment of the Incarnation) He saith to God: Sacrifice and oblation (these empty figures of future goods) Thou wouldst not; but a body Thou hast fitted to Me (for sacrifice). Holocausts for sin did not please Thee. Then, said I, behold I come: at the head of the book it is written of Me: that I should do Thy will, O God (by the sacri-fice of Myself)!" These words constitute the vow of Christ's sacri-fice, that is, the solemn formula in which He vowed to His Heavenly Father, by the Sacrifice of the Cross "to re-establish all things that are in heaven and on earth" (Eph. 1, 10). Therefore, the Apostle adds: "In this will we were sanctified once for all by the Sacrifice of the Body of Jesus Christ," — that is, by the one offering of His bloody atoning sacrifice, which was of infinite value and merit. Christ has acquired for us all grace and sanctification, in obeying with His human will the Divine will of His Father — even to the death of the Cross.

3. Jesus Christ was infinitely worthy of being clothed and adorned with the most eminent dignity of highpriest. — The priest, by his office, is mediator between God and man: it is chiefly by the offering of Sacrifice that he is to glorify God and to reconcile man to Him, and to obtain for man in return the favor and friendship of God, applying to him the fruits and graces of the Sacrifice. [1] To be enabled to exercise, in a perfect manner, the office of mediator, he must also take a medium position, namely, be related and united to God as well as to men, in order to transact the affairs of both properly and successfully. The priest "is ordained for men in all things that appertain to God," to appease God's anger and to draw down His blessing upon the earth: therefore, he must be pleasing in the sight of God by being free from sin and by exalted sanctity; but he is also "ordained for men" to care for their salvation, to pray, to labor and to suffer: hence "he is taken from among men, that he may have compassion on them that are ignorant and that err; because he him-self is also encompassed with infirmity" (Heb. 5, 1—2). In this twofold relation Christ unites in His person, in the most perfect manner, all that can render the priest acceptable to God and power-ful with Him, full of compassion and mercy toward men.

a) Jesus Christ is infinitely holy; therefore, God the Father takes infinite pleasure in Him. "For it was fitting that we should have such a Highpriest, holy, innocent, undefiled, separated from sinners, and made higher than the heavens" (Heb. 7, 26). The whole fulness of the divinity, an inexhaustible treasure of grace and truth, of virtue and wisdom, of holiness and happiness, was bestowed on the soul of Christ — and that already in the first moment of her creation and hypostatic union with "the Eternal Son of the Eternal

---

[1] Offert Deo bonus mediator preces et vota populorum: reportans illis a Deo benedictionem et gratiam (S. Bernard., Tract. de morib. et offic. episcop., c. 3. n. 10). — Cf. S. Thom. 2, 2, q. 86, a. 2.

Father." — By virtue of the hypostatic union the humanity of Christ was deified (*deificata*, θεωθεῖσα), essentially and infinitely sanctified. At the same time, this "grace of union" (*gratia unionis*) is to be considered as the root and germ of all other supernatural privileges and perfections of the human nature of Christ: sanctifying grace, the infused virtues,[1] the gifts of the Holy Ghost, the graces — in superabundance, in the fullest and richest conceivable measure — were the suitable, inamissible and inaugmentable endowment (portion) of the soul of Christ, which by its mystical union with the divinity attained an infinite dignity. In all these privileges — in the hypostatic union, in the Beatific Vision of God, in the fulness of grace — the absolute freedom of Christ from sin is based: the soul of Jesus was not only actually free from all sin, but it was incapable of committing sin, and not susceptible of even the slightest breath or shadow of sin.[2] Thus Christ as man is "the Saint of saints" (Dan. 9, 24). — From this infinite dignity and holiness of our Highpriest, Jesus Christ, proceeds the infinite value of all His labors and sufferings, of all His merits and satisfactions during His mortal life.

b) "We therefore have a great Highpriest, Jesus Christ the Son of God" (Heb. 4, 14), who is most pleasing to God by His infinite majesty and fulness of grace. On the other hand, the perfection of His priestly life and labors was greatly enhanced, in so far as He voluntarily humbled Himself taking the form of a servant, lovingly subjected Himself to the infirmities of fallen man and cheerfully assumed our weaknesses. — This self-renunciation He practised as well for the sake of penance and atonement, as for our example and consolation, that we, "looking on Him, who having joy set before Him endured the shame"(Heb. 12, 2), may neither succumb to the labors and difficulties of our earthly pilgrimage, nor despond amid the fears and anguish of death.[3] The keen air, the cold and

---

[1] Those virtues only are excepted which presuppose or include incompatibility with the *unio hypostatica* and the *visio beatifica*. With regard to the theological controversy, in and how far the *habitus fidei, spei et poenitentiae* may be ascribed to the soul of Christ, cf. Stentrup, S. J., De Verbo incarnato, P. 1, Christolog. thes. 81.

[2] Dives est qui nec hereditario nec proprio unquam debito obnoxius, et ipse justus est et alios justificat Christus (S. Aug. in Joann. tr. 84, n. 2).

[3] Absque dubio congruum fuit, Christum assumere naturam nostram cum defectibus et poenalitatibus, et hoc triplici ex causa, principaliter videlicet propter *pretium* nostrae salutis, propter *exemplum* virtutis et propter *fulcimentum* nostrae fragilitatis. — Propter *pretium* nostrae salutis, quia proposuerat nos redimere *non corruptibilibus auro et argento, sed pretioso sanguine suo* (1 Petr. 1, 18), et animam suam ponere pro animabus nostris. Ad hoc autem non esset idoneus, nisi naturam deficientem et passibilem assumpsisset, et propterea defectus nostros et poenalitates debuit in seipso habere. — Alia etiam ex causa congruum fuit hoc ipsum, videlicet propter *exemplum* virtutis, specialiter autem humilitatis, patientiae et pietatis, quibus mediantibus pervenitur ad coelum, et in quibus Christus voluit nos imitari ipsum secundum illud: "Discite a me, quia mitis sum et humilis corde" (Matth. II, 29). — Tertia ratio est propter *fulcimentum* nostrae fragilitatis, ob quam natura rationalis habet in se difficultatem ad *credendum vera*, et irascibilis ad *sperandum ardua*, et concupiscibilis ad *amandum bona*. Et ideo voluit Christus

heat affected His delicate body; His holy soul was filled with fear and anguish, with sadness and sorrow; He was hungry and thirsty, He travelled and was fatigued, He fled and concealed Himself; He groaned in spirit and was afflicted; He wept with us poor mortals in this vale of tears. Therefore, how animating and encouraging, how refreshing and consoling, is it to glance devoutly at our Redeemer who so lovingly immolated Himself to the sufferings, infirmities and wants of our mortal life. This the apostle teaches when he says: "Wherefore it behooved Him in all things to be made like unto His brethren, that He might become a merciful and faithful Highpriest before God, that He might be a propitiation for the sins of the people. For we have not a Highpriest who cannot have compassion on our infirmities: but one tempted in all things like as we are — without sin. For in that, wherein He Himself hath suffered and been tempted, He is able to succor them also that are tempted. Let us go, therefore, with confidence to the throne of grace, that we may obtain mercy, and find grace in seasonable aid (Heb. 2, 17—18; 4, 15—16).

The heavenly privileges and prerogatives of the humanity of Christ, by which He approached so near to God, as well as the earthly infirmities and miseries which He compassionately shared with us, have contributed to give honor and glory to the Father, (John 8, 49; 14, 23),[1] and also to redeem and sanctify mankind. Christ stooped to us, in order to raise us up; His humiliation is our exaltation, His poverty our riches; His sufferings are our joys, His wounds our cure, His death is our life. Our Lord is not only great, holy and powerful, and therefore infinitely worthy of praise; but also "for us men and for our salvation" He became little, poor, insignificant, and, therefore, infinitely deserving of love. *"Tanto mihi carior, quanto pro me vilior!"* Yes, we have such a Redeemer that the Church in ecstatic, overflowing exaltation of heart can sing: *O felix culpa, quae talem ac tantum meruit habere Redemptorem!* "O happy fault, which has merited such and so great a Redeemer!" "Truly should we be exeedingly joyful over the happy change, in consequence of which we have been transferred from earthly lowliness

---

non tantum nobis similari in natura, sed etiam in defectibus et poenalitatibus ut, manifestando in se *veritatem* humanae naturae, praeberet fulcimentum nostrae rationali ad *credendum;* ostendendo nihilominus immensitatem suae misericordiae per susceptionem nostrae miseriae, praeberet irascibili fulcimentum ad *sperandum;* ostendendo magnitudinem suae benevolentiae, praeberet concupiscibili incitamentum ad *se amandum.* — Et ideo licet incongruum videatur, hujusmodi defectus reperiri in Christo, si per se considerentur; tamen, si ad finem referantur, magna reperitur congruitatis condecentia (S. Bonav. IV, dist. 15, a. 1. q. 1). — Cfr. S. Thom. 3, q. 14, a. 1.

[1] Quoniam Deus est justus et beatus, impassibilis et immortalis, homo vero lapsus est peccator et miser, passibilis et mortalis: necesse fuit, mediatorem Dei et hominum, ut posset hominem reducere ad Deum, cum Deo communicare in justitia et beatitudine, cum homine vero in passibilitate et mortalitate, ut sic habendo mortalitatem transeuntem et beatitudinem permanentem, hominem reduceret de praesenti miseria ad vitam beatam (S. Bonav. Breviloq. P. 4, c. 8).

to the glory of heaven, through the unspeakable mercy of Him who has descended to us, in order to elevate us to Him ; so that He assumed not only the form, but also the condition of our sinful humanity, and that His divinity, incapable of suffering, permitted all the misery of mortal humanity to come upon him." [1]

7. The Death of Jesus Christ on the Cross a True and Real Sacrifice.

Jesus Christ was in His mortal life, as He is now, that He sitteth at the right hand of the throne of majesty in the heavens (Heb. 8, 1), the perfect Mediator, the true and great Highpriest of the human race. Hence it follows that He must have offered a real sacrifice on earth ; for the offering of sacrifice is the first and essential duty of a priest. "For every highpriest is appointed to offer gifts and sacrifices : wherefore it is necessary that he should also have something to offer" (Heb. 8, 3). Christ offered Himself as an unspotted sacrifice unto God (Heb. 9, 14) on the Cross, upon which He, as the Good Shepherd, gave His life for His sheep. To this end the Father had sanctified and sent Him into the world (John 11, 36) at the moment of the Incarnation. God willed, namely, that the redemption and restoration of the human race should be accomplished by the bloody sacrifice of the Cross ; therefore, in loving obedience to the will of His Father, when the hour had come, Jesus Christ offered Himself, His body and blood, upon the altar of the Cross for the life of the world, so that "He Himself was the priest offering the sacrifice as well as the sacrifice offered" (*ipse offerens, ipse et oblatio*). [2] — The death of Christ on the Cross, the offering of His body and the shedding of His blood for the human race, is a sacrifice in the strictest and fullest sense of the word, not in a merely wide or figurative sense, as was His whole life upon earth. This His life constituted the preparation for the sacrificial death of Christ and is justly designated, in a wider sense, as a sacrifice ; for even in those mysteries of Christ which preceded His passion and death, we everywhere find the intention, will and deeds of sacrifice. [3]

1. Holy self-sacrifice forms the seal of the life of Christ on earth : His life was a constant martyrdom, a bloody sacrifice of mortification, an incense-offering of devotion and prayer, a burnt-offering of love for God and men. — Truly, the whole earthly career of Christ from the womb of His Mother to the grave, was a sacrifice of abnegation and self-denial. A vail of mourning shrouded His entire life, bearing the character of severe penance and atonement for a world full of frivolity, sinful, sensual enjoyment and horrible godlessness.

---

[1] St. Leo, First Discourse on the Resurrection of our Lord.

[2] S. August., De civit. Dei, l. 10, c. 20.

[3] Tota vita et conversatio Christi in carne mortali a primo incarnationis instanti usque ad instans suae expirationis in cruce, fuit quasi una continua missa et celebratio, qua se indesinenter obtulit Patri pro nobis voluntate promptissima et affectuosissime oravit pro nobis, et quidquid deliberata voluntate precatus est, impetravit (Dion. Carthus,, Elementat. theolog., propos. 119).

— This painful way began in the crib, to end only on the Cross:
crib and Cross are closely connected with each other. In the crib
Jesus lay as a meek, lovely Infant-God; on the Cross He was suspended, His body torn and bleeding: but in the one situation as well
as in the other, He is the Lamb sacrificed for the sins of the world.
Calvary cast its shadow upon His hidden, silent life at Bethlehem
and Nazareth. "Poor and sorrowful" (Ps. 68, 30) was Jesus
throughout the whole course of his life. Privations, humiliations,
sufferings were His inseparable companions: they surrounded Him
on His entrance into the world, accompanied Him during His earthly
pilgrimage and ascended with Him on the Cross. — Whatever the
world cherishes, seeks and values, all its joys, riches and glory, all
its pomp and grandeur, He despised and disdained; in their stead
He endured poverty, hardships, hostility, contradictions, vexations
innumerable, such as only an unbounded love could choose and endure. As a stranger who had not whereon to lay His head, did the
Lord of Heaven dwell many years upon this earth, — an earth yielding thorns and thistles. At the same time, we must remember that
His pure, delicate body and noble and holy soul were created peculiarly susceptible of suffering, and consequently experienced, a thousand times more than men can imagine, the severity, acuteness and
bitterness of all corporal and spiritual sufferings. — His infancy,
boyhood and youth were passed in retirement and obscurity, in
poverty and self-denial, in painful labor and austere penance; also
the three years of His public life, His ministry among an "unbelieving and perverse generation" (Matt. 17, 16) were filled with
bitterness arising from the inappreciation, ingratitude and persecution on the part of His own nation; and this was all the more
painful to Him, since He had come but to seek and save those who
were lost. He was repudiated, blasphemed and calumniated by the
obdurate Jews, so that before leaving this world, He could apply to
Himself these words of the Prophet: "They have hated Me without
cause" (John 15, 25; cf. Ps. 68, 5), and He could say to His disciples: "If the world hate you, know ye that it hath hated Me before you" (John 15, 18).

An offering of sweetest incensed prayer, ascending to God from
the golden altar that stands before the throne of God (Apoc. 8, 1—4),
was the wonderful life of our Saviour under the form of a servant.
The fire of devotion burned unceasingly with heavenly ardor and
purity in His Sacred Heart. All the days and nights, yea, all the
hours of His poor, humble and painful life He consecrated by prayer,
by the most sublime and powerful prayer that ever pierced the clouds
and mounted to the throne of the Most High.

In fine, the life of Jesus was a most perfect holocaust of the
purest love of God and man. His food was to do the will of His
Heavenly Father (John 4, 34); at the close of His earthly career,
He could say to His Father: "I have glorified Thee on the earth: I
have finished the work which Thou gavest Me to do" (John 17, 4).
Like unto the flame of sacrifice the zeal glowed in His breast for the

house of God and for the honor of His Father, and "consumed" Him as the burning wick consumes the altar taper (John 2, 17). — From this fervent love of God proceeded the flame of His zeal for the conversion and the salvation of mankind.

What our Lord thus did and suffered "in the days of His flesh," during His three and thirty years upon earth, would have been more than sufficient to redeem thousands of worlds, to amass untold treasures of grace and merits; but according to the adorable decree of God, this did not suffice to free us from the slavery of sin and purchase for us the liberty of the children of God; for this the price of the blood and life of Christ was requisite. The justice of God required this ransom for our redemption, and Christ voluntarily, through love, offered Himself to pay it for us; Christ's death on the Cross was to constitute the crown, the conclusion and the completion of the work of redemption. That the death of Christ is a true and real sacrifice is especially taught by the word of God, and has at all times been believed and acknowledged by Christians.

2. From a multiplicity of proofs only a few will be given here.

a) The primary object of the sacrifices of the Old Testament, particularly the principal ones, that is, the bloody sacrifices, was to prefigure and to represent the offering of the life of Jesus by a violent death. Now, if these imperfect figures and representations of the only and truly redeeming death of Christ on the Cross were, without doubt, real sacrifices, must not His death itself have been a real sacrifice, a sacrifice in every sense of the word? The reality, fulfilment and consummation cannot and must not be inferior to the shadow, figure and representation. The holy Pope St. Leo thus very beautifully expresses this thought: "In the public sacrifice was to be fulfilled what in the figurative mystery had long before been promised: that the true Sacrificial Lamb was to supplant the figurative, (ut *uno* expleretur sacrificio variarum *differentia* victimarum) and that in *one* sacrifice the various, manifold sacrifices were to find their accomplishment: for all that which was ordained beforehand by God through Moses relative to the sacrifice of the lamb, predicted the Redeemer and explicitly announced the sacrificial death of Christ. That, therefore, the shadows might depart from the body, and figures cease at the appearance of truth, the old custom was abolished by the new mystery, the victim passed over into the Victim, (hostia in hostiam transit), blood replaced by blood, and the legal celebration found its fulfilment inasmuch as it was changed."[1]

b) What the sacrificial worship of the Old Law prefigured in a mystical sense, the Prophet, enlightened by God, announced beforehand in a precise and touching manner: prophesying the sacrificial character of the passion and death of Jesus Christ. Isaias[2] says ex-

---

[1] Seventh Discourse on the Sufferings of the Lord.

[2] Posuit Dominus in eo iniquitatem omnium nostrum. Oblatus est, quia ipse voluit ... sicut ovis ad occisionem ducetur et quasi agnus coram tondente se obmutescet ... si posuerit pro peccato (as a sin-offering) animam suam, videbit semen longaevum (Is. 53, 4—12).

pressly that Christ would suffer and die for our sins, and that the
death which He would voluntarily undergo for us would be a true
atoning sacrifice: "He was offered because it was His own will."
Then the Prophet compares the Saviour to a sheep led to the slaughter and not opening its mouth, as well as to a lamb dumb before its
shearer: these pathetic symbols are intended to signify that He,
though innocent, would undergo the painful sacrificial death in quiet
resignation and peace. An eternal spiritual generation is designated
as the fruit of His atoning sacrifice, that is, the whole assembly of
the predestined whom no one can number, all those whose names are
written in the Book of Life — they were and they will be saved only
by the redeeming blood of Christ shed for them.

c) In the Old Law a lamb was one of the animals most usually
sacrificed: recall the Paschal Lamb, the daily morning and evening
sacrifice. As Christ was prefigured by these lambs, it is quite natural
that in the New Law He should often be represented and extolled as
the true Lamb, the Lamb without blemish, as our Pasch, as the
Lamb of God; in the Apocalypse of St. John there occurs in many
places the word Lamb *(Agnus)* even as the very name of the God-
Man. The designation of Jesus as the Lamb is, then, characteristic,
and is intended to express that His death is a sacrifice, a real propitiatory sacrifice, — drawing attention, at the same time, to the
heavenly meekness, resignation and patience that He displayed
during His passion. The Prince of the Apostles reminds us of this,
when he says that "The Lord did no sin, neither was guile found in
His mouth. Who, when He was reviled, did not revile: when He
suffered, He threatened not: but delivered Himself to him that
judged Him unjustly" (Peter 2, 22—23). — St. John Baptist alludes
to Christ as "the Lamb of God, who taketh away the sins of the
world,"[1] that is, who reconciles Heaven and earth by shedding
His blood. — St. Paul exhorts us to celebrate the true spiritual
Pasch, since Christ our Pasch is sacrificed.[2] — St. Peter, the
Prince of the Apostles, encourages and exhorts Christians to lead
a holy life in view of the glorious ransom by which they have
been redeemed: "Walk in (holy and wholesome) fear during the
time of your sojourning here. Knowing that you were not redeemed with corruptible things, as gold and silver, but with the
precious blood of Christ, as a lamb unspotted and undefiled"
(1 Peter, 1, 19). Therefore, Christ, absolutely sinless and holy,
is the Lamb, the Victim perfectly faultless and infinitely pleasing to
God, whose blood effaces all sin and effects true reconciliation. —
Writing on these texts of Scripture, St. Leo remarks that "the
reconciliation of the Immaculate Lamb and the fulness of all the
sacraments were imparted to us," and then adds, "Christ offered

---

[1] Ecce Agnus (ὁ ἀμνός — the prophetically foretold lamb as a victim) Dei
ecce qui tollit (ὁ αἴρων — who has the power to take upon Himself and thereby
to take away) peccatum mundi (all the sins of all men). John 1, 29.

[2] Pascha nostrum (our paschal Lamb) immolatus est (ἐτύθη — being slain,
is offered as a bloody sacrifice) Christus (1 Cor. 5, 7).

Himself to the Father as a new and truly reconciling sacrifice,''
and that it was not in the Temple nor within the limits of the
city, but outside of it and the camp that He was crucified, so
that after the old, figurative, immolated sacrifices should cease,
"a new Sacrifice would be placed upon the new altar, and the Cross
of Christ should be the altar not of the Temple, but of the world"
(nova hostia novo imponeretur altari et crux Christi non templi esset
ara, sed mundi. — De pass. Dom. Serm. 8, n. 5).

d) Our Lord Himself declared that He had come "to give His
life a new redemption for many."[1]   Vicarious blood-shedding or
the giving up of life is, indeed, a real sacrifice.   Shortly before His
departure from this world, Christ in His prayer, as Highpriest, called
His death a sanctification, that is, a dedication and offering of Himself for His disciples, to merit for them true sanctity, interior purification from sin and justification : "For them do I sanctify Myself :
that they also may be sanctified in truth."[2] — St. John writes :
"Jesus is the propitiation for our sins : and not for ours only, but
also for those of the whole world."[3]   St. Paul says that we become
justified "through the redemption that is in Christ Jesus, whom God
hath proposed to be a propitiation through faith in His blood."[4]   To
restrain the faithful from sin and to animate them to the practice of
virtue, the Apostle represents to them the intimate and courageous,
tender and generous love of Christ, by which He offered Himself for
us : "Be ye, therefore, followers of God, as most dear children, and
walk in love as Christ also hath loved us and hath given Himself for
us as an oblation and a sacrifice to God for an odor of sweetness"[5]
— In the Epistle to the Hebrews the doctrine of the vicarious and
atoning death of Christ is repeatedly expressed in the clearest and
most emphatic manner.   The Apostle therein proves the dignity and
efficacy of the bloody sacrifice of Christ on the Cross in contrast with
the inefficacious offerings of the Old Testament.   To abolish and remove these inefficient figures, Christ offered "the sacrifice of His
body," the sweet odor of which ascended to heaven, drawing down

---

[1]   Dare animam suam (His soul = His life, His blood, Himself) redemptionem
(λύτρον = money or price of ransom) pro multis (ἀντὶ πολλῶν, representative for
many, who actually obtain the full result or fruit of the redemption in heaven).
Mat. 20, 28.

[2]   Pro eis ego sanctifico meipsum (= in sanctam hostiam me tibi offero et im-
molo in cruce), ut sint et ipsi sanctificati in veritate (Joann. 17, 19).

[3]   Ipse est propitiatio (ἱλασμός=sacrificium expiationis) pro peccatis nostris :
non pro nostris autem tantum, sed etiam pro totius mundi (1 Joann. 2, 2).

[4]   Quem proposuit (προέθετο, publicly erected on the cross) Deus propitiationem
(as a sacrifice of reconciliation ἱλαστήριον) per fidem in sanguine ipsius (Rom. 3,
25).   God gave up His Son and revealed Him on the cross as a propitiatory sacrifice, which He "in His own blood," i. e., by shedding His blood, offered, and in
which we share "by faith" (διὰ τῆς πίστεως).

[5]   Christus dilexit nos et tradidit semetipsum pro nobis oblationem (προσφοράν)
et hostiam (θυσίαν) in odorem suavitatis (Eph. 5, 2). — Christus obtulit sacrificium suavitatis summae pro perfecta Dei placatione (S. Bonav. Breviloq. p. 4, c. 9).

God's favor and grace, procuring for us all salvation and sanctification. "How much more shall the blood of Christ, who by the
Holy Ghost offered Himself unspotted unto God, cleanse our conscience from dead works (that is, from sin), to serve the living God"
(9, 14). "To offer sacrifices for the sins of the people, this Christ
did once, in offering Himself" (7, 27). "But now once at the end
of ages, He hath appeared for the destruction of sin in sacrifice (*per
hostiam suam*); so also Christ was offered once (*oblatus est*) to exhaust the sins of many" (9, 26, 28).

3.   Now, how is Christ's death on the Cross to be understood
as a true sacrifice? In how far does it contain all the constituents
of a sacrifice taken in its strict sense? — Upon the altar of the Cross,
Jesus Christ, the great Highpriest, as the representative of the human
race, dedicated His precious life to the most painful of deaths, thus
worthily to glorify and perfectly propitiate the Divine Majesty, as
well as to regain for man the favor and grace of God.

a) He who was sacrificed on the Cross, was Jesus Christ, the
Man-God and our Highpriest. Hence it was a divine Person, it
was the Son of God Himself who was offered on Mount Calvary; but
He could offer the sacrifice only through His human nature, that is,
by acts of love and obedience, of humility and submission, with
which His holy soul was filled and inflamed. This sacrifice was of an
infinite value and merit, because it proceeded from and was offered
by an infinite Person.

b) That which was offered on the Cross — the Victim — was
also the Son of God according to His human nature; in other words,
it was the human nature, in so far as it was united to the Eternal
Word and through this union possessed of infinite dignity. Thus
Jesus Christ was not only the Priest of His sacrifice, but also the
sacrifice of His priesthood, when He offered Himself, His life, His
body and His blood on the tree of the holy Cross. For according
to St. Peter, "it is the Author of life (*auctor vitae*) you killed"
(Acts 3, 15); according to St. John, "God hath laid down His life
for us"(1 John 3, 16); according to St. Paul, "the Jews crucified the
Lord of Glory" and "God purchased the Church with His own
blood" (1 Cor. 2, 8; Acts 20, 28). [1]

In the Sacrifice of the Cross, therefore, the God-Man [2] is the

---

[1] Absque dubio concedendum est, *Filium Dei* pro nobis fuisse mortuum, et
hoc quidem sibi vere attribuitur *non* secundum naturam *divinam*, sed secundum
humanam . . . Et hoc in nullo derogat divinae dignitati et multum consonat pietati. Nullum enim verbum majoris dignationis resonare potest in auribus cordis
nostri, quam quod unigenitus Dei Filius mortuus fuerit pro nobis debitoribus
mortis. Et ideo non tantum est hoc credendum et asserendum tamquam verum,
sed etiam *frequentissime recolendum* (S. Bonav. III, dist. 21, a. 2, q. 3).

[2] The Son of God alone — not the Father and not the Holy Ghost — is both
Priest and Victim, because and inasmuch as He alone assumed human nature,
which placed Him in a condition to sacrifice and to be sacrificed; but according to
His divine nature, by which He is one with the Father and the Holy Ghost, He receives and accepts the Sacrifice which is perpetually offered to the triune God.

priest offering and, at the same time, the lamb offered : He offers and He is offered according to His human nature. He is Priest and offers, in as far as He acts without restraint and freely gives His life ; He is the Victim and He is offered, inasmuch as He suffers pain and undergoes death, in order to be slain for the honor of God.[1]

c) Since the offering of sacrifice pertains to the priest, it must, consequently, have been accomplished by our Saviour Himself upon Golgotha. — Evidently it did not consist in the physical execution effected by the enemies and tormentors of Jesus, but in the voluntary acceptation and endurance of the bloody death on the part of the Man-God as Highpriest. The executioners and soldiers who lacerated our Lord, wished to kill Him and in reality they did so with violence and cruelty, but in nowise did they sacrifice Him ; they did not perform a work pleasing to God, but rather committed the greatest of outrages.[2] "The Lord took upon Himself what, according to the decree of His will, He hath chosen ; He permitted the hands of the godless to rage against Him, this became of service to Him in the performance of their own transgressions."[3] — Jesus Christ acting as priest on the Cross performed the sacrificial act without compulsion, but of His most free choice He shed His blood amid unspeakable pains, and in prompt obedience gave His infinitely precious life, in order to glorify and to propitiate the majesty of the most High dishonored by sin. — To be a real sacrifice, Christ's passion and death had to be entirely voluntary, that is, to depend upon His human will, to be accepted by it and directed to the divine glory. That this was really the case is frequently and strongly proved in Holy Writ : "Christ was offered because it was His own will" (Isa. 53, 7). — In the first place, the willingness of Christ to undergo His passion and death is evidenced by His allowing sinners to afflict and torment His body, although by His human will He could easily have prevented it ; for without or against His will all the powers of this world and all the rage of hell could not have done Him the slightest harm. When His hour had come, the Saviour voluntarily surrendered Himself into the hands of His enemies and ascended the altar of the Cross ; for by His mere words, "I am He" (John 18, 6), He prostrated the soldiers to the ground, rendered His

---

[1] Nihil mundum (Christus) invenit in hominibus, quod offerret pro hominibus : seipsum obtulit mundam victimam. Felix victima, vera victima, hostia immaculata! Non ergo hoc obtulit, quod nos illi dedimus : immo hoc obtulit, quod a nobis accepit et mundum obtulit. Carnem enim a nobis accepit, hanc obtulit. Sed unde illam accepit? De utero Virginis Mariae, ut mundam offerret pro immundis. Ipse rex, ipse sacerdos : in eo laetemur (S. August. Enarrat. in Ps. 149, n. 6). — Formam servi obtulit (Christus), in hac oblatus est : quia secundum hanc mediator est, in hac sacerdos, in hac sacrificium est (S. August. De civit. Dei, l. x, c. 6).

[2] Passio Christi ex parte occidentium ipsum fuit maleficium, sed ex parte ipsius ex caritate patientis fuit sacrificium. Unde hoc sacrificium ipse Christus obtulisse dicitur, non autem illi qui eum occiderunt (S. Thom. 3, q. 48, a. 3 ad 3).

[3] St. Leo, Eleventh Sermon on the Lord's Passion.

adversaries powerless, and at His petition the Father would have sent "more than twelve legions of angels," consequently, an innumerable host of heavenly warriors to His aid (Matt. 26, 23). But "the Son of the living God" would not ward off the violence committed against Himself: of His own choice and love He entered upon the painful way of the Cross. — Hence sufferings and death were the natural outcome of those cruel torments by which the body and the soul of the Saviour were overwhelmed and consumed; but these natural consequences, — suffering and death — He could likewise have prevented by His own free-will and power. This He refused to do; rather would He drink the chalice of sufferings to the dregs and taste the bitterness of death in all its severity. — With strong voice and loud cry He commended His spirit into the hands of His Heavenly Father (Luke 23, 46), bowed His head and expired, "because He willed it, when He willed it and as He willed it." [1] Why this loud cry? To show His power over death and life; to prove to the world that He possessed the might and strength to ward off death and to preserve His life; that "He died not out of weakness, but by His own might," [2] that is, by His free will and free choice. The effect upon the beholders was, in fact, so great that later on the Pagan Centurion exclaimed: "Indeed, this man was the Son of God!" Thus was accomplished on Golgotha what the Saviour had, beforehand, distinctly foretold: "I lay down My life for My sheep; no man taketh it away from Me, but I lay it down of Myself and I have power to take it up again" (John 10, 15, 18). [3]

The priestly activity and self-sacrifice of our Saviour were first of all accomplished in spirit and in heart, but did not remain interior and invisible, for Christ's intention and will to offer Himself in sacrifice appeared outwardly and revealed itself by the shedding of His blood and the loss of His life, which He could have prevented, but would not prevent.

d) The object and fruit of this bloody sacrifice of Christ was the redemption of the world, the restoration and completion of the supernatural order in the human race, in fact, in the whole creation. For "what else has the Cross of Christ effected, what else does it still effect, than that enmity is destroyed and the world reconciled to God, so that by the sacrifice of the Lamb slain all be led back to true peace?" [4] — To accomplish the redemption, the Lord did not offer a gift of little value, but His own humanity, which in itself is incomparably more valuable than all creation, and which, in union with the divine nature, possesses infinite dignity and majesty. It

---

[1] Quia voluit, quando voluit, quomodo voluit (S. August., De Trinit., 1. 4, n. 16).

[2] Non infirmitate, sed potestate mortuus est (S. August., De nat. et grat. n. 26).

[3] Quia anima Christi non repulit a proprio corpore nocumentum illatum, sed voluit, quod natura corporalis illi nocumento succumberet, dicitur suam animam posuisse vel voluntarie mortuus esse (S. Thom. 3, q. 47, a. 1).

[4] St. Leo, 15th Sermon on the Lord's Passion.

was this august, adorable humanity of Christ that was sacrificed on the Cross, that was "bruised in its infirmity" (Isa. 53, 10), actually to acknowledge and honor the inviolable majesty of the Most High, as well as to appease the anger of God and propitiate His justice. [1] — The fruit of this homage and atonement which Christ offered for us, and in our stead, is profitable to us men ; by means of it He deserved for us the remission of all sin and punishment, as well as the bestowal of every grace and blessing. The majesty and justice of God could not have been glorified in a more brilliant and stirring manner than was done by the unfathomable and incomprehensible self-abasement of the divinely human Highpriest on the Cross. Infinitely worthy was the adoration offered to the Divine Majesty by the Sacrifice of the Cross ; infinitely perfect the satisfaction rendered to the divine justice by the passion and death of Christ ; infinitely abundant also the merit which our Saviour, by giving His life, acquired for man. "What sacrifice was ever holier than that which the true Highpriest offered on the altar of the Cross by the sacrifice of His body ?" [2] Here the Highpriest is infinitely worthy, the gift offered infinitely precious, and the act of offering infinitely valuable ; consequently, it is the absolutely perfect Sacrifice to which all other sacrifices are referred, and from which all other sacrifices draw their significance, power and efficacy. [3]

4. At the touching ceremony of the unveiling of the Cross on Good Friday, the Church three times sings these words to the faithful : *Ecce lignum crucis, in quo salus mundi pependit. Venite, adoremus!* "Behold the wood of the Cross, on which was suspended the Salvation of the world. Come, let us adore !" We will accept

---

[1] Sacrificium proprie dicitur aliquid factum in honorem proprie Deo debitum ad eum placandum. Christus autem *"seipsum obtulit in passione pro nobis"* (S. Aug.) et hoc ipsum quod voluntarie passionem sustinuit, Deo maxime acceptum fuit, utpote ex caritate maxima proveniens. Unde manifestum est quod passio Christi fuerit verum sacrificium (S. Thom. 3, q. 48, a. 3).

[2] St. Leo, 13th Sermon on the Lord's Passion.

[3] Consideremus hujus sacrificii *latitudinem*, qua *universum* in suis complectitur primitiis, et *universo* profuit mundo ; ejus *longitudinem*, quum jam adumbratum fuerit in *Abelis oblatione*, qua de causa Christus *agnus occisus ab origine mundi* dicitur (Apoc. 13, 8), et idem commemorandum sit usque *ad saeculi consummationem;* ejus *altitudinem*, sua enim virtute penetravit *coelos* eosque nobis iterum aperuit ; *profunditatem* effectuum, nam animae maculas radicitus delet et vel ex infernis animas justorum ibi degentium eripuit ; aut etiam ratione *ss. Cordis* Jesu, in quo radicatur. Huic enim Cordi adscribi debet a) tantum pietatis *consilium*, quo nos dilexit usque *in finem* non solum *suae vitae*, sed etiam usque ad *supremam caritatis mensuram* : nam *majorem hac dilectionem nemo habet, ut animam suam ponat quis pro amicis* suis (Joann. 15, 13). Ex illo Corde b) tamquam e fonte manavit sanguis ille pretiosus pro mundi vita ; c) ex amore illius Cordis speciale derivatur pretium hujus sacrificii, quia cum tanto oblatum est amore, ut plus contulerit ad mortem, quam carnifices : nisi enim ille permisisset, nihil hi potuissent. Quare Christus (Joann. 14, 31) ait : *Sed ut cognoscat mundus, quia diligo Patrem . . . surgite, eamus hinc.* Quocirca sacrificium crucis verum est *holocaustum*, cujus ignis erat intensissimus ss. Cordis amor (Hurter, Theol. dogm. Comp. II. [edit. 2], p. 419).

this invitation; therefore, let us tremblingly with reverence and adoration linger a while at the foot of the Cross erected upon Golgotha, the mountain of myrrh and the hill of frankincense (Cant. 4, 6). Upon the mountain of Golgotha the passion of the High-priest was consummated amid incessant sacrificial prayer; hence the place of Christ's crucifixion is a mountain of myrrh, that is, a mountain which became for our Saviour the myrrh of most bitter torments of soul and body — and a hill of frankincense, that is, a hill whence the odor of fragrant devotion and the sacrificial flame of acts of loving atonement ascended without intermission to Heaven from the Sacred Heart of Jesus. — Place yourself in spirit on Golgotha, behold the bleeding sacrificial Lamb and consider whether there was ever sorrow like unto His! For eighteen hours — from the night before to the day of His death — the God-Man was immersed in a fathomless ocean of the bitterest sorrow. How piercing, excruciating and un-endurable were all His pains for His so delicately and nobly consti-tuted body and His most pure and sensitive soul! The incompre-hensible prerogatives of the holy humanity of Jesus served but to sharpen His sense of pain and His confusion; for it was, as it were, framed to taste fully the bitterness of suffering.[1] Along the blood-stained Stations of the Cross, the Divine Sacrificial Lamb was dragged without mercy to the shambles. His soul was overwhelmed with anguish and sorrow, with shame and contumely, His Heart was as molten wax in His body and all His bones were dislocated (Ps. 21, 15), His body struck and beaten, bruised and tortured, shamelessly stripped and scornfully clothed, His face spat upon and defiled, His head pierced with sharppointed thorns, His hands and feet transfixed with cruel nails. "From the soles of the feet to the crown of the head, there is no soundness in Him: wounds and bruises and swelling sores: they are not bound up, nor dressed, nor fomented with oil" (Isa. 1, 6). He that was comely in countenance beyond all the children of men, from whose lips sweetness and benignity flowed, whom God had filled with blessings and anointed with the oil of gladness, — upon Golgotha He became a man of sorrows, a twig in an arid soil, one without form or beauty, a worm and no man, the reproach of men, the outcast of the people, unworthy of esteem, unrecognizable, and, as it were, struck and crushed by God (cf. Ps. 21 and 44; Isa. 53). In suffering and pain, in untold misery, amid the intense pangs of wounds, amid a parching thirst, the innocent Sacrificial Lamb hangs suspended, for three long hours, on the hard wood of the Cross, His blood oozing out in the slow agony of death. The sacrificial ardor with which the Divine Victim is consumed, is that fire which the Lord Himself brought from heaven upon the earth and enkindled — the fire of the love of God and of the neighbor; that fire of love environs His thorn-crowned head, encircling in vivid flames His wounded body, radia-

---

[1] Poenam amarissimam pro nostris peccatis in cruce sustinuit, in proprio cor-pore immaculatissimo, tenerrime ac nobilissime complexionato ideoque maxime perceptivo doloris et summe passivo (Dion. Carthus. Enarrat. in I. Petr. 2, 24).

ting in streams from His pierced members and from His open Heart. At the sight of such inexhaustible sufferings, the Church deeply penetrated and impressed, sings to the tree of the Cross :

> O lovely tree, whose branches wore
> The royal purple of His gore ;
> How glorious does thy body shine,
> Supporting members so divine !

St. Ignatius bids us pray "for sorrow with Christ filled with sorrow, to be bruised with Christ bruised ; to beg for tears, for interior grief at the remembrance of the excessive torments that Christ endured for us." Where may our hard, stony hearts be more readily softened and transported with love and gratitude, with grief and compunction, with constant sorrow for sin, than on Calvary at the sight of the Cross upon which our Saviour shows to us poor, lost creatures a love that shrinks from no sacrifice, that knows no measure and no bounds? "Is the Cross with our dying Lord upon it anything else than the open book of our sins ? Is not Christ He that knew no sin, but was made by God sin for us, as says the Apostle ? (2 Cor. 5, 21.) Alas! if I open this book of the Cross, I read therein all my transgressions ! On beholding the pierced hands, I recognize all my perverse actions ; if I look upon the transfixed feet, I think on the evil ways in which I have strayed ; if I glance upon this body become one wound, I have before me all my effeminacy, all my sensuality ; do I consider the thorn-crowned, bleeding brow, it is a fearful mirror of my vanity, of my sinful ambition ; and this Heart transpierced by the lance — ah ! it denotes my want of love and my unfaithfulness toward God, my hardheartedness and impatience, my implacability towards my neighbor !" [1] "Our Lord bore our sorrows and endured our pains" on the Cross — and yet His boundless love is returned with coldness and indifference, with ingratitude and outrages of all kinds : this pains and wounds His Heart a thousand times more bitterly than all the sufferings of His passion. This should, moreover, impel us to compensate and atone for the despised love of our Redeemer, by gratefully considering and honoring the immensity of His sufferings, by which we bring sweetest consolation to His Heart.

But why this excess of suffering and misery, of humiliation and abandonment, of blood and wounds ? [2] All this was by no means

---

[1] Molitor, Das Gleichniss von den klugen und thörichten Jungfrauen, p. 97.

[2] *Dolor passionis Christi* inter ceteros dolores et passiones fuit *acerbissimus* et *acutissimus*. Et hoc patet, si illa considerentur, quae doloris passionem acerbiorem reddunt. Haec autem sunt *tria*, videlicet *causa passionis* et *modus patiendi* et *conditio patientis*. — Si consideretur causa, ob quam Christus passus est, fuit in eo doloris afflictio magna. Non enim patiebatur pro culpa propria, imo pro aliena ; non pro amicis tantum, sed etiam pro inimicis, et etiam pro his, quos videbat ingratos. — Si autem consideretur *modus patiendi*, fuit in eo passio doloris acerbior, tum propter generalitatem, quia in omnibus membris affligebatur, tum etiam propter continuitatem, quia suspendium ejus continuabatur, et clavi adeo affligebant pendentem, sicut afflixerunt, quando manus ejus et pedes confodiebantur, in quibus

necessary to pay the full price of redemption ; the slightest suffering, each single tear, each single step and grief and sigh of our Saviour sufficed, since all His acts and sufferings were of infinite value on account of the infinite dignity of His person, and, consequently, they were infinitely meritorious and propitiatory before God. — And yet our Lord poured out His precious blood in streams and, so to speak, lavishly in the seven adorable mysteries, namely, of the Circumcision, the Agony, the Scourging, the Crowning with Thorns, the Way of the Cross, the Crucifixion, the Transpiercing of His Sacred Heart ![1] This He did through love of God and man ; for in what is the Divine Majesty more greatly and splendidly glorified, the salvation of mankind more powerfully and efficaciouly accomplished, than by a sacrifice so sorrowful, so bitter and painful as the one the Son of God consummated on the Cross? The greatest mystery of God and Christ (1 Cor. 2, 7 ; Eph. 3, 4), that is, the work of redemption, was in every detail to be perfect as a miracle of divine power, wisdom and love ; and, in effect, it is so profound, so glorious and so bountiful, that even the angels desire to contemplate it (1 Peter 1, 12). Yes, during the long ages of eternity, it will be for angels and for man a subject of unfailing contemplation and never ending adoration, — a subject in the meditation of which all the blessed spirits, with ecstatic jubilation and reverential awe, with ever fresh admiration, will be forever immersed and lost. Hence the Church, on the holy night of Easter, sings in transport of joy : *O mira circa nos tuae pietatis dignatio! O inaestimabilis dilectio caritatis! Ut servum redimeres, Filium tradidisti!* — "O wonderful condescension of Thy goodness to us, O God! O

---

maxima erat afflictio propter nervos et musculos ibidem concurrentes, in quibus praecipue viget sensus. — Si autem consideretur *qualitas* sive *conditio patientis*, maxima erat afflictio propter maximam complexionis aequalitatem et propter sensus vivacitatem. Unde quia nullus potuit ei aequari nec in aequalitate complexionis, nec in vivacitate sensus, dolor illius omnium dolorum fuit acutissimus. — *Et ideo rationes, quae hoc ostendunt, concedamus, et ei gratias, quantas possumus et supra quam possumus, referamus si quo modo donetur nobis, ut tam graviter patienti compatiamur* (S. Bonav. III, dist. 16, a. 1, q. 2). — In Christo patiente fuit *verus dolor* et *sensibilis*, qui causatur ex corporali nocivo, et *dolor interior*, qui causatur ex apprehensione alicujus nocumenti, qui *tristitia* dicitur. *Uterque* autem *dolor* in Christo fuit *maximus* inter *dolores praesentis vitae* (S. Thom. 3, q. 46, a. 6).

[1] Christus pro nobis sanguinem suum fudit *piissime, plenissime* et *acerbissime*. *Piissime* fudit, si consideretur *causa*: nam causa effusionis sui pretiosi sanguinis fuit piissima, quia ipsum fudit ex charitate ferventissima, ex qua voluntarie pro nobis pati voluit.... *Plenissime* fudit, si consideretur *mensura*: quia totum sanguinem effudit, ita ut unica gutta in eo non remaneret.... *Acerbissime* fudit, si consideretur *natura*: nam quanto natura et complexio est nobilior et delicatior, tanto est suae laesionis perceptibilior, et per consequens poena inflicta et ejus sensibilitas est acerbior; sed constat, quod complexio corporis Christi fuit delicatissima, quia Spiritus Sancti artificio de Virginis sanguine formata, et ergo sui sanguinis effusio et poenarum illatio fuit acerbissima, et ideo dicit: Attendite (sc. mentaliter) et videte (sensibiliter), si est dolor similis, sicut dolor meus — quasi diceret: Non (Ludolph. de Saxon. Vita Jesu Christi, II, cap. 64, n. 16).

inestimable favor of love! To redeem the slave, Thou didst give Thy Son!" "O Eternal Wisdom!" — exclaims Blessed Henry Suso — "I realize perfectly that whoever desires a great reward and eternal salvation, exalted science and profound wisdom, whoever would be equal in love and sorrow, have perfect security from all evil and desire to taste Thy bitter passion and receive supernatural sweetness, must keep and bear Thee, O Crucified Jesus, at all times before the eyes of his soul, beholding himself therein as in a mirror, so as to regulate his life according to Thine. Ah! loving Lord, draw me, by means of love and suffering, from all the world to Thee and to Thy Cross; penetrate me most intimately with Thy Cross, so that my soul may enjoy Thee in all Thy glory!"

8. The Fruits of the Sacrifice of the Cross.

The Cross is, as Holy Church sings in her Passion chant, "a tree beautifully adorned, environed with light, a noble tree, selected from all trees, no forest produces its equal in foliage, blossom and fruit." The noble tree (*arbor nobilis*) of the Cross was besprinkled with the blood that gushed forth from the body of the Lamb; hence its branches are full of blossoms of grace and fruits of life — and its foliage, which neither withers nor falls, avails for the salvation of nations. [1] The manifold, blessed fruits of the noble tree of the Cross, "to which was granted the privilege of touching members so holy, of bearing the ransom of the world," should now be considered in all their details.

1. The glory of redemption by the Cross is to the angels a mystery as attractive as it is impenetrable, hence we may conclude, the fruits of redemption must be immeasurably rich and precious. *Ecce lignum crucis!* Behold the Cross — what a sacrifice is there presented! Whose body is thereon immolated! Whose blood is there poured out! Whose life is thereon offered up! It is the body, the blood, the life of the God-Man — therefore the most magnificent sacrificial offering that may be conceived. This infinitely precious sacrifice is presented, after the most perfect manner, in the most perfect sentiments, by the infinitely exalted sacrificing Priest, Jesus Christ, upon the altar of the Cross, to the Most High for the salvation of the whole world. Therefore, inestimable, infinitely rich must be the treasure of grace and salvation purchased at so great and so dear a price, at the price of such a sacrifice. — In fact, through Christ's blood we have not merely redemption from all sin and punishment, but also the fulness and superabundance of all the gifts of grace (Eph. 1, 8—10); by Christ's death God has not only rescued us from the power of darkness, but yet more, translated us to the kingdom of His beloved Son and made us worthy to participate in the heritage of the saints in light (Col. 1, 12—13). Through Christ we have "fulness of grace and gifts" (Rom. 5, 15); for "where sin abounded, grace did more abound" (Rom. 5, 20).

---

[1] Folia ligni ad sanitatem gentium. (Apoc. 22, 2.)

"Through Christ's unspeakable clemency, we have received more and greater gifts than we had lost by the envy of the devil. For those whom the wicked foe had driven from the happiness of their original abode, with them the Son of God has incorporated Himself and placed them at the right hand of the Father." [1] From the dust, from the depth of misery God has raised us and placed us by the side of the angels; He has elevated us to a height, dignity and glory which the heart of man could neither have conceived nor desired. Thus has God, "who is rich in mercy, for His exceeding charity wherewith He loved us, even when we were dead in sins, quickened us together in Christ (by whose grace we are saved), and has raised us up together and has made us sit together in the heavenly places through Christ Jesus, that He might show in the ages to come the abundant riches of His grace (*abundantes divitias gratiae suae*), in His bounty toward us in Christ Jesus" (Eph. 2, 4—7). — What is the frightful abyss of misery and wretchedness from which we have been delivered by the Sacrifice of the Cross? And what are the heavenly gifts with which God, in Christ, has blessed us, according to the riches of His grace which has been imparted to us in superabundance (*secundum divitias gratiae tuae, quae superabundavit in nobis*)? (Eph. 1, 3—8).

2. By the fall of our first parents, the entire human race was plunged into the deepest and most deplorable misery; sin with its bitter consequences, like a crushing weight, lay heavy upon the children of Eve, banished from Paradise. They were spiritually dead, that is, they were deprived of the supernatural life of grace and had forfeited eternal happiness; hence, of themselves, they were absolutely incapable of rendering satisfaction for sin and its punishment and of propitiating the divine justice — they were also just as little capable of regaining and meriting the lost grace of being children of God and heirs to heaven. Without the mercies of the Lord, nothing would have remained for man to do but to pass from the distressing sufferings and trials of time into the hopeless pains and torments of eternity. This lamentable state in which man, full of concupiscence, infected with sin, was subject to temporal and eternal punishment, is justly considered and represented in Scripture as a hard slavery under the tyrannical dominion of Satan.

From all these evils, Christ redeemed poor, unfortunate humanity by the sacrifice of His life; He rendered on the Cross not only ample satisfaction for all the sins of the world, but also regained and merited for us all the gifts of grace. His passion and death possessed atoning and, at the same time, meritorious power and efficacy. By the treasure of satisfaction and merit comprised in the Sacrifice of the Cross, Christ paid for us to the divine justice so glorious a ransom that God delivered us from the slavery of Satan and reinstated us as His children.

3. Jesus Christ suffered and died in order to render satisfaction

---

[1] St. Leo, First Sermon on the Lord's Ascension.

for the sins of the world : — how is this to be more clearly understood? Whoever is in the state of sin has not only incurred a debt, but is, moreover, liable to punishment ; for in sin guilt and punishment (*culpa et poena*) are distinct. Both are evils that press upon sinful man and separate him from God ; man laden with guilt and deserving of punishment, is a stranger to God and remains at a distance from Him, since God's anger and displeasure are resting upon him. If these evils — guilt and punishment — are to be removed from man, if sin is to be utterly effaced, a commensurate satisfaction must, before all, be presented to the divine justice. Now, in what does satisfaction for sin and punishment consist, and in what degree has Christ rendered it by the sacrifice of His passion and death?

a) When man sins he offends God, that is, he violates the rights of God, he does God an injustice by refusing to Him due honor and submission, dishonors the supreme majesty of God, despises His infinite goodness. This places him in a state of guilt, that is, he thereby becomes an object of the divine displeasure and anger — an enemy of God (Rom. 5, 10). How can and how should this guilt be atoned for, that is, how can and how should be repaired the outrage offered to God by the contempt of the honor, esteem and love due to Him — and consequently, in what manner can and should God's displeasure be overcome? To effect this, there is required such a voluntary act, that is, an action or a suffering, that honors the offended majesty of God as much as, or even more than, sin has displeased Him. [1] Satisfaction, therefore, reconciles man with an offended God, that is, it causes God to lay aside His anger and to be ready to forgive the guilt. Satisfaction for the guilt, consequently, is a mark of honor, or rather it is a restitution of honor ; accordingly, a good work will answer the object of satisfaction so much the better the more it is calculated to honor and glorify God. This is the case most especially in sacrifice, since it is the principal act of religion. — From what has been said, it is evident how far and how exceedingly proper the Sacrifice of the Cross of Christ was to effect the atonement demanded by the debt of sin. [2]

Since Christ, through love and obedience to His Father, drained the bitter chalice of His passion and underwent the agony of death for us, He offered to God something far greater and more precious than was required to counterpoise all the offences that the sinful human race had committed and are still committing against Him ; hence God received far more joy and pleasure in the infinitely precious propitiatory Sacrifices of the Cross than the pain and displeasure He experienced from all the sins of mankind. Jesus was

---

[1] Ille proprie satisfacit pro offensa, qui exhibet offenso id, quod aeque vel magis diligit, quam oderit offensam (S. Thom. 3, q. 48, a. 2).

[2] Morte sua quippe uno verissimo sacrificio pro nobis oblato, quidquid culparum erat, unde nos principatus et potestates (the powers of hell) ad luenda supplicia jure detinebant, purgavit, abolevit, exstinxit (S. August., De Trinit., l. 4, c. 13, n. 17).

obedient to His Father unto death — even unto the death of the Cross (Phil. 2, 8), and this His perfect obedience amply compensated for the disobedience of sinful man.   How could the honor of which God was deprived by our sins be more worthily restored than was done on the Cross?   Infinitely great are the honor and adoration offered to the triune God by the bloody self-immolation of the Saviour.   God's inviolable majesty and holiness are there displayed in the clearest light, inasmuch as to acknowledge and propitiate them, the unspeakably perfect humanity of Christ was offered, that is, destroyed and dissolved.   By the voluntary surrender of His precious life to the death of the Cross, the God-man offered infinite honor and glory to the Most High, in order to efface the insults and ignominies with which men had offended and continue to offend the divine Majesty.

b) With the guilt of sin punishment is inseparably connected : and as long as the guilt exists it deserves punishment. — Man laden with sin is a child of wrath (Eph. 2, 3), subject to divine justice, — consequently, condemned to be punished for the sin committed in proportion to the guilt incurred, that is, to be humbled and afflicted. This punishment is either to be undergone (*satispassio*), or the remission of it may be obtained by satisfaction (*satisfactio pro poena*). — Satisfaction takes the place of the punishment to be undergone and remits it ; the punishment must needs be compensated for by an equivalent voluntary service.   Good works, in so far as they are painful and laborious, are most suitable to this end; for the voluntary performance of something hard and difficult is especially well adapted to supply the pain and humiliation inseparably connected with every punishment. — Now, inasmuch as in sacrifice the offering is destroyed and annihilated, sacrifice is most evidently endowed with the power of satisfying for punishment and is, therefore, most peculiarly fitted to supply for the punishment and merit its remission.

If we keep this in view, it will become evident to us why the punishment of sin, which weighs heavily on mankind, cannot be more perfectly compensated for and removed than by the propitiatory sacrifice of the Cross.   What can be more painful and humiliating than to die on a cross between two thieves?   There our Saviour, who is innocence and holiness itself, was immersed in a flood, in an abyss of pain and humiliation : a most bitter ocean of suffering raged around Him.   From the soles of His feet to the crown of His head, His most pure body was but one wound ; covered with blood, cruelly scourged and bruised, He hangs as a victim on the stake of the Cross.   In this manner has He borne "our sorrows"; thus has He suffered and expiated what we had deserved and what we should have undergone. [1]

---

[1] It would be incorrect to say that Christ, the Innocent One, has been literally punished or chastised for us guilty men; for His sufferings and death were no *satispassio*, that is, an involuntary undergoing of the punishment inflicted, as for example, we say of the souls in purgatory, that they have sufficiently satisfied (*satispatiuntur*), but it was a real *satisfactio pro poena*, that is, a voluntary pen-

Christ has, therefore, by His sacrifice on the Cross rendered satisfaction for us: this satisfaction has removed God's displeasure, that is, it has effaced all the debt of sin — and satisfied all the requirements of divine justice, that is, it has delivered us from all the punishment of sin. The sacrificial death of Christ has once more reconciled us with God offended by sin, that is, it has effected this boon that we are no longer objects of the divine displeasure and wrath — and that God, on His part, is prepared to remit our debt and punishment. Thus we have, through the blood of the Saviour, redemption and remission of sins (Eph. 1, 7). "Jesus Christ has loved us and washed us from our sins in His blood" (Apoc. 1, 5). This was accomplished when Christ concluded peace and reconciled us to God by the cross, killing the enmities in Himself (Eph. 2, 15—16), that is, by the sacrifice of His life. Yes, "for when we were enemies, we were reconciled to God by the death of His Son" (Rom. 5, 10). And thus by the blood of the Cross it was brought about that all are united in peace in heaven and upon earth (Col. 1, 20).

4. In addition to and after our reconciliation, the other chief fruit of the tree of the Cross is our restoration to grace. The sacrificial death of Christ had not merely the character of atonement, it was, at the same time, in the highest degree meritorious.[1] Christ by His death on the Cross obtained for us not only forgiveness of sins, but also superabundance of life (John 10, 10) and entrance into the sanctuary of heaven (Heb. 10, 19). He restored the kingdom of God, the supernatural order of grace. It is to the redeeming death of Christ that we owe all and every grace we receive from God — the grace of prayer, the vocation to the true faith, victory over temptations, conversion of the heart, the observance of the Commandments and final perseverance. To each of these graces there is attached, so to speak, a drop of the Precious Blood of Christ; for at the price of His blood has He purchased all graces for us — from the first enlightening of the understanding and the least moving of the will to the consummation of the glory of heaven. Christ has merited for us not only the plenitude of actual graces, but also sanctifying grace, the infused virtues, the gifts and fruits of the Holy Ghost, the heavenly transfiguration of soul and body, — in short, the whole glory of grace of the children of God, which here below is concealed, but which hereafter shall shine with unending

ance, undertaken and suffered out of pure love, which outweighed our punishment and, consequently, obtained for us its full remission. In this sense have the words of the Prophet to be understood: "The chastisement of our peace was upon Him" (*disciplina* pacis nostrae super eum — Is. 53, 5).

[1] To merit is to acquire by some act a right, a claim to recompense, that is, to a good which must in strict justice be given as a reward. While satisfaction (satisfactio) blots out and removes guilt, that is, acquires a claim to pardon and imparts to merit (meritum) a right to reward. One and the same good work has, under different aspects indeed, — both a satisfactory and a meritorious power (vis satisfactoria et meritoria).

brightness. The inexhaustible treasure of grace, the riches of heavenly blessings, the establishment of the Church and its endowment with all the gifts and means of salvation, are fruits that proceed from the tree of the Cross. Thus has God, through the merits of Christ, presented us with the greatest and most precious promises (2 Peter 1, 4). Filled with holy joy and gratitude, the Prince of the Apostles thus exultingly exclaims: "Blessed be the God and Father of our Lord Jesus Christ, who according to His great mercy has regenerated us into a lively hope, by the resurrection of Jesus Christ from the dead — unto an inheritance incorruptible and undefiled, and that cannot fade, reserved in heaven for you" (1 Peter, 1, 4).

5. By His atoning and meritorious sacrificial death, Christ rendered for us all that God, according to the rigor of His justice, required in order to bestow upon us remission of all the guilt of sin and its punishment, and favor us anew with His special benevolence and good pleasure, in consequence of which we are His children and heirs of heaven. — This salvation through Christ is frequently called redemption in Scripture[1]; there we read that we were purchased or ransomed by the blood of Christ. Regarded in this light, the merit and satisfaction of the Sacrifice of the Cross constitutes the ransom required by God and paid by Christ that we might be freed from the bondage of Satan. God accepted the ransom that Christ, from the superabundance of His love, offered for us, as a full payment for our enormous debt, and thus broke the chains of slavery in which we were groaning, and restored us again to the freedom of the children of God.[2] "That great dragon was cast out, the old serpent who seduceth the whole world" (Apoc. 12, 9); he had arrogated to himself dominion over fallen man, God permitting it as a just punishment for sin. The devil exercised his tyranny over men, inasmuch as he tormented and oppressed them by a thousand snares and temptations, by the fear of death and of the torments of hell. Then Christ came to destroy the works of the devil, (that is, sin and

---

[1] Redemptio, λύτρωσις, ἀπολύτρωσις, means loosening, freedom from sin and its consequences or from the slavery of the devil — and, in so far as is done by paying the ransom, means ransoming. (Cf. S. Thom. 3, q. 48, a. 4. — q. 49, a. 2.)

[2] Per peccatum dupliciter homo obligatus erat: *Primo* quidem servitute peccati (John 8, 34. — 2 Petr. 2, 19). Quia igitur diabolus hominem superaverat, inducendo eum ad peccatum, homo servituti diaboli addictus erat. — *Secundo* quantum ad reatum poenae, quo homo erat obligatus secundum Dei justitiam, et hoc est etiam servitus quaedam; ad servitutem enim pertinet, quod aliquis patiatur quod non vult, cum liberi hominis sit uti se ipso ut vult. Quia igitur passio Christi fuit sufficiens et superabundans satisfactio pro peccato et reatu poenae generis humani, ejus passio fuit quasi quoddam *pretium*, per quod liberati sumus ab utraque obligatione. Nam ipsa satisfactio, qua quis satisfacit sive pro se sive pro alio, pretium quoddam dicitur, quo se ipsum vel alium redimit a peccato et a poena (Dan. 4, 24). Christus autem satisfecit non quidem pecuniam dando aut aliquid hujus modi, sed dando id quod fuit maximum, se ipsum sc. pro nobis. Et ideo passio Christi dicitur esse nostra *redemptio* (S. Thomas 3, q. 48, a. 4).

death) (1 John 3, 8), and to cast out the prince of this world (John 12, 30). By the Sacrifice of the Cross He vanquished and subjugated the prince of darkness; hence the apostle says: "Through death, He destroyed him who had the empire of death, that is to say, the devil," and by His death "delivered them who, through fear of death, were all their life-time subject to slavery" (Heb. 2, 14—15). "If, when the Israelites went out of Egypt, the blood of the lamb became the restoration of freedom, and the day upon which the immolation of the victim disarmed the anger of the avenging Angel, became a great and holy feast, how much more should Christian nations rejoice, for whom the Almighty Father hath 'spared not even His own son, but delivered Him up for us all' (Rom. 8, 32), that in the death of Christ we might have the true Pasch and the sole and peculiar sacrifice (*singulare* sacrificium), by which not one nation alone was delivered from the bondage of Pharaoh, but the entire world was snatched from the captivity of Satan." [1] — Christ's dominion over Satan is beautifully expressed by the Church at the solemn Blessing of the Palms, when she prays as follows: "The Palms represent the coming triumph of the Lord over the prince of death; and the olive branches proclaim the advent of a spiritual unction. For that pious multitude (which went forth to meet the Redeemer) knew even then, that these things signified, that the Saviour, compassionating the miseries of all mankind, was to combat with the prince of death, and to triumph over him by His own death. Hence it was, that they offered Him such gifts (palm and olive branches) as would declare both the triumph of His victory and the riches (*pinguedo*) of His mercy. Therefore, the multitude go out to meet the Redeemer with flowers and palms, and pay worthy homage to the triumphant conqueror; the nations proclaim the Son of God with their tongues; and their voices rend the skies in praise of Christ: Hosanna in the highest!"

As Jesus Christ, "the Lion of the tribe of Juda" (Apoc. 5, 5), has conquered the powers of death and hell, He has also obtained for us the grace "to be strong and to overcome the wicked one" (1 John 2, 14), "and to be victorious over the dominion of death, so as to participate in the glorious resurrection with the Lord of life." [2] Hence we praise the Lord who has visited His people and wrought their redemption, that we, being delivered from the hand of our enemies, may serve Him without fear, in holiness and justice all the days of our life (Luke 1, 68—75).

6. The whole work of redemption is an incomprehensible achievement of divine love and mercy. Do not the goodness and humanity of God shine most brightly therein? The Eternal Son of God descended from the kingdom of imperishable glory to our earth, in order here amid brambles and stones to seek the lost, weary, wounded sheep and lead them back to eternal bliss. With

---

[1] St. Leo, Ninth Discourse on the Lord's Passion.

[2] Orat. in bened. Palm.

3

a heavenly self-sacrificing love He gave His life to refresh all that are weary and burdened, to soothe every sorrow, to pour oil and wine into every wound, to remove the sting of death and the terror of the grave — in a word, to free us from all evil and to bestow upon us every good. — This freedom from all suffering and this enjoyment of every happiness will not, of course, be granted to us here below, but in eternity, in the land of the living, where God shall wipe away all tears from our eyes, and where death shall be no more, nor mourning, nor crying, nor sorrow (Apoc. 21, 3—4); we shall fully partake of the blessing of redemption only beyond the grave. — By the Cross the Saviour redeemed us from sin and eternal misery, and with many hardships acquired for us all spiritual and heavenly blessings; hence, according to the wise dispensation of God, the earthly way of the Cross alone will lead us to the eternal full possession of all the gifts of redemption. Since it pleased God to perfect the Author of our salvation by His passion (Heb. 2, 10), and as Christ had to suffer and so to enter into His glory (Luke 24, 26), it is most proper and beneficial that we, too, — His ransomed ones — should enter into the kingdom of heaven through many tribulations. Remove sin, and the bitter waters of earthly sufferings are changed into sweet fountains of grace. To them who love God, all earthly woes serve as means of salvation and sanctification.

> Let us the Cross embrace with love and joy,
> Of fear the curse shall mingle no alloy;
> A blooming Eden from it sprung
> Of Precious Blood from Christ's Heart wrung;
> The thorn-crowned sorrows of this earth
> Give place to rose-crowned joys of heavenly birth.
>
> (Brunner.)

Christ's passion and death have transformed sufferings and have cast a mellow light over the darkness of death and the grave; therefore, the Cross is the joy and sweetness of holy souls. In overflowing love they pray: "To suffer or to die!" — "Not to die, but to suffer!" — "To suffer and to be despised for Thee, O Lord!" Of those who willingly and cheerfully suffer, Blessed Henry Suso says: "I shall be silent on the consolations and heavenly inundations wherewith God often, unknown to men, supports His suffering friends. These persons are, I know not in what manner, as it were already in heaven; what happens or does not happen, what God does in all His creatures or does not do, is altogether to their advantage. Thus the man who knows well how to suffer, is partly recompensed even in time for his sufferings; for in all things he experiences peace and joy, and after death is rewarded with life eternal."[1]

Behold the treasures, the riches and the glory of the fruits of grace, which have ripened on the tree of the Cross, that you may

---

[1] Denifle, Die Schriften des sel. H. Seuse.—Vol. 1, Part 1, p. 138.

embrace and honor it with devotion and love as did the Blessed Henry Suso. "During the night of the eve of May, he usually began by planting a spiritual May-pole, daily paying it honor for a considerable time. Among all the beautiful branches that ever grew, he could find none more like the lovely May-pole than the bough of the holy Cross, which is more blooming with graces and virtues and more finely adorned than all other May-poles. Beneath this May-pole he made six prostrations; each prostration, with its accompanying meditation, formed a desire to deck the spiritual May-pole with the most beautiful productions of summer. He recited and sung from his inmost heart, before the May-pole, the hymn, '*Salve, sancta crux*', in this manner: Hail, heavenly May-pole of Eternal Wisdom, upon which grew the Fruit of Eternal Salvation! At the first prostration, for Thy adornment, I offer red roses with my heart's love this day; at the second, with tiny violets, I offer an humble bow; at the third, with delicate lilies, I offer a pure embrace; at the fourth, with all kinds of beautifully colored and bright flowers that ever the meadows or the woods or the trees or the lowlands or the fertile plains produced during this beautiful month of May, or that ever were or shall be in time to come, my heart presents to Thee a spiritual kiss; at the fifth, with all the gay, merry singing ever executed by the birds during a May-tour, my soul offers Thee unbounded praise; at the sixth, for all the grandeur wherewith a May-pole was ever adorned, I this day raise my heart to Thee, in spiritual song, and I pray Thee, blessed May-pole, that Thou wouldst assist me, so that during this short time I may praise Thee, that I may enjoy Thee, the Fruit of Life, for evermore!"

9. Application and Conception of the Redemption accomplished on the Cross.

1. That with the sacrificial death of the Divine Redeemer on the Cross the work of our redemption was effectually accomplished, is a fundamental truth of faith.[1] — Our Saviour, indeed, during His earthly pilgrimage, from the first moment of His existence until His last breath on the Cross, offered satisfaction and accumulated merits for us, that is, for our redemption. But why does Holy Scripture ascribe the redemption of the world to the death, the blood, the Cross of Christ? Because in accordance with the good pleasure of God and the will of Christ, it was precisely the shedding of His blood and the offering of His life in the sacrifice of the Cross, that were to serve as the appropriate ransom and full price of re-

---

[1] In His ignominious death the satisfactory and meritorious efficacy of Christ reached its full measure, and also accomplished its object: although the Resurrection and Ascension, in a manifold sense, belong to the objective completion (integrity) of the redeeming act of salvation — in so far, namely, as these two glorious mysteries set the seal upon the redemption accomplished in a state of humiliation, and both guarantee and prefigure its eternal valid efficacy.

demption. — The preceding labors, sufferings and prayers, that is, the satisfactions and merits of the whole earthly career of Jesus, belong indeed to the treasure of redemption; but independently of His death they were not offered by Christ and accepted by the Father for the actual redemption, but only in so far as they were to find therein their completion and consummation.[1] "Unless the grain of wheat falling into the ground, die, itself remaineth alone; but if it die, it bringeth forth much fruit" (John 12, 24). These words of our Saviour were marvellously accomplished in His own person: by dying He produced fruits of life and grace in superabundance. His life of redemption reaches its zenith in His sacrificial death; therein the work of redemption was consummated. This the Lord Himself announced, in the presence of heaven and earth, when on the Cross He cried out in a loud voice: *Consummatum est!* "It is consummated!" (John 19, 30).

"All the riches that our Lord has lavished upon us by His holy Incarnation, are beyond the understanding of angels and of men. Hence no one can sufficiently praise and thank our Lord therefor. But, my God, how can we thank Thee as we should for the priceless good which Thou, by Thy wounds, by Thy sufferings, hast bestowed upon us in restoring and healing the breach, which all creatures together could never have remedied? Even the slightest insult offered Thee would have been powerful enough fully to atone for all our indebtedness, yea, for millions of worlds — for innumerable worlds. For the service rendered is measured by the dignity of the person. What shall we, therefore, give Thee in return, sweet Jesus, for the great goodness Thou hast shown us, that out of Thy boundless love and for our sake, Thou, during thirty-three years, didst not pass a single day without suffering, and, finally, Thou didst die a shameful death on the Cross?" (Suso.)

It was by the death of Christ, that the redemption of the human race, the restoration of the supernatural kingdom of God upon earth, were accomplished. On the Cross "the handwriting of the decree that was against us" (Col. 2, 14) was blotted out and destroyed: then God was appeased and the rigor of His justice satisfied, so that the stream of His mercies could again flow without hindrance; then were sin and the curse of sin taken away, and grace and glory once more restored; then was death swallowed up in victory and life resuscitated; then was the power of darkness broken and mankind

---

[1] For an actual ransom it is not sufficient only, that there should be an equivalent price paid, but it must also be destined for the object in question, that is, be offered by him who would redeem and be accepted by him who is to grant the release. Si loquamur de redemptione humani generis quantum ad quantitatem pretii, sic quaelibet passio Christi etiam sine morte suffecisset ad redemptionem humani generis propter infinitam dignitatem personae. Si autem loquamur quantum ad deputationem pretii, sic dicendum est, quod non sunt deputatae ad redemptionem humani generis a Deo Patre et Christo aliae passiones Christi absque morte.... Ideo humanum genus non est redemptum per aliam passionem absque morte (S. Thom. Quodlib. II, a. 2).

delivered from ignominious captivity; then was the abyss of hell closed and the gates of paradise reopened; then Heaven and earth were again united in peace. [1]

With death came also for our Saviour "the night when He could no more work" (John 9, 4) in a meritorious manner. At the moment in which His divine Heart ceased to beat on the Cross, the acquisition of new merits and new atonements for our redemption also ceased: the ransom is neither susceptible nor in need of augmentation. — For our immense debt our divine and bountiful Redeemer has atoned not only sufficiently, but in superabundant measure, out of His overflowing love He paid infinitely more than was required. The treasure of our redemption is infinitely great and, consequently, inexhaustible; it can neither be increased nor diminished. Superabundant, infinitely rich, is the atonement and merit of the death of the Cross, not merely on account of the infinite dignity of the suffering and expiring Redeemer, but also because of the immensity of the love wherewith He suffered and died, as well as on account of the value of the divinely human life which He sacrificed; finally, the extent, the number and the bitterness of the torments and ignominies which He endured, contributed thereto.

The satisfaction offered for us by Christ is, therefore, infinite, that is, far surpassing all sins conceivable: it is a satisfaction beyond which none more bountiful and complete can be thought of. "Far more than we owed has Christ paid for us; in so far as the ocean exceeds a drop of water, does Christ's satisfaction outweigh our indebtedness." [2] The number and greatness of our sins should not, therefore, deprive us of confidence, they should not tempt us to despair: be they ever so great and numerous, — relying on the blood of Christ, we must always hope for mercy and pardon; for Jesus Christ "is the propitiation for our sins, and not for ours only, but also for those of the whole world" (1 John 2, 1). All the sins and all the punishment of sin which God has remitted since the beginning of time or which He will continue to remit until the end of time — He has pardoned and will pardon only because the blood of the divine Lamb flowed in sacrifice on the Cross for their atonement.

The merit acquired for us by Christ is likewise infinite; that is, it is a merit beyond which none greater and more precious can be imagined. Therefore, in consideration of the infinite merits of Christ, we may and we should confidently expect and implore all that is conducive to our salvation; for no gifts and goods imaginable are equal to His merits. All the graces imparted to mortals from

---

[1] Per passionem Christi liberati sumus non solum a peccato totius naturae humanae (from original sin), et quantum ad culpam et quantum ad reatum poenae, ipso solvente pretium pro nobis, sed etiam a peccatis propriis singulorum, qui communicant ejus passioni per fidem et caritatem et fidei sacramenta. Et ideo per passionem Christi *aperta* est nobis *janua regni coelestis* (Hebr. 9, 11). S. Thom. 3,qu. 49, a. 5.

[2] S. Chrysost., Homil. 10 in cap. 5 ad Rom. n. 2.

the beginning of the world, that is, since the fall of man, and that may still be imparted to them until the end of the world, — were and will be imparted only because Christ purchased them at the price of His precious blood. [1]

The numerous host of the blessed in heaven, whom no one can count, are glorious, ripe fruits of the Sacrifice of Christ; because the Lamb was slain and has redeemed them to God, in His blood out of every tribe and tongue and people and nation (Apoc. 5, 9), and in the blood of the Lamb they have washed their robes, so that they are whiter than the newly fallen snow (Apoc. 7, 14). Therefore, they fall down before the Lamb and amid the harmony of celestial harps sing for all eternity the enchanting canticle of praise and thanksgiving: "The Lamb that was slain is worthy to receive power and divinity and wisdom and strength and honor and glory and benediction" (Apoc. 5, 12.)

Incomprehensible and unfathomable are the riches of Christ: from His bleeding wounds and from His transpierced heart all blessings and salvation have come to us. His blood, poured out in sacrifice upon Golgotha, is a fountain of grace, flowing and atoning for, healing and sanctifying all the world, — ever new and ever abundant; it does not diminish, it does not cease to flow, though millions upon millions draw from it grace upon grace, health and strength, light and life and the plenitude of life.

2.   Thus the work of redemption is objectively fulfilled; but it must also be subjectively accomplished and completed in the individual man. — On the Cross Christ merited for us all forgiveness of sin, the grace of sanctification and eternal beatitude; this merit is to be applied to individuals, that by it they may be freed from sin, receive grace and sanctification. Now, what is requisite in order that salvation founded upon the Cross, and placed in the Church within the reach of and offered to all, may be realized in the individual man? The Apostle tells it in these words: "Christ, being consummated, became to all that obey Him, the cause of eternal salvation" (Heb. 5, 9). There is indeed "with the Lord mercy and plentiful redemption" (Ps. 129, 7); but to partake of it and to attain to the imperishable heirship of heaven, obedience to the Lord is demanded, that is, it is required to do all and to comply with all that He has ordained and prescribed. — The obedience requisite for obtaining salvation extends to two things: we must first diligently employ the means of grace instituted and ordained by Christ; and then faithfully co-operate unto the end with the graces received.

---

[1] Those theologians, who are of opinion that the Son of God would have assumed human nature even if Adam had not sinned, refer, as a general thing, all graces, those of our first parents in Paradise (in statu justitiae originalis) and those of the Angels, to Christ as their meritorious cause; consequently, they reject the known distinction of gratia Dei (grace imparted to our first parents before their fall and to the angels without regard to the merits of Christ) and gratia Christi (grace bestowed upon men since the fall in virtue of the merits of Christ). Cf. Mazzella, S. J., De gratia Christi, disp. I, art 1, 2. n. 12.

From the precious blood of Jesus Christ is the heavenly medicine prepared for all : it depends upon us to receive it for the cure of our sickness and infirmities, and thus to be enabled to enjoy eternal health of soul and body. — The fountain of grace that sprang forth upon Golgotha, is open and available to all ; but we must approach it and drink therefrom "that living water," that it may become in us "a fountain of water springing up into life everlasting" (John 4, 14), and that we famish not "in this world's desert land, where there is no way and no water" (Ps. 62, 3). — In the sight of all is the wonderful tree of the Cross planted; but we must pluck and eat of its fruits, in order to live eternally and be able to walk in the strength of this food, unto the holy mountain of God (3 Kings 19, 8).

Christ has given to men the power to be made the sons of God (John 1, 12) and thus to remain ; but so long as we are in this land of probation, there is no infallible security and certainty of salvation. That we may not lose the grace of divine adoption and be excluded from the eternal inheritance of heaven, we should "not receive the grace of God in vain," but we must diligently employ "the acceptable time, the day of salvation" (2 Cor. 6, 1—2), and by good works make sure our predestination. — We must use violence in order to secure the kingdom of heaven, and strive earnestly to enter by the narrow gate ; during the heat and burden of the day, we must cultivate the vineyard of our soul ; we must fight the good fight, keep the faith and win the race so as to gain the crown of justice ; we must suffer with Christ in order to be glorified with Him, and die with Christ in order to live with Him ; we must walk in a manner worthy of God, pleasing Him in all things, fruitful in good works, increasing in the knowledge of God ; by a holy and devout life we should be ready and hasten to the coming of the day of the Lord, so as to be found by Him spotless and without blame ; we should renounce all in order to purchase the hidden treasure, the precious pearl of the kingdom of heaven ; with burning lamps, filled with the oil of charity and good works, we should go forth to meet the Bridegroom, in order to be admitted into the heavenly nuptial chamber. [1]

Therefore, we must watch, pray, labor, suffer and combat, in order to become holy and to secure our salvation. — Eternal life is not merely an inheritance, not merely a pure gift of divine mercy, but a reward also that we must deserve, and a crown of justice which we must win in lawful combat. The superabundant satisfactions and merits of Christ do not exempt us from the obligation that we are under of satisfying God for our sins by performing works of satisfaction and accumulating merits for heaven ; but all our satisfactions have their root and source in Jesus Christ, from whom they draw their efficacy and value, by whom they are presented to

---

[1] Cf. Matth. 2, 12. Luc. 13, 24. Matth. 28, 8. 2 Tim. 4, 8; 2, 11—12. Col. 1, 10. 2 Petr. 3, 12—13. Matth. 13, 44—46; 25, 1.

the Father and through whose mediation they are accepted by the Father. [1] It is precisely in this that the glory and superabundance of the redemption are shown, that Christ our Chief has not only satisfied and merited for us, but has, moreover, acquired for us grace and efficacy, presenting them to us that we ourselves may also in Him, through Him and with Him be enabled to render satisfaction and to merit heaven. [2]

Now, how in the course of time are the plentiful fruits of the redemption, the gifts and graces purchased on the Cross, to be applied to and appropriated by individual man? This is effected in various ways. Some graces God imparts to us without our co-operation; others we obtain only by our co-operation, that is, by disposing ourselves for their reception and employing well the means of grace. Such means of grace are manifold and by God's disposition are found in the Church: on the one hand, the principal ones are prayer and good works; on the other, the Sacraments and the Holy Sacrifice of the Mass. [3] All these means of grace are channels through which the graces merited by Christ flow to us in abundance and in a mysterious manner. Thus has Jesus Christ by the Sacrifice of the Cross won for us an "eternal redemption", and once for all accomplished the regeneration of the world, that is, atoned for all the sins of all men and merited for us every grace.

Consequently, by the Sacrifice of the Cross we expect and obtain full reconciliation and favor in time, as well as happiness and glory in eternity — "*gratiam in praesenti et gloriam in futuro.*" Whosoever separates himself from this Sacrifice; whosoever, through disobedience and unbelief, despises and rejects it, for him "there is left no (other) sacrifice for sins, but a certain dreadful expectation of judgment, and the rage of fire" (Heb. 10, 26). Therefore, with the Church, we joyfully and fervently unite in the hymn:

> The Cross we hail, our only stay!
> In holy hearts fresh grace implant,
> And pardon to the sinner grant!

---

[1] Trid. sess. 14, cap. 8.

[2] Meritum Christi sufficienter operatur ut quaedam causa universalis salutis humanae; sed oportet hanc causam applicari singulis per sacramenta et per fidem formatam, quae per dilectionem operatur. Et ideo requiritur aliquid aliud ad salutem nostram praeter meritum Christi, cujus tamen meritum Christi est causa (S. Thom., De verit., q. 29, a. 7 ad 8).

[3] The holy Apostle Paul, in his Epistle to the Hebrews, does not exclude such a sacrifice as is repeatedly and constantly offered, in order to impart to men the fruits of redemption acquired on the Cross. He therein proves and insists on the uniqueness and the complete adequateness of the bloody sacrifice of Christ only in the sense, that along with it and after it there is and can be no other sacrifice, whose object would be to express the acknowledgment of unatoned guilt, as was the case in the sacrifices of the Old Testament, — or to increase or supply the price of redemption, as though this had been insufficiently or not fully paid for by the Sacrifice of the Cross.

10. Jesus Christ, "a Priest forever according to the order of Melchisedech."

In a short, but magnificent and mystical psalm David prophetically announced that the Messiah would unite in His person both
the regal and priestly dignity; at the same time His priesthood is
more distinctly characterized as eternal, according to the order of
Melchisedech: "The Lord hath sworn, and He will not repent:
Thou art a priest forever according to the order of Melchisedech"
(Ps. 109, 4). St. Paul also ascribes to the Lord "an everlasting
priesthood" *(sempiternum sacerdotium* — Heb. 7, 24). Now if it
be asked in what manner we are to understand the perpetual duration
of the priesthood of Christ, we must then consider the priestly dignity and the exercise of the priestly office.

1. On the Cross Christ exercised His office of Highpriest, to
which at the moment of Incarnation He had been destined and for
which He had been sanctified. After having by the bloody sacrifice
of His life taken away the sins of the world, He sitteth eternally at
the right hand of the Father and dieth no more: thus He retains
His priestly dignity which can never be lost. Of every sainted
bishop the Church sings, God "made him to be a prince in order
that the dignity of the priesthood might belong to him forever;"[1]
for the priestly character is forever indelibly impressed upon the soul
of him who has received ordination. — It must be added that the
power and fruit of the Sacrifice of Christ remains and endures forever. As the Highpriest of the good things to come (Heb. 9, 11),
He has acquired and purchased for us by His bloody sacrifice not
earthly and perishable treasures, but the new, imperishable life of
grace and glory. The priestly dignity as well as the precious
effects of His priestly office never cease, but continue unchanged
for all eternity. These two characteristics are manifest in the
eternal priesthood of Christ, but they do not exhaust it; for it has
a broader and richer capacity, as it, moreover, includes a certain
continuance and permanence of the priestly activity of Jesus Christ.

2. Our glorified Saviour continues His priestly functions, His
redeeming office as mediator for the salvation of mankind, chiefly in
a twofold manner — in heaven by mediatory intercession, and upon
earth by the offering of the Eucharistic Sacrifice: both will endure
until the end of the world, that is, until the last elect soul shall
have entered into the joys of paradise.

That Christ in heaven is our mediator, intercessor and advocate
with the Father, is frequently and clearly expressed in Holy Scripture. Previous to His passion and death, He consoled and encouraged His sorrowful disciples, by promising that when in heaven
He would intercede for them with the Father (John 14, 16), The
Apostle St. Paul says that Christ, after dying and rising again, sitteth at the right hand of God, making intercession for us (Rom.

---

[1] Principem fecit eum, ut sit illi sacerdotii dignitas in aeternum (Introit.
Missae).

8, 34). And elsewhere he says: "Christ has an everlasting priest-hood, whereby He is able to save forever them that come to God by Him ; always living to make intercession for us" (*semper vivens ad interpellandum pro nobis* — Heb. 7, 25). The same truth is ex-pressed in the following words: "Jesus Christ entered into heaven, that He may appear in the presence of God for us" (*ut appareat vultui Dei pro nobis* —(Heb. 9, 24).

That we may the better appreciate the presence of Christ be-fore the face of God for us (ἐμφανισμός) and His everlasting mediato-rial intercession in our behalf (ἔντευξις), we will cast a rapid glance upon the prayer which our Saviour made during His mortal life upon earth. [1]

Prayer occupied the entire life of Jesus: for what else was His sojourn upon earth than an unspeakably holy and mysterious life of prayer, intercession, meditation and contemplation? He prayed in the crib, in the Temple at Jerusalem, during the flight into Egypt, in the house of Nazareth, in the desert. During His public life He frequently retired to secluded places, chiefly to mountains, there to pray and to watch throughout the night in prayer; praying He raised His eyes to heaven before working mir-acles or imparting blessings ; during His prayer, He was gloriously transfigured on the holy Mount ; the whole time of His passion — from the beginning to the end — He continued to offer most humble, fervent sacrificial prayer: He prayed at the Last Supper, on the Mount of Olives and upon the Cross. [2] Thus Jesus entered into the world praying, He prayed while He lived, prayed while He suffered, and it was while praying that He expired. — What sig-nificance, what power and efficacy, His most holy prayer and intercession had for us in the work of redemption! He wished to procure our eternal salvation, not only by satisfaction and merit, but also by prayer; [3] for all the gifts of grace that He merited in His life, in His passion and in His death, He at the same time implored and obtained for us by supplication, laboring thus in

---

[1] Absque dubio decens fuit, Christum orare, maxime *in diebus carnis suae* (Hebr. 5, 7). Ratio autem hujus condecentiae potest quadruplex assignari, vide-licet propter meritum, propter virtutis exemplum, propter veritatis argumentum et propter officium explendum. — Propter *meritum:* quia sua petitione et postu-latione merebatur nobis, qui minus idonei eramus ad susceptionem beneficiorum Dei. — Propter *exemplum:* ut sc. discipulos suos et per consequens alios invitaret ad orationis studium, in cujus exercitio maxime superatur adversarius (Matth. 26, 41). — Propter *veritatis argumentum:* ut ostenderet, se esse verum hominem et vere a Deo missum (Joan. 11, 41). — Propter officium, quia Christus habebat digni-tatem sacerdotis et pontificis ; unde sicut ad ipsius officium pertinebat sacrificium offerre pro peccatis, ita et pro peccatoribus exorare (Hebr. 5, 1; 7, 26). S. Bonav. III. Dist. 17, a. 2, q. 1.

[2] Cf. Luc. 6, 12; 23, 34; 22, 39. Matth. 19, 13; 26, 36. John 11, 41; 17, 1 et seq.

[3] Magna Domini propter salutem nostram benignitas pariter et pietas, ut non contentus quod nos sanguine suo redimeret, adhuc pro nobis amplius et *rogaret* (S. Cyprian., De orat. domin., c. 30).

every possible way for His vineyard (Isa. 5, 4).[1] It was this spirit of prayer animating His Sacred Heart at all times, which in reality made His passion and death, the offering of His body and the shedding of His blood, an atoning and meritorious sacrifice; — prayer is, therefore, the soul of sacrifice. Thus our Saviour through prayer fulfilled the will of God and accomplished His work; through prayer He redeemed the world and saved mankind.

3. But not only during His earthly life did our Lord "with a strong cry and tears offer up prayers and supplications to Him who was able to save Him from death, and He was heard for His reverence" (*pro sua reverentia*, Heb. 5, 7), — but glorified in heaven He is also an advocate and intercessor for men, in order to bring them to the full possession of salvation merited by Him. His heavenly intercession has for its object to procure for individual man the treasures of grace acquired and gathered on the Cross.

On the best grounds we may or should admit, that Christ in heaven really and expressly intercedes for us with the Father. — Why should not the Divine Heart of Jesus, which on earth so often, so earnestly, so constantly prayed and supplicated in our behalf, why should not this Heart also in the glory of heaven present to the Father His wish, His fervent desires for our salvation? This intercession of the glorified Saviour, to whom all dominion and power has been given in heaven and on earth (Matt. 28, 18), is incomparably more perfect, more potent and more efficacious than all the united petitions of all the angels and saints; for it is not merely the divinely human prayer which Christ offered when upon earth and which was always answered (John 11, 42), but it is the prayer of the Eternal Highpriest, who with the price of His blood purchased all those gifts and graces which He desires to obtain for us, and who, consequently, has a just claim to that which He wishes to procure for us and to impart to us. What our Lord thus in virtue of His infinite merits asks, He will infallibly obtain. "Ask (*postula*) of Me and I will give Thee the Gentiles for Thy inheritance, and the utmost parts of the earth for Thy possession" (Ps. 2, 8), says the Father to the Son, who sitteth at His right hand, waiting until His enemies be placed under His feet.

4. To this especial intercession, by which Christ as mediator becomes our advocate with the Father, is moreover added the representation and the offering of the Sacrifice of the Life of the Lord on the Cross, and of the merits He thereby acquired. — Christ appears for us before the face of God, that is, He presents to the Father the wounds He received, the blood He shed and the death

---

[1] Omnia quae pro genere humano impetravit satisfaciendo merendoque, etiam *orando* impetravit, quia his omnibus justitiae titulis remedium hominum operari voluit, quo copiosior esset redemptio ipseque suum erga illos amorem immensum amplius declararet (Arias, Thesaur. inexhaust., tom. I, tr. 3, cap. 14). — Christus exercuit officium sacerdotis merendo nobis, satisfaciendo pro nobis et interpellando pro nobis: hac enim via Deum nobis reconciliavit et nos adduxit ad Deum, quod est munus sacerdotis propriissimum (Salmant., De Incarn., disp. 31, dub. 1, n.11).

which He underwent on the Cross, in order to move Him to impart to us His favor, His mercy and His grace. — In this is found one of the reasons why the Saviour desires to retain for all eternity in His risen body the glorious marks of His wounds. These emblems of His bloody passion and combat represent to the Father what price was given for "the freedom wherewith Christ has made us free" (Gal. 4, 31).[1] These open deep death-wounds now shine as stars with marvellous beauty and brilliance; but they continually proclaim to the Eternal Father that the Heart, the hands and the feet of His Beloved Son were once cruelly transpierced; they repeat loudly and solemnly that the Saviour in lavish profusion shed all His blood in order to ransom us. The sufferings and the wounds of the glorified Saviour appear — as St. Hildegarde declares[2] — before the face of the Father like unto the aurora, which ceases not to increase in splendor until the perfection of day. Or, as Father Faber puts it, God beholds all things in that never-setting red sunset of the Precious Blood, which by His command is forever to be seen hovering on the horizon in all its splendor.

How dear and how precious, therefore, to our soul should be the sight of those glorified wounds of the Lord! They testify that He has written us in His hands and engraved us in His Heart in indelible characters. With gratitude should we gaze upon these sweet tokens of His martyrdom. Yes, for us they are fountains of eternal atonement and mercy, pledges of heavenly goodness and long-animity. In every tribulation and necessity, animated with a confidence full of joy, we should look up to our merciful and faithful Highpriest in heaven; for His Heart is the dwelling-place of eternal gentleness, an abyss of love and clemency. When we sin, we should never despair, for "we have an advocate with the Father, Jesus Christ the just, and He is the propitiation for our sins" (1 John 2, 2).

5. The exercise of the office of mediator and intercessor, explained above, which the God-Man discharges in heaven before the throne of His Father, is a priestly function; for there He propitiates Him in our behalf by virtue of the Sacrifice He once offered for us on the Cross. His heavenly intercession is based upon and supported by the sacrificial merits acquired at the price of His blood, and is, therefore, a priestly function, a priestly intercession (*interpellatio sacerdotalis*).[3] After our Lord had, by the bloody sacrifice

---

[1] In quo non solum fidem firmat, sed etiam devotionem acuit, quod vulnera suscepta pro nobis coelo inferre maluit, abolere noluit, ut Deo Patri nostrae pretia libertatis ostenderet (S. Ambros. in Luc. 1. 10, n. 170).

[2] Ante oculos meos apparet, quid Filius meus propter amorem hominis in mundo passus sit; quoniam nativitas, passio et sepultura, resurrectio et ascensio Unigeniti mei mortem humani generis occiderunt. Unde et ea in coelestibus coram me fulgent, quia eorum non sum oblitus, sed usque ad consummationem saeculi quasi *aurora* ante me in multa claritate apparebunt. (S. Hildegardis, Scivias, lib. 2, vis. 6).

[1] Christus in coelo interpellat et orat pro nobis *idque proprium est Christo, ut tamquam pontifex oret pro nobis;* alii enim Sancti, etiam ii, qui in hac vita

of Himself, atoned for the sins of the people and "obtained an eternal redemption," He entered into the Sanctuary of heaven (Heb. 9, 11—12). There He continually exercises His office of Highpriest, by intercessory supplication, the object of which is to apply and to procure for man, throughout all ages, the fruits of the redeeming sacrifice accomplished on the Cross, that man may obtain salvation and eternal beatitude. This application of the fruits of the Sacrifice of the Cross, by the priestly intercession and oblation of Christ in heaven, may in a certain sense be called the continuation or — according to St. Thomas — the consummation (*consummatio*) of the Sacrifice of the Cross; but we do not intend to assert by this, that the Sacrifice of the Cross was not essentially consummated upon earth. This would be altogether erroneous. For the exercise of the priestly function of mediator in heaven is not in an exact and strict sense a sacrifice. [1] Our Saviour having ascended

---

sacerdotes fuerunt, orant pro nobis in coelo, non tamquam sacerdotes, sed tamquam privati Sancti et amici Dei; non enim amplius funguntur sacerdotio in coelis (Corn. a Lap. in Rom. 7, 25).

[1] With regard to the so-called heavenly sacrifice of Christ, there prevails at present a theological controversy, which, however, in our opinion, refers more to the manner of expression than to the thing itself. As in the Holy Mass the liturgical oblation is annexed to the transient sacrificial act (in *actu* consecrationis), thus Christ with unchangeable sentiments of sacrifice continues in heaven the priestly representation and offering (oblatio) of the Sacrifice once accomplished on the Cross, so as to apply, until the end of time, to all men God's favor and grace. But this heavenly oblation of Christ is no sacrificatio vel immolatio corporis et sanguinis Christi — and, consequently, it is no sacrifice in the real and strict sense as are the Sacrifice of the Cross and that of the Mass. — Therefore, the celebration of the Eucharist is a *verum* sacrificium and not a mere oblatio, since therein, as the Council of Trent says, Christ according to His humanity is offered in an unbloody, but yet true and real manner — incruente *immolatur* (sacrificatur, in statu victimae ponitur hic et nunc). But this last quality *(actualis positio* in statu victimae) is not to be found in the humanity of Christ, inasmuch as it is glorified in heaven, and therefore — because this requisite which is essential for the complete idea of sacrifice is wanting — there can be no question of a heavenly sacrifice in the strict sense of the word. The heavenly interpellatio (ἔντευξις) of Christ is indeed an oblatio *sacerdotalis*, but no actio sacrifica. — *Officii* ratione (Christus vocatur sacerdos *in aeternum*), quia semper apud Patrem in coelis *interpellat* pro nobis. Est enim sacerdotis officium interpellare Deum pro salute eorum, quibus datus est sacerdos. Fungitur autem hoc officio Christus in aeternum, i. e. usque in finem saeculi, donec omnes electos suos adduxerit ad salutem. *Nec vero haec interpellatio est sine oblatione,* quae et ipsa ad sacerdotis officium pertinet; nam continuo seipsum hominem et vulnerum signa, quae passus est, exhibet atque offert Patri pro salute electorum. .... His addi poterat ratio sumpta ab officio *sacrificandi,* quia nimirum Christus Dominus non solum *interpellando* causam electorum suorum etiamnum promovet apud Deum, verum etiam jugiter pro iis *sacrificando.* Sed illud agit continuo per se ipsum; *hoc per ministros ac vicarios suos sacerdotes,* quibus commisit offerendum in Ecclesia, usque at saeculi consummationem, visibile sacrificium corporis et sanguinis sui sub speciebus panis et vini, quod tamen et ipse primus in ultima coena obtulit (Estius, In Epist. ad Hebr. 7, 17; Cf. 7, 25; 8, 2—3; 9, 25). — Est Christus in coelo sacerdos in aeternum non

into heaven does not sacrifice Himself, inasmuch as He is in the glory of the Father, but only inasmuch as He is present on our earthly altars under the sacramental species; in heaven He is not in the state of Sacrificial Lamb, but He reigns there in the splendor of the saints and is there enthroned as King of kings in the radiant glory of victory.

6. Upon earth also does our glorified Saviour continually exercise His office of Highpriest — and that by the accomplishment of a true and real sacrifice; for He is the chief Sacrificial Priest, who upon the altar, by the hands of His duly authorized ministers, ever performs the Eucharistic action of sacrifice. For this reason the Prophet glorifies Him as a priest forever according to the order (*secundum ordinem*) of Melchisedech. In what then is Melchisedech "likened unto the Son of God" (Heb. 7, 3), that is, a figure of the Eternal Highpriest Jesus Christ? Melchisedech was priest and king: according to his name Melchisedech, "King of Justice," and according to his kingdom of Salem, "King of Peace." Christ also in His divine-human dignity is priest and king at one and the same time — and as such the author and source of all supernatural justice, as well as the founder and prince of all true peace in time and eternity; for already David had announced that "in His days shall justice spring up and abundance of peace, till the moon shall be taken away" (Ps. 71, 7). — Holy Scripture makes mention neither of the father nor of the mother of Melchisedech, and portrays him as though he had neither beginning of days nor end of life. — Christ was upon earth according to His humanity, without a father; and He is in heaven, according to His divinity, without a mother; and His priesthood is eternal and imperishable: He is the only priest in His order, having neither predecessor nor successor. — But this figure of Melchisedech would be defective, if he did not prefigure Christ, at the same time, in the essential and truly priestly function, that is, in the offering of sacrifice. But this characteristic also is not wanting. Mechisedech was a priest of the Most High, and as such he presented to Him earthly offerings of bread and wine; thereby prefiguring the new and eternal Sacrifice of the Eucharist, which the eternal and real Melchisedech, Jesus Christ, instituted in the new and eternal Covenant under the sacramental species of bread and wine, and which He will offer until the end of the world. This is the principal reason why it is said of Jesus Christ that He is a priest forever according to the order of Melchisedech.

---

solum dignitate permanente et effectu sacrificii perpetuo, sed etiam continuata quadam functione, non quod sacrificium in coelo offerat, sed quod statim victimae in cruce et totum meritum illius sacrificii Patri pro nobis repraesentat, et ita interpellat pro nobis interpellatione sacerdotali. Unde etiam in coelo victima est, *non quae ibi nunc actu sacrificetur*, sed quae semel est sacrificata et nunc cum omnibus meritis illa oblatione consummatis perseverat et vivit in aeternum (Cardin. Franzelin, De Verbo incarnato, thes. 51, n. 2). —

Cf. in particular Stentrup, S. J., Soteriologia, thes, 81—83.

This twofold priestly function, namely, of intercession in heaven and of offering sacrifice on earth through the application of the healing and sanctifying power of His sacrificial blood and merits, Christ will continue so long as there are men who require help, deliverance from sin and justification, — and, therefore, until Judgment Day, when the number of the saints will be filled and completed, the Heavenly Jerusalem constructed upon and of the living and chosen stones of the elect. — Then, too, when the work of redemption shall have been victoriously and universally accomplished, when the enemies of Christ shall have been placed at His feet and dashed to pieces like the potter's ware, — even then will the Lord, as the glorious Head of the Church triumphant, present to the majesty of the triune God the sacrifice of praise, of adoration and of thanksgiving throughout all eternity!

CHAPTER THE THIRD.

The Unbloody Sacrifice of the Altar.

ARTICLE FIRST.

The Truth and Reality of the Eucharistic Sacrifice.

11. The New Covenant of Grace requires a Perpetual Sacrifice — and that the Sacrifice of the Body and Blood of Christ.

1. The offering of the bloody Sacrifice of the Cross constitutes the conclusion and crowning of the earthly, as well as the foundation of the heavenly, activity and efficacy of Christ for the salvation of mankind. — In the Sacrifice of the Cross all sacrifices prior to the coming of Christ have their fulfilment and by means of it have attained their end. "On the Cross there was but one sacrifice (hostia singularis) offered to God for the redemption of the world, and the death of Christ, the true sacrificial Lamb, announced so many centuries in advance, placed the children of promise in the liberty of faith. Then also was the New Covenant sealed, and the heirs of the eternal kingdom were inscribed with the blood of Christ. Then was evidently effected the transition from the Law to the Gospel, from the Synagogue to the Church, from the many legal sacrifices to the one Sacrifice (a *multis* sacrificiis ad *unam* hostiam), in such a manner that, when the Lord gave up His spirit, the mystical veil which concealed the innermost part of the Temple and its holy mystery from view, was suddenly and violently rent in twain from top to bottom. Then truth abolished the figures (figuras veritas auferebat), and the prophecies became superfluous after their fulfilment."[1] The tearing asunder of the veil before the entrance to the Holy of Holies of the Old Dispensation was a sign that the Old Covenant ceased when the New and eternal Covenant of grace had been instituted in the blood of Christ. With the ending of the Old Covenant, the ancient sacrifices also ceased, because they had become

---

[1] St. Leo, The Seventeenth Discourse on the Lord's Passion.

useless. [1] For when the reality appears, the shadow vanishes; at the rising of the sun, night disappears. *Umbram fugat veritas — Noctem lux eliminat.* — The Sacrifice of the Cross was a transient act, and as such it was accomplished but once, in one place — upon Golgotha — at a stated time — on that memorable and first Good Friday. Only a few persons stood at the foot of the Cross and assisted at this most affecting sacrificial drama; for all others the Sacrifice of the Cross is an historical fact : a thing of long ago and of the past. — Now was there to be no further sacrifice after the death of Christ ? Was Christendom to be without a perpetual sacrifice ? Was Christ, the author and finisher of faith (Heb. 12, 2), not to bequeath to His beloved Church a permanent sacrifice as a heritage ? To say that Christ left the religion He founded without a perpetual sacrifice, is an assertion which of itself appears improbable and will later on be proved utterly false. But before we give proofs from the written and traditional word of God, from which it is as clear as the noon-day sun that the Catholic Church possesses in the celebration of the Eucharist a permanent sacrifice, we will prove how exceedingly proper, yea, how necessary, in a certain sense, for the Christian religion and Church is a perpetual sacrifice, and that precisely the Sacrifice of the Body and Blood of Christ.

a) The offering of sacrifices for the purpose of divine worship, if not of absolute necessity, is, nevertheless, in the highest degree in accordance with human nature and the natural law. Man, being composed of body and soul, cannot express his interior religious life by anything better, cannot give it more powerful and emphatical proof than by sacrifice. Grace does not destroy nature, but improves and sanctifies, ennobles and transforms it ; hence man requires, even in his condition as a child of God and in the kingdom of grace, namely, in Christianity, a visible sacrifice in order to comply with his religious obligations in a manner most consonant with his nature. "Human nature," as the Church says, "requires a visible sacrifice ;" hence God, whose providence arranges all things with so much power and gentleness, would assuredly not leave Christians without a permanent sacrifice which so greatly accords with the inmost wants of a religious heart.

b) Since sacrifice is so well suited to human nature, it is always and everywhere found recorded in history. In the Old Dispensation sacrifices constituted the essence and centre of the entire service. Hence the New Covenant cannot be without sacrifice, since it is the fulfilment and completion of the Old. Now, if the Old Law, which was transient, was invested with so much glory, how much more must the New Law, which is to remain forever, be glorious, that is, endowed and distinguished among other things by a correspond-

---

[1] Quoniam veritate superveniente cessat umbra, et figura praenuntians sortitur finem intentum, quo habito, cessare debet ejus usus et actus : hinc est, quod gratia superveniente, vetera sacramenta et signa *impleta* sunt *pariter* et *sublata* (S. Bonav. Brevil. P. 6, c. 2).

ing sacrificial worship.[1] — In the Old Law there were daily not only bloody, but unbloody sacrifices also. Both kinds were figures of the New Law. Now, as the bloody sacrifices found their fulfilment in the death of Christ on the Cross, in like manner can the figures of the unbloody sacrifices, daily offered, find their realization alone in the fact that in the New Law there exists a perpetual unbloody sacrifice.[2] — In the Old Testament there were sacrifices which prefigured to the Israelites the future Sacrifice of Redemption, placing it before their eyes, thus becoming to them a means of gathering in advance the fruits of the tree of the Cross : hence it is highly proper that the New Law also should have a sacrifice, whose object it is to represent to all generations the Sacrifice of the Cross, accomplished once for all, and evermore to apply to them its graces. — Consequently, we may draw the conclusion that by the New Law Christ did not simply abolish the imperfect sacrificial worship of the Old Law, but changed it into one that was more perfect.

c) The religion instituted by Christ is most perfect and most complete, for it possesses the plenitude of divine truth and grace. In Christianity supernatural revelation has found its consummation, so that a richer and more copious outpouring of the Holy Spirit is not to be expected here below. The Church of Christ is placed in the middle, between the figurative shadow of the Old Law and the final completion of the Heavenly Jerusalem. The Old Dispensation was the preparation and the breaking of the ground for Christianity; and Christianity forms the direct entrance and vestibule leading to the revealed and beatific vision of the eternal truth and beauty to come. — But the perfection of religion necessarily demands a perfect divine worship, that is, the offering of sacrifice ; for sacrifice is the chief and the most excellent act of religion. If the Christian religion had not a perpetual sacrifice, it would not have a perfect divine worship and it would not be complete in every respect ; but it would in an essential point be incomplete and insufficient ; but this is inadmissible. Since the Christian religion is the most perfect, it must possess the most excellent and the most sublime and worthy form of worship, namely, the worship of sacrifice. Where there is no sacrifice, there is no priesthood and no altar : what would Christianity be without sacrifice, priest and altar ?[3]

---

[1] Si enim, quod evacuatur, per gloriam est, multo magis, quod manet, in gloria est (2 Cor. 3, 11).

[2] In promptu est, sacrificia incruenta non minus ac sacrificia cruenta imaginem gerere novi Testamenti ; sacrificia nempe cruenta praesignabant cruentam Christi oblationem in cruce, incruenta vero sacrificium incruentum celebrationis eucharisticae, et ideo sane sacrificia tum cruenta tum incruenta in lege dicta sunt *sancta sanctorum* (Lambrecht, De ss. Missae sacrif., P. 1, cap. 4, 5).

[3] Cum tres intentiones et praecipui actus sint cultus divini ac verae religionis, videlicet honorificentia Dei, impetratio veniarum et adeptio gratiarum, multum deesset cultui Dei, si durante tanta transgressione ac culpa, desit advocatus et sacerdos, ad impetrandum cunctis veniam ac gratiam efficax, utpote Christus (Dion. Carthus., De sacr. altar., art. 10).

d) Christianity is founded on and takes its root in the Sacrifice of the Cross. The holy Sacrifice is the source whence the New Law has emanated with its blessings and graces. As the New Law was instituted and confirmed by sacrifice, it must of necessity be sustained and maintained by a perpetual sacrifice; since the preservation of an object is equivalent to a continued creation, it is dependent upon the same cause as that of its creation. Hence it is not sufficient that the Christian religion and the Church should have as its foundation a sacrifice which was offered once; it must possess a sacrifice which is perpetually repeated as the fundamental support of its permanent existence.

2. The Sacrifice of the New Testament neither can nor may be independent of the Sacrifice of the Cross. From this sacrifice salvation flowed forth to mankind before and after Christ; it, therefore, constitutes the centre point to which all other sacrifices are referred. — The object of the perpetual Sacrifice of the New Covenant cannot be a means of acquiring for us additional merit or of rendering fresh satisfaction for the sins of men, but its sole purpose can be no other than to apply individually to men in need of help and salvation the satisfaction and merits of the Sacrifice of the Cross. — Sacrifice forms the centre point of exterior divine worship and with regard to its perfection stands on a par with it. Now since the New Law so immeasurably excels the Old Law, the former must possess a sacrifice incomparably more noble and more efficacious than did the latter.[1] The difference between the two Testaments must be impressed principally on their respective sacrifices. In the Old Law the exterior and the carnal, the spirit of fear and of bondage prevailed; therefore, the bloody sacrifices offered up by unregenerate man with the consciousness and acknowledgment of unatoned guilt were altogether appropriate; — they appealed to an irritated and avenging God, who punishes sin with death. But for the New Testament is suited not a bloody, but an unbloody sacrifice; for in the New Law the interior and spiritual prevails, we have there the grace and joy of redemption, the spirit of love and of divine adoption.[2] — This unbloody sacrifice must correspond to the perfection of the New Law, which possesses the unfathomable riches and treasures of the grace of Christ, that is, the unbloody Sacrifice must not only represent figuratively the Sacrifice of the Cross, as did the Sacrifices of the Old Testament, but it must really and truly

---

[1] Sacrificium est primarium religionis munus vel potius complementum. Itaque decebat, ut excellentissima religio, qua nulla alia perfectior aut sublimior esse potest (quae quidem naturae humanae sit accommodata) nobilissimum haberet sacrificium, quale est sacrificium Eucharistiae, a quo ipsa religio praecipuam suam excellentiam habet (Lessius, De perfect. divin., 1. 12, c. 14, n. 99).

[2] Dicitur lex mosaica differre ab evangelica, quia illa *figurae,* haec *veritatis* (Hebr. 10, 1); illa lex *poenae,* haec *gratiae* (Rom. 5, 20—21); illa *litteralis,* ista *spiritualis* (2 Cor. 3, 6); illa *occidens,* ista *vivificans;* illa *timoris,* ista *amoris;* illa *servitutis,* ista *libertatis* (Gal. 4, 31); illa *oneris* et ista *facilitatis* (S. Bonavent. Brevil. P. 5, c. 9).

show forth and render present, the Sacrifice once accomplished upon Calvary. Now such a presenting anew of the Sacrifice of the Cross becomes possible only when the offering upon our altars is in no way inferior to the Sacrificial Victim immolated on the Cross — that is, only when in the sanctuary of the Church the Body and Blood of Christ are continually and mystically offered. [1]

3. But how can Christ, who has risen from the dead, who dieth now no more and over whom death shall have no more dominion (Rom. 6, 9), be the gift offered and sacrificed? To all appearances the immortality and glory of our Saviour, who has ascended into heaven, seem insuperable obstacles to a sacrifice: still what is impossible to man is possible with God. His infinite wisdom discovered never suspected means and the way to accomplish what to men was apparently impossible. By virtue of manifold and dazzling miracles our Lord conceals under the appearance of bread and wine upon the altar the grandeur of His glorified humanity, uniting in His adorable person life and death, uniting the condition of a Victim in sacrifice with the possession of heavenly glory in His adorable person. [2]

Since "the Word was made flesh and dwelt among us" — and since "the Lord was seen upon earth and conversed with men" (John 1, 14; Bar. 3, 38), His dwelling among us and His association with us have never ceased. When He ascended into heaven, He would not leave us orphans, He would not deprive us of the joy and consolation of His bodily presence (which is of course perceptible only by the light of faith, because His bodily presence with us is sacramental). He made good His parting words in a marvellous manner: "Behold, I am with you all days, even to the consummation of the world" (Matt. 28, 20). — Jesus wishes to remain in our

---

[1] Congruebat, ut (homines quotidianis peccatis implicati) haberent *oblationem exteriorem;* sed Dominus unica oblatione offerendo se omnes alias oblationes evacuaverat: ergo si non debuit reficere (to restore again), quod destruxerat, debuit dare nobis *illam eandem,* quam obtulit, et non aliam. Ergo sicut *corpus* Christi *verum* fuit oblatum in cruce, ita *sacrificatur in altari* (S. Bonav. 4, dist. 10, p. 1, art. 1, q. 1). — Quoniam tempus gratiae revelatae requirit, quod jam non offeratur *oblatio* qualiscumque, sed *pura, placida* et *plenaria;* et nulla alia oblatio est talis, nisi illa, quae in cruce fuit oblata, scilicet *Christi corpus* et *sanguis;* hinc est, quod necessario oportet in hoc sacramento (Eucharistiae) non tantum figurative, verum etiam veraciter corpus Christi tamquam *oblationem huic tempori debitam* contineri (S. Bonavent., Brevil. P. 6, c. 9). — Cf. Alger., De sacrament., l. 2, c. 3.

[2] Sacrificium Missae quotidie pro vestra reconciliatione, purificatione et salute in ecclesia Deo Patri offertur: nempe tam ardentissime vos dilexi, tam liberalissimum ad vos animum habui, quod non suffecit mihi semel vobis conferri et semel pro vobis offerri, sed in fonte et abysso infinitae sapientiae meae *hunc mysterialissimum modum* inveni ac statui, quo vobis indesinenter adsim et conferar, pro vobisque offerar et ita a vobis manducer, modo vobis tolerabili ac proportionato sub tegumentis panis et vini, non in specie carnis et sanguinis, nec in quantitate propria, ut in ea subsisto, quamvis simul cum ea accipiar (Dion. Carthus., De sacr. alt., art. 7).

midst as a perpetual sacrifice. He is the Head of the triumphant Church above, as well as of the Church militant here below: as He is in heaven, so likewise does He desire to be and abide here upon earth, even in His holy humanity. His presence accords perfectly with the state of the heavenly, as well as with that of the earthly Church here below: therefore, is He bodily present in a different way after the condition of each: in heaven He sitteth at the right hand of God, full of majesty and of glory; upon earth, on the contrary, He abides under the appearances of bread and wine, as a Sacrificial Victim in lowliness and obscurity. So long as the Church continues here below combating and suffering, in labor and tribulation, will Christ abide as a perpetual sacrifice with her; for He Himself will ever be the bright model and inexhaustible source of that life of sacrifice which the Church militant, as a true and worthy Spouse of the Crucified, leads upon earth and will lead unto the heavenly nuptial-day, whose happy dawn will usher in endless joy, crown us with victory and end all suffering. Amid the combat of mortal life, we will, full of consolation and confidence, have recourse to the holy altar, to implore there strength, courage and victory from the Divine Victim. [1]

12. The Prophecies of the Old Law prove the Truth and Reality of the Eucharistic Sacrifice.

Already in the Old Law God announced and predicted by the mouth of His Prophets the unbloody Sacrifice of the New Law.

1. In the first place, we have the figurative priesthood and sacrifice of Melchisedech. The kingly priest Melchisedech appears suddenly in the pages of Holy Writ as a mysterious personage and as suddenly disappears; God conferred upon him the honor of prefiguring the priesthood and the sacrifice of Jesus Christ, inasmuch as both are perpetuated in the New Covenant. — Christ is called "a priest forever according to the order of Melchisedech" (Ps. 109, 4). These words signify that Melchisedech, by the order of his priesthood, that is, by the nature of his sacrifice and by the manner of his offering sacrifice, prefigured the eternal priesthood of Jesus Christ. The eternal priesthood of Jesus Christ must, therefore, correspond to the figurative priesthood of Melchisedech and be similar to it in the nature and manner of its sacrifice. In other words, Jesus Christ must at all times offer His sacrifice in the same manner

---

[1] Magna fiducia adeundus est magnus Pontifex noster, Jesus Filius Dei, qui in aris nostris tamquam in throno gratiae sedet (Hebr. 4, 14—16). Regnat quidem apud coelitos, ex quo devicta morte coelos penetravit, Rex regum et Dominus dominantium; quotidie tamen velut hostia pacifica, quae imis summa reconciliet, ad instaurandum perficiendumque nostrae redemptionis opus offertur. Quae quidem oblatio inexhaustos in nostrum usum et commodum divinae misericordiae thesauros in se continet neque praesentis tantum vitae limitibus circumscribitur ejus fructus et utilitas, sed futuram etiam, alterumque, qui humanis oculis cerni non potest, mundum complectitur (Coll. Lac. 3, 493).

as Melchisedech offered his. The peculiar characteristic of the sacrifice, and, consequently, of the priesthood of Melchisedech consisted merely in this, that he offered bread and wine to the Most High (Gen. 14, 18). Accordingly Christ, as the true and eternal Melchisedech, must also offer a similar sacrifice, and that not merely once, but continually throughout all ages until the consummation of time. But this can be the case only if the daily celebration of the Eucharist under the species of bread and wine is a true and real sacrifice. Christ is "eternal priest according to the order of Melchisedech" only in so far as He, by changing the elements of bread and wine into His body and blood, offers perpetually to the Most High an unbloody sacrifice. — Thus the human figure Melchisedech harmonizes most beautifully with the Divine Original Jesus Christ, saving that the Sacrifice of Christ must be infinitely more perfect than was that of Melchisedech. In fact, Christ offers upon the altar not ordinary bread nor earthly wine, but "the holy bread of eternal life and the chalice of everlasting salvation." "Who," exclaims St. Cyprian, "is more a priest of God, the Most High, than our Lord Jesus Christ, who offered to God the Father a sacrifice, and offered the same as Melchisedech, that is bread and wine — His body, namely, and His blood." [1]

2. On the eternal priesthood and sacrifice of Christ, according to the order of Melchisedech, a marvellously clear light is cast by the grand prophecy of Malachias — the last of the Prophets: — "I have no pleasure in you — saith the Lord of hosts — and I will not receive a gift of your hand. For from the rising of the sun even to the going down, My name is great among the Gentiles, and in every place there is offered to My name a clean oblation" (Malachias 1, 10—11). [2]

The Fathers unanimously teach and the Church herself has formally declared, that the Holy Mass is that "clean oblation", which cannot be sullied by any unworthiness or depravity in him who offers it, and of which the Lord predicted by Malachias, that it would be offered in all places to His name, which would be great among

---

[1] Ep. ad Caecilium, c. 3. — Sacerdos in aeternum Christus Dominus secundum ordinem Melchisedech, panem et vinum obtulit (Antiph. in festo Corpor. Christi).

[2] Non est mihi voluntas in vobis, dicit Dominus exercituum, et munus non suscipiam de manu vestra. Ab ortu enim usque ad occasum magnum est nomen meum in gentibus, et in omni loco sacrificatur et offertur nomini meo oblatio munda, quia magnum est nomen meum in gentibus, dicit Dominus exercituum (Malach. 1, 10—11). The words *magnum est, sacrificatur et offertur* do not relate to the present, but to the future, and to the Christian future, as is evidenced by the context; the Prophets frequently use in their prophecies the present tense instead of the future, because they were accustomed to behold as present the event which, according to time and distance, was to happen in the future. The expressions *ab ortu solis usque ad occasum, in omni loco, in gentibus* (hebr. gojim — not Israelites, but pagan nations), designate the universality or Catholicity of the promised worship and sacrifice, such a universality as is found only in the Christian Church.

the nations."[1] — In the above prophecy (verse the tenth) the annulment and the rejection of the sacrificial worship of the Old Law are clearly and emphatically expressed; then, in verse the eleventh a new worship is foretold and therewith an oblation that is new, unbloody, ineffably pure and to be partaken of, is promised to be offered in all places. By this nothing else can be meant than the celebration of the Holy Eucharist in the Catholic Church.

a) The severe and bitter complaint of the Lord: "I have no pleasure in you," refers to the priests of Levi, who after their return from exile, "as despisers of the divine name," were very careless and irreverent in offering sacrifices; for God complains by the Prophet, that, contrary to the Law, they offered to Him what was "lame and blind and sick." The Lord, therefore, expresses His displeasure at the defective and unclean sacrifices of the priests of Levi; taking an opportunity, at the same time, to announce the total cessation of the sacrificial worship of the Old Testament in these words: "From your hands (that is, from the hands of the priests of Levi) I shall accept no more sacrifices." The true reason why the Lord rejects the Mosaic sacrifices, is not because they were carelessly offered, but because of the fact that an entirely different and new sacrifice was to be offered to Him from the rising to the setting of the sun. "He taketh away the first (the sacrifice of the Old Covenant), that He may establish that which followeth (the Sacrifice of the New Covenant)" (Heb. 10, 9).

b) The ancient sacrificial worship is to be annulled and replaced by a new and better worship. By the worship promised "the name of God will be made great," that is, worshipped and glorified, and that not only in Jerusalem, but "from the rising to the setting of the sun," namely, throughout the entire world; not merely among the Jews, but "among the nations" of the whole earth: in short — "in all places." In contrast to the Mosaic worship, which was confined to one nation and to one place, the new worship is represented as being spread among all nations and throughout the whole world, that is, a true Catholic worship, which is found nowhere but in the Church of Jesus Christ. Hence only Christian worship could have been meant; for the prophecy refers to that time when Christ, as the Prince of Peace, would "rule from sea to sea and from river unto the ends of the earth" — and when "all kings of the earth shall adore Him, when all nations shall serve Him" (Ps. 71, 8, 11).

c) This new, this Christian worship is more minutely characterized as being true and peculiar divine worship. A true and real Sacrifice is promised for the New Dispensation, to replace those offerings which the Lord will no longer accept from the hands of the priests of Aaron, and which, nevertheless, were also real sacrifices. "Not that sacrifice in itself was rejected; for sacrifices were to be found among the Jewish nation and in the Church — but only the manner of offering sacrifice has been changed" (*non genus ob-*

---

[1] Counc. of Trent, Session 22, Chap. 1.

lationum reprobatum est . . . . sed species immutata est tantum).[1]
The words promising the new Sacrifice are as follows : "In all places
there shall be offered a clean oblation (*mincha purum*) to My
name."[2] These words can by no means be figuratively understood
of an oblation not essentially and really a sacrifice, as that of prayer
or any other good work ; for the words clearly and emphatically
express a true and real sacrifice, whether we consider the context or
the words in themselves. — And here the clean oblation of the New
Dispensation is placed in contrast to the unclean sacrifices of the
Old Dispensation ; but the contrast is complete only when there is
question in both cases of sacrifice in its strict sense. — Each word
is so chosen as to designate, not only a real sacrifice in general, but
more particularly and strictly an unbloody sacrifice. This is especially the case with the word *mincha*, which in the holy (liturgical)
mode of speech is invariably employed to indicate the unbloody
sacrifices of eatables. — With the prophecy of this sacrifice is connected the announcement of a new and special priesthood, destined
to offer the new sacrifice ; and with regard to their priestly office
the new ministers of the altar are designated as *Levites* by the same
Prophet Malachias (3, 3—4). Since the new sacrifice is to be
celebrated everywhere, its priests, unlike the Jewish priesthood, do
not belong to one tribe or people, but are chosen by the Lord from
all nations, and by supernatural consecration are fitted and sanctified
for their office. After the Prophet Isaias (66, 18—21) had described
the conversion of the pagan nations and their entrance into the
Christian Church, he continues : "And I will take of them to be
priests and Levites, saith the Lord" — *Et assuman ex eis in sacerdotes et levitas, dicit Dominus.*

---

[1] S. Iren. Adv. haeres., 1. 4, c. 18, n. 2.

[2] Et in omni loco sacrificatur et offertur nomini meo oblatio munda. — The
original text is emphatic ; translated literally it reads thus : Et in omni loco suffi-
mentum oblatum nomini meo, et (incruentum) sacrificium mundum. The words
of the Vulgate sacrificatur et offertur are in the Hebrew muctar muggasch = sacrificium (incruentum) oblatum. Muctar is the participle of hofal and the meaning
of it is rendered in the sense of sacrificium in genere or rather sacrificium incruentum ; for according to its etymology it signifies the sacrificium incensi thuris
vel thymiana = incense-offering. The other participle muggasch = oblatum expresses the presentation. An explanatory addition to the preceding forms the two
concluding words oblatio munda, which in the original text are mincha tehora =
(incruentum) sacrificium mundum. The word mincha has in the Old Testament
one hundred and fifty-four times the specific signification of unbloody sacrifice.
All three words — muctar, muggasch, mincha — occurring in the original text are
often found employed in the liturgical language of the Old Testament, but always
only to signify real sacrifice, *never* to signify interior acts of worship, or such exterior oblations as are not real sacrifices. The sense of the entire text is therefore :
Et in omni loco offertur nomini meo sacrificium, mincha (= incruentum sacrificium) mundum (Cf. Franzelin, De sacrif. th. 10. — Lambrecht, De ss. Miss.
sacrif., Pars 2, cap. 3, 2. — Corluy S. J., Spicilegium dogmatico-biblicum, 2, 398—
408. — Knabenbauer S. J., Commentar. in Prophet. minor. 2, 430—445).

d) From the prophecy just quoted and explained it is now no longer difficult to prove the truth of the Eucharistic Sacrifice. The Prophet announces that there shall be offered in the Christian era throughout the whole earth an unbloody but real sacrifice. — This can mean nothing else than the celebration of the Eucharist: were it not a real sacrifice, then we should be forced to admit that the divine prediction has not been accomplished, — a conclusion that is inadmissible. — The words of the Prophet can not be applied to the Sacrifice of the Cross; for it was offered only in one place and then in a bloody manner, while the sacrifice foretold is an *unbloody* one and offered *everywhere.* On the other hand, in the Holy Sacrifice of the Mass, and in it alone, are found united all those marks by which the Prophet characterizes the promised Sacrifice of the New Law. The new sacrifice is an unbloody oblation of food: is not the Eucharist such, in a marvellous sense? — The sacrifice announced is universal, that is, offered in all places and among all nations: the Sacrifice of the Mass is celebrated wherever the sun shines and the Catholic Church exists — in the Old and in the New World, in the South and at the North, on the hills and in the plains, in the sumptuous cathedral and in the poor village church. — The new sacrifice magnifies the name of the Lord, that is, it contains in itself the most worthy adoration and glorification of the Divine Majesty: it is indeed upon the altar that "all honor and glory" is rendered unto the Holy Trinity. — Finally, the sacrifice in prospective vision is praised, with particular emphasis, as perpetual and perfectly clean: where is this prerogative found in a higher degree than in the Eucharistic Sacrifice? This sacrifice appears not only as exceedingly clean in its exterior celebration and offering, but it is in its very nature and essence so absolutely spotless as to be untarnishable even by the unworthy dispositions of those who offer it; for Christ, the Holy of Holies, is not only the Sacrificial Victim, but also preeminently the Sacrificer at the altar. [1]

3. Already the figurative sacrifice of bread and wine of Melchisedech, as well as the prophecy of Malachias, intimated that the perpetual Sacrifice of the New Dispensation would be a food oblation, and, consequently, that a sacrificial banquet would be connected therewith. This Eucharistic sacrificial repast is beautifully described and clearly announced in an exceedingly mysterious, venerable and affecting Psalm. We allude to Psalm 21. According to the testimony of Holy Scripture, of the Church and of the Fathers, this Psalm is Messianic; and furthermore that it is not only indirectly, but also directly and exclusively Messianic, is taught and

---

[1] Sacrificium consistit partim in actione offerendi, partim in re oblata. Ergo ut sit omnino purum et mundum, non satis est, quod res oblata sit pura, sed praeterea requiritur, ut persona offerens sit pura: quia alioquin actio offerendi non esset omnino pura. Huc refertur illud Malach. 1, 11: "In omni loco sacrificatur et offertur nomini meo oblatio munda" non solum ex parte rei oblatae, sed etiam ex parte principalis offerentis, non tamen ex parte aliorum hominum offerentium (Becanus, Summa theolog. de Sacrific. Miss. p. 1, quaest. 9).

clearly and most satisfactorily proven by almost all Catholic commentators. The Psalm contains a prophetic Gospel relative to the passion of the Lord, and admits of two divisions or parts ; the first part, from verse first to the twenty-second, expresses sorrow, suffering and lament, and unfolds a painful picture of the Crucified Saviour; while the second part, from verse twenty-third to the thirty-second, presents in consoling and bright imagery the abundant fruits of sacrifice and benediction that flow from the passion of the Lord upon Christ Himself and upon those whom He has redeemed. In so far as the latter part of the Psalm refers to our subject, it reads thus :

V. 23. Narrabo nomen tuum fratribus meis: in medio ecclesiae laudabo te.

V. 23. I will declare Thy name to my brethren : in the midst of the Church will I praise Thee.

V. 26. Apud te laus mea in ecclesia magna: vota mea reddam in conspectu timentium eum.

V. 26. With Thee is my praise in a great church: I will pay my vows in the sight of them that fear Him.

V. 27. Edent pauperes et saturabuntur, et laudabunt Dominum, qui requirunt eum : vivent corda eorum in saeculum saeculi.

V. 27. The poor shall eat and shall be filled, and they shall praise the Lord that seek Him : their hearts shall live forever and ever.

V. 28. Reminiscentur et convertentur ad Dominum universi fines terrae : et adorabunt in conspectu ejus universae familiae gentium.

V. 28. All the ends of the earth shall remember, and shall be converted to the Lord: and all the kindreds of the gentiles shall adore in His sight.

V. 29. Quoniam Domini est regnum, et ipse dominabitur gentium.

V. 29. For the kingdom is the Lord's, and He shall have dominion over the nations.

V. 30. Manducaverunt et adoraverunt omnes pingues terrae : in conspectu ejus cadent omnes, qui descendunt in terram.

V. 30. All the fat ones of the earth have eaten and have adored : all they that go down to the earth shall fall before Him.

These words find their full and true meaning only when applied to the Eucharistic Sacrifice and banquet. While the Lord on the Cross is immersed in the lowest depths of torment in body and soul, there gushes forth from His Heart that suffering and agonizing prayer of our Psalm. Then the dark clouds lift at once and disappear ; the morn of the Resurrection dawns clear and brilliant upon His gaze ; all the blessings and glorious results of His passion and death reveal themselves, the future bright and consoling, full of salvation and glory stretches out before Him.   With this blessed perspective presenting itself to His view, the Lord utters the above verses of the Psalm, wherein He predicts a sacrifice and a sacrificial banquet, to which all the inhabitants of the earth are invited.

Verse 23.   All, that have been redeemed by the Sacrifice of the Cross, are "brethren" of Christ and children of God ; as such they constitute the great family of God, namely, the Church, which has been gathered from all nations.   "In the midst of this Church" (*in medio ecclesiae*) Christ, the risen Saviour, abides mystically, perpetually, as the author and source of the joyful tidings that herald to the regenerated "brethren" of Christ the "name" of the triune God.   In the Sanctuary of this Church the glorified Redeemer dwells and lives forevermore, His Eucharistic presence being there as an unfailing source of endless praise to the Almighty.

Verse 26.   After this manner does the Lord promise to glorify His Father "with praises in the great assembly" of the Catholic Church (*in ecclesia magna*).   The crown of this praise is to consist in this that He "would discharge in full His vows" (*vota mea reddam*),[1] that is, that He would uninterruptedly offer a public vow — or thank-offering.[2]   By this offering is understood and meant the Eucharistic peace-offering offered "in presence of those who fear the Lord," who worship His Divine Majesty by faith, love and devotion.   Our Lord here announces that in grateful acknowledgment of His deliverance from suffering and death, He would continually offer the Holy Sacrifice of the Mass, which is not only the eternal and unbloody continuation, but also the sweet fruit of the bitter Sacrifice of the Cross.[3]

Verse 27.   In connection with this Sacrifice there is spread a banquet — the Communion of the admirable Body and Blood of Christ.   To partake of this food of God, to sit at this banquet of love, all indeed are invited ; but among the attending guests, the

[1] Vota — Offering of Vows, that is, peace-offerings made in thanksgiving, in fulfilment of a promise made, in case the petition were granted, when the favor was implored of God.   Along with the peace-offerings were joined banquet-offerings, to which widows and orphans, the poor and needy were invited.

[2] *Vota mea*, i. e. sacrificium N. L., videlicet sacrificium corporis et sanguinis mei, *reddam*, i. e. per sacerdotes meos offerri faciam Domino *in conspectu timentium eum*, i. e. praesentibus atque cernentibus populis Christianis (Dion. Carthus. In Ps. 21, 26).

[3] Vota mea reddam in conspectu timentium eum: per vota intelligenda videntur hoc loco vota sacrificiorum et oblationum juxta illud Is. 19, 21: "Colent eum in hostiis et muneribus; vota vovebunt Domino et reddent." Christus enim cum videret holocaustum mortis suae gratissimum Deo fuisse, videtur quodammodo promisisse, se holocaustum illud per ministros suos frequentissime oblaturum eo quo deceret modo, atque hoc est, quod nunc dicit: "Vota mea reddam in conspectu timentium eum" i. e. per ministros meos, sacerdotes novi Testamenti, assidue immolabo sacrificium Deo gratissimum, idque "in conspectu timentium", i. e. colentium eum ac per hoc verorum fidelium (Bellarminus, In Ps. 21).

honored and preferred are the "poor" in spirit, the humble and the lowly, — in short, all that have emptied their hearts and divested them of the love of the goods of this earth, and who, therefore, hunger and thirst after the imperishable food of heaven. These "poor in spirit will eat" at the table of the Lord and be "filled," that is, they will be strengthened and consoled, be replenished with joy and be loaded with graces; refreshed and regaled with heavenly nourishment, "they will sing praise to the Lord whom they sought," and of whose unspeakable sweetness they have tasted. Therefore, their hearts will live eternally; for whosoever eats of the living and life-giving bread of the Eucharist "will not die forever" (John 6).[1]

Verse 28. Unto this sacrifice and banquet of grace not only is Israel summoned, but from "the ends of the earth" all peoples are thereunto invited. Aroused by the sound of Apostolic preaching, heathen nations, hitherto forgetful of God and estranged from Him, wandering about in error, like lost sheep, shall "be reminded" — shall be renewed in the faith of God and by penance "shall be converted" to God (*reminiscentur et convertentur*); the heathens, at one time "without grace," but "now partakers of it" (1 Peter 2, 10) and belonging to the kingdom of God, will adore "the Lord in spirit and in truth."

Verse 29. The Church of God, the kingdom of grace, which the Lord conquered by His blood, comprises all "nations" and embraces the ends of the earth; for "Christ hath conquered, Christ reigns, Christ governs" by reason of the Sacrifice of His life. *Regnavit a ligno Deus.*

Verse 30. Still, not only the poor, but also the rich, the great and the powerful of the earth (*pingues terrae*) are called to partake of this sacrificial banquet and to adore; yes, every mortal, whose lot it is to return into the "dust" of the earth, will "fall down" in profound reverence before the altar, upon which the majesty of the Eucharistic Redeemer is offered and hidden.

4. During the period of the Old Dispensation a mysterious obscurity hung over all such prophecies; but in the light of Christianity they are made plain. Who does not recognize their glorious fulfilment in the Eucharistic Sacrifice and Communion, which the Catholic Church celebrates in all places and at all times? These prophecies are full of consolation, for they guarantee the truth and divinity of our daily Sacrifice. "Not to themselves, but to you the Prophets have ministered" (1 Peter 1, 12), inasmuch as, urged on

---

[1] *Edent pauperes,* i. e. humiles manducabunt sacramentum altaris, non solum sacramentaliter, sed etiam spiritualiter, et ideo *saturabuntur,* i. e. mentaliter impinguabuntur caritate, gratia, consolatione ac donis Spiritus Sancti, et *laudabunt Dominum* Jesum Christum, qui est in hoc sacramento dator ac donum, *qui requirunt eum* affectu, fide et opere sequendo vestigia ejus; *vivent corda eorum* spirituali vita *in saeculum saeculi,* i. e. sine fine. Nunc enim vivunt per fidem et caritatem, consummatoque cursu praesentis exilii vivent per contemplationem et gloriam. Vivent enim quoniam fontem vitae, sc. Christum, digne recipiunt (Joan. 6, 51 et 52). Dion. Carthus. in Ps. 21, 27.

and enlightened by the Spirit of God, they foretold the salutary Sacrifice and the heavenly banquet of the Eucharist. How great our happiness and how great a grace for us to be able to behold and to enjoy in the bosom of the Church all these promised goods of the Lord! Those enlightened men of ancient times "not receiving the promises, beheld and saluted them from afar off" (Heb. 11, 13): we are in the possession and the enjoyment of all the treasures of Redemption. Hence these words addressed by the Lord to His Apostle are also applicable to us: "Blessed are the eyes that see the things which you see. For I say to you that many prophets and kings have desired to see the things that you see, and have not seen them; and to hear the things that you hear, and have not heard them" (Luke 10, 23—24).

13. The Truth and the Reality of the Eucharistic Sacrifice — proved from the Writings of the New Testament.

That which in the Old Dispensation was prophetically promised by word and figure, has found its wonderful fulfilment and completion in the New Law of Grace, through Jesus Christ who, after suffering death and when leaving the world, bequeathed to His Holy Church as a precious inheritance a clean food-offering and a heavenly sacrificial food. Our Lord "terminated the period of His earthly pilgrimage by a wonderful order" (*sui moras incolatus miro clausit ordine*). Before offering Himself on the Cross in bloody sacrifice, to redeem us from all iniquity and to present to Himself a people acceptable and zealous in the performance of good works (Tit. 2, 14), He had already offered Himself to His Heavenly Father as an unbloody sacrifice under the appearances of bread and wine; as Father of the world to come (Isa. 9, 6), He instituted at the same time the celebration of this unbloody sacrifice for all future ages. The Church says on this subject: "Although Christ, our Lord and God, willed to offer Himself once unto death upon the altar of the Cross, thereon to accomplish an eternal redemption, and because His priesthood was not to cease with His death, He, furthermore, in order to leave to His Church a visible sacrifice, such as human nature requires and demands, did at the Last Supper proclaim Himself the eternally instituted priest, according to the order of Melchisedech, and did offer to God the Father His body and blood under the appearances of bread and wine... To the Apostles, whom He at the same time constituted Priests of the New Dispensation, as well as to their successors in the priesthood, He gave the command to offer this Sacrifice, by the words: 'Do this in commemoration of Me,' as the Catholic Church has at all times held and taught."[1] It is manifestly evident from the words which Christ our Lord employed in celebrating and instituting the Eucharist, that on the night of the Last Supper He did by the consecration of bread and wine perform a true

---

[1] Trid. sess. 22, cap. 1.

and real sacrificial act, and ordained that it be repeated until the consummation of time.⟩

1. The Last Supper was not merely a communion celebration, but also a sacrificial celebration ; for "after partaking of the figurative lamb," our Lord, by His creative omnipotent word, changed the earthly elements of bread and wine into His holy Body and divine Blood, that is, He placed His Body and His Blood in the sacramental state of sacrifice, offered Himself thus to His Father and then gave His Body and His Blood offered in sacrifice to His disciples as food and drink.

a) St. Luke gives the words of consecration thus: "This is the chalice, the new testament in My blood, which (chalice) shall be shed for you ;" St. Matthew: "For this is My blood of the new testament, which shall be shed for many, unto the remission of sins."[1]   Vicariously to shed blood for the atonement of the sins of others, — is an expression frequently employed in Holy Writ to designate sacrifice.   Hence the words of the institution convey this idea: This is the chalice which is offered for you ; this is My blood which is offered for many, in order to blot out sins.   Our Lord, therefore, declares that He presents His sacrificial Blood to His disciples as drink, and that His Blood is offered in sacrifice.   The words of our Lord are (according to the original Greek text) so constituted that they directly and expressly designate the offering of His Blood by a mystical or mysterious shedding in the chalice, and not that of a true and real shedding of His blood on the Cross. — So in order to show that here the sacramental offering of the blood of Christ is meant, reference is made, and very justly, to the use of the verb in the present tense by the Evangelists: "which is shed" ($\dot{\epsilon}\kappa\chi\upsilon\nu\acute{o}\mu\epsilon\nu\upsilon\nu =$ *qui effunditur*); and there is no reason for departing here from the meaning of the present tense.   Now that we must adhere to this meaning is clearly and incontestably proved by the expression employed by St. Luke.   According to it, it is not said that the blood is shed, but that the chalice is poured out ($\tau\grave{o}$ $\pi\upsilon\tau\acute{\eta}\rho\iota\upsilon\nu$. . . . $\tau\grave{o}$ $\dot{\upsilon}\pi\grave{\epsilon}\rho$ $\dot{\upsilon}\mu\hat{\omega}\nu$ $\dot{\epsilon}\kappa\chi\upsilon\nu\acute{o}\mu\epsilon\nu\upsilon\nu = calix$, *qui pro vobis effunditur*).   This figurative mode of speech does not state merely that the contents of the chalice, that is, that the Blood of Christ contained in the chalice, will be somehow or somewhere shed, for example, on the Cross, but, on the contrary, that Christ's Blood will be shed precisely inasmuch as it is present and contained in the chalice — in other words, that it is shed in the

---

[1] Hic est calix novum testamentum in sanguine meo, qui pro vobis fundetur ($\tau\grave{o}$ $\pi\upsilon\tau\acute{\eta}\rho\iota\upsilon\nu$. . . . $\tau\grave{o}$ $\dot{\upsilon}\pi\epsilon\rho$ $\dot{\upsilon}\mu\hat{\omega}\nu$ $\dot{\epsilon}\kappa\chi\upsilon\nu\acute{o}\mu\epsilon\nu\upsilon\nu$).   Luc. 22, 20. — Hic est enim sanguis meus novi testamenti, qui pro multis effundetur in remissionem peccatorum ($\tau\grave{o}$ $\alpha\hat{\iota}\mu\alpha$. . . . $\tau\grave{o}$ $\dot{\epsilon}\kappa\chi\upsilon\nu\acute{o}\mu\epsilon\nu\upsilon\nu$).   Matth. 26, 28.   The original Greek text here designates that also at the consecration of the bread the Eucharistic Sacrifice is directly offered and the Sacrifice of the Cross only indirectly, while reversely the Vulgate has the Sacrifice of the Cross directly and the Eucharistic Sacrifice only indirectly expressed.   The original text and the Vulgate both express the same thing, but in a different manner.   On this subject compare Franzelin De ss. Eucharist. Sacrific., thes. 11.

sacramental state under the appearance of wine. [1] — Our Lord Himself declares unequivocally, that He had shed and poured out His Eucharistic Blood mystically in the chalice, namely, that He had truly offered it to God the Father; consequently, the act of consecration at the Last Supper was a true sacrificial act.

But the blood only cannot be shed, that is, sacrificed, without the body being, at the same time, also sacrificed; body and blood constitute together but one sacrificial gift. The above proof, that Christ at the first celebration of the Eucharist sacrificed His blood, likewise goes to establish the conclusion and the supposition that He also at the same time and in the same manner offered His body, a fact which can be specially proved from the formula of the consecration of the bread.

According to St. Luke our Lord consecrated the bread with the words: "This is My body which is given for you;" St. Paul in the Greek text has the formula: "This is My body which shall be delivered for you." [2] Hence Christ does not say that His body shall be given, or broken, to the disciples, but He declares that His body shall be delivered for ($\dot{v}\pi\dot{\epsilon}\rho$, *pro*) His disciples and "for many unto the remission of sins," as is to be supplied in this place from the formula of the consecration of the wine. Now, the vicarious immolation of the body of Christ for the atonement of sin is indisputably a true sacrifice. The words of our Lord: "This is My body which is given and delivered, or broken, for you," have, therefore, this meaning: This is My body which is sacrificed for you. — The giving or the breaking of the body of Christ in the celebration of the Eucharist is characterized and designated in the present time, not merely as about to take place in the future on the Cross; consequently, there can here be literally meant and understood only the unbloody Sacrifice of the body of Christ in the Eucharist, and not the bloody Sacrifice of the Cross. — This is proved, in the first place, by the use of the present tense: the "body which is given and broken for you" ($\delta\iota\delta\acute{o}\mu\epsilon\nu\sigma\nu = quod\ datur;\ \ \kappa\lambda\acute{\omega}\mu\epsilon\nu\sigma\nu = quod\ frangitur$); for so long as there is no reason to compel us, we dare not depart from the meaning of the present tense in the text. In this instance nothing either requires or justifies us in applying or transferring the present form of the verb to the future Sacrifice of the Cross. On the contrary, there are reasons which preclude such an application. — For, from the circumstance that the shedding of the blood is to be understood in the present time, it necessarily follows that the Sacrifice of the body must be considered also as taking place in the present time. — And the expression of St. Paul, "the body broken for you" (*corpus pro vobis fractum*) is of such a nature that it unequivocally

---

[1] Verum quidem est quod continens ponitur pro contento; quia tamen effusio hic tribuitur *calici* et non sanguini, nisi quatenus calice continetur, necesse est intelligere effusionem, quae tunc fiebat, quando sanguis calice contentus effundebatur, quod erat in coena (Sylvius, In 3, q. 83, a. 1).

[2] Hoc est corpus meum, quod pro vobis datur ($\delta\iota\delta\acute{o}\mu\epsilon\nu\sigma\nu$). Luc. 22, 19. Hoc est corpus meum, quod pro vobis tradetur ($\kappa\lambda\acute{\omega}\mu\epsilon\nu\sigma\nu$). 1 Cor. 11, 24.

designates the Sacrifice of the Eucharist. [1]   The word broken (*frangere*) can in this place be applied only to the body of Christ, inasmuch as, under the appearance of bread, it is presented and eaten as a food ; for only the Eucharistic Body is broken or distributed. The literal meaning of the Apostle is, therefore : This is My body which as food under the appearance of bread is broken for you. — Now, these words necessarily have the same meaning as those of St. Luke : "This is My body which is given for you," that is, sacrificed ; hence they must in like manner express the Sacrifice of the Body of Christ.   The full meaning of the words of St. Paul is accordingly : This is My body which is sacrificed for you in the sacramental state, in which it is given as food. [2]   Thus Christ gave His body, primarily, to His Heavenly Father as a sacrifice for His disciples, and He then distributed to them His Body sacrificed for them to be eaten as food.   By this He accomplished a former prediction : "The bread (of heaven) that I will give (*vobis*) is My flesh for the life of the world" (*pro mundi vita* — Joann. 6, 52).

Hence it is clearly expressed in Holy Scripture that the first celebration of the Eucharist, which our Lord arranged for the eve of His passion, in the presence of His Apostles, was a true Sacrifice and a sacrificial repast. — The Sacrifice was accomplished in the words : "This is My body ; this is My blood ;" for by these words, Christ's body and blood under the appearances of bread and wine were placed in the sacramental state of sacrifice, that is, they were sacrificed to adore and appease the Divine Majesty. — The declaration that this action and change was a true Sacrifice, a real sacrificial act, is contained in the additional words : "which shall be given or broken for you ; — which shall be shed for you and for many."   They designate and testify to this, namely, the sacrifice of the Eucharistic Body taking place at that moment, and likewise the shedding of the Eucharistic Blood then taking place in the chalice ; they designate, therefore, the Body and Blood of Christ under the sacramental appearances as a truly and really sacrificed Body and as a truly and really sacrificed Blood.

b) Christ not only before His death offered Himself in an unbloody manner, but He, moreover, instituted a perpetual unbloody Sacrifice.   This is easily proved.   In the following words : "Do this for a commemoration of Me" (*Hoc facite in meam commemorationem* — Luke 22, 19), the Lord commanded His Apostles and their successors in the priestly dignity (1 Cor. 11, 24—27) to do the same (*hoc*) as He had done, until His return at the end of time, that is, continually to offer the Eucharistic Sacrifice, which He had

---

[1] Cfr. Maldonat., Comment. in Matth. c. 26, v. 26. — Estius, Comment. in cap. 11, Epist. 1, ad Cor. v. 24. — Cornely, S. J. l. c.

[2] Oportet intelligere verba illa de vero corpore, sed sub specie panis, ut sensus sit : Hoc est corpus meum, quod nunc pro vobis in specie panis frangitur, i. e. datur et immolatur Deo (Bellarmin., De Missa, l. 1, c. 12).

just offered in their presence.[1]   By this command, as a natural consequence, He also imparted to them the power of consecration, or of offering sacrifice, that is, He made them priests of the New Law. "Thus our Lord instituted the Eucharistic Sacrifice, and willed to transmit the power to offer it to priests only, to whom it appertains to partake of it and to distribute it to the rest."

2.   Certain circumstances under which the Eucharist was celebrated and instituted by the Lord, serve to develop still further its sacrificial character, and to confirm the proofs already drawn from the words of the institution.

a) Our Saviour named His blood, contained and shed in the chalice, *the blood of the New Testament* (Matt. 26, 28).   The word testament has here a twofold meaning ; namely, covenant and legacy. — Christ is the mediator of a better covenant, which is established on better promises (Heb. 8, 6), and that covenant is the new covenant of grace.

This covenant was formed mainly at the Last Supper and at the same time sealed with Christ's Eucharistic Blood in the chalice ; it then obtained by the shedding of the Blood of Christ its valid and complete confirmation.[2]   Thus Christ's Blood was equally as well in the chalice as on the Cross the Blood of the Covenant, that is, the Blood in which the new Covenant of Grace was established.   Therefore, the Blood of Christ must not only not have first been sacrificed on the Cross, but previously offered in the chalice as sacrificial blood.   This is required by the contrast here evidently made between the establishment of the old and the new covenants ; for the words of our Saviour : "This is My blood, the blood of the new covenant," contain a distinct allusion to the words : "This is the blood of the covenant which the Lord hath made with you" (Exod. 24, 8), the words spoken by Moses after the establishment of the covenant of the Old Law, when he sprinkled the people with blood. At the foot of Mount Sinai, God formed a solemn covenant with the chosen people Israel.   The Lord gave His laws and promises ; the people promised obedience to the instructions and regulations contained in the book of the covenant, and then they were sprinkled with "the blood of the covenant."   This blood of the Old Law was sacrificial blood ; for it was consecrated by the offering of holocausts. — The covenant into which God, through Moses, entered with the Israelites, was only a figure of the new and better covenant which God, through Jesus Christ, formed with mankind.   But in order to be the counterpart and completion of the old covenant, the new covenant had likewise to be established by a sacrifice and to be sealed

---

[1]   Qui (Jesus Christus) formam sacrificii perennis instituens, hostiam se tibi (Deus) primum obtulit, et primus docuit offerri (Liturg. Gallic.).

[2]   Sine dubio in ultima coena praecipue condidit (Christus) testamentum quod suo etiam sanguine tunc incruente immolato sancivit; postea vero in sacrificio cruento omnino stabilivit ac confirmavit (Suarez, In III. S. Thom., disp. 37, sect. 4, n. 15).

with sacrificial blood. Hence it follows that the Eucharistic Blood, which flowed in the chalice for the sealing of the new covenant, was the sacrificial Blood of Jesus Christ shed for the glory of God. This celebration of the Eucharist established by our Lord became, consequently, a true and real sacrifice. — The better covenant, whose author and surety (Heb. 7, 22) Jesus Christ became, is not merely an alliance between God and the regenerated, but, moreover, a legacy.[1] That which Christ bequeathed to us at the Last Supper is nothing else than His sacrificial Body and sacrificial Blood, the Eucharistic Sacrifice together with all the goods and graces of redemption included therein.

b) The paschal lamb of the Old Dispensation was the most expressive and universal figure of the Eucharist.[2] Christ in the Blessed Sacrament is the true paschal lamb, He is our paschal lamb, having taken the place of the ancient. Therefore, the priest during Mass, immediately before his Communion, says the *Agnus Dei*, and before he administers the heavenly Eucharistic Food to the faithful, he says to them in a loud voice: "Behold the Lamb of God!" Ecce Agnus Dei! The ancient paschal lamb unquestionably had the character of sacrifice; the celebration of the Pasch was a sacrificial celebration. Accordingly the Eucharist must also be a true sacrifice; otherwise it would not perfectly correspond to the figurative paschal lamb nor would it fulfil in every respect this excellent type. But the Eucharist is in the most perfect respect the new Paschal Lamb and Easter Banquet of the New Dispensation, — therefore, it is also the true Paschal Lamb that is immolated upon the altar in an unbloody manner, and partaken of as an eternal remembrance of our deliverance from the bondage of sin, and as a perpetual thanksgiving for the wonderful work of redemption. The shadow of the Jewish Pasch disappeared before the brightness of the Eucharistic celebration. *In hac mensa novi Regis — Novum Pascha novae legis — Phase vetus terminat.* "In this Banquet of the new King, the new Paschal Lamb of the New Law puts an end to the ancient pasch." To signify this, our Lord joined directly with the (typical) Paschal celebration of the Old Dispensation the institution of the Eucharist as the Paschal Sacrifice and Banquet of the New Law. First, "He gave to His disciples the lamb and unleavened bread, according to the ordinance of the Law, which had been given to the forefathers." Then He offered Himself as the spotless and blame-

---

[1] Cf. Hebr. 9, 16. 17. — Testamentum is the translation of the Greek διαθήκη = arrangement, disposal, disposition, which may be unilateral disposal of inheritance, or may be effected by mutual agreement (covenant). Therefore Heb. 9, 16, διαθέμενος = testator, a testator. — St. Gaudentius (Sermon 2) calls the Eucharistic Sacrifice "the hereditary gift of the New Testament (*haereditarium munus* novi testamenti), which Christ on the night that He was given over to be crucified, left as a pledge of His presence."

[2] Quamquam multis figuris fuisset Eucharistia sacramentum praefiguratum, *praecipua* tamen ejus *figura* fuit agnus paschalis, cum secundum *omnia* ipsum repraesentaverit (S. Thom. 3, q. 73, a. 6).

4

less sacrificial Lamb in sacrifice to God; and, lastly, He fed His Apostles with His sacrificial flesh, and gave them to drink of His sacrificial Blood. The sacrificial banquet was necessarily preceded by a sacrificial action; for the lamb must be slain before it can be eaten.

3. The doctrine and practice of the Apostles prove that they henceforth celebrated the Eucharist as the Sacrifice of the Christian religion.

a) It is of the Christian altar, upon which the Sacrifice of the Eucharist is offered to God and from which this heavenly sacrificial food is given to the faithful for actual participation, that the following words, which St. Paul addressed to the Hebrews, are often understood: "We have an altar, whereof they have no power to eat who serve the tabernacle,"[1] that is, the Jews; for in order to have the right and privilege to participate by means of Holy Communion in the Eucharistic Sacrifice, they had to cease "to serve the tabernacle," that is, to renounce the Mosaic religion and enter into the Church of the Crucified.

b) The same Apostle "distinctly alludes to the Eucharistic Banquet (*non obscure innuit*), when he says that they who are defiled by partaking of the table of devils, must not partake of the table of the Lord, for by table he each time means the altar."[2] — In the aforesaid passage (1 Cor. 10, 20—21) the heathen sacrificial table and banquet are contrasted with the Eucharistic table and banquet, to show the Christians that it is by no means allowed them "to partake of the table of the Lord and the table of devils; to drink of the chalice of the Lord and the chalice of devils." The contrast between the Eucharistic table and the sacrificial banquets of the heathens is only then completely established, when the Eucharist is considered as a sacrifice of food and as a sacrificial banquet.

c) Finally, when it is recorded in the Acts of the Apostles, that the clergy (prophets and doctors) of the Church of Antioch "were ministering to the Lord,"[3] the celebration of the Sacrifice of the Mass is thereby unmistakably meant; sacrifice being the most worthy service (*oblatio servitutis*) that may and must be rendered to God alone. Therefore, it is evident that the Eucharistic celebration, which is frequently called in Holy Scripture the breaking of bread (*fractio panis*),[4] was in the Apostolic times and Church always regarded and performed as a true sacrificial celebration.

---

[1] Habemus altare (θυσιαστήριον), de quo edere (φαγεῖν) non habent potestatem (ἐξουσίαν), qui tabernaculo deserviunt (Hebr. 13, 10). — Cf. in contrast Stentrup, Soteriologia th. 87.

[2] Trident. sess. 22, cap. 1.

[3] Ministrantibus (λειτουργούντων) illis Domino (Act. 13, 2). The word λειτουργεῖν in the Old and New Testaments is frequently used for the celebration of public worship, principally to mean that of Holy Sacrifice; hence the Greeks usually call the Eucharistic Sacrifice and its celebration λειτουργία.

[4] Acts. 2, 42; 20, 7, 11. 1 Cor. 10, 16.

4. What a marvellous love the Sacred Heart of Jesus has manifested in the institution of the unbloody Sacrifice of the Eucharist![1] How could this divinely human, inconceivable, indescribable love have more touchingly manifested itself? Before the Sacred Heart immersed in the bloody ocean of the bitter pangs of death and broken asunder in death, it burst forth once more in divine radiating flames of love at the celebration of the Eucharistic Sacrifice and Sacrament, just like the gorgeous glow of the setting sun in the horizon. — A short time before His painful and ignominious death, "on the night," says the Gospel, "in which Jesus was betrayed," He bequeathed to us all that is most precious and most adorable in the mystery of the altar.[2] The hour had arrived for Him to depart out of this world, in order that His holy humanity might also take possession of that glory and splendor which He had shared with the Father before the creation of the world. Since He, the Good Shepherd, loved His own who were in the world, He loved them with an eternal love unto the end. Yes, He loved His own to the end, that is, not merely to the end of His life, but to the end of time ; for He will remain upon the Altar for the sake of His own as long as they are pilgrims in this world — wayfarers in this strange land — far from their heavenly country, whither He has preceded them, to prepare mansions for them in the House of His Father. He desires to be and remain with the children of salvation in the mystery of the Eucharist, abiding there for their sakes as a perpetual Victim and as the daily bread of the soul, until the Sacramental Banquet on earth finds its fulfilment in the kingdom of God

---

[1] Omnis sacerdos causas institutionis sacramenti altaris, videlicet cur Christus in coena novissima hoc supervenerandissimum instituerit sacramentum, sapienter atque multoties contempletur. Cujus utique institutionis prima causa est *recordatio totius ardentissimae ac plenissimae dilectionis Christi ad nos.* De qua dilectione ipsemet dixit: Majorem hac caritatem nemo habet, quam ut animam suam ponat pro amicis suis. Haec quippe est summa dilectio, dum quis non sua dona dumtaxat, sed seipsum quoque donat dilecto. Rursus, cum amoris proprietas sit, amantem unire amato, per hoc quod Christus in sacramento se ipsum nobis substantialiter unit, patet ipsius ad nos mutua dilectio ac summa. Toties ergo flammescit spiritus noster ad Deum, totiesque inflammatur ac penetratur, quoties celebramus, quoties sacramentum hoc consecramus ac sumimus, quoties caritatem Christi ad nos recordamur, quoties tantae dilectionis pignus prae oculis habemus, manibus contrectamus, ore suscipimus. Ideo namque Salvator, instituto hoc sacramento, dixit ac jussit sanctis apostolis et in eorum persona sacerdotibus universis : Hoc quotiescumque feceritis, in mei memoriam facietis. Quae utique verba sunt *mirabiliter affectuosa ac dulcia piaeque mentis inflammativa* (Dion. Carthus. De vita Curatorum, art. 15).

[2] Sunt et aliae causae (institutionis Eucharistiae), ut scilicet Christus homo indesinenter et maxime Deum Patrem, imo totam superbeatissimam Trinitatem veneretur tanti sacrificii jugi oblatione, in qua bonitas, caritas, misericordia Dei ad homines, beneficia et promissa ipsius commemorantur, laus, gratiarum actio et reverentia omnium fonti bonorum devotissime exhibentur, humanoque generi multipliciter, imo ineffabiliter subvenitur et *ipsa Ecclesia mirabilissime ditatur, ornatur, munitur* (Dion. Carthus. 4, dist. 8, quaest. 3).

(Luke 22, 15—16), that is, until the time shall come when they will eat and drink at the banquet of heavenly joy and felicity at that table, where the Lord will gird Himself and going about will minister unto them (Luke 22, 29; 12, 37). — He loved His own to the end, that is, to the uttermost bounds, so that He could not love them with greater or more intimate love. [1]   He had nothing more precious at His command than this best of gifts — the Mystery of His Body and Blood, nothing better than His own self with His divinity and humanity, with all the riches and treasures of the redemption. Mount Calvary did not suffice for the ardor of His love, it did not come soon enough for Him.   Before His Blood flowed forth in clear streams from a thousand wounds, He would shed it and have it flow mystically in the chalice; before His Body would be consumed as a fragrant victim on the Cross in the fire of torments, He wished to give and break it for us already at the Last Supper under the appearance of bread.   This unbloody Sacrifice of His Body and Blood, according to the directions of His last will, according to the testament of His Heart inflamed with love, is to be perpetuated to the consummation of the world!

> So great the love for us He bore,
> To torments and death He adds yet more;
> In the Supper Hall, Himself He gives,
> His token of love — with us forever to live.

> Under the appearance of bread and wine,
> He is our food, our nourishment divine;
> On the Cross His life He joyfully gave,
> On the Altar, His same Sacrifice will save.

> Like to the eternal glory of His name,
> His priesthood continues ever the same, —
> In sacrifice to the Father, daily His Sacred Heart
> Prompts Him, Himself to offer on our part!

14. The Proof from Tradition that the Eucharist is a True and Real Sacrifice.

To render our demonstration complete, we will now prove the existence of the Eucharistic Sacrifice from the other source of faith, — namely, divine tradition.   As "the pillar and ground of the truth" (1 Tim. 3, 15) the Catholic Church has always and everywhere believed and taught that the Holy Mass is a true Sacrifice — the sole and perpetual Sacrifice of the New Law.   As the faithful guardian and dispenser of all the means and treasures of the grace

---

[1] Cum dilexisset suos (τοὺς ἰδίους), qui erant in mundo, in finem (εἰς τέλος) dilexit eos (Joan. 13, 1).   Jesus had constantly shown His love to His disciples, whom He left behind in this world, but at His departure out of this world He loved them εἰς τέλος, until the end and the consummation, as much as a God-man could love — giving them the last and greatest proof of His love (τελειοτάτην ἐπεδείξατο τὴν ἀγάπησιν).   S. Cyr. i. h. 1.

of Jesus Christ, she has also at all times preserved and administered
the Eucharistic Sacrifice as her greatest treasure. — In the very
earliest ages of the Church there are to be found very many most
clear and most irrefragable testimonies in favor of the universal and
constant belief of all Christendom in the sacrificial character of the
Eucharist, as well as of its uninterrupted celebration as a sacrifice in
the bosom of the Catholic Church. As the most sublime and wonderful mystery of faith, the daily Sacrifice of the Mass was concealed
with the most anxious care from the eyes and ears of unbelievers
and of the uninitiated, so that the Fathers frequently speak of it in
an obscure and merely suggestive manner; but notwithstanding this
ancient prevalent discipline, there are to be found in their writings
and in the various liturgies so many beautiful expressions relative to
the Eucharist, that we may without difficulty gather therefrom all
the principal teachings of the Church with reference to the Holy
Sacrifice of the Mass.

1. When the Fathers speak of the celebration of the Eucharist,
they often use the expressions sacrifice (*sacrificium, oblatio, hostia,
victima*) and to offer (*sacrificare, immolare, offerre*), priest (*sacerdos*) and altar (*altare, ara*); they, therefore, acknowledge in the
Eucharistic celebration a sacrificing priest, a sacrificial gift, a sacrificial action and a place of sacrifice. But it unquestionably follows
from these words, that they are not to be taken in a wide sense, but
in their strict and literal meaning. —

a) They designate the celebration of the Eucharist often as a
sacrifice of atonement (θυσία τοῦ ἱλασμοῦ, *sacrificium propitiationis*), as
a complete and true sacrifice (*sacrificium plenum et verum*), as the
most sublime and the most true sacrifice (*summum et verissimum
sacrificium*), and as a tremendous sacrifice (φρικτὴ θυσία, *sacrificium
horrendum, tremendum, terribile*).

b) The Eucharistic Sacrifice, which can be celebrated only by
a duly ordained priest, they expressly distinguish from the improperly so called, that is, from the interior and spiritual sacrifice,
which each of the faithful may and should offer.

c) They distinguish the Sacrifice of the Body and Blood of
Christ, which is accomplished by the spiritual sword of the words of
consecration, from participation by Holy Communion in the completed Sacrifice, as well as from the prayers and ceremonies with
which the sacrificial action is accompanied and celebrated.

d) Very often they teach that the perpetual Sacrifice of the
New Covenant has replaced the figurative sacrifices of the Old Law.
They discover in the Sacrifice of the Altar the fulfilment of the
figurative sacrifice of Melchisedech; they behold in the Eucharist
the *clean oblation* predicted by Malachias.

e) When they consider more closely the relation of the Sacrifice
of the Mass to that of the Cross, they say that upon the Altar, as
upon the Cross, there is one and the same sacrificing Priest, one and
the same Sacrificial Victim, but a different mode or action of offer-

ing; for in the unbloody Sacrifice of the Altar the Lamb of God is mystically and sacramentally immolated, in order always to keep alive the remembrance of the bloody Sacrifice of the Cross.

f) They teach that the Eucharistic Sacrifice is offered not only for the living, but also for the dead, and that it procures for all atonement and forgiveness of sins.

g) From those who assist at this Sacrifice, they require the utmost devotion and the most profound reverence; from the celebrating priest, virginity and angelic purity of heart.

For these and similar proofs, we have "a cloud of witnesses" (Heb. 12, 1), but we shall here confine ourselves to a few passages from the Fathers.

A. The Fathers of the East.

Among these proofs we may also reckon the beautiful words said to have been addressed by St. Andrew, Apostle, to the proconsul who ordered him to offer sacrifice to the heathen gods. The Acts of the Martyrdom of this Apostle give them as follows: "Every day I present to God Almighty a living sacrifice. . . . daily I offer to God the Immaculate Lamb upon the Altar of the Cross (that is, upon what takes the place of the Cross). After the faithful have eaten the Flesh of this Immaculate Lamb and drunk of His Blood, He remains whole and living. . . . Although He has been sacrificed and eaten, this Lamb remains uninjured and lives immaculate in His kingdom."[1]

St. Irenaeus († 202) distinctly calls the Eucharist the clean oblation predicted by the Prophet Malachias. "Christ," he writes, "acknowledged (at the Last Supper) the chalice as His Blood and taught the new Sacrifice of the New Covenant, which the Church has received from the Apostles and offers to God throughout the entire world (*et novi Testamenti novam docuit oblationem, quam Ecclesia ab Apostolis accipiens in universo mundo offert Deo*)." "The Jews have not received the Word (*Verbum, λόγος*), which is sacrificed." This Sacrifice, which our Lord commanded to be offered, is accepted by God as a "clean oblation and well pleasing to Him" (*sacrificium purum et acceptum*).[2]

St. Ephrem († 379) — the greatest and most learned Father of the Syrian Church — filled with enthusiasm, extols the inconceivable dignity of the priesthood of the New Law. "O astounding miracle, O unspeakable power, O dread mystery of the priesthood! Spiritual

---

[1] Omnipotenti Deo ego omni die vivum sacrificium offero. . . . Agnum immaculatum quotidie in altari crucis (= quod est loco crucis) Deo offero, cujus carnes postquam fidelis populus manducavit et ejus bibit sanguinem, Agnus immaculatus integer manet et vivus. . . . Postquam immolatus et manducatus est, Agnus integer manet et immaculatus vivit in regno suo (S. Andr. Apost. in epist. Presbyt. Achaiae c. 6). — The authenticity of these Acts is indeed disputed; they are, however, an undeniably ancient and venerable written memorial that reaches back to the third century.

[2] Adv. haeres. 1. 4, c. 17—18.

and holy, sublime and immeasurable office, which Christ, after His coming into this world, gave to us without our meriting it! On bended knees, with tears and sighs, I beg to consider this treasure of the priesthood; I repeat, a treasure for those who preserve it worthily and holily. Yet, shall I attempt to extol the dignity of the priesthood? It exceeds all comprehension and all conception. It was, I believe, in consideration of the priesthood that St. Paul exclaimed: 'O the depth of the riches, of the wisdom and the knowledge of God!' " With respect to the Eucharist, we find in his writings the following passage: "Fire once fell upon the sacrifices of Elias and consumed them. For us the fire[1] of mercy became the sacrifice of life. Fire at one time consumed the sacrifice; but Thy fire, O Lord, we eat at Thy Sacrifice."[2]

Cyrillonas,[3] after Ephrem the most famous of the Syrian poets, repeatedly evidences in a powerful and original manner the Eucharist as a Sacrifice and Sacrament. In his first homily on the Pasch of Christ, he writes: "The Lord prepared a new banquet, inviting to it those of His household. A feast He prepared for His Spouse to satisfy her hunger. He Himself first offered His own Body, and afterward He was slain by man. He pressed it out in the chalice of redemption, and later on the people also pressed it out on the Cross. Upon His head He placed the crown of glorious prophecy. He sharpened the sacrificial knife of the Law, therewith to immolate His own Body as the paschal Lamb. He brought the nations to His banquet and called the tribes to His feast. He clothed Himself with the true priesthood and with the perfect celebration of sacrifice. He stood there and supported Himself through love and held His own Body high up in His hands. His right hand was a holy altar, His uplifted hand a table of mercy. His omnipotence exercised the true priesthood. He consecrated and blessed Himself, He prayed and gave thanks over His own Body. He sacrificed and slew His own self, He bestowed and pressed out His life-giving Blood. — Come, My disciples, thus cries out the Lord, receive Me, I will place Myself in your hands! Behold, here truly do I stand, but at the same time you really and indeed consume Me. Come, My beloved ones, drink also of My Blood, which is the Blood of the New Testament! Drink of the cup of fire, the Blood which inflames all that partake of it, but in order that you may not forget this evening, more precious to you than the day, that you may not forget this hour, in which you have tasted the Divinity, I command you also, My beloved ones, confidants of My mysteries, to do this: the remembrance of this is not to cease among you until the end of the world! Thus, My brethren, shall you do at all times and be mind-

---

[1] The Syrians love to designate the Divinity and especially the Eucharistic presence of the God-Man by the word *"Fire"*.

[2] St. Ephrem, The Incomprehensibility of the Son, chap. 4.

[3] Cf. Bickell concerning him in the "Bibliothek der Kirchenväter", Kempten, 1872.

ful of Me! In My Church let this be My sublime memorial and upon the face of the earth this shall be My Pasch!'' — In a Syrian poem "On Wheat", which in all probability emanated from the same Cyrillonas, we read the words: "Without wheat (which forms the element of the Eucharistic Sacrifice) the altar would be empty, without it the Holy Ghost could not descend (to the consecration of the Eucharist), *without it the priest could not offer the Sacrifice of propitiation*, without it, indeed, no man would be able to appease the Deity."

In a poem on the dedication of a new church, composed by the Syrian Bishop (chorepiscopus) Balaeus[1] (prior to 431), we read: "Enthroned in His house is the Lord, awaiting us that we may enter and implore His mercy. It is not an ordinary dwelling, but a heaven upon earth, because the Lord of heaven resides therein. Instead of angels, holy priests who therein serve the Deity are seen there. The altar is prepared, enveloped in truth; before it stands the priest and enkindles the fire. Bread he takes, but the Body He gives; wine he receives, but Blood he distributes. The altar of stone supports our Hope, the pure priest invokes the Holy Ghost, the assembled faithful unite in the *Sanctus*, the King hears it and allows His mercy to pour down. Upon the earth stands the altar which bears His Body, and in His heavenly kingdom He imparts eternal life and glory."

Isaac of Antioch († between 459 and 461) sings in a poem "On Faith": "I saw the mixed vessel of faith, which was filled with blood instead of wine; and instead of bread the slain body was placed upon the table. I saw the blood and shuddered; the sacrificed body and terror seized me."

According to Didymus "the Blind" of Alexandria († about 395), the Eucharist is that unbloody Sacrifice daily celebrated throughout the world. "Of that which the Lord Himself has given and daily gives to each (bread and wine), each one receives the unbloody Sacrifice offered devoutly and holily ($\pi\rho\sigma\phi\epsilon\rho\omega\mu\acute{\epsilon}\nu\eta\nu$ $\delta\acute{\epsilon}\chi\epsilon\tau\alpha\iota$ $\dot{\alpha}\nu\alpha\iota\mu\alpha\kappa\tau\sigma\nu$ $\theta\upsilon\sigma\acute{\iota}\alpha\nu$)." "Why do we with faith and reverence celebrate the so-much-longed-for and carefully prepared Pasch each year, yea, every day, or rather at every hour, in which we partake of His Body and Blood? They who have been favored with this sublime and eternal mystery know what I say."[2]

Many beautiful and explicit passages relative to the Eucharist are found in the writings of St. Cyril, Bishop of Jerusalem († 386).[3] In the Fifth Mystagogical Lecture, he treats of the Sacrifice of the Mass. In it he instructs the newly baptized ($\nu\epsilon\sigma\phi\acute{\omega}\tau\iota\sigma\tau\sigma\iota$) and explains to them its principal points according to the Rite of the Mass of the Church of Jerusalem, that is, the Liturgy of the Apostle St. James.

---

[1] Cf. Bickell on all the other quotations.

[2] De Trinit. II, c. 7; III, c. 21.

[3] Cf. on this subject Becker in the "Katholik" of 1872 (first half) — pp. 422—449; 641—661.

He calls the time of Sacrifice "a sublimely dread hour," in which, above all, our hearts should be elevated to God. The Mass is "a holy and tremendous Sacrifice," "a holy mystery," "a Sacrifice of reconciliation" — a Sacrifice offered for our sins and for all our wants, for the living and for the dead. "After this spiritual (= mystical, sacramental) Sacrifice, this unbloody worship of God is accomplished (= after the real sacrificial action, the Consecration), over this Sacrifice of reconciliation we implore God[1] to grant universal peace to the churches. . . . and in unison we pray for all who are in need and offer this Sacrifice. For all among us (= in the Communion of the Church), who have already departed this life, we pray, believing that these petitions will be of the greatest benefit to those souls for whom they are offered, while this holy and most sublime Sacrifice is presented on the altar. For the departed, we offer Christ slain for our sins, inasmuch as we reconcile this beneficent God with them as well as with ourselves."[2]

Gregory of Nazianzum († about 390) carefully draws a distinction between Sacrifice in a strict sense, which the priest alone can offer, and sacrifice in a wider sense, which all the faithful can and should present. The interior sacrifice, self-denial, the spirit of self-immolation, is a necessary requisite for the priest, in order worthily to offer the Sacrifice of the Altar. "As I was not ignorant" — thus he speaks — "that no one is worthy of the great God, our Sacrifice and Highpriest, if he has not beforehand presented himself a living and holy sacrifice to the Lord, and rendered to Him a reasonable, acceptable service, if he has not previously offered to God a sacrifice of praise and a contrite heart, the only gifts required of us by the Giver of all good gifts; how could I have dared to offer to Him the visible Sacrifice, the figure of great mysteries?[3] How could I have ventured to bear the name and dignity of a priest, before sanctifying my hands with good works, before accustoming my eyes to regard created things in the proper manner, — in admiration of the Creator and not to the ruin of the creature?"[4]

In the writings of St. Chrysostom († 407), we find many important explanations pertaining to the Sacrifice of the Eucharist. With astonishment he praises the dignity of the Christian priesthood, which "not a man, not an angel, nor an archangel, nor any other created power than the Holy Ghost Himself instituted;" he shows what purity and fear of God are required in order that the priest may worthily celebrate the holy and tremendous Sacrifice. "When you behold how the Lord is sacrificed and laid there, and how the priest stands and prays during the Sacrifice: do you still imagine yourself

[1] Ἐπὶ τῆς θυσίας ἐκείνης τοῦ ἱλασμοῦ παρακαλοῦμεν τὸν θεόν.

[2] Mystag. Catechism, Chap. 8—10.

[3] The external, that is, the real Sacrifice of the Eucharist, which St. Gregory in this place more minutely characterizes as the unbloody representation of the great Sacrifice of the Cross.

[4] Discourse on His Flight, Chap. 95.

to be among men and on this earth?"[1] Those who do not remain
for the conclusion of this holy action, but who irreverently and with
distraction to others leave the church at the time of Communion, are
severely censured by the Saint. He admonishes them in this wise:
"What art thou doing, O man? When the priest stands before the
altar, his hands raised to heaven, invoking the Holy Ghost, that He
come and touch (i. e. change) the gifts lying there, then there reigns
perfect stillness, deep silence; but when the Spirit has granted the
grace, when He has come, when He has touched the gifts on the
altar, when thou perceivest the Lamb immolated and prepared, then
thou makest a noise and disturbance, then thou contendest and
quarrelest."[2] He teaches that on the Cross and on every altar the
sacrificial offering is one and the same — the Divine Lamb Jesus
Christ. "We always offer the same Victim, and not one lamb to-
day and another to-morrow, but always the same one, so that the
Sacrifice is but one. Now, since the Sacrifice is offered everywhere,
are there not also many Christs? By no means, for Christ is only
one and the same in all places, perfect here and perfect everywhere,
— one body. Now, as everywhere, He that is sacrificed is one body
and not many bodies, so also there is but one Sacrifice. Our Highpriest is He who offered the Sacrifice that cleanses us. That which
was then offered, is now still offered; for it is inexhaustible."[3] St.
Chrysostom dates the custom of offering the Sacrifice of the Mass
for the dead back to the Apostles. "It was not in vain," he says,
"that the Apostles ordained that at the tremendous mysteries the
departed should be remembered. They knew that therefrom these
would derive great profit and advantage. For if all the congregation
and the assembly of priests unite, while the dread Sacrifice is going
on at the altar, — why should we not propitiate God by praying in
their behalf? This is to be understood only of those who have died
in the faith."[4] — "Do you desire blood," — says Christ — "then
offer not the blood of animals, but redden My altar with My blood!
What is more awe-inspiring, — but at the same time more loving?
Thus do lovers act. . . . But lovers manifest their liberality by bestowing money and gifts and articles of clothing; never yet has any
one given his blood: but Christ in this manner proved to us His
care and intense love for us. In the Old Law, while men were yet
imperfect, He did indeed accept even the blood, that men used to
offer to idols, in order to detach them from the idols — and this was
indeed a proof of His unutterable love. But in the New Law He
would have this holy action performed in a more tremendous and
magnificent manner, inasmuch as He changed the sacrifice itself,
commanding that He Himself should be sacrificed in place of irrational animals."[5]

---

[1] De sacerdot. l. 6, c. 4.
[2] De coemeter. et cruce n. 3.
[3] In Hebr. hom. 17, n. 3.
[4] In Philipp. hom. 3, n. 4.
[5] 24. Homily on the First Epistle to the Corinthians (10, 17).

B. The Fathers of the West.

St. Cyprian († 258) in various places develops glorious sentiments concerning the Holy Sacrifice of the Mass. He requires the priests to be blameless, devoting themselves by day and by night to things heavenly and spiritual. — According to his teaching, the right to celebrate the Holy Sacrifice constitutes the most beautiful adornment and garland of honor of the Catholic priesthood, and for this reason the deprivation of this privilege was regarded as the most severe and most painful of punishments. [1] The altar is the place in which those members of the Church who are temporarily separated by distance, the living and the dead, remain in constant and most intimate communication with one another. — When the martyr had consummated his testimony for Christ and gained the heavenly crown of victory, the assembly of the faithful had no better offering to make in gratitude to the triune God than that whereby the bloody victory had been obtained, — namely, the Eucharistic Sacrifice. On the anniversary of the martyrdom, the Holy Sacrifice was always repeated. For the other departed the Holy Sacrifice was offered for another intention — to obtain repose for their souls. [2] — The most copious testimonies for the Holy Sacrifice of the Mass are contained in the letter of St. Cyprian to Caecilius. This letter, called by St. Augustine *"liber de sacramento calicis,"* is a classic work in proof of the doctrine of sacrifice. In it the Saint combats the abuse and disorder that had obtained in various parts of Africa of using mere water only in the celebration of the Eucharistic Sacrifice instead of wine mixed with water. At the very beginning of the letter, Jesus Christ, our Lord and God, is called "the Author and Teacher of the Eucharistic Sacrifice." The principal passage (No. 14) is as follows: "If Jesus Christ, our Lord and God, is Himself the Highpriest of God the Father, and if He first offered Himself to the Father as a sacrifice, commanding the same to be done in commemoration of Him, then, in fact, that priest really takes the place of Christ (vice Christi vere fungitur), who imitates what Christ has done, and then offers to God the Father a true and perfect sacrifice (verum et plenum sacrificium), only when he offers the Sacrifice in such a manner as he sees that Christ Himself offered it."

St. Ambrose († 397), that strenuous promoter of the dignity and beauty of divine service, expressed himself in a concise and forcible manner with regard to the Sacrifice of the Altar. "If only an angel would stand at our side and render himself visible, when we are burning incense at the altar, when we are celebrating the Sacrifice (*sacrificium deferentibus*)! For you may not doubt that angels are present, when Christ is there, when Christ is being sacrificed (*immolatur*)" [3] "We saw the Prince of Priests (Christ) coming to us; we saw and heard in what manner He offered His

---

[1] Cfr. Epist. 16. 64. 65. 67.

[2] Epist. 12. 39. 66.

[3] In Luc. lib. 1, n. 28.

Blood for us. We priests imitate Him, as is our right, by offering the Sacrifice for the faithful. Although we are poor in merits, we become worthy of veneration by the Sacrifice. Although at present we do not behold (with our bodily eyes) Christ celebrating, it is still He Himself who is being sacrificed upon earth, when Christ's Body is offered up. Yes, He offers Himself visibly by us, His servants, since His word sanctifies the Sacrifice that is being offered."[1] Here it is plainly stated that upon the altar Christ is not only the Sacrificial Gift, but, moreover, the chief Sacrificer, who through the ministrations of the visible priest performs the Eucharistic Sacrificial action (*ipse offerre manifestatur in nobis*).

Rich in profound instruction on the Sacrifice of the Eucharist are the writings of St. Augustine († 430).[2] "Abraham was then, in truth, blessed by Melchisedech, who was a priest of the Most High God. Of the latter many remarkable things are written in the Epistle to the Hebrews. Then appeared for the first time (figuratively) the Sacrifice which is at present offered by Christians throughout the whole world (*sacrificium quod nunc a Christianis offertur toto orbe terrarum*), and by which is accomplished that which long after this event was said by the Prophet to Christ, who had not yet appeared in the flesh : 'Thou art a priest forever according to the order of Melchisedech.' Can any one still doubt of whom this was said, now when there is nowhere a priesthood and sacrifice according to the order of Aaron, and when everywhere sacrifice is offered through the Highpriest Christ, prefigured by Melchisedech ?"[3] — "To what else do these words refer : 'It is not good for a man but to eat and drink' (Eccl. 8, 15), than to the participation at that table which the Priest and Mediator of the New Law, according to the order of Melchisedech, prepares Himself of His Body and Blood ? For this Sacrifice took the place of all the sacrifices of the Old Law, which were offered as shadows of the future Sacrifice. Hence we recognize in the words of Psalm 39 the voice of the Mediator speaking prophetically : 'Burnt offering and sin-offering Thou didst not require, but a body Thou hast formed unto Me.' For instead of all those sacrifices and oblations, His Body is sacrificed and administered to the participants (*pro illis omnibus sacrificiis et oblationibus corpus ejus offertur et participantibus ministratur*).[4]

St. Gaudentius, Bishop of Brescia, († about 410), has left us several clear testimonies concerning the sacrificial character of the

---

[1] Vidimus principem sacerdotum ad nos venientem, vidimus et audivimus offerentem pro nobis sanguinem suum. Sequimur, ut possumus, sacerdotes, ut offeramus pro populo sacrificium, etsi infirmi merito, tamen honorabiles sacrificio; quia etsi nunc Christus non videtur offerre, tamen ipse offertur in terris, quando Christi corpus offertur; imo ipse offerre manifestatur in nobis, cujus sermo sanctificat sacrificium, quod offertur (In Ps. 38, n. 25).

[2] Cf. Wilden, Die Lehre des hl. Augustin über das Opfer der Eucharistie.

[3] De civit. Dei, l. 16, c. 22; l. 18, c. 7.

[4] De civit. Dei, l. 17, c. 20.

Mass. In the Old Law many figurative lambs were immolated; but in the New Law "One died for all, and the same One in every house of God imparts renewed vigor, inasmuch as He is offered under the appearances of bread and wine, — He imparts life to them that believe, sanctifies them that consecrate, inasmuch as He is consecrated (*in mysterio panis ac vini reficit immolatus, vivificat creditus, consecrantes sanctificat consecratus*)." God purifies and enlightens our hearts for the knowledge of divine mysteries, so that "we comprehend the cause and reason of the heavenly Sacrifice instituted by Christ, in order to return thanks to Him for His ineffable gift (*a Christo instituti sacrificii coelestis causam rationemque noscamus, inenarrabili dono ejus sine fine gratias relaturi*)." [1]

Pope St. Leo the Great († 461) draws an accurate distinction between the general (not the real) and the special (real) priesthood. "The sign of the Cross makes kings of all those who are born again to Christ, but the unction of the Holy Ghost dedicates them as priests, so that all who in spirit and in truth are Christians, independently of the special service of our priestly office (*praeter istam specialem nostri ministerii servitutem*), participate in a royal race and in a priestly dignity. For what is so regal as the spirit which has subjected the body to the dominion of God? And what so priestly as to dedicate to the Lord a clean conscience, and present to Him upon the altar of the heart pure sacrifices of devotion (*vovere Domino conscientiam puram et immaculatas pietatis hostias de altari cordis offerre*)?" [2] He says that Christ at the Last Supper instituted the Sacrifice of the New Testament: "Jesus firmly persevering in His decree, and undaunted in the execution of the will of His Father, brought to an end the Old Testament and founded the new Easter. For as the disciples sat with Him at table, to partake of the mystical supper (*ad edendam mysticam coenam*), while the Jews were deliberating in the Court of Caiphas, in what manner to kill Him, Christ instituted the Sacrament of His Body and Blood, and instructed them as to what kind of victim should be offered to God (*corporis et sanguinis sui ordinans sacramentum docebat, qualis Deo hostia deberet offerri*)." [3] — He also proves that in Christ's Sacrifice the figures of the Old Law found their fulfilment and consummation. "Thou hast drawn all to Thyself, O Lord, for, by the rending of the veil of the temple, the Holy of Holies was taken away from the unworthy highpriests, the figure passed over into the reality, the prophecy into its fulfilment, and the law into the Gospel. All hast Thou drawn to Thyself, O Lord, so that at present when the mystery is accomplished and disclosed (*pleno apertoque sacramento*), the piety of all nations celebrates what formerly in the one temple of Judea was solemnized in figurative symbols (*obumbratis significationibus*). For now the estate of deacons (*ordo levi-*

---

[1] Second Sermon.

[2] Third (fourth) Sermon; Anniversary of Consecration.

[3] Seventh Sermon on the Lord's Passion.

tarum) is more splendid, the dignity of priests (*seniorum*) is greater
and the anointing of bishops (*sacerdotum*) is holier, because Thy
Cross is the source of all blessings, the cause of all graces; by it the
faithful receive strength instead of weakness, honor instead of
ignominy, and life instead of death. Now when the manifold animal
sacrifices have ceased, the one Sacrifice of Thy Body and Blood
supplies the place of all other sacrifices (*omnes differentias hostiarum una corporis et sanguinis tui implet oblatio*); for Thou art the
true Lamb of God, who taketh away the sins of the world, Thou
hast accomplished in Thyself all mysteries, so that in place of all
sacrifices there is one Sacrifice (*sicut unum est pro omni victima
sacrificium*), thus all nations form but one kingdom (the Church)."[1]

2. The foregoing passages from the Fathers are a sufficiently
valid proof of the sacrificial character of the Eucharist. Annexed
to these is another proof, which, if possible, is still more clear and
more convincing. We allude to the proofs from the venerable ancient documents and monuments of ecclesiastical liturgy. — They
contain a rich treasure of the truths of salvation; they are veritable
mines of gold with respect to Catholic dogma. Doctrine constitutes
the root and the soul of both ecclesiastical life and its worship.
There is no point of external life in which the truths of faith are
more directly and more distinctly revealed than in the liturgy of the
Church. Hence these truths can often with certainty be known and
recognized therefrom according to the maxim of Pope Celestine I.:
Legem credendi lex statuit supplicandi[2] — "The liturgical form of
prayer becomes the standard of faith." — With special reference to
our subject, there are a vast number of both Eastern and Western
liturgies and directions for the Mass. By these are meant collections
of formulas of the prayers and rites[3], according to which the Eucharistic Sacrifice has always been celebrated. These liturgies are
in their essence and substance decidedly of Apostolic origin. They
are composed in different languages, and they were for centuries in
daily and public use in various places and among diverse nations —
and, consequently, they denote the universal and constant belief of
Christendom. Now, however variously they may otherwise be
framed, all these liturgical formulas agree perfectly in essentials, so
that they represent in their whole contents the Eucharistic celebration as the true Sacrifice of the Immaculate Lamb, Jesus Christ.

In these liturgical formulas of prayer the Eucharist is designated
a sacrifice, a perpetual sacrifice, a holy sacrifice, a heavenly sacrifice,
a divine sacrifice, a tremendous sacrifice, a sacrifice deserving of

---

[1] Eighth Sermon on the Lord's Passion. — Cf. the Secreta of the Seventh
Sunday after Pentecost: Deus, qui legalium differentiam hostiarum unius sacrificii
perfectione sanxisti, accipe sacrificium a devotis tibi famulis. . . .

[2] Epist. ad Gall. Episc. n. 11.

[3] Liturgiarum nomine intellegi debent Officia seu Rituales libri auctoritate
publica Ecclesiarum scripti, earumque usu comprobati, quibus preces et ritus ad
consecrandam et administrandam Eucharistiam continentur (Renaudot. Liturg.
orient. collect. I, 152).

honor, a reasonable and unbloody sacrifice, a sacrifice for the living and the dead, a sacrifice of praise and thanksgiving; and especially a sacrifice of propitiation and petition. In the Eucharist are offered gifts that are holy, precious, unspeakable, glorious and without blemish; and mysteries are celebrated that are divine, profoundly hidden and full of awful majesty. Christ is styled the Lamb living and as yet slain upon the altar. He is glorified as the Sacrificing Priest and Sacrificial Gift, as well as the Founder of this Sacrifice. They mention a holy altar, which the priest approaches only with a pure conscience, in fear and trembling.

In the liturgy of St. James, for instance, it is said: "Let all mortal flesh be silent, standing there in fear and trembling, let all things of earth vanish from our thoughts; for the King of kings, the Lord of lords, Christ our God, is about to be sacrificed and to be given as food to the faithful. Before Him choirs of angels go, clothed with power and dominion, with faces veiled, chanting the hymn, Alleluia." The Coptic liturgy of St. Cyril directs the priest to say: "Make us worthy, O Lord, to present to Thee this holy, reasonable, spiritual and unbloody Sacrifice for the remission of our sins and for the pardon of the faults of Thy people." To this may be added a passage for the consecration of bishops, found in the Apostolic Constitution (1. VIII, c. 5), which runs thus: "Grant to him, Almighty God, through Jesus Christ, participation in the Holy Ghost, that he may have the power to appoint clerics and to loosen all bonds, and that he may please Thee by a heart meek and pure, steadfast, guileless and blameless, offering to Thee the immaculate and unbloody Sacrifice, which Thou, through Christ, hast instituted as the mystery of the New Law as an agreeable odor to Thee." In a letter to the clergy of Neo-Caesarea, St. Basil assures them that the following prayer was used in all the churches of the East: "Strengthen me, Almighty God, with the power of Thy holy Spirit, and grant that I, invested with the grace of the priesthood, may present myself at Thy holy table to offer to Thee Thy Holy and immaculate Body and Thy precious Blood. I humbly beseech Thee not to turn Thy face from me, but graciously permit these gifts to be offered to Thee by Thy unworthy servant and sinner, as I am. For it is Thou who offerest and who art offered; it is Thou who acceptest this Sacrifice and who art distributed."

3. Thus in the first ages faith the sacrificial character of the Eucharist was expressed in the most striking and unequivocal manner both by the doctrine and practice of the entire Church; but such universal and unchangeable belief of Christianity can rest only on divine revelation, that is, it must proceed from Christ and the Apostles. Our faith, therefore, is that of the first Christians, the faith of Christian antiquity. This fact invariably imparts to the Catholic heart untold satisfaction, in finding the most sacred truths and the treasures of religion sustained by so great an array of witnesses from ecclesiastical antiquity.

4. In conclusion, we will cast a rapid glance upon the Roman Catacombs, in which the doctrine of the Eucharistic Sacrifice, proved from the Fathers and liturgies, rises up to view in picturesque representations and symbolical illustrations.[1] The Catacombs, according to their original plan and destination, were burial places in which the remains of Christians were deposited. In times of persecution they served also as places of refuge, especially for the clergy, and at the same time they were used for divine worship. On the walls and ceilings of these subterranean mortuary chapels, the persecuted Christians inscribed in symbolic pictures, as simple as they were touching, their superhuman faith, hope and charity. In the mysterious language of the Catacombs we may, therefore, read many of the doctrines of faith, emblematically represented as in a pictorial catechism; this is the case also with the Sacrifice of the Mass.

The most ancient and, at the same time, most prominent representation of the Eucharistic service dates from the beginning of the second century, and is found in the so-called "Greek Chapel" in the Catacomb of St. Priscilla. It consists of a continuous fresco cycle, the centre of which exhibits the breaking of the bread (*fractio panis*, ἡ κλάσις τοῦ ἄρτου). As the artist placed this portion of the picture right over the altar, it must be considered as an altar-piece. It represents the liturgical fraction of the consecrated bread, which precedes holy Communion, by the hands of the bishop. — On a semicircular sopha are six persons in a lying position, five men and one woman. At the right of the sopha, i. e., in the place of honor, on a low stool is seated a man, who must be the principal personage, for he alone wears a beard. He is certainly the one who presides, the "chief among the brethren" (ὁ προέστος τῶν ἀδελφῶν), the one who offers the sacrifice, for he holds the bread in his hands, and by his whole demeanor shows that he is about to break it for his companions. Near by at his feet stands a chalice, having the form of a pretty large two-handled goblet; a little further off are two dishes containing two fishes and five loaves, and at both extremities of the scene are baskets filled to the brim with bread. These five loaves, two fishes and seven filled baskets are, doubtless, an allusion to the wonderful multiplication of the loaves and the feeding of the multitude by our divine Saviour, for in this miracle all Christian antiquity recognized a figure of the eucharistic banquet. Near the altar-piece is depicted the typical sacrifice of Abraham, which reminds us of the eucharistic sacrifice. The other scenes surrounding that of the breaking of the bread are symbolical and throw light on the various aspects and effects of the Eucharist as a sacrifice and as holy Communion. It is worthy of remark that it is only in the "Greek Chapel" and in Lucina's crypt that both eucharistic species are

---

[1] Cf. Kraus, Roma Sotterranea. — P. Wolter, Die Römischen Katakomben. — De Richemont, Die neuesten Studien über die Katakomben. — Ott, Die ersten Christen über und unter der Erde.

represented, and that in later paintings the wine is wanting, and in the miracle of the loaves the bread alone appears. The aforesaid highly significant fresco represents that moment of the eucharistic service, when the celebrant divides the consecrated bread, in order to distribute it with the blood of Christ in the chalice to the faithful present. [1]

In the larger chapels there is usually placed on or by the side of a martyr's grave an altar, upon which the Eucharistic Sacrifice was celebrated. The credence-table, on which to place bread and wine, was a niche arranged in the wall or a projecting slab. In addition, many liturgical representations are found. Let us enter the Catacombs of St. Callistus and there consider more closely two Eucharistic paintings.

Upon a three-legged table are depicted three loaves and a fish; near by on the floor are seven baskets filled with bread. What does this mystical representation illustrate? The table can be but the table of the Lord, the table (altar) of the Eucharistic Sacrifice. The fish lying on it is an ancient Christian emblem of "Jesus Christ, the Son of God, the Saviour." As the artist has placed the fish on the table with the loaves of bread, it is natural to imagine his idea was, that Jesus Christ the Divine Fish, under the appearance of bread is truly present and offered on the altar. The seven baskets filled with bread, that surround the table, are doubtless intended to insinuate that it is, at the same time, a dining-table, a table from which the faithful, as St. Paulinus of Nola († 431) says, receive the "true bread and the fish of living waters."

The sacrificial character of the Mass is still more emphatically symbolized in a painting found in the so-called "chapel of the sacrament" of the same cemetery. On the main wall, adjacent to the martyr's grave or the altar, there is painted a three-legged table upon which are represented bread and a fish; along-side of the table stands a man to one side, his right hand extended in blessing above the offerings (fish and bread), while on the opposite side there is seen a female with hands uplifted, praying (*Orans*). Who can fail to see in this picture the representation of the Eucharistic Sacrifice? The man vested in the reddish ascetic-cloak, extending his right hand over the paten, is evidently a priest who blesses, i. e. consecrates the bread, that is, who changes it into the living and divine Fish, into the Body of Jesus Christ, and in this manner offers the Eucharistic Sacrifice. — The figure of the woman in prayer is a common symbol of the virginally pure and maternally fruitful Church, in whose name the priest at the altar celebrates and prays. [2]

---

[1] Cfr. Wilpert, Fractio panis. Freiburg, Herder, 1895.

[2] According to Wilpert's latest explanation, it is not the act or moment of the eucharistic consecration that is depicted in this famous picture, but a realistic appendix to the adjoining scene of the Last Supper; the priest puts forth his hand not to bless or consecrate, but is about to take up the eucharistic food in order to distribute it to the faithful; and the standing figure Orans at the right is the representation of a soul thinking to be in heaven, by which an allusion is made to the effects of holy Communion. See *Fractio panis*, p. 81 and 82.

— In order to show the meaning and object of this picture in a still clearer light, the figurative sacrifice of Abraham is represented on the opposite wall; here this is, as is usually the case, the special type of the Eucharistic Sacrifice, not of the bloody Sacrifice of the Cross. Abraham did indeed sacrifice his son. But in reality the blood of Isaac was not shed; he was only "as if slain" (*tanquam occisus*, Apoc. 5, 6). Abraham "received him for a parable (ἐν παραβολῇ)" from death, that is, as though he had been resuscitated (Heb. 11, 19). By this the unbloody Sacrifice of the altar is prefigured: for here Christ is the Lamb that dieth no more, but liveth eternally, although He is forever mystically immolated (*Agnus, qui numquam moritur immolatus, sed semper vivit occisus*).

These glorious testimonials of the Eucharistic Sacrifice are so much the more precious, because they originated at times in which the situation of Christians was painful and oppressive, as is described in the inscription on the grave of the martyr Alexander in the Catacombs of St. Callistus: "Alexander is not dead, but above the stars, and his body reposes in this grave. Kneeling in order to sacrifice to the true God, he was led to death. O deplorable times, in which we cannot even offer the holy mysteries and safely say our prayers in caves! What is more miserable than life!" — In the quiet enclosure of this city of death, the mysterious sounds of the sublime psalmody of the faithful resounded; here at the graves of the martyrs the Holy Sacrifice was celebrated; here the faithful received the Bread of the strong, and, strong in faith, they hastened to the battle-field of martyrdom, to shed their blood and to die for Christ. To this day the odor of sanctity, the perfume of sacrifice, the spirit of martyrdom emanate from these silent caves and chambers of the Catacombs, in which the venerated traces of the faith and life of the early Christians, throughout the centuries to our own epoch, have been preserved for our joy and consolation. — "Holy Church has received and faithfully retained the blessed inheritance (of the Eucharistic Sacrifice) transmitted to her, mindful of the Divine commission: 'Do this in commemoration of Me!' When the storm of persecution was at its height, she went down into the subterranean Catacombs; she retired into lonely vales and sequestered mountain caves. Amid the silence of night and deep under the ground on rude altars, she performed the mysterious service of the sacrifice of the Lord's Supper, and sent forth her confessors fortified thereby, to give testimony for the Lord in the world before their persecutors, under the sword, on the rack, among wild beasts, into the billows and every kind of torture, and, after His example, to seal their testimony with their blood. The death of the Christian became continually the seed of new confessors to the Cross. And as the Lord had been three days in the grave, and afterward had risen in power and gloriously ascended into heaven; so the Church also, after years of persecution, arose from the bosom of the earth, from the Catacombs and caves, and triumphed over all the powers of the world and hell. Thus risen, the Church went into the cities, villages and valleys and far up mountainous heights, entering into the basilicas, marble temples, grand cathedrals, numberless churches and chapels, built therein altars, and celebrated, as formerly in the stillness of the night, but now in the light of open day, in the presence of the assembled congregations, the heritage of the Lord, the mystery of His Last Supper, the perpetual Sacrifice of His death on the Cross. From this time on, she fulfilled for all ages her mission of carrying to all countries of the world her most holy inheritance. She gathered nation after nation around her altar, celebrated with them, generation after generation, the sacrificial death of the Redeemer, distributed to them the Body of the Lord (and the chalice of His Blood), and thereby accomplished the new and eternal covenant: 'Do this in commemoration of Me,' and fulfilled the testament of the Lord: 'It is consummated!' As the Prophet had predicted, she offered the new and clean, the true and perfect Sacrifice of the New Law everywhere, thus glorifying the name of the Lord in all parts of the globe, from the rising of the sun until the setting thereof" (Geissel).

ARTICLE THE SECOND.

The Essence and the Efficacy of the Eucharistic Sacrifice.

15. The Essential Characteristics of the Eucharistic Sacrifice.

All that we have demonstrated from the written and traditional word of God, the infallible Church has solemnly and formally declared in the Council of Trent, defining that in Holy Mass "a true and real Sacrifice" (*verum et proprium sacrificium*) is offered to the triune God.[1] This revealed truth of salvation is eminently included in the "divine mysteries, which by their nature so far transcend created intelligence, that though divinely revealed to us and comprehended through faith, they yet remain hidden to our eyes by the veil of this very faith, and enveloped in a certain obscurity, as long as we are pilgrims in this mortal life, at a distance from God. Yet reason enlightened by faith, if it inquire diligently, devoutly and prudently, may with the assistance of God obtain a certain and, at the same time, a very profitable insight into these mysteries," and, consequently, into the mystery of the Sacrifice of the Eucharist.[2] Therefore, we should not be contented with the proof that the Mass is a true Sacrifice, but we should endeavor to acquire a fuller and more profound knowledge of this adorable mystery.

In the first place, the question arises as to the essence of the Eucharistic Sacrifice. To answer it, we must show that, and to what extent, in the celebration of the Eucharist are found all the conditions absolutely necessary for a true sacrifice. To every sacrifice, and, consequently, to the Eucharistic Sacrifice, appertain a sacrificial gift, a sacrificing priest and the action of sacrifice.

---

[1] Sess. 22, can. 1.

[2] Vatican. constit. de Fide, cap. 4.

1.   Which is the sacrificial gift in the Holy Mass? The Church has declared that upon the altar precisely the same sacrificial gift (*una eademque hostia*) is offered, as was once offered on the Cross.[1] But Christ, with His holy humanity, with His Body and Blood, was offered on the Cross : consequently, He is likewise the sacrificial gift on our altars ; hence upon them there is nothing less offered than the God-Man Himself.   The Mass is the Sacrifice of the Body and Blood of Christ.   Some theologians[2] have indeed taught, that bread and wine belong also to the matter of the Eucharistic Sacrifice, that is, that besides and with the Body and Blood of Christ they are truly offered in the Holy Mass ; but evidently this is incorrect. Neither the substances nor the appearances of bread and wine constitute a part of the matter of the sacrifice,[3] although they are necessarily required for the celebration of the Eucharistic Sacrifice.   The substances of the bread and wine disappear, in order that, under the species remaining, the Divine Victim of sacrifice may take their place, that is, that they may be changed into the Host of Salvation. The sacramental species render the offering of Christ a visible sacrifice ; they form the sensible, perceptible covering, under which the Body and Blood of Christ are offered. — The Body of Christ, once immolated in a bloody manner, and the Blood of Christ, once shed unto death on the Cross, and consequently the whole Christ, once sacrificed upon Golgotha, by the sacrifice of His Body and the shedding of His Blood (Heb. 10, 10 ; 9, 12), is also on the altar the gift or object of our unbloody sacrifice.   A higher and holier, a better and more precious sacrificial offering, than Christ the Lord, can neither be presented nor imagined.[4]   To possess so glorious a sacrificial Victim is for us an inappreciable grace and it imparts to us unspeakable dignity.

2.   Who offers the Eucharistic Sacrifice ?

a)   It is beyond question, that in the Holy Mass Christ is not only the Victim Sacrificed, but also the Sacrificing Priest (*sacrificium et sacerdos mirabiliter et ineffabiliter constitutus* — Oratio S. Ambros.); for, "as He once offered Himself on the Cross, He now also offers Himself on the altar, but in an unbloody manner and through the ministry of the priests" (*sacerdotum ministerio*).[5] —

---

[1]   Trident. sess. 22, cap. 2.

[2]   Suarez. disp. 75, sect. 1. — Coninck, De sacrament. q. 83, a. 1, d. 4. concl. 3. — Tanner tom. 4, d. 5, q. 9, dub. 2, n. 28.

[3]   Dicendum est, panem et vinum quoad suam *substantiam* nullo modo esse materiam oblatam in sacrificio Missae, sed tantum terminum a quo materiae oblatae; similiter *species* panis et vini non pertinere ad rationem victimae tamquam partem ipsius et proinde non esse rem oblatam (Pasqualigo, De sacrif. Nov. Leg., tr. 1, q. 29—30).

[4]   Sacerdos perpendat, *quid* offerat, videlicet corpus et sanguinem Salvatoris, imo ipsummet Christum, Unigenitum videlicet Dei, qui secundum naturam suam divinam est dignitatis et excellentiae penitus infinitae ; secundum naturam vero suam humanam, ut Verbo aeterno unitam, est toto dignior universo (Dion. Carthus. De vita Curator. art. 15).

[5]   Trident. sess. 22, cap. 2.

Christ in the Eucharist is both the one that sacrifices and the object sacrificed. *Ipse offerens, ipse et oblatio.* As the true Melchisedech, He possesses an imperishable priesthood and unceasingly exercises the priestly office, inasmuch as He daily offers Himself on the altar as a gift and an oblation of sweet odor unto God (Eph. 5, 2), to save those who by Him approach unto God (Heb. 7, 25).

If Christ in the Mass truly makes the offering and this by the visible priest, then it follows that He is the principal celebrant (*offerens principalis*). To be such in reality it does not suffice, that the Lord instituted the Eucharistic Sacrifice and commanded the celebration of it; nor that He imparts power and efficacy to it; He must rather co-operate directly, through His holy humanity, in performing the Eucharistic Sacrifice. He must always and everywhere be found acting as priest wherever Mass is celebrated. Condescending to the words of the visible priest, Christ as invisible Highpriest changes the elements of bread and wine into His Body and Blood, that is, He places His Body and His Blood, His humanity, Himself, in a state of sacrifice. And this action of sacrifice of Himself He, at the same time, directs to the glory of God, to propitiate Him, and also to contribute to the salvation of mankind. — In the celebration of the Eucharistic Sacrifice, the Lord indeed is, in a certain sense, dependent upon the ministry of visible priests; yet He Himself always performs directly and principally the real act of sacrifice. At the celebration of every Mass, Jesus with His soul, with His human will and heart, gives proof anew of His priestly sentiments, His unchangeable love of sacrifice, His inexhaustible devotedness to the honor of God and the salvation of the world. — From what has just been said, we may draw several conclusions. Since Christ on the altar is the direct and principal Offerer, because He Himself by His Highpriestly act celebrates and offers the Eucharistic Sacrifice, therefore, like the Sacrifice of the Cross, the Mass possesses absolutely infinite value and infinite perfection. For the excellence of the Sacrifice depends chiefly upon the merit and dignity of the person who offers it. — Furthermore, it follows that the Eucharist always and everywhere remains the spotless Sacrifice, as the chief Offerer, Jesus Christ, is at all times infinitely holy, although the visible and representative priest be ever so imperfect and unworthy.

b) As the Eternal Highpriest according to the order of Melchisedech Christ does not and will not cease until the consummation of time to offer Himself in the Mass to His Heavenly Father; but now He no longer does so alone in a personal, visible manner, as He did at the Last Supper and upon the Cross, but invisibly and with the assistance of a human representative. Christ is indeed the principal celebrant at the altar, for He has the primary and chief part in the celebration of the Eucharistic Sacrifice; still He does not perform this action alone and without assistance, but employs for it specially authorized servants and instruments, namely, validly ordained priests.

The visible priest acts as the living and free agent of Jesus Christ; therefore, he performs, though only as the instrument of the Lord, but yet in a real manner, the act of consecration or sacrifice at the altar. At his ordination he receives the exalted superhuman and divine power to change the elements of bread and wine into the Body and Blood of Christ, that is, to celebrate Mass; for only God can impart such power. This power, like holy Orders in general, can neither be lost nor destroyed; just as little as the sacerdotal character can be effaced from the soul of the priest, so in like manner, the power of sacrificing cannot be taken away from him. Every validly ordained priest, and only such a one, can offer the Sacrifice of the Eucharist. In this action he always represents the person of Christ and, as an authorized minister, acts in His name. Here the privileged character and dignity of the officiating priest are in contrast with the condition of the faithful, to whom such a heavenly sacrificial power has not been imparted.

c) At the altar, the officiating priest acts not merely as the representative and as the organ of Christ, but also in the name and under the authority of the Church. For the Eucharist is the property of the Catholic Church: to her our Lord bequeathed the Eucharistic Sacrifice, that she might always be able to render to the Most High due honor and glory, as well as to dispense with lavish hand to her needy children the fulness and riches of all blessings. Christ our Lord, in the excess of His divine bounty and goodness, made over to the Church His Body and Blood, Himself with all the treasures of His grace, placing this as an offering in her hands, that she might offer it in sacrifice to God. By the Church we understand all the faithful in so far as they, united to one another and under submission to their lawful Pastor, form but one fold and one kingdom, the one mystical body and the one spouse of Christ. — The entire Church, therefore, offers the Eucharistic Sacrifice; for it is a public and solemn act of worship, which is always celebrated in the name and for the welfare of all the people of God.[1] Now, the Church cannot celebrate without a priest; he is ordained to be the representative of men (*constituitur pro hominibus* — Heb. 5, 1), that is, that he may really celebrate and offer sacrifice in the name of the faithful as mediator between God and the people. — Therefore, at the altar, the priest is the authorized representative of Jesus Christ and of the Church, but in a twofold manner: Jesus Christ, the Divine Highpriest, celebrates by the priest who is His subordinate minister; the Church, on the contrary, celebrates in the person

[1] Datum est hoc sacrificium universae Ecclesiae, ut ipsa illud offerat, quamvis per sacerdotes, quibus potestas offerendi specialiter commissa est, ut dicit Trid.; et ideo sess. 22. cap. 6 addit, Missae omnes, quantumvis privatim dicantur, communes esse censendas, quia a publico Ecclesiae ministro, non pro se tantum, sed pro omnibus fidelibus, qui ad corpus Christi pertinent, celebrantur; dicuntur enim pro eis celebrari, non tantum, quia pro eis offeruntur, sed etiam, quia ipsorum nomine, tanquam eorum sacrificia offeruntur (Suarez disp. 74, sect. 3, n. 1).

of the priest, who is the superior mediator given her by God. When he consecrates, that is, celebrates the Eucharistic Sacrifice, the priest represents, first, the person of Jesus Christ, and then the Church. Then also he acts and speaks in the name of the Church, inasmuch as he performs the remaining acts of divine worship, namely, the ceremonies and liturgical prayers accompanying and surrounding the sacrificial function. — Hence it follows that the Mass prayers are not the private prayers of the priest, but public prayers, that is, the prayers of the Church; and as such there is attached to them a special, efficacious, impetratory character, independent of the disposition of the priest celebrating (*valor ex opere operato*).[1]

The priest, therefore, celebrates in the name of the Church, in the name of the whole Christian people, so that in as far as they are members of the Church, all the faithful at least habitually offer through him as their representative the Eucharistic Sacrifice. For this reason also the Prince of the Apostles calls all Christians "a holy and a kingly priesthood" (1 Peter 2, 5—9), that is, called "to offer up spiritual sacrifices, acceptable to God through Jesus Christ." — The actual participation of each individual faithful in the Eucharistic Sacrifice takes place in different ways and in different degrees, according as their activity and co-operation is merely interior or also exterior.[2] For example, he who assists devoutly at Mass, he who communicates during Mass, he who serves at the altar, he who has a Mass said or who contributes what is necessary for the Sacrifice, participates in a more especial manner in the celebration of the Sacrifice, than he who merely interiorly, that is, without being present in body, unites his intention with the holy Sacrifice and the prayers of the priest at the altar.

3. In what does the sacrificial act of the Eucharistic service properly consist (*sacrificatio vel immolatio hostiae*)?

a) The Eucharistic Sacrificial action (*actio sacrifica*) consists

---

[1] In Missa duo est considerare, sc. *ipsum sacramentum* quod est principale et *orationes* quae in Missa fiunt pro vivis et mortuis. Quantum ergo ad sacramentum non minus valet Missa sacerdotis mali quam boni, quia utrobique idem conficitur sacramentum. *Oratio* etiam quae fit in Missa potest considerari dupliciter: *uno modo* inquantum habet efficaciam ex devotione sacerdotis orantis et sic non est dubium quod Missa melioris sacerdotis magis est fructuosa; *alio modo* inquantum oratio in Missa profertur a sacerdote in *persona totius Ecclesiae,* cujus sacerdos est minister, quod quidem ministerium etiam in peccatoribus manet sicut ministerium Christi. Unde etiam quantum ad hoc est fructuosa non solum oratio sacerdotis peccatoris in Missa, sed etiam omnes ejus orationes, quas facit in ecclesiasticis officiis, in quibus gerit *personam Ecclesiae,* licet ejus orationes privatae non sint fructuosae (S. Thom. 3, q. 82, a. 6).

[2] Cum ad proprie dictum sacrificium offerendum haec duo requirantur: hostiae *immolatio*, hujusque immolationis *oblatio*, improprie dicentur sacrificium offerre, qui sacrificium a sacerdote celebratum interne aut etiam externe in Dei honorem referunt, vel qui aliqua ratione sacerdoti in sacrificii oblatione subveniunt eumque adjuvant (Lambrecht, De ss. Miss. sacrif. pars 3, c. 3, § 3).

in the double consecration, by which the Body and Blood of Christ, under the appearances of bread and wine, are placed in a state of sacrifice and are, therefore, sacrificed. — All the prayers, ceremonies and actions that partly precede and partly follow the consecration in the celebration of the Mass are, consequently, not essential to the Eucharistic Sacrifice. — The oblation-prayers at the Offertory and after the Elevation, the fraction of the consecrated Host and the co-mingling of a particle of it with the Sacred Blood, are important and profoundly significant constituent parts of the ancient, venerable rite prescribed for the Sacrifice by the Church, but in nowise are they integral or essential portions of the sacrificial action instituted by Christ. That the Communion of the faithful who are present is not necessary for the Sacrifice, is admitted by all Catholics. — But the case is quite different with regard to the Communion of the officiating priest. The officiating priest must necessarily communicate at the celebration of the Eucharistic Sacrifice, not merely by reason of a command of the Church, but in virtue of a divine ordinance from Christ Himself. The Communion of the celebrant, therefore, is so necessary, because although it does not appertain to the essence, it is, however, indispensable to the external completeness of the Eucharistic Sacrifice ; for by this Communion the Sacrifice attains its end as a food-offering and, consequently, by it the Sacrifice is in a certain sense perfected and consummated. [1] The celebrating priest must partake of the same sacrificial matter which he has just consecrated, in order that the unity of the visible Sacrifice may in its essence and integrity be perfectly secured. — The so-called Mass of the Presanctified on Good Friday is, therefore, no sacrificial celebration, but only a Communion celebration ; for it is without consecration and consists only of the reception of the Sacrament consecrated on Holy Thursday. This Communion of the priest may be regarded as a continuation and completion of the Mass celebrated on Holy Thursday ; and this throws sufficient light and explanation on the liturgical formulas of prayer occurring in this service. [2]

That the essence of the Eucharistic Sacrifice depends neither wholly nor in part on the Communion of the celebrant, but rests solely and entirely in the consecration, is the most solid and the more general opinion. As is frequently repeated in the ancient

---

[1] Partes alicujus rei compositae aliae sunt *essentiales*, aliae *integrantes :* sine partibus essentialibus res non est talis naturae ; essentia vero rei salva consistit sine partibus integrantibus. Hac distinctione in sacrificio Eucharistiae facta, juxta communem Theologorum sententiam dicimus, in sola Eucharistiae consecratione essentiam sacrificii consistere, et ad integritatem ejus referri utriusque speciei consecratae sumptionem, quae a sacerdote fit in Missa (De Augustinis S. J., De re sacramentaria, lib. 2, p. 3, art. 5).

[2] Aliud est *conficere* sive *consecrare*, aliud est *offerre ;* et quamvis in die Veneris sancto non fiat *confectio*, fit tamen *oblatio*, quia sacerdos corpus in praecedenti die consecratum *offert* in altari (S. Bonav. IV, dist. 12, p. 2, dub. 2).

liturgies and by the Fathers, the Communion of the priest and of the people is a sacrificial banquet, that is, a partaking of the accomplished Sacrifice or the reception of the Lamb of God offered in sacrifice. The sacrificial banquet must, in fact, be preceded by the sacrificial action; only the immolated or sacrificed victim can be partaken of as food. — St. Gregory of Nyssa thus appropriately expresses this truth. "Christ, who is both priest and victim, offered Himself mystically for us in sacrifice. When did He do this? At the Last Supper; for when He gave to the disciples, assembled around Him, His Body to eat and His Blood to drink, He publicly declared that the Sacrifice of the Lamb was already accomplished. The body of the victim to be slain cannot be eaten as long as it is in a natural, living state (ἔμψυχον, *animatum*); as He then gave His disciples His Body to eat and His Blood to drink, His Body was already sacrificed in an unspeakable and inconceivable manner, as it pleased the Lord to perform this mystery by His power."[1] What is here said of the first celebration of the Sacrifice of the Eucharist, naturally holds good with respect to the daily repetition of this unbloody Sacrifice on our altars. The Eucharistic Sacrifice is perfectly the same here, as it was there: its essence consists in the act of the twofold consecration.

b) The mysterious obscurity, in which the mystery of the Eucharist is shrouded from our weak vision, extends particularly to the question, in how far by the act of the dual consecration Christ is really and actually sacrificed. According to the teaching of our holy faith, we must hold firmly that the Eucharist is not merely a simple oblation or a consecrated gift, but much more, truly and properly a Sacrifice. Now for this a sacrificial action, that is, an actual sacrificing (*sacrificatio*), and not a mere offering (*oblatio*), is necessarily required, — a sacrificial action, in which both an interior and an exterior quality are taken into consideration and distinguished. — The interior consists in the disposition of the heart to sacrifice, in the hidden intention of the will to sacrifice, on the part of the priest who celebrates; the exterior, by which the real sacrifice essentially differs from the simple oblation, consists in this, that the offering to God of the sacrificial object, even in its visible form, is accomplished by a change or transformation, corresponding also to the meaning of the Sacrifice. — Conflicting answers are given to the question, whether and how far there takes place a similar change or transformation of the matter of the Eucharistic Sacrifice by the dual consecration, as is essentially the case in every sacrifice. In order to throw some light on this much disputed question — under what aspect the eucharistic consecration is a true sacrificial act — we will here make a few observations.

The Eucharist is a sacrifice wholly peculiar and singular (*sacrificium singulare*), and of a higher and mysterious order.[2] The es-

---

[1] First Sermon for Easter Sunday.

[2] Deus hoc sacrificium instituit modo extraordinario et singulari aliis victimis et sacrificiis non communi (Mastrius disp. 4, q. 4, a. 1, n. 72).

sence of the Eucharistic Sacrifice is of divine institution and, therefore, must not be indiscriminately decided or judged by the same
standard as other known sacrifices. First and above all the peculiarity of the Eucharistic Sacrifice consists in this, that the object
sacrificed is offered under foreign or sacramental species, whilst in
other sacrifices the sensible objects are always offered in their own
natural forms. Another peculiarity is that in the Eucharist the living, glorious God-man is the matter or object of the unbloody sacrifice, although always and everywhere living beings can be sacrificed
only by the actual shedding of their blood and by their immolation.
According to the correct conception of the eucharistic transsubstantiation, there can be no question of the destruction of the bread and
wine, nor of the production of the body and blood of Christ, so that
evidently the explanation of the essence of our sacrifice cannot be
based on either of these suppositions. In like manner, every attempt to prove a real change in the sacrifice of the eucharistic body
must end in failure. Numerically the same glorious Christ, reigning in heaven, is indeed present on the altar, without undergoing
any change in Himself; only the external relation of His humanity
to space and the surroundings is different. On the altar, then, we
have a true and real sacrifice without any real change in the eucharistic victim. So peculiar a sacrifice is rendered possible only by
Christ being offered as a living victim, not in His natural form, but
under the symbolical envelope of the sacramental species. The
Eucharistic Sacrifice takes place simply and merely by Jesus Christ
becoming present, by virtue of the words of consecration, under the
separate species in a state of immolation or death, that is, of sacrifice, so far as external appearances go.[1] — Sacramentally, that is,
according to external signs, the blood of Jesus Christ is separated
from His body, and therefore shed, since by the words of consecration there is designated and effected, on the one hand, the presence
of the body of Christ under the solid species of bread, and, on the
other hand, the presence of His blood under the fluid species of
wine.[2] This sacramental separation of the blood of Christ from His
body, or this mystical immolation of Christ, is fully sufficient for
the actual and symbolical expression of the Saviour's interior intention of sacrificing Himself — that is, for the consummation of a
real sacrifice.[3] Sacrifice is, indeed, an exterior symbolical sign of

---

[1] Exhibetur Christus per modum mortui sub speciebus, quamvis in se non sit
mortuus, et hoc fit ex vi actionis sacrificativae; haec autem exhibitio sufficit ad
protestandum totum id, quod protestari posset realis destructio, nempe totalem
submissionem respectu Dei et recognitionem supremae majestatis (Pasqualigo
tr. 1, q. 43, n. 5).

[2] Quantum est ex vi verborum consecrationis, corpus et sanguis Christi sis-
tuntur et exhibentur seorsum, unum ab altero, sicut in cruce separatus fuit sanguis
a corpore, atque ita Christus mystice et incruente immolatur (Sylvius 3, q. 83,
a. 1, concl. 4.)

[3] Cum Christus sit principalis offerens, dum in se ipso facit repraesentationem
propriae mortis se offerendo Patri, declarat affectum se totum tradentis in obse-

the interior sacrifice; according to this, the mystical shedding of blood on the altar performs the same office as did the real shedding of blood on the cross. The unbloody immolation of the eucharistic victim through the sacramental shedding of blood proves the reality of the sacrifice of Christ under foreign sacramental species. The Eucharist is a mystical, that is, a sacramental and, at the same time, a real or actual sacrifice. — Mystica nobis, Domine, prosit oblatio (Miss. Rom.).

The eucharistic service is not only a true sacrifice, accomplished in the present on the altar, but also, at the same time, the mysterious copy and representation, or renewal, of the past sacrifice of the cross. For the dual consecration should be considered under a twofold aspect; first, in so far as a mystical immolation, it makes the present offering of the body and blood of Christ a real sacrifice; and secondly, inasmuch as it represents in a visible manner the past sacrifice of the cross. [1] It is, therefore, by one and the same thing, namely, by the transsubstantiation of the two elements, that the eucharistic offering acquires the character of an absolute and relative sacrifice, that is, of a true sacrifice in itself, but which, according to its intrinsic nature and constitution, not only relates to the sacrifice of the cross, but also visibly copies it. There was something similar in the bloody sacrifice of the Old Testament. One and the same immolation, or blood-shedding, rendered them not only peculiar sacrifices of the worship then obtaining, but also figures of the future sacrifice of Christ. In the Eucharist a merely mystical shedding of blood suffices to constitute a true sacrifice, for on the altar there is question, not of acquiring the merit of propitiation, but only of applying the fruits of redemption acquired on the cross. For this purpose the Victim actually immolated on Golgotha, with His inexhaustible treasures of merits, is constantly represented and sacrificed to God the Lord, in the eucharistic service through unbloody immolation. — The complete essence of the Eucharistic Sacrifice consists, therefore, in the mystical shedding of blood wrought by the words consecrating both elements; — and, indeed, it consists in this bloodshedding, inasmuch as said blood-shedding is a real expression of the present intention of sacrifice and of the self-offering of Christ taking place on the altar, and, at the same time, in so far as it represents and renews the Sacrifice of the Cross. This conception of the Eucharistic Sacrifice commends itself, not only on account of its

quium Patris, qui est interius sacrificium, atque adeo oblatio externa cum illa repraesentatione mortis declarat hunc affectum et ideo hujusmodi repraesentatio est sufficiens destructio pro sacrificio: nam illa tantum destructio requiritur, quae possit declarare interius sacrificium (Pasqualigo tr. 1, q. 43, n. 4).

[1] Christus Dominus vi consecrationis tanquam verus Agnus et victima sistitur in altari sub speciebus panis et vini, et in quodam statu mortis constituitur, quatenus per spiritualem verborum gladium sub diversis et separatis speciebus immolatur et offertur Deo Patri. — Porro haec mystica, quae vi verborum fit, separatio corporis ac sanguinis, apte separationem cruentam sanguinis a corpore in cruce peractam repraesentat (Puig et Xarrié, De euchar. c. 4, § 1, n. 620).

simplicity and theological foundation, but also because it has a positive basis in the words of the institution of our Lord as well as in the ecclesiastical tradition. The Saviour Himself characterizes the Eucharistic Sacrifice as an unbloody offering, or breaking, of His body, and as a mystical shedding of His blood "for the remission of sins." In agreement with this the ante-tridentine theology always taught, that the formal character of the Sacrifice of the Eucharist consists only in the mystical immolation of Christ through the words of the dual consecration. [1]

4. The priest should frequently reflect that it is God who has called and consecrated him to the exalted office, as a servant of Christ and in the name of the Church, to accomplish and offer the adorable Sacrifice of the Eucharist. The most sublime act of his priestly power consists in the celebration of the Holy Sacrifice, that is, in his power "to call the Lord of Glory with holy words down upon the earth, to bless Him with his lips, to hold Him in his hands, to receive Him into his mouth and to distribute Him to the faithful," whilst at the same time "the angels stand about him in order to honor Him who is sacrificed." Hence the strict obligation incumbent on him to preserve his body and soul pure, and continually to work at his sanctification. "In the Lord", said the Seraphic Francis to his spiritual sons, "I entreat all my brethren, who are priests of the Most High, that, as often as they celebrate Mass, they be spotless and that they thus offer with purity the Sacrifice of the Body and Blood of our Lord Jesus Christ." To animate them still more, he draws their attention to the Virgin who conceived our Lord by the power of the Holy Ghost and who, in the days of His childhood, touched Him with her most pure hands and carried Him in her most pure arms. And in truth, the priest has reason to regard with special veneration that Blessed One, the blessed Mary ever Virgin, of whom was born for us the God present in the Sacrament, and with peculiar fervor to endeavor to make his heart like unto her holy and immaculate heart. As Mary, in a marvellous manner, conceived and gave birth to the Son of God, the priest has received power to call Jesus Christ from heaven to earth. As Mary, standing constantly and to the last at the foot of the Cross, offered Her Divine Son to the Heavenly Father, in like manner does the priest offer Him daily upon the altar of the Cross. As Mary was overshadowed by the Holy Ghost, so are priests, the instruments of the Holy Ghost, to continue in the Church the mystery of the Incarnation for the salvation of men. As Mary gave herself unreservedly to God, the Church requires of her priests a cheerful and self-sacrificing love. As Mary, who conceived the Son of God and carried him in her womb, excelled as a vessel of the Holy Ghost (*vas spirituale*) all creatures in purity of heart, so Christ and the Church require a special purity of heart in the priest who places the Eucharistic Christ upon the altar, carries Him in his hands, receives Him and gives

---

[1] Cfr. Pasqualigo tr. 1, q. 42—44. — Billot, De sacram. 1, 556 seqq.

Him to others, and thus in a more special manner appears as a vessel of the Holy Ghost. This Virgin is, consequently, the honor and joy of all good priests. A priest, inflamed with love for Christ in the Eucharist, clings also with the most tender devotion and truly filial love to the Virgin Mother of God, and such a sentiment obtains for him the special protection of this powerful Virgin. Under her auspices, he is enabled to live a pure life and to celebrate in a holy manner the true Sacrifice of the Body and Blood of our Lord Jesus Christ. His filial piety at all times urges him to implore the holy Virgin to permit him to participate in her profound humility, her exceptional purity and ardent charity. A priest, assiduously intent on this object, will learn from experience that the Mother of the Eternal Word will be propitious to him. [1]

16. The Relation of the Sacrifice of the Mass to the Sacrifice of the Cross.

In the eucharistic celebration are found all the conditions essential to a sacrifice; hence it is a true and real sacrifice. The God-Man — His Body and His Blood — is in reality immolated upon the altar (*immolatur*), and not merely represented and offered (*offertur*) to the Heavenly Father. To the essential characteristics of the Eucharistic Sacrifice belongs its interior peculiar relation to the Sacrifice of the Cross. The sacrifices prior to Christ did indeed prefigure the future Sacrifice of the Cross; but the Sacrifice of the Mass is in an infinitely more perfect manner a copy of the Sacrifice of the Cross accomplished on Calvary. The Eucharist is in its nature a relative sacrifice, that is, a true sacrifice in itself, but which at the same time relates to the Sacrifice of the Cross and objectively represents it. It is in consequence of Christ's institution that this relation to the sacrificial death of Christ is an essential feature of the Mass. Whilst setting this forth, we shall also clearly show the identity of the Sacrifice of the Mass with that of the Cross, as well as the difference that exists between them.

1. Jesus Christ left to His Church in the Eucharist a true and real Sacrifice, "that by means of it that bloody Sacrifice, which He once offered on the Cross, may ever be represented and its remembrance be preserved until the end of the world, and its healing power be applied and spent for the remission of those sins daily committed by us." [2] According to the doctrine of the Church, the Holy Mass

---

[1] Cfr. Neues Pastoralblatt für die Diöc. Augsb., Jahrg. 1876, p. 259.

[2] Visibile sacrificium, quo cruentum illud, semel in cruce peragendum, *repraesentaretur,* ejusque *memoria* in finem usque saeculi permaneret, atque illius *salutaris virtus* in remissionem eorum, quae a nobis quotidie committuntur, peccatorum *applicaretur* (Trid. sess. 22, cap. 1). — According to the teaching of St. Thomas, the essence of the Eucharistic Sacrifice consists in the *immolatio Christi;* therefore, the Sacrifice of the Eucharist is also an imago repraesentativa, repraesentatio, figura quaedam et exemplum dominicae passionis, that is, a living likeness of the Passion of Christ, the actual representation of the Sacrifice of the Cross,

is not a mere memorial of sacrifice (*nuda commemoratio sacrificii in cruce peracti*), but a true memorial sacrifice, that is, a real sacrifice endowed with a commemorative character (*sacrificium commemorativum*). The Mass is not a mere shadowy copy, but the living and essential representation of the Sacrifice of the Cross.

a) That the celebration of the Eucharist is the representation of the sacrificial death of Christ, is evident even from the words of the institution. Our Lord Himself calls the Eucharistic Sacrifice the giving of His Body and the shedding of His Blood. In making choice of these words, He would not merely signify the true Sacrifice of His sacramental Body and Blood, but He would, at the same time, designate that the mode and manner of this Sacrifice by the mystical shedding of blood under the separate species should represent symbolically the violent separation of His body and blood, the real shedding of His blood on the Cross. — He then gives to His Apostles and to their successors in the priestly office the command and the power to celebrate the Eucharist in remembrance of Him. — The Apostle explains and proves this command, by adding that the celebration of the Eucharist is of itself always an actual announcement of the death of Christ and must, therefore, be perpetuated among Christians until our Lord shall return in glory at the consummation of time to judge the world (1 Cor. 11, 26).

b) The sacramental offering of the Body and Blood of Christ on the altar is frequently styled in tradition the figure, the representation, the symbol (*typus, figura, imago, signum, symbolum*) of the passion and sacrificial death of Christ on the Cross. Gaudentius expresses himself happily on this subject: "Christ willed that His benefits should be permanently imparted to us; He willed that souls should be sanctified by the representation of His own passion (*per imaginem propriae passionis*). Therefore, He commissioned His faithful disciples, whom He ordained the first priests of His Church (*quos primos Ecclesiae suae constituit sacerdotes*), unceasingly to celebrate these mysteries of eternal life, which all priests should celebrate in all the churches of the universe until He returns from heaven, in order that the priests themselves and all believing nations also may have a copy (a true representation) of the passion of Christ (*exemplar passionis Christi*) daily before their eyes, may bear it in their hands, receive it into their mouths and hearts — and thus by this celebration the remembrance of our redemption may ever be indelibly impressed on their minds."[1] — St. Gregory the Great writes: "The Eucharistic Sacrifice preserves in a unique manner the soul from eternal perdition, as it renews mystically the death of the only-begotten Son of God (*nobis mortem Unigeniti per mysterium reparat*). For although Christ be risen from the dead, He dieth no

---

and, consequently, it is, moreover, at the same time, the applicatio et participatio fructus dominicae passionis, namely, the application and participation of the fruits of the Sacrifice of the Cross. Cfr. S. Thom. 3, q. 83, a. 1 et 2.

[1] Sermo 2.

more, and death has no longer dominion over Him, yet in His immortal and imperishable life He is sacrificed anew for us in this mystery of sacred oblation (*pro nobis iterum in hoc mysterio sacrae oblationis immolatur*). Let us, therefore, consider attentively all that this Sacrifice (*sacrificium*) is for us, since for the remission of our sins it represents continually the passion of the only-begotten Son of God (*pro absolutione nostra passionem Unigeniti Filii semper imitatur*)."[1] In a similar sense, the words of consecration separately spoken over the bread and wine, which cause Christ's Body and Blood to be present under the separate species, are designated as a spiritual, reasonable and incorporeal sword, by which the Victim is slain upon the altar. Hence St. Gregory of Nazianzum addresses the following petition to Amphilochius: "Delay not to pray for me, when by the word (of consecration) you call down the Word (= the Son of God), when by an unbloody separation you slay the Body and Blood of the Lord with the sacrificial knife of His word (φωνὴν ἔχων τὸ ξίφος)."

c) Finally, how dear to Catholics and how wide-spread among them is devotion to and the hearing of the Holy Mass; they look upon it as a mystical representation, an unbloody celebration of the passion and death of Jesus Christ! — "To our churches Christ could not have given any more effectual or more proper means to preserve the remembrance of our redemption, than His Body and Blood, the price of our ransom. How could we be unmindful of our redemption, when we have before our eyes the Body of Christ mystically sacrificed in death for our salvation, and His Blood shed for our sins? At the very sight of these visible signs (in which we behold with unwavering faith the true Body and Blood of Christ) our hearts should be encouraged to think upon the redemption of the human race, saved by this Body and Blood, and we should be inflamed with devotion and be moved to implore from our inmost heart that God, on account of this holy and precious Sacrifice which in this Body and Blood was once offered for the redemption of mankind, may grant that it profit us for our reconciliation with Himself, and through His mercy for our salvation and beatitude. That this remembrance might remain in constant practice in the Church of Christ, He conferred upon His Apostles the priesthood of the New Law, commanding them to celebrate this Sacrifice: *Do this in commemoration of Me.*" (Ein Vergissmeinnicht, p. 45.)

The words of the Saviour and of the Apostles, the teaching of the Fathers and the prayers of the liturgies, the conviction and acknowledgment of the faithful, place it beyond doubt that the celebration of the Eucharist has also for object to bring before our eyes and to represent to us Christ's sacrificial death, in order that the memory thereof may always be preserved fresh and living in all hearts. [2]

---

[1] Dialog. 1. 4, c. 58.

[2] Notandum, quia quotidianum nostrum sacrificium idem ipsum dicit (S. Chrysostomus) cum eo, quo Christus semel oblatus est in cruce, quantum at ean-

2. A painting or a crucifix may represent the Lord's death on the Cross; but this is a merely figurative and, consequently, an imperfect representation of that divine sacrificial drama, once enacted on Mount Calvary. Quite different, — infinitely more complete and actual, is the bloody sacrifice of Christ represented by the Mass. It is, namely, the real and objective, the living and essential representation of the Sacrifice of Redemption accomplished on the Cross. [1] — The reason for it lies in the inmost nature of the Eucharistic Sacrifice, as it was instituted by Christ. Upon the altar appear the same Priest and the same Victim as upon the Cross. For in the Eucharist Jesus Christ offers Himself, His Body once immolated on the Cross and His Blood once shed on the Cross, with all the merits there acquired, in an unbloody yet in a real and true manner. — We should, moreover, consider the way and manner in which Christ's Body and Blood are to be offered. This consists in the mystical shedding of blood, that is, in the separate consecration of the bread and wine into the Body and Blood of Christ. The separate species, under which Christ's Body and Blood are rendered present by virtue

---

dem veram hic et ibi corporis Christi substantiam: quod vero nostrum quotidianum illius semel oblati dicit esse *exemplum*, i. e. *figuram* vel *formam*, non dicit, ut hic vel ibi essentialiter alium Christum constituat, sed ut eundem in cruce semel, in altari quotidie alio modo immolari et offerri ostendat: ibi in veritate passionis, qua pro nobis occisus est, hic in *figura* et *imitatione passionis ipsius*, qua Christus non iterum vere patitur, sed *ipsius verae memoria passionis* quotidie nobis iteratur.... Non ergo est in ipsius Christi veritate *diversitas*, sed *in ipsius immolationis actione*, quae dum *veram Christi passionem et mortem quadam sua similitudine figurando repraesentat*, nos ad imitationem ipsius passionis invitet et accendat, contra hostem nos roboret et muniat, et a vitiis purgans et virtutibus condecorans, vitae aeternae nos idoneos ac dignos exhibeat (Alger. De sacramentis corp. et sanguin. domin., l. 1, c. 16, n. 109).

[1] Triplex habemus *memoriale passionis*, sc. in *scripto*, in *verbo* et in *sacramento*. — In *scripto*, ut quando passio describitur vel narratur per scripturam, vel quando imaginibus exprimitur; et hoc est *memoriale quasi mortuum* et habet fieri ad visum, qui apprehendit magis de longinquo. — In *verbo*, utpote cum aliquis verbotenus narrat passionem Christi; et illud *partim est vivum, partim mortuum*. *Vivum* est in corde bonorum praedicatorum, sed mortuum in corde tepidorum et malorum; vel *vivum* in corde et cogitatione, *non vivum* in voce; et hoc est ad *auditum*, auditus autem non ita apprehendit de longinquo. — In *sacramento* vero est memoriale, cum ipsum corpus Christi significatur et continetur in specie panis et sanguis in specie vini; et hoc est memoriale *vivum*, quia ipse Christus seipsum ibi praebet, offerens nobis corpus, quod pro nobis fuit occisum, et sanguinem, qui pro nobis fuit effusus, et hoc est ad *gustum*, qui de proximo apprehendit, ut jam *non quasi speculatione*, sed *quadam experientia passionis ejus memores* simus. — Si ergo accendit affectum nostrum passio *descripta*, et amplius ferventer *praedicata;* multo magis inflammare et afficere debet in *hoc sacramento expressa*. Et hoc absque dubio facit, si quis sensum habet et illum convertit ad hoc sacramentum. Ille ergo est, qui ex hoc sacramento efficaciam reportat, qui se convertit; ille vere audit Missam, non qui tantum verba dicit vel audit sine devotione, sed qui ad hoc memoriale totam mentis intentionem convertit (S. Bonav. 4, dist. 12, p. 2, a. 1, q. 1 ad 3).

of the words of consecration, that is, mystically immolated, are symbols of the violent and bloody death of Christ on the Cross.[1] The separation of Christ's Body and Blood takes place on the altar — of course, not in reality, but only in appearance: for the Eucharistic Victim can no longer be slain in a bloody (physical), but only in an unbloody (mystical) manner.[2] This mystical immolation, therefore, in consequence of which the Divine Victim under the two species appears "as if slain" (*tanquam occisus*), is well calculated to represent Christ's Body and Blood in that form of separation which took place on the Cross.[3] By this mystical blood-shedding, which brings the real shedding of blood on the Cross vividly to view, the Eucharistic Sacrifice becomes, in a most perfect manner, a memorial Sacrifice.

The distinct consecration of the elements of bread and wine, the separate representation of the Body and Blood of Christ under the two species, that is, the mystical shedding of blood, is, in virtue of the institution by Christ, absolutely necessary, not merely for the lawful, but also for the valid celebration of the Eucharistic Sacrifice. If culpably or inculpably but one substance is consecrated, then Christ is indeed present under one species, but the Sacrifice is not accomplished, because an essential characteristic and requisite, namely, the twofold consecration, is wanting.[4] Hence it is of divine ordination, that both elements — bread and wine — must always be

---

[1] Consecratio utriusque speciei valet ad repraesentandam passionem Christi, in qua seorsim fuit sanguis a corpore separatus: unde et in forma consecrationis fit mentio de ejus effusione (S. Thom. 3, q. 76, a. 2 ad 1). — Ipsum corpus et sanguis Domini, ut sunt sub illis speciebus (panis et vini), signa sunt ejusdem corporis et sanguinis, ut fuerunt in cruce; repraesentat enim Eucharistia passionem Christi (Bellarm. De sacramento Eucharist., 1. 2, c. 15).

[2] Quod consecratio ex vi verborum ponat sub una specie corpus, non autem sanguinem, et sub altera specie sanguinem, non autem corpus, minime probat, consecrationem esse actionem realiter destructivam Christi, sed solum quod sit mystica mortis ejus repraesentatio: quia consecratio non pertingit ad causandam illam separationem inter corpus et sanguinem Christi in se, sed solum in *sacramento*, h. e. in *signo* et *repraesentatione* (Salmant. disp. 13, dub. 2, n. 38).

[3] Consecratio est maxime expressa significatio sacrificii crucis, quatenus per eam ex vi verborum seorsim ponitur sub specie panis corpus Christi velut occisum et sub specie vini sanguis velut effusus: unde haec separatio, quantum est ex vi verborum, passim dicitur *mystica Christi mactatio et immolatio* (Platelius, Synopsis tot. curs. theol. P. 5, cap. 4, § 6, n. 469).

[4] Ut hoc mysterium absolute et simpliciter sit *verum* sacrificium, prout a Christo est institutum, *essentialiter* requiritur *utriusque* speciei consecratio. . . . quia de essentia hujus sacrificii est *expressa* repraesentatio mortis et passionis Christi; sed haec *intrinsece* requirit consecrationem *utriusque* speciei. . . quando sanguis statim post corpus *separatim* consecratur, quasi in viva imagine repraesentatur *ipsa effusio* sanguinis et consequenter *separatio* animae a corpore, quae ex effusione sanguinis secuta est; nam (ut Scriptura interdum loquitur) vita hominis in sanguine est et ideo solet anima per sanguinem repraesentari (Suarez disp. 75, sect. 6, n. 7). — Cfr. Salmant. De Euch. sacr. disp. 4, dub. 5, n. 92.

5

consecrated, in order that the Eucharistic Sacrifice may take place. Our Lord instituted the unbloody Sacrifice of the Altar in this manner, because He willed that by its very nature it should be a visible representation of the Sacrifice of the Cross, which was accomplished by a violent shedding of blood unto death.

3.   The Holy Mass, accordingly, is a relative Sacrifice which, as a living copy, represents the original of the Sacrifice of the Cross. — Between the two there exists the most perfect unity (oneness), in so far as we consider the Victim and the Priest ; for it is Christ who offers upon the altar His Body and His Blood, consequently, the same gift which He once offered on the Cross. — Still, the Sacrifice of the Mass and that of the Cross differ in several respects. The Church says that the way and manner of offering differs, that is, the sacrificial act is differently constituted (*ratio offerendi diversa* — Trid. sess. 22, cap. 2).[1] On the Cross, the Sacrifice of Christ consisted of the bloody offering of His life and divine self to an actual death : on the altar it consists also in the offering of His holy humanity, but in an unbloody manner, to the mystical sacramental death under the two Eucharistic species. — On Calvary Christ offered Himself in His own natural and human form, and without the assistance of a subordinate priest ; He offers Himself here under the veil of the Sacrament and by the ministry of visible priests. — There the human nature of Christ was susceptible of suffering and death.— The Sacrifice of the Cross, therefore, was infinitely painful.   Here on our altar His human nature is glorified and immortal — the Sacrifice of the Mass, consequently, is a Sacrifice free from pain.   The object of the Sacrifice of the Cross was to obtain the price of the redemption of the world ; the purpose of the Sacrifice of the Mass is to apply to individual man the treasures of grace merited and amassed by the Sacrifice on the Cross. — The bloody Sacrifice of the Cross Christ offered but once, in order to acquire for the redemption of

---

1   In order to judge of the specific and numerical unity, of the dissimilarity of the sacrifices, the sacrificial offering and the sacrificing priest, as well as the sacrificial action must be taken under consideration. — The Sacrifice of the Cross and the Sacrifice of the Mass are identical, that is, they are one and the same sacrifice, inasmuch as on the part of each there is una eademque hostia — idem offerens (Trid.). But, as in the bloody sacrifice the shedding of blood is real and only mystical in the unbloody sacrifice, the sacrificial act is different as well according to number (numero) as according to species (specie). Therefore, the majority of theologians rightly understand the words of the Council of Trent to mean, that "only the manner of offering varies" (sola offerendi ratio diversa = modus sacrificandi diversus, actio sacrifica diversa). — Sacrificium Missae non differt specie aut essentia a sacrificio incruento, quod Christus obtulit in coena, distinguitur tamen numero et quibusdam accidentalibus conditionibus (Suarez disp. 76, sect. 1, n. 2). — In like manner, the daily sacrifices of the altar, in consequence of the continually repeated sacrificial act, differ according to number (numerically), not merely from the Sacrifice of the Cross and from that of the Last Supper, but even from one another, — and only ratione victimae et sacerdotis principaliter offerentis are all these sacrifices identical.   Cfr. Vasquez disp. 222, cap. 2. — Tanner disp. 5. de ss. Euch. et Miss. q. 9, dub. 2. — Pasqualigo, De sacrif. N. L., tr. 1, q. 52.

fallen man an inexhaustible treasure of satisfaction and merits ; the unbloody Sacrifice of the Altar He often offers, in order to apply to us "the fruits of the bloody Sacrifice of the Cross in a most abundant measure."[1] On the Cross, the inexhaustible fountain of eternal redemption was opened ; from the altar it perpetually pours forth its streams into the hearts of men. — Neither amid the glory of heaven nor in His sacramental state can Christ any longer merit, nor can He satisfy any more; for by divine disposition both are possible only in this mortal life, that is, as long as we are pilgrims on earth. The Sacrifice of the Mass, therefore, draws its power and efficacy, its fruit from the Sacrifice of the Cross, that is, Holy Mass applies to us the graces and blessings of Calvary. On the Cross and upon the altar, consequently, there is the same sacrificial fruit ; the distinction consists only in this, that in the former it was merited, and in the latter it is applied.

4. Let us, in conclusion, adduce another difference. The Sacrifice of the Cross was exclusively the Sacrifice of Christ ; the Eucharist is, at the same time, the Sacrifice of the Church and that of Christ — inasmuch as the Church offers it and is offered together with it at the altar. Christ left the Eucharistic Sacrifice to His Church ; it is her chief dower, her glorious mine of wealth, her greatest joy, her all-hallowed sanctuary. At the altar she enters into living communion of sacrifice with Christ ; the Sacrifice of the Mass is offered not alone for the Church, but also by her and through her to the Most High. And this is the principal reason why the Eucharist is and is called the Sacrifice of the Church. — To this is added, moreover, the circumstance that the Church Militant during Holy Mass offers herself and is at the same time offered. Christ has placed Himself in the hands of the Church, that she may offer Him to the Heavenly Father ; with the infinitely meritorious and acceptable sacrifice to God of the Body and Blood of Christ, the Church unites the offering of herself. In union with the sacrifice of Christ the faithful should offer themselves with all their labors, sufferings and prayers, with body and soul. St. Augustine expresses this sentiment in an appropriate manner, when he says : "The whole body of the redeemed, that is, the society and communion of saints (of Christians), is presented to God as a joint sacrifice by the High-priest who in His passion also offered Himself for us in the form of a servant, that we might become the members of so exalted a Head. . . . The Church celebrates this in what is known to the faithful as the Sacrament of the Altar, in which she also is offered while offering it" (*in ea re, quam ipsa offert, ipsa offertur*). And in another place he says, that the Church as the mystical body of Christ "learns to offer herself through Him" (*se ipsam per ipsum discit offerre*).[2] — This truth obtains its most beautiful expression in the

---

[1] Quia fructu dominicae passionis quotidie indigemus, propter quotidianos defectus, quotidie in Ecclesia regulariter hoc sacramentum offertur (S. Thom. 3, q. 83, a. 2).

[2] De civ. Dei 1. 10, c. 6. 20.

prayers and ceremonies of the rite of the Mass : it is signified not only by the mixing of wine with water, but, moreover, by the two sacrificial elements of bread and wine. As the Fathers remark, the bread is made of many grains of wheat and the wine from many grapes ; therefore, the sacrificial bread, as well as the sacrificial wine, is a symbol of the mystical body of Christ, consisting of many members, which in union with the true and natural Body is offered on the altar. [1]

With Christ, in Christ and through Christ, the Church during Mass daily offers herself to the Most High "as a holy, living sacrifice, pleasing unto God" (Rom. 12, 1). — With Christ: at the sight of the Divine Victim, whose Body is daily mystically broken upon the altar and whose Blood is daily mystically shed before our eyes, she is encouraged and animated cheerfully to drink with Him of the chalice of bitter affliction, — to embrace with joy labors and sufferings, persecutions and calumnies. — In Christ: for in Him as her Head, that is, in her most intimate connection and fusion with His Sacrifice, the Church offers herself to tread the rough and lonely, the weary and painful way of the Cross, until she shall have arrived at the heavenly Jerusalem. — Through Christ: for the true and mystical Body of Christ (*corpus verum et mysticum*) constitutes the sole sacrifice, whose sweet odor ascends to Heaven, "through Christ our Lord," through whom alone we may approach to God, and by whom alone we can please Him.

How boundless in goodness, how unspeakably rich in mercies is the Lord in presenting us with so precious a Sacrifice ! Let us also remember how highly favored we are, how enviable is our lot, since the well-beloved Son of the Eternal Father is and will forever remain our Victim, that we may not have to appear before God emptyhanded, but may have a rich and worthy gift to offer Him, and that in union therewith we may offer ourselves also. Since He was once "born and given to us by the Immaculate Virgin" (*nobis natus, nobis datus ex intacta Virgine*), He wished to be always our own. His love can be requited only with love, and His sacrifice only with sacrifice !

5. From all that has hitherto been said concerning the relation of the Sacrifice of the Mass to that of the Cross, it is evident how distasteful and ridiculous is the offensively oft-repeated objection, that the Sacrifice of the Mass undervalues and detracts from the worth and dignity of the Sacrifice of the Cross. The Sacrifice of the Altar is, by its very nature and very object, the living re-presentation of the Sacrifice of the Cross and the perpetual application of its fruits. — Therefore, the Mass does not cast Christ's death on the

---

[1] Quoniam corpus (Christi) mysticum est ex multis aggregatis in unum, talia elementa esse debuerunt, quae ex multis aggregantur in unum; tale autem est panis, quia est ex multis granis puris, tale etiam est vinum, quod est ex multis racemis puris; ideo recte unionem corporis Christi mystici signat (S. Bonavent. IV, dist. 11, p. 2, a. 1, q. 1).

Cross in the shade, but, on the contrary, rather sets it forth in the clearest and most refulgent light. [1] There certainly is not a more glorious testimony to the necessity and profitableness, to the inexhaustible graces and blessings of the bloody Sacrifice of redemption, than precisely this perpetual celebration of the Sacrifice of the Eucharist. At the altar millions draw and drink from the fountain of grace of the Sacrifice of the Cross, without its healing waters ever drying up or becoming diminished. — The bitter sacrificial death of Christ on the Cross should be profoundly engraved upon our minds, and should live unchangeably fresh in our memories and in our hearts. How can this be more easily and surely attained than by the daily celebration of the Eucharist, in which Christ's bloody sacrificial death, with all its blessings, is presented to us so vividly and so touchingly and, indeed, is even, in a certain sense, renewed? Where is the devotion to the passion and death of Christ more highly esteemed and more fervently cultivated, where is the love of the Cross and of the Crucified more strongly inculcated and more fervently practised than in the bosom of the Catholic Church, in which upon thousands of altars the bloody death of Christ is daily celebrated in an unbloody manner, mystically proclaimed and held in constant remembrance? Every altar is a mystical Mount Calvary, upon whose summit waves "the banner of the Cross," at the sight of which the believing soul, deeply moved, entering seriously into herself, exclaims: *Amor meus crucifixus est!* — "My Love is crucified!" But take away the memorial Sacrifice of the altar, and sooner or later the great Sacrifice of atonement, offered on Golgotha nearly nineteen centuries ago, will disappear in a mythical distance, and with it the personality of the Saviour and the entire work of the Redeemer will fall more or less into a deplorable oblivion.

"Ah! my own sweet Good, sovereign Lord and sweet Guest of my soul, I would fain ask yet one more question. Tell me, dear Lord, what advantage is to be derived from the Mass? Is it necessary that every day Thy death should be celebrated anew, for assuredly Thou didst enough for the whole world on Good Friday? Yes, though there had been a thousand worlds, Thou wouldst still have done sufficient for them all! — *Jesus Christ:* This I have done out of My great love, and for mankind have I planned this delightful invention of love; for since men daily need it because of their human frailty, I have willed that that worthy Sacrifice be daily offered anew for the sins and weakness of men, according to the

---

[1] Nulla ratione sacrificium Missae, quod aiunt impii homines, derogat peracto in cruce sacrificio; quinimo ejus merita ac beneficia quam latissime propagat, atque in omnes uberrime diffundit. Siquidem Christus in hoc sacrificio pro iis, quos redemit, omnibus eundem pretiosum sanguinem et vulnera Patri suo ostendit ac offert, quibus ad dexteram ejus in coelis sedens gratiam nobis apud eum conciliat. Utrobique enim sempiterno sacerdotio fungitur, ut possit salvare in perpetuum accedentes per semet ipsum ad Deum, semper vivens ad interpellandum pro nobis (Hebr. 7, 25). Coll. Lac. III, 493.

words of St. Thomas: All the fruitfulness and advantages wrought by God on the day upon which He died, are daily to be found in every Holy Mass, and the same grace is received by all who partake worthily of the worthy Body of our Lord. — Our fervent desires should lead us to have a longing to assist at all the Masses celebrated throughout the world. At every Mass (at which we assist) we should endeavor to receive the Blessed Sacrament, recommending to God in our prayers all whom in our love we bear in mind, whether living or dead. In this manner, we participate not only in the Mass at which we assist, but, moreover, in all the Masses celebrated throughout the world." (Tauler.)

17. The Value of the Eucharistic Sacrifice, as also the Reason and the Manner of its Efficacy. [1]

In the midst of the earthly Paradise stood "the tree of life" (Gen. 2, 9), that is, the tree, the fruit of which was destined to impart to man perpetual youth, strength and beauty. It was a figure of the true tree of life, that stands in the midst of the new paradise, namely, of Holy Church. We are to understand by this true tree of life, first, the Cross of Christ, and then the Eucharist, which imparts fulness of heavenly and imperishable life to all who desire it. We have already investigated the root and the trunk of this tree of life; we must now endeavor to know the quality of its rare and plenteous fruit, "beautiful to behold and agreeable to the taste." This tree of life of the Eucharistic Sacrifice, planted by God in the garden of the Church, rears its blooming top high toward heaven, and spreads wide its shady branches over the earth, dropping down graces and blessings on all men. — The Holy Sacrifice of the Mass may also be considered as the golden bridge uniting heaven and earth, — for while clouds of incense of adoration and thanksgiving rise unceasingly from the altar to the throne of God, the blessed clouds of grace and mercy descend on mankind. *Gloria in excelsis Deo et in terra pax hominibus bonae voluntatis!* — "Glory to God in the highest, and on earth peace to men of good will!" (Luke 2, 14.) This Chant of the Angels, which at the birth of Christ resounded for the first time on the plains of Bethlehem, "as the voice of many waters," echoes and re-echoes throughout all ages, and finds its most splendid fulfilment in the celebration of the Eucharist. In as far as it is a Sacrifice of praise and thanksgiving, the Mass procures all honor and glory to God; inasmuch as it is a Sacrifice of propitiation and petition, it obtains for men the plenitude of peace, that is, of all graces and blessings. [2] That the Sacri-

---

[1] *Valor* sacrificii Missae est ipsa dignitas et virtus, qua pollet, ratione rei oblatae et principalis offerentis. — *Efficacia* est complexus effectuum ejus in se inspectorum et modus quo illos operatur. — *Fructus* est effectus sacrificii quatenus nobis applicatur (Schouppe, Element. theol. dogm., p. 2, c. 3, a. 2, n. 339).

[2] Tibi, Domine, sacrificia dicata reddantur: quae sic ad *honorem nominis tui* deferenda tribuisti, ut eadem *remedia* fieri *nostra* praestares (Secreta Dom. X. post Pent.).

fice of the Mass possesses in reality the above mentioned fourfold
character of praise and thanksgiving, propitiation and petition, that
in these four characteristics it unfolds its efficacy in a striking manner, is evident even from the fact that it not only replaces and transcends the figurative sacrifices of the Old Testament, but also that it
infinitely surpasses them. For as the fulfilment and completion of
the sacrifices prior to Christ, Holy Mass includes in itself all the
goods foreboded by them. [1] Now, in the Old Law different sacrifices
were prescribed for the above-named fourfold object; consequently,
the Eucharistic Sacrifice alone must, in the most perfect manner,
answer all these various objects for which sacrifices were chiefly
offered. [2] The sole and perpetual Sacrifice of the New Testament,
therefore, enables us to cancel all our indebtedness toward God and
to fulfil all our obligations towards Him, to avert from ourselves all
evils and to implore all favors. — However, before we explain that
and how the Holy Mass is the most perfect sacrifice of praise and
the most precious and worthy sacrifice of thanksgiving to God, and
the fullest sacrifice of propitiation and the most powerful sacrifice of
petition for men, some preliminary questions remain to be answered,
relating to the value of the Eucharistic Sacrifice, as also to the
reason and nature of its efficacy.

The value (*valor*) and efficacy (*efficacia*) of sacrifice in general
depend chiefly upon its essence and form. The more excellent and
precious the object sacrificed, the higher the dignity and holiness of
the priest sacrificing, and also, the more perfect his intention and
his sacrificial act, the more valuable in itself and the more efficacious
for the attainment of its object will be the sacrifice. First and chiefly,
we shall consider the person of him who sacrifices, as well as the
way and manner of the sacrifice. As there are more than one person
offering the Eucharistic Sacrifice, who offer it in different ways, we
shall examine and explain its value and efficacy under this aspect.

1. First of all, the Eucharistic Sacrifice is to be considered in
so far as in it Jesus Christ offers Himself, that is, He is not only
the sacrificial gift, but also the most eminent sacrificer. In this
respect the Sacrifice of the Mass is not inferior in value to that of
the Cross: both are equally infinite, equally beyond all estimation
and equally valuable. — The infinite value of the Sacrifice of the
Mass consists, indeed, also in the immensity of the object offered;
but principally in the infinite dignity of the sacrificing Man-God.
The object offered on the altar is the richest and the most glorious,
the very best and the most precious that can be imagined, for it is
Christ Himself, His Body and Blood, His holy humanity, which of

---

[1] Haec oblatio illa est, quae per varias sacrificiorum, naturae et legis tempore,
similitudines figurabatur, utpote quae bona omnia, per illa significata, velut illorum
omnium consummatio et perfectio complectitur (Trident. sess. 22, cap. 1).

[2] Deus, cui, omnium sacrificiorum varietate finita, hostiam nunc offerimus
singularem, adesto votis tua inspiratione conceptis (Liturg. Gallic.). — Legalium
differentiam hostiarum unius sacrificii perfectione sanxisti (Secreta Dom. VII.
post Pent.).

itself, that is, by virtue of its natural and supernatural prerogatives and perfections, is incomparably more noble and valuable than all other creatures, and which by the hypostatic union with the Eternal Word, in which it is offered, even attains and possesses infinite dignity and sublimity above every creature. [1] — But although Christ's precious Blood, which is mystically shed in the chalice, has an infinite, eternal and imperishable value, nevertheless, this of itself would not suffice to impart infinite value to the Eucharistic Sacrifice, since, for this purpose, it is requisite, above all, that the person who celebrates should possess infinite greatness and majesty, as is the case with the God-Man, and with Him alone. — Mary, the ever-blessed Virgin, offered her Son in the Temple and at the foot of the Cross; but, however holy and perfect her sentiments, however acceptable to God her offering may have been, still it was not infinite in value, not infinitely meritorious. The divine dignity and grandeur of the person sacrificing would, on the contrary, impart infinite value to a trifling gift. But since Jesus Christ, the Eternal Son of God and the Splendor of the glory of the Father, offers in the Mass His own self, His own flesh and blood, the Sacrifice of the Altar is in every respect infinitely valuable and precious. [2]

The infinite value of the Eucharistic Sacrifice must be distinguished still more minutely, that is, considered in a twofold sense. First, we may thereby mean the infinite grandeur, excellence and perfection peculiar to the Eucharistic Sacrifice, because Christ is the sacrificing priest and the victim offered. This value, this moral dignity of the Eucharistic Sacrifice, depends upon the grandeur and holiness of Christ; inasmuch as He in the present sacrifices Himself and is sacrificed on the altar. — But if we understand thereby the infinite value of the satisfaction and merit, that is, the infinite price and ransom, the inexhaustible treasure of the redemption contained in the Eucharistic Sacrifice, it also originates from Christ, but not in so far as He now offers Himself on the altar, but in so far as He once offered Himself on the Cross; for by the Eucharistic Sacrificial act Christ can no longer make satisfaction and acquire merit, but merely constantly apply to us the treasure of merit fully acquired on the Cross. [3]

---

[1] Christus secundum quod Deus, est dignitatis prorsus incomparabilis et immensae; secundum assumptam vero humanitatem ut Verbo aeterno unitam et omni gratiarum plenitudine perornatam, dignior est toto universo (Dion. Carthus. in 1. Petr. 2, 6).

[2] Res oblata in hoc sacrificio est infinita et offerens est etiam persona infinita, nempe Christus, qui est principalis offerens, et proinde actio quoque offerendi est infinita, utpote correspondens infinitati offerentis: ergo consurgit sacrificium valoris infiniti; nam non alia ratione sacrificium crucis fuit infinitum, nisi quia res oblata et offerens fuerunt infiniti (Pasqualigo, De sacrif. N. L. tr. 1, q. 117, n. 9).

[3] Omnis efficacia hujus sacrificii debet fundari in aliquo merito et satisfactione Christi, sed non in novo merito et satisfactione, quae Christus habeat incruente offerendo. . . . Christus namque jam non est in statu merendi vel satisfaciendi. . . . ergo fundatur in merito et satisfactione, quae Christus habuit in vita mortali et in cruce consummavit (Suarez disp. 79, sect. 1, n. 10).

Now, if we consider the Eucharistic Sacrifice in itself, that is, the divine dignity of the Sacrificing Priest and Victim, [1] as well as the inscrutable treasures therein enclosed of the fruits of the Sacrifice of the Cross, we then perceive how Holy Mass possesses a value absolutely infinite. As an infinitely valuable and infinitely perfect sacrifice, the Holy Mass evidently possesses also power infinitely great to produce those effects which by Christ's institution belong to it and are peculiar to it. But, it may be asked further, are the effects actually brought forth by the infinitely valuable and efficacious Sacrifice of the Altar, likewise infinite and unlimited, or are they not rather finite and limited ? In order to answer this question, we must consider the Eucharistic Sacrifice in its relation to God, to whom it is offered, and afterward in its relation to man, for whom it is offered.

In sacrifice its relation to God is always the first and the most essential feature, since according to its very nature, sacrifice is an act of religion. Therefore, the Sacrifice of the Mass is primarily to be regarded as an act of divine worship (λατρεία). It serves to honor and glorify God not only in its quality of a sacrifice of praise, adoration and thanksgiving, but also as a sacrifice of propitiation and petition, for God is always honored and glorified, — both when we endeavor to appease His justice and to move His goodness to impart graces to us, and also when we worship His majesty and pay Him our grateful thanks for His liberality. Since the Eucharist, in reference to all these ends, possesses infinite value and infinite power, that is, since it is a Sacrifice infinitely worthy and perfect of adoration, thanksgiving, propitiation and petition, there is given to God on the altar always the greatest possible, that is, infinitely great, homage. If, therefore, we consider the feature of *latria*, or divine worship, which chiefly consists in adoration, praise and thanksgiving, and also in propitiation and petition, then beyond a doubt the celebration of the Eucharistic Sacrifice contains in itself a worship of infinite value and, in fact, renders it to the Most High. In this connection, the Sacrifice of Christ, which in itself is infinite, always displays its full power : — for by the celebration of the Mass the triune God infallibly and at all times receives a truly infinite homage, that is, perfectly worthy adoration, praise and thanksgiving.

But the case is different when the Eucharistic Sacrifice is considered in its relation to man. From this point of view it aims at procuring our salvation and sanctification, and is, consequently, a means of grace, or rather a source of grace, bringing us the riches of heavenly blessings. The Mass, especially as a sacrifice of propitiation and petition, produces for men the operations of grace. Assuredly, acts of propitiation and petition are offered to God in the Mass, but with the intent and purpose that He may be moved by

---

[1] Dignitas carnis Christi non est aestimanda solum secundum carnis naturam, sed secundum personam assumentem, in quantum sc. erat *caro Dei*, ex quo habebat dignitatem infinitam (S. Thom. 3, q. 48, a. 2 ad 3).

reason of the sacrifice of propitiation and petition to restore us again to His favor and to impart to us His gifts. As has already been indicated, the value and dignity, that is, the intrinsic efficacy, of the Eucharistic Sacrifice is infinitely great in this respect also, that is, in appeasing an irritated God and moving His mercy to grant us His benefits. For the entire ransom paid for our redemption, the immense treasure of satisfaction and merit which was acquired on the Cross, are all upon the altar ever presented anew and offered by Christ to His Heavenly Father, that they may be applied to mankind. The Sacrifice of the Mass, accordingly, contains not only a superabundant atonement for the remission of all possible sins and punishments, but also an inexhaustible fund for the purchasing of innumerable graces and goods. Nevertheless, — as it is in the nature of things — the Mass cannot produce for man or in man infinite effects. For positively infinite effects are impossible as to number or magnitude; nor would the finite creature be capable of receiving them. The fruits which the Sacrifice of the Mass obtains for us from God are only finite, that is, restricted to a certain number and determined measure, as is also the case in the Sacrifice of the Cross.[1] The Sacrifice of the Mass, therefore, with respect to man can have only a restricted efficacy, and in its fruits is capable of only a limited application. This restriction and limitation of the fruits of the Eucharistic Sacrifice may be understood in a two-fold sense — intensive and extensive.

The Sacrifice of the Mass does not always produce effects so great and so manifold as the capacity of the recipients would warrant; it acts rather in an intensively limited degree, that is, its effects are restricted to a definite measure, even if they are different in individual cases — sometimes greater, sometimes less. — This is confirmed by the practice of the Church, according to which the Holy Sacrifice is not seldom repeatedly offered for obtaining some benefit, for example, the deliverance of a suffering soul from purgatory, the conversion of a sinner, health of body. If the Eucharistic Sacrifice always yielded the entire efficacy of which it is capable, a single holy Mass would actually suffice to obtain as many and as great blessings as are desired. — Evidently the reason of its limited efficacy does not lie in the essence and value of the Sacrifice, since it possesses infinite power for producing every effect; nor is it solely and alone due to the greater or less susceptibility of the person for whom the fruit of the Sacrifice is applied. This susceptibility, nevertheless, is duly considered therein, for it exerts its influence upon the measure of the fruit of the sacrifice to be obtained; but the final and decisive reason for the more or less plentiful application of the sacrificial graces is the will of Christ, in other words, is to be

---

[1] Quoad efficaciam sacrificium Eucharistiae non potest esse infinitum, cum nec sacrificium crucis hoc habuerit, quia efficacia respicit effectum in re ipsa dandum; non datur autem nec dari potest effectus infinite intensus (Suarez disp. 79, sect. 9).

sought in the positive ordinance of God. [1]   The Sacrifice of the Mass is a means of grace ; for it is intended to convey to us the riches of redemption.   But for this there is need of a positive ordinance on the part of God.   The Eucharistic Sacrifice can communicate graces to us only in as much and in as far as it is destined by God for this purpose.   Now, in the distribution of His gifts, God requires our co-operation ; the better our preparation, the more liberal is He, as a rule, in the dispensation of His graces.   This is the case not only with the Sacraments, but also in regard to the Holy Mass.   The greatness of the fruit of the Sacrifice to be derived by us, therefore, is determined by God, but with regard to the dispositions of those for whom the Mass is offered. — But here above all the good pleasure and the wise providence of God, who lovingly ordains all things, must be taken into consideration ; then the merciful will of the High Priest Jesus Christ, who offers and presents on the altar the price of His Blood to the Heavenly Father for specific effects, more or less great ; finally, also the subjective state of the recipient of the effects of the Sacrifice. [2] — As we are bound to pray without intermission, the Sacrifice also must be offered without ceasing, in order that we may obtain the fruit and the graces desired.   God has so ordained it, because the uninterrupted celebration of the Mass more effectually promotes His honor and our salvation.

b) The other much discussed question is practically of greater importance, namely, whether the effects of the Sacrifice of the Mass considered as to its extension, that is, in relation to the participants, be unlimited, or rather, on the contrary, limited and restricted. — Here we must make a distinction.   The faithful who personally and

---

[1]   Instituit et voluit Christus Deus, ut sacrificium offeratur et prosit ad finitum tantum et certum effectum satisfactionis et impetrationis, a se determinandum ac juxta dispositionem offerentium dispensandum, ut ideo tantum sacrificium frequentius et ferventius offeratur.   Et confirmat hanc doctrinam efficaciter praxis Ecclesiae, quae est infallibilis interpres institutionis Christi: et ipsa ad eundem effectum obtinendum, ut maxime pro eadem anima defuncta multas Missas offerre consuevit, eo ipso indicans, valorem seu fructum unius sacrificii esse finitum et limitatum.   Quodsi enim fructus satisfactorius esset infinitus, ut quamvis poenam majorem et majorem in infinitum delere possit, posset unico sacrificio totum Purgatorium exhauriri, nedum una anima, quamvis gravibus poenis obnoxia, liberari: ad quid ergo tot repetita sacra pro defunctis, etiam unica anima?   Et si fructus impetratorius esset infinitus, ita ut unico sacrificio posset impetrari quodcunque bonum majus et majus in infinitum, certo et infallibiliter, quid opus esset pro eadem re impetranda, v. g. sanitate, serenitate aeris, peste avertenda, multiplicari tot sacra juxta praxim Ecclesiae? (Sporer, Theol. sacram., P. 2, cap. 4, sect. 3, § 3).

[2]   Efficacia sacrificii est limitata ex institutione Christi.   Quia cum consistat in applicatione virtutis sacrificii crucis, unde habet, quod sit applicativum ipsius, habet etiam, quod applicet secundum hanc vel illam mensuram.   Habet autem ex institutione, quod sit applicativum virtutis sacrificii crucis (Trident. sess. 22, cap. 1).   Efficacia ita est determinata, ut tamen habeat operari secundum mensuram dispositionis.   Determinatio non tollit, quin effectus crescat ad mensuram dispositionis.   Unde est veluti duplex determinatio: altera independens a dispositione et altera respiciens dispositionem (Pasqualigo, De sacrific. N. L. tr. 1, q. 119).

actively take part in the Sacrifice, that is, who devoutly assist thereat and unite in the celebration, gain thereby a special sacrificial
fruit. This fruit, obtained by participation in the Sacrifice, is, as is
universally admitted,[1] of unlimited extension, that is, it is applied
undiminished, undecreased to all present, however numerous they
may be. Whether there be many or few assembled around the
altar, — each receives undiminished the whole and full fruit of
grace, corresponding to his zeal, his intention, his devotion and his
piety. — When several priests celebrate, that is, consecrate the same
sacrificial species, as is the case at the ordination of priests and the
consecration of bishops, we have in reality not merely one Sacrifice;
for each of the celebrating priests performs a true sacrificial act and,
consequently, each one's sacrificial act bears fruit entirely equivalent
to that same which would result, had he alone celebrated the Mass.[2]

The question that now engages our attention, relates to another
fruit, namely, to that fruit which, by special application of the
priest, is imparted to some particular person or persons. The question is, does the Sacrifice of the Mass, when it is offered for many,
impart to each the entire fruit, that is, as much fruit as it would have
procured an individual, had it been offered for him alone, — or does
the intensive-limited, sacrificial fruit, divided among the many, thus
become proportionately less for each individual participant, the
greater the number of those for whom the Sacrifice is especially offered?
Some theologians of ancient times, and more still of recent date,
answer the former question in the affirmative and the latter in the
negative, that is, they assert, but probably without solid proof, that
an extensive-unlimited efficacy of the Sacrifice is applied to the
many. The majority of theologians, on the contrary, maintain, with
full right, that the fruit of the Mass is divided among many individuals and becomes thereby proportionately less for each one, the
greater the number of the participants for whom it is offered.[3] —

---

[1] Quod hic fructus non minuatur in singulis ex aliorum consortio, a nemine,
ut arbitror, negari potest (Suarez, disp. 79, sect. 12).

[2] Fructus sacrificii per respectum ad offerentes sive primarios ut sacerdotes,
sive secundarios ut assistentes, potest dici infinitus syncategorematice, i. e. major
et major, si plures et plures fuerint offerentes. Ratio est, quia fructus proportio-
natur offerentium concursui: ergo quo magis augetur vel multiplicatur ille con-
cursus, eo magis augetur et multiplicatur fructus; unde singuli tantum fructum
obtinent, quantum obtinerent, si soli in suo ordine offerrent; et ideo non minorem
fructum recipiunt Neo-mystae consecrantes cum Episcopo (si vere consecrent) ac
si singuli consecrarent seorsim, sicut nec minorem habent mille assistentes sacrificio quam si quilibet assisteret solus. Cujus ratio ulterior est, quod multiplicatis
offerentibus, multiplicantur et oblationes (Henno, de Euchar. sacram. disp. 11,
quaest. 7, concl. 1).

[3] Sententia *communior* et *verior* negat simpliciter hanc infinitatem (exten-
sivam) in Missae sacrificio (Lugo disp. 19, sect. 12, n. 264). — Effectus sacrificii,
respondens oblationi uniuscujusque sacerdotis, quem ipse suo arbitratu potest aliis
per modum operis operati applicare, finitus est; qui proinde diminuitur tanto magis
in singulis, quanto in plures dividitur, ut ex communi contra nonnullos superius

By its nature the Mass could, nevertheless, show forth an extensive-unlimited efficacy, had it been thus ordained by Christ; for it depends wholly on the will of Christ. But that Christ did impart to the Eucharistic Sacrifice such an efficacy, cannot be proved. The opinion and practice of the Church, so important in such matters, is rather the opposite. For centuries, yes, from Apostolic times, the Church approves of and encourages the custom of offering the Mass specially for individuals. Now, it would evidently seem to favor a practice unwise and detrimental to the faithful, if the Mass could procure for hundreds and thousands, yes, for all equally great advantages, as much for the many as for one individual. By the special application in behalf of individuals, an immense amount of fruit would be lost to the remainder of the faithful, who, without reason, would be excluded from this gain. Why, then, should not the Sacrifice of the Mass be continually offered for all, the living as well as the dead?[1] — By the decision of the Church it has been determined, that a priest who receives several stipends and, in return, celebrates but one Mass, sins not only against the commandment of the Church, but also against justice (*contra justitiam*), and, consequently, he is obliged to make restitution. This presupposes that the individuals offering stipends in a case of the kind are actually wronged, that is, that they do not receive as much fruit from the Sacrifice as the exclusive application of the Mass would procure for each individual. — The intrinsic reason consists chiefly in the circumstance, that the sacrificial fruit in question is intensive-limited, that is, the fruit is confined to a certain measure.[2] Now, nothing justifies the assertion that this fruit ever increases by the mere fact of the priest's offering the Mass for several, and that thus this presupposed fruit is communicated undivided to each and every one.[3] —

---

dictum (Tanner tom. IV. disp. 5, quaest. 9, dub. 4, n. 106). — Dicendum est, efficaciam sacrificii quoad fructum medium seu fructum applicabilem a sacerdote esse determinatam seu finitam extensive, ita ut *quo magis extenditur, eo magis minuatur* (Pasqualigo l. c. tr. 1, q. 123).

[1] Si sacrificium tantum prodest omnibus et singulis, quantum si pro uno tantum applicetur, cur non applicantur omnes Missae pro omnibus defunctis, imo et pro omnibus vivis et pro omnibus aliis necessitatibus? (Lugo disp. 19, sect. 12, n. 246.)

[2] Ad illud quod obicitur de sacrificio crucis et altaris, dicendum, quod quamvis idem sit, non tamen utrobique uniformiter; nam in cruce effusum est pretium in *omnimoda plenitudine*, sed in altari habet *effectum determinatum*, cum quotidie assumatur. Et propter hoc prima oblatio non iteratur, sed secunda iteratur (S. Bonav. IV, dist. 45, a. 2, q. 3 ad 4).

[3] Quamvis virtus Christi, qui continetur sub sacramento Eucharistiae, sit *infinita*, tamen *determinatus* est *effectus* ad quem illud sacramentum (also as Sacrifice) *ordinatur*. Unde non oportet quod per unum altaris sacrificium tota poena eorum, qui sunt in purgatorio, expietur, sicut etiam nec per unum sacrificium, quod aliquis offert, liberatur a tota satisfactione debita pro peccatis: unde et quandoque plures missae in satisfactionem unius peccati injunguntur (S. Th. Supplem. q. 71, a. 14 ad 2).

Accordingly, the universal conviction of the Catholic people, that a Mass celebrated exclusively for an individual is of more benefit to him than if it were at the same time offered for others, is entirely founded on truth. — The reasons adduced show that the sacrificial fruit in question, taken in its entirety, is limited as to its extension. We make this remark, because some theologians draw here a distinction between the effects that the Mass produces as a Sacrifice of propitiation, and the effects it operates as a Sacrifice of petition. They are of opinion, namely, that although the fruit of propitiation (*propitiatio*) is limited as to its extension to a certain measure, but not the fruit to be obtained by way of petition.[1] With regard to the latter, they hold the application to be unlimited as to its extension; but the reasons they allege for this merely prove, that this application is possible in virtue of the infinite value of the Eucharistic Sacrifice, but not that it was really intended by Christ and, therefore, actually takes place.[2]

Up to the present time, we have considered the value and efficacy of the Eucharistic Sacrifice, in so far as Christ is not only the victim, but also the sacrificing priest, in other words, in as far as the visible priest accomplishes and offers the Sacrifice as the servant and living instrument of Christ. From this aspect, the Holy Mass is that essential, therefore always and everywhere "clean oblation", which cannot be defiled by any unworthiness or sinfulness either of the celebrating priest or of the faithful assisting thereat, that is, become displeasing to God, or diminished in value or efficacy. Inasmuch as Christ Himself offers His own self by the hands of His visible representative, the value, efficacy and fruit of the Sacrifice of the altar do not depend upon the holiness and devotion of the priest and faithful, but solely and only on the infinite dignity of Christ and the merits which He acquired on the Cross.[3] This is what is meant, when it is said that the Sacrifice of Christ is always pleasing to God and efficacious *ex opere operato*, that is, by virtue of its valid per-

---

[1] Qui non offerunt, ii non aequalem partem accipiunt, si pro pluribus ac si pro uno dumtaxat offerretur . . . *ad satisfactionem* loquor; *ad impetrationem* namque nulla vis minor in sacrificio est, quod pro multis offertur, quam in eo, quod pro uno solo (Canus, De locis theolog., l. 12, c. 13, argum. 10).

[2] Etsi sacrificium ex parte rei oblatae et principalis offerentis, sc. Christi, sit infinitae virtutis, non tamen, ita ejus institutore Christo volente, infinitos producit effectus: secus si finem excipias colendi Deum et supremum latriae actum, qui sane ex qualibet quantumvis crebro repetita divinae victimae oblatione semper Deo exhibetur, superflua esset ejusdem iteratio; semel autem posito quod effectus sacrificii finitus sit, perspicuum jam est, illud plus ei prodesse, cui applicatur, quam aliis: nam aut consideratur tanquam propitiatorium seu satisfactorium et certe pro illo speciatim satisfacit, in cujus debiti solutionem Deo exhibetur, aut consideratur tanquam impetratorium et profecto ad beneficia illi uberius elargienda Deum movet, pro quo nominatim sacerdos divinam hostiam immolans Deum exorat (Bened. XIV. de ss. Missae sacrif. l. 3, c. 21, n. 6).

[3] Nullum catholicum contradicentem invenio ideoque certam existimo hanc veritatem (Suarez disp. 79, sect. 1).

formance without any further human co-operation. This fruit, which has its foundation immediately and solely in Christ and His infinite merits, is the greatest and most precious of the Sacrifice, the essential or real sacrificial fruit: it is always meant, when reference is made to the fruit of the Mass.

2. In the second place, the value and efficacy of the Sacrifice are to be considered, inasmuch as the celebration of it is an act of the united Church, or, in other words, inasmuch as the priest in the name and by the commission of the entire Church performs this sacred function at the altar. The Eucharistic Sacrifice and the prayers of the Breviary form the principal part of public divine worship, which by the ordinance and for the welfare of the Church, is conducted by ministers specially ordained and appointed for this purpose. At the altar the united Church offers and prays through the priest, her representative and delegate; there she presents to God the Sacrifice of praise and thanksgiving, of propitiation and petition. Under this aspect, the value and efficacy of the Sacrifice of the Mass is measured by the dignity, merit and sanctity of the Church. From this it follows that the value of the Eucharistic Sacrifice, inasmuch as the Church offers it, is always finite and limited, for at no time has she been nor can she be infinitely holy. It is self-evident that on the part of the Church the effects which follow the celebration of Mass are always limited as to degree and greatness. It must here be noted, however, that the Church, inasmuch as she offers the Holy Sacrifice and prays through the priest, cannot merit and satisfy, since for this is required a positive action or suffering of a person pleasing to God. But in the celebration of Mass, there is, on the part of the Church, no such positive activity, to which could be attached the power of meriting or satisfying. Accordingly, the celebration of the Eucharistic Sacrifice by the Church has only impetratory power, that is, she can draw down graces and blessings from Heaven only by way of petition.[1]

Holiness is an essential mark of the Church and, therefore, it can never be wanting to her; the Church ever shines in the splendor and adornment of purity, for she is the Spouse of Christ. Consequently, the Sacrifice, offered by her hands, accompanied with many petitions and supplications, is always favorably regarded and received by God, and rewarded by Him with bountiful graces and

---

[1] Quatenus Missa nomine totius Ecclesiae offertur, propitiatorium non habet effectum; nam quamvis sacerdos ab Ecclesiae superioribus deputetur, ut nomine omnium fidelium celebret, omnesque fideles in hanc deputationem saltem implicite consentiant, nihilominus in singulis Missae oblationibus haec Ecclesiae voluntas non existit nisi habitualiter. Atqui nemo potest mereri aut pro peccato satisfacere, nisi quando actu operatur, ac proinde ex illa habituali Ecclesiae oblatione propitiationis fructus profluere nequit... *Ipsa Ecclesia*, Missam per sacerdotem tanquam per suum legatum offerendo, apud Deum *impetrat;* nam hic non obstat defectus voluntatis actualis, siquidem oratio non minus per legatum ac proprio postulantis actu fieri possit (Lambrecht, De ss. Missae sacrif. P. 4, c. 1, § 2. 3).

blessings.   But since the holiness of the Church consists in the sanctity of her members, it is not always and invariably the same, but greater at one period than at another; therefore, the Sacrifice of the Church is also at one time in a greater, at another in a less degree pleasing to God and beneficial to man.[1]

The Church not only offers the Sacrifice, but she moreover unites with its offering various prayers and ceremonies.   The sacrificial rites are carried out in the name of the Church and, therefore, powerfully move God to impart His favors and extend His bounty to the living and the dead.   By reason of the variety of the formulas of the Mass, the impetratory efficacy of the Sacrifice can be increased in an accidental way, and the efficacy be directed in a special manner to different objects. — The sacrificial fruit to be obtained by petition, through the mediation of the Church, is neither as to kind nor degree previously determined and limited.   Therefore, the Church herself in her prayers is accustomed so to express her intentions and desires, that it can be known what benefits she wishes to obtain by the Mass and to whom she wills to apply them.   Hence special prayers are more useful and more beneficial than general ones.[2]   Not only the degree of holiness of the Church, but also the nature of the prayers of the Mass and even of its whole rite exerts accordingly an influence upon the measure and nature of the fruits of the Sacrifice. — From what has been said there follow several interesting consequences.   Among others, that, on the part of the Church, a High Mass solemnly celebrated has greater value and efficacy than merely a low Mass;[3] — and also with regard to the Church's impetratory power a Votive or a Requiem Mass for a special intention is more valuable and efficacious than a Mass harmonizing with the Office of the day.

At a Solemn High Mass the external display is richer and more brilliant than at a low Mass; for at a solemn celebration the Church, in order to elevate the dignity of the Sacrifice, manifests greater pomp, and God is more glorified thereby.   Let us consider the assistants (deacon, sub-deacon, acolytes), the precious vestments and sacred vessels, the greater number of lights, the incensing and the choral singing.   This grander and more solemn celebration of the

---

[1] Purifica nos, misericors Deus: ut *Ecclesiae* tuae preces, quae tibi *gratae* sunt, pia munera deferentes, fiant *expiatis mentibus gratiores* (Secr. in fer. V. post Dom. IV. Quadrag.).

[2] Orationes eo magis et efficacius impetrant, quo sunt magis propriae et expressae (Quarti, In Rubr. Missal. P. I, tit. 5, dub. 7).

[3] Quo solemnior est Missa, nempe cum pluribus assistentibus ministerialiter, cum pluribus cantantibus consuetas preces, cum pluribus luminibus, cum pretiosioribus vestibus sacris, eo magis est fructuosum sacrificium ex parte Ecclesiae offerentis.   Ratio est quia haec omnia augent pompam et majestatem sacrificii atque adeo etiam sensibilem cultum Dei et consequenter augent aestimabilitatem sacrificii et plures actiones satisfactoriae interveniunt.   Efficacia autem sacrificii ex parte Ecclesiae offerentis crescit secundum mensuram aestimabilitatis, quam recipit ab ipsa Ecclesia (Pasqualigo, De sacrif. N. L. tr. 1, q. 131, n. 16).

Sacrifice is more acceptable to God and, therefore, better calculated to prevail upon Him to grant us, in His mercy, the favors we implore; — that is, to impart greater efficacy to the petitions and supplications of the Church.[1]

Votive Masses deviate from the office of the day, and hence may be celebrated only for a reasonable motive and only on certain days. They are offered for special intentions and according to special formulas answering to the particular purposes. These liturgical formulas are, with respect to their contents, that is, their collects and lessons, so arranged, that the desired object or intention, for which the Mass is offered, can be the more easily and more surely attained. From this it follows that the Votive Mass in regard to the special intention possesses a greater impetratory power on the part of the Church than the ordinary Mass of the day.

The same may be said of Requiem Masses.[2] Their whole rite aims so much and so exclusively to implore for the suffering souls comfort, alleviation and abridgment of their pains, as to admit of

---

[1] Dicendum, Missam solemnem esse magis efficacem ad impetrandum pro eo, pro quo sacrificium offertur, quantum est ex parte oblationis Ecclesiae. In Missa solemni interveniunt plura ex parte Ecclesiae offerentis, quae augent majestatem sacrificii et acceptabilitatem apud Deum et quae valde augent cultum et obsequium Deo exhibitum: ergo augent etiam efficaciam ipsius ad impetrandum, quia efficacia impetrandi consistit in eo, quod adsint motiva apta ad movendum Deum ad concedendum, quod petitur. — Supponendum est, quod quando cum hac solemnitate offertur sacrificium ad instantiam alterius, non solum pro ipso offertur nudum sacrificium, sed tota illa solemnitas, quae stat in persona Ecclesiae, ordinatur simul cum sacrificio ad ipsius utilitatem. Quod ex eo constat; nam qui petit offerri pro se sacrificium cum tali solemnitate, nedum petit nudam oblationem, sed etiam illam solemnitatem, et ideo, qui se obligat, nedum se obligat ad sacrificium, sed etiam ad solemnitatem et ad exhibendum Deo hujusmodi cultum cum tota illa pompa in ejusdem beneficium. Deinde cum Ecclesia per suum ministrum applicet sacrificium ad favorem petentis, applicat etiam omnia connexa, cum quibus in persona ipsius offertur, et ideo stante applicatione sacrificii ex determinatione Ecclesiae, remanet etiam applicatus totus cultus, qui consurgit ex pompa et solemnitate sacrificii (Pasqualigo, De sacrif. N. L. tr. 1, q. 131).

[2] Quod Missa de Requiem magis prosit defunctis, quam quaelibet alia Missa, ex eo manifeste constat, quod habet specialem fructum ordinatum ad suffragandum ipsis, quem non habent ceterae Missae. Siquidem cum preces, quae in ipsis recitantur, et totus ritus sit institutus ab Ecclesia pro suffragio defunctorum, et nomine Ecclesiae preces illae Deo offerantur, intervenit ex parte Ecclesiae offerentis aliquis specialis fructus seu suffragium, quod non intervenit in aliis Missis. Et cum Ecclesia sit sancta et Deo accepta, non possunt non esse acceptae preces ipsius et suffragia exhibita pro defuncto. Et proinde Missae de Requiem ex parte Ecclesiae offerentis magis prosunt defunctis (Pasqualigo, De sacrif. N. L. tr. 1, q. 287). — In officio Missae non solum est sacrificium, sed etiam sunt ibi orationes... Ex parte ergo sacrificii oblati Missa aequaliter prodest defuncto, de quocunque dicatur; et hoc est praecipuum quod fit in Missa. Sed ex parte orationum magis prodest illa, in qua sunt orationes ad hoc determinatae. Sed tamen iste defectus recompensari potest per majorem devotionem vel ejus qui dicit Missam vel ejus qui jubet dici vel iterum per intercessionem Sancti, cujus suffragium in Missa imploratur (S. Thom. Supplem. q. 71, a. 9 ad 5).

no Collect whatever for the living. As a tenderly interested Mother, the Church makes every effort to free her suffering children from purgatory and to lead them to eternal rest.

The essential fruit of the Mass has its immediate and only source in the self-immolation of Christ, and is, therefore, independent of the contents of the formulas of the Mass Rite of the Church. Hence there is here question only of the accidental, or subordinate, fruit, arising from the liturgical prayers of the Mass, but added to the essential fruit, and benefitting directly those for whom the Mass is celebrated. Now, if the priest, when obliged to offer a Votive Mass on a day permissible by the rubrics, does not then satisfy his obligation, if he says the Mass of the day, nevertheless, this must be understood of a perfect satisfaction of his obligation, for the essential fruit of the Sacrifice is the same in all Masses, and he is in this case not obliged to make restitution.[1] — We see from several decrees, that the Church is far more reluctant in permitting the Mass of the day to be said instead of the prescribed Votive Mass than instead of a Requiem Mass.[2] The reason for this may be that in Masses for the suffering souls the fruit of the Sacrifice depends chiefly on its satisfactory effect, which is independent of the rite, while in Votive Masses the impetratory fruit is more prominent and principally intended; in this respect the liturgical prayers of the Mass are specially efficacious, particularly when they are, as is the case in the formulas for Votive Masses, chiefly composed with regard to specified intentions.

This efficacy and fruit of the Sacrifice, like the essential sacrificial fruit, is likewise independent of the worthiness or unworthiness of the officiating priest, and it can in regard to him be called *ex opere operato*; but with respect to the Church it is *quasi ex opere operantis*. This impetratory fruit on the part of the Church is entirely wanting in the Mass, when an interdicted priest celebrates it, for such a one cannot offer and pray in the name of the Church.[3]

---

[1] Certum est, quod hujusmodi sacrificantes, dummodo Missam applicent ad finem praescriptum, ad restitutionem minime tenentur, quia fructus principalis et satisfactorius, cui respondet stipendium, aequalis est in Missis omnibus (Cavalieri III, c. 10, n. 19). — This *non satisfacere* in such cases is of itself only a venial sin.

[2] On days that the rubrics do not prohibit, the private votive Mass must always be celebrated, if one be bound to such, since the Church has declared the application of the daily Mass in this case insufficient; while, on the other hand, she declares that the priest fulfils his obligation to the celebration of a non-privileged Mass for the departed even when he adheres to the rite of the day, although the celebration of a Requiem Mass be then allowed, — with two exceptions, however; namely, if the Requiem Mass is expressly desired or required for gaining the indulgence of the privileged altar (S. R. C. 12. Sept. 1840). Hence on all days on which there is an impediment, the private Requiem Mass, but not the private Votive Mass, may always be satisfactorily replaced by celebrating the Mass of the day; for as is evident from some of the decisions of the S. R. C., a dispensation of the Apostolic See is necessarily required, that on these days *oneri Missae votivae satisfieri possit*.

[3] Sacerdos in missa, in *orationibus* quidem loquitur *in persona Ecclesiae*, in

3. Thirdly, the value and efficacy of the Mass are to be considered, inasmuch as its celebration is a personal good work of the officiating priest and of the faithful assisting thereat. The priest who celebrates the Mass and the faithful who participate therein by hearing it, by serving at the altar, by giving a stipend, by procuring the requisite sacred vessels, &c., perform, without doubt, the holiest and most salutary of the acts of divine worship; for the Church herself says, that there "can be no other work so holy and so divine performed by the faithful" than the celebration of the Eucharistic Sacrifice. Considered from this point of view, the value of the Sacrifice of the Mass is evidently only finite, its efficacy only limited and its fruitfulness only a restricted one. — The celebration of the Mass by the priest and the participation of the faithful in this most sacred function have, if the required conditions be complied with, like every other good work, not merely the power to obtain favors and blessings, but to remit the temporal punishment of sin, and also to merit an increase of sanctifying grace and heavenly glory. Of this threefold fruit, the impetratory and satisfactory, but not the meritorious, may be given to and benefit others. For the merit is wholly personal and cannot be transferred to others; whereas we may satisfy for others and obtain by prayer many graces for them.— This fruit originates *ex opere operantis vel operantium*; to gain it in full, one should be in the state of grace, act and pray with a good intention, with faith and reverence. It is evident that this fruit will be so much the more plentiful, the greater the piety and holiness, the love and devotion of the priest and of the faithful.[1] The essential sacrificial fruit (*ex opere operato*) and the Church's impetratory efficacy derived from the liturgy of the Mass cannot indeed be intrinsically either increased or diminished by the good or bad dispositions of the officiating priest, but virtue, holiness and devotion are necessarily demanded of him, that the Mass may, in every respect, be perfect, pleasing to God and rich in blessings.[2]

---

cujus unitate consistit, sed in consecratione sacramenti loquitur in persona Christi, cujus vicem in hoc gerit per ordinis potestatem. Et ideo si sacerdos ab unitate Ecclesiae praecisus missam celebret, quia potestatem ordinis non amittit, consecrat verum corpus et sanguinem Christi, sed quia est ab Ecclesiae unitate separatus, *orationes efficaciam non habent* (S. Thom. 3, q. 82, a. 7 ad 3).

[1] Quo quis melior, melius dispositus, sanctior est, quo ferventius et devotius in Missa pro se et aliis orat, eo plus gratiae et gloriae apud Deum sibi meretur, eoque plus sibi et aliis impetrat et pro peccatis satisfacit (Sporer, Theol. sacram. P. 2, cap. 5, sect. 2, § 2).

[2] Missa a malo sacerdote celebrata aeque valet *ex opere operato*, ac illa quae a bono offertur; item aeque valet vi *orationum*, quatenus eas nomine Ecclesiae sacerdos offerens fundit; at nequaquam, quatenus orat ut privata persona. Etenim certum est, sacerdotis sanctitatem ex hoc capite in fructum impetratorium orationis non parum influere, adeoque sacerdotem bonum et sanctum multo plus prodesse Ecclesiae et fidelibus, pro quibus celebrat, quam improbum aut minus pium (Schouppe, De Euchr. P. 2, c. 3, a. 2, n. 347). — Cf. Chrysostom, 2. Homily on the Second Epistle to Timothy.

All that has been said respecting the dignity and value, the power and efficacy of the Sacrifice of the Mass, demonstrates that in the Holy Mass there is the inexhaustible ocean of the Divine mercies. Admission to this ocean of graces is so easy, and is free to all. God's liberality wills to enrich us with blessed gifts, and fill us with Heaven's blessing; O that our heart were not full of earthly thoughts and worldly attachments! Would that we knew how to esteem and profit by this Eucharistic Sacrifice for our salvation — this "precious pearl", this "hidden treasure" in the field of the Church — how soon should we become enriched with every grace! If the blessed Mystery of the Altar were celebrated in only one place, or the sacred elements could be consecrated by only one priest, with what ardent longing would not all Christians desire to hasten to that spot and to that priest, in order to assist at the celebration! But now many are ordained priests, and Christ is offered on many altars in many places to the end that God's grace and love for men may shine so much the brighter, as the reception of Holy Communion is spread more widely throughout the globe. It is truly distressing and deplorable that, in consequence of our tepidity and sloth, we do not feel ourselves drawn toward God with more ardent desires, although in Him rest all the hope and all the merit of those destined to receive the inheritance of salvation. He is our Sanctifier and Redeemer, He is the source of comfort for the pilgrim in time and the enjoyment of the blessed in eternity. Therefore, with pain and sorrow ought it to be deplored that many pay so little attention to so salutary a mystery, which rejoices Heaven and preserves the whole world! O the inconceivable blindness and hardness of the human heart, not to value more highly so ineffable a gift, and although afforded daily opportunity of hearing Mass, to fall into total indifference in its regard! (Cf. Imitation of Christ, IV, 1.)

18. The Holy Mass — a Sacrifice of Praise and Adoration.[1]

1. It was for Himself that God made all things (Prov. 16, 4), and created all things (Is. 43, 7); therefore it is the end of all creatures to glorify their Creator, therefore the entire creation should form but one choir of joyful praise and exulting adoration of God. All that is in heaven and upon the earth and under the earth should bend the knee before the Lord of all things and praise Him according to the multitude of His greatness (Ps. 150, 2). But how could this be possible? Without measure and without end is His Majesty and praiseworthiness! "Great is the Lord, and exceedingly to be praised, and of His greatness there is no end" (Ps. 144, 3). Numberless are the proofs of His power, of His wisdom and of His love, exhibited in the kingdom of nature, of grace and glory.[2] Hence

---

[1] Laudis tuae, Domine, immolamus hostias — hostias tibi, Domine, laudis offerimus — sacrificium tibi, Domine, laudis offerimus — offerimus tibi, Domine, hostiam placationis et laudis (Sacrament. Gregor.).

[2] Quamvis inter laudare, benedicere et glorificare Deum soleat assignari dis-

"glorify the Lord as much as ever you can, for He will yet far exceed, and His magnificence is wonderful. Blessing the Lord, exalt Him as much as you can, for He is above all praise!" (Ecclus. 43, 32—33.) The works of the Lord do indeed praise Him, and His saints magnify Him (Ps. 144, 10): still, how could the worship of finite creatures be fully worthy of His infinite name? Tempestuous oceans and towering mountains, murmuring brooks and silent valleys, dark forests and smiling plains, fields of waving corn and blooming meadows, singing birds and roaring lions — all join in the full accord, in the marvellous harmony which resounds from one end of creation to the other in honor of the Creator. If we ascend upward from the earth, the heavens show forth the glory of God (Ps. 18, 2): the cerulean hue and the bright sunbeams of the firmament, the flying clouds and the majestic, rolling thunder, the morning flush and the sunset glow, the vivid lightning and the mysterious, quiet reflection of the nightly world of stars announce how great, how unutterably great, how exalted and worthy of all adoration is God our Lord. And beyond the stars — there "the abode of the blessed resounds with canticles of praise to the triune God in unceasing jubilation." The saints of heaven trembling in joyful fear are prostrate in adoration before the throne of the Eternal Father, offering to Him glory and honor throughout eternity (Apoc. 4, 9 — 11). And the Angels — those indescribably beautiful and exalted spirits, those morning stars and first-fruits of creation, those princes of heaven, whose brightness outshines and dims all earthly splendor as the sun eclipses the stars — they, with their wings, cover their countenances before the majesty of God and, trembling with profound love and reverence, sing their never-ending hymn: "Holy, holy, holy!" And finally, the Virgin Mother of God, the glorious Queen of Angels and Saints, — is decked with the plenitude of grace and the ornaments of every virtue, robed in the glory and splendor of heavenly gifts, crowned with dazzling light and radiance. From the pure heart of this Queen of Heaven there issued and shall eternally issue forth the ecstatic joyous chant of the *Magnificat* in homage to the power, holiness and mercy of God; her whole being and life was and is nothing else than an humble and reverential adoration and glorification of God. Yet, however great and how glorious soever in its power the eternal canticle of praise and adoration, in which all creatures in heaven and upon earth unite, — what is it in comparison with the majesty, glory and greatness of Him who alone is great, who is infinitely great? —

---

tinctio, nunc tamen laudationem Dei tam extense accipio, quod benedictionem et glorificationem ejus includit, ut Deum laudare sit bonitatem, virtutem et perfectionem ejus recta intentione proferre atque extollere: sicque laudandus et superlaudandus est Deus in se ipso et in suis operibus, in suis beneficiis ac promissis, in operibus naturae et gratiae ac gloriae, in operibus creationis, reparationis et glorificationis. Etenim justus Dominus in omnibus viis suis et sanctus in omnibus operibus suis, in quibus omnibus excellentia, bonitas, sapientia, omnipotentia et incomprehensibilitas Creatoris relucent (Dion. Carthus. De orat. art. 31).

"Lord," — thus prayed Blessed Henry Suso — "if the Cherubim and Seraphim and the immense number of exalted spirits all praise Thee to the best of their ability, what more can they do to enhance Thy unapproachable, immeasurable merit, than does the most insignificant creature? He that hopes worthily to praise Thee, acts as he who runs after the wind and would seize the shadow."[1] — But shall we by no means be able to render due honor and glory to the Most High? Oh! let us thank the Lord: in the Sacrifice of the Mass He has given us an infinitely perfect means of praising and glorifying Him commensurately with His dignity. Yes, a single holy Mass procures God more honor and praise than all the worship of all the citizens of heaven and of earth can offer Him throughout eternity.

2. The celebration of the Eucharistic Sacrifice, indeed, contains an infinitely perfect adoration of God. Sacrifice by its nature and destination is an act of adoration and glorification of God; it is an efficacious, solemn acknowledgment of the supremacy and dominion of God over all creatures. The more perfect the Sacrifice, the greater the honor rendered to God. From this it follows that the Mass, being a sacrifice of infinite value, includes in itself infinitely worthy praise and adoration of the triune God. Upon the altar it is not merely a man who offers, it is not a mere creature who is offered, but it is the God-Man who offers Himself to the Heavenly Father as a holocaust of adoration and an incense-offering of praise. It is a Divine Person, it is the Son of God, eternal and infinite, like unto the Father and the Holy Ghost, it is Jesus Christ, the first-born of all creatures and the Head of the whole creation, who, in the Mass, according to His humanity, sacrifices and is sacrificed. Could God's majesty and sovereignty be declared and be acknowledged more emphatically than is done upon the altar, where the Son of God, under the sacramental species, conceals, annihilates and humbles to the very depths His most glorious, noble and precious humanity, that is, sacrifices it to the honor of God? — The Mass is then also the representation of the Sacrifice of the Cross. All the honor and glory rendered to the Heavenly Father upon Golgotha is represented and offered anew to Him upon the altar by the mystical sacrifice of His beloved Son, in whom He is eternally well pleased. To honor and glorify the Father, Christ descended to the most profound abyss of abasement, became like unto a leper, as the last of men, like to the decayed root of a tree (Is. 53). His whole life was a life of incomparable adoration, praise and glorification of God. An ardent zeal for the house of God, for the kingdom and the honor of His Father consumed Him. All the prayers, labors and fatigues of His humble life, His painful passion and death, Jesus Christ, in the Mass, ever presents to His Heavenly Father, offers them to Him anew with the same inflamed Heart, with the same reverential submission, as when He was upon earth, in order

---

[1] Denifle, Das geistliche Leben p. 487.

to honor and glorify Him. Therefore, a more worthy adoration, a more profound worship and a greater homage than that offered to God by the sacrifice of Jesus Christ, is impossible and even inconceivable. Holy Mass is an infinitely worthy sacrifice of praise and adoration — consequently, it is the most sublime glorification of the Divine Majesty.

3. But not only does Christ render upon the altar infinite homage and adoration to the Divine Majesty, but through and with His Sacrifice, the Church and we all are enabled perfectly to honor and adore the Most High in spirit and in truth (John 4, 24). The Eucharistic Sacrifice is the property of the Church; she offers it through the priest, in order to render due worship to God in the name of all. In our hands also Christ has placed Himself as a victim, that we may be able to offer a gift to God capable of rendering Him infinite honor and pleasure. Whilst offering the Divine Victim in the Mass, we render to God inexpressible homage and adoration, fully proportionate to His divinity and dominion. — How exceedingly joyful and happy are not the souls that love God at the thought of being able, by the Sacrifice of the Mass, worthily to honor, praise and adore the Lord of heaven and earth! For "to praise God is the sole occupation of the angels and saints in heaven, and of loving souls here upon earth; for them it is the most pleasing and most delightful occupation."[1] The desire of praising God was beautifully expressed by Blessed Henry Suso: "Oh, woe is me! Who will grant to my overflowing heart, that before my death its desire of praising Thee may be fulfilled! Who will obtain for me, that in my own days I may worthily praise this loving Lord, for whom my soul craveth! Ah, my beloved Lord, though I am unworthy to praise Thee, yet my soul desires that heaven may praise Thee with its ravishing beauty, with the splendor of its sun and the brightness of the countless stars in its lofty, transparent firmament. I desire that the beautiful meadows may praise Thee, when under summer skies they clothe themselves in floral beauty and with Nature's grandest and fairest charms. Ah! and may all the sweet thoughts and ardent desires that ever a pure, loving heart experienced in Thy regard, O Lord, when absorbed in the joy and happiness of Thy enlightening Spirit, praise Thee!"[2] Our sweetest occupation and happiest employment should be to magnify God every day and to praise His name forever, yea, forever and ever (Ps. 144, 2). As the Psalmist exhorts us, we will adore the Lord, we will bring praise and honor to the Lord, to the praise of His name (Ps. 28) — and this we will continue to do all the days of our life, in hours of sunshine and of gloom.[3] *Sit laus plena, sit sonora,*

---

[1] Ruysbroek, bei Denifle a. a. O., p. 483.

[2] Denifle a. a. O., p. 485.

[3] Laudabit usque ad mortem anima mea Dominum. Sicut orare convenit civibus militantis ac triumphantis Ecclesiae, magis tamen civibus Ecclesiae militantis, quoniam amplius indigent adjutoriis Dei atque Sanctorum, et in medio

sit jucunda, sit decora mentis jubilatio. Full of devotion be the praise of God, and sweetly sounding in His ears, joyous from mind's gladness, beautiful the heart's exultation! Alas! our praise of God is frequently very imperfect and worthless; therefore, we should unite it with the infinitely perfect praise and adoration which our Head and Mediator, Jesus Christ, presents to His Heavenly Father on the altar. By this union alone is our insignificant worship made holy and meritorious, so as to ascend as clouds of fragrant incense before the face of God. — Then the reflection that God is so often forgotten and despised in the world, His holy name reviled and blasphemed, should deeply wound our hearts and inflame them with holy ardor, in order, as an atonement, to praise and magnify God with greater fervor — especially by celebrating and assisting at the Holy Sacrifice of the Mass. For in the Mass from the rising to the setting of the sun the name of the Lord is infinitely extolled, and there is given to Him the greatest honor and glory. Still not our heart and lips only should praise the Lord, but our life, our whole conduct ought to be a continual praise, a perpetual adoration of God.[1] At all times and in all places we should have God before our eyes, we should realize His blessed presence and, consequently, be profoundly penetrated with the spirit of profound reverence and adoration; then will our prayers be full of recollection and devotion, our works perfect and holy, our conversation circumspect and edifying, our thoughts noble and chaste, our desires pure and heavenly, our whole deportment modest and unassuming.[2]

---

ambulant laqueorum periculisque diversis vallantur et viatores existunt, ita laudare utriusque Ecclesiae civibus ac filiis convenit, potius tamen civibus Ecclesiae triumphantis, qui ad terminum pervenerunt beatum suntque confirmati in bono nec ulli subjacent unquam periculo nec indigent pro seipsis orare: ideo cum incessabili atque plenissima jucunditate laudes et gratiarum actiones suo offerunt Creatori. ...... Majus est Deum laudare quam orare, quia laudare est actus magis angelicus ac coelestis. Laudare quoque Deum est actus simplicior et minus ad commoda sua reflexus quam orare. Verumtamen imperfectis et pusillis magis convenit orationi quam laudationi insistere, quoniam egent purgatione multisque defectuositatibus involvuntur, propter quas ad laudandum Altissimum nondum satis aptati sunt; perfectis vero et contemplativis, quorum conversatio est in coelis, competit laudibus Dei jugiter immorari atque angelicam vitam inchoare ac quantum possibile est continuare in terris; nam et futurae illius beatitudinis suavi praegustu jam recreantur (Dion. Carthus. De orat. art. 31).

[1] Ergo, fratres, non tantum ad sonum attendite: cum laudatis Deum, toti laudate: cantet vox, cantet vita, cantent facta (S. August. Enarrat. in Ps. 148, n. 2).

[2] Meditatio praesentis vitae nostrae in laude Dei esse debet, quia exsultatio sempiterna futurae nostrae vitae laus Dei erit, et nemo potest idoneus fieri futurae vitae, qui non se ad illam modo exercuerit. Modo ergo laudamus Deum: sed et rogamus Deum. Laus nostra laetitiam habet, oratio gemitum. Promissum est nobis aliquid, quod nondum habemus, et quia verax est qui promisit, in spe gaudemus: quia tamen nondum habemus, in desiderio gemimus. Bonum est nobis perseverare in desiderio, donic veniat quod promissum est, et transeat gemitus, succedat sola laudatio (S. August. l. c. n. 1).

19. The Holy Mass — a Sacrifice of Thanksgiving.

Inasmuch as in the Holy Mass we adore, praise and magnify God through and with Christ, we fulfil in a perfect manner that first duty, which as creatures we owe to the Creator. Since God is the origin of all things, He is also the source of every good we possess, that is, He is our first and greatest Benefactor, unto whom it behooveth us to render due thanks. This duty of gratitude toward God we can discharge in no better way than by the celebration of Mass, which by preference and predilection is called the Eucharist, that is, Sacrifice of Thanksgiving. We shall, therefore, clearly show that the Mass is the most perfect, that is, an infinitely valuable sacrifice of thanksgiving for all the graces and favors received from God.

1. Gratitude to benefactors is not only a great and sacred obligation, but also an exceedingly beautiful and precious virtue, which seeks to repay favors freely, lovingly and graciously bestowed. Sincere thankfulness is the mark of a noble soul, rendering one amiable before God and man, while ingratitude is peculiar to a mean and proud spirit, and renders one displeasing to everybody. An humble, childlike disposition sees "in every blossom eternal love bloom"; an arrogant, self-conceited disposition claims everything as its due in strict justice. — The grateful man endeavors to make a return for favors received, first and chiefly by interiorly acknowledging, honoring and esteeming the noble disposition and liberality of the benefactor;[1] then he would express his gratitude also by exteriorly manifesting in word and deed his grateful feelings, thanking his benefactor and doing him good. — There are various circumstances that increase the value of a benefit, and oblige the recipient to still further gratitude. A gift is to be particularly esteemed, when it is a) in itself noble and precious, b) useful to the receiver, and c) frequently and generously bestowed. With regard to the benefactor, two things are to be observed: whether he is a) of exalted dignity, and b) whether he imparts his gifts with very great love. In regard to the recipient, it is to be considered whether a) he is mean and abject, and b) utterly undeserving of the gift, and perhaps has even rendered himself unworthy thereof. All these qualities are combined in the highest degree as to the graces and benefits which we have received and still daily receive from God. Let us, therefore, ever seek more clearly and more fervently to acknowledge the preciousness of the divine gifts, the greatness and love of the Divine Benefactor, and our own wretchedness and unworthiness, so that, by this knowledge, we may be all the more induced faithfully and humbly to prove our gratitude towards God.

Even the natural benefits of God are precious, but far more so are the supernatural, for everything desirable cannot be compared to them (Prov. 8, 11). God bestows these gifts on us, not as though

---

[1] S. Thom. 2, 2, q. 106. a. 3—5

their bestowal would in any way redound to His advantage — for He is, indeed, in Himself infinitely rich and happy, — but to make us happy in time and blessed in eternity. How abundant, durable and salutary to us are these excellent gifts of God! "God who spared not even His own Son, but delivered Him up for us all; how hath He not also with Him given us all things?" (Rom. 8, 32.) The days of our life are like a wreath plaited wholly of graces and benefits by divine love. As fishes in the waves of the ocean, so are we immersed in the divine favors; it would be easier to count the stars of heaven, the snow-flakes in winter, than to enumerate the blessings of ineffable sweetness wherewith God forestalls us (Ps. 20, 4). As the sun never fails to cast his rays upon the earth, as the spring unceasingly bubbles forth from the depths of the earth, so likewise the torrent of divine goodness and liberality will never cease to flow.

The value of these benefits is greatly enhanced by the infinite dignity and majesty, as well as by the immeasurable goodness and mercy of the Divine Giver. The most pure, disinterested and benevolent love of God is the source whence all these indescribable goods flow unto us. "With an everlasting love" — says the Lord — "have I loved thee; therefore have I drawn thee, taking pity on thee" (Jer. 31, 3). St. Paul says that God hath overwhelmed us with heavenly gifts "because of His exceeding charity" (*propter nimiam caritatem suam* — Eph. 2, 4).

What are we, poor, frail, miserable and sinful men, that the Most High should be mindful of us, should turn His Heart toward us, and visit us with His grace? (Ps. 8, 5.) Indeed, we have by our guilt frequently rendered ourselves unworthy of His benefits.

Whenever I calmly and seriously reflect upon all that God has done for me, I must exult in grateful love and exclaim: "What shall I render to the Lord for all the things that He hath rendered to me?" (Ps. 115, 3.) Even if I consecrate myself entirely to Him with all that I am and all that I have, my goods, my life's blood, my body, my soul: how can this be a worthy return for His benefits? (Job 12, 2.) How can an earthly gift, a finite thanksgiving suffice to outweigh and adequately repay the infinitely valuable gifts of God? Lord, I am not worthy of the least of Thy mercies (*minor sum cunctis miserationibus tuis* — Gen. 32, 10), and am unable to offer Thee due thanks for Thy boundless love and liberality.

2. What is impossible to man, God hath made possible; what our weakness cannot perform, we accomplish through Christ our Lord. — "Give to the Most High according to what He hath given to thee" (Ecclus. 35, 12), the Holy Ghost admonishes us; but how can we do this? By thanking God and the Father through Christ (Col. 3, 17), and giving thanks always for all things, in the name of our Lord Jesus Christ (Eph. 5, 20). In the Mass Christ offers Himself with the same infinitely perfect sentiments of gratitude, with which His soul was inflamed upon earth — during His life and

passion, at the Last Supper and on Calvary. This gift of thanksgiving which He offers to His Heavenly Father in return for all the benefits bestowed upon the human race, is the same as the divine oblation on the Cross — namely, His most noble body and most precious blood. Consequently, the Mass is an infinitely meritorious and acceptable Sacrifice of Thanksgiving, perfectly commensurate with all the benefits of God, wherewith heaven and earth are filled. Christ offers the Eucharistic Sacrifice for us, that is, that He may in our stead thank God and supply for the deficiency of our thanksgiving. — With Him and through Him, do we also offer the Sacrifice of thanksgiving, for He has bequeathed it to us as our possession. Through Christ and His Eucharistic Sacrifice, we have become so enriched that we are enabled to present in return to the Heavenly Father a gift inexpressibly glorious and sublime, as a worthy thanksgiving for every good and perfect gift (James 1, 17), which we receive from His hand. Of ourselves we cannot, indeed, render suitable thanks for even the least benefit; but by the Holy Sacrifice of the Mass, we are enabled fully to discharge our entire debt of gratitude, were it even infinite. At the altar we can adequately and worthily thank "the Father of mercies and the God of all consolation," inasmuch as we can take the chalice of salvation and praise the divine name (Ps. 115, 4). — In the liturgical prayers and hymns with which the Church accompanies the Holy Sacrifice, there is expressed most excellently a spirit of the most sincere gratitude and most exalted thanksgiving. The same sentiments should fill our hearts also during the celebration of the Holy Mass. In His well-beloved Son the Heavenly Father has given us all things; we should return all to Him, by offering to Him in Holy Mass in thanksgiving His Divine Son, in whom He is well pleased. The prayer of thanksgiving is a rich source of new gifts. "I will remember the tender mercies of the Lord, the praise of the Lord for all the things that the Lord hath bestowed upon us, and for all the multitude of His good things to the house of Israel (the Church), which He hath given them according to His kindness, and according to the multitude of His mercies" (Is. 63, 7).

3. Do we faithfully profit by the Holy Sacrifice, in order conscientiously to fulfill our duty of gratitude toward God, — or are we like the slothful servant who buried in the earth the talent confided to him? Quite frequently is Holy Mass celebrated and heard to implore new favors of God: but is this done with the intention of discharging a debt of gratitude for benefits received? How earnestly and assiduously should we cultivate the spirit of thanksgiving and prayerful gratitude to God, uniting ourselves to the Eucharistic Sacrifice, in order to make atonement, in some manner, to God for the base and shameful ingratitude wherewith the world so often offends His goodness and irritates His justice! "What is there that I ought to do more to My vineyard, that I have not done to it?" (Is. 5, 4) — thus inquires the Lord with reason. But

ingratitude is the reward of the world; which does not like to and which will not give honor to God. Not only through thought-lessness and indifference, but even by abuse, contempt and disdain of His most noble gifts and graces the world wounds His paternal Heart. To very many Christians may be applied with more reason what Moses complained bitterly of in the conduct of the Israelites: "They have sinned against their God and are a wicked and per-verse generation. Is this the return thou makest to the Lord, O foolish and senseless people? The beloved grew fat and kicked; he grew fat and thick and gross, he forsook God who made him, and departed from God his Saviour" (Deut. 32, 5, 6, 15). As the world is, for the most part, a land of forgetfulness (Ps. 87, 13), a barren desert, in which the venom of ingratitude thrives, we have in this thought a new and powerful incentive fervently to thank God; for "we have received not the spirit of this world, but the Spirit that is of God, that we may know the things that are given us from God" (1 Cor. 2, 12). — Behold the example of the Saints: how their hearts and lips overflowed with grateful sentiments! When the mortified St. Paul of the Cross, so severe to himself, walked through the woods and fields and meadows, all that he saw reminded him of God's goodness. Inflamed with love, he would cry out to the flowers and trees: "Be silent! Be silent! Preach no more!" Once, perceiving a flower by the wayside, he plucked it, and full of joy, showed it to his companion, saying: "Do you not see how the flowers exclaim: Love God! Love God!" And with a radiant countenance, as though he were in an ecstasy, he several times repeated the words: "And why do you not love God?" If the sight of a flower sufficed to inflame the soul of a saint with ecstatic love, should not our hearts burn (Luke 24, 32) with grateful love as incense on glowing coals, or as a lighted taper consuming itself, when we at the foot of the altar devoutly reflect, what wonderful mysteries of divine favor, mercy and condescension are accomplished in the celebration of the Mass? For the Eucharistic Sacrifice is not only our very best and perpetual thanksgiving to God, but, at the same time, it is the living source, whence we can and should un-ceasingly draw the spirit of thanksgiving.[1]

20. The Holy Mass — a Sacrifice of Propitiation.

The object of the Holy Mass, as a Sacrifice of Praise and Thanksgiving, is to glorify God as our Supreme Master and greatest Benefactor: it renders to Him infinite honor and offers Him infinite thanksgiving. Inasmuch as it is a Sacrifice of Propitiation and Petition, its celebration produces the most manifold effects for the welfare and salvation of men. These effects, then, of the Mass flowing to men are properly and by preference called the fruits of the Sacrifice of the Mass. That the Sacrifice of the Cross is not

---

[1] Suscipe, Domine, sacrificium placationis et laudis, quod nos . . . et perducat ad veniam et *in perpetua gratiarum constituat actione* (Sacram. Gregor.).

detracted from by this efficacy, but that rather its inexhaustible virtue
and its fully infinite value are brought out in clearer light, is evident
from the right understanding of the Catholic doctrine. The Church
by no means teaches that the Sacrifice of Christ on the altar adds
new satisfaction or new merits to the treasure of salvation acquired
on the Cross, but she teaches only that the price of our redemption
paid by the Sacrifice of the Cross, being incapable of increase and
inexhaustible in its fulness, is actually applied to and benefits individuals by means of the Sacrifice of the Mass. Christ's treasure of
grace remains always the same; only its application to and realization
in individuals are new, and will continue to be so as long as there
shall be men capable and in need of redemption. The fruits of the
Sacrifice of the Mass are, therefore, in general all those and only
those which were borne by the noble tree of the Cross. What was
acquired on the Cross for the whole human race, is applied to individual man in the Mass, for it is a Sacrifice of propitiation as well
as of petition. The Church expressly teaches "that the Holy Mass
is a true propitiatory Sacrifice and has this efficacy that we find
therein mercy and grace, when we stand in need of assistance," —
and it condems the heresy, "that the Holy Mass is only a Sacrifice
of praise and thanksgiving, but not of propitiation . . . and that it
may not be offered for the living and the departed, for the remission
of sin and of its punishment, for satisfaction and for other necessities."[1] In the first place, we shall here show that the Mass is
truly a Sacrifice of propitiation — and, then, what and how it effects
as a propitiatory sacrifice.

1. Holy Church often emphasizes and with force clearly sets
off both by her teaching and practice the propitiatory character of
the Eucharistic Sacrifice. As already quoted, the Council of Trent
solemnly declares that the Mass is "a true propitiatory sacrifice,"
and in the Roman Catechism also we read that the Mass is "truly a
propitiatory sacrifice, whereby we are reconciled to God and regain
His favor."[2]

a) Since sin entered the world and weighs as a heavy yoke
upon the poor children of Eve, a longing for reconciliation and pardon has obtained everywhere the primary place in sacrificial worship.
"Have mercy on me, O God, according to Thy great mercy,
and according to the multitude of Thy tender mercies blot out my
iniquities!" (Ps. 50, 3.) This is the supreme cry that breaks forth
from the bosom of sinful, yet contrite man, who sorrowfully longs to
be free from debt and punishment. This consciousness of sin, this
desire for redemption, finds its strongest expression in the offering

---

[1] Trident. sess. 22, cap. 2 et can. 3.

[2] Vere propitiatorium sacrificium, quo Deus nobis placatus et propitius redditur (Catech. Roman. P. 2, c. 4, q. 63). — Eucharistia in quantum est sacrificium,
Deum placat: hostiae enim *placant*, et quoniam Deus iratus est, non *affectione*, sed
poenae inflictione: ideo Deum placando non sedat ipsius affectionem, sed remitti
facit *poenae acerbitatem* (S. Bonav. IV, dist. 45, dub. 3).

of sacrifice. Hence in the Old Law propitiatory sacrifices were the most frequent and the most prominent. Now the Mass, being the accomplishment and consummation of all the sacrifices prior to Christ, satisfies all the objects of sacrifice, and, consequently, must also have the character and effect of an atoning sacrifice, that is, must be propitiatory. In this respect the truth and reality of the New Law cannot be inferior to the shadow and figure of the Old Law.

b) Among the effects of the death of Jesus, Scripture often directs particular attention to the effacing of sin, to the redemption from the curse of sin, to the destruction of the handwriting that is against us, to the reconciliation of Heaven and earth. Now, if the Mass as a celebration of our redemption, as a renewal of the death of Christ, as a representation and continuation of the Sacrifice of the Cross,[1] be intended to obtain for individual men the various effects of the sacrificial death of Christ on the Cross, it must then possess a sin-effacing power, and apply to them the satisfaction rendered on the Cross. In other words, the Mass must be a Sacrifice of propitiation. Moreover, our Lord Himself expressly declared at the institution of the Eucharistic Sacrifice, that His Body under the appearance of bread would be broken and delivered, His Blood be shed in the chalice for "the forgiveness of sin."

c) The ancient liturgies,[2] furthermore, the writings of the Fathers most clearly testify to the constant and universal belief of the Church in the propitiatory character of the Sacrifice of the Mass. In the Liturgy of St. James, the priest prays in this manner: "O Lord, may our sacrifice be pleasing to Thee and be sanctified by the Holy Ghost for the atonement of our sins and of the ignorance of the people, and for the repose of those who have fallen asleep. . . Lord, have mercy on us; for in fear and trembling we draw nigh to Thy holy altar, to offer this tremendous and unbloody Sacrifice for our sins and for the ignorance of the people." — In the Liturgy of St. Basil: "According to the abundance of Thy mercy, receive us who

---

[1] Per haec divina mysteria ad novi, quaesumus, testamenti mediatorem Jesum accedamus: et super altaria tua, Domine virtutum, aspersionem sanguinis melius loquentem, quam Abel, *innovemus* (Secreta in festo pret. Sanguinis D. N. J. Chr.). — Suscipe, Domine, hostiam redemptionis humanae — per haec veniat sacramenta redemptionis effectus — benedictio tua, Domine, larga descendat, quae munera nostra . . . nobis sacramentum redemptionis efficiat (Sacrament. Gregor.).

[2] Hostia, quam offerimus, vincula nostrae pravitatis absolvat — haec hostia emundet nostra delicta — hujus sacrificii munus oblatum fragilitatem nostram ab omni malo purget semper — hostias tibi, Domine, placationis offerimus, ut delicta nostra miseratus absolvas — per haec sancta commercia vincula peccatorum nostrorum absolve — suscipe, Domine, sacrificium, cujus te voluisti dignanter immolatione placari — supplices, Domine, te rogamus, ut his sacrificiis peccata nostra mundentur — munera nos, quaesumus, Domine, oblata purificent et te nobis jugiter faciant esse placatum — mystica nobis, Domine, prosit oblatio, quae nos et a reatibus nostris expediat et perpetua salvatione confirmet — iisdem, quibus famulamur, mysteriis mundemur — haec sancta, quae gerimus, et praeteritis nos delictis exuant et futuris (Sacrament. Gregor.).

approach to Thy altar, that we may be worthy to offer Thee gifts and sacrifices for our sins and for those of the people." — St. Augustine declares that "it must not be doubted that the departed receive help by the prayers of the Church and the life-giving Sacrifice"; "for" — he says further on — "thus it has been handed down to us by the Fathers, thus the entire Church observes it for those who have died in the communion of the Body and Blood of Christ, when during the Sacrifice their memento occurs at the prescribed place, prayers are recited and attention is directed to the fact that for them also the Mass is offered."[1] St. Monica at her death had no other desire, no other request to make to her family than that "everywhere, wherever they might be, they would remember her at the altar." The holy Doctor then relates that, after her death, prayers and the Sacrifice of our redemption (*sacrificium pretii nostri*) were offered for her.[2] St. Cyril of Jerusalem calls the Mass "a Sacrifice of reconciliation" and then continues: "For the departed, though even they be sinners (that is, in venial sin), we offer supplications to God, yes, not only supplications, but Christ also who was slain for our sins, thereby for them as well as for ourselves to propitiate the Divine Goodness."[3]

2. The propitiatory power and efficacy of the Sacrifice of the Mass extends, as the Church says, to "sins, punishments, satisfactions." By divine institution the Eucharistic Sacrifice serves to bring about for man forgiveness of mortal and venial sins, and also the remission of the temporal punishment due to sin.

a) The Sacrifice of the Mass cannot directly and immediately cancel mortal sins, but it can only indirectly contribute to their effacement.[4] — Man can be washed and cleansed from the stain of mortal sin only by the infusion, that is, by the first imparting or by the restoration, of sanctifying grace. This grace of justification and, consequently, of forgiveness of mortal sin can, by God's will, be directly obtained only by the reception of baptism or of the sacrament of penance, or by making an act of perfect contrition. The Sacraments were instituted for the justification and sanctification of man; they moreover serve directly to establish and to

---

[1] Orationibus sanctae Ecclesiae et sacrificio salutari et eleemosynis, quae pro eorum spiritibus erogantur, non est dubitandum mortuos adjuvari, ut cum eis misericordius agatur a Domino, quam eorum peccata meruerunt. Hoc enim a Patribus traditum, universa observat Ecclesia, ut pro eis qui in corporis et sanguinis Christi communione defuncti sunt, cum ad ipsum sacrificium loeo suo commemorantur, oretur ac pro illis quoque id offerri commemoretur (Serm. 172, n. 2).

[2] Confess. 1. 9, c. 11—12.

[3] Catech. Mystag. 5, n. 8—10.

[4] Sacrificium Missae vere est propitiatorium, causans aliquo modo ac conferens ad remissionem peccatorum mortalium, justificationem peccatoris ac primam gratiam obtinendam ex opere operato: at non immediate est remissivum peccatorum mortalium (sicut sacramenta Baptismi et Poenitentiae) juxta communissimam Theologorum (Sporer, Theol. sacram. P. 2, cap. 4, sect. 2, § 2).

increase the supernatural life of the soul. Sacrifice, on the contrary, aims principally to promote the worship of God. The Mass, indeed, is also a means of salvation for man; but as such it is not destined directly to impart or bring about the grace of sanctification; consequently, the Sacrifice of the Mass cannot without the medium of another means efface or remove mortal sins.

The propitiatory power and efficacy of the Sacrifice of the Mass is not accurately explained by the mere saying that it procures actual graces, by means of which the sinner is led to true penance and sincere conversion. Such a statement almost totally annuls the distinction that exists between the character of propitiation and the impetratory efficacy of the Sacrifice of the Mass, a distinction which must be strictly adhered to; for as a Sacrifice of propitiation and as a Sacrifice of petition the Mass has different effects, as well as different modes of operation.[1] Namely, in so far as the Mass is a Sacrifice of propitiation, it calms and appeases the righteous anger of God, disarms His justice, and induces the Lord to regard sinful man with favor and mercy. The effect of the atoning power of the Mass, therefore, is to cause God no longer to be angry and to punish, that is, it favorably disposes Him to remit wholly or in part the punishment due to guilty man.[2] This reconciliation and this remission of punishment on the part of God are effected in virtue of Christ's vicarious service or payment (*per modum solutionis*) offered to God for this purpose; for the ransom purchased by Christ with His Blood upon Golgotha for the atonement and satisfaction of sin is always presented anew in the Mass to the Heavenly Father, and this for particular persons, and that He may avert from them their well-merited punishment and impart to them again His mercy more bountifully. Whilst the Mass, as a Sacrifice of propitiation, restrains or disarms God's avenging justice against the sinner, it has, as a Sacrifice of petition, the power, through the divine goodness and liberality, to dispense manifold graces and benefits (*per modum impetrationis*).

Accordingly the Mass as a Sacrifice of atonement helps to cancel mortal sins, inasmuch as, as a Sacrifice of petition, it is an extremely powerful means to effect the grace of true repentance and sincere conversion. Propitiation and petition act in unison in the Mass; they support and perfect each other in order to draw down upon man graces which enlighten and incite him to turn to God by faith, hope, love and sorrow, and to receive worthily the holy Sacraments,

---

[1] Cf. Lugo disp. 19, sect. 9, n. 140—150. — Franzelin, De Sacrificio thes. 13. — Köln. Pastoralblatt Jahrg. 1874, p. 113 etc.

[2] Eucharistia instituta est, ut Ecclesia perpetuum sacrificium haberet, quo peccata nostra expiarentur, et coelestis Pater, sceleribus nostris saepe graviter offensus, ab ira ad misericordiam, a justae animadversionis severitate ad clementiam traduceretur (Catech. Roman. P. 2, cap. 4, q. 55, n. 1). — Est hoc proprie sacrificii effectus, ut per ipsum *placetur* Deus, sicut etiam homo offensam in se commissam remittit propter aliquod obsequium acceptum quod ei exhibetur (S. Thom. 3, q. 49, a. 4).

whereby he is interiorly sanctified and made once more a child of God. This is expresssed by the words: "The Lord, being propitiated by the celebration of the Eucharistic Sacrifice, imparts the grace and gift of penance, remits sins and crimes, be they ever so great."[1] — Above all, God's justice must be propitiated, and only after it has been satisfied, does His mercy impart to sinful man particular graces that dispose him to sorrow and sincere conversion. By the commission of sins, especially if they be numerous and grievous, is God's majesty offended and His avenging justice provoked against the sinner. But among the punishments which the just and holy God inflicts on account of the commission of sin, one of the most severe consists in this that He refuses or deservedly withholds special and more abundant graces. For what St. Bernard says of ingratitude, that "it is like unto a scorching wind which dries up the fountain of divine mercy, the stream of grace, the dew of heaven,"[2] applies to all offences, especially to mortal sins: and these, being a neglect and abuse of grace, are acts of ingratitude towards God, and, therefore, check the more abundant flow of graces which God would otherwise grant to prayer. The refusal of this abundance of grace, so necessary for frail man tainted with sin to enable him to work out his salvation, is certainly a very fatal punishment. For without many and great graces, man will, alas! as is usually to be expected, remain in sin, will commit sin upon sin, and dying in sin, will thus fall into eternal perdition. In this respect the Sacrifice of the Mass exercises its propitiatory power, inasmuch as it reconciles the Divine justice and averts from sinful man the severe punishment of the withdrawal of the abundant helps of grace. — But if by means of the propitiatory power of the Mass, the demands of Divine justice are satisfied and the obstacle removed that prevented the free and full flow of graces from the fountains of the Saviour, then, furthermore, as a Sacrifice of petition the Mass can obtain from the Divine mercy and liberality powerful aids of grace, to enable sinful man to bring forth worthy fruits of penance, to be converted and restored to the life of grace. — The reconciliation, by virtue of the satisfaction of Christ, of the irritated and avenging justice of God must, therefore, precede, that is, previously remove the obstacles and prepare the way, so that the Divine goodness, through Christ's merits and mediation, may be moved to impart those graces which lead man again to the path of salvation and virtue. Accordingly, the Mass contributes indirectly as a propitiatory sacrifice, and directly as a sacrifice of petition, to the effectual acquirement of the implored grace of conversion.[3]

---

[1] Hujus sacrificii oblatione *placatus* Dominus gratiam et donum poenitentiae concedens, crimina et peccata, etiam ingentia, dimittit (Trident. sess. 22, cap. 2).

[2] Ingratitudo inimica est animae, exinanitio meritorum, virtutum dispersio, beneficiorum perditio. Ingratitudo ventus urens, siccans sibi fontem pietatis, rorem misericordiae, fluenta gratiae (S. Bernard. In Cantica serm. 51, n. 6.)

[3] This conception of the subject finds also a support in the authority of the liturgical prayers; compare, for example, the Secret. Dom. XIII. post Pent.: Pro-

This atonement is produced *ex opere operato* by the offering of the Sacrifice of the Mass, but only in a more or less limited measure, dependent chiefly on the will of God, but likewise on the disposition of the sinner. In how far God's justice is placated by a single Mass, and to what extent the punishment of the withdrawal of abundant graces is removed, we know not; for all this depends upon the free ordinance of God, as well as upon the number and gravity of the sins to be atoned for. — Hence it follows that it is not alone useful, but often necessary to offer Holy Mass repeatedly for the same intentions and for the same persons, in order that full satisfaction may be made to God, and that the unhallowed obstacle to the plentiful outpouring of the Divine goodness and liberality may be entirely removed. — When the Divine justice has been appeased by the Mass, then God is again disposed to impart abundant grace, which in punishment of sin He had previously withdrawn. In other words, there is no further obstacle to the impetratory power of the Mass of drawing down abundant graces of conversion into the soul that is in the state of mortal sin. These graces are not always immediately granted, but in God's own time and at His pleasure. However, the sinner must on his part dispose himself to receive them, and must freely co-operate with the graces bestowed. Should he neglect to do this, they remain without effect, and no real repentance and forgiveness of sin follow. Consequently, however capable and efficacious the Sacrifice of the Mass may be to move God to dispense greater and often extraordinary graces,[1] yet the actual conversion and restoration of the person to the state of grace may, through the fault of the individual, result in complete failure. Hence the Church teaches that "by the Sacrifice of the Mass we obtain mercy and grace in due time, when we draw near to God with a sincere heart and perfect faith, with fear and reverence, with compunction and repentance."[2]

b) By the Sacrifice of the Mass, the fruits of the death of Christ are also applied "unto the remission of those sins of which we are daily guilty,"[3] among which are chiefly to be understood venial sins. Only a few theologians have affirmed that the offering of the Sacrifice suffices of itself to efface directly smaller sins and transgressions; the common and correct opinion maintains that venial sins are also, like mortal sins, effaced only indirectly by the salutary efficacy of the Sacrific;[4] for sentiments of sorrow and penance are

---

pitiare, Domine, populo tuo, *propitiare* muneribus: ut hac oblatione *placatus* et indulgentiam nobis *tribuas* et postulata *concedas*.

[1] Oblationibus nostris, quaesumus Domine, placare susceptis: et ad te *nostras etiam rebelles compelle propitius voluntates* (Secreta in Sabb. post Dom. IV. Quadragesimae).

[2] Trident. sess. 22, cap. 2.

[3] Trident. sess. 22, cap. 1.

[4] Dubitatur, an virtute hujus sacrificii possit *immediate* haberi remissio peccaturum venialium. Communis sententia *negat*, quam sequitur Suarez et Vasquez

required to effect the remission of venial sins. — Also smaller faults, infidelities and negligences displease God, excite His disfavor and prevent a more abundant bestowal of His grace. This obstacle must first be removed by the atoning efficacy of the Mass, that God may allow Himself to be moved to awaken in us by special graces that devout, contrite and penitential sentiment which — with or without the reception of the sacrament of penance — is required, and which suffices to efface venial sins. But we should here especially bear in mind, that even venial sins, if frequently and deliberately committed, besides other evil effects following them, prevent the reception of many favors and graces which God's bounty has in reserve for the just, who thereby become weaker and run great risk, during some violent temptation, of plunging into the abyss of mortal sin. Frail man, therefore, for this very reason, too, has great need of a perpetual propitiatory sacrifice, in order that God may not in just punishment for his venial sins refuse unto him the abundant graces he so much needs in order to be preserved from the greatest of all evils — mortal sin. To assist at Mass or to have it celebrated for our intention, is assuredly one of the most available means to obtain in plenteous measure the pardon of venial sins and imperfections.

c) As a Sacrifice of propitiation the Mass has especially the power of satisfying for those temporal punishments which, after the pardon of mortal or venial sins, would otherwise have to be undergone either in this world or in purgatory.[1] The Eucharistic Sacrifice is offered for the living as well as for the dead for the remission of the temporal punishment still due to sin. But while it effects the pardon of sin only indirectly, the Sacrifice directly cancels the temporal punishment of sin, and so cancels it by the vicarious payment (*per modum solutionis*) from out of the treasure of merit and satisfaction that Christ acquired for us upon the Cross.[2] By His infinitely bitter passion and death, our Saviour on Calvary cancelled the penal debts of all men; the ransom there paid He Himself now presents upon the altar to His Heavenly Father for the living and the dead, that they may be released from their justly merited punishment. For upon Golgotha Christ bore our sorrows and the chastisement of our peace was placed upon Him (Is. 53); there He was

---

cum aliis recentioribus, quam ego etiam veram existimo (Lugo disp. 19, sect. 9, n. 152). This view must be adhered to, if we admit the more probable opinion, that in the present order of salvation no venial sin is pardoned to the just without a simultaneous increase of sanctifying grace; for the Mass cannot directly effect the infusion of sanctifying grace. (Cf. Suarez disp. 79, sect. 4—5.)

[1] Sacrificium Missae ex sua institutione habet valorem et vim satisfactivam ad remittendam ex opere operato aliquam poenam temporalem debitam pro peccatis mortalibus et venialibus jam remissis fidelium vivorum et defunctorum. Ita omnes orthodoxi (Sporer, Theol. sacram. P. 2, cap. 4, sect. 2, § 2).

[2] *Immediate* remittit sacrificium poenam peccatis debitam, nimirum *per modum solutionis* jam pro nobis factae in cruce et nobis per sacrificium applicatae, in subjecto tamen capaci, nimirum constituto in gratia (Sporer l. c.).

overwhelmed with shame and bitterness, bruised with pain and torture, that we guilty men might not be visited and humbled under the chastising rod of Divine Justice. This remission of punishment is imparted to us, inasmuch as Christ's passion is placed to our account and applied to us, that is, benefits us.

But the Holy Mass is offered not merely for the remission of punishment, but also as a satisfaction. Temporal punishment still due can be liquidated in a twofold manner: *a*) by real, personal satisfaction (*satisfactio*), that is, by the performance of good deeds, by works of penance, by the voluntary and patient endurance of suffering, all outweighing or equivalent to the punishment due, thus meriting its remission; *b*) by undergoing the punishment itself imposed by God (*satispassio*). The possibility of meriting and of satisfying in a strict sense ceases with death; hence the holy souls in purgatory can only suffer enough, that is, endure their punishment until the requirements of Divine Justice are satisfied and the last farthing has been paid. The living, on the contrary, when in the state of grace, can by prayer, fasting, alms and other penitential works satisfy the Divine justice, that is, merit the remission of those punishments which otherwise they would be obliged to undergo in purgatory. To this distinction Holy Church appears to allude, when she says that the Sacrifice of the Mass is offered "for punishments and satisfactions" (*pro poenis et satisfactionibus*): the propitiatory virtue of the Mass supplies for the punishment otherwise to be undergone by the departed (*poena-satispassio*); but for the living the propitiatory power of the Sacrifice supplies principally for the satisfaction to be rendered (*satisfactio*). For both it removes the last impediment to their entrance into heavenly glory.

If those for whom the Mass is celebrated are susceptible thereof, they always and infallibly receive the satisfactory fruit of the remission of punishment, and this applies not only to the living, but also to the dead.[1] For the rest, it is not known in what degree and measure this punishment is each time cancelled; but it is certain that the punishment due is not always entirely and completely removed by one Mass: for this complete remission not unfrequently the repeated offering of the Mass is required. — To participate in this effect of the Sacrifice, the state of grace and probably also the baptismal character of the recipient are necessarily presupposed. So long as one is in the state of mortal sin and an enemy to God, no punishment whatever, not even the least temporal punishment, can be remitted him. According to the common opinion of theologians, the baptismal character is not only an essential preliminary condition for the valid reception of the other Sacraments, but also for obtaining the remission of temporal punishment by means of the Eucharistic

---

[1] Sacrificium Missae remittit poenam peccatis debitam ex opere *operato*, lege infallibili, adeo, ut fructus hic satisfactorius de lege ordinaria sit infallibilis idque non tantum respectu vivorum capacium, in quo omnes Doctores consentiunt, sed etiam respectu defunctorum secundum communem Theologorum sententiam (Sporer, 1. c.).

Sacrifice (*ex opere operato*). If this opinion be correct, then all the unbaptized, living or dead, are excluded from participation in the aforesaid satisfactory fruit of the Mass.[1] How much of the temporal punishment is remitted, rests wholly in the divine will and decree. According to the well grounded opinion of many theologians,[2] there is so much the more of their punishment remitted unto the living, as they are the better disposed, that is, the more fervently they, by acts of penance, contrition, humility, submission to God and other virtues, render themselves worthy of the divine clemency and compassion.[3] The holy souls are at all times disposed for the obtaining of this fruit; God's wisdom, justice and mercy, however, determine to what extent the Mass shall each time it is offered diminish or abridge their sufferings.

As a propitiatory Sacrifice the Mass has, therefore, the power and, in consequence of the ordinance of Christ, has for object directly and infallibly — that is, in the strictest sense *ex opere operato* — to cancel temporal punishment. But it can also as a Sacrifice of petition bring about the remission of this punishment. This is done, moreover, when by way of petition it obtains assistance and strength for performing penitential works, by which we can satisfy the Divine Majesty and merit the remission of punishment. — According to a tenable and pious opinion, the Mass can also by way of petition directly obtain from the Divine goodness and mercy a gracious remission of punishment.[4] At least the intention and practice of the Church seem to be in favor of this opinion, namely, that in this way we may by prayer and sacrifice implore and obtain the remission of merited punishment. Were this denied, it would be difficult to explain satisfactorily many prayers in the Breviary and in Masses for the dead.[5] Thus the Church implores that the suffering souls "may obtain by pious supplications (*piis supplicationibus*) the par-

---

[1] Quod fructus satisfactionis ex opere operato non communicetur ejusmodi personis (i. e. non baptizatis vel catechumenis), concors est theologorum sententia (Lugo disp. 19, sect. 10, n. 166),

[2] Cfr. Lugo l. c. n. 200 sq. — Pasqualigo, De sacrif. N. L. tr. 1, q. 76.

[3] Quamvis haec oblatio ex sui quantitate sufficiat ad satisfaciendum pro omni poena, tamen fit satisfactoria illis pro quibus offertur vel etiam offerentibus secundum *quantitatem suae devotionis* et non pro tota poena (S. Thom. 3, q. 79, a. 5).

[4] Hoc dubium tractat late Suarez; allegatis utrinque rationibus dicit posse pie sustineri partem *affirmantem*, quam ego etiam *veram* existimo (Lugo disp. 19, sect. 9, n. 158).

[5] Quaestio haec est generalis ad omnes orationes, utrum scilicet praeter satisfactionem ex se respondentem orationi, ut est bonum opus, aliquid etiam respondeat de remissione poenae, *eo quod a Deo petatur remissio:* de ea egi in materia de suffragiis et in affirmantem opinionem consensi illamque probavi, quia Ecclesia videtur id omnino supponere ut certum; ea enim ratione in Sacro pro defunctis habet speciales orationes petentes pro illis eam remissionem. Si autem oratio qua oratio non extingueret *immediate* poenam, sed quatenus est opus poenale et bonum, non essent illae orationes utiles ad effectum, quem Ecclesia intendit (Arriaga, De Euchar. disp. 51, sect. 3).

don which they have always desired." And she has recourse to the
clemency of God, that they who have departed from this transitory
life may, "by the intercession of the ever blessed Virgin and all His
Saints (*beata Maria semper Virgine intercedente cum omnibus sanctis tuis*), arrive at the enjoyment of eternal beatitude."[1]

d) Finally, it is to be attributed to the continual celebration
and propitiatory virtue of the Holy Sacrifice that so many well
merited punishments of God are delayed or even averted from entire
countries and peoples, yea, even from the whole world. — The
multiplicity of sin and of enormous crimes frequently provokes the
divine justice to mete out without delay extraordinary punishments
on men, and to send fearful visitations on a godless and immoral
world. But when the Lord is appeased, He withdraws His threatening
or chastising hand. "The men of Nineve believed in God and
they proclaimed a fast and put on sackcloth from the greatest to the
least. And God saw their works and had mercy with regard to the
evil, which He had said that He would do to them, and He did it
not" (Jon. 3). When Solomon had built the Temple, the Lord
said to him: "I have heard thy prayer, and I have chosen this place
to Myself for a house of sacrifice. If I shut up heaven, and there
fall no rain, or if I give orders, and command the locust to devour
the land, or if I send pestilence among My people, and My people,
upon whom My name is called, being converted, shall make supplication
to Me, and seek out My face, and do penance for their most
wicked ways; then will I hear from heaven and will forgive their
sins and will heal their land" (2 Paralip. 7, 12–14). The severity
of the Divine Judge and Avenger has often been displayed in a terrible
and frightful manner in the Old Law. If now the highly
favored Christian peoples are, for the most part, spared such fearful
visitations, is it perhaps because they do not commit such grievous
crimes? Assuredly not! For behold how the world is inundated
with works of darkness and of the flesh! With frightful fertility
the poisonous weeds of sin sprout out and grow luxuriantly throughout
the earth. Ever longer and darker does the night of unbelief
and of error cast its dismal shadow. Incalculable is the number of
the enemies of the Cross of Christ, who by wallowing in the mire of
sensuality and lust, trample under foot the Precious Blood of their
redemption. The anti-Christian host assail always more and more
audaciously the rock of Peter: and in many ways the abomination
of desolation dwells in the holy place. Is not the earth fairly crushed
under the burthen of crime? Is not the measure of sin filled up?
Is not the world fallen away and estranged from God ripe for judgment?
Why does not the Almighty arm all creatures against those whose
wickedness and arrogance has reached its climax, in order to destroy

---

[1] Oratio duobus modis juvat defunctorum animas: uno modo, ut est opus
quoddam poenale et laboriosum . . ., alio modo ut est *impetratoria,* quod est ipsi
orationi proprium, quomodo etiam Beatorum orationes prosunt nobis et animabus
Purgatorii, licet satisfactoriae non sint (Bellarm. De Purgat. 1. 2, c. 16).

them in His wrath? (Wisdom 5, 18; Ps. 93, 23.) How can the
infinitely holy eye of God behold such godlessness, brook such immorality, without sending fire and sulphur from heaven, or opening
the fountains of the abyss to destroy, from the face of the earth,
man whom He created? (Gen. 6, 5–7.) Why does the Most High
deal so leniently and so tenderly with a world steeped in sensuality,
avarice and pride? Why are the riches of God's goodness and long-
animity not exhausted, and why does He grant to the sinner so long
a respite of grace for penance and amendment of life? For this
favor the world is principally indebted to the propitiatory Sacrifice,
which is offered daily and hourly upon thousands of altars for our
salvation and for that of the whole world (*pro nostra totiusque mundi
salute*). The voice of the Blood of Jesus offered in sacrifice cries
without intermission loudly and powerfully to Heaven — not for
vengeance, as did the blood of Abel, but for pardon, grace and mercy
in behalf of sinful man. — "Look upon the rainbow, and bless Him
that formed it; it is very beautiful in its brightness. It encom-
passeth the heaven about with the circle of its glory; the hands of
the Most High have displayed it" (Ecclus. 43, 12–13). This magnificent vari-colored arch, which unites heaven and earth, is a sign
and pledge of the eternal covenant of peace that God formed with
man. "When I" — thus saith the Lord — "shall cover the sky
with clouds, my bow shall appear in the clouds, and I shall see it,
and shall remember the everlasting covenant, that was made between
God and every living soul of all flesh which is upon the earth"
(Gen. 9, 14, 16). The rainbow symbolizes the Incarnate Son of
God who, as Mediator between Heaven and earth, established peace.
When the Heavenly Father beholds the Blood of His well-beloved
Son which, from the rising of the sun to the going down thereof,
sparkles and glistens in a thousand chalices, then all the dark clouds
of His threatening judgments vanish, and the serene rays of His
gracious countenance shine out again on the world. Therefore, it is
by Christ's Blood in the Mass that the anger of God is daily placated,
the vengeance of the Divine Judge disarmed, that He no more curses
the earth on account of man, whose mind and thoughts are prone to
evil from his youth (Gen. 8, 21). When "this Sacrifice for sins"
shall be no longer celebrated, then "there remains but a certain
dreadful expectation of judgement and the rage of a fire which shall
consume the adversaries" (Heb. 10, 26–27).

3. The atoning virtue and fruit of the Sacrifice of the Mass is
essentially necessary for us, as in many things we all offend (James
3, 2), and, consequently, we must at all times pray for the pardon of
our offences (Matt. 6, 12). — Before we venture, by means of the
Mass as a Sacrifice of petition, to present our desires and concerns
before the throne of God, we should strive, by means of the Mass as
a Sacrifice of propitiation, to appease God's just anger for our sins,
and to disperse the dark threatening clouds of His countenance, so
that He turn to us again His looks of clemency and let the sun of

His love again shine upon us. For the eyes of the Lord are upon the just, and His ears are inclined unto their prayers; whilst His angry look is upon them that do evil. The just cry, and the Lord hears them and delivers them out of all their troubles (Ps. 33, 16—18). If we bear this in mind, we shall understand why the Church in the celebration of Mass, and especially in the secret collects, so frequently implores the Lord for reconciliation.[1] She does not weary, in the course of this holy action, of repeating this cry for reconciliation, and she places it in advance of the petitions for the grace of God. Thus prays the Church, because she well knows and wishes to impress upon her children, that we poor men laden with sins must, before all things, be reconciled to God, and, by turning away the scourges of His anger, be made worthy to participate in His manifold blessings.

How necessary for us is a perpetual Sacrifice of propitiation! Upon Golgotha the fountain of atonement was opened; on the altar it continues to flow; therefrom we can and should draw its waters, so that God may be gracious and merciful unto us, that He may remit our debt and punishment. Is there a greater evil than sin and its fearful punishments? From this evil we can free ourselves by means of the Holy Sacrifice of the Mass; "for God's grace in Jesus's Blood repairs every injury." Precious is the fruit of the Eucharistic propitiatory Sacrifice. Let us remember that God's holiness and justice are equally as infinite and unfathomable as His goodness and mercy; let us reflect how wicked and deserving of punishment is every sin, even the least; let us represent to ourselves how long and severe are the pains of purgatory; let us be thoroughly penetrated with the greatness of our misery and weakness, which causes us to fall so easily into venial sin, thereby burdening ourselves with new debts; let us consider the mystery of the passion and the propitiatory death which Christ endured out of love for us: then our flesh shall be penetrated with a salutary fear of God's inviolable majesty, and we shall tremble at the severity of His judgments; then we shall be cautious and always upon our guard to avoid even slight faults; then, filled with the spirit and fervor of penance, we shall seek ever more and more to purify and sanctify ourselves; then we shall spend carefully and gratefully the blessed time of the Holy Sacrifice, that we may ever wash again our garment white in the Blood of the Lamb. How immeasurably great is the goodness and kindness of God, in making it so easy for us here below to be delivered from sin and its punishment, to the end that after death we may speedily be with Christ!

---

[1] Oblatis *placare* muneribus; *placare* humilitatis nostrae precibus et hostiis; concede *propitius;* sacrificiis praesentibus *placatus* intende; Ecclesiae dona *propitius* intuere; hostias *placationis* offerimus; *propitius* averte; esto *propitius* plebi tuae; tua *propitius* dona sanctifica; a cunctis nos reatibus et periculis *propitiatus* absolve; respice *propitius* ad munera; haec hostia salutaris fiat tuae *propitiatio* majestatis; custodi Ecclesiam tuam *propitiatione* perpetua (Missale Roman.).

Let us daily seek at the altar the efficacious grace of an earnest and sincere spirit of penance. Let us faithfully make use of the great Sacrifice of propitiation, that we may obtain clear light to comprehend how hateful, hideous and ruinous sin is, and that we may possess a more resolute will, in order entirely to break off sinning and wholly to rid ourselves of sin. As often as the Lamb of God, who taketh away the sins of the world, is offered in our presence "for the remission of sin", we should in all humility acknowledge ourselves guilty and deserving of punishment; then we ought ardently to implore that God may, out of regard to this propitiatory Sacrifice, fill us more and more with a tranquil, tender and permanent sorrow for sin, with a holy and wholesome fear of sin, with great delicacy of conscience, with an ineffable uprightness and purity of heart. By means of works of penance, we should again enkindle the ardor of our first fervor in the divine service. For does not this severe admonition of the Lord apply to each one of us: "I have somewhat against thee, because thou hast left thy first charity. Be mindful, therefore, from whence thou art fallen, and do penance and do the first works" (Apoc. 2, 4—5). For this reason, in the Mass, let us daily mingle our tears of sorrow, join our penance and mortifications with the Blood of Jesus in the chalice, in order to make them worthy of God's acceptance and to impart to them full value in the sight of God.

21. The Holy Mass — a Sacrifice of Petition.

Finally, that the Mass is also the most powerful and efficacious Sacrifice of impetration, is incontestably clear from the doctrine and practice of the Church. She has declared that the Holy Mass may not only be offered for the remission of sins and their punishment, of satisfaction due, "but moreover for all other necessities," that is, to obtain whatever we require in the order of grace and salvation. A rapid glance at the various liturgies suffices to convince us that the Holy Mass has always and everywhere been regarded as the most efficacious means to obtain assistance in all the necessities and concerns of life. It now but remains for us to explain in what manner the Holy Mass acts and what it effects as a Sacrifice of petition.

1. As a Sacrifice of petition the Holy Mass produces its effects by way of prayer (*per modum orationis vel impetrationis*);[1] the offering of Mass is, namely, essentially prayer or actual petition, and, therefore, proper to incline the heart of the Heavenly Father to impart to us the riches of His graces and blessings. On the altar Jesus Christ as High Priest offers Himself and intercedes in our behalf, by presenting and offering to the Eternal Father His painful death and all its merits, in order to induce Him to impart His gifts to us. From this aspect, the impetratory fruit of the Eucharistic

---

[1] Sicut oratio ex se et ex proprio officio impetratoria est, sic etiam sacrificium, quod est *quaedam oratio*, ut sic dicam, *realis*, non verbalis, proprie impetratorium est (Bellarm. De Missa l. 2, c. 4).

Sacrifice originates *ex opere operato*; for it has its foundation in the celebration of the Sacrifice, in the acts and merits of Jesus Christ, and not in the devotion of the priest celebrating nor of the faithful for whom it is offered.

Do the impetratory effects follow infallibly, or not? This question is answered in various ways, but the difference lies more in the expression than in the matter itself. The propitiatory efficacy of the Mass is indeed more certain than the impetratory; but the latter also can be called infallible — namely, when all the requisite conditions exist. In case that one or the other of the conditions is wanting, we do not obtain the favors desired. — Above all, it is requisite that the object of our petition be conformable to the will of God, that is, that it should harmonize with the divine economy and the supernatural order of salvation.[1] And frequently this is not the case, inasmuch as the faithful endeavor to obtain special fruits from the Mass; "for we know not what we should pray for as we ought" (Rom. 8, 26).[2] But those graces which our Saviour wills to bestow and apply to us, we always infallibly obtain, provided we place no obstacle in the way: for He wills to procure only such favors for us, as God is disposed to grant us.[3] What Christ asks in our behalf, He always obtains: His will can never be unfulfilled. If He lives always in the glory of the Father, to intercede for us: how much more will He, in His character and office of "merciful and faithful High Priest of God," employ in our behalf His all-powerful aid at that time and hour when He is mystically immolated as a victim upon the altar! Then will He, as "in the days of His flesh," send forth prayer and supplication to God, and "because of His reverence and dignity He shall be heard" (Heb. 5, 7). Yea, the Father always hears Him (John 11, 42); for in the Mass Christ always offers anew to Him the price of His divine-human life, His Blood, His wounds, His love, His obedience, His humility, — in brief, the whole immeasurable treasure of His merits, which He accumulated from the crib to the Cross: should not the Heavenly Father, on beholding the face of His Christ (Ps. 83, 10), for His sake grant us favors and bless us with every heavenly blessing? The Lord does not pray for graces, as we do; He has full claim to them, since He has merited them. For these graces are so much the more the outpouring of the purest goodness and mercy of the Lord, the higher and the more painful the price wherewith He purchased them for us so undeserving of favor.

---

[1] Non habemus de ejusmodi impetratione promissionem absolutam Dei, sed tantum conditionatam, *si nobis, quod recte petimus, secundum divinae providentiae ordinationem, dari expediat* (Sporer, Theol. sacram. P. 2, cap. 4, sect. 1, § 2, n. 238).

[2] Hence the Church prays God: Ut petentibus desiderata concedas, fac eos *quae tibi sunt placita,* postulare (Orat. Dom. IX. post Pent.).

[3] Christus non offert semper in ordine ad illos effectus, quos nos desideramus obtinere, sed solum in ordine ad illos, quos Deus decrevit concedere (Pasqualigo, De sacrif. N. L. tr. 1, q. 133, n. 20).

In order to obtain a superabundance of grace from God through the Eucharistic Sacrifice, the Church, the priest and the faithful offer the Mass, joining their petitions to it. Without doubt the result of the petitions which are borne and supported by virtue of the Eucharistic Sacrifice, is less deceptive than that of a simple prayer.[1] For at the altar it is not we alone who cry from the depths of our misery and poverty to the throne of God, but it is Christ, our Head and Mediator, who prays and offers with us and for us. Yea, we do not merely implore, but at the same time we offer to the Eternal Father the most precious of gifts — the Body and Blood of His well-beloved Son, to move Him, by this offering, to impart to us, according to the extent of His mercies, all manner of blessings. Notwithstanding all this, the grace implored is sometimes denied. But even in this case, we may be confident that the Mass has not been altogether without fruit and effect; in place of the gift desired, we receive another which is better and more profitable for us. Though even we be not heard according to our desire, yet this will conduce to our salvation. "The Lord either gives us that which we ask, or He bestows something else which He knows will be more advantageous to us."[2] — For the sacrificial fruit which, according to our narrow-minded views, we expect, is not always granted, but another more suitable is given to us; thus God does not always give the graces of the Mass at the time we desire them, but at another and better moment, when it pleases Him.[3] "Some gifts are not refused us, but granted later at a more proper time."[4] If, therefore, we place no obstacle in the way, but prepare ourselves worthily, we at all times obtain some salutary fruit by reason of the impetratory power of the Sacrifice of the Mass.

2. In general, it may be said that the Mass as a Sacrifice of petition has precisely the same effects as prayer:[5] both prayer and

---

[1] Orationes muneribus conjunctae multo pluris valent ad impetrandum quam solitariae et sine oblatione. Cum ergo per sacrificium offeratur Deo munus acceptissimum et hostia gratissima, consequenter orationes sacrificio innixae multo pluris valent ad impetrandum. Confirmatur, quia hoc sacrificium vim habet placandi Deum: ergo remoto obice divinae indignationis certum est, orationes reddi majoris efficaciae. Requiritur tamen ad hunc impetrationis effectum oratio seu petitio expressa vel tacita ipsius offerentis seu celebrantis, quia non dicimus impetrare nisi quod petimus (Quarti, De sacrific. Miss. quaest. 2, punct. 6).

[2] Aut dabit quod petimus aut quod nobis noverit esse *utilius* (S. Bernardus, In Quadrag. serm. 5).

[3] Quamvis non semper obtineatur id, quod petitur, *semper* tamen *obtinetur aliquid* vel idem alio tempore opportuno vel aliud quid et prout Deo melius visum fuerit. Ut notant P. P. et D. D. communiter (Sporer, Theol. sacram. P. 2, cap. 4, sect. 2, § 2).

[4] Quaedam non negantur, sed ut congruo dentur tempore *differuntur* (S. August. In Joann. tr. 102).

[5] Hoc sacrificium per modum impetrationis potest habere eosdem effectus, qui habentur per orationem. Quidquid enim Sacerdos potest pro se vel aliis impetrare per orationem extra sacrificium Missae, potest *facilius* multo impetrare

Sacrifice can obtain all gifts for us and avert from us every evil. —
The object of a prayer of petition may also be the fruit of the petition
of the Eucharistic Sacrifice, provided it directly or indirectly promotes God's honor and is beneficial to our salvation. It is chiefly
through the channel of the Mass, that there flow to us supernatural
or spiritual gifts, appertaining to the order of grace; natural and
temporal gifts, whether something spiritual for the soul or something
material for the body, can be petitioned for and obtained only rel-
atively to eternal salvation and subordinately to our final end. [1]

The Sacrifice of the Mass draws down upon the soul the light
and the dew of Heaven, so that all the fruits of the Holy Ghost —
"charity, joy, peace, patience, benignity, goodness, longanimity,
mildness, faith, modesty, continency, chastity" (Gal. 5, 22—23)
therein attain their most beautiful bloom and ripeness. The Mass
obtains grace, strength and courage to perform good works, to overcome the flesh and its concupiscence, to despise the world with its
allurements and threats, to resist the attacks of Satan, to endure not
only patiently, but with joy and thanksgiving to God, the hardships
and troubles, the sufferings and evils of this life, to fight the good
fight, to finish our course and to persevere in the way salvation unto
the end, and thus to bear off the crown of life and of eternal glory. [2]

But not only treasures of grace, not only supernatural and imperishable riches, but temporal benefits and blessings also flow unto
us from the Holy Mass. But as we know not which may the more
surely lead to the possession of heaven, fortune or misfortune, joy
or sorrow, health or sickness, a long or a short life, we ought to
address such petitions to God only conditionally, submitting our will
to His paternal wisdom and goodness. "Commit thy way to the

---

per orationem conjunctam cum sacrificio Missae (Becanus, Summ. theol. schol.,
p. 3, tr. 2, c. 25, q. 13).

[1] Cf. the *Orationes diversae* in the Missal; e. g., Da nobis, quaesumus Domine, piae supplicationis effectum, et *famem* propitiatus averte: ut *mortalium
corda cognoscant*, et te indignante talia flagella prodire, et te miserante cessare. —
Deus in quo vivimus, movemur et sumus: *pluviam* nobis tribue *congruentem;* ut
praesentibus subsidiis sufficienter adjuti *sempiterna fiducialius appetamus*.

[2] Alter hujus sacrificii pretiosissimus effectus est, gratiae omniumque virtutum infusarum in iis, pro quibus offertur, augmentum, non quod homine nihil
operante, dum Sacrum pro ipso fiat, gratia eidem augeatur (hic enim sacramentorum digne perceptorum proprius effectus est), sed quod per illud Deus magna auxilia communicet et sanctas potentesque det inspirationes animabus, pro quibus id
offertur, per quas inspirationes et auxilia excitantur et animantur ad resistendum
tentationibus, ad exercendas virtutes et ad facienda poenitentiae, misericordiae
humilitatisque opera, et ad vitae hujus calamitates ac miserias, hominum persecu-
tiones, morbos et dolores, quos Deus immittit, majore cum resignatione, patientia
ac conformitate cum divina voluntate tolerandos. Et sic homo mirabiles in gratia,
virtutibus infusis et donis Spiritus Sancti progressus facit atque etiam pretiosissimum perseverantiae donum acquirit, qui alius divinissimus est effectus, quem hoc
dignissimum sacrificium operatur in iis, qui diligenter ac devote favoribus per id
communicari solitis utuntur (Arias, Thesaur. inexhaust. I, tr. 4, cap. 8).

Lord and trust in Him, and He will do it" (Ps. 36, 5). You desire by means of the Mass to obtain restoration to health, but instead our Lord gives you the gift of patience and detachment from what is earthly; is not this a more precious gift? In the Missal we find different prayers, prayers for assistance, for safety in dangers, for deliverance from suffering and tribulation; in these prayers, the Church reveals at the same time the spirit in which she prays, subordinating the temporal and earthly to the eternal and heavenly.[1]

These impetratory fruits of the Mass are the more bountifully imparted to us, the more our hearts are open to them, the more worthy they are disposed to receive them;[2] therefore we should prepare our hearts to receive them by a purification of our interior by penance, by withdrawing our affections from earthly things and by inflaming our desires for heavenly goods.

3. The dangers and conflicts of our earthly pilgrimage are manifold. Man's needs are many, his poverty is great. Yet, behold! all they that are weary and heavily laden find at the altar refreshment, security and assistance in all the necessities of soul and body. The Holy Mass is an ocean of all grace: why, then, should any one go from it in want? It is an inexhaustible fountain of blessings, from whose fulness we may, as much as we can and according to our need, draw grace upon grace. By means of this Sacrifice we have become rich in all things, so that no grace is wanting to us (1 Cor. 1, 4—7). Therefore, ought we in all thankfulness and with holy joy make use of the inexhaustible riches of divine mercy, presented to us on the altar and placed at our disposal. But not merely earthly and perishable goods, not merely "the dew of heaven and the fatness of the earth and abundance of corn and wine" (Gen. 27, 28) should we endeavor to acquire, but, above all, we should strive to satisfy the thirst and the desire for supernatural and eternal goods, to enrich ourselves with treasures which "neither the rust nor the moth doth consume, and where thieves do not break through, nor steal" (Matt. 6, 20). Let us pray for that which truly conduces to our salvation and happiness, for that which may advance the kingdom of God

---

[1] Deus, qui in omni re bonum nostrum vult, virtute hujus sacrificii liberat eos, pro quibus offertur, a multis malis poenae, quae ipsorum animabus obessent, et saepe iisdem temporalia bona tuendae vitae statuique christiano necessaria concedit, quando scit ea ipsis ad bene vivendum Deoque cum majore quiete ac stabilitate serviendum profutura. Atque in hoc sensu Ecclesia in communibus suis orationibus, in quibus a Deo per hujus sacrificii virtutem pro ipsis fidelibus petit spiritualium donorum ac divinarum gratiarum abundantiam, postulat etiam, ut eos liberet a temporalibus periculis et damnis et a persecutionibus et adversitatibus utque illis det salutem et fructus terrae. Et in earum multis se declarat, in quo sensu haec temporalia petat, dicens: Da, Domine, famulis tuis salutem mentis et corporis, ut te tota virtute diligant et quae tibi placita sunt, tota dilectione perficiant (Arias 1. c.)

[2] Dicendum est, impetrationem sacrificii esse magis vel minus efficacem juxta majorem vel minorem dispositionem illius, cui impetratur (Pasqualigo, De sacrif. N. L. tr. I, q. 87, n. 5).

within and around us. "It is" — as St. Gregory says — "the Lord's will, that we love Him above all that which He has created, and that we implore Him to grant us eternal, preferably to earthly, goods."[1]

Never should we "separate our prayers from Jesus Christ, who prays for and in us, and unto whom we pray; He prays for us as our High Priest; He prays in us as our Head; we pray to Him as our God."[2] This is done in a perfect manner during the celebration of Holy Mass. Let us, therefore, unite our petitions and supplications with the Sacrifice and the mediation of Jesus Christ. For, supported by His immolation and merits, our prayers will be more availing and efficacious, they will be more speedily and perfectly answered. But our prayer must be properly made; it must be made with faith and confidence, with humility and perseverance, that it may pierce the clouds and, in union with the Eucharistic Sacrifice, ascend to the throne of the Most High. "Reflect how God more readily hears the prayers of the priest during Holy Mass than at any other time. He does indeed at all times impart His graces, as often as they are asked of Him through the merits of Jesus Christ, but during Mass He dispenses them in more abundant measure; for our prayers are then accompanied and supported by the prayers of Jesus Christ, and they acquire through His intercession an incomparably greater efficacy, because Jesus is the High Priest who offers Himself in the Mass to obtain grace for us. The time of the celebration of Mass is the hour in which our Lord sits upon that throne of grace to which, according to the counsel of the Apostle, we should draw near to find mercy and help in all our necessities. The angels too look forward to the time of Holy Mass, in order that the intercession they then make for us may be more availing and acceptable before God ; and what we do not obtain during Holy Mass, we can scarcely expect to be granted us at another time" (St. Alphonsus Liguori).

4. Thus the Holy Sacrifice of the Mass is the most profound and significant expression of all our petitions and intercessions in spiritual and temporal concerns. We offer it when weighed down by adversity of all kinds, imploring therein consolation and assistance from Him who for our sake underwent so much sorrow and pain. We offer it when the Lord in His just anger, provoked by our sins, visits us with His chastisements, strikes our fields with drouth, destroys our crops by rain and flood, and we implore from His paternal Goodness that He would in due season give to our lands needed sunshine and rain. When the Angel of Death moves amongst us in times of contagion, we offer the Holy Mass, imploring therein of the Lord of life and death that He would stay the horrors of death. In behalf of the faithful who in the presence of God and of the

---

[1] De magis Dominus quam ea quae condidit, vult amari, aeterna potius quam terrena postulari (Moral. 1. 15, c. 20).

[2] Orat *pro nobis* ut sacerdos noster; orat *in nobis* ut caput nostrum; oratur *a nobis* ut Deus noster (S. Aug. Enarrat. in Ps. 85 n. 1).

Church engage in the sacred bond of matrimony, we offer the Holy Sacrifice, therein imploring for them the grace of fidelity and love and all the blessings of a Christian union throughout life and until death shall part them. We offer it when our young Levites are chosen for the service of the altar of the Lord by the imposition of hands; and when those selected from among the priests are consecrated to the office of chief shepherd, we therein implore for them the assistance of the great Shepherd of souls (1 Peter 2, 25), that in word and deed they may be good shepherds and worthy dispensers of the mysteries of God, and be able to stand in judgment on the day of reckoning. We offer it for our brethren whom our Lord has called from this world, imploring therein from the Judge of the living and the dead, that He may be merciful to their souls and grant them eternal rest. We offer it for all the faithful, that God may impart to them grace and blessing and admit them to the eternal kingdom of heaven. (Cf. Geissel I, p. 460 et seqq.)

22. The Participants of the Fruits of the Mass.

The principal purpose of the Eucharistic Sacrifice is to render to God due worship of adoration and thanksgiving, of propitiation and petition;[1] at the same time, it is also offered for men and it benefits them. Among the effects flowing from the Mass, those graces, those spiritual advantages and blessings, those temporal gifts and favors which God bestows by reason of the Sacrifice offered, are in a more restricted sense called sacrificial fruits.[2] As a rule, the application of the fruit is meant, when it is said that the Mass is offered for some particular person. It is evident that herein the propitiatory and supplicatory character of the Mass is to be chiefly considered, since, as a Sacrifice of petition and propitiation, it procures for man the fulness of blessings; considered, therefore, in this twofold character, the Sacrifice of the Mass is in a strict sense offered

---

[1] Sacrificium Missae principaliter et universaliter semper offerendum est ad finem colendi Deum: non quidem semper ad solum finem latreuticum, sistendo solum in intentione colendi Deum in recognitionem supremi ejus dominii, in actu signato, absit; sed simul etiam ad finem eucharisticum, impetratorium et satisfactorium. Quemcunque enim ex his finem expresse intendas, eo ipso etiam implicite, imo in ipso actu exercito etiam intendis et exerces cultum divinum soli Deo debitum. An non etiam, si sacrificio tuo Deo gratias agis pro beneficiis acceptis, supplicas pro nobis accipiendis, deprecaris remissionem peccatorum: in actu exercito et ipso facto Deo divinum cultum exhibes, ejus supremum in te dominium, potestatem, eminentiam tuamque humillimam submissionem, dependentiam, indigentiam contestaris? Quis enim peccata remittit nisi solus Deus? Quis beneficia et bona salutaria ad ultimum finem aeternae beatitudinis conferre potest efficienter nisi solus Deus? *Laudandus esses et laudabilis valde, mi sacerdos, si praedictos fines omnes semper explicite et expresse intenderes et bene applicares tanquam fidelis dispensator* (Sporer, Theol. sacram. P. 2, cap. 5, sect. 3, § 1).

[2] Fructus sacrificii sunt ipsa *bona*, quae sacrificium oblatum vel potius ratione et intuitu sacrificii oblati motus ipse Deus confert offerenti et iis pro quibus offertur (Sporer, Theol. sacram. P. 2, cap. 4, sect. 2, § 1).

for the needy.[1] — To offer Mass for some one may be understood
also to mean, but rarely, to offer it in the name and in the place of
another.   In this sense, the Mass may likewise, in so far as it is a
Sacrifice of adoration and thanksgiving, be offered for, i. e., in the
place of others, without any sacrificial fruits being especially applied
to them or falling to their share.   The adoration and thanksgiving
offered to God by Christ in the Mass is, indeed, beneficial to men
also, but only in as far as the adoration and thanksgiving of the
Eucharistic Sacrifice supplies for the defects that invariably accompany their imperfect adoration and thanksgiving.   On the contrary,
as a Sacrifice of propitiation and petition, the Mass tends in quite a
different manner to the benefit and advantage of persons for whom
it is offered ; for by its propitiatory and impetratory efficacy it procures for them benefits and graces of all kinds.   These blessings
accruing to man we have in view, when treating of participation in
the fruits of the Sacrifice and of its participants.

We have previously mentioned the different sources whence the
fruits of the Mass flow and descend upon man.   Here we shall
chiefly treat of the participation in the essential sacrificial fruit (*ex
opere operato*), which has its source directly from Christ as the Chief
Priest.   This principal fruit of the Sacrifice is shared in by different
participants and is gained by them in different ways.   Among the
complicated questions which have been discussed on this subject, the
following one occupies the first place.   On what does the participation in the designated sacrificial fruit depend — and who then participates therein ?   Some[2] hold that all have a share in this sacrificial fruit who in any manner co-operate in the Sacrifice of the
Mass — whether or not the Mass be offered for them ; others,[3] on
the contrary, are of opinion, and justly, that the Sacrifice (*ex opere
operato*) benefits persons only in so far as it is offered for them.[4]   In
reality both conditions usually concur, that is, it is always at least
in a general way offered for those who themselves offer it or who
offer it along with them ; thus far both requisite conditions, therefore, may conduce to secure said sacrificial fruit.   In this fruit there
share the entire Church, the faithful who actually take part in the
Mass, the celebrating priest, and they to whom the priest especially
applies the fruit of the Mass.

i.   The sacrificial fruit, which falls to the share of the whole
Church, is called the general fruit (*fructus generalis vel generalissi-
mus*).   It has a twofold source : first, the offering of Christ, inasmuch as He offers Himself for the Church ; and then the offering of

---

[1]   Sacrificium sub hac duplici ratione — quatenus propitiatorium et impetratorium est — fructum aliquem seu effectum habere potest praeter ipsum cultum, et
ideo sub his rationibus *proprie* offertur pro aliquo (Suarez disp. 78, sect. 1, n. 1).

[2]   Suarez disp. 79, sect. 8.

[3]   Pasqualigo, De sacrif. N. L., q. 57. — Stentrup, Soteriologia, th. 101.

[4]   Eucharistia effectum sacramenti habet in eo qui sumit, effectum autem sacrificii in eo qui *offert* vel in his pro quibus *offertur* (S. Thom. 3, q. 79, a. 5).

the Church, inasmuch as she also offers the Mass herself through the priest for her own welfare. Both sources flow into each other and pour out a stream of blessings throughout the Church and unto all her children.

a) Every holy Sacrifice of the Mass has its efficacy and advantage for the whole Church — for all that are incorporated in the mystical Body of Christ and still need to be assisted by grace, whether they be numbered among the living or the dead. And, indeed, in a less degree, and indirectly at least, this general fruit is diffused even among those without the pale of the Church, who, though out of it, are called and required to enter or return into its bosom. The chalice of the Precious Blood rises daily from the altar heavenward, in order that all men may come to the knowledge of the truth and be saved (1 Tim. 2, 1—4). Jesus Christ is the Redeemer of the world (John 3, 17); for He shed His Blood and underwent the torments of the Cross, to obtain for all men without exception the forgiveness of sin, grace and eternal happiness. Without intermission and in all places there gushes forth and flows this universal wellspring of grace and of salvation of the Sacrifice of the Cross in the Mass, whose blessings benefit the entire world. It is, moreover, to this Holy Sacrifice, as a very sun of grace, that these words of the Psalmist are applicable: "His going out is from the end of heaven — and his circuit even to the end thereof, and there is no one that can hide himself from the heat" (Ps. 18, 7). Yea, unto thousands of hearts, that are unaware of it, there radiate from the altar rays of supernal light, to enlighten and to lead back the stray sheep to Christ, the great Shepherd and Bishop of souls (1 Peter 2, 25), into His sheepfold, to the maternal home of the one true Church, in which the treasures of all the ways of grace and its gifts are unfolded to them and placed at their disposal.

Far more abundantly and more richly still, certainly, is the blessing of the Mass poured out over the Church militant on earth and suffering in purgatory; for the Mass is, by the will and institution of Christ, the property of the Church. It is for the welfare and benefit of the Church that the daily Sacrifice was instituted, and for this end it is principally offered. The general fruit accruing from the Mass is applied, in the first place, for the common welfare of the Church, that is, it is bestowed on the Church in its entirety, inasmuch as the Church is a divine work and institution, the kingdom and Spouse of Christ. With His heart's blood Christ acquired the Church (Apoc. 20, 28); upon the altar He continually renews, in an unbloody manner, the bloody Sacrifice of Golgotha for His Church, so as always gloriously to present her — without spot or wrinkle, holy and immaculate (Eph. 5, 25—27). By virtue of the Blood of the Lamb (Apoc. 12, 11), that daily flows in the chalice, the Church gains the victory over her enemies, and invariably comes forth triumphant from her combat with the gates of hell and the anti-Christian powers of the world. In the Sacrifice of the Altar, Christ comes forward as mediator and advocate with God in behalf of the Church, to sustain and exalt her in all her necessities and tribulations, to humble her enemies and put them to confusion.   From this we may conclude, that those members of the mystical body of Christ have a particularly large share in this universal sacrificial fruit, who chiefly contribute to the common weal of the Church — namely, the pastors and teachers of the Church (Pope, bishops and priests).   It behooves them principally to promote the glory and holiness of the Church; they stand in great need of supernatural light, of strength and endurance, courageously to persevere in the distressing combats which they are almost constantly obliged to wage in behalf of the flock of Christ which is confided to them, for the unity and freedom, for the treasures of faith and grace of the Catholic Church.   The guardians and protectors of the Spouse of Christ, therefore, experience, in the first place, the salutary influence and the beneficent effects of the Eucharistic Sacrifice bestowed on them in order that they may ever prove themselves servants of God by much patience in tribulation, in necessities, in distresses, in stripes, in prisons, in watchings, in weariness . . . . in the word of truth, through the power of God, by the armor of justice (2 Cor. 6, 4—13).

In what this fruit of the Sacrifice actually consists, and whether it extends to each individual member of the Church, cannot be positively determined.   Some theologians[1] are of opinion that the general sacrificial fruit includes not only those blessings obtained by way of petition, but also a satisfactory effect, namely, the remission of temporal punishment due to sin — and, moreover, a remission more or less abundantly imparted to all the members of the Church who are disposed to receive it.

b) Christ, the invisible Priest, therefore, continually offers Himself for the entire Church by the hands and through the ministry of the visible priest.   The latter, at the same time, stands at the altar in the name and by the commission of the Church.   The Church offers and prays by the lips of the priest who, in every Mass, is her delegate and mediator with God for all her children upon earth and in purgatory.   As she, the holy and well-beloved Spouse of Christ, is ever acceptable to God, her petitions, especially when united to the Mass, are always answered; hence, in consideration of the Sacrifice and prayer of the Church, the Most High day after day pours out the richest blessings upon her needy children.   In the liturgical prayers of the Mass, mention is usually made of those gifts and graces which the Church desires to obtain, by means of the Mass, for herself in general or for individual members in particular.   Thus, for example, she implores the Almighty during the celebration of Mass for the grace "that, after overcoming all attacks and errors,

---

[1] Valentia, Comment. theol. IV, disp. 6, quaest. 11, punct. 1. — Vasquez, In III, disp. 231, cap. 6. — Gotti, Theol. schol. dogm. tr. 8 de Euch., quaest. 2, dub. 1, § 3. — Tanner, Theol. schol. IV, disp. 5, quaest. 9, dub. 4, n. 98. — Cf. in particular Stentrup, l. c. thes. 112.

she may serve God with perfect liberty" and "be able to enjoy undisturbed devotion."

c) Christ and the Church offer the Mass continually for the body of the faithful. Therefore, the general fruit of the Sacrifice benefits the Catholic people simply because the priest exercises his ministry at the altar as prescribed; for this a special and express application on his part is not required. — Excommunicated persons who are excluded from the Church, do not share in the general sacrificial fruit; those of the faithful who are in the state of mortal sin, participate proportionately in a much less degree than do persons in the state of grace, who are more intimately incorporated in the mystical body of Christ. The better the faithful dispose themselves by virtue and piety, the more closely they unite themselves to the Mass and the more perfectly they co-operate in its offering, the more abundant will be their share in the general sacrificial fruit of the Church. — For this reason, it is a pious custom and a very salutary practice of many Christians each morning in spirit to commend themselves to and to include themselves in all the Masses that may be celebrated at all hours of the day throughout the world; for they thereby draw upon themselves in greater abundance the blessing and fruit of the Holy Sacrifice. [1]

How great and inestimable in this respect also is the happiness of being of the household of Christ and one of the fellow-citizens of the Saints (Eph. 2, 19), that is, a believing, faithful and obedient child of the Catholic Church, in the communication of grace with Christ! Whoever remains a spiritually living member of God's great family, spread all over the earth, can draw his full share of the stream of blessings and mercies that is daily poured out over the Church from Masses innumerable. Again, how consoling to the heart is the thought: Even were I to die on the most isolated spot of the earth, forgotten by everybody, — Holy Church, my spiritual Mother, forgets me not; for upon thousands of altars, she prays and offers for my poor soul also Christ's Precious Reconciling Blood, let-

---

[1] Die quadam, cum (sancta Mechtildis) prae debilitate longius ire non valens, Missam in ambitu audiret, ingemuit, conquerendo se Deo esse remotam. Cui Dominus statim respondit: "Ubicunque tu es, ego sum." Tunc illa requisivit, si aliquid obesset quod homines de longe Missam audirent. Cui Dominus: "Bonum est ut homo praesens sit; quod dum nullo modo potest, sic tamen prope sit, ut verba valeat audire, quia secundum quod Apostolus dicit: Sermo Dei vivus est et efficax et penetrabilis (Hebr. 4, 12). Verbum enim Dei animam vivificat, infundens ei spirituale gaudium, sicut etiam apparet in hominibus laicis et idiotis, qui licet non intelligant quae leguntur, sentiunt tamen gaudium Spiritus, et inde ad poenitentiam animantur. Verbum etiam Dei efficacem reddit animam ad virtutes et quaeque bona, et penetrat eam, omnia ejus interiora illustrando. Sed cum infirmitate vel obedientia vel alia rationabili de causa praepeditur, ubicunque tunc homo est, ibi eidem praesens et cum illo sum... dico tibi: qui Missam devote et studiose audierit, in extremis ejus tot nobiles Sanctorum meorum personas in ejus consolationem et defensionem, ad animam ejus cum honore deducendam, sibi transmittam, quot Missas in terris audivit" (S. Mechtild., Lib. special. grat. p. 3, c. 19).

ting it trickle down into the flames of purgatory in order to relieve
or abridge my painful banishment in that abode of suffering.

2. All the members of the Church do not gain in the same
manner and measure this general sacrificial fruit. Those of the faithful who personally co-operate in the celebration of Mass, who share
in the offering of the Sacrifice and who thus, in a certain sense,
appear as joint celebrants (*co-offerentes*), obtain without doubt a
greater share of heavenly blessings, and this not only *ex opere operantis*, but even *ex opere operato*. [1] These graces, imparted to the
faithful who co-operate in the Sacrifice, are termed the special fruit
(*fructus specialis*). — Among the various ways of participating by
personal co-operation in the offering of the Sacrifice, is chiefly to be
mentioned the assisting at Holy Mass. Whoever assists at Mass
with reverence and devotion, enters into the closest and most intimate connection with the Sacrifice, because as the priest prays and
offers the Mass, such a one joins his prayers, praying and offering
with the priest — and because in addition to this, the Church also
prays and offers for all there present. The faithful who worthily
assist at Mass, gain thereby a special sacrificial fruit, more or less
abundant according to the measure of their co-operation, their
worthiness and devotion. Justly, therefore, is the devout attendance
at Mass regarded as one of the most efficacious means to draw on
ourselves and others the fulness of spiritual and temporal blessings. [2]
The Mass is a spiritual mine of gold, where we may dig and enrich

---

[1] That on all the faithful who, through and with the priest, actually offer the
Sacrifice, an impetratory and satisfactory fruit *ex opere operato* from the Sacrifice
is bestowed, Suarez holds (Disp. 79, sect. 8, n. 5) as a "devout and reliable opinion." Lugo remarks thereon: Haec sententia probabilis est et deservit ad com-
mendandam magis utilitatem audiendi Missam, — but adds: sed non video firmum
fundamentum ad eam persuadendam. — He believes that there is no well founded
reason for the assertion, that to them who assist at Mass is granted a *remissio
poenae residuae ex opere operato;* on the contrary, he regards it as established,
that the assistants receive a fruit *ex opere operato, quatenus per modum saltem
impetrationis sacerdos offert specialiter pro circumstantibus* (Disp. 19, sect. 11, n.
230—238). — Cf. on this also Arriaga tom. VII, disp. 53, sect. 3.

[2] *Magna dignitas* est, quam Deus homini christiano Missam cum spiritu
devotioneque audienti impertit, et *magna valdeque mira sunt bona*, quae is sic
illam audiens lucratur. Quantae dignitatis, gloriae utilitatisque homini christiano
est, quod Deo Patri donum offert ac munus infiniti valoris, et quod illi infinite
gratum est, et quo ipsum placat propitiumque reddit, si peccatis iratus est, voluntatem ejus conciliat, summamque ei voluptatem affert et in ejus amore ac gratia
crescit, familiarior eidem Domino fit, majorem cum ipso amicitiam contrahit, no-
vos ab illius liberalitate favores, dona et gratias percipit, et ab eodem suorum
bonorum desideriorum complementum consequitur, quoque non soli sibi tantum
bonum procurat, sed etiam a Deo ingentia bona ac misericordias pro omnibus illis
impetrare potest, pro quibus idem sacrificium vult offerre ? Nam Missam audiendo,
quemadmodum offert sacrificium corporis et sanguinis Christi pro seipso, sic etiam
potest illud offerre pro omnibus iis, quibus bene vult, et omnibus magno adiumento
erit pro anima proque salute ac vita temporali, quae animae bono conducit (Arias,
Thesaur. inexhaust. II, tr. 7, cap. 7).

ourselves with little labor; it is a treasure-house inexhaustible in its riches, that is ever open to us and to which we can always gain admittance. But where are our faith and love? Do we esteem and make use of this overflowing fountain of heavenly blessings? Is the holy hour of Mass, so full of graces, what is dearest to us and the most precious portion of the day? Do we consider the celebration of the Holy Mass, or assisting thereat, as the highest and most important action of our daily duty? We have in this certainly much to lament, much to atone for. Holy Mass should be the treasure, the joy and comfort of our life.

3. While the whole Church receives the general fruit of the Mass, and the assisting faithful the particular fruit, the very special or personal fruit (*fructus specialissimus vel individualis*) is imparted to the celebrant.[1] This is easy to understand. The priest has the closest and most prominent part in the celebration of Mass. By virtue of his ordination, he is empowered and called to celebrate, in the name of Christ and of the Church, the holy Sacrifice. He is not only the real offerer, but according to the will of Christ and in the name of the Church he also expressly offers the Sacrifice for himself: should not then the Mass, as a Sacrifice of propitiation and petition, be rich in graces and blessings for him? It is a never-failing fountain of salvation, open more especially to the celebrant than to any one else. Therefore, he cannot fail to be enriched in quite a signal manner with the blessings of Heaven, if, besides approaching the altar in the state of grace, he, moreover, celebrates with attention and devotion.[2] This personal sacerdotal fruit the celebrant receives by simply performing his sacrificial duty in the proper manner. No special application or wish to gain this fruit of the Sacrifice is required, its source is not in the priest's devout sentiments, which are only a necessary condition to gain this fruit in a more plentiful measure. — For this reason also, it is of vital importance that the

---

[1] The worthy celebration of Mass is, indeed, in the highest degree meritorious, satisfactory and impetratory for the priest ex opere *operantis*. The fructus specialissimus, on the contrary, of which there is question here, is ex opere *operato*. — Some theologians (for example, Suarez, Henriquez, Amicus, Laymann) assert, that the priest has also the fruit ex opere *operato*, inasmuch as he offers the Sacrifice (quatenus *offert*); others more correctly affirm (for instance, Vasquez, Coninck, Isambert, Pasqualigo), that it is granted to him because the Mass also is specially offered for him (quatenus *pro ipso offertur*). — The opinion that the fructus specialissimus of the celebrant and the fructus specialis of the assisting faithful cannot be applied to others, is better founded than the contrary view. Cf. Pasqualigo, De sacrif. N. L. tr. 1, q. 99, 115. — Stentrup l. c. thes. 113.

[2] Nemo plus utilitatis recipit ex sanctissimo Missae sacrificio, quam sacerdos ipse qui offert; nemo enim tam est propinquus, intimus et, ut sic loquar, practicus et totalis executor tanti operis, tam Deo placiti, tam ex sese naturaque sua fructiferi, tam ad miserationes liberalitatesque divinas evocandas ac emungendas instituti; nemo tam illimitatus et arbitrarius dispensator atque arbiter tanti thesauri fructuumque ac effectuum ejus quam sacerdos (Druzbicki, Tract. de effect. fruct. et applicat. ss. Missae sacrif. cap. 8).

priest do his utmost to prepare well for the daily celebration of Mass. If he wishes to obtain at the altar the many and great graces of which he stands in need for the discharge of his responsible office in an edifying manner, he must endeavor to lead a spotless life and ever celebrate the Divine Mysteries with ardent love. The Church admonishes him to use every exertion and care always to celebrate the Holy Sacrifice with the utmost purity and devotion. Before approaching the altar, let him ask himself the following questions[1]: How sinful, how full of imperfection, how slothful am I in the service of God, I who venture to offer the Holy Sacrifice? How unspeakably exalted, glorious and precious is the Divine Victim, who is about to rest in my hands and in my heart? How inconceivably sublime the greatness and the majesty of the Most High, whom I am expected to honor and glorify by the celebration of Mass? How manifold, how weighty are the cares and tribulations of the Church and of her children, for which they expect help and assistance by the power of the Eucharistic Sacrifice? — Such reflections will inflame the soul with love and devotion.

4. Finally, there proceeds moreover from the Mass a propitiatory and impetratory fruit (*ex opere operato*), which is imparted to those for whom the priest, in a special manner, celebrates Holy Mass —and this fruit is called the ministerial or mediatorial fruit (*fructus ministerialis vel medius*). Inasmuch as the priest is a servant of Christ and a dispenser of the mysteries of God (1 Cor. 4, 1), he has not only the power to offer the Sacrifice, but also to determine to whom the fruit of the Sacrifice should be applied. With regard to the ministerial fruit of the Sacrifice, the priest can freely dispose of it in his own favor or in favor of others, but to the celebrant and to him only does it appertain to make the special application of the

---

[1] In omni sacrificio *quatuor* sunt pensanda, ut puta *quis, quid, cui* et *quare*. Ideo antequam celebremus aut communicemus, perpendamus haec omnia. Imprimis unusquisque attendat, *quis* sit, i. e. quam fragilis, defectuosus, indignus et reus: ac per hoc indignissimum se recognoscat sicque pro viribus ad communionem seu celebrationem se praeparet ac suo modo se dignificare Deo auxiliante conetur. Secundo consideret *quid*, i. e. quale et quantum sit sacrificium istud, in quo Christus Deus et homo offertur; et ita cum ingenti humilitate, filiali amore, reverentia praecordiali, puritate praecipua, charitateque fervida progrediatur ad Sancta sanctorum. Tertio penset, *cui* fit ista oblatio, ut puta Deo Patri, Regi ac Domino majestatis immensae, cui cum omni sinceritate, humilitate, attentione, diligentia adstare et immolare oportet. Nam et oblatio sacrificii hujus opus est valde privilegiatum, ad cujus dignam executionem devotio requiritur actualis et esse in charitate, quam qui habuerit, ceteris non carebit virtutibus. Quarto advertat, *quare*, i. e. propter quas causas institutum sit et immoletur sacrificium istud, videlicet pro communi bono totius Ecclesiae, pro vivis et mortuis, pro ereptione ab omni periculo et peccato, pro virtutum et gratiae incremento, pro pace patriae et omni rationabili causa. Idcirco cum pro tot tantisque causis nequaquam sit segniter deprecandum nec tepide offerendum, satagamus cum grandi instantia integroque affectu sancti fervoris celebrare ac celebrando aut communicando orare (Dion. Carthus. in hymn. "Verbum supernum" enarrat.).

Mass.[1] — The power and the right of especially offering the Holy Sacrifice for others, of applying its fruits in their behalf by special intention, is inviolably imparted to the priest at his ordination. And the obligation of celebrating the Mass for such special obligation can arise from various causes. It arises in general from the order of ecclesiastical authority, or the free consent of the priest, who, on receiving an alms or some stipend *(eleemosyna vel stipendium)*, obliges himself thereto.[2] That such a special application of the sacrificial fruit is lawful, useful and salutary, is manifest not only from the nature of the Sacrifice considered in itself, but also from the constant practice from ancient times and the explicit teaching of the Church. From the very beginning it has always been the practice of the Church to offer Holy Mass for individual persons and for certain intentions. Thus pastors are strictly obliged on Sundays and holidays to celebrate Holy Mass for the flock committed to their care. The assertion that the special application of the Mass for certain persons or certain classes of people is of no special advantage to them, has been condemned by the Church.[3]

As this application of the sacrificial fruit is exclusively an act of the power received at the ordination of the priest, it can always be validly *(valide)* made for all that are capable or in need of the effects of the Mass; but in order that it may be lawfully *(licite)* done, no prohibition of the Church must intervene or be opposed to the application. By the will of Christ, the Eucharistic Sacrifice is the property of the Church; He has commanded it to be celebrated by her and in her. The highest ecclesiastical authority, consequently, has the power to limit and regulate more definitely the right of application. Therefore the question still remains to be considered, namely, in behalf of what persons may the priest celebrate Holy Mass with a special intention, that is, to whom especially may he apply the ministerial sacrificial fruit? To answer this question, we must distinguish several classes of persons, among the living as well as among the departed.

a) The living are either members of the Catholic Church or outside of her communion.

α) The members of the Church are either in the state of grace or in the state of sin: for either class the Holy Mass may be offered. The just members of the Church, animated by an active charity, are alone disposed to gain in their fulness the fruits of the Mass; for the participation in the Mass is so much the greater, the more in-

---

[1] Dicendum est, sacrificium determinari, ut huic potius prosit speciali modo quam illi, ab ipso offerente, quatenus determinat offerre pro hoc vel pro illo, et in hoc consistere *applicationem*, qua dicitur *applicari* (Pasqualigo, De sacrif. N. L. tr. 1, q. 161, n. 1).

[2] Sacerdos non accipit pecuniam quasi pretium consecrationis Eucharistiae aut Missae decantandae (hoc enim esset simoniacum), sed quasi stipendium (gift, alms) suae sustentationis (S. Thom. 2, 2, q. 100, a. 2 ad 2.)

[3] Cfr. Prop. 30 of the Constitution Auctorem fidei of Aug. 28, 1794.

timate is one's communion with Christ and the Church. — To the
dead members of the Church, that is, to those of the faithful who are
deprived of the life of grace, who are spiritually dead through mortal
sin, not all the fruits of the Sacrifice can be applied; for as long as
they are enemies of God, no temporal punishment can be remitted
them. The chief and the weightiest need they have, and which
oppresses them and from which they should be freed by the propitiatory virtue of the Mass, is the need entailed by sin. The Sacrifice of the Mass will, above all, obtain for them the mercy and reconciliation of God, light and strength from on high, so that with a
resolute will they may be enabled to abandon the path of sin, sincerely turn to God and be restored to the life of grace. — Moreover,
for baptized children who have not as yet attained the use of reason,
the Mass can be celebrated, but only as a Sacrifice of petition, and
not of propitiation.

b) If we pass over to those persons who are outside of the
Church and are separated from her visible communion, there is no
doubt that, at least indirectly and in a general way, they are included in the Sacrifice, since the Mass is celebrated for the conversion
of Jews and pagans, the extirpation of heresy and schism, to obtain
and promote the increase and exaltation of the kingdom of God.
The first object in this is, indeed, the welfare of the Church; while,
at the same time, the greatest benefit and advantage accrues from
the Mass to those who receive the grace of becoming children of the
true Church. — On the contrary, according to the positive definitions
of the Church, the direct and special application of the Mass is not
permitted so unconditionally to all classes of persons. Thus it is
strictly forbidden to offer the Holy Sacrifice for those excommunicated persons who are not tolerated, but are to be avoided
(*excommunicati vitandi*), and this prohibition holds good so long as
the ban of excommunication has not been removed by absolution.
According to some theologians, on the contrary, such an application
for the excommunicated who are tolerated is regarded not only as
valid, but also as permitted. — The Holy Sacrifice may be lawfully
offered, but only under certain restrictions, for schismatics and heretics, as well as for the unbaptized or unbelievers (Jews, Turks,
heathens). And in so doing everything is to be avoided that would
cause scandal or offence to the Christian people. The Holy Mass
may be offered for schismatics and heretics first and chiefly to obtain
their conversion, that is, with the intention of appeasing the anger
of God in their regard, as well as of obtaining for them from the
goodness of God various graces and benefits, whereby they may the
more easily work out their salvation, be brought to the knowledge
of the true faith and into communion with the Church. [1]

---

[1] Proposito dubio: Utrum possit aut debeat celebrari Missa ac percipi eleemosyna *pro Graeco-schismatico*, qui enixe oret atque instet, ut Missa applicetur pro
se sive in ecclesia adstante sive extra ecclesiam manente? S. Congr. Officii die
19. April. 1837 respondit: *Juxta exposita non licet, nisi constet expresse, eleemo-*

b) The salutary and saving influence of the Holy Sacrifice extends even beyond the tomb. Can and may the Holy Mass be offered for all the departed?

They who have departed out of this world have either entered heaven, where they rejoice in happiness and reign in glory — or they are buried in the abyss of hell, whence there is no redemption; or they sojourn in the abode of purification until they are purified in the pain of fire and in the fire of pains, until cleansed from all defilement and found worthy to appear before the face of God.

a) It is for the last only of these three classes of deceased persons that the Mass can strictly be offered and according to apostolical tradition[1] is truly offered.[2] The Syriac Bishop Balæus, who lived toward the end of the fourth and the beginning of the fifth century, proves that prayer and sacrifice are useful to the departed. "It is evident to all reasonable minds, that the faithful departed have the benefit of the Church vigils and of the Sacrifice of the Mass and of the incense of propitiation, when the priest is mindful of them at the altar. Then the citizens of heaven rejoice, and they that live upon earth are gladdened, and the departed, too, exult, for they are summoned in order to be refreshed by the heavenly Sacrifice." The suffering souls, who are helplessly suffering and enduring pains in purgatory, stand in great need of the propitiatory Sacrifice of the Mass, that the divine justice may be induced to abridge their tedious punishment, or alleviate their intense sufferings. The Church has declared, that the Mass most especially (*potissimum*) procures help and relief for the faithful departed.[3] The Sacrifice of the Altar, accordingly, is the most effectual, all-sufficient and sure means of obtaining for the suffering souls in purgatory comfort and refreshment; for it helps them more than prayers and indulgences, more than fasting, alms and night-vigils, more than works of charity, mercy and piety which the living may offer for the departed. As these suffering souls are always in the best dispositions, the Holy

---

synam a schismatico praeberi ad impetrandam conversionem ad veram fidem. Quam resolutionem P. M. Gregorius XVI. approbavit.

Proposito dubio: Utrum liceat sacerdotibus Missam celebrare *pro Turcarum aliorumque infidelium intentione,* et ab iis eleemosynam pro Missae applicatione accipere? S. Congr. Officii die 12. Julii 1865 respondit: *Affirmative, dummodo non adsit scandalum, ac nihil in Missa specialiter addatur, et quoad intentionem constet, nihil mali aut erroris aut superstitionis in infidelibus eleemosynam offerentibus subesse.*

[1] Trident. sess. 22, cap. 2.

[2] Cum alia sacramenta non prosint post mortem, unde est, quod hoc sacramentum altaris prodest? — Dicendum, quod aliorum sacramentorum dispensatio respicit actum *in persona* vel *circa personam,* sicut patet in baptismo, et ideo non potest baptizari, nisi qui praesto est in aquam mergi; sed *sacrificium* est actus *pro persona.* Et quoniam actus *in personam* requirit personam actu existentem, sed *pro persona* non; sicut Christus obtulit se Patri pro illis, qui fuerunt et qui futuri sunt, sic sacrificium prodest *his qui finierunt vitam* (S. Bonav. IV, dist. 45, dub. 3).

[3] Trident. sess. 25 de Purgat.

Mass, in all probability, is never without effect when said for them. This is all we know, the rest is entirely enveloped in great darkness, for it is hidden from us, in what measure and to what extent the Holy Sacrifice each time abridges or relieves the sufferings of a poor soul. How soon such a soul may be released from purgatory depends upon the will of God, whose justice is equally as infinite and impenetrable as His mercy. Therefore it is not useless, but rather necessary, to have the Holy Sacrifice repeatedly offered for one and the same soul, to assist it all the more speedily and surely to enter into possession of heaven. This is true also of the so-called privileged Mass, in which, by virtue of the privileged altar, there is added a plenary indulgence to the fruit of the Sacrifice for the benefit of the soul in behalf of whom the Mass is celebrated; for the real effect of such an indulgence, which can be applied to the departed only by way of petition, remains yet subject to the merciful acceptance of God.

Of the different effects of the Mass, the faithful departed can receive but a single one, namely, the remission of the temporal punishment by satisfying the Divine Justice. — These punishments are the last impediments which withhold them from entering into the longed-for rest and joy of their Lord. As a Sacrifice of propitiation, the Mass disarms God's justice, resting heavily upon these souls, and cancels the punishments to be undergone by them. — As a Sacrifice of petition, the Mass may also contribute to the alleviation and deliverance of the suffering souls: on the one hand, by procuring for them from the goodness of God a gracious release from punishment; on the other, by obtaining many graces, whereby the living are incited and animated to offer constantly for the departed penitential works, indulgences and prayers.[1]

In a general way, the Church in her liturgy offers and prays for "all the faithful departed" and for "all resting in Christ" — and, therefore, in behalf of all the souls suffering in purgatory. For important reasons the special or direct application of the Mass is far more limited in regard to the departed than to the living. It depends on whether the person died in or out of the communion of the Church. All who in life and at death were in visible communion with the Church, are after death considered as connected in a living manner with the Church, that is, if not already in heaven, at least

---

[1] Constat inter omnes doctores catholicos, sacrificium Missae vere prodesse defunctis, nedum quatenus satisfactorium, sed etiam ut est impetratorium, ut colligitur ex Trident. sess. 22, cap. 2, et ex praxi Ecclesiae, quae orat in sacrificio pro defunctis, etiam pro illis, quibus non applicatur fructus satisfactionis ex opere operato, et quia praescribit, ut oretur pro illis in secundo *Memento* post consecrationem, propter solum fructum impetrationis, quia tunc facta est jam applicatio et distributio fructus satisfactionis ex opere operato (Quarti, In Rubr. Missal. p. 1, tit. 5, dub. 6). — According to the opinion of this author, the Mass as a Sacrifice of petition can benefit the departed only indirectly, quia per orationes sacrificio innixas impetramus a Deo, ut excitet fideles ad offerenda sacrificia et suffragia pro defunctis vel indulgentias, quibus immediate liberantur a poenis.

as being on the sure way to eternal blessedness, namely, in the place of purification. Therefore, she allows the Holy Sacrifice to be celebrated for all that have died in her fold. — The case is quite different with respect to those who have departed not as members of the Catholic Church. It is, indeed, possible that they were separated without fault of their own from the visible communion of the Church, that they died in the state of grace and, consequently, were saved; the judgment of this the Church leaves to God. As a visible society, she judges according to external facts; outwardly they did not belong to her — the only true and saving Church. The Church cannot, then, recognize and treat as her own those who previous to their death were not in a visible manner her children. Such would be the case if she permitted them to share in her public prayers and sacrifices, in her ceremonies and marks of honor. To these common spiritual treasures they only have a claim who were and who remained children of the Church until death, and that not merely in the sight of God, but also before man. In all justice, therefore, the Church forbids every kind of funereal celebration, foundation Masses and application of Mass for those who have died outside of her visible communion — that is, for all deceased non-Catholics, whether members of sects or unbelievers. Were she to act otherwise, she would endanger the dogma of her exclusive truth and authority, and open both door and gate to indifference in matters of faith.[1] — As long as heretics and unbelievers are alive, the Sacrifice of the Mass may be offered for them, to obtain in their behalf the grace of conversion. With their death their conversion ceases to be possible: hence the difference in the ecclesiastical regulation which permits the celebrant's application of the fruit of the Mass, on the one hand, for living non-Catholics and, on the other, forbids it to deceased non-Catholics. Recently it was attempted to make a distinction between public and private application for departed non-Catholics, and to represent the latter application as permissible. But this distinction has no foundation in the law and, therefore, appears unreliable (*Ubi lex non distinguit, neque nos distinguere debemus* — Where the law makes no distinction, neither ought we). The opinion of the lawfulness of applying the Mass in this case is, therefore, at least insecure and doubtful.[2] The Church has prohibited every special application of the Mass and its celebration for deceased non-Catholics for weighty reasons; therefore, she is not responsible for the injury

---

[1] Cf. the Brief of Gregory XVI. of Feb. 16, 1842, to the Bishop of Augsburg, and that of July 9, 1842, to the Benedictine Abbot of the Bavarian Monastery of Scheyern. — To the question: An liceat in die anniversarii obitus principissae ad Protestantium sectam pertinentis celebrare Missam in levamen defunctorum regiae familiae? was replied by the S. R. C. of May 23, 1859: Non licere, et detur exemplum epistolae in forma Brevis die 9. Julii 1842 s. m. Gregorii XVI.

[2] For such as die in manifest heresy (*in manifesta haeresi*) Mass may not be said, even if the application were known only to the priest and the giver of the stipend (C. S. O. April 7, 1875).

that the separation from her visible communion may have entailed even beyond the tomb. As to the rest, deceased non-Catholics are not totally deprived of the blessed influence of the Mass; for prayers and the Mass also are offered in general for them, and when Mass is celebrated for all the suffering souls, they also derive advantage therefrom.

None the less true is it, that the children of the Catholic Church in life and after death enjoy many graces and special advantages, from which non-Catholics are excluded. This is an unmerited blessing and an inappreciable privilege for which we should be most grateful to God. At the same time we ought to "praise and magnify His infinite goodness and benignity, by which we are enabled to make satisfaction for one another," — and for the reason that in the Sacrifice of the Mass principally He has given us such an excellent and efficacious means of procuring untold comfort, relief and solace in behalf of the suffering souls in their painful banishment. The ingenious love of the Church has appointed a special solemnity for the comfort and peace of these souls. For centuries on All-Souls' Day she stands in robes of mourning at the altar and at the tomb. It is a mournful day; but one on which Masses for the dead are multiplied, when prayers and sighs are more fervent, the faithful more recollected and better disposed, when streams of grace descend to the sufferers in purgatory, when heaven throws open its gates to them, and signs of peace hover over the abyss. Oh, that is a blessed day! Though the darkness that envelops us be ever so dense and to us impenetrable, yet from thousands of altars shines the light of the glorified Body of Christ, casting its rays into heaven, into the very face of the infinitely just Father, causing it to be lit up in friendly and gracious clemency, and, from the throne of God, it reflects its rays downward into the darkness of the subterranean prison, in order that the perpetual light of the heavenly home may shine upon them.[1]

b) For the reprobate the Holy Sacrifice cannot and may not in any manner whatever be offered: for them there is neither redemption (*in inferno nulla est redemptio*) nor alleviation of their torments.[2] As withered branches they are completely severed from the true vine, Jesus Christ; for all eternity they are excluded from the communion of the Saints. Their torments in the ocean of fire and brimstone are not alleviated, even by a drop of cold water; no single ray of light or of hope ever penetrates the dark abode of hell.

---

[1] Cf. P. Keel, Die jenseitige Welt, 1. Buch (Das Fegfeuer), p. 156 &c.

[2] Mitigatio poenae damnatorum dupliciter potest intelligi: aut quantum ad *taxationem* et *inflictionem* poenae et sic absque dubio est ibi mitigatio, quia divina justitia non totum exigit, pro eo quod, ejus pietate interveniente, aliquam partem poenae infligendo remittit. — Alio modo potest intelligi mitigatio *post* poenae taxationem et inflictionem, et hoc modo nulla cadit mitigatio a divina misericordia, quia *ex tunc claudit eis Dominus viscera pietatis* (S. Bonav. IV, dist. 46, a. 1, q. 2).

Equally unlawful is it to celebrate Mass for children who have not reached the age of reason and who have died without baptism. Whatever their eternal destiny may be, this much is certain that they are irrevocably excluded, not only from the bliss of heaven, but in general from all participation in the supernatural goods which Christ acquired for the human race, and which are applied to individual men mainly through the Sacrifice of the Mass.

c) In contrast with the reprobate, whom, in their eternal separation from Christ, grace can neither reach nor influence, "the spirits of the just made perfect" in heaven are most intimately united to Him and, consequently, stand in no need of the help of grace. The blessed dwell in the land of the living, where they are free from all evil and in full possession of all the riches of the Lord. From this the reason is clear, why the Sacrifice of the Mass can never properly (*proprie*) be offered for them.[1] They are free from all guilt of sin and its punishment; therefore, the Mass as a sacrifice of propitiation cannot be offered for them. Moreover, since their essential glory cannot be increased, for it remains unchangeably the same, Mass cannot be celebrated even as a sacrifice of petition for them in this respect, that is, to obtain for them an increase of their essential glory. Now, although the Mass may not be offered to the Saints, or in reality for them, still the celebration of it conduces in various ways to their honor and glory.

Inasmuch as the Mass is a sacrifice of praise and thanksgiving, it may in a certain sense be celebrated or heard for the blessed, that is, in their name for the purpose of praising and thanking God for the gifts of grace and glory which He has bountifully bestowed upon them.[2] For this the blessed rejoice; for the Mass is a more glorious homage of praise and of thanksgiving to the Lord than that which the combined choirs of the blessed and of the angels could render

---

[1] *Pro Beatis* sacrificium non dicitur offerri nisi *improprie.* Potest quidem offerri in gratiarum actionem pro beneficiis in Sanctos collatis; potest etiam offerri ad impetrandam gloriam et venerationem alicujus Sancti in terra: hoc tamen non sufficit ut dicamus offerri Missam pro tali Sancto, quia hoc videtur significare imperfectionem et indigentiam in illo, pro quo offertur. . . . Quando ergo apud aliquos antiquos reperitur ille modus loquendi, quod offerimus *pro* Sanctis, explicandus est in sensu *minus proprio,* quod vel offerimus loco illorum, h. e. ad agendas gratias pro beneficiis a Deo in eos collatis, quas gratias ipsi libenter agerent; vel quod offerimus, ut redundet in eorum honorem, quem sensum significant illa verba Missae: ut illis proficiat ad honorem, nobis autem ad salutem; vel denique quod illos invocamus in oblatione sacrificii, ut ipsi pro nobis intercedant, quem etiam sensum significat Ecclesia in verbis sequentibus: et illi pro nobis intercedere dignentur in coelis, quorum memoriam agimus in terris; et eundem sensum expressit Concil. Trident. sess. 22, cap. 3 (Lugo disp. 19, sect. 10, n. 192). — Cfr. Ejus auxilio tua beneficia capiamus, *pro quo* tibi laudis hostias immolamus (Secr. in festo s. Barthol. Apost.).

[2] Laudis hostia, Domine, *quam pro sancto Ignatio gratias agentes obtulimus,* ad perpetuam nos majestatis tuae laudationem, ejus intercessione, perducat (Postcomm. in festo s. Ignatii Conf.).

Him, and it is, therefore, a means of responding to their ardent desires of ever more and more glorifying God. — The blessed also rejoice that their graces and virtues, their actions and miracles, their combats and victories, their power and greatness afford us an opportunity and give us matter worthily to praise and honor God, the bestower of all holiness, by the celebration of the Eucharistic Sacrifice.[1]

As a Sacrifice of petition, the Mass may also be celebrated with the intention of promoting on earth the greater glory of the blessed. But offered in this way, the Mass is not so much for the advantage of the Saints, to whom the increase of external glory brings no real profit, but rather for us men, for we are thereby enriched with spiritual favors. The fruit that God in this case imparts by reason of the Sacrifice offered by way of petition, consists of graces by which the faithful are animated and spurred on to honor, invoke and imitate the Saints. The diffusion of the veneration of the Saints on earth brings great blessings to man, and to the blessed in heaven new joy, since thereby the Most Blessed Trinity is glorified, the communion of Saints made active, the life of the Church enhanced and the salvation of the faithful promoted.

These effects, which the Mass produces with regard to the blessed in heaven, that is, for their honor and joy, proceed simply from the celebration of the Mass offered with an appropriate intention. The Church has connected with the Divine Sacrifice a copious rite, in which the veneration of the Saints finds manifold expression. The liturgy of the Divine Sacrifice, in which their names occur, their intercession is invoked and the example of their virtues is set forth to us, already in itself sheds great glory on the blessed friends of God and children of the Church — the Saints of heaven.[2] This is especially the case with regard to the festal and votive Masses, composed expressly to honor individual Saints or whole classes of them. In the collects of these Masses, the intercession of the Saints holds a prominent place; in the *Secreta* and Post-Communion prayers, it is brought in the closest connection with the Sacrifice. Very frequently the petition is addressed directly to God, as follows, that He may through the intercession, by the merits, through the merits and intercession, through the intercessory merits of the Saints,[3]

---

[1] Ad sacra mysteria celebranda trahat te *laus Dei* et *Sanctorum,* cum non habeamus, quo possimus Deum et Sanctos pro sua dignitate laudare quam Christum sacramentaliter Deo Patri offerre et immolare (S. Bonav. tr. de praep. ad Miss. c. 1, § 4, n. 15).

[2] In manibus est hostia (θυσία) et omnia parata prostant: adsunt angeli, archangeli, adest Filius Dei: cum tanto horrore adstant omnes, adstant illi clamantes omnibus silentibus. . . . Quid putas, pro martyribus offerri, quod nominentur in illa hora? Licet martyres sint, etiam pro martyribus *magnus honos nominari* Domino praesente, dum mors perficitur illa, horrendum sacrificium, ineffabilia mysteria (S. Chrysost. Homil. 21 in Act. Apost., n. 4).

[3] Ejus meritis et precibus; ejus suffragantibus meritis; ejus exemplo et intercessione; ejus patrocinio; ejus interventione; intercessionis ejus auxilio; ejus

whom we honor and whose feast we celebrate, take us under His merciful protection, or favorably receive the Sacrifice of the Church and of the faithful, and abundantly grant them its fruits. — Often the petition addressed directly to God runs thus, that He grant that this or another particular Saint may be our constant intercessor, obtain pardon for us, assist us by his prayers, that we may partake of his assistance, be supported by his intercession and be defended by his protection. — In these liturgical prayers the intercession of the Saints is placed in a dual relation to the Eucharistic Sacrifice. On the one hand, the petition is frequently repeated, that the Sacrifice, inasmuch as it is offered by us sinful men, may, through the merits and intercession of the Saints, be more pleasing to the Divine Majesty and more advantageous to us;[1] on the other hand, the intercession of the Saints is again implored after a manner more intimately connected with the Holy Sacrifice offered in their honor and to their memory[2] — or to speak more correctly, the intercession of the Saints is invoked because of the efficacy of the Holy Sacrifice; and this is but proper, since the Saints possess and exercise the right of intercession in our favor only by the power of Christ and of His Sacrifice. For whatever the Saints are and can do, they hold and accomplish in virtue of the Sacrifice of Christ, renewed upon the altar in an unbloody manner. By virtue of this Sacrifice they became holy and persevered in holiness until the end of their life; by its virtue they overcame themselves, the world and the devil; by its virtue they entered, rich in merits, into the glory of heaven, where they have become intercessors in our behalf; by its virtue God listens to their petitions, hence the confidence which we have in the merits and intercession of the Saints and with which we invoke their intercession, is based upon the efficacy of this Sacrifice. It is but proper then, indeed, that in offering the Eucharistic Sacrifice unto the honor of God and His Saints and for our own salvation, we acknowledge and confess this; and this we do by beseeching the Heavenly Father, unto whom the Mass is offered, that

---

meritis et intercessione; ejus intercedentibus meritis: ejus interventu; intercedentibus sanctis Martyribus; ejus supplicatione; ejus suffragiis &c.

[1] Oblationes populi tui, quaesumus Domine, beati Jacobi Apostoli passio beata conciliet: et quae nostris non aptae sunt meritis, fiant tibi placitae ejus deprecatione (Secr. in festo s. Jacobi Apost.). — Munera, quae conscientiae nostrae praepediuntur obstaculis, sanctorum Apostolorum meritis grata reddantur (Secr. in Vigilia ss. Ap. Sim. et Jud.). — Sanctifica, quaesumus Domine, oblata libamina; et beatae Dei genitricis Mariae saluberrima intercessione, nobis salutaria fore concede (Secr. in festo B. M. V. de Monte Carmelo). — Ut nobis, Domine, tua sacrificia dent salutem: beatus Confessor tuus Augustinus et Pontifex, quaesumus, precator accedat (Postcomm. in festo s. August.).

[2] Dum eorum merita recolimus, patrocinia sentiamus; quorum solemnia celebramus, eorum orationibus adjuvemur; cujus natalitia colimus, de ejusdem etiam protectione gaudeamus; quorum gloriamur triumphis, protegamur auxiliis; quae pro illorum veneranda gerimus passione, nobis proficiat ad medelam; quorum festa solemniter celebramus, continuis foveamur auxiliis etc.

He would deign, by virtue of this Sacrifice, to make us share in the intercession of the Saints, and, in view of the merits they have acquired by their union with the self-same Sacrifice and through their intercession, the efficacy of which is derived from this Sacrifice, to grant us His powerful protection. Want of confidence in the Divine Mercy cannot be associated with such a petition, based as it is upon the Sacrifice of His infinite love and goodness. On the contrary: such a petition serves to promote the honor of Christ, since we thereby acknowledge and confess that it is Himself who has glorified the Saints by the power of His Sacrifice; yet more, this petition conduces to the praise of the Saints, who, by the grace of the Sacrifice of Christ, have offered themselves for Christ and, consequently, now reign with Him and are our intercessors.[1] Thus, while the celebration of Mass covers the Saints of heaven with honor and glory, it confers on us men, in need of assistance, every spiritual advantage.[2]

ARTICLE THE THIRD.

What Place the Eucharistic Sacrifice Holds in the Organization of the Church; Its Meaning There and Purport.

23. The Holy Sacrifice of the Mass—The Centre of Catholic Worship.

It yet remains for us to explain at least briefly the central position and fundamental signification pertaining to the Holy Sacrifice of the Mass in the Catholic Church, instituted for the salvation of souls.[3] Thence it will be seen that it is of vital importance for the very life and operation of the Church.

1. The Catholic Church is the great institute of salvation, founded by Christ for the entire world and for all time: as such she has the sublime mission and task to continue and accomplish throughout all ages the work of Christ's redemption by the conversion and salvation of all nations. God wills that all men by means of the Church and in the Church should receive heavenly light and life, and come to the knowledge of the truth and be saved (I Tim. 2, 4.). For this purpose the Lord is and remains with His Church; in her He lives and acts all days until the end of the world. In sacramental truth and reality the God-man continues always His mediatorship on earth by the ministry of His Church. As He redeemed mankind especially by the bloody Sacrifice of the Cross, so He carries out the work of redemption in His Church chiefly by the unbloody Sacrifice of the Altar, since it is the essential representation and mystical

---

[1] Cf. Augsburger Pastoralblatt 1876, p. 277.

[2] Illis proficiat ad honorem, nobis autem ad salutem; quod pro illius gloria celebramus, nobis prosit ad veniam; quae pro illius celebrata sunt gloria, nobis proficiat ad medelam etc.

[3] Tolle hoc sacramentum de Ecclesia, et quid erit in mundo nisi error et infidelitas? Sed per hoc sacramentum stat Ecclesia, roboratur fides, viget christiana religio et divinus cultus (S. Bonav. tr. de praepar. ad Miss. c. 1, § 1, n. 3).

renewal of the world's redeeming Sacrifice of the Cross. This the Church concisely and appropriately expresses, when it says of the Mass: *Quoties hujus hostiae commemoratio celebratur, opus nostrae redemptionis exercetur,*[1]—that is, as often as this memorial Sacrifice is celebrated, the work of the redemption is performed. These simple words not merely express that by the Eucharistic Sacrifice the fruits of the Sacrifice of the Cross are bestowed on men in regard to the redemption taken subjectively, but they also declare that all the features of the work of the redemption, taken in its objective sense, are mystically renewed and represented on the altar.[2] All this is done already by the mere accomplishment of the Sacrifice at the consecration, but still more strikingly in the ecclesiastical rite which accompanies the sacrificial action, that is, in the liturgical celebration of Mass. From a twofold aspect, the Mass represents the entire work of redemption; for in the Eucharistic service the three offices, as well as the different mysteries of Christ are represented.

a) Christ redeemed the world, as Supreme Teacher inasmuch He announced the truths of faith; as Highpriest, inasmuch as He established peace between heaven and earth and regained for us the gifts of grace; as Divine King, inasmuch as He founded a kingdom which, although in this world, is not of this world — a supernatural kingdom of truth, of grace and of love, wherein He reigns over hearts. Christ continues to exercise His office of teacher, of priest and of shepherd over the whole world in the Holy Sacrifice of the Mass. As in the earthly life of Christ, so likewise in the Eucharistic Sacrifice, the sacerdotal operation of the Lord holds the prominent place; for the radiant central and culminating portion of the Mass lies in the the Canon, in the course of which the real sacrificial act is accomplished, which secures for us reconciliation and mercy. — Before our Saviour died in sacrifice on the Cross, He taught the divine truth by word and deed; corresponding to this in the Holy Sacrifice of the Mass, the oblation—His mystical death—is preceded by a preparation or an interior service, in which the prophetic-teaching of Christ is represented and repeated, that we may be filled with the light and wisdom of faith. "For the ministry of Jesus Christ continues to live throughout all time, and in the Holy Sacrifice of the Mass moves around the earth to serve ignorant and erring humanity. In the Holy Sacrifice, wherein Christ appears as the victim which upon the altar of the cross allowed itself to be consumed by the torments of death, is seen here also as the Heavenly Teacher of men. As victim, He is veiled under the material appearances of bread and wine. His voice is concealed and yet ever present by the voice of His messengers in Holy Scripture: in the Epistles and the

---

[1] Orat. secret. Dom. IX. post Pent.—Dicitur exerceri, non tantum secundum *repraesentationem,* sed etiam secundum *efficaciam,* quia nobis applicatur (Suarez in S. Thom. 3, q. 83, a. 1.)

[2] In celebratione hujus mysterii attenditur *repraesentatio* dominicae passionis et participatio fructus ejus (S. Thom. 3, q. 83, a. 2).

7

Gospels'' (Eberhard). And, finally, as the Saviour by His sacrificial death entered into glory, as He established by means of the Cross His supernatural kingdom and eternal dominion, thus the act of Consecration or Sacrifice in the Mass is followed by Holy Communion, as the completion and conclusion of the Holy Mass, and, by means of Holy Communion, Christ as a meek king takes possession of our hearts, and as Prince of Peace extends and consolidates the kingdom of God, the dominion of grace and love in our souls.

b) The work of redemption considered historically, namely, in its gracious beginning, in its blessed progress and in its glorious completion, is also in this aspect represented in the Eucharistic Sacrifice, for it is a living memorial of all the wonders and mysteries which the redeeming love of the triune God wrought for the salvation of man. *Memoriam fecit mirabilium suorum, misericors et miserator Dominus; escam dedit timentibus se* (Ps. 110, 4—5). The joyful, sorrowful and glorious mysteries of the Incarnation, life, death and glory of the Saviour of the world are placed before the eyes of faith in the celebration of Mass. To the presence of the Lord on the altar in the unbloody Sacrifice of the Mass, the words of the prophet may be applied: *Ecce Salvator tuus venit: ecce merces ejus cum eo, et opus ejus coram illo.* — "Behold thy Saviour cometh: behold His reward is with Him, and His work before Him" (Isa. 62, 11). Yes, the God-Man comes on the altar to sacrifice Himself for us; but where He is present, there also appears the work and the price of the redemption accomplished by Him;—with Him both are inseparably united.

In the Mass, first of all, Christ's painful and bloody death on the Cross is celebrated and represented. Now, as in Christ's sacrificial death on the Cross all the other mysteries of redemption partly culminate and partly have their root, so must they also meet and come together in the unbloody Sacrifice of the Altar, since it is the living and real representation of the bloody Sacrifice of the Cross.[1] By the separate consecration of bread and wine, Christ's Body and Blood are offered under the symbol of death; therefore, the altar becomes Mount Calvary, the Cross saturated with His Blood.

The wonders of the Incarnation,—of Bethlehem—are likewise repeated: the altar becomes the crib, the Infant Jesus lies concealed therein in the humble little Host.

Nor is less renewed in mysterious reality upon the altar all that transpired of the life of Christ, from Bethlehem to Golgatha. In the intervening period "three and thirty years of the Lord's earthly pilgrimage elapsed, such years as had never before been seen on earth, years that shone out in brighter light, resplendent with grace and benediction, truth and mercy, crowned by the presence, the dwelling and journeyings of the Son of God here below" (Eberhard).

---

[1] Missae sacrificium est expressa quaedam et viva imago passionis Christi et consequenter incarnationis et aliorum Christi mysteriorum, quibus nihil altius et excellentius operatus est Deus (Suarez disp. 76, sect. 2).

This silent, humble, hidden, obedient, adorable life of prayer and sacrifice is continued by the Saviour until the end of time under the veil of the Eucharistic species for the honor of God and the welfare of man. Finally, the Eucharistic Sacrifice is also a memorial of the glory of the Lord — of His Resurrection and Ascension.[1] As the risen, transfigured Saviour appeared unto His own, saying confidently to them : "Peace be to you ; it is I, fear not," so He now is and remains with us, near us and in our midst in His concealed glory and with His painless wounds, to console, to rejoice, to bless and to protect us.

We thus behold in the Eucharistic Sacrifice not only the glorious crown of the great work of redemption, but we have also there the summary and renewal of those adorable mysteries of profound annihilation and supreme glory, which Christ once accomplished upon earth for the love of us and for our redemption. In a manner as simple as it is grand, the celebration of Mass places before the eyes of the faithful the way in which our Lord descended from the heights of heaven to visit us, through the mercies of our God (Luke 1, 78); how He did not abhor the Virgin's womb (*non horruisti Virginis uterum—Te Deum*) and the hard manger (*praesepe non abhorruit— Hymn. Eccl.*); how as a giant He entered with joy and hastened with exultation through the thorny career of our redemption (Ps. 18, 6); how He dwelt and walked among men under the humble appearance of a servant, teaching, healing, doing good, bestowing blessings; how He, finally, descended to the lowest depths of sorrow and disgrace, and from the shadows of the tomb raised Himself to the brightest glory of heaven.

These holy mysteries, contained as in their germ in the Eucharistic Sacrifice, are fully developed and beautifully shown forth in the sacrificial rite of the Church; for in the course of the year the formulas of the Mass, alternating in due order, severally place before us and prominently represent in turn the mysteries of the great redemption. The Eucharistic Sacrifice is most intimately connected with the celebration of the ecclesiastical year; for the Holy Sacrifice finds therein its full illustration. The cycle of feast-days and holy seasons casts its refulgence and its shadows upon the altar: the silent longing and joyful anticipations of Advent, the heartfelt blessedness and the delicious peace of soul of the lovely Christmas night, the serious penitential spirit and the sentiments of bitter regret of Lent, the unspeakable sorrows and the gloom and mourning of Holy Week, the cheering glory and the Alleluias of Eastertide, the joy and supernal happiness of the grace of the Octave of Pentecost find in

---

[1] Resurrectio et ascensio Domini eo ipso commemoratur, quod Christus sub speciebus panis et vini praesens est immortalis et gloriosus, prouti est post resurrectionem et ascensionem : ideoque in oratione post consecrationem dicitur, Missae sacrificium offerri in memoriam passionis, nec non ab inferis resurrectionis, sed et in coelos gloriosae ascensionis Domini nostri Jesu Christi (Müller, Theol. moral., l. 3, tit. 1, § 15, n. 11).

the liturgical celebration of Mass appropriate and touching expression. At the altar our ears are greeted at one time with the sound of doleful lamentation, at another, with the tones of joy and praise; we there behold the priest now in the color of love or of hope, and again in that of joy or of sorrow.

2. The work of redemption accomplished by Christ on the Cross is always included in a lively manner and mystically represented in the Eucharistic Sacrifice, in order to render due honor and worship to God, as well as to apply to man all the benefits and blessings of redemption. From this it follows that the Eucharistic Sacrifice must be the centre, the heart and soul of the entire liturgy, that is, of divine worship and the dispensing of grace. The principal object of the liturgical activity and efficiency of the Church consists in rendering to God in the highest all honor, adoration and glory, and to obtain for man on earth reconciliation, remission of sin and sanctification. In the liturgy praise and thanksgiving ascend to Heaven, blessing and grace descend upon earth; in the liturgy man elevates himself to God and God descends to men. The liturgy daily procures and maintains the supernatural relation, the reciprocal intercourse, the mystical communion of life and love between Heaven and earth, between God and men. This aforesaid object is most perfectly attained by the celebration of Mass,—which excels and eclipses all other acts of worship.[1] These acts are numerous and manifold; for in her liturgical worship the Church has always bestowed her heavenly treasures of grace, in form more beautiful and with a hand more lavish and has exteriorly revealed more fully and universally her interior plenitude of life. In the beauty and splendor of her liturgy, she appears as that new and heavenly Jerusalem, which the Evangelist St. John saw descending from Heaven as a bride richly adorned (Apoc. 21, 2); therein she appears as the spouse of the King, betrothed to the Lord (2 Cor. 11, 2), standing at the right hand of the King, in garments of gold, clothed round about with variety of splendor (Ps. 44, 10—14): yet the most brilliant diadem and the most precious jewel of her rich, her divine bridal attire is the exalted and elevating sacrifice of the altar.—It forms not merely the crown of her liturgy; but is also, in a certain sense, its vivifying root and noble stock. Catholic worship possesses, so to speak, the Eucharistic stamp, the Eucharistic color and the Eucharistic perfume, since all acts of worship are referred proximately or remotely to the Eucharistic Sacrifice, or are joined to it, drawing thence fresh life, power of attraction and consecration. Without the Sacrifice this noble worship would be impoverished and stunted, would fade and die away, as is evident from non-Catholic denominations. This unrivalled supremacy the Eucharistic Sacrifice

---

[1] In the liturgy the Eucharistic and Communion service are often designated by the words veneranda, sacrosancta *commercia*—and the Incarnation as admirabile *commercium*, to signify that by both these mysteries a real commerce and exchange is negotiated between Heaven and earth, between God and men. Cf. Secret. in Nativ. Dom. et in Domin. XVIII. post Pent.

obtains throughout the entire sphere of religious worship. To show this more in detail let us, in the first place, consider the divine service, that is, those acts of divine worship which relate principally to the honor of God; and secondly, the dispensation of grace, that is, those acts of worship which directly and chiefly relate to the sanctification of man.

a) The celebration of Holy Mass is the most worthy and the most perfect divine service; for it procures to the Most High a worship and a veneration which millions of worlds would be incapable of rendering Him.[1] The Eucharistic Sacrifice is of itself the most glorious chant to the the praise and glory of the triune God. It is the summary of divine worship; for it is our highest adoration and best thanksgiving, our most efficacious propitiation and most powerful petition. The duty of praising God, of thanking Him, of rendering Him due honor and satisfaction, and of petitioning Him, can and must be complied with also by prayer; but how naked, poor and deficient would be this divine service, if we had not the Sacrifice of the Altar, whereby the name of the Lord is magnified and glorified among all nations! (Mal. i, 11.) This unique Sacrifice infinitely excels in value and dignity, in power and efficacy all the many prayers of the Church and of the faithful. — Christ offers Himself on the altar by our hands and we should, as intimately united with Him as the branches are with the vine, enter wholly into His sentiments, and unite ourselves to His Sacrifice. It is only by such a union that our praise, thanksgiving, petition and atonement become meritorious and pleasing in the sight of God. The ivy-vine left to itself can but creep on the ground and must miserably decay; but if planted near a tree, it finds a support, it clings to it and climbs upwards. In like manner our divine worship would be of itself very weak and imperfect, and would hardly rise above the dust of the earth; but when in union with the worship of the Sacrifice of Christ it ascends even to Heaven. At the celebration of Mass, we say: "Behold, O Heavenly Father, to Thee we owe infinite praise on account of Thy infinite majesty; because of Thy numberless graces and benefits, we owe infinite thanks; for the innumerable offences we have committed against Thee, we owe infinite atonement; and because of our manifold needs and dangers, we owe the tribute of our humble supplication; but all our acts of praise, of thanksgiving, of atonement and of supplication, how miserable are they not, and how unworthy to be offered to Thee! Still we unite them to the Sacrifice of praise, thanksgiving, propitiation and peti-

---

[1] Alia institutionis hujus sacramenti causa est quotidiana et jugis honoratio et glorificatio Dei Patris, imo totius superbeatissimae Trinitatis, quia in hujus sacramenti celebratione ac sumptione magnalia et beneficia Dei recoluntur, gratiarum actio Deo offertur, bonitas et majestas Omnipotentis laudatur et multiplex honor Altissimo quotidie exhibetur: imo per hujus sacramenti celebrationem ac sumptionem cultus christianae religionis praecipue conservatur, fideles ad ecclesiam conveniunt, confitentur, coadunantur. Estque sacramentum hoc *incomparabile et pretiosissimum Ecclesiae militantis clenodium* (Dion. Carthus. De vita Curator. art. 15).

tion of Thy Son Jesus Christ, infinitely pleasing to Thee, with which
we offer them to Thee, imploring Thee that for His sake Thou wilt
graciously accept this our unworthy homage, with all that we are
and have, and be merciful and favorable to us!" [1]

Since in the Eucharistic Sacrifice the divine history of the
Redeemer and of His redemption are mystically represented, the
Holy Mass, too, takes precedence in the ecclesiastical festivals. What
the sun in the heavens is to all nature, shedding light and imparting
warmth, the Eucharistic Sacrifice is in the house of God, beautifying
and adorning its every feast with celestial splendor. Wherefore the
Church of Christ celebrates the mysteries of grace by the Eucharistic
Sacrifice, unto which the faithful unite their acts of adoration, praise,
thanksgiving, petition, love and admiration. We likewise celebrate
the mysteries, the privileges, the graces, the virtues, the glories,
the power and goodness of the Virgin Mother of God by the Holy
Sacrifice of the Mass. In what way do we most worthily celebrate
the annual commemoration of the Saints? By offering the Eucharistic Sacrifice in order to praise and thank God, because He is
wonderful in His Saints, because He has adorned them with the
greatest diversity of graces, virtues and miracles, crowned them
with honor and glory, and given them to us as bright models and
powerful patrons. Thus the Eucharistic Sacrifice, like a gold ring,
moves around the liturgical cycle of the holy feasts and seasons. On
the most pleasant of all feasts, namely on Christmas, "when the
heavens are overflowing with honey, and true joy hath come to us
from on high," the Church permits her priests to celebrate three
Masses, in order to express more perfectly her exceeding exultation
over "this day of the new redemption of the ancient reconciliation
and eternal bliss." [2] — On sorrowful Good Friday, on the contrary,
when the Church with deepest compassion is entirely absorbed in
her meditation and contemplation of the Cross and of her Divine
Spouse, dying in torments for the sins of the world — on this great
day of mourning, the Church, so to speak, forgets what is dearest
and most precious to her, namely, the joy and consolation of the

---

[1]   Martin, Das christliche Leben p. 275.

[2]   In die Nativitatis plures Missae celebrantur propter triplicem Christi nativitatem. Quarum una est *aeterna*, quae quantum ad nos est occulta, et ideo, una
Missa cantatur in nocte, in cujus Introitu dicitur: "Dominus dixit ad me! Filius
meus es tu — ego hodie genui te." — Alia est *temporalis*, sed *spiritualis*, qua sc.
Christus oritur tanquam lucifer in cordibus (2 Petr. 1, 19) et propter hoc cantatur
Missa in aurora, in cujus Introitu dicitur: "Lux fulgebit hodie super nos."—Tertia
est nativitas Christi *temporalis* et *corporalis*, secundum quam visibilis nobis processit ex utero virginali carne indutus et ob hoc cantatur tertia Missa in clara luce, in
cujus Introitu dicitur: "Puer natus est nobis."—Licet e converso posset dici quod
nativitas aeterna secundum se est in plena luce et ob hoc in Evangelio tertiae
Missae fit mentio de nativitate aeterna.—Secundum autem nativitatem corporalem
ad litteram natus est de nocte in signum quod veniebat ad tenebras infirmitatis
nostrae, unde et in Missa nocturna dicitur Evangelium de corporali Christi nativitate (S. Thom. 3, q. 83, a. 2 ad 2).

Holy Sacrifice, denying herself the chalice of refreshment and salvation in view of the bitter cup of sorrow which her Divine Spouse drank upon Golgotha.[1]

Finally, all that the faithful do for and give to His service, is referred principally to the worthy celebration of the Eucharistic Sacrifice. For what purpose are all those magnificent churches and altars built, dedicated and furnished with every imaginable adornment that art and nature can produce? Principally for the celebration of Holy Mass. For what purpose are the gold and silver sacred vessels and the magnificent vestments? Chiefly for the celebration of the Mass. For what purpose the lights that burn on the altar, the flowers that exhale their perfume, the clouds of incense that fill the sanctuary — for what else than to honor and to place before our eyes the majesty of the Eucharistic Sacrifice?

It must not be forgotten, in fine, that the Eucharistic Sacrifice is an inexhaustible source of holy thoughts and pious emotions — always refreshing, comforting and quickening both mind and heart.[2]

---

[1] In hoc sacramento recolitur passio Christi, secundum quod ejus effectus ad fideles derivatur, sed tempore passionis recolitur passio Christi secundum hoc quod in ipso capite nostro fuit perfecta, quod quidem factum est semel, quotidie autem fructum dominicae passionis fideles percipiunt, et ideo illa commemoratio fit semel in anno, haec autem quotidie et propter fructum et propter jugem memoriam. . . Veniente veritate cessat figura. Hoc autem sacramentum est figura quaedam et exemplum dominicae passionis. Et ideo in die quo ipsa passio Domini recolitur, prout realiter gesta est, non celebratur consecratio hujus sacramenti. Ne tamen Ecclesia ea etiam die sit sine fructu passionis per hoc sacramentum nobis exhibito, corpus Christi consecratum die praecedenti reservatur sumendum illo die, non autem sanguis propter periculum, et quia sanguis specialius est imago dominicae passionis. Nec verum est quod quidam dicunt, quod per immisionem particulae corporis Christi in vinum convertatur vinum in sanguinem. Hoc enim aliter fieri non potest quam per consecrationem factam sub debita forma verborum (S. Thom. 3, q. 83, a. 2 ad 1—2).

[2] Hoc Ecclesiae sacramentum, quoniam assidua sui repraesentatione memoriam innovat, fidem auget, spem roborat, charitatem confirmat, non superfluum, sed valde necessarium est. . . . Solvit quidem et plene tollit peccata mundi Agnus Dei in cruce immolatus; nec tamen idcirco, ut dixi, superfluus est in altari oblatus. Et ut in teipso hoc dicas, adverte quicumque haec legis, teque ipsum interroga, quando magis movearis, si tamen quod profiteris firmiter credis, utrum quando dicitur: Christus olim inter homines apparuit; an quando dicitur: Christus nunc inter homines conversatur; quando dicitur: Olim in cruce pependit; an quando dicitur: Nunc in altari offertur: utrum, inquam, te magis moveat et ad admirandum et amandum accendat ejus praedicata absentia quam *demonstrata praesentia?* Sed scio quia non diffiteris, quod verum est, magis humana corda moveri praesentibus quam absentibus rebus. . . . Movetur igitur magis ad praesentem quam ad absentem, movetur magis ad visum quam ad auditum Christum, movetur ad admirandum, movetur ad amandum, quo amore amanti generatur remissio peccatorum. . . Non est ergo superfluum Christi corporis et sanguinis sacramentum, quo vivacior memoria excitatur, quo ferventior dilectio provocatur, quo plenior peccatorum remissio comparatur. Non est superfluum, quia non tantum per id quod Deus est, sed etiam per id quod homo est, nobiscum est usque ad consummationem saeculi (Petrus Venerab. Tractatus contra Petrobrusianos [Migne tom. 189, p. 813]).

At the altar all the rays of heavenly truth and grace meet as in a focus: who is there that can approach this glowing hearth, without being inflamed with ardent devotion and fervent love of God ? The altar on which the God-Man day after day offers Himself before our eyes and by our hands, is the holy hearth where faith, hope and love are enkindled and inflamed, where the spirit of prayer in enlivened and devotion is aroused and ascends to Heaven itself. "The fire on the altar shall always burn," God said in the Old Law (Lev. 6, 12). But in reality it is upon our altars that God has enkindled a fire that shall never be extinguished. All the mysteries and truths hidden in the Sacrifice of the Mass and which appeal to the heart with a wonderful force from the altar, call forth the spirit and words of prayer. Is it difficult to raise ourselves in thought to Heaven, to lift our mind to God, although the earth as a leaden weight ever drags us downward, when in the Mass Heaven descends to us, when our God and Redeemer stands before us, humbly veiled under the appearances of bread and wine? Christ descends under the mean appearances of material food, with which our thoughts and cares are concerned, that silently and gently He may wean us from those thoughts and cares, and raise our hearts heavenward. We are in a wonderland of mysteries, where under the shadow of foreign appearances the Manna of life eternal grows and the waters of salvation rush along. Our Lord and Saviour is there awaiting the tribute of our adoration. Behold! the Church raises aloft the Cross of the Redeemer, crying unto us: "You are poor sinners, altogether destitute of honor before God," and she points out to us the avenging hand of justice raised above our life and our sins. Then we strike our breast; our conscience awakes, accuses and convicts us, so that we exclaim: Through my fault! And we bow our head under the weight of the reproaches and accusations of our thoughts. But we do not sink into the abyss of despair. The night, through the mercy of God, has become light. For "Peace to men of good will" the angels sang; and over the Cross this peace embraced impending justice and disarmed it. We have before us Christ's Body and Blood, which prove to us the great love of God and wrest from our hearts a thanksgiving full of joy.[1] As our Saviour has given us the most encouraging assurance in the words: "If you ask the Father anything in My name, He will give it to you" (John 16, 23), our courage must then be boundless, when we hold in our hands Christ, the well-beloved Son Himself, when we pray to Him and He Himself prays for us. Then our gaze falls upon the great community of those who are united with us at the sacred family table of Jesus Christ, upon His holy Church, upon our brothers and sisters gone

---

[1] Vere dignum et justum est. . . . tibi debitam servitutem per ministerii hujus impletionem (Sacrificial celebration) persolvere, quia non solum peccantibus veniam tribuis, sed etiam praemia petentibus impertiris. Et quod perpeti malis operibus promeremur, magnifica pietate depellis, ut nos ad tuae reverentiae cultum et terrore cogas et amore perducas (Sacrament. Gregor).

before us and detained in the purification and expiation of purgatory, upon all for whom Christ died. Our heart, enlarged to embrace them all in view of the love of Christ, includes them in our prayers. Thus naturally prayers crowd each other within us and on our lips. Prayer finds forcible expression in the numerous ceremonies performed by the priest: in bowing, kissing the altar, in the sign of the Cross, in genuflecting and in many other symbolical actions. The Church would do violence to herself and act contrary to the current of her feelings, if she did not thus in a variety of ways reveal the spirit of prayer. Who would not be moved on beholding in the spirit of faith our wounded Saviour stretched on the hard wood of the Cross, His body bruised and torn, His blood poured out, and all the love blazing out from His wounds? Hence it is not surprising if these lively sentiments burst forth into unceasing prayers and into a multitude of ceremonies surrounding the Holy Sacrifice, down even to the color of the sacerdotal vestments. These are not mere empty forms, they are whole-souled customs, in which the ever youthful and fresh emotions of our Church find expression. These noble and holy sentiments manifest themselves in the ancient prayers and chants woven into the Rite of the Mass: in prayers which for their sublime simplicity cannot be surpassed, in choral singing, which resounds through the halls of the Church as melodies from a better world. They are prayers and chants that bloom in an eternal youth, ever full of the vigor of life, ever attractive as does all that emanates from the mind of the highly gifted human soul when filled with God.[1]

b) Among the ordinances for the dispensation of grace which principally and immediately relate to the sanctification of man, the Holy Sacrifice of the Mass holds, in many respects, the most prominent place. This is based on the relation which the Sacrifice of the Mass bears to the Sacrifice of the Cross. The Sacrifice of the Cross is the original source of all grace; for from the Sacrifice of the Cross all the blessings of redemption proceed and all the means of grace draw their virtue and efficacy. Now, in the Sacrifice of the Mass the inexhaustible source of grace and salvation of the Sacrifice of the Cross is transferred from the past to the present, from a distance it is brought nearest to us. For this reason and under this aspect, the Eucharistic Sacrifice can, in a certain sense, be designated as the source of the grace-giving sacraments and sacramentals. [2]

---

[1] Cf. Eberhard, Kanzelvorträge 1, 369 etc.

[2] Missae sacrificium non quidem uti sacramenta, immediate institutum est ut gratiam ex opere operato conferat, sed fontem constituit unde sacramenta vim suam hauriunt, et thesaurum bonorum, quibus miseriae fidelium ex omni parte subvenitur: hic obtinent peccatores gratiam sese disponendi ad conversionem, hic succurritur insufficientiae adorationis et gratiarum actionis quas Deo offerimus, hic satisfit pro peccatis, hic impetrantur quaecunque bona sive temporalia sive spiritualia. Atque idcirco, quemadmodum sacrificium crucis est opus salutis nostrae consummativum et prima origo omnis santitatis et justitiae, ita sacrificium Missae est praecipuum medium meritorum crucis applicativum et proinde totius oeconomiae gratiae centrum (Lambrecht, De ss. Missae sacrificio p. 5, c. 1, § 4).

If we consider the Sacrifice of the Mass chiefly as a means of grace,[1] it is inferior, indeed, to the Sacraments, inasmuch as it cannot, as they do, directly efface sin and impart sanctifying grace; but in other respects the Sacrifice excels them, since by the Sacraments only certain graces and those merely for the recipient are obtained, while the Mass can obtain directly or at least indirectly all divine graces and blessings, and those not only for the one who celebrates, but also for others, in whose behalf it is celebrated.[2] Consequently, the efficacy of the Mass is more universal and comprehensive than that of the Sacraments. The Eucharistic Sacrifice is truly a means of salvation; for it has great power to avert all evil from us and to procure for us all goods, all kinds of benefits and blessings. The Mass reconciles God's justice and leads us to the treasury of graces, by which we are disposed worthily to receive the Sacraments and to obtain sacramental graces. In this manner the Eucharistic Sacrifice tends to the possession, increase and preservation of sacramental grace; but in how far has it its origin in the Holy Sacrifice?

The chief blessing of grace is contained in the holy Sacraments. The Sacraments are "stars that light up the firmament of fallen humanity, well-springs in the desert of the pilgrimage of life, miracles of the love of God, mercies of Jesus Christ." They obtain those graces which correspond to and relieve the general constant necessities of Christian life. Their efficacy consists essentially in removing the curse of sin and in infusing into the soul the grace of sanctification. They were instituted by Jesus Christ to produce and awaken, to preserve and strengthen, to heal and restore, to increase and perfect the higher, supernatural life of the soul, that mystical life of grace of the children of God. The Sacrifice of the Cross is the primary source, which, at the altar in the Mass, gushes forth anew day by day, to re-fill continually the channels of the Sacraments which bring to us the saving waters of redemption. Inasmuch as on the altar the same Sacrifice is offered as was offered on the Cross, we may designate the Mass also as the Sacrificial source whence flow the Sacramental streams of grace and salvation.[3] Or the Mass may be regarded as a daily rising sun of grace, whose pure, white rays of light are refracted sevenfold in the Sacraments, and thus form

---

[1] Alia causa institutionis Eucharistiae est copiosa et multiplex et misercordissima subventio indigentiae nostrae. Hujus quippe dignissimi celebratio ac sumptio sacramenti est nobis quotidianum contra quotidiana nostra peccata remedium, infirmitatis ac fragilitatis nostrae praesidium ac munimen, paupertatis nostrae ditatio, passionum dejectio, expugnatio vitiorum, confirmatio et auctio gratiarum: imo ineffabiles utilitates ex hoc sacramento nostris proveniunt animabus (Dion. Carthus. De vita Curator., art. 15).

[2] Suarez disp. 76, sect. 3, n. 4.

[3] Vere ac necessario (Eucharistia) *fons* omnium gratiarum dicenda est, cum fontem ipsum coelestium charismatum et donorum, omniumque sacramentorum auctorem, Christum Dominum, admirabili modo in se contineat, a quo, tanquam a fonte, ad alia sacramenta, quidquid, boni et perfectionis habent, derivatur (Catech. Rom. p. 2, cap. 4, q. 40, n. 2).

the golden peace-bow which connect the riches of Heaven with the poverty of the earth. — The relation of the Sacraments to the Sacrifice of Christ is mystically indicated, inasmuch as from the pierced Heart of the Saviour on the Cross flowed forth a stream of water and of blood. The water flowing from the side of Christ symbolizes the water of baptism, which cleanses from sin; the stream of blood refers to the blood of Christ, wherewith the soul in the Sacrament of the Altar is nourished and strengthened unto life eternal. In these two Sacraments the others are comprised, since Baptism is the beginning, the Eucharist the term and consummation of them all. Hence by the flow of blood and water from the Heart of the Crucified is mystically indicated that the Sacraments draw their power from the sacrificial death of Christ on the Cross, and consequently, also from the renewal of this sacrificial death on the altar in the Mass.

The Sacramentals are also means of salvation, but in a weaker sense and in an essentially different manner from the Sacraments. The Sacramentals have been instituted by the Church. As the divine institution of salvation, the Church has received from Christ the mission and the power to impart in full measure not merely to man, but also to nature the blessings of redemption, and to make all things new. We know that in consequence of sin the entire creation is in mourning and misery, enslaved and liable to perish — and, therefore, longs to be freed from the thraldom of corruption and, along with the children of God, to be glorified in liberty (Rom. 8, 19). This final renovation and transformation of all creation is begun, or anticipated, by the use of the Sacramentals, which are destined to remove as far as possible the consequences and misery of sin, not merely among men, but throughout the domain of created nature; for this also pertains to perfect redemption, and, therefore, belongs to the effacing of the guilt of sin and to the interior sanctification, which is effected by the Sacraments. Through the merits and intercession of the Church, the Sacramentals acquire a special power to remove the curse of sin, to destroy the dominion of Satan or to render it harmless, to free from manifold wants, to impart temporal welfare and blessings, to obtain for us the divine protection and assistance, to dedicate and sanctify persons and objects destined to the service of God.

The Sacramentals are divided into exorcisms, blessings and consecrations; their salutary effects extend to mankind and to the work of their hands, as well as to objects of nature. The Church employs her exorcisms over man and irrational creatures, to expel from them the influence of the evil spirit who by sin has obtained power to injure and ruin us and our belongings. Man and objects in nature withdrawn from evil influence are then dedicated and sanctified for the service of the Lord. The blessings obtain for man both spiritually and corporally and for all that belongs to him or serves to his use, the divine protection against evil and the divine favor for all that is good and salutary. — The Church blesses and consecrates to God not alone persons, but also inanimate things: thus she blesses or dedicates, or consecrates churches, cemeteries, altars and bells, crosses and pictures, candles and incense, water and oil, the vessels and articles for Holy Mass, the vestments of the priest, candles for the feast of the Purification, the ashes of Lent, the palms of Holy Week, etc. She blesses what is necessary for the support of the body: food and medicine, cattle and the fruits of the field; as well as the requirements of human society: weapons and tools, houses and ships, bridges and streets. In brief — there is scarcely an important requisite of the natural and supernatural life to which the Church denies the protection and blessing of her Sacramentals.[1] Like the Sacraments the Sacramentals are also connected with the Eucharistic Sacrifice and source of blessings, from which they, in a certain sense, draw their salutary efficacy; for on the altar in the Holy Mass that stream of blood and water from Golgotha continues to flow, in whose flood the earth, the sea, the starry firmament, in a word, the universe is cleansed, that is, touched with the blessing of Redemption and led on to its future transformation: *Unda manat et cruor: terra, pontus, astra, mundus quo lavantur flumine!* (Hymn. Eccl.).

Therefore, while Christ's Sacrifice is the fountain-head of all the blessings of redemption, the Sacraments and Sacramentals should be regarded as brooks and rivulets which convey to all who are well disposed the inexhaustible blessings of that Sacrifice. This connection of the sacramental means of salvation with the Holy Mass is expressed and sanctioned in various ways in the liturgy of the Church. At the ordination of priests, the Church says: *Sacerdotem oportet offerre, benedicere, baptizare* . . . — "It behooves the priest to offer Sacrifice, to bless, to baptize . . . ," and at the consecration of bishops, she says: *Episcopum oportet . . . consecrare, offerre . . .* — "It behooves the bishop to consecrate, to offer sacrifice."[2] Here the power of offering sacrifice is placed in the closest relation with the power of blessing and consecrating. The administration of the Sacraments and the Sacramentals is intrusted to the same persons (priests and bishops), who are called and authorized to offer the Eucharistic Sacrifice; for the power of administering the Sacraments and the Sacramentals has, so to speak, its source in the higher and more eminent power of celebrating Mass. Because priests and bishops offer sacrifice, they can and may in the name of Christ and of the Church dispense graces and blessings: the power of blessing is, so to speak, the outcome and extension of the power of offering sacrifice, an accessory to the divine service.—The connection of the sacramental graces and the means of grace with the Eucharistic Sacrifice is, moreover indicated by the fact that many liturgical formulas of blessing are inserted in the Missal, — and still more so and especially by the regulation of the Church requiring that the

---

[1] Cf. Laurent, Christolog. Predigten 11, 100—103.

[2] Pontif. Roman.

administration of the Sacraments and Sacramentals should take place, as much as possible, in connection with the Mass. Thus the Sacrament of the Altar is consummated and prepared during the celebration of Mass and should also, as much as possible, be then received and administered.[1] Minor Orders and especially the holy Orders are conferred on clerics at the altar and during the celebration of Mass. In connection with the Mass the material of many Sacraments is blessed ; — thus baptismal water on Holy Saturday and on the eve of Pentecost, the holy oils on Holy Thursday.[2] Immediately before Mass the blessing of the candles, of the ashes and palms takes place. The coronation of the Pope, the clothing and profession of religious persons, the annointing of kings, the consecration of churches and altars are rites and ceremonies most closely connected with the celebration of Mass.—In the Eucharistic Sacrifice originates also the sacredness and sublime dignity of the Catholic priesthood, which imprints on the soul at ordination the ineffaceable sacerdotal character. The grades by which the ministers of the Church step by step ascend to the highest, that is, to the episcopal dignity, are chiefly distinguished according to the power concerning the Sacrifice of the Mass. The first, namely, Minor Orders, empower the cleric with a more remote participation in the service of the altar ; while the sub-deaconate and deaconship have closer intercourse with the Holy Sacrifice and permit a closer assistance in its celebration. The

---

[1] The interior relation between the Sacrifice and the Sacrament of the Eucharist finds a manifold expression in the liturgy. Wherever possible the Communion is to be given *intra missam* statim post communionem sacerdotis celebrantis, and only ex rationabili causa is it to be administered *extra missam.* In the latter case the stole of the priest to be used is not always white, but it should be of the color of the actual Officium diei, that is of the color corresponding to the Mass of the day, so that at least by the color of the stole the Holy Communion may be characterized as participatio sacrificii, as the partaking of the Sacrificial Food (Rituale Romanum et S. R. C. 12. Mart. 1836). — The time of day for distributing Communion (except per modum viatici) appears to be limited to the hours when (vi *rubricae* vel *indulti*) it is permitted to celebrate Mass (ab aurora usque ad meridiem). S. R. C. 7. Sept. 1816. According to St. Alphonsus (1. 6. n. 252) the sententia communis formerly went so far as to say that the distribution of Holy Communion per se loquendo was permitted at any time of the day — except noctu et sub vesperis, i. e. in extrema diei parte.—On the feast of Christmas as the midnight Mass (post mediam noctem) Holy Communion may be distributed only in places where an Apostolic indult expressly allows it, or an existing custom sanctions it (S. R. C. 23. Mart. 1866 ; — 3. Dec. 1701 et 16. Febr. 1781). — In Holy Week from the time that the Blessed Sacrament is removed on Holy Thursday until the Communion of the High Mass on Holy Saturday the Eucharist may not be given to those who are in good health (those who are grievously ill may receive it per modum viatici). After the High Mass of Holy Saturday it may be given everywhere, but during that Mass only in such places in which the custom of receiving it prevails (consuetudo) (S. R. C. 23. Sept. 1837 et 7. Sept. 1850).

[2] The Mass in question is called in the Sacramentary of St. Gregory Missa chrismalis. As it was preceded by a Missa ad reconciliationem poenitentium and followed by a Missa serotina vel vespertina, the feria V. in Coena Domini belonged formerly to the poly-liturgical days.

priest possesses the power to change bread and wine into the Body and Blood of Christ, that is, to celebrate the Sacrifice of the New Covenant, which imparts to him an indescribably sublime dignity. Finally, the bishop is raised and exalted above the simple priest, in this that he possesses this heavenly power of sacrifice not only for himself, but also to communicate it to others, and propagate it by the sacramental ordination of priests.

3. The Eucharistic Sacrifice is, therefore, the soul or life of the entire divine worship, the sun that illumines all religious celebrations, the heart that gives pulse to all sacramental cult, the fountain-head of the whole ecclesiastical life of grace — in short, it is the centre of the Catholic liturgy. If the Catholic liturgy is a mighty stream, with its sweet salutary waters cleansing, sanctifying, vivifying, fructifying, beautifying, transforming, inundating the entire Church, all this is due to the holy fountain of the Mass, which ceases not to flow on the altar, and to diffuse the vigor of life throughout all the members of the mystical body of Christ. Every grace, every consecration, every blessing issues from the depths of the Sacrifice of Christ. Under the influence of the celestial light and supernal heat which radiate anew daily from that sun of grace, the Eucharistic Sacrifice, all creation tends towards its final consummation and eternal transfiguration.

The Sacrifice of the Mass is and remains the centre of the Christian religion, the sun of spiritual exercises, the heart of devotion and the soul of piety. Hence "that ever new, never-failing power by which the Holy Sacrifice of the Mass attracts all Catholic hearts and gathers Catholic nations around its altars. Already before the dawn of day, before the morning flush enters our churches, the bells ring out their summons to the Holy Sacrifice; and soon here and there a light appears at the window; over the crisp snow steps are hastening to the house of God, whilst the moon still looks down from heaven. 'Happy does he rise at early dawn who strives after what is good!' Everywhere the Holy Mass retains this magnetic power of attraction, whether celebrated within the marble walls of St. Peter's at Rome, in gorgeous vestments, amid thousands of brilliant lights, encompassed with the master-pieces of Christian art and adorned with its fairest festal robe of flowers and blossoms; or whether it be celebrated without pomp in a poor wooden shed, or under a canopy of branches of trees, erected by the hands of the new converts around the missionary celebrating the holy mysteries; — a striking proof that Catholics do not worship the exterior but the substance, and that it is not the charm of religious pageantry but the reality which attracts them. Who has not from childhood the sweetest and purest recollections of the celebration of the Mass, even though he witnessed it in only a poor village church! And this magnetic attraction is not of to-day, nor was it but of yesterday, nor will it perhaps to-morrow die away. It is not the fictitious power of novelty. More than fifteen centuries ago the Holy Sacrifice drew our fore-fathers around the altar with a power that overcame all the terrors of persecution, which often broke in upon the peaceful celebration of Holy Mass. Thus St. Dionysius of Alexandria, who lived in the third century, relates: 'Though hunted after and persecuted by everybody, even then we did not omit the celebration of the Holy Sacrifice. In every place, wherever we, torn from each other, bore our numerous trials, the field, the desert, the ship, the habitations of animals served us as temples for the celebration of the Holy Sacrifice.' When the storm of persecution raged throughout the whole world, the stream of grace and benediction poured from the Holy Mass celebrated in the Catacombs, or underground caverns; just as at a much later period this Holy Sacrifice, persecuted by Protestantism, took refuge in the garrets. But even in this dire extremity the attractive power of the Mass was not weakened. Catholics went down into underground dens, into the Catacombs, and climbed up under the rafters of houses, to pray for those whose hatred had driven what was most holy to them to the most wretched nooks, and who were giving themselves airs in edifices reared by Catholic piety.''[1]

What should not the Holy Sacrifice, therefore, be for us priests, and what should not we priests be for the Holy Sacrifice? The priesthood was instituted for the Eucharist. Our priestly life is made up of duties connected with it. To this end we have been chosen out of the world and separated from it. The seal of Jesus Christ is stamped upon us; the spirit and the ways of the world, and even the permissible things of the world should be for us what they are not for others. By the chisel of the Holy Ghost an invisible character has been engraved on our soul, in order that we may forever be the property of the Blessed Sacrament. What are we, and what should we be? Once only did Mary draw the Eternal Word down from heaven, whilst every day we priests draw Him down from heaven to earth. She carried Jesus in her arms until He had reached the age of boyhood, but for us He prolongs His childhood throughout our lifetime. Can we look into the face of our Mother and tell her that in this respect we are greater than she was, and not think on the sanctity that our awe-inspiring office requires of us? Oh, how happy would the long martyrdom of our spiritual life be, if we but aspired to priestly holiness! The attraction of the Eucharist should be our vocation, our ecclesiastical spirit, our joy. The fires of hell can not in all eternity burn out the sacerdotal character imprinted on our soul in ordination; but the splendors of heaven will make that sacred character shine out with so much the greater lustre.[2]

24. The Holy Sacrifice of the Mass — the School and the Source whence Catholic Life receives its Spirit of Sacrifice.

The Holy Sacrifice of the Mass is the soul and the heart of the liturgy of the Church; it is the mystical chalice which presents to

---

[1] Eberhard, Kanzelvorträge I, 317.

[2] Cf. F. Faber, The Blessed Sacrament.

our lips the sweet fruit of the passion of the God-Man — that is, grace. Hence we may conclude what influence the Mass must and will have upon true Christian life, and upon all striving after perfection. The impious world, estranged from God, seated in wickedness (1 John 5, 19), has a desolate aspect; it resembles a sterile, barren wilderness, "devoid of fruit and divested of flowers." But in the midst of this desert stands the Church like unto a blooming, fruitful oasis, like a paradise of God, wherein dwell joy and gladness, thanksgiving and the ringing hymn of praise (Isa. 51, 3). To the delight of God and of the angels, this garden of the Church, planted by the Lord, shines with the most beautiful and the most fragrant variety of flowers, with the abundance of heavenly blossoms and fruits. Ravishingly beautiful is this garden, where "bloom the violets of humility, the lilies of purity shine brightly, and the roses of martyrdom glow." But whence do these noble, heavenly plants draw their life's sap, their nourishment, their growth, their perfume and their bright colors? Chiefly from the Eucharistic Sacrifice and fountain of grace. The fountains of the Saviour which in the garden of the Church unceasingly flow on thousands of altars, irrigate and fructify the soil, refresh and strengthen the tender shoots, and cause the seed of virtue to blossom and ripen. If the just man flourishes like the palm and is likened unto a tree planted near the running waters, and producing fruit in due season, all this is to be attributed principally to the stream of grace issuing from the Sacrifice of the Mass. Where, on the contrary, the altar has been buried under ruins, and the Eucharistic source of grace has been obstructed, there all growth of higher virtue and heroic perfection languishes, withers and dies. — That Christ's Sacrifice, celebrated day after day, is the deep mystical source of all fulness of virtue in the Church, will appear evident, when we show that Christian perfection must be acquired and be preserved by the spirit of sacrifice — and that the supernatural, heroic spirit of sacrifice can be drawn only from the fountain of the perennial Sacrifice of the Mass.

a) Christ's doctrine and example prove that every true Christian life must be a life of perpetual sacrifice, a life of self-denial and mortification. To live in a Christian manner is to follow the teaching of Jesus — and what else is this teaching than the Word from the Cross? (1 Cor. 1, 17.) "If any man will come after Me, let him deny himself, and take up his cross daily, and follow Me" (Luke 9, 23) — in this saying the Lord included all His Commandments and encouraged us to imitate Him; for the Christian life is a copy and imitation of the life of Jesus on earth, which in its whole course from the crib to the Cross was one great, uninterrupted sacrifice. This life of sacrifice of Christ Christians must imitate and imprint on their own lives; for He has given us an example that we may follow in His footsteps (1 Peter 2, 21), and as He walked, must we also follow (1 John 2, 6), that we may be conformed to His image

(Rom. 8, 9) and bear in ourselves His heavenly likeness (1 Cor. 15, 49). — That the life of the Christian must be a life of perpetual sacrifice is evident from its very nature. The Christian life consists essentially in loving God and the neighbor. Now, this mode of life can endure, be developed and attain the mastery, only when the inordinate love of the world and of self is destroyed in our hearts, that is, unremittingly sacrificed under the immolating knife of interior and exterior mortification. This latter demands a constant renunciation in the use of earthly goods and in the enjoyment of worldly* pleasures, as well as a courageous endurance of temporal hardships and privations. In order that heavenly flames of everlasting love may burn brightly and purely and transform the life of the soul with supernatural beauty and holiness, all earthly love must be extinguished, nature prone to evil must be overcome, selfishness must be uprooted, and every worldly attachment must be sacrificed. — But this is not yet sufficient. To become perfect we must do and suffer much for God, we must by interior recollection of mind walk continually in the presence of God, in all confidence communing with Him, following as much as possible on every occasion the inspirations and suggestions of divine grace. All this is hard, very hard indeed, for the natural man; it costs combat, self-denial and exertion. It is only by dint of labor and energy that the reign of sin and sensuality is destroyed in the heart — and in its place the kingdom of grace and of the love of God is established and developed. The spirit of sacrifice is, therefore, the chief element, the touchstone of all true virtue and holiness. Self-sacrifice is absolutely necessary for solid asceticism, for the perfection of the love of God and of the neighbor. Ever true is the golden axiom: *Tantum proficies, quantum tibi vim intuleris* — "The greater the violence thou offerest to thyself, the greater the progress thou wilt make."[1] In order to ascend from a lower to a higher degree of the love of God, it is not merely sufficient to pray and to nourish devout affections, but much painstaking and self-renunciation are requisite. Whether you are a beginner in the way of purification, or have made some progress in the illuminate way, or are a proficient in the unitive way, always and everywhere you must offer in sacrifice yourself and whatever you possess; you cannot stand still for a moment on the road of self-immolation. "Lord, how often shall I resign myself, and in what things shall I leave myself?" — thus the faithful soul inquires, and the Lord replies to her that the sacrifice of self must be uninterrupted and universal: "Always and at all times; as in little things, so also in great. I make no exception, but will have thee to be found in all things divested of thyself."[2] If you would truly live as a disciple of the Crucified, you must be crucified to the world and the world must be crucified to you (Gal. 6, 14), you must die daily to the world and to yourself, your life must be a perpetual death —

---

[1] De imit. Christi l. 1, c. 25.

[2] Ibid. l. 3, c. 37.

scias pro certo, quia morientem te oportet ducere vitam.[3] "The life
of man upon earth is a warfare" — *Militia est vita hominis super
terram* (Job. 7, 1). In this Christian warfare many a hard and fearful battle must be fought against visible and invisible enemies; you
will have much to dispense with and in many things to deny yourself, much to bear and much to undergo. "Thou must be willing,
for the love of God, to suffer all things, viz., labors and sorrows,
temptations and vexations, anxieties, necessities, infirmities, injus-
tices, contradictions, censure, manifold humiliations, confusions,
corrections and contempts. These sufferings help to acquire virtue;
these prove the soldier of Christ, these prepare a heavenly crown."[1]
This combat against sensuality, pride and the concupiscence of the
eyes, against the temptations of the world and the assaults of the
devil lasts during our whole life: it is a warfare for all time — from
the beginning to the end.

b) The daily carrying of the cross, the holy hatred of self and
the Christian renunciation of the world, in short, the constant life
of sacrifice, which makes the Christian perfect and produces saints,
is something so far removed from earth, so far surpassing all natural
understanding and strength, that it is only from the heart, wounds
and sacrifice of Jesus that we can receive the light, power and
strength requisite for such a life. Such superhuman love of the
cross, such a spirit and power of sacrifice, is a plant which not corrupt nature, but only the soil of grace can produce and cause to
fructify. It needs ever to be refreshed with the dew of Heaven and
the water of life, that it may not unhappily wither and die. The
inspirations and helps of grace for constant self-sacrifice issue, therefore, principally from the altar, where Christ every day and at every
hour gives Himself up for us as an offering and a sacrifice (Eph. 5,
2). Day after day the Church offers the Body and Blood of Christ,
and in union with this Divine Sacrifice she also immolates herself;
the faithful assisting at Mass offer themselves likewise "in the spirit
of humility and with a contrite heart." This spiritual self-sacrifice
of the Church and of her children, which at the altar is made by the
will, must then be realized in life "by the burden and heat of the
day," by deeds. The Christian life is formed and developed according to the model and by the power of the Sacrifice of Christ
upon the altar. The Eucharistic Sacrifice trains and forms, gives
strength and urges to the life of sacrifice; for it is the school and the
source of the disposition and courage necessary to lead such a life.

1. The worthy celebration of Mass, as well as the devout
attendance thereat, independently of the graces to be obtained, belongs to the chief means of virtue; for the liturgy of the Mass is by
its nature calculated to impress and to move deeply all those who
take part in it with faith and attention, to excite and awaken in the
celebrant and the faithful present pious thoughts and feelings, whole-

---

[3]   Ibid. 1. 2, c. 12.
[1]   De imit. Christi l. 3, c. 35.

some affections and resolutions and acts acceptable to God of the different virtues. The Eucharistic Sacrifice is so constituted as to be a school, in which the most manifold virtues are awakened and nourished, strengthened and purified. From the altar proceeds the impulse to all striving after the higher virtues, after a life of perfection.

a) We must make progress in the way of salvation, we must grow in the knowledge and love of Jesus Christ; but where else shall we find more incitement to piety, where purer, healthier and more strengthening food of soul for a virtuous, for a religious life than in the Sacrifice of the Mass? Faith, hope and charity, humility and meekness, obedience and patience, gratitude and resignation, self-denial and renunciation, in a word — all the virtues bloom in the heavenly atmosphere which surrounds the altar during Mass. For in the Mass, our Lord mystically accomplishes, in the presence of the faithful, the entire work of redemption — offers His life of sacrifice and His sacrificial death — and He thus appears in the closest proximity to us as the brightest and the most affecting Model of all virtue and holiness. [1] Could the God-Man practise and reveal His ardent and cheerful love of sacrifice, His humility and His obedience, His love of poverty, mortification and obscurity in a more striking manner than He does in the Eucharistic Sacrifice? Our Lord once showed St. Mechtilde a large ring which surrounded Himself and her own soul; this ring contained seven precious stones, signifying the sevenfold manner in which the Lord is present in the Holy Sacrifice for our salvation. He comes, namely, upon the altar in so great humility that no one is so lowly, that the Lord will not stoop down to him, if the man only desire Him; with so much patience that there is no sinner or enemy, with whom He does not bear, and to whom He will not grant full discharge of his sins, if he only seeks to be reconciled with Him; — with such love, that no one is so cold or hardened, whose heart He will not inflame and soften, if he but will it; — with such boundless generosity, that no one is so poor whom He will not immensely enrich; as a food so sweet and so pleasant, that no one is so sick or famished as not to be invigorated and fully satiated thereby; — with such brightness, that no heart is so blinded and obscured, as not to be enlightened and purified by His presence; finally, with such plenitude of holiness and grace, that there is no one so slothful and so distracted, as not to be aroused and inspired to devotion by His love. [2]

b) The Eucharistic Sacrifice is the most glorious crown of the great work of salvation and, at the same time, the living memorial of all the mysteries of Christ. All that is mysterious and divine, majestic and sublime, affecting and moving, blissful and consoling,

---

[1] Agnoscite quod agitis. *Imitamini quod tractatis:* quatenus mortis dominicae mysterium celebrantes, mortificare membra vestra a vitiis et concupiscentiis omnibus procuretis (Pontif. Rom., De ordinatione Presbyteri).

[2] Liber specialis gratiae p. 3, cap. 18.

instructive and edifying, in religion, in the Incarnation, in the Catholic Church and her holy year, all this is combined and enclosed in the liturgy of the Mass as in a focus. Whosoever considers this devoutly in the spirit of a lively faith cannot fail to grow strong and increase in virtue and merit.

Above all, the Eucharistic Sacrifice brings vividly before the mind the passion and death of Christ, the God-Man.[1] Amidst the joys of Christmas and the triumph of Easter, Mount Calvary with its eternal seriousness remains the central point of all sacrificial celebration ; the *Confiteor* and the *Kyrie eleison* are never suppressed from the Mass by the chant of the Alleluja. Hence it follows that the faithful when hearing Mass should, above all, devoutly dwell upon and revere the passion and death of Jesus. No time is more proper for this devout meditation than the sacred time of Mass, when the Lamb of God is mystically immolated before our eyes. Assuredly it is not difficult during the celebration of Mass to place one's self beneath the Cross and embrace it ; for the vestments of the priest, the crucifix on the altar, the many signs of the Cross, the mingling of the water and wine, the separate elements of bread and wine, the elevating of the sacrificial offerings, the breaking of the Host, the different goings to and fro and movements of the celebrant at the altar, in short, the entire rite of the Mass represents the various mysteries of the passion, reminding us what numerous and bitter sufferings Christ endured for us, giving His life and dying the most cruel death for us. At every Mass place yourself in spirit at the foot of the Cross with the sorrowful Mother of God, with the virginal disciple St. John and the penitent St. Magdalen, and there represent to yourself the precious Blood of Jesus trickling down upon you, think of the pains and wounds of Jesus, of the vinegar and gall, the nails and the lance ; and how can you remain cold and unconcerned? Should not your soul, at the thought of such awful mysteries as were accomplished on Mount Calvary — even for your sake — and which are mystically renewed upon the altar, tremble with holy fear, and your heart be inflamed with love, contrition and gratitude ?[2] In the wounds and pains of Jesus there is a countless num-

---

[1] Quia consacramentales et concorporales sumus Christo, licet non vera, sed imaginaria passione in seipso immoletur, vera tamen et non imaginaria passione in membris suis immolatur, quando nos, qui in memoriam passionis suae sacramentum tantae suae pietatis agimus sacrificando ipsum, flendo et cor nostrum vera compunctione atterendo, mortem tam pii et dilecti Domini et Patris annuntiamus (Alger. De sacrament. corp. et sang. domin., lib. 1, c. 16, n. 115).

[2] In sacrificio altaris magnus ignis devotionis et dilectionis exigitur, quia ibi est tota nostra salus. Certe indevotissimus est sacerdos, qui ibi non conteritur, ubi Filius Altissimi ante Patris oculos immolatur. Sane sacerdos devotus et prudens, dum mensae divinae assistit, nihil cogitat, nisi Christum Jesum et hunc crucifixum. Ponit ante oculos cordis sui Christi humilitatem et patientiam, Christi angustias et dolores ; Christi opprobria, sputa, flagella, lanceam, crucem, mortem devote et sollicite recolit, et se in ipsa memoria passionis dominicae crucifigit (Petr. Blesens. Serm. 56).

ber of reproaches to us for our cowardice and sloth in the service of God, for the inconstancy of our will, for our aversion to trials, privations and humiliations. "Daily the Holy Mass displays before our eyes the tree of the Cross with its arms raised heavenward, its withered branches bearing the sweet fruit of the Body of Christ. Mount Calvary spreads itself out above the altar before our eyes, and the cup of the chalice receives anew the Blood of Jesus Christ. But then few witnessed the bloody Mass which Jesus Christ, the High Priest, celebrated Himself visibly on the altar of Calvary; ah, fewer still stood there to partake of the blessings that proceed from the Cross. At that time when men were wanting, nature herself performed the funeral rites for Him. The earth quaked, as if moved with compassion, the rocks were rent. The cracking of the rocks tolled His knell. The brightness of day veiled itself in universal darkness, dark curtains hung in front of the bright temple of creation, and the sun, concealing his countenance, joined the funeral procession. This mourning throughout the vast temple of inanimate creation is indeed sublime in its grandeur and most awfully impressive in its beauty. More beautiful still, viewed with the eyes of the soul, are the obsequies which take place in the Sacrifice of Holy Mass. By the institution of Holy Mass, that sacrifice which is offered in all times, and which traces its course with the sun around the earth from East to West, every Christian is privileged to look upon this Sacrifice of the Lord, to join in His funeral procession, and to be overwhelmed at the foot of the Cross with sentiments of contrition, gratitude and love. Now it is that the Lord rends the hearts of stone, now it is that sorrow for sins fills the souls and clothes them in mourning, now man's interior revives in the meditation on the nameless sufferings and death of Christ. Thus is Christ's death daily placed before the hearts and eyes of Catholics. They gaze upon the open Book of His wounds and His death; Holy Mass itself proclaims His death. And this language is understood by all Christians who have not wholly given up the practice of their faith. This the peasantry understand; when they join their hands, hardened by toil, and lean them on the pews, and when they recite the rosary, they represent to themselves in their prayers the mysteries of Christ's presentation, passion and death. The fervent were wont at all times, even in the early ages of the Church, to meditate profoundly on the passion of Christ. Thus the amiable Dominican, Henry Suso, relates of his simple mother, that she once told him, that for thirty years she had never assisted at Mass without dwelling upon the Passion of Christ and without being moved to tears by its consideration. But we are not to imagine that the Sacrifice of the Mass, which leads us deeply into the mysteries and places us beneath the Cross of Christ, is an obstacle to the ordinary active life, that it engenders only sentiments appertaining to the contemplative life, that it enervates the will and mind for the daily life, and causes us to underrate and to neglect the duties of our state of life. Not at all, the Holy Sacrifice of the Mass refers us unceasingly to the hard, prosaic, practical life. It invites the Christian to bring with him to the holy sacrifice the burdens and trials of life, to offer himself to God together with his cross in union with Christ. It inspires and persuades us to exemplify in our own conduct the spirit of sacrifice of Jesus Christ, so that our entire life may be animated with the resolution of making every necessary sacrifice. Such is the greatness and the grandeur of the Holy Mass. It leads us in its mysteries up to the very gates of heaven and, at the same time, embraces the humblest duties and hardships of daily life."[1] "As often as thou sayest or hearest Mass, it ought to appear to thee as great and as new and as delightful, as if Christ had that very same day for the first time descended into the Virgin's womb and become man, or, hanging on the Cross, was suffering and dying for the salvation of mankind."[2]

Thus the frequent and devout participation in the Holy Sacrifice of the Mass is a school spurring us on to the practice of every virtue and perfection. In this school shall we be instructed in the science of salvation and of the Saints, only when the liturgy of the Mass is not for us a closed book sealed with seven seals, but when we penetrate through the shell into the kernel, and understand what mysteries are therein concealed, and what is the meaning of the rite of the sacrifice and of its prayers and ceremonies.

2. The Holy Mass is not only a school which directs us and incites us to the practice of the different virtues, it is also an inexhaustible fountain from which gushes forth grace and strength necessary to lead the life of sacrifice enjoined on the Church militant and her children unto the end of the earthly pilgrimage, when all sorrow shall be changed into joy, and the brief combat be followed by an eternal triumph in heaven.

a) Unto the end of time, as St. Augustine says,[3] the history of the Church will oscillate between the "persecution of the world and the consolations of God;" during all time the Church continues here below on her pilgrimage, rejoicing in hope and patient in tribulation (Rom. 12, 12) — until the miseries of this life are over. She ever lives a life of sacrifice, from the beginning she shines in the color of sacrifice; for her apparel is red, and her garments like those worn by them that tread in the wine-press (Isa. 63, 2).— The life of sacrifice of the Church is mainly revealed in a two-fold aspect — the sacrifice of love and the sacrifice of suffering. When Jesus was asleep in death on the Cross, the Church came forth from the open wound of His transpierced Heart: she then inherited from her Divine Spouse, as her most beautiful bridal ornament, that excess of love and of suffering, which animated and flooded the divine Heart of Jesus at His death. On the day of her espousals with the Crucified Son of God, she was adorned on Calvary with a bridal

---

[1] Eberhard, Kanzelvorträge I, 338.

[2] De imit. Christi 1. 4, c. 2.

[3] De civit. Dei l. 18, c. 51.

crown of thorns, and veiled in the festal garment of sacrifice. These her bridal ornaments she will not lay aside, until she has finished her course of sacrifice through gloomy and dreary time, and has reached the bright, happy eternity, where at last the heavenly wedding-feast shall forever be celebrated in imperishable glory and endless hymns of victory.

a) "Jesus went about doing good and healing" (Acts 10, 38) — these words comprise the entire earthly life of our Lord; they also express the action and operation of the Church, which is nothing else than Christ continuing to live and operate through His representative organ. Like the Redeemer, the Church is also "an image of the divine goodness" (Wisdom 7, 26), of the merciful and communicative love of God. That great canticle of love — of the purest, most noble-minded and most generous self-sacrificing love —, which was entoned on the Cross by the Saviour, resounds in His Church throughout all times and countries. The spirit of the Lord continues to hover over the Church; He has anointed and sent her to announce glad tidings to the poor and to heal the contrite of heart (Luke 4, 18). As it is natural for the sun to give forth light and heat, so it is the peculiar mission of the Catholic Church to give refreshment to and to make happy "all that labor and are heavily burdened." Always and everywhere she is occupied in alleviating sorrow, pouring oil and wine into wounds, drying up tears, consoling the afflicted, succoring the abandoned, bringing to all peace and salvation. With maternal solicitude she is intent on relieving the corporal wants, the earthly miseries and the many troubles of mankind; she seeks to comfort and to gladden with the gifts and services of corporal mercy the poor and the sick, the feeble and the infirm. "Where was there ever a corporal misery to which the Church did not lend a nursing and a healing hand? Where has she not lovingly devoted herself to raise up the mourning and withering plants? Where was ever the plague of infection too great for the Church to encounter, capable of driving her from the scene in order to leave the field to the enemy of life? To relieve the distress of the most fearful epidemics she has ever offered her best and noblest forces. The Church has ever taken under her care the whole life of the body, from birth to death, with all its wants and miseries. The whole course of the life of man, of which Holy Scripture says, 'great labor is created for men, until the day of their burial' (Ecclus. 40, 1), she has comforted under the wings of her charity." (Eberhard.) — But far more intent is the Church in relieving spiritual misery, in awakening to a life of grace those who are spiritually dead, in healing the wounds and infirmities of the soul, in withdrawing man from eternal woe and perdition, in nourishing hearts desirous of salvation with the pure, the strong and the heavenly food of divine truth and grace. [1]

---

[1] Non sicut secularis beneficentia, corporales dumtaxat necessitates sublevat Ecclesia; verum, ad exemplum benignissimi Salvatoris, omnem semper curam et operam contulit, ut *duplicis substantiae totum cibaret hominem* (Collect. Lacens. IV, p. 355).

The entire history of the Church is one of inexhaustible mercy and charity. [1] Who could enumerate them all — the grand institutions of Christian charity, the Orders, the Congregations and Societies of Christian love and mercy, which age after age have sprung up in the soil of the Church of God, and flourished unto the boundless blessing and comfort of poor, suffering humanity? There is no kind of suffering, no form of bodily or spiritual misery that has not found and does not find alleviation and relief through these religious associations which, according to the wants of the times, have sprung up like blossoms on the ever green tree of life of the Church under the inspiration of the spirit of God. The Church sends forth her missionaries to deliver the poor heathen from the darkness and the shadows of death; by instruction and education she leads the youth to Christ; to orphaned and abandoned children she is a tender, loving and solicitous mother; she strives to bring back the erring to the way of truth and the fallen to the way of virtue; to the sick and to the imprisoned, the suffering, the distressed and the unhappy, she is an angel of love and consolation. — Along with the supernatural and overflowing good of the redemption, the Church has also brought temporal blessings, true civilization and genuine love of mankind. She has broken the chains of the slave, restored womanhood and childhood to their rightful dignity, and purified, ennobled and consecrated with the blessings of heaven all the circumstances of man's temporal life. "The Church, which sows broadcast the spiritual seed of the Word of God, and ploughs up the soil of souls with the plough of the Cross of Christ, took up also the material hoe and spade, and drove the plough over the fields. She has cleared forests, drained marshes, brought cheerfulness into desolate places, and changed earthly deserts into blooming gardens. And where the earth produced nothing, she by her mercy sheared the poverty of the wilderness of its terrors. Upon the eternal snow-capped Alpine summits flourish her works of charity. There in a desert of snow stand her monasteries, like plants of Heaven, to refresh with generous shelter and nourishment the traveller journeying through the dreary waste" (Eberhard).

Thus has the Church renewed and changed the face of the earth. But this she could effect only because she is the focus of the heavenly fire of love, which Christ brought and kindled upon the dark, cold and dreary world. Truly, such heroic deeds of corporal and spiritual mercy, with which the Church has at all times filled the earth, could have been performed only by a charity that is patient and kind, that seeketh not itself, that endureth all things, hopeth all things, believeth all things, expecteth all things (1 Cor. 13, 7), and sacrifices all it possesses and its own self besides (2 Cor. 12, 15). Who can enumerate the sacrifices which the Church has had to make in order to accomplish the mission of peace confided to

---

[1] Cf. Bauer, Die Kirche als Mutter der leiblichen und geistlichen Barmherzigkeit. Donauwörth 1876.

her by Christ! "Unless the grain of seed fall into the ground and die, itself remaineth alone; but if it die, it bringeth forth much fruit" (John 12, 24) — these words apply no less to the Church than to our Lord. For the Church is the most munificent benefactress of humanity; but the blessings she dispenses and the works of mercy she exercises cost her most noble children the greatest sacrifices; it costs them the sacrifice of their worldly goods, of honors and pleasures, of their liberty and health, of their will and the affections of the heart, of the pleasures and comforts of life, yea, even of life itself. It is only through a virginal priesthood freed from family ties, and only through poor, chaste and obedient religious, that the Church is enabled to bring and to disseminate throughout the world the spiritual and temporal blessings of Christianity. Those, indeed, who are called to labor and to accomplish much in the world, to preserve many from its corruption and to rescue them from it, must in their sentiments be raised above the world and in heart be sincerely detached from it; they must be dead to it and to all its vain and transient show; while, on the other hand, they must by a lively faith and continual devotion commune with God, walk in holy recollection and solitude of heart, and by persevering prayer and meditation keep united with God, that they may lead an unworldly, heavenly life, a life of uninterrupted penance and prayer, a life of perfect sacrifice.

This heroism, this fulness of a love that renounces the world and sacrifices itself, is to be found only within the bosom of the Catholic Church, since it is only within her pale that these fountains of the Saviour flow, whence streams forth that energy of life and love into weak human hearts, in order to strengthen and animate them to a life of superhuman sacrifice. The manifold societies and institutions of Christian charity and good works, which the spirit of sacrifice has at all times founded in the Church, are precious fruits of the Eucharistic Tree of Life. Wherever the sacrificial altar has been destroyed or broken down, such institutions are no longer seen, or at least they do not thrive, but merely eke out a scanty and miserable existence.[1] For only where such works and services of benevolence are undertaken out of love of God and permeated with the sweet spirit of sacrifice, will they bear the impress of a higher motive, receive the benediction of Heaven, and attract and win the hearts of men. Where, on the contrary, society independently of religion fosters similar works and "without God and without Christ," they degenerate into secular or social institutions, and are regarded merely as means for obtaining subsistence, emolument, wealth, temporal rewards or advantages. Wherever religious faith, Christian hope and a holy spirit of self-sacrifice no longer exist in a community to inflame and enlarge the heart, there base, chilling egotism spreads its baneful blight throughout all ranks and conditions of life.[2]

---

[1] Cf. Allies, Formation and development of Christianity.

[2] Multa sane videre est a secularibus viris ad miserorum levamen tentata, sed

b) Although the Catholic Church by such grand creations of love for mankind, by such glorious proofs and results of her Christian charity, which fill every unprejudiced observer with astonishment, lavishes blessings on the world, still she has to endure in the world and from the world scorn and affliction, imprisonment and chains, contumely and death (Heb. 11), to tread the thorny path of suffering and drink the bitter chalice of suffering and sacrifice. At the very time she becomes for the world a holocaust of love, the same world makes her the victim of its persecution, — in this respect also she follows, step by step, in the blood-stained footprints of her Divine Spouse. Men, devoid of all gratitude and feeling, pierced the hands, the feet and the Heart of Jesus: those hands dripping with nought but graces and mercies; those feet that were weary and sore in seeking the lost sheep; that Heart wholly inflamed with heavenly charity, on fire with love and consuming itself in sacrifice for sinners. The Saviour led His people out of Egypt, sustained them with bread from heaven, refreshed them with sweet waters from the rock and gave them a royal sceptre; — and in return what did His people do to Him? They made a cross for their Saviour, with a lance they pierced His side, they loaded Him with blows and stripes, they drenched Him with vinegar and gall, they implanted a crown of thorns on His head.[1] The Church is treated in the same manner. Our Lord bequeathed to her the heritage of His sufferings; yea, it is He Himself who continues to suffer in His Church, it is He Himself who is persecuted in His Church (Acts. 9, 4). She is the Spouse of Jesus Christ — the Crucified One; but as the true Spouse of a thorn-crowned King, she appears only in the ornaments of sufferings, inasmuch as likewise ladened with the cross and with brow encircled with a crown of thorns, she too journeys through many tribulations to the glory of heaven. The passion of the Lord is continually repeated and renewed throughout the life and history of the Church: at all times there are to be found dishonorable traitors, false accusers, unjust judges, cruel tormentors, bloody executioners; and whenever the warfare is against the Church, Herod and Pilate become fast friends. The Church must here below pass through her Holy Week, must endure a bloody sweat on the Mount of Olives, and upon Calvary she must abide the torment of the Cross; she must struggle and combat, labor and suffer, endure and bleed, in a word, she must constantly lead a life of more or less painful sacrifices. It is the same mystery of the Cross, which operates and manifests itself in the life of Christ as in the life of the Church. The bloody and unbloody martyrdom is a prominent feature and a special characteristic of the Catholic Church, by which she resembles her Divine Master and Founder, and is distinguished from all religious sects.

---

quae parum prospere successerunt; nam sola charitas, quam non gignit et inspirat nisi Christi fides, intelligit super egenum et pauperem (Concil. Avenion. **a.** 1848 l. c.).

[1] Cf. The *Improperia* of the liturgy of Good Friday.

The Lord Himself frequently and emphatically predicted this martyrdom to His Church and all true Christians, and prepared them for it, by prophetically announcing that, "for His sake" and "in His name", they would suffer from the world hatred, persecution, accusations, chains and imprisonment, torments and tortures, and every manner of death. "They will lay hands on you and persecute you, delivering you up to the synagogues and into prisons, dragging you before kings and governors for My name's sake . . . and it shall happen unto you for a testimony" (Luke 21, 12).

Let the world rage and nations threaten, let people devise vain things, let the princes of the earth rise and come together against Christ and His Church (Ps. 2, 1—3), the Church, however, always looks with confidence to the future; for the roaring of the waters does not terrify her (Ps. 45, 4—5) and the powers of hell do not prevail against her.[1] *Per crucem ad lucem* — the way of the Cross leads to the joys of victory; through want and death triumph is reached. As in the earthly life of Christ, so in the life of the Church warfare and toil, sorrow and pain predominate; but just as Christ, even in the days of His humiliation and the abasement of His divinity under the form of a servant, revealed His power and divine glory, so also in the history of the Church militant brilliant victories and glorious triumphs are not wanting. Since judgment has been passed upon the world and the prince of the world has been cast out (John 12, 31), the Church is and remains, even in chains and amid oppression, the moral ruling power of the world. But as the Church is not a kingdom of this world, so also her combats, her victories and triumphs are not of an earthly character. She combats and conquers, as did Christ, by the apparent folly and weakness of the Cross; by apparent defeats she attains triumph,[2] — and, as often as the world would chant her funeral dirge, she raises anew her head, triumphant in the joyful consciousness of her imperishable life, and looking down on her enemies and persecutors mouldering in the dust, she each time exultingly entones her canticle of thanksgiving: "Let us sing to the Lord; for He is gloriously magnified: the horse and the rider he hath thrown into the sea!" (Exodus 15, 1.) — The glory of the victories of the Church consists here on earth principally in her indestructible duration in spite of the assaults and persecutions of all epochs, in her interior inexhaustible plenitude of life and power of sanctification, in her external growth and development, in her sovereignty over hearts, in the bestowal of spiritual blessings and heavenly consolations, in the promotion of the temporal welfare and the true happiness of mankind. The complete victory, the eternal triumph, the fulness of glory will, according to divine promise, be the lot of the Church only beyond this world, in the next life, in the Heavenly Jerusalem.

---

[1] Cfr. S. Bern. in Cant. serm. 79, n. 4.

[2] Ecclesiam tuam inter adversa crescere tribuisti, ut cum putaretur oppressa, tunc potius praevaleret exaltata, dum simul et experientiam fidei declarat afflictio, et victoriosissima semper perseverat te adjuvante devotio (Sacrament. Gregor.).

Here below the Church glories only in the Cross of her Lord Jesus Christ (Gal. 6, 14), and she will know nothing but Jesus Christ and Him crucified (1 Cor. 2, 2). But because she adores and preaches, sacrifices and dispenses Jesus Christ crucified, it behooves her in her own life and operation also to copy, portray and represent Him Crucified. The glorious history of the martyrdom of the Church testifies that the Christians, with heavenly peace and meekness, with quiet resignation and cheerful countenance, with great unflinching courage, yea, often even amid exquisite torture and frightful torments, broke out into hymns of praise and thanksgiving, esteeming themselves happy to be permitted to suffer outrages and persecution for the name of Jesus. This heroism, this cheerfulness in their sacrifice they drew mainly from the Sacrifice and Sacrament of the Eucharist; for the Church says, that on the altar is offered that Sacrifice in which all martyrdom has its origin and source,[1] and that the Lord by His wonderful mysteries imparted to the martyrs that invincible strength and grace, by which they in their bloody combat triumphed over the pains and terrors of a violent death.[2] The intimate and striking connection between Christian martyrdom and the Eucharistic Sacrifice is symbolically expressed by the enclosing of the relics of the martyrs in the altar on which Mass is celebrated.

Thus the Catholic Church, as a whole, leads a life of constant sacrifice, — a life spent in deeds of mercy and in acts of charity, as well as a life full of combats and sufferings — in loving her enemies, doing good to those who hate her, blessing those who curse her, and praying for those who calumniate her (Luke 6, 27—28). The heavenly strength needed to accomplish this she draws from "the divine mysteries of the altar, by which she is continually fed and nourished."[3] As long as the Church wanders upon the earth, — this abode of sorrow, tribulation and misery, — Christ wills to remain with her as a Victim of sacrifice to be daily immolated in her midst in a mysterious manner, in order to imbue her continually with the spirit of martyrdom, with the spirit of cheerful endurance and privation. Inasmuch as the Church offers herself in the Mass with Christ, "she takes along with her from the Holy Sacrifice a two-fold resolution and a two-fold strength: the resolution and strength to bear and practise in patience and ready obedience whatever God may

---

[1] In tuorum, Domine, pretiosa morte justorum *sacrificium illud* offerimus, de quo martyrium sumpsit omne principium (Secret. fer. V. p. Dom. III. Quadrag.). — Quatenus martyres pro fratribus sanguinem suum fuderunt, hactenus talia exhibuerunt, qualia de *mensa dominica* perceperunt (S. Aug. in Joann. tr. 84, n. 2).

[2] Pro sanctorum tuorum Basilidis . . . sanguine venerando hostias tibi, Domine, solemniter immolamus: tua mirabilia pertractantes; per quem talis est perfecta victoria (Secret. in festo ss. Martyr. Basilidis, Cyrini . . . 12. Jun.). The Codex Rhemensis of the liber Sacramentorum of St. Gregory the Great has instead of "per quem" sc. Dominum the reading "per quae" sc. mirabilia. Cf. the Remarks of Hugo Menardus on the above sermon in Migne tom. 78, 393.

[3] Sacrificia, Domine, immolamus, quibus Ecclesia tua mirabiliter et pascitur et nutritur (Secret. fer. IV. p. Pascha).

decree in her regard, to be content in every state, in every circumstance of life, to be content in suffering, patient in death, to offer life and death to God; then the resolution and the strength freely and lovingly to offer sacrifices, and to sacrifice herself for the brethren. Blessed be that Divine service which puts into practice this two-fold offering of obedience and of a willing love, and with it turns even our own wretched life into a divine service. Blessed be our altars, upon which Heaven itself descends in obedience and love, in order then to pour itself out over the discontented, complaining and selfish world. The world accepts all these benefits and sacrifices without inquiring where grows the tree that furnishes this heavenly fruit. The world idly suffers itself to be fairly inundated with blessings, without asking where the fountain of these blessings is, just like the Egyptians who allow the Nile to irrigate their lands, without inquiring for its source. Where is the source of all this self-sacrifice? In our churches, on our altars, in the Holy Sacrifice of the Mass. There day after day the boundless sacrificing love of Christ reveals itself. Thence gushes forth the strength into the poor human nature to sacrifice itself also. Therefore also the higher and nobler souls thirst after this Holy Sacrifice. The living fountain of blessings would be closed, were the Holy Sacrifice abolished from among the faithful. Where the Holy Sacrifice no longer exists, there also has disappeared the grand Catholic spirit of self-sacrifice and love. To us has come down the Sacrifice of the Cross and along with it, as our heritage, the mystery of our own sacrifice, the mystery and the strength of patience and obedience as also of the freely self-sacrificing love. Let us, therefore, go to assist at the Holy Sacrifice of the Mass, daily offering as a sacrifice to Jesus, who offers Himself therein for us, ourselves, our thoughts, words and actions, our joys and our sufferings" (Eberhard).

b) The sacrificial life of the Church can assume form and manifest itself only in its members, the individual faithful. But the life and actions of the children of God will bear the character of sacrifice in a degree so much the higher, the more they are filled and penetrated with the spirit of Christ and of His Church, that is, the better, the more virtuous, the more perfect, the more holy they are. Holiness essentially consists in the intention and will to sacrifice one's self, in actual sacrifice and suffering. Without the spirit of sacrifice perfection and holiness can neither be attained, nor preserved, nor increased. However varied the interior and exterior life of the Saints of God, all agree in this that their whole life and their deeds bear the character of sacrifice, the stamp of self-sacrifice.

The immense multitude of the Saints is composed of martyrs and confessors.[1] The martyrs sacrificed themselves once, inasmuch

---

[1] In toto mundo lilia pacis pullulare coeperunt, et Ecclesia mater jam martyrum purpura decorata, confessorum quoque candore adornari gaudebat. Non enim in uno tantum loco fulsit gratia, sed ad finem usque orbis terrarum vernantia spectacula ager plenus benedictione pandebat. Nam et deserta in ubertatem versa

"as they imitated Christ in their death, shedding their blood for Him;" the confessors sacrificed themselves in an unbloody manner, but countless times, by the heroic practice of all virtues and by the constant discharge of all the duties of their state and calling, until they peacefully slept in the Lord. Both — martyrs and confessors — were, therefore, for Christ's sake prepared to die daily, and were accounted as sheep for the slaughter (Rom. 8, 36). They are all children of Holy Church; wherefore Venerable Bede exclaims: "O Mother truly blessed, who adorns the glorious blood of the victorious martyrs and clothes the immaculate purity of the pure confessors! To her crown are wanting neither roses nor lilies." [1]

Self-sacrifice [2] was the vocation and the office, the life and the death of the Apostles: they left all to become all to all and to gain all to Christ; like their Divine Master, they gave their life for the brethren and planted the Church in their blood.

The host of the martyrs shines in the blood of the Lamb and in their own — *Martyrum candidatus exercitus.* The martyrs triumphed over all human weakness and over all human and diabolical malice and cruelty, inasmuch as they passed through great tribulation and confessed Christ in life and in death, and sacrificed themselves for the name of Jesus, that from their blood might spring forth abundant Christian seed, and a plenteous harvest ripen for the granaries of the Heavenly Father.

The confessors who belonged to all ranks of life, — were they not all copies of the Divine Victim, even though they were not permitted to shed their blood? Their whole life was a "cross and a martyrdom;" [3] for they "of whom the world was not worthy," were "crucified to the world, and the world was crucified to them." Their life was spent in serving God in uninterrupted devotion and severe penance, in great poverty and in arduous labors; as the fruit of their life of sacrifice, they left to their fellow-men the good odor of their sanctity, the lustre of their example and the efficacy of their prayers.

And the holy virgins renounced all earthly love, in order to

---

infusionem pinguedinis supernae dum acciperent, in jucunditate floruerunt (Hugo de s. Victor., De vanit. mundi 1. 4).

[1] O beatam Ecclesiam nostram, quam sic honor divinae dignationis illuminat, quam temporibus nostris gloriosus martyrum sanguis illustrat. Erat ante in operibus fratrum candida; nunc facta est in martyrum cruore purpurea; floribus ejus nec lilia nec rosae desunt. Certent nunc singuli ad utriusque honoris amplissimam dignitatem. Accipiant coronas vel de opere candidas, vel de passione purpureas. In coelestibus castris et pax et acies habent flores suos, quibus miles Christi ob gloriam coronetur (S. Cyprian. Epist. 8 [10]. Ad martyres et confessores).

[2] Cf. Laurent, Christol. Predigten II, 111 etc.

[3] Of St. Martin the Church sings: O sanctissima anima, quam etsi gladius persecutoris non abstulit, *palmam* tamen *martyrii* non amisit. — Genus martyrii est spiritu facta carnis mortificare, illo nimirum, quo membra caeduntur ferro, horrore quidem mitius, sed diuturnitate molestius (S. Bernard. in Cantica serm. 30, n. 11).

consecrate themselves entirely to the heavenly love of their Divine Spouse and "to follow the Lamb whithersoever He goeth;" they kept themselves pure in body and soul, to serve undisturbed the Lord of heaven and earth, the King of their heart, and to please Him alone. With St. Agnes they joyfully exclaimed: "To Him am I espoused, whose beauty the sun and moon admire," — and on their lips was incessantly the favorite saying of St. Cecilia: "My heart and my body shall remain undefiled, that I may not be put to shame!" The heavenly flower of virginity and purity, consecrated to God, they were able to preserve fresh and unsullied only by watering it with the dew of never-ceasing prayer, and hedging it around with the thorns of constant mortification, that is, by a life of unceasing sacrifice.

These great and honored Saints, who shine in the celestial firmament of the Church as numerous as the stars of heaven, by their light and brilliancy proclaim the glory of God, who "is wonderful in His Saints," and the fame of the Catholic Church, in whose bosom they became saints. They are the ripest, the most precious fruit of the precious Blood which sparkles in the chalice on the altar. No saint would be possible, if the Church did not possess the Eucharistic Sacrifice and Banquet; for from the living, heavenly fountain of sacrifice alone flow the power, the courage, the inspiration and the endurance necessary for the sacrifices required for a life of holiness.[1] For such a plenitude of heroic virtue, such a zeal for self-renunciation, such an unreserved devotedness in the service of God and our neighbor, such a universal and uninterrupted self-sacrifice, as is comprised in Christian sanctity, can develop and thrive only in the fertile, well-watered soil of the Church, where the waters of salvation and grace flow unceasingly from the altar into open and willing hearts, to enliven and refresh them, to inure and to strengthen them in a life and death of cheerful sacrifice.

Besides these eminent saints the Church at all times possesses a countless number of other noble and perfect souls, whose lives are stamped with a spirit of sacrifice, far beyond what is required by the Divine Commandments. God alone knows and counts the number of magnanimous and noble souls,[2] who in the sanctuary of the cloister or in the world have led and lead lives detached from the world; consecrated to God, and full of sacrifices incomprehensible to the natural man. At no period in her existence did the Catholic Church ever cease to oppose to the prevailing passions of avarice, inordinate enjoyment, effeminacy and sensuality, the example of generous renunciation of the world, of voluntary mortification of the flesh, of a self-sacrificing love of God and of the neighbor. Hence we find within her pale, ever springing up and flourishing, religious Orders and Congregations whose members, by their own free choice

---

[1] Sacrosancta mysteria, in quibus omnis sanctitatis fontem constituisti, nos quoque in veritate sanctificent (Secret. festi s. Ignatii Confessoris, 31. Jul.).

[2] Animae *sublimiores* (Pontif. Roman.).

and with a holy emulation, break off and cast aside all worldly ties, in order that they may follow unimpeded the suffering, persecuted, crucified Jesus, and in perfect obedience, in holy poverty, in virginal purity, may climb the heights of sanctity, and raise themselves to an intimate union with God, the Supreme Good. Some lead in the retirement and seclusion of the cloister lives of devout contemplation, of angelic purity and heroic austerities, in order to make atonement to the Divine Majesty for a world steeped in sin, and to invoke upon guilty man the mercies of Heaven. Others, along with the endeavor to sanctify themselves by renouncing the world, by prayer, labor and penance, engage in diverse kinds of exterior works for the salvation of their fellow-men. The contemplative as well as the active religious Orders can blossom and flourish on the Tree of Life of the Church, only because it is watered and made fruitful by the fountain of the Eucharistic Sacrifice.

The human heart, left to itself and to its inclinations, does not attain to such heroic sacrifices. The mysterious Sacrifice of the Eucharist alone creates and illumines the mystery of the Catholic life of sacrifice.[1] The Sacrifice of the Altar with its sacramental food furnishes us with the key wherewith to explain all the heroism, all the sanctity in the Church: by this we can understand the martyr and the confessor, the apostle and the missionary, the Carmelite, the Trappist and the Sister of Charity. On this altar, "that source of holy love, grow the lilies of virginity, which unreservedly and forever espouse the Lord; here hearts derive the courage to become poor with Jesus poor in the manger; here they learn to love the brethren as He has loved them, and draw the strength that enables them to sacrifice themselves in the service of the poor and the sick. Where the Blessed Sacrament is wanting, there also is wanting the inspiring power of the love that creates saints, and stoops even to the most degraded outcast, to raise him up again. Here all wounds are healed, all noble resolutions mature; from this proceed all the deeds of a holy heroism, overcoming the world. The faithful soul will never depart thence without hearing mysterious voices, without obtaining supernatural strength, without carrying away an ardent longing for the place of her rest, which constantly attracts her thither, where her God, her Supreme Good is" (Hettinger). It is at the altar-steps that there awakens in the heart of the young man the generous resolution to bid adieu to the world and home with its pleasures and charms, to travel to foreign lands, among savage nations and amid untold hardships, privations and dangers, in order to carry to poor heathens the glad tidings of salvation. — At the sight

---

[1] Our spiritual or metaphoric sacrifices, prayers, thanksgivings, alms, sacred chants, preachings, obedience, humility, martyrdom, good works, are only a dependence, an appendix, an extension, a consequence, an echo of the Eucharistic Sacrifice, which combines all their varieties as well as the varieties of the material sacrifices (Blot, Marie Réparatrice et l'Eucharistie p. 207. Paris 1863).

of the Lamb of God immolated on the altar, thousands of virgins[1] derive courage and energy to tread under foot the world and its allurements, to sacrifice to the Lord wealth, beauty and the charms of youth, to choose a life of self-denial and of the Cross. They do indeed love parents, brothers and sisters, but Jesus, whom they love more than father and mother, has called them, and cheerfully responding to his call, they lay hold of the veil and the crown of thorns, saying: "I will renounce all things for the love of Christ, to serve Him in the person of the poor and the sick." In the hospitals, in the prisons, in the insane asylums, we behold what treasures of patient charity and of cheerful devotedness are bestowed for the relief and consolation of poor, oppressed and afflicted humanity. Charity in the garb of religion, which from voluntary choice visits such dwellings of misery and suffering, not merely transitorily, but chooses them as its constant place of abode, even choosing such a life among the poor and miserable as its own — such a charity gives more than bread, more than gold : it sacrifices liberty, health and life to serve Christ whom it beholds with the eye of faith concealed beneath the rags of the poor stretched on the bed of sickness. To the altar, to the wedding-feast of the Lamb does the Church lead "her chosen virginal souls, who out of voluntary, devoted love, have sacrificed themselves wholly to Him, who here daily celebrate anew their espousals with the Divine Bridegroom, and who ask nothing else of Him than this, as the greatest of His favors, to be permitted to sacrifice themselves as He did for the brethren. There the sublime and holy love of sacrifice is daily enkindled anew, for sacrifice is love and in sacrifice does love prove itself. This holy love of sacrifice has not only erected hospitals for the poor and the abandoned, it has imprisoned itself with captives in their infected abodes, it has, like Sandoval and Blessed Peter Claver, become forever a slave of the slaves. Where was there ever a creature so unfortunate, so miserable and lamentable, so forsaken and such an outcast, into whose wretched hovel this holy love of sacrifice would not enter, in order to embrace him and kiss his ulcers, at whose wretched couch it would not kneel as a cheerful, helping servant, in order to wash his feet? Such a charity has gone begging for the love of God at the doors of the wealthy, and bestowed the alms received upon the famishing. It is this love of sacrifice, which becomes a child with the child, in order to lead the hearts of

---

[1] St. Ambrose relates that a noble virgin, when urged by her parents and relatives to marry, fled to the altar. Where could the virgin find a better place than the one in which the Sacrifice of Virginity is offered (*ubi sacrificium virginitatis offertur*)? She stood at the altar of God — a sacrifice of virginal chastity (*stabat ad aram Dei pudoris hostia, victima castitatis*) — and begged that the priest might with the altar-cloth as with a holy bridal veil envelope her head and consecrate her a spouse of Christ. "This is the most beautiful bridal veil" — she exclaimed — "upon which Christ is daily offered" (*plus tale decet flammeum, in quo caput omnium Christus quotidie consecratur*). Cfr. S. Ambr. De virgin. 1. 1, c. 11, n. 65.

8

children to their Saviour, which, forgetting its learning, becomes weak with the weak, mourns with those who are in sorrow, becomes all things to all, in order to gain all to Christ" (Hettinger).

3. No pen is able to describe the ardent zeal, the generosity, the energy, the purity of heart and greatness of soul, the magnanimity and meekness, the patience and self-denial — in short, the spirit and love of sacrifice which have flowed forth from the altar for more than eighteen centuries, and made of millions of the children of the Church living holy sacrifices, pleasing unto God (Rom. 12, 1). We too should aspire to be of the number of these her good children, who constitute her crown and joy (Phil. 4, 1); we should make ourselves a sacrifice unto God and for our fellow-men by leading a pure and chaste, an active and patient, a devout and charitable life — a life of sacrifice. Can the life of the true children of God and of the Church in an anti-Christian age and in a world estranged from God be anything than a life of continual sacrifice? "All that will live godly in Christ, shall suffer persecution" (2 Tim. 3, 12). Only in the glow of fire does incense exhale its sweet odors, only in the crucible does gold acquire all its purity and lustre; thus also must we be tested, purified and proved in the crucible of suffering and tribulation, that the fruitful seeds of virtue may blossom in us, and that we may attain eternal joy and glory, "A faithful saying: for, if we be dead with Christ, we shall also reign with Him" (2 Tim. 2, 11—12). Above all, persevering courage and patient love are necessary to enable us to support the many sacrifices, little and great, that all go to make up the cross placed on our shoulders and to be borne during our pilgrimage through life. We should not painfully drag along our daily cross, but we ought to embrace it with courage and cheerfulness, for it then loses its weight, severity and bitterness — and turns out to be for us a source of blessed peace and undisturbed joy. Since we are the children of God, a chosen generation, a holy and kingly priesthood (1 Peter 2, 9), our aim and conduct in life should glow and shine with a courageous, active, patient love of sacrifice, until we have offered in the service of God and of the neighbor all our strength and goods, and the sacrifice of our own self shall be consummated. Such a life of sacrifice is, indeed, hard and painful to nature, but by the grace of God it becomes sweet and pleasing. The Sacrifice of Christ fortifies and strengthens unto patient endurance; from the altar peace and joy, comfort and refreshment daily flow to us.

The way of sacrifice is the royal road which leads to true life and whose outcome is glorious; yea, even amidst the hardships, difficulties and tribulations of this way, the Lord replenishes and refreshes the generous soul with hidden sweetness, with heavenly consolation and peace, so that she, under the vivifying breath of grace, daily renews her strength, takes flight as that of the eagle, runs and grows not weary, flies and needs no rest (Isa. 40, 31). Man "still combats, strives, suffers here on earth; therefore is he drawn to his Redeemer, who appears to him not in the splendor of His glory, but in unspeakable humiliation, who is present to him in sacrifice, whose descent upon the altar is an objective, a real memorial of His passion. Thus the sinful, guilty human heart, having its God near it, requires that He should not appear as the just God avenging sin, but as the Victim who hath borne our infirmities and taken away our sorrows, upon whom the Father hath laid the iniquity of us all! (Isa. 53, 6.) Thus the weak, sorrow-stricken human heart requires it, that, as long as trial and mourning, sin and temptation are our portion in this life, we may be able to look to the Highpriest who, tried in all things, 'hath compassion on our frailty.'

"Again it is not all humiliation without prospect, nor all sorrow without hope, for it is the glorified Christ whom we behold present in His sanctuary, and therefore we behold in His glory the pledge of our transfiguration in good season. As in the life of the Church the gloom of Good Friday and the joys of Easter, as in the life of every individual sorrow and hope of salvation, the daily need and confidence of redemption, follow upon and blend with each other, so Christ is here present poor and humble, as He was once in the manger, and again He is here on the throne of His majesty and glory; for it is He that hath overcome the world, who, elevated upon the Cross, draws all hearts to Himself, before whom all creatures bow down in adoration. Here is our Golgotha, where we grieve beneath the Cross, and our Thabor, where we build tabernacles to receive the peace of Heaven, dread Gethsemani and Easter morn, mystical death and the fountain of life. Thus our Saviour is here, invisible and yet visible, a hidden God and yet evident to our eyes. For in this Sacrament there has appeared for us all the goodness and kindness of our God (Tit. 3, 4). Thus the human heart needs not mere humiliation, not mere grief, and again not mere exaltation, not all joy. For this earthly life is neither the one nor the other. But in Him, the Friend and Spouse of souls, who suffered all that man endures and yet much more, who in grief silently and yet so audibly speaks words of encouragement to us, in the glorified Redeemer, who cries out to us: 'Have confidence, I have overcome the world' (John 16, 33), in Him the soul learns to understand the real meaning of life, and from Him she receives resolution and strength to immolate herself also with the Sacrifice offered on the altar. Now she comprehends the Holy Sacrifice as the root and crown of all that is great, noble-minded and sacred in mankind; now she takes pleasure in returning love for love, life for life, in giving herself in sacrifice unto Him who first offered Himself and all things in sacrifice for her. Thus the altar becomes the sanctuary of the Church, the fountain of living water from which flows all that is grand and sublime, all that is glorious and divine over the wide world. Upon the altar where the First-Born among His brethren dwells on His Cross and on His throne, mankind beholds its model, its future, its whole history;

here mankind understands all its sufferings, lays them on the altar, where the Man of Sorrows blesses them and turns them into benefits; here mankind understands all its joys, for His exaltation is man's exaltation, His victory man's victory; in the beauty of His body, once wearied of struggle and torn by torments, mankind beholds the image of its own glory" (Hettinger).

The joyful, the sorrowful and the glorious mysteries, which are represented and celebrated on the altar in the Eucharist, become so many figures of our own life, as it begins and as it passes upon earth and as it projects into eternity. For life is made up of joy and sorsow, which lead on to eternal glory. Alternate joys and sorrows, consolations and trials, hopes and visitations make up our life, until all earthly joy and sorrow cease, until what is mortal is absorbed by what is immortal and transfigured in the glory of Heaven. — At the same time we find at the altar powerful assistance and support always to preserve humility and gratitude amid joys and sorrows, and never to lose patience and endurance in the midst of pains and trials. — "The love of Christ urgeth us," inflames and animates us to make every sacrifice; hence with the Apostle we exclaim in all confidence: "Who then shall separate us from the love of Christ? Shall tribulation? or distress? or famine? or nakedness? or danger? or persecution? or the sword? In all these things we overcome ($ὑπερνικῶμεν$, *supervincimus*) because of Him that hath loved us. For I am sure that ... no creature shall be able to separate us from the love of God, which is in Christ Jesus our Lord" (Rom. 8, 35—39).

BOOK II.

Liturgical and Ascetical Part.

CHAPTER THE FIRST.

Preparation for the Holy Sacrifice of the Mass.

25. Preliminary Remarks

In the Eucharistic Sacrifice the Catholic Church possesses the *sun* of her divine worship, as well as the *heart* of her life of grace and virtue, her supreme good, her greatest wealth and her most precious treasure. Hence she has ever exerted all her energy and care to celebrate this sublime and exalted mystery of faith in the most worthy manner.[1] Christ Himself instituted and ordained merely the essential sacrificial act; but all that appertains to the liturgical development, representation and investment of the divine sacrificial action, He left to His Church directed and enlightened by the Holy Ghost.[2] The sublime and inspiring sacrificial Rite, created by the Church, is not a purely human production, but a work of art and a masterly achievement accomplished with the divine assistance, — a sacred edifice, so beautiful, so harmonious, so wonderful, so complete in its entirety as well as in its component parts, that the invisible hand of a heavenly wisdom, which directed the erection and execution of it, cannot be mistaken and should not be heedlessly overlooked. However, before entering upon the consideration of the ancient and venerable sanctuary of the liturgy of the Sacrifice of the Mass, the most important subjects of worship are briefly to be treated, namely, those most closely relating to the Sacrifice, and required by the ecclesiastical law for the becoming celebration of the Sacrifice. The special explanation of the different kinds of vestments and vessels used in the Mass may be preceded by some general preliminary remarks.

1. It pertains to the Church to regulate and to prescribe all that concerns the liturgy: it is our duty obediently to comply with

---

[1] Hoc sacramentum cum omni diligentia est consecrandum. Et quantum istud opus et hoc sacramentum praecellit alia opera, tantum negligentia in hoc praeponderat aliis negligentiis (S. Bonav. IV, dist. 11, p. 2, a. 1, q. 3 ad 8).

[2] Quaedam spectant ad hujus sacramenti *necessitatem* et *integritatem*, et talia Christus per se tradidit: quaedam ad *solemnitatem*, et haec Ecclesia superaddit; haec autem non sunt diminuentia, sed salvantia illa quae sunt de integritate sacramenti.... Additio harum solemnitatum est pro excitanda devotione et arctanda intentione, est etiam tertio propter expressiorem significationem (S. Bonav. IV, dist. 12, p. 1, dub. 5).

her injunctions and to submit our judgment and our inclinations to her ever wise regulations. Therefore in the matter of procuring liturgical objects, neither the private taste nor the wishes of the individual, nor the fancy of a changing fashion should be taken as guide, but at all times the prescriptions and wishes of the Church, the approved traditions and customs of her practice must be followed and carried out as minutely as possible. The Church desires and wills that all articles of worship, as to material and form, be as perfect as possible, that is, that they answer the requirements of Christian art as well as the practical demands of the liturgy. The materials employed for purposes of divine worship should be not only genuine and solid, but also — as far as practicable — precious, rich and excellent. The precious material, moreover, should have a form correspondingly beautiful, ornamental and artistic, as well as practicably suitable to its purpose. — But why does the Church have so much at heart "the beauty of the house of God and the place where His (Eucharistic) glory dwelleth" (Ps. 25, 8), why does she delight in the display of pomp, riches, splendor in the house of God and at divine worship — especially at the altar during the celebration of the most Holy Sacrifice?

In answer to this question, the heart of the devout Catholic will demand no lengthy reply; a mere glance at the altar suffices and explains all, convinces him that it is just as it should be, that it ought not to be otherwise, — a glance at the altar upon which day after day heaven with its majesty and grace descends in Holy Mass. The mysteries of the Eucharistic Sacrifice are so exalted and sublime, so holy and so divine, that for their worthy celebration nothing can be too precious. — With His precious blood the Immaculate Lamb of God purchased and ransomed us: this world-redeeming blood, this inestimable ransom, compared with which all transitory things are but nought, all the treasures of the earth but vain dust and ashes, — this precious blood poured out so abundantly and lavishly, flows daily on the altar and fills the chalice: should not man then gladly and cheerfully offer whatever is noblest, most magnificent and most beautiful in the productions of nature and the creations of art, in order to celebrate as worthily as possible this sublime, heavenly Sacrifice? Are gold and silver and the precious stones of the earth perhaps too valuable for the Eucharistic worship, at the celebration of which the children of the Church militant emulate the glorious choirs of the blessed spirits, who before the throne of God and of the Lamb throughout eternity sing the new canticle, the hymn of adoration: "To Him that sitteth on the throne, and to the Lamb, benediction and honor and glory and power for ever and ever"? (Apoc. 5, 9—13.) — Were the heavens to open and the King of Glory to appear in visible splendor upon the altar, with what ornaments and with what wealth would we not adorn the house of God in order properly to receive Him? Now, the fact that upon the altar He veils His glory under the mean and humble sacramental appearances, comes to us and remains with us in such profound concealment, abasement and humiliation, is assuredly no reason for honoring Him less; — on the contrary, the more He abases and conceals Himself for the love of us, the more fervent should the gratitude of His children be intent on decorating His altars with all they have at their command of the most costly and precious. — The King of Glory, who is infinitely rich on His throne in heaven, descends daily into the poor and mean appearances of bread, in order to enrich us with graces and bless us with all His gifts: should not, then, gratitude urge us to devote all the wealth our poverty can gather together, in order to offer suitable worship to Him in His Eucharistic poverty?

All the gold, all the magnificence of the fields, the earth and its fulness is the property of the Lord, which He has given over for the use of man; therefore, it is proper that man should again place at the Lord's feet the richest and most splendid gifts, as the holy Kings with princely liberality offered Him gold, frankincense and myrrh. — God, the Creator of all things, has assuredly no need of the gifts that the creature does or can offer Him (Ps. 15, 2); but for us it is necessary and profitable that we again consecrate to Him that which He first gave us, in order thereby to pay tribute of honor due to His majesty and supreme dominion, to declare to Him our absolute dependence on Him and our submission to Him, to prove our love and gratitude, to increase our merit and to work out our salvation;[1] for "in the sight of the divine mercy all that is dedicated and offered to God has the value of the purest gold, which He, in His own good time, will reward with eternal joys."[2] Devotion and the spirit of sacrifice are evidenced in the rich adornment of divine worship; God takes delight therein.[3] When Mary Magdalen anointed the feet of our Lord, in the house of the Pharisee, with the most delicate spikenard, He praised her for it: "She hath wrought a good work upon Me" (Matt. 26, 10). After His death His body was embalmed with precious ointments. Our Lord, therefore, willed that His body during His mortal life should be honored; consequently, He now wishes that His most holy body in the Eucharist should be treated with reverence, that His Eucharistic dwelling should be

---

[1] Cum laude nostra non egeas, grata tibi tamen est tuorum devotio famulorum; nec te augent nostra praeconia, sed nobis proficiunt ad salutem (Sacrament. Gregor.).

[2] Fullerton, Louisa de Carvajal.

[3] Cultus exterior in vasis sacris, in apparatu altaris et ministrorum ejus semper quidem sanctus, sed pro dierum vel temporum diversa ratione interdum splendidior est. Auro et argento, lapidibus pretiosis pro posse fidelium singulis in locis splendet festiva devotio, quae cum in saecularibus ambitionis insignia sint, in ecclesiasticis et divinis rebus pietatis officia sunt; non quia Deum, qui spiritus est, plus aurea quam lutea, plus gemmata quam nuda delectent corpora, sed quia homines, quod diligunt, cum Deo libenter offerunt, dilectione Dei, qua illud a se separant, quidquid illud sit, Deo pretiosum efficiunt (Rupert. Tuitiens. De divin. offic. 1. 2, c. 23).

adorned and magnificently prepared, that the church and the altar should be conspicuous by their splendor and beauty. — The Lord Himself promised, that in the New Law He would fill the house of God with His glory, and with a far greater glory than was that of the old Temple of Jerusalem (Aggeus 2, 8—10); now if the people of Israel "joyfully and in the simplicity of their heart offered all these things" (1 Paral. 29, 9—17), to build unto the Lord of Hosts a magnificent temple, how much more should the highly favored children of the Church make every effort and exertion duly to honor the God and Saviour concealed in the Sacrament, since He, out of love for them, so graciously and so benevolently abases Himself on the altar.

Splendor and wealth of ornament serve, therefore, in the first place to glorify God, and, moreover, to promote the edification and salvation of men. When precious vessels and vestments are used in the celebration of the divine service, then the Christian faithful are in a more striking and lively manner impressed with the sublimity and adorableness of the mysteries celebrated; those present find themselves lifted up above the common daily life, penetrated with a holy awe and reverence for heavenly things, more devoutly and seriously disposed, edified in heart and refreshed in mind. For this reason the Church also celebrates her divine worship with more pomp, in order to awaken and foster in the faithful the utmost esteem and reverence for the marvellous mysteries of Christ's Sacrifice. "His temples are the most beautiful of artistic edifices and the richest and the most splendid of buildings; His altars are of precious stones, His tabernacles are masterpieces of artistic carving; His sacred vessels are of gold and silver, adorned with gems; His altar-cloths and corporals are of fine and clean linen, ornamented with embroidery; as the king is surrounded by his courtiers, here Christ is surrounded with the images of His saints; He is served by priests and ministers in festive garments, amid the splendor of lights, the sheen of variegated flowers and the sweet perfume of incense, amid melodious chants, the harmony of the organ and the ringing of bells."[1] Thus has the Church at all times loved to adorn the sanctuary of the Lord with all that riches and magnificence can furnish. But her solicitude in this respect has never in any wise caused her to neglect those living temples of God, the poor and the suffering. She knows that Christ is assisted and cared for in the person of His needy brethren; hence she has called into existence benevolent foundations, institutions and confraternities without number for the exercise of all the works of mercy. She knows furthermore that a devout, moral and learned clergy serves as the most beautiful ornament of the house of God; hence to form such a body she spares no sacrifice, no effort. But the best and most perfect consists in doing the one and not omitting the other. Thus does the Church act, not only lovingly embracing and nursing Christ in the person of the poor and needy,

---

[1] Laurent, Christol. Predigten I, 658.

but also, as far as possible, honoring and glorifying Him in His
Eucharistic life and Sacrifice,[1] her zeal consuming her not only for
the holiness of her ministers, but also for the splendor of His sanctuary and worship. Already in the first ages, the faithful of the Church
made rich presents for the service of the altar. But when Christians
were in great want, or when the persecutors of the Christians threatened to rob the sanctuary of its treasures, then the ruler of the
Church distributed these treasures in alms to the poor, as, for example, is evident from the history of the martyrdom of St. Lawrence.[2]

If, therefore, the Church has ever been concerned, that in the
house of God "marble should shine, gold should glisten from the
ceilings, the altar be adorned with precious stones," only religious
ignorance or indifference can accuse her of excess and extravagance.
Certainly it cannot be too much deplored that the house of the Most
High is, alas! frequently more wretched, poorer and more miserably
furnished than the dwellings of His servants and of the faithful. —
If, as is the case in certain religious Orders, through poverty and the
love of poverty, sacred vessels and vestments of little value are used
at Divine Service, no censure or blame is to be attached; but if it be
done through avarice, carelessness and neglect, then it is a sign of
utter disregard and of want of reverence for the Most Holy. The
religious life of him who has no love and no zeal for the adornment
of the sanctuary, must be very stunted and lukewarm. He who in-
veighs against the expense incurred for the adornment of the house
of God and for divine worship, imitates the conduct of Judas. That
unhappy disciple became incensed and offended, when Magdalen
anointed the head and feet of Jesus with precious spikenard, and
exclaimed: "Why was not this ointment sold for three hundred pence
(about $42) and given to the poor?" Under the cloak of charity-
giving, the hypocrite concealed a base avarice. For he said this,
remarks the Gospel, not because he cared for the poor, but because
he was a thief and had no faith in Jesus nor love for Him (John 12,
1—6). As a rule, those of the faithful who possess an ardent and
most practical love of their neighbor, are also the most generous and
cheerful contributors to the splendor and rich adornment of the
house of God.

Where means and circumstances do not permit much outlay for
display in divine worship, at least care can and should be taken,
that all things pertaining to divine worship be kept, as far as pos-

---

[1] Dum auro et lapidibus et sericis vestibus honoratur Christus in altaris
apparatu, poterat et hoc dari pauperibus, sed non ideo jure ornatus mensae Domini
reprehenditur, cujus habitus, dum est incultus, non sine culpa eorum despicitur,
qui illam ornare posse videntur (Rupert. Tuitiens. l. c. l. 2, c. 23).

[2] Facultates Ecclesiae, quas requiris, in coelestes thesauros manus pauperum
deportaverunt — thus spoke the glorious Deacon to the Pagan tyrant. — St. Ambrose enumerates the reasons which make it justifiable to place sacred vessels (vasa
mystica s. initiata) under the hammer or to melt and sell them. — Cf. De offic.
ministr. l. 2, c. 28.

sible, neat and clean: to let them lie in dust and dirt, to use them in a torn and neglected condition for the celebration of the Holy Mass, is highly unbecoming, irreverent and more or less sinful. The sacred vessels and vestments cannot always and everywhere be had rich and precious, but at all times they can and should be entirely clean and sufficiently beautiful.[1]

2. How perfect soever be the articles destined for the Holy Sacrifice as to their intrinsic value, their artistic decorations and beauty, they are not yet fit to be used for divine worship; most of them require a previous blessing or consecration, in order to be fit for their exalted and sublime destination.[2] Whatever is intended to be brought into direct and intimate connection with the Holy Sacrifice, must first be withdrawn from profane use and be especially dedicated to the service of the Most High, that is, it must be made a sacred object (*res sacra*).[3] — By means of the blessing and prayers of the Church, liturgical objects are not only made sacred, but they, moreover, become capable of producing various salutary effects on those who devoutly use them and come in contact with them. — These blessed or consecrated objects are, so to speak, transferred from the domain of nature into the kingdom of grace, and become the special property of God; thus they have in themselves something divine, on account of which due religious veneration is to be shown them.[4] They must in no wise be irreverently treated, nor ever be

---

[1] Adverti volumus, nos verba facere non de sumptuositate et sacrorum templorum magnificentia nec de divite et pretiosa supellectili; non enim nos latet, haec non omnibus in locis haberi posse, sed decentiam et munditiam desideramus, quas nemini detrectare licet, quia etiam cum paupertate bene convenire et componi possunt (Benedict. XIV. Encycl. *Annus*, d. 19. Febr. 1749).

[2] In this place is not meant the benedictio invocativa, but the benedictio *constitutiva*. If an anointing with chrism or holy oil is at the same time applied, then it is called consecration. The consecration (benedictio constitutiva, resp. consecratio) differs essentially from the invocative benediction, in that it impresses upon persons and objects a higher supernatural character, that is, it places them permanently in the state of sanctified and religious articles, by which they are in a special manner consecrated to the service of God. According to an ancient mode of expression, the Church nearly always uses in formulas of blessing (even when there is no holy unction) the words benedicere, sanctificare et *consecrare*, for example, at the benedictio indumentorum — mapparum — corporalium. Cf. Carli, Bibliotheca liturg. s. v. benedictio.

[3] In his quae circumstant hoc sacramentum, duo considerantur: quorum unum pertinet ad repraesentationem eorum quae circa dominicam passionem sunt acta; aliud autem pertinet ad reverentiam hujus sacramenti, in quo Christus secundum veritatem continetur, et non solum in figura. Unde et *consecrationes* adhibentur his rebus quae veniunt in usum hujus sacramenti tum propter sacramenti *reverentiam*, tum ad repraesentandum *effectum sanctitatis* quae ex passione Christi provenit (Hebr. 13, 12). S. Thom. 3, q. 83, a. 3.

[4] Ex hoc quod aliquid deputatur ad cultum Dei, efficitur quoddam divinum; et sic ei quaedam reverentia debetur, quae refertur in Deum (S. Thom. 2, 2, q. 99, a. 1).

employed for profane uses,[1] but should always be regarded, used and kept with great reverence; as to the manner of using and dealing with them (touching and washing them), the Church has laid down directions which are to be conscientiously observed.[2] — The formula prescribed by the Church in her ritual for the blessing or consecration of these objects must precede their use at the Holy Sacrifice, and cannot be supplied by such use.[3] Inasmuch as the objects blessed for divine worship are brought more or less closely in connection with the holy mysteries of the Mass, they acquire besides by their use in divine worship a sacred character.

3. Finally, we are to consider the religious-symbolical meaning of the objects used in divine worship; this point should not be passed over or questioned. From many of the liturgical prayers it is evident that according to the intent and spirit of the Church a mystical or deeper meaning is to be attached to objects used in divine worship, by which they become a silent but eloquent sermon, announcing holy truths and wholesome doctrines. The Church loves this symbolical conception of the objects used in her worship; therefore she employs points of similarity that present themselves — their destination, name, material, color and use, as well as the historical reminiscences connected therewith, in order to express and inculcate the mysteries of the life of Christ, truths of faith, admonitions to virtue and holiness.

Thus in the service of the altar nothing is insignificant, nothing is to be regarded as such, but everything, even the very least, is of great moment when viewed, as it should be, in the light of faith and reason.[4] Therefore, the faithful, and still more the priests, should show esteem and veneration, should manifest a noble dis-

---

[1] Semel Deo dicatum non est ad usus humanos ulterius transferendum (Regula jur. 51 in VI).

[2] Jure ipso naturali prohibemur nos facere quidquid in injuriam vel irreverentiam harum rerum cedere potest, quod pertinet ad quemdam earum honorem ac reverentiam. . . . Speciali jure positivo et ecclesiastico quaedam sunt prohibita fieri circa hujusmodi res sacras ob reverentiam earum, quae si fiant, sacrilegium erit, saltem contra jus positivum (Suarez disp. 81, sect. 8, n. 2. 4).

[3] The permanent sanctification and consecration to purposes of divine worship, as is required for the blessed articles of divine cult both from a religious point of view and by ecclesiastical law, is an effect which, according to the ordinance of the Church, can be produced only by using the formulas prescribed in the ritual for this purpose. Cfr. Quarti, In Rubr. Missal., p. 2, tit. 1, sect. 2, dub. 3. — Reperitur apud Antonelli de Regimine Ecclesiae Episcopalis lib. 1, c. 17 haec assertio: Si sacerdos bona fide celebraverit cum vestimentis nondum benedictis, poterunt alii sacrdotes cum iisdem rite celebrare, quia per primam celebrationem bona fide factam consecrata seu benedicta remanserunt. Quaeritur an hoc in praxi sequi tuto liceat? S. R. C. in una S. Hippolyti 31. Aug. 1867 respondit: Negative.

[4] Cum exterior cultus sit pietatis internae splendor et ad hanc refovendam non modicum conferat, omnibus Christi ministris commendamus, ut omnia et singula, quae de ritibus sacris ab Ecclesia decreta sunt, religiose observent (Coll. Lac. IV, 478).

position of sacrifice in all that relates to the house of God and its adornment, and for all that is more or less closely connected with the Eucharistic Sacrifice.[1] The priest Nepotian may serve as a model to all. In his life he despised himself, poverty he chose for his personal most beautiful ornament, therefore, he was the more zealous in adorning the Church. A mind devoted to God is attentive to the least thing as well as to the greatest, knowing well that even an idle word must be accounted for. Thus Nepotian took care that the altar should be spotless, the walls free from dust, the floors well swept, the sacristy clean, the sacred vessels shining brightly; in a word, his solicitude, which took in all the ceremonies, neglected no duty, little or great. The basilicas and places of assembly at the graves of the martyrs, he decorated with flowers, branches and evergreen, so that the labor and anxiety of the priest appeared in whatsoever regarded the arrangement and exterior magnificence of the Church.[2]

26. The Christian Altar.[3]

The Sacrifice must be offered somewhere; for the celebration of the adorable mysteries of the Body and Blood of Christ a sanctified place is without any doubt proper. Dedicated churches and chapels constitute the more remote place of sacrifice; the immediate place of sacrifice is the consecrated altar. With special permission, Holy Mass may be celebrated outside of a sanctuary, for instance, in the open air, in dwellings, in prisons. On the other hand, it would be with greater difficulty permitted, and this only in extreme necessity and most exceptionally, to celebrate without a consecrated altar-

---

1 Curam habeas diligentem de munditia et nitore paramentorum altaris et sacrorum vasorum, ut cum omni honore et diligentia tractetur ille, qui est Angelis et Archangelis tremendus et honorandus (S. Bonav. tr. de praepar. ad Miss. c. 1, § 2).

2 S. Hieron. Epist. 60 ad Heliodorum n. 12.

3 The exalted destiny and dignity of the Christian altar, although not exhaustively expressed by the different appellations, is yet sufficiently indicated. As it is principally the place for the Eucharistic Sacrifice and Sacrament, the Fathers employ, after the example of Holy Scripture (Hebr. 13, 10; 1 Cor. 10, 21), as a rule the name θυσιαστήριον, *altare*, seldom *ara* — or τράπεζα, *mensa*, of which the former refers more to the sacrificial action, and the latter, on the contrary, to the Sacrificial Banquet. — Various predicates, moreover, for the most part exalt the holiness and venerableness of the altar; for example, the τράπεζα is characterized as ἁγία, θεία, φοβερά, πνευματική, βασιλική; the mensa as sacra, mystica, tremenda, divina, regia, spiritualis, coelestis, immortalis. The word altare is frequently abbreviated, especially by the poets, into altar; again it is extended into altarium. Altare ab altitudine nominatur, quasi *alta ara*, writes St. Isidore of Seville (Etymolog. 1. 4, c. 4). — Appellations which occur more rarely are, for instance, memoria (memorial-place of a saint); sepulchrum (burial-place); martyrium, confessio (place of confession) — inasmuch as the altar covered the body of a martyr. Already at an early epoch the altar received the name of a saint, because it enclosed his remains or was at least dedicated to him. Thus St. Augustine mentions a memoria s. Stephani and a mensa Cypriani.

stone.[1] If the word *altar* be understood in a wider sense, and be meant only to designate in general a place on which the Eucharistic species are deposited, then it is evident that Mass may never and nowhere be celebrated without an altar.[2] Thus in the case of the martyr Lucian of Antioch († 312), who used his own breast as an altar on which to offer Holy Mass. Shortly before his death on the feast of the Epiphany he celebrated Holy Mass in presence of the imprisoned Christians; as there was no altar there, he said: "My breast is the altar, and you who surround me are the temple." He then offered the Holy Sacrifice on his breast, and then gave Holy Communion to those gathered around him. — Since the altar is so intimately connected with the sacrificial action, we see it referred to in history before mention is made of a temple; only where there is no sacrifice, can there also be no question of an altar. We will here consider principally the most important liturgical features of the altar.[3]

1. The first and most venerable altar, upon which the Lord Himself instituted the Eucharistic Sacrifice, was a wooden table; it is still preserved in the Cathedral of Rome — namely, in the church of St. John Lateran. — When St. Peter had won over the Senator Pudens and his family to Christianity, the holy Apostle took up his permanent residence in his house.[4] There also the Prince of the Apostles offered the Sacrifice of the Body and Blood of Christ, and that on a wooden altar which the saintly Pope Silvester I. (314 —335) removed from the Church of St. Pudenziana to the Basilica of St. John Lateran, where encased in marble it is still to be seen; it is exclusively reserved for the Pope to celebrate thereon the Holy Sacrifice. — Conformably to these models many altars in early Christian times were of wood, and had likewise the form of a table.

---

[1] In hoc sacramento continetur ille, qui est totius sanctitatis causa, et ideo omnia quae ad consecrationem hujus sacramenti pertinent, etiam consecrata sunt, sicut ipsi sacerdotes consecrantes et ministri et vestes et vasa et omnia hujusmodi, et ideo etiam debet in altari et in domo consecrata celebrari hoc sacramentum. — Si autem necessitas adsit vel propter destructionem ecclesiarum in aliqua terra vel in itinere constitutis, licet etiam in locis non consecratis celebrare, dummodo habeant altare portatile consecratum et alia hujusmodi, quae ad consecrationem hujus mysterii requiruntur (S. Thom. IV, dist. 13, q. 1, a. 2, sol. 5).

[2] Victimam in altari ponere, est reipsa illam Deo offerre, et quia vi consecrationis fit, ut corpus Christi et sanguis incipiat reipsa esse super altare, mediante manu sacerdotis, ideo verbis consecrationis vera et solemnis oblatio celebratur. Neque his repugnat, quod aliquando sine altari celebratum est sacrificium. Nam non disputamus hic de altari lapideo; sed *id omne vocamus altare, ubi recipitur victima per verba consecrationis effectu* (Bellarm. De Missa, l. 1, c. 27).

[3] Cf. Jakob, Die Kunst im Dienste der Kirche. 4. Aufl. Landshut 1885. — Schmid, Der christliche Altar. Regensburg 1871.

[4] About the middle of the second century, the house of this venerable senator was turned into a church by the holy Pope Pius I. (140—155), which, on account of a daughter of Pudens, bears the name S. Pudenziana, and is still the title of a cardinal.

This form characterizes the Eucharist not merely as a sacrifice, but moreover as a sacrificial banquet or as sacrificial food. In the distracted times of persecution, wooden altars for the Sacrifice could the more easily and the more quickly be moved from place to place. The use of the wooden altar was, in a measure, retained until the 6th century, but its use never formed the rule. For, from the time of the Apostles, stone was employed and anointed for the purpose of thereon celebrating the holy Sacrifice. Pope Evaristus († 105), to whom is ascribed the division of Rome into parishes under the direction of individual priests, it is said, ordered the erection and dedication of altars of stone, and Silvester I. merely renewed this law.[1] — In the Catacombs, as a rule, the martyr's grave, covered with a stone slab or with a large stone projecting from its side, formed the altar for the celebration of the Sacrificial Mysteries. This form of altar reminds us of the stone on which the martyred Body of Christ reposed when in the sepulchre, and, consequently, of the death of Christ. — Christian altars were, therefore, formerly made of wood and sometimes of stone; they were in the shape sometimes of a table and sometimes of a coffin. The Rite and place of the Eucharistic Sacrifice naturally brought it about that, as a rule, only tables or graves (that is, coffins) were selected as the places of sacrifice. The top or surface of the table and of the tomb are similarly flat, whilst the lower part of the table is open and that of the tomb is closed.

Even during times of bloody persecution, and still more since the Christians came forth from their dark underground caves, from the silent Catacombs, the faithful ever strove, at the cost of great sacrifices, to erect to the Most High glorious and magnificent churches, and, above all, to put up in them the most artistic altars of the most precious materials, as is becoming to their exalted dignity and their sublime destination. The principal parts of the altar are the lower portion and the stone-slab, upon which the host and chalice are consecrated; the remainder is an addition artistically ornamented, which throughout the different ages has assumed manifold forms.

2. Without the approbation of the bishop an altar can neither be erected nor broken up. The decree of the Church ordering that the altar be of natural stone,[2] is based on practical and symbolical reasons.[3] — The altar is either immovable (*altare fixum, immobile*),

---

[1] Cf. Offic. dedic. Basilic. Petri et Pauli 18. Nov. lect. 5.

[2] The expressions used in the general rubrics of the Mass (tit. 20) altare lapideum and ara lapidea mean, that the *whole* altar should be of *stone*. The different parts which constitute the essential stability of the altar, must be made of natural stone. This is the case especially with the slab which closes the grave of the relics (sepulchrum, confessio), and also with those parts of the support (of the slab), which are connected with the table of the altar by means of mortar, and are consecrated together with it by anointing.

[3] Dicendum, quod, sicut legitur (De consecr. dist. 1, c. 31), "altaria, si non fuerint *lapidea*, chrismatis unctione non consecrentur." Quod quidem competit *significationi* hujus sacramenti, tum quia altare significat Christum: dicitur autem

or movable (portable, *altare portabile, mobile*).[1] An immovable altar necessarily consists of three parts: the altar-slab or altar-table (*tabula, mensa*), the lower part (*stipes, basis, titulus*), and the relic-grave or sepulchre (*sepulchrum*). — The stone altar-slab should not be made up of several pieces of stone joined together, but must be one entire stone; otherwise it is not fit to be consecrated. On account of its sublime use and as a symbol of Christ (the corner-stone), the altar-stone should not only possess solidity, but also entirety.[2] As a rule, five crosses are cut into the altar-stone, one on each of the four corners and one in the centre. The lower part on which the altar rests is formed either of stone pillars, which give it the appearance of a table, or it is constructed of stone-work,[3] which imparts to the altar more of the form of a tomb. — The receptacle, that is, the opening or cavity into which the case containing the relics is placed, can be made on the surface of the altar-slab or (in a threefold manner) in the lower part.[4] — By a portable altar we understand a four-cornered stone-slab (*ara lapidea*), in which a cavity for the relics is cut out;[5] this altar-stone must at least be sufficiently large to allow the Host and the greater part of the chalice to rest upon it. It is placed upon the provisional altar-table, or, if it is to remain there in use for any length of time, it is so placed into the wood or stone of the altar-table as to be near its front edge, and easily noticeable. This altar-stone can be taken from the altar-table and placed elsewhere without losing its consecration, as would

---

(1 Cor. 10, 3): "*Petra* autem erat Christus;" tum etiam quia corpus Christi in sepulchro lapideo fuit reconditum. — Competit etiam quoad *usum* sacramenti. Lapis enim et solidus est et de facili potest inveniri ubique (S. Thom. 3, q. 83, a. 3 ad 5).

[1] The essential difference between the immovable and the movable altar consists in this, that the former is usually composed of an extended stone slab and a stone foundation, both of which are not only cemented together, but also consecrated and connected together as a whole by the anointing of the bishop, so that they can not again be separated without losing the consecration. The latter altar, however, consists only of a simple, usually a small, stone slab, which is consecrated by itself and which can be inserted, according to pleasure, into any substructure and thence removed without losing the consecration.

[2] Si tamquam altare fixum consecrandum sit, rite construi debet cum tota mensa ex *uno* et *integro lapide* juxta canonicas praescriptiones (S. R. C. 29. Aug. 1885; — 20. Mart. 1891).

[3] S. R. C. 7. Aug. 1875 in una Cuneen. ad 2 respondit: "Ut altare consecrandum sit lapideum, oportet, ut etiam in ejus stipite *saltem latera* seu *columellae*, quibus mensa sustentatur, sint *ex lapide*."

[4] In medio tabulae altaris a parte superiori; — in stipite a parte anteriori; in stipite a parte posteriori; in medio summitatis stipitis (Pont. Roman.).

[5] The receptacle for the holy relics of a portable altar must be placed in the upper side or surface of the stone, and, as a matter of course, be closed with a small stone, as this closing constitutes an essential part of the altar. Reliquiae condendae sunt in sepulchro intra lapidem effosso et claudendae cum parvo operculo ex *lapide* etiam confecto. (S. R. C. 31. Aug. 1867.) The prescribed small stone may not be replaced by wood, hard putty or sealing wax.

be the case with the immovable altar, whose table and base are united into one inseparable whole not only by cement, but likewise by the holy anointings of the consecration. — The altar should be elevated; for it is indeed a mystical Mount Calvary. This applies especially to the main altar, up to which several steps should ascend.[1] — Whenever practicable, the altar, as well as the body of the entire church, should face to the East; for Christians have ever loved to pray toward the East, and in so doing they would think of Jesus Christ as the Orient from on High and the Sun of Justice.

3. The altar must be consecrated.[2] The consecration of an

---

[1] Altar steps — desirable for practical and symbolical reasons — occur at quite an early period and have been in general use since the sixth century. Many expressions of the most ancient Ordines Romani (for example, ascendere ad altare — altior vel superior gradus) have reference to the elevation of the altar. These steps should be so constructed as to be ascended on three sides; the highest (the platform, suppedaneum, piedrella, pradella) should be of such length and width that the priest may conveniently genuflect thereon. For Solemn High Mass several steps are required, so that the rank in the hierarchy of those who officiate may be observable by the different standing places of the celebrant (in suppedaneo), of the deacon (in gradu medio), and of the sub-deacon (in plano). — Wooden or marble railings (cancelli) should remind us of the holiness of the altar, should protect it from desecration and prevent the entrance of the laity. Terribilis est locus iste! (Gen. c. 28.)

[2] The consecration of the altar, in all probability, had its origin in the most ancient, perhaps in apostolic, times, although positive proofs of this consecration can be obtained only from the fourth century. Thus does St. Gregory of Nyssa († about 395) express himself in an exhortation on the Epiphany: "This holy altar at which we stand is in its nature an ordinary stone, different in nothing from the other stone-slabs wherewith our walls are built and with which our floors are covered. But since it is dedicated to the service of God and has been blessed, it is a holy table, a spotless altar, not to be touched by all, but only by priests and by them, moreover, with holy dread." — The consecration of the altar, although not altogether necessary, is yet highly expedient, and, therefore, since the earliest times it has been strictly prescribed by the Church. Not the altar-stone in its natural state, but the one alone which by consecration has been raised to a higher order, that is, only the sanctified altar-stone, is a suitable, worthy place of sacrifice, as well as an appropriate symbol of Jesus Christ. Domum Dei decet sanctitudo. Therefore, the altar dedicated to God exhorts the faithful to participate with devout mind and heart in the Eucharistic service, and at the same time it possesses a mysterious power to infuse into susceptible souls pious and fervent sentiments. — Ecclesia et altare et alia hujusmodi inanimata consecrantur, non quia sint gratiae susceptiva, sed quia ex consecratione adipiscuntur quamdam spiritualem virtutem, per quam apta redduntur divino cultui, ut scil. homines devotionem quamdam exinde percipiant, ut sint paratiores ad divina, nisi hoc propter irreverentiam impediatur (S. Thom. 3, q. 83, a. 3 ad 3).

The bishop alone can jure ordinario consecrate altars. The stationary altar thereby receives the name of a mystery (titulus altaris) or of a saint (patronus altaris). In a consecrated or merely blessed church newly erected altars may be consecrated by themselves. (S. R. C. 12. Sept. 1857.) On the other hand, it is not permitted to consecrate a new church, unless at the same time an altar, that is, the high-altar (altare majus), be constructed as a fixed altar and consecrated at the altar can be performed either separately or in connection with that of the church. In the latter case, and this is the rule, the two consecrations are unified one with the other, as if to represent (in the church consecration) the intimate communion of life of the mystical Body, and (in the altar consecration) of the real Body of Christ. [1] — Considering the fulness and the splendor of the ceremonies, the chants and prayers, the consecration of a church is, indeed, the grandest and most magnificent of all the consecrations; the consecration of the altar being the most splendid part of the ceremony. The Rite of its consecration embraces mystical prayers and chants, ceremonies and symbols, sprinkling with holy water and incensing, anointings and blessings. [2] — The enclosing in the altar of the relics

---

same time. (S. R. C. 19. Sept. 1665.) However, if a church that has already a consecrated high-altar is to be consecrated anew, then another altar must be consecrated with the church. (S. R. C. 31. Aug. 1872.) — The remaining altars of a consecrated church may be altaria *mobilia*, but exteriorly in form and decoration should resemble stationary altars. (S. R. C. 10. Nov. 1612.)

[1] *Ecclesia* ipsa materialis rationabiliter *consecratur* ad repraesentandam sanctificationem spiritualem, qua Ecclesia fidelium consecrata est per passionem Domini nostri, insuper et ad sanctitatem significandam, quae requiritur in iis, qui sacramenta ecclesiastica ministrant, similiter et suscipere ibidem debent, ut eo reverentius tractent hujusmodi mysteria, quo locus ipse religiosior est et veneratior. Per altare vero significatur ipse Christus. . . . et ipsa *consecratio altaris* designat ipsius Christi perfectissimam sanctitatem. . . . Quoniam autem Ecclesiae catholicae sanctimonia ex Christi sanctitate derivatur et pendet (nam haec fons est primarius totius ecclesiasticae sanctificationis), idcirco nunquam ecclesia sine altari consecratur. E diverso tamen interdum consecratur altare cum reliquiis Sanctorum in eo reconditis (quemadmodum et ipsorum Beatorum vita in Christo est abscondita) sine consecratione ecclesiae.

[2] In consequence of the consecration the altar-table and the lower part of the altar, together with the receptacle of relics and the small stone closing it, form one solidly connected and consecrated whole. If this connection is severed, or if one of these essential constituents of the altar is essentially injured, then the altar is profaned, and is, therefore, no longer a fit place for the offering of sacrifice. Such a profanation can occur in diverse ways. 1) By taking away the relics, or by injuring or merely momentarily opening the receptacle of the relics. Contrary to the opinion of ancient authors (Quarti, Vasquez, Coninck), the enclosure and the presence of the relics are to be regarded as essential to the validity of the consecration of the altar. As a pledge for the genuineness and identity of the relics therein contained the enclosure of the receptacle must be inviolable, and its permanence must be beyond all doubt (S. R. C. 23. Febr. 1884). The loosened cover can or should be fastened again with mortar blessed for the purpose, and that either by the bishop or a sub-delegated priest (S. R. C. 25. Sept. 1875; 3. Sept. 1879; 18. Maii 1883). — 2) By a considerable crack (fractio enormis) of the altar-table or of the body of the altar. In this we are to consider not only the material size, but also the special anointing or consecration of the broken piece. According to many authors the altar-table is to be considered as profaned, if even only a small piece containing one of the anointed crosses is broken, or if a stone connected by anointing with the altar-table is loosened. Aliqua altaria portatilia, licet nec sepulchrum fuerit violatum nec enormis fractura adsit, *tenui scissura* laborant, quae per medium integrum lapidem decurrit. Quaeritur an per ejusmodi tenuem scissu-

of the martyrs constitutes one of the chief ceremonies in the rite of consecration.[1] It is profoundly significant. For they who sacrificed their lives and gloriously shed their blood for Christ, should rest at the foot of the altar, whereon is celebrated Christ's Sacrifice that infused into them the heroism and the strength of martyrdom. The entombing of martyrs in or under the altar designates their close resemblance to the Lamb of God, as it took place in suffering and now consists in glory. "Rightly do the souls of the just rest beneath the altar, since on it the Body of the Lord is immolated. Quite properly by reason of a certain fellowship in suffering, so to speak, (*pro quodam consortio*) do the martyrs receive burial in the place where the death of the Lord is daily commemorated (*ubi mors Domini quotidie celebratur*);"[2] for in honor and with the assistance of the Divine Lamb did they shed their blood, inasmuch as they freely and cheerfully familiarized themselves with His sacrifice and death, suffering and dying with Christ, in order to reign and triumph with Him in glory. When St. Ambrose discovered the bodies of the Martyrs Gervasius and Protasius, he placed them under the altar. In an animated discourse to the people, he said among other things: "The triumphal sacrifices are to be placed where the propitiatory Sacrifice of Christ is commemorated. Upon the altar is He that suffered for us all; beneath the altar are they who by His sufferings were redeemed. . . the martyrs are entitled to this resting place."[3]

---

ram ad instar fili altare exsecratum censendum sit? R. *affirmative* (S. R. C. 31. Aug. 1867). — 3) By every, however small, or even momentary separation of the altar-table from the body of the altar, because in a fixed altar the connection established by consecration between the two parts, being therefore essential, is thereby destroyed (S. R. C. 23. Febr. 1884). On the other hand, the whole fixed altar may be transported to another part of the church, provided both parts remain uninterruptedly united. Non est verum, consecrari altare ut immobile respectu *loci*, sed respectu *suarum partium* seu ut fixum et firmum in se ipso per unionem partium (Quarti, In rubr. Miss. p. 1, tit. 20, dub. 5).

[1] In order that the celebrant may in all truthfulness at the first kissing of the altar, after the prayers said at the foot of the altar, be able to say the prescribed words per merita Sanctorum tuorum, *quorum reliquiae* hic sunt, the relics of several saints must be therein enclosed. These relics should be genuine, that is, members or portions of holy bodies; not clothing, girdles, cloths, instruments of martyrdom, etc. Finally, they must be relics of at least two martyrs, to which, however, relics of holy confessors — especially of those in whose honor the church or altar is dedicated — may be added. (Cfr. S. R. C. 6. Oct. 1837 and 13. April 1867). — Relics of our Lord (particles of the holy Cross) and of those who are only beatified may not be inserted (without a special privilege).

[2] Serm. 221, n. 1 (inter serm. supposititios s. August.).

[3] Succedant victimae triumphales in locum, ubi Christus hostia est. Sed ille *super* altare, qui pro omnibus passus est; isti *sub* altari; qui illius redempti sunt passione. Hunc ego locum praedestinaveram mihi; dignum est enim, ut ibi requiescat sacerdos, ubi offerre consuevit: sed cedo sacris victimis dexteram portionem; locus iste martyribus debebatur. Condamus ergo reliquias sacrosanctas et dignis aedibus invehamus, totumque diem fida devotione celebremus (S. Ambr. Epistol. 22, n. 13).

By their burial there, the vision of St. John is represented and realized in the Church upon earth; in the Heavenly Jerusalem, he "saw under the altar the souls of them that were slain for the word of God and for the testimony which they held" (Apoc. 6, 9). Thus the Church also describes the blessed, heavenly portion and lot of the Holy Innocents, those "blossoms of martyrdom" and "tender flock of victims" of Christ, by saying of them in a wonderfully lovely picture, that, "standing before the altar in simplicity and innocence, they play with palms and crowns."

The placing of relics in the altar is performed with much solemnity, according to a formula of the Ritual, very similar to the burial of the bodies of the martyrs (*depositio martyrum*). On the day previous to the consecration of the church and altar, the relics are taken to the church in a vessel expressly prepared. Three grains of incense are enclosed with them; before the relics, where two candles must be burning, the clergy recite the Matins and Lauds of the Office of the Martyrs in question.[1] On the day of the consecration the relics are carried in solemn procession with cross, lights and incense, first around the church and then into the church. At the same time responses and antiphons are sung; the Church calling out to the Saints: "Arise from your abodes, ye Saints of God; proceed to the place of your destination; sanctify all the places through which you pass, bless the people and preserve us sinful men in peace!" Amid clouds of incense, amid prayer and singing, they are placed in the receptacle anointed with chrism, and the opening is closed. After depositing the relics, the text already begun of the mysterious vision of the Apocalypse (6, 9—11), is sung and the Saints are invoked: "Under God's altar you have received your seat, ye Saints of God; intercede for us with our Lord Jesus Christ!" — The mortal remains of the Saints are "inestimable treasures", "more valuable than gold and precious stones," pearls more noble than those found in the depths of the ocean. In their possession the Church has an earnest of the intercession of the Saints at the throne of God; and hence from their relics there streams forth spiritual and corporal help, salvation and blessing.

4. Like the entire temple, so its centre especially, namely, the holy altar, in its construction and adornment, presents a wealth of deep symbolism; for it is the representation and expression of various mysteries.

a) In the prayers for the consecration of the altar reference is made to the Holy of Holies of the Old Law, to the stone-altar of Jacob, to the place which the blood of Abel sprinkled, to the spot where Isaac was to be immolated, to the altar on which Melchisedech offered sacrifice, and to that which Moses built; — our altar, therefore, recalls the places of sacrifice on which the figurative sac-

---

[1] Celebrandae sunt vigiliae ante reliquias ipsas et canendi nocturni et matutinae laudes in honorem Sanctorum, quorum reliquiae sunt recondendae (Pontif. Rom.). The Commune Martyrum is recited — cum oratione de Communi sine expresso nomine. Cfr. S. R. C. 6. Oct. 1837; 13. Apr. 1867.

rifices were offered up. — It is also a figure of that venerable table at which Christ celebrated the Eucharistic Sacrifice and Banquet; it also bears allusion, moreover, to the sepulchre in which the wounded and sacrificed Body of Christ reposed, and likewise to the Cross,[1] where in the fulness of time the bloody sacrifice of the Redemption was accomplished, and is the mystical Golgotha upon which the Sacrifice of the Cross is mystically shown forth and renewed. — The altar, as "the seat of the Body and Blood of Christ"[2] is, moreover, both a figure of the heavenly throne upon which the Lamb of God rests, and of that altar in heaven, beneath which repose, as so many sacrificial trophies, those "who were put to death for the sake of the Word," awaiting their perfect glorification (Apoc. 5, 6; 6, 9; 7, 17). — The altar chiefly symbolizes the God-Man Himself, in whom and through whom alone we can present to God acceptable sacrifices and prayers.[3] Since the altar symbolically represents Christ and His eternal Highpriesthood,[4] the one to be erected should very appropriately be of stone, even if possible be made of precious stones. The altar-stone is intended to represent Christ, that living foundation and altar-stone[5] which imparts to the spiritual edifice of the Church its existence and strength, its immovable firmness and imperishable duration. Christ is that "living stone" which was "rejected" by an unbelieving and corrupt world, but "chosen

---

[1] Sicut celebratio hujus sacramenti est imago repraesentativa passionis Christi, ita altare est repraesentativum crucis ipsius, in qua Christus in propria specie immolatus est (S. Thom. 3, q. 83, a. 1 ad 2).

[2] Quid est enim altare, nisi sedes corporis et sanguinis Christi? (Optat. Milevit., De schism. Donat. l. 6, n. 1).

[3] Altare quidem sanctae Ecclesiae ipse est Christus, teste Joanne, qui in Apocalypsi sua altare aureum se vidisse perhibet, stans ante thronum, in quo et per quem oblationes fidelium Deo Patri consecrantur (Pontif. Roman. de Ordin. Subdiaconi). — Altare, quod chrismate delibutum Domini nostri Jesu Christi, qui altare, hostia et sacerdos noster est, figuram exprimit (Off. dedicat. Basilic. ss. Salv. 9. Nov. Lect. 4)

[4] Forma corporis altare est et corpus Christi est in altari (De sacrament. l. 4, c. 2, n. 7). Quid est altare nisi forma corporis Christi? (Ibid. l. 5, c. 2, n. 7). — In this writing, which in all probability does not belong to St. Ambrose, but yet does not appertain to a much later date, the altar is, therefore, called forma, that is, figura, symbol of the Body of Christ, because Christ offers on it His Body and by His Body a perpetual sacrifice to the Father. — Sicut Christus fuit non solum sacerdos, sed etiam hostia sive sacrificium, sic etiam fuit templum et *altare:* templum quidem, nam in eo specialissime habitavit Deus; *altare* vero, quia in eo fusus est sanguis, quo ipse aspersus: quare sicut templum et altare sunt loca, in quibus specialiter colitur Deus, sic etiam Christus dicitur saltem metaphorice templum et altare Dei, quia in illo exhibitus Deo fuit cultus omnium excellentissimus (Salmant. De incarn. disp. 31, dub. 1, n. 8).

[5] Te, Redemptor mundi, exoramus, ut lapidem istum seu mensam.... consecrare et sanctificare digneris... et sacri hujus mysterii sicut institutor, ita etiam ut sanctificator appare, qui *angularem lapidem et saxum sine manibus abscissum nominari voluisti* (Pontif. Roman., De altar. portat. consecratione).

and honored of God" (1 Peter 2, 4). Since He, as chief corner-stone, imparts salvation and life to the faithful, so also is He as "a stone of stumbling" and "a rock of scandal" (1 Peter 2, 8) to the unbelieving unto perdition; for "whosoever shall fall on this stone, shall be broken; but on whomsoever it shall fall, it shall grind him to powder" (Matt. 21, 44). — Like the stone walls surrounding the stone altar, the faithful, as "living stones", that is, filled with and enlivened by the Holy Ghost, should cling always more closely to Christ, the primeval life-giving rock, and be built up into a spiritual temple for a holy service of sacrifice (1 Peter 2, 4—5), that, being daily the more firmly established in Christ and in all virtue, they may grow up to eternal salvation — from earth to heaven — where faith shall be transformed into vision. The faithful are living and chosen stones, taken from the quarries of earth, "hewn by the salutary strokes of the hammer and much chiseling" (*scalpri salubris ictibus et tunsione plurima — Hymn. Eccl.*), in order that they may be joined together in the magnificent edifice of the Heavenly Jerusalem.[1] At the consecration of the altar, holy chrism (balm mixed with oil) is freely poured over the surface of the stone, as a sign that the altar represents Christ, "the Eternal Blessed One", "the Anointed" with "the blissful oil" of the Holy Ghost, from whose wounds flows the saving ointment of all graces.

b) There are just grounds for attributing a moral signification to the altar.[2] The sanctified Christian is a temple of God, a dwelling

---

[1] Deus, qui de vivis et electis lapidibus aeternum majestati tuae praeparas habitaculum, auxiliare populo tuo (Postcomm. in dedicat. Eccles.).

[2] St. Polycarp (Epistle to the Philippians, chap. 4) calls widows an altar of God (inasmuch as they had consecrated themselves to God and to His holy service), and St. Ambrose designates the virgins espoused to God as altaria quae (Deo) dedicantur. — Te nunc, Domine, deprecor, ut supra hanc domum tuam (that is, the virgins who consecrate themselves to Thee), supra haec altaria, quae hodie dedicantur, supra hos lapides spiritales, quibus sensibile tibi in singulis templum sacratur, quotidianus praesul intendas, orationesque servorum tuorum, quae in hoc loco funduntur, divina tua suscipias misericordia. . . Cum ad illam respicis hostiam salutarem, per quam peccatum mundi hujus aboletur, respicias etiam ad has piae hostias castitatis et diuturno eas tuearis auxilio, ut fiant tibi in odorem suavitatis hostiae acceptabiles (S. Ambros. Exhortat. virginit. n. 94). "Mercy elevates the faithful to priests and to priestly dignity. The altar of the Benevolent God Himself has erected, not of stone, but of a material more precious than heaven, that is, of rational souls. This altar consists of the poor, that is, of the mystical body, of the mystical members of Christ. This altar is even more terrible than the altar of the house of God. If the latter altar is wonderful, because, although built of stone, it yet becomes holy by the Body of our Lord, whom it lodges, then the former is holy likewise, because it is itself the (mystical) Body of the Lord. This altar you can behold erected everywhere, on the street and in the market-place; on it you can offer at any hour; for here also a sacrifice is accomplished. And just as the priest stands at the altar and calls down the Holy Ghost, you also may call down the Divine Spirit, not indeed by words, but by works. Nothing so maintains and inflames the fire of the spirit as does the oil of mercy, when it is plenteously poured out. Therefore, when you behold a poor person, believe that you see an altar of sacrifice." (Cf. St. Chrysostom, 20th Homily on the Second Epistle to the Corinthians.)

of the Holy Ghost, a spiritual sanctuary (1 Cor. 3, 16. — Eph. 2, 22); therefore, the heart can be symbolized by the altar, that is, it can be regarded as a spiritual altar of sacrifice upon which we continually "immolate our earthly inclinations and desires, presenting to God our Lord prayers, resolutions and works, inflamed and burning with the fire of charity.[1] Upon the altar of our heart we must offer to God the gold of charity, the incense of devotion and the myrrh of mortification; there we must sacrifice ourselves and all that we have as a holocaust "unto an odor of sweetness."[2] These ideas are expressed by the Church herself in a magnificent Preface used at the consecration of the altar: "Upon this altar, therefore, let there be the worship of innocence, let pride be sacrificed, anger annihilated, luxury and all lust destroyed, and let there be offered instead of turtle-doves the sacrifice of chastity, and instead of young pigeons the sacrifice of innocence."[3] — The high altar (*altare* from *altus; ara* from αἴρω, I lift up) symbolically teaches the Christian that his heart must tend heavenward, and strive after what is above, where Christ reigns at the right hand of the Father; that his heart must have noble aspirations, be raised above all that is earthly, and be greater and higher than the world, in order that the Most High may in all things be glorified.

5. "Mine eyes shall be open and mine ears attentive to the prayer of him that shall pray in this place. I have chosen and sanctified this place, that My name may be there forever, and that Mine eyes and My heart may abide there always."[4] This chosen, this blessed place of grace, in which the ancient and faithful promise of the Lord is most perfectly and wonderfully verified to the end of the world, is the Catholic church, the House of God, and in it principally the place of sacrifice with the tabernacle. Therefore, at the consecration of the altar the antiphon is sung: "The Lord hath sanctified His dwelling (*tabernaculum*); for this is the House of God, wherein His name is invoked of whom it is written: And My name shall be there, saith the Lord." Just as the altar is like the place of sacrifice, so it is also the throne of grace and of the love of the Eucharistic Saviour. There the Name is, that is, the Lord in

---

[1] *Per altare cor nostrum intellegitur,* quod est in medio corporis, sicut altare in medio ecclesiae. Ignis semper ardebit in altari, quia charitas semper fervebit in corde nostro (Durand. Ration. 1. 1, c. 2, n. 11—12).

[2] Justi qui spiritum Dei habent, . . . fide, quae charitate inflammatur, in *altari mentis* suae spirituales Deo hostias immolant, quo in genere bonae omnes et honestae actiones, quas ad Dei gloriam referunt, numerandae sunt (Catech. Rom. p. 2, c. 7, q. 22).

[3] Sit in hoc ergo altari innocentiae cultus, immoletur superbia, iracundia juguletur, luxuria omnisque libido feriatur; offeratur pro turturibus sacrificium castitatis et pro pullis columbarum innocentiae sacrificium (Pontif. Rom. De altar. consecratione).

[4] Elegi et sanctificavi locum istum, ut sit nomen meum ibi in sempiternum et permaneant oculi mei et cor meum ibi cunctis diebus (2 Paralip 7, 15—16).

His infinite majesty, though veiled under the sacramental species, to offer for us to His Heavenly Father to the end of time the Sacrifice of praise and reconciliation; there His eyes and heart, inasmuch as He remains with us as the Good Shepherd, watch to direct and protect us in all dangers, difficulties and combats, and to console and cheer us in all the hardships, wants and sufferings of our earthly pilgrimage. The Lord fills this house with His glory, and His peace will He give in this place (4 Kings 6, 12).

The altar, upon which the Eucharistic God and King is enthroned, is for all devout and faithful souls a most sacred place and a most happy heaven upon earth, the dearest home and the most blissful paradise. The unbroken stillness, the solemn dim light, the mystic glow of the sanctuary lamp, the familiar nearness, the blessed presence of the Eucharistic Saviour — often enable the weary soul at the foot of the altar to enjoy a foretaste of heavenly bliss and a supermundane peace, while the restless world without is full of noise and tumult, fatiguing and torturing itself in its feverish race for gain and in the pursuit of pleasure. Here the Lord hath set up His shepherd's tent, whence He dispenses grace, joy, peace, consolation and bliss into the hearts that are still struggling in fear and want with the sorrows and hardships of this perishable life. Here is the river of the water of life which, pure as crystal, proceeds from the throne of God and the Lamb (Apoc. 22, 1). — May the altar in this valley of tears be always thy favorite place of delights! Behold! there Jesus has prepared for thee a fresh and green, a shady and well-watered pasture to refresh and comfort thee; there nothing can be wanting to thee that can insure thy salvation and thy peace. Is the altar dearer and more precious to thee than all things else? Is that ardent longing and consuming home-sickness of the Royal Psalmist after the Sanctuary of the Lord also the sentiment of thy soul? "How lovely are thy tabernacles, O Lord of hosts! My soul longeth and fainteth for the courts of the Lord. My heart and my flesh have rejoiced in the living God. For the sparrow hath found herself a house, and the turtle-dove a nest for herself where she may repose her young; — I (find) Thy altars, O Lord of hosts, my king and my God! As the hart panteth after the fountains of water, so does my soul aspire unto Thee, O God! My soul hath thirsted after the strong living God; when shall I come and appear before the face of God? One thing I have asked of the Lord, this will I seek after, that I may dwell in the house of the Lord all the days of my life, that I may see the delight of the Lord and visit His temple. For He hath hidden me in His tabernacle; in the day of evils He hath protected me in the secret place of His tabernacle. O how great is the multitude of Thy sweetness, O Lord, which Thou hast wrought for them that hope in Thee, in the sight of the sons of men! Thou shalt hide them in the secret of Thy face from the disturbance of men, — Thou shalt protect them in Thy tabernacle from the contradiction of tongues."[1]

[1] Cfr. Ps. 84, 2—4; 41, 2—3; 26, 4—5; 30, 20—21.

27. The Dressing and the Decoration of the Altar.

The purpose and the dignity of the altar require that it should, as far as possible, not only be of precious materials and artistically constructed and solemnly consecrated, but also correspondingly fitted up and decorated.[1]   At the consecration of the altar, the bishop blesses the cloths, ornaments and other articles used on the altar, that they may be fit "for divine service and for the celebration of the sacred Mysteries" (*divinis cultibus et sacris mysteriis*).   While the priests of the Church clothe and decorate the altar, the following verses are sung: "Surround, ye Levites, the altar of the Lord God, clothe it with spotless vesture and sing ye a new hymn, saying: Alleluja!"   Circumdate, Levitae, altare Domini Dei, *vestite vestimentis albis*, estote et vos canentes hymnum novum, dicentes: Alleluja!   "The Lord hath clothed thee with the mantle of gladness and crowned thee.   And He hath adorned thee with holy ornaments." *Induit* te Dominus *tunica jucunditatis* et imposuit tibi coronam. Et ornavit te ornamentis sanctis. — While Mass is being celebrated, nothing is to be placed on the altar, but what is required for the sacrifice or useful for the adornment of the place of sacrifice.[2]   In dressing the altar special regard must be paid to the various seasons and feasts of the ecclesiastical year.   With respect to the liturgical fitting up of the altar, as is partly prescribed and partly recommended by the Church, the following points are principally to be considered.[3]

I.   The altar must be covered with three clean and blessed linen cloths.[4]   The two under cloths, which may consist of a single one folded, should cover at least the entire surface of the altar, while the upper and finer cloth should reach almost to the ground on the right and left sides of the altar.[5]   Immediately on the altar-stone, which has been anointed with chrism, is placed the *Chrismale*, that is, a linen cloth saturated with wax (*pannus lineus ceratus*); it serves as a substratum for the altar-cloths and protects them from the dampness of the altar-stone.[6]   As all the remaining white material des-

---

[1]   Already St. Ambrose speaks (De myster. c. 8, n. 43) of a sacrosanctum altare *compositum*, that is, prepared and adorned for the offering of sacrifice.

[2]   Altare sit coopertum mundis linteis, saltem tribus diversis.   Et desuper nihil ponatur nisi reliquiae ac res sacrae et pro sacrificio opportunae (Pontif. Roman. Ordo ad Synodum).

[3]   Cf. Vorschriften des hl. Karl Borromäus über Gestalt, Form und Material der Cultgegenstände der Kirche.   Trier 1874.

[4]   The Pontif. Roman. has in the rubrics for the consecration of a church: Ministri ponunt super altare Chrismale. . . . deinde vestiunt altare tobaleis et ornamentis *benedictis*.

[5]   Altare operiatur *tribus mappis* seu *tobaleis mundis*, ab Episcopo vel alio habente potestatem *benedictis*, superiori saltem oblonga, quae usque at terram pertingat, duabus aliis brevioribus vel una duplicata (Rubr. gen. tit. 20).

[6]   When no service is going on, in order to protect the altar-cloths from dust there should be a cover of colored wool or silk (tela stragula, vesperale, vesperal-

tined for the service of the altar (corporals, palls, purificators, — albs, amices, finger-towels), so also the altar-cloths must be made of linen, that is, of flax or hemp; every other material (for example, cotton, muslin), although it may equal linen in quality, firmness and beauty, is strictly forbidden.[1]

The Eucharistic Sacrifice has never been celebrated without suitable covering for the altar-table; and the altar-cloths are probably of Apostolic origin.[2] Early mention is made of their use; St. Optatus, Bishop of Mileve in Numidia († after 384), presupposes that their use is universally known, exclaiming: "Who among the faithful are ignorant of the fact that in the celebration of the Divine Mystery the wooden altar is covered with a linen cloth?"[3]

The reasons for this strictly enjoined triple covering of the Eucharistic table are founded partly on the propriety and necessity of securing cleanliness for the altar itself, and of preventing any profanation of the Precious Blood in the event of its being spilled, and partly on the symbolical signification of the altar and the altar-cloths. The altar symbolizes Christ, the source of all graces, and the dressing of the altar with white, clean linen cloths reminds us of the linen cloths in which the Body of Christ was wrapped while resting in the tomb. — The linen cloths, moreover, also symbolize the mystical members of Christ, that is, the faithful of God, by whom the Lord (symbolized by the altar) is surrounded as with precious garments, according to the words of the Psalmist: "The Lord hath reigned, He is clothed with beauty" (Ps. 92, 1). St. John also in his Revelations saw the Son of Man girded round about with a golden girdle, which signifies the hosts of the saints.[4] Of Christ it is

---

cover) spread over the entire surface of the altar. It is improper, and not allowed, instead of this cover to place a thrice folded oil-cloth on the altar and to leave it constantly there, even during the celebration of Mass, at which time only the middle portion is removed or rolled up, so that the Corporal may be spread out.

[1] The general decree of the Congregation of Rites, May 19, 1819 — strictly prescribes the exlusive use of bleached linen (*linum et cannabis*) for making the aforesaid religious articles, partly in view of ancient custom, partly with regard to the mystic symbolism and signification of linen; for the Church attaches much importance to these two points.

[2] The more ancient writers use various names to designate the altar-cloths; for example, pallae, velamina, indumenta, vela, pallia, mensalia, mappae, tobaleae. According to Anastasius, Pope Sylvester I. (314—335) promulgated an ordinance with regard to the material required, that is, he ordained that the Sacrifice should be offered, not on a silk or colored cloth, but only on a white linen cloth (non in serico neque in panno tincto. . . . nisi tantum in linteo ex terreno lino procreato). From the very earliest times linen was generally used for symbolical and practical reasons to cover the altar, though even, through devotion, more precious materials were occasionally chosen. The number of altar-cloths was not always and everywhere the same; from the sixteenth century three have been prescribed. Since the ninth century, we meet with formulas for blessing them.

[3] Quis fidelium nescit, in peragendis mysteriis ipsa ligna linteamine cooperiri? (De schismat. Donat. l. 6, n. 1).

[4] Altaris pallae et corporalia sunt membra Christi, scilicet fideles Dei, quibus

likewise said: "Behold, the Lord cometh with the baptized, His saints" (Jud. 1, 14); they are, thus to speak, the garment of His body, the girdle of His breast, the brilliant crown on His head. But if the saints constitute Christ's holy attire and garment of honor, we may recognize in the use of the three altar-cloths an allusion to the threefold division of the mystical body of Christ; namely, the Church militant, suffering and triumphant. To express this symbolical meaning of the altar-cloths the bleached linen is well adapted; for according to Holy Scripture "fine linen glittering and white are the justifications of the saints" (Apoc. 19, 8). White linen represents cleanness of heart and purity of life: this can be only laboriously acquired and preserved by constant prayer, watching and mortification, as precious linen is prepared with much labor.

The altar is covered and adorned with linen cloths throughout the entire year — until Holy Thursday, when after Holy Mass the stripping of the altars (*denudatio altarium*) takes place, thus introducing the liturgical celebration of Good Friday. Until Holy Saturday the altars remain stripped of all ornament and of their usual covering. The touching ceremony of the stripping of the altars symbolizes not only the grief of the Church at the death of her Divine Spouse, but it also reminds us of the shameful stripping of Christ's most pure body of its garments, as well as of His cruel abandonment and desolation during His passion.

2. If the front (*frons*) of the altar display in its design neither art nor beauty, it should be covered and adorned with an antipendium,[1] that is, with a curtain of precious material, corresponding,

---

Dominus quasi vestimentis pretiosis circumdatur, ut ait Psalmista: Dominus regnavit, decorem indutus est. Beatus quoque Joannes in Apocalypsi vidit Filium hominis praecinctum zona aurea, i. e., Sanctorum caterva (Pontif. Rom. De ordinat. Subdiacon.).

[1] The ornamentation and covering of the altar in front (as well as on the two sides) was, from the earliest epoch, made of metallic plates, or of cloth, or of stone or wood, and was partly movable and partly immovable. The Cerem. Episc. desires for great feasts pallia *aurea* vel *argentea* (raised work embossed) aut *serica* auro perpulchre contexta (gold brocade), coloris festivitate congruentis (l. 1, c. 12, n. 11). — These hangings are mentioned under different names; for example, circitoria, laminae, petala, platoniae, tabulae, coopertorium, frontale; moreover, the words frequently occurring in the papal ceremonial: vestes altaris, in altari, super altare, have reference probably to the cloths which surrounded and adorned the altar-table — not in reality to colored altar-cloths. The appellation *antependium* (= velum ante pendens) originated also during the Middle Age. The rubrics use the name which likewise occurred in the Middle Age of *pallium* = envelop, covering, mantle. Observandum est, ut mensa Christi, i. e. altare, ubi corpus dominicum consecratur, ubi sanguis ejus hauritur, ubi Sanctorum reliquiae reconduntur, ubi preces et vota populi in conspectu Dei a sacerdote offeruntur, cum omni veneratione honoretur: et mundissimis linteis et *palliis* diligentissime cooperiatur, nihilque super eo ponatur, nisi capsae cum Sanctorum reliquiis et quatuor Evangelia (Ivon. Carnot. Decret. p. 2, c. 132). — The antependium must not be blessed.

as far as possible, in its color to the Office of the day,[1] and bearing pious emblems, suitably illustrating the Eucharistic Sacrifice.

3. Since the Holy Sacrifice must never be celebrated without light, that is, without burning candles, there must be some (two, four or six) candlesticks on the altar;[2] these (six) candlesticks should not be equal in height, but should rise toward the middle of the altar in gradation, so that those placed next to the Cross may be the tallest.[3] They should be of metal or of wood, of beautiful form, and should be kept clean and bright.[4]

4. In the middle of the altar there must be a Crucifix, that is, a cross with an image of the Crucified, so placed that it may easily be seen by the priest and people.[5] The small Crucifix, which is generally carved on the door of the tabernacle, or a simple cross without the figure will not answer. If in the construction of the altar, our Lord crucified be represented in painting, in stone — or in sculpture — and set forth as the prominent and main picture of

---

[1] Altare pallio quoque ornetur coloris, quoad fieri potest, diei festo vel officio convenientis (Rubr. gener. Miss. tit. 20).

[2] The position of the candlesticks should be, according to the rubrics of the Missal super altare, and according to the Ceremoniale in planitie altaris. It is nevertheless recommended to place them outside of the altar-cloths on a step or a stool. Candlesticks on the wall separated from the altar do not suffice (S. R. C. 16. Sept. 1865).

[3] Cerem. Episcop. 1. 1, c. 12, n. 11. — This rubric, which recommends the gradual elevation of the candlesticks toward the middle of the altar, is usually not regarded as of precept; still the S. R. C. on Dec. 24, 1849, answered: melius esse servare regulam Ceremonialis.

[4] The present custom of placing the candlesticks (candelabra, phari, cereostata, ceroferaria) on the altar, dates from the tenth century; previously to this period they were usually placed on the sides and around the altar. The candelabra were generally of a considerable size and frequently of precious metal (gold and silver, also of copper and brass with silver ornaments).

[5] Pes crucis aequet altitudinem vicinorum candelabrorum et crux ipsa tota candelabris superemineat cum imagine sanctissimi Crucifixi (Cerem. Episc. 1. 1, c. 12, n. 11). — Since the fifth century the altar-cross has been in use in many places, but it was not universally prescribed: moreover, it was not always placed over the altar, but often affixed in front or at the side of the altar. In the thirteenth century there was always a "cross on the altar between (two) candlesticks." (Cfr. Innoc. III. De alt. myst., 1. 2, c. 21. — Durand. Ration. 1. 1, c. 3, n. 31.) — In the West also since the twelfth century the Crucified was no longer represented as a king, but as the Man of Sorrows (with a crown of thorns and with falling arms). The image of our Crucified Redeemer appertains to the necessary altar ornaments and, therefore, it should be artistic and beautiful. That it may answer its purpose, the altar-cross should be of suitable size and occupy an elevated position. It is more important than all the representations of the Saints; hence the place of honor is given it in the middle of the mensa between the candlesticks. — The blessing of the altar-cross is not prescribed, but it may be done privately by any priest. (S. R. C. 12. Jul. 1704; 12. Aug. 1854.) — Because the altar-cross is necessary for the adornment of the altar, it may be affixed to the upper part of the tabernacle or immediately in front of the tabernacle door.

the altar, or if the Blessed Sacrament is exposed, then a Crucifix on the altar is not necessary; it may or may not, according to the custom of individual churches, be placed there.[1]

The Cross must be on the altar, to remind and to place before the eyes of the celebrant and of the faithful there present, the passion of Christ, of which the Mass is the living picture and the true representation.[2] The altar represents Mount Calvary, and as Calvary it should be adorned with the Cross, to which while celebrating Mass the priest must often raise his eyes,[3] bow and make genuflections.[4] The devout, pious and earnest look at the image of the Crucified, of that grand, holy representation of the passion of the Lord is at all times — but especially during the time of Holy Mass — exceedingly profitable and advantageous to the soul. What rich treasures of patience and resignation, of meekness and fortitude, of consolation and encouragement have for more than eighteen centuries been imparted to thousands by the simple, silent, contemplative look at the Crucifix, at the suffering and crucified Saviour! "This is my highest wisdom," thus spoke St. Bernard, "to know Jesus and Him crucified!" "Give me my book," exclaimed in broken accents St. Philip Benitius, — "give me my book!" he cried, until those around him, comprehending his meaning, presented to him a Crucifix upon which his eye rested. "This is my book," the saint then exclaimed, as he pressed it to his heart and lips with love and reverence, "I have read therein during the whole course of my life, and with this book I shall close my life." Yea, in life and at death the Cross should be our favorite book. In order that we may ever gratefully remember the love and the sufferings of our Redeemer, the Cross is placed not only on the altar, but in Catholic countries it is everywhere erected and brought before the eyes of the faithful; in the valleys and on the mountains, at home and in the field, on the wayside and in the streets. Therefore, do not grow weary or despondent, but "look on Jesus, who endured the cross, and now sitteth on the right hand of the throne of God" (Heb. 11, 13; 12, 2—3).

5. Of three altar-cards only the middle and largest one, which should be placed at the foot of the altar-cross,[5] is prescribed by the

---

[1] S. R. C. die 2. Sept. 1741.

[2] Ab aspectu crucis sacerdoti celebranti passio Christi in memoriam revocatur, cujus passionis viva imago et realis repraesentatio hoc sacrificium est, mortem cruentam Salvatoris nostri incruente exprimens, tanquam idem sacrificium, quod in cruce oblatum est, quamvis diverso modo offeratur (Bona, **Rer.** liturg. 1. 1, c. 25, n. 8).

[3] Denegatur ab aliquibus ecclesiasticis obligatio *crucem aspiciendi*, dum a rubrica sacerdoti celebranti injungitur in Missa *oculorum elevatio:* quid dicendum de hujusmodi opinione? Resp.: Juxta rubricas in elevatione oculorum *crucem esse aspiciendam* (S. R. C. 22. Juli 1848).

[4] Quoniam imago Christi introducta est ad repraesentandum eum, qui pro nobis crucifixus est, nec offert se nobis *pro se,* sed *pro illo;* ideo omnis reverentia, quae ei offertur, exhibetur Christo (S. Bonav. III, dist. 9, a. 1, q. 2).

[5] At crucis pedem ponatur tabella Secretorum appellata (Rubr. gen. tit. 20).

rubrics; the two smaller ones, set up on either side, have been introduced by general usage. All three should have the prayers printed in legible type and have neat frames.[1]

6. A cushion (*cussinus*) serves as a support for the Missal or, what is more practical, a wooden stand *(pulpitum)* neatly carved. The Missal itself should, as far as possible, be perfect, beautiful and handsomely bound.

7. On the altar relics and images of the saints find a proper place.[2] It has never been the habit of the Church to suffer the precious remains of her glorified children to remain in the ground or in a grave, but she takes them up and puts them in a place worthy of them, that is, she places and exposes them on the altar for veneration. This action of the Church admonishes us that the saints in heaven have won the crown of life, only because they were nourished and strengthened with the fruit and food of the Sacrifice of the Altar; for, like so many fresh blooming branches of the olive tree, the children of the Church surround the Sacrificial banquet-table of the Lord.[3]

It is also befitting to place on the altar images of the saints, especially of those in whose honor the altar is consecrated.[4] By their

---

[1] The Canon or Secret Cards were gradually introduced only since the sixteenth century. To assist the memory of the celebrant, or to spare him inconvenient search and the reading over of many prayers from the Missal, they began to print "the Angels' Hymn, the Nicene Creed, the formula and words of Consecration and several other things," especially the secret prayers (hence the name chartula vel tabella cum *secretis,* tabella secretorum); they were printed at first on a single leaf, and later on several leaves. These were then pasted on wood, framed nicely and placed opposite the celebrant, so that he could easily read them. — If the Blessed Sacrament is exposed, the Canon Cards should be removed from the altar (except during Mass). (S. R. C. 20. Dec. 1864.)

[2] Sacrae Reliquiae et imagines.... disponi poterunt alternatim inter ipsa candelabra (Ceremon. Episc. 1. 1, cap. 12, n. 12). — It is forbidden to place them in such a manner that the tabernacle containing the Most Blessed Sacrament should serve them as a basis (pro basi). (S. R. C. 3. Apr. 1821.) On March 12, 1836, this prohibition was also extended to relics of the holy Cross or to any other instrument of the passion of our Lord. — If the Blessed Sacrament is exposed, there should be no images or relics of the saints placed on the altar, lest they withdraw the mind from the adoration of the Holy of holies. (S. R. C. 2. Sept. 1741.—May 19, 1838.— Dec. 7, 1844). — Only the images of adoring angels may then be used on the altar.

[3] Sicut novellae olivarum, Ecclesiae filii sint in circuitu mensae Domini (Ant. in Vesp. ss. corp. Chr.). Cfr. Ps. 127, 3.

[4] The picture above the altar, or altar-piece, is intended to make known to the faithful what saint is the titular of the altar, that is, in whose honor the altar is consecrated. Without an apostolic indult the titular picture may not be removed from the altar and replaced by the picture of another saint. (S. R. C. 27. Aug. 1836 et 11. Mart. 1837.) — The pictures and relics of the blessed, that is, of those who are only beatified, may be placed or exposed on the altar only in those places, in which it is expressly permitted to erect altars or to have the Mass and Office in their honor (Decr. Alex. VII. die 27. Sept. 1659. — S. R. C. 17. Apr. 1660).

images the saints descend; as it were, from heaven on the earth, and
live and move in our midst, speak to us in mysterious language,
entertain us with their glorious examples of virtue, excite in us good
thoughts and pious resolutions, animate and encourage us to follow
them, with the assistance of grace, in the toilsome path of virtue,
and courageously to persevere until we shall have finished our course
and shall have happily attained unto our blessed destiny in heaven.[1]

8. To decorate the altars, especially on great feasts, with
flowers is an ancient, venerable, devout and praiseworthy custom,
and, therefore, approved of by the Church.[2] — Artificial as well
as natural flowers may serve to adorn the altar;[3] but the latter
are preferable.[4] The artificial flowers should be imitations of the

---

[1] Quoties imagines Sanctorum oculis corporeis intuemur, toties eorum actus
et sanctitatem ad imitandum memoriae oculis meditemur (Pontif. Rom. De bened.
imagin.). — *Imaginum* introductio in Ecclesia non fuit absque rationabili causa.
Introductae enim fuerunt propter triplicem causam, videlicet propter *simplicium
ruditatem*, propter *affectuum tarditatem* et propter *memoriae labilitatem.* — Propter *simplicium ruditatem* inventae sunt, ut simplices, qui non possunt scripturas
legere, in hujusmodi sculpturis et picturis tanquam in scripturis apertius possint
sacramenta nostrae fidei legere. — Propter *affectus tarditatem* similiter introductae
sunt, videl. ut homines, qui non excitantur ad devotionem in his quae pro nobis
Christus gessit, dum illa aure percipiunt, saltem excitentur, dum eadem in figuris
et picturis tanquam praesentia oculis corporeis cernunt. Plus enim excitatur
affectus noster per ea quae videt, quam per ea quae audit. — Propter *memoriae
labilitatem*, quia ea quae audiuntur solum, facilius traduntur oblivioni, quam ea
quae videntur. Frequenter enim verificatur in multis illud quod consuevit dici:
verbum intrat per unam aurem et exit per aliam. *Praeterea*, non semper est
praesto, qui beneficia nobis praestita ad memoriam reducat per verba. Ideo dispensatione Dei factum est, ut imagines fierent praecipue in ecclesiis, ut videntes
eas recordemur de beneficiis nobis impensis et Sanctorum operibus virtuosis (S.
Bonav. III, dist. 9, a. 1, q. 2).

[2] Cfr. Merkle, Augsburg.Pastoralblatt, Jahrg. 1876, p. 289 etc. — Since flowers
as well as relics and pictures of the saints appertain to the festive decoration of
altars, they should not be used when Mass is celebrated in black or purple. (Cfr.
Cerem. Episc. 1. 2, c. 9, n. 1; — 1. 2, c. 13, n. 2.)

[3] Vascula cum flosculis frondibusque odoriferis (natural flowers) seu serico
contextis (also flowers made of silk) studiose ornata adhiberi poterunt (Cerem.
Episc. 1. 1, c. 12, n. 12). — These vases containing flowers, as well as other ornaments, should not be placed either on the tabernacle or in front of the tabernacle
door. An *ante ostiolum* tabernaculi ss. Sacr. retineri possit *vas florum* vel *quid
simile*, quod praedictum *occupet ostiolum* cum imagine Domini nostri in eodem
insculpata? Resp.: Negative, posse tamen in *humiliori et decentiori loco* (S. R.
C. 22. Jan. 1701). — The placing of the middle Canon Card, prescribed, before the
door of the tabernacle is often unavoidable and, moreover, it does not appear to be
forbidden by the above-quoted decree.

[4] Etsi vasa cum flosculis serico contextis adornando altari bene inservire
queant, flores tamen horti frondesque odoriferae melius convenire videntur (Conc.
prov. Prag. a. 1860, tit. 5, c. 4). — The altar should not be overladen, but decorated
with taste. Garden and field flowers, as well as flowers from the woods and meadows, may be employed for its adornment. Artificial flowers should always be
manufactured of precious material (silk, gold, silver). Great care is requisite to

natural, and should be well made and be kept clean; for thus only can they, in a measure, supply the place of fragrant, bright, fresh flowers. Faded and worn out imitations are never to be suffered on the altar.

Fresh, bright and fragrant flowers growing in pots add to the decorations of the altar, making it beautiful and pleasing and, consequently, greatly contribute to enhance the celebration of the feast and to the edification of the people. A holy religious, the Capuchin Francis Borgia, used to say: "God has left us from Paradise three things: the stars, the flowers and the eyes of a child." In fact, flowers have in God's creation a place entirely their own; they are on the globe of the earth what the stars are in the canopy of heaven — uneffaced traces of a former world, the earthly Paradise, the least affected by the curse of sin. In the splendor of their colors, in their fragrance, they are revelations of the beauty and goodness of God, emblems of His benevolence, images of His first, true designs (Isa. 25, 1). For all these reasons, flowers, besides lighted candles and incense, have their liturgical meaning, and are used to adorn the divine service.[1] By their fine and elegant forms and lovely colors they possess a peculiar charm to please and captivate both the heart and the senses, not without impressing us more deeply. These beautifully colored creatures are wonderfully formed by the light from the mud of the ground and colorless water. Truly! flowers, those lilies of the field, which neither spin nor weave, and yet are so splendidly arrayed — by the purity and perfection of their attire give us to understand that they are the handiwork of that Creator who created Paradise, from which they come, and that they have been left, as it were, to us as a remembrance thereof.[2]

There is also a symbolical reason for adorning altars with flowers. Flowers possess a language all their own, they have a higher meaning; they are evident emblems of spiritual things. This is expressed in the Church liturgy itself. On the fourth Sunday in Lent (*Laetare*) the Holy Father blesses in Rome a golden rose with solemn prayer, anoints it with chrism, besprinkles it with perfumes and holy water, and incenses it.[3] He prays at the same time, that God, who is the joy and happiness of all the faithful, may be pleased to bless and sanctify in its beauty and fragrance this rose, which we hold in our hands as a sign of spiritual joy; that His people, delivered

---

prevent all kind of danger and inconvenience that might easily result from decorating the altar with natural and artificial flowers. (Cfr. Rütter, Die Pflanzenwelt als Schmuck des Heiligthums und Frohnleichnamsfestes. Regensburg 1883.—Reiners, Die Pflanze als Symbol und Schmuck im Heiligthume. Regensburg 1886.)

[1] Laurent, Mariol. Pr. II, 232.

[2] Cf. Berthold, Das Naturschöne, p. 84.

[3] With respect to the blessing of the rosa aurea mixta cum balsamo et musco (balsam, musk), which is a symbol of celestial happiness, quia rosa prae ceteris floribus colore delectat et recreat suavi odore, — cfr. Quarti, De benedict. tit. II, sect. 2; Moroni, Dizionario s. v. Rosa d'oro, vol. LIX, 111—149.

from the captivity of Babylon, through the grace of His Only-Begotten Son, may even now partake of the happiness of the heavenly Jerusalem. Therefore, since the Church on this day to the honor of His name gives expression to her joy, may He grant her true and perfect joy and devotion, in order that she may by the fruit of good works shed forth a balmy odor like unto the perfume of that flower, who, springing from the root of Jesse, is called the flower of the field and the lily of the vale. If a Catholic prince deserving of such a gift is present, the flower is presented to him, with the words: "Receive from our hands the rose, which signifies the joy of the heavenly and earthly Jerusalem, that is, of the Church triumphant and militant, and which guides all the faithful to that lovely Flower, the joy and crown of all the saints. Accept it that you may be more and more enriched with every virtue in Christ our Lord, like unto the rose planted along the streams." Flowers may also, on account of their grace and loveliness, serve as emblems of the festive joy wherewith we should long for the altar of Christ, the Author of all true joy. *Flores sunt signa laetitiae.* Thus the adorning of the altar with flowers appears as a symbolical expression of that joy in which we may exclaim with the Psalmist: "How lovely are Thy tabernacles, O Lord of hosts! I have loved the place where Thy glory dwelleth."

Flowers also symbolize those supernatural prerogatives, graces and virtues with which the soul should be adorned; for the saints bloom as the lily and they are in the presence of God as the odor of balsam. Flowers, by reason of their freshness and beauty which they receive from the sun and which they turn towards it, are emblems of that innocence and holiness we derive from Christ, the Sun of Justice, and with which we again glorify Him as the Sun of our spiritual life. — The flowers on the altar signify, moreover, that the blossoms of grace, prayer and virtue unfold in the supernatural light and in the heavenly warmth which radiates from the sun of the Eucharistic Sacrifice. The flowers of the altar, at the same time, admonish us to make of our heart a garden for God with the flowers of virtue, so that Christ, who feeds among the lilies, may find His delight therein; for nothing gives Him so much joy as a heart adorned with the blossoms of purity. — The flowers with which we ornament the altars on great feasts, therefore, symbolize the souls of the faithful, who adorn their interior with faith and with the grace of the Divine Victim, in order to receive the King of Glory and offer to Him their homage. In this connection, the Holy Ghost says to us: "Send forth flowers, as the lily, and yield a perfume and bring forth leaves in grace and praise with canticles and bless the Lord in His works" (Ecclus. 39, 19).

It should, then, be a loving occupation for us to adorn the church, to decorate the altar and to enhance the beauty of divine worship with fresh and fragrant flowers. God is thereby honored, pious people are rejoiced and edified. On this subject we have a beautiful model in the Blessed Henry Suso. "When delightful summer came round and the delicate flowers appeared for the first time, he refrained from culling or even from touching them until the day had arrived on which he would gather them to greet his spiritual love, the gentle, the all-fair and lovely Maiden, the divine Mother. Thus he gathered the flowers with many a tender aspiration, and carried them to his cell to weave them into a wreath; he then went to the choir or to the chapel of our Lady and, kneeling humbly before her statue, he placed the lovely crown upon her head with the request: that since she is the loveliest of flowers and the summer-joy of his young heart, she would not despise the first flowers of her servant."[1]

The altar is here on earth the most holy and the most venerable of all places — our Bethlehem and Nazareth, our Thabor and Golgotha. To do honor to Him who here sacrifices Himself for us and who so graciously deigns to dwell among us, all the splendor and decoration of the temple lend their service. The altar, therefore, should be the most beautiful of all, and the pastor should have at heart, in a special manner, its adornment, so that he may in truth be able to say: *Domine, dilexi decorum domus tuae et locum habitationis gloriae tuae* — "O Lord, I have loved the beauty of Thy house and the place where Thy glory dwelleth" (Ps. 25, 8).

28. The Chalice and its Appurtenances.

Among the necessary requisites for the celebration of the Eucharistic Sacrifice is to be enumerated the chalice[2], together with

---

[1] Denifle, Die Schriften des sel. Heinrich Seuse. 1. Abth., p. 162.

[2] Calix, a deep cup for drinking, goblet, chalice, (also with its contents). Through Christ the chalice received a new, sacred destiny; hence natalis calicis an ancient designation for Holy Thursday. The Biblical name is ποτήριον — or ποτήριον τῆς εὐλογίας (1 Cor. 10, 16), or ποτήριον Κυρίου (ibid. 10, 21 and 11, 27). More modern names are: calix sanctus, vas sacrum, vas dominicum, vas mysticum, vasculum, poculum sanctum. The chalice is necessary for the celebration of sacrifice, and was, therefore, always and everywhere in use. As to the material and form of the chalice which our Lord used at the institution of the Eucharist, we have no reliable information; for the models preserved at Valencia and Genoa are assuredly not authentic. The three parts of the chalice (cuppa=goblet; nodus= knob or handle; pes=foot) were in different periods of art formed differently (for example, Roman, Gothic chalices). The nature of the thing and historic proof place it beyond a doubt, that from the earliest epoch endeavors were made to have the sacred vessels manufactured of precious material, mostly of gold and silver and artistically ornamented. Chalices were frequently enamelled and set with pearls and gems (calices gemmei). In order to preserve the gold and silver vessels from pillage, St. Lawrence used them for the support of the poor. Prudentius makes a Pagan persecutor say, that among the Christians it is customary: libent ut *auro* antistites.—*Argenteis* scyphis ferunt—Fumare sacrum sanguinem—*Auro*que nocturnis sacris—Adstare fixos cereos (Peristeph. 11, 68. sqq). Of Urban I. (220–230) the Liber Pontificalis mentions: Hic fecit ministeria sacrata omnia *argentea* et patenas argenteas 25 posuit, that is, he had all the sacred vessels made of silver

9

its appurtenances (the paten, pall, corporal, purificator, burse, veil and cruets).

1. The chalice and paten occupy the first place of honor[1] among the sacred vessels; for in the chalice the infinitely Precious Blood of Christ is consecrated,[2] and on the paten the glorious Body of the Lord is placed.[3]

a) Considering the sublime use to which these vessels are put and their sacredness, the Church has ordained that they be made only of the best, the most noble and the most precious metals. Brittle, unsafe and inferior materials are not to be used in their construction—such as, glass, which breaks easily; wood, which is porous and which would absorb the precious Blood; brass and copper, given to rust and verdigris; lead and iron, on account of their little value. The chalice proper, that is, the cup, must be of gold or silver; only in an exceptional case, that is, on account of poverty, are chalices of pewter allowed. If the cup be of silver or pewter, then at least the interior of it must be gilt with gold.[4] The paten[5] must be of the same material as the cup (*cuppa*) of the chalice, also gilt with gold. The outer rim of the round paten must be thin and sharp so that chance fragments of the Sacred Host may the more easily and surely be gathered up therewith; the inner cavity should be shallow and without border, so that the particles of the Sacred Host may easily be conveyed into the chalice. — Both chalice and

---

and he donated twenty-five silver patens. — Chalices of glass were also used in some places, but probably only exceptionally and chiefly in cases of necessity. Nihil illo ditius qui sanguinem (Christi) portat in *vitro*—writes St. Jerome of Bishop Exuperius of Toulouse, who had distributed all he possessed to the poor. Chalices of wood, bone, clay, stone, brass, copper, pewter were condemned by many Synods, already towards the end of the tenth century, although their use did not altogether cease.—In the primitive Church there were various kinds of chalices; for example, calices ministeriales, communicales, majores (for the Communion of the laity); c. offertorii, in which the deacons poured the wine presented by the people; c. pendentiles, which hung in the Church for ornament; c. ansati, appensorii, with handles; c. imaginati, with images; c. literati, with inscriptions. With respect to these and other names cfr. Du Saussay, Panopol. sacerd., p. 1, l. 8.

[1] Vasa, quibus praecipue nostra sacramenta imponuntur et consecrantur, *calices* sunt et *patenae*. Calix dicitur a graeco, quod est κύλιξ; patena a patendo, quod patula sit (Walafr. Strab. De exord. et increment. c. 25).

[2] Optatus of Mileve calls chalices bearers of the Blood of Christ — Christi sanguinis portatores (De schism. Donat. l. 6, n. 2).

[3] At the consecration of the paten the bishop prays God "to sanctify it, so as to break on it the body of Christ" (sanctificet hanc patenam ad *confringendum* in ea corpus D. N. I. Ch.). For many centuries the holy bread has no longer been broken over the paten, but over the chalice (cfr. Durand. Ration. l. 4, c. 51, n. 1—4.)

[4] The making of chalices and patens of copper (cuprum) or brass (aurichalcum) was declared an abuse and therefore forbidden (S. R. C. 16. Mart. 1876).

[5] The Patena (from patere=vas late patens, an open vessel broader than deep) was probably used even in apostolic times for the offering of Sacrifice. For preserving the Chrism there were formerly the so-called patenae chrismales, which evidently were larger and deeper.

paten should always be kept scrupulously clean and bright; it is proper that when not in use they be not kept uncovered, but be enclosed in a case.

b) As mere art or richness of material cannot make them worthy of the service of the altar, they require to be consecrated with the divine blessing, in order to be made fit for use in the celebration of the Holy Sacrifice.[1] Therefore, the chalice and paten may be used at the Holy Sacrifice only after they have been rendered sacred by consecration. As the ceremony includes anointing with holy chrism, their consecration belongs exclusively to the bishop.— It must precede their use at Holy Mass, and cannot be supplied thereby; the consecration is lost, if the chalice or paten has become unfit for its purpose (for example, if broken or fractured) or if the interior be regilt.[2]—Both chalice and paten are properly anointed with holy chrism. Chrism is composed of balm mingled with olive oil and, consequently, it is a symbol of the sweet-scented, enlightening, healing, comforting and strengthening grace of the Holy Ghost. In the chalice the Sacrificial Blood flows, and on the paten rests the Body of Christ, who was anointed by God with the oil of gladness above His fellows (Ps. 44, 8); from the wounds of the Eucharistic Victim gushes forth all the heavenly perfume of grace, all reconciliation and mercy, all peace and joy in the holy Ghost.—To the consecrated vessels a sacred character is imparted; they are withdrawn from profane use, removed from the service of man and specially dedicated to the service of the Most High. The sacred, venerable vessels (*vasa sacra*) which come into immediate communication with the Most Holy cannot, therefore, — at least not without special permission—be touched by the laity.[3]

---

[1] Quod *arte* vel *metalli natura* effici non potest altaribus tuis dignum, fiat tua *benedictione* sanctificatum (Pontif. Rom., De Pat. et Calic. consecrat).

[2] If the foot of the chalice is not broken off, but only loosely screwed (in a calix tornatilis), then the cup does not lose its consecration. The sacred vessels— at least those of silver—are not desecrated, if by degrees they lose their gilding; on the other hand, re-gilding makes a new consecration necessary (S. R. C. 14. Jun. 1845). Totus calix deauratus per modum unius consecratur, et ideo, quamvis aurum amittatur, argenteus calix consecratus manet, quia licet inunctio vel consecratio versetur circa superficiem, tamen simpliciter totum consecratur. Quando vero postea nova deauratio superadditur, requiritur nova consecratio, quia id, quod additur, nullo modo consecratum erat. Nec dici potest, manere consecratum ex sola adjunctione ad aliud . . . quia id, quod per deaurationem additur, *principalius* est, non solum quia est nobilior materia, sed maxime, quia in ea fit contactus corporis et sanguinis Domini (Suarez disp. 81, sect. 7, n. 3).

[3] The discipline of the Church with regard to this point was not always and everywhere the same. The Liber Pontificalis attributes to Pope Xystus I., in the beginning of the second century (115—125 ?), the ordinance that only ministri should touch the vessels consecrated to God (ministeria sacrata). Among these "ministers" deacons and sub-deacons are to be understood.—So long as the sacred vessels really contain the Eucharist, they can be touched by the priest only, and at most by the deacon.—It is permitted the sub-deacon to handle the sacred vessels

c) The mystical meaning of these two vessels is to be found chiefly in the formula of their consecration and in the use that is made of them. The chalice accordingly recalls to our mind that sanctified chalice (*calix sacratus*) of Melchisedech, which the Lord God once filled with grace. — Again it reminds us of the Sacred Heart of Jesus; for that Divine Heart is the laboratory in which the blood of our redemption was prepared, and also the source whence this blood of all redeeming merit was so abundantly and lavishly poured out, and daily fills the chalice on our altars. In the sacrificial cup of the Sacred Heart of Jesus is contained the Precious Blood of our redemption. Into and from this Sacred Heart once flowed and will flow for all eternity that precious Blood which purchased, ransomed and redeemed us. — The paten reminds us of the gold and silver plates of the Old Testament upon which, according to the Lord's direction, various gifts (of wheaten-meal) were brought to the altar. — As the immediate and actual bearer of the Sacred Host (*corporis Christi pretiosum ferculum*), the paten represents the tree of the Cross upon which Christ voluntarily underwent death for us (*in patibulo crucis elegit immolari*) and His martyred body hung. — By its form it is also emblematic of the heart[1] enlarging and dilating itself in holy love and charity, with which priest and people go to meet and receive the Eucharistic Victim (*patena — cor patens vel amplum latitudine charitatis — Innocent III. l. 6, c. 1*). — Finally the chalice and the paten jointly represent the sepulchre, within whose dark recesses the Lord reposed in death after accomplishing the great and painful work of redemption; for the Church prays, that these vessels, "by the grace of the Holy Ghost, may become a new sepulchre (*novum sepulchrum*) for the Body and Blood of the Lord."[2]

---

on certain occasions even before they are purified and, therefore, they may still contain some particles of the Eucharist; thus, for example, he may carry the chalice, not yet purified, which was used at the first or second Mass on Christmas Day. — The empty and purified altar-vessels may now be handled by all clerics. The same right is by privilege or legitimate custom granted to all male and even female religious who act as sacristans. — For lay-sacristans of larger churches this permission should be obtained from the bishop; and in smaller churches the priest should himself, as much as practicable, take care of and arrange the chalice.

[1] Patena, quae dicitur a patendo, cor latum et amplum signat: super hanc patenam, i. e. super latitudinem caritatis sacrificium justitiae debet offerri, ut holocaustum animae pingue fiat (Innoc. III. 1. 2, c. 59).

[2] That the holy, sacred vessels be made of gold or at least be gold-gilt, is also recommended for symbolical reasons. — Gold, as the most excellent and precious of the metals, is a symbol of what is noblest of a higher order, that is, of the heavenly and divine. (Cf. Cant. 5, 11. — Apoc. 21, 18). On the altar, therefore, gold indicates the supernatural character, the divine grandeur and excellence of the Sacrifice. — The Magi presented Christ with gold (aurum regium), ut ostendatur Regis potentia: thus the golden or gold-gilt sacred vessels denote the royal dignity and power of our Divine High-priest. — As the noblest of the metals, gold, finally, symbolizes the heavenly wisdom and love with which Christ offers Himself for us on the altar.

2. We will now speak of the corporal, upon which the most holy Body of Christ and the chalice of His Blood are consecrated; and also of the pall which serves as a covering for the chalice. Originally the pall was not distinct from the corporal, but formed one and the same piece with it; for a linen cloth, which was much larger than our corporals, served as a cloth whereon to repose the Sacred Hosts and at the same time to envelop and cover the chalice.[1] Since the twelfth century[2] it has been customary to make this linen cloth—our present corporal—smaller and to use it only to place the Host and chalice thereon ; while for the covering of the chalice a separate and independent linen—our pall—has been employed.[3]

a) The corporal must not be interwoven in the centre with threads of silk or gold, but must be throughout pure white linen, and be blessed as also the pall by a bishop or by some one thereunto empowered. The corporal as well as the pall may have in front a small embroidered cross.

At the present the palls that are perfectly plain deserve the preference, that is, palls consisting of a piece of linen folded in two. It is also permissible to have embroidered or woven on the upper surface of the pall decorations (for example, representations of the pelican, of the Lamb with the banner of the Cross bearing the name of Jesus); but they must not be in black, nor contain symbols of

---

[1] Pallium (=mantle, over-garment) and palla (=long, wide over-garment) were formerly in a more extended sense (=envelop, covering) generally used for the designation of various cloths that cover the altar, especially the objects for the sacrifice. Pallium is still the proper liturgical name of that covering which adorns the upper part of the altar. The altar cloths were called pallae altaris. As a distinction from these the other wider linen cloth, which spread over the entire surface of the altar,—immediately held and covered the oblations was called pallium corporale, often palla dominica, palla corporalis, but generally only corporale. From this large altar-piece proceeded our present corporal and chalice-pall (parva palla— in lieu of the more extensive corporal-palls). At the close of the thirteenth century (see Durandus) the names corporal and pall were distinguished and used just as at present. The chalice pall is also called animetta (little soul) and in the Mozarabic Ritual filiola (little daughter), as it formed the inmost, part of the folded corporal and was only a piece of it. Among the Carthusians the old (somewhat inconvenient) practice of covering the chalice with the corporal, is maintained to the present day. The Theatines use in addition to the corporal a small linen pall, on which the Sacred Host is held (cfr. Quarti, In Rubr. Miss. p. 2, tit. 1, sect. 3, dub. 4.—Krazer Sect. 3, art. 3, cap. 2. § 103).

[2] Duplex est palla, quae dicitur corporale: una quam diaconus super altare totam extendit ; altera, quam super calicem plicatam imponit (Innocent. III. 1. 2, cap. 56).

[3] With regard to its origin the pall is still considered a portion of the corporal; hence corporal and pall are blessed with one and the same formula, in which they are designated in the singular number as *linteamen*, which serves ad tegendum involvendumque Corpus et Sanguinem D. N. I. Chr. (cfr. Pontif. Rom. De benedict. corporalium). This formula must always be recited unchanged in the singular, and it is not allowed to bless the palla without the corporale (S.R.C. 4. Sept. 1880).

death.[1] Black covers for the chalice are forbidden and consequently, if still in use, are to be put aside.

Since the corporal and pall come into such close contact with the Sacred Body and Blood of Christ, and are so intimately connected with the sacred vessels—the chalice and paten—they should ever be found spotlessly clean and white; and to this end they require to be frequently and carefully washed,[2] and always handled with care and reverence.[3]

b) The linen corporal, upon which rests the Adorable Body of Christ, reminds us of the swathing-bands of the Child Jesus in the crib, which were crimsoned with the blood of the Circumcision, and also of the fine linen shroud in which the martyred Body of Christ was wrapped and laid in the tomb.[4] The linen winding-sheet, which shrouded "our Treasure, the Ransom of Captives,"[5] bears the imprint of the passion of the Saviour, the traces of His painful, bleeding wounds, and is still venerated in the Holy Chapel, (as it is

---

[1] An non obstantibus decretis a S. R. C. editis, uti liceat palla a parte superiori panno serico cooperta et auro contexta? Resp. Permitti posse, dummodo palla linea subnexa calicem cooperiat, ac pannus superior non sit nigri coloris aut referat aliqua mortis signa (S. R. C. 10. Jan. 1852). This decree, which merely tolerates such palls (as were formerly forbidden, Jan. 22, 1701), has not yet been received into the authentic collection.

[2] Linteamina, corporalia, pallae et alia altaris indumenta integra sint et mundissima, et saepe abluantur per personas a canonibus deputatas (scil. quoad corporalia et pallas, per ipsum sacerdotem, ubi subdiaconus non adest), ad reverentiam et praesentiam Salvatoris nostri et totius curiae coelestis, quam huic Sacramento conficiendo et confecto non dubium est interesse (Coll. Lacens. tom. III, 932).

[3] Corporals, palls and purificators may after being used at the Holy Sacrifice and before their first washing be handled only by persons to whom the privilege of touching the consecrated vessels is permitted. — The first washing of these three linen cloths must always be done by a cleric of the higher orders, that is, by a sub-deacon, deacon or priest; afterwards they may be thoroughly washed by lay persons. The water is to be poured into the Sacrarium. — Certum est, corporalia, pallas et purificatoria etiam benedicta, antequam fuerint adhibita ad sacrum usum, posse ab omnibus contingi, etiam a laicis et feminis, quia prohibetur contactus vel ratione *unctionis sacri chrismatis* vel ratione *specierum consecratarum;* neutra autem ratio ex praedictis militat in casu nostro. Similiter quando post sacrum usum fuerunt lota, antequam iterum adhibeantur ad sacrum usum, possunt licite ab omnibus tangi, quia moraliter censentur ac si essent nova (Quarti, In rubr. Miss. p. 2, tit. 1, sect. 3, dub. 6).

[4] Panni in quibus corpus Christi consecratur, repraesentant sindonem mundam qua corpus Christi involutum est, et ideo sicut illa *linea* fuit, ita non licet nisi in pannis *lineis* corpus Christi consecrare. — *Linum* etiam competit huic sacramento et propter *puritatem,* quia ex eo panni candidissimi et facile mundabiles fiunt, et propter multiplicem *tunsionem* lini qua paratur ad hoc ut ex eo fiat pannus candidus, quae competit ad significandam *passionem* Christi; unde non deceret de pannis sericis corporale et pallas altaris esse, quamvis sint pretiosiores, neque de panno lineo tincto, quamvis sit pulchrior (S. Thom. IV, dist. 13, q. 1, a. 2, sol. 3, ad 3).

[5] O admirabilis sindon! in qua involutus est thesaurus noster, redemptio captivorum (Offic. sacrat. sindon. D. N. I. Ch.).

called), of Turin as a precious relic of our Lord.[1] The head of Jesus was wrapped in a separate linen cloth—the designated napkin (*sudarium*—Joann. 20, 6–7);—referring to this covering, the Church prays at the blessing of the corporal and pall, that they "may be made, by the grace of the Holy Ghost, a new napkin (*novum sudarium*) for the Body and Blood of our Redeemer." — The fine white linen, of which the corporals and palls are made, symbolizes, moreover, the most pure Body of Christ in the incarnation, in His passion and in His transfiguration. Linen is a product of the earth, prepared with much care, and made shining and white after much labor. The Son of God, as the New Adam, has also taken His body from the immaculate, untainted earth of the virginal bosom of Mary — and only by His painful passion and death was His body fitted for the blessed glory of the resurrection and heavenly bliss. The sight of the linen corporal and pall is, therefore, calculated to awaken in us the remembrance of the pure Body of Christ sacrificed, once capable of suffering and mortal, but now transfigured in glory and immortal, and to excite us to the consideration of the Incarnation, Passion and Resurrection of Christ. — The white glossy linen is, finally, a figure of the purity of heart or the spiritual ornaments[2] with which the faithful should be attired, that they may present themselves worthy guests at the Sacrificial Banquet of the Lamb and in all due disposition receive the holy Body of Jesus Christ.[3]

The symbolical meaning of the four named requisites for the Holy Sacrifice can be construed in a somewhat different manner: the chalice may be considered as the sepulchre, the paten as the stone wherewith it was closed; the corporal, the winding-sheet in which

---

[1] Permansit hactenus integra sindon illa, quae corporis Christi delibuta unguento, in sepulchro posita fuit, veluti operimentum et stratum, cui etiam imago Christi in sepulchro jacentis impressa est asservaturque summo honore in ecclesia Taurinensi (Gretser, De Sancta Cruce l. 1, cap. 97).

[2] In tribus, quae perducunt corporale *lineum* ad candorem, intelliguntur tria, quae faciunt ad nostram mundificationem. — Primo enim lavatur, secundo torquetur, tertio exsiccatur. Sic qui ad suscipiendum Dominum nostrum mundus vult fieri, primo debet per aquam lacrymarum lavari, secundo per opera poenitentiae torqueri, tertio per fervorem amoris Dei a carnalium desideriorum humore siccari (B. Albert. serm. 15. de ss. Euch. sacram).

[3] To the objection: Sicut aurum pretiosius est inter materias vasorum, ita panni serici pretiosiores sunt inter alios pannos. Ergo sicut calix fit de auro, ita pallae altaris debent de serico fieri, et non solum de panno lineo St. Thomas answers: Dicendum, quod ubi potuit *sine periculo* fieri, Ecclesia statuit circa hoc sacramentum *id quod expressius repraesentat passionem Christi*. Non erat autem tantum periculum circa corpus, quod ponitur in corporali, sicut circa sanguinem, qui continetur in calice. Et ideo licet calix non fit de petra, corporale tamen fit de panno lineo, quo corpus Christi fuit involutum ... Competit etiam pannus lineus propter sui munditiam ad significandam conscientiae puritatem, et propter multiplicem laborem, quo talis pannus praeparatur, ad significandam Christi passionem (3, q. 83, a. 3, ad 7).

the holy body was wrapped, and the pall, the napkin which bound up the blood-stained head of Jesus. [1]

3.   The purificator [2] is a small linen cloth which is used at the Holy Sacrifice for cleansing and wiping the chalice, as well as the mouth and fingers of the celebrant after Communion, and to wipe off the paten before the consecrated Host is placed upon it. [3] That it may the more easily be distinguished from the other cloths, a small cross should be embroidered in its centre. The purificator may, but need not be blessed. (S. R. C. 7. Sept. 1816).

4.   The Burse [4] and the Chalice-veil. — The corporal must not be allowed to remain lying on the altar, nor be carried in the bare hands, but it must be placed in a special case, which is usually called the burse. [5] The burse should be open only at one end and be conveniently large enough to enclose the corporal within it. The exterior covering of the burse, on which sacred emblems may be wrought, must correspond as to material and color with the vestments of the Mass; [6] the interior may be lined with silk or fine white linen.—It is proper to use precious material for the making of the burse; because it serves as an ornament to the chalice and as a receptacle for the blessed and very sacred linen within, namely the corporal. [7] The chalice-veil, [8] with which the chalice and paten are

---

[1]   Duplex est palla, quae dicitur corporale, una scilicet, quam diaconus super altare extendit; altera, quam super calicem plicatam imponit, significantes duo linteamina, quibus Joseph corpus Christi involvit. *Extensa* repraesentat sindonem, qua corpus fuit in sepulchro involutum, et inde corporale vocatur; *plicata* super calicem posita sudarium, quo caput ejus fuit separatim involutum (Durand. Ration. 1. 4, c. 29, n. 4).

[2]   Writers of the Middle Age and the Ordines Romani do not allude to the purificator; yet the Ordo Rom. XIV. mentions a pannus tersorius, which served for purification. The Greeks use for cleansing the chalice and paten the holy sponge (ἡ ἁγία σπογγία).

[3]   Since the purificator is intended for the cleansing of holy things, the rubrics expressly require that it should be kept clean (purificatorium *mundum*).

[4]   It was introduced toward the close of the Middle Age, ut corporale cautius et decentius deferretur (Krazer). It is called pera (πήρα, wallet), theca, (θήκη, envelop, cover, case) and mostly bursa (money-bag from the Greek βύρσα, drawn-off skin, hide).

[5]   S. R. C. 27. Febr. 1847.

[6]   Super velo ponit (sacerdos) *bursam coloris paramentorum*, intus habentem corporale plicatum (Miss. Rom. Rit. celebr. Miss. tit. 1, n. 1).

[7]   The burse, therefore, should not be a simple covering, that is, merely laid on the corporal, or a lid with a pocket sewed to the upper portion, but rather a double cover of strong card-board forming a quadrangle, the three sides of which are sewed together in such wise that into the fourth open side the folded corporal may easily be pushed and taken therefrom.

[8]   Velum=cover, cloth, veil. The velum calicis and the velum humerale of the sub-deacon at High Mass must be of the liturgical color of the Mass. Velum autem celebrantis in expositione ss. Sacramenti nunquam alius nisi coloris *albi* sit; prout vela ciborii (that is, the Ciborium Cover) quoque, necnon bursae et baldachini deferendo Venerabili Sacramento inservientes ex *albi* coloris panno confecta sint

covered up to the time of the Offertory and after the Communion,[1] should be of silk[2] and correspond in color to the Office of the day. Although a cross upon it is not prescribed, the veil is almost universally decorated with this sacred emblem. It should not be thick and stiff, but soft, that it may the more easily be spread over the chalice and folded again.[3]—The object of covering the chalice with a veil is to express due reverence for this sacred vessel ; it may also relate to the obscurity, profundity and incomprehensibility of the mystery of the Eucharistic Sacrifice.

5. To the above mentioned articles may, moreover, be added some others, such as the cruets, finger-bowl, the small spoon, the bell.

The cruets,[4] of which the Church makes use for presenting the wine and water for the Eucharistic Sacrifice of the Blood of Christ,[5] may be made of metal (gold, silver, pewter);[6] but it is more appropriate to make them of crystal or of glass,[7] as these are more easily kept clean, and the wine is more readily distinguished. If they are made of metal, they should be distinctly marked on the covers respectively V and A, in order to prevent any mistake of taking the water for the wine.—They should be brought to the altar on a plate or small basin (*pelvicula*).[8] Both cruets and basin should be

oportet (Conc. Prag. a. 1860, tit. 5, c. 7, n. 2).—The sub-deacon uses the humeral-veil to carry the chalice, (the veil of which has previously been removed), from the credence table to the altar, and to hold the paten covered in his hands from the Offertory to the end of the Pater noster.

[1] If the veil is rather small, it should be arranged so that at least the front of the chalice, exposed to view, may be entirely covered (S. R. C. 12. Jan. 1669).

[2] Cum velo *serico* (Miss. Rom. Rit. celebr. tit. 1, n. 1). — The word sericus= silken, originated from the circumstance that the inhabitants of Serer (a people in the East of Asia) chiefly manufactured this material.

[3] The blessing of the chalice-veil and burse is not prescribed, but is proper.

[4] The name now is use is ampulla (diminutive of amphora; properly amp[h]orula, also amporla, ampurla, ampulla; from αμφί, utrinque, and φέρω, porto—because this vessel had two handles to carry it by)=a vessel with a small neck and two handles, a small flask—and *urceolus* (from urceus)=a little pitcher. More ancient designations are: amula; scyphus (σκύφος)=bowl, goblet; lagoena= flask ; phiala (φιάλη)=cup, beaker; in the Ord. Rom. it is termed also fons.

[5] As long as the faithful brought wine for the Sacrifice, it was collected in two larger vessels (amae from ἄμη, bucket). From this a smaller vessel was filled (amula offertoria vel oblatoria) and from the first the deacon poured out the wine through a strainer (colum vinarium, colatorium) into the chalice for Mass. Archidiaconus sumit amulam pontificis de subdiacono oblationario et refundit in calicem super colatorium (Ordo Rom. III. n. 13). After the offerings of wine ceased, the present cruets replaced these larger vessels.

[6] An uti liceat in Missae sacrificio ampullis *aureis* vel *argenteis?* Resp.: Tolerandum esse consuetudinem (S. R. C. 28. Apr. 1866).

[7] Ampullae *vitreae* vini et aquae cum pelvicula (Miss. Rom. Rubr. gener. lit. 20).

[8] These vessels were formerly—and even in the sixteenth century—carried with bare hands by the acolytes to the altar; but the Cerem. Episc. has the rubric: Acolythus . . . curam habebit portandi ampullas sive urceolos vini et aquae super aliquo parvo bacili (basin) pariter dispositos (L. 1, c. 11, n. 10).

always kept clean and bright.[1]— The small spoon which is used in many places to take the water from the cruet and to pour it into the wine, is neither prescribed nor forbidden by the Church.[2] If the water cruet is provided with a tube for pouring out, then the danger of mingling too much water with the wine is as much obviated as by the use of a small spoon.

For a considerable time the Church has been using a little altar-bell,[3] to call the attention of those present to the most sacred portions of the Mass: such as the Sanctus, Elevation,[4] Communion, and to animate their devotion. They are either hand or mural bells; their form and their ornamentation should differ from that of bells intended for profane use. Already in the Middle Age, at the moment of the Elevation a signal from a "small bell" was given to the faithful assisting, in order that "the attention of the people might be aroused, and they be admonished to adore Christ in spirit and in truth, in the sacrament, which would now be shown to them."[5]

All these latter articles which serve for the ornamentation and equipment of the most sacred of all Church vessels—the consecrated chalice—, are to be handled with religious care and devotion, and should be kept clean and in good condition. *Sancta sancte tractanda.*[6]

---

[1] For the washing of the hands, already at an early period (about the fifth century), special tankards and a basin (aquamanile, vas manuale, aquamanus, aquamanualis, agmanilis), to receive the water were employed, and a cloth was used for wiping the hands (manutergium, manutergiolum). — For the washing of the hands at four different times during solemn Pontifical High Mass (before vesting, after the reading of the Offertorium, after the incensing of the offerings, and after Communion) a larger cruet (buccale) and a larger basin (lanx) of a precious metal are required (Cfr. Cerem. Episc. 1. 1, c. 11, n. 11–12).

[2] S. R. C. 9. Sept. 1850 ad 15.—6. Febr. 1858.—The Cerem. Roman. prescribes (lib. 2, tit. 2, c. 15) that in the Solemn Pontifical Mass of the Pope, at the Offertory the water be mixed in the chalice with a small golden spoon. Already in the Middle Age a spoon was occasionally used by the priests for the same purpose. Cf. Zaccaria, Onomast. rituale, s. v. cochlear.—In the Greek liturgy a gold or silver spoon (λαβίς), forming a cross at the handle, has been used from the most remote times to remove the particles placed in the chalice and to distribute them to the communicants.

[3] They have always had different names, for example, campanula=a small bell; cymbalum=a cymbal, gong; tintinnabulum=a small bell, tingling bell.

[4] The rubrics prescribe that the signal be given with the bell only at the Sanctus and at the Elevation (Miss. Rom. Rubr. celebr. tit. 7, n. 8.—tit. 8, n. 6).

[5] Tewtsch Rational über das Ambt hl. mess (1535) c. 14, n. 4.

[6] Religionis christianae excellentia postulat, in cultu divino nihil adhiberi, nisi divina majestate dignum, sacramentorum sanctitati atque fidelium pietati congruum. — Post animarum salutem nihil sacerdotali sollicitudine dignius, quam rerum et aedium sacrarum cura, in quibus Deus ipse absconditus habitat et christiana plebs verbo Dei et sacramentis pascitur. In ecclesiis omnia munda sint et nitida: curent igitur rectores, ne pulvere aut alio squalore obsordescant non solum altaria et sacra supellex, sed insuper pavimenta, parietes et tecta fornicata (the arches).—Coll. Lac. III, 1181–1193.

29. The Sacerdotal Vestments.

1. "He (the high-priest Simon) shone forth in his day as the morning star amid lowering clouds, and as the moon with the fulness of her beauty. And as the sun in his glory, so did he shine in the temple of God. And as the rainbow shedding its light in the brilliant clouds, and as the blooming of roses in the spring time, and as the lilies on the banks near the waters, and as the sweet frankincense on the summer air. As a bright fire, and frankincense aflame. As a massy vessel of gold, adorned with precious stones. As an olive-tree budding forth, and a cypress-tree rearing itself on high, like unto such was he, when he put on the robe of glory and was clothed with the perfection of power. When he went up to the holy altar, he honored the vesture of holiness" (Ecclus. 50, 6—12). With these inspired words Jesus, the son of Sirach, depicts the appearance which the high-priest of the Old Law presented to the eyes of the people, when he entered the sanctuary in his festal attire. Now, if God even in the Old Law, which was but a weak figure of the wonderful mysteries of the New Covenant, prescribed such beautiful, such rich garments for the liturgical functions, "that Aaron and his sons shall use them when they go into the tabernacle of the testimony, or when they approach to the altar to minister in the sanctuary, lest being guilty of iniquity they die" (Exod. 28, 43); how much more is it the Lord's will, that His beloved Spouse (Holy Church) should appear at the altar robed in magnificence and splendor, whenever she celebrates that adorable Sacrifice and spreads the Table of the Lord whereat even here below, in this country of her exile, is had a foretaste of those joys which she is to enjoy forever in her heavenly country with the Lamb!

To the believing eye and mind it would appear as a desecration of what is most holy, an outrage against the Divine Mysteries for one to attempt to offer the Holy Sacrifice at the altar in the ordinary everyday dress. The holiness of the house of God and the altar, the sublimity of the Sacrificial action[1] and the dignity of the Christian priesthood demand for the celebration of the Mass special and venerable vestments, altogether distinct from the ordinary dress. Since a distinction in garment at the sacred functions — especially at the Holy Sacrifice — is so necessary, and founded in the nature of things and is, moreover, most appropriate, both the Old Law and the New Law prescribe a special clothing in their liturgy. The

---

[1] Pertinet ad splendorem et decorem cujusvis sacri ministerii, et praesertim tanti sacrificii, ut non fiat tantum veste vulgari et communi, sed ut ipso exteriori apparatu et sacris indumentis indicetur, actionem illam non esse communem et vulgarem, sed sacram. Etenim si absque sacris indumentis communi modo et vulgari fieret, vilesceret quodammodo, praesertim apud homines rudes et sensibiles, qui non facile distinguunt pretiosum a vili; igitur ad decorem et debitum honorem hujus sacrificii conveniens fuit institutio sacrarum vestium (Suarez disp. 83, sect. 2, n. 2).

Council of Trent declares, that the use of vestments in Holy Church rests on "Apostolic prescription and tradition." This is, indeed, to be understood as follows. In the primitive ages of Christianity, the apparel for Divine Worship did not differ from the clothing of ordinary life;[1] but it was distinguished from the profane clothing in being as rich and as beautiful as possible, and in being allowed to be worn only at the celebration of the Divine Mysteries.[2] In the course of time and gradually the most complete and striking difference arose between the liturgical and civilian dress. The more ancient forms were preserved up to the sixteenth and seventeenth centuries. From this epoch regard for tradition greatly decreased, and the clear understanding of the object and symbolism of ecclesiastical vestments was lost; the Church authorities left the manufacture of these articles to the prevailing industrialism and to individual tastes; and the oft-repeated decrees of the Church were inadequate to counteract the decadence. Hence it came to pass that in many places the vestments destined for Divine Worship answered as little to the requirements of the liturgy as to those of art. Above all, the liturgical vestments should be restored to their flowing, folded and ample form. A general return to more worthy forms cannot be effected by an imitation (according to fancy) of ancient patterns prevalent at various periods, but only by once more following the ordinances of the Church.

The form of the church vestments should be those that have been traditional and in general use; therefore, those of the West should be Roman in form. Only with permission of the Pope is a change allowable.[3] If, for instance, we would wish to introduce

---

[1] Patres nostri in illis quoad *formam* vestibus sacram celebrarunt Liturgiam, quibus per quinque saecula et reliqui laici in imperio Romano et longiori tempore clerici in foro erant induti. Unice dabant operam Antistites, ut vestes *liturgicae candidiores, nitidiores* ac tandem *pretiosiores* essent vestibus communibus et usitatis; ut *venustiores* tantum Romanorum, Graecorum et Orientalium habitus, iique maxima ex parte *talares* adhiberentur ad sacrificium, prout illius dignitas omnino exigebat (Krazer Sect. 3, art. 5, cap. 2, § 139).

[2] The prohibition of Pope Stephen I. († 257), to wear church apparel in civic life (Instituit, ut sacerdotes et diaconi nusquam sacris vestibus nisi in ecclesia uterentur — Breviar. Rom. lect. 9, 2. Aug.), is only a renewed inculcation of an ancient custom then overlooked by some ecclesiastics. "Neither in the East nor in the West did the liturgical vestments differ altogether from those used at that epoch in ordinary life, still less were they different from the patriarchal clothing as to form, as is indicated by the similarity of names. On the other hand, from all investigations we are to draw a two-fold conclusion. First, that not every garment, nor every change of form consequent upon the decay of discipline, was employed in the liturgy; but certain definite garments appropriate to the holy functions and of a most befitting form were selected. Secondly, that these garments served for divine service alone, and were therefore richly adorned (Jakob, Die Kunst im Dienste der Kirche, p. 321).

[3] S. R. C. 21. Aug. 1863. — Cf. Pastoralblatt für die Diöcese Ermland, Jahrgang 1875, S. 95.

again the so-called gothic form of chasubles, the Holy See, that is, the Sacred Congregation of Rites, must be informed of this design, together with the reasons therefor. In the making of vestments excellent and appropriate patterns should be insisted on, that is, smallness, stiffness and deformity should be avoided.

With regard to the material of the vestments, the amice and alb must be of linen. — Silk and woolen cinctures corresponding to the color of the day are permitted; but the Church justly prefers them to be of white linen.[1] — It is not allowed to have on the lower hem or on the sleeves of the alb transparent lace showing a colored foundation.[2] — For the vestments themselves,[3] that is, for vestments corresponding to the liturgical colors, among which chasuble, stole and maniple are reckoned, no particular material is prescribed. But all common material is forbidden, such as is worn in every day life; for example, linen and cotton, also a material that is half linen and half cotton (cotton cambric);[4] finally, wool. A sort of material also is forbidden in which fine threads of glass (*vitrum in filamenta subtilissima redactum*) are substituted for threads of gold or silver (as glass brocade).[5] However, that material is not prohibited in which the long threads are of cotton (or even of linen or wool) and the cross threads are of silk.[6] The fabrics, (especially those of gold,

---

[1] An sacerdotes in sacrificio Missae uti possint cingulo *serico?* Resp.: Congruentius uti cingulo *lineo* (S. R. C. 22. Jan. 1701). — Posse uti cingulo *coloris paramentorum* (8. Jun. 1709). — Nihil obstare, quominus cingula *lanea* adhiberi possint (23. Dec. 1862). — White cinctures are always liturgical, and for practical reasons we are always recommended to use them, although it is necessary to have them more frequently washed than colored cinctures; for the changing of cinctures is thereby avoided, if, for example, after a Requiem Mass another function is to be performed (benedictio mulieris, churching of women, &c.), when the use of a black cincture would be out of place and inappropriate.

[2] S. R. C. 17. Aug. 1833. — Yet it appears (as may be seen even in Rome) that, in consequence of a contrary custom, at least on the sleeves a colored ornament may be suffered under a transparent lace. Cfr. Patroni tratt. 2, lezion. 5, n. 44. — Such a violet ornament is conceded to bishops, and a red one to cardinals. Cfr. Stella, Instit. liturg. p. 52.

[3] To the sacred vestments, which in the rubrics are usually called sacra indumenta, sacra paramenta, or simply paramenta (that is, vestments), in a stricter sense belong the chasuble, the cope, the stole, the maniple, the dalmatic, the tunicella and the humeral-veil. Whoever is robed in one or more of these vestments, is called in the rubrics really and simply paratus. In a more comprehensive sense, however, the amice, alb and cincture are also included in the sacra paramenta. — Cf. Bourbon, Introd. aux cérém. rom. p. 113.

[4] S. R. C. 22. Sept. 1837.

[5] S. R. C. 11. Sept. 1847. — The reason for this prohibition lies not only in the danger of glass (as glass threads easily break into small splinters and might fall into the chalice), but also and principally in consideration of the little value of glass (*vilitas* materiae). Cf. S. R. C. 14. Jul. 1141. Therefore, trimmings made of glass beads are forbidden, as well as those made of fine spun glass thread.

[6] S. R. C. 23. Mart. 1835; 23. Mart. 1882.

silver and silk) of which the chasuble, stole and maniple should be made, are, therefore, more precious than the materials found in garments worn in daily life.

All that is precious belongs to the Lord and should serve to promote His glory; therefore, the Church would have not only rich vessels, but also handsome vestments for the service of the altar. The richness and the value of the sacred vestments betoken and awaken due reverence for Divine service, and set forth before the faithful the incomprehensible grandeur and holiness of the mysteries of the Eucharistic Sacrifice. — Vestments for Divine worship become sacred in a special manner by reason of the blessing of the Church imparted to them, and of their religious symbolical meaning.

2. All the vestments for Mass (cincture included) must be blessed before being used.[1] This blessing of the vestments has, in all probability, been in practice since the first ages; nowadays it is strictly enjoined, and is to be done by a bishop or a priest especially empowered thereto. — By this blessing (benedictio *constitutiva*) the altar-vestments are in a special manner consecrated to God and His service, that is, they become sacred things (*res sacrae*), and should be regarded and treated with reverence. — This blessing is retained as long as the vestments preserve their original shape and are suitable for use.[2] Worn out vestments and those no longer fit for divine service, should not be put to profane uses, but be burned, and the ashes are to be thrown into the *Sacrarium*.[3] — The blessing is imparted to the vestments by means of prayer, the sign of the cross and sprinkling with holy water, and, at the same time, special graces are invoked for the wearers of the blessed garments; for the Church petitions not only, that the Lord may "with the dew of His grace

---

[1] Vestimenta ecclesiastica, quibus Domino ministratur, et *sacrata* debent esse et honesta (Cap. 42. de consecr. dist. 1). From the circumstance that the blessing of the vestments for divine worship is mentioned for the first time in the fourth century, it in nowise follows that it was not previously practised; whether at that epoch it was already obligatory or merely optional, is immaterial. This blessing is reserved to the bishop. The bishops may only in virtue of an apostolic indult, generally granted to them by the so-called Quinquennial-Faculties, delegate priests (whether they hold an ecclesiastical dignity or not) to bless the vestments and the other necessary articles for the Holy Sacrifice (S. R. C. 16. Mai. 1744). — But the delegated priest may not use the formula of blessing specially reserved to the bishop in the Roman Pontifical, but he must take the ordinary formula to be found in the Missal. Religious superiors, as a rule, have also the privilege of blessing vestments, but only for their own churches and convents (S. R. C. 13. Mart. 1632). Whether vestments, that is, all objects in general used for divine service, when made of material forbidden by the Church, can validly be blessed, is disputed.

[2] The sacred vestments lose their blessing, when they are so torn or so worn out as to be unsuitable for divine service, and when another vestment is made out of them, v. g., an amice out of an alb. When they are mended, the blessing is lost only in case such a part of it is separated from it as to render it unfit for use. v. g., if an arm were taken out of an alb.

[3] Vasa sacra et vestimenta sacerdotalia nolite negotiari aut tabernario (pawn-broker) in pignus dare (Pontif. Roman. Ordo ad Synodum).

and abundant blessing cleanse, sanctify and consecrate these sacerdotal vestments, to the end that they may become fit for the service of God and the holy mysteries," but also that the priests "robed in them may be protected against all the assaults or temptations of the evil spirits, and may exercise the holy mysteries devoutly, fervently and worthily, persevere in God's service, remain subject to God in peace and devotion — and appear before the face of God holy, immaculate, without reproach and obtain the assistance of Divine mercy."

3. The sacred vestments enjoy another religious feature by means of the mystic-symbolical (mysterious) meaning which the Church ascribes to them, and which should be ascribed to them in the meaning of the Church.[1] In the Divine worship, in the service of God there is nothing merely exterior: all is figurative and expressive of the interior, there all is "spirit and life". The Church endeavors, namely, to spiritualize and transform, so to speak, corporeal things by means of higher, supernatural relations, in order to direct the observing, reflecting mind of the faithful to what is invisible, divine and eternal. — This is also the case with the liturgical vestments, which thus acquire the significance and virtue of a picture; for they indicate not only in general the majesty of the Eucharistic Sacrifice, but they express, in a special way, manifold mysteries that excite and nourish devotion. The sacred vestments are full of salutary instruction and admonition for all that will comprehend their meaning and attend to their language. Even if they were not originally introduced on account of this symbolism, the Church afterward justly ascribed to them a higher and mystical meaning, inasmuch as she made use, for example, of the name and origin, the color and destination, the usage and form, as well as the method and manner of putting on and wearing the vestments, in order to express mysteries of the life of Christ and of faith, and moral admonitions.[2] The symbolical conception and meaning of the litur-

---

[1] Quis ignorat, necesse esse, ut in publicum prodiens munerique et ministerio venerando vacans non solum vestiatur, verum et modeste et decore vestiatur. En itaque causam naturalem et physicam vestium, quibus presbyteri in obeundis sacris muneribus induuntur. Verum postquam sanctae matri Ecclesiae placuit, singularem illis usum assignare, formamque praescribere easque alio quam ministerii tempore adhibere vetuit, ac denique easdem certarum ceremoniarum pompa tradere, particularibusque precibus benedicere incepit, profecto tanquam res sacrae ac symbolicae considerandae sunt. At ridiculus sane mihi foret ille, qui rejectis omnibus symbolicis et mysticis significationibus hic solum causas naturales physicas et necessitatis reperiri contenderet, universosque mysticos conceptus debiles ac inanes judicaret (Languet, De vero Ecclesiae sensu circa sacrarum caerimoniarum usum § 33).

[2] De indumentis sacerdotalibus ... diligenter considerandum est, quid in moribus sacerdotum significet illa varietas vestium, quid fulgor auri, quid nitor gemmarum, cum *nihil* ibi debeat esse *ratione carens*, sed forma sanctitatis et omnium imago virtutum. Sicut enim bona domus in ipso vestibulo agnoscitur, sic Christi sacerdos cultu sacrarum vestium ostendit exterius, qualis apud se esse

gical vestments is, therefore, fully justified and established.[1] This symbolism, in general, is twofold — namely, allegorical and moral.[2]

　　The Eucharistic Sacrifice is the living representation and mystical renewal of the Sacrifice of the Cross; accordingly, the vestments have reference to the different garments with which Christ was clothed in His passion, or to the instruments of torture wherewith He was tormented and reviled. — The vestments for the Mass recall to mind different scenes in the passion of our Lord. This difference of course here exists, that the vestment which serves to adorn the celebrant as a garment of honor and joy, was once the cause of most bitter confusion and keenest suffering to our crucified Saviour.[3] This allegorical interpretation of the sacred vestments is not expressed in the prayers of the Church; therefore, in considering this subject we must have recourse to the opinion of liturgical and ascetical authors, who differ more or less in their views. The most generally accepted allegorical explanation of the sacerdotal vestments for Mass is the following. — The amice may remind us of the shameful veiling of the eyes and face of Jesus by the Jews, who at the same time struck Him on the head and in the face, saying derisively: "Prophesy to us, Christ, who struck Thee?" and uttering many other blasphemies against Him. — The alb reminds us that Jesus Christ, the Eternal Wisdom, was clothed in mockery as a fool in a white garment by Herod and his court. — The cincture recalls the cords with

debeat interius. . . . In ornamentis . . . et sublimitas sacerdotii commendatur et sacerdotum casta dignitas significatur, quatenus per exteriorem habitum discant quales intra se debeant esse, qui vices illius veri summique Pontificis gerant, in quo fuit omnis plenitudo virtutum, quam profitentur exteriora ornamenta membrorum (Ivon. Carnot. Serm. 3).

　　[1] Ex vestibus omnibus recte compositis resultat gravis quidam et decens ornatus sacerdotis ad sacrificandum accedentis, quod in hujusmodi vestimentis primum omnium considerari debuit; nam hoc est veluti primum fundamentum et litteralis ratio horum indumentorum. Sed ultra hoc habent haec omnia optimas et sacras significationes, tum in ordine ad mores, tum in ordine ad Christi passionem (Suarez disp. 82, sect. 2, n. 3).

　　[2] Singulis vestibus liturgicis significatio *mystica* inest; quatenus his Christi repraesentatur passio et ejusdem designantur virtutes, quibus exornari sacerdotem par est, ut dum munere Christi personam gerit, moribus etiam similitudinem Christi referat, pleneque Christum indutus, in Christum veluti transformatus videatur. Ideo duplicem significationem vestes sacrae exhibent, quae quidem praeprimis ministris, sed etiam populo bene perspecta esse deberet, nempe *allegoricam, quae respicit Christi passionem, et moralem, quae spectat virtutes sacerdotales* (Müller, Theol. mor., l. 3, tit. 1, § 31).

　　[3] Here also the words of Cardinal Toledo find their application. Among the reasons for the institution of the Sacrifice of the Mass he gives in the fourth place the following: ut Christus ostenderet unionem amoris indissolubilem, quam habet cum sua Ecclesia. Una enim caro fit sponsi et sponsae; unde Christus voluit idem poculum, quod in cruce gustaverat, Ecclesiae dare; sed sub specie altera et incruentum *ac suave, tota amaritudine sibi reservata* (In Summ. theol. s. Thom. enarrat. De sacrif. Miss. controv. 1, art. 3).

which our Lord was bound, when taken captive by the soldiers in the garden of olives, in order to drag Him to the slaughter as a lamb not opening His mouth, and also the ropes which tied His innocent all-powerful hands to the pillar at the scourging, and, finally, the thongs wherewith His immaculate flesh was scourged and torn amid frightful torture. — The maniple refers to the fetters with which the hands of our Lord, as those of a malefactor, were bound. — The stole indicates the heavy burden of the Cross, which the exhausted Victim voluntarily and patiently carried on the way to His crucifixion. — The chasuble brings to our mind the purple robe of mockery wherewith the soldiers, after they had crowned Him with thorns, covered the mangled body of Jesus, reviling His regal dignity by kneeling in mockery before Him. Viewed in this light, the sacerdotal vestments recall to us in what manner the Saviour on His "way" to glory drank from "the torrent", that is, from the bitter flood of sufferings, labors and humiliations (Ps. 109, 7); in putting them on or when beholding them, we should awaken most ardent sentiments of love, compassion, sorrow, gratitude, hope, amazement, resignation and compunction.[1]

In a moral sense the vestments designate the different virtues with which the celebrant should be clothed and adorned after the example of the invisible High Priest, Jesus Christ, whom he represents at the altar. This meaning of the vestments is expressed in the liturgy in a manifold way, and it can, therefore, be surely ascertained from the words with which they are bestowed at the ordination, and taken off at the degradation, as well as from the prayers the celebrant has to recite when putting them on before Mass. Accordingly, it will here be shown more minutely what moral lessons and admonitions are inculcated according to the spirit of the Church by the six vestments used by the priest at Mass; namely the amice, alb, cincture, maniple, stole and chasuble.

a) The amice[2] is put on first.[3] It is a linen envelop which

---

[1] Cum haec indumenta signa sint eorum, quae Christus pro nobis perpessus est, varii actus a sacerdote, dum illis induitur, eliciendi sunt, amoris, doloris, gratitudinis et intensissimi desiderii ejus patientiam et humilitatem imitandi in doloribus, afflictionibus, opprobriis aliisque adversitatibus sustinendis (Bona, Tract. ascet. de Missa, c. 5, § 2).

[2] Amictus from amicio (amb and jacio) = to throw around, to envelop. Se amicire and amiciri was the identical word for throwing about or putting on the outer garment, while induere was employed for the putting on of a garment and vesture for clothing the body. Hence amictus = the throwing around of a garment; meton. the cloak = the garment serving as a cloak, the outer robe; transferred to head-wrap. Rarer designations: humerale, superhumerale = shoulder covering. In the Ord. Rom. the name anaboladium (ἀναβολάδιον, to throw about the shoulders, — cfr. Ital. Gen. 49, 11) in corrupt forms (anabolajum, anagolajum, ambolagium, anagolai, anagolagi) is often used.

[3] According to the most ancient Ord. Rom. the amice was put on after the alb and cincture, — until about the twelfth century. Amalarius, however, mentions the present practice in the ninth century. Amictus est *primum* vestimentum nostrum, quo collum undique cingimus (De eccles. offic. 1. 2, c. 17).

covers, in the first place, the head, then the neck and shoulders; in the middle of it a cross is wrought, which is to be kissed in putting it on and taking it off.[1] — The amice has been in use since about the eighth century; it appears that up to that date Mass was celebrated with neck uncovered.[2] At any rate already in the twelfth century the amice covered not only the neck and shoulders, but also the head; however, at the beginning of Mass it was allowed to fall back upon the shoulders, and it is still done in some Orders of monks.[3] The rite at the ordination of subdeacons reminds us of this practice, when the bishop covers the head of the ordained with the amice; and also the manner of putting it on, when, according to the directions of the rubrics, the amice is first placed on the head and thence drawn down to the neck and put over the shoulders.

One meaning of the amice rests on the ancient custom of covering the head with it, and on the circumstance that in remembrance thereof the amice must still be placed on the head, before it is put on the neck and shoulders. The meaning of this rite is explained by the Church herself in the prayer which is to be recited by the celebrant when he puts on the amice: "Place, O Lord, on my head the helmet of salvation, that I may overcome the assaults of Satan."[4] The question arises, what is to be understood by this helmet of salvation (*galea salutis*), with which the priest at the altar should be armed against the attacks of Satan. The expression is taken from Holy Scripture, which also contains its meaning. When the Apostle St. Paul exhorts Christians to put on the armor of God, to resist the attacks of Satan, he urges them "to take unto them the helmet of salvation" (*galeam salutis assumite* — Ephes. 6, 17).[5]

---

[1] Missal. Rom. Rit. celebr. Miss. tit. 1, n. 3. — This kiss is prescribed both for the putting on and the taking off of the maniple and stole, and is to be regarded as a mark of reverence (actus reverentialis) toward these vestments blessed for divine service, to which a cross is affixed.

[2] Si vetusta documenta, si priscas picturas, si antiqua vitra consulamus, sacerdotes usque ad saeculum VII. et VIII. nonnisi *nudo* in *collo* conspicimus (Krazer Sect. III, art. 6, c. 1, § 162).

[3] Honorius of Autun († 1120) writes (Gemma animae 1. 1, c. 201), that the priest covers with the amice *caput* et collum et humeros.

[4] Impone, Domine, capiti meo *galeam salutis* (= impart to me the victorious hope of securing salvation, that is, heaven), ad expugnandos diabolicos incursus. The bishop prays: Pone, Domine, *galeam salutis* in capite meo ad expugnandas omnes diabolicas fraudes: inimicorum omnium versutias superando (Missale Roman.). — Already in Tertullian (De veland. virgin. c. 15) we meet a passage relative to these prayers: Pura virginitas ... confugit ad *velamen capitis*, quasi ad *galeam* contra tentationes.

[5] Quaenam est haec galea? Dico "galeam salutis", i. e. galeam, quae est ipsa salus. Galea ergo militis Christiani est salus allata a Christo et *sperata* a Christianis, h. e. *spes salutis:* ita enim se explicat Apostolus I. Thessal. 5, 8. Ecce *spem salutis* vocat *galeam.* Sicut enim galea principem corporis partem, puta caput ipsum, a quo cetera membra totusque homo pendet, tuetur et communit, ita spes salutis et gloriae coelestis ac immortalis servat et communit caput, i. e.

In another place he says Christians should "be sober, having on the breast-plate of faith and charity, and for a helmet the hope of salvation" (*induti loricam fidei et charitatis et galeam spem salutis —* I Thess. 5, 8). The protecting helmet[1] and, consequently, the amice also which covers the head in a similar manner, are accordingly symbolical of Christian hope; for "hope" in the goods of grace and glory acquired and promised to us by Christ is a powerful weapon of protection against "our adversary the devil who, as a roaring lion, goeth about seeking whom he may devour" (I Peter 5, 8). Truly, the supernatural virtue of hope is our protection and shield in combat against all the enemies of salvation! "They that hope in the Lord shall renew their strength, they shall take wings as the eagles, they shall run and not be weary, they shall walk and not faint" (Isa. 40, 31). These words are the most beautiful triumphal hymn of hope. Before the goal is reached, natural strength exhausts and wears out itself — helplessly breaks down. On the contrary, they that trust in the Lord, instead of growing weary, gain fresh strength, and strive in their eagle flight to reach the loftiest and most difficult goal : Their firmness and courage remaining undaunted in every circumstance of life.[2] The contemplation of heaven, the hope of a better life, the longing for the eternal goods and joys, confidence in the blood of Christ and in the strength of grace — in short, genuine Christian hope elevates the soul above all that is earthly and perishable, fills the heart with joyful enthusiasm, strengthens and animates the will to resist valiantly and perseveringly all the attacks of the devil, as well as all the seductions and the threats of the world. — Hope unto "an inheritance incorruptible and undefiled, and that fadeth not, reserved in heaven for us" (I Peter 1, 4) is our sheet-anchor of safety on the stormy sea of life, lifts us up to behold with unfailing eye the grand and glorious destiny that awaits us hereafter, "and amid the manifold vicissitudes of this life ever inclines our hearts where true joys are to be found," assisting us "so to pass on through temporal goods that we may not forfeit those which are eternal" — *ut sic transeamus per bona temporalia, ut non amittamus aeterna* (Orat. Eccl.). Hope in the eternal and blessed life to come

---

hominis cogitationes, fines et intentiones. *Spes* ergo quasi *galea* caput nostrum symbolicum, puta finem et intentionem, armat et communit : *primo*, quia facit, ut ultimus noster finis et intentio sit Deus, fruitio Dei, salus et beatitudo aeterna, eoque refert omnes alios nostros fines et intentiones ac consequenter reliqua omnia cogitata, dicta et facta nostra ; *secundo*, quia facit, ut homo cogitans bona illa immensa, quae consecuturum se sperat, alias omnes cogitationes a diabolo suggestas repellat, hacque cogitatione et spe ardua quaevis aggrediatur et animose cum hoste confligat, proponens sibi gloriam illam speratam, quae victorem manet (Cornel. a Lapid. i. h. l.).

[1] Helmet, old German hĕlm = covering, protector, from old G. helan = to conceal, to cover, to hide ; Greek περικεφαλαία, a covering that envelops the entire head.

[2] Cf. Knabenbauer, S. J., Erklärung des Propheten Isaias a. a. O.

is a precious treasure in the heart of the Christian, of which the world cannot rob him; by means of this hope he feels happy and strong amid all kinds of sufferings, combats and tribulations. Joyful in his hope, he exclaims: "The Lord is my light and my salvation, whom shall I fear? The Lord is the protector of my life: of whom shall I be afraid? My enemies that trouble me, have themselves been weakened, and have fallen. If armies in camp should stand together against me, my heart shall not fear. If a battle should rise up against me, in this will I be confident!" (Ps. 26, 1—3.) Unshaken in faith and all confident in God, animated with every hope of his salvation, he will "walk upon the asp and the basilisk, and trample under foot the lion and the dragon" (Ps. 90, 13). — Therefore, lively hope, firm confidence in God is that armor of protection which the priest prays for in putting on the amice, that he may victoriously overcome all the attacks and temptations of the Evil One — especially during Mass. — Such a petition is most appropriate before beginning Holy Mass.[1] Although the devil is ever lying in wait for man to destroy or at least to weaken in him the life of faith and hope, yet it is more particularly at the time of the Holy Sacrifice that he seeks to confuse the soul by all manner of suggestions and distractions, in order to rob her of devotion and of the fruits of the Sacrifice. The amice now admonishes the priest to arm and to prepare himself to encounter this danger. — Therefore, this great and firm confidence with which he should approach the altar, is a means of attracting to himself an abundance of graces and blessings from the inexhaustible ocean of the Divine Goodness. Finally, unwavering confidence is necessary for the priest to enable him, a poor sinner, to venture to ascend the altar and to hold in his hands and receive into his heart the Most Holy, in whose presence the angels and archangels are filled with awe.

Originally the amice was intended to cover the bareness of the neck and to preserve the voice clear so as to enable it properly to sing the praises of God.[2] With regard to this circumstance, the Church, in the second place, considers the amice also as a symbol of self-control over one's speech, in which is comprised, in a certain sense, the sum of mortification. — At the ordination of the subdeacon, the bishop says to him: "Receive the amice, by which the restraint of the tongue is signified."[3] The putting on of the amice contains, therefore, the symbolical warning to the priest to take this resolution: "I will take heed to my ways, that I sin not with my tongue!" — *Custodiam vias meas, ut non delinquam in lingua*

---

[1] Cfr. De Ponte, De christian. homin. perfectione IV, tr. 2, cap. 10, § 1.

[2] Adverterunt Antistites, non raro ex denudato collo *raucedinem* contrahere sacerdotem, ita ut libera voce Dei laudes personare non valeret, unde collum cooperire sive *amicire* coeperunt (Krazer l. c.).

[3] Accipe amictum, per quem designatur *castigatio vocis* (Pontif. Rom. De ordinat. Subdiac.). — Quia *vocem tuam non castigasti*, ideo amictum a te auferimus (Pontif. Rom. Degradat. ab ordine Subdiac.).

mea (Ps. 38, 2). And indeed, in order not to sin with the tongue, one must attend to all his ways, that is, order and regulate by mortification his whole conduct, both his interior and exterior life, "for out of the abundance of the heart the mouth speaketh" (Matt. 12, 34). Words are the expression of the hidden life of the soul; he only can control his tongue who perfectly controls his interior. Therefore, the Apostle St. James sees in the guarding and bridling of the tongue not only something very difficult, but, moreover, a sign of great perfection; for he writes: "If any man offend not in word, the same is a perfect man" (James 3, 2).[1] And yet "Who does not offend by his tongue?" — *Quis est, qui non delinquerit in lingua sua?* (Eccl. 10, 17.) To master our tongue, we must at the proper time practise a silence holy and pleasing to God, we must be intent on recollection of mind and live in God's presence. "It is good to await in silence the salvation of God" — *Bonum est, praestolari cum silentio salutare Dei* (Lam. 3, 26). And on the other hand, he who would lead an interior life, a life hidden with Christ in God, and would become a spiritual man, a man of prayer, must, above all, bridle his tongue, avoid talkativeness, speak more with God than with men.

These two meanings of the amice mutually complete each other, since they are united to one another as means and object. Both are expressed in the words of the Psalmist, who says of the devout man, that "he shall sit solitary and hold his peace: because he has taken it up upon himself" — *Sedebit solitarius et tacebit, quia levavit super se* (Lam. 3, 28). The interior life, which is secluded and silent, quiet and mortified, disposes man to forget the outside world, to look up to God with the pure eyes of faith, to elevate his heart and mind, by the virtue of hope, to heavenly things and desires. Only that priest is able worthily to celebrate the Adorable Sacrifice, who is not immersed in the business and turmoil of the world, who is neither distracted nor dissipated in mind, but is recollected in himself and in God, who does not cling to the earth, but rises upward on the wings of hope. — As soon, therefore, as the priest has put the amice on his head, neck and shoulders, he should close up all entrance to everything foreign, preserve a holy silence and a profound recollection, carefully guard his eyes, with a reverent deportment approach the altar, and perform his sacred functions, as the mystical language of the amice admonishes him to do.[2]

---

[1] Non excessisse in verbo signum est magnae custodiae cordis, magnae sapientiae mentis, magnae perfectionis interioris (Dion. Carthus. l. c.).

[2] Obiter etiam monentur sacerdotes, a momento, quo amictum sibi imponunt, debere maximam, quam possint, modestiam oculorum servare, cum e sacristia exeunt et redeunt ad eam, et multo adhuc majorem, quamdiu sunt apud ipsum altare, ut eos semper demissos habeant neque huc illucve convertant nisi quantum necesse est ut videant quod faciunt, nec aliud quidquam aspiciant, ne eis eveniat, quod Jeremias conqueritur, dicens: "Oculus meus depraedatus est animam meam" et "mors ascendit per fenestras," quae subtrahit attentionem ac devotionem cordis

b) After the Amice comes the Alb.[1]   In the first ages of
Christianity the alb, then a garment worn in ordinary life, was
adopted into the divine service; mention of it is made for the first
time in the fourth century (in the 41. Canon of the alleged Fourth
Synod of Carthage 398) as a particular liturgical garment.   From
the beginning down to the present time it has been a wide white
linen robe full of folds, reaching down to the feet and covering the
whole body.[2] — The principal symbolical meaning of the alb, based
on its color and material, is easily recognized and, moreover, clearly
expressed in the prayer which the priest recites when putting it on:
"Purify me, O Lord, from all stain and cleanse my heart, that
washed in the Blood of the Lamb I may enjoy eternal delights."[3] —

(De Ponte, 1. c.). — Amictus significat, oportere mentem in aeternae dumtaxat salutis rerumqe coelestium consideratione fixam habere, ab omnibus curis rerum
caducarum amotam, et contra quoscunque hostium incursus spe et fiducia in Deum
tamquam galea salutari communitam (Bona, Tract. ascet. de Missa c. 5, § 2).

[1] The ordinary names for this vestment refer chiefly to its color, material,
size: *alba* sc. vestis = a white garment; *linea* sc. tunica = a tunic of linen or flax;
talaris sc. tunica (ποδήρης) = a long garment, reaching to the ankles; *camisia* = a
linen covering, worn next to the body, a shirt (Ital. camicia, from cama = a short,
low bed). — Linea dalmatica, quam dicimus *Albam* (Ord. Rom. III, n. 6). — Sequitur poderis, quae vulgo *Alba* dicitur (Pseudo-Alcuin. De divin. offic. c. 39). —
Postea (sc. post amictum) camisiam induimus, quam Albam vocamus (Amal. De
eccl. offic. 1. 2, c. 18). — Poderis est sacerdotalis linea, corpori adstricta usque ad
pedes descendens, unde et nuncupatur.   Haec vulgo camisia vocatur (S. Isidor.
Hisp. Etymolog. 1. 19, c. 21). — Formerly the Friars Minor also wore the alb,
which, however, was somewhat shorter and from which later on proceeded the
superpelliceum and rochettum.   Albas gerere, esse in albis, esse albati — these expressions were often applied to the clerics, and imply that they perform liturgical
functions (cfr. Du Saussay, Panopl. sacerdot. p. 1, 1. 2).

[2] In the Middle Age the amice, alb and cincture were frequently made of silk,
as well as richly ornamented with gold and silver.   Already from the ninth century
it became customary to put precious decorations on the edge of the alb.   As a rule,
on the different hems of the alb one or several stripes were sowed (clavus or lorum,
hence Albae monolores, dilores etc.) of purple or gold material or of colored silk
embroidery. — In place of these decorations on the edge of the alb, different kinds
of lace have been substituted since the sixteenth century, principally the beautiful, strong and durable Belgium laces, and afterward all manner of imitations of
them, down to the objectionable tulle and cotton lace. — Another ornamentation of
the alb was for a long time (from the eleventh until the seventeenth century) the
so-called parura or paratura (from parare = to adorn).   The parura were colored
adornments about one foot in length, sewed on four points of the alb (in front, at
the back and on both sides) and on the amice.   These five decorations, being generally red, answered as symbols of the five wounds of our Lord (hence they were
also called plagae or plagulae). — Both the stripes on the hem and the parura were
merely sewed on, so that in washing they could easily be removed.   If lace is used
on the hem, care should be taken, that it be handsome, rich, durable and not too
wide, as it should always be regarded only as a mere accessory. (Cf. Hefele,
Beiträge II, 172 &c.)

[3] *Dealba* me, Domine, et *munda* cor meum, ut in sanguine Agni *dealbatus*
gaudiis perfruar sempiternis.

Accordingly, the alb is a symbol of that spotless innocence and perfect purity with which the priest should appear at the altar, that he may be accounted worthy to partake with the blessed who are clothed in snow-white garments, in the never-ending joy and felicity of the heavenly nuptial feast. For they only who have washed their robes white in the Blood of the Lamb, stand "before the throne of God and serve Him day and night in His temple" (Apoc. 7, 14, 15). And the Saviour says: "He that shall overcome shall thus be clothed in white garments, and I will not blot his name out of the book of life, and I will confess his name before My Father, and before His angels" (Apoc. 3, 5). Holy Scripture itself looks upon white linen as emblematic of sanctity; for of the transfigured Spouse of Christ (the glorious Church), who is called to the eternal nuptials of the Lamb, it is said: "And it is granted to her that she should clothe herself with fine linen glittering and white. For the fine linen are the justifications (*justificationes*) of the saints" (Apoc. 19, 8).[1]

With regard to this symbolism the following points of resemblance deserve special notice. Linen does not naturally possess its brilliant whiteness, but acquires it chiefly by being washed and bleached in the rain and sun. Is not this the case with the whiteness and brilliancy of purity of life?[2] Brilliantly white, that is, perfectly pure, chaste and holy does the soul become only by many austerities, much self-denial and mortification, also only by the heavenly dew and bright rays of grace.[3] In the form of a servant,

---

[1] Byssus repraesentat purissimam et innocentissimam conversationem Sanctorum, quae in tribulatione and persecutione magis enitescit et resplendet, perinde ac byssus, h. e. linum praestantissimum injuria, i. e. maceratione, tunsione, carminatione semper melius, puta purius, candidius et splendidius evadit (Cornel. a Lapid. i. h. 1.).

[2] Hunc candorem et pulchritudinem sacerdotes non ex seipsis habent, sed ex gratia et misericordia Dei propter Christi merita, sicut illi Sancti, de quibus in Apocalypsi (7, 14) dicitur, "quod lavissent stolas suas et dealbassent illas in sanguine Agni." Qui sanguis applicatur per sacramenta et exercitia bonorum operum, lavando animas a culpis ac dealbando eas splendore praestantium virtutum. Et cum Agnus ipse sanguinem suum effuderit ingentibus cruciatibus, ut eo lavaremur ac dealbaremur, aequum est, nos quoque aliquem sustinere laborem et mortificationem, sine qua candor ille et pulchritudo non obtinetur. Ac propterea Alba est linea et alba, quae multis lotionibus et percussionibus ad suum pervenit candorem, ut intelligatur, etiam animae candorem obtinendum esse laboriosis et poenam aliquam afferentibus operibus, lacrymis, orationibus et mortificationibus. Horum omnium merito meminerit sacerdos, cum ipsam Albam induit (De Ponte 1. c. § 2).

[3] Tunica byssina est quae graece ποδήρης, i. e. talaris appellatur, quia a collo usque ad talos extenditur. ... Haec ob speciem candoris nomen Albae sortitur, quo munditiam significat ministrorum Dei. ... Caro hominis munditiam quam ex natura non habet, studio bono adnitente acquirit per gratiam, ut secundum Apostolum minister Christi corpus suum castiget et in servitutem redigat (1 Cor. 9), quemadmodum byssus vel linum candorem, quem ex natura non habet, per studium et industriam multis tunsionibus et quasi quadam vexatione attritum acquirit (Hugo de S. Vict. De Sacram. 1. 2, p. 4, c. 2).

amid untold hardships, by a bloody sweat the Son of God acquired
for us the jewel of holiness; He shed all His blood to cleanse us
from sin; therefore, it is but just, that we should endeavor by prayer
and tears, by works of penance and self-denial, to preserve unspotted
or to regain the perfect purity, innocence and beauty of the soul.
No labor should be deemed too difficult, no struggle too painful, no
sacrifice too great to cleanse ourselves more and more "in the blood
of the Lamb," until our soul becomes "more spotless than the snow,
whiter than milk, fairer than the sapphire" (Lam. 4, 7). For
"blessed are they that wash their robes white in the blood of the
Lamb, that they may have a right to the tree of life (that is, to the
Beatific Vision of God), and enter in by the gates into the (heavenly) city" (Apoc. 22, 14).

The spotless white alb, therefore, daily admonishes the priest
so to live, to watch and pray, that he may each time approach the
holy altar with a pure mind, with an unblemished heart, with an
untrammelled spirit, with holy joy and a secret longing. To ascend
the mountain of the Lord and to stand in the holy place, where even
the heavenly spirits tremble, the priest must be "innocent in hands
and clean of heart" (Ps. 23, 3—4), "holy in body and in spirit"
(1 Cor. 7, 34); then will he receive at the altar most abundant
blessings from the Lord and mercy from God his Saviour (Ps. 23, 5).
Therefore, should he earnestly and indefatigably strive by exercises
of piety and works of charity, by self-denial and a penitential spirit,
by watchfulness and humility to persevere and advance in the grace
of God, to make progress in virtue and holiness, and purify his heart
more and more not only from sin, but also from worldly, faulty and
dangerous inclinations and attachments. [1]

---

[1] Non sufficit Omnipotenti laus et honor oris, nisi ex sinceritate et devotione
prodeat mentis virtuosisque actibus decoretur. Si igitur, o sacerdos, sapienter at-
tendas, quanta sit hujus excellentia, sanctitas ac dignitas sacramenti, confestim
fateberis, te non posse cor tuum sufficienter ad ejus susceptionem disponere neque
pro suscepta communione satis posse regratiari; etiamsi mille vixeris annis et die
ac nocte sine interruptione ac cessatione totis viribus te praeparares ad celebrandum
et gratias ageres pro susceptione ac collatione muneris tanti. Quid itaque restat,
nisi ut omne quod tibi in his possibile est facias et tamen nihil condignum te fecisse
recognoscas per respectum ad incomparabilem excellentiam sacramenti.... Cum
ergo quotidie aut frequenter sis celebrans, oportet te indesinenter omni hora die ac
nocte esse sollicitum, providum ac ferventem, ne quid culpae inveniatur in te, per
quam indignus aut minus dignus ad celebrandum existas, aut ingratus seu minus
gratus de beneficiis tantis. Erubesce mente non pura, corde frigido, sine reverentia, sanctitate et fervore ad Sancta Sanctorum accedere, fonti infinitae munditiae te unire, Unigenitum Dei suscipere, Deum ac judicem tuum sine debita
veneratione tractare; imo quo frequentius celebras, eo devotius magisque timorate,
reverenter et amorose te habere satage. Jugiter ergo dic tibi ipsi in corde tuo:
Ecce hodie aut in brevi Deo celebrabis propitio, aut celebrasti: ubi est praeparatio
et gratiarum actio tua? ubi profectus et fructus tanti mysterii? (Dion. Carth. De
sacram. altar. art. 15.)

c) The cincture,[1] that is, the girdle, is necessary to gather up the long and broad alb, that it may be fitted closely to the body.[2] — The cincture should be tied around the loins,[3] for by this act is expressed its higher and symbolical meaning, which is evident from the prayer recited by the priest while tying the alb about the body: "Gird me, O Lord, with the cincture of purity, and extinguish in my loins the fires of concupiscence, that the virtue of continence and chastity may abide within me."[4]

To gird one's self or the loins is a figurative expression often repeated in Holy Scripture (Luke 12, 15 — Eph. 6, 14), and the saying has a manifold signification.

Laborers, warriors, pilgrims were wont to gird themselves in order to gather up their loose, wide garments and hold them securely. They were then freer in their movements, more at ease and, consequently, the better prepared for labor,[5] battle or travel. Now, the Christian life is justly represented as a time of labor, of combat, of pilgrimage. — "The life of man upon earth is a warfare, and his days are like the days of a hireling. As a servant longeth for the shade, and as the hireling for the end of his work" (Job 7, 1—2). The Christian is "a laborer in the vineyard of the Lord, where he must bear the heat and burden of the day," in order to gain an eternal reward (Matt. 20). — He must, therefore, "as a good soldier of Christ Jesus, please Him to whom he hath engaged himself, and must strive for the mastery" (2 Tim. 2, 4—5), that he may be victorious over Satan, the world and the flesh. — Finally, he is also upon earth as "a stranger and pilgrim" (1 Peter 2, 11), having here no permanent abode, but traveling onward to his true, eternal home in the next world. A frivolous, distracted and worldly mind is as great an encumbrance to the Christian laborer, combatant and pilgrim, as would be to the earthly a loose and wide garment;

---

[1] In Holy Scripture and in ecclesiastical language the words cingulum — balteus — zona (ζώνη) are employed without distinction to designate a girth or girdle, fastened around the waist in order to hold together flowing garments, thereby facilitating movement and activity.

[2] Alba sine zona vel cingulo commode et decenter gestari nequit, unde rituales scriptores etiam vetustissimi zonam cum alba et amictu inseparabili recensione conjunxerunt (De Saussay, P. 1, l. 3, c. 6).

[3] Exhinc cingulo cingitur, quod in Lege balteus, apud Graecos zona dicitur. Per cingulum, quod circa *lumbos* praecingitur et, alba ne diffluat et gressum impediat, adstringitur, mentis custodia accipitur, qua luxuria restringitur (Honor. August. Gemma animae l. 1, c. 203).

[4] Praecinge me, Domine, *cingulo puritatis*, et extingue in lumbis meis humorem libidinis: ut maneat in me virtus continentiae et castitatis. — Cingulum puritatis = grant me the grace and virtue of crushing all carnal emotions, symbolized by the girdle, that is, by girding the loins, so as to maintain purity of heart, that is, to preserve it inviolate.

[5] Cinctio opera significat: tunc enim se quisque cingit, cum operaturus est (S. August. Enarr. in Ps. 92, n. 3).

therefore, as St. Peter says, the Christian must "have the loins of his mind girt up" (1 Peter 1, 13),[1] that is, he must recollect himself and keep safeguarded all the faculties of his mind for the business and combat of salvation, to enable him also to persevere in his painful and dangerous pilgrimage through this vale of tears to his true country in heaven. To gird one's self means, therefore, to arm one's self; the girding of the loins (*praecinctio lumborum*) is a sign of preparation and readiness for combat, as much as of manly strength.

In as far as the loins are considered as the principal seat of sexual desires, the girding of them symbolizes especially the subjugation of the flesh by mortification and self-denial. For precisely in the crucifixion of the rebellious flesh, in the bridling of the sensual appetites, the spiritual vigor and manliness of the Christian laborer, combatant and pilgrim are proved in the most striking manner. — As a stranger and pilgrim, whose true home is with his Father in heaven, the Christian must lead a heavenly life on earth; he must not suffer himself to be immersed in the base things of an earthly life, nor be taken up with worldly gratification and enjoyments, but he must with all his energy resist the seductive allurements of earthly desires and passions, in order to preserve the robe of innocence undefiled. The fervent Christian unceasingly mortifies his sensual inclinations, ever walks on with loins girded and with his lamp burning, sober and watchful, in dread of the reckoning to come and in expectation of the blessed hope at the coming of the Lord (Tit. 2, 12—13).

The cincture, therefore, enjoins upon the priest the same virtue for which the Church prays in a Lenten hymn: "Let us tame our body by abstemiousness, that our heart may turn aside from the things that foment evil desires, and may remain undefiled by sin." Clothed in a white garment and girt about the loins does the priest stand at the altar; for he is to "serve the Lord with a chaste body and please Him with a clean heart." Virginal chastity is the most precious pearl, the brightest jewel in the crown of sacerdotal virtues.[2] Nothing equals in value and dignity a pure soul resplendent with the

---

[1] Lumbi *mentis* sunt voluntas seu affectus et intellectus, ex quibus procedunt cogitationes malae et desideria prava. Lumbi vero *carnis* sunt, ex quibus prodeunt carnales concupiscentiae et opera impudica: et utrique lumbi sunt praecingendi, i. e. coarctandi ab illicitis cogitationibus et operibus. Cinctorium primorum est divinae legis meditatio assidua, quae fit per studium sacrae Scripturae; cinctorium secundorum est justitia, quae fit per rigorem disciplinae: et ita per primum fluxus cogitationum et desideriorum inutilium reprimitur in mente; per secundum fluxus concupiscentiarum carnalium et operum restringitur in carne (Ludolph. de Saxon. Vita I. Chr. P. 2, c. 47, n. 1).

[2] Cingulum jam a primis temporibus in Ecclesiam induxit *necessitas*, aurum dein et gemmas addidit *religio*. Ita enim sacras zonas antiquitus fuisse exornatas deprehendimus (Krazer Sect. III, art. 6, cap. 2, § 167). — As formerly the girdle was frequently handsomely made and decorated, it served as an ornament. Herein is found a symbolical allusion to the beauty of virginal purity.

brilliancy of chastity.[1]   Such a soul is an object of delight to heaven and earth; God and His holy angels look down on it with joy.   The chaste, pure heart is resplendent in the brightness of the Son of God, rivalling the azure of heaven and the light of the stars, it is fertile in holy thoughts, sentiments and affections; it dwells in the beauty of peace, in the tabernacles of confidence and in wealthy rest (Isa. 32, 18).   Holy purity is not only the brilliant, spotless virtue of the soul, but, moreover, the ornament of the body; for it ennobles and transforms this earthly covering of flesh with supernatural and heavenly perfume.   It is, therefore, the most beautiful adornment of the priestly heart, which should be all aglow with the fire of divine love. It is for a virginally pure priesthood to offer the all-pure Sacrifice of the virginal body of Jesus Christ; "the Host exhaling the perfume of virginal holiness" (*hostia virgineo fragrans odore* — Secr. in fest. S. Cathar. Senen.) should also be consecrated and offered, handled and distributed by pure virginal hands. — The delicate and heavenly blossom of purity of heart can be preserved untarnished only amid the thorns of mortification and the renunciation of the world.[2]   The priest who would walk unsullied through the dusty path of this life, must ever have his loins girt, that is, he must live in holy austerity and sobriety, in humble watchfulness and caution, and in constant recollection and devotion.   For this he gathers the requisite supernatural strength at the altar; for the offering of the Eucharistic Sacrifice not merely obliges him to a pure, mortified life, but, at the same time, gives birth to and nourishes within him a life dead to this world.   The Sacrifice of the Altar is holy and sanctifying, — therefore, it is the consolation, the joy and the strength of the devout priest.   Daily is granted him the inestimable grace of being refreshed with the wheat of the elect and of drinking the wine that springeth forth virgins (Zach. 9, 17).[3]

---

[1]   Omnis ponderatio non est digna continentis animae (Eccli. 26, 20). — O *quam pulchra* est casta generatio cum claritate!   (Sapient. 4, 1.)

[2]   The purity of the body, this precious fruit of holy baptism and of the Sacrament of the Altar, is the object of many and ardent petitions, which the Church— especially in the hymns of the Office — puts into the mouth of the priest; for example: Absint faces libidinis; ne foeda sit vel lubrica compago nostri corporis; ne corpus adstet sordidum; discedat omne lubricum, phantasma noctis exsulet; sit pura nobis castitas; motus pravos atterat; aufer calorem noxium; carnis terat superbiam; castique, recti ac sobrii vigilate; ne manus oculive peccent lubrici, ne noxa corpus inquinet.

[3]   Ulterius pergit singuli hujus significatio, quod etiam colligat et contineat partes Albae superfluas, ne per terram trahatur aut ministerium impediat.   Et hoc nomine significat prudentem et cautam mortificationem non solum in illicitis, sed etiam in licitis, cum non sunt ei, quod tunc fit, accommodata.   Sanctitas enim est sicut Alba adeo longa et lata, ut complectatur varia genera cogitationum, affectuum et curarum, et quidem bonarum et sanctarum.   At cogitationes et curae, quae in alio tempore et loco bonae sunt, non semper sunt aptae in altari et tempore Missae.   Quare opus est, illas praecingere et colligere, ne impediant.   Tempus enim illud destinatum est ad orandum et sacrificandum, non autem ad studendum,

d) The maniple[1] became gradually since the tenth century an ecclesiastical vestment, which, corresponding in material and color to the stole and chasuble, is worn on the left[2] arm. In the middle part of the maniple there must be a cross, which is to be kissed when vesting and unvesting; it also has usually a cross at each end. The maniple is at present the distinctive garment worn in divine service by the subdeacon,[3] who has to cleanse the consecrated vessels, wash the sacred linens and minister at the Holy Sacrifice.

The mystical meaning of the maniple may be taken from some liturgical texts. In putting it on before Mass, the priest says: "May I be worthy to bear the maniple of weeping and sorrow, that with exultation I may receive the reward of labor."[4] The bishop presents the maniple to the newly ordained subdeacon with the words: "Receive the maniple, by which the fruit of good works is designated."[5]

---

concionandum aut negotium aliud agendum, quod extra illum locum et tempus esset licitum (De Ponte l. c.).

[1] The name manipulus (from manus and pleo, therefore, properly a handful, a bundle) came into general use only since the eleventh century, while previously other designations were more in vogue, for example: mantile = a linen cloth, which was actually used for wiping the hands after meals, or often served also as a napkin placed before the breast at table; mappula = a small apron; sudarium = a towel or handkerchief; fanon (fanulus) = cloth, little cloth, in the dictionaries of the Middle Age = hantfan, hantvan. — These names express the original form and use of the maniple. In the beginning it was not an ornament for wear, but a small linen cloth for wiping and cleansing the face and hands. — Quartum mappula s. mantile sacerdotis indumentum est, quod vulgo phanonem vocant, quod ab hoc eorum tunc *manibus* tenetur, quando missae officium agitur, ut *paratos ad ministerium mensae Domini* populus conspiciat (Raban. Maur. De Cleric. instit. c. 18). — Mappulae in sinistra manu ferendae (Ord. Rom. VI, n. 1). — The fourth article of the vestments is called the manipula or phanon, that is, a handkerchief which is placed on the left arm (Tewtsch Rational, Kap. 2, n. 5).

[2] According to the liturgists of the Middle Age, the maniple symbolizes the penance and sweat of the present life, represented by the left side, namely, the left arm. — The real and natural reason for the constant practice of wearing the maniple on the left arm, is in order that the right arm and the right hand may remain free and undisturbed in the performance of their functions.

[3] As the alb, so likewise the maniple was formerly worn by all clerics and even by unordained monks (in choir). Quamdiu manipulus *sudarii* vel *mappulae* loco fuit, tribui necessario debuit omnibus, qui alba induti suam Ecclesiae operam exhibebant. Ast ubi singulare ornamentum evasit manipulus, tunc Subdiaconis ut *specialis nota* in eorum *ordinatione* quibusdam in Ecclesiis fuit data, aliis antiquo mori insistentibus (Krazer Sect. III, disquis. 3, c. 1, § 211).

[4] Merear, Domine, portare *manipulum fletus et doloris*, ut cum exsultatione recipiam mercedem laboris. The bishop prays: Merear, precor Domine, manipulum portare mente *flebili*, ut cum exsultatione portionem accipiam cum justis.

[5] Accipe manipulum, per quem designantur *fructus bonorum operum* (Pontific. Rom. De ordin. Subd.). Depone manipulum, quia per *fructus bonorum operum*, quos designat, non expugnasti spirituales insidias inimici (Pontific. Rom. Degrad. ab ordin. Subd.).

The symbolical meaning of the maniple here alluded to is probably based on the circumstance, that originally it served the celebrant to wipe off perspiration and tears during the celebration of Mass, but sprang principally from a passage in the Psalms, in which the word *"manipulus"* is mentioned in the sense of a sheaf of wheat.—"They that sow in tears shall reap in joy. Going they went and wept, casting their seed; but coming they shall come with joyfulness, carrying their sheaves (*manipulos suos*)."[1] Consequently, the maniple symbolizes, on the one hand, penitential tears and grief, the toil and hardships of sowing, the suffering and the combating, the work and labors of this perishable life; on the other, the fruit of good works and sheaves full of merit, as well as the abundant harvest of happiness and joy, of peace and rest reaped in eternity. The thoroughly Christian life and still more the thoroughly priestly life is here below in exile and "upon the banks of the rivers of Babylon" principally in "labor and sorrow" (Ps. 136, 1; 89, 10); and though weeping must go on to the evening of life, yet on the morning of eternity joy and gladness will break forth. "Thou hast turned for me my mourning into joy, thou hast cut my sack-cloth, and hast compassed me with gladness" (Ps. 29, 12); "for that which is at present momentary and light of our tribulation, worketh for us above measure exceedingly an eternal weight of glory" (2 Cor. 4, 17). — The wail of sorrow in sowing will give place to the sounds of the harvest-songs of joy. "He who soweth in blessings, shall also reap of blessings" (2 Cor. 9, 6). Therefore, be indefatigable in sowing the good seed, scatter abroad the seed of good works, — works of love, of penance, of piety, of spiritual and corporal mercy, — sow this seed amid sweat and tears, in storm and showers, in rain and cold: for behold! the day will soon come, when the ears will be

---

[1] *Qui seminant in lacrimis*, i. e. qui modo in luctu poenitentiae seu lacrimis devotionis se ipsos exercent, qui temporales delectationes contemnunt et corde contrito et humiliato Deo ministrant, isti *in exsultatione metent* bona gratiae in praesenti et fructum gloriae in futuro: "bonorum enim laborum gloriosus est fructus" (Sap. 3, 15). Porro quinque sunt genera lacrimarum: primae lacrimae sunt pro indulgentia propriae culpae et hae mundant a sorde peccati; secundae sunt pro timore futuri judicii et gehennae et istae refrigerant ab ardore concupiscentiae retrahuntque ab omni iniquitate; tertiae sunt pro incolatu praesentis exsilii, quae potant animam sitientem; quartae pro defectibus proximorum et istae impinguant plangentem; quintae sunt pro desiderio patriae, quae animam omni bono fecundant. — *Euntes* electi Dei per viam vitae praesentis *ibant* per viam mandatorum Altissimi et *flebant mittentes semina sua*, h. e. opera meritoria facientes: quae opera dicta sunt semina, quoniam sicut ex semine nascitur fructus, sic ex operibus bonis oritur fructus vitae aeternae, infusio consolationis divinae. Mittunt igitur semina sua, i. e. opera bona ante se mittunt, cumulum meritorum colligunt quem in Christo abscondunt (Matth. 6, 20; Gal. 6, 9). *Venientes* autem ad Christi tribunal *venient cum exsultatione*, h. e. cum secura et laeta conscientia, *portantes manipulos suos*, i. e. opera virtuosa quae collegerunt: "Opera enim illorum sequuntur illos" (Apoc. 14, 13). Dion. Carthus. in Ps. 125, 5—6.

ripe, the sheaves be full and garnered in the granaries of the Heavenly Father; the day that knows no evening, the day of the most gladsome, blessed harvest jubilation, the unspeakably bright day of eternity, that shines on the saints in imperishable splendor! Then the Lord will wipe away all tears; and mourning and crying and sorrow shall be no more (Apoc. 21, 4). Thus the maniple is a symbolical expression of that exalted truth which the Lord expressed in the words: "Blessed are they that mourn; for they shall be comforted" (Matt. 5, 5).

Since the maniple denotes "weeping and sorrow", it is used in Holy Mass, where the Sacrifice of the Cross is renewed and where the sufferings and the cruel and bitter death of Jesus Christ are represented; as a rule, it is not worn outside of the Mass, because no sorrow can compare with the sorrow which Christ endured on the Cross, a sorrow which should penetrate our hearts during Holy Mass. [1]

At the altar the priest should be filled and penetrated with sorrow and compunction, with regret for his own sins and those of others, with grief for the tribulations of the Church, for the loss of so many souls, and with sympathy for the passion of Christ; thence he should daily draw strength to persevere in the labors and trials of life, to bear with cheerfulness all the hardships of his vocation, to overcome all difficulties and obstacles in the practice of good works, so that he may once attain the reward

---

[1] So long as the broad chasuble covered the entire body and also the arms of the celebrant, the mappula was put on last of all the vestments, after the chasuble had been rolled up above the arms (Cfr. Ord. Rom. I, II, III). — Ad *extremum* sacerdos fanonem in sinistrum brachium ponit, qui et mappula et sudarium vocatur, per quod *olim* sudor et narium sordes extergebantur. Per hoc poenitentia intelligitur, qua quotidiani excessus labes extergitur. Hoc in *sinistro* brachio gestatur, quia in *praesenti* tempore tantum vita nostra poenitentia emundatur (Honor. Augustod. Gemma anim. 1. 1, c. 208). — Of this ancient practice the present rubric of the Missal reminds us, which accords to the bishop celebrating (except at Requiem Masses) the distinction of putting the maniple on with greater solemnity at the altar — after the absolutio in the preparatory prayers. There is in this action also a symbolical admonition to the bishop to be a guiding-light to his whole flock by his apostolic labors, sufferings and combats. — Priests and levites wear the maniple out of Mass by way of exception; for example, at functions on Good Friday (but not at the uncovering and adoration of the Cross) and on Holy Saturday. According to a general rule, the ministri sacri wear the maniple whenever they sing the Epistle or Gospel, for instance, at the blessing of the palms, — the deacon wears it at the blessing of bells. To the priest applies the rubric: Dum Celebrans utitur pluviali, *semper* deponit manipulum (Rubr. gener. Miss. tit. 19, 4). This rule, however, suffers an exception, when the blessing of the Palms takes place without ministri sacri. In this case the celebrant wears the maniple with the cope, but only until after the reading of the Gospel at this blessing. (Cfr. Memoriale Rituum Bened. XIII.)

of eternal joy.[1]   Of this the maniple reminds and admonishes him.[2]

e) The Stole.   In Holy Scripture and universally in ancient times, the stole signified in general every kind of dress, every outfit and adornment of the body with garments, often too, in a limited sense, a magnificent, costly dress, a festal robe, a splendid raiment. Since the ninth century the name *stola* has been gradually restricted to an article of liturgical vestment, which had been a long time in use previous to that date and had until then borne the name of *Orarium*.[3]   The ecclesiastical *Orarium* was originally a small band, a long linen strip, which was loosely suspended from the left shoulder; it was the distinctive badge of the deacon, who served at the Holy Table, and was used to wipe the mouth and face.[4]   Already in the seventh century the *Orarium*, worn by deacons, priests and bishops — but in different ways, — had only a symbolical character; hence it began to be made of precious material and to be richly adorned.

At the present time the stole is a long silk strip, as wide as the hand, adorned at each end and in the middle with a cross. The stole should be worn only by those who are strictly members of the hierarchy, that is, by deacons, priests and bishops,[5] and then only in cases in which the rubrics prescribe its use, or a lawful custom sanctions or at least tolerates it.   Of itself the stole is not a mark of

---

[1]   Post vitam istam brevissimam boni sacerdotes a Deo gloriosissimam sortientur coronam, ineffabilem jucunditatem, superplenam mensuram, mercedem aeternam, tam de propriis meritis, quam pro meritis gregis sui et omnium, quibus bene agendi causa fuerunt, quorum omnium beatitudo et gloria redundabit copiose et gloriose in eos, si jam debitum sui impleverint officii.   Quemadmodum enim hi, qui aliis causa perditionis sunt, Christo odibilissimi exstant, et durissime ac terribilissime recipientur, judicabuntur ac damnabuntur ab eo, ita et qui aliis sunt causa conversionis ac salutis, amabilissimi Christo consistunt, et jucundissime ac benevolentissime suscipientur ac remunerabuntur ab ipso, tanquam veri sui vicarii, cordiales amici atque cooperatores idonei (Dion. Carthus. De vita Curatorum art. 68).

[2]   Dicere possumus, manipulum significare virtutem zeli, h. e. tristitiam et dolorem de peccatis propriis et alienis, in quantum honori Dei et animarum saluti adversantur, cum sancta quadam contra ea indignatione et ferventi ea disturbandi et expellendi desiderio.   Peccata propria dissolvuntur lacrimis, gemitibus et contritionis actibus et poenitudinis, qui disponunt hominem ad hoc sacrificium digne offerendum.   Aliena peccata sunt etiam removenda, orando cum lacrimis et sacrificium pro eorum remissione offerendo (De Ponte l. c. § 3).

[3]   Quintum (vestimentum) est, quod Orarium dicitur, licet hoc *quidam* Stolam vocent (Raban. Maur. [† 853] De institut. Clericor., l. 1, cap. 19).

[4]   Orarium is more correctly derived from *os* = face, mouth, than from *orare* = to pray, or from *ora* = a border.   Mention is made of the Orarium as a church vestment for the first time about the middle of the fourth century in the Synod of Laodicea.   Yet it remained for several centuries more a profane garment. (Cf. Prudent. Peristephan. I, v. 86).

[5]   After the example of the Council of Laodicea (in the fourth century), the use of the stole was always prohibited to clerics in Minor Orders (among whom originally sub-deacons were also included).

ecclesiastical jurisdiction, but a sacred decoration to be worn during certain functions.[1] It is principally intended to be worn when graces and blessings are dispensed; therefore, it is used, for example, at Mass, as well as at all functions which appertain directly to the Eucharist, the source of every grace and blessing, in administering the Sacraments and in performing the Sacramentals. — The deacon, priest and bishop wear the stole each in a peculiarly different way. The deacon places it over the left shoulder and fastens its ends together under the right arm. When the priest is robed in the alb, he places the stole around his neck and ties it with the cincture in the form of a cross[2] on his breast; but if he wears the surplice, the stole is allowed to hang straight down on both sides.[3] The bishop who already wears a cross on his breast (the pectoral), to distinguish him from the priest, — also wears the two ends of the stole hanging loosely down over the alb.[4]

The symbolical meaning of the stole may be known from certain ecclesiastical prayers. The bishop gives to the newly ordained deacon the stole in these words: "Receive this shining white stole from the hand of God; fulfil your ministry; for God is powerful to increase His grace in you."[5] While the bishop places the two parts

---

[1] Orarium, quod necessitas induxit, brevi *singulare* Episcoporum, Presbyterorum et Diaconorum evasit *ornamentum*, dignitatis et jurisdictionis *symbolum*, coepitque primo *coloribus* et *auro* ornari, dein non amplius ex lino, sed ex *serico* aliaque pretiosa confici materia (Krazer Sect. III, art. 6, cap. 4, § 173). — In consequence of this view the stole was in former times more frequently worn as a mark of spiritual dignity and authority, than is now permitted. According to the present discipline of the Church, the stole may not be worn according to caprice to indicate in the wearer the habitual possession of the potestas ordinis vel jurisdictionis, but, as a rule, it is intended merely to signify the actual use of this power, that is, to accompany the performance of certain liturgical functions. (Cfr. Bourbon, Introduction aux cérém. rom. p. 138—146. — De Conny, Des usages et des abus en matière de cérémonies chap. 6).

[2] S. R. C. 30. Sept. 1679. According to this decree the right end of the stole must be placed over the left end. — A Spanish Synod held at Braga (675) says: Signum in suo pectore praeparet crucis.

[3] Diaconus habet stolam in *sinistro* humero in signum, quod applicatur in *ministerium* in ipsis sacramentis; sed sacerdoti in *utroque* humero ponitur stola, ut ostendatur quod ei *plena potestas* dispensandi sacramenta datur, non ut ministro alterius et ideo stola descendit usque at inferiora (Supplem. q. 40, a. 7).

[4] As the praecipuum insigne sacerdotii the stole ever adorned the recipients of the Sacrament of Holy Order (deacons, priests, bishops); but at the same time in order to indicate the varied degree of sacramental power and grace, it was and is at ordination placed on them in different ways. Till about the twelfth century the stole was worn by the deacon over the dalmatic and across the left shoulder, hanging free in front and at the back, as with the Greeks the deacon still wears the ὡράριον. In the twelfth century it became the custom to lay on the deacon at his ordination first the stole and then the dalmatic. — Priests and bishops have always worn the stole in the manner now in use.

[5] Accipe stolam candidam (= radiant, splendid garment, as a symbol of the sublime service) de manu Dei: adimple *ministerium* tuum; potens enim est Deus,

of the stole in the form of a cross on the new priest, he says: "Take upon you the yoke of the Lord; for His yoke is sweet and His burden light."[1] When vesting for Mass, the priest puts on the stole, saying: "Give me anew, O Lord, the robe of immortality, which I have lost by the prevarication of our first parent, and although I am unworthy to approach Thy Holy Mysteries, may I yet merit eternal joy."[2]

In comparing the aforesaid texts, we find that the stole has a twofold, a threefold meaning. Inasmuch as it is placed around the neck and rests on the nape of the neck, it symbolizes the yoke and the burden of the service of the sanctuary;[3] inasmuch as with the ancients it was a special garment of honor, and inasmuch as it is now with us a sacred ornament, the stole represents also the robe of innocence[4] required for the worthy administration of the spiritual office, as well as that garment of glory with which the good and faithful servant will be clothed by the Lord as an eternal reward.[5]

In the first place, the stole is a symbol of the arduous, but at the same time blessed and honorable, ministry exercised in the sanctuary of the Lord. The ecclesiastical administration is a duty to which the ordained members of the hierarchy should perseveringly

---

ut augeat tibi *gratiam* suam (from God proceeds the office as also the fulness of grace for the office) (De ordinat. Diaconi).

[1] Accipe *jugum Domini :* jugum enim ejus suave est et onus ejus leve (De ordin. Presbyt.). — *Signum Domini* per hanc stolam turpiter abjecisti, ideoque ipsam a te amovemus, quem inhabilem reddimus ad omne sacerdotale officium exercendum (Degrad. ab ordin. Presbyt.).

[2] Redde mihi, Domine, *stolam immortalitatis,* quam perdidi in praevaricatione primi parentis: et quamvis indignus accedo ad tuum sacrum mysterium, merear tamen gaudium sempiternum (Miss. Rom.).

[3] Deinde (sacerdos) circumdat collum suum *stola,* quae et *orarium* dicitur, per quam obedientia Evangelii intelligitur. Evangelium quippe est suave Domini jugum, obedientia vero lorum; quasi ergo sacerdos ad jugum Christi loris ligatur, dum collum ejus stola circumdatur (Honor. Augustod. Gemma anim. 1. 1, c. 204).— Orarium, i. e. stola, dicitur eo quod oratoribus, i. e. praedicatoribus concedatur. Admonet illum, qui illo induitur, ut memor sit, sub jugo Christi, quod leve et suave est, se esse constitutum (Pseudo-Alcuin. De divin. offic. c. 39). — The Fourth Synod of Toledo (633) remarks, that the deacon must wear the Orarium on the left shoulder, propterea quod orat, i. e. praedicat.

[4] Per stolam quoque innocentia exprimitur, quae in primo homine amissa, per vitulum saginatum occisum recipitur. Beati qui hanc stolam a criminum labe custodiunt vel maculatam lacrimis lavant, quia illorum potestas est in ligno vitae, — sc. in Christo amissam gloriam possidebunt (Honor. Augustod. 1. c., c. 205). — The stole is also considered as a symbol of innocence at the degradation of deacons: Stolam candidam, quam acceperas immaculatam in conspectu Domini perferendam, qui non sic cognito mysterio exemplum conversationis tuae fidelibus praebuisti, ut plebs dicata Christi nomine posset exinde imitationem acquirere, juste a te amovemus, omne diaconatus officium tibi prohibentes.

[5] Stola, praesertim candida et splendida, in Scriptura symbolum est gloriae, immortalitatis ac felicitatis (Cornel. a Lapide in Apocal. 6, 11).

10

devote themselves in order to promote the honor of God and the welfare of the faithful. This service of the Lord, this busy life spent
in the care of souls, is a yoke and a burden: a burden which would
be terrible for the shoulders of angels even, a burden from which the
very saints fled in dread and terror. The faithful performance of
the pastoral office, the preaching of the word of God, the celebration
and dispensation of the mysteries of salvation, the preservation of
discipline and good morals in congregations, the training and direction of the faithful, especially of youth, in the way of salvation, the
care of the poor and sick, the preventing or suppression of scandals
and dangers from the flock entrusted to one's care costs much labor
and hardship, many sufferings and combats, many exertions and
sacrifices (*jugum* Domini). The yoke, that is, the office of bishop
and of priest, is heavier than the ministry of the deacon, therefore,
they wear the stole on both shoulders. — But the sacerdotal vocation,
with all the labors and responsibilities attaching to the life of a
priest, is lightened and sweetened by the mighty grace of the Lord
(jugum ejus est *suave* et onus ejus *leve;* potens enim est Deus, ut
augeat tibi *gratiam* suam). Whom the Lord chooses as His servant,
him He helps to carry the burden; for a precious, a full, an overflowing measure of heavenly grace and consolation, the great and
countless graces of his calling, the Lord has in reserve for the priest.
He that has a vocation, delights in and loves the duties of his ministry; therefore, it is not an oppressive weight for him, but a light
and sweet burden, which he joyfully carries, though it may require
on his part much bodily exertion and many spiritual combats. From
the bottom of his heart he prays with the Psalmist: "Better, O Lord,
is one day in Thy courts above thousands" in the world; "rather
would I" be "an abject" unknown and forgotten in the world, than
amid abundance and honors "dwell in the tabernacles of sinners."
The sufferings of the priest are great, but equally great, yea, far
greater, are his joys. For as the good priest "abounds in the sufferings of Christ, so also through Christ does his comfort abound." —
"I am filled with comfort; I exceedingly abound in all my tribulation," he says with the Apostle of the Gentiles. — The service of
Christ and of His Church is not only the greatest joy, but also the
highest honor and distinction for the priest. The service of the altar
is the most sublime office, it is the summit and crown of all dignities
upon earth. *Deo servire regnare est* — "To serve God is to reign"
in the noblest sense of the word; therefore, the glorious martyr St.
Agatha said to the heathen tyrant: "The service of Christ is the
highest nobility and consummate freedom" — *Summa ingenuitas
ista est, in qua servitus Christi comprobatur.* Truly, it is sweet to
serve God, despising the world! "It is a great honor, a great glory
to serve Thee, O Lord, and to despise all things for Thee. For they
who willingly subject themselves to Thy most holy service, shall have
a great grace. They shall find the most sweet consolation of the
Holy Ghost, who for love of Thee have cast away all carnal delight.

They shall gain great freedom of mind, who for Thy name enter upon the narrow way and neglect all worldly care. O pleasant and delightful *service* of God, which makes a man truly free and holy! O sacred state of religious bondage, which makes men equal to angels, pleasing to God, terrible to the devils, and commendable to all the faithful! O service worthy to be embraced and always to be wished for, which leads to the supreme good and procures a joy that will never end!" (Imit. of Christ.)

The stole reminds us also of the garment of sanctity,[1] in which the priest should serve God and be a shining light to men; — and also of the garment of glory which will eventually be his in reward of his fidelity in the service of God.[2] For both — the garment of grace as well as that of glory — constitute the robe of immortality (*stola immortalitatis*), which Adam forfeited for himself and his descendants, but which now, on account of the blood and merits of Christ, will be restored by God to His humble, obedient servants. Though the priest be frail and wretched, the grace of God renders him capable and worthy of meriting the reward of eternal happiness in the service of the altar and in dispensing the mysteries of Christ. How pure and enlarged must be the heart, how blameless and unselfish the life of the priest, who is placed so high on the candlestick, that he may serve as a model of all that is good, forcibly combat vice and eloquently proclaim the praises of virtue! To feed the entrusted flock by good example and to draw them to Christ, is for him a duty of his state and office.[3] To him the admonition of the Apostle applies: "Be thou an example of the faithful, in word, in conversation, in charity, in faith, in chastity,"[4] and in all things show thyself an example of good works."[5] The priest will exercise his sublime and perilous office with so much the greater success and blessings, the more virtuous he is, the more perfectly he walks before and leads the faithful in the way of holiness. — If he carefully preserves until death the robe of grace and holiness, which he lost

---

[1] The stola prima (Luke 15, 22), that is, the best and most distinguished garment which the father put on his prodigal son, is a figure of sanctifying grace.

[2] Sacerdos Stolam induens, detersa vitiorum labe, innocentiae decorem sibi adesse debere praedicat, quo idoneus efficiatur tam sublimi mysterio rite perficiendo, ut deinde inveniatur dignus aeternae gloriae stola indui cum Sanctis illis, qui visi sunt ante thronum Dei stare amicti stolis albis, cujus stolae gloriosae demum obtinendae haec stola sacerdotalis symbolum est atque nota (Clichtoveus, Elucidator. ecclesiastic. l. 3, n. 13).

[3] Abundet in eo totius forma virtutis, auctoritas modesta, pudor constans, innocentiae puritas et spiritualis observantia disciplinae. In moribus ejus praecepta tua fulgeant, ut suae castitatis exemplo imitationem sanctam plebs acquirat (Pontif. Rom. De ordin. Diacon.). — Sit odor vitae tuae delectamentum Ecclesiae Christi, ut praedicatione atque exemplo aedifices domum, id est, familiam Dei (Pontif. Rom. De ordin. Presbyt.).

[4] Exemplum est fidelium in verbo, in conversatione, in caritate, in fide, in castitate (1 Tim. 4, 12).

[5] In omnibus teipsum praebe exemplum bonorum operum (Tit. 2, 7).

througn Adam, but triumphantly regained through Christ, it will be to him a pledge of a blessed and glorious immortality. Great, greater than words can tell, is the reward laid up in heaven for the zealous shepherd of souls. When Christ, the Prince of Pastors, shall appear in glory, the good priest "shall receive a never-fading crown of righteousness" (1 Peter 5, 4). For "then they that are enlightened shall shine as the brightness of the firmament, and they that instruct many to justice, as stars for all eternity." From the highest heavens our glorified Saviour addresses to the zealous priest in the midst of his sufferings and labors these consoling words : "I know thy works and thy labor and thy patience and how thou canst not bear them that are evil . . . and hast not fainted. — Because thou hast kept the word of thy patience, I will also keep thee from the hour of temptation. . . Behold, I come quickly, hold fast that which thou hast, that no man take thy crown. He that shall overcome, I will make him a pillar in the temple of my God, and he shall go out no more, and I will write upon him the name of my God. — I know thy tribulation and thy poverty, but thou art rich. . . Fear none of those things which thou shalt suffer. . . *Be thou faithful unto death, and I will give thee the crown of life.*" (Apoc. 2, 3; 3, 10—11; 2, 9—10).

f) The principal vestment of the celebrant is the chasuble (*casula, planeta*).[1] Originally the chasuble was an outer garment which fell about the priest and completely enveloped him. The chasuble had an opening in the middle by which it was allowed to come down on the shoulders. As these cloak- and bell-shaped[2] chasubles had much about them which was inconvenient, they began in the eleventh century to shorten or open them at both sides for a freer use of the arms, and this alteration gave the form of the so-called Gothic chasubles, which were still common in the sixteenth century. Although from this period more and more was cut away from the chasuble, it yet remained up to the eighteenth century

---

[1] This vestment had its origin in the Roman paenula (Greek, φαινόλης, φελόνης), It was a circular, closed over-garment, worn especially when travelling, as well as in the city during cold and inclement weather. In the first ten centuries after Christ it is frequently mentioned by the name of casula and planeta as a garment of ordinary life. These two names designate the original use of the chasuble : casula (= a small hut, from casa, a little house) refers to its size and width, — planeta, m. (πλανήτης = sidus errans, stella erratica, wandering star) to its moveableness. — From the wide, flowing appearance of this garment two historic usages are explained, which are still prescribed by the rubrics : the way and mode of taking off during divine service the planeta plicata, and the custom at the Elevation (cum ss. Sacramentum *elevatur* — Cerem. Episc. l. 1, c. 9, n. 5; — l. 2, c. 8, n. 69) of raising up a little the edge of the chasuble.

[2] Septimum sacerdotale indumentum est, quod casulam vocant; dicta est autem per diminutionem a casa, eo quod totum hominem tegat quasi *minor casa*, hanc Graeci planetam, πλανήτην, vocant (because the border, so to speak. trails about). Haec supremum omnium indumentorum est, et cetera omnia interius per suum munimem tegit et servat (Raban. Maur. De Instit. Cleric. l. 1, c. 21).

tolerably long and full of folds, but alas! since that time the vest-ment has been replaced by a chasuble of still shorter and less grace-ful pattern.[1]

The symbolical meaning of the chasuble may be known from the formula of ordination and from the Missal. When the bishop places the folded chasuble on the back of the newly ordained priest, he says: "Receive the priestly garment, by which love is under-stood; for God is powerful to increase in you charity and a perfect work."[2] Afterward, when fully unfolding the chasuble, he says: "With the garment of innocence may the Lord clothe thee."[3] — When putting on the vestment, the priest says: "O Lord, Thou who hast said: 'My yoke is sweet and My burden light,' grant that I may carry this yoke and burden in such a manner as to obtain Thy grace."[4]

As the chasuble is the principal vestment of the priest,[5] it should be sufficiently wide and large to cover and protect all his other ap-parel; it should, moreover, be made of precious material and be suitably ornamented, for thereby it is fitted symbolically to express holy love.[6] Divine love, or charity, is the most excellent, the first, the greatest and the most precious of all the virtues. As a queen she reigns supreme over all the other virtues by her sublimity, dig-nity and majesty. She is the mother, the soul and the life of the remaining virtues, to which she imparts true value and higher con-secration; for without it no virtue and no virtuous deed is merito-rious for heaven and eternity. All other gifts and privileges are of no avail to man, if this one — namely, charity — be wanting (1 Cor. 13, 1—4). Charity renders fruitful, ennobles, beautifies and trans-forms the entire religious and moral life of man. "Charity never falleth away" — *Caritas nunquam excidit* (1 Cor. 13, 8). Faith gives place to vision, hope is absorbed in possession and enjoyment,

---

[1] Cf. Archiv für christliche Kunst, Jahrg. 1888 und 1891.

[2] Accipe *vestem sacerdotalem*, per quam *caritas* intelligitur: potens est enim Deus, ut augeat tibi caritatem et opus perfectum (Pontif. Rom. De ordin. Presbyt.). — *Veste sacerdotali caritatem signante* te merito exspoliamus, quia *ipsam* et omnem *innocentiam* exuisti (Pontif. Rom. Degrad. ab ordin. Presbyt.).

[3] *Stola innocentiae* induat te Dominus (Pontif. Rom. De ordin. Presbyt.).

[4] Domine, qui dixisti: *Jugum meum* suave est, et *onus meum* leve: fac, ut istud portare sic valeam, quod consequar tuam gratiam (Miss. Rom.).

[5] Although the chasuble was formerly a common robe (generale indumentum [Amal.] — communis vestis [Ivo Carnot.]) of the clerics, still for many centuries it has been regarded in a special sense as vestis *sacerdotalis* (Pontif. Rom.), and as a vestment intended exclusively for the Holy Sacrifice, since the priest at his ordi-nation is solemnly invested therewith, and it is to be worn only at the altar.

[6] Casula, quae ultima est vestium magisque splendida ac pretiosa et reliquas tegit, significat virtutem caritatis, quae reliquis virtutibus est excelsior, quibus et honorem affert, eas defendit ac protegit, comitando eas in earum actionibus, ut perfectae sint. "Caritas enim, ut ait Apostolus (1 Cor. 13, 7), omnia credit, omnia sperat, omnia sustinet," et ad omnia valet, ita ut sine ea res omnes sint imperfec-tae, cum ea autem suam omnes habeant perfectionem (De Ponte l. c. § 4).

love alone remains, but in its highest perfection and transformation.[1] Charity is the bond of perfection: it includes all the virtues, it is full of mercy, benignity, humility, modesty, patience (Col. 3, 12—14), it is kind, it beareth all things, believeth all things, endureth all things (1 Cor. 13, 4—7).

The two parts of the vestment may more particularly signify the love of God and the neighbor, which are one and the same virtue. The priest is the representative of the love of Christ — *vicarius amoris Christi*. Magnanimous, self-sacrificing, self-forgetting charity constitutes the good shepherd. Tender and strong love is the very soul of apostolic labors, the very nerve-centre of all priestly activity. Ardent love of Christ and of the neighbor is the source of zeal for souls.[2] The zealous priest lives entirely for his neighbor, because he belongs entirely to the Crucified. *Totus est proximi, quia totus est Crucifixi.* To serve God and to sacrifice one's self for God, to do good to one's neighbor and to devote one's self to him — such is the vocation of the priest. To become a holocaust of love in the service of God and for the salvation of men is assuredly difficult and painful to nature; therefore, the genuine life of a priest is and ever will be a yoke and a burden.[3] But divine grace and love help to make this yoke easy and this burden light.[4] Love is something great; it is, in fact, the only great good, for love alone can make every burden light and accepts with equanimity all the vicissitudes of life. It alone carries every burden without being burdened; it alone makes all that is bitter sweet and pleasant to the taste.[5] *Amor leve facit omne onerosum, et omne amarum dulce efficit.* He that loves God flies to his end, hastens forward with a joyful heart, for he is free and does not allow himself to be kept back by

---

[1] Caritas non evacuatur per gloriae perfectionem, sed eadem numero manet (S. Thom. 1, 2, q. 67, a. 6).

[2] Dicendum, quod zelus ex *intensione amoris* provenit (S. Thom. 1, 2, q. 28, a. 4).

[3] Because the vestment also covered the shoulders, it answered (like the stole) as a symbol of the *jugum* Domini — and as such was often ornamented with the cross, either on the back or in front, or (like the so-called Borromeo-chasuble) both in front and at the back at the same time.

[4] Ultimum indumentum est casula seu planeta, quae ex omnium sententia caritatem significat, quae cunctis virtutibus supereminet, easque protegit et illustrat... Tamen ut constat ex oratione quae dicitur, cum casula induitur, etiam *jugum* Domini significat, sed diversa fortasse ratione; nam stola significat jugum Christi, planeta *jugum amoris:* illa patientiam et fortitudinem, quae ad jugum illud ferendum necessaria est, haec vero *suavitatem* et *dulcedinem jugi* hujus, quae ex caritate provenit, significat (Suarez l. c. n. 4).

[5] *Omnia fiunt facilia caritati*, cui uni Christi sarcina levis est (Matth. 11, 30) — aut ea una est sarcina ipsa quae levis est. Secundum hoc dictum est: "Et praecepta ejus gravia non sunt" (1 Joann. 5, 3), ut cui gravia sunt, consideret, non potuisse divinitus dici "gravia non sunt," nisi quia potest esse cordis affectus cui gravia non sunt, et petat quo destituitur, ut impleat quod jubetur (S. Aug. De natura et gratia c. 69, n. 83).

anything whatever. Love feels no burden, it regards no difficulty. By the unction of grace crosses lose their severity and thorns their points. To the priest great and efficacious graces are abundantly imparted by God, who increases His love in His servant and (through love) the perfect work (*potens est enim Deus, ut augeat tibi carita-tem et opus perfectum*). Now, in order to make his ministry pleasing to God and to obtain fulness of grace, he must bear the yoke and burden of the Lord with love, that is, if not with sweet facility, at least with patience and perseverance. He implores the divine assistance to this effect, when putting on the chasuble before Mass (*fac, ut istud — sc. jugum et onus — portare s i c valeam, quod consequar tuam gratiam*). — The love of the neighbor, represented by the back of the chasuble, the priest must exercise chiefly in administering the Sacrament of Penance; but in order to purify others from sin and reconcile them with God, he should be pure himself, confirmed in virtue and by his holiness of life be pleasing to God. Therefore, at the ordination the bishop, after imparting to him the power of forgiving sins, and when unfolding the chasuble until then folded on his back, prays that the Lord may clothe him with the garment of innocence and purity (*Stola innocentiae induat te Dominus*).

The chasuble is worn during the Sacrifice of the Mass: on the altar is the furnace of celestial love, there it is that the Lord enkindles the divine fire upon earth, that at least some sparks of divine love may penetrate our cold hearts and inflame them with its ardor. Here it was that the heart of a St. Philip Neri glowed so strongly, that he frequently broke out into the words: "If Thou, O God, who art so loving and so amiable, wouldst be loved by us, why then didst Thou give us but one heart, and that one so small?" Here in the furnace of love the priest should daily dip his whole life, his actions and sufferings, his hopes and struggles, that they all may be borne and animated by the spirit of charity. Then will he exclaim with St. Francis de Sales: "O God, what a sweet and honorable labor for me it is to serve souls!"

The color of the vestment varies according to the times; for love impels to the performance of manifold acts and affections of virtue.[1] It is full of invention and, as far as possible, it endeavors

---

[1] Quemadmodum casula inter reliqua ornamenta singularem exigit colorem, unum ex quinque juxta diversitatem temporis . . . ita caritas varios induit affectus, nunc laetitiae et gaudii ob Dei magnalia, et gratitudinis propter ejus beneficia; nunc patientiae et fortitudinis, ut se ad martyria magnosque labores offerat; nunc heroicos exercet actus spei, tum cum orat, tum cum egregium aliquod facinus aggreditur aut se in aliqua videt pressura constitutam; nunc exercet actus fidei, ex se quidem obscuros, sed illustratos amore supplente cognitionis defectum; ac denique affectus exercet tristitiae et fletus propter sua peccata et miserias aut etiam aliena, aut propter adversa, quae ejus dilectus est in passione perpessus, aut propter exsilium, quo detinetur, optans illum in sua gloria videre. Hac affectuum varietate potest ac merito debet exornare se sacerdos diversis temporibus, ut suum digne offerat sacrificium (De Ponte l. c.).

to have one become all to all, to save all and gain them to Christ (1 Cor. 9, 22); it rejoices with them that rejoice and weeps with them that weep (Rom. 12, 15).

4. The priest ascends the altar to perform by offering the Eucharistic Sacrifice the most divine and sublime function, to accomplish the grandest and most awful mystery, to exercise in the most perfect manner the office of mediator between God and man, to give to God, as a representative of Christ and a servant of the Church, the greatest glory, as well as to procure for man the most abundant blessings. The sacred vestments with which he is then attired cause him to appear exteriorly before the eyes of all in all his dignity, in his sublime and divine calling. At the same time the precious and mystical vestments admonish him, with what great virtues his soul should be adorned, with what heavenly thoughts, sentiments and affections his heart should be possessed, how far he should soar by his holiness above the faithful, in order that he may as worthily as possible offer the Divine Victim to the Most High.[1] This spiritual adornment should never be wanting to the priest at the altar, in order that his interior and exterior may harmonize, please God and edify men.[2] "Take heed to thyself, and see what kind of ministry has been delivered to thee by the imposition of the bishop's hands. Lo! thou art made a priest, and art consecrated to say Mass: see now, that in due time thou faithfully and devoutly offer up sacrifice to God, and that thou behave thyself in such manner as to be without reproof. *Thou hast not lightened thy burthen, but art now bound with a stricter band of discipline, and art obliged to a greater perfection of sanctity.* The priest ought to be adorned with all virtues, and to give example of a good life to others. His conversation should not be with the vulgar and common ways of men, but with the angels in heaven, or with perfect men upon earth. The priest clad in his sacred vestments is Christ's vice-gerent, to pray to God for himself and for all the people, in a suppliant and humble manner. He has before him and behind him the sign of the Cross of the Lord, that he may always remember the passion of Christ. He bears

---

[1] Omnis ornatus exterior sacerdotum significat, qualis debeat interior esse ejus ornatus, quamque prae populo eminere et effulgere eum oporteat (Cornel. a Lapide in Exod. 28, 43). — Vestes, quibus corpus exterius decoratur, sunt virtutes, quibus interius homo perornatur (Honor. Augustod. Gemma anim. l. 1, c. 198).

[2] En quantarum virtutum vestis ipsa sacerdotalis indicium est! Quam dives igitur erit, quam pulcher, quam splendidus, quam gratus et acceptus oculis divinae majestatis, si hac adornatus panoplia sacerdos rem divinam acturus ad altare accedit! Dum antistes mysticas vestes benedicit, eas inter orandum appellat "insignia sacerdotalis gloriae" ... Licet ad reverentiam divinis mysteriis sacrificioque simul et sacerdotio conciliandam voluerit Deus, ut tanto cum externi etiam ornatus decore procedat sacerdos ad coelestis muneris dispensationem, tamen sacer hic apparatus, ornatus monimentum est, panopliae scil. virtutum, quibus altari se sistens sacerdos praeditus esse debet: hoc ejus verum decus est, honor singularis, perfecta gloria et perennis corona (Du Saussay P. 1, l. 6, c. 15).

the cross before him in his vestment, that he may diligently behold
the footsteps of Christ, and fervently endeavor to follow them. He
is marked with a cross behind, that he mildly suffer, for God's sake,
whatsoever adversities may befall him from others. He wears the
cross before him, that he may bewail his own sins; and behind him,
that through compassion he may lament the sins of others, and
know that he is placed, as it were, a mediator between God and the
sinner. Neither ought he to cease from prayer and the holy oblation, till he be favored with the grace and mercy which he implores.
When the priest celebrates, he honors God, he rejoices the angels,
he edifies the Church, he helps the living, he obtains rest for the
dead, and makes himself partaker of all that is good" (Imit. of
Christ, l. 4, c. 5).

30. The Liturgical Colors.

1. As in the Old, so also in the New Law there are different
liturgical colors which impart to the vestments not only splendor,
beauty and variety, but also a religious symbolical meaning. The
rich, deep symbolism of the colors was the determining reason, why
the Church selected and prescribed various colors for the different
feasts and seasons, as well as for special functions of the holy year.[1]
Until the Middle Age the white color was, if not exclusively, yet
constantly used for religious feasts and as a symbol of joy. In the
twelfth century the practice of using different colors was already
pretty well developed;[2] but not until the epoch of the newly revised
edition of the Missal in the sixteenth century was the selection of
the liturgical colors finally determined and settled. The five colors
prescribed by the Church in her liturgy, to the exclusion of all other
colors,[3] are the following: white, red, green, purple and black.[4] —

[1] Paramenta Altaris, Celebrantis et Ministrorum *debent* esse coloris convenientis Officio et Missae diei, secundum usum Romanae Ecclesiae (Missal. Rom. Rubr.
gener. tit. 18, n. 1). — Non licet in Missae celebratione aliisque ecclesiasticis func-
tionibus adhibere paramenta etiam pretiosa, quae non correspondeant coloribus a
rubrica praescriptis (S. R. C. 19. Dec. 1829). — Servetur strictim rubrica quoad
colorem paramentorum (S. R. C. 12. Nov. 1831).

[2] Innocent III. (1198—1216) counts, according to the variety of feasts and
days, four principal colors (white, red, green, black); the later fifth color, that is,
violet, is regarded by him as secondary to black. Quattuor sunt principales colores, quibus secundum proprietates dierum sacras vestes Ecclesia Romana distinguit:
albus, rubeus, niger et viridis. Ad hos quattuor ceteri referuntur: ad rubeum colorem coccineus (scarlet), ad nigrum violaceus, ad viridem croceus (saffron). De
sacr. alt. myst. l. 1, c. 65. — In Durandus (Ration. l. 3, c. 18) violet appears already
in general use. — The Fourteenth Roman Ordo, which is of the fourteenth century,
contains also these words: Sancta Romana Ecclesia quinque coloribus utitur in
sacris vestibus, videlicet, albo, rubeo, viridi, violaceo et nigro. *Quidam autem
duos hos ultimos pro uno reputant* (c. 49).

[3] On the Sundays Gaudete (in Advent) and Laetare (in Lent) the vestments
used in the Missa solemnis should be "rose-colored" (coloris rosacei), in order to
enhance the solemnity and express joy by means of this lighter violet, which is so
close to the red. Cfr. Cerem. Episc. l. 2, c. 13. 20.

[4] Ecclesia quinque coloribus uti consuevit: albo, rubeo, viridi, violaceo et

Yellow (*color flavus*) and cerulean blue (*color caeruleus*) are positively forbidden.[1] Gold colored vestments (*paramenta coloris aurei*) are also excluded from the use of the Church; but vestments composed entirely or for the most part of real gold cloth (*paramenta revera ex auro maxima ex parte contexta*) may be tolerated or permitted to take the place of white, red and green vestments. — The Church has, moreover, expressed her disapproval of so combining colors in one and the same vestment, that one principal or fundamental color (*color primarius et praedominans*) is scarcely or not at all recognizable.[2] Likewise the indiscriminate use for two colors of double-colored vestments is interdicted, for example, a white chasuble with a red cross, to answer for a red as well as for a white vestment; such different colored vestments are tolerated for one color only, to be so decided upon, that the middle part of the vestment is to be regarded merely as ornamental.[3] — Finally, the use of purple instead of black is forbidden in Masses of Requiem.[4] — Consequently, in order to preserve the sacred symbolism of color, the Church has always declared against confounding, as also against combining, the liturgical colors.

2. "Simple light unfolds its beams in an extraordinary variety of hue, inasmuch as it admits of the most varied degrees of intensity and attenuation, and is refracted into an incalculable number of colors."[5] Colors are produced by the varied refraction of the rays of light, and, like light itself, stand in an intimate and mysterious relation to the inner spiritual life of man. Light and color, among all material things, are the nearest related to the spiritual. "The sentiments awakened in us by the particular colors are similar to the contrasts between light and darkness. The bright vivid colors act by inciting and rejoicing us, while the dark, sombre colors depress the spirits and produce the effect of darkness." The colors are not only symbols of different mysteries, truths, thoughts, feelings, sentiments, but they also exert a more or less powerful influence over

nigro (Missal. Rom. Rubr. gen. tit. 18, n. 1). — White and red are the only real festal colors, and are intended for the different feasts; while green and violet, as a rule, are used only on Sundays and week-days, and black is intended for the Good Friday services, and is used also in the liturgy for the departed.

[1] In some dioceses in Spain it is permitted, or rather obligatory, in virtue of a special papal privilege, to use sky-blue vestments at all the Masses of the Immaculate Conception, whether of the feast itself, or votive (S. R. C. 12. Febr. 1884).

[2] S. R. C. 23. Sept. 1837 ad dub. 8, n. 2.

[3] In chasubles of this description uniformity of color is wanting, wherefore they are not approved; their use (in poorer churches) can at most be tolerated only until they are worn out.

[4] Missae defunctorum celebrandae sunt omnino in paramentis *nigris* adeo ut violacea adhiberi nequeant, nisi in casu, quo die 2. Novembris SS. Euchar. sacramentum publicae fidelium adorationi sit expositum pro solemni Oratione 40 Horarum, prout cautum est in Decreto sacrae hujus Congregationis diei 16. Septembris anni 1801 (Decret. Urbis et Orbis S. R. C. 27. Jun. 1868).

[5] Berthold, Das Naturschöne S. 28.

the understanding and mind, on the life of the soul and heart. Now, this universally known and acknowledged fact is employed by the Church, inasmuch as she makes use of the symbolism of colors in her liturgy for her exalted and holy purposes, for carrying out her divine service.[1]

The Church possesses in her bosom an inexhaustible, fertile life of faith and grace; this interior life she would reveal exteriorly by the variety and splendor of the liturgical colors, so as to produce and nourish in the hearts of the faithful heavenly thoughts and representations, holy affections and resolutions. Yea, inexhaustibly rich and manifold is the life of the Church. "As in the material world outside the seasons come and go, so also the Church gathers her children around her, and at the foot of the altar in the sanctuary of the immutable One she lives with them through the changing seasons of the ecclesiastical year. In the beginning of the ecclesiastical year, she prepares the hearts of the faithful for the approaching advent of the promised Redeemer; with the shepherds, she leads her children to the crib in the stable, there to celebrate at the holy hour of midnight the merciful birth of our Saviour amid the hymns of the angels (Luke 2, 14). She celebrates the feast of the Circumcision of the Redeemer, in whom all prophecy is fulfilled. With her children she accompanies to Bethlehem the Wise Men guided by the star from the East, there to adore, to make offerings to, and to kneel before the acknowledged God-man and King of the world (Matt. 2, 11). She follows the Divine Saviour in His flight into Egypt and on His return therefrom; and later on, in His public life, she accompanies her Lord and Master in His journeyings, as He preaches His divine doctrine; and from Sunday to Sunday, she is a witness of His teachings and miracles, as though He were visible on earth with us. On Palm Sunday, she solemnly enters Jerusalem with Him, strewing His way with green branches and chanting Hosannas to Him (Mark 11, 8—10). Along with Him she celebrates His last supper in the midst of His Apostles; she accompanies Him in His sorrowful journey to the Garden of Gethsemani, to His unjust judges and persecutors, and on His last journey to Golgotha; there she sees Him expire on the cross, bowing His head; and she follows Him in mourning to the sepulchre where friends have buried Him. After three days she celebrates with joyful Alleluja the Christian vernal feast, the glorious Resurrection of the Lord; she follows Him risen from the dead to the Mount of Olives, whence forty days after He ascends gloriously into heaven in the presence of His disciples; she awaits with His faithful ones the descent of the Holy Ghost and His bountiful outpouring of grace and blessing for the founding of the infant Church; on Trinity Sunday she attests her faith in the fundamental doctrine of her religion, the belief in the Ever Blessed Trinity, God the Father, God the Son, and God the Holy Ghost; and the

---

[1] Colorum varietas adspectabilis quandam animo injicit mysterii celebrandi praesensionem, quae pietatem excitet foveatque plurimum (Guyet, Heortol. 1. 3, c.29).

feast of Corpus Christi, the feast confessing His living presence in
the Most Holy Sacrament of the Altar, she makes resplendent with
solemn procession and with all the grandeur and magnificence that
the approaching summer enables her to display.   In addition to these
festivals of the Lord, the Church also celebrates the anniversary
feasts of His most blessed Mother, from her Immaculate Conception
and birth to her glorious Assumption into heaven, as days commemorative of the sublime graces which she herself received from God
and which we too have shared and received through her; likewise
she commemorates the special feasts of the Apostles, martyrs, confessors and virgins and of all His saints, in remembrance of the
triumphs that they, by their heroic combats, have, with the assistance of His grace, achieved in life and death, bequeathing them to
us in many moving examples for our imitation.   Finally, when in
the material world without the closing autumn season robs the
forests of their foliage, and dying nature sinks into the icy embrace
of winter, the Church brings to an end the Christian year in her
temples with the feast of All Souls, the commemorative day of all
those who, dying in the Lord, have passed out from the Church
militant into the Church suffering, and she implores the Lord with
devout supplication to grant rest unto them, and that He receive
them into the Church triumphant to enjoy a blessed eternity with
Him.[1]   Thus does a life that is warm, fresh and complete pulsate
in the heart of the Church.   This life the Church seeks to inculcate
on all her children during the course of the ecclesiastical year, by
means of her liturgy.   This is the object of the varied splendor of
the colors of the vestments, with which she has adorned the blooming wreath of her holy feasts and days; for the liturgical colors have
a language of their own, by which they point out the spiritual, the
divine and the eternal.

3.   In the following pages we shall briefly state the symbolical
meaning of each of the colors the Church uses at the altar.

a) White is the color of light and, therefore, symbolical of the
lustre and glory of the light, that is, of radiant purity, innocence
and holiness, as also of heavenly joy, bliss and transfiguration. —
White is the robe of the baptized, who in the laver of regeneration
are washed from the blemish of every sin; this robe they should
wear untarnished and unspotted unto the judgment-seat of Jesus
Christ, in order that they may be adorned with the radiant garment
of glory. — To those who in the combat against sin persevere victoriously to the end of life, is made in the Apocalypse (3, 5) the
promise that they shall be clothed in white garments, that is, rewarded with the possession of the eternal happiness and the glory of
heaven — *Qui vicerit, vestietur vestimentis albis.*[2]   In the radiant

---

[1] Geissel, Schriften und Reden II, 387.

[2] Vestis alba sive splendida notat candorem et splendorem gloriae coelestis,
ad quam anhelamus, quamque ambimus velut ejus candidati, ut illa semper nostris
oculis et menti obversetur, itaque ineamus vitam sanctam et coelestem (Cornel. a
Lapide, in Eccles. 9, 8).

light of an eternal day that will never wane shines the heavenly
Jerusalem; for it is made bright with the splendor of God and that
light is the Lamb (Apoc. 21, 23). At the transfiguration on Mount
Thabor, the face of Jesus shone out bright as the sun, and His garments became white and shining (*vestitus ejus albus et refulgens*)
as the sunlit snow (Matt. 17; Luke 9). Whenever God's angels
have appeared to mortals here below, they invariably have manifested
themselves clothed in bright and radiant vesture (Matt. 28, 3; Luke
2, 9); the multitude of the elect stand before the throne of God and
the Lamb clothed in white garments (*amicti stolis albis* — Apoc. 7,
9).[1] — Many of the saints were often during life and after death
seen surrounded with a heavenly splendor. Thus, for example, it is
related of the holy Father St. Benedict, that his mien was so amiable, his deportment so angelic, and the splendor which environed
him so great, that one would have supposed he was not a being living upon earth, but in heaven. The pale, emaciated face of St.
Lidwina shone after her death with a supermundane brightness; her
whole appearance was that of an angel.

Now, at the celebration of the Eucharistic Sacrifice "the Lord
inclines the heavens and comes down" (*inclinavit coelos et descendit*
— Ps. 17, 10) upon the altar with His hosts, with all His love and
bounty, with all His treasures and graces, in order to make a heaven
of our poor earth; the celebration of this celestial Sacrifice the priest
should always perform with angelic purity and joyfulness. And in
order to signify this, the white color is never to be entirely wanting
at the altar, some parts at least of the priestly vestments (the amice
and alb) must always be white.[2] *Omni tempore sint vestimenta tua
candida* (Ecclus. 9, 8). At certain times, for particular reasons,
the entire robing of the priest and chalice must be white. This is
generally prescribed on those feasts and days when the characteristics
of heavenly purity, joy and glory are to be prominently represented
and expressed.

Thus all the joyful and glorious mysteries of our Lord and Saviour Jesus Christ are celebrated in white festive colors; for what
other color would be more appropriate, for example, for Christmas,
for Epiphany, Easter, the Ascension, Corpus Christi? The Church
celebrates at midnight the birth of our Divine Redeemer, on holy
Christmas night. This blessed night is brighter than the brightest
day, for it knows no obscurity, no darkness, no sorrow, no tribulation. It floods the world with a stream of light and joy; it is replete
with joy above all other feasts, since in addition to its Heavenly

---

[1] Stola alba Sanctorum significat 1) conscientiae puritatem, castitatem et
candorem; 2) inde consequentem serenitatem, hilaritatem et laetitiam; 3) felicitatem et gloriam (Cornel. a Lapide l. c.).

[2] Ideo ministri Christi vel Ecclesiae in albis vestibus ministrant, quia Angeli,
aeterni Regis ministri, in albis apparebant. Per albas itaque vestes admonentur,
ut Angelos Dei ministros per castitatis munditiam in Christi servitio imitentur
(Honor. Augustod. Gemma anim. l. 1, c. 198).

Gift, it brings intimate and heartfelt joy to every household, a joy which, like a pleasant odor, refreshes the heart. — On the Feast of the Epiphany we are reminded of that wonderful star, which "in beauty and brilliancy surpassed the sun," and which shone brightly into the hearts of the Wise Men, filling them with extraordinary joy. For us also this beautiful feast is a day of rejoicing. Since here below in the luminous obscurity of faith we know God, we pray in the celebration of this feast for the grace to be led in the next life to the clear and blessed vision of His eternal glory. — Easter is radiant with the glory of the Risen Saviour. At no other time of the ecclesiastical year do the church bells ring out so solemnly, does the singing sound more joyous; and the Alleluja is never-ending; the house of God is resplendent with the most beautiful decorations, and the priests ascend the altar, clad in the most festal vestments. Upon all who were permitted to see the Risen Lord, there was poured forth a stream of cheerfulness and happiness, of peace and consolation. Therefore, we also sincerely unite in joy over this great honor of our Lord. — The Ascension is likewise a day of rejoicing and triumph.[1] *Ascendit Deus in jubilo* (Ps. 46, 6). This day is the close of the Lord's earthly pilgrimage; a bright cloud conceals Him from the gaze of the Apostles, as triumphant "He mounteth above the heaven of heavens" (*ascendit super coelum coeli* — Ps. 67, 34), to the highest heaven, where, "crowned with glory," He sits at the right hand of the Father. "And the Apostles adoring went back into Jerusalem with great joy" (Luke 24, 52), and we also rejoice on this day, mindful of the consoling promise of Christ: "In my Father's house there are many mansions... I go to prepare a place for you. I will come again, and will take you to myself, that where I am, you also may be" (John 14, 2—3). — Finally, is not the triumphant and glorious Feast of Corpus Christi a day of over-flowing joy, a day of unspeakable bliss, a day of the most rapturous exultation? It would seem on this glorious Feast as though the world had never fallen. The Church militant on earth thrills with joyous emotion, just as the rock threatens to tremble before the mighty waves of the ocean; for the time being she forgets her banishment and her state of combat. Sin appears forgotten; tears flow indeed, but are shed rather out of rapture than for penance. It is like the soul's first day in heaven, or as though earth itself had been converted into a heaven, from sheer joy in the most holy Sacrament. It is a day on which we cannot stand still, but must move about in procession.[2]

White is, in like manner, used on feasts commemorating the mysteries of the life of the Blessed Virgin Mary Mother of God, be-

---

[1] Solemnitas ista *gloriosa* est et, ut ita dicam, *gaudiosa*, in qua et singularis Christo gloria et nobis specialis laetitia exhibetur. Consummatio enim et adimpletio est reliquarum solemnitatum et felix clausula totius itinerarii Filii Dei (S. Bernard. In Ascens. Dom. serm. 2, n. 1).

[2] Cf. Father Faber, The Blessed Sacrament.

ginning with that of her Immaculate Conception and continuing
until her glorious Assumption into heaven. For Mary is the miraculous flower, a heavenly lily of dazzling whiteness, wholly beautiful
and without blemish; the beautiful month of May with its blossoms
and wealth of flowers, is a symbol of that abundance of graces and
virtues with which she is adorned. In her dazzling light all the
saints pale. Save the majesty of God no splendor equals hers;
clothed in the light of the sun (Apoc. 12, 1), she has all the blessed
spirits as a glittering crown of stars around her head, and all the
saints as the moon-light at her feet. She shines in the beauty of the
Daughter of God, in the dignity of Mother of God, in the charms
of Spouse of God. She is "the bright morning star," "the bearer
of light of the Eternal Day;" "the gentle Queen of Heaven," "the
pure, tender and loving Mother," "the most lovely heavenly Lady."
"To her gentle care and maternal sweetness" we recommend ourselves on her feasts, that she may be "a companion and protectress
to us against the evil one, until through the heavenly portals we
reach eternal felicity."[1] We cry to Mary, "the Star of the Sea":
Mites fac et castos! Vitam praesta puram! — "Make us meek
and chaste! Grant that our life be pure!"

White, moreover, harmonizes admirably with the character of
the feasts of the angels. The holy angels, those blessed heavenly
spirits, are unspeakably pure: pure in the perfection of their beautiful being, pure in the treasures of divine grace. They bask in the
very rays of divine glory; and they reflect as clear, bright mirrors
the image of God Himself. Even down into our earthly darkness
does this angel light dart its rays: the angels are heavenly messengers, showing us the way of life unto eternal light. They are "our
brethren with praise and joy in eternal bliss, and accompany and
protect us at all times" (H. Suso). O dear Angel mine, lead me on
through joy and sorrow, through want and death to heavenly bliss!

White is, finally, the color of all those saints who are not martyrs, of the confessors, holy women and virgins. All these "walk
with Christ in white, because they are worthy" (Apoc. 3, 4). They
all either remained pure, inasmuch as they walked the dusty paths
of earth unsullied, and never lost the precious and resplendent robe
of baptismal innocence; — or, after having fallen into sin, they
again became pure, because, as penitents, they washed the stains of
their soul in the Blood of the Lamb and in the tears of repentance.
But all — both those that ever remained pure and those who again
became pure — "now flower as lilies before the Lord and bloom
eternally" (Osee 14, 6).

The white color of the vestments admonishes the faithful to
appear in the house of God clad with the bright garment of grace
and purity, to assist at divine worship with heartfelt joy and gratitude; for it is meet to praise God with holy joy and to render Him
thanks for the wonderful light of truth and grace unto which He has

---

[1] Denifle, Die Schriften des seligen Heinrich Seuse, 1. Abthlg.

called us, and for the greatness and glory of the Redemption which
has fallen to our share.

b) The red color is the strongest, the most sprightly and gorgeous of all the colors.[1] "When the white ray of light is refracted
on material objects, it becomes colored and assumes one of the seven
colors of the rainbow, of which red — the original color of the rose
— is the fullest and most conspicuous" (Laurent). "White is the
color of light; red is the color of the most glaring light — of fire.
White beamed forth from the Lord on Thabor, when He showed
Himself as King of Eternal Light; He stands in red at the prae-
torium of the governor, when aflame with love and in the scarlet of
wounds He enters the combat. St. John beheld Him in flowing
white garment in the midst of the seven golden candlesticks (Apoc.
1, 13), as the King of eternal glory; the same St. John sees Him
robed in red, when He appears in triumph as conqueror. 'He was
clothed,' says the holy Seer of Patmos, 'with a garment sprinkled
with blood. The armies that are in heaven followed Him on white
horses, clothed in fine linen and clean. He shall rule the nations
with a rod of iron and He treadeth the wine-press of the fierceness
of the wrath of God Almighty' " (Apoc. 19, 13—15).[2]

As the color of flame and blood, red represents the ardent, consuming fire of love which the Holy Ghost enkindles in the heart
(Rom. 5, 5); it is emblematic of that generous, conquering love
which yields up in martyrdom the greatest and dearest of all earthly
blessings, namely, life itself, — and triumphs in death. As the sun
sets in the bright red glow of the evening, so also love flames up
powerfully in the bloody martyrdom. For "love is as strong as
death, as hard as hell; the lamps thereof are fire and flames, many
waters cannot quench it" (Cant. 8, 6). Without suffering there is
no love. Love is shown and proved to be most heroic by the cheerful endurance of the torments of death, and by the shedding of one's
blood.[3] For "greater love than this no man hath, that a man lay

---

[1] Red is also the color of the purple, in which kings and princes clothed
themselves; therefore, red purple answers as a symbol of royal majesty, of princely
power and dignity. Formerly Christ on the Cross was often represented as a triumphant conqueror, adorned with the regal crown and the purple mantle, the
emblem of royal power (regnavit a ligno Deus). The Pope frequently wears red
purple garments as a peculiar distinction, notably on Good Friday (Papa luget in
purpura). But for many centuries red purple has been the distinctive color of the
highest dignitaries in the Church, that is, of the cardinals who, consequently, are
called Patres purpurati. Merito purpura Cardinalibus quasi regibus data, cujus
color in galero eximiae caritatis est symbolum, cujus igne ita ardere debent, ut
semper pro defensione et bono Ecclesiae sanguinem fundere sint parati (S. Antonin.
Sum. p. 3, tit. 1. Cf. Piazza, L'Iride sacra spiegata nei colori degli abiti ecclesiastici, cap. 15—16. — Moroni, Dizionario di erudizione storico-ecclesiastica, s. v.
Porpora).

[2] Breiteneicher, Die Passion des Gottmenschen II, 69.

[3] Caritas tunc maxima est in hac vita, quando pro illa *ipsa contemnitur vita*
(S. Aug. De natura et gratia c. 70, n. 84).

down his life for his friends," and "in this we have known the charity of God, because He hath laid down His life for us" (John 15, 13; 1 John 3, 16). In the order of nature, man has nothing more precious than life; for "all that he hath he will give for his life" (Job. 2, 4). Therefore, the sacrifice of life, martyrdom, is the most perfect proof of love.

Red is the liturgical vestment for the feasts of the Finding and Exaltation of the Holy Cross, as well as for the feasts of the Passion of our Lord, which for the most part fall on the Fridays of Lent; for on all these feasts Christ's saving blood shed in torrents and the excessive love of His Sacred Heart are offered to the soul's consideration. The Cross is the place of sacrifice, that is, the altar (*ara crucis*), on which the propitiatory Sacrifice was offered up for the sins of the world; it was entirely covered with blood. The remaining instruments of the Passion (the thorns, the nails, the lance) were sprinkled and crimsoned with blood. In the mystery of His passion the Lord appears with dyed garments (*tinctis vestibus*) as a combating hero, who has gloriously finished His combat for our freedom and gained the victory by His blood (Isa. 63, 1). In the imperishable and roseate adornment of His bleeding wounds, our Lord reveals the inextinguishable flames of love that burn for us in His merciful Heart. "Behold and consider the rose of the bloody passion, how it glows as a mark of the most ardent love. Love and suffering contend with each other: love, to burn more; suffering, to bleed more. The rose of love would be crimsoned in suffering, and the rose of suffering would glow in the fires of love. Behold, how in this rosy attire our best Vine bloomed, Jesus crimsoned with blood! Consider His whole body, and see if you do not recognize the bloom of the blood-red rose! Look at one hand and then at the other, do you not observe the red rose in each? Behold one foot and then the other, are they not rose-colored? Contemplate the pierced side, the rose is not wanting there. O what a stream of blood flowed from the deep wounds of His sacred body! In this fount (of His sacred body) our rose is dyed and glows in deepest crimson hues; for most ardently did love's fires burn where suffering revealed itself in crimson red. In the greatness of the torment you behold the greatness of love. The Rose glitters with a twofold light before you — it is fiery in its love, and blood-red in its suffering. By the flames of love suffering is purpled; for if there were no love, there would not be this suffering. And again — from this blood-red of torment love radiates in its fulness and glory." [1]

Red is also used on the feasts of the saints who gloriously shed their blood for the Lord and manifested a love that surrenders up body and life itself, a love stronger than death and the torments of death. [2] — To this class belong the Apostles who "planted the Church

[1] Cf. Breviar. Rom. Lect. II. Noct. in festo ss. 5 Vulnerum D. N. I. Chr. — S. Bonav. Vitis mystica c. 17—22.

[2] Quod martyribus datur color rubeus, fit propter eorum corpora, ut repraesentet sanguinem ab eis effusum mereri purpuram et regnum coeleste. Quocirca veri-

in their blood;" then the martyrs, countless multitudes of whom trod in the blood-stained foot-prints of the Saviour, and are now glorified in their own blood and in the blood of the Lamb;[1] finally, the martyred virgins who preserved victorious fidelity to their Divine Spouse by their constancy in faith as well as by their chaste life, inasmuch as they offered and consecrated to Him together with the lily of their virginity the rose of martyrdom, so that it cannot be decided, whether their wedding garment shines more brightly on account of their snow-white purity, or on account of their rose-colored martyrdom.[2] Therefore, the red rose, because of the color of blood, is considered the flower of the martyrs. Thus the Church sings on the Feast of Holy Innocents: "Hail, blossoms of martyrdom; the persecutors of Christ robbed you of the morning light of life, as the fury of the raging storm destroys the opening rosebuds."

Red is also the color of Whitsunday. "On this great feast the Church displays in her service the utmost splendor; priest and altar are clothed in crimson red, as emblematic of the ardent flames of the Spirit of God, who descended visibly upon the Apostles, and since then upon millions and millions of souls. They are effulgent rays proceeding from 'the face of God,' brilliant in faith and ardent in love" (Wolter). In the form of tongues of fire the Holy Ghost descended upon the disciples, that they might be fluent in words and glowing with love (*verbis ut essent proflui et caritate fervidi*). And the Holy Ghost still continues ever to strew the fiery sparks of heavenly love upon the earth and in the hearts of men, to create them anew and to fill them with the courage of self-sacrifice. — At the same time, Pentecost is the birthday of the Catholic Church, which as the holy city of God upon the summit of the mountain rises towering high from the ocean of blood shed by the Lord and His martyrs. The Church has always been gloriously honored by the testimony of martyrs and made fruitful in their blood.

As the Divine Bridegroom is "white and ruddy" *(candidus et rubicundus* — Cant. 5, 10),[3] His spouse, the human soul, should

---

simile est, etiam in coelo dotem claritatis, quae erit in corporibus Martyrum, ita candidam fore, ut simul sit rubea, sive vermiculata ex candido et purpureo (Cornel. a Lapide, in Apoc. 7, 9).

[1] The Church sings of the Martyrs: *Rubri* nam *fluido sanguine,* laureis — Ditantur bene fulgidis. In the liturgy there are also some saints honored as martyrs, although they did not die a violent death. To these the red, that is, the color similar to fire, applies, inasmuch as they were penetrated with the fire of the Holy Spirit and of love, and, therefore, courageously persevered in the furnace of tribulation and persecution until death.

[3] Martyrdom, as proof and evidence of the most perfect love, is more excellent than virginity and is, therefore, preferred to it in the liturgy. Ecclesia praefert Martyres Virginibus tum in ordine, quem servat in Communi Sanctorum, tum in Martyrologio, tum in Litaniis et commemorationibus, tum in hoc ritu, quo in festis Virginum et Martyrum non albo, sed *rubeo* colore utitur (Quarti, Comment. in Rubr. Miss. p. 1, tit. 18, dub. 5).

[3] Christus *candidus* et splendidus est ob puritatem innocentiae et splendorem

also shine resplendent in the delicate white of purity and in the fiery red of divine love, which when commingled make up the lovely rosy garment of grace. O charming heavenly attire of grace in a soul! Brilliant beauty that adorns and delights the garden of God! Who would not desire this adornment, covet this beauty, this roseate raiment of the soul! Thy soul must shine in the rose-colored garment of purity, love and grace, if thou wouldst be admitted to the heavenly wedding-feast. — Red also reminds thee of the great accounting-day, of the dreadful day of judgment. Behold, the Son of man comes on bright, shining clouds; He comes surrounded by the brilliant heavenly court; He comes with great power and majesty. Like the blood-red radiant·rising sun, He appears in the purple clouds of the eternal heavens, in the purple rays of the holy Cross, in the purple splendor of His radiant wounds. The Cross will shine in the heavens, and will cast frightful blood-red rays on the wicked. On the body of the Judge of the world His sacred wounds will shine as fiery purple and terrify all who have rendered His precious blood fruitless and trampled it under foot.

c) Green is a medium between the strong and the weak colors; therefore, it is the most refreshing and the most soothing of colors to the eye. Everywhere, when spring awakens, country and meadow, hill and dale grow green and bud forth, blossom and exhale sweet odors; all nature develops new life and growth, decks herself out in fresh and lovely verdure and gives promise of plenteous harvest. According to the general opinion and also in the liturgy, green is, therefore, a symbol of hope.[1]

Green harmonizes with the nature of the Church. She is a mighty tree, which rears its head majestically heavenward, spreads its shady branches and leaves covering the earth with blessings, displaying its richest blossoms in all their beauty, and producing an abundant harvest of precious fruits of grace and virtue. She is the well-watered garden of the Lord; Christ, the Good Shepherd, leads His flock to pasture on its ever-green meadows, waters and refreshes them at the fountains of the ever-fresh and living waters of grace. Thus the Church here below grows green and blooms, increases and ripens on her way to her eternal consummation.

---

sanctitatis, qua ex purissima Virgine natus sanctissimus exstitit; *rubicundus* propter passionem, qua sanguine suo fuit purpuratus (Cornel. a Lapide in Cant. Cantic. 1. c.).

[1] This symbolical conception of green may be established in various ways. In winter the pleasant green of springtime is the subject of our confidence, and when it appears, it becomes for us an earnest of an abundant harvest. — Just as green refreshes and revives the eye in a high degree, so it is especially the virtue of hope that cheers and encourages, consoles and rejoices us (*spe gaudentes*, in tribulationibus patientes, Rom. 12, 12). — In nature green is a sign of life and, therefore, it becomes in the higher order the symbol of the life of grace and glory, which constitutes the principal object of Christian hope (gloriamur in *spe gloriae* filiorum Dei, Rom. 5, 2; in *spem vitae aeternae*, quam repromisit Deus, Tit. 1, 2). Hence the Church prays: Mentis perustae vulnera — Munda *virore gratiae;* and of Easter Sunday she sings: Dies venit, dies tua, — In qua *reflorent* omnia.

The Church is robed in green garments to express her joyous, vivid hope, of coming to the ever delightful and ever-green pastures of the celestial paradise,[1] of possessing the incorruptible inheritance and the never-fading crown of glory in heaven (1 Peter 1, 4; 5, 4). In the heavenly Jerusalem the blessed eat of the tree of life, whose never-falling leaves are for the healing of the nations (Apoc. 22, 2); there shall the Lamb lead them to the fountains of the waters of life (Apoc. 7, 17).

For the reason that green holds an intermediate place between the bright and the dark colors, it is used in the Church service on days, which have, on the one hand, no special festal and joyful character, but which, on the other, are moreover not days appointed for penance and mourning. To this class belong the Sundays and week-days after the Octave of the Epiphany until Septuagesima and from the Octave of Pentecost until Advent.[2] — When after the Feast of the Epiphany we see green used at the altar, we should re-awaken and re-animate the virtue of Christian hope in our heart; for the green vestments are a consoling pledge of the hope of eternal salvation, that has been regained for us by Christ's merciful Birth and Manifestation, by the revelation of His goodness and love for men. — The ecclesiastical season after Pentecost represents the journeying of the children of God to their true country in heaven. "Years fly with the rapidity of an arrow, one after another, and centuries follow one another in never-ending succession; but their term of years comes and goes only because He guides and directs it in its course, whose glance encompasses all the centuries of time (Ecclus. 36, 19), that in their rapid flight the years of time may announce that there is One who was before all time and who exists unto all ages (42, 21), the King of Ages (1 Tim. 1, 17), whose throne is forever and ever (Heb. 1, 8) and whose kingdom endureth throughout all generations (Ps. 144, 13). Everything under the sun is changeable and must perish, because He who endureth forever, wills that it should perish. Man, too, may not remain upon earth. Created out of nothing, his life is short and filled with labors and his end is painful, and after all nothing remains to him but the tomb (Job 17, 1. — Wisdom 2, 1—2). A creature of yesterday, he passes as a shadow moving and changing, until after a few short days he dies (Job 14, 2, 5); but his life is so brief, that he may acknowledge that there is One, the Lord of Life, who has set for him this short period (14, 5), so that he may not forget the unchangeable on account of the changeable, and attach his heart to the goods that are dust like himself. It is appointed for him once to die (Heb. 9, 27); but he dies only when and because He that rules also over death (Ps. 67,

---

[1] Constituat te Christus Filius Dei vivi intra *paradisi sui semper amoena virentia* (Ordo commendat. animae).

[2] The Sundays named are, therefore, called Dominicae *virides*. Cfr. Angel. Rocca, Thesaurus pontif. sacrarumque antiquit. I, 75: An summo Pontifici sacrum facienti conveniat uti sacris vestibus colore *viridi* affectis.

21), suffers him to die, so that he may understand that only through the Lord, the Conqueror of Death (1 Cor. 15, 42), power has been taken from death and from the fear of death (Heb. 2, 15), that the Master of the harvest of men sows the corruptible body in corruption only that it may again arise in incorruption (1 Cor. 15, 42), and that all that proceed from Adam and who by sin have become subject to death (Rom. 5, 12), only by death and the grace of God can come to Him in His eternal tabernacles, where He will wipe away every tear from their eyes, and where there will be no more sadness, nor sorrow, nor pain, nor death any more (Apoc. 21, 3—4)" (Geissel). This earthly pilgrimage is, indeed, beset with hardships, difficulties, privations and temptations, and yet abounding in consolation and joy by reason of the unfailing expectation of eternal rest, of final victory and of never-ending triumph in our heavenly country. And by "this hope is our salvation and our joy" (Rom. 8, 24; 12, 12): it mitigates the sorrow of the present time and brings along with it the consolation of a happier future. Deprived of this hope we should be the most miserable of men (1 Cor. 15, 19). — During the period after Pentecost the Church wears green vestments, in order to fill us in faith with all joy and peace, so that we may abound in hope and the power of the Holy Ghost (Rom. 15, 13): for to us in our pilgrimage, hope for the goods of the Lord in the land of the living is a guiding-star, a pilgrim's staff and a support.

d) Purple belongs to the subdued colors, but it is somewhat enlivened by red. Inasmuch as the violet-color resembles the dark grey of ashes, it inculcates an earnest spirit of penance and a true penitential disposition; but in so far as it is like the dark coloring of the violet (violaceus from viola), which modestly conceals itself amid the grass of the field, in the vale and wood from human eye, blooming and yielding its perfume but for its Creator, it may be considered as an emblem of unpretentious humility, of holy retirement, of well tempered sorrow, of a sorrowful longing and sighing after heaven.[1] The dark, serious violet, therefore, bespeaks sadness; though not a complete and universal sadness, but one that is moderated and tempered with rays of joy.[2] Consequently, violet is a

---

[1] The symbolism of violet may also be rendered in a somewhat different way. Inasmuch as violet is dark blue, it symbolizes in general sorrow and grief (for it produces a dark blue shadow upon the face); — and inasmuch as it is violet blue, it indicates at the same time, that this penitential sadness and sorrow proceeds from an humble and humbled heart (for violet is symbolical of humility and of the humble).

[2] In former times violet was rarely used, for example, on the Feast of Holy Innocents and on Laetare Sunday, because black was regarded as a penitential color; since the end of the thirteenth century, the present more strict distinction between violet and black has been gradually developed. The Ordo Rom. XIV, c. 53 has the following rubric in reference to the use of black in the fourteenth century: Colore *nigro* utitur (s. Romana Ecclesia) feria sexta in Parasceve, in Missis defunctorum et in processionibus, quas Romanus Pontifex nudis pedibus facit. Sciendum tamen est quod diebus, quibus est usus nigri coloris, uti violaceo non est inconveniens.

fitting emblem of that holy sadness pleasing to God, which produces a spirit of penance steadfast unto salvation (*quae secundum Deum tristitia est, poenitentiam in salutem stabilem operatur* — 2 Corinth. 7, 10), and also of that laudable sorrow felt by the soul in being obliged to remain far from the Lord, in a world foreign to her, and daily, yea, hourly endangering her salvation. The soul penetrated with this sorrow does indeed frequently exclaim: "Who shall deliver me from the body of this death?" (Rom. 7, 24) — or: "Woe is me: that my sojourning is prolonged!" (Ps. 119, 5); but her sorrow, her sadness is not without its consolation and sweetness.

From what has been said the liturgical use of violet vestments on certain days of the ecclesiastical year can easily be explained. In general, the color is worn on those days that bear the serious character of penance. The penitential color used is intended to represent and proclaim to the eye the penitential sentiments, the holy grief and ardent supplications of the Church. The days for violet are, in the first place, the Ember days (excepting those of Pentecost week) and the vigils, as well as the days appointed for the greater penitential procession (*Litaniae majores*) on St. Mark's Day and on the three days termed Rogation Days (*Rogationes*) before the Ascension. Violet reminds the faithful on these days that they should be intent upon appeasing the justice of God by penance, cleansing their hearts from sin; that they should fervently implore God to free them from famine and tribulation, and turn away from them calamities and divine judgments. — The dark sombre violet color is intended principally for the seasons of Advent and Lent. The observance of Advent is, indeed, enlivened with manifold tones of ever increasing joyousness, since we have the comforting certainty that our Lord Himself will come and redeem us, and that we shall soon behold His glory full of grace and truth. — Nevertheless, Advent prominently bears the stamp of a holy penitential grief, and of a sorrowful and longing desire for redemption from sin and its oppressive misery. The chief duty during the season of Advent is to employ its days in cleansing perfectly the heart and in preparing a worthy dwelling-place for the coming Saviour. *Ab alto Jesus promicat*, — from on high Jesus already sends the first rays of His splendor to greet us; He cries out to the soul: "Be zealous, therefore, and do penance. Behold, I stand at the gate and knock. If any man shall hear My voice and open to Me the door, I will come unto him and I will sup with him and he with Me" (Apoc. 3, 19—20). — The violet color in which the Church robes herself from Septuagesima Sunday, or Ash Wednesday until Easter, forcibly admonishes us to consecrate this penitential season to the spirit of mortification and to works of penance. We should then faithfully consider, devoutly reverence and generously embrace the mystery of the cross; we should sincerely acknowledge, contritely detest and atone for our sins, correct our frivolous, sensual, slothful life, and to this end indulge in "words, food, drink, sleep, jokes more sparingly, and be more watchful;'' by means of prayer, meditation, fasting we should be converted with our whole heart to God from the vanity and the turmoil of the world, to God, who is so good and a God of mercy (Joel 2, 12—13). The dark penitential color shows us that we must still abide far removed from the heavenly Zion on the rivers of Babylon — meditating, praying, weeping, and longing for the eternal home. "What are we here on earth? Exiles, captives, a prey to every danger met with in Babylon. If we love our true country, if our heart longs to see it again, then we must break with all the allurements offered by this foreign land, we must reject the cup of forbidden pleasure with which it intoxicates so many of our captive brethren. It invites us to its joys and pleasures, but our harps should be left suspended on the willows of its accursed rivers, until the signal for our return to Jerusalem shall be given (Ps. 125). They would tempt us at least to sing the songs of Zion in the unholy land, as though our heart could be moved with joy far away from our true home, although we know that this would bring on us eternal banishment; but 'how could we sing the songs of the Lord in a strange land?' (Ps. 136). The Church endeavors to inspire us with these sentiments during the long days of our tribulation; she draws our attention to the dangers that menace us, which are partly within our own selves, partly in the outer world." (Guéranger).

e) Black is a color essentially the opposite of white: the series of all colors and of all combinations of colors is limited by the white on the one side, and by the black on the other; in these two the distinction of colors is suspended. Black is, therefore, the color of extinct life, of the absence of the light of joy, of death and the tomb, — consequently, it is symbolical of that most profound, sorrowful mourning such as death produces.[1] Clothed in black garments the Church bewails the death of her Divine Spouse on Good Friday; she stands at the grave and at the altar arrayed in black, when praying and offering Sacrifice for her departed children.[2]

Good Friday is the day commemorative of the sufferings and death of the Lord — and, therefore, of the entire ecclesiastical year the day of most profound grief and sorrow. Then it is that the house of God is a house of mourning, and the divine worship a worship of mourning. The altars are bare and unadorned; lamentations and sorrowful psalms alone are heard. All that the Church says and does, — her entire Good Friday liturgy breathes but affliction and grief. For on this day the Divine Victim shed His blood on the Cross for the sins of the world; the heavens were then overshadowed

---

[1] Hence nigrae (sc. vestes) = mourning robes, as albae (sc. vestes) = solemn and festal robes.

[2] The wearing of black garments is prescribed for the clergy. This color constantly reminds them of their obligation to lead a life dead to the world and retired from it, a life that is mortified and hidden with Christ in God. "Black garments should be a sign of a pure, white soul," writes St. Jerome to the monk Rusticus.

with a black pall of mourning, the earth, too, mourned, shaken to its very foundations. "At the Last Supper our Lord clothed Himself in white, when He girt Himself with the white linen cloth and washed the feet of His disciples. This was a sign of peace. In the judgment hall of Pilate He was clad in red, when the soldiers placed the scarlet cloak about Him: and this was a sign of blood and of reconciliation by blood. But on Calvary He is shrouded in black by the darkness of the sun, and this is the sign of grief and of approaching death. For now is come the all-important hour, the hour of which God Himself had spoken ages before by the Prophet Ezechiel: 'I will cover the heavens, when Thou shalt be put out, and I will make the stars thereof dark. I will make all the lights of heaven to mourn over Thee and I will cause darkness over the land, saith the Lord God'" (Ezech. 32, 7—8). The annual commemoration of the bloody death of Jesus is at all times a day of pain, a day of sorrow, a day of silent grief for us, because our salvation proceeded only from His wounds, our life sprung only from His death — and because our sins inflicted these wounds, caused His death. Justly, therefore, does the Church on Good Friday robe herself in the color of death and mourning, and prostrate herself in profound adoration, in meditation full of bitter grief before the Cross on which was suspended the salvation of the world.[1]

Black is also the color of the liturgy for the dead. The Church is a loving mother; she does not abandon or forget her children even after death, but she even accompanies them with her mourning service (Exsequiae) to the grave and follows them beyond the grave unto the other world, unto eternity. She knows not whether the faithful departed may immediately be admitted to the eternal light, to enjoy the Beatific Vision (Ps. 35, 10), or whether they have yet to abide for awhile in darkness and in the shadow of death (Isa. 9, 2). The latter is generally the case; for the majority at their departure from this life are not perfectly cleansed from every defilement contracted from intercourse with the living and by reason of human frailty (*per fragilitatem carnis humana conversatione*). Therefore, is the passage to an unknown eternity and to the severe judgment-seat of an irritated and just God fraught with fear so grave and so awful. By the black color at the funeral service the Church would admonish the living to have compassion and mercy on the poor suffering souls, who can no longer merit of themselves by good deeds, prayer and penance, and by their suffrages to mitigate their pains and assist them to gain speedy admission to the vision of eternal light.[2]

---

[1] Justum est ut hi, pro quibus passus est (Dominus) impassibilis, cum omni hujus saeculi tempore, tum praecipue in die suae passionis ei compatiantur, pro se dolenti condoleant, pro se tristanti tristitiae vicem rependant, amore pro se morientis in hac potissimum die ab omni carnis delectatione semetipsos commortificent (Pseudo-Alcuin. c. 18).

[2] The case is quite different with regard to children, the little ones whom God takes to Himself. They die wearing the unsullied garment of baptismal in-

31. The Use and Meaning of Light at the Holy Sacrifice of the Mass.

1. Light is strictly (*sub gravi*) prescribed for the celebration of Holy Mass. According to the decree of the Church wax-candles must burn on the altar during Mass.[1] The wax should be pure, unadulterated and, as a general rule, white — even on the Feriae of Advent and Lent; only in exceptional cases are candles of unbleached or yellow wax becoming.[2] For centuries the Church has used and prescribed pure beeswax[3] as the material for the liturgical candles:[4] this was and is still done chiefly for mystical reasons.[5]

nocence and enter immediately into heavenly glory. Therefore, they are not interred with the expression of mourning, but of joy: the priest wearing a white stole.

[1] On account of exceptional local circumstances the Missionaries in Oceanica were permitted, when it was not possible to procure wax, to celebrate either without light, or to make use of oil, or to use candles manufactured from refined fish grease (the so-called sperm or star-candles). S. R. C. 7. Sept. 1850. — Stearine candles (στέαρ, standing or solid grease) are forbidden except in case of necessity (S. R. C. 16. Sept. 1843—7. Sept. 1850). Oil-lights are also excluded from the altar. Nulla lumina nisi *cerea* vel supra mensam altaris vel eidem quomodocunque imminentia adhibeantur (S. R. C. in decr. gen. 31. Mart. 1821). — In private low Masses neither more nor less than two candles should burn; in such Masses only a bishop may have four candles (S. R. C. 19. Jul. 1659). For solemn Masses (the High Mass as well the parochial and conventual Mass on feast-days) more (at least four or six) candles should burn (S. R. C. 6. Febr. 1858). — The lights should burn from the beginning of Mass until the reading of the last Gospel is completed. They should be lighted beginning at the Gospel side (nobiliori parte) (S. R. C. 12. Aug. 1854). Electric lights may be used to illuminate the church, but not for purposes of divine worship. To the question: Utrum lux electrica adhiberi possit in ecclesiis? the Sacred Congregation of Rites replied, June 4. 1895: Ad cultum—negative; ad depellendas autem tenebras ecclesiasque splendidius illuminandas — affirmative; cauto tamen, ne modus speciem prae se ferat theatralem.

[2] The rubrics distinguish between white wax (cera *alba*) and ordinary wax (cera *communis*), that is, yellow wax (cera flava). According to the Cerem. Episcop. the latter must be used at the Tenebrae of Holy Week (on the altar and for the triangle) and at the Missa Praesanctificatorum (but not in the procession) on Good Friday, as also at the Office for the Dead. (Cerem. Episc. 1. 2, c. 22, n. 4.—1. 2, c. 25, n. 30.—1. 2, c. 10, n. 4).—The candles for the altar must not necessarily, but may be blessed on Candlemas Day or at any other time.

[3] In all countries home-made beeswax may be used for Church purposes. From careful chemical and physical analysis it is evident that beeswax is entirely different from every other wax-like substance (vegetable or earth-wax).

[4] The candles blessed on Candlemas Day and the Paschal Candle likewise must also be of wax. Domine sancte . . . qui omnia ex nihilo creasti et jussu tuo *per opera apum* hunc liquorum ad perfectionem *cerei* pervenire fecisti (Bened. Candel. in festo Purificat. B. M. V.).—Suscipe, sancte Pater, incensi hujus sacrificium vespertinum, quod tibi in hac Cerei oblatione solemni . . . de *operibus apum* sacrosancta reddit Ecclesia (Bened. Cerei in Sabbat. sanct).—In the rubrics, for the designation of the liturgical candles we meet with the words cerei, candelae ex cera, candelae cerae, candelae cereae, funalia cerea etc.

[5] Wax candles are so strictly prescribed, that not even for poor churches may an exception be made (S. R. C. 10. Dec. 1857). Several congruent reasons, in

The burning candle is intended to represent the God-Man, Jesus Christ; it is perfectly fitted for this object only when its light is nourished by excellent, pure wax. The bright flame above represents the Divinity of Christ; the candle proper symbolizes His humanity, the wick concealed within the candle is a figure of His soul, the wax itself, which is the product of the virginal bee, is an emblem of Christ's most pure body.[1] The working bee, which even in ancient times was regarded as a type of virginity,[2] gathers and forms the wax from odoriferous blossoms and calyxes of flowers. Being the fruit of virgin bees and fragrant flowers the noble, pure wax is, therefore, an excellent figure of the most pure and holy flesh which the Son of God assumed from the virginal bosom of Mary the Immaculate Spouse of the Holy Ghost, who was replenished with the good odor of every grace and virtue. — By its sweet scent the wax candle, moreover, represents the *bonus odor Christi*, that is, the plenitude of grace and virtue, the infinite holiness of Christ. — Furthermore, the lighted candle designates very beautifully "the hearts of the faithful, fragrant with virtue, pure, loving the divine Sun and illumined by it, while the unclean and smoky tallow candle, composed of animal matter, is a picture of the sinner." (Wolter.)

2. Since the times of the Apostles the Church has made use of lights in the ceremonies of her divine worship. The liturgical use of light has its origin neither solely nor chiefly in the accidental necessity of dispelling darkness, in order to celebrate the Holy Mysteries, as, for example, at divine worship in the Catacombs, where circumstances rendered light necessary. The candle-light on the altar may indeed suitably remind us of the dreadful days of bloody persecution and combats for the faith, which compelled the Christians to celebrate the holy Sacrifice at night or in subterranean caves; but it would be erroneous to regard the burning of lights at divine service as a remnant of the necessary lighting up to remove material darkness, or merely as an historic reminiscence of that early period. The real reason for the use of lights in the ceremonies of divine worship is far more profound, — being the harmony of light with the nature of the liturgy, or the promotion of the object of the liturgy by means of light. For light contributes in a special man-

addition to symbolism, favor the use of beeswax. Beeswax is (compared with stearine and grease) a noble product of the vegetable kingdom, and is distinguished as such by its value, purity and pleasant odor (lumina ceratis adolentur *odora papyris*—S. Paulin.). Hence wax has at all times been employed in the liturgy, and been donated by the faithful for divine worship. In this respect the Church will not allow of any innovation. (Cf. the two interesting articles by Mühlbauer, on the subject of stearic candles, Geschichte und Bedeutung der Wachslichter S. 202 ff.)

[1] Recte cereus Christum significat propter tria, quae in eo sunt: lychnum namque animam, cera corpus et lumen divinitatem significat (Durand. Rational. 1. 4, c. 80, n. 6).

[2] Digna virginitas quae apibus comparetur: sic laboriosa, sic pudica, sic continens (S. Ambr. de Virginib. 1. 1, c. 8, n. 40).

ner to the embellishment of divine worship, and contains in itself an abundant fund of symbolism; — it is an ornament to the worship and, at the same time, the symbol of religious, supernatural mysteries.[1] This higher signification and purpose of light in divine worship cannot be questioned; for at all times it has been declared in the Church and by the Church in unequivocal terms. Already in the books of Holy Writ we come across the figurative meaning of light in a thousand places. The Fathers often call attention to the mystical sense of light in its liturgical use. Thus St. Jerome (†420) says, that at the reading of the Gospel, when the sun is shining bright (*sole rutilante*) lights are lit, but in nowise to dispel darkness, but to give expression to the joy of the heart (*non utique ad fugandas tenebras, sed ad signum laetitiae demonstrandum*).[2] St. Paulinus, Bishop of Nola, († about 431), relates that in the church lamps and sweet-scented wax candles were burning, that "day itself might be brightened up with a heavenly splendor." The prayers recited at the blessing of candles, of the Paschal fire and of the Paschal candle prove, as also many hymns of the Breviary render evidence, that the Church regards and employs light as a symbol to portray the manifold ideas and truths of our holy religion. Thus on Candlemas Day she implores God graciously "to grant that as the candles lighted with visible fire (*luminaria igne visibile accensa*) dispel the darkness of night, so in like manner our hearts, enlightened by invisible fire, that is, by the resplendent light of the Holy Ghost (*corda nostra invisibili igne, id est, Sancti Spiritus splendore illustrata*), may be delivered from all blindness of sin and with the purified eyes of the spirit be enabled to perceive what is pleasing to Him and conducive to our salvation, in order that, after the dark and dangerous combats of this earthly life (*post hujus saeculi caliginosa discrimina*), we may come to the possession of immortal light" (*ad lucem indeficientem*). At the blessing of the fire on Holy Saturday the Church prays to God, "the Eternal Light and Creator of all light," that He would bless this light, so that we "may be thereby inflamed with love and be enlightened by the fire of the divine brightness." The large Paschal candle is a symbol of the majesty and glory of the Risen Redeemer, who by the brilliancy of His light has banished from the world the darkness that enveloped it.

3. In order to comprehend the varied symbolism of light, we must consider its natural qualities and effects. To us the origin, essence and effects of physical light are altogether mysterious and enveloped in unfathomable obscurity. Light appears to be rather

---

[1] In blessed candles the sacramental character is also worthy of notice. They are, namely, not merely religious symbols, signifying something supernatural; but, moreover, holy objects, which—in their way—effect something supernatural, in that they obtain for us by reason and in virtue of the prayers of the Church, divine blessing and protection, chiefly against the spirits of darkness, that we may know, fulfil and obtain the mysteries signified by light.

[2] Lib. contra Vigilant. cap. 7.

spiritual than corporeal and, consequently, exercises also a powerful influence over the spirit and mind; its effect is encouraging, cheering and exhilarating. "Therefore, God has imparted it to the sun, moon and stars, in order to give us light by day and by night; and just as the sun is like the friendly face of our Father in heaven which He causes to shine on the earth, so also is the moon as the eye of a heavenly Mother calmly and benignly looking down upon us; and the stars are as the glances of heavenly brethren encouraging us to praise the Great Father of all." (Laurent).

Light from a great number of wax candles is naturally best suited to shed grandeur and beauty on the celebration of divine worship, as well as to excite in those present higher sentiments; for their soft, quiet, mysterious light pours rays of life, of joy, of hope, of comfort, of happiness throughout the house of God and over the divine service. On the contrary, the grief and affliction of the Church are manifest when amid the Lamentations of the mournful Tenebrae during Holy Week, light after light is extinguished, until finally the last one disappears behind the altar, and darkness reigns supreme in the temple of God.

Among the things that fall under the senses light is the purest, the most agreeable, the most delicate, the most ethereal: it is called the smile of heaven, the beauty of earth, the joy of nature, the life of objects, the blossom of colors, and is the delight of the eye and of the soul.[1] So rich in advantages is the visible earthly light. It is therefore, the most appropriate symbol of the beauty and glory, of the purity and brightness of the invisible world of spirit and grace. While darkness is a picture of paganism, that is, of ignorance, of error, of unbelief, of sin, of godlessness, of desolation and despair, light is considered an image of Christianity, that is, of truth, of grace, of faith, of wisdom, of virtue, of consolation and benediction, all of which emanate from heaven and lead thereunto. In this comprehensive sense the words of the Prince of the Apostles are to be understood: "Out of darkness into His marvelous light hath God called us" (I Peter 2, 9).

In the first place, light symbolizes the Divine nature and essence; for "God is light and in Him there is no darkness" (1 John 1, 5), "He hath put on praise and beauty, He is clothed with light as with a garment"(Ps. 103, 1–2), "He dwelleth in light inaccessible" (1 Tim. 6, 16) and is "the Father of lights" (James 1, 17). God is the eternal, uncreated light, that is, an unfathomable ocean of truth and wisdom, of love and sanctity, of beauty and felicity, of majesty and glory. God is, moreover, the Creator and the source of all material and spiritual, of all natural and supernatural light.

What the sun is for the material world, the God-Man Jesus Christ is for the spiritual world, for the kingdom of grace and glory. He is the "Light of light" (*lumen de lumine*), "the brightness of His Father's glory" (Heb. 1, 3), "the brightness of eternal light"

---

[1] Cf. Scheeben, Die Herrlichkeiten der göttlichen Gnade, 3. Buch, 1 Hauptst.

(Wisdom 7, 26), "a light to the revelation of the Gentiles, and the glory of the people Israel" (Luke 2, 31), "the Star of Jacob" (Numbers 22, 16), "the bright morning star" (Apoc. 22, 16), "the light of the world" (John 12, 46), "the lamp of the heavenly Jerusalem" (Apoc. 21, 23), "the morning star that knows no setting," "the true sun that shines with unfading splendor." Light also represents the glory of the Only-Begotten of the Father and the reflection of this glory in the plenitude of truth and grace (John 1, 14), which through Him — the Author and End of salvation — has been imparted to mankind. "As the angels and the stars, the army of the Lord, are nothing else than the visible splendor, the radiant garment of His invisible being, so also Holy Scripture, to designate the manner of His revelation and of His gracious operations, makes use of no image more preferably than that of light, and is inexhaustible in presenting this image repeatedly under new aspects" (Grimm).

Nothing is more familiar to us, than to speak of the light of truth and of grace. Light enlightens the eyes and renders the things of this world visible: the truth of faith shows us a new, more beautiful and supernatural world, gives us an insight into the most profound mysteries of God, unveils the beauty and the splendor of the kingdom of grace and glory, which is infinitely more marvelous than all the grandeur of the wondrous world of stars. By means of revealed truth God Himself enlightens, — God, who by His word caused His light to shine out of darkness into our hearts, to give the light of the knowledge of the glory of God, in the face of Christ Jesus (2 Cor. 4, 6). — In a manner none the less excellent does the light represent the essence and the efficacy of grace, which is called by the Fathers "the light of God." The flame of light is mysterious, pure, beautiful, lovely, radiant, full of brightness and warmth; divine grace is also a mystery, it removes the stains of sin from the soul and imparts purity, beauty and brilliance, it fills the understanding with knowledge and wisdom, the will with power and strength, the heart with love and joy.

From Christ's fulness of light we should draw light and receive His truth and grace into our hearts, that we "may be transformed from glory to glory into a like image of the Lord" (2 Cor. 3, 18), and be made "light in the Lord" (Eph. 5, 8), "children of the light and of the day" (1 Thess. 5, 5). Consequently, light is also the emblem of the true disciple of Jesus Christ, who walks in the light as Christ is in the light (1 John 1, 7); it is the symbol of the new life of God's children illumined with the splendor of virtue and purity of life. For "the path of the just, as a shining light, goeth forward and increaseth even unto the perfect day" (Proverbs 4, 18). "Whosoever lives devoutly and chastely in the Church, striving for what is above and not for what is of the earth, is as a light from heaven, and while preserving in himself the brightness of a holy life, shines like unto a star, to lead many into the way of the Lord."[1] In a more particular manner the three divine virtues of

---

[1] St. Leo, Third Discourse on the Feast of the Lord's Circumcision.

faith, hope and charity are very beautifully represented by burning candles. The brightness of the flame indicates faith, which is a lamp to our feet and a light to our paths (Ps. 118, 105); the constant flaring up of the flame is an image of Christian hope, which keeps its glance fixed immovably above, directing all its aspirations to supernatural goods; the glow of the flame which gradually consumes the wick and the wax, represents love, a love which sacrifices all that it has, all the powers of soul and body in the service of God. — The flame of the candle, ascending silently, pure and warm, is also an emblem of adoration and devotion, on the wings of which the heart flies above all that is earthly, and peacefully reposes in the bosom of God. — Finally, the glory of heaven is also represented under the figure of light : the eternal unfading light enlightens the saints of heaven. *Lux perpetua lucebit Sanctis tuis, Domine, et aeternitas temporum.* "To him that shall overcome." saith the Lord, "I will give the morning-star" (Apoc. 2, 28), that is, the light of heavenly glory, the Beatific Vision of God. He that casts off the works of darkness and puts on the armor of light, he that is enlightened in heart and mind, aglow with the fire of the Holy Ghost and inflamed with heavenly desires, producing fruits of light in all goodness, justice and truth, will, after the dangerous darkness of this life, attain to imperishable light and to the feast of eternal brightness (*ad perpetuae claritatis festa*).

4. This comprehensive and profound symbolism confirms and explains the manifold use of light in the liturgy. The Church performs her divine services in the splendor of lights. In general this indicates that Jesus Christ, the true light, is the object of her divine worship and the author of the dispensation of her graces. — The wax candles which burn during Holy Mass proclaim that Christ appears on the altar as the mystical sun of grace, to diffuse light and life, joy, consolation and blessing into all susceptible hearts. The lighted candles consume themselves, as they brightly burn, and thus represent the sacrificing love of Jesus, who offers Himself on the altar in the Eucharistic Sacrifice, in order to impart to man the interior light of grace and the eternal light of life. The candles on the altar designate the manifold graces flowing from the Sacrifice, by which the Lord enlightens the soul with holy knowledge, fills it with salutary strength and animates it with a heavenly joy. — The burning candles, moreover, admonish us to celebrate or to assist at the Holy Sacrifice with lively devotion and ardent love; the sight of these mystical lights should awaken in us quiet, serious and holy joy and happiness of soul. The light of the candles shows us that on the altar glows the very focus of divine love, into whose ardors we should day by day dip our poor heart, that it may be transformed into a flame of love, and that, as "bright examples of sincere Christian living, without reproach, in the midst of a depraved generation, we may shine before the world as lights from heaven" (Phil. 2, 15—16), and thus by a fervent and virtuous career glorify God and edify our

neighbor.[1] So intimate, so instructive and elevating is the liturgical use of the light; it helps us to assist at and celebrate the divine worship with proper sentiments of interior enlightenment, with a corresponding heartfelt fervor.

32. The Language Used in the Celebration of the Holy Mass.

1. All the requisites for the celebration of the Eucharistic Sacrifice have been selected with especial care, and nothing has been adopted but what has been found best suited unto this end. This applies also to the language in which the Holy Sacrifice is celebrated ; for the liturgical language should correspond to its liturgical object. The Mass considered in itself could assuredly be celebrated in any language, but by the Providence of God the Latin language has become, and still continues to be of all languages the most widely diffused for divine worship.[2] The very ancient practice of the Church of celebrating Mass in the West, not in the living

---

[1] Liturgists of the Middle Age find also in the number two, that is, in the two rows of altar-candles — to the right and left from the Crucifix — a mystical, symbolical reference. According to them the lights divided equally on the two sides of the altar symbolize that the light and joy of faith was brought to the two ancient nations, namely, to the Jews and Pagans, hence to the entire world by Jesus Christ crucified, that is, by the Sacrifice of the Cross and the "Word from the Cross," of which the altar-cross placed in the midst of the lights reminds us. — The multiplication of lights at Solemn High Mass enhances the celebration and denotes the increased joy of the feast (Christmas joy, Easter joy, &c.), which has its peculiar reason and object in the mystery that is celebrated. The devout visiting of the Blessed Sacrament and the faithful devout celebration of divine worship is, in the course of the ecclesiastical year, an ever fresh source of holy and heartfelt joy.

[2] Whether the Apostles celebrated the Holy Sacrifice in the language of each individual nation or only in the Aramean (Syro-Chaldaic), Greek and Latin languages cannot be determined with certainty. In any case, from the first four centuries no liturgy can be shown composed in any other than the three languages of the inscription of the Cross. In the West, for example, in Italy, in Germany, in Spain, in France, in England, Latin was at all times the liturgical language. Toward the end of the ninth century Pope John VIII. (872—882) permitted the Moravian Slavs, converted by Sts. Cyril and Methodius, to celebrate the liturgy in their (Slavonic or Glagolitic) native language, and that probably in order to prevent their apostasy to the Greek Schism. In the East also the Church later on permitted some schismatics and heretics, who had returned to the unity of the Church (for instance, the Copts, Armenians, Ethiopians), to retain their native language in the liturgy. At present there are twelve languages used in the Catholic liturgy; namely, 1. Latin, 2. Greek, 3. Syriac, 4. Chaldaic, 5. Arabian, 6. Ethiopian, 7. Glagolitic, 8. Ruthenian, 9. Bulgarian, 10. Armenian, 11. Coptic, 12. Roumanian. With the exception of Roumanian, all these languages used in the liturgy have for a considerable time no longer been the living languages of the people, but only dead languages. The united Roumanians alone make use of the living mother-tongue in the liturgy; this is not expressly permitted by Rome, but is merely tolerated. (Cf. Bartak, Versuch, die liturgische Sprache der Kirche vom dogmatischen, historischen und pastorellen Standpunkte zu beleuchten. Königgrätz, 1875.)

language of the country, but in a dead language, that is, in Latin, for the most part a language unintelligible to the people, has since the twelfth century to the present epoch been frequently made the subject of attack.[1] Such attacks originated principally in an heretical, schismatical, proudly national spirit hostile to the Church, or in a superficial and false enlightenment, in a shallow and arid rationalism entirely destitute of the perception and understanding of the essence and object of the Catholic liturgy, especially of the profoundly mystical sacrifice. In the attempt to suppress the Latin language of the liturgy and to replace it by the vernacular, there was a more or less premeditated scheme to undermine Catholic unity, to loosen the bond of union with Rome, to weaken the Catholic spirit, to destroy the humility and simplicity of faith. Therefore, the Apostolic See at all times most persistently and inflexibly resisted such innovations; for it is an invariable principle of the Church never to alter the ancient liturgical language, but inviolably to adhere to it, even though it be no longer the living language spoken or understood by the people. — The Church likewise, when introducing the Roman liturgy among newly converted nations, has for many centuries permitted the Latin language only.[2] — She excommunicates all those who presume to declare the vernacular to be the necessary or the only permissible language for the liturgy;[3] she stigmatizes as impertinent effrontery for any one to censure or combat the retention of the Latin language for divine worship.[4] This is just; for, as St. Augustine remarks, "to question what the united Church practises as a rule is the most daring madness."[5] In all such general decrees and usages appertaining to divine worship, the Church is directed and preserved from injurious blunders by the Holy Ghost.[6] Instead of censuring the Church on account of her practice,

---

[1] Opponents of the Latin language of worship were, as a rule, heretics, schismatics and rationalistic Catholics; for example, the Albigensians, the so-called Reformers, the Jansenists, the Gallicans, the Josephites, the so-called German and the Old Catholics.

[2] Concludendum, constantem firmamque disciplinam esse, ne Missae idioma mutetur, etsi mutet lingua vernacula: sed eo sermone Missa celebretur, quo celebrata est ab initio, etiamsi ea lingua exoleverit apud vulgus, ejusque peritiam viri docti dumtaxat habeant. Est autem Apostolicae Sedis in recenti populorum conversione ad fidem pro variis circumstantiis vel permittere vernaculae linguae usum in divinis officiis celebrandis, sed vere affirmari potest, S. Sedem propensiorum esse in illam partem, ut ex recens conversis ad fidem, habiliore qui sint ingenio, seligantur et latinis potius literis erudiantur, quam ut facultas concedatur, adhibendi in Missae celebratione vulgarem linguam. (Benedict. XIV. De Missa sacrific., 1. 2, c. 2, n. 14.)

[3] Trident. sess. 22, can. 9.

[4] Bulla "Auctorem fidei" 1794. prop. 33. 66.

[5] Quod universa frequentat Ecclesia, quin ita faciendum sit, disputare, insolentissimae insaniae est. (S. Aug. Epist. 54 ad Januar.)

[6] In things relating to divine worship St. Thomas makes use of the prescription and custom of the Church as a conclusive argument, to refute various objec-

that has endured more than a thousand years, of conducting her liturgical worship in a dead language, we should rather acknowledge and admire her supernatural wisdom ; she counts her experiences by centuries : ours we can enumerate only by days.

The Church is moved by interests most sacred to maintain and to introduce wherever she is spread in the world and receives new nations into her pale, the Latin as the common language of her liturgy. This conduct on her part does not rest on a discipline of secrecy. The Church does not wish to conceal her mysteries from the faithful. It is rather her very ardent desire that her children should understand all the wealth and beauty of her divine worship ; hence she obliges and admonishes her priests to unfold[1] to the people the meaning of the celebration of the mystical Sacrifice by clearly and devoutly explaining from time to time the holy Sacrifice of the Mass with all its ceremonies and prayers in the school-room and in the church, in the catechetical instructions and in sermons.[2] After the fathers of the Council of Trent had subjected the objection raised to the Latin tongue in Church service to thorough examination, they unanimously declared that, although the Mass embodied a vast amount of religious instruction, they still deemed it inexpedient that the Holy Sacrifice should be everywhere (*passim*) celebrated in the vernacular ; that, on the contrary, everywhere the rite (custom) authorized by the Holy Roman Church should be maintained. But in order that the sheep of Christ may not hunger and the children may not ask for bread without there being some one to break it unto them, the Council commands pastors of souls, that during the celebration of Mass they frequently explain some part of what has been read in the Mass, and that especially on Sundays and holidays they give instruction of some mystery of this most Holy Sacrifice.[3] — The Church acts thus, because she is persuaded that an unchangeable and universal language for divine worship prevents, on the one hand, much harm and danger, and, on the other hand, offers numerous advantages for her liturgical object, as well as for her activity and efficiency in general. These advantages are so great, that the profit the people might in a certain respect and in some cases derive from understanding the language used in the

tions. Contra est, quod ea quae per Ecclesiam statuuntur, ab ipso Christo ordinantur. In contrarium est Ecclesiae consuetudo, *quae errare non potest*, utpote a Spiritu sancto instructa. (3, q. 83, a. 3 et 5.)

[1] Quisque vestrum expositionem Symboli et Orationis dominicae juxta orthodoxorum Patrum traditionis penes se habeat easque atque Orationes Missarum et Epistolas, Evangelia et Canonem bene *intelligat*, ex quibus *praedicando* populum sibi commissum sedulo instruat et maxime non bene credentem. (Pontif. Roman. Ordo ad Synodum.)

[2] Vehementer cupimus, ut animarum moderatores commissos sibi greges saepe ac diligenter doceant divini hujus sacrificii dignitatem ac praestantiam uberrimosque fructus, qui in pie ac devote sacris adstantes deriventur. (Coll. Lac. III, 496.)

[3] Trident. sess. 22, cap. 8.

11

divine service, bears no comparison thereunto, and is far surpassed thereby; besides said profit may be secured in some better and more sure way and thus be easily compensated. [1]

2. Latin is the language almost universally employed in the divine service all over the Catholic world; other cult languages are comparatively but little disseminated. Only the most weighty reasons will be given here for the use of the Latin language in the liturgy of the holy Sacrifice of the Mass.

a) The Latin language is consecrated by the mystic inscription attached to the Cross, as well as sanctified by the usage of nearly two thousand years, and hence it is most closely interwoven with the primitive Roman Catholic liturgy of the holy Sacrifice. The inscription on the Cross: "Jesus of Nazareth, King of the Jews," was written in Hebrew, Greek and Latin (John 19, 19, 20). These were the three principal languages of that epoch, and by divine dispensation they were, so to say, destined and consecrated on the Cross for the liturgical use of the Church. Through the inscription on the Cross they proclaimed to the whole world the dignity, power and glory of the Redeemer, the royalty and dominion of grace which He acquired by His bloody death; at the altar these languages continue to live throughout all ages, and serve to announce and to celebrate until the end of time the death of Christ for our redemption, whereby the reign of grace is ever more widely extended and firmly established, the kingdom of peace progresses ever more towards its happy consummation. In the first centuries these three languages were employed predominantly, if not exclusively, in the liturgical service.

Of these three languages the Latin at an early date gained the precedence; for, being the language of the Roman world, it became throughout the West with the spread of Christianity also the language of the liturgy. Divine Providence selected Rome as the centre of the Catholic Church; from Rome the messengers of the faith were sent forth in all directions to spread the light of the Gospel. Along with the grace of Christianity, together with the Catholic faith and its divine worship the western nations also received Latin as the Church-language; for in that tongue the Holy Mysteries were always celebrated, though the nations recently converted spoke a different language and did not understand Latin. Thus the language of the Mother Roman Church became the common language of worship of all her daughters, the Catholic Christian Churches established from Rome in the West. — In the beginning Latin was understood and spoken in many localities by the people, but it continued to be the liturgical language even after it had been superseded by other tongues in civil life, and had ceased to be the language of the people and of the country. — For centuries the Latin language has ceased to be spoken in the daily life and intercourse of the world, but it will continue to live immortal by ecclesiastical usage and in the

---

[1] Illa utilitas et incerta est et multis periculis exposita et alio securiori et sufficiente modo suppleri potest. (Suarez, disp. 83, sect. I, n. 21.)

sanctuary of divine worship unto the consummation of ages. The most sacred reminiscences, the history and the acts of the Catholic Church are intimately connected with it. From the beginning of Christianity the sublime mystery of the Mass was celebrated, the sacramental means of grace were administered, God was glorified, men were sanctified and led to salvation in this language. It is without doubt elevating and inspiring to offer sacrifice and pray in the very language and in the very words, whose forcible yet sweet tones once resounded in the mouths of the primitive Christians and our forefathers in the dark depths of the Catacombs, in the golden areas of the ancient basilicas, and in the sumptuous cathedrals of the Middle Age. In the Latin language of divine worship innumerable saints, bishops and priests of all times have offered sacrifice, prayed and sung ; in it the most magnificent liturgical formulas are composed — prayers of incomparable beauty and "marvellous hymns, which echo throughout the vaults of Catholic churches, now resounding in great exaltation or sung in soft strains of sweet joy, now weeping in sorrow, at another time lamenting in sympathetic grief for Christ." Should not this ancient Latin language of divine service, so venerable and hallowed in its origin and use, be extremely dear and precious to us, so that we would not for any price give it up or be deprived of it at the celebration of Holy Mass?

b) The Latin language is better suited than the languages of different countries to the celebration of divine worship, not only because it is very perfect, but furthermore because, as a so-called dead language, it has the incomparable merit of being at the same time unchangeable and mysterious. The genus of the Latin language possesses great perfection : it is distinguished for its dignity and gravity, clearness and precision, for its richness and euphony. It is, therefore, often difficult to render the complete sense, and still more difficult, and sometimes utterly impossible, to bring out in a translation the beauty, the strength, the dignity, the unction, the depth and the wealth of thought of the original Latin. To convince one's self of this, one should compare, for example, the various translations of the Mass prayers and sequences with the Latin text. In addition to all this, Latin is the language *Urbis et Orbis* (the language of the world), the official Church language, the language of communication between the Pope and the Bishops, the language of the Councils and of theological science. Because of such advantages it is eminently fitted to be used the world over as the language of the Catholic Church in the celebration of her divine worship.

Latin survives no longer in the converse of the common people, but in the sanctuary of the Church. As a so-called dead [1] language,

---

[1] The Oriental churches also reject the principle, that the vernacular language of a country or people should be used in the celebration of Holy Mass. This is proved by the most decisive facts. The united and the schismatical Greeks celebrate the Holy Sacrifice in the ancient Greek, which the people do not understand.

it is unchangeable, while the languages of the people undergo constant improvement and remodelling, and are ever liable to go on progressing and altering. What would become of liturgical books, if, with time and the changes of the vernacular, they were subjected to perpetual change and reconstruction? By such necessary, incessant remodelling and alteration of the liturgical formulas of prayer, the original text and context would lose not only much of their incomparable force and beauty, but often — notwithstanding strict surveillance on the part of the Church — would be disfigured and spoiled by circumlocutions, interpolations, omissions, incorrectness, errors and misrepresentations. Hence it would be impossible to preserve and maintain uniformity of divine worship at different times among even one and the same people, much less throughout the world. All these inconveniences are obviated by the use of an unchangeable language for divine worship. In the unchangeableness of the Latin for divine worship the Roman Missal appears as an intangible and inviolable sanctuary, deserving of admiration and profound respect.

Since the Latin language has been withdrawn from daily life, from the ordinary intercourse of mankind, since it is not heard on the street or in the market-place, it possesses in the eyes of the faithful a holy, venerable, mystic character. Under this aspect also it is eminently suited for the celebration of the Holy Sacrifice of the Mass, which in itself comprises many mysteries. The celebration of this mystic Sacrifice fittingly calls for a language elevated, majestic, dignified and consecrated; religious sentiment demands this, and the Latin tongue answers this requirement. — Just as the silent saying of the Canon, so also the use of a sanctified cult language, different from that of profane intercourse, points to the unfathomable and unspeakable depth of the mystery of the altar, and protects it against contempt and desecration. The majesty of the divine worship depends, indeed, chiefly on the devout, dignified and reverential

---

The Abyssinians and Armenians celebrate Holy Mass respectively in the ancient Ethiopian and the ancient Armenian, understood only by the learned. The same holds good with regard to the Syrians and Egyptians, who celebrate Holy Mass in the ancient Syrian, and also with regard to the Melchites and Georgians (Caucasian province) who at Holy Mass make use of the ancient Greek. The same is observed by the Russians, although Greek is not the language of the people, who speak only a Slavonian dialect. Here we may also refer to the practice of the Church in the Old Law. Up to the time of Christ and the Apostles, the ancient Hebrew was the language of the Patriarchs, the cult language, although no longer understood by the Jewish nation, who after the Babylonian Captivity made use of the Syro-Chaldaic idiom. It was this divine worship in the ancient Hebrew that our Lord and His disciples attended, thus actually approving a language for divine worship that was not the language of the people. Neither the Lord nor His Apostles designated or censured this as an abuse. The use of a particular cult language, differing from the ordinary current and spoken language, was, therefore, practised for a long time in the Church of the Old Testament, and was unequivocally approved of by the conduct of our Saviour and of His Apostles. (Cf. Augsburg. Pastoralblatt, Jahrg. 1877, S. 166.)

demeanor of the celebrant; but the liturgical language contributes also its share thereunto, and a foreign language is suitable, in a measure, to veil the defects and repulsive routine of many a priest, and to prevent them from appearing so glaring. Thus the Latin language — elevated above the time and place of every day life, — is a mystic veil for the Adorable mysteries of the Holy Sacrifice, which here below we acknowledge only in the clear obscurity of faith, but whose clear vision shall be our portion in heaven as a recompense for our humble faith.

The use of the Latin language in nowise prevents the faithful from participating in the fruits of the Sacrifice, notwithstanding assertions to the contrary. The demand that the Mass should everywhere be celebrated in the vernacular, is based for the most part on ignorance, or on an entire misconception of the real nature and object of the Eucharistic Sacrifice. The liturgy of the Holy Sacrifice contains "much that is instructive" (*magnam eruditionem* — Trident.), but instruction is by no means its principal object. The altar is not a pulpit, the Holy Mass is not primarily a doctrinal lecture or an instruction to the people. The Sacrifice is essentially a liturgical action performed by the priest for propitiating and glorifying God, as well as for the salvation of the faithful. In this sacrifice the Christian people should take a lively part, full of profit to themselves, and they should in spiritual union with the celebrating priest — *plus medullis cordis quam labiis vocis* — more with the heart than with the lips — join in prayer and sacrifice. And this is not possible for them to do without some understanding of the liturgical celebration; for "although devotion consists principally in an abundance of devout sentiments and, consequently, belongs more to the heart than to the understanding, there is, however, no perfect devotion without the enlightenment of the understanding. But in order to acquire the requisite knowledge to join in devout union with the priest celebrating the Mass, various means are at the disposal of Catholics; the celebration of the Church service in the vernacular is not at all requisite therefore, and would oftentimes prove of little or no avail. By means of oral teaching, with the aid of books of instruction and devotion, every Christian may obtain a sufficient knowledge of the liturgy of the Holy Sacrifice, of the prayers which the priest recites at the altar. For this purpose the mere recital of formulas of prayer in the vernacular by the celebrant would not suffice: for in many cases, for example, in large churches, at High Mass, or when several priests celebrate at the same time, it would be impossible, or at least disedifying, to pray so loud at the altar that all present could distinctly hear and understand the words of the officiating priest. Even if they did understand the words which the priest sings or recites at the altar, but little would be attained for the real understanding of the sense; for the formulas of the Mass, taken principally from Holy Scripture, are often mystical and difficult to comprehend; the mere rendering of them into the vernacular would not always disclose the hidden meaning, and the translation might often be the occasion of misconceptions, of misunderstandings, it might arouse the desire for disputation and dangerous hyper-criticism.

When man subjects science and any perfection whatever totally to God, his devotion is thereby increased;[1] therefore, a clear, profound, comprehensive knowledge of the Holy Sacrifice and its prayers is without doubt very useful and greatly to be recommended. The prayers of the Church are to be preferred to all private prayers; they are the sweetest manna, the most solid nourishment of the soul. Therefore, it is very desirable that the faithful should assiduously strive to increase more and more their knowledge of the precious treasure of the liturgical prayers, to the end that they may join their voices in prayer the more intimately and perfectly with the voice of the Church at the altar. The mere understanding of the prayers which the priest utters or sings does not assuredly suffice to enable us to share abundantly in the advantages and the fruits of the Sacrifice of the Mass. The most perfect disposition for this is a lively faith, fervent love, sincere compunction, profound reverence and devotion, humility of heart, a longing for mercy and help. Such devout sentiments may exist independently of the knowledge of the particular Mass prayers, and are produced by the worthy, holy and mysterious Sacrifice, which, having a varied symbolical character, possesses, therefore, a peculiar, significant and eloquent language of its own. This language can be perfectly understood only by him who, by previous instruction, has learned the purpose and meaning of the ceremonies of the Church. — Latin is, therefore, no hindrance to the Catholic Christian, preventing him from deriving from the source of the liturgy of the Holy Sacrifice life, light and warmth, in order to nourish his piety and devotion. It serves rather to awaken a holy awe and reverence in his heart in the presence of the obscure mysteries of the Divine Sacrifice.

c) As a universal language of worship, Latin is an admirable means not only of presenting, but also of preserving and promoting the unity and harmony of the Church in divine worship, in divine faith, and in conduct.

a) The unity of the liturgy for all time and place can be perfectly maintained only inasmuch as it is always and everywhere celebrated in the same language. By the introduction of the various national languages, the uniformity and harmony of Catholic worship would be imperilled and, in a measure, rendered impossible. How beautiful and sublime is that uniform celebration of the Holy Sacrifice in the Catholic Church from the rising to the setting of the sun! Thus every priest is enabled to celebrate Mass, over the whole world, no matter what country he visits. And "how consoling is it not for a devout Catholic, whilst dwelling in a foreign land in the midst of strangers, hearing no sounds but those of an unknown tongue, to be

---

[1] S. Thom. 2, 2, qu. 82, a. 3 ad 3.

able at least when assisting at the celebration of divine service, to hear again the words of a language which, as the accents of a second mother-tongue he has listened to from childhood in his native country? He feels then as though he were in a spiritual home, in a universal fatherland of the faith, and for the moment he forgets that he is dwelling in a strange place." [1] Thus travel on our altars "the same prayers in the same language all around the globe. When the sun rises and the morning flush shows itself on the mountain tops, we awaken, and the celebration of Mass begins with these same prayers and continues until noon. Then other countries have their morning, and take up the same Sacrifice with the same prayers. And when in the evening the sun sinks beneath the horizon, it rises in another part of the globe, and the same Sacrifice is there repeated with its identical prayers." [2]

b) The unity of the liturgical language and of the divine worship in the Church is, therefore, a very efficient means for preserving the integrity of faith. [3] The liturgy is, indeed, the main channel by which dogmatic tradition is transmitted; [4] dogma is the root of all ecclesiastical life, of discipline and of worship. Worship is developed out of the doctrine of faith; in the liturgical prayers, in the rites and ceremonies of the Church the truths of Catholic faith find their expression, and can be established and proved therefrom. [5] But the more fixed, unchangeable and inviolable the liturgical formula of prayer is, the better it is adapted to preserve intact and to transmit unimpaired the original deposit of faith. Therefore, all the primitive liturgies proclaim and prove that our faith is in perfect harmony with that of the first ages of the Church.

---

[1] Martin, Das christliche Leben, S. 286.

[2] Eberhard, Kanzelvorträge I, 372.

[3] Cum *legem credendi statuat lex supplicandi*, proindeque libri liturgici non minus doctrinae fontes sint quam pietatis, summopere optandum est, ut, quemadmodum per fidei unitatem miro splendore lucet Ecclesia, ita per ritus et precum uniformitatem omnium oculis effulgeat. Ideoque eamdem ac Ecclesia Romana, omnium Ecclesiarum magistra materque, fidem habentes, eamdem disciplinam et eundem officii divini modum habeamus. (Concil. prov. Aquens. a. 1850, tit. XI, cap. 2. — Collect. Lacens. IV, p. 1004.)

[4] Cfr. Zaccaria, Bibliotheca ritualis I, diss. 2. De usu librorum liturgicorum in rebus theologicis. — Lapini, La Liturgia, p. 2, lezion. 15—18.

[5] Hence the theological axiom: *Legem credendi lex statuit supplicandi*, regarding which De la Hogue (Tract. de Eccles. c. 5, q. 1) writes: Merito quidem urgetur ad permulta dogmata confirmanda. Sic ex exorcismis supra baptizandos, confirmatur peccati originalis dogma; ex doxologia, qua terminantur omnes psalmi, doctrina mysterii Trinitatis; ex ritu externo adorationis Eucharistiae exhibito realis Christi praesentia; ex omnibus orationibus necessitas gratiae ad bonum operandum; ex precibus, quae ab antiquioribus saeculis pro defunctis funduntur, dogma purgatorii. In his et similibus causis, ubi ex mente Ecclesiae et publico omnium fidelium sensu, tam notoria est arctissima, quae inter universalem praxim Ecclesiae et dogma reperitur connexio, non minus vere quam energice dicitur: *Lex orandi, lex credendi.*

c) Unity of liturgical language and the consequent uniformity of divine worship form, finally, a strong bond for uniting indissolubly the churches dispersed all over the world, among themselves and with their common centre — the Roman Church, the chief and Mother-Church of them all. The bond of a universal language of worship, which embraces the head and the members of the Church, supports and promotes everywhere the unity and the common life and operation of the Church. History confirms this; for it proves that a difference of liturgies, that is, the introduction of national languages into the liturgy, frequently gave or threatened to give rise to heresy and schism. We need only recall to mind the eastern nations, which, for the most part, have a ritual of their own and in the liturgy make use of a language different from the Latin.

While, therefore, the use of the various national languages for divine service is peculiar to the sects and to national churches, the use of the Latin as the common language for divine worship harmonizes perfectly with the essence, the object and the workings of the Catholic Church. In her bosom we behold how the Holy Ghost has "gathered all the nations from out of the babel of tongues into the unity of faith." Being formed of "all nations and tribes and peoples and tongues," she constitutes but one family of God, one kingdom of Christ, a kingdom not of this world, but exalted above every nation of the earth. Therefore, it is proper that the Church, when celebrating divine worship, when offering the divine Sacrifice, should make use not of the language of some one single country or nation, but of a language that is universal, consecrated and sanctified. Thus at the altar it is a figure of the heavenly Jerusalem, where all the angels and saints in unison (*una voce*) sing their "Holy, holy, holy" and Alleluja.

CHAPTER THE SECOND.

The Rite of the Holy Sacrifice of the Mass.

33. Preliminary Remarks.

1. Countless goods, incomprehensible wonders and mysteries are contained in the Holy Sacrifice of the Mass. This holy Sacrifice is too great, too precious and too glorious to be adequately expressed in words or to receive an appropriate name: it surpasses all created knowledge, it is unspeakably grand and sublime. Since the mind of man is too limited and his language too feeble to express perfectly the Mystery of the Eucharistic Sacrifice, there have been even from the most ancient times a number of titles bestowed upon it, each of which, however, brings into prominence but some one side of the mystery, yet not one of them exhausts its unfathomably deep and rich contents.[1] Among these names that of *Missa* (Mass) deserves

---

[1] Nomen dictum quasi notamen (characteristic, mark), quod nobis vocabulo suo res notas efficiat. Nisi enim nomen scieris, cognitio rerum perit (S. Isidor.

a more particular explanation, as it is almost the only one employed since the early part of the Middle Age to designate the Eucharistic Sacrifice.

The word *Missa* (= missio, i. e. dimissio, ἀπόλυσις)[1] denotes the solemn dismissal or the departure of those present after the conclusion of divine service; this signification it even now retains in the well known concluding formula given: *Ite, missâ est* — "Go, it is the dismissal." As long as the old baptismal and penitential discipline was in force, a twofold dismissal took place at the Eucharistic Sacrifice: the catechumens and the penitents were permitted to assist along with the faithful assembled at divine worship and to be present at the readings or discourses, but were formally dismissed after the Gospel, or the sermon;[2] the faithful only were allowed to assist at the celebration proper of the Sacrifice, and to them also the

---

Etymolog. 1. 1, c. 7, n. 1). — Such names are, for example, collecta; dominicum; memoriale; communio; oblatio; — λειτουργία, εὐχαριστία, θυσία, λατρεία, σύναξις, μυσταγωγία, οἰκονομία. — Cfr. Bona, Rer. liturg. 1. 1, c. 3.

[1] Altogether untenable and, therefore, universally rejected is the etymological tracing of the word Missa from the Hebrew (Deuter. 16, 10 missah = tributum, oblatio), or from the Greek (μύησις = initiatio, mystica doctrina), or from the German (Mess = festum, congregatio). — Missa is also not to be taken as a participle of mitto, to which the substantive concio or congregatio (concio vel congregatio missa, i. e. dimissa est) or oblatio (oblatio missa, i. e. transmissa est ad Deum) would have to be supplied; Missa is rather a later Latin substantive for missio, as similar derivative words often occur, for example, remissa = remissio; collecta = collectio; ingressa = ingressio; oblata = oblatio; accessa = accessio; confessa = confessio. As a substantive Missa was used in a manifold sense. It designated in the first place the dismissal at the close of divine service and also of secular assemblies; for the holy Bishop Avitus of Vienne writes (about the year 500) to the Burgundian King Gundobald, that it was customary in churches and in judgment-halls to cry out missa est, when the people were dismissed (in ecclesiis palatiisque sive praetoriis *missa fieri pronunciatur*, cum populus ab observatione dimittitur). Furthermore, the word Missa was employed to designate the entire *Officium divinum*, as well as the separate readings and prayers during it; for example, missae matutinae, was the name given to Matins; Vespers were called missae vespertinae. In the Middle Age we meet the word Missa in the signification of feast and annual fair, as celebration of the sacrifice was the principal part of the festivity, and as the people flocked together at the festivals for buying and selling. The view already advanced and recently defended by Müller in his pamphlet "Missa, Ursprung und Bedeutung der Benennung," that Missa is an ancient Latin sacrificial name and originally signified the same as oblatio, is unfounded. Cfr. Bellarmin. De Missa, 1. 1, c. 1. — Benedict. XIV. De sacr. Miss. sacrif. 1. 2, c. 1. — Cfr. especially P. Rottmanner, O. S. B., in the "Tübinger Quartalschrift" 1889.

[2] Missa (dismissal), tempore sacrificii, est quando catechumeni foras mittuntur, clamante levita: "Si quis catechumenus remansit, exeat foras," et inde missa, quia sacramentis altaris interesse non possunt, qui nondum regenerati noscuntur (S. Isidor. Etymol. 1. 6, c. 19, n. 4.)— Missa (the dismissal) catechumenorum fiebat ante actionem Sacramentorum: missa (the dismissal) fidelium post confectionem et participationem eorundem Sacramentorum (mysteries). Flor. Diac. De expos. Miss. n. 131.

dismissal was formally announced at the conclusion of the service. The rite of the dismissal with blessing and prayer was called *missa*, and the term, in the first place, found its way into the language of the people, and later on was written and introduced into the liturgical public Church service in the celebration of the divine Sacrifice, which was introduced and concluded with the dismissal.

The name *Missa*, which in the beginning, therefore, signified the dismissal from divine service of persons assisting thereat, was thus transferred to the celebration of divine worship itself. This without doubt occurred already at an early period; but when this first happened cannot be historically ascertained. A certain proof for the use of the expression *Missa* in the meaning of the liturgical celebration of the divine Sacrifice is first met with in the writings of St. Ambrose († 397)[1]; from his manner of speaking, it is evident that the word *Missa* was at that epoch not a newly coined expression, but a traditional designation of the celebration of the Eucharistic Sacrifice.

The transfer of the expression *Missa* to designate the most holy and sublime Sacrifice is at first sight strange indeed, but is, however, susceptible of explanation. At the period when the name *Missa* was first applied to the celebration of the Eucharistic Mystery, the strictest discipline of secrecy was in force. This mode of calling the Holy Sacrifice was well fitted to conceal the holy mysteries from the uninitiated. Therefore, the dismissals in use at that period are not to be regarded as implying "unessential ruling of Church discipline," but as important acts, which were conducted with a certain degree of solemnity. After an appropriate prayer of thanksgiving and blessing the dismissal was liturgically announced by the deacon's exclaiming: *Ite, missa est*. The first dismissal which was intended for the uninitiated, characterized the subsequent celebration as mysterious, and gave to those who remained to understand what purity was required to assist at the Sacrifice and to receive the sacrificial food. Not less venerable was the liturgical dismissal of the faithful; they were thereby admonished not to depart from the house of God without permission and not to return to the daily duties of their calling, until they had rendered unto God the honor and adoration due Him, and had been enriched with the fulness of heavenly gifts and blessings.[2]

---

[1] Sequenti die (erat autem Dominica), post lectiones (sc. sacrae Scripturae) atque tractatum (sc. expositionem lectionis vel concionem), dimissis catechumenis, symbolum aliquibus competentibus in baptisteriis tradebam basilicae. Illic nuntiatum est mihi comperto quod ad Portianam basilicam de palatio decanos (= lictores) misissent et vela suspenderent, populi partem eo pergere. Ego tamen mansi in munere, *Missam* facere coepi. Dum *offero*, raptum cognovi a populo Castulum quemdam (S. Ambr. Epistol. 20, n. 4—5).

[2] The Latins have given this name (Missa) to the Sacrifice, because, when the time of the offering was reached, the catechumens, the penitents and the possessed, and at the end all the faithful, were dismissed by a solemn proclamation. . . . This

In addition to this explanation, the best founded and the most widely spread, there is still another that deserves mention, one which was held in esteem especially by the liturgists of the Middle Age. It runs thus — the Eucharistic Sacrifice is called *Missa*, because in it there is a sending forth (*missa = transmissio*) from earth to heaven and from heaven to earth. — The Church sends up to the throne of God by the ministry of the priest the Eucharistic Sacrifice and prayers, and the necessities and desires of the faithful; God in return sends down upon men the riches of heavenly grace and blessing. — Or we may put it in a different way: Christ is sent into the world by the Father as a sacrifice, and in turn He is sent back again to heaven by the faithful as a sacrifice, in order to reconcile us to the Father and to procure for us all blessings.[1] This signification of the *Missa* is implied by the very nature of the thing, and thus far undoubtedly contains truth; but this point of view probably did not determine the selection of the expression *Missa* to designate the Holy Sacrifice: in other words, the faithful of the first ages did not choose the word *Missa* to express that in the Sacrifice the above mentioned mission or sending forth from God to man and from man to God takes place; it was only later that this was so understood and explained.[2]

2. Jesus Christ Himself offered the first Eucharistic Sacrifice in the Supper Room of Jerusalem, and this in close connection with the eating of the Paschal Lamb of the Old Testament.[3] At the same time He ordered the celebration of this Sacrifice in His Church for

---

solemn exclusion of these three kinds of persons inspired the people with an exalted idea of the holy mysteries, because it showed them how great a purity is requisite to assist thereat, and much more still to participate therein. The dismissal of the faithful at the end of the service was not less venerable: because it gave them to understand that they should not go out of the church without leave, and that the Church did not dismiss her children until she had filled them with veneration for the majesty of the holy mysteries and the graces accompanying their reception; so that they returned to their ordinary occupations, bearing in mind that the Church, which had dismissed them, admonished them thereby to perform them as religiously as their vocation called for, and with the spirit with which they were filled (Bossuet, Sur les prières de la Messe. Oeuvres complètes IV [Bar-le-Duc 1870], q. 447).

[1] Sacrosanctum altaris mysterium idcirco missa dicitur, quia ad placationem et solutionem inimicitiarum (Ephes. 5), quae erant inter Deum et homines, sola valens et idonea *missio* est (Rupert. Tuitiens. De divin. off. l. 2, c. 10). — Dicitur autem Missa a mittendo, et repraesentat *legationem* inter homines et Deum; Deus enim mittit Filium suum Christum in altare, et iterum mittit Ecclesia fidelis eundem Christum ad Patrem, ut pro nobis intercedat (S. Bonavent. Expos. Miss. c. 2). — Missa dicitur, quia in hoc officio repraesentatur *missio Christi* a sinu Patris in mundum redimendum, i. e. incarnatio, et *missio Christi* a mundo ad Patrem placandum, scilicet passio (Sicardus, Mitral., l. 3, c. 1).

[2] Prima etymologia *verior* videtur, altera *ad pietatem propensior* (Benedict. XIV. De Miss. sacrif. l. 2, c. 1, n. 5).

[3] Bickell, Messe und Pascha. Mainz 1872.

all times, when He gave to the Apostles and their successors in the priestly office the command and the power to do the same as He had done. After the example and by the order of Christ, the Apostles celebrated everywhere on their missionary journeys the Eucharistic Sacrifice. In all probability they did not celebrate it for the first time previous to Whitsunday, but they most likely did so on that grand day, when the Holy Ghost descended on the infant Church;[1] this view is made evident by the fact that the Holy Ghost performs forever the mystery of the Consecration as He once did the mystery of the Incarnation. Christ's example was the norm for the Apostles; at the celebration of the Sacrifice they did, first, only that which Christ had done before. According to His directions and under the inspiration of the Holy Ghost they observed other things besides, namely, according to circumstances of time and place, to the simple, essential act of sacrifice they added various prayers and observances, in order to celebrate the Holy Mysteries as worthily and as edifyingly as possible. Those constituent portions of the sacrificial rite, which are found in all the ancient liturgies, have incontestably their origin from Apostolic times and tradition; such, for example, as the preparatory prayers, the readings from Holy Scripture, the Psalms, the offering of bread and wine mixed with water, the supplications for the living and the dead, the Offertory prayers and the words added to those of the Consecration, the reference to the death and resurrection of Christ, the Lord's Prayer, the sign of the Cross, the kiss of peace, the fraction and distribution of the Host, the thanksgiving after Communion. The Apostles, who had been instructed by the Lord Himself in the mysteries of the kingdom of God, and were filled with the Holy Ghost, assuredly observed a fixed order in the daily celebration of the Holy Sacrifice, although they did not establish and bequeath a written liturgy.[2] — The first offering of the Holy Sacrifice by our Lord was the rule and the model for the Apostles; and the essential and fundamental features of the sacri-

---

[1] The *first Mass* said by an apostle was not celebrated before the Resurrection, nor before the Ascension, nor before Pentecost. Mary d'Agreda assigns the day of the octave for this; but the most common and most probable opinion assigns the very day on which the Holy Ghost came down. Did He come down before or after the consecration? According to Theophile Raynaud (De prima Missa sect. 2, c. 6), it took place only after the communion of the faithful; but is it not preferable to suppose, as St. Proclus, patriarch of Constantinople, seems to do, that the sanctifying Spirit descended before the consecration, which took place and always takes place by His virtue? (Blot, Marie Réparatrice et l'Eucharistie p. 200—201. — Cf. Bona, Rer. liturg. 1. 1, c. 5.)

[2] Probst, Bickell, Funke and others state that the so-called Clementine Liturgy (the 8th Book of the Apostolic Constitution) with some slight peculiarities was used in the entire Church, — from the days of the Apostles until the fourth century: not until this epoch did the various liturgies of the eastern and western churches proceed by reform from this one primitive liturgy. Historic as well as intrinsic reasons rather oppose than approve of this view. Cf. Thalhofer, Liturgik, I, 334 etc. — Krazer, sect. 1, c. 1—4.

ficial rite, introduced and enlarged upon by the Apostles, were preserved with fidelity and reverence in the churches founded by them and their successors; but in the course of time, according as it was deemed necessary or expedient, it was always more and more developed, enriched and perfected, yet after a different manner, in the various churches of the East and West. "The Lord never ceases to be present to His beloved Spouse the Church, never fails to be at her side in her office of teaching and to accompany her in her operation with His blessing," — consequently, He had the power, as He also had the will, to bequeath to the chiefs and shepherds of the Church the right to give to the Sacrifice instituted by Himself the most natural and the wisest development and the best adapted form, that is, to give it due liturgical form and solemnity.

Thus there originated in different places, at different times and among different nations also different liturgies, that is, ecclesiastical formulas for the celebration of the Eucharistic Sacrifice. In the main features, in the essential points of the Sacrifice, all these various rites of the Mass agree; but in the rest they all differ more or less, both in substance as well as in construction.[1] With regard to their origin and their affinity, they may be divided into different classes; in general they are divided into two extensive groups — the liturgies of the East and the liturgies of the West. This division is warranted and well grounded, for the Eastern liturgies are characteristically distinguished from those of the West, not only by reason of their country and language, but also because of their spirit, contents and form. The liturgies of the East have a more stable, unchangeable character, since the same divine praises, the same petitions and thanksgivings are nearly always repeated; they present very little variety in the daily celebration of the ecclesiastical year. The liturgies of the West, on the contrary, exhibit a greater variety, fresh life and constant progress, for the celebration of the ecclesiastical feasts and seasons is most intimately connected and interwoven with the Holy Sacrifice. While the Oriental liturgies, for the most part, contain more lengthy prayers, a greater abundance of symbolical customs and acts, the Western, and especially the Roman-Latin rite,

---

[1] In celebrando sacrosancto Missae sacrificio omnes Orientis et Occidentis Ecclesiae modum quemdam in summa communem ab initio habuere; singulae tamen ritus aliquos singulares ac diversos. Haec omnibus semper communia: nempe lectiones sacrarum Scripturarum initio Liturgiae; psalmorum aliorumque canticorum recitatio; oblatio panis et vini aqua mixti; consecratio utriusque verbis Christi Domini cum benedictione ac signo crucis a sacerdote facta; oratio Dominica et sacra communio cum gratiarum actione. At designatio certarum ex Scriptura lectionum; psalmorum aliarumque precum numerus et definitio; ministrorum ritus praeter eos, qui sunt ex institutione divina, — haec omnia pro locis ac temporibus varia exstiterunt (Mabillon, De Liturg. Gallic. l. 1, cap. 2). — Non errare illos reputamus, qui rituum et ceremoniarum *varietatem* inter ipsa rerum christianarum *primordia* jam esse natam suspicantur. Fieri enim potuit, ut Apostoli gravissimis de causis in *diversis* partibus et provinciis pro captu et ingenio populorum *diversas* rogarent leges, *diversas* ordinarent ceremonias (Krazer sect. 1, c. 1, § 2).

is marked by a significant brevity, as well as by a dignified simplicity and a marvellous sublimity in word and action.

3. While the liturgies of the East are very numerous, there are but few in the West. The principal are the Mozarabic, the ancient Gallic, the Ambrosian [1] and Roman liturgies. The last named has

---

[1] The Mozarabic Liturgy is also called the Gothic-Spanish, Isidorian and Toledian. The expression Mozarabic probably denotes that this was the liturgy of the Arabianized, that is, of the Christians resident in Spain under Arab power and mingling with the Arabs. It bears much resemblance to the ancient Gallic Liturgy, and appears to have originated from it. Probably it was in use from the beginning among the Christians in Spain, and gradually gave place to the Roman Liturgy, so that at the close of the fifteenth century at Toledo alone, and that only in six churches of the city, was the Mozarabic rite celebrated on great feasts. Cardinal Ximenes († 1517) founded a college of thirteen priests at Toledo, who were obliged daily to celebrate according to the Mozarabic Rite. In the beautiful chapel ad Corpus Christi, which Ximenes built in the Cathedral of Toledo, the Office is until now daily recited and Holy Mass celebrated according to the Mozarabic Rite. Besides this in two parish churches in Toledo — namely, in that of St. Mark and that of Sts. Justa and Rufina — the Holy Sacrifice is celebrated according to the Mozarabic Liturgy, — but only on Sundays and feast-days. Also at Salamanca there is in the cathedral a chapel — St. Salvador's, in which the priest on sixteen stated days of the year has to observe the Mozarabic Mass Rite. Cf. Theologisch-praktische Quartalschrift von Linz 1879, S. 35 etc. — The ancient Gallic Rite was observed in Gaul until the end of the eighth century, when it was replaced by the Roman. The ancient Gallic Liturgy, now nowhere in use, harmonizes to a great extent with the Mozarabic. Both have the same Introit, called in the Mozarabic Liturgy officium, in the ancient Gallic antiphona ad praelegendum. Then follows the Gloria, which in the Gallic Liturgy is often replaced by the Benedictus, for this reason the oration that follows it is called collectio post prophetiam, while, on the contrary, in the Mozarabic it is styled post Gloria. Both have the salutation: Dominus sit semper vobiscum. After the three Lessons and the Offertory there follow in both Liturgies seven prayers: a) The Oration *Missa*, so called because it is the first in the actual Mass, that is, in the Mass of the faithful (formerly called praefatio ad missam); b) the *alia* oratio (A. G. collectio); c) the Oratio *post nomina*, that is, after the reading of the Diptychs; d) the Oratio *ad pacem*, that is, before the kiss of peace; e) the Inlatio (A. G. contestatio vel immolatio = Preface); f) the prayer *post pridie* (A. G. post mysterium), that is, after the Elevation; g) the prayer *post orationem dominicam*. Both have the blessing before the Communion. The Mozarabic Rite has an elevatio hostiae at the Creed, the Pater noster with responsories after each petition, the fraction of the Host in nine specially named parts. — The Ambrosian Rite still partly in use in Milan (so called because St. Ambrose enriched and completed it) harmonizes with the Roman as to essentials, and is to be regarded as its daughter or sister. In both prevails the same connection between the changeable and unchangeable constituent parts, the same structure of prayers, the same brevity, vigor and precision, the same wealth of thought. The variations are insignificant; thus, for example, the succession of the parts is somewhat changed in the Ambrosian Rite, in that the Credo comes after the Offertory, the Pater noster is recited after the fractio hostiae, and the washing of the hands immediately precedes the Consecration; the regulation of the liturgical colors is also somewhat different. — Cf. Liturgia Mozarabica (Migne tom. 85). — Mabillon, De Liturgia Gallic. 1. 3 (Migne tom. 72). — Mozarabische und ambrosianische Liturgie in der Bibliothek der Kirchenväter. Kempten 1877.

at all times had the precedence, and is now found in all parts of the world.   Already Pope Innocent I. (402—417), in writing to Decentius, Bishop of Gubbio, about ritual matters, traces the origin of the Roman liturgy to the Prince of the Apostles: "Who does not know," he writes, "that what has been handed down by Peter, the Prince of the Apostles, to the Roman Church is still observed unto this day, and must be observed by all?"   St. Peter, consequently, must be regarded (in a more general sense) as the founder of the Roman liturgy, for the method of celebration followed and introduced by him[1] was, without doubt, the essential and permanent foundation for its later development and form.   "This liturgy, as yet a tender plant, was brought by St. Peter, the Prince of the Church, into the garden of the Roman Church, where by his nursing care and that of his successors, assisted by the Holy Ghost, it has grown to a large tree, and although the trunk has long ago attained its full growth, it nevertheless shoots forth in every century new branches and new blossoms" (Kössing). — The most ancient written inventories of the Roman liturgy we possess in three Sacramentaries, which bear the names of Pope Leo I. (440—461), Gelasius I. (492—496) and Gregory I. (590—604) (*Sacramentarium Leonianum, Gelasianum, Gregorianum*).[2]   These Sacramentaries contain a precious treasure

---

[1]   *Istum ordinem ab apostolis et ab apostolicis viris traditum Romana tenet ecclesia* et per totum paene Occidentem omnes ecclesiae eandem traditionem servant (Raban. Maur. De clericor. institut. 1. 1, c. 33). — Inter *Occidentis* Liturgias potissimum sibi locum vindicat *Romana*, quam saltem quoad praecipuas partes a Petro Apostolorum principe processisse constans et perpetua *Ecclesiae Romanae* est traditio.   Id Decentio Eugubino *Innocentius I.*, id Profuturo Braccarensi episcopo *Vigilius* in suis contestantur epistolis (Krazer sect. 2, c. 2, § 25).

[2]   Sacramentarium (= liber sacramentorum vel mysteriorum, the book for the celebration of the mysteries) was in the West until far into the Middle Age the name of the liturgical book containing the prayers to be recited by the priest only in the celebration of Mass and in the administration of the sacraments and sacramentals, v. g., the Orationes and Prefaces with the Canon, the rite of administering baptism and holy orders,and the blessing of the holy oils. — The parts to be sung by the choir (at the Introit, after the Epistle, at the Offertory and at the Communion) were in another book, which was called in early times Antiphonarium, and later Graduale. — The complete list of the readings from the Bible was called Comes, Companion, that is, Guide for the liturgical Scripture lessons of the whole ecclesiastical year.   If the sections for the readings from the Bible were taken according to the order of the Comes not merely by their first words, but according to the whole text, they were called *Lectionaries* or *Plenaries;* and these contained the whole course in full (plene, pleniter) and were used until the seventh century. These Lectionaries were often divided into two books — the Epistolarium and the Evangelarium.   Since the tenth century the parts for reading and singing were partly externally connected with the Sacramentarium, and partly internally and organically blended with the contents of the Sacramentarium to form the complete Missal (Missale plenum vel plenarium), which did not come into exclusive and general use until the thirteenth century. — The rubrics were given in the so-called Ordines Romani, from which they afterward were taken up into the liturgical books. — (Cf. Zaccaria, Biblioth. ritual. I, 26 sqq. — Thalhofer, Liturgik I, 33 etc. — Ebner, Quellen und Forschungen S. 359 etc.)

of liturgical traditions, which date from the most ancient period of the Roman Church.　The above named Popes deserve well of the liturgy, inasmuch as they faithfully preserved the ancient formulas, and, at the same time, enriched and perfected them with additions suitable to the times.　Our Missal is principally derived from the Sacramentary of St. Gregory the Great.　Under him the Canon of the Mass received its last addition.　The rest of the constituent parts of the Roman liturgy of the Mass (the Introit, the Kyrie, the Gloria, the Collect, the Epistle, the Gradual, the Gospel, the Secreta, the Preface, the Pater Noster, the Communion and the Post-Communion) date back at least to the fifth or even the fourth century.　Toward the close of the Middle Age the Missals were much disfigured by particular changes and unsuitable additions, so that there was urgent need of a reform.　This was accomplished under the Popes Pius V. (1560—1572), Clement VIII. (1592—1605) and Urban VIII. (1623 —1644), who carefully revised and corrected the Missal.[1]　Thus the Gregorian Rite was, as far as possible, restored to its original purity, simplicity and dignity, while at the same time the desired unity of divine worship was brought about.

4.　Thus has the Church in the course of time set the jewel of the Holy Sacrifice in the most magnificent manner with heavenly wisdom and skill for the praise of God and the edification of the faithful, by surrounding it with the precious decorations of holy prayers, of holy hymns, lessons and ceremonies.[2]　She has enveloped the celebration of the adorable Sacrifice in a mystic veil, in order to fill the hearts and minds of the faithful with religious awe and profound reverence, and to urge them to earnest, pious contemplation and

---

[1] The holy Pope Pius V., whom the Church honors as an instrument chosen by God ad conterendos Ecclesiae hostes et ad divinum cultum reparandum, forbade in the bull of July 14, 1570, any one to add or omit or change anything in the Missal that had recently been published by him. At the same time he suppressed all other Missals; those only might be retained, which had been in use for more than two hundred years. Thus, for example, the Carmelites, the Carthusians and the Dominicans retained their ancient rite, as also the Mozarabic and Milan liturgies have remained in use in some churches until this day.

[2] Olim non tanto exterioris apparatu decoris Missarum solemnia celebrabantur, nec ab uno quolibet haec omnis religiosi obsequii gloria consummata et perpolita est. Pontifices quippe sacri, splendida Romanae sedis luminaria, sicut diversis temporibus affulserunt, ita paulatim studii sui claritate, venustatem hujus salutaris officii perfecerunt. Et sicut traditum a Domino per Moysen sacrificii veteris ordinem praecipue David et Salomon (III. Reg. 7) sacerdotum et levitarum ministerio (I. Paral. 23), cantorum multiplici numero, psalmorum divinorum tripudio, templi vel altaris illustri gloria, sacrorumque multitudine vasorum splendidius amplificaverunt, sic traditum a Domino mirabilem novi sacrificii ritum per primos Apostolos sancta Romana Ecclesia suscipiens, religiosa fide amplexata est, fideli cura conservavit, diligenti apparatu exornavit... Studiosa divinae legis Ecclesia Romana paulatim protulit de thesauro suo nova pietatis monumenta, et quoddam velut ex auro lapidibusque pretiosis religiosi officii sancto sacrificio fabrefecit diadema (Rupert. Tuitiens. De divin. offic. l. 2, c. 21).

meditation. The beauty, the worth and the perfection of the Roman liturgy of the Mass are universally acknowledged and admired. Father Faber styles the Church's Rite of the Holy Sacrifice "the most beautiful thing this side of heaven," and, as he remarks, "it came forth out of the grand mind of the Church, and lifted us out of earth and out of self, and wrapped us round in a cloud of mystical sweetness and the sublimities of a more than angelic liturgy, and purified us almost without ourselves, and charmed us with celestial charming, so that our very senses seem to find vision, hearing, fragrance, taste and touch, beyond what earth can give." The Church prayers of the liturgy are superior to all other prayers; no "human genius can hope to attain their beauty and sublimity. In these two qualities, the Mass differs from all other offices in a remarkable manner. It has not merely flights of eloquence and poetry strikingly displayed in particular prayers, but it is sustained throughout in the higher sphere, to which its divine purpose naturally raises it. If we examine each prayer separately, it is perfect; perfect in construction, perfect in thought, and perfect in expression. If we consider the manner in which they are brought together, we are struck with the brevity of each, with the sudden but beautiful transitions, and the almost stanza-like effect, with which they succeed one another, forming a lyrical composition of surpassing beauty. If we take the entire service, as a whole, it is constructed with the most admirable symmetry, proportioned in its parts with perfect judgment and so exquisitely arranged, as to excite and preserve an unbroken interest in the sacred action. No doubt, to give full force and value to this sacred rite, its entire ceremonial is to be considered. The assistants, with their noble vestments, the chant, the incense, the more varied ceremonies which belong to a solemn Mass, are all calculated to increase veneration and admiration. But still, the essential beauties remain, whether the holy rite be performed under the golden vault of St. Peter's, with all the pomp and circumstance befitting its celebration by the Sovereign Pontiff, or in a wretched wigwam, erected in haste by some poor savages for their missionary" (Wiseman). — "That overruling influence of the Spirit of God, that directs even in secondary matters the affairs of the visible Church, nowhere else appears so marked and evident as in the arrangement of the rite of the Holy Mass, which, although only monumental, yet in its present state forms such a beautiful, perfect whole, yea, a splendid work, that it excites the admiration of every reflecting mind. Even the bitterest adversaries of the Church do not deny it; unprejudiced, aesthetic judges of good taste admit that even from their own standpoint the Mass is to be classed as one of the greatest masterpieces ever composed. Thus the momentous sacrifice is encompassed with magnificent ceremonies: it is our duty to study to penetrate more and more into their meaning, and to expound what we have learned to the people according to their capacity" (Oswald). — The Roman liturgy has for some centuries been a complete masterpiece of art,

wonderful in the harmony and union of its parts. The most sacred
and venerable prayers and chants, breathing religious fervor and
tenderness, follow most ingeniously upon one another, and together
with the most appropriate and significant actions and ceremonies,
form a beautiful whole, serving as a protecting garment and a worthy
ornament to the divine mystery of the Holy Sacrifice. Their language, for its kind and object, cannot be surpassed;[1] for it is biblical,
ancient, simple, grave, dignified, solid, full of the spirit of faith,
humility and devotion, and penetrated with the perfume of piety
and holiness.

5. This glorious rite of the Sacrifice of the Mass is an unfailing
mine of religious instruction and edification; it is like an immensely
rich mine, where always new gold veins are disclosed to the search-
ing look. Even if we were to devote our entire life to considering
in our meditations and prayers the mystical liturgy of the Mass,
there would still remain for our heart and mind new treasures, still
new riches would reveal themselves and new beauties would be disclosed. And yet though it be so deep and impenetrable as to prove
inexhaustible to even the greatest contemplative saint, it is, at the
same time, so clear and easy of comprehension, that the most art-
less child as well as the most simple of the faithful finds therein
light, incentive, strength and nourishment for his religious life.
But is this precious liturgical treasure valued and turned to good
account, as it deserves to be, by the ministers of the Church, in other
words, do they study it for their own sanctification and make it
available to the faithful in the school, in catechetical instructions
and sermons?[2] "The liturgy is a constant mysterious sermon, but
it is by the mouth of the priest that the laity must learn to understand its language. Without liturgical instruction the participation
of the faithful in the functions of divine worship will be in many
instances only external and mechanical. The mighty stream of the

---

[1] What Bossuet says of the Christian language in general, applies in the highest degree to the liturgical language: "It is not addressed to the senses, but to the
soul, whose food it is" — "verbum nutritorium animarum" (Origen. in Matth.
n. 85). "Like the body of Jesus Christ, who made Himself the bread of our souls,
it must not be dazzling, for His word must participate in the humility of His flesh,
and as in His flesh lowliness is mingled with greatness, so in it every thing is
grand and every thing is lowly, every thing is rich and every thing is poor" (Bossuet, Panégyrique de Saint Paul).

[2] Sacrorum rituum leges, quae rubricarum nomine censentur, presbyteri accurate addiscant, apprimeque calleant ac attentissime servent; nec illos commen-
tarios, qui de istis sacris ritibus a piis et eruditis viris conscripti sunt, legere
omittant, dictasque ceremonias frequenter inter Missarum celebrationem exponere,
ut earum sanctitas et significatio ab omnibus agnoscantur (Coll. Lac. III, p. 644).
— There are few priests, even among those who exercise the sacred ministry, who
have nothing to reproach themselves with in this matter. This is the cause of the
ignorance among the people of one of the most interesting parts of the Catholic
worship, and of the disgust or indifference of many for the mysteries or sacraments
of our holy religion (Gousset, Théol. mor. II, 28).

ecclesiastical year flows by, the faithful stand on its bank, they look on, and of its waters they receive but a few drops which the waves of themselves cast upon the shore" (Amberger).

In order to discover the true and full meaning of the rite of the Mass, we must view it from the proper standpoint, and be guided by those correct maxims which give the sense of the liturgical words and actions.[1] — It is self-evident that that unecclesiastical view is to be rejected which, while discarding all the higher and mystical sense, seeks to explain the mysterious liturgy after a mere natural or historic manner, by trying to ascribe all ceremonies exclusively to reasons of necessity, expedience and propriety.[2] — Yet, on the other hand, in the mystical explanation of the liturgy the opposite mistake is to be avoided, which consists in giving arbitrary explanations without regard to the intentions of the Church, and in indulging in silly trifles and affected subtleties.[3] — The Church herself applies symbolical meanings in her liturgy; therefore, in explaining the liturgy we must, above all things, attend to what the Church would express by her ceremonies.[4] "Since by reason of his nature man is so constituted that without exterior aid he cannot easily rise to the contemplation of divine things, the Church, as a devoted Mother, has, therefore, introduced into her liturgy certain usages, as, for example, that some portions of the Mass should be recited in a low tone, others in a loud tone of voice. In like manner certain ceremonies, for instance, the mystical blessings, the use of lights, incense, vestments and many things of that nature, she employs by Apostolic prescription and tradition, in order both to manifest thereby the majesty of the great Sacrifice, as well as to animate the minds of the faithful by these visible signs of religion and piety to the consideration of the sublime mysteries hidden within this Sacrifice."[5]

---

[1] Cfr. Languet, De vero Ecclesiae sensu circa sacrarum ceremoniarum usum. — Assemani, De ritibus sacris (Migne, Curs. theolog. compl. 26). — Lebrun, Explication de la Messe, Préface n. IV. — VI.

[2] Thus writes Claudius de Vert († 1708) in his celebrated work: Explication simple, littérale et historique des Cérémonies de l'Eglise IV (Paris 1706—1713).

[3] Blessed J. M. Thomasius (Tomasi) of the Order of the Theatines († 1. Jan. 1713), writes on this subject (Op. VII, 185): Concerning the mystical or moral senses of the Mass we should be somewhat sparing, because many things are intended to signify something, ... whilst many others, rather the most part, are instituted not to signify anything in particular, but from decorum, for good order and religious propriety, ... and to look for a mystical and spiritual sense in every little thing, would not be in accordance with the intentions of those who instituted it.

[4] Sunt quidem quam plurimae caeremoniae et usu et origine mysticae. Concedo tamen, et alias esse, quae exordium et institutionem suam necessitati, commodo et decoro debent. Imo nec diffiteor, quamplures auctores nimio indoctae pietatis zelo adductos extra justi tramites vagatos fuisse, dum sibi mysteria, parabolas, symbola iis in caeremoniis fabricarunt, quibus certe talia adjungere Ecclesia numquam in mente habuit (Languet l. c, § 2).

[5] Trid. sess. 22, cap. 5.

The ceremonies of the liturgy of the Mass, accordingly, have in general for their purpose a twofold object : in the first place they are intended to enhance and adorn the celebration of Mass, to serve for the honor and the worship of God; then, too, they are designed as a means to place before the eyes of the faithful in a lively manner the sublimity, the holiness and the efficacy of the Sacrifice, that the faithful, being thereby moved to sentiments of devotion, may be better disposed in heart to glorify God and to obtain grace.   Now the honor of God and the sanctification of man invariably constitute the principal object of all liturgical acts, — and this, consequently, in their explanation must be always kept in the foreground; whatever is instructive therein is merely subordinate, and should be made to serve the main object.[1] — The different ceremonies may, according to their object and signification, be more succinctly grouped into three classes.[2]

a) All the ceremonies of Mass conduce to the order, beauty and adornment of divine worship.   Now while some ceremonies, nay, even many, have yet a higher mystical meaning, others are prescribed merely to invest the celebration of divine worship with decorum, dignity and reverence.   The latter ceremonies are based merely on a just regard to propriety, decorum and suitableness.   To this class belongs, for example, the prescription that the priest approach the altar with downcast eyes and measured step; that he place the left hand on his breast when making the sign of the Cross; that he turn toward the faithful, when greeting or blessing them.[3]

b) Most of the ceremonies are outward forms of worship, that is, they are the outcome of an interior emotion, expressions of religious thought and sentiments.[4]   Among these are the different positions and movements of the body, of the members of the body, for example, the bending of the knee, the striking of the breast, the bowing of the body and the head, the raising up and the joining of the hands.   Such acts are outward signs which express, accompany and awaken devout sentiments of the heart; for instance, sentiments

---

[1] Finis omnium caeremoniarum et verborum, quae ab Ecclesia (Apostolis eorumque successoribus) instituta sunt in administratione sacramentorum et nominatim sacrificii eucharistici, potissimum duplex est; *proxime* ut res ipsa essentialis quae agitur, distinctius declarata velut ob oculos ponatur atque convenienti majestate et externo cultu condecoretur, *consequentur* deinde ut excitetur et foveatur congruentior dispositio ac devotio in animis fidelium ad cultum Deo exhibendum et majorem fructum percipiendum (Cardin. Franzelin, De Sacramento Eucharistiae thes. VII).

[2] Cfr. Suarez disp. 84, sect. 1.

[3] Primo quaedam ex caeremoniis Missae inductae sunt solum, ut hoc sacrum mysterium *debita honestate, modestia et reverentia* peragatur ; unde constat, hujusmodi caeremonias non solum convenientes, sed moraliter etiam esse necessarias et ideo summa prudentia esse ab Ecclesia institutas (Suarez l. c., n. 2).

[4] Secundo sunt aliae caeremoniae institutae *per se primo propter exteriores actus latriae exercendos*, quae etiam convenientissime institutae sunt (Suarez l. c., n. 3).

of adoration, humility, desire, sorrow and confidence. "They who pray, bend the knee, raise the hands or prostrate themselves to the ground, thereby expressing outwardly what they feel inwardly. Their invisible will and the intention of their heart is indeed known to God, and their interior sentiments need not be made known to Him by such signs; but by their means we are to pray and sigh more humbly and more ardently; and although these bodily motions are made through a previous impulse of the heart, nevertheless, the emotion of the heart is, I know not how, again increased by these exterior signs, which it had produced, and the interior devotion, which preceded them, grows more intense through the exterior devotion which it had brought forth."[1]

c) A third group is prescribed especially because of their symbolical signification; these ceremonies are destined prominently to indicate the mysteries of Christian faith and life.[2] To this class, for example, belong the mixing of wine and water, the washing of the hands at the Offertory, the placing of the hands over the oblation before the Consecration, the breaking of the Host and the dropping of a small particle of it into the chalice, the frequent making of the sign of the Cross, the use of lights and incense.

Accordingly the ceremonies of the liturgy in the intention of the Church serve not merely for the proper, the worthy and the edifying celebration of the Sacrifice, but also for the exterior honor of God, of the Eucharistic Saviour, of the saints, of relics and pictures, as well as for the symbolical expression of the different mysteries. These different objects do not exclude one another, but are often united together in one and the same liturgical act, for example, sometimes in the use of the sign of the Cross, the honor paid the Cross. Along with the natural reason and object of a ceremony the Church not unfrequently combines a higher, mystical sense.[3]

---

[1] S. Aug. De cura pro mortuis gerenda c. 5, n. 7. — Exercentur ab hominibus quaedam *sensibilia* opera, non quibus Deum excitent, sed quibus seipsos provocent in divina, sicut prostrationes, genuflexiones, vocales clamores et cantus, quae non fiunt, quasi Deus his indigeat, quia omnia novit et cujus voluntas est immutabilis et qui affectum mentis et etiam motum corporis non propter se acceptat, sed propter nos facimus, ut per haec sensibilia opera intentio nostra dirigatur in Deum et affectio ascendatur; simul etiam per hoc Deum profitemur animae et corporis auctorem, cui et spiritualia et corporalia obsequia exhibemus (S. Thom., C. gent. l. 3, c. 119).

[2] Tertio sunt aliae caeremoniae, *quae specialiter sunt propter significationem* (*moralem vel mysticam*) institutae, non quod non pertineat etiam ad ornatum, neque quod cultum etiam aliquem non contineant, sed quod *principaliter propter significationem* ordinatae sint (Suarez l. c., n. 4).

[3] In the ceremonies, even in those which seem the least important, there is nothing that has not its reason, and often a very deep meaning. Christian symbolism is something admirable for those who are able to understand it. It is God with His infinite perfections and His grandeurs, it is the Church with her doctrines and her history made evident to the eyes of our infirmity (Mgr. Guibert, Lettre à son clergé sur les études ecclésiastiques, 2. Oct. 1851).

Finally, we must not overlook in the ceremonies their sacramental character, which consists in this that they in their own way produce spiritual effects and obtain divine grace.

6. Catholic ceremonies, therefore, are not the relics of heathen or Jewish customs, but Apostolic and ecclesiastical ordinances, forms of worship created and pervaded by a higher spirit. Consequently, the priest should highly esteem and love them, and therefore perform them with punctuality and dignity. St. Teresa was ready to sacrifice her life for even the least ceremony of the Church. In the service of the Almighty, in the most Holy Sacrifice of the Mass even the smallest thing has its meaning and importance; and, therefore, the Church has so exactly and minutely regulated by her rubrics the entire deportment of the priest at the altar. Whosoever conscientiously complies with these ecclesiastical regulations, has the special merit of practising the virtue of obedience in all his actions and movements when celebrating. To all applies the admonition of the Apostle: "Glorify and bear God in your body!" (1 Cor. 6, 20.) — A modest demeanor and a becoming exterior, regulated according to the requirements of reason and faith, honors God, edifies our neighbor and promotes our own spiritual life. Therefore, the priest at the altar should, above all, not neglect the exterior. In his whole deportment should be reflected his faith, his reverence, his recollection of mind, his heartfelt devotion.[1] "What great care is to be taken to celebrate Holy Mass with all religious solemnity and devotion, every one will easily understand, when he reflects that in Holy Scripture a curse is pronounced upon those who do the work of God negligently.[2] Since we must confess that the faithful can perform no action so holy and so divine as this adorable mystery, in which that life-giving Victim, which has reconciled us with God the Father, is daily offered by the priest on the altar. It is, then, self-evident that all pains and care should be taken to perform this Sacrifice with the greatest purity of heart and with all the marks of ex-

---

[1] Tanta gravitate, tanto religionis cultu (sacerdotes) Missae sacrificium celebrent, ut per visibilem ministri pietatem invisibilia aeterni sacerdotis mysteria conspiciantur. Nihil igitur obiter in hac divina actione, nihil perfunctorie, nihil praecipitanter, nihil inconditis gestibus, omnia vero graviter, omnia secundum ordinem fiant, juxta receptos et approbatos Ecclesiae ritus, qui vel in minimis sine peccato negligi, omitti vel mutari haud possunt (Concil. prov. Quebec. II, a. 1854).

[2] Ex consideratione infinitae bonitatis, majestatis et excellentiae Dei, ex intuitione quoque totius miseriae, vilitatis, culpae ac indigentiae nostrae exhibeamus nos Deo in omni suo obsequio, in oratione praesertim et psalmodia, maxime vero in *celebratione* cum omni ac profundissima humilitate, compunctione, reverentia, attentione, custodia ac fervore, et ante horarum, orationum et psalmodiae inceptionem recolligamus cor nostrum et simplificemus ac stabiliamus illud in Deo, ejus incircumscriptibilem dignitatem, praesentiam, misericordiam justitiamque pensando, proprias quoque miserias et offensas efficaciter ponderando et aggravando, et ita *singula verba sacra quasi ex proprio affectu cum attentione et gustu interno distincte pronuntiemus* (Dion. Carthus. De laude vitae solitariae art. 21).

terior devotion and piety.''[1] The priest at the altar should render to God in the name of the Church a homage of the highest veneration: in the first place, interiorly by acts of faith, of hope, love, humility, contrition, praise, thanksgiving and petition; then also exteriorly by bows, by genuflections, by striking his breast, raising his hands and eyes, kissing the altar and many other ceremonies.[2] All these acts should be performed with devotion, reverence and dignity in the presence of God and of His holy angels, otherwise they become occasions of distraction, of scandal and of all manner of irreverence.[3]

From historical and, at the same time, from objective reasons the liturgical celebration of the Mass may be divided into two parts — 1) into the general, preparatory divine service (*Missa catechumenorum*) and 2) into the particular, real sacrificial worship (*Missa fidelium*), which admits of a three-fold subdivision (the Offertory, the Consecration and the Communion).[4]

FIRST SECTION.

The Preparatory Divine Service.

What is most holy must be treated in a holy manner; therefore, a careful preparation for the mystery of the Divine Sacrifice is required. The whole career, the entire life and conduct of the priest should be a remote, uninterrupted preparation for Holy Mass;[5] but

---

[1] Trident. sess. 22, decret. de observandis et evitandis in celebr. Miss.

[2] Cogitemus nos sub conspectu Dei stare. Placendum est divinis oculis et *habitu corporis et modo vocis* (S. Cyprian. De Orat. domin. c. 3). — Quia ex duplici natura compositi sumus, intellectuali sc. et sensibili, duplicem adorationem Deo offerimus: sc. *spiritualem*, quae consistit in interiori mentis devotione, et *corporalem*, quae consistit in exteriori corporis humiliatione. — Et quia in omnibus actibus latriae id quod est exterius, refertur ad id quod est interius, sicut ad principalius, ideo ipsa *exterior* adoratio fit propter *interiorem*, ut videlicet per signa humilitatis, quae corporaliter exhibemus, excitetur noster affectus ad subjiciendum se Deo, quia connaturale est nobis, ut per sensibilia ad intelligibilia procedamus (S. Thom. 2, 2, q. 84, a. 2).

[3] Presbyter=*senior*, non propter senectutem, sed propter dignitatem, honorem et sapientiam, quia quicunque presbyter est, *sapiens* esse debet, ut *intelligat* ea quae legit: intelligat orationes, quas dicit et diurnis temporibus et nocturnis; intelligat ea quae cantat in Missa (Pseudo-Alcuin. cap. 36).

[4] In hoc sacramento totum mysterium nostrae salutis comprehenditur, ideo prae ceteris sacramentis cum majori solemnitate agitur. Ante celebrationem hujus mysterii primo quidem praemittitur *praeparatio* quaedam ad digne agenda ea, quae sequuntur... Consequenter acceditur ad *celebrationem mysterii*, quod quidem et offertur ut sacrificium et consecratur et sumitur ut sacramentum. Unde primo peragitur *oblatio;* secundo *consecratio* oblatae materiae; tertio ejusdem *perceptio* (S. Thom. 3, q. 83, a. 4).

[5] Generalis dispositio ad celebrandum est ea diligentia, qua incumbere sacerdotes debemus, ut vita nostra et conversatio respondeat sanctitati atque amplitudini mysteriorum, quae celebramus. Et haec est principalis magisque necessaria prae-

when the hour for Mass is near, he has an immediate and special preparation to make, that is, by religious acts, by the exercise of mental and vocal prayer,[1] to dispose his soul and to excite his heart to devotion.[2] In a touching manner does the venerable John of Avila exhort one thereto. He thus writes: "It is indeed the most powerful means to arouse a man, to make this serious reflection: I am going to perform the holy Consecration, to hold God in my hands, to converse with Him and to receive Him into my heart. Who will not be inflamed with love by making the reflection to himself: I am on the point of receiving the Infinite Goodness? Who does not tremble and shudder out of a loving awe toward Him, before whom the heavenly Powers themselves shudder and tremble? Who does not tremble with the fear of offending Him, and does not tremble with the desire to praise and serve Him? Who does not experience sorrow, confusion and remorse for having offended the Divine Master, whom he beholds before him? Who is not filled with confidence by such a pledge? Who does not endeavor — having such a Viaticum with him in the desert of this world — to do penance? In short, such a meditation, dictated by the spirit of God, entirely transforms man, and carries him away and beside himself, — at one time by a sense of reverence, now by love, again by other powerful emotions. How cautious should we not be to keep ourselves wholly and unreservedly for Christ, who so greatly honors us, as to descend unto us

---

paratio: adeo ut omnino requiratur, ut *tota sacerdotis vita praeparatio sit ad digne celebrandum*, et in omni re tam circumspecte agat, ut paratus esse ad offerendum semper dici possit, utque in omnibus, quae dixerit ac fecerit, *recordetur sese hodie celebrasse, et cras celebraturum* (Anton. de Molina, Instructio sacerdotum tr. 4, c. 6).

[1] Optimum consilium est, ut sacerdos omnino rejectis curis et cogitationibus saeculi immediate ante Missam *orationi vacet*, i. e. mentali, quae maxime fervorem et devotionem excitat (Quarti, In rubr. Miss. p. 2, tit. 1, n. 1).

[2] *Tota vita sacerdotis timorati cupientis celebrare devote, debet esse continua praeparatio incessabilisque dispositio ad celebrandum condigne*, ita ut diligentissime vitet, quidquid impedimentum est celebrationis devotae ac fervidae, et quidquid ad eam disponit ac confert viriliter apprehendat et exsequatur, ita tamen, ut hora celebrationis instante, per *specialia* et *peculiaria* quaedam exercitia devotionalia orationum, meditationum, psalmodiarum, contritionis, confessionis et satisfactionis ad instantem celebrationem se praeparet (Dionys. Carthus. De particul. judicio dialog. art. 34). — Ad celebrandum meritorie sufficit et item requiritur, quod celebrans existat in caritate et ex caritate ad celebrandum moveatur ac procedat, quae interior motio sit promptitudo aliqua voluntatis ad opus illud cultus divini. Celebratio namque est actus tam privilegiatus, divinus ac eminens, quod ad eam exigitur actualis devotio, quae caritatem ejusque actum et quandam Dei contemplationem aut saltem considerationem includit. Christus quippe sacramenti hujus frequentationem, h. e. celebrationem instituendo praecepit Apostolis et in eorum persona cunctis presbyteris: "Haec quotiescunque feceritis, in mei memoriam facietis," h. e. in commemorationem amorosam ac devotam eximiae caritatis meae ad vos et acerbissimae meae passionis pro vobis... Tenetur ergo sacerdos in celebratione bonam et specialem timoratamque diligentiam adhibere, ut attente, devote ac reverenter se habeat et se a distractione compescat (Id. De sacram. altar. art. 17).

and place Himself in our hands, when the words of Consecration are pronounced!"[1]

After this private preparation[2] the priest proceeds to the altar,

---

[1] Cfr. Schermer, Geistliche Briefe des ehrw. Juan de Avila I, 47—55.

[2] The preparatory prayers recommended by the fact that the Church has received them into the Missale Romanum, deserve the preference over others and should, therefore, never be omitted. The above mentioned five Psalms contain and awaken every affection (faith, hope, confidence, love, desire, devotion, humility, sorrow, compunction, gratitude, resignation, self-offering), that disposes the priest for the worthy and fruitful celebration of Mass. The Antiphon: "Remember not, O Lord, our (mine and the nation's) offences nor those of our parents and take not revenge of our sins" (according to Tob. 3, 3), is a prayer of atonement that imparts corresponding expression to the sentiment of sinfulness and unworthiness, with which the soul of the priest should be animated at this moment. — Psalm 83 has a priviledged position in the liturgy among the hymns which glorify the Eucharistic mysteries: fervently and with deep feelings of devotion it expresses the sentiments of the priestly heart, which longs for the altar, to place there in Jesus's Heart and wounds all his labors, sufferings and joys, thence also to draw strength for the earthly pilgrimage which conducts through this valley of tears to our heavenly home and to glory. — Psalm 84 has by preference become an Advent and Christmas hymn in the Church. It contains gratitude for redemption about to begin, petitions for the completion of redemption and for perfect sanctification (for mercy, favor and peace, for freedom from the assaults of sensuality and self-love, and for the diminution of daily faults, &c.), and concludes with the joyful confidence of obtaining the fruits of salvation at the altar in all their fulness. — Psalm 85 is an humble and ardent prayer of petition. Feeling his indigence and dependence on God, in consideration of the goodness and power of his Master, the priest implores strength against his perverse inclinations and protection against external enemies, as well as assistance for the worthy performance of the most holy, sublime and divine action of his office at the altar. — Psalm 115 imparts earnest and enthusiastic expression to the celebrant's intention of thanksgiving, that is, to his grateful sacrificial joy and joyful self-sacrifice in the service of God. — Psalm 129 is a heartrending penitential hymn, full of humility and contrition, of hope and confidence in the mercy of God and in the superabundant redemption, the source of which is daily disclosed anew on the altar for the atonement of sin. — The following Versicles and Responsories continue the supplication for favor and mercy, and the perfect application of the "copiosa redemptio" prepared at the altar, and the orations contain petitions for light, for purifying and inflaming the heart by the light and fire of the Holy Spirit, ut veniens Dominus noster Jesus Christus *paratam* sibi in nobis inveniat *mansionem*. — This praeparatio ad Missam was in use as to its essential parts already in the eleventh century. Presbyter, cum se parat ad Missam, juxta Romanam consuetudinem decantat (recites) hos Psalmos: Quam dilecta (83), Benedixisti (84), Inclina Domine (85), Credidi (115); deinde Κύριε ἐλέησον, Pater noster, cum precibus et oratione pro peccatis, videlicet ut intus et exterius summo sacerdoti placere valeat, quem cum sacratissima oblatione sibi omnibusque christianis placare desiderat (Microlog. c. 1). Decanta cum devotione illos quinque psalmos (83, 84, 85, 115, 129) cum suis versiculis et orationibus. Dicas etiam, si tempus suppetit, orationem illam "Summe Sacerdos", quae valde efficax est et devota. Postea procedens ad altare recole Christum euntem ad crucem et fige cor ad ea, quae in passione gesta sunt; legas clare et distincte ea, quae legenda sunt, non multiplicando collectas nimias nec alia legendo ex devotione vel proprio arbitrio, quam quod a sanctis Patribus institutum est (S. Bonav. tr. de praepar. ad Miss. c. 2, n. 2).

to offer the Holy Sacrifice. The first principal division of the Mass liturgy, which extends from the prayers said at the foot of the altar to the Offertory, bears also a preparatory character; it may be considered as the public and common preparation of the priest and the people for the actual celebration of the Holy Mysteries.

The prayers, hymns and readings which compose this introductory and preparatory divine service, aim principally at purifying the heart and enlightening the mind, at animating the faith and exciting devotion, in order that all present may be placed in the proper dispositions and thus be able to offer worthily the most Holy Sacrifice to the Most High.

34. Introductory Prayers.

These prayers[1] include Psalm XLII., the Confiteor and two prayers for the perfect cleansing of the heart. This part of the rite as far as the Introit may be called the general introduction to the celebration of Mass; for priest and people therein seek mainly, by humble petition and supplication for mercy and pardon, duly to prepare themselves, so as to approach the altar with perfect purity of heart and worthily to celebrate or assist at the Holy Sacrifice.

1. The priest[2] unfolds the corporal entirely, places thereon the covered chalice,[3] opens the Missal,[4] bows at the middle of the altar

---

[1] These prayers were the last developed of the various portions of the preparatory part of the Mass, for they are first mentioned only since the eleventh century. Preparatory prayers were indeed recited at a much earlier period; but they were not so rigorously prescribed, and did not belong so strictly to the Mass liturgy, as they were generally said in the sacristy or on the way to the altar, while the choir sang the Introit Psalm. All known liturgies begin with a kind of confession of guilt. In former times the formulas differed greatly: the present Confiteor appears to have been in general use since the thirteenth century. The assertion that Pope Celestine I. (422—432) gave the Psalm Judica its present position, is entirely untenable. Cf. Bona, Rer. liturg. 1. 2, c. II, § 1—8.

[2] Clothed in sacred vestments, the priest when advancing to the altar must also have his head covered — as a mark of his dignity and authority; for the rubric that directs the priest *capite cooperto* to go to the altar, is of precept (S. R. C. 14, Jun. 1845). From the time that the amice no longer served this purpose, the biretta gradually became the prescribed liturgical covering for the head. In Italy the biretta used at liturgical functions must have only three corners or points (in remembrance of the Most Holy Trinity), because in that country the doctor's biretta is four-cornered. (S. R. C. 7. Dec. 1844.) In other countries, on the contrary, for instance, in Germany, Spain, France, the United States, four-cornered birettas — in the form of a cross — have always been used and are, therefore, permitted also at ecclesiastical functions. Cfr. Bouvry, Expositio rubricarum II, 196 sq.

[3] Sacerdos extendit corporale super medium altaris, ubi est ara consecrata, et super corporale collocat *calicem velo coopertum:* totus autem calix saltem quoad partem anteriorem debet esse coopertus, dum recitatur ea pars Missae, quae dicitur catechumenorum, ut postea in Missa fidelium discooperiatur, quia revelari debent fidelibus magis expresse arcana passionis Christi mysteria (Quarti, in rubr. Miss. p. 2, tit. 2, n. 2).

[4] An in Missis *privatis* permitti possit ministro aperire Missale et invenire

to the altar-cross,[1] descends and remains standing at the foot of the altar — as at the threshold of the Most Holy. "How terrible is this place! This is no other than the house of God and the gate of heaven!" (Gen. 28, 17.) In his interior the priest hears, as it were, a voice saying to him: "Come not hither, put off the shoes from thy feet, for the ground whereon thou standest, is holy ground." (Exod. 3, 5.) He remembers the words of St. Chrysostom: "When the priest calls upon the Holy Ghost and offers the tremendous Sacrifice: tell me in what rank should we place him? What purity shall we require of him, what reverence? Then reflect how those hands should be constituted which perform such services! What should that tongue be which pronounces such words! At this moment the very angels encompass the priest, and the whole choir of the heavenly powers lend their presence. and take up the entire space around the altar, to honor Him who lies thereon in Sacrifice. Therefore, the priest should be as pure and as holy as though he were himself in heaven among those sublime beings."[2] With what holy thoughts and sentiments should not his soul be filled at this moment? On the one side, God expects due honor from the Sacrifice, the Church militant claims the blessings of the altar, and the suffering souls in purgatory are thirsting for the refreshing stream of the blood of the Sacrifice: thus the priest is drawn to the altar by love, vocation and duty.[3] On the other hand he is reminded of the infinite sanctity of the Sacrifice, of his fearful responsibility, of his sinfulness and unworthiness, of his faults and infidelities: and thus he is kept back from the altar by the consciousness of guilt, by a holy and salutary fear.[4] In this interior struggle of contrary

---

missam? Resp.: Negative et serventur rubricae (S. R. C. 7. Sept. 1816). — Sacerdos Missale aperiens et ex eo divina mysteria populo annuntians denotat Christum, qui solus dignus est inventus aperire librum et solvere signacula ejus (Apoc. 5, 9). Quarti, 1. c. p. 2, tit. 2, n. 5.

[1] According to the S. R. C. 12. Nov. 1831 the celebrant must adhere exactly and strictly to the rubrics, which prescribe only in two cases a bow to the cross on the altar: on reaching the middle, that is, when leaving the middle of the altar — before descending for the prayer at the foot of the altar (facta primum cruci reverentia), and when he himself carries the Missal before the Gospel to the other side (caput cruci inclinat).

[2] De sacerdotio 1. 3, c. 4; 1. 6, c. 4.

[3] Cum celebrare sit tam privilegiatum ac dignissimum opus, Dei Patris omnipotentis, imo totius superexcellentissimae Trinitatis praecipue honorativum, passionisque Christi et ceterorem ipsius mysteriorum ac beneficiorum eximie recordativum, totius quoque Ecclesiae, imo vivorum ac mortuorum potissime subventivum, admonendi sunt sacerdotes, ut *quotidie* celebrare non cessent, nisi speciale occurrat obstaculum; imo sic conversari, taliter proficere satagant, quod ad celebrandum quotidie, quantum humana sinit fragilitas, suo modo sint digni (Dion. Carthus. De sacram. altar. serm. 5).

[4] Cum sacerdos est absque peccato mortali et in proposito bono, non habens legitimum impedimentum, et non ex reverentia, sed ex negligentia celebrare omittit, tunc, quantum in ipso est, privat sanctam Trinitatem laude et gloria, angelos

feelings he signs himself with the holy sign of the Cross and recites alternately with the acolyte, who represents the congregation, [1] the Forty-second Psalm, wherein the sentiments of his soul find their full expression.

a) The holy sign of the Cross. [2] — The priest makes what is known as the large or Latin cross upon himself, bringing his open hand from the forehead to the breast and from the left to the right shoulder, [3] saying at the same time the words: *In nomine Patris et*

---

laetitia, peccatores venia, justos subsidio et gratia, in purgatorio existentes refrigerio, Ecclesiam Christi spirituali beneficio — et se ipsum medicina et remedio contra infirmitates et quotidiana peccata, quia, sicut ait Ambrosius (De sacr. 1. 4, c. 6, n. 28), si "quotiescunque effunditur sanguis Christi, toties in remissionem peccatorum effunditur, debeo illum semper accipere, ut semper mihi peccata dimittantur; qui semper pecco, semper debeo habere medicinam." — Item, privat se omnibus talibus provenientibus ex sacra communione, quae sunt peccatorum remissio, fomitis mitigatio, mentis illuminatio, interior refectio, Christi et corporis ejus mystici incorporatio; virtutum roboratio, contra diabolum armatio, fidei certitudo, elevatio spei, excitatio caritatis, augmentatio devotionis et conversatio angelorum. — Item, non complet sibi injunctum magnae dignitatis obsequium nec officium exercet debitae servitutis Dei (Jer. 48, 10). — Item, contemnit Christi praeceptum de observantia hujus sacramenti (Joan. 6, 54). — Item, abicit viaticum suae peregrinationis, exponens se periculo mortis, quia, nisi recipiat alimentum corporis Christi et vitae vegetationem, efficitur sicut aridum membrum, ad quod non transmittitur corporalis cibi nutrimentum. — Ultimo, quantum in se est, evacuat divinum cultum et latriam Creatori debitam sicut ingratus de beneficiis Dei. Ergo, quantum potes, toto conatu per exercitium boni operis, lacrimarum contritionem et devotionis flammam expelle a te omnem torporem et negligentiam, ne inveniaris respuere tantorum charismatum dona (S. Bonav. tr. de praepar. ad Miss. c. 1, § 3, n. 9).

[1] Our acolytes (Mass or altar servers) actually attend to the important duties of the minor clerics; they act and speak (respond) in the name of the faithful. The pastor should see that they behave with modesty, recollection and reverence, that they perform their task with devotion and with hands joined, pronounce the words correctly and distinctly, and that they be cleanly attired. — In Missis privatis sufficit unum habere ministrum, qui gerit personam totius populi catholici, ex cujus persona sacerdoti *pluraliter* respondet (S. Thom. 3, q. 83, a. 5 ad 12.)

[2] Cfr. Gretser, De sancta cruce 1. 3, c. 1—65, in which the kinds, the constant and repeated use, the mysteries and blessings of the sign of the Cross are explained in detail.

[3] In former times it was also made with three or two fingers (in allusion to the Trinity or to the two natures in Christ). The Greeks carry the hand from the right to the left shoulder, as appears to have been practised at the time of Innocent III. († 1216) and generally also in the Roman Church (quia Christus a Judaeis transivit ad Gentes — De sacro alt. myst. 1. 2, c. 45). It is made with the right hand, because the right hand has precedence over the left. Hoc rudis illa liberorum aetas docetur, qui si porrigant sinistram (quippe qui nesciunt quid sit inter dextram et sinistram suam), illico parentes dextram poscunt. The pretty little hand, dicunt Germani (Gretser 1. c. c. 2). — The so-called Latin cross appears to have come into vogue only since the eighth century; previously the Sign of the Cross was usually impressed on the forehead with the thumb, more rarely also on the breast or on the mouth.

Filii et Spiritus sancti. Amen. "In the name of the Father and of the Son and of the Holy Ghost. Amen."

The venerable custom of making the Sign of the Cross over persons and things has, without doubt, its origin from Apostolic times; some even trace it to Christ our Lord Himself who, according to a devout opinion, blessed at His Ascension into heaven the disciples with His hands in the form of a cross.[1] The very ancient use of the Sign of the Cross is proved from the universal testimony of the Fathers and ecclesiastical writers. Tertullian writes at the beginning of the third century: "At every step, in coming in and going out, when putting on our garments and shoes, when washing, when at table, when lighting a candle, on going to bed, when sitting down, at every work we perform, we Christians mark the forehead with the Sign of the Cross" (*frontem crucis signaculo terimus*).[2] — The sign of the Cross forms one of the most important features of the liturgy; for it is employed in the celebration of the Sacrifice, in the administration of the Sacraments, in all exorcisms, consecrations and blessings.

The making of the sign of the Cross, or the signing of one's self with the Cross is a profoundly significant and, at the same time, an efficacious act. — It is first, full of holy mystery, of wholesome instructions and admonitions. The sign of the Cross is a symbolical expression of the principal mysteries of Christianity, a confession of the Catholic faith. It reminds us of the Crucified, of the price of our redemption and of the value of our soul; it enkindles love of God, strengthens hope, animates us to follow Christ on the way of the Cross; it indicates that in the Cross we are to find our honor, our salvation and our life; that we should prefer "the folly and weakness of the Cross" to all the wisdom and power of the world, that, as disciples of the Crucified, we should combat under the banner of the Cross and by this sign triumph over all our enemies. — As to the different meanings inherent in the sign of the Cross, often the one or the other is more clearly pronounced and more emphasized by the accompanying words; for the words and actions of the liturgy harmonize with each other, mutually supply and explain each other. This is also the case in the universally known formula: "In the name of the Father and of the Son and of the Holy Ghost. Amen," which in the plainest manner sets forth the mystery of the Most Holy Trinity symbolized in the sign of the Cross. St. Francis de Sales writes on this subject:[3] "We raise the

---

[1] "Elevatis manibus suis benedixit eis" (Luc. 24, 50) — sc. forsitan signum crucis super eos formando et verba benedictionis aliqua proferendo, ut et ipsi sic facerent aliis (Dion. Carth. i. h. l.). — Potest pie et probabiliter credi Christum non utcunque manus elevasse, sed in signum crucis vel certe in aëre crucem describendo, sicut nunc est in usu Ecclesiae, quem ex apostolica traditione manasse testatur s. Basilius, Liber de Spiritu Sancto c. 37 (Suarez disp. 51, sect. 2, n. 5).

[2] De corona militis c. 3.

[3] L'étendard de la s. croix, liv. 3, ch. 1.

hand first to the forehead, saying: 'In the name of the Father', to signify that the Father is the first person of the Most Holy Trinity, of whom the Son is begotten and from whom the Holy Ghost proceeds. Then saying: 'and the Son,' the hand is lowered to the breast, to express that the Son proceeds from the Father, who sent Him down to the womb of the Virgin. Then the hand is moved from the left shoulder or side to the right, while saying: 'and of the Holy Ghost,' thereby signifying that the Holy Ghost, as the third person of the Holy Trinity, proceeds from the Father and the Son, that He is the love that unites both, and that we, through His grace, partake of the fruits of the Passion. Accordingly, the sign of the Cross is a brief declaration of our faith in the three great mysteries: namely, of our faith in the Blessed Trinity, in the Passion of Christ and in the forgiveness of sin, by which we pass from the left side of curse to the right of blessing. [1]

Exceedingly great, therefore, is the efficacy of the holy Sign of the Cross which, likened by the Fathers to the true Cross of Christ, is not unfrequently termed by them the cause of our salvation. — The Cross is the source of all graces and blessings; it is likewise the weapon and the armor of our defence against the evil spirit; for it is the glorious sign of the victory of Christ over sin, death and hell. [2] Wherefore the Church prays: *Per signum crucis de inimicis nostris libera nos, Deus noster!* and she cries out to the evil spirits: *Ecce crucem Domini, fugite partes adversae* — "Behold the Cross of the Lord, begone ye adverse powers; for the Lion of the tribe of Juda hath overthrown you!" — This superior power, which has ever been ascribed to the Sign of the Cross, depends for its efficacy neither solely, nor mainly on the faith and confidence wherewith it is made, but also, and that principally, on the ordinance of God, who, on account of the honor and merits of the Crucified, has imparted to the Sign of the Cross such salutary efficacy. This efficacy is, of course, the greater and the more meritorious in its results, if it be made with a believing, devout disposition, with recollection of mind and devotion of heart, with love toward the Crucified and with confidence in Christ's death on the Cross. [3]

Certainly it is highly proper that the most sacred act of Sacrifice

---

[1] In signo crucis sanctissimae Trinitatis mysterium, admiranda Verbi divini incarnatio, Christi Domini passio, remissio peccatorum et vita aeterna repraesentantur . . .; sive enim formando crucem proferantur illa verba: "In nomine Patris et Filii et Spiritus Sancti. Amen," sive non proferantur, semper animo mysterium sacrosanctae Trinitatis et incarnationis objicitur (Gretser l. c. c. 4).

[2] Signum crucis diabolo valde formidolosum est (Robert. Paulul. De offic. eccles. 1. 2, c. 20). — Diabolus super omnia abhorret memoriam passionis et figuram crucis, per quam sumus a potestate ejus liberati (S. Bonav. 3, dist. 19, a. 1, q. 3).

[3] Confert ad effectus crucis *pietas* et *probitas operantis:* cum enim signum crucis sit tacita quaedam Christi crucifixi invocatio, sequitur, eo fore efficacius, quo ex majori caritatis fervore processit, sicut et ipsa invocatio, quae corde vel ore perficitur, tanto aptior est ad impetrandum, quanto melior et Deo carior est is, qui invocavit (Gretser l. c. c. 62).

should begin with the equally significant as well as merciful Sign of the Cross. As he invokes the triune God, the priest signs himself with the Sign of the Cross, to express by word and action, that "in the name," that is, by the commission, with the power and the assisting grace of the three divine persons, as well as to promote the honor and glory "of the Father and of the Son and of the Holy Ghost" he intends to celebrate Mass, this mystical representation and renewal of the Sacrifice of the Cross, — to implore for himself at the same time protection and security against the snares of Satan, as well as help and assistance from on high for the devout celebration of the Sacrifice. The concluding word *Amen* has here a twofold meaning: on the one side, it expresses his desire that the petitions included and mentioned in signing himself with the Sign of the Cross may be fulfilled; on the other hand, it confirms and seals the good intention excited within him by the accompanying words in honor of the Most Holy Trinity.

b) *The Antiphon*[1] *of the Forty-second Psalm.* — By this is understood the verse: *Introibo ad altare Dei: ad Deum qui laetificat juventutem meam* — "I will go up to the altar of God: to God who giveth joy to my youth." This verse introduces and concludes the psalm. This antiphon contains the fundamental thought of the aforesaid psalm which should here have the prominent place, and hereby indicates the special point of view in which it is to be taken and recited, that is, it gives the key to the liturgical and mystical understanding of the psalm with regard to its application to the celebration of Mass. It expresses the sentiment which animates the priest: it powerfully attracts him to the altar. He longs to ascend to the altar of God, there to perform his holy office, to draw near to the Lord God and to be united to Him and, by this union with the Eucharistic Saviour, cheerfully and joyfully to be strengthened in the interior life. This longing and desire for the holy place and for the celebration of the Sacrifice is expressed three times.[2] By the

---

[1] Ἀντίφωνος = resounding against, answering replying; hence Ἀντίφωνα = responsive sound, singing opposite, alternate chant. "Antiphona" (= cantus antiphonus) signifies, according to its etymology and original meaning, a singing, in which two choirs deliver separate verses alternately (antiphonatim) and, as it were, respond to each other. Quaedam in Ecclesia canebantur olim alternis vicibus, ut etiam modo fit; alia verbo simul et adunatis choris. Primum canendi modum veteres appellarunt ἀντίφωνον ὑμνωδίαν, alterum σύμφωνον (Praefat. in Antiphon. S. Gregorii M.). At present the name Antiphona is usually employed in another sense; namely, to designate a verse, a sentence or a phrase, by which the psalms and canticles are begun end ended.

[2] *Introibo ad altare Dei*, quod est in ecclesia materiali et manufacta, quatenus sacramenta Christi recipiam oblationemve faciam, nec subsistam in ipso altari, sed *introibo*, mentis affectu et debito cultu, *ad Deum qui laetificat juventutem meam,* non corporalem et exteriorem, sed spiritualem ac interiorem, qui non veterascit cum corpore, sed indesinenter virescit per gratiam, donec ad patriam anima sancta transferatur. Haec ergo *juventus* est spiritualis profectus in gratia Dei; hanc Deus *laetificat,* dum anima corde jucundo et fervido Domino servit (Dion. Carthus. In Ps. 42, 4).

words: "to God who giveth joy to my youth," the priest may, indeed, also acknowledge that from his early days God has been his delight and bestowed on him a thousand joys; but the term youth (*juventus*) is here to be understood first and chiefly of the supernatural and spiritual new life which is obtained by regeneration in the grace of the Holy Ghost. By grace the old man of sin (Rom. 6, 6) is destroyed in us and the newness of life in the Holy Ghost (Col. 3, 9) is created. This life of grace and of spirit, ever young and imperishable, is nourished and refreshed at the altar by the Holy Sacrifice and its banquet. Whoever approaches the altar as a spiritually new-born child, that is, full of holy simplicity, innocence and purity of mind, his youthfulness of spirit, that is, his fervor and cheerfulness in the service of God, or his young (that is still tender, weak) life of grace daily grows and waxes strong under the blessed influence of the Divine Sacrifice and Sacrament. [1]

c) The Forty-second Psalm.

1. Judica me, Deus, et discerne causam meam de gente non sancta, ab homine iniquo et doloso erue me.

1. Judge me, O God, and distinguish my cause from the nation that is not holy, deliver me from the unjust and deceitful man.

2. Quia tu es, Deus, fortitudo mea: quare me repulisti et quare tristis incedo, dum affligit me inimicus?

2. For Thou, O God, art my strength: why hast Thou cast me off? and why go I sorrowful whilst the enemy afflicteth me?

3. Emitte lucem tuam et veritatem tuam: ipsa me deduxerunt et adduxerunt in montem sanctum tuum, et in tabernacula tua.

3. Send forth Thy light and Thy truth: they have led me and brought me unto Thy holy hill, and into Thy tabernacles.

4. Et introibo ad altare Dei: ad Deum, qui laetificat juventutem meam.

4. And I will go in unto the Altar of God: unto God, who giveth joy to my youth.

5. Confitebor tibi in cithara, Deus, Deus meus: quare tristis es, anima mea, et quare conturbas me?

5. I will praise Thee upon the harp, O God, my God: why art thou sad, O my soul? and why dost thou disquiet me?

Spera in Deo, quoniam adhuc confitebor illi: "salutare vultus mei et Deus meus."

Hope thou in God, for I will yet praise Him: "the salvation of my countenance, and my God."

---

[1] Cfr. the Antiphon: Introibo ad altare Dei: sumam Christum qui renovat juventutem meam (In festo corp. Chr.). By means of the sanctifying and blessed effects of the Eucharist "youth," that is, the soul's supernatural life is renewed

This little hymn of David is a prayer petitioning God (v. 1–3), followed by a holy resolution (v. 4), and concluded with an act of resignation and confidence in God (v. 5). It depicts the situation and sentiments of David, who had been driven from Jerusalem by the revolt of Absalom, and was grievously harassed by his enemies. The separation from the holy tabernacle distresses him most of all, and appears to him as a punishment of God; hence he sorrowfully longs after a return to the sanctuary of the Lord. There he will glorify God by sacrifices of praise and thanksgiving; in conclusion he encourages himself to a cheerful confidence in God, to a reliance on prompt assistance.

The principal reason for incorporating this psalm into the prayers recited at the foot of the altar at the beginning of Mass is, without doubt, contained in the fourth verse: *Et introibo ad altare Dei . . . .,*[1] which serves at the same time as an antiphon, that is, gives a pointer to the mystical and ascetical comprehension of the holy hymn in its liturgical position and application. The sorrowful longing, humble fear, touching plaint, joyful hope seek and find an affecting expression in this psalm. Its prominent tone is one of joy and happiness in God; for the expectation of salvation, the fervor of faith and hope triumph at last over every sorrow and sadness — and exult joyously in the *Gloria Patri* and in the repetition of the antiphon *Introibo.*[2]

1. The priest is on the point of ascending the altar: the solemnity of the moment affects him in a lively manner. The world around him is immersed in wickedness, is full of deceit and violence, in his own interior even there is strife, a combat of the spirit against the flesh. Hence he implores God to protect his good and holy cause against a godless and deceitful world; to assist him to come off victorious over the "old man," that is, over the concupiscence of the flesh, over all perverse inclinations and attachments.

---

and refreshed. While the Lord on the altar satisfies your desires with supernatural goods, your youth, your life is renewed in fresh strength, so that, like the eagle, you may take flight heavenward (renovabitur ut aquilae juventus tua — Ps. 102, 5).

[1] This verse is also recited with propriety in those Masses in which the Psalm itself is omitted. The Mozarabic Rite has this Psalm with the Antiphon Introibo in the prayers at the foot of the altar and the Antiphon in addition again before the Illatio (that is, the Preface.) The Milan Liturgy has in the prayer at the foot of the altar merely the Antiphon Introibo without the Psalm Judica.

[2] Antiphona (Introibo) repetitur, ut intellegatur, quanta firmitate et constantia incohandum et prosequendum sit hoc opus intendentibus intrare ad altare Dei ejusque praesentiae assistere, qua renovetur, quod fuerat inveteratum, et restituatur nobis *juventus spiritualis,* quae est *fervor spiritus et laetitia* ex eo oriens, repetitur etiam, ut intellegamus, Missam nec dicendam nec audiendam esse solum ex consuetudine, cum quadam tepiditate, animo abjecto, taedioso ac tristi, quasi grave sit et molestum, tempus in ea re consumere, sed potius audiendam et legendam esse recenti quadam, delectatione et spirituali impulsu, quasi illa esset prima, resistendo taedio spiritus quod tunc aggredi nos audet (De Ponte l. c.).

12

2. The priest is aware of his own weakness; he knows that God alone is his "strength" and "girds him with power" (Ps. 17, 33), that only God's nearness and assistance can avert defeat in this his warfare against enemies within and without. Besides the combats to be sustained against temptations, the passions and daily faults, there are frequently added either as a punishment for sin or as a trial and purification of the soul — the painful apprehension of being abandoned by God; the distressing state of spiritual disgust, dryness and darkness. In such a condition, presenting the strongest and most justifiable reasons for sorrow, all adversaries appear to gather renewed strength; hence the touching plaint: "Why go I sorrowful whilst the enemy afflicteth me?"

3. Still the ray of a bright hope lights up even the darkest night of desolation and anxiety: the priest supplicates the Lord, who imparts to him the blissful light of truth, for grace and devotion; the Lord is his comfort and his guide, who conducts him to the sanctuary, to the mystical Calvary and to the eucharistic tabernacle.

4. Lovely, indeed, are the tabernacles of the Lord of Hosts. Confiding in the mercy of God, the celebrant, cheered and encouraged, will ascend the steps of the altar, where "the Bread of Life" imparts to him an unalterable youth of mind and blissful immortality, fills his whole life with fresh vigor and joy in the Lord, so that "the inward man is renewed day by day, though the outward man be corrupted" (worn out) (2 Cor. 4, 16) by the labors, difficulties and combats of the priestly vocation.

5. Again a feeling of sadness and anxiety is felt, but the strength of holy hope overcomes it all. This hope is not confounding; it shows him in God the source of light, salvation and peace. For all these graces the priest will gratefully praise and glorify the Lord during the day and all the days of his life.

d) The little Doxology[1] as a rule forms, according to ecclesi-

---

[1] Doxologia *minor* vel *parva* (from δόξα and λόγος = speech of praise, formula of glorification), the Gloria Patri is called in distinction from the Gloria in Excelsis, which is called doxologia *major* vel *magna*. Already in Holy Scripture we meet at one time with shorter, and at other times with longer doxologies (Rom. 11, 36; 16, 27. Apoc. 5, 13). In the Fathers we come across a great variety of doxologie formulas, with which, as a rule, they close their homilies. The conclusion of the liturgical prayers and the concluding stanza of the Church hymns are usually a glorification of the triune God. The Gloria Patri occurs in the Responsories of the Nocturns and Hours, at the end of the Psalms and Canticles; we wish thereby to confess the eternal equality of essence of the three Divine Persons, and to glorify and adore the Most Blessed Trinity. The simple Old Testament formula, "God be praised," is accordingly enlarged and transformed in the Gloria Patri to a specifically Christian doxology. The first half of the little doxology is copied from the baptismal formula, and it dates in all probability from apostolic times, but it had previous to the Arian heresy a manifold form or composition (Gloria Patri et Filio cum Spiritu sancto, — vel per Filium in Spiritu sancto). In its present form, with the annex sicut erat . . . . the Gloria Patri was

astical ordinance, the conclusion of the Psalms. It runs thus: *Gloria Patri et Filio et Spiritui sancto, — sicut erat in principio, et nunc, et semper, et in saecula saeculorum. Amen.* — "Glory be to the Father, and to the Son, and to the Holy Ghost. As it was in the beginning, is now, and ever shall be, world without end. Amen." By these sublime words we acknowledge, in union with the angels and saints of heaven, the truth of the adorable mystery of the Trinity — the unity of essence and the Three Persons in the Trinity — expressing at the same time our profound homage, the highest praise, the most joyful thanks, the most faithful and efficacious love towards the Most Holy Trinity. Many other praises, consecrated by their origin and by custom, ascend daily and hourly from earth to Heaven. The sublime *Gloria in excelsis* in the Mass, the marvelous, soul-stirring *Te Deum*, the incomparable *Magnificat*, the thrice repeated *Sanctus*, the joyful *Benedictus*, the many beautiful chants of the Psalter, the numerous touching Church hymns and canticles: what sublime, ravishing, heaven-penetrating praises of God! But they all are but the development of the brief, yet comprehensive *Gloria Patri*. The most genial Christian thinker, the most celebrated theologian can discover nothing greater or higher than what the most simple Christian stammers daily in the few words of the *Gloria Patri*. What lofty sentiments, what devotion and enthusiasm should there not be awakened in me by the reflection! Not I alone repeat this *Gloria Patri et Filio et Spiritui sancto*; but millions of brethren are at this moment offering the homage of their hearts to the infinitely great God in the self-same words![1] — When we say *Gloria Patri*, we bow the head as a sign of that reverence due the infinite majesty and greatness of God, as well as in acknowledgment of our own lowliness and unworthiness. As this manner of praise expresses and calls to mind the final object of all sacrifices and prayers, that is, the glorification of the triune God, it is advisable when reciting it to recollect one's self anew, to

---

quoted for the first time at the Second Council of Vaison (529), and that with the remark that it was thus, as a general thing, everywhere recited. The addition sicut erat in principio, expressing the eternal equality and unity of essence of the Son with the Father, is a protest against the heresy of Arius, and thus, in consequence of the combat against this heresy in the West, it has found universal acceptance; for the Greeks do not make use of it. — In the fifth and sixth centuries the custom was introduced everywhere in the West of concluding each separate Psalm with the little doxology. Quoniam psalmorum usus antiquior est quam lex gratiae, ut propriam ejus perfectionem participaret, et ita fieret (ut ita dicam) psalmus consummatus, non sine speciali Dei providentia factum est, ut ex institutione Ecclesiae in fine uniscujusque psalmi adderetur Trinitatis confessio et glorificatio per illa verba: Gloria Patri . . . (Suarez, De religione tr. IV, 1. 4, c. 2, n. 4). — According to an ordinance of the Fourth Council of Toledo (633) the little doxology in the Mozarabic Liturgy is as follows: Gloria et honor (cfr. Ps. 28, 2) Patri et Filio et Spiritui sancto in saecula saeculorum. Amen. (Cfr. Lüft, Liturgik II, 81 etc. — Augsburger Pastoralblatt, Jahrg, 1863, S. 290 etc.)

[1] Cf. Martin, Die Schönheiten des Rosenkranzes, S. 59 ff.

renew and enliven the good intention, our attention and fervor. This chant of praise should not only ascend heavenward from our heart and lips, but it ought, moreover, to form the motto of our whole life: all our thoughts, intentions and efforts, all our actions and our conduct, our life, our death should be a joyful and grateful *Gloria Patri et Filio et Spiritui sancto*, so that "the charity of God (the Father) and the grace of our Lord Jesus Christ and the communication of the Holy Ghost may be with us all" (2. Cor. 13, 13). *Spes nostra, salus nostra, honor noster, O beata Trinitas!* — "Our hope, our salvation, our honor art Thou, O most blessed Trinity!" "When you repeat the Glory be to the Father," writes St. Alphonsus, [1] "you may make various mental aspirations, for example, acts of faith and thanksgiving, of joy at the felicity of God, and of desire to honor Him and to suffer for His honor and glory. As often as St. Mary Magdalen de Pazzi recited the 'Gloria Patri,' she made the intention, at every inclination of the head, to offer it to our Lord as a sacrifice of herself for the holy faith; and this practice she followed with so much fervor, that at times she would grow pale, because it so impressed her, as though she were really about to be beheaded."

The *Gloria Patri* with the Psalm *Judica* is omitted in all Requiem Masses and in all the Passiontide Masses from Passion Sunday to Holy Saturday. On Holy Saturday, "the great and holy Sabbath," the Sacrifice formerly was not celebrated; now the Mass of the Resurrection night is anticipated on that day, and the Forty-second Psalm is resumed, as the celebration really no longer properly belongs to Passiontide. The reason for its omission is justly founded on the contents of the Psalm, and on the character of the Masses. For this Psalm seeks to banish sorrow and sadness from the soul (*quare tristis es, anima mea, et quare conturbas me?*), to awaken a joyful mood in him who prays; therefore, it is proper to omit the Psalm at a time when the heart should be penetrated with profound sorrow, painful sadness and intense compassion, as is supposed to prevail in Requiem Masses and the Masses of Passiontide. [2]

2) The central and chief part of the prayers said at the foot of the altar is composed of the *Confiteor*, which is introduced by a passage from the Psalm (Ps. 123, 8) and is concluded by what is known as the *Absolution*.

a) The verse: *Adjutorium nostrum in nomine Domini — qui fecit coelum et terram* — "Our help is in the name of the Lord, — who made heaven and earth," at which the priest signs himself with the sign of the Cross, may be regarded as a transition, that is, as referring as well to what precedes as to what follows. In connection with the desire and purpose previously expressed of drawing

---

[1] The true Spouse of Christ, c. 24, § 3.

[2] The Carthusians, Dominicans and Carmelites never use the Psalm Judica in the prayers at the foot of the altar (cf. Romsée, Oper. liturg. IV, p. 353 sqq.).

nigh to the Lord on the altar and of applying the mind to the Holy Sacrifice, it signifies that in carrying out this purpose we depend on and confide in the unlimited power and goodness of God. For since we are deeply conscious of our nothingness, our weakness and unworthiness, our unwavering hope in and our longing for the Holy Sacrifice are founded solely on the power and love of God, who has created us, as well as on the mercies and merits of Christ, who died on the Cross for us and acquired for us all the helps of grace, as we intimate in signing ourselves with the Cross. Our misery is so great that, of our own strength, we cannot even think anything conducive to our salvation, and without the grace of the Holy Ghost we cannot even pronounce worthily the holy name of Jesus (2 Cor. 3, 5; 12, 3); how much more will we have need of help from on high, and of a greater and more powerful assistance, in order that we may worthily and meritoriously discharge the most sublime and holy function — the Sacrifice of the Mass!

However, if the verse of the Psalm be considered as an introduction or transition to the *Confiteor* which follows, then it means that the Almighty alone can relieve our poverty and misery, and remit our sins and the punishment due to them — and that we may with confidence expect favor and pardon, "because with the Lord there is mercy and with Him plentiful redemption" (Ps. 129, 7), which issues forth on the Cross of Christ and which flows unto us from the Cross (sign of the Cross). [1]

b) *The general confession of sins (Confiteor).* — At the foot of the altar the priest is incited to humble, contrite self-accusation and to earnest supplication for the forgiveness of all sins. Only he who "is innocent in hands and clean of heart" (*innocens manibus et mundo corde*), may approach the altar, "go up to the mountain of the Lord and stand in His holy place" (Ps. 23, 3–4). In order worthily to represent here "the High Priest Jesus Christ, the holy, innocent, undefiled, separated from sinners and made higher than the heavens" (Heb. 7, 26), the priest should be adorned with all blamelessness, purity and sanctity of life. But despite his careful preparation, he knows and feels himself to be still far removed from such purity. The dignity, the knowledge and the fulness of grace bestowed upon him also aggravates in him slight sins and infidelities of which he may be guilty in the service of God; light faults and negligences become grave evils in his eyes, when he weighs them in the scales of the sanctuary, and even "for sins forgiven he is not without fear." [2] *Quo magis pius in me Dominus, tanto magis ego*

---

[1] In like manner the Adjutorium nostrum . . . . is placed before the Confiteor of Prime and Complin. With this petition the Church begins all her blessings: for for she would thereby humbly and gratefully confess the Almighty Creator as the fountain and source of all blessing and salvation, while the Sign of the Cross then made refers to the merits of the death of Christ, for the sake of which all gifts are imparted to us. In the Psalms and at Prime after the lectio brevis the Sign of the Cross is not made at this verse.

[2] De propitiato peccato noli esse sine metu (Eccli. 5, 5).

impius! Hence he has every reason, before beginning the great act of Sacrifice, an act filling the very angels even with admiration, reverence and awe, to make a public confession of guilt, to approach the altar only in the spirit of the deepest sorrow and compunction, and to implore heavenly and earthly intercession.

Confiteor Deo omnipotenti, beatae Mariae semper Virgini, beato Michaeli Archangelo, beato Joanni Baptistae, sanctis Apostolis Petro et Paulo, omnibus Sanctis, et vobis fratres: quia peccavi nimis cogitatione, verbo et opere: (*percutit sibi pectus ter, dicens*) mea culpa, mea culpa, mea maxima culpa. Ideo precor beatam Mariam semper Virginem, beatum Michaelem Archangelum, beatum Joannem Baptistam, sanctos Apostolos Petrum et Paulum, omnes Sanctos, et vos fratres, orare pro me ad Dominum Deum nostrum.

I confess to almighty God, to blessed Mary ever Virgin, to blessed Michael the Archangel, to blessed John Baptist, to the holy Apostles Peter and Paul, to all the saints, and to you, brethren, that I have sinned exceedingly, in thought, word and deed, (*here he strikes his breast three times, saying*) through my fault, through my fault, through my most grievous fault. Therefore I beseech the blessed Mary, ever Virgin, blessed Michael the Archangel, blessed John Baptist, the holy Apostles Peter and Paul, all the saints, and you, brethren, to pray to the Lord our God for me.

The *Confiteor* is an open avowal of compunction of heart, a contrite and penitential prayer which should cleanse the soul from even the slightest stains of guilt and from all sinful defects.[1] But in order that its recital, together with the threefold striking of the breast, may prove cleansing and salutary to the soul, it must in truth be the outpouring of a contrite spirit, proceeding from the depths of a heart touched with love and sorrow.[2]

---

[1] The Confiteor with the tunsio pectoris may not in a real, but only in a more general sense be called a Sacramental, having power to cancel venial sins. While the devout use of the real Sacramentals (for example, the holy water) impetrates, in virtue of the prayer and blessing of the Church, the dispositions required for the forgiveness of venial sins (for example, sentiments of compunction, affections of love and sorrow), the confessio generalis and tunsio pectoris contribute towards the freeing from venial sins, only in as far as they include the acts of penance, sorrow, love and humility by which the just obtain remission of venial sins.

[2] *Summa sollicitudine providendum est, ne tale officium sine actuali et fervida devotione inchoetur.* Nam virtus principii in his, quae sequuntur, relucet ac permanet, et modicus defectus in principio, magnus efficitur in processu. Debet ergo confessionem ante altare cum magna attentione facere sacerdos, non ex consuetudine arida, ut exterior humiliatio corporis et tunsio pectoris vera sint signa interioris humiliationis atque mentalis redargutionis sui ipsius. Debet etiam cordialiter

The *Confiteor* is divided into two clearly distinct parts: for it contains an acknowledgment of sin, as well as a petition to the blessed and the faithful to intercede in our behalf with the Lord our God. The confession of guilt is made not only before Almighty God, but also in presence of the blessed in heaven and the faithful upon earth. Before them, we humble and debase ourselves, and chiefly, that they may be the better disposed to become by their powerful intercession and mediation, which we afterward implore, our support before God and our help to obtain from Him more perfect pardon.[1] In every Mass the intercession of the saints is repeatedly invoked, and God is besought for grace with confidence in their prayers and merits. "God has wished that we should pray to the saints and they should pray for us, in order that the faint-hearted may gain confidence to receive through worthy intercessors that which they do not dare ask of themselves or could not obtain by their own prayers; and so that humility may be preserved in those who pray, the dignity of the saints be made manifest, and finally, that in all the members of the body of Christ love and unity may be revealed, so that the lower creatures may confidently look up to those higher placed and implore their assistance, and these latter in return may in all love and kindness condescend unto them."[2] It is in the divine economy that[3] the saints be our helpers, protectors and intercessors; and they are to be regarded as such especially when we poor sinners, conscious of our unworthiness and weakness, desire to approach the throne of the Almighty, in order to be delivered from the misery of sin. Therefore, it is highly proper that we humble ourselves by self-accusation before the saints in heaven, as well as in presence of the faithful on earth and implore their

---

affectare, ut alii orent pro se, et per preces aliorum auxilium sibi affuturum sperare, pie atque humiliter credens alios meliores et apud Deum magis auditos quam se (Dion. Carthus. Expos. Miss. art. 7).

[1] Debet unusquisque orationes aliorum humiliter ac ferventer appetere et eos ut pro se orent rogare. Quo enim alios humilius atque ferventius ut pro nobis orent rogamus, eo capaciores efficimur fructus orationis illorum (Dion. Carthus. In ep. Jac. 5, 16).

[2] S. Bonav. Brevil. V, 10.

[3] Deus decrevit et voluit, quod Sanctos rogaremus, triplici ex causa, sc. propter *nostram inopiam, Sanctorum gloriam et Dei reverentiam.* — Propter *inopiam* in *merendo*, ut ubi nostra non suppeterent merita, patrocinentur aliena; propter inopiam in *contemplando*, ut qui non possumus summam lucem aspicere in re, aspiciamus in Sanctis; propter inopiam in *amando*, quia miser homo se magis sentit affici circa unum Sanctum quam etiam circa Deum. Ideo compassus *nostrae inopiae* voluit, nos rogare Sanctos. — Secunda causa est *Sanctorum gloria:* quia Deus vult Sanctos suos glorificare, vult per eos miracula facere in corporibus et salutem in animabus, ut ipsos laudemus, et hoc non tantum per supremos Sanctos, sed etiam infimos; unde sicut aliquis sanatur corporaliter invocando Linum et non Petrum, alius e converso; sic et spiritualiter. — Tertia causa est *Dei reverentia*, ut peccator, qui Deum offendit, quasi non audeat Deum in propria persona adire, sed amicorum patrocinium implorare (S. Bonav. IV, dist. 45, a. 3, q. 3).

mediation with God. Besides the saints whose names are mentioned in the *Confiteor*, no others are to be expressly named without the sanction of the Holy See. [1]

a) *The Blessed Mary ever Virgin*, Mother of God, is always named in the Liturgy in the first place — before all the angels and saints, — and her name which, after the name of Jesus, is the sweetest, the most powerful and the most holy, is invariably distinguished by some honorable title which celebrates and expresses her ineffable privileges of grace and glory, chiefly her incomparable virginity and her dignity of the Divine Maternity. For us Mary is the "Mother of Divine grace," "the Mother of mercy," "the Refuge of Sinners," "our dear Lady, our Mediatrix, our Intercessor," "our Life, our Sweetness and our Hope;" "she obtains for us the clemency of the Father at Christ's throne of grace," and "as the Mother of divine clemency she imparts salvation to her servants," for "God has taken her out of this world, that she may stand before His throne in heaven, an unfailing intercessor in behalf of us poor sinners."

b) *The blessed Michael the Archangel.* [2] The angels have their position in the liturgy immediately after their Queen, Mary the Mother of God, and hence before all the saints. They constitute in God's creation a marvellously glorious, brilliant kingdom; they are sublime spirits, full of wisdom and power, full of splendor and beauty. As children of the same Heavenly Father, they are also our brethren and they form along with us one family of God. They take a manifold, active part in the work of redemption, in the preservation and extension of the Church of God, as well as in her combats and victories; themselves not in need of redemption, they are altogether ministering spirits, sent to minister for them who shall receive the inheritance of salvation (Heb. 1, 14): consequently, they rejoice over the conversion of sinners and over the perseverance of the just (Luke 15, 7). — St. Michael is one of the three angels whose name and deeds Holy Scripture records, and he is, indeed, the chief of all the heavenly spirits, the prince of the angelic hosts, the leader of all the choirs of angels. [3] He is the angelic warrior,

---

[1] Some religious orders have the privilege of mentioning the name of their founder after the Princes of the Apostles. (Cf. S. R. C. 13. Febr. 1666.)

[2] The name *Archangelus* (Archangel) does not denote that Michael belongs to the second last order of the Angels, who are thus called, but that he (as Gabriel and Raphael) in the rank of the Angels in general occupies a higher place, that is, is placed above the lowest orders of mere Angels. (Cf. de la Cerda S. J., De excellentia coelestium spirituum c. 49).

[3] In the Office of the Church St. Michael is called princeps gloriosissimus, princeps militiae Angelorum, praepositus paradisi. Michael dicitur Archangelus, non quod sit de ordine Archangelorum, sed quia omnium Angelorum caput et dux est (Molanus, De histor. ss. Imag. 1. 3, c. 39). — Multi jam valde probabiliter censent, Michaelem tum naturae, tum gratiae et gloriae dignitate esse absolute primum et principem omnium omnino Angelorum (Cornel. a Lapide, in Daniel. c. 10).

who handles the sword of the power and of the justice of God; he hurls the rebellious spirits into the abyss, and he still continues to battle victoriously with the old dragon of hell and his adherents in behalf of the Church and of individual souls. [1] In the Old Law he was the protector of the Synagogue, and now he is the defender of the Church and of the reigning Pontiff. In the Middle Age, that age of faith, the valiant Archangel was highly honored by noble and peasant as the guardian and patron of the German nation. Many churches bear his name, and in his honor two feasts are celebrated (May 8th and September 29th.)

c) *Blessed John the Baptist* [2] is the glorious precursor of our Lord, the mighty preacher of penance in the desert, the greatest prophet, yea more than a prophet (Matt. 11, 9), since "with his finger he pointed Him out, who taketh away the sins of the world, while the other seers, with prophetic spirit, merely predicted the Light of the World that was to appear" (Hymn. Eccles.). The Church celebrates the holy and glad day of his birth (June 24), as well as his saintly and glorious martyrdom (August 29). [3]

---

[1] Cf. Stengelius O. S. B., S. Michaelis principatus, apparitiones, templa, cultus et miracula.

[2] Cf. Medini, De s. Joannis Bapt. relativa dignitate et sanctitate. Venetiis 1890. — Bazy, S. Jean-Baptiste. Paris 1880.

[3] Since St. John the Baptist stands in the middle, between the Old and the New Law — terminus Legis et initium Evangelii (S. Thom. 3, qu. 38, a. 1 ad 2), he is considered at one time to belong to the Old, at another to the New Testament. It would in all probability be more correct to place him (with St. Thomas, Suarez, Guyet, Benedict XIV. and others) in the New Dispensation. Joannes pertinet ad *novum* Testamentum (S. Thom. 2, 2, qu. 174, a. 4 ad 3). "Since the peculiarity of the Old Dispensation consists in the expectation of the promised Messiah, then must he who not merely expects the Redeemer, but beholds Him present, be considered to appertain not to the Old, but to the New Testament," writes Suarez. (Cf. disp. 24, sect. 6, n. 3-4.) — St. Joseph is not named in the Confiteor and in some other formulas in which the names of several saints are given. A reason for this may be found in the fact that the liturgical veneration of the holy Patriarch was not developed until later on, while the formulas of prayer in question originated at an earlier epoch. This later and gradual growth of the Church's devotion to St. Joseph, harmonizes wonderfully with his mysteriously hidden and retired life. At present he is honored as the Patron of the Universal Church, and shines as a resplendent constellation in the firmament of the Saints. Suarez affirms as a devout and established opinion, that the Foster-Father of Christ and the Spouse of the blessed Virgin excelled all the other Saints — therefore, even St. John the Baptist and the Apostles — in grace and glory (disp. 8, sect. 2, n. 5-6). In the Litany of the Saints "St. Joseph, consequently, is named after John the Baptist, because the latter is a martyr; while he is mentioned before the Apostles, because he is a Patriarch" (Benedict. XIV. De beatif. l. 4, p. 2, c. 20, n. 48). By the established order of names in the Litany, as well as by the distinction of feasts and their celebration, the Church does not intend to decide and pronounce judgment with regard to the greatness, that is, the difference of grace, of merit and of glory of the individual saints. To the question: Quis erat melior, utrum Petrus an Joannes? the seraphic doctor replies: Quis eorum apud Deum finaliter fuerit

d) The holy Apostles Peter and Paul. St. Peter was the representative and vicegerent of Christ upon earth, endowed with the highest power and dignity, to open to the sheep and lambs of the Lord the pastures and the holy fountains of life (*Vitae recludit pascua et fontes sacros* — Hymn. Eccles.). — St. Paul was Christ's chosen instrument for the propagation of the Gospel, the teacher of the nations, the apostle of the world and the ideal of an Apostle in his labors and sufferings. In the liturgy the names of the two princes of the Apostles are inseparably connected with each other. "Glorious princes of the earth," sings the Church, "as their mutual love joined them together in life, so in death they were not separated from each other!"

The position of the body corresponds to the meaning of the *Confiteor* and serves, on the one side, to express, after a perfect manner, the interior penitential disposition, and, on the other hand, to intensify it and stimulate it the more. The profound inclination of the body, the joining of the hands and the striking of the breast,[1] all betoken that humble position and disposition of a poor sinner who, laden with sin and full of compunction, stands before His Judge to implore grace and mercy. — The priest does not presume to raise his eyes to Heaven, but in deep confusion and profoundly inclined, he casts them to the earth, debasing himself before the offended Majesty of God, since he is but dust and ashes (Gen. 18, 27). — The joining of the hands indicates recollection of mind and a spirit of devotion, the surrendering of one's self up to God and a repose in God, the mistrust of one's own strength and a confident supplication for grace and mercy. — The striking of the breast, that is, of the sinful heart, is a very natural symbolical sign of a penitential spirit: it includes a sincere acknowledgment of guilt, of sorrow and displeasure for sin committed, the will to make satisfaction and to undergo punishment for sin heartily repented of.[2] The striking of the breast means that the heart concealed within is the cause of sin and deserving, therefore, to be punished, bruised and humbled;[3]

---

carior, hoc melius sciemus in gloria et melius est expectare, quam hic temere definire. Hoc tantum dixisse sufficiat, quia ille altior est in coelis, qui finaliter majorem caritatem habuit in terris et hoc dico quantum ad magnitudinem *praemii substantialis.* Nam quantum ad *decorem aureolae,* quae respondet continentiae virginali, non est inconveniens, Joannem (Evangelistam) Petro praeponi (S. Bonav. III, dist. 32, q. 6).

[1] This threefold gesture is beautifully expressed in the Dies irae: Oro supplex (= joining of the hands) et acclinis (= profund inclination of the body), cor contritum quasi cinis (= striking of the breast).

[2] Tunsio pectoris 1. symbolum est *confessionis* peccati, quod scilicet confitens fateatur peccati sui causam non esse aliam quam cor, appetitum et voluntatem suam in pectore latentem; 2. eadem est symbolum *contritionis,* indicat enim, cor esse contusum et contritum; 3. eadem symbolum est *satisfactionis* et *vindictae,* percutit enim pectus, ut illud reum affligat et puniat (Cornel. a Lapide, in Luc. 18, 13).

[3] Pectus percutimus, signantes videlicet, quod nequiter egimus, displicere nobis, ac ideo antequam Deus feriat, id nos in nobis ipsis ferire, et antequam ultio

that the insolent pride of the sinful heart is to be broken and destroyed, in order that God may create a new, clean heart within the penitent breast.—The striking of the breast three times signifies, in general, the intensity, the sincerity and the vehemence of our contrition ; in a stricter sense it may be understood as the suitable accompaniment and confirmation of guilt thrice acknowledged, each time with increased fervor (*mea culpa, mea culpa, mea maxima culpa*), and it may, moreover, be referred to the three kinds of sin (in thought, word and deed) of which we accuse ourselves. [1]

c) The forgiveness of guilt is dependent upon the acknowledgment of the sin: "I have acknowledged my sin to Thee (O God), and my injustice I have not concealed. I said: 'I will confess against myself my injustice to the Lord,' and Thou hast forgiven the wickedness of my sin." (Ps. 31, 5). The priest has publicly acknowledged, and in a most humble posture, his guiltiness not merely before God, but also before the angels, the saints and the faithful, to move them to intercede with God for him, and thus by means of joint supplication the more readily to obtain his forgiveness. [2] Those present accede to his desires and they beg for him by the mouth of the server mercy and favor (*Misereatur*). — Then the server also in the name of the faithful recites the *Confiteor*, that they, too, by the intercession of the saints and of the priest may obtain favor, that is, be cleansed from the guilt of sin in order to have a share in the fruits of the Holy Sacrifice. After the *Confiteor* of the server, the priest likewise intercedes for the faithful, in pronouncing the formula known as the *Absolution*, [3] which is as follows:

---

extrema veniat, commissum poenitentia digna punire (Nicolaus I. ad consulta Bulgar. n. 54). — Tunsio pectoris obtritio (a crushing) cordis (S. Aug. Enarr. II. in Ps. 31, n. 11. — Cfr. in Ps. 141, n. 19. — in Ps. 137, n. 2. — Sermo 67, n. 1).

[1] Cum vice quadam (S. Mechtildis) ad Missam iret, vidit Dominum de coelo in candidissima veste descendentem et dicentem: Cum homines ad ecclesiam properant, poenitentia, pectoris tunsione et confessione se deberent praeparare; sic meae divinae claritati possent obviare, et eam in se recipere, quae per hujus vestis candorem declaratur (S. Mechtild. Lib. special. grat. p. 3, c. 19).

[2] "Confess, therefore, your sins one to another; and pray for one another, that you may be saved; for the continual prayer of a just man availeth much" (James, 5, 16).

[2] *Absolutio* — the principal signification of this word is, on the one hand, freeing and acquittal; on the other, conclusion and completion. It often occurs in the liturgy, and is not always easy of explanation. Thus in Matins certain formulas of prayer after the Psalms and before the Lessons are called *absolutiones*, either ab *absoluta* prece, that is, as conclusion of the Psalmody, or because the name was transferred from the third formula (A vinculis peccatorum nostrorum *absolvat* nos . . . Domine), which contains a petition for the cleansing of the heart, to the two others. — The intercessions, made at the catafalque (or tomb) for the departed by prayers and Sacramentals, are also called *absolutio*, as they seek to obtain the deliverance of the suffering souls from the pains of purgatory, and usually conclude with the prayer *Absolve*. — The expression ad *absolutionem*

Misereatur vestri omnipotens Deus, et dimissis peccatis vestris, perducat vos ad vitam aeternam. Amen.

(Signat se signo crucis, dicens:)

Indulgentiam, absolutionem et remissionem peccatorun nostrorum, tribuat nobis omnipotens et misericors Dominus. Amen.

May Almighty God be merciful unto you, and, forgiving you your sins, bring you to life everlasting. Amen.

(Making the sign of the Cross, he says:)

May the Almighty and merciful Lord grant us pardon, absolution, and remission of our sins. Amen.

The priest accordingly prays,[1] that God would deign by virtue of His almighty power (*omnipotens*) to impart to the faithful the fulness of His mercy (*misereatur*), forgive all their sins (*dimissis peccatis*) and thus raise them up from spiritual death to the life of grace, and conduct them to the eternal life hereafter (*perducat vos ad vitam aeternam*).

Then the "almighty" Lord, who "reveals His power most gloriously by sparing the sinner and by exercising mercy," and the "merciful" Lord, "whose property it is always to show mercy and to spare," is again implored to grant us all (*nobis*) His gracious favor and kind forgiveness, the full remission of sin (*indulgentiam*), that is, absolution of guilt (*absolutionem*) and remission of punishment due (*remissionem*).[2] — The accompanying sign of the Cross indicates Christ's atoning sacrificial death, from which flows unto us all forgiveness of sin.

Profoundly significant and well established is the connection apparent in many prayers of the Church between the power and the mercy of God (*omnipotens et misericors Dominus*); for upon God's absolute fulness of power are based His unbounded mercy, clemency,

---

capituli, which is still found in Prime before the lectio brevis, probably signifies that in ancient times, "at the close of the assembly for chapter" after the foregoing prayers, a spiritual reading was made in convents and that the supplement or second part of Prime — the so-called officium *capituli*, not held in the choir but in the chapter-room — was concluded by a short lecture.

[1] The deprecative formula Misereatur and Indulgentiam is designated in the Ordo Missae by the name Absolutio. But in this place it does not mean a judicial absolution, but only an intercessory prayer, a petition, a desire for God to remit sins; hence this Absolutio must be carefully distinguished from the Absolutio *sacramentalis*, which in those who are properly disposed infallibiliter et ex opere operato effaces and removes sin. But the above deprecatory formula is said before the sacramental absolution, in order to dispose the penitent for the reception of the sacramental grace.

[2] The words indulgentia, remissio are often used synonymously; combined they doubtless denote more forcibly the full remission of sin. An attempt has been made and can be made to distinguish more minutely their respective meaning; but a well founded basis for this distinction is wanting.

compassion, mildness and longanimity toward His sinful creatures. "God has mercy upon all, because He can do all things," because, "being Lord of all, He makes Himself gracious to all;" "as Master of power He judges with tranquillity and with great favor disposes of us" and "He spares all, because all are His." [1] — God's mercy is proved in relieving our wants, frailties and shortcomings, in delivering or preserving us from the misery and the evil of sin. All this God can do, because He is almighty, because His power is without end and without bounds. Yes, God's power is principally manifested in the exercise of His mercy, whereby He comes to the assistance of His weak and needy creature. The conversion and justification of the sinner, the production of sanctifying grace in the soul, is, in a certain sense, a greater work than the creation of heaven and earth, — hence a glorious work of divine power. [2] "In accordance with the greatness of God is, therefore, His mercy" (Eccli. 2, 23). "God is rich in pardoning and in displaying His bounty; for His mercy is almighty and His omnipotence is merciful; so great is the goodness of His omnipotence and the omnipotence of His goodness, that there is no guilt that He will not or cannot pardon to one who is converted to Him." [3]

3. The conclusion of the prayer at the foot of the altar is made up of two orations, which are introduced by some verses of the Psalms. The priest recites these concluding prayers in silence, the one while ascending the steps of the altar, the other after reaching it; he says them specially for himself, [4] to obtain of God the grace of perfect cleanliness and purity of heart for the worthy celebration of the most holy Sacrifice.

a) Sin disturbs all peace in life and vitiates all the sources of joy; therefore, there is no greater happiness nor sweeter consolation than to be delivered from the evil and burden of sin. By mutual intercessory prayer hope of pardon gains new strength and is uppermost, but the consciousness of sinfulness has not as yet entirely left the celebrant; therefore, he recites the verses of the Psalms [5] which

---

[1] Misereris omnium, *quia omnia potes.* — Ob hoc, quod omnium Dominus es, omnibus te parcere facis. — Tu autem Dominator virtutis, cum tranquillitate judicas, et cum magna reverentia disponis nos: subest enim tibi, cum volueris posse. — Parcis autem omnibus, quoniam tua sunt, Domine, qui amas animas (Sapient. 11, 24; 12, 16–18; 11–27).

[2] S. Thom. 1, 2. q. 113, a. 9.

[3] *Multus est* (Deus) *ad ignoscendum* (He forgives often and much). (Is. 55, 7). — In hoc multo nihil deest, in quo *et omnipotens misericordia* et *omnipotentia misericors est.* Tanta est autem et benignitas omnipotentiae et omnipotentia benignitatis in Deo, ut *nihil* sit quod nolit aut non possit relaxare converso (S. Fulgent. Epist. 7, ad Venantium n. 6).

[4] That both of these prayers refer to the celebrant only is apparent from not only their being recited in silence, but also their wording or contents, for the first treats of the entrance into the "Holy of holies" of the New Testament which is the privilege of priests only, and the second implores the forgiveness of all sins for the celebrant (indulgere digneris omnia peccata *mea*). Cf. Lebrun p. 1, a. 7.

[5] Ps. 84, 7–8; 101, 2.

follow the *"Absolution,"* no longer as he did the *Confiteor*, with a profound but with a middling or moderate inclination of the body, which at the same time expresses both confidence and reverence.

V. Deus tu conversus vivificabis nos.

R. Et plebs tua laetabitur in te.

V. Ostende nobis, Domine, misericordiam tuam.

R. Et salutare tuum da nobis.

V. Domine, exaudi orationem meam.

R. Et clamor meus ad te veniat.

V. Thou, O God, being turned toward us, wilt enliven us.

R. And Thy people will rejoice in Thee.

V. Show us, O Lord, Thy mercy.

R. And grant us Thy salvation.

V. O Lord, hear my prayer.

R. And let my cry come unto Thee.

God is irritated and turns away from us, when we sin; but if we repent and acknowledge our guilt, He again favorably turns toward us, giving back to us His grace and mercy (*Deus tu conversus*), as the Living God, as the Giver of life, from whom we draw anew joyful courage and fresh life (*vivificabis nos*). — After receiving fuller reconciliation with God and a more abundant life of grace from Him, the heart finds its peace, joy and felicity in God, it rejoices and exults in God, its Saviour (*et plebs tua laetabitur in te*). This joy which we experience in the possession of present happiness, as well as in the prospect of future glory, is still imperfect and incomplete, indeed; for we shall be filled with a glorified and an unspeakable joy only in the next life; there our happiness shall be perfect, and no one shall take it away from us (John 17, 13).

In order that we may attain this happy end, we beg our Lord that He deign to extend to us His mercy and to let it rule over us (*ostende nobis, Domine, misericordiam tuam*); to send us our salvation, that is, Jesus, our Light and our Life on the altar (*salutare tuum da nobis*). It was after this salvation from God, that is, after the Saviour, that the saints of the Old Law yearned, for they saw and saluted the promises only from a distance (Heb. 11, 13). More privileged, far happier are the children of the Church, for they can daily hasten to the altars of the Lord, and thence draw and drink to their hearts' content from the perennial living fountains of the Saviour.

Before the priest ascends the steps of the altar, he expresses the desire that all his petitions, supplications and cries for help may find their way to the ears of God and be answered by Him. A holy vehemence, devout impetuosity and an ardent fervor of heart is a powerful voice (*clamor*), penetrating to the throne of God and drawing down the fulness of heavenly blessings.[1]

---

[1] Frigus caritatis, silentium cordis est; *flagrantia caritatis, clamor cordis.* Si

b) To the above verse from the Psalms is annexed the salutation: *Dominus vobiscum* — "The Lord be with you" — *Et cum
Spiritu tuo*—"And with thy spirit," and this immediately introduces
the two concluding orations of the prayers said at the foot of the
altar. This mutual salutation between the priest and people is
frequently repeated during the celebration of Mass.[1] Both as to its
meaning and partly as to its wording it is taken from Holy Scripture;
and because of its beautiful, profound signification it was not only
received at an early date into the liturgy of the West, but is also
frequently used. — When the priest says: "The Lord be with you"
— he desires and prays, in virtue of his mediatorial office, that God
would especially bless and favor those whom he addresses with this
salutation, that He would graciously dwell, act, and reign in them,
and impart to them His powerful help and assistance. This explains
why the priest so often repeats these words in the Mass. For the
grace of the Lord is the first requisite for the worthy celebration of
the Holy Sacrifice. But since this action needs constant grace, there
is need of constant and earnest prayer for this grace. Therefore, in
the course of the Mass, the priest repeatedly desires that God may
be with those who assist at the Holy Sacrifice, and, on the other
hand, those present wish that "the Lord may be with his spirit."—
This salutation includes all the good that the Church can desire for
her children. Where the Lord is, there He is present with His
truth and grace, with His favor and help, with His love and His
mercy, with His blessing and peace. To have Him with us who is
our God, our Creator, our Redeemer, our Comforter, our felicity and
supreme good and last end, our one and all, — what can be better,
greater, more full of bliss? If we bear this in mind, then will it
become clear to us, why the Church during the Holy Sacrifice so

---

semper manet caritas, semper clamas (S. Aug. Enarr. in Ps. 37, n. 14). — Deus non
vocis, sed cordis auditor est; nec admonendus est clamoribus, qui cogitationes
hominum videt (S. Cyprian. De Orat. domin. c. 4). — *Clamor meus* — sc. mentalis,
i. e. ardens affectio desideriumque coeleste; seu clamor vocalis, qui est magni ac
sancti desiderii nuntius — *ad te veniat* — tibi acceptus sit, tibi complaceat, et
attendatur ac impleatur a te; venit enim clamor noster ad Dominum non loco, sed
acceptatione (Dion. Carthus. in Ps. 101).

[1] This formula of salutation in the present rite of the Mass does not occur
seven times, as is often erroneously asserted, but eight times. The priest in saying
it turns four times to the people (before the Collect, before the Offertory, before
and after the Post-Communion), unless he has the people before him in consequence of the situation of the altar; the remaining four times (during the prayer
at the foot of the altar, before the Gospel, before the Preface and before the last
Gospel), it being neither proper nor necessary, the turning to the people is, therefore, omitted. — In the primitive ages the altar generally was so placed that the
celebrant had his face toward the people and, therefore, he had no occasion to turn
around. From this circumstance it may have arisen that in the Ambrosian and
Mozarabic Rites the celebrant never turns to the congregation when pronouncing
this salutation. The Mozarabic formula is invariably as follows: Dominus *sit
semper* vobiscum — Et cum spiritu tuo.

often puts in our mouth the words *Dominus vobiscum*, — and the more we take this to heart, the less risk shall we run of repeating its words in a thoughtless manner. If we truly and sincerely wish that the Lord may be present in the hearts of the faithful, will not our own heart, then, necessarily ardently yearn also for the Lord, and be fit to receive Him, whom the faithful wish to be in our heart? Where there is an ardent longing for the Lord, the Lord enters there with His grace; and such a desire should be excited, maintained and augmented in us by the frequent repetition of the salutation and petition: "The Lord be with you" — "And with thy spirit."[1]

c) By this formula of salutation, both priest and people implore the assistance of divine grace to enter on devout prayer, to which all are now invited by the Oremus — "let us pray" given out in the hearing of all.[2] Not until after saying *Oremus* does the priest stand erect in order to ascend the altar, this mystical Mount Calvary, on which He as Moses on Sinah stands nearer to the Lord God than do the people who are present.[3] Therefore, while ascending to the altar, the priest continues his supplication that greater purity be granted him, reciting secretly the following prayer:[4]

Aufer a nobis, quaesumus Domine, iniquitates nostras: ut ad sancta sanctorum, puris mereamur mentibus introire. Per Christum Dominum nostrum. Amen.	Take away from us our iniquities, we beseech Thee, O Lord, that we may be worthy to enter with pure minds into the Holy of Holies. Through Christ our Lord. Amen.

The Lord has promised: "I have blotted out (*delevi*) thy iniquities as a cloud, and thy sins as a mist" (Isa. 44, 22). Therefore, the priest invokes Him, that, in His compassionate mercy, He would cleanse his soul more and more from all iniquity, from all defilement and the remains of sin, from all evil inclinations and attachments, that, being made whiter than snow (Ps. 50, 9), he

---

[1] Cf. Augsburger Pastoralblatt, Jahrg. 1876, p. 249 etc.

[2] In the Mozarabic Liturgy of the Mass the formula *Oremus* is said or sung at high Mass only twice (namely, before the threefold cry agios [ἅγιος], which differs from the Trisagium proper [Sanctus], and before the prayer which introduces the Paternoster). Among the Greeks the deacon always cries out: "Let us pray to the Lord" (τοῦ Κυρίου δεηθῶμεν).

[3] Quanto sacerdotes et clerici ampliori, singulariori ac diviniori a Christo ornati et exaltati sunt potestate, auctoritate, gradu, ordine et honore, tanto omnino decet et opus est, ut Christo sint gratiores, subjectiores et puriores (Dion. Carthus. De vita Curatorum art. 68).

[4] The Sacrament. Gelasian. contains this prayer among the Orat. et preces a Quinquagesima usque Quadrag. with some slight change: Aufer a nobis, Domine, quaesumus, iniquitates nostras, ut ad sancta sanctorum puris mereamur *sensibus* introire.

may be worthy to go into the true *Holy of Holies*[1] of the new Covenant of grace, that is, to enter the place of sacrifice, there to offer the Eucharistic oblation. The *Holy of Holies* of the Old Law, which the high-priest alone was permitted to enter, and that but once a year, with the sacrificial blood of the animals, was a feeble figure of the Holy of Holies of the New Testament, into which entrance is open daily, even to the humble priest; for day after day Jesus Christ, the *Holy of Holies (Sanctus sanctorum)*, offers Himself there by His own hands, to gain for us admission into the *Holy of Holies* of heaven.[2]

d) The desire of being entirely free from sin and from all the misery of sin, again finds expression in the following prayer which the priest says while bowing down moderately before the altar and resting his joined hands thereon.

Oramus te, Domine, per merita Sanctorum tuorum, quorum reliquiae hic sunt, et omnium Sanctorum ut indulgere digneris omnia peccata mea. Amen.	We beseech Thee, O Lord, by the merits of Thy saints, whose relics are here, and of all the saints, that Thou wouldst vouchsafe to forgive me all my sins. Amen.

The petition for perfect purification from all sin is here further supported and strengthened, — namely, by the invoking of the merits of the saints, by the placing of the hands on the altar and by the kissing of the altar. Aware of his own unworthiness, the priest bases his petition for the remission of all sins and all punishment due to them, on the merits and satisfactions of all the saints and especially of those martyrs, whose relics are deposited within the altar. This confidence and reliance are expressed by word (*per merita Sanctorum*) and by act; for the priest places his joined hands on the dressed altar, which is the figure of Christ and the saints, thereby to show that he does not rely on his own strength, but on Christ and the saints, and that, relying upon their merits, he hopes for and implores of God the remission of all his sins. — In oder to share more abundantly in the heavenly treasures of grace merited and obtained by Christ and by the saints with Christ's assistance,

---

[1] Eusebius in his History of the Church (l. 10, c. 4) uses the same expression to designate the altar τὸ τῶν ἁγίων ἅγιον = sanctum sanctorum.

[2] Inter alias legis gratiae excellentias ea est valde admirabilis, quod in sacrificio *summam praestantiam* cum *summa frequentia* conjungat. Nam in mundo omne pretiosum, ut dicitur, est rarum. . . . Olim *summus sacerdos semel tantum in anno* ingrediebatur in Sancta sanctorum, ubi erat propitiatorium, ad orandum pro se, pro familia sua et pro omni populo, offerens sacrificium thymiamatis, quod ponebat super prunas, et nullus hominum poterat cum eo ingredi, aut assistere ei, quod ille faciebat. Nunc autem *quilibet sacerdos* etiam ex minoribus potest *quotidie* ingredi in Sancta sanctorum Ecclesiae et orare coram propitiatorio, Christo Jesu, pro se et pro toto populo, licetque aliis ipsum comitari et omnibus fidelium ei assistere (De Ponte, De christ. homin. perfectione IV, tr. 2, c. 15).

the celebrant devoutly kisses the altar in the middle when saying the words: *quorum reliquiae hic sunt* — "whose relics are here (preserved)." As the accompanying words show, this kissing refers chiefly to the relics concealed in the altar, that is, to the martyrs and other saints, whose earthly remains at the consecration of the altar were placed there;[1] and, in the next place, it refers generally also to all the saints, who are mentioned at the same time (*et omnium Sanctorum*), and above all to Christ — the Head, the Crown and the King of all the saints — of whom the altar is and will ever be the symbol. By kissing the altar, enriched with relics, the priest would evince his love and veneration for the Church triumphant, for Christ and all the saints, and he would thereby animate anew and confirm his communion with them. — How exceedingly consoling this supernatural communication between earth and heaven, this communion of life and of goods between the glorified children of the Church who are reigning in heaven, and the wretched children of Eve still in their earthly pilgrimage, struggling amid want and hardship! And how could we, without overflowing with gratitude and joy, be mindful of the glorious treasures that the blood of Jesus Christ, the tears and sorrows of the Blessed Mother, the works of charity and penance which all the saints have acquired for our benefit? This reflection and this sentiment take possession of the priest on his first arriving at the altar, and he kisses it, to testify his love, esteem and reverence for His Heavenly Benefactor.

35. The Incensing of the Altar.

At the solemn High Mass (*Missa solemnis*)[2] immediately after the prayers at the foot of the altar, the incensing takes place.[3] The

---

[1] The ordinance of Pope Felix I. (about 270), to celebrate the Holy Sacrifice of the Mass "over the tombs of the martyrs," merely confirmed a long existing custom. Later on the remains of the saints were transferred from their place of burial and placed in the interior of newly erected altars. The place in which the martyrs were interred, that is, the altar built over their tomb and also the church which enclosed it, were usually called confessio (μαρτύριον, place of confession) or memoria (memorial). The remains of the saints on earth may also be regarded under various aspects and, therefore, they received from the Fathers different names, for example, reliquiae (λείψανα), pignora, patrocinia, sanctuaria, beneficia, cineres, xenia, insignia, exuviae Sanctorum. With respect to the close connection of devotion to relics and the Eucharistic Sacrifice cf. also Prudent. Peristephan. III, 211 sqq. — V, 515 sqq. — XI, 169 sqq.

[2] By Missa *solemnis* is to be understood here in a stricter sense only that and every high Mass, in which the ministri sacri (deacon and sub-deacon) participate; for the incensing, according to a later decree, is a rite pertaining exclusively to the high Mass celebrated with deacon and sub-deacon, and may never be omitted therein (not even in Missis ferialibus Quadragesimae). (S. R. C. 19. Aug. 1651; 14. Jun. 1845; 29. Nov. 1856.) But since in many churches no ministri sacri are present, several dioceses have obtained an Apostolic Indult, which at least occurrentibus solemnioribus festis permits also for the Missa cantata the customary incensing to take place. (Cf. Bourbon, Introduct. aux cérém. rom. p. 330 ss.)

[3] In the East the incensing of the altar at the beginning of Mass was intro-

explanation of this rite may be prefaced by a few remarks concerning the use and symbolism of incense in general.

1. By the express command of God [1] in the Old Law incense was already frequently used for liturgical purposes. Then indeed incense might be offered only to the Lord, might be burned only in honor of Jehovah. Incense was "holy to the Lord;" the Lord Himself minutely directed how it was to be prepared and mixed, where and how often it was to be burned (Exodus 30, 1 etc.). In the sanctuary, which was separated by a veil from the Holy of Holies, stood the altar for the offering of incense; on this altar every day, morning and night, a special incense-offering had to be made to the Lord. Also at the great propitiatory sacrifice on the feast of reconciliation and at the offering of the show-bread, incense (*thus lucidissimum*) was accepted and burned as an additional gift. — The Fathers unanimously teach that the Wise Men from the East, by the offering of incense intended symbolically to adore the Child Jesus, "the King of the Jews," as the God concealed and revealed under the garb of earthly lowliness.[2] Incense found a place in Christian worship already at an early date,[3] and was more universally used especially from the time of the fourth century,[4] when divine wor-

duced already in the fourth century; for Pseudo-Denis the Areopagite writes: "After the bishop has recited at the altar of God the holy prayer, he commences the incensing of the altar and walks around the entire circumference of the sacred place" (The Hierarchy of the Church III, 2). — In the West, on the contrary, mention is first made of the incensing of the altar before the Introit about the middle of the twelfth century. The Ordo Rom. XI, n. 18, namely, directs: Ascendens Pontifex ... ad altare, facit confessionem, osculatur Evangelium ... et intrat ad altare, et inclinato capite dicit orationem, qua peracta osculatur altare ... accipit capsam et ponit incensum in thuribulum et *incensat altare* et archidiaconus retinet planetam, ne impediatur. — In quibusdam ecclesiis sacerdos ad altare accedens statim thurificat (Robert. Paulul. De offic. eccles. 1. 2, c. 14).

1 Voluit Deus hos odores sibi adoleri, non quod odoratu thymiamatis delectetur, cum nullum habeat odoratum ... sed quia magnus inter homines censetur honor, suaves cuipiam apponere vel suffumigare odores: hinc Deus, qui cum hominibus humano more agit, voluit eosdem ad sui cultum coram se adoleri. Sic omnium gentium consuetudine et ritu *thuris et odorum incensio attributa est Deo;* hinc poëtae "thuris honores" vocant honores divinos, et tres Magi haec tria munera dederunt Christo, scilicet: "aurum regi, *thura Deo,* myrrhamque sepulto." Unde et nos christiani thurificamus Deo (Cornel. a Lapide in Exod. 30, 1).

2 Per ista tria munerum genera in uno eodemque Christo et *divina majestas* et regia potestas et humana mortalitas intimatur. *Thus* enim ad *sacrificium,* aurum pertinet ad tributum, myrrha ad sepulturam pertinet mortuorum (S. Fulgent. Sermo 4).

3 Among the heathens also incense was prominently destined for sacrifice; the devil wished to have the same marks of honor shown to him by the idolaters as God required of His people. To offer incense to the pagan gods was always reckoned among Christians as apostasy from the faith.

4 The first positive proof with respect to the liturgical use of incense in the West is found in St. Ambrose. When, namely, this holy Doctor of the Church speaks of the apparition of the angel to Zachary (Luke 1, 5—25), he adds: "May

ship began to be more freely and more splendidly developed. The present liturgical practice in the use of incense was perfectly developed in the West only during the Middle Age. In the Greek liturgies there is far more frequent mention of incense than in the Latin Rite. — At divine service only pure incense is to be employed; the best comes from Africa, where it is obtained from the boswellia (incense-tree).[1] To the incense other odoriferous substances, for instance, rosin or herbs, may be added, but only in a considerably smaller quantity.[2]

The burning in the religious service of this precious, noble and fragrant incense is a splendid rite, which not only contributes much solemnity to the celebration of divine worship, but also symbolically represents the mysteries of faith and the virtues of the Christian life.[3] The symbolism of incense consists essentially in this, that the grains of incense are dissolved by the heat of the coals, thereby diffusing a sweet odor which ascends heavenward in fragrant clouds, filling the sanctuary and the whole church. Consequently, the liturgical incensation, that is, only the lighted, burning incense (*incensum sc. thus*), has in reality a symbolical meaning, and this meaning is lost, if there be no odor arising from the incense, or the glow of fire be wanting, or if burning coals are not used (*prunae ardentes* — Pontif. Rom).

The fragrant incense, burning in the fire, has, as it were, been created as a symbol, as a solemn expression of the interior sentiments of sacrifice[4] and of prayer acceptable to God. The perfume of a plant is its most delicate and most noble part, and, so to speak, "its hidden, sleeping vitality," for example, the fragrance of the balm-tree, the rose and the violet. Hence incense exhales and breathes

---

we also, when incensing the altar (nobis *adolentibus* altaria) and when offering the Holy Sacrifice, have an angel at our side."

[1] Incense is a resinous gum which oozes from the bark of a tree, dries in the air, is collected by scraping it from the bark and is used in commerce.

[2] Materies, quae adhibetur, vel solum et purum thus esse debet *suavis odoris;* vel si aliqua addantur, advertatur, ut *quantitas thuris longe superet* (Ceremon. Episcop. 1. 1, c. 23, n. 3). — Incense is sold in the form of grains or as a powder.

[3] The Tridentine Council places the incensing at divine worship (thymiama) expressly among the visibilia religionis et pietatis signa, which incite and elevate the mind to the devout contemplation of heavenly things (Sess. 22, cap. 5). — Cf. Kölner Pastoralbl. Jahrg. 1875, S. 17 etc.

[4] The Latin and Greek name of incense (*thus*, θυμίαμα from θύειν = to offer, but originally to dissolve into smoke, fumigating) indicates its intimate connection with the Sacrifice. Since incense is destroyed and consumed in the fire, there are found in it all the requisite elements for a sacrifice (material and form), and if the legitimate institution is added, then it is a real sacrifice. This was the case in the Old Law. In the New Law, on the contrary, the burning of incense is only a ceremony prescribed by the Church, which serves for the liturgical adornment and symbolism of the Eucharistic Sacrifice. — Sometimes thymiama (from θυμιάω, I light) is taken as perfumes in a wider sense, and mentioned separately from real incense (thus) (cf. Pontif. Rom. De benedict. signi).

forth its inmost soul when it is consumed in the fire and dissolved in fragrant clouds of smoke, that rise heavenward. It thereby symbolizes, first, man's spirit of sacrifice or his life of sacrifice, for he consumes himself with all his faculties in the fire of love for the honor and service of God. Then the odor of incense which arises from the burning grains and ascends in its fragrance, also symbolizes prayer. Prayer is the surrender of the soul to God, the elevation of the mind and spirit to Heaven, the aspiration of the heart toward goods invisible and eternal. If the grains of incense be cast on burning coals, a pleasant odor will arise; if the heart, like unto a glowing coal, is set on fire with the flames of divine love and ardent devotion, then our prayer will free itself from all that is earthly, and will ascend to the Lord as a sweet and precious perfume, that is to say, our prayer will be received with favor and pleasure and will be answered by Him.[1] Hence the Psalmist exclaims: *Dirigatur, Domine, oratio mea sicut incensum in conspectu tuo!* — "Let my prayer be directed as incense in Thy sight, O Lord!" (Ps. 140, 2.) Scripture represents the prayers of the saints under the figure of golden vials full of sweet odors,[2] which the ancients bear in their hands, standing before the throne of the Lamb (*habentes singuli phialas aureas plenas odoramentorum, quae sunt orationes Sanctorum* — Apoc. 5, 8). Adoration, praises, thanksgivings and petitions, like odoriferous incense, penetrate to the heavenly Holy of Holies — as far as the throne of the Almighty.

From the original meaning of incense another naturally suggests itself. The "smoke of agreeable odors," symbolizing sacrifice and prayer, or, rather, sacrifice and prayer themselves excite the divine pleasure and mercy, and draw down upon us God's grace; hence divine grace also is figured by the odor of incense (*bonus odor gratiae*). While the odor of ascending incense denotes devout sacrifice and prayer penetrating to heaven, the clouds of incense floating round about signify the effects of prayer and sacrifice, — namely, the sweet odor of grace descending from Heaven or issuing from Christ on the altar.[3] Prayer ascends and God's mercy descends.

The fragrant clouds of incense are for the priest and people also

---

[1] Thuribulum est cor humanum, ignis caritas, thus oratio: sicut thus cum igne in thuribulo *redolet* et sursum *ascendit,* sic oratio cum caritate in corde ultra omnia pigmenta (aromatics, perfumes) fragrescit (Sicard 1. 1, c. 13).

[2] Orationes Sanctorum comparantur hic suffitui, non cuivis, sed odoramentorum 1. quia oratio instar thuris sursum ascendit; 2. quia sicut thus odoratum ita orationes Sanctorum Deum oblectant; 3. uti thus foetorem, ita oratio peccatum abigit Deique iram mitigat; 4. thymiama fiebat ex aromatibus contusis: sic oratio ex animo mortificato et humili procedere debet; 5. thymiama in igne adolebatur; ita oratio in igne tribulationum exardescit (Cornel. a Lapide, in Exod. 30, 34).

[3] Cf. the prayer at the incensing of the offerings: Incensum istud a te benedictum, *ascendat* ad te, Domine: et *descendat* super nos misericordia tua (Miss. Rom.). — Vespertina oratio ascendat ad te, Domine — et descendat super nos misericordia tua (Breviar. Roman.).

an admonition so to live as to become, by sacrifice and the spirit of prayer, by the wealth of grace and virtue, by devotion of heart and piety, a spiritual "good odor of Christ" (*Christi bonus odor* — 2 Cor. 2, 15),[1] in order to give joy to heaven and earth.[2]

The very nature of the thing itself indicates in the burning of the grains of incense chiefly a symbol of adoration, or rather of the sacrifice as the most perfect act and expression of adoration; but it is to be observed, that in the intention of the Church incense is not exclusively employed to render the highest honor due to God alone, that is, to manifest interior adoration in a solemn manner, but also generally to denote religious veneration towards that which is holy. Therefore, besides the Most Blessed Sacrament, the relics and images of the saints, the Book of the Gospels, the celebrant, the clergy and the people are incensed.

At Solemn High Mass the incense is blessed,[3] that is, made a holy object consecrated to God. Blessed incense is a Sacramental: as such it not merely signifies something ennobled and mystical, but it has also (in its way) supernatural effects.

In consequence of this blessing, it is evident that the incense appears expressly and perfectly as a holy and religious symbol. The symbolism of incense is indeed founded in its very nature, and is clearly set forth in its use at divine worship, which already, in a certain way, imparts a consecration to it; but it is really perfected and forcibly expressed, in the first place, by the blessing of the

---

[1] Per thuribulum cor humanum competenter notatur... habens ignem caritatis et thus devotionis sive suavissimae orationis seu bonorum exemplorum sursum tendentium, quod per fumum inde resultantem notatur. Sicut enim thus in *igne* thuribuli *suaviter redolet* et *sursum ascendit*, ita *opus bonum* vel *oratio* ex *caritate* ultra omnia thymiamata *fragrat* (Durand. 1. 4, c. 6, n. 6).

[2] Res sacras, ut Dei et Sanctorum basilicas, variis suavissimorum odorum replere generibus, optimum ac Deo honorificum est — sic enim *internam* erga eum *reverentiam testamur*, quod Ecclesia, festis praesertim solemnioribus, eo fine faciendum instituit; cumque templa sic suave olentia ingredimur, puros ac sanctos odores illos percipiendo, debemus ex his perceptis mentem ad coelestia meditanda sursum erigere, orationem nostram sicut incensum ad Deum dirigere et ad virtutis exercitium nos excitare, ut sic bonus odor Christi simus in omni loco (Philipp. a. SS. Trinit. Theol. myst. 1, p. 1, tr. 2, art. 5).

[3] Incense, as a rule (even coram exposito), must be blessed when put into the thurible. The blessing must be omitted when the Most Holy Sacrament alone is to be incensed, for example, at Expositions or Processions of the Blessed Sacrament, because in this instance incense is regarded merely as a symbol, and not as a Sacramental. In the Mass of the Presanctified on Good Friday the blessing of the incense is likewise omitted as a sign of mourning, although in addition to the Consecrated Host the altar also is incensed. The petition for blessing the incense is addressed (by the deacon) to the celebrant in reverential words; if he be a priest, the formula is as follows: Benedicite, Pater reverende; if a bishop: Benedicite, Pater reverendissime; if a cardinal: Benedicite, Pater eminentissime. — The priest must always stand when putting the incense into the thurible. (Cf. Ceremon. Episc. l. 1, c. 23, n. 18; l. 2, c. 22, n. 11. — Quarti l. c. dub. 2.)

Church, for the incense (like ashes and palm) appears only when blessed in the complete light of a holy and mystical symbol.

As a Sacramental incense is, then, a means to secure the divine protection and blessing. By virtue of the sign of the Cross and the blessing of the Church incense is especially made efficacious for expelling or keeping at a distance Satan from the soul, and for affording us a powerful protection against the deceit and malice, the snares and the attacks of evil spirits, a protection we greatly need at the altar and during the celebration of the Holy Mysteries. Before the incense is burned on the altar that is about to be consecrated, the bishop prays Almighty God, that He "would deign to look down upon this incense, that He would bless and sanctify it, to the end that all sicknesses and infirmities, as well as every snare of the Evil One may flee from its sweet odor, and that the creature (man) redeemed by the precious Blood of Christ may never be wounded by the bite of the infernal serpent."[1] — Blessed incense produces yet another effect: it is used for the blessing of persons and of things. For with the clouds of incense is diffused the power of the blessing which the Church pronounces and desires to impart; they draw all who are incensed into a sanctified atmosphere.

From what has just been explained concerning the symbolism and efficacy of incense, the purport and meaning of the different incensings in particular is easily inferred.

3. The ascending clouds of the fragrant incense clothe the celebration of divine worship with additional majesty, pomp and solemnity; therefore has the Church honored and distinguished many of her liturgical functions by the use of incense, — among the number the highest and most important of all, the solemn celebration of the Holy Sacrifice of the Mass, in quite a prominent and profoundly significant manner. The light clouds of incense soaring heavenward envelop the altar and fill the sanctuary throughout with their agreeable fragrance, most befittingly express and recommend the majesty of so great a Sacrifice, and make the earthly appear more evidently a copy of the heavenly altar (Apoc. 8, 3). — The incensation takes place at the beginning of the general divine service, that is, between the prayers at the foot of the altar and the Introit, as well as at the beginning of the special sacrificial service, namely, during the Offertory; also at the culminating point of each of these principal parts of the Mass, namely, at the Gospel wherein the Lord is teacher, and at the Consecration when He appears in sacrifice on the altar. The cloud of incense is also symbolical of the appearance, that is, of the presence of the Lord in the Blessed Sacrament and in His word; for already in the Old Covenant the glory of the Lord

---

[1] Domine Deus omnipotens ... dignare respicere, benedicere et sanctificare hanc creaturam incensi, ut omnes languores omnesque infirmitates atque *insidiae inimici* odorem ejus sentientes effugiant et separentur a plasmate tuo, quod pretioso Filii tui sanguine redemisti, ut nunquam laedatur a morsu *iniqui serpentis* (Pontific. Roman. De ecclesiae dedicatione).

appeared in the cloud of the Tabernacle (Exodus 40, 32; Leviticus 16, 2; Paralip. 5, 13), and on the great Day of Atonement the high-priest enveloped the Holy of Holies of the Old Testament with clouds of incense in token of Jehovah's revelation on that most sacred spot.

The first incensing at High Mass may be regarded as a solemn conclusion of the preparatory prayers at the foot of the altar; the rite is simple and is performed without any accompanying prayer. The celebrant places incense three times on the glowing coals, while saying: *Ab illo benedicaris — in cujus honore — cremaberis. — Amen.*[1] "Be thou blessed by Him in whose honor thou wilt be consumed. Amen." Only after these words does he make the sign of the Cross over the burning grains of incense. This formula of blessing declares the principal object of the incensing — the glorification of the divine name. Incense is used at divine worship because of its exquisite odor, not to afford man a sensuous gratification, but to evince profound reverence toward the divine mysteries. In the first place, the Crucifix on the altar, or the Blessed Sacrament,[2] is honored by incense, that is, due adoration is offered to the Lord in His image or in His Sacrament. — If the Blessed Sacrament be not exposed, then the relics or images of the saints on the altar are incensed. This incensing is an eminent sign of veneration paid to the blessed in heaven, who diffuse an agreeable odor like unto cinnamon and sweet-smelling balm and like precious myrrh (Ecclus. 24, 20); then as a mark of honor it ought to move them to obtain, by their powerful intercession, mercy for us at the throne of God and a favorable answer to our petitions. The priest, having just ascended the altar, and relying upon the intercession of the saints, has just prayed to God for perfect purity of heart: the fragrant clouds of incense which envelop the altar are now emblematical of the aforesaid prayers and merits of the saints, and, consequently, express in a symbolical manner the same petition that had immediately before been presented in words, that is, the petition for the assistance of the saints. — The altar solemnly consecrated by the bishop and enriched with relics, is the most sacred place of sacrifice — *Sancta sanctorum*

---

[1] In former editions of the Ceremon. Episcop. we read in hono*rem* (l. 1, c. 23, n. 1); but the new editio *typica* (Ratisbonae 1886) has in hono*re*. The original and correct mode of reading is without doubt in cujus *honore*. — The Vulgate, the ancient liturgies and the entire vulgar-Latin literature construe the proposition (to the question where? or why?) frequently in the ablative instead of in the accusative. Clichtoveus gives the fourth stanza of the hymn Iste confessor thus: Unde nunc noster chorus *in honore* — Ipsius hymnum canit hunc libenter. In the liturgy for Good Friday the Church sings: Ecce enim propter lignum venit gaudium *in universo mundo.* — The Ord. Rom. XIV, c. 71, has the formula: Ab ipso sanctificeris, in cujus honore cremaberis.

[2] Sacerdos dum incensum ponit in thuribulo stare debet; ab eodem vero Ss. Eucharistiae Sacramentum thurificandum est triplici ductu, sed genibus flexis et tam ante quam post incensationem profunda facta capitis inclinatione (S. R. C. 26. Mart. 1859 in una Tarnov.). — But every *ductus* thuribuli is performed duplici *ictu* (S. R. C. 22. Mart. 1862).

— and is to be regarded and revered with religious awe. The incensing of the altar symbolizes and calls to mind the sublime holiness of the consecrated altar. — The blessed clouds of incense, therefore, not merely admonish us, but also obtain for us from above the necessary assistance to enter with a pure intention into the Holy of Holies, to stand at the altar and to celebrate the Most Holy Sacrifice with a devout heart. — The fragrant clouds of smoking incense signify, at the same time, that this Sacrifice, by the power of the Holy Ghost, will ascend to Heaven as a "sweet odor" and be for us the source of all spiritual odors of grace.[1] — Finally, the celebrant himself, and he alone as the visible representative of the invisible Highpriest, Jesus Christ, receives by the threefold incensing the veneration due to his sacred character.

The incensing at the beginning of Mass is intended mainly for the altar,[2] which by the Heaven-blest fumes of mystic incense pervading its surrounding atmosphere is characterized, distinguished and honored as the holy and venerated place of sacrifice and adoration. — The ceremony of incensing, so solemn, so significant and so edifying, should also move those present to devout and holy sentiments, and, as incense is consumed by the heat of the coals, should inspire them at the same time with the thought that their life should, amid the fire and flames of love, like unto a precious holocaust, be dedicated to the honor and service of God.

36. The Introit.[3]

1. Over many of the formulas for Mass we meet with an inscription which requires a brief explanation; it is said, for example, *Statio ad S. Petrum* = Station at the Church of St. Peter; *Statio ad S. Caeciliam* = Station ad St. Caecilia's. These words indicate the church wherein, before the exile of the Popes at Avignon, on the aforesaid Saint's day the Divine Sacrifice was offered up after the clergy and laity had gone in solemn procession to the Station Church, where the procession halted (statio), and the Divine Sacrifice was offered. These stations were, therefore, a particular kind of religious assembly, arranged for fixed days and certain churches of the city of

---

[1] Domine sancte... respice ad hujus altaris tui holocaustum, quod non igne visibili probetur, sed infusum sancti Spiritus tui gratia in odorem suavitatis ascendat et legitime se sumentibus Eucharistia medicabilis fiat ad vitamque proficiat sempiternam (Pontific. Roman. De ecclesiae dedicat. seu consecrat.).

[2] The altar, as far as is convenient, is incensed all around, and the rear of the altar also toward the six symmetrically arranged candlesticks (incensat altare, ter ducens thuribulum aequali distantia, *prout distribuuntur candelabra* — Missal. Rom.); the candlesticks are, therefore, not incensed. Cf. Lebrun p. 1, art. 9.

[3] The Introit is called in the Ambrosian Rite ingressa, in the Mozarabic officium and in the old Gallican praelegere or antiphona ad praelegendum. Amalarius writes: Officium quod dicitur introitus Missae, habet initium a prima antiphona, quae dicitur Introitus, et finitur in oratione, quae a sacerdote dicitur ante lectionem (De eccles. offic. l. 3, c. 5).

Rome, wherein was to be celebrated divine service in a solemn manner.[1] The complete celebration of the Station was threefold : the assembling in a certain church, the procession to the Station Church, and the holding of divine worship therein. — Clergy and laity, in the first place, assembled in a church in which the religious celebration was opened by the singing of Psalms and by a prayer of the celebrant. This preparatory assembly was called *Collecta*.[2] Thence they proceeded processionally to the Station Church : the banner of the Cross was carried at the head of the procession, on the way Psalms were chanted, and on nearing the church the Litany of the Saints, whence the processions received the name of *Litaniae*.[3] In the Church of the Station there was usually a homily delivered (by the Pope) and the Holy Sacrifice was celebrated.

The Stations were often accompanied by the observance of fasting[4] and of penitential practices; such penitential Stations took place during Advent and Lent, on the Ember days and vigils, — occasionally also at special times, when there was question of averting the chastisements and visitations of God, for instance, pestilence, famine and war. — There were also held joyful Stations, for example, such as fell on Sundays and feast-days, or which were instituted for the annual commemoration of the more famous saints.

---

[1] *Statio* hoc loco sumitur pro *concursu populi ad locum indictum*, i. e. ad ecclesiam, in qua processio clericorum consistit statis diebus ad statas preces faciendas. Antiquus quippe in Urbe ritus est, ut certis diebus clerus Romanus in unam aliquam ecclesiam conveniat supplicationis causa, ubi sacra fiunt aliaque divina officia. Cleri Romani processio in illas stationes duplex est, *solemnis* aut *privata*. Haec fit, cum unusquisque privatim in locum indictum se recipit; solemnis vero, cum solemni more, decantando litanias aliasque preces, Pontifex aliique omnes eo sese recipiunt. Processiones solemnes praecedit *Collecta*, i. e. coadunatio clericorum in una ecclesia, ut ex ea, quasi agmine facto, in locum stationis procedatur; sic dicta, quod in eo loco clerus cum populo *colligatur* ad faciendam processionem solemnem. Et quia in loco, ubi fit Collecta, oratio super populum funditur ante processionem, inde fit, quod ejusmodi *orationes* etiam *Collectae* appellantur, quoniam super *Collectam populi* fiunt, dum colligitur, ut procedat de una ecclesia in aliam ad Stationem faciendam, ut loquitur Micrologus in cap. 3 (Mabillon, in Ordinem Romanum commentarius praevius V).

[2] Thus, for example, on Ember Wednesday: Feria IV. *statio* ad Sanctam Mariam Majorem. Fit *collecta* ad Sanctum Petrum ad Vincula in Eudoxia (Ordo Roman. XI, n. 10).

[3] The expression Litaniae (Λιτανεία=rogatio, supplicatio) originally designated every prayer of supplication, but later on especially public prayers, in which the saints were invoked and which were recited at processions (preces, quibus invocatione Dei et Sanctorum desideratam nobis divinae propitiationis abundantiam efficacius impetramus — *Quarti*), and, therefore, also these penitential and supplicatory prayers at processions. The simple invocation Kyrie eleison joined thereto is also called Litania or Letania, for example, in the Rule of St. Benedict and in the Roman Ordines.

[4] Therefore statio is also a designation for fasting; dies stationum also = fast-days.

Stations in the seven principal churches of Rome were particularly frequent;[1] for in them were deposited the holy bodies of celebrated martyrs, and they were large enough to give admission to an extraordinary number of the faithful. — Originally the Station Churches were not definitely assigned for the particular days: announcements were made each time where the next Station would take place. St. Gregory the Great enhanced the solemnity of the Stations, limited them to specified days, attached them permanently to certain churches, and had them inscribed in the *Sacramentarium*, from which they were afterward copied into the Roman Missal.[2] — The present arrangement of the Stations, in its main points, comes from him; only a few churches received their Station-days from the Popes of a later epoch.[3] — After the removal of their place of residence to Avignon (1305, or 1309) the Popes no longer took part in the Stations. With the exception of the absence of the Pope, divine worship is still held in the Station Churches, and with greater solemnity; on the specified days, especially in Lent, large assemblies gather in the Station Churches, to venerate the relics there exposed and to gain the indulgence of the Stations. — The greater penitential processions (*Litaniae majores*) on St. Mark's Day (April 25) and the minor penitential processions (*Litaniae minores*) made through the fields on the three days before the Ascension, evidently resemble the ancient Station solemnities.

As Tertullian supposes it to be universally known,[4] the word *Statio*[5] passed from the language of the military into that of the

---

[1] They were called: 1. S. Giovanni in Laterano, 2. S. Pietro in Vaticano, 3. S. Maria Maggiore, 4. S. Paolo fuori le mura, 5. S. Lorenzo fuori le mura, 6. S. Croce in Gerusalemme, 7. S. Sebastiano fuori le mura. The Basilica of St. Sebastian was also originally a Station Church, but it has not been used as such for several centuries, perhaps on account of the great distance from the city. (Cf. P. Ausserer, Pilgerführer oder Wegweiser nach Rom S. 42 etc. — A. de Waal, Die Wallfahrt zu den sieben Hauptkirchen Roms S. 6 etc.)

[2] Litanias, stationes et ecclesiasticum officium auxit (Brev. Rom. 12. Mart.). Stationes per Basilicas et Martyrium Coemeteria ordinavit: et sequebatur exercitus Domini Gregorium praeeuntem. Ductor coelestis militiae arma spiritualia proferebat. — Cf. Grisar S. J. in der Innsbrucker Theol. Zeitschrift 1885, S. 561 etc.

[3] At present there are still 111 Station-Devotions held, which are distributed among 87 days and 44 churches; frequently in one day several are kept (2—3), and the Stations recur often in one and the same church during the course of the year.

[4] Si statio de *militari* exemplo nomen accipit (nam et *militia Dei* sumus), utique nulla laetitia sive tristitia obveniens castris, stationes militum rescindit. Nam laetitia libentius, tristitia sollicitius administrabit disciplinam (Tertullian. De Orat. c. 19).

[5] Statio = the standing, the quiet and firm standing; especially = the guard, the watch, the watch-guard, the field-watch. — Statio primo et per se significat actum standi seu permanendi ad certum tempus in locis sacris orandi causa et publicos conventus fidelium ad orationem. — Secundo minus proprie significat loca seu templa, in quibus statio habetur. — Tertio significat orationem ipsam, quae fit in eisdem locis. — Tandem significat indulgentiam ibi orantibus concessam (Quarti, De Procession. sect. 2, punct. 14).

Church: the above mentioned assemblies and practices of the Christians were called *Stationes*, because they bore a certain resemblance to the service of the sentinels. As "good soldiers of Jesus Christ" the faithful of those ancient times wished to keep guard, so to speak, in the house of God, in order to protect themselves against the snares and assaults of the infernal adversary; and to this end they persevered in fasting, prayer, reading, the recitation of the Psalms and the celebration of the Eucharist until None, namely, until three o'clock in the afternoon, in holy recollection (*perstabant*). In this manner did they confirm and strengthen themselves, in order not to hesitate and waver in life's struggles and sufferings, but to "put on the armor of God," that is, "to take the shield of faith, the helmet of salvation and the sword of the spirit, which is the word of God; by all prayer and supplication, praying at all times in the spirit, and in the same watching with all instance and supplication for all the saints — (Christians)" (Eph. 6, 11—18).

2. While at all times the unchangeable prayers at the foot of the altar form the general introduction to the whole celebration of the Mass, the variable Introit begins in a special manner the first, that is, the principal changeable part of its liturgy. This part does not directly touch upon the Sacrifice, but serves merely to prepare the way for the actual Sacrifice, by infusing into the minds of those present such holy thoughts, devout affections and good resolutions, as dispose them for the worthy celebration of the Divine Mysteries. Accordingly, it consists, on the one hand, of reading and instruction calculated to enliven and strengthen the faith; and, on the other hand, of prayer and chant to awaken and nourish devotion[1]: for faith and devotion are, above all, required to derive fruit from the celebration of the Holy Mysteries.[2] These prayers, Psalms and readings of the Introit vary principally according to the course and character of the ecclesiastical year; for they are intended to give suitable expression to the idea of the ecclesiastical celebration of the day or feast, which principally induces the offering of the Holy Sacrifice and is intimately connected therewith.

a) In its present form the Introit[3] is a Psalm abbreviated as much as possible; for it consists of psalm-verses with a *Gloria Patri*, which (like entire Psalms usually are) is introduced and concluded with an Antiphon.[4] — The Antiphon is generally taken from the

---

[1] Introitus laudem Dei continet et ad honorem Altissimi cum modulatione *cantatur*, quatenus universorum adstantium corda in Dei amorem sanctamque devotionem excitentur et accendantur, ac per hoc toti sequenti officio cum fervore alacri jucunditate intersint (Dion. Carthus. Expos. Missae art. 8).

[2] Cf. in the Canon the words: quorum tibi *fides* cognita est et nota *devotio*.

[3] Introitus = entrance, entering, introduction; then = beginning, prelude. — Interim (during the prayer at the foot of the altar) cantatur Antiphona ad Introitum, quae ab *introitu* sacerdotis *ad altare* hoc nomen meruit habere (Microlog. c. 1).

[4] The word Introitus has, in addition to the above, a still more varied signification in the liturgy. a) In the first place and originally, it signifies the solemn

Psalter, often too from other books of the Old or New Testament, and only in a few instances is it composed expressly by the Church herself.[1] The Antiphon is, as a rule, though not in every case, followed by the beginning (the first verse) of a Psalm.[2] — During the joyful Eastertide generally two, occasionally three, *Allelujas* are added to the Antiphon. In those Masses which do not have the Psalm *Judica*, the *Gloria Patri* is omitted after the verse of the Psalm. In the Gloria Patri, this solemn praise of the Blessed Trinity, there resounds an air of joy; hence it is omitted in the Masses of Passiontide and of Holy Week as well as in the Masses for the dead, in order to indicate the profound sorrow, affliction and grief of the Church.[3]

The Mass of Holy Saturday and the principal Mass of the vigil of Pentecost, that is, the one which is preceded by the Prophecies (with or without the blessing of baptismal water) have no Introit.[4] The reason of this may be, that the foregoing chants, prayers and lessons were regarded as taking the place of the usual introductory Psalm, and consequently a further introductory chant could well be omitted.[5] On these days the preliminary solemnities constituted a

---

entrance of the celebrant into the church, the going from the sacristy to the altar; b) derivatively, the whole alternate chant of the choir, which comprises a greater number of Psalm-verses in addition to an Antiphon which was chanted at the entrance of the celebrant, or c) at times the Antiphon alone appertaining to this choir-chant, and d) in a more comprehensive sense, the Antiphon and Psalm-verse together with the Kyrie, Gloria and Collect.

[1] The Antiphons taken from the Psalms are called Introitus *regulares*, the others Introitus *irregulares*. Cfr. Durand. 1. 4, c. 5.

[2] In many, especially in the newer, Mass formulas, not the first, but another appropriate Psalm-verse has been selected, for example, in the Missa de Sacrat. Spinea Corona D. N. I. Chr., de S. Ignatio Conf., de S. Francisco de Hieronymo. — If the first verse of a Psalm forms the Antiphon, then the next verse is added, for instance, Dominica XII. et XV. p. Pent., Missa votiva pro infirmis. — One and the same Antiphon is in different Masses often accompanied with different Psalm-verses, for example, the Antiphon Gaudeamus omnes in Domino on the feast of the Assumption of the Blessed Virgin Mary and on the feast of All Saints. Only seldom, for instance, in the Requiem Mass and on the feast of St. Francis Xavier, two verses of the Psalm follow the Antiphon. Cfr. Guyet, Heortologia 1. 3, c. 25, q. 2).

[3] The hymnus *glorificationis* essentially bears the impress of the joyous, and, therefore, as vox laetitiae et laudis (Rupert v. Deutz) must be partly or wholly silent in the liturgy of the sorrowful season. De responsoriis "Gloria Patri" subtrahimus et apud quosdam ad Missas quoque cum Introitu officii non dicitur (Rup. Tuit. V, 2).

[4] The other Masses of the vigil of Pentecost have an Introit; on the Easter vigil, on the contrary, the low Mass also is without an Introit, in this case such a one may be celebrated ex privilegio only (S. R. C. 22. Jul. 1848).

[5] Totus Introitus fuit omissus, ubi vel processio Missam antecessit vel officium quodpiam ante Missam fuit celebratum, quem morem hodiedum adhuc in Vigiliis Paschae et Pentecostes observari conspicimus. Introitus enim ad id solum institutus erat, ut populum occuparet, dum Celebrans veniebat ad altare; cum autem

whole or joint service with the Mass; hence the Ordinance of the Church laid down that one and the same celebrant should discharge the entire function, namely, the Mass together with the blessings.[1]

Whilst the priest is saying the first words of the Introit, he makes the sign of the Cross, because the Introit forms the beginning of the variable Mass formula, that is, of the particular day or festal celebration.[2] — In Requiem Masses the celebrant does not make the sign of the Cross on himself, but over the Missal (*super librum quasi aliquem benedicens* — Rubr.), at the same time imploring from the Lord eternal rest and perpetual light for the departed souls; this sign of the Cross is, without doubt, not intended for the book, but for the suffering souls, that is, it would indicate that the fulness of the blessing of the Sacrifice may fall to their share. — The Introit is read on the Epistle side (*cornu Epistolae*), namely, on the left side of the altar,[3] and with the hands joined before the breast, to signify and to manifest the priest's prayerful disposition.

b) It yet remains for us to specify and explain more minutely the object and meaning of the Introit. As it is the introduction to the celebration of the particular feast or day, the Introit belongs to the variable component parts of the Mass-Rite, and is to be considered under the same aspect as the Gradual, Offertory and Communion verse.

These four pieces[4] belong to the chants, with which the choir, in the name of the people, accompany the sublime, divine tragedy of the Eucharistic Sacrifice. In their present form they are but brief remnants of longer chants, which consisted of whole Psalms or of an indefinite number of verses of the Psalms, and which were rendered while the priest was going to the altar (*Introitus*), or after the reading of the Epistle (*Graduale*), or while the faithful were presenting their offerings (*Offertorium*), or while they received Holy Communion (*Communio*). At the beginning of the fifth century

---

his diebus populus jam esset congregatus, et **Pontifex** de fontibus sive de baptisterio ad altare transiret, dum Litaniae vel Kyrie eleison canerentur, hinc illis finitis statim, "Gloria in excelsis" intonabat (Krazer Sect. IV, art. 1, cap. 1, § 217).

[1] S. R. C. 1. Sept. 1838.

[2] Therefore, some Masses and Sundays also were named after the initial words of their respective Introit. Thus the Masses for the dead are called Requiem, and the Votive Mass in honor of the Blessed Virgin Mary in Advent Rorate; the first five Sundays of Lent Invocavit, Reminiscere, Oculi, Laetare, Judica, — and the first four Sundays after Easter Quasimodo, Misericordias Domini, Jubilate, Cantate and the sixth Exaudi.

[3] Since the fifteenth century the right and left sides of the altar have been named and considered with regard to the Crucifix placed in the centre, while previously — from the standing-place of the celebrant — precisely the opposite denomination was in practice. Cfr. Benedict. XIV. De Missae sacrific. l. 2, c. 4, n. 1.

[4] For those parts of the Missal that are to be sung, as well as for the Antiphons and Responsories of the Breviary, the text of Itala (version of Scripture), somewhat differing from our Vulgate, is used, because the original and unalterable mode of chanting had always been intimately connected with it.

these chants were already introduced into the Roman Church, but not all at the same time: the Communion chant was probably the most ancient, while the Introit Psalm was the latest.[1] St. Gregory the Great had already abridged these choral chants, as may be seen from his Antiphonarium; they were later on simplified still more, such as they are at present to be found in the Missal.

Evidently these Psalms, or passages from the Psalms, did not find their way into each of the Mass formulas by chance or by mere fancy, but were inserted after judicious selection. The ecclesiastical year with its feasts and holy seasons, or the special, extraordinary occasion or intention of the Mass, suggested and determined their adoption. — The celebration of Mass is most intimately connected and interwoven with the mystical, marvellously arranged cycle of the holy year: *Sacrificium* and *Officium*, Missal and Breviary, mutually harmonize and complete each other, and both together make up the entire and perfect liturgical celebration of the holy days and seasons. Like the Breviary of the priest, the formula of the Mass is also intended to impress and represent from all sides the idea of the feast or the fundamental thoughts of the Sundays and week days.[2] Hence it follows that the changeable chants of the Mass formulas were selected with a view to the appropriate celebration of the feast or day; this should always be had in mind as a guiding principle, in ascribing a natural, suitable and edifying liturgical relation and meaning to the choral chants taken from Scripture.[3]

What has just been said is especially applicable to the Introit.

---

[1] The introduction of Psalm-singing at the beginning of Mass is ascribed to Pope Celestine I. (422—432). He ordained that for the beginning of Mass an entire Psalm or at least the greater part of a Psalm should be sung "antiphonatim", that is, alternately by two choirs. Hic multa constituta fecit et constituit, ut psalmi David 150 ante sacrificium psallerentur antiphonatim (in two choirs) ab omnibus, quod ante non fiebat, nisi tantum epistola b. Pauli recitabatur et sanctum evangelium (Lib. pontif. ed. Duch. I, 230). Coelestinus Papa psalmos ad introitum Missae cantari instituit. De quibus Gregorius Papa postea Antiphonas (sung alternately) ad introitum Missae modulando composuit. Unde adhuc primus versus ejusdem psalmi ad introitum cantatur, qui olim totus ad introitum cantabatur (Honor. Augustod. Gemma animae l. 1, c. 87). — Probst seeks to prove, that Gelasius I. (492 to 496) was the first to order the antiphonal psalm-chants as an introduction to the celebration of the Mass (cf. Die abendländische Messe § 36). — The Ordo Roman. VII, n. 2 makes the first mention of the Antiphona ad Introitum.

[2] In addition to the Mass formulas found in the Proprium Missarum de tempore, in the Proprium Missarum de Sanctis and in the Commune Sanctorum, that is, besides the Masses celebrated *secundum* ordinem Officii, there is still a number of Masses celebrated *extra* ordinem Officii, — namely, Requiem and Votive Masses. In these the contents of the changeable formula are not regulated by the course of the ecclesiastical year, but according to the special intention for which the Sacrifice is principally offered.

[3] In this all constraint and subtlety are to be avoided. In order correctly to conceive and explain each Psalm-verse in its connection with the entire Mass formula, it will, in many cases, be necessary, or at least to the purpose, to represent to one's self the contents of the entire Psalm.

Throughout its contents it is as full and varied as the liturgical year of the Church: joy, jubilation, sadness, sorrow, lamentation, hope, longing of the soul, fear, praise, thanksgiving, petition, deprecation, — in short, every religious sentiment with which the soul should be filled in the course of the ecclesiastical year, finds in the Introit brief and forcible expression. The Introit "seems intended to be the key-note to the whole service; which being one in its essence, yet adapts itself to all our wants, whether of propitiation or of thanksgiving, whether of evils to be averted or of blessings to be gained. Sometimes this introductory verse is loud and joyous, — *Gaudeamus omnes in Domino*; sometimes low and plaintive, — *Miserere mihi, Domine, quoniam tribulor;* in the Paschal solemnity the *Alleluia* rings through it all, like a peal of cheerful bells; in Passion-tide, even the *Gloria Patri* is silent, and it falls melancholy and dull; when a saint is commemorated, the nature of his virtues and triumphs is at once proclaimed; if it be a festival of Our Lord, the mystery which it celebrates is solemnly announced" (Wiseman).

The Introit strikes the tone and note proper for the ecclesiastical day and Mass[1]: the chord thus struck sounds again after shorter or longer intervals, — in the Gradual as well as in the Offertory and Communion. As the variable prayers and didactical readings also harmonize with these pieces of chant, there pervades throughout the whole Mass a uniform fundamental tone, namely, the idea of the feast or the thought of the day.

3. The ecclesiastical year begins with Advent; the time of the expectation of salvation, the time of preparation for the coming of the Lord and His redemption. The redeeming advent of the Lord is principally threefold: His descent on earth in the mystery of the Incarnation, His entrance into hearts by grace and His return again to judge mankind at the end of time. "The first Advent is humble and hidden, the second is secret and full of love, the third will be public and full of terror."[2] In the liturgy the first advent of Christ in His birth in the stable of Bethlehem is principally celebrated; as the season of Advent advances, the sentiments of the Church go on increasing in joy and longing, and thus find their corresponding expression in the Introit of the four Sunday Masses.

On the First Sunday of Advent the Church prays:

---

[1] *Introitus* Missae cum *magna devotione* cantandus est sive legendus, et ipsa cordis affectio ad Deum sollicite dirigenda. Et quia dispersio cordis ad alia devotionem hanc tollit, propterea sacerdos, antequam Missam inchoat, debet Introitum legendum praescire, et dicenda atque agenda in promptu praenoscere, ne talia quaerendo distractionem et indevotionem incurrat (Dion. Carthus. l. c.).

[2] Primus adventus fuit occultus et humilis; secundus est secretus et amabilis; tertius erit manifestus et terribilis. In primo enim venit ad nos, ut in secundo veniret in nos; in secundo venit in nos, ne in tertio veniret contra nos. In primo adventu fecit misericordiam; in secundo dat gratiam; in tertio dabit gloriam (Petr. Blesens. Serm. 3 de Adventu Domini).

Ps. 24.—Ad te levavi animam meam; Deus meus, in te confido, non erubescam; neque irrideant me inimici mei: etenim universi, qui te exspectant, non confundentur.

To Thee have I lifted up my soul; in Thee, O my God, I put my trust: let me not be ashamed. Neither let mine enemies laugh at me: for none of them that wait on Thee shall be confounded.

Ps. ib. — Vias tuas, Domine, demonstra mihi: et semitas tuas edoce me.

Show, O Lord, Thy ways to me, and teach me Thy paths.

V. Gloria Patri.

Glory be to the Father.

On this Sunday the Gospel reminds us of the end of the world, of the coming of the Judge of the World in all majesty; hence we raise our hearts and minds above the perishable things of this world and look up to God, our last end, and to Christ, "the eternal light of the faithful" (*aeterna lux credentium*). Full of confidence in God, we implore His assistance and protection against all the adversaries of salvation, His direction and guidance likewise to walk in the way of virtue and in the path of perfection, so that we may be able hopefully to look forward to the advent of the Judge of the World.

On the Second Sunday of Advent:

Is. 30. — Populus Sion: ecce Dominus veniet ad salvandum gentes: et auditam faciet Dominus gloriam vocis suae in laetitia cordis vestri.

People of Sion, behold the Lord will come to save the Gentiles: and the Lord will make the glory of His voice heard to the joy of your hearts.

Ps. 79. — Qui regis Israel, intende: qui deducis, velut ovem, Joseph.

Give ear, O Thou that rulest Israel: Thou that leadest Joseph like a sheep.

V. Gloria Patri.

Glory be to the Father.

Joy increases with the promise made that the Lord Himself will come to redeem us. As the Good Shepherd He will come upon earth to seek and to save the lost sheep: "I will feed my sheep" — thus He says — "and I will cause them to lie down. I will seek that which was lost; and that which was driven away, I will bring back again; I will strengthen that which was weak" (Ezech. 34, 15—16). This utterance of the Good Shepherd so full of sweetness and power ought to console, encourage and rejoice our poor hearts.

On the Third Sunday of Advent:

Phil. 4. — Gaudete in Domino semper: iterum dico, gaudete. Modestia vestra nota sit omnibus hominibus: Dominus enim prope est. Nihil solliciti sitis, sed in omni oratione petitiones vestrae innotescant apud Deum.

Rejoice in the Lord always; again, I say, rejoice. Let your modesty be known to all men: the Lord is nigh. Be nothing solicitous: but in everything by prayer and supplication with thanksgiving let your petitions be made known to God.

13

Ps. 84.—Benedixisti, Domine, terram tuam: avertisti captivitatem Jacob.	O Lord, Thou hast blest Thy land; Thou hast turned away the captivity of Jacob.
V. Gloria Patri.	Glory be to the Father.

The heart quickens and pulsates more joyfully now that "the Lord is already so near" (*Prope est jam Dominus*); consoled and filled with confidence, we may cast all our cares and troubles on the Lord, since He watches over us with a paternal love, shielding and defending us. He will come to break the chains of sin and of the passions, and to impart to us the blessing of redemption.

Finally, the Introit for the Fourth Sunday of Advent runs thus:

Is. 45.— Rorate coeli desuper, et nubes pluant justum: aperiatur terra et germinet Salvatorem.	Drop down dew, ye heavens, from above and let the clouds rain the just: let the earth be opened and bud forth a Saviour.
Ps. 18. — Coeli enarrant gloriam Dei et opera manuum ejus annuntiat firmamentum.	The heavens show forth the glory of God and the firmament declareth the works of His hands.
V. Gloria Patri.	Glory be to the Father.

The longing for the Saviour, who is to come, reaches the highest point: in the words of the Prophet the Church addresses her Advent cry to Heaven and earth, that they give unto us the Promised Redeemer. Soon "He shall come down like rain upon the fleece and as showers falling gently upon the earth" (Ps. 71, 6). Like unto a wonderfully refreshing rain, descending on and watering a burnt up land, will the Lord by His word and by the graces of His redemption raise up and make happy the weary, wounded hearts. Like "the flower of the field and the lily of the valley," He will bud forth from the earth, that is, He will come forth from Mary's virginal pure womb. The work of the Incarnation reflects the perfection and the glory of God a thousand times more resplendently than does the firmament with its innumerable starry worlds.

On the Vigil of Christmas the Church announces to us:

Ex. 16. — Hodie scietis, quia veniet Dominus, et salvabit nos: et mane videbitis gloriam ejus.	This day you shall know, that the Lord will come, and save us: and in the morning you shall see His glory.
Ps. 23. — Domini est terra, et plenitudo ejus: orbis terrarum et universi, qui habitant in eo.	The earth is the Lord's, and the fulness thereof: the world and all that dwell therein.
V. Gloria Patri.	Glory be to the Father.

In these words[1] does the Church proclaim the early appearance

---

[1] The biblical text (Exodus 16, 6—7) is as follows: Vespere scietis, quod Dominus eduxerit vos de terra Aegypti, et mane videbitis gloriam Domini. — Thus Moses and Aaron announced to the people of Israel the downpour of Manna. The Church now freely employs this passage of the Bible to announce to us the true Manna and Bread of Angels, that is, the Son of God become man.

of the Saviour so ardently longed for. He comes under the form of a poor babe, although He is the Lord and Owner of the universe.

Regard for the newly baptized converts had the greatest influence on the contents of the liturgy for the Easter Week.[1] The Resurrection of the Lord is a figure of the spiritual resurrection of the soul from death and from the grave of sin to the glory of the new life of grace. Now while the Introit of the feast of Easter places the glory and the beauty of the Risen Saviour before our eyes, the Introits of Easter Week present in picturesque language to the contemplation of the soul the blessed effects and graces of holy baptism. This celebration is included on Low Sunday, the Introit of which is as follows:

1 Petr. 2. — Quasi modo geniti infantes, alleluja: rationabiles, sine dolo lac concupiscite. Alleluja, alleluja, alleluja.	As new born babes, Alleluja, desire the rational milk without guile. Alleluja, Alleluja, Alleluja.
Ps. 80. — Exsultate Deo adjutori nostro: jubilate Deo Jacob.	Rejoice to God our helper: sing aloud to the God of Jacob.
V. Gloria Patri.	Glory be to the Father.

The above admonition of the Prince of the Apostles applies not only to the newly baptized, the first Communicants, and the newly converted, but in general to all Christians who have been regenerated by the holy Sacrament of Baptism, and who must become as children in order to enter into the kingdom of heaven. Christians should become children in a spiritual manner, that is, be full of innocence, simplicity, guilelessness, purity, docility, humility and obedience. That they may grow in all Christian knowledge, virtue and perfection, they must have conceived a lively and earnest desire for the "spiritual and pure milk,"[2] namely, for the pure, healthy and sweet nourishment of the spirit, which the Church offers to them in the treasures of her truth and grace. For the bestowal of such blessings we should rejoice and give thanks to God.

The Introit for the Feast of the Immaculate Conception runs thus:

Is. 61. — Gaudens gaudebo in Domino, et exsultavit anima mea in Deo meo: quia induit me vestimentis salutis: et indumento justitiae circumdedit me, quasi sponsam ornatam monilibus suis.	I will greatly rejoice in the Lord, and my soul shall be joyful in my God: for He hath clothed me with the garments of salvation: and with the robe of justice He hath covered me as a bride adorned with her jewels.

---

[1] *Baptismalia* celebrantur officia (Durand. Ration. 1. 4, c. 94).

[2] In the West for centuries it was the custom to present to the newly baptized a mixture of milk and honey to drink (mellis et lactis societas — Tertull. adv. Marc. 1. 1, c. 15), to indicate thereby the spiritual infancy (ad infantiae significationem — Hieron.) obtained by their regeneration, and to express, that by baptism they were introduced into the true "land flowing with milk and honey," that is, into the Catholic Church. (Cf. the Introit in fer. II. p. Pascha).

Ps. 29.—Exaltabo te, Domine, quoniam suscepisti me: nec delectasti inimicos meos super me.

I will extol Thee, O Lord, for Thou hast upheld me: and hast not made mine enemies to rejoice over me.

V. Gloria Patri.

Glory be to the Father.

These verses make up a hymn of thanksgiving, of praise, of triumph in the mouth of Mary, the Immaculate Virgin and Mother of God. As the Immaculate One conceived without sin, she was enriched with the fulness of gifts, graces and virtues. In the first moment of her existence she found favor with the Lord, who endowed her with power to crush the head of the infernal serpent, and to gain a complete victory over the prince of darkness.

On the Feast of Holy Confessors the Church sings at the Introit:

Ps. 61.—Justus ut palma florebit, sicut cedrus Libani multiplicabitur: plantatus in domo Domini, in atriis domus Dei nostri.

The just shall flourish like the palm, like the cedar of Libanus he shall be multiplied; having been planted in the house of the Lord, in the courts of the house of our God.

Ps. ib. — Bonum est confiteri Domino: et psallere nomini tuo, Altissime.

It is good to give praise to the Lord: and to sing to Thy name, O Most High!

V. Gloria Patri.

Glory be to the Father.

This Antiphon depicts in an excellent manner the life of the just on earth, as full of graces and virtues, and their imperishable glory in heaven. The palm, as the queen of trees, presents in its majestic height, widespreading branches and evergreen foliage an admirable figure of the holy life of the just man, elevated in spirit above all that is grovelling and low, ever rejoicing in the sunshine of eternal truth, and constantly tending upward from the perishable to the imperishable, from earth to heaven.—The other simile of the cedar, which with its massive, apparently indestructible and fragrant growth towers aloft, the pride of Mount Libanus, completes the comparison in a charming and lovely manner by the traits of its strength, and of its durability. God's saints, planted by the Heavenly Father within the "portals of the house of God," that is, in the well-watered garden of the Church, grow and strive heavenward in the sunshine of peace as well as amid the storms of temptation, where "in the house of God," that is, in the kingdom of undisturbed splendor and glory, they flourish ever green and blossom eternally.[1] Therefore, it is our pleasant and wholesome duty gratefully to praise and magnify the Most High, who is so wonderful in His saints.

Requiem Masses have the following Introit:

Requiem aeternam dona eis, Domine: et lux perpetua luceat eis.

Grant them eternal rest, O Lord, and let perpetual light shine upon them.

---

[1] Cf. Reischl zu Psalm 91. — Eberhard, Kanzelvorträge II, 449.

Ps. 64. — Te decet hymnus Deus in Sion, et tibi reddetur votum in Jerusalem: exaudi orationem meam, ad te omnis caro veniet.	A hymn becometh Thee, O God, in Sion; and a vow shall be paid to Thee in Jerusalem. O hear my prayer; all flesh shall come to Thee.
Requiem aeternam. . .	Grant them eternal rest. . .

The principal object of the Requiem Mass is to implore for the suffering souls eternal rest and perpetual light, that is, rest in the bosom of God and the light of heavenly glory. — On the lips of the suffering souls in purgatory, this verse of the Psalm expresses their longing to be allowed admission to sing to the Lord in the heavenly Sion the blessed hymn of praise and thanksgiving, and there to be enabled perfectly to fulfil their vow to God, the first and irrevocable vow made, the baptismal vow (*votum*). They made this vow already at the beginning of their earthly pilgrimage; but they shall fulfil it perfectly only in their true home, in the heavenly Jerusalem, in God's city of the perfect and the glorified. The supplication for entrance into the kingdom of eternal peace, the Lord will grant so much the sooner, since "all flesh", that is, the whole human family, "is to come to Him"; for it is His will that all men attain salvation and reach heaven.

37. The Kyrie. [1]

1. After the Introit the priest returns to the middle of the altar[2] and recites the *Kyrie eleison*[3] (= *Domine miserere*, "Lord, have mercy"), that is, alternately with the acolyte he nine times addresses fervent petitions for mercy to the triune God. The *Kyrie* is a cry for help of touching humility and simplicity, one proceeding naturally and directly from the heart, that is in want, suffering and distress; hence we come across it in many parts of the Old and the New Testaments, and formerly it resounded thousands of times from the mouths of the people supplicating God in penitential procession. — The *Kyrie* chant was sung originally in Rome by the clergy and people, later on by two choirs that repeated it alternately until the celebrant gave the sign to cease.[4] The custom of invoking

---

1 The Kyrie must be recited by the priest at all Masses without exception — hence also on Holy Saturday.

2 Very appropriately this prayer of supplication is said before the image of the Crucified, while in former times it was recited on the Epistle side (as is still observed at the solemn High Mass).

3 This cry is derived from the Greek, where it is as follows: Κύριε ἐλέησον. The latter word is the imperative of the aorist of ἐλεέω = *misereor*, and in the Latin Church language it is read *eleison;* for the Church favors Itacism, that is, she pronounces η as *i* (for example, Παράκλητος = Paráclitus). Besides, as it is read according to the Greek accent, the *i* is short and the word e-lé-ï-son has four, not three syllables. The mode of writing eleyson is incorrect. (Cfr. Stadler, Ordo divini officii, P. II, cap. 1, sect. 2, § 105.)

4 The Kyrie chant is, of course, differently arranged in all the liturgies of the East and West. As the Second Council of Vaison (529) says, it was at that time the

the Divine Mercy nine consecutive times in the Roman liturgy has been practised and prescribed since the eleventh century.

2. The frequent repetition of the *Kyrie* denotes in general the ardor, perseverance and importunity with which, impelled by the consciousness of our sinfulness and unworthiness, we implore mercy and assistance; then there is also therein a still higher, mystical and hidden meaning; wherefore the number three is thrice repeated. The three Divine Persons are separately and consecutively invoked: first, the Father by the *Kyrie eleison;* then, the Son by the *Christe eleison;* and, finally, the Holy Ghost by the *Kyrie eleison.* The invocation of each of the Divine Persons is repeated exactly three times, to signify that with each of the Divine Persons the two others are at least virtually invoked,[1] since by the fact of their mystical indwelling in one another (*circuminsessio*, περιχώρησις) all three of the Divine Persons are and live eternally in one another.[2] Other meanings, founded rather in devotion than otherwise, have still been given to this ninefold cry for mercy; thus, for instance, the ninefold signification of the *Kyrie* is devoutly thought to refer to the nine kinds of sins and wants, or it has been said that thereby we express our desire of union with the nine choirs of angels.[3]

---

universal custom to recite the Kyrie at Holy Mass *frequentius* cum grandi affectu et compunctione. — St. Gregory the Great writes to Bishop John of Syracuse concerning the divergence existing in his time in regard to the Kyrie chant in the Roman and Greek Churches: "The Greeks recite the 'Kyrie eleison' all together, but with us the clerics say it, while the people answer; we also recite 'Christe eleison' as often, which the Greeks do not." (Cfr. Bona, Rer. liturg. 1. 2, c. 4, § 1.) — In the Ambrosian Liturgy the priest alone recites the Kyrie eleison three times, and that at three stated intervals (namely, after the Gloria, after the Gospel and after the Communion).—Formerly the Kyrie was omitted at Rome in the Mass itself, if it had immediately before been said in the Litany. Thus it was still practised in the twelfth century. Kyrie non dicitur propter Litaniam processionis, ubi dictum est Kyrie (Ord. Roman. XI, n. 63).

[1] Quoniam unus est Patris et Filii Spiritus, necesse est ut dum invocatur Pater aut Filius, in Patre et Filio etiam ille qui unus est utriusque Spiritus invocetur (S. Fulgent. Contra Fabian. fragm. 31).

[2] Secunda pars praeparationis continet commemorationem praesentis miseriae, dum misericordia petitur, dicendo: "Kyrie eleison", ter quidem pro persona Patris; ter autem pro persona Filii, cum dicitur: "Christe eleison", et ter pro persona Spiritus sancti, cum subditur: "Kyrie eleison", contra triplicem miseriam ignorantiae, culpae et poenae, vel *ad significandum, quod omnes personae sunt in se invicem* (S. Thom. 3, q. 83, a. 4).

[3] Singulis in Trinitate personis ternam miseriam, nimirum culpae, poenae et defectus bonorum spiritualium exponimus, ut oculis misericordiae suae nos respicientes auferre dignentur a nobis miseriam culpae indulgendo, miseriam poenae auferendo afflictiones, miseriam defectus donando spiritualia, quibus maxime indigemus; atque ita ss. Trinitatis misericordia novem choris Angelorum aliquando consociemur. Ut autem attentius et devotius haec verba proferamus, expedit speciatim meminisse culparum nostrarum in prima harum vocum recitatione, poenarum et afflictionum in secunda, ac defectum in tertia (Van der Burg, Brevis elucidatio totius Missae cap. 2, § 4).

3. The *Kyrie* is the only short prayer in Mass rite in Greek that is now retained. The principal reason for this may be that the common supplication of the people to God for help passed already in the earliest times from the Eastern into the Western Church, in which on account of its frequent use the *Kyrie* became universally known and loved; hence the reason why this ancient and venerable form of supplication was not translated into Latin. In addition to the Greek *Kyrie*, the Hebrew expressions *Amen, Alleluia, Sabaoth, Hosanna* appear in the Latin Mass prayers, and thus in the celebration of the unbloody Sacrifice are found still united those three languages which proclaimed to the world in the glorious title on the Cross Jesus Christ's Kingdom, sovereignty of grace and dignity (John 19, 19).[1]

The *Kyrie*, as an expression of our wants, is never omitted in the celebration of Mass, and has a very appropriate place in its rite; whilst, on the one hand, it follows the Introit quite naturally, it forms, on the other hand, a suitable preparation for the Collect, or for the Gloria. The Introit expresses — sometimes in a vein of joy and praise, again in a strain of tender pity, wailing or humble supplication — such thoughts and sentiments as should principally occupy the soul at the daily celebration of Mass, that is, it serves as an introduction to the special feast or day. At the remembrance of this celebration we are so overpowered by the conviction of our own unworthiness, weakness and indigence, that our heart is involuntarily compelled to break out into the oft-repeated supplications of the *Kyrie*, since God's mercy alone can make us worthy of celebrating the holy mysteries and days in a proper manner.

The special celebration of the day opened with the Introit gives us then an opportunity at once to present our particular intentions and petitions to the Lord: here the *Kyrie* is best adapted to place the soul in suitable dispositions for prayer and to prepare it for the reception of the divine gifts.[2] Humility, confidence and desire constitute the key to the treasury, to the riches of divine mercy. Now precisely in the repeated cry of the *Kyrie* is expressed the humble acknowledgment of one's own misery, as well as one's firm confidence in the divine mercy and ardent desire for divine help. It, therefore, disposes us for the recitation of the collects that follow it, that is, for the prayer of petition coming from the consciousness of our own

---

[1] Ecclesia latina merito et satis convenienter retinet voces aliquas, tum graecas, tum hebraicas, eisque utitur in Missa, in Officio, in Litaniis etc., praesertim *Kyrie eleison*, i. e. Domine miserere. *Primo* quia habent peculiarem quandam emphasim, et ob frequentem usum aeque intelliguntur ac voces latinae. *Secundo* retinentur ob venerationem antiquitatis. *Tertio* ad indicandam Ecclesiae catholicae unitatem, praesertim ex populis hebraeis, latinis et graecis, quorum omnium litteris conscriptus fuit titulus crucis Christi (Quarti, De Litaniis Sanctorum, s. 1, pct. 6).

[2] Ideo et *Kyrie eleison* cantatur, ut subsequens oratio sacerdotis exaudiatur (Honor. Augustod. Gemma animae, l. 1, c. 92. — Cfr. Amalar. De eccles. offic. l. 3, c. 6).

need and based upon the infinite mercy of God. "By considering our own wretchedness, we are taught to pray for what we need; by the meditating on the Divine Mercy we are admonished with what fervent desires we should present our petitions. On these two wings — the misery of man and the mercy of our Divine Redeemer — prayer ascends heavenwards." — With humility and confidence, therefore, we should repeat the *Kyrie,* and in this disposition "go to the throne of grace, that we may obtain mercy and find grace in seasonable aid" (Heb. 4, 16).[1]

The *Kyrie* is, moreover, a fitting preface to the *Gloria;* filled with joy and gratitude at the very thought of the graces and favors of our merciful God, we are impelled to bless His holy name. "The *Kyrie eleison,* — that cry for mercy which is to be found in every liturgy of East and West, — seems introduced as if to give grander effect to the outburst of joy and praise which succeeds it in the *Gloria in excelsis*; it is a deepening of our humiliation, that our triumph may be the better felt" (Wiseman).

4. As long as we children of Eve are constrained to remain in this vale of tears weeping and mourning, in exile and misery (*in exsilio*), no prayer is so necessary, none so befitting our condition as the *Kyrie,* this heartfelt appeal, this humble cry for mercy to the triune God,[2] who is compassionate and merciful, long suffering and

---

[1] In omni Dei obsequio, praesertim in oratione et laude divina, duo nobis consideranda incumbunt, videlicet *Dei misericordia et nostra miseria.* Intelligo autem pro misericordia Dei omnia, quae ad bonitatem ejus respiciunt, scilicet caritatem ejus et liberalitatem et patientiam super nos. Per nostram vero miseriam universa intellego, quae nostram imperfectionem, culpam et fragilitatem concernunt. Haec igitur intente nobis pensanda sunt, quatenus ex contemplatione divinae bonitatis atque clementiae respiremus et cum fiducia ad thronum gratiae accedamus, in plenitudine fidei, certissime agnoscentes, quia quidquid oraverimus Patrem in nomine Filii, dabitur nobis, si tamen perseveranter infatigabiliterque pulsemus. Dici non valet, quantum omnipotenti Deo perseverans ac fiducialis oratio placeat. Ex consideratione vero nostrae miseriae humiliemur et displiceamus nobis vilesque simus in oculis nostris... Sic ergo sacrosancta Ecclesia convenienter instituit, ut post *Introitum,* in quo *laus Dei* cantata est, ad nos ipsos redeamus et Dei misericordiam imploremus dicentes: *Kyrie eleison,* i. e. Domine miserere. Et dicitur novies, quatenus nostram imperfectionem novies profitentes ad perfectionem ac societatem novem ordinum Angelorum perducamur (Dion. Carthus. Exposit. Missae art. 9).

[2] Inter omnia verba deprecativa verbum hoc *Miserere* videtur efficacissimum et insuperabile esse et Omnipotenti quodammodo praevalere. Nam quidquid dicenti *Miserere* dixerit Deus, ipse orans opponere potest et dicere: *Miserere.* Si dixerit Deus: "Impius es et omni misericordia mea indignus," respondeat miser: *Miserere.* Nam quia indignus sum, imo indignissimus et quasi infinite indignior, quam ego ipse comprehendere valeo, ideo dico et oro: *Miserere mei.* Et quidquid huic orationi objiciatur, scil. quod non oro ex zelo justitiae, ex caritatis affectu, idem verbum resumam dicamque: *Miserere.* Etenim quia ex zelo justitiae et caritate non oro, peto ut mihi miserrimo miserearis et des mihi ex zelo justitiae atque ex caritate et ut tibi placeat orare. A tua justitia ad misericordiam tuam confugio, quae in infinitum major est omni malitia et miseria mea: ideo *miserere mei,* a cujus verbi prolatione numquam cessabo (Dion. Carthus. De orat. art. 27).

plenteous in mercy (Ps. 102, 8). "Man born of woman, living for a short time, is filled with many miseries" (Job 14, 1), "all his days are full of sorrows and miseries" (Eccl. 2, 23): who can enumerate them — the sins, the temptations, the dangers, the defects, the weaknesses, the sufferings, the wants, the diseases, the cares, the adversities, the hardships and the tribulations that here below surround man and oppress his heart? Freedom and redemption, protection and assistance, consolation and refreshment poor man finds only with God, who is good and whose mercy endureth forever (Ps. 117, 1). "As a father hath compassion on his children, so hath the Lord compassion on them that fear Him; for He knoweth our frame and He remembereth that we are dust" (Ps. 102, 13—14). "The mercy of God will follow us all the days of our life" (Ps. 22, 6): and like unto an ever visible star, a never-setting star in the heavens, it sheds its gentle and consoling rays upon us, in the morning as well as in the evening of life. But in order that the plenitude of Divine Mercy may descend upon us, the cry of the *Kyrie* must proceed from a heart penetrated with a lively sense of its poverty and misery. [1]

38. The Gloria.

1. After the Kyrie not unfrequently follows the *Gloria in excelsis Deo*; it is called the great or greater Doxology, because in comparison with the *Gloria Patri* it contains ampler and fuller praise of the triune God; it is called the Hymn of the Angels,[2] because its opening words were sung by a host of heavenly spirits on the plains of Bethlehem on the night of the birth of Christ.

The compiler of this ancient hymn, that is, of the part added to the words of the angels, cannot be historically ascertained; only this much is undoubtedly certain, that the *Gloria* is not of Latin, but of Greek origin, and that it came from the East.[3] The Latin text, therefore, is not the original one, but a somewhat free translation or a re-arrangement of the original Greek text, which for good reasons is ascribed to St. Hilary of Poitiers, Doctor of the Church († 366).

---

[1] Constat ex his, cum quanta humilitate et affectione contritioneque cordis haec sacratissima verba Kyrie eleison dicenda sint, non cursorie, sed morose, quatenus presbyter omne genus peccati sibi indulgeri desideret, et tanto haec verba *ferventius* dicat quanto ea *saepius* iterat. Nam et ideo saepius iterantur, ut semper devotius explicentur (Dion. Carthus. Exposit. Missae art. 9).

[2] If the Gloria is called hymnus angelicus, the Te Deum hymnus SS. Ambrosii et Augustini, the Preface hymnus gloriae, then the word hymnus is not used as a technical term, but mainly in the general sense of a chant or a song of praise; for, in a stricter sense, by a church-hymn is understood a spiritual canticle expressing religious sentiments in a concise form, and composed, or at least adapted, for public liturgical use.

[3] In a somewhat altered composition, but which in all probability is the original, we find the Great Doxology already in the Apostolic Constitutions (1. 8, c. 47) as an ecclesiastical morning prayer.

In the Orient it was customary in the third century to make use of the great Doxology in the liturgy, but not at the Eucharistic Sacrificial celebration, and only as a morning hymn in the Little Hours of the Divine Office. Even now it is not recited at Mass by the Greeks; but only the words of the Angels — without further additions — are to be met with in some Oriental Mass liturgies, for instance, in that of St. James, where they are repeated three times.

With regard to the insertion of the Gloria into the Roman Mass liturgy, we have only obscure and uncertain accounts.[1] The use of the Gloria was originally and for a long period rather restricted: it served by preference for the expression of Christmas joy and the Easter chant of exultation.[2] Until nearly the close of the eleventh century the rubrics of the Gregorian Sacramentary prevailed, which granted or prescribed the recitation of the Gloria by the bishop on all Sundays and feast-days; by the priest, on the contrary, only at Easter. But from that time this privilege of the bishops was extended also to priests. Since the revision of the Missal under Pope Pius V. († 1572) the following rule holds good: as often as the Te Deum occurs in the Matins of the Office, the Gloria is said in the Mass corresponding to the Office; but if the Ambrosian Hymn is omitted in the Office, then in the Mass of the day the Angels' Hymn is not to be recited. And if on Holy Thursday[3] and Holy Saturday[4]

---

[1] According to the Liber Pontificalis, Pope Telesphorus († 136 or 138) prescribed the Angels' Hymn for Christmas night; and Pope Symmachus († 514) for Sundays and the feasts of Martyrs. Telesphorus constituit, ut ... Natali Domini noctu Missae celebrarentur ... et *ante sacrificium* hymnus diceretur angelicus, h. e. *Gloria in excelsis Deo.* — Symmachus constituit, ut omne die dominica vel natalicia martyrum *Gloria in excelsis* hymnus diceretur (Duch. 1, 129. 263). — About the middle of the eleventh century, the ordinance of Sacr. Gregor. was still in force: Dicitur Gloria in excelsis Deo — si episcopus fuerit, tantummodo die dominico sive diebus festis; a presbyteris autem minime dicitur nisi solo in Pascha. — (Cfr. Bern. Augiens. [† 1048], Libell. de quibusdam rebus ad Missae officium pertinentibus cap. 2.)

[2] Until the ninth century the Gloria, as the Te Deum at present, was sung in solemn thanksgivings. Since the eleventh century at the Introit, Kyrie, Gloria, Sanctus and Agnus Dei there occur manifold so-called tropes, that is, all manner of explanatory and amplified additions with an abundance of melody. These insertions or adornments of the liturgical text, as a rule, took place only on feast-days and were often collected into separate books (libri troparii vel troponari). (Cf. L. Gautier, Histoire de la poésie liturgique.) — An amplified Gloria — Gloria *Marianum* — was still recited here and there at the epoch of the revision of the Missal, in spite of the issued prohibition; therefore, in the Ordo Missae of the Roman Missal, after the Gloria the express ordinance was inserted: Sic (that is, as it is given in the Missal and without addition) dicitur Gloria in excelsis Deo, etiam in Missis beatae Mariae, quando dicendum est.

[3] Ob Eucharistiae institutionem est, quod in hac die, cum omnes horae sint flebiles, *sola Missa est solemnis*, tanquam in suo natali, sc. in die suae institutionis (Ludolph. de Saxon. Vita Jesu Christi p. 2, c. 56, n. 2).

[4] In Missarum solemniis "*Gloria in excelsis Deo*" canitur: hoc quippe pro baptizandis agitur, ut nimirum illucescente jam resurrectionis gloria in morte

the Gloria is sung at High Mass, although the Te Deum is omitted at Matins, it is only an apparent exception of the rule laid down; for the Mass of these two days deviates from their mournful Office, that is, it has a joyful and festive character. The Gloria and the Te Deum are enthusiastic, sublime chants of joy and exultation, expressive of festal rejoicing; hence both are omitted on days and in seasons mainly devoted to mourning and penance, or which at least are without a festive character.[1]

2. The great Doxology is as follows:

Gloria in excelsis Deo, et in terra pax hominibus bonae voluntatis.

Glory be to God on high, and on earth peace to men of good will.

Laudamus te: benedicimus te: adoramus te: glorificamus te: gratias agimus tibi propter magnam gloriam tuam: Domine Deus, Rex coelestis, Deus Pater omnipotens.

We praise Thee, we bless Thee, we adore Thee, we glorify Thee. We give thanks to Thee for Thy great glory, O Lord God, heavenly King, God the Father Almighty.

Domine, Fili unigenite, Jesu Christe: Domine Deus, Agnus Dei, Filius Patris. Qui tollis peccata mundi, miserere nobis. Qui tollis peccata mundi, suscipe deprecationem nostram. Qui sedes ad dexteram Patris, miserere nobis.

O Lord Jesus Christ, the only-begotten Son, O Lord God, Lamb of God, Son of the Father, who takest away the sins of the world, have mercy on us. Who takest away the sins of the world, receive our prayers. Who sitteth at the right hand of the Father, have mercy on us.

Quoniam tu solus Sanctus, tu solus Dominus, tu solus Altissimus, Jesu Christe, cum sancto Spiritu, in gloria Dei Patris. Amen.

For Thou only art holy, Thou only art the Lord, Thou only, O Jesus Christ, together with the Holy Ghost, art most high in the glory of God the Father. Amen.

Domini baptizari videantur, ideoque Missa, quae intra ipsum diem prohibetur, nocte celebrari praecipitur... Unde et eadem Missa simul videtur esse quodammodo quadragesimalis atque paschalis, dum postquam *Alleluja* canitur, mox etiam *Tractus*, qui Quadragesimae proprius est, adhibetur (S. Petr. Damian. De celebrand. Vigil. c. 4).

[1] Micrologus (c. 2) wrote at the close of the eleventh century: In omni festo, quod plenum habet officium, excepto intra Adventum Domini et Septuagesimam et natali Innocentium tam *presbyter* quam episcopus "Gloria in excelsis" dicunt. Quod etiam numquam post meridiem legitur dicendum nisi in Coena Domini, ubi chrisma conficitur et in sabbatis Paschae et Pentecostes. According to Amalarius (1. 4, c. 30), the Gloria was omitted during Advent about the ninth century in aliquibus locis. The same statement is made by Honorius of Autun († 1145) in the

The Gloria is the sublime triumphal chant of redemption, which partly first resounded from the choir of the heavenly hosts, and partly was an outpouring from the heart of the Church: choirs of angels entoned it at the birth of the Saviour, the Church — initiated in the mysteries of God — has continued and completed it.[1] On the plains of Bethlehem the heavenly notes of the "*Gloria in excelsis*" resounded[2] — they pealed forth with the sublimity and power of tones of "thunder", full and melodious as "the roaring of many waters." "When God laid the foundation of the earth, the morning stars praised Him in unison, and the angels made a joyful melody" (Job 38, 4—7): but this rejoicing was silenced when man sinned, and all that was saved for man on earth of holy sentiment and disposition, all that accompanied man as the only gleam of light throughout the darkness of ages, was the hope and the desire of a Redeemer. The Saviour's birth was the happy hour that summoned the angels again to rejoice: their hymn of jubilant praise to the Most High resounded on the air of this fallen world, amidst its longing sighs and lament. More quickening and refreshing to a desolate world was that chant of the angels than ever were fast falling raindrops to a parched up earth. What it now needs and desires — all, all, is contained in the words: "Glory be to God in the Highest: and on earth peace to men of good will!" (Luke 2, 14.)[3] The

---

twelfth century (cfr. Gemma animae 1. 3, c. 1). — In the Roman Church, on the contrary, the Sundays of Advent were celebrated in a festive manner until toward the close of the twelfth century — with white vestments and the Angels' Hymn (cf. Ord. Roman. XI, n. 4). From this date Rome took up also, on this point, the practice that had for a long time existed in other churches, ut hymnus angelicus *laetius solemniusque* Dominici natalis die repeteretur.

[1] Hymnum angelicum, in quo paucis verbis quaedam ab angelis circa nativitatem dominicam in laudem Dei sunt prolata, sequentes ss. Patres ad communem sanctae et individuae Trinitatis laudationem dulcissimas et congruentissimas dictiones addiderunt, ut sicut ejus principium a coelestibus est ordinatum ministris, ita etiam tota ejus series divinis esset plena mysteriis (Walafrid. Strabo c. 22).

[2] Cf. Grimm, Geschichte der Kindheit Jesu S. 281 etc. — Father Faber, Bethlehem.

[3] Gloria in altissimis Deo et in terra pax hominibus bonae voluntatis (ἐν ἀνθρώποις εὐδοκίας — Luc. 2, 14). The angelic hymn of praise is to be considered not as a wish but as an assertion, and, therefore, not ἔστω, *sit*, but ἐστίν, *est*, is to be understood. By the birth, that is, by the person and the whole work of the Saviour infinite glory is given to God reigning in heaven, and on earth peace, that is, the fulness of all the supernatural goods of salvation, to men, on whom, instead of anger, the divine good will or pleasure (εὐδοκία, bona voluntas Dei — cf. Ps. 5, 13; 50, 20) now again rests. In their liturgical use the angels' words form a chant of praise, intoned by the Church or by us, and may then properly be considered as a wish (*sit*). Here, indeed, there is question of the subjective realization and individual application of that which in the angelic hymn is represented as already realized and accomplished. In like manner, we may refer the words bonae voluntatis also to the good will of men redeemed, effected by the divine favor and grace; this good disposition, this desire of salvation is indispensable, if we wish to draw down on ourselves the divine pleasure and the plenitude of peace.

angels glorify the Child in the crib. With His birth honor is restored to God and peace to men. And this makes the angels rejoice greatly. When at Bethlehem, amid the silence of the midnight hour, the flower from the root of Jesse came forth and bloomed, visible to mortal eye, filling the world with its fragrance, then could the heavens open, then did the angels sing melodies, such as the listening earth had never heard before — melodies as might be sung only to grace a triumph wherein the Eternal God celebrated the victories of His own boundless love. The heavenly harmony filled all creation. The heavenly harmony penetrated into the very depths of the ocean, and the waves of the glorious music were wafted even over the mountain tops. Even the forests ceased their murmuring in the night wind and listened, and the streams, in which the stars glittered, flowed still more silently, that they might hear the heavenly melody.

Gloria in excelsis Deo, et in terra pax hominibus bonae voluntatis! — "Glory be to God in the highest, and on earth peace to men of good will!" Thus do we joyfully sing at the celebration of Mass in unison with the choir of heavenly hosts; for it is at the altar that this joyful message of the angel has its perfect and mysterious fulfilment. There all due honor and the highest glory are rendered unto God; for an infinite person — the God-Man Jesus Christ — debases, humbles and sacrifices Himself to the praise, acknowledgment and adoration of the Divine Majesty. There is imparted true peace to man; for Christ, by His sacrifice, purchased for us reconciliation, pardon, favor and happiness. — The initial words *Gloria Deo et pax hominibus* constitute the theme of the entire hymn. The Gloria is a chant of praise, thanksgiving and petition; for the praise of God is interrupted by thanksgiving and petition, which are likewise acts of adoration and contribute to proclaim the divine glory.

Gloria in excelsis Deo! — "Glory be to God in the highest!" The heavenly hosts never weary of praising and magnifying God; St. John in a vision heard the heavenly chant: "Let us be glad and rejoice and give glory to Him, the Lord our God, the Almighty" (demus gloriam ei — Apoc. 19, 7). In this grand hymn, in this eternal canticle of praise once heard on the plains of Bethlehem, all creation, and especially man, should unite. In praise of the Most High do the stars twinkle, the flowers bloom, the ocean is agitated, the birds sing; but by far more precious still and exalted is the praise which man in prayer consciously and freely presents to God. Hence out of the fulness of our heart we cry to the Lord: *Laudamus te*[1]—

---

[1] At the words laudare, benedicere, adorare, glorificare the varied meaning and the proper succession is worthy of consideration. The most general idea, contained in all four expressions, is that of honoring; for they denote religious veneration, but each in a different manner. Laus and benedictio are marks of honor which consist in acknowledging, extolling and announcing the perfections, privileges, virtues and merits of others with heart and mouth. Laus Dei est sapida

"We praise Thee." Yes, let us praise the Lord, for He is great and exceedingly worthy of praise, and of His greatness there is no end (Ps. 144, 3). Let us proclaim aloud, let us with heart and lips exalt His infinite power and majesty, His never-failing goodness and mercy, His boundless holiness and justice, His impenetrable ways and decrees! Matter for praise of Him can never fail us, when we contemplate the beauty and the glory of the divine essence, the number and the greatness of the divine works, wonders and mercies. It is the sweet duty and blessed vocation of the priest always to praise God — seven times a day to withdraw from the world and in the hours of prayer to chant the praises of the Lord.[1]

Benedicimus te — "We bless Thee."[2] The blessing, that is, the praising of God is a spirited and sublime praise, proceeding from the overflowing sentiments of the heart, and which we offer to the Lord chiefly to acknowledge Him as the source of all blessings, graces, gifts and mercies imparted to us. The consideration of the divine mercies inflames the heart to bless the name of the Lord, who above all is deserving of praise.[3] To the praise of the Most High

---

quaedam cognitio majestatis et perfectionis divinae, ejusque per verba interiora et exteriora magnificatio et exaltatio (Alvarez de Paz, De studio orationis 1. 4, p. 3, c. 14). Laudare and benedicere are indeed often used without distinction, but here their signification may be somewhat distinct; for benedicere (= to praise) expresses an intensive, corroborated and increased praise, as is evident from the liturgical-doxological formula Benedictus Deus (εὐλογητὸς ὁ θεός) = "May God be highly praised." Through the liturgical use of this formula, the word benedictus has obtained a certain solemnity, and in the Old Testament it is almost always, as well as in the New, where it occurs in eight passages, employed only with reference to God (Rom. 8, 5, of Christ as God). Not merely in degree, but essentially different from laus and benedictio, is adoratio, that is, adoration. In this restricted meaning adorare is to be taken, as it otherwise often designates, religious veneration in general. If to the knowledge and confession of the infinite majesty of God a corresponding subjection is added, then laus and benedictio become adoratio, that is, adoration. — The word glorificare (= to exalt, to ennoble) includes a further quality: it designates a special laudare, benedicere et adorare, that is, such as brings about among other persons glory for the one that is praised, extolled and adored. Gloria idem fere est quod honorifica laus; addit enim effectum quemdam, quem laus efficit in aliis, scil. bonam existimationem de re laudata. Est enim gloria clara cum laude notitia; unde glorificare aliquem nihil aliud est quam eum ita laudare, ut apud alios bona ejus existimatio inde oriatur (cfr. Suarez disp. 51, sect. 1, n. 1—4).

[1] Non est laboriosa, sed amabilis et optanda servitus, in Dei laudibus perpetuo assistere (Beda Venerab. 1. 1, homil. 9).

[2] Cfr. S. August. Enarrat. in Ps. 66, n. 1. — Benedicimus Deum, in quantum ejus bonitatem corde recognoscimus et ore confitemur (S. Thom. in ep. ad Rom. c. 1, lect. 7).

[3] *Benedicimus te* = bonum de te vel tibi dicimus. Nos benedicimus Deo, et Deus benedicit nobis, sed differenter valde. Nam benedictio Dei est collatio munerum divinorum et multiplicatio eorundem; benedictio igitur Dei est causa bonitatis et gratiae et sanctitatis in nobis. Benedictio vero, qua nos Deum benedicimus, est quaedam professio, qua omnia bona Deo adscribimus tanquam fonti bonitatis et sanctitatis ac gratiae (Dion. Carthus. Exposit. Missae art. 10).

St. Paul, the Apostle of the Gentiles, exhorts us: "Let the word of Christ dwell in you abundantly, in all wisdom, teaching and admonishing one another in psalms, hymns and spiritual canticles, singing in grace in your hearts to God" (Col. 3, 16). "Singing and making melody in your hearts to the Lord" (Eph. 5, 19) for all gifts and favors conferred.

Adoramus te — "We adore Thee." Adoration in itself is far more sublime than the praise and the extolling of God; for it is that supreme honor which may not be given to a mere creature, but which is due and may be rendered only to the Divine Majesty. It is by adoration that man worships his God, as the infinitely perfect Being, before whom all that is created vanishes as a mere nothing. Adoration is peculiarly the prayer of the angels and the saints in heaven. And we also in this vale of tears, being animated with holy joy and fear, should "adore and fall down and weep before the Lord that made us" (Ps. 94, 6), so that heaven and earth may form together a choir of humble joyous adoration.

Glorificamus te — "We glorify Thee." The Lord for His own honor and glory hath created all things (Prov. 16, 4); the faithful hath He called, redeemed and sanctified, that they may be to the praise of the glory of His grace (Eph. 1, 6). Every creature is in its way destined to glorify God. All that we do should be done for the greater glory of God, should tend to promote God's honor — *Omnia ad majorem Dei gloriam* —; we principally proclaim God's glory by praising Him, exalting Him and adoring Him. Namely, inasmuch as we praise, exalt and adore God, we bear a public testimony to His power, wisdom and goodness, acknowledge His absolute perfection and supreme dominion, spread His fame and His honor, make known "His name, how admirable it is on the earth, for His magnificence is elevated above the heavens" (Ps. 8, 2).[1] The Psalmist admonishes us to do this: "Bring unto the Lord glory and honor, bring to the Lord glory unto His name, adore ye the Lord in His holy court!" (Ps. 28, 2.)

Now the hymn of praise, exaltation and adoration of the Gloria changes to a canticle of thanksgiving of almost ecstatic joy: *Gratias agimus tibi propter magnam gloriam tuam* — "We give Thee thanks for Thy great glory."[2] These words have a wonderful and profound depth of meaning, springing as they do from an ardent and pure love of God. We thank God for gifts and benefits received; but how

---

[1] *Glorificamus te.* Dicimur Deum sanctificare vel magnificare, dum ei in sanctitate et aequitate servimus sicque eum magnum et sanctum esse ostendimus. Sic quoque Deum glorificamus, dum nomen ipsius aliis manifestamus, ac per hoc ipsum famosum et in animo aliorum gloriosum efficimus (Dion. Carthus. l. c.).

[2] The words propter magnam gloriam tuam may likewise be referred to the four foregoing expressions, and thus the "great glory" of the heavenly Father may be indicated as the reason and object of our praise as well as of our adoration and glorification, but even then it needs to be explained how and how far we may also *thank* God "on account of His great glory."

can we thank Him because of His great glory ?   Many seek to solve
the difficulty here presented, and they would have, for example, the
Incarnation or the mercy of God to be understood to be the glory
and the magnificence that inspire our grateful thanks.[1]   This acceptation of the meaning is evidently too restricted, for the expression glory is here to be taken in its most comprehensive sense : it
refers to the internal as well as to the external glory or glorification
of God.   We, therefore, thank God because of His great glory,
which from all eternity He has in Himself and of Himself ; we,
moreover, thank Him, and that principally, by reason of that great
glory which He has procured and continues to procure for Himself
in time by the works of His hands.

God is in Himself, that is, according to His nature, infinitely
glorious, infinitely worthy of glory, absolutely glorious, the uncreated glory itself.   This interior, eternally unchangeable and
impenetrable glory of God, we must admire, praise, adore; it may
also be a subject of gratitude for us, inasmuch as by the perfect love
of God, the divine glory becomes in a manner our property and the
source of holy joy to us.[2]   For this love of benevolence unites us
most intimately with God.   "He that abideth in charity, abideth in
Him" (1 John 4, 16).   "He who is joined to the Lord, is one spirit
(unus spiritus) with Him" (1 Cor. 6, 17).   In consequence of this
love of union we regard the goods of God as our own, and we rejoice
at the infinite perfection, happiness and glory of God more than over
our own welfare and happiness, since we should love God more than
ourselves.   Therefore, the love of God in the heavenly bliss is such
that "the greatest happiness of the blessed does not spring from the
joy over their own possession of the highest Good, but consists in the
joy experienced over the happiness and glory which God possesses,
and one's own perfection also rejoices the spirit still more, because
it is pleasing to God and tends to His honor, rather than because
that perfection is pleasing to self and redounds to one's own
honor."[3]   Nothing pleases and delights the loving soul more than
the consideration of the infinite majesty, beauty, goodness, holiness,
wisdom, power and mercy of God; therefore, it is not surprising
that the soul breaks out into a joyous chant of thanksgiving because
of the great, that is, the eternal and infinite glory of God.

---

[1]   In the Irish Stowe-Missal (of the 7th or 8th century) we read: Gratias agimus
tibi propter magnam misericordiam tuam.

[2]   Gaudium est quies animi in bono suo jam adepto.   Bonum autem proprium
non solum est quod quisque in se habet, sed etiam *quod habet in aliis sibi con-
junctis*.   Aspicies ergo Dominum ut benignissimum et dilectissimum Patrem tuum,
a quo genitus es, et (ut speras) ad aeternam haereditatem efficaciter vocatus, et
omnia ejus bona propria reputabis.   Gaudebis de omnibus perfectionibus Dei tui,
ut de ejus sapientia, bonitate et potentia et reliquis, ut de bonis benignissimi Patris
tui.   Et sufficiat tibi, quod ipse sit infinite beatus et dives adeoque exsultes de gloria
ejus (Alvarez de Paz, De studio orationis l. 6, p. 3, c. 12, exercit. 11).

[3]   Scheeben, Handbuch der Dogmatik I, 742.

Still our thanks have reference principally to the exterior glory of God, wherewith heaven and earth are filled. The rays of the glory of the Creator and Redeemer strike us everywhere. In the works of His power, the magnanimous deeds of His love and mercy, the Lord has exteriorly revealed His interior glory hidden in inaccessible light. If God acts outwardly, He glorifies Himself and He cannot but glorify Himself; but this self-glorification of God redounds to man's profit and advantage, and constitutes our happiness and our bliss.[1] God's glory is our salvation; that which gives God glory, gives us an abundance of graces and blessings. — Consider the creation of heaven and earth, the preservation and government of the world, the Incarnation, the life, the passion and death, the resurrection and ascension of Jesus Christ, the sending of the Holy Spirit, the institution of the Eucharistic Sacrifice and of the holy Sacraments, the guidance of the Church throughout the storms and conflicts of all ages, the sanctification and happiness of man, the future transformation of the world; all these works have for their object, first of all, the glory and honor of the Most High, and, at the same time, secure the welfare and salvation of man. "All is for the sake of the elect;" the elect are themselves "for the praise of the divine glory" (1 Cor. 2, 23; Eph. 1, 12). Our supreme good, that is, our eternal happiness, is the highest glory of God: nowhere is God more glorified than in heaven, where the blessed contemplate, enjoy, love, praise and glorify forever face to face His infinite goodness and beauty.[2] The thanksgiving offered to the Lord on account of His great glory, accordingly, has reference principally to the marvellous works and ways of God in the kingdom of nature, of grace and of glory, and from which flows our happiness, exaltation and beatitude.[3] The Church does not say: We thank Thee, O

---

[1] Deus "omnia operatus est propter se," h. e. operatus est omnia ad hoc, ut suam bonitatem, sapientiam, potentiam, magnificentiam, gloriam etc. creaturis ostenderet et communicaret, quod est *bonum creaturarum, non Dei.* Deus enim ex hac sui communicatione nihil acquisivit, cum nihil ei addi possit (unde et gloria, qua eum glorificant homines, Angeli et creaturae omnes, nihil ei addit, cum ipse in se habeat gloriam increatam et infinitam); sed creaturae suam essentiam, proprietates, dotes, omneque bonum suum hauserunt a Deo (Cornel. a Lapide, in Proverb. Salom. 16, 4).

[2] Dei glorificatio completur ipsa exaltatione et beatitudine Sanctorum, seu potius ipsa exaltatio et beatitudo Sanctorum est suprema Dei gloria objectiva et formalis, quod Deus ut summum bonum a creatura per visionem, amorem et inde consequentem beatitudinem in perpetuas aeternitates possidetur (Franzelin, De Deo uno thes. 29).

[3] Dum Deus spectat suam summam gloriam, eo ipso necessario spectat et intendit summum bonum nostrum, quia summa ejus gloria est summum bonum nostrum et summum bonum nostrum non potest esse nisi summa ejus gloria. Unde *non minus Deo gratias agere debemus, quod quaerat gloriam suam, quam quod quaerat salutem nostram, quia gloria ejus est nostra salus.* Hoc in Hymno angelico Ecclesia innuit, cum ait: "Gratias agimus tibi propter magnam gloriam tuam;" beneficia enim ipsius in nos sunt gloria ejus (Lessius, De perfect. divin. l. 14, c. 3.)

Lord, for Thy many benefits or mercies, — but she expresses herself in terms exceedingly beautiful and ingenious: "We thank Thee for Thy great glory;" this expression of thanks made choice of by her manifests the purest love of benevolence, — a love forgetful of self and interested only in what regards the honor of the Lord. — Praise and thanks are addressed to the first of the Divine Persons — to "God the Lord, the Heavenly King, to God the Father Almighty," who is just in all His ways and holy in all His works, and whose kingdom is a kingdom for all eternity, whose dominion extends from generation to generation (Ps. 144, 13, 17).

From the heights of the holy and enthusiastic praise of God the Gloria descends to the depths of the humble prayer of supplication; now follows a more detailed amplification of these words of the angels: "*In terra pax hominibus bonae voluntatis!*" — "On earth peace to men of good will!" Peace and reconciliation with God proceed from the Child in the manger, who by His death on the Cross established peace and reconciliation between heaven and earth (Col. 1, 20). Heaven and earth are reconciled: — this rejoices the angels, who bring the tidings down to the plains of Bethlehem, to the Child lying in the manger, precisely that He may suffer and die; in the fulness of their joy they sing: "Peace to men on earth!" Jesus Christ is peace (Mich. 5, 1), the Prince of Peace (Is. 9, 6): He restored to the world peace that was forfeited. This peace includes all the blessed effects of Redemption, a peace that is the sweet and heavenly fruit of justification, and a peace imparted to all whose will is truly good, that is, given to those subject and united to God in love. This His peace, which the world can neither bestow nor take away, the Lord has bequeathed to us, and He wills to impart it to us chiefly by means of His daily Sacrifice. Let us hasten with a yearning for salvation to the altar: there we find the Divine Child as the Victim, and with the Child we find peace — peace for time and eternity, God's peace, peace of soul, peace of heart. That heavenly peace-offering of the altar "relieves sorrows, quickens our hearts to sentiments of gratitude, love and heavenly joy."

There is, as says St. Leo in his sixth sermon for Christmas, nothing in the treasury of the divine bounty better than peace, which at the birth of our Lord was praised by the chant of the angels. This peace is "the rest of the blessed and their abiding-place for eternity." Here below it is never perfectly imparted to us: we are ever sighing under the pressure and suffering of tribulation, in the midst of which we must incessantly have recourse to the mercy of the Lord. Thus amid the loud jubilant strains of the Gloria, we are reminded of our sinfulness, frailty and poverty; for on the outburst of ardent praise follows again the cry of entreaty, expressed in most fervent and heartfelt terms. The petition is addressed to Jesus Christ,[1] and the most moving reasons are set forth for Him to hear our prayer and to listen to the voice of our supplication (Ps. 129, 2).

---

[1] Dominus Christus, qui nos *exaudit* cum Patre, orare pro nobis dignatus est ad Patrem. Quid felicitate nostra certius, quando ille pro nobis orat, qui dat quod

Domine, Fili unigenite, Jesu Christe: Domine Deus, Agnus Dei, Filius Patris — "O Lord Jesus Christ, the only-begotten Son, O Lord God, Lamb of God, Son of the Father." With this invocation the Church exhausts herself in extolling her Heavenly Chief and Spouse: she exalts His Divinity and sovereignty over all creatures; she praises Him as the only-begotten Son, whom the Father begot before the morning-star, that is, before all time (Ps. 109, 3), and in whom He is eternally well pleased (Matt. 17, 5); she celebrates Him as the Divine Victim for the honor of God and the salvation of the world; she combines all His divinely human perfections and privileges in the name of Jesus (= Saviour, Redeemer), and Christ (= the Anointed, that is, the highest Prophet, Priest and King).[1]

Qui tollis peccata mundi, miserere nobis — "Who takest away the sins of the world, have mercy on us." In torrents and to the last drop did Christ shed His precious Blood for the atonement and the cleansing of all sins, which unceasingly deluged the world and provoked God's justice to punish. The Son of God assumed a truly human heart, making it the throne of mercy, aye, allowing it to be opened and pierced with a lance, in order to show mercy and compassion on our weaknesses, wants and errors.

Qui tollis peccata mundi, suscipe deprecationem[2] nostram — "Who takest away the sins of the world, receive our supplication." Almost the same words are repeated; for the Church is greatly moved by the mercy and condescension of our Divine Saviour, who has loved us and washed our sins in His Blood (Apoc. 1, 5). Since He has given Himself for all as a propitiatory sacrifice, He will also attend to the petitions of them that fear Him, and He will save them (Ps. 144, 19).

---

orat? Est enim Christus homo et Deus: orat ut homo; dat, quod orat, ut Deus (S. Aug. Sermo 217, n. 1). — Petere et orare competit Christo secundum naturam assumptam, sed *posse implere* debetur ei secundum naturam assumentem (S. Bonav. III, dist. 17, a. 2, q. 1).

[1] Clarificatio nominis Christi est manifestatio cognitionis habitae de Christo, qua cognoscitur esse *Dei Filius* et *Christus* et *Jesus*, et quodlibet istorum est nomen super omne nomen. Nam *Filius Dei* nominat personam in *una* natura; *Christus* autem et *Jesus* nominant personam in *duabus* naturis; sed Christus nominat personam in *humana* natura relata ad divinam, quia dicitur *unctus*. *Jesus* autem nominat personam in *divina* natura relata ad humanam, quia *Jesus* dicitur Salvator esse et ideo in nomine *Jesu* Christi debet omne genu curvari (Phil. 2, 10), sicut in nomine *Filii Dei* (St. Bonav. III, dist. 18, dub. 2).

[2] Deprecatio = the solicitous, urgent, earnest petition and = the petition to avert, the petition for grace and pardon. — Precationem et deprecationem, multi nostri hoc idem putant, et hoc quotidiano usu jam omnino praevaluit. Qui autem distinctius latine locuti sunt, precationibus utebantur in optandis bonis, deprecationibus vero in devitandis malis. Precari enim dicebant esse precando bona optare; imprecari mala, quod vulgo jam dicitur maledicere; deprecari autem, mala precando depellere (S. Aug. Epistol. 149, al. 59, n. 13 ad Paulin.).

Qui sedes ad dexteram Patris, miserere nobis — "Who sitteth
at the right hand of the Father, have mercy on us." In the Holy
of Holies in heaven Christ reigns at the right of the Father, that is,
He excels, even according to His human nature, all creatures in
dignity, power and plenitude of grace, He shares in the fullest measure in the power, sovereignty and glory of God. In His heavenly
exaltation and glorification He is not only our all-powerful mediator
and advocate with the Father, but also our most merciful God and
Master, who is ever ready with divine power and clemency to forgive us, to succor us in every want and to assist us in every danger.[1]

In the beginning of the Gloria, full of pious enthusiasm, we
present the Lord our God our homage and our thanks; mindful of
our constant necessities, we then address the most ardent supplication to Jesus Christ who died, who also rose from the dead, who
sitteth at the right hand of God, who also intercedes for us (Rom.
8, 34); this cry for mercy and for a favorable hearing is changed, at
the end, into spirited tones of joy, — the Gloria now peals forth in
powerful, sublime harmony of praise to the triune God.

Quoniam tu solus[2] *Sanctus, tu solus Dominus, tu solus Altissimus, Jesu Christe, cum sancto Spiritu in gloria Dei Patris. Amen*—
"For Thou only art holy, Thou only art the Lord, Thou only, O
Jesus Christ, together with the Holy Ghost, art most high in the
glory of God the Father. Amen." The more profoundly Jesus

---

[1] Propter errorem Arii vitandum, ne videamur Christum credere creaturam, et
ne videamur ejus potestatem minuere, qua potest omnia, ejus petimus *miseratio-
nem*, non *orationem* (S. Bonav. IV, dist. 45, a. 3, q. 1).

[2] The word solus may relate either to the preceding subject tu or to the following predicate Sanctus, Dominus, Altissimus: "Thou alone art (with the Holy
Ghost and the Father) the holy, the Lord, the most high," or "Thou art (with the
Holy Ghost and the Father) the only (essentially) holy, the only Lord, the only
highest." If tu and solus are combined together, then naturally only the creatures,
but not the two other Divine Persons, are excluded from the possession of the predicate. Non dicimus absolute, quod solus Filius sit Altissimus, sed quod sit Altissimus cum sancto Spiritu in gloria Dei Patris (S. Thom. 1, q. 31, a. 4 ad 4). A passage parallel to solus and Sanctus combined together, is found in the prayer of our
Saviour to His Father: Haec est vita aeterna, ut cognoscant te, *solum Deum verum*.
—"This is eternal life, that they may know Thee, the only true God" (John 17, 3).—
Divinae naturae propria attribuuntur Filio Dei, cum ipse *solus Sanctus, solus Dominus* et *solus Altissimus* esse enuntiatur. In quibus quidem tribus Filii Dei
celebrationibus particula "solus" non excludit reliquas duas divinas personas,
Patrem, inquam, et Spiritum Sanctum, quin potius eas includit, cum illa tria praedicata *Sanctus, Dominus* et *Altissimus* sint essentialia et divinitatis concernant
substantiam. . . . Ex quo protinus evadit dilucidum, particulam illam "solus"
naturas alias a divina, ut angelicam et humanam, hic excludere. Non enim angelus aut homo secundum eam rationem sanctus est, qua dicitur Deus sanctus,
quandoquidem Deus est absolute Sanctus, Dominus et Altissimus, natura sanctitatem habens, dominatum et altitudinem, et ex se Angelus autem et homo non
suapte natura neque ex se sanctimoniam habet, dominium et celsitudinem, sed
participatione et sola gratia quadamque a Deo dependentia, perinde atque aër et
aqua claritatem mutuantur a sole per se lucido (Clichtov. Elucidat. 1. 3).

Christ has debased and humbled Himself for us and for our salvation, so much the more joyfully and gratefully do we chant these words, so replete with an enthusiastic confession of His absolute holiness, sovereignty and majesty, that is, of His divinity. "The All Holy, the Lord God, the Most High" — these titles are frequently used in Holy Scripture to designate the true God. The Father, the Son and the Holy Ghost are (of and through themselves, that is, by their essence) "the only Holy,"[1] "the only (boundless) Lord" and "the only Most High."[2] — Jesus Christ is "the (infinitely) Holy One," and, therefore, the source and prototype of all created holiness; even in His humanity are to be found all the treasures of grace and virtue. — He is still "the Lord",[3] that is, the absolute proprietor, sovereign and judge of the universe; He is the blessed and the only Powerful (*solus potens*), the King of kings and the Lord of lords (1 Tim. 6, 15), whom all creatures serve and to whom man in particular owes the most profound reverence and submission. Also as man Christ is our Lord; for "He came and paid the ransom, He shed His Blood and bought the earth."[4] — He is "the Most High," since by reason of His divine greatness, grandeur and majesty He infinitely excels all created things. His holy humanity also is exalted and glorified above all things; for God raised Him from the dead and placed Him at His right hand in heaven, above all kingdoms, above all power and might and sovereignty and every name that is mentioned, not only in this world, but also in the world to come. And God hath put all things under His feet, and He hath made Him Head over all the Church, which is His body (Eph. 1, 20–23).

Thus ends the glorious hymn of praise with a joyous look to heaven and to the glorious majesty of the triune God: we exult, because the Son of God possesses with the Holy Ghost the same glory which the Father has from eternity. "Every tongue should confess that the Lord Jesus Christ is in the glory of God the Father" (*in gloria Dei Patris*) (Phil. 2, 11).

3. While the priest recites the Gloria, he stands erect at the middle of the altar with hands joined: only a few simple ceremonies are prescribed to emphasize and to give stress to certain particular words of the text. At the words *Gloria in excelsis*, the priest, without raising his eyes at the time, extends and elevates his hands to

---

[1] Like Dominus et Altissimus the word Sanctus also is not to be taken here as an adjective, but as a substantive: it designates Him, whose whole essence is holiness and from whom proceeds all created holiness.

[2] Cf. Ps. 82, 19: Et cognoscant, quia nomen tibi *Dominus;* tu *solus Altissimus* in omni terra — "Let them know that the Lord is Thy name, — Thou alone art the Most High over all the earth."

[3] Nomen et ratio Domini *soli* omnipotenti *Deo* plene, summe, pure ac proprie competit, quippe qui solus universale, primordiale, independens ac nulli subjectum habet dominium (Dion. Carthus. in Luc. 1, 68).

[4] Venit Redemptor et dedit pretium; fudit sanguinem suum, emit orbem terrarum (S. Aug. Enarrat. in Ps. 95, n. 5).

the shoulders, thus giving vent to his eagerness, enthusiasm and longing to praise and to magnify God. At *Deo* he again joins his hands and bows his head profoundly toward the Crucifix on the altar (or toward the Blessed Sacrament when exposed); for "holy and terrible is the name of God" (*sanctum et terribile nomen ejus* — Ps. 110, 9). This profound inclination of the head is several times repeated, to express the interior acts of adoration (*adoramus te*), of gratitude (*gratias agimus tibi*), of petition (*suscipe deprecationem nostram*), of reverence (*Jesu Christe*), and to give expression to these acts of homage not merely in words, but also by the body in bowing the head. At the last words of the Gloria the celebrant signs himself with the sign of the Cross, — principally to close the sublime hymn in a suitable and worthy manner. But as the sign of the Cross is of itself a symbolical representation of the Trinity, it may also be referred to the glory of the Holy Trinity expressed in the concluding words of the hymn; for the acknowledgment of the three Divine Persons is often, although not always, accompanied with the sign of the Cross.[1]

4. This Hymn of the Angels should be recited and sung with angelic devotion.[2] During it we should unite in heart and lips with the choirs of the heavenly hosts, who daily assemble around the altar and never grow weary of chanting God's praise and our happiness, as they once sang at the crib of the new-born Saviour. There the blessed spirits themselves sang for us the hymn, to teach us how we should thank the Lord for having raised us up, poor sinful creatures, from the dust, and for having destined us to occupy the thrones of their fallen brethren in the other world, to whom God vouchsafed neither time nor grace for repentance.[3]

---

[1] Litania Kyrie eleison finita, dirigens se Pontifex contra populum incipit *Gloria in excelsis Deo* et statim regyrat se (he turns around) ad Orientem (to the altar) usquedum finiatur (Ordo Roman. 1, n. 9). This turning of the celebrant while entoning to the people, which probably was meant to invite and summon them to praise God, was no longer customary in the ninth century. According to Amalarius († 857) the Gloria was entoned while facing the East (that is, toward the altar, where our Lord is), but on the Epistle side (cfr. De ecclesiast. offic. 1. 3, c. 8). — Later on it was judged more suitable to recite the Angels' Hymn before the image of the Crucified in the middle of the altar (cfr. Durand. Rational. 1. 4, c. 13, n. 1).

[2] Hoc angelicum canticum cum magna cordis laetitia ac devotione dulcissima est cantandum sive legendum, quod fieri nequit, nisi intellectus in contemplatione Dei stabiliter atque sincere firmetur. Quanto enim verba fuerint diviniora, tanto ampliorem advertentiam et elevationem mentis puriorem requirunt; quo etiam sensus divinorum verborum affectuosior est atque profundior, eo modica cordis distractio vehementius nocet ac impedit. Postremo quum Deus attente orandus sit, attentius tamen laudandus est, et tanto attentius quanto majus ac dignius est Deum laudare quam orare (Dion. Carthus. Exposit. Missae art. 10).

[3] Quaedam dicuntur a choro, quae pertinent ad populum, quorum quaedam chorus *totaliter* prosequitur, quae scil. toti populo inspirantur; quaedam vero populus prosequitur *sacerdote inchoante*, qui personam Dei gerit, in signum quod talia pervenerunt ad populum ex revelatione divina, sicut fides et gloria coelestis,

"In this hymn we are reminded of the marvellous joys which happened to the whole world, when God sent to condemned man a Saviour from heaven. This hymn the Church of God likewise sings with great joy, like unto that joy which any man might in all reason experience on favorably and bounteously receiving what he stood in great need of, for which he had entertained an ardent desire and for which he had earnestly and suppliantly prayed. As though our cries to God had just now been heard and we had but just obtained from God the fulfilment of our desires, the priest begins with great joy to praise God: "Honor and glory be to God in the highest," — and the choir, in the place of the entire congregation, who can no longer restrain their hearts overflowing with exultation, unite with the priest, and with lips and heart they jointly sing the praises of God, who has acted so mercifully toward us, praising and extolling His graces in many joyful words" (Ein Vergissmeinnicht S. 65).

"No composition ever lent itself more perfectly (than the Gloria) to the musician's skill; none ever afforded better play to the rich and rapid succession of every mode, gay and grave; none better supplied the slow and entreating cadence, or the full and powerful chorus. In the simple Gregorian chant, or in the pure religious harmonies of Palestrina, it is truly 'the hymn of the Angels' " (Wiseman).

The glorious Apostle and Protector of Rome — St. Philip Neri — on the day of his death, namely, on the feast of Corpus Christi (May 26, 1595), at a very early hour celebrated a low Mass. At the *Gloria in excelsis,* he was suddenly rapt in ecstasy and he began to sing; full of devotion and jubilation of heart, in a clear, loud voice, he sang the "Angels' Hymn" from the beginning to the end, as though he had already departed from earth and was rejoicing among the choirs of the blessed spirits.

39. The Collect.

After the Gloria, or the Kyrie, follows the principal prayer, that is, the peculiar prayer of the day or of the feast, and which, as a rule, is called the Collect.[1] It has here an appropriate place in the arrangement of the Mass rite; for by the humble and confident cry for mercy in the Kyrie, as well as by the praising of the divine power and goodness in the Gloria, we have placed ourselves in the sentiments befitting prayer, that is, disposed ourselves to receive

---

et ideo sacerdos inchoat Symbolum fidei et Gloria in excelsis Deo (S. Thom. 3, q. 83, a. 4 ad 6).

[1] In the Roman Missal the heading of this prayer is *Oratio,* whereby it is in an eminent sense characterized as a prayer. The name Collecta is ascribed to it in the summarized exposition of the Mass Rite (Ritus celebr. Miss. tit. 11, n. 1). To the proper prayer of the day there are generally added some others; they too are called Collectae, whether prescribed by the rubrics and decrees (Orationes *prae-scriptae*) or ordered (Orationes *imperatae* sc. a Superiore) by ecclesiastical super-iors (Pope or Bishop), or on certain days of lower rite, when they are added by the celebrant (ex privata devotione) to the others (Orationes *votivae*).

from God a favorable answer to our petitions. "The Lord hath had regard to the prayer of the humble, and He hath not despised their petitions" (Ps. 101, 18); "the prayer of the humble and the meek hath always pleased Him" (Judith 9, 16), "it pierceth the clouds and till it come nigh, he will not be comforted and he will not depart until the Most High behold" (Ecclus. 35, 21), that is, until the prayer is answered. The Collects are prayers of petition,[1] in which the Church by the mouth of the priest presents to God her maternal desires and interests, in order to obtain for her children the special gifts and graces corresponding to the different feasts and times of the holy year. The Collect, although but a small portion of the liturgy of the Mass, presents, nevertheless, in several respects some very important and interesting features.

1. The name *Collecta*.[2]

The single formulas for Mass are uniformly arranged according to a determined rule; hence they all have in the same way differently named prayers. The first prayer comes before the Epistle and is called *Oratio*, or *Collecta* (collected prayer); the second forms the conclusion of the *Offertorium* and is called *Secreta* (silent prayer); the third and last follows the Communion and is called *Postcommunio* (Communion prayer). — The Collect now engages our attention, and the origin and meaning of this somewhat peculiar name will first be explained.

The word *Collecta*[3] frequently designated in former times the religious assembly or congregation of the faithful for the exercises of divine service, and principally for the Sacrifice of the Mass; then it was made to designate the celebration of divine worship itself, — of the ordinary morning and night prayer, the prayer in choir, of the Holy Sacrifice. *Collecta* was the name especially given to the preparatory divine service held on the Station days in a particular

---

[1] In officio Missae est *ordinatissima mixtio* commemorationis divinae excellentiae, quam laudamus, et recognitionis nostrae miseriae, pro qua oramus; nam post *Confessionem* ante altare, in qua nostram profitemur miseriam, inchoatur *Introitus*, qui est cantus laudis divinae, et statim subjunguntur *Kyrie eleison*, in quo rursus humiliamus nos ipsos, nostram miseriam declarantes. Hoc finito ad Dei laudem convertimur, dicentes *Gloria in excelsis Deo*, quo completo *Oratio* sequitur, in qua denuo consideramus nos ipsos et misericordiam imploramus miseriae nostrae (Dion. Carthus. Expos. Missae art. 11).

[2] Sequitur oratio prima, quam *Collectam* dicunt (Ordo Roman. II, n. 6). — Prima oratio dicitur aliquando *Oratio*, aliquando *Collecta* (Amalar. [† 857] Eclog. n. 23). — *Oratio* sive *Collecta* statim subsequitur, quamtumvis Collecta *proprie* vocetur oratio illa, quae fit in processione, cum populus et universus clerus ab una ecclesia procedit ad alteram (Beleth. c. 37).

[3] Collecta (from colligere = to collect or to gather) is a substantive form instead of collectio. In the Vulgate and the Fathers Collecta is also the name of the (public) gathering of alms and charity. (Cfr. 1 Cor. 16, 2.) — The corresponding Greek word *synaxis* (σύναξις from συνάγω) is also frequently used to denote the assemblies of the faithful for divine worship, the celebration of the Eucharistic Sacrifice, and especially Holy Communion.

church, which preceded the procession to the Station Church. At this preliminary celebration the blessing and the concluding prayer of the celebrant, namely, the *Oratio ad Collectam*, that is, the prayer at the religious gathering, formed the principal part. The longer term *Oratio ad Collectam* was then abbreviated and merely the word *Collecta* was used to designate the prayer, thus transferring the name of the whole to the principal part. Now, if the name Collect was originally given to that prayer which was addressed to the assembled people at the preparatory service of the Station celebration (*super populum collectum*), then it was evident that the first Mass prayer to be said soon after in the Station Church should likewise be called Collect, since it also was a prayer at the Collect, that is, at the assembly and celebration of divine worship.[1] — With this historical interpretation are found to harmonize naturally certain other explanations, which are often unjustifiably advanced and emphasized on their own merits alone, that is, without regard to the historic origin and foundation of the term *Collecta*.

Like the Mass prayers in general, this prayer before the Epistle is not merely a private prayer of the priest, but a liturgical one, that is, a public prayer which the celebrant recites in the name and by the commission, as well as according to the ordinance of the Church, and with a special intention for the welfare of the whole Christian people.[2] The priest stands at the altar as mediator between God and man, he there presents the desires and interests of all before the throne of God. To him applies what is said of the Prophet Jeremias: "This is a lover of his brethren and of the people Israel, this is he that prayeth much for the people and for all the city" (2 Mac. 15, 14). The faithful assisting at the Sacrifice are of one heart and one soul, they pray interiorly and unite with the priest who, as their representative, gathers up and collects, so to say, their supplications and desires to present them before the God of holiness (*vota populi colligit*).[3] The celebrant is the angel of the Lord who puts the holy incense, namely, the devout prayers of fervent Christians, into the golden chalice of his heart, whence they sweetly ascend to the throne of the Most High (Apoc. 8, 3—4).

As a collective prayer, the Collect is still to be considered under another aspect. It is considered, namely, as a prayer which in comprehensive brevity (*compendiosa brevitate*) embodies the most

---

[1] *Collectam* proprie dici volunt eam orationem, quae olim super populum fieri solebat, quando collectus in unum erat cum universo Clero in una Ecclesia, ut ad aliam procederet, in qua Statio celebranda erat. Ex quo fieri potuit, ut ad reliquas hujusmodi orationes *Collectae* nomen dimanarit (Bona, Rer. liturg. 1. 2, c. 5, § 3).

[2] Oratio *publica* est, quae a ministris Ecclesiae pro populo manifeste ac solemniter funditur, quam oportet non solum esse mentalem, sed etiam vocalem (Dion. Carthus. IV, dist. 15, q. 6).

[3] Orationes, quae circa principium Missae dicuntur, *Collectae* vocantur eo quod sacerdos, qui fungitur ad Deum legatione pro populo *petitiones omnium in eis colligat et concludat* (Innocent. III., De sacr. altar. myster. 1. 2, c. 27).

important petitions, that is, the sum or idea of all that we, in consideration of the day's celebration, especially seek to obtain from God.[1] With this feature of the Collect its place in the Divine Office harmonizes perfectly; it returns almost in every Hour[2] and in such a way that the whole of the prayer preceding it finds therein a short and solemn conclusion. It is, therefore, the peculiar prayer of the day, that is, the prayer in which the Church repeatedly expresses what is nearest to her heart and what she principally desires for her children.

Finally, some persons — and indeed in a manner more edifying than solid — discover in the word *Collecta* an admonition for priest and people to gather and keep all their senses and thoughts collected together, in order to offer to God in profound recollection of spirit (*collectis animis*) the supplications comprised in the prayer.[3] — Collect is, therefore, an ingenious, deeply significant term for the first prayer of Holy Mass: the name itself recalls the beautiful Station solemnities of early Christian ages, at the same time it characterizes the Oration as a liturgical prayer of the priest, draws attention to the rich contents embodied in its few words and, moreover, reminds us of the pious disposition of soul required for its recitation.[4]

2.　The Liturgical Kissing of the Altar.[5]

---

[1] This name of *Collects*, in fine, has its origin in the fact that the words, of which they are composed, are taken from all that is most touching and beautiful in Holy Scripture, in the treasures of tradition, or even in the lives of the saints, whose feasts are celebrated; it is a wonderful epitome, a substantial abridgment which sums up everything (Pichenot, Les Collectes p. 8).

[2] Prime and Complin have — as liturgical morning and evening prayers — always the same Oration, and in the Vespers of Lent the Oratio super populum is recited.

[3] Sequitur oratio, quae *Collecta* dicitur eo quod omnes adstantes Missae se *debeant devote colligere* et cum sacerdote fideliter orare (S. Bonav. Exp. Miss. c. 2).

[4] Brevis haec oratio ideo *Collecta* dicitur, quia populo in unum congregato et collecto recitatur, vel quia sacerdos legatione apud Deum pro omnibus fungens omnium vota in unum colligit, vel quia ex selectis s. Scripturae et Ecclesiae verbis compendiosa brevitate colligitur, vel quia omnes collectis animis affectus suos et mentem ad Deum attollunt (Bona l. c.).

[5] Already the most ancient Roman Ordos and all the Missals of the Middle Age prescribe the kissing of the altar several times during the celebration of the Eucharistic Sacrifice. The unauthorized assertion that the kissing of the altar in this manner at the celebration of Mass is, "without doubt, repeated too frequently" (Lüft, Liturgik II, 542), is absolutely to be rejected; for the present ordinance and practice of the Church, according to which the celebrant kisses the altar quite often, is based on the signification of this liturgical osculum. As the specially dedicated place of sacrifice, as the resting-place of the Body and Blood of Christ, as the tomb of the relics of the martyrs and as the symbol of Christ, our Divine Victim, the altar is incontestably the most excellent and the holiest part of the Church and, therefore, deserving of all the veneration rendered by the kissing. — This liturgical kiss does not merely apply to the sanctified place of sacrifice, but principally to the invisible Victim and Sacrificing Priest, whom the altar symbol-

The Collect is introduced by the kissing of the altar, the mutual salutation and the invitation to prayer. — After the celebrant at the conclusion of the Gloria has made the sign of the Cross on himself, he immediately, without joining his hands,[1] kisses the altar in the middle, because the holy stone is there which represents Jesus Christ, the living Head and Corner-stone of the Church, and also because principally in this place rest the relics of the martyrs. In the kissing of the altar we may distinguish a twofold meaning: first of all, it is a sign and expression of benevolent love; and then, a proof of reverence and devotedness. Hence the special meaning of kissing the altar at this part of the Mass is now evident. In a full sense, the altar is a symbol of Christ and the saints united with Him in glory; it represents the triumphant Church in heaven as a whole; to it belong Christ as the Head and the elect as His members. Now, since the priest stands at the altar as a mediator between heaven and earth, he, therefore, first salutes with the altar-kiss the triumphant Church, to tender to it his love and reverence,[2] then by the *Dominus vobiscum* the Church militant in words that call down upon the latter salvation and blessing.

3. The Priest's Salutation.

With hands joined before his breast and with downcast eyes, the priest with grave and measured step turns (on his right) toward the people; then, while slowly extending and joining the hands,[3] in the person of those present he salutes the entire Church with the benediction: *Dominus vobiscum* — "The Lord be with you." This motion of the hands, which is repeated in precisely the same manner at the *Oremus*, harmonizes perfectly with the meaning of the words spoken. The extending of the hands expresses the ardent longing and the earnest desire of the priest, that the blessing he invokes may be bestowed; the joining of the hands signifies that the priest humbly mistrusts his own strength and confidently abandons himself to the Lord.

---

ically indicates. If the priest thinks of this, he will be touched by this ceremony and incited to devotion, and will joyfully often repeat the kissing of the altar, in order, in his own name and in the name of the faithful, anew to present to our Saviour sacrificing Himself for us, due love, veneration and gratitude (cf. Augsburger Pastoralbl. Jahrg. 1879, S. 265 etc.).

[1] In like manner the hands must not be joined after the Sign of the Cross at the end of the Credo and Sanctus (S. R. C. 12. Nov. 1831).

[2] The priest kisses the altar each time before turning to the people, and, with the words *Dominus vobiscum*, wishing the people to their very face, as it were, the divine blessing in a more impressive manner. He would, namely — for thus also may this rite be interpreted — not turn to the people, without having previously evinced toward the sanctuary this reverence, and he would at the same time indicate that all the help and all the blessings of grace that he wishes to the people present, must come from the altar and from our union with the Saviour sacrificing Himself upon it.

[3] Without raising them.

This formula of well-wishing dates back to the Old Testament. In the book of Ruth it is related, that Booz greeted his reapers in the field with the words: "The Lord be with you,"[1] and that they answered him: "The Lord bless thee." To the blessed Virgin the Archangel Gabriel said: *Dominus tecum* — "The Lord (is) with thee" (Luke 1, 28).—The aforesaid mutual salutation[2] is frequently repeated during the celebration of Mass (eight times), in order constantly to excite, increase and awaken afresh the spiritual union and the communion of prayer during the Holy Sacrifice between the priest and the people. As the meaning of this general formula of salutation is uncommonly copious, its special signification must be explained according to the place and connection in which it occurs. Where the Lord is, there He produces the most happy results, there He imparts manifold gifts, graces and blessings. By the formula *Dominus vobiscum* are wished all the goods, which are connected with the presence of the Lord.

Inasmuch as the priest before the Collect expresses his wish, that the Lord come into the hearts of the people, he at the same time intends to implore for the faithful the assistance of the grace, light and strength necessary for a good and perfect prayer.[3] The words *Dominus vobiscum* in this place are, consequently, a request for the assistance of divine grace, to enable the faithful to pray efficaciously and to ask for what is proper, since all our sufficiency is from God, and without Christ we can do nothing profitable for salvation (2 Cor. 3, 5; John 15, 5). Prayer presupposes the assistance of divine grace, without which its practice is not possible. "We know not what we should pray for as we ought;" therefore "the Spirit must help our infirmity." Yes, the Holy Ghost Himself "asketh for us with unspeakable groanings" (Rom. 8, 26), that is, He awakens in us the desire to pray, He urges us to pray, He grants us devotion and perseverance in prayer, He renders our prayer pleasing and meritorious in the sight of God.[4] "The spirit of grace and of supplication" (*spiritus gratiae et precum* — Zach. 12, 10), which the Lord pours

---

[1] Booz veniebat de Bethlehem dixitque messoribus: Dominus vobiscum. Qui responderunt ei: Benedicat tibi Dominus (Ruth 2, 4).

[2] At the recitation of the Divine Office only the priest and deacon (but not the sub-deacon) may say the Dominus vobiscum before and after the prayer; by this is signified that here there is question of a canonical salutation, which presupposes the Sacrament of Order on the part of him who pronounces the blessing.

[3] Dominus vobiscum, i. e. gratiam vobis infundat devote mecum orandi et sacra verba digne atque salubriter audiendi, et haec verba ex libro Ruth sumpta videntur, suntque affectuose a sacerdote dicenda, velut a mediatore inter Deum et populum, secundum exigentiam caritatis fraternae, quae in sacerdotibus exuberantior esse debet (Dion. Carthus. Expos. Missae art. 11).

[4] Illo modo recte accipitur, quo solet significari per efficientem id quod efficitur, i. e. gemere, desiderare et postulare nos faciat Spiritus sanctus, dum scilicet gemendi atque postulari cordibus nostris inspirat affectum (S. Fulgent. Contra Fabian. fragm. 5).

out over His Church, is, indeed, a great and precious gift, since prayer itself is the source of so many blessings.

In addition to the grace of prayer, which is here principally and first of all desired, the salutatory blessing of the priest comprises numberless other graces; for when the Lord enters into a pure and penitent heart, at the same time all good things come along with Him — riches, glory, peace, joy and happiness. When our Lord is with us, He imparts the desire and the relish for all that is good; strength in all combats and persecutions, consolation in all sufferings and encouragement in all temptations. The possession, the grace and the love of God, the soul's familiar intercourse and confident communion with God constitute a boundless treasure for man. Whoever lives and perseveres in this intimate union with God, may with confidence exclaim in the words of David: "Though I should walk in the midst of the shadow of death, I will fear no evil, for Thou, O Lord, art with me" (Ps. 22, 4). Therefore, the priest could not wish anything better to the faithful than what is included in the greeting *Dominus vobiscum*; for "blessed is the nation whose God is the Lord; the people whom He hath chosen for His inheritance" (Ps. 32, 12).

And how do the people respond to this greeting of the priest? By the mouth of the acolyte, they answer with the corresponding greeting: *Et cum spiritu tuo* — "And with thy spirit."[1] The same or a similar wish for a blessing St. Paul frequently employed in his Epistles.[2] Out of gratitude for the imparted salutation and blessing, the people express the wish that the Lord would with His enlightening and strengthening grace replenish and penetrate the spirit[3] of

---

[1] In a profoundly significant manner does St. Chrysostom refer the word *spiritus* — spirit — to the divine πνεῦμα, imparted at the ordination by the imposition of hands. "If the Holy Ghost were not in this your common father and teacher, you would not recently, when he ascended this holy chair and wished you all peace, have cried out with one accord: *And with thy spirit.* Thus you cry out to him, not only when he ascends his throne, when he speaks to you and prays for you, but also when he stands at this holy altar, to offer the dread Sacrifice. He does not touch that which lies on the altar before wishing you the grace of our Lord and before you have replied to him: *And with thy spirit.* By this cry you are reminded that he who stands at the altar does nothing, and that the gifts, that repose thereon, are not the merits of a man, but that the grace of the Holy Ghost is present and, descending on all, accomplishes this mysterious Sacrifice. We see indeed a man, but God it is who acts through him. Nothing human takes place at this holy altar" (First Homily for the Feast of Pentecost, Number 4).

[2] Dominus Jesus Christus *cum spiritu tuo* (2 Tim. 4, 22). — Gratia Domini nostri Jesu Christi *cum spiritu vestro* (Gal. 6, 22).

[3] Nec vacat mysterio, quod sacerdoti dicenti: *"Dominus vobiscum"* non respondeatur: "Et tecum," sed: *"Et cum spiritu tuo,"* quod verbum est majoris momenti magisque spirituale, quasi respondentes optent, Dominum implere spiritum ejus devotione, ut magno fervore pro omnibus oret, ita ut ejus oratio non solum lingua proferatur, sed multo magis corde et spiritu (De Ponte, De christ. hom. perfect. IV, tr. 2, c. 11, § 2).

the celebrant, that he may, as a man of God, as a truly spiritual man, be enabled to present in a worthy manner the petitions and supplications of the whole Church. The priest does indeed greatly stand in need of the assistance of this grace, when he is standing at the altar; for "holy is this place, where he prays for the transgressions and sins of the people" — *Locus iste sanctus est, in quo orat sacerdos pro delictis et peccatis populi.* In that he prays and offers as a minister of the Church, he discharges the most exalted duty that the Church has to fulfil toward God. The priest appears at the altar by commission of the Church, the immaculate Spouse of Christ, there to recite for the welfare and salvation of the living and the dead those venerable prayers which she herself, inspired by the Holy Ghost, has composed and prescribed. Now, if we are already obliged to prepare our soul carefully for every private prayer, how much more is this necessary for the prayers of the Mass: how great then should be the celebrant's recollection of mind, devotion and fervor of heart, that he may offer up worthily such holy, such sublime words to the Most High![1]

"The Lord be with thy spirit," — this wish also reminds the priest of the solemn hour, when on receiving the tonsure he made the offering of the adornment of his hair as a figure of his renunciation thenceforth, for the love of Jesus Christ, of all the goods and joys of this world — as he cheerfully uttered the words: *Dominus pars haereditatis meae et calicis mei* — "The Lord is the portion of my inheritance and of my cup" (Ps. 15, 5). Then it was that "the lines fell to him in goodly places, and his inheritance became goodly to him;" for then the Lord became his sole possession, his precious legacy, his fortune and property, his reward. All this the priest cannot but remember, whenever he hears this salutation from the lips of the people: he cannot but renew, on his part, his promise to consecrate himself entirely to the Lord, and wish that he should ever remain the Lord's special property and possession, in order that he may be a true cleric in the fullest sense of the term.

The bishop salutes the faithful (as does the priest) during Holy Mass with the *Dominus vobiscum*; except that in this place (that is, before the Collect) the bishop's salutation on those days on which the Gloria is said, is: *Pax vobis* "Peace be to you!"[2] The connec-

---

[1] Quamvis oratio boni sacerdotis efficacior sit ad impetrandum quam mali, tamen oratio, imo et totum officium mali sacerdotis virtutem sortitur et ad impetrandum fit efficax, in quantum sacerdos talis orat et agit in persona totius Ecclesiae. Praeterea quamvis ubique et semper Deus ab omni christiano reverenter et pure atque sollicite exorandus consistat, a sacerdote tamen in Missa tanto ardentius sinceriusque orandus est, quanto causa orandi est major et ipsum officium dignius, persona quoque Christo vicinior, ut puta mediator Dei et plebis (Dion. Carthus. l. c.).

[2] Postea salutans populum Pontifex dicit *"Pax vobiscum"* sive *"Pax vobis"*. Respond. *"Et cum spiritu tuo"* (Ordo Rom. II, n. 6). Before the Offertory it says n. 9: Salutat episcopus populum dicens: *Dominus vobiscum.* — The words Pax vobis were regarded, even in the tenth century, as a festive, joyful formula of

tion between this salutation and the Hymn of the Angels should not be passed over: the bishop invokes that peace which is announced in the Gloria.[1] Therefore, as it was the privilege of the bishop to recite the Hymn of the Angels on all Sundays and feast-days, while the same was permitted to priests only at Easter, in like manner, the bishops alone were allowed to salute the faithful immediately after the Gloria with the *Pax vobis*. From the end of the eleventh century the recitation of the Gloria ceased, indeed, to be the exclusive privilege of bishops, as priests were then placed on the same footing as they in this matter; but the greeting of the people with *Pax vobis* was, nevertheless, reserved to them as a peculiar distinction. The formula *Pax vobis* has a certain preference over *Dominus vobiscum*; this preference does not lie in its contents, but in the fact that the Lord Himself had frequently this salutation *Pax vobis* on His lips and thereby sanctified it. Therefore, if the bishop salutes the faithful with *Pax vobis*, he hereby manifests himself in a special manner as the representative of the Lord who, after His Resurrection, said to His disciples: "Peace be to you!"[2] As successors of the Apostles, bishops also possess (in addition to other privileges) a greater power of dispensing graces and blessings than priests enjoy; for they possess the plenitude of the power of Order for the administration and dispensation of the heavenly treasures of grace. This sublime and more complete power of blessing, connected with the bishop's consecration and dignity, is very appropriately exhibited by the bishop's saluting the faithful at the commencement of Mass with the *Pax vobis*, as well as at the end of Mass in the concluding benediction by the threefold sign of the Cross. — The salutation of peace *Pax vobis*, which the bishop, after the example of Christ and the Apostles, utters on certain days in the Mass, contains in itself the plenitude of every good. — However, salvation and blessing for time and eternity are also essentially comprised in the *Dominus vobiscum:* for where our Lord is, there also is His peace.[3]

---

salutation and were, therefore, not used on penitential days. The Ordo Rom. XIV, c. 79 (written before the middle of the fourteenth century) contains the rubric: Ante orationem non dicit: *Pax vobis*, sed tantum: *Dominus vobiscum*, et sic in omnibus feriis et dominicis tam Quadragesimae quam et Adventus, exceptis Dominica *Gaudete* et *Laetare*.

[1] Episcopus celebrans in festis in prima salutatione dicit: "*Pax vobis*", quod post resurrectionem discipulis dixit Dominus, cujus personam repraesentat praecipue Episcopus (S. Thom. 3, q. 83, a. 5 ad 6).

[2] Pontifex salutationem praemittit ad populum dicens: Pax vobis; illius utens eulogio, cujus fungitur pontificio. Minor autem sacerdos ait: Dominus vobiscum. Ut episcopus se ostendat Christi vicarium, prima vice dicit: Pax vobis. Quoniam haec fuit prima vox Christi ad discipulos, cum eis post resurrectionem apparuit. Ad instar vero sacerdotum ceterorum dicit postea: Dominus vobiscum; ut se unum ex ipsis ostendat (Innoc. III., De sacr. alt. myst. 1. 2, c. 24). — Cfr. Sicard. Mitral. 1. 3, c. 2.

[3] The Greeks always use indiscriminately the formula: "Peace be to all" (εἰρήνη πᾶσιν), to which the congregation answer: "And with thy spirit."

Both the sacerdotal and the episcopal salutation come from the lips of the representative of Christ, not as some mere empty wish, but as a blessing spoken with the efficacy of higher power, containing within itself supernatural strength; so that in reality it imparts the good it expresses to all whose hearts are susceptible of it. The Lord stands at the door and knocks; to any one who hears His voice and opens the door to Him, He will come and enter with His peace (Apoc. 3, 20).

If the mutual salutation is realized, if priest and people are animated and moved by the silent wafting of grace, if they are closely united to God and to one another, then in the Collects they will so express the desire and longing of their hearts as to deserve to be favorably heard.[1] Prayer in common penetrates more powerfully to Heaven,[2] as it was expressly recommended by our Divine Saviour and received from Him a special promise (Matt. 18, 19–20). Therefore, there now follows the invitation of the priest to common prayer.

4. The *Oremus.*

Standing at the Epistle side of the altar, the priest humbly and reverently bows his head to the Crucifix upon the altar, extends his hands and presently joins them again, while saying the word: *Oremus* — "Let us pray!" This is an invitation to pray in common, which the priest directs both to himself and to those present.[3] "Let us pray!" Thus the priest invites all; we are not merely to utter words with the lips, but to honor God we must raise heart and mind to Him. We will pour out our heart to the Lord, acknowledge our poverty and misery, and expect and implore from God, the all-merciful and the all-powerful, salvation and help in all our necessities! That this prayer of the Mass should be made in common, is indicated not only by the name *Collect* and the word *Oremus*, but, moreover, by the priest's speaking aloud. For the priest prays aloud to call the attention of the faithful to join at least mentally with him in his prayer and to pray along with him. Prayer is the liturgical accompaniment of the Sacrifice. The best and the most profitable participation in the Holy Sacrifice consists in that those present follow the priest step by step, jointly praying and offering with him.[4] — "The greeting of the priest to the people has for its

---

[1] Sola est oratio, quae Deum vincit (Tertull. De Oratione c. 29).

[2] Post introitum sacerdotis ad altare litaniae aguntur a clero, ut generalis oratio praeveniat specialem sacerdotis; subsequitur autem oratio sacerdotis et pacifica primum salutatione populum salutans, pacis responsum ab illo accipit, ut vera concordia et caritatis pura devotio facilius postulata impetret ab eo, qui corda aspicit et interna dijudicat (Raban. Maur. De clericor. institut. 1. 1, c. 33).

[3] Non *oro*, sed *oremus* dicit, quia vocem totius Ecclesiae exprimit (Honor. Augustod. 1. 1, c. 93).

[4] Sacerdos salutatione praemissa dicit *Oremus*, ubi oraturus alios hortatur ut secum orent. Tunc ejus pro nobis maxime suscipitur oratio, si nostra ei jungatur devotio. . . . Oportet ergo ut et in Missa et in ceteris officiis cor nostrum jungamus cum voce sacerdotis (Robert. Paulul. De offic. eccles. c. 15).

purpose to encourage them, attracting and directing their hearts to prayer. And it is meant for us all. For prayer in church is not a simple act of one alone, nor is it for one alone, but it is *Collecta*, that is, a joint prayer said by the entire congregation of the faithful and in behalf of the whole congregation. Although but one pronounces the words, yet all the others should with heart and mind pray with him. Therefore, we are reminded of the Lord, that we may seriously recollect ourselves, and put aside all levity and frivolous thoughts, for we are in the presence of the greatest and the most powerful of Lords, treating with Him and beseeching Him who is our Master, who has power over our life and death, over fortune and misfortune, who has the power to cast both our soul and body, into eternal fire, as He says Himself, but who is also bountiful and merciful, and who will gladly bestow upon us all the good which we earnestly and with firm confidence ask of Him. — Consequently, every Christian should be attentive to the greeting: *The Lord be with you,* — and to the admonition : *Let us pray.* Then we should, as members of God's Church, unite in prayer also. Whoever does not understand the words of the prayer, can indeed in general be mindful of God and beseech Him graciously to receive the prayer of His Church, and grant to us who are on earth what is needful and profitable for soul and body, — through Christ our Lord." (Ein Vergissmeinnicht S. 67—68).

The liturgical prayers are recited partly standing and partly kneeling. Anciently[1] it was customary on the Sundays of the year and during the whole of Eastertide to pray standing.[2] The standing up should remind us of the Lord's glorious Resurrection and admonish us of life eternal. On these days the invitation to common prayer has always been made by the simple formula *Oremus*. And although we stand up at the prayers, we ought at the same time to abase ourselves in humility of heart before the face of the Lord. — During the seasons, when the spirit of penance should be more prominent, it is befitting to manifest even exteriorly by genuflecting the interior humility and reverence of the heart.[3] Hence, for ex-

---

[1] The various methods of prayer in use among Christians already in the most ancient times, Prudentius (Cathermerin. II, v. 48 sqq.) has collected very beautifully in the following lines :

Te, Christe, solum novimus :
Te mente pura et simplici,
Te voce, te cantu pio,
Rogare curvato genu,
Flendo et canendo discimus.

In them is expressed the inmost prayer of the heart, which is the requisite foundation of every other mode of prayer, mente pura et simplici ; vocal prayer without singing, voce, and with singing, canto pio ; prayer with genuflection, curvato genu, and prayer with singing and tears, flendo et canendo. Cf. *Arevalo* l. c. (Migne LIX, p. 789).

[2] On Sundays we consider it improper to pray kneeling (de geniculis). The same privilege we enjoy from Easter until Pentecost (Tertull. De corona militis c. 3).

[3] Cfr. Honor. Augustod. Gemma animae 1. 1, c. 117. — In Quadragesima ideo

14

ample, it is that on the Ember Days, as well as on other days that have several lessons and prayers (Wednesday after *Laetare* Sunday, Wednesday of Holy Week, Good Friday, Holy Saturday and the Vigil of Whitsunday), almost all have prayers which are introduced by the words *Flectamus genua* (= let us bend the knees) and the answer *Levate* (= arise).[1] Before we address our petitions to the thrice holy God, we will yet abase and humble ourselves profoundly in the consciousness of our guilt and sinfulness, and also to express our repentance and contrition.

Frequently a double *Oremus* occurred in the Mass: the first with an addition of for whom and for what the prayer should be made; the second, before the prayer proper. This original form is still maintained in the liturgy of Good Friday at the great or solemn intercessory prayers which date from the first ages. The Church shows herself therein as the loving Mother of the entire human race, inasmuch as she prays at the foot of the Cross for the redemption of the whole world.

5. Contents of the Collects.

After this introduction follows the Collect itself, a prayer distinguished as much for the beauty and perfection of its form as for the copiousness and depth of its contents. The Collects are prayers of petition: the numberless needs and necessities of soul and body form the substance of the supplications therein expressed. In them we seek to obtain all manner of favors and blessings, and implore the averting of every evil. The Collects indeed ask of God no more than what is petitioned for in the Lord's Prayer; but the object of these petitions is presented in the most copious and varied expressions. Thus we pray for the grace to serve God, to let the light of divine faith shine in our works, in the name of Christ to become rich in good works, to know well our duty and to be strengthened in its fulfilment, to become interiorly changed and renewed according to the image of our Saviour, to be supported by His continual help and to be confirmed in all righteousness, to grow strong spiritually and corporally so as to be able to overcome every evil, to be rescued from all sufferings and tribulations, to be safeguarded against all perverting error, to draw down upon ourselves by purity of body and mind the good pleasure of Heaven, to abhor all that is unchristian,

---

ad Missam *Flectamus genua* dicimus, quia corpus et animam in poenitentia nos humiliare innuimus.

[1] Formerly the deacon said the Flectamus genua (upon which all present prayed kneeling for some time in silence) as well as the Levate. According to the present rite the priest recites the Oremus, the deacon Flectamus genua (when all except the celebrant bend the knee), and the subdeacon the Levate. But if the priest says the Flectamus genua, he must also genuflect; the acolyte in that case answers Levate. The reason for this difference is that in the latter case the celebrant considers himself among those whom he summons to genuflect, while in the former case it suffices for the deacon to unite in genuflecting, to which he invites those present (with the exception of the celebrant). Cf. Quarti, Comment. in Rubr. Missal. p. 1, tit. 17, n. 3.

and faithfully to observe the divine Commandments, to love the Commandments of God and to long for His promises, to understand and put in practice what is right and perfect, to be enabled to serve God in undisturbed and pure cheerfulness, to grow in every virtue, to walk in accordance with God's pleasure — thereby to arrive at the enjoyment of the Beatific Vision, at the happy enjoyment of an imperishable life, at never-ending joys, at the fulness of eternal life, to obtain the heavenly goods.

Each Collect contains a special petition. The reason for imploring precisely this or that favor lies in the variety of days, seasons and feasts, in the special motive for and the character of the celebration of the Mass. In the liturgical cycle of feasts the sacred history and the entire work of Redemption are repeated and renewed. The Church celebrates the mysteries of Christ and of His blessed Mother, as well as the anniversaries of His saints, so that they may become for priest and people a school and a source of supernatural life. By reason of the plenitude of its truths and of the stream of grace flowing throughout its channel, the ecclesiastical year should induce and enable us so to employ the shortness of time, that we may happily arrive at the blissful life of eternity. At the same time the weekdays and the Sundays, the feast-days and the holidays, during the course of the holy year, should constantly bring before our soul other truths and mysteries, and continually secure for us new graces. For this practical purpose the simple dogmatical teaching of the feasts and times will liturgically clothe and impress in the most attractive and most dissimilar ways the truth therein embodied. This is done especially by those parts of the Mass, which change in the greatest and ever fresh diversity, — therefore, also by the Collects, in which the Church implores those graces precisely which are appropriate to the season, that is, corresponding to the spirit of the ecclesiastical year, to the different festal seasons and festivals, inasmuch as they enable us to celebrate the holy year to our profit and advantage, to lead an interior life in harmony therewith, and to manifest its spiritual fruit in our conduct.

6. The Form of the Collects.

The Collect is, therefore, a prayer of petition for the peculiar grace of the day: but in what form is this petition clothed? Amid all the variety and diversity of the Collects there still prevails a certain uniformity in their construction, which shows that they have been composed after a specified and general rule. The petition is not simply presented to God by itself, but is supported by other kinds or acts of prayer, in order that it may be made so much the more fervent and efficacious. Praise, adoration, thanksgiving — in short, all kinds of prayer are finally resolved in petitions: for petitions are for us in our present state the most important and necessary mode of prayer. Hence petition also forms the peculiar essence of the Collects. But by what other acts is this petition usually accompanied? St. Paul mentions — and probably here there is question of public worship — supplications (urgent entreaty, to which a powerful motive is added, that the prayer may be heard the sooner), prayers, petitions and thanksgivings.[1] These four methods of prayer are not only found alternately in the course of the celebration of the Holy Sacrifice, but they are, for the most part, combined in each Collect,[2] and form these acts into a perfect and most effectual prayer of petition. The person praying must approach God, draw nigh unto God, elevate himself to God (*oratio*); and then present his petitions (*postulatio*), and to obtain more speedily what is asked for, he joins to it his motives: one of which is on the part of the petitioner gratitude or thanksgiving (*gratiarum actio*); for in so far as we are grateful for benefits received, do we obtain graces yet more plentifully;[3] — but the most efficient means for having our petitions granted, is to beg them of God by the merits and intercession of Jesus Christ: hence the concluding words "through Christ our Lord," words which express the entreaty (*obsecratio*).

The Collect for Whitsunday, for example, is as follows:

Deus (*oratio*), qui hodierna die corda fidelium sancti Spiritus illustratione docuisti (*gratiarum actio*), da nobis in eodem Spiritu recta sapere et de ejus semper consolatione gaudere (*postulatio*). Per Dominum nostrum. . . . (*obsecratio*).

O God (*elevation of the soul*), who to-day by the light of the Holy Ghost didst instruct the hearts of the faithful (*thanksgiving*), give us by the same Holy Spirit a love for what is right and just and a constant enjoyment of His comforts (*petition*). Through our Lord Jesus Christ. . . . (*supplication*).

---

[1] Obsecro primum omnium fieri obsecrationes, orationes, postulationes, gratiarum actiones pro omnibus ¡hominibus (1 Tim. 2, 1). These expressions of the Apostle are differently interpreted. (Cfr. S. Thom. 2, 2, q. 83, a. 17. — Suarez, De Relig. tr. 4, 1. 2, c. 3, n. 3—8.) — St. Augustine finds indicated in them the whole course of the Mass. Aliqua singulorum istorum proprietas inquirenda est, sed ad eam liquido pervenire difficile est: multa quippe hinc dici possunt, quae improbanda non sint. Sed eligo in his verbis hoc intelligere, quod omnis vel paene omnis frequentat Ecclesia, ut *precationes* (sc. obsecrationes) accipiamus dictas, quas facimus in celebratione Sacramentorum, antequam illud quod est in Domini mensa incipiat benedici; *orationes*, cum benedicitur et sanctificatur et ad distribuendum comminuitur, quam totam petitionem fere omnis Ecclesia dominica oratione concludit. . . *Interpellationes* (sc. postulationes) fiunt, cum populus benedicitur: tunc enim antistites velut advocati susceptos suos (their clients) per manus impositionem misericordissimae offerunt potestati. Omnibus peractis et participato tanto sacramento, *gratiarum actio* cuncta concludit, quam in his etiam verbis ultimam commendavit Apostolus (S. Aug. Epist. 149, al. 59, n. 15—16 ad Paulin.).

[2] S. Thom. 1. c. — Guyet, Heortol. 1. 3, c. 2, q. 4. The oratio (elevation of the mind to God) is usually contained in the words Domine or Deus or Domine Deus or Omnipotens et misericors Deus; the gratiarum actio in the mention of some benefit of God; the postulatio in the expressions: concede, da, largire, praesta, tribue; the obsecratio in the concluding formula: per Dominum nostrum. . .

[3] De acceptis beneficiis gratias agentes, meremnr accipere potiora ut in Collecta dicitur (S. Thom. 1. c.). — Gratiarum actio est orationis completio et integralis

Thus the Church complies with the admonition of the Apostle: "In every thing by prayer and supplication with thanksgiving let your petitions be made known to God."[1]

The prayers may be addressed to the holy and indivisible Trinity or to any one of the Divine Persons: when the latter is done, it is self-evident that the other two Persons are not excluded, but rather virtually included, and to make this obvious they are, as a rule, expressly mentioned. It is the same with respect to the Collects. Whether they be directed to the Father or to the Son, there follows at any rate at the conclusion an explicit confession and solemn acknowledgment of the holy Trinity.[2]

The Collects were originally and without exception and are now usually addressed to the Father. For the Father is the first Person of the Blessed Trinity and as such He is, in a manner, the original source not only of the divine nature which from all eternity He imparts to the Son and with the Son to the Holy Ghost,[3] but of all created things. To the Father are principally attributed (appropriated) power and majesty, revealed in the creation of the world; the Father has sent us His only-begotten Son, and together with Him He has given us all things. — Jesus Christ Himself offered His whole life, actions, sufferings and especially His prayers to God the Father. The Saviour in His prayer to God was not only our advocate, but also our model in prayer — our leader in prayer. He always prayed to His Father, "to show that the Father is His origin, from whom He from eternity receives His divine nature and by whom His human nature also was created, and from whom it received all the good that it possessed." — Inasmuch as the Church when praying has usually recourse to the Father, she in this respect follows not merely the example but, moreover, the teaching of Christ, who said to His Apostles: "Amen, amen I say to you, if you ask the Father anything in My name, He will give it to you" (John 16, 23). In this a further reason is indicated why the Col-

___

pars ejus, per quam tam ipsa oratio Deo fusa exaudibilis redditur, quam sequentibus orationibus via ac praeparatio exauditionis aperitur. Qui enim gratus est de acceptis et de minoribus regratiatur, majoribus donis efficitur dignus (Dion. Carthus. De oratione art. 3).

[1] In omni oratione et obsecratione cum gratiarum actione petitiones vestrae innotescant apud Deum (Philipp. 4, 6).

[2] Neque enim praejudicium Filio vel sancto Spiritui comparatur, dum ad *Patris* personam precatio ab offerente dirigitur; cujus consummatio, dum Filii et Spiritus sancti complectitur nomen, ostendit nullum esse in Trinitate discrimen. Quia dum ad solius Patris personam honoris sermo dirigitur, bene credentis fide *tota Trinitas* honoratur, et cum ad Patrem litantis destinatur intentio, sacrificii munus *omni Trinitati* uno eodemque offertur litantis officio (S. Fulgent. [† 533], Ad Monim. 1. 2, c. 5).

[3] *Patrem* sancta Ecclesia in precibus poscit, quem esse originem Filii et Spiritus sancti recta credulitate cognovit. Ideo autem nomine Filii et Spiritus sancti orationes precesque consummat, ut sanctam Trinitatem unius esse naturae ac majestatis ostendat (S. Fulgent. Contra Fabian. fragm. 29).

lects, for the most part, are addressed to the Father. Our petitions should be presented "in the name of Jesus." Jesus is the Mediator through whom all our prayers and supplications ascend to Heaven, and through whom as well do all graces and merits descend upon earth; hence for the sake of the Son we pray to the Father who sent Him, by concluding the Collects with these words "through our Lord Jesus Christ." This rule is especially observed at Holy Mass, in which the Son offers Himself to the Heavenly Father.

Some of the Collects are addressed to the second Person of the divine Trinity, because they have a particular and closer relation to the mystery of the Incarnation or to the Incarnate Word.[1] On the other hand, we do not find in our Missal a single Collect addressed to the Holy Ghost; while in the liturgy there are other prayers to the Holy Ghost and hymns in His honor, wherein He is invoked and glorified as God.[2]

The form of the conclusion of the Collect is modified in a five-fold manner, according as the Collect is addressed to the Father or to the Son — and according as in a Collect addressed to the Father mention is made in any way of the second or third Divine Person.[3]

---

[1] For example, the prayer to the Most Blessed Sacrament, on the feast of the Invention of the Cross, on several feasts of the Passion and of St. Joseph.

[2] Tota Trinitas una et eadem adoratione colenda est, puta unus Deus, cum in ipsis personis sit una numero majestas et deitas; nihilominus cum unaquaeque increata persona sit in se vere subsistens persona, potest unusquisque fidelis preces suas specialiter dirigere ad quamlibet divinam personam et eam secundum se specialiter exorare, non tamen cum actuali aliarum personarum exclusione, quasi ipsa sola sit adoranda. Hinc in Missae Officio orationes Ecclesiae ad Patrem specialiter effunduntur, interdum ad Filium, ut cum dicimus: "Fidelium Deus omnium Conditor et Redemptor," communiter vero ad Patrem, tanquam ad totius Trinitatis principium, i. e. primam fontalem personam a nullo manantem; sic et aliquae laudes, orationes, hymni, sequentiae ad Spiritum sanctum specialiter depromuntur (Dion. Carthus. Elementat. theolog. prop. 128).

[3] The prayers to the Father usually conclude: Per Dominum nostrum J. Chr...; those to the Son always: Qui vivis et regnas cum Deo Patre... Sometimes the Collects addressed to the Father conclude: Per *eundem* Dominum... (when, for instance, the Son was mentioned at the beginning or in the middle), or: Qui tecum vivit et regnat... (if this mention is made at the conclusion). This naming of the Son may be done by the words Christus, Verbum, Unigenitus, Salvator etc. or also merely according to the sense. (S. R. C. 11. Mart. 1820). When the person of the Holy Ghost is mentioned directly and actually, as is not the case in such expressions as spiritus dilectionis, fortitudinis, fervoris, adoptionis, gratiae salutaris, the concluding formula is: .... in unitate *ejusdem* Spiritus sancti... (S. R. C. 12. Nov. 1831). — But in order to obtain these modifications of the conclusions, the naming of the Son or of the Holy Ghost must not merely be in one of the preceding Orations, but it must be found in the last, to which the conclusion is attached. (S. R. C. 23. Mai.1835; 8. Apr. 1865). — Outside of the Divine Office and the Mass all Orations have the shorter concluding formula: Per (eundem) Christum Dominum nostrum or Qui vivis et regnas in (or per omnia) saecula saeculorum, if in the liturgical books the longer one is not expressly ordered, as, for example, in the Litany of the Saints (S. R. C. 20. Dec. 1864). — When several prayers occur, only

The usual form of conclusion is as follows : *Per Dominum nostrum Jesum Christum Filium tuum, qui tecum vivit et regnat in unitate Spiritus sancti Deus : per omnia saecula saeculorum.*—"Through our Lord Jesus Christ Thy Son, who with Thee in the unity of the Holy Ghost liveth and reigneth forever and ever." Thus the Collects end and thus they rise to a magnificent praise of the Most Holy Trinity. How solemn, how overpowering, how grand are these concluding words! With what courage and confidence, with what consolation and consciousness of victory should they fill us! "Were it not for the intercession of our Mediator, without doubt, the cry of our supplication would go up unheard in the presence of God."[1] The Church prays with a lively faith in the mediatorship of Jesus and an unshaken confidence in His merits; as Christ has merited for us all grace, He has, therefore, secured a favorable answer also to our prayers. For Christ's sake we are favored and blessed by God. Whenever God looks upon the face of His Anointed, in whom He is eternally well pleased, He will through Christ[2] and for the sake of Christ graciously receive our petitions and graciously hear them, by pouring out upon us His abundant mercies and blessings.[3]

---

the first (to which, however, at times another sub *una* conclusione is joined), and the last have a special concluding formula. The Oremus also is prefaced to the first and second Mass orations, while in the Divine Office all the prayers are introduced with this cry, as here the Antiphon together with the Versicle is inserted between the separate orations. — As the prayers are addressed to the omniscient God, in them only the simple or also the double proper names may be employed (for example, Joanna Francisca, Petrus Coelestinus) and similar designations of saints, as express their dignity (for example, Apostolus, Martyr, Confessor, Virgo — but never Vidua, because this is not a title of honor). To them may also be added the names Joannes *Chrysostomus* and Petrus *Chrysologus;* for nomina Chrysostomi et Chrysologi adjectiva potius sunt et vel facundiam vel vim et efficaciam divini sermonis recensitis Sanctis quasi supernaturali inditam virtute designant. (S. R. C. 8. Mart. 1825. — 7. Dec. 1844 ad 9.) — All other surnames, of what nature soever (*cognomina,* for example, de Matha, a Cruce, Benitius, Nonnatus, Quintus — and *patria,* for instance, de Cortona, de Paula, Nepomucenus, with the exception of Maria *Magdalena*), must be omitted, as they are necessary only *for us* to distinguish the saints one from another. The name rex and regina may be added, but not of the kingdom over which the saints have reigned (for example, Danorum, Scotiae). (S. R. C. 22. Dec. 1629; 23. Jun. 1736. Cfr. Guyet. Heortol. 1. 3, c. 2, q. 5. — Cavalieri, Oper. liturg. t. II, c. 38. — Beleth, Ration. c. 54).

[1] Adjutor quaeritur, ut desiderium exaudiatur, quia nisi pro nobis interpellatio mediatoris intercederet, ab aure Dei procul dubio nostrarum precum voces silerent (S. Greg. Moralium 1. 22, c. 17).

[2] Patri dicimus orantes "Per Dominum nostrum J. Chr. Filium tuum" poscentes, ut *per ipsum faciat* quod oramus, per quem nos facere dignatus est ut essemus. Omnia enim Pater per Filium fecit et facit, quia *unus Dominus J. Chr. per quem omnia* — 1 Cor. 8, 6 (S. Fulgent. contra Fabian. fragm. 31).

[3] *Per Dominum nostrum Jesum Christum* — hoc est, per ipsius dignitatem et per virtutem ejus et efficaciam et per ejus meritum et per intercessionem orationemque ejus. Quae omnia significat hoc verbum omniaque sub eo Ecclesia comprehendit, allegans omnes titulos, quos Christus habet, ut omnes ejus orationes ab aeterno Patre exaudiantur et impleantur (Arias, Thesaur. inexhaust. 1, tr. 3, cap. 16).

In our prayers, therefore, we put our trust and reliance in the power and goodness, in the merits and mercy of our Head and High-priest Jesus Christ, who "liveth and reigneth" — *vivit et regnat.* [1] "The Lord of life died," thus sings the Church in the sequence for Easter, therefore, "He liveth and reigneth" — *Dux vitae mortuus regnat vivus.* Jesus is the Good Shepherd who offered His life for His sheep and He truly rose again, — "who was dead and He now liveth forever and ever" (Apoc. 1, 18). Christ lives in the light of heavenly glory, in heaven He hath "an everlasting priesthood whereby He is able also to save forever them that come to God by Him, always living to make intercession for us" (Heb. 7, 24–25). Christ is "immortal," He is "the Son of the living God," "He bears life within Himself" and He is for the creature "the inexhaustible fountain of life." All life of grace and truth in souls proceeds from Christ, the "living foundation-stone" of holy Church. But Christ not only lives, but He reigns and rules as the "Blessed and the only mighty One, as the King of kings, and the Lord of lords" (1 Tim. 6, 15). All power has been given to Him in heaven and on earth: He possesses plenitude of power, to lead men into the kingdom of grace and glory. The Heavenly Father said to Him on the day of His Ascension: "Sit Thou at My right hand, until I make Thy enemies Thy footstool" (Ps. 109, 1–2). After Christ had drunk from the fountain of suffering and humiliation, He raised His head aloft, and He now possesses triumphantly in glory the throne and the kingdom of eternity, He reigns as King of glory, in order to favor and make happy those who are His own, — but the enemies of His Church "to rule with a rod of iron and to break in pieces like a potter's vessel" (Ps. 2, 9). The greatness of the Lord is a warrant to us of the terror of His judgment, but it is also a guarantee to us of the bounty of His goodness and the fulness of His grace. Hence, as often as we conclude the petitions which we address to the Father of mercies, and the God of all consolation, with the overwhelming expression of our formula, we are reminded of the infinite power, the eternal sovereignty and glory of Jesus Christ which He possesses with the Father and the Holy Ghost; and is not this thought well calculated to raise up our spirits and console us, to strengthen and encourage us, as well as to fill us with humility and holy fear! "Thy (Christ's) kingdom is a kingdom of ages, and Thy dominion endureth throughout all generations" (Ps. 144, 13). Jesus Christ is, moreover, the King of hearts: may His kingdom, the kingdom of grace and love, become daily more firmly established within us! With the most intimate and the most self-sacrificing love we will give ourselves to Jesus and cling to Him: He is indeed infinitely amiable and full of love. May Jesus live and reign in our hearts!

---

[1] Omnes fere orationes finiunter obsecratione illa: Per Dominum nostrum Jesum Christum . . ., expressa item mentione regni aeterni duraturi, ut inde crescat fervor et fiducia, cum orationes innitantur meritis Jesu Christi et speretur regnum aeternum in ejus societate (De Ponte l. c.).

The "*Amen*," that the acolyte says at the end of the Collect, in the name of the people,[1] is a solemn expression of the wish that the petitions offered be graciously heard and fulfilled : "So be it done!" This word occurs even in the Old Testament, especially in its divine worship ; and on account of its antiquity and solemnity, and for the reason of its frequent use also by our Lord, the term is highly venerable and has, therefore, been adopted, without being translated, into her liturgy by the Church.[2] "This word was so frequently on the lips of our Saviour, that it pleased the Holy Ghost (*ut Spiritui Sancto placuerit*), to preserve it in the Church of God."[3] In the New Testament our Lord willingly employs it in His exhortations, and that at the beginning of sentences, to arouse the attention of His hearers, and forcibly to emphasize and impress some thought.[4] At the conclusion of prayers, of blessings, of creeds, of doxologies and hymns it is at one time the expression of the ardent desire of the heart (= *fiat*, γένοιτο, be it so); at another the formula of solemn confirmation, attestation and consent (= *verum est*, ἀληθῶς, it is so).[5] Such is its |meaning in the liturgy, and to this meaning entirely corresponds the grave and solemn manner in which it is sung by the choir at the conclusion of the *Gloria* and *Credo*. The concluding *Amen* is, therefore, a repetition and confirmation of the petitions which have been presented in the Collects; it is an expression of the ardent desire and confident hope of being favorably heard by God.[6]

---

[1] In the first centuries the entire congregation responded. Already St. Justin Martyr writes in his first Apology (chap. 67), that all the congregation join in the liturgical prayers and thanksgivings, by saying "Amen." St. Jerome says of the Roman Basilicas: ad similitudinem coelestis tonitrui *Amen* reboat (Commentar. in epist. ad Galat. 1. 2). — *Amen* hebraeum est, quod ad omnem sacerdotis orationem seu benedictionem respondet populus fidelium (Raban. Maur. De clericor. institut. 1. 1, c. 33). — *Amen* confirmatio est orationis a populo (Pseudo-Alcuin. De divin. offic. c. 40).

[2] Duo verba *Amen* et *Alleluja* nec Graecis nec Latinis nec barbaris licet in suam linguam omnino transferre vel alia lingua enuntiare. Nam quamvis interpretari possint, propter sanctiorum tamen auctoritatem servata est ab Apostolis in iis propriae linguae antiquitas. Tanto enim sacra sunt nomina, ut etiam Joannes in Apocalypsi referat se Spiritu revelante vidisse et audivisse vocem coelestis exercitus tamquam vocem aquarum multarum et tonitruum validorum dicentium *Amen* et *Alleluja:* ac per hoc sic oportet *in terris utraque dici sicut in coelo resonat* (S. Isidor. Etymol. 1. 6, c. 19, n. 20—21).

[3] Catech. Rom. P. 4, c. 17, q. 3, n. 1.

[4] Christus geminavit dixitque *"Amen, Amen"* ad ostendendam rei gravitatem, sublimitatem et certitudinem (Corn. a Lap. in Joannem 3, 3).

[5] In Hebrew the Amen as an adjective signifies reliable, faithful, true, firm; as a substantive: fidelity, truth ; as an adverb: truly, assuredly. (Cf. Hundhausen, Das erste Pontificalschreiben Petri S. 404).

[6] Omnes respondent *Amen*, h. e. *utinam fiat, sicut petis*, et *ita verum est, sicut dixisti.* In quo solo verbo continetur, quidquid sacerdos pluribus dixit, et tanto affectu verbum illud dici potest, ut non minus promereatur unico illo verbo prolato, quam si protulisset omnia. Deus enim Dominus noster non tam verborum multitudinem respicit, quam fervorem affectuum (De Ponte, 1. c).

It is as though the people would make those desires, which the priest in the name of all has offered at the throne of God, still more efficient and, as it were, put their seal upon them by answering: *"Amen,"* that is, *be it done, be it as you have asked.*[1] Would that we may always pronounce this short, but truly significant and venerable word with all recollection of mind and fervor of heart, as do the angels in heaven (Apoc. 7, 12).

7.   How the Collects are to be said.

According to the prescription of the Church, during the recitation of the Collects the hands of the priest are to be extended and elevated before the breast — but in such wise, that the ends of the fingers do not reach beyond the breadth and height of the shoulders.[2] This rubric leaves room for no extravagant and unbecoming gestures. "If we pray with modesty and humility, we recommend our petitions to God far better, inasmuch as we do not raise our hands too high, but only moderately and becomingly."[3] This position of the body in praying, namely, the extending and raising of the hands, is very proper and well calculated to increase devotion in him who prays, and also to edify those present; it is, at the same time, so natural and expressive, that it has always been customary at prayer among all nations. Amalek fought against Israel. When Moses raised his hands, Israel was victorious; but when he allowed them to fall ever so little, Amalek triumphed.[4] And Solomon placed himself before the altar of the Lord in the presence of the people of Israel and extended his hands towards heaven.[4] David cries out: "Hear, O Lord, the voice of my supplication, when I pray to Thee; when I lift up my hands to Thy holy temple" (Ps. 27, 2). The adorable hands of Jesus were also extended and elevated on the Cross, when along with His bloody sacrifice He offered prayers and intercession for the whole world. This divine Model the primitive Christians had before their eyes and imitated when they so ardently loved to pray with arms outstretched in the form of a cross.[5] "The ancient christian representation of the cross

---

[1] Amen est orationis signaculum fructuosum et animi recollectivum. Dicendo enim "Amen," anima summatim fertur ad omnia praeinducta et renovatur affectio impetrandi, sicque oratio cum fervore finita pleniorem sortitur effectum (Dion. Carthus. in S. Matth. cap. 6).

[2] Digitorum summitas humerorum altitudinem distantiamque non excedat. On this Lohner remarks: Unde colligitur, in altum elevatos digitos esse debere et non in aequali cum palma altitudine constitutos et quasi jacentes, ut multi faciunt. Sed et distantia manuum cum decore servanda est (De sacrif. Miss. p. 6, tit. 5).

[3] . . . ne ipsis quidem manibus sublimius elatis, sed temperate et probe elatis (Tertull. De Orat. c. 17).

[4] Cf. Exodus 17, 8—11.

[4] 3 Kings 8, 22.

[5] Non ausa est cohibere poena *palmas — In morem crucis ad Patrem levandas* (Prudent. Peristephanon, hymn. VI, v. 106—107).

by means of the arms extended for prayer, is both the most respectable as to number, and the most beautiful and significant as to symbolism. For hundreds of paintings, tombstones, enamels and sculpturings of the Catacombs represent the blessed in heaven and the faithful on earth praying with arms extended in the form of the cross. 'We have the command,' writes St. Maximus, 'to pray with uplifted hands, so that even by our corporal bearing we may confess the passion of the Lord.' And St. Peter Chrysologus remarks: 'Does not he who extends his hands, pray even by the position of his body?' — through Jesus Christ or in the name of the Crucified. When, therefore, in the first ages the clergy and faithful in general were accustomed to pray with outstretched arms, and when the martyrs often even suffered and died in this posture, they thereby confessed the Saviour extended on the Cross, and presented His merits to the Heavenly Father." [1]

The manner in which the priest according to the rubrics must now hold his hands at the altar, presents no longer indeed the form of the cross, as was the case in the ancient Christian mode of prayer, but the position of his uplifted hands can and should still remind us of our Saviour praying and sacrificing Himself upon the Cross. [2] — The extending of the hands is, so to speak, an embracing, a collecting together of all the wants and concerns, desires and necessities of the faithful. The elevating of the hands denotes and promotes the uplifting of the heart to God, [3] the soaring of the soul above the earthly to the heavenly, the rising to that which is above, where Christ ascended with arms extended. The sedate position of the hands extended and raised is a sign of the ardent desire for help, an expression of the fervor and urgency wherewith the petitions are presented, a symbol of confidence and an assurance of being favorably heard. Thus the priest stands at the altar — and from the depths of this earth of suffering, of poverty, he cries to the Lord and stretches out his hands for rescue and redemption, which must come from above. If he then at the concluding formula of the Collect again joins his hands, he thereby manifests the sentiments of ardent devotion, the humble disavowal of his own strength, the devout desire to give himself entirely to the Lord and to rest in the Lord;— he also acknowledges the union and combination of all gifts in God, the Supreme Good, whence as from the fountain and source of all graces every gift comes to us through Jesus Christ. [4]

---

[1] P. Wolter, O. S. B., Die römischen Katakomben, II, 43.

[2] Passis quondam sublatisque brachiis orabant, *ut statum, quo Christus oravit in cruce, imitarentur.* Consultius vero existimavit Ecclesia, si ad eum modum, quo nunc utimur, Collectae recitarentur, ne veteri retenta consuetudine orandi passis extensisque brachiis, inconcinnis et ridiculis figuris aperiretur locus (Benedict XIV. De Miss. sacrif. 1. 2, c. 6, n. 5).

[3] *Levat* sacerdos manus orando ad designandum, quod oratio ejus dirigitur pro populo ad Deum (Thren. 3, 41. Ex. 17, 11). S. Thom. 3, qu. 83, a. 5 ad 5.

[4] Manuum junctio significat omnium bonorum a Deo fluentium in ipso unitatem et conjunctionem (Durand. Ration. 1. 4, c. 7, n. 5).

"Now some brief mention should be made as to what direction of the heavens we are to turn while at prayer. But since there are four cardinal points of the heavens, who will not admit at once that the direction of the rising sun is evidently the one towards which we should turn when at prayer, in token that the soul looks to the rising of the true light (that is, to Jesus Christ)?"[1] As is still evident from many other testimonies from the Fathers, it was an ancient custom to turn toward the East when praying; accordingly, as a rule, the Church with the main altar was built in this direction, so that the priest and the faithful might when at prayer look toward the rising of the sun. The principal symbolical reasons for this are, according to St. Thomas,[2] the three following. First, the position of the person who prays is considered in reference to the Divine Majesty, revealed to us in the movement of the heavens; this movement of the heavens takes place from the East. — Secondly, we seek to express by this posture that we desire to return to Paradise, which was situated in the East. — Thirdly, we turn in that direction because we thereby think of Jesus Christ who is the true light of the world and is, therefore, called the Orient (*Oriens*), that is, the Rising Sun of Justice, and who at His second coming, as Judge of the living and the dead, will appear "as lightning coming out of the east and passing even into the west" (Matt. 24, 27).

8. The Antiquity, the Number and the Value of the Collects.

From Apostolic times a number of prayers and supplications were offered at the celebration of the Holy Sacrifice; naturally their form gradually developed. In our Missals may be found Collects which date from primitive ages. The saintly Popes Leo I. (440—461), Gelasius (492—496) and Gregory I. (590—604) deserve great credit for not only having faithfully preserved the treasure of traditional prayers, but also for having added new ones. The most of our Collects, therefore, are venerable for their antiquity and their use throughout many centuries.

Until far into the Middle Age, till about the twelfth century, the Roman Church was accustomed in every Mass to recite but one Collect before the Epistle. However, in the eleventh century this original practice was in many instances departed from in other churches in which several prayers were recited; only the consecrated number of seven was not to be exceeded.[3] With the development of

---

1 Origen, On Prayer, chap. 32.

2 2, 2, qu. 84, a. 3 ad 3.

3 Amalarius (d. c. 847) attests in the praefatio altera to his principal work, that even in his time some juxta affectum recited two or three Collects, although in Rome only one (unam tantum) was said — even on Sundays upon which the feast of a saint fell. Micrologus (in the eleventh century) defends this antiqua vel romana traditio, but adds these remarks: Sed hoc jam pauci observant, imo plures in tantum orationes multiplicant, ut auditores suos sibi ingratos efficiant et populum Dei potius avertant quam ad sacrificandum alliciant. Hoc autem sapientioribus multum displicet, qui etsi aliquando antiquam traditionem aliis morigerando

the liturgical calendar, a fixed law was gradually formed regulating the number of prayers to be said at Mass. Since the thirteenth century the prescribed number of prayers has been determined according to the respective rank (*ritus*), also according to the dignity (*dignitas*) and to the solemnity (*solemnitas*) of the feasts of the ecclesiastical year. The greater the feast, the more deeply recollected we should enter into the spirit of it, the more we should concentrate all our thoughts and sentiments upon the mystery celebrated; hence for the feasts of the highest rank (*duplex*) only one Collect is properly appointed.[1] — The celebration of a feast of an inferior rite (*semiduplex*) is of less importance; hence other commemorations and interests may and should find expression in our prayer, which is then offered at the throne of God generally in the consecrated number of three. — The lowest rite (*simplex*) allows the priest to go beyond the consecrated number of three and to present to the Lord various needs in the number of the five wounds of Jesus, or of the seven petitions of the Our Father.[2] As often as the rubrics leave the priest free to add, according to his pleasure, one or more prayers to those prescribed, he must take care that the number be an uneven one.[3] For this symbolizes the indivisibility of the Supreme Being and the unity of the Church. The number of seven should not be exceeded: in the first place, because our Lord who taught us to pray, compiled all that we require for soul and body in seven petitions, then too, that those present may not become weary and annoyed on account of the length of the Mass.

As to the value of the prayers of the Mass, but one opinion can be expressed in their regard: as to form and contents they are incomparable and unequalled models of prayer. The language of

---

excedunt, in ipsa tamen sua excessione modum tenere et aliquam rationem attendere solent. Unde et in Missa, etsi non semper una tantum oratione sint contenti, septenarium tamen numerum in orationibus raro excedunt. . . . . Hoc autem summopere solent observare, ut in Missa aut unam, tres aut quinque aut septem orationes dicant (De eccles. observat. c. 4). — Debet dici *una* oratio, sicut una epistola et unum evangelium, propter fidei unitatem . . . sed ex Patrum institutionibus quandoque dicuntur tres vel quinque vel septem. Praetor hos numeros alius est, non dico reprehensibilis, sed extraordinarius. . . . Pares non sunt dicendae, quia "numero Deus impare gaudet". . . Quotcunque dicantur, sola prima conclusione debita terminentur (Sicard. [† 1215], Mitral. 1. 3, c. 2).

[1] Oratio est explicativa desiderii. Sed desiderium tanto est sanctius, quanto magis ad unum restringitur, secundum illud Ps. 26, 4: "*Unum* petii a Domino, *hanc* requiram" (S. Thom. 2, 2, qu. 83, a. 14).

[2] Quadt, Die Liturgie der Quatembertage S. 81—84.

[3] The priest is, however, not bound, in simplicibus, feriis et votivis to add another prayer, so that the numerus *impar* may be observed (S. R. C. 2. Dec. 1684). — Regarding the Missa quotidiana for the departed curandum est, ut orationes sint numero *impares* (S. R. C. 2. Sept. 1741). Quod si in quotidianis Missis pro defunctis plures addere orationes celebranti placuerit, uti rubricae potestatem faciunt, id fieri potest tantum in Missis *lectis*, *impari* cum aliis praescriptis servato numero et orationi pro omnibus defunctis postremo loco assignato (S. R. C. 30. Jun. 1896).

the Collects is calm, simple and plain, yet not without ornament;
their contents exceedingly rich and profoundly dogmatic. One need
but reflect in devout meditation on the text of a Collect, and he will
discover what a wealth of sublime thoughts and holy emotions is
embodied in those brief, substantial words. It is, therefore, very
difficult, often even impossible in a translation to render these
prayers without impairing their full meaning and weakening their
force. That profound connoisseur of the Roman liturgy, Cardinal
Wiseman, writes on this subject: "There is a fragrance, a true incense in those ancient prayers which seems to rise from the lips, and
to wind upwards in soft, balmy clouds upon which angels may
recline and thence look down upon us, as we utter them. They
seem worthy to be caught up in a higher sphere, and to be heaped
upon the altar above, at which an angel ministers. They partake
of all the solemnity and all the stateliness of the places in which
they were first recited: they retain the echoes of the gloomy
Catacomb, they still resound with the jubilee of gilded basilicas,
they keep the harmonious reverberations of lofty groined vaults . . .
Nothing can be more perfect in structure, more solid in substance,
more elegant in conception, or more terse in diction, than the
Collects, especially those of the Sundays and of Lent. They belong
essentially to the traditional deposits of the Church. In fact, there
is hardly a Collect in which some singular beauty of thought, some
happy turn of phrase, is not to be found. Each is almost invariably
composed of two parts, which may be called the recital and the
petition. The first contains either a declaration of our wants, or a
plea for mercy, or for a favorable hearing. Nothing strikes one so
much as the noble and appropriate terms in which the Deity is
addressed, and the sublime greatness in which His attributes are
described. The petition itself is ever most solemn, devout and
fervent; often containing depth of thought which would supply
materials for a long meditation. . . . If any one thinks that these
prayers, so easy in appearance, require no great power to imitate
them, let him try to compose a few, and he will soon find their
inferiority to the old ones; he will see that it is far from easy to put
so much meaning into such a small compass, and still more difficult
to come up to the beauty and greatness of thought generally con-
densed in the ancient form."[1] The Collects are, therefore, to be
reckoned among the most precious liturgical treasures of the
Church: they are masterly, unsurpassable prayers, distinguished
alike for their solid force and pithy brevity, as for their fragrant
charm and imperishable freshness.

9. Examples.

The petition contained in the Collect is, as a rule, taken from
and based on the Mass of each day. This is made evident in the
various feasts of the ecclesiastical year. The Saviour of the world
is born to us — this is the mystery, this is the great joy of the holy

---

[1] Essays.

Christmas night. To honor the threefold birth of Jesus Christ, (of God the Father, of the Virgin Mary and in the hearts of the faithful) the Holy Sacrifice is offered three times to the glorious Trinity (*in nocte, in aurora, in die*). Now what are the desires and petitions of the Church on this great feast? In the first Collect she implores of God, who "enlighteneth this most holy night with the brightness of Him who is the true light, to grant that we who have known the mysteries of this light of earth, may likewise come to the enjoyment of it in heaven." In the prayer of the second Mass the Church addresses to Almighty God the petition that He would "grant to us, who are flooded (perfundimur) by the new light of the Word made flesh, the grace that this light may be so reflected by our actions, as it shines through faith in our mind" (*hoc in nostro resplendeat opere, quod per fidem fulget in mente*). The Collect of the third Mass contains the petition that "the new birth in the flesh of Thy only-begotten Son may free us, whom the ancient slavery holds under the yoke of sin." On the feast of the Ascension, we beg of God the grace which elevates us above all that is earthly and effects that "we also may with our mind dwell among heavenly things" (*ipsi quoque mente in coelestibus habitemus*). — On the feast of the Sacred Heart of Jesus, the Church begs that "the earthly and temporal celebration (*actu*), as well as the heavenly and eternal fruit (*fructu*) of the benefits of this love-inflamed Heart may be our joy and felicity" (*delectemur*) — and, in order the more easily to be heard, she represents to the Almighty "that the most Sacred Heart of His beloved Son is our glory and that we recall out of gratitude the chief benefits of its love towards us" (*recolimus*).[1]

In the Masses in honor of the Saints, the subject of the petition is in general, that, by their example and merit, by their doctrine and intercession, we may be raised to a spiritual life, make progress therein and attain eternal joys; that we may enjoy their mediation, their protection and their intercession; that, animated by their example, we may be converted to God, produce worthy fruits of penance, despise all that is earthly, temporal and perishable, and, on the contrary, long for and strive after all that is heavenly, eternal and imperishable, fly the lust of the world and come to God, walk in the simplicity and innocence of heart, endure all adversity with constant patience; that we may love what they loved, do what they taught, imitate what they have done and obtain what they possess. — Frequently the prayer of the Church prays for their imitation in a particular virtue, for example, love of our neighbor, constancy in faith, confidence in God, the spirit of prayer, mortification; — or a special protection, for instance, against the malice of the devil, against enslavement of soul by the body, for the extinguishing of evil desires, for the ruling of the tongue, for Holy Communion and

---

[1] Concede, quaesumus, omnipotens Deus: ut, qui in sanctissimo dilecti Filii tui Corde gloriantes, praecipua in nos caritatis ejus *beneficia* recolimus: eorum pariter et *actu* delectemur, et *fructu*.

the overcoming of the Evil One at the hour of death. The occasion for petitioning for such special graces and virtues is usually based upon some fact, on a miracle or some prominent characteristic feature of the life of the Saint whose feast is celebrated. Thus the Church prays to Almighty God on the Nativity of St. John Baptist, that He would grant "His people the grace of spiritual joys, and direct the minds of all the faithful into the way of eternal salvation." On the feast of St. Thomas of Aquin, the Collect is as follows: "O God, who by the wonderful learning of blessed Thomas, Thy confessor, dost illustrate Thy Church, and by his holy works dost render her fertile; grant, we beseech Thee, that we may perceive with our mind what he taught and, in our lives, fulfil by our imitation what he practised." On the feast of St. Teresa we beseech God to give us the grace, "to be nourished with the food of her heavenly doctrine, and taught by the affection of her pious devotion."

On the Sundays of Advent we implore the Lord "to arouse His power and come; that by His protection we may deserve to be freed from the imminent dangers of our sins, and be saved by His redeeming aid;" "to stir up our hearts to prepare the way for His only-begotten Son, that we may be enabled to serve Him with minds purified by His coming;" "that He would bend His ear to our prayers, and enlighten the darkness of our minds by the grace of His visitation;" "that He would exert His power and come, and succor us by His great might, that by the assistance of His grace, what by our sins is delayed may be hastened by His indulgent mercy."

The Collects of the Lenten liturgy have reference almost always to the same subject; for they generally implore the grace to worthily and profitably employ this solemn time of penance, so as to make it available for the sincere practice and sanctification of fasting. With an astonishing variety this petition is expressed in an ever new and changeable form. Thus, for example, the Church prays that "our mind, chastened by the mortification of the body, may, by the ardor of its desires for God, shine brightly in His sight (*desiderio fulgeat*); that the faithful who by abstinence mortify their body, may by the fruit of good works become quickened in spirit;" "that God, who understands our utter helplessness, may protect us from within and without, that our body may be safeguarded from all that may injure it, and our mind purified from evil thoughts;" "that, by abstaining from material food, we may also refrain from pernicious lusts;" "that, fervently persevering in fasting and prayer, we may be delivered from the enemies of both soul and body;" "that the chastisement which we have inflicted on the body may serve to the strengthening and fortifying of the soul" (*ad nostrarum vegetationem transeat animarum*); that "amidst the sufferings that we have deserved and that oppress us, we may be enabled to breathe more freely through the consolations of divine grace;" "that our fast may be pleasing to the Lord, make us worthy of divine grace and lead us to the fountains of eternal salvation."

The second half of the ecclesiastical year — the time from Pentecost to Advent — represents the pilgrimage of the children of God to their eternal home, their heavenly country: this pilgrimage is indeed accompanied with hardship and labor, but is also full of hope and consolation.[1] We feel that we are "pilgrims and strangers, hailing from afar, look towards the promises" and "we seek a better heavenly country — the city which God hath prepared for us" (Heb. 11, 13-16). There we live "in expectation of the blessed hope and coming of the glory of the great God and our Saviour Jesus Christ" (Tit. 2, 13). Therefore, in the Collects of this time, the Church prays that God, the strength of all that hope in Him, may send us the help of His grace, that, in the fulfilment of His Commandments, we may please Him by thought and by deed; that God may grant that we may always revere His holy name with filial love and fear, since He never withdraws His benign protection from those whom He has firmly established in His unchanging love; that God would multiply His mercies to us, that guided by Him we may make use of temporal goods in such a manner as not to lose those which are eternal; that under the guidance of God, the world may be ruled peacefully and the Church may enjoy undisturbed devotion; that God, who has prepared invisible goods for all who love Him, may pour into our hearts the fire of His charity, that, by loving Him in all things and above all things, we may obtain His promises which surpass all understanding; that God's infallible providence may avert from us all that is hurtful and grant us all that is profitable for us; that God may give us the spirit of always knowing and accomplishing what is right and just; that God, who in the abundance of His goodness grants to us more than we merit or even desire, may pour out His mercies upon us, so that He may pardon what fills our conscience with dread, and add those gifts which we do not venture to ask in prayer; that He would give us an increase of faith, hope and charity, and in order that we may attain unto the happiness He has promised, He may fill us with love for His holy commandments; that grace may always forestall and accompany us, and urge us onward to perseverance in the practice of good works. — Faithful children, who are as yet pilgrims at a distance from their true home, suffering and combating,[2] assuredly can ask or desire nothing better than what is expressed in these Sunday prayers.

---

[1] Deliciae spiritus nostri divina cantica, ubi et fletus sine gaudio non est. Fideli homini et peregrino in saeculo nulla est jucundior recordatio quam civitatis illius unde peregrinatur; sed recordatio civitatis in peregrinatione non est sine dolore atque suspirio. Spes tamen certa reditus nostri etiam peregrinando tristes consolatur et exhortatur (S. Aug. Enarr. in Ps. 145, n. 1).

[2] Ab octavis Pentecostes usque Adventum Domini (Ecclesia) recolit *tempus peregrinationis*. In hoc est nobis perpetua pugna et lucta adversus tres infestissimos hostes, mundum videlicet, carnem et diabolum. Mundus est hostis sophisticus, caro hostis domesticus, diabolus hostis antiquus. Nullus tamen istorum hostis est efficacior ad nocendum quam inimicus noster familiaris, scil. caro, quam fove-

40. The Readings from the Bible in general. The Epistle.

1. The general preparatory part of the holy Sacrifice is drawing near its end. Now follow the readings from the Bible which are connected with each other by various forms of chant, and are often crowned by the Creed. — What signification have the readings from Holy Scripture in the organism of the Sacrifice? In the Mass the Saviour's entire work of redemption is shown forth and carried out (*opus nostrae redemptionis exercetur* — *Secr.*); the celebration of the Mass embraces in its several parts the whole operation of the Redeemer. As the Lord exercised during His mortal life the office of mediator, thus He continues to exercise it in His Church, — and that in a sacramental manner. Christ came as mediator between God and man, to reconcile and unite Heaven and earth with each other. God "sent His Son to save the world" and "to bring godliness and the promise of the life which is to come" (John 3, 17. 1 Tim. 4, 8). "Christ has come from God unto wisdom and unto justice and unto sanctification and redemption,"[1] that is, as Redeemer He is not only the source of grace and sanctification, but also of enlightenment in all truth for mankind.

The first office of the Redeemer consisted in teaching the truth and the law of God — exteriorly by the words which fell from His lips, and interiorly by the light which He infused into the hearts. Already the Prophet remarks, that in the days of the Messiah "the earth shall be filled with the knowledge of the Lord, as the covering waters of the sea" (Isa. 11, 9). The Spirit of God hovered over the Saviour, anointed Him and sent Him "to preach the gospel to the poor" (Luke 4, 18). Christ came into the world to give testimony to the truth, and He taught the way of God in truth (John 18, 37. Matt. 22, 16). In Him were "hidden all the treasures of wisdom and knowledge" and "the fulness of His grace we have all received" (Col. 2, 3. John 1, 14–16). Only after the Lord had as teacher of truth shown the way to heaven, did He die on the Cross the death of reconciliation, in order to unite man again in grace and love with God. Now all this is repeated in the Holy Sacrifice of the Mass. Before the Saviour descends on the altar at the Consecration as a mystical Victim, He speaks words of eternal life to us, — and that, first, by His prophets and apostles, then through Himself. The Epistle and Gospel come before the sacrificial action. In this arrangement is revealed the profound and interior connection between the teaching of truth and the mystery of the altar, between the word of God and the Divine Eternal Word, who was made flesh and who under the Eucharistic veil is again present and dwells

---

mus indumentis et reficimus alimentis, — cui tanquam jumento tria debentur : cibus ne deficiat, onus ut mansuescat, virga ut non indirecte, sed directe incedat (Beleth., Rational. c. 56).

[1] Christus factus est nobis sapientia a Deo et justitia et sanctificatio et redemptio (1 Cor 1, 30).

among us. The sacramental God-Man is not merely the life, but also the way and the truth for us men (John 14, 6): only where the fountain of grace of the Eucharistic Sacrifice flows, does the truth of Christ shine forth in full and undimmed splendor. The altar of grace and the pulpit of truth are sanctuaries intimately connected: they are in the same house of God, and the priest who offers the Sacrifice also proclaims the heavenly doctrine. The Church, therefore, most appropriately combines the reading of the prophetical and evangelical word with the celebration of the Eucharistic Sacrifice, which is eminently termed "the mystery of faith."[1] The announcement of the truth precedes the accomplishment of the Sacrifice; for knowledge is the beginning of salvation. The living word of God is the seed whence proceeds the imperishable life of faith, which here below is perfected by grace and in the next life is transformed into glory.

The Church with predilection and preference employs in her liturgy Scriptural words, because they are especially holy and venerable, efficacious and full of grace: they are, indeed, the words of God — words that have the Holy Ghost for their author. These words are supernatural, heavenly and divine. Therefore, are they so well adapted to manifest to the Lord our sentiments, desires, petitions and interests. To commune with God in prayer, to praise Him, to thank Him, to supplicate Him, to pour out to Him in chant our heart's joys and plaints, we can find no words more befitting than those which God Himself has put into our mouth, and inspired through His "Holy Spirit who within us beseeches Heaven in our behalf with unutterable groanings." In this way we have in the preceding part of the Mass already frequently prayed in God's words; but in the readings now following we have the word of God, by which He speaks to us and instructs us in all doctrine and truth. — "The Spirit searcheth all things; yea, the deep things of God" (1 Cor. 2, 10); hence the writings inspired by Him are of wonderful depth and inexhaustibleness, full of spirit and power, full of light and life. They teach the science of the Saints and show unto us the kingdom of God. They afford us material immeasurably abundant "for growth in grace and in the knowledge of our Lord and Saviour Jesus Christ" (2 Peter 3, 18). How dear and precious should they, then, be to our hearts! "For what things soever were written, were written for our instruction: that through patience and the comfort of the Scriptures, we might have hope" (Rom. 15, 4). Yes, an abundance of consolations do we draw from the word of God, which, with all its truth and graces, with all its promises and threats, remains forever and is accomplished, whilst this perishable world is as grass, and its glory as the flower of grass; — "the grass is with-

---

[1] Instructio fidei is duplex: una quae fit noviter imbuendis, scil. catechumenis et talis instructio fit circa baptismum. — Alia autem est instructio, qua instruitur fidelis populus, qui communicat huic mysterio et talis instructio fit in hoc sacramento et tamen ab hac instructione non repelluntur etiam catechumeni et infideles (S. Thom. 3, q. 83, a. 4 ad 4).

out, and the flower thereof is fallen off'' (1 Peter, 24–25). In the midst of a world fallen away from Christianity and hostile to the Church, amid all the sufferings and persecutions that oppress us, amid the storms that rage around us, the imperishable word of God, which does not pass away, though even heaven and earth should pass away, encourages and raises us up, and imparts life eternal to all who receive it with faith and docility. Since the Church has included in her formula for Mass readings from the Bible, we may daily place ourselves at the table of God, to nourish and strengthen ourselves with the heavenly bread of the revealed truths of salvation.

2.   It is incontestable, that from Apostolic times the canonical, or holy Books have been read aloud at the assemblies of divine worship, and principally at the celebration of the Eucharistic Sacrifice.[1] For a long time it belonged to the bishop, as the chief liturgist, to select what, how many and how long were the parts of Scripture which were to be read. St. Justin Martyr († 166 or 167), who describes the order of divine worship among the Christians, says, that at the Sunday assemblies the writings of the Apostles (that is, the Books of the New Testament) or the writings of the Prophets were read, as long a time as was permitted (μέχρις ἐγχωρεῖ).[2] With the gradual development of the liturgical year, the distribution of the extracts to be read was evolved more and more according to certain aspects, until finally (in the 16th century) the present arrangement of the Epistles and Gospels for the Missal was decided upon by the Church. In this matter St. Jerome, who by order of Pope Damasus I. (366—384), completed, corrected and perfected the traditional arrangement of the biblical extracts for the Mass, deserves great credit.

Now what rule was followed in the choice and arrangement of the Biblical readings? The Epistles and the Gospels bear the closest and most intimate connection with the course and spirit of the ecclesiastical year: the Church's selection, therefore, was made in conformity with the celebration of the feast or day. Indeed, among the variable parts of the Mass formula, the lessons selected from Holy Scripture, which are instructive, occupy the principal place. In them, as a rule, the idea of the ecclesiastical time finds its most perfect expression. Together with this the standpoint is given and marked out, which is to be taken in understanding and explaining these lessons.

---

[1] In the first four centuries the liturgical celebration of Mass began with the reading of Scripture, at which the different books of the Bible were read (as they are still in the Breviary) serially (in continua serie). (Cf. the 124 sermons of St. Augustine on the Gospel of St. John and St. John Chrysostom's homilies on the Epistles of St. Paul). For the highest feasts there were chosen already from the beginning appropriate passages, that is, such passages as had reference to the mysteries celebrated. With the progressive evolution of the ecclesiastical year the lectio continua was replaced by a series of biblical extracts arranged for the various feasts and festal seasons.

[2] First Apology chap. 67.

3. According to a general rule that has few exceptions, every Mass formula has two Biblical readings,[1] the first of which is called the Epistle[2] and the other the Gospel. Leaving out the four Gospels and the Psalms — the first reading may be taken from any part of the Old and New Testaments; but generally, for example, on all the Sundays of the year, the Epistle is taken from the writings of the Apostles. Hence it is that the name *Epistola*, that is, letter, was used to designate the first Pericope, even when it was not taken from the Epistles of the Apostles, but from some other part of Holy Scripture.[3] And from the fact that this Pericope was not sung in former times, but only read,[4] it is still called in the superscription or heading of the Missal *Lectio*, that is, lesson,[5] — having coupled with the term a reference to the book from which the lesson is taken.[6]

---

[1] In the Mozarabic and Ambrosian Liturgies the Gospel is usually preceded by two lectures (generally one from the Old, the other from the New Testament). — On Ember Saturdays there were formerly, according to the Roman Rite, twelve lessons read by twelve lectors (that is, six lessons, first in Latin and then in Greek); hence in the ancient liturgical books these Saturdays are called Sabbata duodecim lectionum s. in duodecim lectionibus. At present they still retain the six lessons (five from the Old Testament and one from the New) before the Gospel, while Ember Wednesdays have but two. In the Pope's High Mass the Epistle and Gospel are still sung both in Latin and Greek.

[2] Notandum est, non omnia verba ex s. Scriptura esse desumpta, sed *initium* fere semper et interdum etiam *finem* ab Ecclesia dumtaxat additum esse, ut convenientius inchoetur aut claudatur Epistola. Hinc Epistolae desumptae ex s. Paulo initium vox "fratres" et finis frequenter "in Christo Jesu Domino nostro". Si vero ex aliorum Apostolorum Epistolis sumatur, vox "carissimi"; si ex Prophetis, verba "in illo tempore" ab initio praeponuntur, et in fine non raro verba "dicit Dominus omnipotens" subjunguntur (Lohner, De ss. Miss. sacrif. p. VI, tit. 6).

[3] Because this first reading was more frequently taken from St. Paul's epistles, it was called also ἀπόστολος to distinguish it from εὐαγγέλιον. Under the former term were included not only the epistles of the apostles, but also the Acts of the Apostles and the Apocalypse. Postmodum dicitur Oratio; deinde sequitur Apostolus (Sacr. Gregor).

[4] *Lectio* dicitur quia non cantatur ut psalmus vel hymnus, sed *legitur* tantum. Illic enim modulatio, hic sola pronuntiatio quaeritur (Isidor. Hispal. Etymolog. 1. 6, c. 19, n. 9).

[5] The present mode of delivering the Epistle is a tone between singing and simple reading: it is a manner of singing in which the whole text is delivered in a monotone tone (tono recto) without modulation (except at an interrogation the voice descends half a tone, but in the last syllable it returns to the dominant tone). The rubrics designate this as chanting. Subdiaconus *cantat* Epistolam alta voce. (Cer. Episc. 1. 2, c. 8, n. 40). The ancient liturgists called it *choraliter legere* (reading in a choral manner). — The reading or singing tone of the Gospel is somewhat more melodious and, therefore, more festive.

[6] For example, Lectio Epistolae B. Pauli . . ., Lectio libri Exodi, Lectio libri Regum, Lectio Danielis Prophetae. In regard to the superscription Lectio libri Sapientiae it is to be observed, that to it are given not merely extracts from the Book of Wisdom itself, but also portions from the Book of Jesus the son of Sirach (Ecclesiasticus), from the Preacher (Ecclesiastes), from the Canticle of Canticles

As according to the present custom the *Lector* is appointed to read the first lesson from the Old Testament on Good Friday, thus he had formerly also, perhaps up to the fifth century [1] — charge of reading the Epistle; but from that time forward the solemn reading of the Epistle was assigned to the Subdeacon, who only since the fourteenth century was especially empowered [2] thereto by the handing to him at his ordination, according to the ritual, of the Book of the Epistles, while it is the office of the Deacon [3] to sing the Gospel. [4] In ancient churches, in the space between the sanctuary and the nave of the church, there stood the *Ambo*, that is, an immovable tribune or oblong pulpit, which was ascended by a few steps. If a church had two Ambos, as has, for example, St. Mary's in *Cosmedin* at Rome, then one served for the reading of the Gospel and the other for that of the Epistle. If there was but one Ambo, then the Gospel was read from the highest step and the Epistle from a lower one. [5] Thus the prominence due the Gospel over the Epistle

---

(Cantic. Canticor.) and from Proverbs (Proverbia): all these taken together are called by the Fathers and in the liturgy Books of Wisdom (libri Sapientiales). (Cf. Gutberlet, Das Buch der Weisheit S. 2).

[1] Cf. Reuter, Das Subdiakonat S. 177 etc.

[2] In the 13th century Durandus answers the question, quare subdiaconus legit lectiones ad Missam, cum non reperiatur hoc sibi competere vel ex nomine vel ex ministerio sibi concesso? (Ration. 1. 2, c. 8, n. 4.)

[3] Antiquioribus temporibus *Lectorum* ordo legendo Evangelio fuit destinatus. Verum saeculo IV. visum est Patribus nostris, reverentiam et venerationem *Evangelio* debitam omnino exigere, ut tantum munus non amplius Lectoribus, qui jam ut plurimum ex puerili aetate eligebantur, sed ministris sacris, saltem *Diaconis* committeretur, qui ad sacerdotalem dignitatem proxime accedebant (Krazer Sect. 4, a, 1, c. 5, § 235). — The handing of the Book of the Gospels, however, came into use only gradually after the tenth century at the ordination of the deacon. (Cfr. Amalar. De ecclesiast. offic. 1. 2, c. 11—12. — Morin. De sacris ordinat. p. 3, exercitat. 9, c. 1; — exercitat. 12, c. 2).

[4] In former times the lectors were even allowed to read the Gospel. St. Cyprian mentions this when speaking of the confessors Aurelius and Celerinus whom he had ordained lectors (about 250; cf. Epist. 38, 39). In a High Mass without the assistance of the ministri sacri a lector in surplice sings the Epistle (Rubr. Miss, p. 2, tit. 6, n. 8). On the 23rd of April, 1875, the S. R. C. gave this answer: Quum Missa cantatur sine ministris et nullus est clericus inserviens qui superpelliceo indutus Epistolam decantet juxta Rubricas, *satius* erit quod ipsa Epistola legatur sine cantu ab ipso Celebrante; nunquam vero in Ecclesiis monialium decantetur ab una ex eis. Accordingly, it is indeed more proper (satius), that the celebrant in the said High Mass should merely read the Epistle, but he is not forbidden to sing it. The priest in this matter should conform to the ordinance, that is, to the general practice of the diocese. — Only in a case of actual necessity (in casu absolutae et praecisae necessitatis) may a superior permit a cleric who is not in a higher order, to vest as subdeacon (however, without maniple, paratus *absque manipulo*) and sing the Epistle in a Missa solemnis, and to perform the remaining functions of a subdeacon (S. R. C. 15. Jul. 1698).

[5] The word ἄμβων is deduced from ἀναβαίνω, ἀμβαίνω = ascend; other designations: βῆμα, πύργος, suggestus, pulpitum, tribunal, auditorium, dictorium, lectorium

was and is now expressed both by the manner of delivery and by the person of the reader and the place of reading. — The subordination of the Epistle to the Gospel[1] is signified likewise by the position which both occupy in the rite of the Mass: the Gospel is preceded by the Epistle. Now in answering the question, what is the reason and object of this arrangement, the relation of the Epistle to the Gospel will be placed in a clear light.

The Old and New Testaments, with all the books appertaining to them, possess the same divine character, the same divine dignity and authority, inasmuch as they have God for their author, and are inspired by the Holy Ghost, and are, therefore, in a true and full sense the word of God; but in other respects a certain distinction of rank can and must be given to them. That which the Holy Ghost imparts through the medium of the inspired writers can be more or less important, the manner of communication be more or less perfect. In this respect, the superiority of the New Testament over the Old Testament is manifest, and again in the New Testament itself the four Gospels take precedence of the Acts of the Apostles, the Apostolic Epistles and the Apocalypse. For there prevails in the great work of salvation of the divine revelation a constant and gradual progression. All that whose foundation was laid in the Old Dispensation, was brought to perfection in Christ and His Apostles. The Old Testament is included, realized, developed and completed in the New. The summit and crown of the supernatural revelation consists in this that God spoke to us not only by the Prophets and Apostles, but also through His only-begotten Son (Heb, 1, 1 etc.). The Prophets and Apostles were, indeed, organs of the Holy Ghost, who announced through them heavenly truths; still they were and remained only men, only human messengers of salvation. Jesus Christ, on the contrary, is a Divine Person; He is truth itself; He is the true light of the world; all His words, works and miracles are eminently divine works and actions, full of divine spirit and life, of infinite truth and depth.[2] The Gospel places before our eyes the life

(Lettner). The ambo was a smaller or larger platform, that served for the solemn reading of the Holy Scriptures, the announcement of divine worship, etc. In the Basilica of St. Clement at Rome are to be found three ambos, as there is, beside the ambo for the Epistle, another marble stand arranged for the Old Testament lessons.

[1] From the most ancient times (cf. Ord. Rom. I, n. 10), it is customary to sit with head covered in choir at the solemn reading of the Epistle, whilst from the beginning the Gospel was listened to standing and with head uncovered. — Although the subdeacon no longer (as was formerly done till towards the end of the Middle Age) reads the Epistle to the people from the Ambo, but at the left side turned towards the altar, he must, nevertheless, both before and after reading it make a genuflection (in plano) in the middle of the altar. — The subdeacon receives the blessing from the celebrant, who represents Christ, only after he has finished reading, because the Old Law, symbolized by the Epistle, was fulfilled, or annulled by Christ (Mat. 5, 17-20); the deacon, on the contrary, is blessed by the celebrant before he reads the Gospel, because the Gospel is derived from Christ (cf. Durand. l. 4, c. 17).

[2] Cf. Heinrich, Dogmat. Theologie I, 764 etc.

of Jesus Christ, the word and the example of the Eternal Wisdom
made flesh; in it appears the God-man Himself — teaching and
acting, suffering and triumphing — while in the Epistles the Holy
Ghost speaks to us, instructs and admonishes us only by His human
messengers and servants.   Hence it is usually said,[1] that the instruction of the people takes place at first in the Epistle, in a preparatory
and imperfect manner through the doctrine of the Prophets and
Apostles, but that the faithful are more perfectly instructed through
the teachings of Christ as contained in the Gospel.[2]   The Epistle,
therefore, is read before the Gospel because it is subordinate to it,
prepares for it, paves the way for it, that is, leads to the understanding of it.[3]   Both readings harmonize with one another and mutually
complete each other, — they would express a common thought, or at
least kindred ideas.   But as the subject or the mystery of the
ecclesiastical celebration appears more closely and more fully exposed
at one time in the Epistle, at another time in the Gospel, it may in
general be said that both readings mutually explain and throw light
on each other, so as to constitute together a whole.[4]   On the feast of
the Most Holy Trinity, for example, the Apostle in his grand Epistle
extols and glorifies[5] the impenetrable secrets of the Divinity, while
in the Gospel[6] the adorable mystery of three persons in God, which
forms the groundwork of faith and is its crown, is clearly and
distinctly set forth.   The Epistle of Whitsunday[7] announces and
describes in detail the coming of the Holy Ghost, while the Gospel[8]
contains the promise of the Comforter and of His blessed gifts of
grace.

Many of the Epistles are taken from the Old Testament, and for
the following reasons.   The Old Testament is a great divine
testimony to Christ and to His kingdom; every thing in it is

---

[1] Instructio fidelis populi *dispositive* quidem fit per doctrinam prophetarum et
apostolorum, quae in Ecclesia legitur per lectores et subdiaconos; — *perfecte* autem
populus instruitur per doctrinam Christi in Evangelio contentam, quae a summis
ministris legitur, scilicet a diaconibus (S. Thom. 3, qu. 83, a. 4).

[2] Epistolarum doctrina respectu evangelicae doctrinae, quae immediate a
Christo profluxit, est imperfecta et ordinatur ad eam sicut ad finem.   Intellectus
namque Epistolarum disponit ad intellectum Evangeliorum; propterea Epistola
ante Evangelium legitur (Dion. Carthus. Expositio Missae art. 12). — According to
the liturgies of the Middle Age, the Epistle precedes the Gospel, because it
represents the Law and the Prophets, or the efficacy of the Precursor of Christ, or
the preaching of the seventy-two disciples, who prepared the way for the Saviour.

[3] Anteponitur in ordine quod inferius est dignitate, ut ex minoribus animus
audientium ad majora proficiat et gradatim ab imis ad summa conscendat (Walaf.
Strabo cap. 23).

[4] Cf. Veith, Dikaiosyne oder die Epistelreihe des Kirchenjahres in ihrem Ver-
hältnisse zu den Evangelien.   Wien 1874.

[5] Rom. 11, 33—36.

[6] Matt. 28, 18—20.

[7] Acts of the Apostles, 2, 1—11.

[8] John 14, 23—31.

prophetical of Christ and of the Church, whether given in express words or in types, that is, in figurative personages, facts and customs. Now the Church loves to explain and apply typically (spiritually) the Old Testament. Whenever she found in it some striking prophecy of a New Testament mystery or event, she incorporated it if possible as an Epistle in the Mass, as a supplement and explanation of the Gospel. For example, on the Epiphany the Church celebrates the revelation of the divine Glory of Jesus Christ, and that in three events which the Antiphon of the Benedictus combines: "This day the Church is espoused to the Heavenly Bridegroom, because Christ washed away her sins in the Jordan; the Wise Men hasten with gifts to the nuptials of the King; and the guests rejoice at the changing of water into wine." The apparition of God at the baptism of Christ, the call of the Wise Men by the star, and the change of the water into wine constitute, therefore, the subject of the feast of the Epiphany; but the mystery of the marvellous star is celebrated with particular joy and detail, while the two other facts receive but a passing notice. Accordingly, the Epistle contains[1] a magnificent prophecy and description of the wonderful glory of the new kingdom of grace; heathen kings and nations pour in from the four quarters of the earth, to be received into the bosom of the Church and to walk in her light. The Gospel[2] shows us the beginning of the fulfilment of what is predicted by the Epistle: kings come from heathen lands, they come with precious and mystical presents, to pay their homage to and adore the Divine Child, and in reward of their faithful obedience they are enriched with the light of faith and grace. In like manner, most of the Masses in honor of the Mother of God have Epistles from the Old Testament, and these have preferably been selected from the Books of Wisdom. To the same class belong the Epistles of the feasts of the holy Guardian Angels, of St. John the Evangelist, of St. Mary Magdalen and of others.

Another reason why the Church inserted in the liturgy of the Mass lessons from the Old Testament is found in the following reflection.[3] In the Old Law salvation had not yet appeared and the light had not as yet arisen, but darkness and the shadow of death enveloped all nations; it was a time of anxious and painful expectancy, a time of sighing and longing for redemption. Lessons taken from this dark period are well fitted to impress the character of penance on those days on which they are used. This explains why the Church on all ferial days, from Ash-Wednesday until Tuesday in Holy Week, makes use exclusively of lessons from the Old Testament. They are intended to awaken, to nourish and to strengthen within us a true penitential spirit; for, like so many voices from the ages before Christ, they impressively admonish us that by sin we

---

[1] Isa. 60, 1—6.

[2] Matt. 2, 1—12.

[3] Cf. Quadt, Liturgie der Quatembertage S. 45—47.

have become estranged from God and have strayed back into the ancient night and cold of death. — On those days which have Old Testament lessons in a greater number, such as the Wednesdays and the Saturdays of Ember Weeks,[1] the earnest spirit of penance is still more deeply stamped. Coming down to us from Apostolic times the Ember days are, according to their original intent and purpose, days of penance, whereon we are expected by prayer, fasting and alms, to purify and to sanctify our souls, as well as days of thanksgiving and petition for the blessings of the past or coming season. Later on they became also Ordination Days, because they were specially suitable for the conferring of Holy Orders.

4. At the conclusion of the Epistle the acolyte, in the name of the people, answers: *Deo gratias!*—"*Thanks be to God!*" What is more befitting than that we should thank the Lord from the bottom of our heart for the divine instruction which He has imparted to us by the mouth of His messenger? In the Epistle Almighty God, so to speak, sends a letter, a writing from heaven, to us miserable creatures:[2] should we not with faith and reverence receive His words which are of infinite dignity, power and depth of meaning, and obey them with cheerfulness and alacrity? Every word emanating from the mouth of God is supernatural and heavenly food for the life of the soul. Holy Scripture more than any other book is fit "to instruct us unto salvation, to teach, to reprove, to correct, to indoctrinate in justice, that the man of God may be perfect, furnished unto every good work" (2 Tim. 3, 15—17). By means of the biblical readings the minister of God plants and waters the field of our heart; let us be grateful for this, and the Lord will then give the increase, so that the heavenly seed of their living word may germinate and thrive, blossom and produce fruit — thirty, sixty and a hundredfold.[3] But in order that this fruit of salvation may ripen, that is, in order that we may advance in the holy love of God and in every Christian virtue unto perfection, we must not only receive and preserve the divine word with a good, yea, with a perfect heart, but we must persevere in patience amid all sufferings and contradictions, amid all temptations and combats, — *fructum afferunt in patientia.*

It is peculiar to the Christian always to return thanks to God through Christ our Lord, who has revealed Himself unto us full of truth and grace, who in the character of a penitent has taken our place and submitted to the death of the Cross, who is our Mediator and Advocate with the Father. Hence the words *Deo gratias* were

---

[1] Only on the Wednesday of the Pentecost Ember Week are there two New Testament lessons; the reason is, because the penitential character of this Ember Week is in many respects superseded by the festal spirit of the octave.

[2] Sunt et Angeli cives nostri: sed quia nos peregrinamur, laboramus, illi autem in civitate exspectant adventum nostrum. Et de illa civitate, unde peregrinamur, *literae* nobis venerunt: ipsae sunt *Scripturae*, quae nos hortantur, ut bene vivamus (S. Aug. In Ps. 90 serm. 2, n. 1).

[3] 1 Cor. 3, 6—9. Matt. 13, 3 etc.

at the time of the persecution of the Christians the watchword or the
mark by which, as a short profession of faith, the *Ostiarius* (the
door-keeper) recognized those as Catholic Christians who sought
admission into the place of public worship. At the same time there
was comprised in this expression of gratitude a confession of the
sentiments with which the Christians were urged to assist at divine
worship, and how they regarded this as a grace from God. No
wonder that the words *Deo gratias* crept into the liturgy, and that
they occur so frequently therein.[1]

41. The Intermediary Chant (Graduale, Alleluja, Tractus, Sequentia).

The Church has assigned to the choir the task of executing, in
the name of the congregation, the various parts that are to be sung.
These are very appropriately and skilfully inserted in the liturgy of
the Mass, for sacred chant is productive of many wholesome results;[2]
it makes divine worship more solemn and more majestic, elevates
the mind, exhilarates the heart, renders the disposition more peaceable, inclines to devotion, excites to piety, softens to mildness and
compunction of spirit, produces a flow of tears and raises a desire of
amendment, enables the soul to soar above the earth and all that is
earthly and to lose itself in heavenly meditation. St. Augustine
depicts the powerful impression made by the chant of the Ambrosian
Hymns upon his soul: "How I wept, O Lord, amid Thy hymns and
chants, greatly moved by the voices of Thy sweetly singing Church!
They poured themselves into my ears — these voices, and like drops
Thy truth penetrated my heart: the fervor of devotion was awakened,
tears flowed, and ah, how happy I was then!"[3] Thus the choir
chants at the celebration of Mass, by a pleasing variety, drive away
weariness, and keep the participation of the faithful in the divine
service ever lively and on the alert. Formerly they had a larger
scope and were in the form of responsories or alternate singing,
directed according to a certain rule of repetition and conducted by
precentors and the choir. — The chant which follows the Epistle and
precedes the Gospel is an intermediate and connecting link between
these two biblical readings.

Said intervening chant is of varied composition at the different
periods of the ecclesiastical year, and accordingly bears different
names. The Gradual at times occurs by itself alone; but for the
most part it is connected with an addition, namely, the (minor)

---

[1] Circumcelliones insultare nobis audent, quia fratres, cum vident homines,
"Deo gratias" dicunt (S. Aug. in Ps. 132 ennarr. n. 6). The formula of thanks
"Deo gratias" — τῷ Θεῷ χάρις — is found already in St. Paul (cf. 1 Cor. 15, 57;
2 Cor. 2, 14).

[2] Psallendi utilitas tristia corda consolatur, gratiores mentes facit, fastidiosos
oblectat, inertes exsuscitat, peccatores ad lamenta invitat. Nam quamvis dura sint
carnalium corda, statim ut psalmi dulcedo insonuerit, ad affectum pietatis animum
eorum inflectit (S. Isidor, Hispal. Sentent. 1. 3, c. 7, n, 31).

[3] S. Aug. Confession. 1. 9, c. 6.

Alleluja or the Tract. Sometimes the Gradual, or the Alleluja, or the Tract, is followed by the so-called Sequence. For a period the Gradual is entirely replaced by the so-called major Alleluja, and once (on Good Friday) by the Tract.

1. The Gradual. The word *Graduale*[1] comes from *gradus* = step. To distinguish the Responsory that occurs between the Epistle and the Gospel from the Responsories of the Divine Office, it was (later on) called *Graduale* from the place in which it was sung: for the leading singer who intoned the longer Psalm-chant after the Epistle and sang it alternately with the choir, stood (in the Roman Church) on an elevated step, that is, on the same step of the Ambo from which the Epistle[2] had previously been read.[3]

The Apostolic Constitutions (l. 2, c. 57) already prescribe a chant of Psalms after the reading from the Old Testament. St. Augustine several times mentions that between the Apostolic reading (Epistle) and the Gospel an entire Psalm should be sung in responses.[4] Thus in this place whole Psalms were sung until the fifth century; but in the Antiphonarium of St. Gregory the Great this Psalm-chant is reduced to a few verses, as is now-a-days the case in our Missal. Even in its present abridgment the Gradual chant has preserved its previous responsory form; for all the Graduale consists of two parts, the first retains the name *Responso-*

---

[1] The original designation was: Responsum, Responsorium, Responsorium graduale, Responsorius (sc. cantus vel psalmus). The name Responsorium (from respondere), that is, alternate singing, expresses the way and manner of the singing, namely, quod uno canente chorus consonando *respondet* (Isidor. De offic. eccles. l. 1, c. 8). Accordingly, the responsory-hymn consists of two parts — of the Responsorium proper (R.) and the Versus (V.). Often (but not always) the other explanation holds good, by which Responsorium would designate a chant of the choir answering the contents of the preceding reading, quia lectioni convenire et quodammodo *respondere* debet (Benedict. XIV. De sacros. Missae sacrif. l. 2, c. 5, n. 15). Responsoria dicuntur a respondendo. Tristia namque tristibus, et laeta laetis debemus succinere lectionibus (Rupert. Tuitiens. De divin. offic. l. 1, c. 15).

[2] Subdiaconus ascendit in ambonem (— non tamen in superiorem gradum, quem solus solet ascendere qui Evangelium lecturus est — Ordo Rom. II, n. 7) et legit (sc. Epistolam). Postquam legerit, cantor cum cantatorio (Antiphon or Gradual) ascendit et dicit Responsum (Ordo Rom. I, n. 10). — Non tamen ascendit superius, sed stat in eodem loco, ubi et lector, et solus inchoat Responsorium et cuncti in choro respondent et idem solus Versum Responsorii cantat (Ordo Rom. II, n. 7). — Lectionem quae legitur post sessionem, sequitur cantus, qui vocatur responsorius (Amalar. De ecclesiast. offic. l. 3, c. 11. — Cfr. Eclog. Amalar. in Ord. Rom. n. 14).

[3] According to others this chant was called Graduale, because it was sung while the deacon with his attendants went from the altar to the steps (gradus) of the choir-stand and ascended them, in order to sing the Gospel. (Cf. Bellarm. De Missa l. 2, c. 16.)

[4] Primam lectionem audivimus Apostoli. Deinde cantavimus *Psalmum*. Post haec evangelica lectio decem leprosos mundatos nobis ostendit et unum ex eis alienigenam gratias agentem mundatori suo (S. Aug. Sermo 176, n. 1).

rium, the other bears the title of *Versus* (V).[1] In most cases both parts are taken from the Psalms, not unfrequently passages from other books of the Old and New Testaments are used; only a few times do we meet with texts which are not from the Bible.[2] Thus do we find everywhere in the liturgy "words of Holy Scripture which the Church with a delicacy of thought has appropriately selected and causes, like so many brilliant gems, to glisten in her divine service."

The object and meaning of the Gradual, or chant after the Epistle, can generally be easily seen and determined, if we take into consideration that this choir chant with the three other variable chants (*Introitus, Offertorium, Communio*), forms a whole which bears the impress or idea of the ecclesiastical year, that is, gives in various ways expression to the fundamental thought of the celebration of the liturgical day or feast, which thought, like a red string, is drawn through each Mass formula. Thoughts, sentiments and resolutions similar to those of the Introit are again expressed afresh or amplified in the chant that comes between the readings, that we may be ever more and more penetrated with the spirit of the day's celebration, may dive ever more and more deeply into the mystery which is to be made glorious by the offering of the Holy Sacrifice. — Hence is made evident the intimate connection between the Gradual chant and the two Scriptural lessons which it binds together. The lessons (Epistle and Gospel), as well as the Gradual chant which comes between them, are selected with regard to one and the same idea of the ecclesiastical time or liturgical celebration; accordingly, as to their contents, there must exist some relationship between them. The readings and the chant harmonize with one another: in both the peculiarity of each ecclesiastical celebration is reflected, but in a different way, according as the character of an instructive reading or an inspiring chant demands.[3] In the reading God descends to us, speaks to us, makes known His mysteries and His will to us, addresses exhortations and admonitions to us, terrifies us by threats and consoles us with His promises; in the chant, on the contrary, we soar upwards to God, make known our devotion and fervor, we praise, thank, love and admire, implore, lament and

---

[1] Formam habet Responsorii Graduale, imo et Responsorium semper appellatur in Antiphonario S. Gregorii, et frequentius a Radulpho et aliis rituum interpretibus. Unde sicut Responsorii duae sunt partes, ita et Gradualis: prior una, quae ipsa *Responsorii* nomen retinet, posterior altera huic cohaerens et annexa, quae *Versus* dicitur (Guyet. Heortolog. l. 3, c. 25, q. 3).

[2] This is the case, for example, in the Gradual of the feast of the Seven Dolors of the Blessed Virgin Mary: Dolorosa et lacrymabilis... and in the Gradual: Benedicta et venerabilis..., which occurs in many Masses of the Blessed Virgin Mary. Here also belongs the first part (Responsorium) of the Gradual in Requiem Masses: Requiem aeternam...

[3] In lectione auditores pascuntur, sed in cantu quasi aratro compunctionis corda conscinduntur; habet enim musica quamdam vim ad flectendum animum (Sicard. Mitral. l. 3, c. 3).

rejoice. — This harmonious blending of instructive readings with
affective singing brings along a beneficial variation in the divine
service. — In the Gradual chant we give appropriate expression to
our lofty dispositions, we utter sentiments of joy or sorrow, various
impressions and resolutions which have been awakened in us by the
day's celebration and by the Mass in general, as well as by the
reading in particular.[1] In a certain sense, then, we may say that
the intermediate chant is an echo, a dying away sound of the
Epistle and a suitable transition to the Gospel. In order, then, to
expound thoroughly the meaning of the Gradual chant, it must
always be conceived and explained in its twofold relation — to the
preceding Epistle and the following Gospel.

The Gradual for the Feast of the Holy Innocents runs thus:

Ps. 123. Anima nostra, sicut passer, erepta est de laqueo venantium.

V. Laqueus contritus est, et nos liberati sumus: adjutorium nostrum in nomine Domini, qui fecit coelum et terram.

Ps. 123. Our soul hath been delivered as a sparrow out of the snare of the fowlers.

V. The snare is broken, and we are delivered: our help is in the name of the Lord, who made heaven and earth.

As a "tender flock of little victims" the holy Innocents were
immolated for Christ and for the sake of Christ: in return, a lot of
eternal blessedness has been awarded them. Filled with jubilant
gratitude they praise in the words of the Gradual aforesaid this
glorious lot which was prepared for them by the Almighty Lord and
Creator: the Almighty has cut the cunningly laid net of the bloody
tyrant, and thus they escaped the snares of the world, the combat
and wants of this earthly life. This Gradual, so to speak, re-echoes
the Epistle,[2] wherein St. John relates how — in a heavenly vision —
he beheld and heard singing before the throne of God all the chaste
and virginal souls, that were purchased from among men, as the
first-fruits unto God and the Lamb, and who sang, therefore, a new
canticle which no one else can sing. The Gospel narrates[3] in words
of sublime and touching simplicity how these tender and unspotted
little victims were cruelly murdered for the Infant Jesus.

The Feast of the Guardian Angels has the following Gradual:

Ps. 90. Angelis suis Deus mandavit de te, ut custodiant te in omnibus viis tuis.

V. In manibus portabunt te, ne unquam offendas ad lapidem pedem tuum.

Ps. 90. He hath given His angels charge over thee, to keep thee in all thy ways.

V. In their hands they shall bear thee up, lest thou dash thy foot against a stone.

---

[1] Utraque Gradualis pars, perinde atque Introitus, modo invitationem et exhortationem continet, modo collaudationem et congratulationem, nonnumquam prosopopoeiam vel apostrophen, saepissime vero omnium narrationem aut invocationem (Guyet l. c.).

[2] Apoc. 14, 1—5.   [3] Matt. 2, 13—18.

The Gradual here pictures in beautiful imagery the Guardian Angels carrying the souls entrusted to them, as priceless treasures in their hands. In all the ways and by-paths they watch over and lovingly and unwearingly care for their wards, that they may not strike against a stone, that is, that amid the dangers and scandals and seductive examples of the world they may suffer no injury. Corresponding to this the Epistle [1] describes the protecting care of the holy Angels, as well as the veneration which we owe to them. In the Gospel of the feast,[2] our Lord Himself shows what a frightful sin it is to scandalize little children, for there in energetic words He calls attention to their being always protected by Angels of light, who at all times behold the face of the Heavenly Father.

2. *The Gradual with the Alleluja Verse (Versus Allelujaticus).* — It is only seldom, that is, on some ferial days in Lent, that the Gradual is sung or recited alone; usually it has an appendix, which, according to the tenor of the ecclesiastical celebration, bears the impress of joy or of sorrow. Expressive of joy is the so-called Minor Alleluja, which is generally added to the Gradual throughout the year. It consists of two Allelujas, a verse and another Alleluja; hence it is often called the Alleluja verse.[3] In this addition the Gradual expands and rises into a joyful chant, which, like a streak of lightening, thrills through the soul.[4] The verse, between the three Allelujas, is in its contents frequently not a mere continuation, but rather a clearer development and a more perfect expression of the thoughts contained in the Gradual. The reason of this is due, in a measure, to the fact that in selecting the verse the Church gave herself freer scope. While she compiled the Gradual mostly always wholly from the Psalms, she did not adhere so strictly to this rule in the composition of the Alleluja Verse, but in its make-up often employed therein other Bible texts also: indeed and especially in

---

[1] Exod. 23, 20—23.

[2] Matt. 18, 1—10.

[3] *Alleluja* canimus, quoniam ad laudes angelicas in hoc itinere festinamus; *Versus,* quoniam sic euntes, laborantes, festinantes ad Dominum revertimur, unde et Versus cantantes ad Orientem nos convertimur; et attende, quod Alleluja, prius summotenus dictum, praesentis contemplationis gaudium repraesentat, sed postea repetitum cum jubilo gaudium designat aeternum et tam angelorum quam beatarum animarum convivium. Unde et hoc hebraicum nomen in officio remanet peregrinum, quoniam gaudium illud peregrinatur ab hac vita et nos a Domino peregrinamur. Congrue igitur *post Graduale* cantatur, quia post actionem sequitur contemplatio, post *luctum poenitentiae canticum laetitiae,* post irriguum dilationis magnitudo consolationis, quoniam ... qui seminant in lacrymis, in exsultatione metent. Congrue quoque in Alleluja jubilamus (= we continue to sing the last syllable with varied melodious turns), ut mens illuc rapiatur, ubi Sancti exsultabunt in gloria et laetabuntur in cubilibus suis (Ps. 149), quod gaudium nec potest verbis exprimi nec omnino taceri: non exprimitur propter magnitudinem, non tacetur propter amorem (Sicard. Mitral. 1. 3, c. 3).

[4] Versus nihil sinistrum aut triste, sed totum jucundum et dulce debent sonare (Innoc. III. 1. 2, c. 33).

Masses celebrated in honor of the Saints, more than thirty of these
verses are not taken from Scripture, but are of ecclesiastical origin.
In this way it was easier to designate more minutely and to mark
more distinctly the subject of the day's celebration.   Verses thus
composed by the Church are, for example, the following.   On the
Assumption of the Blessed Virgin: *Assumpta est Maria in coelum,
gaudet exercitus Angelorum* — "Mary is taken up into heaven, the
angelic host rejoices."   On the feast of St. Lawrence: *Levita Lauren-
tius bonum opus operatus est, qui per signum crucis caecos illuminavit*
— "Lawrence the Deacon wrought a good work, for he by the sign
of the Cross gave sight to the blind."   On the feast of St. Francis of
Assisi: *Franciscus, pauper et humilis, coelum dives ingreditur, hymnis coelestibus honoratur* — "Francis, poor and humble, entereth
rich into heaven, and is honored with ecclesiastical hymns."

The Gradual with the Alleluja chant for the Feast of the Most
Holy Name of Jesus:

Ps. 105. Salvos fac nos, Domine Deus noster, et congrega
nos de nationibus: ut confiteamur
nomini sancto tuo, et gloriemur
in gloria tua.

V. Is. 63. Tu Domine, Pater
noster et Redemptor noster, a
saeculo Nomen tuum.

Alleluja, Alleluja.

V. Ps. 144. Laudem Domini
loquetur os meum, et benedicat
omnis caro Nomen sanctum ejus.

Alleluja.

Ps. 105. Save us, O Lord,
our God, and gather us from
among the nations: that we may
give thanks to Thy holy Name,
and may glory in Thy praise.

V. Is. 63. Thou, O Lord,
art our Father, our Redeemer,
from everlasting is Thy Name.

Alleluja, Alleluja.

V. Ps. 144. My mouth shall
speak the praise of the Lord, and
let all flesh bless His holy Name.

Alleluja.

The adorable Name of Jesus is "light, food, medicine," "honey
to the mouth, music to the ear, joy to the heart:"[1] it is the sweetest,
the most powerful, and the most glorious of all names.   Now,
throughout the Gradual unto the glory of this blessed Name resounds
praise and a thanksgiving full of love, — and this chant of praise
proceeds from the heart and mouth of the ransomed and privileged
children of God.   In full accord with it is the Epistle,[2] which
announces to us that no other name than the Name of Jesus can
bring us salvation and redemption, and the Gospel, too,[3] which
proclaims to us that the Lord received this heavenly Name when for
the first time He shed His blood for us. — On the Feast of Christ's
Transfiguration the following intermediary chant is heard:

---

[1] Nomen Jesus lux, cibus, medicina. Lucet praedicatum, pascit recogitatum,
invocatum lenit et ungit. . . . Jesus mel in ore, in aure melos, in corde jubilus (S.
Bernard. In Cantica serm. 15, n. 5. 6).

[2] Acts. 4, 8—12.

[3] Luke 2, 21.

Ps. 44. Speciosus forma prae filiis hominum: diffusa est gratia in labiis tuis.

V. Eructavit cor meum verbum bonum; dico ego: "Opera mea regi."

Alleluja, Alleluja.

V. Sap. 7. Candor est lucis aeternae, speculum sine macula, et imago bonitatis illius.

Alleluja.

Ps. 44. Thou art beautiful above the sons of men: grace is poured abroad in Thy lips.

V. My heart hath uttered a good word: "I speak my works to the King."

Alleluja, Alleluja.

V. Wis. 7. He is the brightness of eternal light; the unspotted mirror and the image of His goodness.

Alleluja.

The Gospel [1] of the Feast of Thabor unveils to us the radiant glory of God, which at other times the Saviour always concealed under the lowly appearance of a servant; in the Epistle [2] the Prince of the Apostles narrates how on "the holy mountain" he had seen the resplendent glory of His Master and had heard the Heavenly Father's voice "amid the brightness of His splendor." Now whilst the Divine Spouse stands revealed to the eyes of His Church in radiant splendor and loveliness, how could she better pour out the enthusiastic and ravishing sentiments of her joyous feast, than she does in the aforesaid Gradual chant?

In the Mass of a feast (*Vultum tuum*) in honor of a Virgin we find the following Gradual chant:

Ps. 44. Concupivit Rex decorem tuum, quoniam ipse est Dominus Deus tuus.

V. Audi filia, et vide, et inclina aurem tuam.

Alleluja, Alleluja.

V. Haec est virgo sapiens, et una de numero prudentum.

Alleluja.

Ps. 44. The King shall greatly desire thy beauty: for He is the Lord thy God.

V. Hearken, O daughter, see, and incline thy ear.

Alleluja, Alleluja.

V. This is a wise virgin, and one of the number of the prudent.

Alleluja.

The corresponding Epistle [3] depicts the privileges, the glory and the blessedness of virginity embraced and vowed out of the love of God: the virgin strives to be holy in body and mind, in order to be able to serve and to please the Lord with an undivided heart. It is with the light of faith that she sees and contemplates the attractions of this angelic life; why should she not willingly and humbly follow the call of grace, inviting her thereto? This call is expressed

---

[1] Matt. 17, 1—9.

[2] 2 Peter 1, 16—19.

[3] 1 Cor. 7, 25—34.

15

in the Gradual with the assurance that the Lord Himself yearns for the soul adorned with such supernatural beauty of virtue. Thus runs the verse between the Allelujas. Wise and prudent is the virgin who dedicates and surrenders herself entirely and unreservedly to the Lord. The Gospel[1] shows us the prudent virgin, representing her either as renouncing all things to obtain "the hidden treasure and the precious pearl" of the heavenly kingdom, or as going forth to meet the Heavenly Spouse with her lamp filled with oil and lighted, in order to celebrate the eternal nuptials.

The Gradual for the First Sunday after Pentecost:

Ps. 40. Ego dixi: Domine miserere mei: sana animam meam, quia peccavi tibi.

V. Beatus qui intelligit super egenum et pauperem: in die mala liberabit eum Dominus.

Alleluja, Alleluja.

V. Verba mea auribus percipe, Domine, intellige clamorem meum.

Alleluja.

Ps. 40. I said: O Lord, be Thou merciful to me: heal my soul, for I have sinned against Thee.

V. Blessed is he that understandeth concerning the needy and the poor: the Lord will deliver him in the evil day.

Alleluja, Alleluja.

V. Ps. 5. Give ear, O Lord, to my words, understand my cry.

Alleluja.

Whosoever lovingly understands the sufferings, the wants, the poverty of his brethren; whosoever kindheartedly compassionates the sorrow-stricken and the abandoned, will, as a reward in the evil day, in the hour of dire distress be graciously freed by the Lord and be refreshed with heavenly consolation. This Gradual most significantly unites the Epistle and Gospel of the Sunday. The former depicts[2] in sublime words the essence and greatness of God's love for us and our love for God and our neighbor; the latter[3] recommends to us the virtues of mercy, meekness, forgiveness and love towards all our fellow-men.

The Gradual of a Votive Mass for the Sick is as follows:

Ps. 6. Miserere mihi, Domine, quoniam infirmus sum: sana me, Domine.

V. Conturbata sunt omnia ossa mea: et anima mea turbata est valde.

Alleluja, Alleluja.

Ps. 6. Have mercy on me, O Lord, for I am weak: heal me, O Lord!

V. All my bones are troubled: and my soul is troubled exceedingly.

Alleluja, Alleluja.

---

[1] Matt. 13, 44—52; 25, 1—13.

[2] 1 John 4, 8—21.

[3] Luke 6, 36—40.

Ps. 101. Domine, exaudi orationem meam: et clamor meus
ad te perveniat.

Alleluja.

Vs. Ps. 101. Hear, O Lord,
my prayer: and let my cry come
to Thee.

Alleluja.

Tormented by sufferings of body and soul, the invalid cries from his bed of pain to his God and Lord for health and cure. This urgent and confident appeal for assistance forms a suitable intermediate link between the readings. In the Epistle[1] the Apostle encourages us to receive the grace imparted by anointing, that is, by Extreme Unction, whereby "the merciful kindness of God" alleviates suffering, healing all manners of wounds and frailties. The words of the Centurion in the Gospel[2] recall the boundless healing power of Christ, as well as the blessings and graces of the holy Viaticum.

3. *The Gradual with the Tract.* — At certain times the joyful Alleluja chant after the Gradual is silent, and its place is supplied by the Tract, which is of entirely different tenor. Whilst the Gradual with the annexed Alleluja assumes the form of a spirited hymn of joy, it goes over in the superadded Tract into a chant of a grave, mournful and penitential character.

Tractus is a musical term; it relates primarily not to the contents, but to the manner of delivery, that is, to the mode of singing. The peculiar, characteristic manner of singing called Tract consisted in this, that all the verses were continuously sung by one singer, that is, without the choir interrupting him by responding — and this was done in a slow, protracted measure.[3] This uniform and measured way of chanting is — in contrast to the animated alternate singing of the Gradual and Alleluja Verse — evidently suited for the expression of holy sorrow and penitential sentiments. For this reason the Tract has replaced the jubilant Alleluja, and already become long ago the peculiar characteristic of the Lenten rite: it occurs only on days especially devoted to quiet reflection upon one's interior, to exercises of prayer and of mortification, to works of penance and fervent prayer for divine grace and mercy. What the sombre purple is to the eye on these days of earnest sorrow and

---

[1] James 5, 13—16.

[2] Matt. 8, 5—13.

[3] Tractus = the drawing, the extension, the slow movement of the words; tractim = in one strain, drawn, extended, slowly. — We find the Tract already in the most ancient Roman Ordos. Cantor dicit Responsum. Si fuerit tempus ut dicat Alleluja, bene; sin autem, *Tractum;* sin minus, tantummodo Responsum (Ordo Roman. I, n. 10). — Saeculo decimo complures sibi persuaserunt, quod *tractim* canere nihil aliud significaret, quam cunctanter lento et tristi tono canere; hinc jusserunt, ut non amplius *unus,* sed plures et quidem *bini* Tractum alternis canerent vicibus, ea tantum servata lege, ne *chorus* eos interrumperet (Krazer Sect. 4, art. 1, cap. 4, § 234). — Tractus dicitur a *trahendo,* vel quia lente et lugubriter cantatur, vel quia olim tractim et sine interruptione a cantore canebatur (De Carpo, Biblioth. liturg. p. 1, a. 2).

penance, the touching chant of the Tract is to the ear — a sigh of penitential grief. — The Tract is a continuation or amplication of the Gradual, and according to its contents harmonizes with it: at times it expresses quietly sentiments of joy, of hope and confidence; but more frequently, however, it utters the prayer, the supplication, the plaint of a heart oppressed with distress and suffering, with contrition and love of God. — The Tract is nearly always taken from Holy Scripture, especially from the Psalter; often various biblical texts are freely joined together; only seldom is it partly or wholly of ecclesiastical origin. Sometimes it is longer, at others shorter; it always comprises — with but few exceptions — more than two verses, on three occasions (on the first Sunday of Lent, Palm Sunday and Good Friday) almost an entire Psalm. — Not all those days have a Tract on which the joyful Alleluja chant is omitted; it rather serves to distinguish certain more strict penitential days from others, or to bring the festive expression of some Masses more into harmony with the spirit of Lent. The most sorrowful day of the year — Good Friday — has a double Tract, while at other times but one is used.[1]

The Mondays, Wednesdays and Fridays in Lent were from the earliest period the most prominent as well as the strictest days of penance;[2] hence they have a tract especially arranged for penitents and, with the exception of Wednesday in Holy Week, the Tract is always the same.

It is as follows:

Ps. 102. Domine, non secundum peccata nostra, quae fecimus nos: neque secundum iniquitates nostras retribuas nobis.

V. Ps. 76. Domine, ne memineris iniquitatum nostrarum antiquarum: cito anticipent nos misericordiae tuae, quia pauperes facti sumus nimis.

Ps. 102. O Lord, deal not with us according to our sins: nor reward us according to our iniquities.

V. Ps. 78. Remember not, O Lord, our former iniquities: let Thy mercies speedily prevent us, for we are become exceedingly poor.

---

[1] On Ember Saturdays the Tract follows the Epistle only, and thus closes the five chants (Graduals), that are annexed to the five preceding lessons and are, thus to speak, regarded as one single Gradual. Rupert of Deutz remarks on this circumstance, that on Ember Saturdays and on Wednesday in Holy Week, after the Epistle, as well as on Good Friday after the (two) lessons, not the Gradual with the Tract, but merely the Tract without the Gradual follows, whereby the expression of penitential sorrow is augmented in the highest degree (De divin. off. 1. 5, c. 13).

[2] They are called feriae legitimae, that is, official penitential days, the observance of which was transplanted from the East to the West. The mystical reasons taken from the symbolical number for selecting the feriae legitimae (fer. II. IV. VI.), on which in Lent is prescribed also the Office of the Dead, the Gradual Psalms and the Penitential Psalms for the choir, are given by Quadt, Die Liturgie der Quatembertage S. 111—112.

V. (*Ad hunc versum genu-flectitur.*) Adjuva nos, Deus salutaris noster: et propter gloriam nominis tui, Domine, libera nos; et propitius esto peccatis nostris, propter nomen tuum.

V. (Genuflect.) Help us, O God, our Saviour: and for the glory of Thy name, O Lord, deliver us; and forgive us our sins for Thy name's sake.

This Tract is a fervent supplication for mercy, for the pardon of sin and for obtaining the assistance of grace to persevere in a life of virtue.[1] When we sinned, we "loved vanity and sought lying," we abandoned the fountain of living water and dug for ourselves broken cisterns: thus by sin we have become poor and wretched beyond expression. This we feel and acknowledge, humbled to the earth by the consciousness of guilt and pierced with sorrow; but cheered by hope, we cry to God for His mercy, which always outweighs the severity of His justice, and we implore the remission of the sins which we have committed, and a merciful preservation from fresh falls. For all this we pray, not indeed relying on our merits, but for the sake of the honor and name of God, that is, that God may thereby be glorified and praised. But to make our cry of supplication and our petition still more pressing, we bend the knee at the last verse in token of the most profound humility and of the most sorrowful compunction.

The Votive Mass of the Holy Ghost, when celebrated after Septuagesima, has the following chant between the Epistle,[2] which treats of the imparting of the Holy Spirit by the sacrament of Confirmation, and the Gospel,[3] which contains the promise of the Holy Ghost from the lips of the Lord.

Graduale. Ps. 32. Beata gens, cujus est Dominus Deus eorum: populus, quem elegit Dominus in haereditatem sibi.

Gradual. Ps. 32. Blessed is the nation whose God is the Lord: the people whom He hath chosen for His inheritance.

V. Verbo Domini coeli firmati sunt: et Spiritu oris ejus omnis virtus eorum.

V. By the Word of the Lord the heavens were established, and all the power of them by the Spirit of His mouth.

Tractus. Ps. 103. Emitte Spiritum tuum et creabuntur: et renovabis faciem terrae.

Tract. Ps. 103. Thou shalt send forth thy Spirit and they shall be created: and thou shalt renew the face of the earth.

---

[1] Admiranda est virtus orationis versuum horum et omnino saluberrimum est mentali affectu cum attentione ingenti, cum praecordiali sapore hos sacros versus depromere, quoniam possibilius foret coelum et terram perire quam talem orationem inefficacem existere (Dion. Carthus. in Ps. 78. 8).

[2] Acts 8, 14—17.

[3] John 14, 23—31.

V. O quam bonus et suavis est, Domine, Spiritus tuus in nobis!

V. (Hic genuflectitur.) Veni sancte Spiritus, reple tuorum corda fidelium: et tui amoris in eis ignem accende.

V. O how good and sweet is, O Lord, Thy Spirit within us.

V. (Here genuflect.) Come, O Holy Ghost, fill the hearts of Thy faithful, and kindle in them the fire of Thy love.

The Gradual praises as happy the people that know and serve God, whose Head and King is, therefore, God the Lord. It then announces that by "the word" of the Lord the heavens were created and by His "Spirit" the splendor and adornment of the starry firmament and of the whole creation were accomplished; for in this verse the Fathers find an indication of the mystery of the Holy Trinity: in the term "Lord" of the Father, in the term "Word" of the Son, and in the term "Breath" of the Holy Ghost.

The Tract implores for the sending of the Spirit Creator, that He may renew not only the face of the earth by awakening the life of nature, but also the face of the human world by the light of truth and the power of grace, until all things be perfected and transformed. Inasmuch, then, as we consider the Holy Ghost as the source of spiritual joys, sweetnesses and consolations, we beseech Him to forestall us with the blessings of His goodness, and to enkindle in us the pure flame of heavenly love.

All the Mass formulas for the departed souls have the same unchangeable chant after the Epistle:

Graduale. Requiem aeternam dona eis, Domine: et lux perpetua luceat eis.

V. Ps. iii. In memoria aeterna erit justus: ab auditione mala non timebit.

Tractus. Absolve, Domine, animas omnium fidelium defunctorum ab omni vinculo delictorum.

V. Et gratia tua illis succurrente, mereantur evadere judicium ultionis.

V. Et lucis aeternae beatitudine perfrui.

Gradual. Eternal rest grant unto them, O Lord: and let perpetual light shine upon them.

V. Ps. iii. The just shall be in everlasting remembrance: he shall not fear the evil hearing.

Tract. Release, O Lord, the souls of all the faithful departed from the bonds of their sins.

V. And by the assistance of Thy grace may they escape the sentence of condemnation.

V. And enjoy the bliss of eternal light.

The ecclesiastical time has no influence whatever on the Requiem Mass which is ever uniformly the same, and it has, therefore, throughout the entire year a Gradual with a Tract,[1] which —

---

[1] Tam Graduale quam Tractus in Missis defunctorum nullam unquam mutationem subeunt; adeo luctuosa officia sunt Missae de Requiem, quae nobis objiciunt

with the exception of an inserted verse from the Psalms — was composed by the Church herself. As a tender solicitous Mother she begs of God the Father, that He would vouchsafe to take His and her suffering children out of purgatory into the peace of heaven and into the light of glory. The Church is encouraged thus to pray and intercede, because the souls that are expiating in purgatory, led here below God-fearing and devout lives: the just will live eternally in blessed remembrance, and he needs not fear the "very worst notice" of the sentence of condemnation from the lips of the Judge of the world. — She then implores the Lord to remove the last obstacle to glory; and whilst suddenly representing to herself these souls at the moment of their departure from the body and out of this world, she entreats for them a favorable judgment, that they may soon be admitted to the possession of eternal joys.

The Alleluja and Tract are, therefore, at different times annexed to the ordinary Gradual, in order to express the various interior sentiments of the Church. Although the times of Advent and Lent are in many respects liturgically framed alike, yet there is a distinction made with regard to the Alleluja. Advent is of a character partly grave and partly joyful; it is indeed still night, but the first rays of the dawn and of the Sun about to rise already chase away the dark shadows — *Ab alto Jesus promicat.* On the four Sundays of Advent, the sombre hue of the purple vestments of the Church announces the penitential spirit of the holy season, while the Alleluja after the Gradual gives expression to the joyful expectation.[1] The Church stamps this season with the seal both of her joy and of her anxious solicitude; she intermingles the Alleluja amid her sighs, knowing well that "joy will drown all sorrow on that night which is brighter than the clearest day."

The case is entirely different with respect to the period from Septuagesima until Easter.[2] This is the greatest and the strictest penitential season of the Church : hence the Alleluja is totally withheld from her lips.[3] She is quite overwhelmed with sorrow and a holy sadness. She accompanies her Divine Spouse step by step on His bloody journey of suffering; she sighs and weeps over the malice and bitterness of sin, which runs riot everywhere on the earth,

---

Purgatorii animas a facie Dei projectas, in immanissimis tormentorum generibus excruciatas, ut aptae haud sint suscipere vel intermixta admittere laetitiae signa, unde et respuunt vocem Alleluja (Cavalieri, Oper. liturg. III, c. 10, n. 3).

[1] Quamvis cum gaudio boni servi spectent, adventum Domini sui, tamen maximum gaudium recolunt in praesentia ejus (Amalar. De eccles. offic. 1. 4, c. 30). — Adventus partim est laetitiae, quia *Alleluja* dicitur et cantus in jucunditate cantatur; partim tristitiae, quia *Te Deum, Gloria in excelsis* et *Ite Missa est* reticentur (Radulph. Tungren. De canon. observantia prop. 16).

[2] Cfr. Ivon. Carnot. serm. 12 de Septuagesima.

[3] Alleluja certis quidem diebus cantamus, sed omni die cogitamus. Si enim hoc verbo significatur laus Dei, etsi non in ore carnis, certe in ore cordis — *"semper laus ejus in ore meo"* — Ps. 33, 2 (S. Aug. Enarr. in Ps. 106, n. 1).

cursed by the Lord.   As faithful children of the Church we should heed her admonition and exercise ourselves in works of penance. Our hearts, sullied by sin and the love of the world, we should bathe in the tears of sorrow and compunction before we presume to permit that hymn of pure souls, the Alleluja, to again cross our lips.[1]   Sinners that we are, do we not in our poverty famish here in exile, far from the haven of true peace ?   Yes, the new happy Jerusalem is our true home; it constitutes, already now, for us life's greatest joy and the heart's never-to-be-forgotten love.   The remembrance of the eternal Sion awakens profound sadness in the soul, and the tears of homesickness are never dried from the eyes, since we are pilgrims in a foreign land and are sitting by the rivers of the worldly Babylon.[2] This Babylon invites to enjoyment and sensuality, to play and to frivolity, and with its cup of deceitful pleasure it seeks ever to intoxicate one and all.   And right here it is necessary to withstand temptation, to save one's self from corruption.   We must not allow ourselves to be carried away in the torrent of vain perishable things, nor to be swept away into the vortex of sensuality and passion, but, reflecting and praying, we must remain on the shore and weep tears of desire for the celestial Sion.   How could we sing a joyful hymn in a strange land ?   The Alleluja — that chant of the heavenly Jerusalem — ceases, therefore, to resound during the season of Lent, which so deeply impresses our hearts with consciousness of the misery of our earthly banishment and pilgrimage; the modest, humble and tranquil melody of the Tract alone expresses our silent grief, our longing, our petition to be heard, our lament and hope.[3]   Yet we lovingly cling to the jubilant Alleluja chant, and only reluctantly separate ourselves from it; and this we express at the Vespers on the Saturday preceding Septuagesima,[4] by repeating twice the Alleluja

---

[1] Cfr. Regul. s. Benedicti c. 15. Speciale caput s. Benedictus instituit de *Alleluja*, tanquam de voce divina vereque angelica nec nisi ab Angelis aut certe ab hominibus vitae puritate angelicos spiritus imitantibus decantanda (Martene, Regul. commentata l. c.).

[2] Quid sunt flumina Babylonis, nisi fluxus labilis vitae mundanorum, qui nunquam requiescit et ad mare mortis aeternae perducit? Ille ergo sedet super flumina Babylonis, qui intra seipsum recollectus, mente considerat inquietum et amarum statum vitae mundanorum. Quod cum quis consideraverit et recordatus fuerit, quanta sit quies quantaque gloria Sion, scil. civitatis supernae, dum se in Babylone videt peregrinum, statim ad fletum et lacrymas consurgit (Ayguanus [Ord. Carm. † 1416] in Ps. 136).

[3] Cuncti *tractus* fletum et tristitiam in humilitate sonorum denuntiant. Tristitiae tempus exigit, ut Alleluja, quod laetantium carmen est, intermitteretur. Bene ergo tractus, qui interim pro Alleluja cantatur, altitudinem atque excellentiam gaudii, gravi succentu et modestis declinat incessibus (Rup. Tuit. De div. off. l. 4, c. 6).

[4] According to the prescription of St. Benedict the Alleluja was sung usque ad caput Quadragesimae, that is, until the first Sunday of Lent; this was customary in many Orders of Monks (Benedictines and Cistercians) for a long period, and it is still in use in the Ambrosian Rite. Thus writes Radulph of Rivo, Dean of Tun-

after the *Benedicamus Domino* and *Deo gratias*.[1] And after that it resounds no more within the hallowed precincts of the sanctuary, until it is again introduced with a certain solemnity and intoned in the High Mass on the vigil of the feast of Easter. Then after the Epistle the Alleluja forms the beginning of the Gradual chant, and is sung three times alternately by the priest and the choir, the tone rising at each Alleluja. As Easter dawns, not only the Tract but also the Gradual must now be laid aside; the joyful peal of the Alleluja during Eastertide appears never to cease.

4. The major Alleluja (without Gradual). — The Hebrew word *Alleluia* signifies litterally: "Praise the Lord!"[2] And because it has a peculiar meaning and dignity, a force of expression and emphasis peculiarly its own, it has not been translated into other languages.[3] Thus in the cry of the Alleluja are the tongues of all nations lifted up in unison to praise and adore God even here on earth with one voice and one sound, as will most perfectly be done in the world to come.[4] The blessed inhabitants of the heavenly

---

gern († 1403): Benedictini et Ambrosiani servant Alleluja usque ad Dominicam Quadragesimae (De canon. observantia, prop. 16). — The Breviary ascribes the present practice to St. Gregory the Great: constituit, ut extra id tempus, quod continetur Septuagesima et Pascha, Alleluja diceretur.

[1] In the Middle Age were sung on the eve of Septuagesima as a farewell to the Alleluja Antiphons, Hymns and Sequences, filled with childlike naïveté and simplicity (cf. Guéranger, Le temps de la Septuagésime, p. 121 s. — Mone, Latein. Hymnen I, 86 etc. — Sicard. Mitral. 1. 6, c. 1).

[2] In view of the joy and consolation found in the pious death (mors pia vel sacra) of the Christian (Beati mortui, qui in Domino moriuntur — Apoc. 14, 13), the Alleluja formerly was sung even in the liturgy of the dead; this is still the case among the Greeks who even during Quadragesima do not omit the Alleluja. From Rome St. Jerome writes (Ad Oceanum ep. 77), that at the funeral obsequies of Fabiola "Psalms were sung and the Allelujas resounding aloft re-echoed throughout the gilded ceilings of the temples (sonabant psalmi et aurata tecta templorum reboans in sublime quatiebat *Alleluja*). — Even outside of divine worship in the primitive times of Christianity, the chant of the Alleluja was very common. Thus St. Jerome remarks, that young children even had been trained to sing the Alleluja balbutiente lingua, and that in the fields of Bethlehem this chant might everywhere be heard (Quocunque te verteris, arator stivam tenens *Alleluja* decantat). Seamen sang the Alleluja amid the echoes of the shore (responsantibus ripis — Sidon. Apollin. 1. 2, ep. 10). In many places it was customary by this word to call the inmates of the convent to the hours of common prayer.

[3] Illud advertendum, multo majorem vim apud Hebraeos habere hanc vocem *Alleluja* quam apud Latinos *Laudate Deum;* hoc est enim exhortantis vel excitantis ad Deo laudes reddendas: at Alleluja vim potius habet interjectionis quam verbi, et vehementem sonat affectum acclamantis prae gaudio et ex laude Dei exsultantis atque in jubilum vocemque laetitiae erumpentis (Bona, De divin. Psalm. c. 16, § 7, n. 7). — Alleluja vox hebraica est et sonat "laudate Dominum" vel "laus Deo", cum gaudii tamen laetitiaeque plenitudine (Carli, Biblioth. liturg. s. h. v.).

[4] Rectissime et pulcherrime generalis sanctae Ecclesiae mos inolevit, ut hoc divinae laudationis carmen propter reverentiam primae auctoritatis a cunctis per orbem fidelibus hebraea voce cantetur. Quod ideo fit, ut per talis consonantiam

Jerusalem — who are the angels and saints — sing without ceasing
or intermission their endless Alleluja, as already Tobias (13, 21–22)
announced in prophetic vision: "The gates of Jerusalem shall be
built of sapphire and of emerald and all the wall thereof round about
of precious stones. All its streets shall be paved with white and
clean stones, and *Alleluja* shall be sung in its streets" (*per vicos
ejus Alleluja cantabitur*). The virginal Prophet and beloved Disciple describes a vision which he beheld in heaven: "After these
things I heard, as it were, the voice of many multitudes in heaven,
saying: Alleluja. Salvation and power and glory is to our God.
And I heard the voice of many waters, and as the voice of great
thunders, saying: Alleluja! for the Lord our God the Almighty hath
reigned. Let us be glad and rejoice, and give glory to Him; for the
marriage of the Lamb is come, and His wife hath prepared herself"
(Apoc. 19, 1. 6. 7). The souls of the blessed in heaven overflow
with joy and happiness; hence their language becomes a canticle of
praise. "The saints shall rejoice in glory; they shall be joyful in
their beds. The high praises of God shall be in their mouth" (Ps.
149, 5—6). Thus they continue for all eternity in heaven, what
upon earth was their delight and felicity; for the Church sings in an
Antiphon: *In velamento clamabant Sancti tui, Domine: Alleluja,
Alleluja, Alleluja* — "When clothed with mortality, Thy Saints,
O Lord, cried out: Alleluja, Alleluja, Alleluja."

The literal meaning of the word Alleluja (hallĕlū = praise,
iah = God) is no longer clearly felt; in the mouth of the Church
the word Alleluja becomes transformed and perpetuated as a powerful cry of joy and exultation, and especially of happy Easter jubilation.[1] The Church on earth is midway between the Synagogue and

---

devotionis admoneatur Ecclesia, quia et nunc in una fidei confessione ac dilectione
Christi consistere debeat, et ad illam in futuro patriam festinare, in qua nulla diversitas mentium, nulla est dissonantia linguarum (Beda Venerabilis 1. 2, hom. 10).

[1] Quinquagesima (the fifty days of Eastertide) ab ipso dominicae resurrectionis die inchoare et gaudiis potius laudibusque divinis quam jejuniis (Patres nostri)
voluerunt esse celebrem, quatenus annuis ejus festis dulcius admoneremur, desiderium nostrum ad obtinenda festa, semper accendere fixumque tenere, quia non in
tempore mortalitatis hujus, sed in aeternitate futurae incorruptionis vera nobis
quaerenda felicitas, vera est invenienda solemnitas, ubi cessantibus cunctis lan-
guoribus tota in Dei visione ac laude vita geritur — juxta hoc quod propheta corde
pariter et carne in Deum vivum exsultans ajebat: "Beati qui habitant in domo tua,
Domine; in saecula saeculorum laudabunt te" (Ps. 83). Unde merito Quinquage-
simae diebus in memoriam hujus nostrae quietissimae ac felicissimae actionis
crebrius ac *festivius* Alleluja canere solemus (Bed. Venerab. 1. 2, homil. 10). —
Dum s. Gertrudis cum devotione et intentione omnes vires et sensus tam interiores
quam exteriores extenderet, et se ad cantandum Matutinas in gloriam Dominicae
resurrectionis praepararet, dum imponeretur Invitatorium *Alleluja*, dixit ad Dominum: "Doce me, instructor benignissime, quali devotione te laudare possim per
Alleluja, quod toties in festo isto repetitur." Respondit Dominus: "Convenientissime poteris me per *Alleluja* collaudare in unione laudis supercoelestium qui
per idem jugiter collaudant in coelis." Et adjecit Dominus: "Nota igitur quod in

the heavenly Jerusalem: accordingly the cry of the Alleluja resounds more frequently in the divine worship than it did in the service of the Old Law, but yet not with us, as it peals forth in the Church Triumphant without interruption. This "cry of triumphant praise and salvation" (Ps. 117, 15), which descended from heaven to our poor earth, resounds in the liturgy principally from Holy Saturday until the Saturday after Pentecost; for this great octave of weeks (called Eastertide at one season and Whitsuntide at another) is throughout of a joyful nature. The celebration of holy Eastertide is nothing else than the triumph of the Redeemer and the Redemption, that is, the celebration of the victory over sin, death and hell. Here all in the liturgy refers to the eternal blessed life of glory, upon which Christ has entered and which He has acquired for us. The three joyful and most glorious mysteries — namely, the Resurrection and Ascension of Christ, as well as the descent of the Holy Ghost, are sources of true and lasting joy, so that for a time we seem to forget the combats and labors of our earthly pilgrimage, the place of our banishment, and full of joy and gratitude we chime in the Alleluja of the citizens of heaven, without ever becoming weary of repeating it again and again. The Alleluja is the outpouring of that grand Easter joy with which our hearts are filled to overflowing; it is the festive song, the exultant cry over the happiness and the glory of our Redemption.

What is the form of the Alleluja chant after the Epistle during Eastertide ? While the Gradual is still retained during Easter-week, it is omitted on the Saturday before Low Sunday, and thenceforth until the feast of Holy Trinity two Allelujas are sung (as Antiphons) followed by two verses, each with an Alleluja. "The Gradual as a canticle of mourning is omitted at Eastertide, and the Alleluja is repeated almost without measure, to note that salvation has been, by the death and resurrection of Christ, purchased for us and the way to eternal joys has been opened, where with all the blessed we shall sing to our Lord an eternal Alleluja." (Ein Vergissmeinnicht S. 78). — On the feast of Christ's Ascension the Epistle and Gospel narrate the glorious entrance of the world's Redeemer into His eternal glory and beatitude. The intermediate chant likewise announces this triumphant and solemn entrance of Christ.

Alleluja, Alleluja.	Alleluja, Alleluja.
V. Ps. 46. Ascendit Deus in jubilatione, et Dominus in voce tubae. Alleluja.	V. Ps. 46. God hath ascended with jubilee, and the Lord with the sound of trumpet. Alleluja.
V. Ps. 67. Dominus in Sina in sancto; ascendens in altum, captivam duxit captivitatem. Alleluja.	V. Ps. 67. The Lord is among them in Sinai, in the holy place; He hath ascended on high, and hath led captivity captive. Alleluja.

illa dictione *Alleluja* omnes vocales inveniuntur praeter solam vocalem *o*, quae dolorem signat, et pro illa duplicatur prima, scil. vocalis *a*." (S. Gertrud. Legat. divinae pietatis l. 4, c. 27).

When in His painful struggle with the powers of darkness, the Lord had by the humility of the Cross overcome Satan and his power, He entered victoriously and gloriously into the Holy of Holies of Heaven, which is the true Sinai, the throne of His divine glory revealing itself; the angelic choirs rejoiced and exulted, when the King of Glory came up "leading captivity captive," namely, bringing with Him the just and devout of ancient times, whom He delivered as the prize of victory from Limbo, and introduced into the kingdom of eternal light as captives of His redeeming and blissful love. That the Gradual is still continued during Easter-week appears strange. Is not the liturgy of the Easter vigil already radiant with the splendor of light and fire, does it not resound throughout with the joyous exultation of the Resurrection? Does not the Church cry out during the entire week: *Haec dies, quam fecit Dominus: exsultemus et laetemur in ea* — "This is the day, that the Lord hath made; let us rejoice and be glad thereon"? (Ps. 117, 24.)[1] Assuredly it is so; already during the night of the Resurrection does our Lord turn our lament into joy, unloosen our garb of penance and gird us with bliss (Ps. 29, 12). During the first thousand years of Christianity the Church had a special reason for inserting the Gradual throughout the octave of Easter; this reason lay in the peculiar form of divine worship at that time. It had reference almost exclusively to the newly baptized, who on Holy Saturday by means of the laver of regeneration had risen to a new life; during the entire week they were instructed in the truths and mysteries of the Christian religion, and went about wearing white robes all the while in token of the innocence and holiness acquired in baptism.[2] On Saturday the baptismal solemnities were ended and the white garment was laid aside.[3] Like the rest of the liturgical celebration, the Gradual of Easter-week was also arranged with special regard to the neophytes.[4] This is beyond a doubt; but the difficulty is to determine more minutely what in reality was the purpose and meaning of the Gradual for the newly baptized.

---

[1] Merito cantatur hic versiculus in die Paschae tam frequenter, quoniam Christus, sol justitiae, candor lucis aeternae, lux lucis et fons luminis, qui erat in die Parasceves passionis caligine obscuratus atque in monumento lapideo tanquam densissima nube absconditus, in die Paschae de sepulcro glorificatus, candidus et rubicundus processit, illuminans mundum, noctem infidelitatis et tenebras ignorantiae de cordibus discipulorum ejiciens (Dion. Carthus. in Ps. 117, 23).

[2] In the Gregorian Sacramentary all the days of Easter week are designated as feriae in Albis.

[3] As the practice varied in the different churches, this did not take place in many localities until Sunday; hence we still have the name Sabbatum in Albis and Dominica in Albis scil. depositis. In ancient liturgical books the octave day of the feast of Easter is also called Dominica post Albas (depositas).

[4] Graduale, quod est *cantus laborantium in hac peregrinatione,* jam dictum est ad hos dies resurrectionis usque in Pentecosten non pertinere, sed *propter baptizatos* per hanc hebdomadam in officiis additum esse (Rupert. Tuit., De divin. offic. l. 8, c. 1).

The Gradual lies midway between the mournful Tract and the exultant Alleluja : it denotes the laborious and difficult pilgrimage of the children of God through life to their heavenly country.[1] Therefore, at one time the Gradual is connected with the Tract, at another with the Alleluja, — according as the sufferings and pains of penance or the consolations and hopes of future eternal rest predominate in our earthly pilgrimage.[2] At certain times the Gradual is entirely omitted or it gives place to the Tract, for the reason that grief of soul has reached its profoundest depths, as on Good Friday, or is displaced by the Alleluja, because the soul, as it were, forgets the earth and can but rejoice with the blessed of heaven, as during Eastertide. When, therefore, the Church still sang the Gradual in Easter-week, this was for the newly baptized a significant admonition for them to note, that, during the whole term of their earthly pilgrimage, they must ever advance in the midst of labors and combats from virtue to virtue, until the day of perfect redemption and eternal transformation shall have dawned for them.[3] The time for the happy consummation of their pilgrimage and arrival in the heavenly Jerusalem was symbolized by the Saturday, on which day the Gradual was omitted. This Saturday was the octave-day of solemn baptism; but the octave symbolized eternal beatitude. — To this we may add the following reflection. The time of Septuagesima in a wider sense, that is, the days from Septuagesima Sunday until Easter, are accounted by all liturgists of the Middle Age as a reminder of the Seventy Years Captivity, during which the Jews sat on the banks of the rivers of Babylon and wept, mindful of their home in Sion. This Babylonian exile is itself a figure of our life upon earth, where we are sojourning at a distance from the face of the Lord, sighing for the perfect liberty, in the heavenly Jerusalem, of the children of God. All those days on which the Alleluja is silent belong to the time of Septuagesima, which is intended, in the first place, to represent symbolically to us the Babylonian Captivity and then, furthermore, the life of man as an exile in this world. Frequently Easter-Week also is comprised in Septuagesima; for including it up to Septuagesima Sunday and counting backwards, we have precisely seventy days; but it is difficult to see how the jubilant

---

[1] Graduale significat non jam requiem remuneratorum, sed *laborem operantium* (Rupert. Tuit. l. 1, c. 24).

[2] Post lectionem cantatur a choro *Graduale*, quod significat profectum vitae, et *Alleluja*, quod significat spiritualem exsultationem, vel *Tractus* in officiis luctuosis, quod significat spiritualem gemitum : haec enim consequi debent in populo ex praedicta doctrina (S. Thom. 3, q. 83, a. 4).

[3] In hoc quidem tempore peregrinationis nostrae ad *solatium viatici* dicimus Alleluja : modo nobis Alleluja canticum est viatoris, tendimus autem per viam laboriosam ad quietam patriam, ubi retractis omnibus actionibus non remanebit nisi Alleluja (S. Aug. Sermo 255, n. 1). — Graduale illi convenit, qui necdum ascendit de virtute in virtutem, sed in convalle plorationis positus, jam tamen ascensiones in corde suo disposuit — Ps. 83 (Rupert. Tuit. l. c.).

Easter-Week could have the same meaning and purpose as the foregoing period of penance.[1] Only in a very limited sense can there be admitted a certain kind of connection between the liturgy of Easter-Week and Septuagesima, — namely, in as far as the Saturday in its character as the octave-day symbolizes the eternal rest and liberty of the children of God. On the feast of Easter the Church celebrates the glory and beauty of the Risen Saviour, as well as the spiritual resurrection of the newly baptized from the death of sin to the life of grace. This festive idea finds its realization and further development in the liturgy of the entire Easter-Octave, which is but a prolonged festal celebration, forming but one joyful day, as the Antiphon of the Gradual continually announces: "This is the day which the Lord hath made: let us be glad and rejoice thereon!" The different effects of baptismal grace just received by the neophytes are brought before the eyes of the newly baptized with reference to the figurative guidance and deliverance of the chosen people in the Old Law; these effects of grace find their fulfilment in this, that after the pilgrimage of this life the newly baptized will be allowed to enter the kingdom of glory. The Saturday, on which the celebration of the Easter-Octave ends, announces at the very beginning of the Introit of Mass, how "God led His people amid triumph and His chosen ones in the midst of rejoicing"[2] from the land of banishment and introduces them to the mansions of eternal joy — in this sense it indicates the end of our exile on earth. — This idea is, therefore, in perfect harmony with the direction that the Gradual be sung during the whole of Easter-Week, because the main feature of the celebration of these days had reference to the newly baptized: they were thereby to be admonished that their joy would be perfect only when they would be permitted to behold and possess God in the heavenly Sion. The ancient baptismal rite has long since fallen into disuse, but the Gradual in Easter-Week has been retained. On Easter Saturday the Gradual gives place to the major Alleluja which, strictly speaking ushers in the Eastertide.

5. *The Sequence.* — On certain days the Alleluja's joyful praise[3] or the mournful melody of the Tract continues to resound in a prolonged canticle, which is universally called Sequence *(Sequentia)*: the sentiment of joy or sorrow already awakened finds its greatest intensity and its fullest expression in the Sequence. How did the Sequences originate, and at what time were they inserted in the liturgy? Already before the ninth century it was customary to continue singing melodiously the last syllable of the Alleluja (ia), without any further text. To this harmonious series of many notes

---

[1] Rupert of Deutz considers this assertion as preposterous, and adds: Quis enim dies indignius captivitatem significare videtur, quam ille, quo victo captivatore Dominus resurrexit? (L. 4, c. 1.)

[2] Eduxit Dominus populum suum in exsultatione: et electos suos in laetitia (Ps. 104, 43).

[3] Post Alleluja *Sequentia jubilatur* (Consuetud. Cluniac. 1. 1, c. 43).

to one syllable, that is, to this textless melody, different names were given, for example, *Neuma, Jubilus, Jubilatio, Sequentia*.[1] Such *Neumae* (songs without words) are an exultation and a shouting of the soul carried away with holy enthusiasm; they indicate the transcendent joy of the blessed, which is endless and unspeakable ; — for so surpassingly great and above all measure is the happines of heaven, that the feeble language of poor mortals has not words adequately to express it.[2] In the ninth century various hymnal verses began to be set to these joyful airs, and to them the name Sequence was then transferred.[3] The first composition of such chants as well as their introduction into the celebration of Mass is ascribed to St. Notker (*Balbulus*, the Stammerer) of St. Gall († 912); "at the time his equal was not to be found, he was a vessel of the Holy Ghost" and "favored by God with the gift of divine praise for the edification of the faithful." Such religious poems soon won great public praise and were extensively circulated; they increased to that extent, that (exclusive of Septuagesima time) every Sunday and almost every feast had a Sequence. Among many inappropriate compositions, not a few excellent chants, full of lyrical animation, are to be found. The revised Roman Missal has retained but five Sequences, which serve to distinguish particular feasts (Easter, Whitsuntide, Corpus Christi and the bi-annual feast of the Seven Dolors of the Mother of God, also the Sequence for Requiem Masses). Even though the authors of the Sequences cannot always be assigned with certainty,[4] nevertheless, these hymns "proved how completely in those golden ages of devotion men might be the tongues of the Church, so to

---

[1] This extension of the Alleluja according to Cardinal Bona (Rer. lit. II, c. 6, § 5) is called Sequence, quia est quaedam veluti *sequela et appendix cantici Alleluja*, quae sine verbis post ipsum sequitur. Probably sequentia is = regulated succession or series (cfr. Boëth., De Arithmetica 1. 1, c. 10 et c. 23).

[2] Pneumata, quae in Alleluja fiunt, jubilum significant, qui fit, cum mens aliquando sic in Deum afficitur et dulcedine quadam ineffabili liquescit, ut quod sentit, plene effari non possit. *Beatus populus, qui scit jubilationem* (Ps. 88), id est, qui saepe experitur et praegustat hanc dulcedinem, et sic interius movetur, ut quod praesentit nec dicere sufficiat nec possit tacere (Robert. Paulul. De offic. eccl. 1. 2, c. 19. — Cfr. S. Aug. Enarr. in Ps. 99, n. 4).

[3] The other name for these hymns is Prosa. It is meant to indicate that in the Sequences neither metrical rules nor a homogeneous arrangement of stanzas are strictly observed, as is the case with actual hymns (cf. Clichtoveus, Elucidator. eccl. 1. 4).

[4] In all probability the Easter Sequence Victimae paschali is erroneously ascribed to St. Peter Damian († 1072); in an Einsiedeln manuscript (Schubiger, Sängerschule von St. Gallen S. 91 etc.) of the eleventh century, the court chaplain of Conrad II., Wipo of Burgundy, is mentioned as its author. — The Pentecost Sequence Veni Sancte Spiritus is said to have been composed by King Robert of France († 1031), or by Innocent III. († 1216). — St. Thomas († 1274) sang the Sequence on the feast of Corpus Christi. — It is said that the Stabat Mater was composed by Jacopone da Todi († about 1306), and the Dies irae by Thomas of Celano († about 1255).

speak, and express her holiest feelings" (Wiseman). The five Sequences of our Missal belong incontestably to the most glorious and most sublime creations of the hymnology of the Church; they are variegated but equally fragrant blossoms "of Christian poetry, of that poetry, forsooth, which sings on earth the mysteries of heaven and prepares us for the canticles of eternity" (Guéranger); each of them has its peculiar beauties and excellencies.[1] — "After the Alleluja the Sequence is sung; they are too long to be quoted here, but the greater part of them and especially those for ancient and great feasts are very lovely and Christian chants. Would to God that all Christians had these beautiful Sequences as beautiful and as lovely in their own languages as they are in Latin!" (Ein Vergissmeinnicht S. 79.)

a) The Easter Sequence *Victimae paschali*, which in the Middle Age found numerous imitations, is a *dulce canticum dramatis*, a sweet dramatical chant, in the form of a dialogue, that sings the praises of the glorious Resurrection of the Saviour. In the first place, the Christians are therein exhorted to offer, out of gratitude, sacrifices of praise to our true Easter-Lamb, Jesus Christ: why? Christ the Lamb of God was immolated to purchase and redeem the sheep; Christ the Good Shepherd, innocence itself, laid down His life for His flock, that He might reconcile the guilty to His Father. Death and life struggled together, engaged in a marvelous combat: the Prince of Life, who had died, reigns in the imperishable life of glory. Then Mary Magdalene is appealed to as an eye-witness of the Resurrection; and she is questioned: *Dic nobis, Maria, quid vidisti in via?* — "Tell us, O Mary, what thou hast seen in the way?" She testifies to and bases her answer on the Lord's Resurrection: "I saw the tomb of the Living One and the glory of the Resuscitated; as witnesses of this, I beheld the Angels, the napkin and the linen cloths." And triumphantly she adds: *Surrexit Christus spes mea* — "Christ, my hope, is risen," and she announces to the Apostles that the Risen One will go before them into Galilee. Upon this assertion follows the joyful acknowledgment of the faithful: *Scimus Christus surrexisse a mortuis vere* — "We know that Christ is truly risen from the dead." This Easter hymn concludes with the fervent petition, that the King of Glory, who has overcome the sting of death, may have mercy on us (*tu nobis victor Rex miserere*).

b) The Sequence for Whitsunday, *Veni sancte Spiritus*, can have come but from a heart wholly inflamed with the fire of the Holy Ghost. It is an incomparable hymn, breathing of the sweetness of Paradise, and regaling us with heaven's sweet fragrance. Only the soul when buried in deep recollection can suspect and taste what wealth of deep thought and affections this Pentecost hymn contains, and that, too, in a form remarkable as much for beauty as for

---

[1] Cf. Gihr, Die Sequenzen des römischen Messbuches dogmatisch und ascetisch erklärt. Freiburg 1887.

brevity.[1] The entire hymn is an ardent and devout supplication to the Holy Ghost, in which, on the one hand, His mysterious, blissful imparting of grace is depicted in a manner uncommonly tender and charmimg, and, on the other hand, also the wants and indigence of our earthly pilgrimage is represented in a manner exceedingly simple and touching. The Holy Ghost is called by the Church: *Digitus paternae dexterae* — "The finger of God's right hand," that is, the Treasurer and Dispenser of all the gifts and graces which Christ has merited for us. But He not only donates to our poverty His riches, but He comes Himself and dwells in a sanctified soul as in His living temple: He thus becomes in it "a fountain of water, springing up into life everlasting" (John 4, 14). How beautifully expressed is the strong and ardent desire for the joyful coming of the Holy Ghost into the soul, in the four consecutive invocations[2]: "*Veni*"— "Come", O Holy Ghost! And why these supplications and sighs, why this passionate desire? Because the Holy Ghost is "the Father of the poor, Dispenser of gifts, the Light of hearts;" because He is "the best Consoler, the gracious Guest, the sweet Refreshment of the soul;" because He is "our Rest in labor, our Alleviation in heat and our Solace in weeping." — "O most blessed Light," continues the Church in her prayer to the Holy Ghost, "fill the inmost hearts of Thy faithful! Without Thy will there is nothing in man, nothing harmless." And because our wretchedness is unspeakably great and manifold, the Church goes on imploring for her children: "Wash what is soiled, water what is parched, heal what is wounded. Bend what is stiff, warm what is cold, guide what is astray." As at the beginning, she repeats at the close with equal ardor and earnestness four consecutive times the petition: "*Da*" — "Give", O Holy Ghost! "Give to Thy faithful confiding in Thee Thy seven-

---

[1] Omni commendatione superior est, tum ob miram ejus suavitatem cum facilitate apertissima, tum ob gratam ejus brevitatem cum ubertate et copia sententiarum, tum denique ob concinnam ejus in contextu venustatem, qua opposita inter se aptissimo nexu compacta cernuntur. Crediderimque facile, auctorem ipsum (quisquis is fuerit) cum hanc contexuit orationem, coelesti quadam dulcedine fuisse perfusum interius, qua Spiritu sancto auctore tantam eructavit verbis adeo succinctis suavitatem (Clichtov. Elucidat. eccles. 1. 4).

[2] To this Sequence also apply the beautiful words, written by Denis the Carthusian in reference to the hymn Veni Creator Spiritus: Hunc hymnum cum omni puritate et elevatione mentis ad superdulcissimum Spiritum sanctum cantemus. Cumque nihil impedit nos a desiderata plenitudine susceptionis Spiritus sancti et exuberantia charismatum ejus, nisi negligentiae nostrae, distractiones corporeae et vitia, praesertim sensuales affectus, satagamus haec omnia evitare ac erubescamus, Dominum illum majestatis immensae, hospitem sanctitatis atque munditiae penitus infinitae, invitare ad visitandum, ingrediendum et inhabitandum corda nostra adhuc imparata ac sordida. Mente ergo contrita, recollecta, affectuosa invocemus, laudemus, adoremus Spiritum sanctum. Toto corde afficiamur ad eum, cujus omnia attributa, proprietates et nomina dulcedinem redolent, amabilissima exstant consolationemque largiuntur (Hymn. aliq. veter. eccles. Enarratio).

fold gifts. Give them the merit of virtue; give a happy end, give them never-ending joy."

c) The *Lauda Sion*, the Sequence for the feast of Corpus Christi, belongs to those "quasi-inspired hymns, in which the Church combines the precision of dogmatic teaching with a grace and sweetness of sound more like unto an echo from heaven than the song of mere earthly poetry" (Faber). St. Thomas, the Angel of the Schools, is the author of this hymn of praise to the adorable Sacrifice and Sacrament of the Altar; he reveals therein the profound learning of a cherub, as well as the inflamed love of a seraph; with a clearness and a penetration of thought only equalled by ardor of feeling he unveils the hidden, unfathomable riches, beauties and sweetnesses of the Holy Eucharist, which is our heaven in this vale of tears and sin. "One of the most useful literary productions of St. Thomas, in which the Church even now takes great delight, is the Office of the Blessed Sacrament, which on the occasion of the institution of the feast of Corpus Christi, Pope Urban IV. engaged St. Thomas to compose. Not only are the psalms and antiphons, lessons and responsories chosen by him replete with the most beautiful and fruitful references to the mystery of the Altar, but also the hymns composed by him, as the *Pange lingua*, *Sacris Solemniis*, *Verbum supernum* and *Lauda Sion*, are full of fervor and devotion and pearls beyond price in the hymnal treasury of the Church. The same grand mind, that like the whale dived down into the lowest depths of the sea of Christian speculation, and like the lion destroyed with fiery strength the errors against faith, soared like the eagle into the greatest heights of Christian poetry. No element pertaining to the Deity was foreign to him."[1] Incomparably beautiful and heartfelt are the concluding words, wherein the Church prays to the Saviour as the Good Shepherd concealed in the Sacrament, that He would here below guide the sheep purchased with His precious blood, protect them and finally lead them to the evergreen pastures of Paradise.

> O Jesus, our Good Shepherd, have mercy on us;
> Deign to feed us, to protect us;
> Deign to make us see good things
> In the land of the living.

> Thou who knowest and canst do all things;
> Who here feedest us mortals,
> Grant that we may be Thy guests in heaven,
> The co-heirs and companions of its holy citizens.

d) How touching, how affecting is the *Stabat Mater*, this doleful lamentation on the Sorrowful Mother of God! At first the Sequence depicts the overwhelming anguish and indescribable compassion (*compassio*) of the Virgin Mother with the bitter sufferings and death of her Divine Son; she had to become the Mother of Sorrows, because her Son was the Man of Sorrows. She stood at

---

[1] Laurent, Hagiolog. Pr. II, 388.

the foot of the Cross wholly plunged in grief (*dolorosa*) and bathed in tears (*lacrymosa*), while her Son was shedding all His blood on the Cross; — but she *stood* there as the valiant woman and as the Queen of Martyrs (*stabat*). "Who, unmoved, can behold her bewailing her Son?" — Therefore, the loving soul implores the Sorrowful Mother, that she would permit us to realize and share her grief. "Holy Mother, grant that the wounds of the Crucified may be deeply impressed in my heart." — "Grant that I may be wounded by His wounds, that I may be inebriated with His Cross and with the blood of thy Son." — Finally, there follows a supplication to Christ for the full fruit of His redeeming sufferings: "When my body shall die, then grant that the glory of Paradise be given to my soul!"[1]

e) The grandest, the most magnificent hymn of the Church is the chant for the funeral rites, the world-renowned and never sufficiently admired *Dies irae*. "Remarkable for majesty, sublimity and affective power in language of the most childlike simplicity and expressiveness through its realistic illustration and great poetical value, its words fall upon the soul as claps of thunder. Very appropriate to its contents is also the choice of the three-versed stanza, with the touching pause in its movement." (Lüft.) As to contents and form this hymn is a perfect work of art; the judgment of all connoisseurs designates it as the most sublime composition that human genius ever produced in this style of poetry.[2] The terrors of the general judgment, before which all the vain pride of this world shall sink into dust and ashes, are depicted in this chant for the dead in lines of such dread sublimity and grand simplicity, that the soul spontaneously imagines herself removed to the gates of eternity, and already beforehand feels penetrated with the woes and dread of that day of tribulation and anguish, of lamentation and misery. "What trembling, what trepidation shall there be, when the Omniscient

---

[1] The Stabat mater dolorosa is outwardly simple in form and versification: and this, indeed, is precisely the mark of true poetry, which with little outward show, almost unadorned, attains the highest object, and understands how to place in the most simple form the richest contents. If we abstract from its form in order to briefly grasp the contents of the beautiful Sequence, we observe that they also are very simply arranged. The first, second and fourth stanzas in a few words unfold the historical event which took place beneath the Cross, according to St. John (19, 25) and St. Luke (23, 35). The remaining stanzas, on the contrary, contain reflections, affections, petitions and resolutions, that the passion and death of Christ may, in view of the sorrows of His holy Mother, not be devoid of fruit for us, but may impart to us vigor in life, comfort in suffering, and in the end be to us the source of bliss... Happily and beautifully does the form bear out the context in this poem. The solemn, sonorous beginning places us at once in the mournfulness of the occasion. How resigned is the language in the resolutions, how gentle in the petitions, how melodious when announcing in advance the happiness of Paradise, in the last stanza in which the soul longs for heaven!" (Kröll, Kanzelreden II, 870 etc.)

[2] Cf. Oswald, Eschatologie, 3. Abschn., 3. Hauptst., No. 6.

Judge shall appear, about to judge all things most rigorously! When the Judge shall take His seat, all that is hidden, shall be revealed, and no crime shall be left unpunished. The trumpet will sound its wonderful blast throughout the graves of earth, and shall compel all mankind before the throne of the Judge. Death and nature will stand aghast, when the creature shall arise to answer its Judge." — The contemplation of so terrifying a spectacle draws from sinful man in alarm the exclamation: "What shall I, poor wretch, be pleading? Who for me be interceding, When the just are mercy needing?" There is nothing left for him to do than to have recourse to the mercy of the "King of dreadful majesty." This is done in the following heartfelt, humble, childlike and trustful appeal for grace and favor: "Think, kind Jesus, my salvation Caused Thy wondrous Incarnation — Leave me not to reprobation. Faint and weary Thou has sought me, On the Cross of suffering bought me; Shall such grace in vain be brought me? Righteous Judge of Retribution, Grant Thy gift of absolution Ere that Reck'ning Day's conclusion." The concluding petition is for all the faithful departed: "O good Lord Jesus, give rest unto them."

The insertion in their respective Masses of the last two Sequences (*Stabat Mater* and *Dies irae*) belongs to a later period and, strictly considered, is to be regarded as a departure from the general rule; for from the beginning, Sequences were throughout festive and joyful chants which followed the Alleluja and replaced the sounds of jubilant praise without text. The *Dies irae* always follows the Tract, while the *Stabat Mater* is either appended to the Tract or to the Alleluja Canticle. To both Sequences are the words of Wiseman applicable: "Even when the Church mourns, she must have her song — attuned in a deeper key, but still enlivening sorrow itself with hope." Singing always introduces a cheerful, enlivening and refreshing element into the divine service, even though the service bears the grave character of a holy grief.[1]

If we compare the varied form and composition of the chant intervening between the Epistle and Gospel, we cannot but admire with what refined delicacy the Church understands how to indicate and set forth the manifold dispositions and shades of the soul's interior life, from the most profound sorrow to the height of joy — as is evident from the contents as well as from the form and melody of the pieces of chant chosen by her. And thus the soul becomes ever

---

[1] Defunctorum Missae et neumate et ipso Alleluja carent, et nihilominus Sequentia quadam, quae simul maeroris et aliqualis gaudii argumentum est, easdem condecorat Ecclesia in symbolum consolationis, quam defunctorum animae inter purgatorii gemitus habent super securitate de sua aeterna beatitudine, praxis instar, quam servat Ecclesia in Sabbato sancto, in quo tractum unit cum Alleluja, ut semiplenam laetitiam ostendat ac paschale gaudium in spe proxima. Quae Sequentia etiam alia habet commoda, majus scilicet defunctorum suffragium et commiserationem ac nostram admonitionem super novissimis (Cavalieri III, c. 10, n. 6).

more worthily prepared and disposed to receive the word of God, now about to be announced in the Gospel.[1]

42. The Gospel.

The second Scriptural reading during Holy Mass is called the Gospel. It constitutes, especially when solemnly sung at High Mass, the brightest portion and the pinnacle of the first part of the Mass. The word Gospel is here employed in the strictest sense, and according to this interpretation it designates a pericope (περικοπή), that is, a part or fragment, selected from what is known as the four Gospels for appropriate liturgical purposes. — In the New Testament, as a rule, it has a far more comprehensive and detailed meaning. *Evangelium* (εὐαγγέλιον) signifies the same as good, joyful tidings. Joyful tidings in its sublimest sense is the entire revelation of God in and through Christ; it is the fulness of all truth and grace, which Christ brought into the world. These joyful tidings of salvation and peace resounded first from the mouth of angels to the devout shepherds of Bethlehem: "Behold, I bring you good tidings *(evangelizo)* of great joy, that shall be to all the people; for this day is born to you a Saviour, who is Christ the Lord, in the city of David" (Luke 2, 11). Our Saviour Himself testifies, that the Holy Ghost anointed and sent Him to announce good tidings to the poor *(evangelizare pauperibus)*, to heal the contrite of heart, to preach deliverance to the captives, and give sight to the blind (Luke 4, 18). Justly, therefore, is the work of redemption called the Gospel, that is, good and joyful tidings.[2] For is it not a joy to be delivered from the bondage of sin and Satan, to have been rescued from the depth of misery, the abyss of endless torment and insupportable darkness? Is it not an ecstatic joy to be blessed with the fulness of peace, with the abundance of grace and glory by the Father of mercies and the God of all consolation (2 Cor. 1, 3), who in giving us His Son has given us all things? Is it not an unspeakably joyful announcement, that God Himself descended from His own happiness to our wretchedness in human form, to redeem us, and that from on high He visited us, to enlighten all that sat in darkness and in the shadow of

---

[1] Ideo non ab apostolica vel evangelica lectione, quod majus esse constat, Missa inchoatur, sed potius canendo et psallendo, quatenus dulcedo suavitatis corda audientium prius demulceat, et sic post modulationem suavis cantilenae in spiritualibus rebus populus per compunctionem mentis intentus, salutifera Evangelii verba ardenti affectu suscipiat (Pseudo-Alcuin. De divin offic. c. 40). — The Alleluja chant denotes the joy of the heart in view of the glad tidings of the Gospel. Alleluja ante lectionem evangelicam a cantore interponitur, ut laudetur ab omnibus, cujus gratia salvantur omnes, quasi dicat. Quia verba Evangelii salutem conferentia mox audituri estis, *laudate Dominum*, cujus beneficio hanc gratiam percipere meruistis (l. c.).

[2] Lex nova est perfecte et simpliciter *evangelium*, i. e. bona annuntiatio, quia annuntiat maxima bona, scil. coelestia, spiritualia et aeterna (S. Thom. in ep. ad Galat. c. 1, lect. 2).

death? Is there an event more joyful than that the King of Heaven was born of a virgin, in order to recall lost man to the celestial kingdom? Since the grace and the benignity of God have appeared to all men, it behooveth them all to be glad and to rejoice in God their Saviour. — Yes, happy are we to whom salvation has appeared, and to whom God has given the greatest and the most precious promises, which the saints from the Old Dispensation could salute only from a distance! The redemption which Christ accomplished shed immeasurable blessings upon the earth; for the poor human race it became an endless source of unutterable joy and of superhuman consolation.

How precious, therefore, must the holy Gospels be to us, in which are recorded by God's own hand the wonderful deeds and mysteries of redemption! The words of the Gospel are words of eternal wisdom, of the Word creating and redeeming the world, who, as He contained within Himself and revealed the fulness of the Deity even in the form of a slave, so also in the simplicity of human language and human actions, in parables intelligible to children, but also publicly and without figures, has taught the plenitude of divine truth and science; and, as in the beginning He called into existence the whole natural world, so He likewise gave being to the whole supernatural world of Christianity until its consummation in eternity through short and simple words, but words full of infinite meaning and creative power, and preserves it continually, and in this sense also supports all things by the word of His power.

The value of the Gospels consists principally in the fact that they give us so perfect, so plain and so living a picture of the person, of the conversation and actions, of the life and passion of our Divine Saviour, by the description of chosen eye-witnesses, and what is infinitely more significant, through the inspiration of the Holy Ghost, in such wise as no oral tradition would be able to do.[1] Grace flowed from the lips of Jesus, and a divine beauty transfigured His countenance; now in the Gospel we continue to hear "the sweetness of His words"[2] and to look at His face full of heavenly benignity and majesty. To recognize the picture of the Saviour in the fulness of its beauty and glory and to keep it, the heart lovingly requires, indeed, a special light of grace and an exquisite purity of soul. For "God who commanded the light to shine out of darkness, hath Himself shone in our hearts, to give the light of the knowledge of the glory of God, in the face of Christ Jesus" (2 Cor. 4, 6).

The readings from the Gospel at Mass serve not merely for instruction and edification, but are at the same time a liturgical action by which religious veneration and homage are paid to the word and truth of God — hence to God Himself, who is present in His word, so to speak, as our teacher. This explains the splendid wreath of

---

[1] Heinrich, Dogmat. Theol. I, 772. 734.

[2] *Os Christi Evangelium est.* In coelo sedet, sed in terra loqui non cessat (S. Aug. Sermo 85, n. 1).

customs, full of meaning, wherewith the reading of the Gospel especially at the solemn celebration of Mass is surrounded and distinguished. Next to the Body and Blood of the Lord in the Most Holy Sacrament and the grace of the Holy Ghost, the Church esteems nothing so sublime and so holy as the word of God in the holy Gospel. To the Gospel are paid the honors of a divine service: when it is solemnly chanted, it is enveloped with the splendor of lights and the fragrance of incense.

1. *Liturgical Preparation for Announcing the Gospel.*

To announce the words of eternal life at the Holy Sacrifice, is an exalted and sublime office (*praedicare, praeconare, κηρύσσειν*). The solemn reading of the Gospel at divine service, therefore, belongs since the fourth century to the deacon, or to the priest, but both must specially prepare themselves that they may be worthy to lend, as it were, their heart and mouth to the Lord for the announcement of His heavenly truth. "Praised be the Lord forever, that He does not disdain to make something so insignificant an instrument for something so sublime, and — although He is God — to speak by means of a tongue of flesh, and to raise up man to be an instrument of the divine voice and an interpreter of the Holy Ghost."[1] Suitable preparation for announcing the divine word consists in a perfect purification and sanctification of heart and mouth. Indeed, the soul should not only be free from all sin, from all base, earthly and selfish motives, but should, moreover, be sanctified by blessing from above. To this effect two prayers are now recited — the one for purification, the other for the bestowal of the blessing. The priest stands in the middle of the altar, raising his eyes aloft, as if "to the mountain whence assistance comes," he soon lowers them again; with body profoundly inclined and with hands joined, but without resting them on the altar, he prays:

Munda cor meum ac labia mea, omnipotens Deus, qui labia Isaiae Prophetae calculo mundasti ignito: ita me tua grata miseratione dignare, ut sanctum Evangelium tuum digne valeam nuntiare. Per Christum Dominum nostrum. Amen.

Jube, Domine, benedicere!

Dominus sit in corde meo, et in labiis meis, ut digne et competenter annuntiem Evangelium suum. Amen.

Cleanse my heart and my lips, O Almighty God, who didst cleanse the lips of the Prophet Isaias with a burning coal: vouchsafe so to cleanse me by Thy gracious mercy, that I may be able worthily to proclaim Thy holy Gospel. Through Christ our Lord. Amen.

Give me Thy blessing, O Lord!

The Lord be in my heart and on my lips, that I may worthily and in a becoming manner announce His holy Gospel. Amen.

---

[1] Schermer, Die Werke des ehrw. Juan de Avila I, 117.

First comes the petition for interior purification (*Munda cor meum*). A thought of frequent occurrence with the Fathers is, that the soul should receive the word and truth of God with a purity similar to that of the Blessed Eucharist. Only in a clear fountain is the image of the sun reflected: in like manner, it is only in a perfectly pure heart that the light of heavenly truth can be reflected fully and unobscured. Wisdom enters not into an unclean soul nor does it dwell in a body subject to sin.[1] How difficult it is to walk undefiled on the dusty path of this earthly life! The heart is not only sullied by sin — but its purity is likewise dimmed and lessened by passion, distraction, earthly inclinations and worldly attachments. Hence the humble petition of the priest, that the Lord would purify anew his heart; for only a stainless heart is a vessel worthy of divine truth and wisdom. This purity of the inner man is the first and principal requisite; but this is not all — the lips also which pronounce words so holy must be pure (*Munda . . . labia mea*). "For the lips of the priest shall keep knowledge, and they shall seek the law at his mouth; because he is the Angel of the Lord of hosts" (Mal. 2, 7). The mouth of the priest is consecrated for heavenly mysteries, hence no profane sound should proceed therefrom. But with what ease and levity does not the talkative tongue sin, if we endeavor not with all our might to master it. Incalculable is the multitude of the sins of the tongue. Hence the priest is fully aware of how necessary it is, that his lips be purified anew from all stains of idle, worldly and sinful talk. For interior and exterior, that is, for a general, perfect cleansing the priest prays before he sets about announcing God's word. — This petition has its foundation and development in a symbolical reference to a mysterious event in the life of the Prophet Isaias.[2] He relates his call, consecration and mission to exercise the office of a prophet. In a marvellous vision he beheld the glory of the God of hosts and heard the canticle of the angels in His praise; filled with holy awe, he acknowledged and confessed his sinfulness and unworthiness. Then a seraph took from the heavenly altar of incense a live coal, touched therewith the lips of the Prophet, burning away all its defilement, saying these words: "Behold! this hath touched thy lips, and thy iniquities shall be taken away, and thy sin shall be cleansed." Then only did Isaias say: "Lo, here am I, send me!" — The live coal in the Prophet's vision is a symbol of grace and of its efficacy. Grace is like unto a spiritual fire which so consumes and destroys all earthly dross in the soul, that it becomes more brilliant and radiant than the finest gold and silver. The fire of the grace of the Holy Ghost not only purifies the heart, but also enlightens the mind with exalted wisdom and inflames the soul with heavenly love.

---

[1] Wisdom 1, 4.

[2] Isa. 6, 5 etc.

"Give me Thy blessing, O Lord!"[1] This blessing asked for is twofold: that the Lord would be in the purified heart as well as on the purified lips of the priest. If the Lord be in the heart of the priest, then will he worthily (*digne*) announce the tidings of salvation, that is, with uninterrupted recollection and attention, with a holy joy and zeal, with profound humility and reverence. If the Lord be on his lips, then will the priest announce the Gospel competently (*competenter*), that is, in a proper manner, clearly and distinctly, with power and energy, so that all may be edified.[2] Prepared after this manner, the priest is a pure channel which receives within itself the salutary waters of the Gospel in a clear state from the fountain-source of the Holy Ghost, and then conveys them into the hearts of the faithful.

2. *Delivery of the Gospel.*

After the above preparatory prayers the priest goes from the middle to the right of the altar, where the Missal must be placed in a manner differing from that in which it was at the reading of the Epistle. The back of the book must not be parallel with the back of the altar, but it is to be turned diagonally towards the corner (*cornu*) of the altar, so that the priest, when reading the Gospel, is half turned toward the people (*semiversus*) and looks northward. In this position the priest reads or sings the Gospel; of which the beginning, middle and conclusion are now to be considered.

a) The opening formula comprises the mutual salutation and the announcement of the Gospel to be read.

What graces do priest and people mutually wish each other in this place by the well known salutation *Dominus vobiscum — Et cum spiritu tuo?* Here there is question that the word of God be correctly understood, that it be embraced with faith and faithfully followed. For the Lord says by the prophet: "As the rain and snow

---

[1] Jube, Domine, benedicere, that is: "Be pleased to bless, O Lord." Jubere in this formula, much used in the liturgy, in order to express the petition with more humble modesty and reverence, has the signification of velle or dignari = deign. The deacon says: Jube *Domne* benedicere, because he does not ask the blessing immediately from God, the Absolute Master (Dominus), but from the priest (Domnus). The name Dominus was given to God the Lord alone, while the abbreviated word Domnus was a distinguished title bestowed upon personages high in authority. In the Litany of the Saints the Pope is called *Domnus* Apostolicus. From Domnus originated the form Dom and Don. Also among the Greeks there is a difference between Κύριος (= Dominus, Deus) and Κύρις (= domnus). (Cf. Bona, De Psalm. divin. c. 16, § 14, n. 5.) — Sacerdos ad altare ratione excellentissimi ministerii, quod exercet, aptus non videtur alium quam Deum in superiorem agnoscere, et ideo sicut ratione pontificiae dignitatis Papae et episcopalis Episcopo, dum ad Matutinum in choro lectionem legunt, datum est dicere *Jube Domine* et non *Domne*, ita idipsum datum est *sacerdoti celebranti* (Cavalieri II, c. 34).

[2] Monendi sunt sacerdotes, ut internae devotioni etiam *externam* conjungant, ita ut majori pausa et distinctione, quam alia, quae clara voce dicunter, Evangelium pronuntient, quia est verbum Verbi et sapientia incarnatae Sapientiae. Et quidem praemissis tot diligentiis et petita attentione populi valde indecens esset, sanctissima verba praecipitare (Quarti, Comm. in Rubr. Miss. p. 2, tit. 6, n. 2).

come down from heaven, and return no more thither, but soak the earth, and water it, and make it to spring, and give seed to the sower, and bread to the eater: so shall My word be which shall go forth from My mouth: it shall not return to Me void, but it shall do whatsoever I please, and shall prosper in the things for which I sent it" (Isa. 55, 10—11). It does not suffice that the sound of the word penetrates our ears; but still more necessary is it that the Spirit of Truth together with His unction and heavenly light of grace should teach us interiorly, in order that we may be able to understand and to love the wonderful sublimity and depth as well as the unfathomable riches of the Gospel. Furthermore, it is for the Spirit of God, with His mysterious power, to move and attract us, that we may unreservedly subject and abandon ourselves to the divine word in thought, in will and in deed. A lively, clear and ardent faith is a precious gift which God bestows upon us, and, at the same time, a virtue which we must acquire and increase. By the mutual salutation, therefore, priest and people implore for each other the grace of the Lord, that is, light and love to embrace and to obey the divine truths with a cheerful faith.[1] May this wish of a blessing be ever fulfilled in us and at the same time excite within us a relish, an ardent desire for the heavenly bread of the divine word — the purest, the most wholesome and strengthening nourishment of the soul!

The Gospel extract to be read is announced in simple words. If the pericope begins with the first words of one of the four Gospels, which is rarely the case, the heading is, for instance: *Initium sancti Evangelii secundum Matthaeum* = "The beginning of the Holy Gospel according to St. Matthew" (for example, on the festival of the Nativity of the Blessed Virgin Mary).[2] If the extract to be read is taken from the context that follows the beginning of the Gospel, which as a rule is the case, then the announcement runs thus: *Sequentia*[3] *sancti Evangelii secundum Matthaeum* . . . = "Continuation of the Holy Gospel, according to St. Matthew . . ." The acolyte thereupon answers in the name of the people: *Gloria tibi, Domine!* — "Glory be to Thee, O Lord!" When the good tidings

---

[1] Doctrina sine adjuvante gratia, quamvis infundatur auribus, ad cor nunquam descendit: foris quidem perstrepit, sed interius nil proficit. Tunc autem Dei sermo infusus auribus ad cordis intima pervenit, quando Dei gratia mentem interius ut intelligat tangit. Sicut enim quosdam flamma caritatis suae Deus illuminat, ut *vitaliter sapiant*, ita quosdam frigidos torpentesque deserit, ut sine sensu persistant (S. Isidor. Hispal. Sentent. 1. 3, c. 10, n. 1—2).

[2] The headings of the Gospels are very ancient, but they are of ecclesiastical origin. They appropriately express that one and the same Gospel of Jesus Christ was written under the inspiration of the Holy Ghost by the Evangelists in a fourfold manner. This is comprised in the little word *secundum* = according. — Evangelistae, quum sint quatuor, non tam quatuor Evangelia, quam *unum quatuor* (Quartetto) varietate pulcherrima consonum ediderunt (Beda Vener. Prooem. in Luc.).

[3] Vox *Sequentia* non singularis est numeri, sed *pluralis*, significatque *ea, quae sequuntur* in textu Evangelistae (Guyet. Heortolog. 1. 3, c. 27, q. 2).

are announced — how can we then do otherwise than break forth in words of praise to our Lord ? He has revealed Himself to us in an altogether incomparable manner, preferring us to millions who still remain in darkness.[1]

At the above words the priest with his thumb imprints a cross on the first words of the Gospel extract, then on his forehead, mouth and breast. The Sign of the Cross made on the book[2] is to express that the whole Gospel, the whole doctrine and the whole work of salvation is comprised and contained in the one mystery of the Cross, that is, in the bloody sacrificial death of the God-Man, undergone for the redemption of the world. Hence St. Paul calls the Gospel simply "the word of the Cross," and although he had been taken up and ravished to the third heaven, where he saw and heard things not given to man to utter, yet he wished to know and to preach nothing else than Jesus Christ and Him crucified: his only glory he sought in the Cross of Christ, in which is our salvation, our life and our resurrection. The mystery of the Cross which is to the world a scandal and a folly, but to us the power and wisdom of God, includes in itself all other mysteries of Christianity, of the Christian faith and life. The Cross shows forth the love, wisdom and providence of God, who through the Cross offers to us again the friendship and heirship of God, imparts strength in all tribulations and assaults. The Cross teaches all Christian virtues: renunciation of the world and of self, humility, obedience, faith, patience, hope, love of God and of our neighbor. The Cross with which the Gospel in the Missal is signed, is intended to remind us of all this. — On their forehead, mouth and breast[3] the priest and the faithful make the Sign of the Cross, in order to express by a beautiful symbolism, that they wish to bear and preserve the doctrine of the Cross and of the Crucified in their mind, on their lips and in their heart, and that

---

[1] Respondet populus: *Gloria tibi, Domine.* In Evangelio agitur de gloria Dei et nostra, scil. quod diabolum vicit et victor ad gloriam Dei Patris ascendit; quod nos redemit et nobis majora promisit. Audientes igitur Evangelii mentionem, nos ad Orientem vertimus et exclamamus in laudem Creatoris: *Gloria tibi, Domine* — quasi dicamus: Quod in Evangelio praedicatur, et nos credimus et speramus, nobis proficiat, nobis eveniat, sine fine permaneat. Et exinde: Non nobis, Domine, non nobis, sed nomini tuo inest et inerit gloria, et ita populus glorificat Deum qui misit nobis verbum salutis et fecit redemptionem plebis suae, juxta quod in act. Apost. (11, 18) dicitur: Et glorificaverunt Deum (Sicard. Mitral. 1. 3, c. 4).

[2] This is not a benedictio libri, but merely a symbolical *signatio* of it. — Libro crucem imprimit sacerdos, tanquam si dixerit: hic est *liber Crucifixi* (Beleth. Rational. c. 39).

[3] The Ecloga Amalarii Abb. in Ord. Rom. mentions here only the signatio frontis, and the Ord. Rom. II, n. 8, has in addition the signatio pectoris. But already Honorius Augustod. wrote in the first half of the twelfth century: Per *cordis* signationem fides verbi accipitur; per *oris* signationem confessio Christi intelligitur; per *frontis* signationem operatio Evangelii exprimitur (Gemma animae 1. 1, c. 23). — In pectoris signo fides et in oris signo confessio, in frontis signo intelligitur operatio, quasi dicat: Signo me in fronte, ore et pectore, quia crucem Christi non erubesco, sed praedico et credo (Sicard. [† 1215] Mitral. 1. 3, c. 4).

they are not ashamed to proclaim freely and cheerfully to the world both by word and deed the glory of the Cross of Christ. — For the priest, who is to preach Christ crucified, this Sign of the Cross is at the same time a serious admonition to lead a life hidden with Christ in God, to be attached with Christ to the Cross and to be crucified to the world. All sincere and true Gospel preaching is only the sublime voice of the Precious Blood. Our Lord Himself once revealed to Blessed Angela of Foligno, that the word of the Gospel penetrates powerfully to the soul only when it proceeds from lips reddened with His Precious Blood.

But since the Cross is not only a significant, but also an efficacious sign, it can here be also conceived principally as a protection and a defence against the Evil One, to prevent his coming and snatching the seed of the divine word out of our hearts.[1]

b) The Gospel Pericope.

As has been said above and proved by examples, each Gospel is selected with regard to the ecclesiastical year with its cycle of feasts and holy seasons. Indeed, the Gospel excels in meaning and importance all the other variable constituent parts of the Mass formula;[2] it gives most perfect expression to the fundamental thought of the day's celebration, to the special intent and application of the Sacrifice of the Mass. The Gospel is to be explained in harmony with the other portions of the Mass which are to be read and sung; but in order that the true and entire sense may be obtained, the Gospel must repeatedly be explained allegorically or in a liturgically mystical manner.[3]

The prominent position and sublime signification of the Gospel is clearly evident in the ecclesiastical rite.

a) The Gospel is read on the right side of the altar in contrast

---

[1] In order to obtain this grace, they formerly signed themselves again with the holy Cross after the reading of the Gospel. Perlecto Evangelio, *iterum* se signo sanctae crucis populus *munire* festinat (Ordo Rom. II, n. 8). — Debet quilibet *post* Evangelium se signo crucis *munire* contra diabolum, qui Evangelio lecto confestim insidiatur, ne capiat in nobis sermo (lest the word of God may take root in our hearts). (Sicard. Mitral. l. 3, c. 4.)

[2] Sanctum Evangelium principale est omnium, quae dicuntur ad Missae officium. Sicut enim caput praeeminet corpori, et illi cetera membra subserviunt, sic Evangelium toti officio praeeminet et omnia, quae ibi leguntur vel canuntur, *intellectuali ratione* illi consentiunt (Rupert. Tuitiens. De divin. offic. l. 1, c. 37).

[3] Exaggerated is the assertion, that "the Evangelical Pericope appears as a pure, bright precious stone, in which the idea of each day is depicted in wonderful clearness" (Kindhäusser); for frequently the *sensus accommodatius* or the mystical reference of the Gospel to the mysterious life of the Church is not so clear to the eye, but deeply hidden, and, therefore, it is not always easily discerned. If we would at all times adhere merely to the literal explanation, then the Pericope would often be too superficially conceived, and its signification in the ecclesiastical year would not be grasped according to the sense of the Church. This, for example, applies to many of the Sunday Gospels after Pentecost. (Cf. Benger III, 981 etc. — Seisl S. J., Die Geleise des Kirchenjahres. Regensburg 1875.)

to the left, as the right side is generally regarded as the more honorable. As the church and altar, in consequence of a very ancient custom, were usually built to face the East, the book on the Gospel side is so placed as to be turned toward the North,[1] and in this there is a mystical meaning.[2] For as the beautiful life of Nature in the warm sunny South is a symbol of the higher life of grace, so the reverse in Nature is the dark and frigid North, which is considered to have an evil significance and to symbolize the kingdom of the Evil One.[3] The dormant, snow-bound regions of the North, enchained in the death grip of Winter's frosts, represent in a suitable manner the dreary and lifeless condition, the unfruitful and desolate existence of heathenism, which, in its forgetfulness of God and estrangement from Him, had rudely destroyed in human hearts the germs of grace and virtue, and hardened the cheerless hearts in an icy egotism. But now the Gospel is read toward the North, as a sign that the good tidings of Heaven have changed the icy night and coldness of mankind into the mild warmth of Summer, and awakened them to an imperishable spiritual spring of grace and mind.[4] Cold and dark was it on the globe of the earth; but when Christ the Lord, who dissolved the curse and brought blessing, arose on the horizon as the Sun of Justice, then were the hearts of men warmed and enlightened. The winter was over, the storms had dispersed; a joyful spring-time of the knowledge and love of God set in on the earth, where the Lord had enkindled the heavenly fire. "The Church", says St. Peter Chrysologus in his sermon on the parable of the mustard seed, "the Church is the odoriferous garden of unfading blossoms, which by the ploughshare of the Gospel has been carefully extended over

---

[1] Formerly the deacon read the Gospel looking toward the South (ad quam partem viri solent confluere). Thus it is prescribed in the very ancient Ordo Roman. II, n. 8. Still Honorius Augustodunensis (Gemma animae l. 1, c. 22) already in the beginning of the twelfth century remarks, that the deacon, when reading the Gospel, should turn no longer secundum Ordinem to the South, but secundum solitum morem to the North.

[2] The assertion is erroneous, that the ordinance of reading the Gospel at the right side of the altar has its origin exclusively in a reason of necessity — in the circumstance, namely, that the left side of the altar must be left free for the sacrificial gifts, that is, for the presentation of the sacrificial elements. For this, it would suffice to remove the Missal only after the reading of the Gospel. The present rubric has its origin, therefore, in a higher or mystical reason.

[3] Isa. 14, 13. — Jer. 1, 14; 4, 6.

[4] Verba Evangelii levita pronuntiaturus contra septentrionem faciem vertit, ut ostendat verbum Dei et annuntiationem Spiritus Sancti contra eum dirigi, qui semper Spiritui Sancto contrarius existit et in nullo ei communicat. . . Sicut enim per austrum, qui ventus est calidus et leniter flat, Spiritus Sanctus designatur, qui corda quae tangit ad amorem dilectionis inflammat, ita et per aquilonem, qui durus et frigidus est, diabolus intelligitur, qui eos quos possidet ab amore caritatis atque dilectionis torpentes et frigidos reddit. Quod enim per aquilonem diabolus designetur, ostendit propheta dicens: O Lucifer, qui dicebas in corde tuo: "Sedebo in lateribus aquilonis. . ." — Is. 14, 13 (Pseudo-Alcuin. De divin. offic. c. 40).

the entire world, which has been hedged in with the thorny hedges of discipline, has been cleansed of all poisonous weeds by the industry of the Apostles, and adorned with the plants of the faithful, with the lilies of the virgins, with the roses of the martyrs and the evergreens of the confessors." The Gospel's bright rays change rugged winter into gentle spring; how could snow and ice otherwise but melt before these heavenly rays? "The Lord shall send out His word, and shall melt them; His wind shall blow, — and the waters shall run" (Ps. 147, 18). In this world, indeed, the gentle breezes of spring do not perpetually blow; but frequently violent storms arise, light and darkness still combat each other. There is the blissful light of the Gospel, our star of hope, pointing to the constant peace and unclouded glory of Paradise. "To the Christian mind life upon earth, surrounded as it is with misery and want, often appears as a winter, so dreary, so dark, that hope alone makes patient endurance possible. And this hope? It points to approaching spring, to a time of 'refreshment' (Apoc. 3, 20), that will forever abolish on earth the reign of sin, renewing and transforming the face of the earth into the peace and joy of God."

b) In like manner, it is not without a deeper meaning, that all present stand when listening to the Gospel.[1] This rite, in all probability, dates from the time of the Apostles and has a manifold meaning. By the act of standing up at the Gospel, we would first testify that "the Gospel of the peace and of the glory of the blessed God" fills us with "great joy", and that the truth of Christ has made us truly free and brought us spiritual resurrection; for by "the sword of the Spirit, which is the word of God" (Eph. 6, 17), the fetters of slavery, the bonds of sin and passion are cut asunder. — Furthermore, standing is a mark and a practical proof of the profound reverence, esteem and attention due to the word of Jesus Christ. — Finally, to stand is the posture of the servant in the presence of his master. In the Gospel Christ our Lord appears as our teacher: and by the fact that we receive His word standing, we express our obedience and our readiness to serve Him; we avow our alacrity and willingness to do all that He requires of us and recommends to us, in order that we may be not merely hearers, but also doers of His Commandments and Counsels.[2]

---

[1] In the Liber Pontificalis we read, that the holy Pope Anastasius I. (399—401) prescribed or rather inculcated anew to the priests the very ancient custom of standing at the reading of the Gospel (Constit. Apost. 1. 2, c. 57). Hic constituit, ut quotiescunque Evangelia sancta recitantur, sacerdotes non sederent, sed *curvi starent*. According to a pseudo-Isidorian letter (in opposition to an abuse which had crept in) he ordained, "that while the holy Gospels were read in the church, the priest and all present should not remain seated, but reverently bow . . . and stand, while attentively listening to and devoutly honoring the words of the Lord."

[2] Martene gives (Regula commentat. c. 11) the following reasons for standing during the reading of the Gospel: a) Honor et reverentia s. Evangelii; b) quod non deceat alios sedere stante s. Evangelii lectore, qui "Domini nostri Jesu Christi personam gerit" (Rupert. 1. 2, in regul. s. Ben.); c) ut hac nostri corporis disposi-

At solemn High Mass the reading of the Gospel is distinguished and honored by the splendor of lighted tapers and the fragrance of incense.

c) During the singing of the Gospel, the two acolytes hold lighted torches and stand one on each side of the book. St. Jerome already defended the higher meaning of this very ancient custom of lighting candles at the Gospel, inasmuch as he insists that thereby we should give expression to the joy and jubilation of our hearts at the good tidings of salvation. — Above all, the light by its brightness and its glow symbolizes Jesus Christ, the Sun that knows no setting and the Light of the City of God as well on earth as in heaven. By means of the Gospel Christ is the light of the world; by the Gospel God has called us to the wonderful light of Christian truth and grace. In this dark vale of the earth "Thy word is a lamp to my feet, and a light to my paths" (Ps. 118, 105). "And wheresoever in the world the word of God does not shine and enlighten, profound darkness hovers over the ways of man and over man himself. For then not only the security as to how to act aright, but even the whence and the whither — that is, the origin and end of our pilgrimage, all this is for reason left to itself alone enveloped in darkness. This darkness is enlightened and becomes marvellously bright through the word of God; by this word the ground on which we stand becomes clear, and the way we have to follow to reach our destiny is made manifest. From the word of God beams a secure light to guide us amid the various directions and helps, as well as amid the various wants, obstacles and dangers we meet on this path so stern and so difficult to be determined" (R...chl). — The light used at the Gospel contains the same admonition that is expressed in these words of the Lord: "So let your light shine before men, that they may see your good works, and glorify your Father who is in heaven" (Matt. 5, 16). By the Gospel we should become as light in the Lord and shine always as children of light, by producing fruits of light in all goodness, justice and truth. If, enlightened and filled with fervor by the light of the Gospel, we lead a life all resplendent with the brightness of virtue and purity, we shall then pass from the darkness of this earth to the kingdom of unclouded brilliance, where the morning star of glory will rise in our heart — "that Morning Star which knows no setting" (*Lucifer ille, qui nescit occasum*).

d) The incensing[1] at the Gospel is also rich in symbolism.[2]

---

tione demonstremus, nos tanquam veros Dei servos ad ejus, quae proferuntur, exsequenda mandata semper esse paratos.

[1] Sicard of Cremona († 1215) mentions the incensing of the Book of the Gospels. Exinde (after signing himself with the Cross) librum diaconus thurificat (Mitral. 1. 3, c. 4). — The incensing of the celebrant, after reading the Gospel, is first mentioned in the Ordo Rom. V, n. 7. Subdiaconus accipiat a diacono Evangelia, et exhibeat ea ad deosculandum episcopo, quibus exosculatis exhibeatur ei, et *incensorium*.

[2] In the Middle Age the celebrant, whilst putting incense into the censer, at

In the first place, the incensing of the Book of the Gospels is to be regarded as an act of holy reverence, a religious mark of honor paid to "the words of eternal life," which the Lord here speaks to us. — The fragrant clouds that envelop the book call to mind how by the announcement of the Gospel is spread abroad and around the good odor of the pre-eminent knowledge of Jesus Christ. "Thanks be to God, who always maketh us triumph in Christ Jesus, and manifesteth the odor of His knowledge[1] by us in every place. For we are the good odor of Christ unto God, in them that are saved. . . the odor of life unto life" (2 Cor. 2, 14—16). The incense furthermore admonishes us, with what heavenly ardor of devotion the words of the Gospel should be announced by the deacon and also by the priest, and be listened to by the faithful and laid up in their hearts. — As the bright flame of the lighted taper is an image of a pure life, so the sweet fragrance of incense also symbolizes, finally, a virtuous, God-fearing life. Christ's doctrine and grace should make of us a good odor unto God and men. This will be the case if, by innocence and purity, by mildness and mercy, by humility and meekness, by constancy and patience, by mortification and austerity, on the one hand, we propitiate and give pleasure to God, and, on the other, edify and console our neighbor. To lead so pure a life of sacrifice is for all the children of the Church an obligation so much the more sacred, the more the pestilential atmosphere of impurity, the more fetid the moral corruption and decay, the more the infernal exhalations of horrible vices and abominations arise day and night from the whitened sepulchre of a corrupt world, and provoke the lightning of divine punishment! Virtue, indeed, exhales a sweet and a refreshing perfume; to prove this, the Lord has often wonderfully effected that the bodies of the saints in their life-time or after their death exhaled a sweet scent, altogether supernatural and heavenly.[2] The body of St. Peter of Alcantara remained, after the soul had departed, still supported by his brethren in a kneeling posture, with hands raised heavenward; the cell was filled with a marvellously sweet odor, a celestial light surrounded the venerable remains, and the ravishing melodies of the angelic choirs filled the air with their glorious strains. His body, which had previously been emaciated and worn out, withered and wasted from continual mortification, bronzed by the air and the heat of the sun, suddenly became dazzling white and slightly rosy, like the flesh of a delicate child, and emitted a bright light; but his eyes especially, which during life had been so carefully guarded, sparkled like two precious stones of

---

this place frequently said these words: Odore coelestis inspirationis suae accendat et impleat Dominus corda nostra ad audienda et implenda Evangelii sui praecepta.

[1] *Odor* notitiae is, according to St. Thomas, notitia de Deo, quae habetur per fidem, et illuminat intellectum et *delectat affectum* — therefore, a loving, fervent, blissful knowledge of the Divine Mysteries. (Cfr. In Epist. II ad Cor. c. 2, lect. 3.)

[2] Cfr. Ribet, La Mystique divine II, chap. 27.

rare beauty. Would that our hearts and conduct should become ever more and more adorned with bright and fragrant virtues![1]

c) *The Conclusion.*

When the reading of the Gospel has ended, the acolyte answers in the name of the people: *Laus tibi, Christe!* — "Praise be to Thee, O Christ!"[2] The priest kisses the initial words of the extract just read, saying at the same time: *Per evangelica dicta deleantur nostra delicta* — "By virtue of the words of the Gospel may our sins be blotted out." Thus the reading of the holy Gospel is closed not only with a chant of thanksgiving, but moreover with a kiss and a prayer.[3]

Jesus Christ teaches the science of salvation and points out the way of life, — on the one hand, by His word and example, announced to us by the Gospel, and, on the other hand, by the interior voice of grace which so sweetly and powerfully speaks to the heart. Joyfully moved by a feeling of heartfelt gratitude for the blessed truth and grace of the Gospel, the faithful break forth into words of praise and glorification, saying: "Praise be to Thee, O Christ!" This con-

---

[1] Habent et mores *colores* suos, habent et *odores* (S. Bern. in cant. serm. 71, n. 1).

[2] Formerly the answer was Amen or Deo gratias or Benedictus, qui venit in nomine Domini. Lecto Evangelio quisque dicere debet *Amen*. Vel ut alii volunt, recitato Evangelio, statim dicamus oportet *Deo gratias*, quemadmodum post quamlibet lectionem sive capitulum. Sed melius est ut dicatur *Amen* ac nos cruce contra diabolum muniamus, ne ipse sermones Domini ex pectore nostro rapiat (Beleth. [† about 1165], Rational. c. 39. — Cfr. Sicard. 1. 3, c. 4). — Already St. Benedict prescribes in his Rule (chap. 11): Legat abbas lectionem de Evangelio, cum honore et tremore, stantibus omnibus. Qua perlecta respondeant omnes *Amen*. Here Amen mainly denotes devout assent.

[3] The Book of the Gospels, or rather, the sacred text of the Gospels in general, represents our divine Saviour Himself and was, therefore, ever (the same as the images of Christ) a subject of religious veneration. The manifold ceremonies at the reading of the Evangelical Pericope are likewise so many symbols and signs of veneration for the holy Gospels and of grateful joy at the glad tidings of salvation. The kissing of the Gospel after it has been read, is also the expression and, so to speak, the seal of these sentiments. Formerly it was customary, to present to all present the Book of the Gospels (in some places closed, in others open) to be kissed. (Cf. Ordo Rom. II, n. 8.) Under Pope Honorius III. (1216—1227) this was forbidden. According to the present practice one person only kisses the Gospel, and that, as a rule, is the celebrant. But if a prelate (that is, the Pope, a cardinal, a nuncio, the patriarch, the archbishop and the bishop of the diocese) assist at the Mass, the Book is kissed only by him (and if there are more than one, by the highest in dignity). (Cfr. Cerem. Episc. 1. 1, c. 30.) — In Requiem Masses the introductory benediction formula (Jube . . . Dominus sit . . .) and at the close of the Gospel the kiss with the accompanying words (Per evangelica . . .) are omitted. The Church evidently wishes to respond to the just exigencies of human nature, when in Requiem Masses for the departed she avoids exterior signs of joy and, therefore, omits such rites and prayers (as those just mentioned), which denote joyful sentiments and impart to the holy action a more festive disposition, or which tend to impart a blessing to the living. (Cf. Quarti, Comment. in Rubr. Miss. p. 2, tit. 13, n. 1.)

16

cluding formula corresponds in sentiment to the introductory formula: "Glory be to Thee, O Lord!", just as the kiss of the book and the signing of it with the Cross also harmonize with each other.

What is the meaning of kissing the Gospel? After having tasted and experienced in the Gospel how sweet the Lord is, how faultless His doctrine, how good and refreshing His consolations and promises, the heart of the priest overflows with happiness and joy, and he kisses the words of eternal life, in order to testify his profound reverence, his great and ardent love for them. This liturgical kiss, therefore, expresses what is contained in the verses of the Psalm: "More to be desired than gold and many precious stones are the words of the Lord; and sweeter than honey and the honeycomb. Greatly purified by fire is Thy word, O Lord, and Thy servant is exceedingly pleased therewith. Yes, I love Thy Commandments more than gold and precious stones; they are the delight of my heart; in my exile, they have become to me a canticle. I opened my mouth and I sighed; for I long for Thy Commandments."[1] "What the world values most is threefold: riches, whose principal representative and symbol is gold; beauty, represented by precious stones; and pleasure, symbolized by the honeycomb. Yet nothing of all that the earth can bestow is comparable to the joy and refreshment imparted by the word of God" (Reischl). The Gospel bestows that heavenly wisdom of which Solomon says: "I preferred her before kingdoms and thrones, and esteemed riches nothing in comparison of her. Neither did I compare unto her any precious stone: for all gold, in comparison to her, is as a little sand, and silver in respect to her shall be counted as clay. I loved her above health and beauty, and chose to have her instead of light; for her light cannot be put out" (Wisdom 7, 8—10).

If the Gospel is taken into the heart and preserved therein, with all that esteem and submission, love and joy, which the kissing of the book denotes, then is the Gospel also able "to blot out our sins." It is self-evident that no such power of effacing sin may be ascribed to the words of the Gospel, as is peculiar to the forms of the Sacraments of Baptism and Penance: they are only a kind of Sacramental in a more general sense and have, therefore, assuredly a great power of awakening and promoting that disposition of soul by which venial sins are effaced, or which prepares for and renders one worthy of receiving the Sacraments. — The word of God, which is accompanied by the interior working of grace, exercises a redeeming, healing and sanctifying influence on man when he is properly disposed, by exciting faith, hope and charity, fear and contrition, conversion and amendment of life. It is not only a powerful means of clearing the soul of the excrescence of sin and imperfection, but it possesses, moreover, other beneficial effects besides. "Are not My words as a fire, saith the Lord, and as a hammer that breaketh the rock in pieces?" (Jer. 23, 29.) Yea, the words of the Lord are spirit and

---

[1] Cf. Ps. 18 and 118.

life: they are powerful, two-edged, penetrating. When Christ on the road to Emmaus "opened" the meaning to the two disciples of "the Scriptures, their hearts burned within them." The word of God has a marvellous power for enlightening the eyes, for imparting wisdom to the lowly and the humble, for rejoicing the heart and refreshing the soul. In like manner, may the living and quickening word of God, which abides forever, impart to us "salvation and protection," [1] may it purify, consecrate and sanctify our souls ever more and more. For "the Gospel is the power of God unto salvation to every one that believeth" (Rom. 1, 16). [2]

43. The Creed.

1. On certain days and feasts, the announcement of the good tidings of salvation is followed by the solemn profession of faith, the heart full of joy and gratitude exclaiming *Credo* — "I believe." When the *Credo* occurs, it forms the answer and the echo to the voice of God, who has spoken to us by His prophets and apostles, yea, by His own Son. The liturgical Symbol in the Holy Mass is as follows:

Credo in unum Deum, Patrem omnipotentem, factorem coeli et terrae, visibilium omnium et invisibilium. Et in unum Dominum Jesum Christum, Filium Dei unigenitum. Et ex Patre natum ante omnia saecula. Deum de Deo, lumen de lumine, Deum verum de Deo vero. Genitum, non factum, consubstantialem Patri: per quem omnia facta sunt. Qui propter nos homines, et propter nostram salutem descendit de coelis. (Hic genuflectitur.) *Et incarnatus est de Spiritu sancto ex Maria Virgine: Et homo factus est.* Crucifixus etiam pro nobis: sub Pontio Pi-

I believe in one God, the Father Almighty, Maker of heaven and earth, and of all things visible and invisible. And in one Lord Jesus Christ, the only-begotten Son of God; born of the Father before all ages: God of God, light of light, true God of true God; begotten not made, consubstantial to the Father; by whom all things were made. Who for us men and for our salvation came down from heaven; (Here make a genuflection.) *and became incarnate by the Holy Ghost, of the Virgin Mary; and was made man.* He was crucified also for us, suffered

---

[1] Cf. the Benediction in the third Nocturn: Evangelica lectio sit nobis *salus et protectio*. (Cfr. S. Ambr. Enarr. in Ps. 39, n. 16.)

[2] Verbum Dei animam vivificat, infundens ei spirituale gaudium, sicut etiam apparet in hominibus laicis et idiotis, qui licet non intelligant quae leguntur, sentiunt tamen gaudium Spiritus et inde ad poenitentiam animantur. Verbum etiam Dei efficacem reddit animam ad virtutes et quaecunque bona et penetrat eam omnia ejus interiora illustrando (S. Mechtild., Lib. spec. grat. p. 3, c. 19).

lato passus et sepultus est. Et
resurrexit tertia die, secundum
Scripturas. Et ascendit in coelum: sedet ad dexteram Patris.
Et iterum venturus est cum gloria judicare vivos et mortuos:
cujus regni non erit finis. Et in
Spiritum sanctum, Dominum et
vivificantem: qui ex Patre Filio-
que procedit. Qui cum Patre et
Filio simul adoratur et conglorificatur: qui locutus est per Pro-
phetas. Et unam sanctam catholicam et apostolicam Ecclesiam.
Confiteor unum baptisma in remissionem peccatorum. Et ex-
pecto resurrectionem mortuorum.
Et vitam venturi saeculi. Amen.

under Pontius Pilate, and was
buried. And the third day he
rose again according to the
Scriptures; and ascended into
heaven, sitteth at the right hand
of the Father; and he is to come
again with glory to judge the
living and the dead; of whose
kingdom there shall be no end.
And in the Holy Ghost, the Lord
and giver of life, who proceedeth
from the Father and the Son,
who together with the Father
and the Son is adored and glorified; who spoke by the prophets.
And one holy Catholic and
Apostolic Church. I confess
one Baptism for the remission of
sins. And I expect the resurrection of the dead, and the life of
the world to come.

There are a great number of ecclesiastical Symbols of faith
(symbola fidei). They contain the principal points of all dogmas
united in pregnant brevity[1] and hence such Symbols of belief serve
for the profession (*professio*) of communion of faith with the
Church.[2] The first in origin and the simplest is the Apostles'
Creed, which most probably is of strictly apostolical origin, and
forms the basis of the others, as all later symbols are only a greater
or less development and extension thereof.[3] — Next to the Apostles'
Creed (*symbolum Apostolorum*), the so-called *Nicene-Constantino-*

---

[1] Symbolum est regula fidei brevis et grandis: brevis numero verborum, grandis pondere sententiarum (S. Aug. Sermo 59, n. 1).

[2] Symbolum (σύμβολον)= mark, characteristic, true sign, by which a person
may be recognized or be identified. By the profession of faith the faithful are
distinguished from heretics and unbelievers. — Beati Apostoli Ecclesiae Dei, quam
adversus militiam diabolici furoris armabant, mysterium symboli tradiderunt, ut
quia sub uno Christi nomine credentium erat futura diversitas, *signaculum symboli* inter fideles perfidosque secerneret et alienus a fide atque hostis appareret
Ecclesiae (S. Maxim. Taurin. Homil. 83 de traditione symboli). — Symbolum per
linguam graecam *signum* vel *collatio* interpretatur. Discessuri enim Apostoli ad
evangelizandum in gentibus hoc sibi praedicationis *signum* vel *indicium* posuerunt
(S. Isidor. Etymol. 1. 6, c. 19, n. 57).

[3] Cf. Blume S. J., Das apostolische Glaubensbekenntniss. Freiburg 1893. —
P. Suitbert Bäumer O. S. B., Das apostolische Glaubensbekenntniss. Mainz 1893.

politan Creed (*symbolum Patrum*) holds the most prominent place. This Creed is called Nicene, because the definition of the first General Council of Nice (325) regarding the divinity of the Son is therein almost literally recorded; it is called Constantinopolitan because, although not first arranged in this order by the Second Ecumenical Council of Constantinople (381), it was, however, there received and confirmed as Catholic. The fact that not only the divinity of the Father, but also the divinity of the Son and of the Holy Ghost are so expressly and emphatically emphasized in this symbol of faith, rendered this Creed particularly suited for the solemn profession of the true faith at divine worship; — mainly in opposition to the Arian and the Macedonian heresies, which chiefly occasioned its admission into the sacrificial liturgy of the East, in the beginning of the sixth century.

After this action of the Orient, the great National Council of Toledo (589), in Spain, resolved and decreed that in the Mozarabic Rite, immediately before the *Pater noster*, the profession of faith of Constantinople should be recited aloud by all the people.[1] Toward the end of the eight century, the same Creed was incorporated in the constituent portions of the Mass rite in France and Germany.[2]— Far more difficult is it to state the period when the Roman Church began to recite or to sing the *Credo* during Mass. Since apparently contradictory testimonies on this point exist in the ancient documents, liturgists, consequently, differ greatly in their opinions. According to the lucid and reliable information of the Abbot Berno of Reichenau[3] († 1048), the general admission of the *Credo* into the Roman Mass Rite took place only at the commencement of the eleventh century,[4] and that, indeed, by Pope Benedict VIII. at the

---

[1] In the Mozarabic celebration of Mass the priest says: Fidem, quam corde credimus, ore autem dicamus. He then elevates the Sacred Host so that it may be seen by the people, and holding it over the chalice, he recites the Symbol alternately with the choir or assistants. Its recitation, therefore, is here an act of immediate preparation for Holy Communion.

[2] *Symbolum* quoque fidei catholicae recte in Missarum solemniis post Evangelium recensetur, ut per sanctum Exangelium *"corde credatur ad justitiam"*, per Symbolum autem *"ore confessio fiat in salutem"*. Et notandum, Graecos illud Symbolum, quod nos ad imitationem eorum intra Missas assumimus, potius quam alia in cantilenae dulcedinem ideo transtulisse, quia Constantinopolitani concilii proprium est, et fortasse aptius videbatur modulis sonorum quam Nicaenum, quod tempore prius est, et ut *contra haereticorum venena in ipsis etiam sacramentorum celebrationibus medicamenta* apud regiae suae urbis sedem confecta *fidelium devotio replicaret.* Ab ipsis ergo ad Romanos ille usus creditur pervenisse; sed apud Gallos et Germanos post dejectionem Felicis (Bishop of Urgel) haeretici (Adoptianists), sub gloriosissimo Carolo Francorum rectore damnati, idem Symbolum *latius* et *crebrius* in Missarum coepit officiis iterari (Walafrid. Strabo [† 849] De exord. et increm. c. 23).

[3] In his document De quibusdam rebus ad Missae officium pertinentibus (c. 2) he mentions what he witnessed during his sojourn in Rome.

[4] Of his opinion are, for example, Baronius, Bona, Menardus, Lupus, Gavantus, Renaudot, Bellotte, Mari, Lesley, Zaccaria.

instigation and request of the Emperor Henry II. On the 14th of February, 1014, which fell that year on Sunday, Henry II. was anointed and crowned Emperor in St. Peter's Church. During the High Mass at his coronation, the devout Emperor noticed that the *Credo* had not been sung, as was customary throughout Christendom; inquiring the cause, he was informed that the Roman Church, which had never departed from the Catholic faith and had never been corrupted by heresy, had no necessity for such a profession of faith. But the Emperor requested as a coronation gift to him and for the edification of the faithful, who from all parts of the world flocked to Rome, that the Pope would prescribe the insertion of the profession of faith into the solemn High Mass, and the Pope deemed it advisable to introduce into Rome a custom which henceforth for all times would be a testimony of the lively faith of the holy Emperor and which, in consequence, would enkindle this ardor of faith in thousands of hearts.[1]

The rite for the recitation of the Creed is simple. Its recitation in a loud voice invites all present to unite in heart and mind with the priest, and joyfully to repeat the Creed with him. At the first words, the hands of the priest are raised and extended, to evince the joyful, believing, adoring sentiments of the heart. — During its recitation, the hands remain joined before the breast: this devout attitude corresponds with the humble homage and the confiding abandonment of oneself to the absolute truth and veracity of God, and with the perfect submission of the will and of the understanding to the infinite majesty and sovereignty of God, as enjoined in obedience to faith. — The three different inclinations of the head at the words *Deum — Jesum Christum — simul adoratur*, that is, at the confession of faith in the Father, the Son and the Holy Ghost, express due reverence to the three Divine Persons. — The words: *Et incarnatus* . . . are accompanied by a genuflection, slowly made in order appropriately to revere and glorify the Incarnation, this mystery of God's inconceivable condescension and self-annihilation.[2] — At the last words (*et vitam venturi saeculi*), the priest makes the Sign of the Cross. This Sign of the Cross has been variously interpreted: it can be understood as referring to the entire Symbol, or merely to the words immediately preceding. In the former case it is evident how appropriate it is to conclude and seal the *Credo* with the Sign of the Cross, because the latter is not only a brief profession of our faith, but also our shield and buckler against all the adver-

---

[1] Laurent. Hagiol. Pr. II, 167.

[2] If the celebrant, the deacon and subdeacon are seated, while these words are sung by the choir, as a rule, they make only a profound bow with head uncovered. But at Christmas and at the Annunciation (when the latter feast is transferred, in ipsa die translationis — S. R. C. 25. Sept. 1706) they must rise from their seats and kneel down on the lowest step of the altar, on the Epistle side, (utroque genu cum capitis inclinatione), because on these days the mystery of the Incarnation is celebrated in a special manner. (S. R. C. 11. Jun. 1701; 23. Mai. 1846.)

saries and dangers of our faith.[1] — With this signification we can easily harmonize the other, which places the Sign of the Cross in special relation to the concluding words: *"and the life of the world to come."* According to this, it would here signify the fundamental truth, that only the royal road of the Cross, the way of sorrow and suffering, leads to the home of imperishable joys. Besides this allusion, that the way of the Cross is the path to eternal glory, it contains the admonition that the Sign of the resplendent Cross will appear in the heavens with Christ at His second coming to judge the world.

While in the Greek the Symbol of faith is placed after the kiss of peace which follows the Offertory, the Roman liturgy orders its recitation after the Gospel, and whereas in the former the Creed is a permanent, constituent part of every Mass celebrated, it occurs in the latter liturgy only on certain days as a mark of special distinction. The *Credo* has assuredly in the make-up of the Roman liturgy for Mass the most suitable position. It makes no difference whether it be regarded as the end of the first or as the beginning of the second principal division of the Mass, it is in any case the most proper medium and connecting link between the two parts. As the blossom and fruit of the preceding Scriptural readings[2] it forms, on the one hand, the conclusion of the general divine Service; but on the other hand, it is also the foundation-stone and the basis for the special sacrificial celebration about to begin, which is called in a special manner the "mystery of faith" (*mysterium fidei*).

2. Since, therefore, only certain Masses are distinguished and privileged above others by the solemn profession of faith, the question remains to be answered,[3] which were the reasons for admitting the Symbol into the sacrificial rite.[4] As a rule, liturgists classify under three heads the principal reasons for the recitation of the Symbol, and these they designate by the words *Mysterium — Doctrina — Solemnitas.*

a. Accordingly, the first principal reason lies in the mystery celebrated. The *Credo* is recited, namely, on certain days and

---

[1] Signaculum crucis virtutem passionis Christi ostendit. Hoc ergo quando fronte imprimitur, christianus *munitur*. Quando contra imminens periculum opponitur, adversaria virtus *fugatur*. Primum ad arma, secundum ad tela; primum ad defensionem, secundum ad impugnationem (Hugo de s. Vict. De Sacrament. 1. 2, p. 9, c. 8).

[2] Quia Christo credimus tanquam divinae veritati (Joan. 8, 46), lecto Evangelio, symbolum fidei cantatur, in quo populus ostendit se per fidem Christi doctrinae assentire (S. Thom. 2, q. 83, a. 4).

[3] Cf. Cavalieri V, c. 12, n. 9—64. — Quadt, Die Liturgie der Quatembertage S. 64—65, 72—77.

[4] From the statement of Innocent III. (De sacr. alt. myst. 1. 2, c. 51) it follows, that already in the twelfth century certain rubrics had obtained regarding the recitation or omission of the Credo on certain days. The practice was, and continued to be, widely different until the liturgical development was concluded in the revision and the new edition of the Missal under Pius V.

feasts whose historical foundation or dogmatic subject is contained in the Symbol, that is, one of the mysteries expressly mentioned therein or at least acknowledged as therein included.[1] Since the celebration of divine worship on such days is consecrated to the commemoration and to the honor of a special mystery of faith, it is proper to confess this mystery by the solemn singing or the recitation aloud of the *Credo*. Among such days are reckoned:

a. All Sundays.[2] — Sunday is sanctified by reason of many mysteries recited in the Symbol and is devoted to their commemoration. The celebration of Sunday is pre-eminently ordained to honor the triune God; this veneration is rendered to the Adorable Trinity not merely because of the infinite majesty and glory of the divine Persons, but also on account of the great works of their power and love for the salvation of men. A number of these great works were wrought on the first day of the week, which day corresponds to our Sunday: for on this day was commenced the creation of the world in the beginning of time; and also, in the fulness of time, the new creation of the fallen world was accomplished by Christ's resurrection[3] and the sending of the Holy Ghost. With greater probability, it is held that on this day Jesus Christ was born, and at the Circumcision shed His first blood, receiving the sweet name of Jesus. It is, therefore, not alone the resurrection of the Lord, but, at the same time, other mysteries besides, which induced and occasioned the recitation of the *Credo* on Sunday. — The day of the Lord reminds and admonishes us not only to profess the faith with heart and mouth, but also to tend with earnest hope and childlike love towards God as our last end and supreme good, — consequently, to make ready to enter into that rest (Heb. 4, 11), which has no end; for this is the full meaning of the expression "to believe in God" (*credere in Deum*).

b) The feasts of the Most Holy Trinity and Whitsunday, as well as all the feasts of Jesus Christ and of His Blessed Mother Mary. — In the *Credo* we proclaim the name and glory of the three Divine Persons, who are therein expressly mentioned and confessed. — Through His joyful, sorrowful and glorious mysteries, which are celebrated during the course of the ecclesiastical year and are mentioned in the Creed, Jesus Christ has become the "author and finisher," as well as the most comprehensive object "of our faith" (Heb. 12, 2). In these mystical joys, sorrows and glories, the Blessed Mary, Virgin Mother of God, is inseparably connected and united with her Son; therefore, some special days are feasts of Mary as well as of Jesus. The Blessed Virgin is also praised by the Church

---

[1] According to John Beleth, the Credo was recited in the twelfth century in eorum tantummodo festis, quorum in Symbolo fit mentio (Rational. c. 40).

[2] Suarez, De relig. tr. II, 1. 2, c. 5, n. 8—14. — Bona, De divin. Psalm. c. 16, § 18.

[3] Primo dierum omnium — quo mundus exstat conditus — vel quo resurgens Conditor — nos morte victa liberat (S. Gregor. M.).

as the Queen of Apostles and of Apostolic Doctors, as she who has destroyed all heresies.[1]

c) The feasts of the Holy Angels.—The reason is found in the mention made of them in the words "the invisible world" (*invisibilium*), by which the angels are understood. — The recitation of the *Credo* in the Masses of the angels can be still further based on their mission and calling; for they are "all ministering spirits, sent to minister for them who shall receive the inheritance of salvation" (Heb. 1, 14). As messengers of God, the angels appear active in carrying out the work of redemption, in which they most heartily take part. They announce to man the decrees and revelations of God. An angel brings to Mary the joyful tidings that she is to become the Mother of the Saviour. About the Saviour angels ascend and descend: they appear at His birth, at His resurrection and ascension — and they will accompany Him on His return to judge the world. They labor untiringly for the extension and progress of the kingdom of God upon earth; to the Church they are a heavenly, protecting guard in all her sufferings and combats with the powers of hell and the hatred of the world.

d) The Feast of All Saints. — The *Credo* on this day has for its reason the article of faith of "the one, holy, Catholic and Apostolic Church," whose triumphant, glorious members are the blessed in heaven. In addition to this, we find very many among the saints to whom the Credo is already given for other reasons.

e) The celebration of the Dedication of the Church and its anniversary. — This day also may be brought into relation with the above-mentioned article of the Symbol; for the material house of God is a figure of the Church Militant and Triumphant, of the kingdom of Christ on earth and in heaven.

b) The second principal reason for the recitation of the Symbol is designated by the word doctrine. For this reason the honor of the Creed is bestowed upon the principal and secondary feasts[2] of the Apostles, Evangelists and Doctors of the Church.

a) The Symbol contains the doctrine taught by the Apostles, and it mentions expressly as one of the four marks of the true Church that she is Apostolic. The Apostles introduced into the world the Church instituted by Christ and they spread it over the whole earth. They were the organs of the Holy Ghost and the infallible bearers of revelation; they announced all that Christ did and suffered for our salvation.[3]

b) By the hands of Evangelists the Holy Ghost Himself wrote down the history of redemption, the tidings of salvation of the king-

---

[1] Gaude, Maria Virgo, cunctas haereses sola interemisti in universo mundo (Antiph. Eccles.).

[2] Yet only inasmuch as they are celebrated sub ritu duplici.

[3] Isti (scil. Apostoli) sunt viri sancti, quos elegit Dominus in caritate non ficta, et dedit illis gloriam sempiternam: *quorum doctrina fulget Ecclesia, ut sole luna* (Breviar. Roman.).

dom of Christ, the doctrines and facts, the mysteries and means of grace of our faith; these writings of the holy Gospels were handed over and entrusted to the Church as a precious treasure.

c) The Doctors of the Church are chosen and glorious men, of whom "nations shall declare the wisdom, and the Church shall show forth the praise" (Ecclus. 39, 14). With the depth of their knowledge corresponded the height of their sanctity. Enlightened with light from above and inflamed with ardor for the truth, they have in their conversation and writings gradually developed, confirmed and defended the doctrine of Christ against the attacks of error and calumny.[1]

These choirs of saints shall shine as the brightness of the firmament and as stars for all eternity (Dan. 12, 3), because they have illumined the whole world with the light of faith: what then is more appropriate than that glory be shed on their feasts by the recitation in the Mass of the joyful and solemn profession of faith?

All the other saints — martyrs and confessors, holy women and sacred virgins — possessed indeed the virtue of faith in an heroic degree, and some of them even merited for themselves the immortal honor to extend the faith, yet in this respect they are outranked by the Apostles, the Evangelists and the Doctors of the Church, and in the Mass of their feast the *Credo* is properly left out. [4]

d) Only on the feast of St. Mary Magdalen does the Church make an exception: besides the most holy Mother of God, to St. Mary Magdalen alone among all the female saints is the distinction of the recitation of the Creed on her feast accorded. Why is this? Probably because Magdalen — after the Mother of God — first beheld the Risen Saviour and as an eye-witness of His resurrection, she was sent by Him to the Apostles as the first promulgator of the mystery of His resurrection. Mary Magdalen went to the disciples and announced to them: "I have seen the Lord, and these things He said to me" (John 20, 18). St. Jerome in the life of St. Marcella writes: "Mary Magdalen, on account of her fervor and the ardor of her faith, received the name of one 'standing on a high tower,'[3] and she was found worthy, the first of all even before the Apostles, of beholding the Risen Lord."

---

[1] At present the following Saints are venerated as Doctors of the Church: 1. Athanasius; 2. Basil the Great; 3. Gregory of Nazianzum; 4. John Chrysostom; 5. Ambrose; 6. Jerome; 7. Augustine; 8. Gregory the Great; 9. Thomas of Aquin; 10. Bonaventure; 11. Anselm; 12. Isidore of Seville; 13. Peter Chrysologus; 14. Leo the Great; 15. Peter Damian; 16. Bernard; 17. Hilary; 18. Alphonsus Maria de Liguori; 19. Francis de Sales; 20. Cyril of Jerusalem; 21. Cyril of Alexandria; 22. John Damascene; 23. Venerable Bede. (Cfr. Bened. XIV. De serv. Dei beatif. l. 4, p. 2, c. 11 et 12. — Acta sanctae sedis VI, 289 sqq.)

[2] Hence the Memorial Verse:

D A credit; M V C, per se, non credit.

D = Doctores, A = Apostoli, M = Martyres, V = Virgines et Viduae, C = Confessores.

[3] Magdalena from Migdol = the observatory or the tower.

c) The third reason for inserting the *Credo* in the ritual of the Mass is some special solemnity, that is, the profession of faith is often sung or recited publicly to enhance the exterior splendor of the feast or Mass. According to this rule, the following feasts or Masses are entitled to the Creed:

a) The so-called Patronal feasts, that is, the feast of the principal Patron of the church and of the place.[1] The patron of a church is that saint under whose invocation and in whose honor the church has been erected and dedicated. Since the church has received its name (its title) from this saint, he is usually called in liturgical language the Titular of the church, even if he be not at the same time the patron of the place. Moreover, the title of a church is not always that of a saint or an angel, but is taken from some mystery, for example, that of the holy Trinity, or from the five sacred wounds of Christ. — By the patron of the place, on the other hand, we understand that saint who is chosen as the special intercessor or protector of a parish, a diocese, a province or a kingdom and who is invoked, honored and celebrated as such.[2]

b) The Mass of the feast of a saint in that church in which the body or at least a notable relic (*reliquia insignis*)[3] is preserved. — Besides this may also be reckoned the solemn High Mass, which "on account of an extraordinary concourse of people" (*missa solemnis ob extraordinarium populi concursum*) is celebrated in honor of the saint who has a special altar in the church.

c) The solemn Votive Masses which, on general and important occasions, are celebrated by order or with permission of the bishop; those only have no *Credo* which are sung on ordinary week days in purple vestments.

---

[1] *Titularis* sive *patronus ecclesiae* is dicitur, sub cujus nomine seu titulo ecclesia fundata est et a quo appellatur. *Patronus* autem *loci* proprie is est, quem certa civitas, dioecesis, provincia, regnum etc. delegit velut singularem ad Deum patronum (S. R. C. 9. Mai. 1857).

[2] Churches, therefore, have either titular feasts in a stricter sense, or patronal feasts; places, on the contrary, have only patronal feasts. There is a distinction between patronus vel titulus *principalis* and patronus vel titulus *minus principalis s. secundarius*. The Symbol properly is only for the chief (festum primarium), but not for the secondary feast (festum secundarium) of the principal patron or principal patrons, as only the principal feast sub ritu dupl. I. cl. cum oct. is celebrated. The feast of the patronus vel titulus *minus principalis* is usually celebrated only sub ritu dupl. maj. vel min., and that without octave, and has, therefore, no Credo. (Cf. S. R. C. 2. Dec. 1684; 15. Sept. 1691; 22. Aug. 1744.) — The regular priests recite the Credo also on the principal feast of their founder, but not of the other Saints of their Order (S. R. C. 12. Mart. 1836; 22. Jul. 1848).

[3] As notable relics of a Saint are considered, for example, the head, an arm or leg, if they are entire, that is, consisting of both bones, and every other portion, in which the martyr specially suffered, provided it is still entire and not too small, and is regularly approved by the bishop. The integrity of a relic may also be restored by the artificial joining of the separate fragments of a member. — A hand, a foot, a thigh bone or shin bone alone does not answer as reliquia *insignis s. major* (S. R. C. 13. Jan. 1631. S. C. Indulg. 12. Jun. 1822).

The octave is nothing else than the continuation and completion of the celebration of the feast; therefore, if a feast has a *Credo*, the whole octave of the feast receives also this distinction. If feasts that have no Credo fall during such an octave or on a Sunday, they then receive it on account of the day on which they are celebrated.

Thus the Church has, according to well established principles, prescribed the *Credo*, as a special distinction of the feasts and days, only in such Masses whose character has a most intimate and close relation to the profession of faith.

3. The profession of faith, proclaimed so loudly and solemnly at the Holy Sacrifice, should always emanate from hearts replete with joy and gratitude to God. Inappreciably great is the grace of the Catholic faith. How touchingly does St. Francis de Sales write on this subject: "O God, the beauty of our faith so ravishes me that I die of love, and it seems to me that the precious gift God has therewith made to me, I should preserve in a heart wholly penetrated with the sweet odor of devotion. Be grateful for this divine splendor, which so mercifully sheds its rays into my heart, that I acknowledge the more clearly the greatness and desirable sweetness of faith, the longer I associate with those who have no faith." And with what enthusiasm does the Apostle describe the combats and victories of men of faith![1] "By faith they became heroes in the conflict; by faith subdued kingdoms, wrought justice, obtained promises, stopped the mouths of lions, quenched the violence of fire. Persecuted, oppressed, maltreated, they wandered in deserts, in mountains, in the caves and dens of the earth, — of whom the world was not worthy; but, strong in faith, their spirit did not succumb." Millions of martyrs have endured pain and derision, imprisonment and chains, fire and sword, torture and death — strong in faith and sacrificing themselves cheerfully for the faith. The "unbelieving and perverse generation" (Matt. 17, 16) of this world cannot understand the superhuman power and endurance, the imperturbable frankness and fortitude, the invincible meekness and magnanimity infused by faith. "This is the victory which overcometh the world, our faith" (1 John 5, 4). Such firmness, nobility of heart, strength of character, contempt of the world and of death are produced by faith only when it is animated and enlivened by love, when it rules our life, our thoughts and desires, our actions and sufferings. The lively, ardent and strong faith is a noble, heavenly plant which blossoms and thrives only in the soil of an humble and pure heart; by the scorching winds of pride it is blighted, and it is choked up in the mire of voluptuousness. Consequently, the precious treasure of faith must be carefully safeguarded; for only a life of faith conducts to the glory of the Lord. Therefore, "may the God of hope fill you with all joy and peace in believing" (Rom. 15, 13). "Sprouting from heaven and descending to earth, faith unites earth with heaven; coming forth from out of the boundless ocean of eternal light, its rays

---

[1] Heb. 11, 4—10.

penetrate the dark night which envelops man, made of dust, enlightening his pathway through the darksome vale of life. What was man before this heavenly light penetrated darkness, when the nations were still sitting in the shadow of death (Luke 1, 79; Ps. 106, 10; Matt. 4, 16), and what would the child of earth be, even now, were he not enlightened from a higher world? What a sad, what a dark picture humanity presents without faith! — The light of faith dawns, and where previously there ruled but folly and passion, and strife and fear and darkness and ruin, there are now found truth and virtue and peace and light and life eternal. — Faith brings to man consolation, instruction, warning, confidence, fortitude and self-denial on his journey through life; faith inspires him with courage and hope in death; and faith accompanies him beyond the tomb to a blissful immortality, and in the more beautiful land of light and glory it removes the dark veil from his eyes, and enables him to behold his God face to face. — Thus the holy, Christian faith is to man a true heavenly messenger, that religion sends before him to prepare his way. Again, faith is, in fact, a brilliant star, which serves him as an unfailing guide on his dangerous passage to his heavenly country. Faith is to him an angel, who supports him in his arms, a strong defence and refuge in every danger. Thus faith renders us truly happy here and hereafter" (Geissel III, 123).

SECOND SECTION.
The Sacrificial Celebration Proper.[1]

The part thus far explained of the rite of the Mass is very properly prescribed to purify the heart and to enlighten the mind as well as to enliven faith and to excite devotion. Now after the proper dispositions have been formed in priest and people by means of pious considerations and fervent resolutions, by devout sentiments and affections, that is, after they have been duly prepared, the special celebration of the Eucharistic Sacrifice begins. Since this holy mystery is not only offered and consecrated as a sacrifice, but also received as a sacrament, the representation of the real sacrificial service is naturally divided, as it were, into three distinct parts:

I. The Oblation, that is, the offering of the sacrificial elements.

II. The Consecration, that is, the accomplishment of the sacrificial action.

III. The Communion, that is, the participation in the accomplished Sacrifice.

---

[1] This portion is often called by liturgists of the Middle Age Missa in a strict sense (proprie, proprio nomine, strictim). Secunda pars Missae, quae proprie Missa appellata est, proxime sequitur... Haec pars Missae, ut Missam appellamus totum officium ab Introitu usque ad "Ite missa est," si strictim accipiatur, proprio nomine Missa appellata est (Beleth. Ration. c. 43). — Missa vocatur ab eo loco, ubi incipit sacerdos Deo sacrificium offerre, usque ad *Ite missa est* (Hildeb. Turon. De exposit. Missae).

The Offertory, Consecration and Communion are the principal parts of Holy Mass: they are intimately connected with one another, but are not of equal significance, importance or necessity in the accomplishment of the Sacrifice.

The sacrificial act proper (*sacrificatio vel immolatio corporis et sanguinis Christi*) is accomplished in the Consecration, which, therefore, forms the centre and summit of the Mass.

In the second place (according to rank) comes the Communion of the officiating priest, which belongs, although not to the essence, yet to the completeness of the Eucharistic Sacrifice.

Less important and significant than these two parts is the Offertory, in which the elements of bread and wine, requisite for the accomplishment of the Eucharistic Sacrifice, are dedicated and offered to God.

In the Oblation, therefore, the Sacrifice is prepared, at the Consecration it is really accomplished, and during the Communion it is entirely concluded and finished.

FIRST ARTICLE.

The Offertory.

44. Preliminary Remarks.

1. The prayers and ceremonies of the Offertory constitute a most appropriate, although not an essentially necessary preparation for the sacrificial action accomplished at the moment of Consecration. To comprehend the true sense and the abundant contents of the rite and prayers of the Offertory, the following points should be considered.

The words and the rite of the oblation before the Consecration relate to a twofold object — namely, to the elements of bread and wine, and also to Christ's Body and Blood. In the first place, the oblation (*oblatio*) relates to the Eucharistic elements: the bread and wine are withdrawn from common use, consecrated to God and previously sanctified, that they may be in a manner prepared and made fit for their unspeakably exalted destiny. We give up all claim to these earthly gifts and offer them to the Most High, with the intention and desire that He would change them in the course of the Sacrifice into the most holy Body and Blood of Christ. Accordingly, this portion of the Mass rite includes manifold petitions to the Most High, that He graciously accept and bless or consecrate the bread and wine offered.[1] — Yet the Offertory has not exclusively for its object the mere elements of bread and wine, but also the real object of the Sacrifice, the true and only Sacrifice of the New Law, that is, the Body and Blood of Christ, which by Consecration take the place

---

[1] During the Middle Age many prayers were expressly said during the Offertory for the consecration of the elements. Sanctifica †, quaesumus Domine Deus, hanc oblationem, ut nos Unigeniti corpus (or sanguis) fiat. — Oblatum tibi, Domine, munus sanctifica, ut nobis unigeniti Filii tui D. N. J. C. corpus et sanguis fiat. (Cf. Ebner, Quellen und Forschungen S. 296 etc.)

of the former substances of bread and wine, and thus become present on the altar.[1] The Church, therefore, does not wait until the change of substance has taken place to offer to the Divine Majesty the Divine Victim; — no, she already now offers the real Victim to the Divine Majesty, regarding, as it were, the approaching Consecration of the sacrificial elements as if already passed.[2] The offering (*oblatio*) of the sacrificial gifts may precede and follow the accomplishment of the actual sacrificial act (*immolatio, sacrificatio*), as in our rite for Mass, in which a similar oblation repeatedly takes place, on the one hand, for the glorification of the divine name, on the other, for the salvation of the living and of the dead. From this point of view it can be explained why the Church already designates her Oblation by such names (*immaculata hostia, calix salutaris, sancta sacrificia illibata, sacrificium laudis, etc.*), as in their full sense are applicable only to Christ's sacrificial Body and Blood, — and why by reason of this Oblation she expects as great effects and fruits as can by no means be ascribed to the offering of some bread and wine, but only to the offering of the Divine Victim.

From the liturgical prayers of the Offertory, therefore, we may by no means conclude that the offering of the elements of bread and wine is a real sacrifice or constitutes a part of the Eucharistic Sacrifice.[3] Only Jesus Christ, present on our altars under both species as

---

[1] Respondeo, illam oblationem panis et vini, quae fit in Missa, non esse oblationem sacrificativam, sed simplicem oblationem, qua offertur materia, ex qua facienda est hostia sacrificanda... Dicitur autem panis *hostia*, quia in ipso tanquam in materia, ex qua facienda est, praeexistit hostia et quia ipsam repraesentat: unde cum nondum sit praesens hostia, offertur Deo simplici oblatione tanquam praeparatoria in pane tanquam in typo. Quia cum sit futura panis spiritualis et vestita accidentibus panis, assumitur panis ut materia praevia tanquam typus illius (Pasqualigo, De sacrific. N. L. tr. 1, q. 30, n. 8).

[2] This view is not opposed to the meaning of the Offertory prayers, which are here considered; for even according to the ordinary mode of speaking the demonstrative pronoun (*hic*, this) in general refers to things near the person speaking. Now such things can either really and perceptibly be near (demonstratio ad *sensum*), or be merely represented as present and thought to be present (demonstratio ad *intellectum*). All Middle Age scholastics acknowledge this distinction in explaining the words of Consecration. Pronomen *hoc* facit demonstrationem ad intellectum et ad sensum simul, sic intelligendo, quod demonstrat aliquid quod est objectum intellectus et aliquid quod est objectum sensus (Richard. a Med. IV, dist. 8, a. 3, q. 1). The expressions: *hanc* hostiam, *hanc* oblationem, *hoc* sacrificium etc., that often occur in the Offertory prayers before the Consecration, may, therefore, grammatically be equally as readily referred to Christ's Body and Blood that seem in the light of the spirit and of faith as already present, as to the bread and wine which the celebrant beholds with his corporeal eyes immediately before him. (Cf., for example, the Secreta: *Haec* oblatio, Domine quaesumus, ab omnibus nos purget offensis, *quae* in ara crucis etiam totius mundi tulit offensam (Missa vot. de s. Cruce).

[3] Dico, hanc oblationem nullo modo pertinere ad substantiam hujus sacrificii, neque ut essentialem partem neque ut integralem, sed tantum esse ceremonialem quamdam praeparationem ab Ecclesia institutam ad conciliandam devotionem et reverentiam animosque fidelium excitandos ad mysterium ipsum peragendum (Suarez disp. 75, sect. 3, n. 1).

symbols of His death, is the perpetual Sacrifice of the Catholic Church, our real and true Sacrifice. "As soon as Christ, by virtue of the Consecration, has descended from heaven, as soon as He has taken up His abode with us under the humble appearances of bread and wine, He offers Himself to His Father a clean oblation, amid a sin-stained human race, shows His wounds to His Father and holds up His death before Him, and in His wounds and death exhibits all His obedience, all His humiliations and His love. And we, fully conscious of our unworthiness, take up this clean oblation with a thrill of joy and offer it to the Father. The offering of the bread and wine, which previously takes place in Holy Mass, removes the bread and the wine from ordinary use and dedicates them to God, that He may change this inefficacious offering into the true oblation that worketh salvation. This offering of bread and wine should serve to prepare us and to raise our hearts to the Lord, who is to appear and to whom the prayers of the Church already beforehand refer, and whom the Church meets with rejoicings, as she, in the spirit of meditation, beholds Him approaching: 'Blessed is He, that cometh in the name of the Lord. Hosanna in the highest!' But when He does come, it is not in the splendor of His glory that He appears, but enveloped under the images of His passion and death, and environed with the most painful, heart-rending reminiscences." (Eberhard I, 337.)

Until far into the thirteenth century the Roman Church had in this portion of the Mass rite only the Offertory chant (*Offertorium*) of the choir and the secret oblation prayer of the priest (*Oratio super oblata* = Secreta)[1]: all the other intervening prayers of the Offertory were admitted only after this epoch into the Roman rite,[2] after they had already been adopted by other churches. "All the prayers connected with the Offertory are remarkably short; but they are full of vigor and of feeling; there is in them a most heavenly and sublime simplicity, a mild and tender pathos" (Wiseman). — All these prayers collectively were in former times not improperly styled the minor Canon (*canon minor*), as their contents indicate they were in many ways connected with the great, that is, with the real Canon.

45. The Offertory Chant.

1. The Offertory is introduced by the kissing of the altar and the mutual salutation: *Dominus vobiscum — Et cum Spiritu tuo.*[3]

---

[1] Circa oblationem duo aguntur: scil. laus populi in cantu offertorii, per quod significatur laetitia offerentium, — et oratio sacerdotis, qui petit ut oblatio populi sit Deo accepta (1 Par 29, 17). S. Thom. 3, q. 83, a. 4.

[2] Romanus Ordo nullam orationem instituit post Offerendam ante Secretam (Microlog. c. 11). The prayers now prescribed we meet for the first time in Ordo Rom. XIV, c. 53. Perfect unity in regard to the rite and prayers at the offering of the Sacrificial Elements was restored only in the sixteenth century by the publication of the newly revised Missal. (Cf. Krazer sect. 4, art. 1, c. 8, § 250).

[3] Quartum officium (= distinctio, part) Offertorium vel Offerenda vocatur, quod incipit a *Dominus vobiscum.* Consuetudo est quod cum nuper ad operarios.

By these words priest and people reciprocally express the desire that
the Lord would assist them by His grace, aid and power, in order
that with lively faith and with proper dispositions they may celebrate
the Eucharistic Sacrifice, and in union therewith offer themselves
to the Most High as an acceptable gift. The nearer the moment of
the Sacrifice approaches, the more urgently do we require assistance
from above.

The *Oremus*, which the priest then says, relates not merely to
the Offertory chant, but also to the whole series of prayers that are
said during the Offertory. All present are thereby exhorted to unite
with the celebrant in sentiments of devotion, in a spirit of recollection, with attention, with heartfelt fervor, and, in union with him,
to pray and make the offering in silence; for the interior sentiments
of prayer and sacrifice alone impart to our offering true and full
value in the sight of God.

After this the priest recites an Antiphon, which in the Missal
is called *Offertorium*.[1] From Apostolic times until about the eleventh
century, there was always a procession at the Offertory during the
celebration of the Holy Mysteries. All the faithful who were to be
admitted at the Table of the Lord — and only these — were authorized and at the same time bound at the Offertory to offer their gifts.
The rite of this offering differed at various places and times. To the
altar and at the Offertory, for the most part, bread and wine alone
could be brought as offering; from these gifts the materials for the
Sacrifice were selected.[2] The procession at the Offertory of the

---

ingredimur, eos salutemus. Sic, secundum quosdam, cum de uno officio ad aliud
transitum facimus (that is, at the beginning of a new part of the Mass), salutationem
praemittimus (Sicard. 1. 3, c. 5). — Lecto Evangelio populus offert, chorus cantat,
sacerdos suscipit, Deoque corde et ore et manibus repraesentat et incurvatur et orat.
Officium igitur, quod nos dicimus Offerendam, ab eo loco inchoatur, ubi post Evangelium sacerdos dicit *Dominus vobiscum* et finitur in eo loco, ubi excelsa voce
dicit: *Per omnia saecula saeculorum* (Hildeb. Turon. De exposit. Missae).

[1] The word Offertorium designates in a more comprehensive sense also the so-
called Little Canon, that is, all the prayers and rites of the Offertory until the
conclusion of the Secreta. Already in the Ord. Rom. the Antiphon in question is
called Offertorium, and it is distinguished from the added verses (Canitur offertorium cum versibus — Ord. II, n. 9). The word Offertorium, which is found only
in Church Latin, had previously several other meanings. Thus in old documents
it designated, for example, the *book* in which the Offertory chants were contained,
then the Sacrificial Gifts themselves. Pontifex, *Offertorio* lecto, ... accipit
offertorium (the lighted candles) ab omnibus ordinatis (Pontif. Roman. De
ordinat. Presbyt.).

[2] According to an ancient custom and an ecclesiastical ordinance, the faithful
formerly offered in more or less close reference to the Eucharistic Sacrifice all
manner of material gifts (oblationes, προσφοραί), to defray the expenses of the divine
service, as well as for the maintenance of the clergy and the poor. Thus they
offered, for example, corn, fruit, grapes, milk, honey, wax, oil, later on money
also. The offering of such objects, however, could not be made at the same time
as that of the bread and wine, which served for Consecration, but it was done generally before or after Holy Mass in a particular place in the church, or also in the

clergy and people was accompanied with singing, to excite and enliven a joyful disposition in the givers, since God "loveth a cheerful giver." The question arising in later times of the period of the introduction of the chant at the Offertory cannot be answered.[1] Its particular development is ascribed to St. Gregory the Great. In his Antiphonary the Offertory chant consists of an antiphon and several verses. The whole Antiphon was first entirely sung, and then partly repeated after several verses. It was a responsorial chant sung in two choirs. When, after the twelfth century, the ancient custom at the Offertory gradually disappeared,[2] the Psalm chant was abridged; in our Missal there remains thereof only the antiphon designated by the name *Offertorium*, which the priest recites immediately before offering the sacrificial gifts, but it is still sung by the choir now as in former times during the Offertory.

2. The *Offertorium* at present is a shorter or longer verse, generally taken from the Psalms, sometimes from the other books of Holy Scripture, and only a few are composed by the Church herself. As to its contents, it in nowise, as the name[3] would seem to imply, relates to the Oblation. It rather constantly changes during the

---

house of the bishop. These religious offerings were already in themselves a meritorious and satisfactory act of virtue; in addition to this, they who offered them would thereby participate in the Eucharistic Sacrifice and gain the Eucharistic Sacrificial fruits in more abundant measure. In this twofold connection the oblations of the faithful served pro remedio vel pro redemptione animae, that is, to efface sin, as is often expressed in the old documents. From this ancient custom there was gradually developed the present practice, in existence for many centuries, of giving Mass stipends for the special application of the so-called ministerial sacrificial fruits. — Of the loaves presented a portion only was ordinarily blessed and at the close of the celebration distributed to the non-communicants, later on to all present, or sent to the absent as a mark of union with the Church, — the socalled Eulogies, εὐλογία, benedictio, panis benedictus, ἀντίδωρον (substitute for Holy Communion). Among the Greeks Eulogies are still in use.

[1] *Offertorium*, quod inter offerendum cantatur, quamvis a prioris populi consuetudine in usum christianorum venisse dicatur, tamen quis specialiter addiderit officiis nostris, aperte non legimus, sicut et de Antiphona, quae ad communionem dicitur, possumus fateri: cum vere credamus priscis temporibus Patres sanctos *silentio* obtulisse vel communicasse, quod etiam hactenus in Sabbato sancti Paschae observamus (Walafrid. Strabo c. 23).

[2] Remains of these are the offerings still in use at Requiem Masses and the festal offerings practised in many congregations; likewise the offering of a lighted candle when receiving Holy Orders, as well as the presentation of two large lighted candles, of two loaves and two small casks of wine at the Consecration of a bishop and at the Benediction of an abbot. Cf. Pontif. Rom.

[3] Oblationes offeruntur a populo et *Offertorium* cantatur a clero, quod ex ipsa causa vocabulum sumpsit quasi *offerentium canticum* (Raban. Maur. De clericor. institut. l. 1, c. 33). — Dicto Symbolo cantatur Offertorium sive Offerenda, ut aliqui dicunt. Appellatur autem *Offertorium* ab offerendo, quia tunc *offerimus*. Sed necessario hic considerandum est, *tria* omnino esse quae offerre debemus: primo nosmetipsos, ac deinde ea quae sacrificio sunt necessaria, scil. panem, vinum et aquam, et si qua sunt alia sacrificio apta (Beleth, Ration. c. 41).

course of the ecclesiastical year, and gives expression to the dominant thought of the celebration of the day or Mass, — and has, therefore, precisely the same significance and purpose as have the foregoing Introit and Gradual chants. The same spirit that pervades these two choral chants, resounds again in the Offertory, strengthens the festal dispositions, awakens thoughts and feelings anew, with which we should offer or assist at the Sacrifice.

The Offertory of the Epiphany depicts in glowing terms how princes and peoples pour in from all countries, humbly to worship the new-born King of kings and to offer presents to Him:

Ps. 71. Reges Tharsis et insulae munera offerent: reges Arabum et Saba dona adducent: et adorabunt eum omnes reges terrae, omnes gentes servient ei.

Ps. 71. The kings of Tharsis and the islands shall offer presents: the kings of the Arabians and of Saba shall bring gifts: and all kings of the earth shall adore Him, all nations shall serve Him.

On the Feast of the most blessed Virgin Mary of Mount Carmel the Church implores in the Offertory:

Recordare, Virgo Mater, in conspectu Dei, ut loquaris pro nobis bona, et ut avertat indignationem suam a nobis.

Be mindful, O Virgin Mother, to plead for us before God, that He may turn away His anger from us.

In the Votive Mass for a happy death the Offertory is as follows :

Ps. 30. In te speravi, Domine, dixi: Tu es Deus meus, in manibus tuis tempora mea.

Ps. 30. In Thee, O Lord, have I hoped: Thou art my God, my lots are in Thy hands.

The following Offertory read in Requiem Masses deserves a very special notice :

Domine, Jesu Christe, Rex gloriae, libera animas omnium fidelium defunctorum de poenis inferni et de profundo lacu: libera eas de ore leonis, ne absorbeat eas tartarus, ne cadant in obscurum: sed signifer sanctus Michael repraesentet eas in lucem sanctam: Quam olim Abrahae promisisti et semini ejus.

Lord Jesus Christ, King of glory, deliver the souls of the faithful departed from the flames of hell, and from the deep pit. Deliver them from the lion's mouth, lest hell swallow them, lest they fall into darkness: and let the standard-bearer, St. Michael, bring them into the holy light: Which thou hast promised of old to Abraham and his posterity.

V. Hostias et preces tibi, Domine, laudis offerimus : tu suscipe pro animabus illis, quarum hodie memoriam facimus: fac eas, Domine, de morte transire ad vitam: Quam olim Abrahae promisisti et semini ejus.

V. We offer Thee, O Lord, a sacrifice of praise and prayers: accept them in behalf of the souls we commemorate this day: and let them pass from death to life. Which Thou didst promise of old to Abraham and his posterity.

This is the only Offertory which has retained its original form: it consists of an antiphon, a verse and the concluding antiphonal words repeated. The text is difficult to understand — hence such variously interpreted meanings are given to it. The two most probable explanations given are the following.

The difficulties of this beautiful prayer lie in those expressions from which it appears as if the Church implores redemption of the departed from hell,[1] or begs the preservation of the departed souls from hell.[2] But such a prayer, according to Catholic dogma, is inadmissible, and is, therefore, not uttered in such a sense by the Church. *In inferno nulla est redemptio* — the sufferings of the damned in hell can neither cease nor be diminished. The suffering souls in purgatory, on the contrary, are immutably confirmed in the grace and the love of God, and secure of their eternal bliss. Now, how are these petitions, at first sight somewhat strange, how are these petitions of the Offertory of the Masses of the dead to be understood?

The Church — thus say many theologians[3] — the Church, it is self-evident, prays and offers the Sacrifice only for those departed souls who have still to suffer in the place of purification. For these she implores for deliverance from their torments and admission to the glory of heaven. All the expressions of the Offertory are, consequently, to be understood of the pains of purgatory — and not of those of hell. This interpretation can, of course, be adhered to; yet it appears to do violence to the text and to destroy its highly poetical character. However keen and painful the sufferings of purgatory, yet they are altogether far less severe than the torments of hell. Now, since the Church is accustomed to impress her dogmas clearly and accurately upon her liturgy, we may not readily admit that she employs such strong expressions to designate the punishment of purgatory. Least of all do these words adapt themselves to this view: *ne absorbeat eas tartarus, ne cadant in obscurum; fac eas de morte transire ad vitam.* Now is it not using violence to understand the words *ne absorbeat* (may not swallow them up) and *ne cadant* (lest they fall), words that evidently refer to a primarily threatening danger, as meaning a prolonged sojourn in purgatory?[4]

---

[1] *Libera* animas omnium fidelium defunctorum *de* poenis inferni et de profundo lacu, de ore leonis.

[2] Ne *absorbeat* eas tartarus, ne *cadant* in obscurum.

[3] For example, Valentia, Gavanti, Benedict XIV., Sporer, Lejeune, Kössing, Rösler C. ss. Red., Thalhofer.

[4] Dum dicis: *libera eas de poenis inferni,* hoc ipso dicis: libera eas igne Purgatorii, qui idem cum igne infernali est; *a profundo lacu,* a carcere nimirum sub terra abdito, ubi detentae expiantur animae piorum. *Ne absorbeat eas tartarus,* i. e. ne eas amplius et diutius profundi illius carceris cavernae et vincula remorentur, nec inferni poenae tanquam fauces quaedam belluae immanis, saevae ac truculentae detineant. *Ne cadant in obscurum* vult dicere: ne post hoc sacrificium factum et oblatum permittas adhuc eas in obscuris terrae carceribus cruciari

And where else is purgatory designated by the expression *mors* (death)? — Hence the following explanation is to be preferred, as it not only recommends itself by intrinsic reasons, but is also accepted and defended by many theologians of both ancient and modern times.[1]

According to this view the Offertory for the dead contains petitions to be preserved from the pains of hell. The Church can pray that her deceased children be preserved from being cast into the abyss of hell, because in so praying she does not thereby imagine them as then suffering in purgatory, but as struggling in the agony of death, when the soul is on the point of leaving the body and of appearing before the judgment-seat of God, — and, therefore, still in danger of being lost. The Church employs this method of prayer, because it is not only calculated to effect the alleviation and abridgment of their sufferings, but also presents other advantages besides. — The Catholic liturgy, as to form and contents, bears almost throughout the impress of true poetry.[2] Special vigor and life are infused in the liturgy by the dramatic element which consists in this that the mysteries of Sacred History of the past are, so to speak, rendered present and so celebrated as though they were but just now about to take place before our eyes. This we perceive in the celebration of Advent, Christmas and Holy Week. The same poetical, dramatical character dominates in many ways in the liturgy for the dead. The Church in the latter calls, so to speak, the dead back to life, that is, to the hour of death, which decided their eternal destiny; she represents to herself the departed at that moment, when in the presence of death, they could still prepare for the divine judgment.[3]

---

et quasi denuo in Purgatorii poenas incurrere. *Sed signifer sanctus Michael repraesentet eas in lucem sanctam,* i. e. fac, ut per hoc sacrificium poenas debitas exsolvant in totum, ac proinde eas plene mundatus Michael sistat in patria coelesti. Ita explicat I. Azor. tom. I, 1. 10, c. 22, q. 8 eumque alias explicationes afferens sequitur Dicastillo tr. 5, disp. 2, n. 101 (Gobat, Alphabet. sacrificant. n. 172–176).

[1] For example, Suarez, Sardagna, Pasqualigo, Tournely, Habert, Merati, Wiseman, Franzelin, Jungmann, Oswald. — Cavalieri, as a rule, is cited only in the first edition, but erroneously; for in several passages he approves the second manner of explanation, for instance, tom. III, c. 10: Ecclesia Deo repraesentat animas in purgatorio, ac si tunc e vita discessurae forent easque quasi inspicit *in actu agoniae.*

[2] Cf. Wiseman, Ceremonies of Holy Week in the Papal Chapel.

[3] *Toto illo funeris et exsequiarum decursu,* qui aliquando post plures ab obitu dies absolvitur, nobis veluti praesens ob oculos ponitur terribile illud ac plenum horroris momentum, quo animus a corpore abstrahitur et ad Dei tribunal adducitur, quo anteactae vitae rationem supremo Judici reddit et extremam sententiam in summo adhuc timore ac metu positus praestolatur, quae sibi aut sempiternae felicitatis requiem aut sempiterni supplicii locum decernat. Id vero non alia de causa fieri credendum est, quam ut Deum severum judicem veluti coram intuentes et animam fratris nostri veluti in ipso adhuc judicio aestuantem, tum majore animi demissione et ardentiori pietatis affectu divinae misericordiae pro illius aeterna salute supplicemus, tum etiam ut in tremendi illius judicii contemplatione, quod

And, therefore, the liturgy of the dead acquires something of the grand and sublime and affecting. Now the Offertory of the Masses for the dead is in perfect harmony with all this: for the Offertory has the same highly poetical character. Several of its expressions, for instance, refer to the moment of death, which is to decide one's eternal lot; they represent the departed to us as they are at the time of their death-agony, surrounded by wicked enemies, and on the brink of a frightful precipice, which threatens to swallow them up. The Church accordingly then prays to the Lord to preserve her children, who are in such imminent danger, "from the pains of hell and from the deep abyss, and to deliver them from the fierce lion's mouth, lest hell swallow them up and lest they sink into darkness." Such petitions are the more appropriate and touching, because they are made just at the Offertory, that is, during the procession then taking place. We then unite our gifts and prayers with the Sacrifice of the Altar, and accompany with this outfit the departing soul before God's judgment-seat, that she may experience the goodness and clemency of the Lord, and be permitted to pass "from the temporal death of the body into the eternal life of glory" (*de morte ad vitam*).[1]

This method of prayer is profitable — for the living as well as for the departed.[2] The living are filled with holy gravity and wholesome fear, when the severity of divine judgment and the punishments of sin are thus presented to the soul in so vivid and dreadful a manner. For the faithful departed this prayer of the Church is a very efficacious means for alleviating their pains: it procures for them rest, consolation and release from purgatory.[3]

nos etiam esse aliquando subituros certo scimus, diutius immorantibus, altiores in nobis radices agat divinae majestatis timor ac reverentia (Orsi O. P., De liturg. S. Spiritus invocat. c. 5, n. 3).

[1] Ecclesia in Offertorio duo petit: ut animae defunctorum liberentur a poenis inferni et ut perducantur ad gloriam, ut constat ex illis verbis: *Sed signifer sanctus Michael repraesentet eas in lucem sanctam*, et rursus: *Fac eas, Domine, de morte transire ad vitam*. Et ideo in illa oratione non considerat statum animarum, in quo de praesenti sunt, sed repraesentat exitum illarum e corpore, et tanquam sisterentur tunc ante tribunal Dei, precatur, ut liberentur a poenis inferni *praeservative*, h. e. ne damnentur, sed perducantur in Paradisum, et ideo cum primum sit jam factum, ordinatur oratio ad obtinendum secundum atque adeo *ad liberationem a poenis Purgatorii* (Pasqualigo, De sacrific. N. L. tr. 1, q. 156, n. 11).

[2] Sacerdos non orat proprie, ut animae jam exutae corpore ac a Deo judicatae liberentur ab inferno ac de morte ad vitam transeant (hoc enim vanum esset), sed, ut magis commoveat adstantes, per prosopopoeiam repraesentat sibi ac populo illas animas quasi jamjam egressuras e corpore ac divino judicio repraesentandas, et proponit ob oculos pericula, in quibus in illo articulo versantur, et pro illis quasi in eo statu constitutis Deo supplicat, ut eas liberet, quod nullo modo frustra fit. Nam et multum confert ad concitandos adstantium animos ad pietatem et horrorem divini judicii, et illae preces etiam apud Deum habent suum effectum, quatenus ex intentione Ecclesiae et sacerdotum funduntur, ut per eas Deus liberet eas animas a poenis Purgatorii, si iis forte detinentur (Coninck q. 83, a. 5, n. 262).

[3] Very insecure and uncertain is the devout belief, that God "in view of our prayers and especially the future prayers and Sacrifices of the Church, which He

This conception[1] of the meaning of the Offertory for the dead may be elucidated and established by many other prayers which the Church offers for the faithful departed and for the dying.[2] Thus, for example, the prayer recited on the day of death or of burial contains a petition to be preserved from the pains of hell. "O God... we implore for the soul of Thy servant, whom Thou hast this day called out of this transitory life, that Thou wouldst not deliver it into the hands of the enemy (*ut non tradas eam in manus inimici*), and that Thou wouldst eternally be mindful of it and cause it to be received by Thy holy angels and have it admitted to its true country of Paradise: that since it hath believed in Thee it may not be forced to undergo the torments of hell (*ut non poenas inferni sustineat*), but be admitted to partake of eternal joys."[3] The purport and

---

in His goodness foresees, will impart to the dying sinner sorrow and repentance, in order to abtain the salvation of his soul." (Cf. Katholik, Jahrg. 1874, I, 171). — Oratur pro animabus purgatorii secundum quandam repraesentationem: repraesentat enim Ecclesia statum illarum animarum in eo puncto, in quo a corpore exeunt et ad judicium feruntur, et hoc modo intercedit pro illis et orat: *ne absorbeat eas tartarus* et similia, sicut etiam nunc, quando Christi adventum repraesentat, orat: *Rorate coeli desuper*, et in die resurrectionis: *Haec dies quam fecit Dominus*, etc. Neque est inutilis talis oratio aut repraesentatio, tum *quia viventibus potest esse utilis*, ut periculum illius momenti, in quo judicandi sunt, sibi proponant, tum etiam *quia cedit in verum Dei cultum*, quem Ecclesia confitetur et recognoscit ut supremum animarum judicem et patrem misericordiae, qui orationibus placari potest, tum denique, *quia potest esse utilis animabus defunctis*, vel ut propter has Ecclesiae orationes aliquid poenae eis remittatur, vel etiam *fortasse*, ut propter tales orationes Ecclesiae praevisas, quando ab hac vita decedunt, a Deo recipiant auxilium et dispositionem, secundum quam benigne et misericorditer possint judicari. Hunc vero esse Ecclesiae sensum in citatis verbis, constat ex illis: *Fac eas, Domine, de morte transire ad vitam;* illa enim non possunt intelligi de *morte secunda*, quae est infernus, quia ab illa nullus potest ad vitam transire; intelliguntur ergo vel de *morte corporali* vel de *morte peccati* (Suarez disp. 83, sect. 1, n. 29).

[1] Altogether without foundation is the objection, that liberare never signifies preservation from an impending evil, but always deliverance or redemption from an evil that has already taken place; for frequently in her liturgy the Church prays: ut a cunctis malis *imminentibus* liberemur, ut ab *instantibus* malis et *a morte perpetua* liberemur, etc. The expression liberare, therefore, necessarily does not presuppose the entanglement in an evil, but solely the being threatened therewith. (Cfr. S. Aug. Enarrat. in Ps. 85, n. 18; Serm. 134, n. 2). — The word defunctus can be taken in the present participial signification = "dying", as in St. Irenaeus (I, 21, 5) mortuus occurs in the sense of moriens. (Cf. Kaulen, Handbuch der Vulgata S. 195.)

[2] The Subvenite, Sancti Dei..., which is to be recited immediately after a person's death, (egressa anima de corpore), was formerly recited during the agony. Cf. the lect. 6 for the feast of St. Dominic (Aug. 4th).

[3] At the Obsequies the Church prays for the departed and already judged soul: *Non intres in judicium* cum servo tuo, Domine.... Non ergo eum, quaesumus, tua *judicialis sententia* premat, quem tibi vera supplicatio fidei christianae commendat: sed gratia tua illi succurrente, mereatur *evadere judicium ultionis*, qui dum viveret, insignitus est signaculo sanctae Trinitatis (Rit. Rom. De Exsequiis).

words of the magnificent *Commendatio animae* in many respects
correspond to our Offertory; the priest prays therein for the Christian
struggling in the agony of death (*cum in agone sui exitus anima
anxiatur*): "Deliver, O Lord, the soul of Thy servant (*libera*) from
the pains of hell (*a poenis inferni*) and from the power of Satan;
let it not experience any of the terrors of darkness (*quod horret in
tenebris*); let the legions of the infernal abyss (*legiones tartareae*)
be confounded; may Christ preserve it from torments and eternal
death (*a cruciatu et ab aeterna morte liberet*); may St. Michael the
Archangel, who deserved to be placed at the head of the heavenly
hosts, receive it (*qui militiae coelestis meruit principatum*); may all
the angels of God meet it and conduct it into the Heavenly
Jerusalem." [1]

46. The Sacrificial Elements.

Wheaten bread (*panis triticeus*) and wine of the grapes (*vinum
de vite*) are the two elements which are necessary for the accomplishment of the Eucharistic Sacrifice; hence they are frequently called
the matter of the Holy Sacrifice. This mode of speech, however,
must not be misunderstood. It does not say that bread and wine
belong to the Eucharistic offerings, that is, in the same way that the
Body and Blood of Christ in their real sense are offered. As on the
Cross, so on the altar Jesus Christ alone is our Victim. The substances of bread and wine appertain to the Eucharistic Sacrifice,
inasmuch as they are changed into Christ's Body and Blood; the

---

[1] The words os leonis = the jaws of the lion, that is, of Satan, designate hell.
St. Peter calls the devil a "roaring lion" (leo rugiens), who seeks to devour souls,
that is, totally to destroy them. There are points of comparison in the watchfulness, the violent strength and rage, as well as in the extreme cruelty and rapacity
of the lion and of the devil (cf. 1 Peter 5, 8). In another passage (2 Peter 2, 4)
he designates the place of punishment of the damned by the words infernus and
tartarus, writing, that "God spared not the angels that sinned: but delivered them,
drawn down by infernal ropes to the lower hell, unto the torments, to be reserved
unto judgment" (rudentibus *inferni* detractos in *tartarum* tradidit cruciandos).
By the words: Ad *infernum* detraheris in *profundum laci* (Is. 14, 15), which apply
to the chief of the fallen angels, hell is likewise designated. — St. Michael is the
"Standard Bearer" (signifer), that is, the prince and leader of the angelic choirs,
who protect the faithful in the agony of death against the attacks of the infernal
spirits and conduct the souls that have faithfully struggled into the heavenly
Paradise. Hence the Church sings in an Antiphon: Archangele Michael, constitui
te *principem super omnes animas suscipiendas* — "Archangel Michael, thee have
I constituted as prince, to receive all souls." — The promise of salvation (of eternal
light and life) was repeatedly made to Abraham as the "Father of Believers" and
to his spiritual children. The earthly Chanaan promised him (Gen. 12, 7; 17, 8),
"the land of promise" was a type (figure) of the true Chanaan, that is, of the kingdom of God here below and in heaven (Hebr. 11, 8—12). Terra promissionis erat
figura regni coelestis seu patriae et quies illius figura fuit quietis beatorum in coelis
(Dion. Carthus. in Ps. 94, 11). Cf. also God's word to Abraham: Ego merces tua
magna nimis (Gen. 15, 1).

species of bread and wine serving to make the offering of the Body and Blood of Christ a visible sacrifice. From the close relation in which the elements of bread and wine stand to the Eucharistic Sacrificial Mystery, it follows with what great care and reverence they should be handled even before their consecration.

1. Our Lord and Saviour, at the first celebration of the Eucharistic Sacrifice, consecrated bread and wine and prescribed the use of these elements for the accomplishment of the unbloody Sacrifice in His Church for all future time. Christ indeed freely and out of His good pleasure chose bread and wine for this sacred purpose; but since His divine wisdom orders all things sweetly, there are certainly some reasons which show the suitableness of these sacrificial elements. The Eucharist is not only a sacrifice, but it is also a sacrament; under both of these points of view bread and wine are manifestly proper for their high destiny.[1] — In this place only the fitness of these gifts for the purpose of the Eucharistic Sacrifice is chiefly to be considered. "When God united the human soul with the body, thereby imparting life to the body, He, for the support of this life within us, directed us to the natural life without, and in the beginning ordered us to draw the nourishment of our life from the vegetable kingdom. In the state of man's innocence, the trees of Paradise yielded spontaneously for man their fruits, substantial and succulent, delightful to the taste and aromatic; but after his fall, banished from Paradise to the earth under a curse and of itself yielding but thorns and thistles, man has been obliged to wrest support from the earth by hard labor in the sweat of his brow. The grain of wheat, which is the fat of the land, and the grape, which ripens in the sun, in a manner contain the marrow and blood of the earth, are also intended mainly to renew man's substance and to refresh his blood, and are, therefore, the chief means for the nourishment of his life. — Nowhere do these grow wild, but in all places they thrive only by man's careful and laborious cultivation; and when he has harvested the ears and gathered in the grapes, it is still by renewed labor that he must prepare them for food and drink. — If, therefore, on the one hand, bread and wine are gifts of God, they are, on the other, products of man; the sweat of his brow cleaves to

---

[1] Si quaeratur, cur panis et vinum sint hujus sacramenti materia, dicendum, quod principalis causa *institutio* est *divina*, cujus institutionis *multiplex* est *ratio*. *Primo* ex parte usus sacramenti, quoniam panis et vinum communius in cibum et potum proveniunt, sicque per ea in spiritualem refectionem manuducimur magis apte. *Secundo* ex sacramenti effectu, quia panis prae ceteris cibis sustentat corpus et vinum laetificat cor. Ita et hoc sacramentum magis laetificat et sustentat caritate inebriatos, quam alia sacramenta. *Tertio* ex ritu celebrationis, quoniam duo ista tractantur mundius ac frequentius, quam cetera alimenta. *Quarto* ex significatione duplicis rei sacramenti istius. Panis namque ex multis granis conficitur et vinum ex multis acinis confluit, quod competit ad significandum corpus Christi verum ac mysterium. *Quinto* ex repraesentatione ejus, quod praecessit. Grana namque in area conculcantur, panis in fornace decoquitur et vinum in torculari exprimitur, et ita per ea Christi passio designatur (Dion. Carthus. IV, dist. 11, q. 3).

them, before they are changed into his flesh and blood. Hence they are eminently suited as gifts of man to God; in presenting them we offer to God our fatigue and labor, and in the offering of these gifts we bring to God, so to speak, our flesh and blood, our body and life. Therefore, before our Lord can give and leave us His Flesh and Blood as a sacrifice, we must offer to Him bread and wine, in that we separate and withdraw these articles from the ordinary wants of life, and reserve and sanctify them for Him for His Sacrifice. Consequently, in ancient times the Church permitted the faithful in general to bring bread and wine to the house of God and to place them on the altar, and the priest accepted them as well for the Sacrifice as for his daily support."[1] — Ears of wheat and bunches of grapes are the most noble and most valuable products of the vegetable world; they compose, so to speak, the flesh and blood of the earth. These "firstlings of God's creatures and gifts"[2] represent, therefore, nature in her entirety, which is in a manner offered to God in the oblations of bread and wine, obtained one from the ears of wheat, the other from the grapes. — The offering of bread and wine then symbolizes also the donation of man himself and of his life; for bread and wine are the most excellent means of nourishment, that serve to support and strengthen corporal life.[3] Therefore, the Psalmist says (Ps. 103, 14—15): "The Lord bringeth bread out of the earth for the service of men, and wine that it may cheer the heart of man." Thus the gifts of bread and wine serve symbolically to represent the offering to God of all created things, as required of man. In the bread and wine, man offers himself and all that he is.[4] — It may then be inferred that the separate species of bread and wine are suited to represent the separation of the Blood from the Body of Christ, the painful death of Christ, Christ's bloody sacrifice on the Cross.[5]

---

[1]   Laurent, Christol. Predigten II, 67.

[2]   *Primitiae* ex Dei creaturis, *primitiae* munerum Dei (S. Iren. Adv. haeres. 1. 4, c. 17, n. 5).

[3]   Prima causa (for the offering of bread, wine and water) est, quia inter omnia humanae vitae sustentandae necessaria, haec tria sunt mundiora et utiliora et magis necessaria, propterea potius debuerunt apponi quam alia, et in id quod mundius est et utilius omnibus et super omnia ad vitam aeternam capessendam magis necessarium, transferri et transformari, i. e. in corpus Christi et sanguinem (Lib. de canone mystici libam. c. 2). This little work is no longer ascribed to John of Cornwallis, but to Richard, a Premonstratentian of the monastery of Wedinghausen (diocese of Cologne).

[4]   On the words of the Canon, qui tibi offerunt *pro* se suisque omnibus, Robert Paululus remarks, the small word *"pro"* hoc sensu non inconvenienter accipitur, ut haec, scil. panem et vinum quae in victu vitae animalis principalia sunt, offerendo seipsos et sua omnia, i. e. totum victum suum offerre dicantur. Praecipua quippe illius portio sunt et totum figurant (De offic. eccles. 1. 2, c. 29).

[5]   Eucharistia praeteritae Christi passionis signum est, et corporis a sanguine separati repraesentatio: at panis corpus exsangue, vinum sanguinem in passione Salvatoris *fusum* aptissime repraesentat (Contenson. Theologia mentis et cordis 1. 11, par. 2, diss. 2, c. 2, spec. 1).

2. The Church requires that the matter used for the Consecration be not only valid and as far as possible genuine, but, moreover, that it be permissible and as far as possible perfect. — The bread destined for the sacrificial action must have been made of pure wheaten flour, that has been mixed with natural water and baked in the fire; and that the bread be pure, whole and fresh. — The sacrificial wine of the vine must have been pressed from ripe grapes, fully fermented, not soured, nor settled, nor artificially composed; as to the color and taste, it may be red or white, strong or light, naturally sweet or tart. With regard to the color, it is to be remarked that, although red wine symbolizes more perfectly than the white the Blood of Christ, still white wine is to be preferred, because in its use at the altar cleanliness can more easily be observed. — Another prescription respecting the sacrificial elements is that the bread is required to be unleavened and the wine to be mixed with a little water. The use of unleavened bread and the mixing of wine with water have a higher meaning, and are, therefore, strictly prescribed by the Church; although they are not required for the validity, yet they are absolutely required for the lawfulness of the Consecration.

a) The bread should be unleavened.[1] This is a strict ordinance of the Church for the priests of the Latin rite, while on the united Greeks[2] it is as strictly enjoined, according to an old custom, to consecrate only in leavened bread.[3] Unleavened and leavened bread

---

[1] Azymus panis = panis sine fermento (instead of fervimentum = fermentation, fermenting mixture, leaven, ζύμη) vel non fermentatus, from ἄζυμος, Substantive azymon = unleavened bread. The second syllable is made short by Prudentius and others. — Bread raised with leaven, leavened bread, is called by Isid. (Etymol. l. 20, c. 2, n. 15) panis fermentacius, i. e. fermentis confectus, also p. fermentalis vel fermentatus. — In omnibus Scripturis invenimus panem indifferenter dici, sive fuerit azymus sive fuerit fermentatus (Humbert. Adversus Graecor. calumnias n. 12).

[2] In the East the Armenians and Syro-Maronites (like the Latins) use unleavened bread.

[3] Among the Greeks it appears that leavened sacrificial bread, from the most ancient times, was exclusively or at least generally used. The historic question has not as yet been solved, what kind of bread the Western Church used for the Sacrifice during the first ten centuries. Three different views prevail regarding it among Catholic theologians since the seventeenth century, when the controversy was most animated. P. Sirmond S. J. († 1651) in his Disquisitio de azymo, semperne in usu altaris fuerit apud Latinos defended the assertion (in its universality at any rate exaggerated and incorrect), that the Western Church in the middle of the ninth century consecrated exclusively leavened bread. Christopher Lupus O. S. Aug. († 1681) first opposed this opinion. But as its chief opponent Mabillon O. S. B. († 1707) came forth, who principally in his Dissertatio de pane eucharistico azymo ac fermentato defended the diametrically opposite opinion, namely, that in the West the constant and general use of unleavened sacrificial bread had prevailed (among the Apostles only, he admits the partial use of leavened bread). Cardinal Bona O. Cist. († 1674) takes a middle view, employing the inconclusive arguments used by both opponents, to make it probable, that the Roman Church until late in

are equally valid matter of the Sacrifice: the one as well as the other
has its peculiar mystical signification. Yet there are more numerous
and better reasons for the usage prevalent in the Latin Church; hence
the rite of the latter is to be preferred. These reasons are principally the following:

a) The example of Christ at the institution of the Eucharist.
The Saviour kept "on the first day of unleavened bread" the Pasch
with His disciples — therefore, at the time in which the Jews,
according to the ordinance of the law, were obliged to have nothing
leavened in the house or to partake of it. Consequently, it is generally admitted that Christ[1] consecrated unleavened bread.[2] Although
the words of the Lord to His Apostles and their successors commanding them to do the same as He had done at the Last Supper, may
not have been a formal command to consecrate unleavened bread,
still it is evident that in so grave and sacred a matter the example
of Christ should not easily be departed from. To depart from it,
the Church has not the slightest reason; on the contrary, she has
every reason to retain the use of unleavened bread after the example
of Christ, since in many respects the unleavened merits a preference
to the leavened bread.

b) The unleavened bread symbolizes very appropriately the
Eucharistic Victim and the Eucharistic Food of the soul. The
leaven penetrates and soon leavens the entire mass of flour in which
it is mixed, changing it into savory bread; from this point of view
the Saviour (Matt. 13, 33) calls the Divine Truth and Grace a
heavenly leaven that transforms mankind. — Otherwise leaven is
usually employed in an evil sense.[3] Namely, it displaces the flour
in its working, that is, in its fermentation works decomposition or
decay; therefore, it serves as a figure of the unclean, the perverse
and the corrupted.[4] — Unleavened bread, on the contrary, which has

---

the ninth century permitted the use of leavened as well as of unleavened sacrificial
bread. The views of Mabillon and Bona since that epoch have had the greater
number of adherents. On the side of Mabillon are, for example, Martene, Macedo,
Ciampini, Cabassutius, Boucat, Berti, Simmonet, Sandini; on Bona's side, for
example, Tournely, Witasse, Bocquillot, Grancolas, Graveson, Natalis Alexander.

[1] Credimus panem illum, quem primum Dominus in coena mystica in mysterium corporis sui consecravit, *infermentatum* fuisse, maxime cum in tempore
paschae nullum fermentum cuiquam vesci, sed nec in domo habere ulli licebat
(Raban. Maur. De cleric. instit. 1. 1, c. 31).

[2] Even though our Saviour had anticipated the Paschal meal, which can by
no means be proved, the use of leavened bread would not in consequence follow. —
"The first day of the unleavened bread was the fourteenth Nisan, that is, the feast
of Easter began on the eve. The leavened bread that remained was already collected on the evening of the thirteenth Nisan and burnt on the fourteenth before
noon" (cf. Schanz, Commentar über das Evangelium des hl. Matthäus S. 508 etc.).

[3] Fermentum significat caritatem propter *aliquem effectum*, quia scil. panem
facit sapidiorem et majorem; sed corruptionem significat *ex ipsa ratione suae
speciei* (S. Thom. 3, q. 74, a. 4 ad 3. — Cfr. Humbert. n. 30).

[4] In fermento duo possunt considerari. Primo *sapor*, quem tribuit pani, et
secundum hoc per fermentum significatur sapientia Dei, per quam omnia quae sunt

undergone no such process of fermentation, is a symbol of purity and cleanliness. Accordingly, only unleavened bread can appropriately indicate the superhuman holiness and purity of the Eucharistic Victim, as well as the incomparable purity and incorruption of the Eucharistic Food of the soul.

c) Inasmuch as unleavened bread calls to our mind, how unspeakably pure and bright the transfigured Body of Christ is, at the same time it also reminds us of the purity of heart and body with which we should approach the Table of the Lord and receive the Food of Angels. According to the counsel of the Apostle (1 Cor. 5, 7–8) we must purge out the old leaven of sin and passion, of wickedness and wantonness, that we may be "a new paste, as we are unleavened" and be enabled, when thus sanctified, to partake of the immaculate Flesh of the Eucharistic Victim. These thoughts are beautifully expressed in the Paschal Hymn which says: "Christ is our paschal sacrifice, while for unleavened bread we need but heart sincere and purpose true" (*pura puris mentibus sinceritatis azyma*).[1]

b) To the sacrificial wine a small quantity of natural water must be added, according to Apostolic ordinance and the strict discipline of the Church. As this commingling is a holy ceremony, it must take place at the altar before the Oblation and be made in the chalice itself. Even a drop answers the purpose. It is, moreover, advisable and always safe to pour but a little water[2] into the chalice, that the wine be not too much weakened and thus perhaps be

---

hominis sapida redduntur; secundo in fermento potest considerari *corruptio*, et secundum hoc per fermentum potest intelligi uno modo peccatum, alio modo homo peccator (S. Thom. in I. ad Cor. c. 5, lect. 2).

[1] Unleavened bread is also different in appearance and taste from the daily bread that we eat; hence it is suitable, by its appearance to indicate, that under the Eucharistic veil no ordinary bread, but the true and living Bread of Heaven is concealed, that preserves the spiritual life of grace and ensures the blessed life of immortality. — The unleavened bread, which was eaten with the Paschal lamb and bitter herbs, is called "bread of tribulation" (panis afflictionis — Deut. 16, 3), because it was a reminder of the labors and oppression endured in Egypt; in this it also symbolizes the Eucharistic Banquet celebrated in memory of the bitter passion and death of Christ. Cf. Algerus, De sacramentis corp. et sang. dominici, 1. 2, c. 10. — The ferment that penetrates and invigorates the mass of meal, is indeed a figure of the divinity, clothing itself with human nature, but panis est proprie sacramentum *corporis* Christi, quod sine corruptione conceptum est, magis quam *divinitatis* ipsius (S. Thom. 3, q. 74, a. 4).

[2] The Florentinum gives: aqua *modicissima* and *paululum* aquae; the rubric: *parum* aquae. Hence the well known adage: quanto *paucior*, tanto potior. "Although the reasons for the mingling of the water are so manifest, that without mortal sin it may not be omitted, yet the Sacrament exists when it is not done. But priests should be attentive that, as in Holy Mass water must be taken with the wine, yet only a little must be added. For according to the opinion and judgment of ecclesiastical commentators, this water is changed into wine" (Catech. Roman. p. 2, c. 4, q. 16). — Vino consecrando miscenda est aqua naturalis tantum et modica, et per modum sacrae ceremoniae, ad altare et in calice (Sporer, Theol. sacrament. p. 2, c. 3, sect. 2, § 3).

spoiled. This mixture is so important and, therefore, so strictly prescribed, that it would never be allowed for a priest to begin the Holy Sacrifice, if he foresaw that no water could be procured. Profoundly significant are the reasons that favor the fitness of this ecclesiastical ordinance and practice.

a) *The example of the Saviour.* That the Lord at the institution of the Eucharist consecrated wine mixed with water, is beyond a doubt. And in favor of this is the circumstance, that the addition of water to the wine at the Paschal meal was a permanent and universally practised custom from which the Lord surely did not depart.[1] The ancient liturgies and holy Fathers are unanimous in asserting that the Saviour mingled the Eucharistic chalice with water.[2] Thus from the time of the Apostles the Church has everywhere and at all times faithfully followed after the example of her Divine Master, and has ever consecrated only wine mixed with water. She regarded it, as St. Cyprian writes in his letter to Caecilius, as proper that at the mixing and offering of the chalice of the Lord, she should observe the true tradition thereof, in order that at His glorious and triumphant return He may find us adhering strictly to that whereunto He had exhorted us, observing what He had taught and doing what He had done.

Besides this historical reason there are also mystical and symbolical reasons.[3]

b) The wine destined to be changed into the Blood of Christ is mixed with water at the altar, that by these two elements the blood and water which flowed, on the Cross, from the wound in the side of Christ may be represented.[4] — The piercing and opening of the Heart of Jesus, with the stream of blood and water issuing there-

---

[1] As a rule, red wine mingled with water was used for the Paschal celebration: . . . τὸ ποτήριον ἐξ οἴνου καὶ ὕδατος (Const. apostol. 1. 8, c. 12).

[2] The mingling of the wine with water is not de necessitate sacramenti neque praecepti divini, but only de necessitate praecepti *ecclesiastici*, that is, *apostolici*. With the Fathers, in Councils and liturgies the Eucharistic Chalice, that is, its contents (before the Consecration), has, for example, the following denominations: κρᾶσις, κρᾶμα, ποτήριον κεκραμένον, calix mixtus, temperamentum calicis, poculum aquae et vini, calix dominicus vino mixtus, calix vini et aquae plenus, vinum aqua mixtum, calix dominicus vino et aqua permixtus, mixtum, temperatum.

[3] Sicut propter imitationem magis exactam, et propter mysterium Ecclesia latina praecipit consecrationem in *azymo*, sic propter eamdem imitationem, et propter mysterium Ecclesia universalis praecipit consecrationem in *vino* non puro, sed *lymphato* (Lugo l. c.).

[4] It is the better established and the more general opinion, that the right side of the Saviour (together with His Sacred Heart) was opened by the lance. Dominus meus Jesus post cetera inaestimabilis suae erga me beneficia pietatis, etiam *dextrum* sibi propter me passus est latus fodi : quod videlicet nonnisi de *dextera* mihi propinare vellet, nonnisi in *dextera* locum parare refugii. Utinam ego talis merear esse columba, quae in foramine petrae habitet et in foramine lateris *dextri* (S. Bernard. In Ps. 90, serm. 7, n. 15).

from, is a wonderful event[1] and, at the same time, one full of mystical meaning, which should in a very special manner engage the
attention of men; for the Evangelist, in speaking of it, mentions this
passage of the Prophet: "They shall look on him whom they have
pierced" (John 19, 37; Zach. 12, 10). For this occurrence proves
not only the truth and reality of the sacrificial death of Christ, but
it, moreover, involves a profound symbolism; for the stream of blood
and water which proceeded from the wounded Heart of Jesus symbolizes all the graces and blessings that flow to us from the passion
and death of Christ. The water, namely, symbolizes Baptism,
which is the laver of purification and regeneration; the blood signifies the Eucharist, the fountain of reconciliation and strength unto
life eternal. But since Baptism is the beginning, the Eucharist, the
end and complement of the remaining sacraments, they are all included in these two principal ones. The outpouring of blood and
water from the pierced side of the Redeemer, therefore, symbolically
expresses that all the sacraments have their origin in His sacrificial
death, that is, that they derive from it their power and plenitude of
grace. — But the Church is the only lawful possessor and administra-
tor of the sacraments, by virtue of which she in her members is ever
undergoing purification and sanctification, enlivened and fructified:
hence the holy Fathers behold in the pierced Heart of Jesus also the
divine origin of the Church. They say that from the opened side
and breast of the second Adam, while slumbering in death, the new
Eve, that is, the Church, was formed and came forth.[2] In the Office
of the Sacred Lance and Nails it is said: "Thou, O Lance, hast
opened to the world the life-giving side, whence came forth the holy
Church." Thus from the pierced Heart of Jesus, that is, from the
stream of blood and water proceeding therefrom, the pure, immaculate Church was born, and thence the inexhaustable fountain of her
graces originated. — The rite of the mixing of wine and water in the
chalice can and should remind us of these mysteries.

  c) The commingling of wine and water in the chalice refers
also to that intimate, mystical relationship existing between Christ
and His Church.[3] Under this meaning, the noble, precious element
of the wine, considered as to its qualities and effects, as well as

---

  [1] In this outpouring of blood and water from a heart that beat no longer, the
holy Fathers behold a great miracle. Contumelia a Judaeis illata in signum prodiit,
quia de corpore exstincto sanguis verus et aqua pura *miraculose* manavit (Ludolph.
de Saxon. p. 2, c. 64, n. 13). — Cfr. Officium ss. Cordis D. N. J. Ch. — Bucceroni
S. J., Commentarii in cultum ss. cordis Jesu. Parisiis 1880.

  [2] Sopor ille viri (Adam — Gen. 2, 21) mors erat Christi, cujus exanimis in
cruce pendentis latus lancea perforatum est atque inde sanguis et aqua profluxit
(Joan. 19, 34): quae sacramenta esse novimus, quibus aedificatur Ecclesia (S. Aug.
de civit. Dei l. 22, c. 17).

  [3] Consulte a prioribus statutum est, ne vinum in sacrificio sine aquae admix-
tione offeratur, ut videlicet per hoc significetur, populos qui secundum Joannem
(Apoc. 17, 15) aquae sunt, a Christo, cujus sanguis in calice est, dividi non debere
(Walafr. Strabo, de exord. et increm. c. 16).

viewed as to the approaching consecration into the Blood of Christ, is taken as a symbol of the God-Man; while the running, flowing water is a speaking figure of unstable, perishable man.[1] "The waters which thou sawest," said the Angel to John, "are peoples and nations" (Apoc. 17, 15). Like wave on wave nations, one on the other, press upon the stream of time; like billows chasing and rolling on one another, and lost in the deep, generations of men rise, one on another, to sink again in turn into the grave of eternity. The drops of water which have been poured into the chalice no longer exist of themselves, but they are diffused in and incorporated into the wine, partaking of its qualities. Similar is the union of the faithful with Christ[2]: by virtue of this union a change takes place in them and they are made partakers of the divine nature, that is, by sanctifying grace they are made children of God, and by the bestowal of heavenly glory they become heirs of God. For from the Head, Jesus Christ, who is filled with all the treasures of the divinity, the unction of grace flows down to His members, descending even to the hem and extremity of the garment of the Church (Ps. 132, 2), so that she becomes wholly penetrated with the precious flow of heavenly gifts. — We are to understand by the commingling of wine and water before the Oblation, first of all, the sacrificial Communion between Christ and the Church, that is, this ceremony is intended to place before our eyes that Christ as the Head, in union with the Church, as His mystical body, offers sacrifice and is offered in sacrifice at the celebration of Mass. — Hereby, at the same time, is indicated that unspeakably intimate and exalted relation, which is realized and perfected between the children of the Church and our Redeemer by the Sacrifice and Sacrament of the Eucharist. This is that supernatural espousal of which the Apostle wrote to the Christians of Corinth: "I have espoused you to one husband, that I may present you a chaste virgin to Christ" (2 Cor. 11, 2). It commences here below in sanctifying grace and is consummated above in eternal glory.

d) Finally, our rite is calculated to symbolize, moreover, that mystery by which the divine and human natures are united together in one person, namely, the Incarnation of the Eternal Word. This mystery is the root and source of all and of every supernatural relation of man with God in time and eternity.

3. To the matter of the Sacrifice, already before its oblation, are due the most scrupulous care and the greatest reverence, as is evident from their more remote preparation.[3] Every precaution

---

[1] Unda *fluens*, homo *praeteriens* (Hildeb. Turon. Vers. de myster. Missae).

[2] Cum aqua in vinum convertitur, significatur, quod populus Christo incorporatur (S. Thom. 3, q. 74, a. 8 ad 2). — Aqua significat populum, qui est insipidus, et sapidus fit per conjunctionem cum Sapientia, Christo, sicut aqua, cum adjungitur vino (S. Bonav. IV, dist. 11, p. 2, a. 1, q. 3 ad 6).

[3] The bread selected for the Consecration was generally called *oblata* or *hostia.* The figure and size were not prescribed in the first centuries, but left to the judg-

must be taken to procure genuine and freshly made hosts, to procure
genuine pure wine for the Sacrifice of the Altar. Let us recall the
epoch of the Middle Age, so full of faith. Then it was that devout
princes and princesses esteemed it high honor to be allowed to prepare and to provide the bread and wine for the Holy Sacrifice.[1] In
convents the preparation of the sacrificial bread was even accompanied with religious solemnity and with a kind of divine service.
Thus was it prepared in the world-renowned Benedictine Abbey of
Cluny.[2] At prescribed hours the monks performed manual labor;
but that they might also be sanctified in the midst of their occupations, they worked amid the singing of Psalms. But of all manual
labor especial care was bestowed upon the preparation of the bread
for the Sacrifice. It was amidst the singing of Psalms that the seed
destined for it was confided to the earth and the ripe grain gathered;
amid the praises of divine power and love, grain after grain was

---

ment of the celebrant and people, prout erat cuique studium atque devotio in
religione divina (Bernold. Constant.). Si de primis Ecclesiae saeculis agitur,
quando ipsae populi oblationes immolabantur, perspicuum est, alia tum forma non
fuisse, quam quae panum erat oblatorum. Integri enim ac solidi, ut oblati fuerant,
consecrabantur consecratique in partes ad distribuendum comminuebantur (Sir-
mondus, Disquis. de azymo c. 4). In reference to the example of our Saviour, who
consecrated a loaf (a cake, a slice, a round) of the unleavened Paschal bread, the
round form had even at a very early period the preference, the more so as it is regarded as a symbol of perfection. Already St. Epiphanius († 403) mentions, that
the Eucharistic Sarificial bread is of a round form (στρογγυλοειδής — The Anchor c.
57). In the Middle Age it received names that allude to its circular form, for
example, corona oblationum, circulus, rotula panis, panis rotularis. According to
an ordinance of the Sixteenth Synod of Toledo (693), the sacrificial bread should
be specially and carefully prepared, be white and of moderate size; finally, not a
piece, but whole loaves were to be consecrated (panis integer et nitidus, qui ex
studio fuerit praeparatus, neque grande aliquid, seu modica tantum oblata). It was
already then baked in iron moulds, provided with symbolical pictures and Scriptural signs (host-irons, ferrum oblatorium, ferrum oblatarum, ferramentum charac-
teratum). Moreover, in the eleventh century the consecrated breads were still so
large, that they had to be broken and divided for the Communion of the faithful
(*particulae*). Tenues oblatas ex simila (of the finest wheaten flour) praeparatas
integras et sanas sacris altaribus superponimus et ex ipsis post consecrationem
fractis cum populo communicamur (Humbert. Card. [† c. 1064], Advers. Graec.
calumn. n. 33). From this time on they gradually became smaller and thinner,
until they received the present (coin) form. As a rule, now only hosts that are whole
may be distributed; but the name particulae, that has clung to them, still reminds
us of the ancient practice of the breaking of bread. — Decet revera panem *candi-
dissimum* esse et *mundissimum*, si facultas non defuerit, qui transferri debet in
splendidissimum corpus Agni immaculati (Algerus, De sacram. corp. et sang. dom.
l. 2, c. 9). — Cfr. Mabillon, Acta SS. O. S. B. tom. III, praef. n. 57—60. — Gerbert,
Vetus Liturgia Alemannica, p. 1, disp. 4, c. 3.

[1] S. Wenceslaus summa religione sacerdotes veneratus suis manibus triticum
serebat et vinum exprimebat, quibus in Missae sacrificio uterentur (Brev. Rom.)

[2] Cfr. Consuetud. Cluniac. 1. 3, c. 13 (De hostiis qualiter fiant). — Krazer,
Sect. 3, art. 2, c. 3.

17

selected, carefully washed, and carried in a special sack to the mill
by one of the most exemplary monks. There he first washed the
two mill-stones, covered them from top to bottom with cloths, robed
himself in white, and then, with veiled face so that his eyes alone
were uncovered, he began to grind the wheat. With similar care the
sieve was then washed and the flour sifted. To prepare the bread
from the flour was the duty of the highest official of the monastic
church; two monks and a recently admitted brother, with no less
care shared the holy labor with him. Being well washed and clothed
in white garments, they baked the hosts in a blessed vessel. — It is
very proper that persons consecrated to God prepare with all devotedness and reverence the bread for the Holy Sacrifice, regarding this
preparation as a work of love and of conscience.

47. The Offering of the Host.

The next preparation of the elements of the Sacrifice takes place
during the Mass itself,[1] — and it includes the separation, the dedication and the blessing of the bread and wine for the exalted end to
which they are destined. This preliminary sanctification of the
Eucharistic elements, if not essentially necessary, is yet in the highest degree just and proper.[2] The earthly elements are to be taken
from the sphere of nature into the higher order of grace, that is, they
are to become holy things, before the Holy Ghost changes them into
the Body and Blood of Christ. — And it has in its favor the example
of Jesus Himself, who at the Last Supper, in His character of Highpriest, taking the bread and the chalice with wine "in His holy and
venerable hands," and "raising His eyes to heaven, blessed, as He
gave thanks" to the Almighty Father, the earthly gifts of bread and
wine, that is, He as Man fervently prayed — for that moment and for
all future time — that the elements be changed, a change which He
as God together with the Father and the Holy Ghost would effect
not only then, but as often as the words of Consecration would be
pronounced as prescribed.[3] — The Church, therefore, imitates the

---

[1] The preparation of the offering, that is, the pouring of the wine into the
chalice and the mixing of water in it, took place, in the Middle Age, usually before
the prayers at the foot of the altar, that is, immediately after the priest had ascended the altar, and also the bread and the wine were then often offered to God
not one after the other, but both together by a single prayer. Cf. the present rite
of the Dominicans.

[2] Per prolationem sacrorum verborum et signa crucis panis et vinum *aptantur*
et *quasi meliorantur*, ut sint *condigna* materia, quae in corpus et sanguinem
Christi convertatur. Si enim vestes et templum ac vasa ecclesiae benedicuntur et
sanctificantur, ut sint apta instrumenta divini obsequii, quanto *rationabilius* est,
panem et vinum ante consecrationem benedici, ut sint *apta* materia transsubstan-
tiationis supermirabilis atque divinae. Nam et aliorum sacramentorum materiae
propter reverentiam sacramenti ante usum suum sanctificantur, ut aqua baptismi
vel chrisma seu oleum (Dion. Carthus. Expos. Missae art. 18).

[3] The Lord celebrated the Pasch of the New Testament by blessing (εὐλογήσας,
benedicens) the bread and the chalice, as also by giving thanks (εὐχαριστήσας, gra-

Saviour, when in the course of the sacrificial celebration up to the time of the Consecration, she repeatedly blesses the Eucharistic elements, and implores of God their acceptance, sanctification and transformation.

The Offertory of the elements begins with the offering of the Host, wherein we may distinguish the act and the prayer of the Oblation.

I. *The Act of Oblation.*

The priest takes the paten with the Host resting thereon and elevates it, that is, he offers it as a sacrificial gift to the Lord God "who dwells in the highest," and he does this by holding it, as it were, before His eyes, and joining to it the supplication, that the Lord would graciously accept it.[1] The raising of the Host is intended to express the act of presentation. At the same time, the priest, as is conformable to the first words of the accompanying prayer, raises his eyes to the Crucifix on the altar and lowers them again almost immediately; this harmonizes with the rest of the oblation prayer, wherein he is mindful of his unworthiness and first of all offers it for his own sins. — After the conclusion of the prayer, the celebrant makes with the paten and Host the Sign of the Cross over the place on which the Host is to be placed.[2] This ceremony is intended to

tias agens) to God the Father. Both words εὐλογεῖν and εὐχαριστεῖν are not simply synonymous, but are often used to designate one and the same prayer, in so far as the blessing therein contained is connected with thanksgiving. At all events by this εὐλογεῖν or εὐχαριστεῖν we must not understand merely the uttering of the words of consecration; for there is thereby designated another act entirely different from the consecration, that is, a preparatory prayer of blessing and thanksgiving preceding the consecration, the conclusion of which are the words of the consecration. This presanctification of the elements was wholly appropriate, since their species remained after the consecration, and, in like manner, the thanksgiving also was appropriate before and during the performance of a mystery equally glorious for God as beneficial for men. (Cf. Knabenbauer ad Matth. 26, 26, and Cornely ad 1 Cor. 10, 16 and 11, 24.)

[1] In oblatione panis et vini dicuntur aliquae orationes valde tenerae, devotae ac sanctae a sacerdote, quasi spiritualiter *habente in manibus thus lucidissimum et panes propositionis* (Lev. 24, 7), qui in mensa Domini offeruntur. Et quamvis sacerdos satisfaciat, orationes illas eo affectu dicens, quem ipsa verba insinuant, bene ad ea attentus, tamen magis adhuc specialiter quum accipit Patenam cum hostia in manibus, debet spiritualiter in ea cor proprium ponere et corda omnium circumstantium, imo et omnium fidelium, ut ea etiam Deo offerat cum ea celsissima intentione, quod quemadmodum hostiam illam offert, quae est purus panis, ut ejus substantiâ destructâ convertatur in corpus ipsius Christi, ita cor suum et omnium fidelium offerat, ut in eis destruat quidquid terrenum est, et convertat ac per amorem et imitationem transformet in ipsum Christum, ita ut desinant esse quod erant et vivere more antiquo, incipiant autem esse et vivere sicut ipse omnium Redemptor (De Ponte, De christ. hom. perf. IV, tr. 2, c. 12, § 1).

[2] There is, moreover, already a cross cut in the altar-stone and anointed with chrism, when the altar was consecrated, in the very place (the middle of the altar) where the host is placed. Quod sacerdos oblata in altari deponit super crucem in consecratione altaris cum chrismate factam, hic est Christus, qui carnem suam cruci affixit (Sicardus, Mitrale l. 3, c. 6).

bring before the mind in a striking manner that the Cross and altar are holy places, where, though, indeed, after a different manner, one and the same Sacrifice was once and is now offered. The very same Body that hung upon the Cross, is laid on the altar; as the Cross was once deemed worthy to bear the atoning Sacrifice for the world, so is now the altar.

2. *The Oblation Prayer.*

Suscipe, sancte Pater, omnipotens aeterne Deus, hanc immaculatam hostiam, quam ego indignus famulus tuus offero tibi Deo meo vivo et vero, pro innumerabilibus peccatis et offensionibus et negligentiis meis, et pro omnibus circumstantibus, sed et pro omnibus fidelibus Christianis, vivis atque defunctis: ut mihi et illis proficiat ad salutem in vitam aeternam. Amen.	Accept, O holy Father, Almighty and eternal God, this unspotted Host, which I Thy unworthy servant offer unto Thee, my living and true God, for my innumerable sins, offences and negligences and for all here present; as also for all faithful Christians, both living and dead, that it may avail both me and them for salvation unto life everlasting. Amen.

This prayer, which is as terse in composition as it is rich in thought, affords an answer to various questions that may be asked with regard to the Eucharistic Sacrifice. — Who is to receive and accept the Host? — "The holy Father, the Almighty, eternal God."[1] The Church in the Mass generally addresses herself to God the Father, in order to unite herself to the Saviour, who on the altar offers Himself to His heavenly Father. In the full and complete sense God alone deserves the name of Father, as Christ says: "Call none your father upon earth; for one is your Father, who is in heaven" (Matt. 23, 9). Yes, God is our Father; we are and we are called His children. Through His only-begotten Son, Jesus Christ, He has conferred upon us the dignity as well as the goods and privileges of children of God. What love has He not thereby shown us! God is not merely the best and the most liberal of fathers, but He is also the infinitely "holy Father". Thus does the Saviour call Him in His sacrificial prayer as Highpriest (John 17, 11). Therefore, as His children, it is incumbent on us to be, after the Saviour's example, holy in all our conduct; for we should be perfect as is our Father in heaven (Matt. 5, 48). — God, whom we may with confidence call our Father, is, moreover, the "Almighty, eternal God," to whom, on account of His majesty and glory, the sacrifice of the

---

[1] Pensa, *cui offeras*, utpote Deo Patri omnipotenti et aeterno, ex cujus bonitatis, dilectionis, pietatis, munificentiae ac beneficiorum contemplatione debes vehementi dilectione accendi, atque ex consideratione suae majestatis et aequitatis debes reverentiali timore et omni humiliatione tui ipsius repleri. Hinc ante celebrationem et in ea debes bonitatem, caritatem, liberaliter et misericordiam Dei Patris ad homines intueri, mirari et honorare (Dion. Carthus. De sacr. altar. art. 16).

most profound reverence and humble subjection is due; finally, He is the "living and the true God," to whom alone sacrifice may and should be offered. In the liturgy the Lord is often designated as the living and true God,[1] in contradistinction to the inanimate and false gods, which are vain, powerless and full of deception. The priest offers to the "living and true God," who created heaven and earth. The "living" God is life itself, the eternal and increated life, the source of all life: because from Him proceeds both natural and supernatural life, the life of grace and glory in the world of angels and of men. In God and from God all things live and move; out of Him there is but death. The "true" God is truth itself, the primordial and purest truth, the fountain-head of all truth. St. John writes: "We know that the Son of God is come, and has given us understanding that we may know the true God, and may be in His true Son. This (Christ) is the true Son of God and life eternal. Little children keep yourselves from idols" (1 John 5, 20—21).

What is offered to God the Father ? — An "unspotted Host" — *immaculata hostia.*[2] By this expression the Eucharistic Sacrificial Body of Christ, as well as the Eucharistic Sacrificial bread is to be understood. That the term *unspotted Host* is not exclusively applied to the bread there present, but is to be referred also to the Body of the Lord soon to be present under the appearance of bread, is clearly evident from the context, as also from the comparison of this prayer with other oblation prayers, recited before the Consecration. Only the Body of Christ is that unspotted Host, which secures for us atonement of sin and salvation, for which supplication is made.[3] — The Church, therefore, looks on the bread resting on the paten and chosen for the Consecration, as already consecrated, and in offering it has already Christ's Body in view. Hence the priest already before (as later after) the Consecration calls the gift that he offers immaculate, unspotted; for Christ is the absolutely pure, holy and faultless Victim. The unspotted Host on the altar is, therefore, that "clean oblation" — *oblatio munda* — announced by the Prophet Malachias. — This offering of the Body of Christ is, in a measure, to be distinguished from the offering which takes place after the Consecration, and the difference consists in this, that here at the same time the bread is still presented and dedicated to the Lord God with

---

[1] Conversi estis ad Deum a simulacris, servire *Deo vivo et vero* (1 Thess. 1, 9).

[2] This spotlessness is frequently commented upon in the liturgy, because it is the first and essential requisite, in order that the Sacrificial Gift may be acceptable to God.

[3] *Panis* non est immaculata illa hostia pro expiatione peccatorum oblata, sed *solus Christus.* Itaque sensus horum verborum hic est: Suscipe, sancte Pater, immaculatam hostiam, quam ego indignus servus tuus ex hoc pane per mirabilem conversionem confecturus sum et tibi oblaturus. . . . Unde sacerdos in Offertorio orat Deum, ut acceptet hostiam a se ex hoc pane conficiendam et offerendam, et ut victima ex pane conficienda prosit sibi et aliis. Atque simul per caerimoniam illam sacrat Deo materiam remotam sacrificii ad sacrificium eucharistiae decentius peragendum (Antoine, de sacrif. Missae q. 2).

the desire that He would accept it for the purpose of consecration, that is, that He would bring the oblation of the bread to its final termination by the Consecration. Consequently, the expression *unspotted Host* can and ought to be understood of the sacrificial bread lying on the paten,[1] which is wholly faultless in consequence of the care taken in the selection of the prescribed materials and in its preparation. To two things therefore, namely, to the Sacrificial Body of the Lord, in spirit regarded as already present, and to the sacrificial bread soon to be changed, which is present in reality, the eye and heart of the priest are directed, while he raises on the paten the "unspotted Host" imploring its favorable acceptance by the heavenly Father.

Who performs the offering? — The priest who acknowledges himself an unworthy servant of God. The priest is God's servant. The Lord, who "raiseth up the needy from the earth, and lifteth up the poor from the dunghill, that He may place him with princes, with the princes of His people" (Ps. 112, 7—8), — the Lord hath called him into His sanctuary, that he may serve Him there all the days of his life. But it is especially at the altar that the priest is penetrated with a sense of his unworthiness to discharge this honorable and sublime service. The humblest office in the house of God is more exalted than the greatest wordly position. Now when the priest considers his misery and frailty, his ingratitude and sinfulness, how painfully should he not realize that he is quite unworthy to serve the Most High and, above all, in the most holy Mystery of the Altar?

For whom does the priest offer the Sacrifice? — In the first place, for himself, then for all present and, finally, for all Christians. — The celebrant, therefore, first offers the unspotted Host as a sacrifice of propitiation for his own sins, to obtain remission of all guilt and punishment; upon the altar there is, indeed, the very Body in which the Saviour bore our sins on the Cross and atoned for them by His death (1 Peter 2, 24). The priest knows full well that he is not (as he should be) holy, innocent, undefiled, separated from sinners, but that he is encompassed with infirmity; therefore, must he, in the first place, offer sacrifice for his own sins and afterward for those of his people (Heb. 7, 26).[2] He confesses his sins and faults

---

[1] After the Consecration not only the Body and Blood of Christ, but also the figurative bread and wine offerings of Melchisedech are designated as immaculata hostia. Bishop Odo of Cambrai († 1113) remarks in respect to this designation (Exposit. in Canon. Miss. dist. 3): "Ab immaculata (Virgine) sumpta est haec hostia, ideo et ipsa immaculata. Et hoc loco admonemur quod panis appositus altari debet esse candidissimus et in quo nulla possit inspici macula, ut hoc appareat in figura, quod praedicatur de substantia, ut pura et immaculata videatur exterius figura, cujus substantia dicitur interius pura et immaculata.

[2] Christus Dominus noster, qui aeternitate sacerdotii sui omnes tibi (Deo) servientes sanctificat sacerdotes, quoniam mortali carne circumdati, ita quotidianis peccatorum remissionibus indigemus, ut non solum pro populo, sed etiam pro nobis (sacerdotibus) ejusdem te Pontificis sanguis exoret (Sacrament. Gregor.).

and negligences to be "innumerable".[1] *Delicta quis intelligit?* (Ps. 18, 13.) Who can understand and take a note of all sins?[2] The possibilities of failing and stumbling are incalculably numerous. Who is not terrified at the facility and at the danger of committing sin! Even the just man falls seven times a day, and we all fail in many things. The more brightly the light of grace shines in the soul and the more delicate the conscience grows, the more clearly does man perceive the errors and guilt, the remissness and imperfections, the deliberate and indeliberate faults of his life.[3] Though even his sins be but trivial, they are still many and in their number lurks the danger. See you not how the little drops swell the streams and tear up the earth? All the sins incident to the very living of this wretched life of ours, the priest would daily atone for and efface

---

[1] Tu Christi sacerdos considera temetipsum, *quis sis*, h. e. quam defectuosus et fragilis in natura . . . quam culpabilis in vita, quam *innumerabilibus* vicibus quotidie peccans, saltem in venialibus, per omissionem et commissionem, per interiorum et exteriorum incustodiam sensuum, per irrefrenationem linguae, per inexemplaritatem et scandalum, per cogitationes inutiles, per distractiones, levitates, negligentias etiam in divinis, per immoderantias cibi ac potus, per inordinatas circa quaecunque creata affectiones. In his et consimilibus multis adverte te quotidie toties esse culpabilem ac peccantem, ut *nequeas numerare*, nec singula possis attendere, imo exorare indigeas et exclamare ad Dominum: *Delicta quis intelligit? Ab occultis meis munda me* (Dion. Carthus, De sacramento altaris serm. 3).

[2] P. Roothaan S. J. distinguishes in his Annotations to the Exercitia spiritualia of St. Ignatius the peccata et offensiones et negligentiae of our Oblation prayer in the following manner: a) *Peccata* quaevis, seu gravia seu levia, sive cogitationis sint, sive verborum sive operum sive etiam omissionis. Peccata, intelligo *culpas proprie sic dictas*. b) *Offensiones, culpae minus proprie dictae, seu involuntariae,* in quas scilicet offendere fragilitatem nostram in tot tamque variis vitae hujus casibus pronum est, ferme ut per viam salebrosam incedenti frequenter offendere seu impingere vel nolenti accidit. Et tamen, cautius incedendo, *offensiones* hujusmodi minuere Dei famulus potest et debet. c) *Negligentiae eae, quae ad rationem quidem peccati omissionis non pertingunt*, sed in actiones nostras irrepere, easque si minus vitiare omnino, tamen imperfectas minusque acceptas Deo reddere solent, suntque profecto innumerae, sive *intentionis* puritatem et intensionem spectes sive *modos* omnes, quibus actiones nostras ornari ac perfici in Dei conspectu decet, pro mensura luminis et gratiae nobis a Domino communicatae.

[3] Impossibile credo secundum statum viatoris, quod aliquis unum diem vel septimanam transeat sine remorsu venialis; tamen quod totum annum transeat, hoc habeo magis pro impossibili, et vix credo, quod fuerit hoc donum in aliquo nisi in Christo et ejus Matre; et ideo unusquisque vel habet conscientiam vel debet habere et omni hora petere: *Dimitte nobis* etc. Vix enim est, quod homo aliquamdiu sit in vita ista sine veniali, tum propter *frequentiam*, quia strepitus vitiorum et peccatorum venialium semper insonant auribus cordis nostri; tum propter *ignorantiam*, quia in multis venialiter peccamus et ignoramus, et non consideramus; tum propter *adhaerentiam*, quoniam venialia ista sunt magnae adhaerentiae, maxime quando habetur affectio circa aliquod terrenum: et ideo, quantumcumque sit perfectus, corde debet recognoscere et ore confiteri, se peccatorem esse. (S. Bonav. IV, dist. 17, p. 2, a. 2, q. 1 ad 4.)

by the Sacrifice of the Altar.[1] — The priest, in the second place, offers and prays expressly for all present, that is, for all those who are devoutly assisting at the divine service and who are uniting in the Holy Sacrifice; such persons, consequently, partake of a more special and abundant share in the fruits of the Sacrifice. — Like the loving, solicitous Mother she is, the Church forgets none of her children; she, therefore, permits the priest to offer and pray for all the faithful who belong to the communion of saints and who still stand in need of assistance, consequently, for all her children, whether "this present world yet retains them in the flesh or the world to come has already received them stripped of their mortal bodies," — whether they still are combating on earth or suffering in purgatory.

For what purpose is the Sacrifice offered? — That to all "it may be available unto eternal life," that is, that the Sacrifice may apply to them the benefits and blessings of Redemption, not merely for time, but for all eternity. Salvation (*salus*) is the ideal and the sum of all the good things that Christ brought into the world, for we acquire possession of these goods when we obtain salvation. This salvation begins for us here below in receiving pardon, and is completed in the other world in beatitude. Now, on the altar there flows the universal and inexhaustible fountain of salvation, whence all spiritual gifts come to us. Hence the priest prays that the Eucharistic Sacrifice may be unto all so efficacious a means of salvation, that they may attain to glory of soul and body in eternity.[2]

48. The Offering of the Chalice.

In a manner similar to the Host, the chalice also is dedicated and offered to the Heavenly Father;[3] but the offering is preceded by the preparation.

---

[1] Non solum lavit Christus nos a peccatis nostris in sanguine suo, quando sanguinem suum dedit in cruce pro nobis, vel quando unusquisque nostrum mysterio sacrosanctae passionis illius baptismo aquae ablutus est, verum etiam *quotidie* tollit peccata mundi. Lavat itaque nos a peccatis nostris quotidie in sanguine suo, *cum ejusdem beatae passionis* ad altare *memoria* replicatur, *cum panis et vini creatura in sacramentum carnis et sanguinis ejus ineffabili Spiritus sanctificatione transfertur,* sicque corpus et sanguis illius non infidelium manibus ad perniciem ipsorum funditur et occiditur, sed fidelium ore suam sumitur in salutem (Beda Venerab. lib. 1, homil. 14).

[2] After the offering of the host the paten, when the Mass is not a solemn one, is concealed under the corporal until after the Pater noster (cf. Microl. c. 10). In solemn Masses, however, the subdeacon holds the paten enveloped in the veil that hangs from his shoulders. The original and peculiar reason for keeping it thus covered is, because the paten (as also the chalice), being a blessed and sacred object, should, as far as possible, be withdrawn from profane gaze (cf. Lebrun p. 3, a. 6).

[3] That the Oblation prayer of the chalice is always addressed to the Father, is manifest from the Mozarabic Missal, in which the prayer is as follows: Offerimus tibi, Domine, Jesu Christi *Filii tui* calicem humiliter implorantes clementiam tuam, ut ante conspectum divinae majestatis tuae cum odore suavitatis ascendat. Per eundem Chr. (Migne 85, 528).

1. Preparation of the Chalice.

a) This comprises the pouring of the wine into the chalice, as well as the mixing of it with a little water which was previously blessed by the Sign of the Cross.[1] The symbol of mixing the wine and water is here to be considered, in order to arrive at the reason and the meaning of the use of the Sign of the Cross, which is omitted only in Requiem Masses. — It is asked why the Sign of the Cross is made over the water only and not over the wine, and why in Requiem Masses the blessing of the water also is omitted. The most reliable explanation rests on the symbolical meaning to be found in the mingling of the wine and water. The wine symbolizes Christ, who has no need of a blessing and to whom no advantage accrues from His union with the people; hence the wine is not blessed. The water symbolizes the faithful, who greatly need divine grace and to whom accrues, from their union with Christ, the greatest gain. This is expressed by the use of the Sign of the Cross that is made over the water before it is mingled with the wine.[2] The Sign of the Cross, therefore, does not apply so much to the water itself, as to the people signified by the water.[3] — This, consequently, explains why the Sign of the Cross is omitted in Requiem Masses. The whole Requiem Mass rite, for instance, aims at giving to the departed souls the greatest possible assistance, hence much is omitted which refers to that fruit which those present, namely, the living, generally derive from the Mass. Thus, for example, the celebrant at the Introit makes the Sign of the Cross not over himself, but over the book, which here in a certain way represents the suffering souls, and at the conclusion of the Mass he does not bestow the blessing on those present. For the same reason, at the Offertory he omits to bless the water, that is, the people symbolized by the water.

b) The prayer recited at the mixing of the water with the wine is as follows:

Deus, qui humanae substantiae dignitatem mirabiliter condidisti, et mirabilius reformasti: da nobis per hujus aquae et vini mysterium, ejus divinitatis esse	O God, who in creating human nature, hast wonderfully dignified it, and still more wonderfully reformed it: grant that by the mystery of this water and wine,

[1] John Beleth (in the twelfth century) writes on the subject: Tum vero aqua benedicitur, quando admiscetur vino; sed haudquaquam vinum, quoniam peculiarem suam exspectat benedictionem (Rationale c. 41).

[2] Vinum in hoc loco Christum significat, qui nulla eget benedictione; aqua populum qui in hac vita nequit esse sine peccato, propter quod indiget benedictione Dei, ut reddatur dignus ad unionem cum Christo. Ad hoc igitur significandum aqua benedicitur, quando vino admiscetur (Durand. 1. 4, c. 30, n. 21).

[3] The former rite had not this signification; it was differently constituted, as the cross was not made over the water, but the water was poured into the chalice in the form of a cross: Archdiaconus infundit (aquam) faciens crucem (= in modum crucis) in calice (Ordo Rom. I, n. 14). — The Ordo Rom. XIV, c. 72, had the rubric: demum (after pouring the water into the wine) signat super calicem semel.

consortes, qui humanitatis nostrae fieri dignatus est particeps, Jesus Christus, Filius tuus, Dominus noster; Qui tecum vivit et regnat in unitate Spiritus Sancti, Deus: per omnia saecula saeculorum. Amen.

we may be made partakers of the divine nature of Him, who vouchsafed to become partaker of our human nature, namely, Jesus Christ, our Lord Thy Son, who liveth and reigneth with Thee in the unity of the Holy Ghost, one God, world without end. Amen.

The foregoing prayer, which occurs in the ancient Sacramentaries as a Christmas Collect,[1] contains in part the mystical meaning of the mingling of the water and wine. In it we beg for that participation in the divine nature of which St. Peter writes: "By Christ He hath given us very great and precious promises, that by these we may be made partakers of the divine nature (*divinae consortes naturae*)" (2 Peter 1, 4). This participation in the divine nature is an exceedingly consoling and elevating mystery. It consists in this, that poor, frail human nature, by the communication of heavenly gifts and graces, is elevated to a supernatural state, endowed with inestimable riches and clothed with incomparable beauty. Hence the holy Fathers speak of a deification of man (*deificatio*), whereby they understand a supernatural, mystical, blissful union with and resemblance to God. "They in whom the Holy Ghost dwells become deified" (θεοποιοῦνται).[2] The virgin martyr Agnes referred to these gifts of grace when, full of enthusiasm, she spoke of her heavenly Spouse: "With sparkling and glittering gems hath He covered my breast, with golden garments hath He clothed me, with artistic and precious jewels hath He adorned me, — and, moreover, He hath shown me incomparable treasures, which are to be mine, if I remain true to Him." — To participate in the divine life, in the divine glory of Jesus Christ, we, therefore, pray, saying: *per hujus aquae et vini mysterium*, that is, by the mystery which is represented by the present mingling of water and wine. This mystery is manifold: at one time it represents the Incarnation, as also the passion and death of the Saviour (the issue of water and blood from Christ's pierced Heart), — hence the beginning and the conclusion of the work of redemption. These two mysteries are the original source of all grace for us: only because the Son of God assumed human nature and sacrificed His life in death for us, have we been made the children of God, co-heirs and associates in the glory of Jesus Christ. — Another mystery (signified in the mixing of wine and water) is the mystical union of the faithful with Christ — principally as accomplished in the reception of the Eucharist.[3] By this union with the

---

[1] Self-evidently these words are there wanting per hujus aquae et vini mysterium.

[2] S. Athanas. Epist. 1 ad Serap. n. 24.

[3] Under the form of bread the Body is given to thee, and under the form of wine the Blood is given to thee, that, by partaking of the Body and Blood of Christ,

Head, divine life diffuses itself throughout the members, as from the stock of the vine the vivifying and fructifying sap flows on to the branches. The more intimately we become incorporated with Christ by means of the holy Sacrament, the nearer we draw to the fountain of all graces, and the more plentifully are they diffused in our soul.

That we may be the more readily heard, we gratefully acknowledge, in support and confirmation of the above petition, the exceedingly great mercy the Lord has shown us in the boon both of our creation and of our redemption.[1] Therefore, we implore that the work which God has wonderfully begun, He may mercifully complete in us by imparting to us the divine life of grace here below and of glory hereafter.[2] In a wonderful manner did God make the dignity of man's being: He made man the king of the visible world, setting him but a little below the angels, with honor and glory He crowned him; for He did not leave human nature in Paradise in its lowliness, poverty and imperfection, but He enriched and adorned it with supernatural gifts. From this blissful height man precipitated himself into the depth of sin and misery; then God in a still more wonderful manner restored him and raised him up from his fall. God's love, wisdom and power are incomparably more gloriously displayed in the redemption than in the creation of the world. *Nihil nobis nasci profuit, nisi redimi profuisset*, sings the Church. "Of what avail would it have been for us to be born, unless the regeneration had been added?"

2. The Oblation of the Chalice.

a) The Act of Offering. — The priest raises the chalice, as though he would present it to God; but here the celebrant does not cast down his eyes, as at the offering of the Host, but he keeps them fixed on the Crucifix all the while that he is offering the chalice. The reason lies in the accompanying offering prayer, with which this raising of the eyes harmonizes, since the prayer contains the petition that the sacrificial offering "may ascend as an agreeable odor" to the throne of the Most High, and since, moreover, the offering prayer does not peculiarly and expressly remind the celebrant

---

thou mayst become one body and blood with Him (σύσσωμος καὶ σύναιμος αὐτοῦ). In this manner we also become Christ-bearers, in that His Body and Blood are distributed throughout our members. Therefore, according to the blessed Peter, we become partakers of the divine nature (S. Cyrill. Hierosol. IV, Cat. mystag. n. 3).

[1] Ipse erit *reformator* tuus, qui fuit *formator* tuus (S. Aug. Enarr. in Ps. 103, n. 4). — Duo sunt, quae principaliter attendere debet humana circumspectio: dignitatem suae conditionis et excellentiam suae reformationis. Dignitatem suae conditionis, ut peccare timeat; excellentiam redemptionis, ut gratiae redimentis ingratus non existat (Ivon. Carnot. serm. 22).

[2] Grace is the beginning, the principle and the root of glory, and glory is the completion, the blossom and the fruit of grace. Gratia et gloria ad idem genus referuntur; quia *gratia* nihil aliud est quam quaedam *inchoatio gloriae* in nobis (S. Thom. 2, 2, q. 24, a. 3 ad 2).

of his unworthiness. Before the priest puts down the chalice,[1] he makes the Sign of the Cross with it over the altar, to signify that in the chalice and upon the altar that same Precious Blood is offered which was shed on the wood of the holy Cross.

b) The Offering Prayer.

Offerimus tibi, Domine, calicem salutaris, tuam deprecantes clementiam, ut in conspectu divinae majestatis tuae, pro nostra et totius mundi salute cum odore suavitatis ascendat. Amen.	We offer unto Thee, O Lord, the Chalice of salvation, beseeching Thy clemency, that it may ascend before Thy divine Majesty, as a sweet odor for our salvation, and for that of the whole world. Amen.

As the above prayer shows, "the Chalice of salvation"[2] is here offered. Although the Chalice now contains merely the wine mixed with water, it is yet called the chalice of salvation, that is, a chalice bringing salvation, for the reason that the sacrificial wine will soon be changed into the sacrificial Blood of Christ. — In the offering of the chalice there is, at the same time, contained the petition that the Lord would change the wine into Christ's Blood, and graciously and agreeably accept this Blood from our hands.[3] These two ideas are comprised in the words that "the Chalice may ascend as a sweet odor" to Heaven. Only the consecrated chalice is truly a "chalice of salvation," as it contains that divine Blood which was shed on the Cross as a sacrifice and a ransom.[4] The chalice becomes the

---

[1] During the Middle Age the chalice was (not as now put behind the host, but) placed to the right, that is, towards the Epistle side, near the host, by which was symbolically indicated, that blood and water flowed from the right side of our Lord. Ita juxta Romanum Ordinem in altari (panis et vinum aqua mixtum) componenda sunt, ut oblata (i. e. hostia) in corporali posita, calix ad *dextrum latus oblatae* ponatur, quasi sanguinem Domini'suscepturus, quem de latere dominico profluxisse credimus (Microl., De eccles. observat. cap. 10). — This practice continued in the Roman Church until the fifteenth century, while in other places the present rite was introduced still earlier, ut Christi stantis ante crucem memoria haberetur, or rather, ob majorem *securitatem*, ne calix tam facile effundi posset. — Ista sacramenta modo vario ponuntur in ara—; Oblati panis dextra tenet calicem — In cruce pendentis quoniam latus Omnipotentis — *Dextrum* sanguinem vulnere fudit aquam. — Non reprehendendum si panis in *anteriori* — Parte locatur, habens posterius calicem. — Illius ordo prior tenet intuitum rationis — Posteriorque favet usibus Ecclesiae (Hildeb. Turon. Versus de myster. Missae).

[2] Cf. Ps. 115, 4. Calix salutaris (ποτήριον σωτηρίου) = chalice of safety or of salvation, salutary chalice, calix salutifer.

[3] According to an Ordo Missae of the beginning of the twelfth century the priest says here — hence before the consecration — at the offering of the chalice: Offerimus tibi, Domine, Jesu Christi Filii tui *sanguinem*. Humiliter imploramus clementiam tuam, ut ante conspectu (!) divinae majestatis tuae cum odore suavitatis accedat (!).

[4] Orat sacerdos, ut calix oblatus "in conspectu divinae majestatis cum odore suavitatis ascendat," cum *illo scil. mystico odore, qui ex ipso calice, cum conse-*

sacrificial cup in which the Precious Blood of Christ, this source of salvation and life, gushes forth new and fresh every day. In the chalice we offer that sacred Blood which once flowed through the members of the Saviour's body, and which gave Him strength to love, to labor and to suffer for us, — that divine Blood which throughout eternity flows in and out of the Heart of Jesus. In the chalice is offered that Blood which has brought eternal salvation to all the elect; for in heaven the blessed stand around the throne of the Lamb of God, singing unto Him: "Thou wast slain, and hast redeemed us to God in Thy Blood out of every tribe and tongue and people and nation, and hast made us to our God a kingdom and priests, and we shall reign on the earth" (Apoc. 5, 10).

Who offers the Chalice of salvation? *Offerimus* — "we offer", says the priest here, while at the offering of the Host he said *Offero* — "I offer". It makes no great difference, whether the singular or plural number be used. The priest stands at the altar as the representative and authorized agent of the Church; therefore, he offers the Host, as well as the Chalice, in the name of all the faithful, and they, especially those who are present, offer in conjunction with the priest.[1] This participation of the faithful in the celebration of the Eucharistic Sacrifice is now made expressly prominent, when it is said in the plural: "We offer", and this is frequently the case in the Canon. — But why just at the offering of the Chalice is the cooperation of the faithful expressed? The reason for it we find usually in the incident where by the mingling of the water with the wine in the Chalice, the union of the faithful with Christ in the Communion of Sacrifice has just been symbolically represented, and this union is, therefore, now suitably expressed in the offering of the Chalice. It is also affirmed, that the plural *offerimus* — "we offer", refers to the priest and deacon, who in Solemn High Masses offers the Chalice with the celebrant and recites the prayer with him.[2]

---

cratus fuerit, suavissime exspirat (Bona, Rer. lit. 1. 2, c. 9, § 5). It is only the chalice changed into Christ's Blood that is truly an odor suavitatis (ὀσμὴ εὐωδίας).

[1] St. Cyprian says, that the Christians assemble in common with the brethren and celebrate with the priest of God the Divine Sacrifice (in unum cum fratribus convenimus et *sacrificia divina cum Dei sacerdote celebramus*. — Cfr. De Orat. domin. c. 4). Already the apostle (1 Cor. 10, 16) writes: "The chalice of benediction which we bless," that is, consecrate; in this the faithful are included, who assist at the Sacrifice, and, by the Amen they say, make the prayers of the priest, as it were, their own.

[2] The deacon is at the same time the representative of the people and the consecrated assistant of the priest; in the first quality, he brings to the priest the matter of the Sacrifice; in the second, he supports the priest in the oblation of the chalice and assists him, after the completion of the Sacrifice, in the distribution of the sacrificial food, so that the last function has its foundation in the first (Scheeben III, 607). — Paratus debet esse diaconus progredi cum sacerdote ad sacrificium altaris, ad martyrium, ad evangelizandum. Experire certe utrum idoneum ministrum elegeris, cui commisisti Dominici (corporis et) sanguinis consecrationem — non ad conficiendum, sed ad assistendum. Quia sicut secretarius altaris particeps

We offer the Chalice "for our salvation and for that of the whole world." Holy Mass is, in the first place, a means of grace and salvation for the children of the Church, who most of all receive in bountiful measure of the fruit of the Sacrifice. But they who do not belong to the communion of the Church, are by no means entirely excluded from the blessing of the Sacrifice. The Church prays and offers that all may be saved, and may attain unto the knowledge of the truth. Countless blessings daily flow from the altar and diffuse themselves over the vast expanse of the earth. In the Mass, as on the Cross, Christ is, moreover, "the propitiation for our sins, and not for our sins only, but for those also of the whole world" (1 John 2, 2). If this "sacrifice for sin" were no longer left us, what else would remain for the world "but a certain dreadful expectation of judgment, and the rage of a fire which shall consume the adversaries?" (Heb. 10, 27.) Although the Lord sees that "great as is the wickedness of men on the earth, and that all the thought of their heart is bent upon evil at all times," yet He no longer says: "I will destroy man, whom I have created, from the face of the earth" (Gen. 6, 5—7); for He promised, that no flood should henceforth come to destroy all flesh, and that He would no more curse the earth on account of man (Gen. 9, 15). But why? Because the Lord God "scents the sweet savor of the Sacrifice" (Gen. 8, 21), that is offered daily on thousands and thousands of altars "for the salvation of the world."[1] Unceasingly does the Church offer "Christ's Sacrifice from the rising to the setting of the sun, every day and at every hour, without interruption and without end. As the sun moves around the earth, and as he advances in his course, shedding light and life, so also in the same round with him daily travels the Holy Sacrifice of the Mass, diffusing around the earth as it is offered up spiritual life in the Church and in its members. At the morning's dawn, priests ascend the altar to offer the Holy Sacrifice, hour after hour other priests succeed them and to these others still in every country wherein the Church has followers, and the offering of Sacrifice goes on until the daily cycle is completed and to the last link is joined the first in the sacrificial chain and the perpetual Sacrifice continues anew. This is the true eternal fire that is never extinguished, the sacrificial fire which burns day and night in the sanctuary in honor of the Almighty. This is the eternal Highpriesthood, the perpetually offered Sacrifice of the Highpriest. Without ceasing does it go up to Heaven, and without ceasing does God come down to the altar to become present in the Sacrament for our sakes, that

---

est confectionis Eucharistiae cum sacerdote; non quia sumat vel conficiat nec quod hoc sine eo non possit fieri, sed *quia celebrius et in majori reverentia conficitur corpus Domini cum praesentia, ministerio et testimonio illius* (Petr. Cantor. Verbum abbreviat. c. 60).

[1] Odor suavitatis (= odor suavissimus) is a figurative expression, often occurring in the Old Testament. "To ascend as a pleasing odor" is to say, that God takes pleasure in the offering and graciously receives it.

we all and each one in particular may be partakers of this Sacrifice, and with it and in it of the whole plenitude of grace. Unceasingly does the Holy Sacrifice of the Mass fasten an eternally new bond between heaven and earth, between God and man. Truly the Holy Sacrifice of the Mass is a worship of God, such as He is deserving of, a divinely ordained, true and perfect divine service of adoration and subjection to God, of contrition and reconciliation, of praise and thanksgiving, and of the glorification of the Saviour invisibly and yet visibly enthroned among us on the altar; a divine service ever renewed and continued to the end of the world, when He shall come again in judgment amid the clouds of heaven with power and majesty" (Geissel).

49. The Self-offering of the Priest and Faithful.

1. Bread and wine are now on the altar, set apart from profane use and dedicated to the service of the Sacrifice; soon their substance will disappear, and under their appearances Christ's Body and Blood will be offered. In union with this divine Sacrifice, we should offer ourselves with all that we are and have. Where Christ, the Head, offers Himself, there the members of His mystical Body must also be offered together with Him. Thus the Church prays, that God would sanctify not only the elements of bread and wine just offered, but that He would also, by the Eucharistic Sacrifice, make us wholly worthy to be presented to Him as an eternal sacrificial gift.[1] This self-offering of the Christian people, united to Christ's Sacrifice, has indeed been already symbolically effected in the previous offering of the wine mixed with water; but now the self-offering is to be made especially and expressly for the purpose of awakening and enlivening the more in the heart the sentiments of self-sacrifice. On this disposition the worthiness of the self-offering principally here depends: it imparts, first of all, to the offering of ourselves true value and the proper consecration, making of it an act of virtue pleasing to God and rich in blessing for ourselves. — This interior sentiment of prayer and of self-sacrifice is also a necessary requisite, then, to fit us to offer in a proper manner the Sacrifice of the Altar. For God favorably receives the Sacrifice from our hands and for our salvation, only when we present ourselves in the sanctuary, animated with pious and devout sentiments.

2. Therefore, the priest now in the name of all the faithful offering with him recites the following prayer of offering, during which in sentiments of humble compunction he makes a moderate inclination of the body, and, to express fervent supplication, he supports his joined hands on the altar.

---

[1] Sanctifica, quaesumus Domine Deus noster, per tui sancti nominis invocationem hujus oblationis hostiam, et *per eam nosmetipsos tibi perfice munus aeternum* (Secreta in festo ss. Trinit.).

In spiritu humilitatis et in animo contrito suscipiamur a te, Domine; et sic fiat sacrificium nostrum in conspectu tuo hodie, ut placeat tibi, Domine Deus.	O Lord, accept us, animated with a spirit of humility and contrition of heart; and grant that the Sacrifice we offer in Thy sight, this day, may be pleasing to Thee, O Lord God.

In order perfectly to appreciate the full sense of these words, and to recite them in the proper spirit, we should remember by whom and in what place they were spoken for the first time. They are taken from a longer, humble, penitential prayer, recited by the three young men in the Babylonian furnace. Since, faithful to God's law, they would not adore the statue of the king, they were cast into a furnace heated seven-fold. Praising God, they walked about in the flames which did them not the least harm. And because they were prevented from offering exterior legal sacrifices, they offer themselves as a propitiatory sacrifice for their sins and for those of their people, in order to obtain mercy. "In a contrite heart and humble spirit let us be accepted (*in animo contrito et spiritu humilitatis suscipiamur*); so let our sacrifice be made in Thy sight this day, that it may please Thee (*sic fiat sacrificium nostrum in conspectu tuo hodie, ut placeat tibi*)" (Dan. 3, 39—40). In similar words, the celebrant here prays that the Lord would graciously receive him and the faithful people, for the sake of their humble, penitential sentiments, as a spiritual sacrifice; and if so accepted, then the Eucharistic Sacrifice, when offered by them, in the sight of God, with these dispositions will be such as God will behold and accept with pleasure from their hands.

The three young men were ready to offer their lives cheerfully in sacrifice to God by a bloody martyrdom; after their example we should present ourselves to God to suffer a life of perpetual sacrifice and an unbloody martyrdom. "As gold in the furnace He hath proved them and as a victim of a holocaust He hath received them" (Wis. 3, 6). Thus should we also, filled with humility and compunction, offer ourselves to God as a holocaust in the furnace of suffering and tribulation, of persecution and temptations. A sacrifice to God is an afflicted spirit; a contrite and humbled heart He does not despise (Ps. 50, 19). Yes, a heart penetrated with penitential love and sorrow, a mind bowed down with compunction will always be favorably received and accepted by the Lord. It is the best disposition that we should bring with us to the altar. When the Lord breathed forth His spirit amid the darkness that enshrouded Mount Calvary, many of the beholders were seized with such fear and sorrow, that they returned to their homes striking their breast (Luke 23, 48). Should not we also be penetrated with regret and contrition, with a penitential sorrow, as often as we celebrate in the Mass the remembrance of Christ's bloody death? "During this holy

function," writes St. Gregory the Great,[1] "we must offer ourselves
with compunction of heart as a sacrifice; for when we commemorate
the mystery of the passion of our Lord, we must imitate that which
we celebrate. The Mass will be a sacrifice for us to God, when we
have made an offering of ourselves. But we should, moreover, after
retirement from prayer, endeavor as far as we are able with God's
assistance, to keep our mind in recollection and renewed strength,
so that passing thoughts may not distract it, nor vain joy find its
way into the heart, and that thus our soul may not, by carelessness
and fickleness, again lose the spirit of compunction it has acquired."
Our entire life should be a cheerful, uninterrupted offertory. We
should present ourselves in body and soul[2] as a living sacrifice, holy,
pleasing to God (Rom. 12, 1). "All the prayers and acts of divine
worship, all the charitable and benevolent works, all the practices
of mortification and penance, all the labor and fatigue, all the trials
and sufferings of her militant children; all the pains and torments,
all the patience and longing of her children suffering in the other
world; all the virtues and merits, all the holiness and glory of her
children already in heaven; the fruitful sweat of the Apostles, the
vivifying blood of the martyrs, the devout tears of the anchorets, the
chaste, loving sighs of the virgins, the great deeds and still greater
fortitude of all the saints, — all these the Church places on her
Divine Victim, all these she pours into the chalice of His holy sacrificial Blood" (Laurent).

The Holy Mass is the great heart of the whole body of the
Church: whatever the Church, with her members, believes and hopes
and loves and suffers and cares and prays for, all this she collects in
Holy Mass into the common heart, and in and with the selfsame
Sacrifice she carries it up to the throne of God. Whatever moves
and affects the soul in joy and sorrow, in prosperity and adversity, in
distress and death — we place upon the altar during the Holy Sacrifice of the Mass, we place it directly upon the Heart of our Redeemer
who is present, and we are sure of consolation and relief. Yes, all
the children of the Church should unite in the offering, all the faithful should be incorporated into and offered along with the one, great
and eternal Sacrifice. To all the events in the life of her children
the Church would, by this Sacrifice, impart consecration, and there-

---

[1] Dial. IV, c. 59.

[2] Quid, fratres, nos offerimus aut quid retribuimus Domino pro omnibus quae
retribuit nobis? Christus pro nobis obtulit hostiam pretiosiorem quam habuit,
nimirum qua pretiosior esse non potuit — et nos ergo faciamus quod possumus,
optimum quod habemus offerentes, quod sumus utique *nosmetipsi.* Ille seipsum
obtulit: tu quis es qui teipsum offerre cuncteris? Quis mihi tribuat, ut oblationem
meam dignetur majestas tanta suscipere? Duo minuta habeo, Domine, corpus et
animam dico: utinam haec tibi perfecte possim in sacrificium laudis offerre! Bonum enim mihi longeque gloriosius atque utilius est, ut tibi magis offerar, quam ut
deserar mihi ipsi. Nam ad meipsum anima mea conturbatur, in te vero exsultabit
spiritus meus, si tibi veraciter offeratur (S. Bernard. De Purific. B. M. serm. 3, n. 3).

by increase the happiness of her children, alleviate their distress, bless and sanctify their whole life and their death, so that at all times they may live unto the Lord and die in the Lord (Rom. 14, 8).[1]

50. The Oblation Invocation.[2]

The so-called Invocation,[3] that is, the prayer that, by the operation of the Holy Ghost, the Eucharistic Sacrificial gifts may be transubstantiated, is found in all liturgies. But in the Greek and in the Oriental it follows the act of Consecration; in the Roman it has its place among the oblation prayers, which precede the Consecration. Simple, yet expressive and majestic, are the ceremonies and words of this Invocation, that is, of the supplication that the Holy Ghost would deign to bless and change the sacrificial elements. — Just before, at the offering of himself, the priest took a posture full of humility; but now he again raises his person and lifts up his head, and in an erect posture he solemnly invokes the Holy Ghost, whilst looking heavenward, raising, extending, and then immediately joining his hands before his breast, and at the word *benedic* (bless), making at the same time the Sign of the Cross over the chalice and Host.[4] While this ceremony symbolically represents the act of blessing implored of the Holy Ghost and consecrates the gifts, the raising of the eyes and the motion of the hands denote longing and desire for the descent of the Holy Ghost from on high, and for His benediction.

Veni Sanctificator, omnipotens aeterne Deus, et bene†dic hoc sacrificium tuo sancto nomini praeparatum.

Come, the Sanctifier, O Almighty and eternal God, and bless† this sacrifice, prepared for the glory of Thy holy name.

That this Invocation is directed to the Holy Ghost[5] is beyond doubt.[6] He is called Sanctificator (the Sanctifier) in the language

---

[1] Cf. Geissel, Schriften und Reden I, 461 etc.

[2] Cf. Hoppe, Die Epiklesis S. 248—273. — Franz, Die eucharistische Wandlung II, 187 etc.

[3] By the word ἐπίκλησις (from ἐπικαλέω) = invocation, a liturgical prayer is designated, which implores the consecration of the sacrificial elements and the imparting of the sacrificial fruits by the Holy Ghost, or at least through the Holy Ghost.

[4] In celebratione quisque calicem et oblata non circulo aut digitorum vacillatione, ut quidam faciunt, sed junctis et extensis digitis cruce signet sicque benedicat (Pontif. Roman, Ordo ad Synodum).

[5] Mitte, Domine, quaesumus, *Spiritum Sanctum*, qui et haec munera praesentia nostra *tuum* nobis *efficiat sacramentum*, et ad hoc percipiendum nostra corda purificet (Sacrament. Leonian.).

[6] In the Mozarabic Missal this prayer is as follows: Veni *sancte* Spiritus sanctificator: *sanctifica* hoc sacrificium de manibus meis tibi praeparatum (Migne 85, 113). In the sacramentary manuscripts of the Middle Age it is, for instance, given as follows: Veni sanctificator omnium, S. Spiritus, et sanctifica hoc praesens sacrificium ab indignis manibus praeparatum et descende in hanc hostiam invisibiliter, sicut in patrum hostias visibiliter descendisti.

of the Church to distinguish Him from the Father and the Son, because and inasmuch as the imparting of all sanctifying graces and charismatical gifts belongs and is ascribed to Him. — From this prayer it is clearly evident that up to the present the Sacrifice has been but "prepared". For its object there is assigned the glorification of the divine "name", that is, the acknowledgment and the praise of the infinite majesty and perfection of God. Only by honoring and adoring God do we obtain His gifts and graces; only inasmuch as we seek God's honor and glory, do we secure our well-being and salvation. — Of the Sacrifice it is here especially said, that it is prepared in order to glorify and magnify among the nations the "name" of the Holy Ghost; for the Holy Ghost, with the Father and the Son, is one and the same "almighty, eternal God," to whom alone sacrifice is due. — The concluding words implore the blessing of the Holy Ghost over the gifts of bread and wine. To understand this petition, three questions must be answered: What does *benedicere* (to bless) in general mean? What blessing is here asked? Why is this blessing expected only from the Holy Ghost?

Benedicere properly means to speak well, to say what is good. This can be done in many ways: if one already possesses the good that is said of him, then *benedicere* is to exalt, to magnify, to praise, to glorify the possessor; if a person (or thing) does not as yet possess the good, but if the speaker by his words wishes to procure it for him or to give it to him, then *benedicere* means speaking well for some one, wishing him something good, blessing him. In this we must especially distinguish as to the one who speaks the words of blessing. The blessing word of God is efficacious and all-powerful, it is an actual benefit and infallibly imparts good to the creature. — The liturgical blessing of the Church also is never without fruit, but it is always a "good wish imparting sanctification and good gifts;"[1] for Christ has commissioned her with full power to bless. — Finally, the simple faithful also may bless, that is, impart good by desire and prayer,[2] but this blessing is evidently not always crowned with success.[3]

---

[1] Benedictio est sanctificationis et gratiarum *votiva collatio* (S. Ambros. De benedict. patr. c. 2).

[2] Dividi solet benedictio etiam in ecclesiasticam et laicam. *Ecclesiastica* vim habet ex meritis et intercessione Ecclesiae, et ex institutione ejusdem Ecclesiae competit solum ministris sacris, videlicet episcopis vel aliis sacerdotibus. — Benedictio vero *laica* vim habet ex merito personali eam conferentis: unde peti solet benedictio a viris sanctis vel etiam fundatur in auctoritate naturali, sicut ea quae confertur a parentibus suis filiis et utraque dici solet benedictio *privata*, quatenus confertur privata auctoritate; e contra benedictio ecclesiastica dicitur *publica*, quatenus confertur publica Ecclesiae auctoritate (Quarti, De bened. t. 1, s. 1, d. 2).

[3] Benedicere est *bonum dicere*. Contingit autem bonum dicere *tripliciter*. Uno modo *enuntiando*, puta cum quis bonum alterius laudat. — Alio modo *imperando*, et sic benedicere per auctoritatem est proprium Dei, cujus imperio bonum ad creaturas derivatur; ministerium autem pertinet ad ministros Dei, qui nomen Domini super populum invocant. — Tertio benedicit quis *optando*, et secundum hoc

In this place there is question especially of the blessing of consecration, which is to be effected by the descent of the Holy Spirit. No higher blessing can assuredly be imparted to the gifts prepared, than that they be consecrated, that is, changed into the Body and Blood of Christ by the almighty power of the Holy Ghost. The material elements of the Sacrifice receive the most perfect blessing imaginable, in that they become Christ's Body and Blood offered in sacrifice, which again on their part are sources of blessing, that is, of life and salvation to us.[1] It is for the gracious presence of the Divine Victim and for the plenitude of blessing flowing from His wounds — that the priest prays, while with the Sign of the Cross he blesses and sanctifies the gifts on the altar. Since he implores of the Holy Spirit the miracle of the Eucharistic Consecration, he invokes the Holy Ghost as the "almighty, eternal God" who, by reason of His unlimited power, can bestow and impart every blessing.

Why, finally, is the third Person of the Deity — the Holy Ghost — invoked, to change the material elements by His almighty blessing into heavenly sacrificial gifts? The proximate reason lies in the analogy which the Consecration bears to the Incarnation. The great similarity and manifold relation between the accomplishment of the Eucharist on the altar and the mystery of the Incarnation of the Son of God in the bosom of the Immaculate Virgin Mary are often commented on by the Fathers, and are expressed also in the liturgy.[2] — The Incarnation is, in a manner, renewed and enlarged in the Eucharistic Consecration — and that at all times as well as in numberless places.[3] In like manner and for the same reason is it that the miracles of the Incarnation and Consecration are ascribed to the efficacy of the Holy Ghost.[4] This happens because both mysteries,

benedicere est bonum alicui velle et quasi bonum pro aliquo precari (S. Thom. in Epist. ad Rom. c. 12, lect. 3).

[1] The Eucharist is blessing (benedictio, εὐλογία) in its highest meaning.

[2] Thus, for example, on the feast of Corpus Christi the Christmas Preface and the concluding stanza Jesu, tibi sit gloria — Qui natus es de virgine are prescribed. Altari tuo, Domine, superposita munera Spiritus Sanctus assumat, qui hodie beatae Mariae viscera splendoribus suae virtutis replevit (Sacr. Gregor.).

[3] St. Chrysostom compares (De beato Philog. hom. 6) altar and crib, remarking that on them the Body of Christ reposes no longer wrapped in swaddling bands, but wholly reclothed by the Holy Ghost (πνεύματι πανταχόθεν ἁγίω περιστελλόμενον). — An instrument customary in the Greek liturgy and known by the name of star (ἀστήρ, ἀστερίσκος) also reminds us of the Incarnation. It consists of two intersecting arcs turned downwards. Assuredly the asterisk serves, in the first place, as a protecting cover for the Eucharistic Bread, that — especially after the Consecration — it may not be touched by the velum spread over it; at the same time it symbolizes by its appearance the star that stood over the place where the Child Jesus lay. When, therefore, the priest has incensed the asterisk, and placed it on the discus under the veil, he says: καὶ ἐλθὼν ὁ ἀστὴρ ἔστη ἐπάνω οὗ ἦν τὸ παιδίον (et veniens stella adstitit ubi erat puer).

[4] Quando congruentius quam ad consecrandum sacrificium corporis Christi sancta Ecclesia (quae corpus est Christi) *Spiritus sancti* deposcat *adventum*, quae ipsum caput suum secundum carnem de Spiritu sancto noverit natum? (S. Fulgent. Ad Monim. 1. 2, c. 10.)

being works of divine favor and love, as well as works full of infinite purity and holiness, have a special resemblance to the peculiar character of the Holy Ghost, who is personal love and sanctity.[1] Therefore, although in reality all the three Divine Persons[2] accomplish the act of Consecration, yet it is most frequently ascribed to the power of the Holy Ghost.[3] As it is said in the Creed, that the Son of God "became incarnate by the Holy Ghost, of the Virgin Mary," we also acknowledge that the Holy Ghost, by His creative power as "Lord and Dispenser of life," changes the inanimate elements of bread and wine into Christ's Body and Blood. "How shall this be done," says the holy Virgin, "because I know not man?" The Archangel Gabriel, answering, said to her: "The Holy Ghost shall come upon thee, and the power of the Most High shall overshadow thee." "And now you ask: How shall the bread become the Body of Christ, and the wine, mingled with water, become the Blood of Christ? And I also answer you: The Holy Ghost shall overshadow each and shall effect that which is beyond language and conception."[4] "We invoke our merciful God, that He would send down the Holy Ghost upon the gifts before us, we invoke Him that He change the bread into the Body of Christ and the wine into the Blood of Christ. Whatever the Holy Ghost but touches is sanctified and changed. That which lies on the altar as an offering is holy after it has received the descent of the Holy Ghost."[5] — "You must believe that which was announced is now done by the fire of the Holy Ghost (*per ignem divini Spiritus id effectum quod annuntiatum est credas*): for what you receive is the Body of that heavenly bread and the Blood of that holy vine. When Christ gave the consecrated bread and the consecrated wine to His disciples, He said: 'This is My Body! This is My Blood!' Let us, therefore, — I beseech you — accept the word of Him whom we have (heretofore in other in-

---

[1] Opus incarnationis manifestativum est divinae *bonitatis* et *caritatis:* sed hoc appropriatur Spiritui sancto. . . In incarnatione fuit copiosissima *divinae bonitatis effusio* (S. Bonav. III, dist. 4, a. 1, q. 1). — Quoniam *liberalitas* Spiritui Sancto appropriatur et *sanctificatio Virginis*, in qua peracta fuit Verbi conceptio, hinc est, quod licet opus illud sit a tota Trinitate, per *appropriationem* tamen dicitur Virgo concepisse de Spiritu sancto (S. Bonav. Brevil. IV, c. 3).

[2] Sanctifica, quaesumus, *Domine Deus noster*, per *Unigeniti tui* virtutem hujus oblationis hostiam, et cooperante *Spiritu sancto*, per eam nosmetipsos tibi perfice munus aeternum (Sacram. Gregor.).

[3] The golden or silver vessel for the preservation of the Holy of Holies had often, in ancient Christian times, the form of a dove, and was, therefore, called columba, περιστερά, περιστέριον. This dove-like vessel indicated in a realistic manner, that the blessed Body of Christ, concealed therein, was formed by the Holy Ghost (Sanctusque columbae — Spiritus in specie Christum vestivit honore — Sedulius), and was, at the same time, a symbol of Christ (Tu mihi, Christe, *columba potens* — Sanguine pasta cui cedit avis — the bird nourished with blood [eagle] is a symbol of Satan. — Prudent. Cathem. III, 166).

[4] S. Joan. Damasc. De fide orthod. 1. 4, c. 13.

[5] S. Cyrill. Hieros. Catech. myst. V, n. 7. 19.

stances) believed! Truth hath no commerce with lying (*nescit mendacium Veritas*)!"[1]

The Holy Ghost, consequently, effects the presence of the Body and Blood of Christ, and one that is full of grace — in view of the salvation of the faithful, and inasmuch as they are to draw therefrom the fulness of graces, light, purification, sanctification, strength and fervor. Hence it is certainly not without a deeper signification that almost all the preparatory prayers of the priest for Holy Mass, as given in the Missal and recommended by the Church, invoke the Holy Ghost.[2]

51. The Incensing of the Sacrificial Gifts at Solemn High Mass.

1. The oblation-rites considered up to this point (*in Missa solemni*) are followed most beautifully and symbolically by the incensing,[3] which has been observed in the Roman liturgy in this part of the Mass since the eleventh or twelfth century.[4] This incensing partly differs from the one that took place at the Introit of the Mass, since it has a richer rite and a more significant symbolism. When we go into particulars, we shall see that this exalted and grand ceremony is a poetical development and extension of the preceding Offertory.[5]

First, by virtue of the Sign of the Cross and an impressive prayer for its blessing, the incense is made a Sacramental, that is, something holy, which has not only a holy meaning, but also a wholesome effect. While the priest puts the grains of incense on the live coals, he says:

---

[1] S. Gaudent. Serm. 2.

[2] We mean the concluding prayers of the Preparation: Aures tuae pietatis... Ure igne S. Spiritus, etc. — In the very ancient Oratio s. Ambrosii, that has been likewise inserted in the Missal, among the preparatory prayers of the priest we read: Peto clementiam tuam, Domine, ut descendat super panem tibi sacrificandum plenitudo tuae benedictionis et sanctificatio tuae divinitatis. *Descendat etiam, Domine, illa Sancti Spiritus tui invisibilis incomprehensibilisque majestas* sicut quondam in patrum hostias descendebat, *qui et oblationes nostras Corpus et Sanguinem tuum efficiat* et me indignum sacerdotem doceat tantum tractare mysterium cum cordis puritate. This prayer is originally from St. Anselm (Or. 29).

[3] "Otherwise the incensing follows after the offering of the bread and wine, thus on great feast days at High Mass during the Little Canon it enhances the devotion of the faithful" (Tewtsch Rational Kap. 8, § 4).

[4] Romanus Ordo praecipit, ut incensum semper praecedat Evangelium, cum ad altare sive in ambonem portatur; non autem concedit, ut oblatio in altari thurificetur, quod et Amalarius in prologo libri sui de Officiis Romanos devitare fatetur, *quamvis modo a pluribus, imo paene ab omnibus usurpetur* (Microlog. De eccles. observat. c. 9. — Cfr. Krazer Sect. IV, art. 1, cap. 8, § 251).

[5] Cf. Köln. Pastoralbl. 1875, No. 2. 3.

Per intercessionem beati Michaelis Archangeli stantis a dextris altaris incensi, et omnium electorum suorum, incensum istud dignetur Dominus bene†dicere, et in odorem suavitatis accipere. Per Christum Dominum nostrum. Amen.

By the intercession of blessed Michael the Archangel, standing at the right hand of the Altar of Incense, and of all His elect, may the Lord vouchsafe to bless† this incense, and receive it as an odor of sweetness. Through Christ our Lord. Amen.

The prayers of the Church are always heard. In this instance she prays verbally and with the Sign of the Cross, that the Lord would bless the incense and graciously accept it as a thing dedicated to His service.[1] To obtain a fuller answer to her petition, the Church has recourse to the intercession and mediation of the holy Archangel Michael and all the elect of God. The name of St. Michael[2] occurs in the *Confiteor* and it is again mentioned in this place, because he is at the head of the angelic choirs, and, at the same time, the heavenly protector of the Church on earth. It certainly is proper that the Church at the moment when there is question of a favorable reception of her offering, symbolized by the incense, should invoke her great and powerful protector in heaven, St. Michael, for his assistance and intercession. This is all the more appropriate, because by incensing the sacrificial gifts, she would emulate the celestial choirs in paying homage to the Divine Lamb on the throne; for when the earthly altar of the Church is enveloped in clouds of incense, it is in the eyes of all truly indeed a figure of the heavenly Holy of Holies, which is perpetually fragrant with the prayers of the blessed. — St. Michael stands at the right hand of the altar of incense, that is, he presents before the face of God in golden censers the incense of prayer and sacrifice. On Mount Gargano St. Michael appeared with a censer in his hand, on the spot where a church was to be built; hence it is said of him in the Office of the Church: "The angel stood before the altar of the temple, having a golden censer in his hand;" an unmistakable allusion is here made to the vision of the heavenly altar which St. John saw (Apoc. 8, 3–4).

The sacrificial gifts — the bread and the wine mixed with water

---

[1] Incense is also a material offering made to the Lord in connection with the Eucharistic Sacrifice. This connection of the incensing with our Sacrifice is, according to some, mentioned in Mal. 1, 11, where the Hebrew word, rendered by sacrificatur, is properly = suffitur.

[2] On account of the addition stantis a dextris altaris incensi, which in St. Luke, 1, 11—19 is stated literally of the Archangel Gabriel, there is to be found in many of the more ancient Missals the name of Gabriel instead of Michael; therefore, many liturgists would have this prayer thus changed. But they are mistaken. For well established reasons the Church adheres to the name of Michael; she will here invoke the Archangel Michael. The name of Michael is, consequently, not from oversight or by mistake placed in this benediction prayer, but that of Gabriel would be (cf. S. R. C. 25. Sept. 1705).

— are first incensed by swinging the censer three times in the form of a cross and then three times in the form of a circle over the Host and chalice,[1] while the following prayer is recited:

Incensum istud, a te bene-dictum, ascendat ad te, Domine: et descendat super nos miseri-cordia tua.	May this incense which Thou hast blessed, O Lord, ascend to Thee, and may Thy mercy descend upon us.

The rite and prayer constitute the symbolical representation of the previous offering. The separation and dedication of the sacrificial gifts consists in this, that they are enveloped in a holy atmosphere by the swinging of the censer, containing the fragrant, hallowed incense, in the form of a cross and in the form of a circle. —The grains of incense, consumed in the fire and ascending heavenward as an agreeable sacrificial odor, also symbolically express the petition, that the substance of the material elements, by the fire of the Holy Ghost, be changed into the Divine Victim, under the appearances of bread and wine.[2] — The incense, ascending in clouds and descending upon the faithful and spreading round about, indicates that the Eucharistic Sacrifice may be accepted for the salvation of the faithful and of the whole world.

2. Thus by the incensing a hallowed circle has been drawn around the sacrificial gifts; the incensing is now continued and extended to the Crucifix on the altar, or the Blessed Sacrament, to the relics or images of the saints, to the altar itself, to the celebrant together with his attendants, to the clergy and people present. This incensing rite is but the further representation and development of the oblation ideas which were just before expressed in the prayer: "May this incense which Thou hast blessed, O Lord, ascend to Thee, and may Thy mercy descend upon us."

The burning, fragrant incense, which goes up in light clouds, symbolizes the Eucharistic Sacrifice[3]; and also the oblation prayers

---

[1] Sicut per altare significatur Christus, ita etiam et quidem expressius per Oblata in Christi corpus et sanguinem convertenda, et idcirco sicut in thurifica-tione altaris per odorem, qui inde emanat, significatur effectus gratiae, qui a Christo derivatur ad fideles, ita in hac thurificatione, qua incensantur Oblata, per odorem inde emanantem significatur *effectus uberrimus gratiarum ex sacrificio provenien-tium*, in quo Christus est hostia. Ducitur autem thuribulum primo per modum crucis, quia fructus gratiarum hujus sacrificii incruenti a sacrificio crucis tanquam a fonte proveniunt; secundo etiam ter ducitur circumcirca a dextris et a sinistris, ut indicetur, nos usquequaque adjuvari virtute sacrificii in prosperis et adversis (Quarti, Comment. in Rubr. Miss. p. 2, tit. 7, n. 10).

[2] *Sacrificia*, Domine, tuis oblata conspectibus, *ignis ille divinus absumat*, qui discipulorum Christi Filii tui per Spiritum sanctum corda succendit (Orat. se-cret. fer. VI. p. Pent.).

[3] Eucharistia vocatur *incensum* vel *thymiama*. Primo, quia continet Christi corpus quasi hostiam Deo in ara crucis igne caritatis incensam, quae quasi thymiama odorem suavissimum Deo exhalavit, quo ejus iram placavit eumque hominibus reconciliavit. Secundo, quia Eucharistia conficitur et conditur sacris precibus,

connected therewith, in which the celebrant's interior dispositions and those of the devout participants manifest themselves.[1] This is clearly evinced by the verses of the Psalm which accompany the sacred ceremony of incensing. — By the three swings of the censer (*ductu triplici*) the prayer and sacrifice of adoration are offered to the three Divine Persons, either in the figure of the Crucifix or in the Blessed Sacrament.[2] — Relics and images are incensed,[3] to honor the saints and, at the same time, to express thereby the desire we entertain that our sacrifice and prayers, supported by their powerful intercession, may be favorably received, that is, be made the more pleasing to God and profitable to ourselves. — The clouds of incense which envelop the altar from all sides, indicate that, at the moment of Consecration, it becomes a mystical Mount Calvary, a mysterious mountain of myrrh and hill of frankincense (Cant. 4, 6), from which ascend to heaven the sweetest odor of sacrifice and the most delightful perfume of prayer. — The words said while incensing the Cross and altar are as follows (Ps. 140, 2—4):

Dirigatur, Domine, oratio mea, sicut incensum, in conspectu tuo: elevatio manuum mearum sacrificium vespertinum. Pone, Domine, custodiam ori meo, et ostium circumstantiae labiis meis: ut non declinet cor meum	Let my prayer, O Lord, be directed as incense in Thy sight: and the lifting up of my hands as the evening sacrifice. Set a watch, O Lord, before my mouth, and a door round about my lips. That my heart may not incline

quae sunt thymiama Deo... Denique Eucharistia vocatur *incensum*, quia non tantum repraesentat, sed et re ipsa continet Christum in ara crucis pro nobis incensum, i. e. dolore et amore tostum Deoque sacrificatum (Cornel. a Lapide in Malach. 1, 11).

[1] Thymiama sunt ignitae orationes, suspiria et vota tam sacerdotum quam fidelium, dum Eucharistiam vel consecrant et conficiunt, vel sumunt et manducant (Cornel. a Lapide l. c.).

[2] When the Blessed Sacrament is not exposed, the Cross on the altar forms the principal visible object and is, therefore, the first to be incensed after the offerings; coram exposito it should not be incensed in case it should, according to the custom of some places, be on the altar. The Blessed Sacrament enclosed in the tabernacle is not incensed, but it is adored before and after the incensing of the Crucifix by the genuflection of the celebrant and the ministri.

[3] As a distinction from the Cross on the altar, they are incensed only ductu *duplici* (first, those on the Gospel side, then those on the Epistle side); the inclinations of the head which precede are not made to them, but to the Cross. — Pictures painted on the wall of the altar are not incensed, but only pictures or statues placed on the altar (though even no relics are enclosed in them). — If relics, besides pictures of the saints, are on the altar, the relics only, and not the pictures, are incensed. If at Christmastide the image of the Divine Infant, and at Eastertide that of the Risen Saviour be exposed for public veneration in a prominent place of the altar (principi loco super altari), then it must likewise be incensed after the Cross on the altar *triplici* ductu. (Cfr. S. R. C. 15. Febr. 1873.)

in verba malitiae, ad excusandas excusationes in peccatis.[1]	to evil words, to make excuses in sins.

David, an exile in the wilderness and, therefore, far removed from the sanctuary in Jerusalem, begs of the Lord that He would deign to receive his prayerful pleading, made with uplifted hands, with the same favor as He received the evening incense and food-offering which terminated the daily sacrificial service. But well aware that God willingly answers the prayer of man, only when it proceeds from clean lips and a pure heart, he utters the additional petition: Guard and protect my mouth, close my lips, that I sin not with my tongue — and if through weakness I have sinned in the past, grant by Thy powerful grace, that at least my heart may not swerve from the straight path, and that it may not, for the purpose of self-justification, still add, through excessive pride, excuse to excuse for sin. — Incomparably more profound and abundant is the meaning which these words of the Psalm have in the mouth of the incensing priest. While fragrant clouds of incense envelop the altar and ascend on high, the celebrant implores above all and most fervently that his sacrificial prayers and those of the faithful may, in union with Christ's most holy Sacrifice, ascend direct to the throne of God as an odor equally agreeable and precious, and that they may draw down upon those who are praying and sacrificing the divine good pleasure.[2] To this petition the following additional one is

---

[1] *"Dirigatur, Domine, oratio mea"* = ascendat, coelos penetret, tibi perfecte complaceat — *"sicut incensum"* in Lege dirigebatur ad te et fumando ascendit ac tibi prae ceteris sacrificiis placuit, non propter seipsum, sed ex devotione offerentis — *"in conspectu tuo"* referri potest ad utrumque horum, videl. ut oratio dirigatur in conspectu Dei sicut incensum; dicebatur autem incensum oblatio quae *tota* incendebatur et comburebatur ad Dei honorem, per quod designatur obsequium perfectorum, qui *se totos* mancipant Deo seque *totaliter* abnegant et relinquunt. — *"Elevatio manuum mearum"* = exaltatio desideriorum meorum ad superna, directio operum meorum ad divina, erectio manuum mearum corporalium ex cordis elevatione procedens seu ordinata ad illam virtualiter sit coram te, Domine, *"sacrificium vespertinum"*, quatenus ita placeat tibi, sicut placebat sacrificium vespertinum seu ultimum quolibet die, quoniam videlicet offerebatur agnus ad vesperam, cujus immolatio erat figura immolationis Agni Dei sive Christi in cruce. Unde Christus in cruce pendens dicere poterat: "Elevatio manuum mearum sacrificium vespertinum." —*"Pone, Domine, custodiam ori meo"* = da mihi gratiam custodiendi os meum, ne loquar vel taceam inordinate, sed, dum tempus est loquendi, prudenter atque utiliter loquar; dum vero tempus tacendi affuerit, moderate ac laudabiliter taceam. Pone quoque *"ostium circumstantiae"* = clausuram discretam *"labiis meis"* = ut tum et taliter labia mea ad loquendum aperiam et ad tacendum recludam, quando, quo loco et qualiter oportet aut expedit, ut sim in utroque discretus et fructuosus. *"Non declines"* (Missale: *"ut non declinet"*) = non inclinari seu moveri permittas *"cor meum in verba malitiae"* = ut verba maligna effundat, videl. *"ad excusandas"* = excusatorie proferendas *"excusationes in peccatis"* = mihi objectis et a me perpetratis (Dion. Carthus. Comment. in Ps. 140).

[2] Declinante jam die in vesperum Dominus in cruce animam deposuit recepturus, non amisit invitus. . . Illud ergo est sacrificium vespertinum, passio Domini,

appropriately joined, that the Lord would Himself, by His grace, assist those present to attain and preserve the interior disposition, which, before all, is requisite to render prayer acceptable to God. If prayer is to ascend in a manner agreeable to God as a spiritual odor of sacrifice, then it should proceed from a heart and from lips that are not profaned by worldly and sinful conversation, or that have, at least, by a sincere, humble and contrite confession of sins been purified anew. He who has sinned, must beware of alleging all kinds of pretexts and plausible reasons in excuse and in palliation of his evil conduct. The tongue sins with great facility and in manifold ways: when it speaks at a time in which it should be silent, or when it is silent when it should speak; it sins in the matter and in the manner of its speech. It is very difficult to govern and control perfectly this unruly member, the tongue; hence the priest prays for the assistance of God's grace, to which, however, must be added one's energetic co-operation.

If in the previous act of incensing, the petition for a gracious acceptance of the Sacrifice and of prayer assumed the character of a striking symbolism under the figure of smoking incense, then the additional act (of incensing the celebrant, clergy and people) is principally a symbolic expression of the desire that the divine mercy may sweetly and plentifully descend on all assisting at Holy Mass. Inasmuch as the fragrant clouds of incense penetrate everywhere and from the altar spread throughout the entire house of God, they symbolize the sweet fruit of the Sacrifice and of prayer, that is, the divine good pleasure and complacency, the divine benediction of grace. Grace is dispensed from the Sacrifice, first to the priest and through his ministrations to the faithful. This idea is conveyed in the ceremony of incensing, first, the celebrant, then the clergy and finally the faithful.[1] — At the same time the incensing of persons co-operating in and assisting at the Sacrifice contains, moreover, a lesson and an admonition to them ever to be mindful of their priestly dignity, of their nobility as members of Christ and temples of the Holy Ghost, that by their conduct they may spread everywhere the good odor of piety and godliness. — That this incensing is also to be understood as a mark of honor, as a religious distinction in favor of all those who are incensed, is self-evident from what has been

---

crux Domini, oblatio victimae salutaris, holocaustum acceptum Deo. Illud sacrificium *vespertinum* fecit in resurrectione munus *matutinum*. Oratio ergo pure directa de corde fideli tanquam de ara sancta surgit incensum. Nihil est delectabilius odore Domini: sic oleant omnes qui credunt (S. Aug. Enarr. in Ps. 140, n. 5).

[1] Ritus incensandi eos, qui Missae assistunt in choro et in ecclesia, laudabilis et conveniens est: tum quia laudabile est, moderatum honorem exhibere iis, qui Missae deserviunt et assistunt, tanquam Christi fidelibus; tum ob significationem, quia pie exprimitur, virtutum odorem a Christo derivari ad fideles officio ministrorum secundum illud (2 Cor. 2, 14): "Odorem notitiae suae spargit per nos in omni loco." Et ideo, ut docet S. Thom. (3, q. 83, a. 5 ad 2), undique thurificato altari, per quod Christus designatur, thurificantur omnes per ordinem (Quarti, l. c. tit. 4, sect. 1, dub. 3).

said of the signification and use of incense in general. When the priest returns the censer to the deacon, he says: *Accendat in nobis Dominus ignem sui amoris, et flammam aeternae caritatis. Amen.* — "May the Lord enkindle within us the fire of His love and the flame of eternal charity. Amen." With these words the celebrant finally expresses the desire that Christ the Lord would, by the grace of His Sacrifice, enkindle in all that inflamed and ardent love which is the real and deepest source whence rises aloft the incense-offering of prayer, with a right intention, without being misled by worldly-mindedness, as also with constant devotion; without being carried away by sinful distractions.[1] And this wish the Lord will assuredly fulfil, since He Himself came to bring this pure, heavenly fire upon the earth, and He desires nothing more than that it be kindled in all hearts and that it continue to burn without ever being extinguished (Luke 12, 49).

52. The Washing of the Hands.

1. Before the priest puts on the sacred vestments, he should wash his hands in the sacristy: profound reverence for the divine mysteries, which should be celebrated with perfectly clean hands, dictates this regulation. Already at this washing, which is based mainly on propriety and decorum, the priest prays for a higher purification,[2] that is, for purity of soul as well as of body, that he be found fit worthily to serve the Lord. — After the offering, or the incensing of the sacrificial gifts, there is prescribed another washing of the hands, or rather of the consecrated fingers. This washing dates from the earliest antiquity, and its origin is doubtless traceable not merely to natural reasons of necessity and propriety, but also mainly to motives of higher consideration. After receiving in his hands the offerings of the people, the celebrant found it necessary to cleanse his hands again by washing them, and especially the fingers which were to touch the Most Blessed Sacrament[3]; neverthe-

---

[1] Mystica sunt vas, thus, ignis, quia vase notatur — mens pia, thure preces, igne supernus amor.

[2] Da, Domine, virtutem (strength of grace) manibus meis (to me at the washing of the hands) ad abstergendam *omnem* maculam: ut *sine pollutione mentis et corporis* valeam tibi servire (Missal. Roman.). — Prior Gerhoch of Reichersberg († 1169), explaining Psalm twenty-fifth, remarks that at the washing of the hands in praeparatione divinae servitutis the following prayer should be recited: Largire sensibus nostris, omnipotens Pater, ut sicut *exterius* abluuntur inquinamenta manuum, sic a te mundentur *interius* pollutiones mentium et crescat in nobis augmentum omnium sanctarum virtutum.

[3] Consummata oblatione sacerdos lavat manus, et tergit cum mundissimo linteolo, quod sibi soli ad hoc est deputatum, cavens postea *ne aliud quid tangat* cum digitis, quibus Domini corpus tangendum est (Constit. Hirsaug. s. Gengenbac. l. 1, c. 84 — of the eleventh century). — Aliqua pretiosa tractare non consuevimus nisi manibus ablutis; unde indecens videtur quod ad tantum sacramentum aliquis accedat manibus etiam corporaliter inquinatis (S. Thom. 3, q. 83, a. 5 ad 1).

less, the symbolical signification of this action has ever been and is mainly taken into consideration.[1] The mystical sense of this rite of handwashing is easy to comprehend. The hand has ever been considered as the principal instrument, as the privileged member within which the power and activity of man are concentrated and, therefore, by which, in a certain manner, the whole man is represented.[2] The outward washing of the hands, or rather of the fingertips, consequently, symbolizes the interior purification and cleansing of the whole man from all that sullies the soul and body; the circumstance of washing in reality only the tips of the consecrated fingers (both thumbs and both forefingers), is usually supposed to signify that the officiating priest should cleanse his heart and preserve it undefiled from even the slightest faults, yea, even from the shadow of sin.[3] The Apostolic Constitutions (1. VIII, c. 11) already behold in the handwashing at Mass "a symbol of the purity of souls dedicated to God." St. Cyril of Jerusalem says, that the washing of the hands evidently "designates the purity and blamelessness of our actions."[4] — But who can say: "My heart is clean, I am pure from sin"? (Prov. 20, 9.) For in the sight of God no man living shall be justified (Ps. 142, 2). And yet the priest should appear at the altar for the Holy Sacrifice holy and spotless, pure and blameless, and without blemish in soul or body. Now, the further the holy action proceeds, the nearer the most holy moment of Consecration approaches, the more powerfully does the priest feel his unworthiness, the more his desire for greater purity is increased. As an expression of this sentiment and disposition, he now washes his hands, just as at the beginning of Mass, at the foot of the altar, he cleansed and prepared his soul by a contrite acknowledgment of his guilt.

2. The verses of the Psalm that he recites in the meantime, express clearly the more profound meaning of the liturgical handwashing: the priest openly avows his purpose of celebrating the

---

[1] Profound reverence for the Holy Mysteries made the washing of hands a necessity at this place, so long as the people were accustomed to bring offerings. Lavat sacerdos manus suas more priorum sacerdotum, *ut extersae sint a tactu communium rerum atque terreno pane.* Quae lavatio manus munditiam cordis significat per lacrymas et compunctiones (Amalar. De eccles. off. 1. 3, c. 19). — Quod ideo ab antiquis Patribus decretum fertur, ut pontifex, qui coelestem panem accepturus est, *a terreno pane,* quem jam a laicis accepit, *manus lavando expurget* (Ordo Rom. IV, n. 9).

[2] Ablutio manuum sufficit ad significandam *perfectam* mundationem; cum enim manus sit organum organorum, *omnia opera* attribuuntur *manibus* (S. Thom. 3, q. 83, a. 5 ad 1). — Aristotle writes: ἡ χείρ ὄργανόν ἐστιν ὀργάνων.

[3] Cum sacerdos manus suas alias (i. e. ante Missam) laverit (ut intelligatur, quod sit a gravioribus mundus), nunc solum lavat digitorum extremitates, significans desiderium se purificandi etiam *a culpis levioribus, praecipue si in aliquas esset lapsus post Missam inchoatam,* et hoc spiritu lotio haec adhibetur (De Ponte, De christ. hom. perfect. IV, tr. 2, c. 12, § 1).

[4] Catech. mystag. V, n. 2.

spotless Sacrifice of the Lamb with the utmost possible purity and devotion of heart (Ps. 25, 6—12).

Lavabo inter innocentes manus meas: et circumdabo altare tuum, Domine.	I will wash my hands among the innocent: and I will compass Thine altar, O Lord.
Ut audiam vocem laudis: et enarrem universa mirabilia tua.	That I may hear the voice of praise, and tell of all Thy wondrous works.
Domine, dilexi decorem domus tuae: et locum habitationis gloriae tuae.	O Lord, I have loved the beauty of Thy house, and the place where Thy glory dwelleth.
Ne perdas cum impiis, Deus, animam meam: et cum viris sanguinum vitam meam.	Take not away my soul, O God, with the wicked, nor my life with men of blood.
In quorum manibus iniquitates sunt: dextera eorum repleta est muneribus.	In whose hands are iniquities: their right hand is filled with gifts.
Ego autem in innocentia mea ingressus sum: redime me et miserere mei.	But as for me, I have walked in my innocence: redeem me, and be merciful unto me.
Pes meus stetit in directo: in ecclesiis benedicam te, Domine.	My foot hath stood in the right way: in the churches I will bless Thee, O Lord.
Gloria Patri.	Glory be to the Father, etc.

"Among the innocent I will wash my hands" — how can the priest pray thus? Does he not live in the midst of the world, where by reason of human frailty, carelessness and attachment to earthly things, the lustre of the soul's purity is in a greater or less degree most easily tarnished? Such is, in truth, the case, and a good priest feels convinced of it; but he is also daily intent on destroying within his heart the love of the world, sensuality and all selfishness, in order that his soul may be purified more and more in the fountain of the Precious Blood of Jesus and in the stream of tears of penance and sorrow. Hence he may well protest, that in his innocence he would wash his hands,[1] and thus with pure hands "advance to the altar." Yes, it behooves those hands to be clean which he is to raise in supplication and prayer to God; clean must be the hands

---

[1] Dicat devotus ac dignus Christi sacerdos: *Lavabo*, quando at celebrationem accessurus sum, *inter innocentes*, i. e. cum sanctis ac veris sacerdotibus N. L., quorum est nulli nocere, sed verbis et exemplis cunctis prodesse, *manus meas*, non solum corporales, quibus Christi sacramenta tractabo, sed etiam affectus, cogitationes et opera: istas lavabo in confessione, quoniam teste Scriptura omnia in confessione lavantur (Dion. Carthus. In Ps. 25).

that are to touch, to offer and to dispense the most holy, spotless Victim.[1]

The priest in the midst of the Sacrifice lingers awhile at the altar, "to listen" with blissful joy to the hymns of praise and thanksgiving, that resound from the lips of the faithful — to join in the jubilant choir and "to announce" all the "wonderful ways and works" of divine power and love.

Above all he loves "the pomp and grandeur" of the house of God; his heart clings to the place where the Lord dwells in His Eucharistic glory. He is consumed with zeal for the house of the Lord; he adorns it as worthily and as splendidly as possible, since the King of Glory does not disdain to dwell so silently and so hidden near us and among us. The place where the Saviour has built His throne of grace, is in this wide, dreary world the pleasure-garden and the favorite resort of the priest; thither does he flee to find consolation for his soul, peace and refreshment amid the woes, miseries and turmoil of life. At the foot of the altar there flows for him a bright and clear stream of pure joys; he there spends the most delightful hours, he gathers there the most precious graces.

It is his care to lead a faultless and godly life; he seeks and cultivates an interior and familiar intercourse with the Lord "in the privacy of His tabernacle of grace;" he has nothing in common with a world forgetful of God, and he shuns its ways; hence, abounding in confidence in God, he may beg of the Lord to preserve his "soul" and his "life" from the perdition which befalls all the "godless", who through deceit and violence practise all manner of wickedness, trampling upon justice and the rights of their fellow-men.

"Blameless and without stain" does he endeavor to live; hence he hopes that "deliverance and mercy" may be his share.

Confidence in God is conscious of victory. Assured of being heard, the priest, full of gratitude, exclaims: "My foot hath stood in the direct way," that is, snatched from the abyss of danger and sufferings, I stand on a firm and safe plain, — or I dwell in the direct paths of grace and virtue, leading to God. Both are gifts of the Lord; hence he promises "to extol" His favors and goodness in union with the pious all the days of his life.[2]

---

[1] Quodsi patena et calix non solum esse debent pretiosa, ex auro scilicet vel argento, sed etiam mundissima a quocunque pulvere et macula, eo quod sanctissimum corpus et sanguinem Salvatoris contingant, quanto erit magis rationi consentaneum, sacerdotes habere manus mundas a pravis operibus, linguam a verbis ineptis, et pectus suum a malis desideriis et cogitationibus, et sese purificare ab omni immunditia, etiam valde parva (De Ponte l. c., tr. 2, c. 6, § 1).

[2] Ecce ex psalmo isto sententioso et splendido audivimus, quid ad christianum perfectum pertineat. Si igitur aliquid horum in nobis invenimus, Deo gratias referamus et ad perfectionem feramur. Si autem praedictae perfectiones viri perfecti longe a nobis sunt, ingemiscamus, emendemus atque juxta verbum gloriosi Apostoli cum timore et tremore nostram operemur salutem (Dion. Carthus. [† 1471] Comment. in Ps. 25).

53. The Prayer Suscipe, Sancta Trinitas.

After the washing of the hands, which is performed at the Epistle side,[1] the priest returns to the middle of the altar; full of confidence he raises his eyes to the Crucifix, presently lowering them again; he then bows with humility and reverence, places his joined hands on the altar, and recites in this suppliant posture[2] the following short oblation-prayer, rich in thoughts[3]:

Suscipe, sancta Trinitas, hanc oblationem, quam tibi offerimus ob memoriam passionis, resurrectionis et ascensionis Jesu Christi Domini nostri: et in honorem beatae Mariae semper Virginis, et beati Joannis Baptistae, et sanctorum Apostolorum Petri et Pauli, et istorum, et omnium sanctorum : ut illis proficiat ad honorem, nobis autem ad salutem: et illi pro nobis intercedere dignentur in coelis, quorum memoriam agimus in terris. Per eundem Christum Dominum nostrum. Amen.	Receive, O Holy Trinity, this Oblation, which we offer unto Thee, in memory of the Passion, Resurrection, and Ascension of our Lord Jesus Christ, and in honor of the blessed Mary ever Virgin, of blessed John the Baptist, of the holy Apostles Peter and Paul, of these and of all the Saints; that it may be to their honor and to our salvation: and may they vouchsafe to intercede for us in heaven, whose memory we celebrate on earth. Through the same Christ our Lord. — Amen.

In this prayer the previous oblation of the Host and chalice is not simply repeated or continued, but developed and perfected by the incorporation of new aspects. While the first two Oblation-prayers were directed to the Father, and the Invocation was made to the Holy Ghost, the Church now turns to the Holy Trinity and offers to it the Sacrifice prepared on the altar. Host and chalice are here jointly offered, and that under a new aspect: it contains a short allusion to the relation which the Eucharistic Sacrifice bears to the mysteries of the life of Christ, as well as to the saints of heaven.

The Mass is celebrated in memory (*ob memoriam*) of the entire

---

[1] On this side, during the Middle Age, there was often attached to the altar the Sacrarium (piscina, lavacrum, lavatorium, perfusorium, θάλασσα), which served not only to receive the remains of holy objects become useless, for instance, ashes, and to secure them against desecration, but, at the same time, answered for the washing of the hands of the priest at the Offertory and after Holy Communion.

[2] Quod sacerdos manus interdum jungit et se inclinat, est suppliciter et humiliter orantis, et designat humilitatem et obedientiam Christi, ex qua passus est (S. Thom. 3, q. 83, a. 5 ad 5).

[3] These prayers during the Middle Age were often somewhat differently expressed, and were recited neither in all the churches nor at all Masses. In the Eleventh century they were said, according to Micrologus, non ex aliquo Ordine, sed ex ecclesiastica consuetudine (De eccles. observ. c. 11).

work of the redemption, the principal parts of which are here expressly and prominently set forth, as is also done immediately after the Elevation. In His Passion[1] the immaculate Victim was immolated; in the Resurrection He was glorified, and in the Ascension He was raised to the throne of God, in order to effect our redemption and to perfect our salvation. On the altar not only the sorrowful, but also the glorious mysteries of the life of Christ are represented and renewed. There Christ, who "was dead and now lives eternally" in heaven (Apoc. 1, 18), offers Himself.

It is self-evident that the Sacrifice of the Mass can and may be offered solely to the triune God,[2] and not to the saints; the offering of it, however, serves not merely to render supreme adoration and glory to God, but it also serves as an honorable commemoration (*in honorem*)[3] of the saints, whose memory we celebrate at the altar (*memoriam agimus*). — By an ecclesiastical ordinance, which, indeed, dates back to Apostolic times, frequent mention is made of the saints during the celebration of Mass: by this great honor and distinction are evidently shown them, since they are remembered at the altar, and their names honorably mentioned at the Sacrifice. This we intend to express by saying, that we offer this Sacrifice "in their honor" (*in honorem*). — But the contents of the prayer are not exhausted thereby; for it says further on that the Sacrifice is offered

---

[1] Quoties celebratio corporis et sanguinis Domini agitur, non equidem Christum iterum occidimus, sed mortem ejus in ipsa et per ipsam celebrationem memoramus, estque *ipsa celebratio passionis Christi quaedam commemoratio.* Commemoratio autem passionis Christi ipsam passionem significat. Celebratio igitur corporis et sanguinis Domini passionis Christi est signum (Guitmund, De corp. et sang. Dom. verit. 1. 2).

[2] Omne cujuslibet honorificentiae et *sacrificii* salutaris obsequium et Patri et Filio et Spiritui sancto, h. e. *sanctae Trinitati* ab Ecclesia catholica pariter exhibetur (S. Fulgent. Ad Monim. 1. 2, c. 5).

[3] The latest edition of the Missal, approved by S. R. C., gives the following reading: in *honorem*. And this justly. According to the sense and form these words constitute a parallel clause to the preceding ob memoriam and are afterward paraphrased by the formula: quorum memoriam agimus. In honorem is, therefore, = memoriam venerantes, as in the Canon, and not tautological with the following: ut illis proficiat ad honorem, as is asserted by many following Lebrun, who gives the preference to the other reading in honore and would have it restored. We remark, on the contrary, that both formulas in honorem and in honore in vulgar Latin can have and often do have the same meaning. But in this prayer the reading in *honorem* is, therefore, to be preferred, because it harmonizes more beautifully with the parallel ob *memoriam.* — The sense of this expression in honorem is clearly paraphrased in the Postcommun. in Vigil. omn. Sanctor.: Sacramentis, Domine, et gaudiis optatae celebratis expletis: quaesumus, ut eorum precibus adjuvemur, *quorum recordationibus exhibentur.* — By a decree since issued this controversy has been finally settled (Dub. III). In Ordine Missae post Lavabo in Oratione "Suscipe sancta Trinitas" plures recentiores Rubricistae graves dicunt loco "*in honorem B. M. semper V.*" esse legendum "*in honore B. M.*" etc. — Estne horum sententia sequenda et correctio hoc in loco Missalis facienda? — Ad III. Legendum: in *honorem* (S. R. C. 25. Mai. 1877).

18

"to serve for the honor of the saints." These words, indeed, signify the fruit accruing to the denizens of heaven through the Holy Sacrifice; the Mass being also offered to obtain for the saints the spread of their veneration on earth. We, therefore, offer the Sacrifice and pray that the saints may be ever more and more honored and glorified on earth — *ut illis proficiat ad honorem*.[1] This means that we offer sacrifice and pray, not so much in behalf of the saints, as for ourselves; for it is to our own benefit and advantage, if greater honor be shown to the saints. Inasmuch as we honor and glorify the saints during and through the Holy Sacrifice of the Mass, we advance thereby our own welfare (*nobis ad salutem*), and that in a greater degree, since in this way we obtain for ourselves the powerful intercession of the saints *(illi pro nobis intercedere dignentur in coelis)*. For, since we celebrate upon earth the memory of the citizens of heaven, we would thereby incline them to be more favorably disposed to interest themselves in our behalf with God. — Moreover, the blessed rejoice when we offer Holy Mass to God as a Sacrifice of praise and thanksgiving in their name, that is, when we offer it to God to praise and thank Him for all the benefits, for the grace and the glory they have received from Him.

The saints mentioned by name are the same as in the *Confiteor*, with the exception of the Archangel Michael, who, however, in Solemn High Mass is named immediately before the blessing of the incense. Then is said: *et istorum et omnium Sanctorum* — "and of these and of all the saints." Who are to be understood by "these" (saints)? According to the present context of the prayer, the most simple and natural meaning put, is to refer the demonstrative pronoun (*isti*) to the previously mentioned saints, that is, to regard it as comprising them all, so that the translation should be: "of the saints just mentioned and of all the saints." Formerly, it may have been a word of the rubrics, and may have signified that in this place still other saints may or should be mentioned, for example, those whose relics repose in the altar or are exposed upon it, or whose feast was celebrated, or who were honored as special patrons. But all, that is, the glorification of the saints on earth, by our commemoration and the Sacrifice itself, on the one hand, and our own benefit, by the same Sacrifice and by their intercession, on the other hand, we hope for and obtain "through Christ our Lord," the one Mediator, who crowns the blessed in glory and leads us to felicity.[2]

---

[1] Sancti orationibus nostris non indigent, pro eo quod cum sint perfecte beati, omnia eis ad vota succedunt, sed nos potius eorum orationibus indigemus, quos, cum miseri simus, undique mala multa perturbant. Unde quod in plerisque orationibus continetur, *prosit* videl. vel *proficiat huic sancto* vel *tali* talis *oblatio ad gloriam* vel *honorem*, ita sane debet intelligi, ut ad hoc prosit, quod magis ac magis a fidelibus *glorificetur in terris* aut etiam *honoretur*, licet plerique reputent non indignum, Sanctorum gloriam (sc. accidentalem) usque ad judicium augmentari ac Ecclesiam interim sane posse augmentum glorificationis eorum optare (Innocent. III. Regest. 1, 5, ep. 121).

[2] Quidquid Sanctorum tuorum meritis adhibemus, ad *tuam* laudem recurrit et gloriam, qui in eorum semper es virtute mirabilis (Sacram. Leon.).

54. The Orate Fratres and the Secreta.

1. The purer and the more perfect the disposition, recollection and fervor of the priest and of the faithful present, so much the more acceptably does the Sacrifice rise from their hands to the throne of God. In order to support and inflame each other mutually, the celebrant and the people uniting with him in the Sacrifice keep up reciprocally an active and lively intercourse with each other; hence the priest frequently salutes the people and invites them to pray with him, and the people chime in through their representative, the acolyte or choir, in the priest's prayer. — After the *Suscipe sancta Trinitas* has been concluded, the priest again summons all the faithful to unite with him in common prayer, in order that their common Sacrifice may be so much the more favorably received by God. For the priest kisses the altar, rises, and turning toward the people and with downcast eyes, extending his hands and again joining them, — he says the words: *Orate fratres* — *"Brethren pray"*, in a somewhat audible voice (*voce aliquantulum elata*), so as to be heard by the acolyte and those standing near by; then while again turning to the altar, he continues in silence: *ut meum ac vestrum sacrificium acceptabile fiat apud Deum Patrem omnipotentem* — *"that my sacrifice and yours may be acceptable to God the Father Almighty."* [1]

The priest here addresses all the faithful as *"brethren"*, [2] without distinction of state or sex. By their regeneration in baptism all Christians are children of God and of the Church; they form one great, grand and holy family of God and they are all brethren among

[1] Sacerdos versus ad populum *orare moneat*, conversusque ad altare secretam orationem dicat (Joann. Abrincens. Lib. de offic. eccles.). — Erectus presbyter populum *hortatur ad orandum*, et ipse post finitam Secretam, Praefationem orditur in Canonem (Microl., De eccles. observat. c. 11). — This invitation to prayer was, accordingly, in the eleventh century in general use; the oldest Ordines Romani have for it only the short formula Orate (Ordo II, n. 9) or Orate pro me (Orde VI, n. 10), while in Ordo XIV it runs thus: Orate fratres etc. — Since the words ut meum ac vestrum . . . form only an explanatory clause, that is, assign more minutely the purpose and object of the prayer (Orate), they were formerly (as is still the case, for example, among the Dominicans and Carthusians) not recited at all, and later on merely in silence.

[2] This mode of expression is genuinely Christian. Fratres, ἀδελφοί, viri fratres, brethren, fraternitas, ἀδελφότης, brotherhood — in the mouth of the Apostles and Fathers frequently designate the members of the Church, who by the same sacrament (Baptism) were regenerated and are nourished at the same table (the Eucharist) to life eternal, and are united with one another by the bond of the same faith, the same hope, the same charity (cf. Justin. Mart. Apolog. I, c. 65). — Omnes qui jam de hoc mundo recesserunt sive qui adhuc versantur in mundo sive qui futuri sunt usque ad finem saeculi credentes in Christo *fratres esse veraciter* constat, utpote una baptismatis regeneratione in Christo renatos, unius matris Ecclesiae uberibus educatos, unius fidei vinculo tanquam dulcissimae fraternitatis affinitate connexos, ad unam eandemque coelestis regni haereditatem ab eodem piissimo Patre Deo pia adoptione vocatos. Debemus itaque omnia quae nobis accidunt *fraterno affectu* invicem communicare, i. e. in adversis pariter contristari et in prosperis communiter congratulari (Pseudo-Alcuin c. 18).

each other, unto whom it is granted to say: "Our Father, who art in heaven." "All you are brethren" and "one is your Father who is in heaven" (Matt. 28, 8—9), says our Saviour. As brethren, all Christians should, above all at the Eucharistic Sacrifice and communion, have but one heart and one soul, and pray for and with one another.

In addressing the faithful the priest says: "my Sacrifice and yours." The Eucharist is the Sacrifice of the whole Church; it is not exclusively the priest's Sacrifice, but the property of the faithful also.[1] They partake in a variety of ways and in different degrees in the offering of the Eucharistic Sacrifice, while the priest in their name and for their benefit alone completes the sacrificial action itself.[2] Thus priest and people are at the altar bound together in a communion of sacrifice; and they offer not only the Host and chalice, but themselves also.

In compliance with the invitation of the priest, the acolyte[3] answers in the name of the faithful:

| Suscipiat Dominus sacrificium de manibus tuis ad laudem et gloriam nominis sui, ad utilitatem quoque nostram totiusque Ecclesiae suae sanctae. | May the Lord receive the Sacrifice from thy hands, to the praise and glory of His name, to our benefit, and to that of all His holy Church. |

The priest answers in a low voice: *Amen* — "So be it," whereby he expresses his assent to the devout desires of the faithful.

Although the faithful unite in offering the Holy Sacrifice, still they make mention here only of the act of the celebrant, inasmuch as they pray, that the Lord would favorably receive this Sacrifice "from his hands". This is proper, for it indicates that the priest, as the servant and organ of Christ, alone performs the sacrificial act itself; for only his hands are anointed and consecrated to offer sacri-

---

[1] This idea is often expressed in the Secreta, for example, Suscipe munera populorum tuorum, munera exsultantis Ecclesiae; accepta tibi sit sacratae plebis oblatio; plebis tuae dona sanctifica. The expressions munera, dona, oblationes, fidelium preces cum oblationibus hostiarum etc. in the original and actual sense referred to the material oblations of the people; they are still entirely true, although their signification has changed.

[2] Merito sacerdos ad populum dicit: *meum ac vestrum* sacrificium. Et laudandus esses, mi sacerdos, qui facta reflexione super ejusmodi verba, ex vera humilitate cogitares, esse complures e laicis praesentes, qui majori pietate ac puritate animi Deo offerunt hoc ss. sacrificium, quam tu, minister ordinarius et insignitus charactere sacerdotali. Sed haec in aurem (Sporer, Theolog. sacrament. p. 2, c. 5, sect. 2, § 4, n. 3).

[3] As the rubrics give no precise rule, many rubricists insist that the server should answer at once; others, on the contrary, maintain that he should not do so until the priest has turned to the altar and finished his formula. The Suscipiat is of later origin, and is not recited on Good Friday. Before the revision of the Missal, in the sixteenth century, various formulas were in use (cf. Martene, De antiq. Eccles. ritibus l. 1, c. 4, a. 7).

fice. Only from priestly hands, which exhale the mystical perfume of the chalice and Host, does the Sacrifice ascend agreeably before the face of God.[1]

This prayer expresses the object and purpose of the Sacrifice of the Mass. On the one hand, the Sacrifice is offered for the honor and praise of God, to adore and glorify His infinite majesty; on the other, it is offered to be for us and the whole Church an inexhaustible source of all goods and gifts.[2]

2. The *Orate fratres* here takes the place of the customary *Oremus* and introduces us to the prayer called the *Secreta*. As this was, in ancient times, the only oblation-prayer in the Roman rite, the *Oremus* at the beginning of the Offertory answered as an introductory formula.[3] The prayer received the name of *Secreta* from the method and manner of its recitation, namely, from the circumstance that from time immemorial[4] it has been said in an inaudible voice (*secreto*). Justly, therefore, is *Secreta* translated silent prayer or silent dedicatory prayer.[5]

[1] Ut sacerdos pro causa, pro qua celebrat, exaudiri mereatur, taliter vivere sicque Deo dignissimo familiaris et carus esse conetur, ut mediator idoneus inter Deum et populum esse possit. Est nempe sacerdos inter Deum et populum medius, quoniam ea, quae populi sunt, scil. preces, vota et dona, repraesentat et immolat Deo. Ea quoque, quae Dei sunt, ut puta gratiam et sacramenta, impetrat, dispensat seu tribuit populo. Debet ergo *sacerdos populo in omnibus esse exemplaris* et *Deo dilectus ac familiaris* (Dion. Carthus. Exposit. Miss. art. 4).

[2] Sicut *gloriam divinae potentiae* munera pro Sanctis oblata testantur: sic *nobis effectum*, Domine, *tuae salvationis* impendant (Secr. in festo ss. Mart. Viti, Modesti atque Cresc. 15. Jun.). — Simul Christus semel se in cruce visibiliter obtulit Deo Patri pro nostra reconciliatione, gratia et salute, ita instituit se quotidie in hoc sacramento invisibiliter pro eisdem causis usque in finem saeculi immolandum, consecrandum, tractandum, sumendum, edendum ad maximum et excellentissimum Dei honorem, laudem et gloriam, totiusque suae ad nos dilectionis, pietatis, munificentiae commemorationem et regratiationem, ob multiplices quoque animarum nostrarum profectus, opes et gratias, ineffabiliter grandes et copiosas (Dion. Carthus. Elementat. theolog. prop. 135).

[3] "Before the Secreta some priests say Dominus vobiscum — Oremus, others do not, after saying it before the Offertory and from this on the prayer is continued without interruption" (Tewtsch Rational Kap. 8, § 6).

[4] The former customary denomination (for example, in the Gregorian Sacramentary) Oratio *super oblata* (sc. panem et vinum) only makes its oblation feature more striking, and does not make it apparent whether this prayer was originally (up to the ninth century) recited aloud or in a low tone. In the Ambrosian Ritual it is always said aloud. Beleth writes: Secreta dicitur, quia *secrete* pronuntiatur, cum tamen olim *alta* voce diceretur (Ration. c. 44). — Composito sacrificio sacerdos orationem *sub silentio* recitat (Honor. August. 1. c., c. 40). — "While the Offertory is sung, the priest reads the little Canon, called the silent Mass or the secret of the Mass, which is recited in a low tone until the Preface, especially the prayer Secreta, in the same Canon. The great Canon is likewise considered a low Mass, before the words of Consecration, which are said in perfect silence and with marked secrecy" (Tewtsch Rational Kap. 8, § 2).

[5] *Secreta* ideo nominatur, quia *secreto* (silently) dicitur... Quod omnibus licet simul agere, i. e. gratias referre Deo, hoc acclamatur; quod ad solum sacerdo-

In regard to their construction, number, succession and concluding form, the *Secreta* harmonize perfectly with the Collects which
are said before the Epistle, but as to their contents the *Secreta* are
entirely distinct from them. The Collects and *Secreta* equally are
prayers of petition, but the object prayed for is generally different.

The Sacrifice is not referred to in the prayers of the Collects,
which but ask some special grace respecting the mystery of the day
celebrated; the *Secreta*, on the contrary, are oblation-prayers,
prayers that contain almost the same thoughts as those expressed in
the *Offertorium*. In the whole oblation rite, and hence in the
Secreta also are current throughout two closely connected petitions:
one the petition, that the sacrificial gifts prepared on the altar be
accepted, be blessed, dedicated, be sanctified and consecrated[1]; then
the petition that the abundant and manifold graces of the Sacrifice
be bestowed.[2] Both petitions at one time are united, while at another each is separately presented; frequently God is implored for
reconciliation, so that the propitiatory feature holds a prominent
place therein. — But this does not sufficiently characterize the contents of the *Secreta*. They belong to the changeable parts of the
liturgy of the Mass, that is, they are in touch and in intimate connection with the day's celebration, which has an influence on their
form. The petitions contained in the *Secreta* are inspired not merely respectively to and by the special day's sacrificial celebration, but
they are, moreover, in various ways influenced, suggested, supported
by it and based thereon. Hence in the *Secreta* the spirit and the
sense of the mysteries of the ecclesiastical year are found incorporated
and blended in the most beautiful harmony and in abundant variety
with oblation petitions, which generally concern the same object.
In spite of their great similarity in general the *Secreta* are not uniform, but present in their arrangement and contents the most
attractive and agreeable variety. The fruitful and inexhaustible
eloquence of the heavenly wisdom of the Church is herein clearly
manifested.

The *Secreta* for Whitsunday is as follows:

Munera, quaesumus Domine, oblata sanctifica: et corda nostra sancti Spiritus illustratione emunda.	Sanctify, we beseech Thee, O Lord, these oblations, and purify our hearts by the light of the Holy Ghost.

---

tem pertinet, i. e. immolatio panis et vini, *secreto* agitur (Amalar. De eccles. offic.
l. 3, c. 20). This signification of the name is found throughout the Middle Age
liturgists. Utterly without foundation is the assertion, that the prayers in question
are called Secretae — eo quod super materiam ex fidelium oblationibus *separatam*
et *secretam* recitantur. The name *Arcana* also indicates the low tone.

[1] Secreta dicitur, eo quod *secretam* orationem dat episcopus super oblationem,
ut velit respicere Deus super oblationem propositam, et deputare eam futurae con-
secrationi. Notum est enim, ideo secretam orationem facere super oblatam, ut
possit ex ea fieri corpus Domini (Amalarii Ecloga in Ord. Rom. n. 24).

[2] Sacerdos orat *voce submissa*, petens a Deo effectum et fructum acceptatio-
nemque oblationis exhibitae, benedictionem quoque oblatae materiae, sicut patere
potest consideranti diversas Secretas (Dion. Carthus. Expos. Miss. art. 14).

The *Secreta* for the Feast of Corpus Christi:

Ecclesiae tuae, quaesumus Domine, unitatis et pacis propitius dona concede: quae sub oblatis muneribus mystice designantur.

Mercifully grant Thy Church, O Lord, we beseech Thee, the gifts of unity and peace, which are mystically represented in these offerings.

For the Feast of St. Philip Neri:

Sacrificiis praesentibus, quaesumus Domine, intende placatus: et praesta, ut illo nos igne Spiritus Sanctus inflammet, quo beati Philippi cor mirabiliter penetravit.

We beseech Thee, O Lord, to look favorably on this present Sacrifice and to grant, that the Holy Ghost may inflame us with that fire, wherewith in a wonderful manner He filled the heart of the blessed Philip.

After the priest has recited the *Secreta* reverently in silence, in ending the last prayer, he raises his voice, saying aloud or singing: *per omnia saecula saeculorum* — "world without end." To this majestic conclusion the acolyte or choir answers in the name of the people *Amen*, that is, may what the priest has implored in secret of God be granted and fulfilled in every respect.[1] "When the priest sings, the faithful can assuredly do nothing better than to assent to the priest's words, even if they do not understand them, — than to pray for what the priest prays, even if they do not exactly know what it is. This was done by the first Christians, especially at the time when the liturgy was handed down only by mere vocal tradition, and even for a long time after; they restricted themselves to answering "so be it" after the priest had prayed in silence, thus making an act of faith, really sublime in its simplicity; as if they said: we know not what is best for us, but God knows it; now the Church has prayed, for in her name and by her commission the priest has prayed; the Church has placed on his lips the prayers which he has recited, — we assent thereto, whatsoever they may contain, — we can desire nothing better than what the Church desires, we can say nothing better than what the Church utters, hence 'be it so' — '*Amen*'." — Thus the silent *Secreta* glide over into the loud Preface; what now follows after the Oblation can be considered only as forming "an introduction and a soaring up to the mystery." And is it not a lesson for us "to suffer in silence and to return thanks aloud?"

---

[1] Officium, quod nos dicimus *Offerenda*, ab illo loco inchoatur, ubi sacerdos dicit "*Dominus vobiscum*", et finitur, ubi excelsa voce dicit "*Per omnia saecula saeculorum*". Ideo *excelse* novissimum profertur, ut audiatur a populo et populi responsione (sc. *Amen*) confirmetur oratio (Amalarius, De eccles. offic. 1. 3, c. 19). — Sacerdos excitat attentionem populi dicendo: "Dominus vobiscum" et exspectat assensum dicentium: "Amen". Et ideo etiam in his quae secrete dicuntur, publice praemittit: "Dominus vobiscum" et subjungit: "Per omnia saecula saeculorum" (S. Thom. 3, q. 83, a. 4 ad 6).

The Consecration.

The Eucharistic Celebration advances: we are drawing nigh to the most important part — the sacrificial action proper. The rite thus far explained was already exceedingly grand, holy, full of mystery; yet incomparably more sublime, more glorious and more venerable are the prayers and actions that encompass the Consecration. What now follows, therefore, constitutes the golden centre of the whole of the Mass liturgy. First comes the Preface, which by its animated, elevated and grand soaring forms a worthy transition and introduction to the Canon, that is, to the innermost and mysterious sanctuary of the liturgical Sacrificial Celebration.

55. The Preface. [1]

Holy Scripture informs us that Jesus Christ "gave thanks" to His Heavenly Father before consecrating the bread and wine, that is, before He changed them into His Body and Blood. Who could fail to understand, even at the first glance, that the Church too herein follows the example of her Divine Lord and Master, from the fact that at the Eucharistic Celebration she places before the act of Consecration the Preface, an incomparably elevated chant of praise and thanksgiving to God? For the Preface bears the closest relation to the Consecration, with which liturgically it forms a whole.[2] As its position indicates and its name signifies,[3] the Preface is the prologue, that is, the introduction to the Canon, the prelude to and preparation for the accomplishment of the mystical action of Sacrifice.

To trace the origin and introduction of the Preface[4] in the

---

[1] Praefatio = the words spoken before a religious action, the introductory words, the proem.

[2] The Sacrament. Gelas. has, not after, but already before the Preface the inscription: Incipit *Canon* actionis. The pronouncing of the words of Consecration — the εὐχαριστεῖν in an eminent sense — forms the crown, the pinnacle and the conclusion of the εὐχαριστία, that is, of the liturgical thanksgiving contained in the Preface.

[3] Haec pars Missae vulgato nomine *Praefatio* dicitur, i. e. *praelocutio ante praecipuam orationem*, sacrorum mysteriorum consummativam et in Canone contentam. Ut enim in principio operis ipsorum auctorum praefationes ponuntur, introductoriae ad totam operis materiam intelligendam, et in orationibus oratorum prooemia sunt et exordia ante causae narrationem, quibus captetur auditorum benevolentia reddanturque attenti ad ea, quae dicturus est orator: ita, si magna licet componere parvis, in hoc divinissimo celebrando sacrificio haec oratio quasi *prologus* quidam est et *praelocutio* sequentis Canonis, captans ipsius Dei in nos benevolentiam. In ea enim praeloquitur sacerdos *gratias* et *laudes Deo*, ut praeparatus hujusmodi laudatione aptius possit ac melius ad consecrandum Christi corpus pervenire (Clichtov. Elucidator. ecclesiast. 1. 3).

[4] In the Mozarabic Missal it is called *inlatio (illatio)*, either ob donorum illationem seu hostiae oblationem (Du Cange), or quia ex verbis fidelium *infert* sacerdos, vere dignum et justum esse, Deo omnipotenti gratias agere, ipsumque laudare et praedicare (Bona). In the old Gallican rite it is inscribed *Contestatio*

sacrificial rite, one must go back to the days of the Apostles; this is evident from the testimony of the holy Fathers, and especially from the most ancient liturgies, not a single one of which can be found without a Preface. The oriental liturgies have had from the beginning until the present time but a single Preface. In the West, on the contrary, the number of Prefaces, even at an early date, increased to such a degree, that before the time of St. Gregory the Great almost every formula of Mass contained a separate Preface.[1] It is probable that St. Gregory himself reduced this immense number to ten. It was under Urban II. (1088 to 1099) that the Preface of our Lady's Masses was added.[2] Therefore, the present eleven Prefaces in the Roman Missal date back to the eleventh century.

According to their text and melody the Prefaces belong to the most solemn, sublime and touching chants of the Church; they are the purest poetry, flowing from the inspiration of the Holy Ghost. The Church is the divinely enlightened proclaimer of the Eternal, she is the Bride of Christ ever in communication with Him, and this communication is a never-ending nuptial celebration in sacrifice and prayer: therefore, speech becomes on her lips a poem, a canticle, having throughout a poetical feature. Amid the chant of angels the Lord came into the world, and He entered on His passion and death when the chant was ended (Matt. 26, 30). This shows how the Church should celebrate her representation of the life and actions of her Lord from beginning to end; her sacred poetry should also be sacred chant.[3] — In explaining the Preface, we distinguish three parts: the introduction, the body and the conclusion. While the introduction always remains the same, the main part or body of the Preface changes according to the feasts and times of the ecclesiastical year.

---

or *Immolatio,* quia in ea sacerdos audita voce populi vel cleri sive ministri asserentis dignum et justum esse Deo gratias agere, *contestatur* veram esse hanc populi assertionem; tum solemni gratiarum actione se et fideles disponit ad tremenda mysteria, quibus Christi corpus *immolatur* (Bona, Rer. lit. 1. 2, c. 10, § 1). Inlatio and Immolatio, in all probability, were originally designations (titles) of the entire central portion of the Mass, which commences with the Preface and includes the sacrificial action.

[1] The Sacram. Leon. contains 267 Prefaces, although those from January to April are wanting; of the Gelasian. but 56 still remain. Also from the time of St. Gregory the Great until the thirteenth century, it was customary to add to the Missal — as a general thing, only in the Appendix — numerous Prefaces. — Albinus (Alcuinus) *Praefationes* etsi non Gregorianas, ecclesiasticae tamen celebritati idoneas, collegit (Microl. c. 60).

[2] According to the statement of a contemporary writer, it was sung for the first time at a Solemn Pontifical Mass by Pope Urban, during a Synod held at Guastalla (1094). As its composer is named at one time Pope Urban II. himself, at another, St. Bruno, founder of the Carthusians. (Cf. P. Tappert, Der hl. Bruno in seinem Leben und Wirken S. 163—166.)

[3] Cf. Jakob, Die Kunst im Dienste der Kirche S. 343—346.

1. The ordinary Preface (*Praefatio communis*) is the one for all Masses to which no special Preface is assigned.

a) The Introduction consists of three Versicles with corresponding Responses.

V. Dominus vobiscum.	V. The Lord be with you.
R. Et cum spiritu tuo.	R. And with thy spirit.
V. Sursum corda.	V. Lift up your hearts.
R. Habemus ad Dominum.	R. We lift them up unto the Lord.
V. Gratias agamus Domino Deo nostro.	V. Let us give thanks unto the Lord our God.
V. Dignum et justum est.	R. It is meet and just.

The usual salutation and invocation of blessing of the *Dominus vobiscum etc.* between priest and people also introduces the Preface. Probably nowhere is this more opportune than here, when the accomplishment of the Holy Mysteries is so near at hand. Priest[1] and faithful at this moment greatly require the help of the Lord and assistance from on high. Only when the heavenly breath of grace pervades the soul sweetly and powerfully, is the soul enabled to rid itself of earthly defilement, to raise itself above the baseness of earth and soar upward, in order to join in the chant of praise of the blessed spirits. Who will give me the wings of the dove, that I may fly and be at rest (Ps. 54, 7) in undisturbed contemplation of the sacrificial mysteries enacted on the altar? God only, from whom every good gift cometh. Recollection of mind and fervor of devotion are gifts of the Lord. — Why does not the priest now turn toward the people, when saluting them? He has after the *Orate fratres*, like Moses on Mount Sinai, entered into the holy cloud,[2] and, therefore, he henceforth communes "face to face" with the Lord; henceforth he has eyes and mind directed only to the altar, and the faithful will behold his countenance again only after the marvels of Consecration and Communion have been consummated.[3]

Upon the salutation, *Dominus vobiscum*, follows the reminder from the priest for the people to raise their hearts,[4] and from the

---

[1] *Dominus vobiscum* — tunc enim praesentia Dei et illuminatio gratiae ejus tanto amplius necessaria est, quanto ea, quae restant, magis ardua sunt (Dion. Carthus. Exposit. Missae art. 14).

[2] Moses was beloved of God and men; the Lord brought him into a cloud (induxit illum *in nubem*) (Ecclus. 45, 1—5).

[3] Quando dicimus "*Pax vobiscum*" sive "*Dominus vobiscum*", quod est salutatio, ad populum sumus versi. Quos salutamus, eis faciem praesentamus, excepto in uno, quod est in praeparatione hymni ante "*Te igitur*". Ibi jam occupati circa altare, ita ut congruentius sit uno modo versos nos esse, quam retro adspicere, ad insinuandam *intentionem devotissimam*, quam habemus in offerendo sacrificio (Amalarius, De eccles. offic. 1. 3, c. 9).

[4] In hoc sacramento et *major devotio* requiritur quam in aliis sacramentis propter hoc quod in hoc sacramento totus Christus continetur, et etiam *communior,*

faithful comes the answer and assurance to the priest that it has been done.[1] At the words *Sursum corda*[2] the priest raises his hands, in order by this gesture to manifest and accentuate the inward soaring of the mind and his desire to give himself wholly to the Lord. By this movement of the hands is expressed the longing for that which is exalted above us, that is, for the heavenly and eternal. Thus the Church complies with the invitation of the Prophet: *Levemus corda nostra cum manibus ad Dominum in coelos* — "Let us raise our hearts together with our hands to the Lord in heaven" (Lam. 3, 41). The hymn of the Church contains a like sentiment: *Mentes manusque tollimus* — "Minds and hands we raise — we bear aloft — to the Lord." To the Saviour who has preceded us to heaven and who is awaiting us on the heavenly throne, we cry out with holy enthusiasm: *Sis meta nostris cordibus*, that is, be Thou, O Jesus, the desire of our hearts, and the object of our longing and striving! — *Sursum corda!* "Lift up your hearts!"[3] The meaning of these words is most comprehensive: they signify that we should withdraw all the faculties of our soul from what is earthly, and consecrate them exclusively to intercourse with God and divine things. For this is, above all, necessary to turn mind and spirit from worldly objects and to close them to distracting thoughts, so as to be immersed with all one's might and attention in holy meditations.[4] If the mind be penetrated with a higher light from above,

---

quia in hoc sacramento requiritur devotio totius populi, pro quo sacrificium offertur et non solum percipientium sacramentum, sicut in aliis sacramentis (S. Thom. 3, q. 83. a. 4 ad 5).

[1] Sicut sacerdos jussit eos sursum corda tenere, sic se habere profitentur (Raban. Maur. De sacr. ordin. c. 19). — Audis quotidie, homo fidelis: *"Sursum cor"*, et quasi contrarium audias, tu mergis in terram cor tuum (S. Aug. Serm. 311, n. 15).

[2] Rightly wrote St. Augustine: Quotidie per universum orbem humanum genus *una paene voce* respondet, *sursum corda se habere* ad Dominum (De vera relig. c. 3).

[3] Audi: "Sursum cor", sed *ad* Dominum, non *contra* Dominum. Omnes superbi sursum cor habent, sed contra Dominum. Si autem vis tu vere sursum cor habere, *ad* Dominum habe. Si enim ad Dominum habueris cor sursum, ipse tenet cor tuum, ne cadat in terram (S. Aug. Serm. 25, n. 2). — Nemo potest cogitare nisi de thesauro suo et quodam *cordis itinere* divitias suas sequi. Si ergo in terra obruuntur, ima petit cor; si autem in coelo reservantur, sursum erit cor. Si ergo volunt facere christiani, quod norunt se etiam profiteri (neque enim hoc omnes qui audiunt noverunt atque utinam non frustra noverint qui noverunt): qui ergo vult cor sursum habere, ibi, ibi ponat quod amat, et in terra positus carne, cum Christo habitet corde, et sicut ecclesiam praecessit caput ejus, sic christianum praecedat cor ejus. Quomodo membra itura sunt quo praecessit caput Christus, sic iterum resurgens iturus est quo nunc praecesserit cor hominis. Eamus ergo hinc ex qua parte possumus; sequetur totum nostrum, quo praecesserit aliquid nostrum. Domus terrena ruinosa est; domus coelestis aeterna est. Quo venire disponimus, ante migremus (S. Aug. Serm. 86, n. 1).

[4] Volens sacerdos populum ad divina mysteria praeparare, excitando eum ad laudem divinam, invitat eundem ad laudandum Altissimum; ideo addit. *Sursum*

then the will also will be incited to devotion. The heart becomes
aglow with holy love of God, and disengages itself from the bonds of
worldly inclinations and desires, that enchain it in the dust; it rouses
itself from its sluggish indolence and tepidity, that it may with holy
ardor soar heavenward with all its powers. "Hearts on high!"[1]
This applies principally to the time of Mass. It, of course, requires
serious effort on our part to raise mind and spirit on high, and keep
them recollected and disengaged from what is earthly and perishable; human frailty and the inconstancy of man being so very great.[2]
To persevere in undisturbed recollection and communion with God,
is possible only to a soul that daily endeavors to divest itself of all
earthly dross and bonds, and labors to attain a permanent direction
upward. Hence the words of the Apostle: "Our conversation is in
heaven" (Phil. 3, 20). What does this imply? That we should
not grovel like worms in the dust, but like the birds in the air we
ought to soar in spirit heavenward; we should not burthen and
oppress our hearts with the thoughts and desires, with the cares and
pleasures of this life, but we should so divest ourselves of the earthly
and of the love of perishable goods, that our soul may aspire with
ease to Heaven with lively hope and ardent desire. "Mind the
things that are above, and seek for what is above" — this is the
wisdom of Christian life. The *Sursum corda*, therefore, admonishes
us, especially at the Sacrifice of the Mass, to have our mind occupied
with heavenly things only and to be intent upon them. "No one
should be present in such a manner, that, although he may say with
the lips: 'We have lifted our hearts to the Lord,' his thoughts are
directed to the cares of this life. We should indeed think of God at
all times; but if this be impossible, on account of human frailty, we
should take it to heart most especially at least during the Holy
Sacrifice."[3]

---

corda! Non enim laudare valemus Deum sincere ac digne, nisi contemplando
divina, ad quod necesse est inferiora et sensibilia ista relinquere, mentisque oculum
divinorum considerationi infigere, et *hoc in praesenti officio summe requiritur,
maxime in hoc loco, quoniam sacramentum istud totaliter divinum et spirituale
ac abditum est* (Dion. Carthus. 1. c.).

[1] Quaedam corda *sursum* sunt, quaedam semetipsa *deorsum* demerserunt.
Deorsum sunt illa corda, quae configurantur huic saeculo; sursum vero sunt illa,
quae conversationem suam habent in coelo. Deorsum sunt, quae terrena sapiunt;
sursum sunt, quae jugiter meditantur coelestia; secundum id ergo, cui per amorem
conjungitur, cor hominis sursum ac deorsum esse judicatur. Et recte extra semetipsum esse dicitur, quando ad exteriora et transitoria haec expetenda dilabitur.
Tunc autem ad semetipsum revertitur, quando ea quae ad suam salutem pertinent
meditatur. Sunt ergo quaedam, quae amando et cogitando cor hominis deorsum
premitur, scissumque per varia dissipatur, — et sunt iterum quaedam, quae amando
et meditando sursum elevatur et ad semetipsum colligitur (Hugo de s. Vict. De
vanitate mundi 1. 2).

[2] Quantis conatibus corda levare necesse est, quae quidem (ut miserabiliter
satis in libro propriae experientiae legimus) et corruptio corporis aggravat et terrena inhabitatio deprimit (S. Bern. in Ascens. Dom. serm. 5, n. 2).

[3] St. Cyril of Jerusalem, Mystag. Catechism n. 4. — Cf. also Denifle, Die
Schriften des sel. Heinrich Seuse I. Bd., 1. Abth. S. 42—44.

St. Martin is a striking example in this respect. The Church says of him in his Office: "With eyes and hands raised toward heaven, he never let his mighty spirit slacken in prayer."[1] His life of constant prayer and attention to the presence of God reached its highest degree of perfection during the celebration of Holy Mass. In a sacristy intended especially for his use, he carefully prepared himself for the divine service: when he afterward approached the altar, he appeared as an angel of the Lord, rapt in devotion and inflamed with love. Once when raising his hands during the Holy Sacrifice, they shone with crimsoned light and appeared adorned with precious jewels. At another time his head was environed with bright rays, as though his spirit had soared heavenward.[2]

The more estranged the soul becomes from frivolity and the distractions of the world, the more she rises above all created things, the more clearly and profoundly also will she perceive that God is the eternal love and the fountain-source of all that is good: she thereby becomes penetrated with a lively sense of grateful praise to Him. To this sentiment the priest gives expression in the words: "Let us give thanks to the Lord God!" At the same time joining his hands before his breast, and when saying "to our God" (*Deo nostro*), he raises his eyes and bows his head reverently toward the Crucifix. The faithful reply in the person of the acolyte: "It is meet and just."[3] Countless and inestimable are the benefits wherewith the Lord has overwhelmed us, and for which we owe Him a debt of gratitude. If the heart be deeply moved with grateful love toward God, it breaks forth spontaneously into an exultant hymn of praise: the most solemn thanksgiving resounds in the jubilant strains of the *Te Deum*. The whole Preface is, consequently, but a magnificent rendition of the words: *Gratias agamus Domino Deo nostro!*

b) The Body of the Preface. The priest standing in a reverential posture, with uplifted hands and elevated heart, continues (on ordinary days) to say or sing the following hymn of praise and thanksgiving:[4]

---

[1] Oculis ac manibus in coelum semper intentus, invictum ab oratione spiritum non relaxabat (Antiph. eccl.).

[2] Cf. Sulpicius Severus, Third Dialogue, chap. 10, and Second Dialogue, chap. 2.

[3] The Versicles of the introductory formula just explained date from apostolic times — proof of this is found in all the ancient liturgies and in the Fathers; for in these we meet the above introductory formula, — and with a considerable degree of agreement in the words employed. St. Cyprian was already acquainted with the name Preface. Quando stamus ad orationem, vigilare et incumbere ad preces toto corde debemus. Cogitatio omnis carnalis et saecularis abscedat nec quidquam tunc animus quam id solum cogitet quod precatur. Ideo et sacerdos ante Orationem (before the Canon) *Praefatione* praemissa parat fratrum mentes dicendo: "*Sursum corda*", ut dum respondet plebs: "*Habemus ad Dominum*", admoneatur, nihil aliud se quam Dominum cogitare debere (S. Cypr. De Orat. dom. c. 31).

[4] Postea (after the Oblation) cantatur Missa a sacerdote, qui postquam loquitur ad populum de elevatione cordis ad Deum exhortaturque eos ad *gratias agendas*

Vere dignum et justum est, aequum et salutare, nos tibi semper et ubique gratias agere: Domine sancte, Pater omnipotens, aeterne Deus: per Christum Dominum nostrum. Per quem majestatem tuam laudant Angeli, adorant Dominationes, tremunt Potestates. Coeli coelorumque Virtutes, ac beata Seraphim, socia exsultatione concelebrant. Cum quibus et nostras voces, ut admitti jubeas deprecamur, supplici confessione dicentes: — —.	It is truly meet and just, right and salutary, that we should always, and in all places, give thanks to Thee, O Holy Lord, Father Almighty, eternal God, through Christ our Lord: by whom the angels praise Thy majesty, the dominations adore it, the powers tremble before it, the heavens and the heavenly virtues, and the blessed seraphim, exultingly celebrate it in common. Together with whom we beseech Thee, that we may be admitted to join our voices in suppliant confession, saying: — —.

The priest resumes the words of the people, — confirms and develops them, inasmuch as he calls special attention to the great importance as well as to the whole extent of the obligation of returning thanks to God: "It is truly meet and just, right and salutary, — that we should always and in all places give thanks to God the Lord."

Four reasons are cited, which here clearly manifest the importance and necessity of gratitude.

a) That we give thanks, is meet — (*dignum*) — with respect to God and ourselves, that is, the practice of giving thanks acknowledges and glorifies the dignity of God, on the one hand; and, on the other, it argues and enhances, at the same time, the dignity of man. For, inasmuch as when we return thanks to God, we acknowledge Him as the source of all good, we glorify His majesty and fatherly love, we magnify His greatness and goodness, that is, we give to God what His dignity demands of us. — This manifestation of our gratitude also contributes to our moral dignity, revealing the beauty and nobility of the soul. Gratitude is the sign of a noble heart, while ingratitude is the mark of a mean soul. Fervent thanksgiving belongs to Christian perfection. The more perfect and devout, the more humble and pure the soul, the more will it be filled with the spirit of gratitude. The saints, when upon earth, never wearied thanking God, and unceasing thanksgiving is their blessed occupation in eternity.

Domino, *laudibus os implet* rogatque ut ipse omnipotens Deus Pater, cui deserviunt coelestes potestates, sua gratia illorum vocibus jubeat humanas associari confessiones, quam deprecationem mox subsequitur laus ex angelicis et humanis cantibus confecta (Raban. Maur. De clericor. institut. 1. 1, c. 33). — Oratione secreta completa, sacerdos *"Vere dignum"* devota mente dulcique voce proferat (Joann. Abrinc. De offic. eccles.).

b) To thank God is but just (*justum*), that is, a claim and a duty of justice (in a wide sense). Gratitude is allied with justice: for it is the will and the endeavor to return and repay, as far as possible, the benefits received. He who possesses strict justice, will also entertain grateful sentiments, that is, he will strive to reward the benefactor. God expressly exacts gratitude from us as a tribute which we owe to Him; frequently and strongly does Holy Writ inculcate this duty of proving ourselves grateful to the Lord our God. "In all things give thanks; for this is the will of God in Christ Jesus" (1 Thess. 5, 18). "Giving thanks always for all things, in the name of our Lord Jesus Christ to God and the Father" (Eph. 5, 20).

c) To thank God is right (*aequum*), that is, it is becoming and proper from reasons of propriety. After considering our relations to God, gratitude appears in the highest degree an act of equity, which performs more than what is required according to strict justice and law. Reflect on the excessive goodness of God toward you and the riches of His mercy, wherewith He daily visits you: is it then requiring too much, that your heart should be inflamed with an ardent, a strong and grateful love, that your lips should overflow with the praises of the Divine goodness which accompanies you in all your ways? What is more proper and right than that, by a grateful return of love and fervent thanksgiving, you repay, as far as you are able, the favors you receive of God, who has no need of your gifts?

d) To thank God, finally, is, moreover, salutary (*salutare*), that is, promotes the temporal and eternal welfare, inasmuch as it enriches the soul with great blessings and precious graces.[1] Gratitude opens to us the treasures of the divine liberality. Inasmuch as we sincerely thank God for benefits received, we draw down new and more special graces upon ourselves. God takes complacency in a grateful heart; nothing shall be wanting to it. Hence gratitude is salutary, profitable and rich in blessings; while ingratitude is a scorching wind that dries up the spring of divine goodness, the dew of heavenly mercy and the streams of grace. "The gifts of grace cannot abound or flow in us, because we are ungrateful to the Giver; and because we do not return them all to the fountain-head. For grace will ever be given him who dutifully returns thanks. Be grateful then for the least, and thou shalt be worthy to receive greater things" (Imit. of Chr. II, 10).

To cultivate a spirit of gratitude toward God is, therefore, a practice "truly meet and just, right and salutary": but how far must we go — what is the extent of this thanksgiving? This is

---

[1] Optima ratio impetrandi a Deo donum perseverantiae et pertingendi ad salutem et beatitudinem, est *jugis gratiarum actio*. Haec enim est inchoatio vitae coelestis, haec est stimulus ad iter hoc in coelum usque jugiter prosequendum; haec est tácita invocatio Dei, quae novam et continuam ab eo gratiam elicit et provocat (Corn. a Lapide, Comment. in Apocal. 7, 12).

made known by the words, that we "should always and in all places"
(*semper et ubique*) give thanks.   There is no time or place in which
we should not from the fulness of our heart say: *Deo gratias!* —
"Thanks be to God!"   Even in the hour of tribulation and in the
night of adversity, even when on the couch of suffering and in a
home of direst poverty, gratitude towards God should never be silent
on our lips or in our heart.[1]   When St. Elizabeth on a cold winter's
night wandered about an outcast and forsaken, she entered a Fran-
ciscan church and had the *Te Deum* sung, to thank the Lord for
the tribulations wherewith He had in His mercy visited her.   Hence
do you also repeat with the Psalmist: "I will praise the Lord at all
times; His praise shall be always in my mouth" (Ps. 33, 2).

The words "O holy Lord, Father Almighty, eternal God" refer
to the first Person of the Deity: they express the majesty and glory
of the Father, and should likewise incite us to fervent thanksgiving.
But are we, poor, frail creatures, able appropriately and adequately
to thank the holy, the almighty and the eternal God?   "Through
Christ our Lord" — answers the Church.   Christ is our mediator:
through Him do all gifts and graces descend upon us "from the
Father of Lights" — and through Him must our gratitude and praise
ascend to God.[2]   This should be done especially during the celebration of Holy Mass: we should place all our grateful sentiments and
prayers in the Eucharistic Chalice, by means of which we can present
to God a thanksgiving, of all the most worthy and meritorious, because it is infinitely perfect.

The Saviour enthroned at the right hand of God is as man the
Head also of all the angelic choirs.   They constitute a part of the
eternal kingdom of God, whose glorious King is Jesus Christ.   The
risen Saviour is exalted above every creature and placed "above
every name that is named not only in this world, but also in the
one to come, — and He hath subjected all things under His feet and
He hath made Him head over all the Church" (Eph. 1, 21—22).
To Him "the angels and powers and virtues are made subject"
(1 Peter 3, 22).

According to the common teaching (founded upon Scripture and
tradition) the angels are divided into nine distinct choirs.[3]   Revela-

---

[1]   Christiani non sumus nisi propter futurum saeculum: nemo praesentia bona
speret, nemo sibi promittat felicitatem mundi, quia christianus est, sed utatur
felicitate praesenti, ut potest, quomodo potest, quando potest, quantum potest.
Cum adest, consolationi Dei gratias agat; cum deest, justitiae Dei gratias agat:
Ubique sit gratus, nunquam ingratus: et Patri consolanti et blandienti gratus sit;
et Patri emendanti et flagellanti et disciplinam danti gratus sit; amat enim ille
semper, sive blandiatur sive minetur (S. Aug. Enarrat, in Ps. 91, n. 1).

[2]   Eodem ordine debet gratiarum actio in Deum recurrere, quo gratiae a Deo
in nos deveniunt, quod quidem est *per Jesum Christum* (S. Thom. In Epist. ad
Rom. c. 1, lect. 5).

[3]   The gradations of the angelic world are principally based on natural perfections, but especially in the varied gifts of grace and offices of the angels. That
among the angels generally there are higher and lower orders, is de fide; that there

tion gives no further particulars as to the peculiar nature or the special offices of the different orders of angels. We can, therefore, entertain only more or less probable opinions or conjectures concerning them.[1] To penetrate more deeply into the wonderful mysteries of the angelic world is reserved for the beatific vision in heaven. Yet already here below — how beautiful and attractive to the eye of faith is that grand, brilliant, angelic world! Like shining stars the angels surround the throne of the Most High; they bask in the rays of the divine glory and contemplate the abyss of the divine essence. Those sublime spirits overflow with light, love and happiness; jubilation, praise and thanksgiving ascend unceasingly from their midst up to the throne of God. The Preface reveals to us but a glimpse of that jubilant kingdom of the angels, for it further on declares: "through whom the angels praise Thy majesty..." The blessed spirits also present their homages to God "through Jesus Christ" — their Head and Mediator.[2] By angels[3] are not here to be understood all the angelic spirits in general, as is otherwise frequently the case when angels are mentioned, but those angels only who belong to the lowest choir. As is evident from what follows, several choirs are to be mentioned by name. The Dominations in a manner annihilate themselves and adore the majesty of the Creator (*adorant Dominationes*), as no mortal is capable of doing. The Powers, those mighty spirits of heaven, tremble in profound humility and reverential awe (*tremunt Potestates*) before the grandeur of the Divine Majesty[4]: "they serve the Lord in fear and sing to Him with

---

are but nine choirs of angels — no more and no less — is not so certain, still it is the teaching of tradition. Holy Scripture mentions nine choirs of angels, and since the ninth century we meet with the enumeration of them in the most ancient liturgies and in the Fathers. According to St. Gregory the Great (Hom. 34 in Evangel.) their order is: 1. Angeli (Angels); 2. Archangeli (Archangels); 3. Virtutes (Virtues); 4. Potestates (Powers); 5. Principatus (Principalities); 6. Dominationes (Dominations); 7. Throni (Thrones); 8. Cherubim (Cherubim); 9. Seraphim (Seraphim). The two lowest and the three highest are enumerated in the same order by all, while the four middle ones are differently grouped by others. In the Prefaces all the choirs — with the exception of the Principatus — are mentioned by name. In the Ordo commendat. animae likewise the eight choirs are mentioned, in which, however, the Virtutes are passed over. (Cf. Petavius, De Angelis l. 2, c. 3—5).

[1] Quid inter se distent... dicant qui possunt, si tamen possunt probare, quod dicunt; ego me ista ignorare confiteor (S. Aug. Enchirid. c. 58).

[2] Et "ipsum (Christum) dedit (Deus Pater) caput supra omnem Ecclesiam", scilicet tam *militantem*, quae est hominum in praesenti viventium, quam *triumphantem*, quae est ex hominibus et Angelis in patria (S. Thom. In Epist. ad Ephes. c. 1, lect. 8).

[3] The generic name *Angelus* (ἄγγελος, nuntius) is employed in other Prefaces also to designate the lowest choir.

[4] Tremor autem nihil poenae, sed reverentiae castique timoris plurimum significat; constat enim, timorem castum et reverentialem haerere in coelitibus et "permanere in saeculum saeculi" (Ps. 18, 10) et "*tremere Potestates*", in curia angelica non postremas, dum in luce atque oculis divinae majestatis humillime

trembling." It is a joyous, blissful reverence, that penetrates these glorious heavenly spirits.[1]

Moreover "the heavens and the heavenly virtues and the blessed Seraphim exultingly celebrate in common" the majesty of God. All the choirs of the angels are not specially mentioned, but they are included in the word heaven (*coeli*)[2]; for this word does not here denote the visible heaven, but the blessed citizens and princes of the invisible heaven in general. Then there are yet two choirs of angels expressly mentioned: the Powers (*Virtutes*) and the Seraphim (*Seraphim*). The latter constitute the highest choir of the angelic kingdom and are emphatically called blessed,[3] because they burn and glow with an incomparable love of God.

Thus the exceedingly blessed hosts of heavenly spirits are eternally immersed in the loving and praising vision of the glory of God; they are never weary of celebrating and blessing the glory of their Creator. Now, in the sacred hour of the Sacrifice, we rise and ascend in spirit above the lowliness of the earthly and soar to the heights of the heavenly Jerusalem, which "is constructed of living stones, which towers on high and is surrounded as a bride by thousands and tens of thousands of angels." But how dare we join in

---

stratae et abjectae contremiscunt et pavent ad nutum ejus (Corder. Comm. in libr. Job c. 26, v. 11). — Cum igitur in coelestibus tanta sit devotio laudantium, veneratio adorantium, tremor admirantium, consideret haec homo, cui dictum est: Quid superbit terra? (Flor. Diac. De actione Missar. n. 27). — Contemplare majestatem et item justitiam Dei altissimi, quatenus timorate in cunctis te habeas. Si enim columnae coeli pavent in conspectu ejus et si angelici spiritus cum reverentiali tremore Deo assistunt, intendunt, deserviunt, cum quanta sollicitudine atque custodia cordis, timoreque mentis nos pauperes Deo adstare et sacrificare oportet? (Dion. Carthus. Expos. Miss. art. 4.)

[1] Divinam majestatem non solum Angeli, Dominationes et Potestates laudant, adorant, tremunt, sed etiam coeli et coelorum Virtutes et Seraphim *concelebrant*, i. e. in commune celebrant, concordi devotione et commune gaudio laudant (Flor. Diacon. n. 28). — The expression coeli is often used to designate the angelic choir of the Thrones, or also = the heavenly abode, in which case by virtutes coelorum the heavenly spirits in general are understood (hoc nomine omnes coelestes spiritus nonnunquam generaliter appellari solent — Flor. Diac. n. 30). Here five, or rather, six choirs of angels are mentioned; in other Prefaces Angeli et Archangeli, Throni et Dominationes — or Angeli et Archangeli, Cherubim quoque ac Seraphim — and once (on Whitsunday) all the angels are comprised in the words supernae Virtutes atque angelicae Potestates.

[2] In the majority of Prefaces the choirs of angels not expressly mentioned are designated by the words omnis militia coelestis exercitus. — Instead of socia (= allied) exsultatione (properly = exulting, rejoicing) concelebrant (= extol, glorify) once is given *una* voce dicentes. — Omnes ordines majestatem Dei Patris per Christum *juncta* exsultatione aequaliter concelebrant (Raban. Maur. De sacr. ord. c. 19). — Concentus in coelo angelicus totus est unisonus, totus consonus, quia projectus est inde antiquus ille disturbator coelestis harmoniae (Gerhoh. Reichersp. in Ps. 25).

[3] They are called *beata* Seraphim, because, according to a general rule, indeclinable substantives are regarded as neuter.

the angels' glorious hymn of praise? Our adoration being so very lowly, contemptible and unworthy. Penetrated with this sentiment of our total unworthiness, we, therefore, implore of God that He would suffer us to join our feeble voices with the angelic choirs[1] — and in all humility we praise the glory of the triune God and the glory of the Redeemer in the *Sanctus*.[2]

c) The End of the Preface.

Sanctus, Sanctus, Sanctus, Dominus Deus Sabaoth.	Holy, holy, holy, Lord God of Hosts.
Pleni sunt coeli et terra gloria tua.	Heaven and earth are full of Thy glory.
Hosanna in excelsis.	Hosanna in the highest.
Benedictus qui venit in nomine Domini.	Blessed is He that cometh in the name of the Lord.
Hosanna in excelsis.	Hosanna in the highest.

This exceedingly sublime hymn of praise[3] is made up of words taken from Holy Scripture,[4] and consists of two parts. The first half contains the glorification of the Holy Trinity by the angels of heaven; the second half consists of the welcoming of the Saviour by the mouth of the faithful on earth.[5] With regard to the first part,

---

[1] Haec est supplicatio nostra, ut ipse coelestis Pater per Christum Filium suum, per quem nos ei gratias de omnibus agimus, dignetur admittere voces nostras et jungere vocibus ordinum Angelorum (Raban. Maur. 1. c.).

[2] Humility, which accompanies our chant of praise *(supplex confessio)*, is also manifested in the corporeal bearing, that is, in the moderate inclination of the body when reciting the Thrice Holy. Cf. the original concluding stanza of the Saturday Vesper Hymn (of St. Ambrose), in which we read: Te nostra *supplex gloria* (praising) — per cuncta laudet saecula.

[3] The Second Council of Vaison (529) deemed it proper to renew the ordinance, that this hymn must be sung at *all* Masses. Ut in *omnibus* Missis sive matutinis sive quadragesimalibus vel quae in defunctorum commemorationibus fiunt, semper "*Sanctus, Sanctus, Sanctus*" eo ordine, quo ad Missas publicas dici debeat: quia *tam dulcis et desiderabilis vox, etiamsi diu noctuque posset dici, fastidium non potest generare* (Can. 111).

[4] Audeo dicere: ut bene ab homine laudetur Deus, laudavit se ipse Deus, et quia dignatus est laudare se, ideo invenit homo quemadmodum laudet eum. . . Spiritu suo implevit servos suos, ut laudarent eum, et quoniam Spiritus ejus in servis ejus laudat eum, quid aliud quam ipse se laudat? (S. Aug. Enarr. in Ps. 144, n. 1.)

[5] Vox *angelorum* Trinitatis et unitatis in Deo commendat arcanum; vox *hominum* divinitatis et humanitatis in Christo personat sacramentum (Innocent. III. 1. 2, c. 61). — Circa consecrationem, quae supernaturali virtute agitur, excitatur populus ad devotionem in praefatione; unde et monetur *sursum habere corda ad Dominum*, et ideo, finita praefatione, populus devote laudat divinitatem Christi cum angelis dicens: *Sanctus, Sanctus, Sanctus*, et humanitatem cum pueris dicens: *Benedictus qui venit*. . . (S. Thom. 3, q. 83, a. 4).

this magnifying of the Lord God of Hosts is termed the *Thrice Holy* (*Trisagium*)[1] or *Hymn of the Seraphim*, or *of the Angels* (*Hymnus seraphicus* vel *angelicus*)[2]; and the second part of the hymn is designated the *Victorious* or *Triumphal Chant* (*Hymnus triumphalis*, ἐπινίκιος). The *Trisagium* is found whole or in part in all the liturgies; in ancient times it was sung also by the congregation.[3]

The first part of the hymn, with some slight alterations, is taken from the grand description of a vision of the Prophet Isaias[4]: "And the Seraphim cried one to another, and said: Holy, holy, holy, the Lord God of hosts, all the earth is full of Thy glory. And the lintels of the doors (of the Temple) were moved at the voice of him that cried, and the house was filled with smoke (that is, with the cloud of the glory of light)." St. John the Apostle also heard the celestial canticle: "Holy, holy, holy, Lord God Almighty" (Apoc. 4, 8). As is evident from the universal doctrine of the Fathers and from several passages of Holy Scripture itself, the thrice repeating of the word "Holy" is intended, not merely to proclaim emphatically the holiness of God, but rather to indicate the threefold personality of God: it is a hymn of praise to the adorable Trinity.[5] Since in God's

---

[1] Trisagium (τρισάγιον) is also the name given to the enlarged Biblical Thrice Holy: Sanctus *Deus*, sanctus *Fortis*, sanctus *Immortalis*, miserere nobis! "Holy God, the holy Strong, the holy Immortal, have mercy on us!" It is modeled after the psalm-verse (41, 3) Sitivit anima mea ad *Deum, fortem, vivum* — "My soul has thirsted after the strong, the living God" (that is, the Immortal), and it is only a paraphrase for Holy Father, Holy Son and Holy Ghost. This Trisagium is recited in the ferial-prayers of Prime and is sung in Latin and Greek in the liturgy of Good Friday. (Cf. S. Joann. Damasc. Epistola de Hymno Trisagio.)

[2] The designation "Hymn of the Cherubim" (χερουβικός) also occurs; for they and all the other angels sing the Trisagion, although Isaias mentions only the Seraphim. (Cf. the Te Deum.)

[3] In the Pontifical the ordinance is ascribed to Pope Sixtus I. (119—128), "that the congregation should, when the priest begins the Canon (actionem) of the Mass, sing the hymn: Holy, Holy, Holy is the Lord God of Sabaoth." In the Mozarabic Liturgy we read, that the Thrice Holy is that aeterna laudatio, quae in coelestibus sine defectu psallitur ab Angelis et hic solemniter decantatur *a populis*. — Ubi expedita contestatione *omnis populus "Sanctus"* in Dei laudem proclamavit (S. Gregor. Turon. De mirac. S. Martini 1. 2, c. 14). — With the people naturally sang also the choir, and in many places the priest likewise, who in the Frankish Capitularies of the eighth and ninth centuries was often forbidden to begin the Canon before the close of the hymn, for example, *Te igitur* non inchoent sacerdotes, nisi post angelicum hymnum finitum. — Ut Secreta presbyteri non inchoent antequam *"Sanctus"* finiatur, sed cum populo *"Sanctus"* cantent. (Cfr. Martene, De antiq. Eccl. ritibus 1. 1, c, 4, a. 7).

[4] Is. 6, 3: Sanctus, Sanctus, Sanctus Dominus Deus exercituum, plena est omnis terra gloria ejus. The liturgical text is an address to God; it has according to the ancient biblical translation instead of exercituum the Hebrew word Sabaoth, which has been retained only in three passages in our Vulgate, and instead of the biblical omnis terra it gives coeli et terra. — Ad ipsum Deum dicitur gratulando (Flor. Diac. n. 37).

[5] Domine Deus dulcissime, sanctitas tua ineffabilis est: de qua quodammodo magis quam de aliis perfectionibus gloriaris. Seraphim ut te collaudent, *ter*

sanctity His infinite perfection, beauty and glory shine forth most resplendently, He is in the language of revelation and of the Church very often praised as "the Holy One". The divine holiness is uncreated, immense, unchangeable: the infinitely pure, luminous, spiritual being of God is holiness itself. God is the "only Holy One", and from God the supernal splendor of holiness is reflected over all the world of angels and of men: His is the type and the source of all created holiness.

In the holiness of the triune God is celebrated His interior and eternal glory, which of itself is invisible to us. This uncreated glory of the Lord of Hosts is unveiled in the works of creation and redemption; for "heaven and earth" (*coeli et terra*), the sum of all creation, the visible and the invisible world, bear witness to the glory of God. "Heaven and earth" are full of "His glory", that is, of proofs of the power and greatness, of the goodness and mercy of God: hence they announce and proclaim His greatness, His unspeakably great glory.[1]

To the praise of the triune God follows the jubilant salutation of the Redeemer, who will soon appear mystically on the altar "in the fulness of mercy."[2] The hymn concludes with the triumphal chant with which the Saviour was welcomed by the multitudes as Prince of Peace and Conqueror of Death at His solemn entrance into Jerusalem, and with which He is now again saluted at His coming on the altar: "Hosanna in the highest! Blessed is He that cometh in the name of the Lord! Hosanna in the highest!" The original verse of the Psalm, from which this acclamation is taken, is somewhat different: "O Lord save me! O Lord, give me success! — Blessed is He that cometh in the name of the Lord!"[3] The first

---

sanctum vocant, non tantum ut *personarum Trinitatem* indicent, sed ut te omnino sanctum et pelagus sanctitatis insinuent (Alvar. de Paz, De studio orationis 1. 3, p. 3, dec. 6, contempl. 53).

[1] Tria laudant: personarum trinitatem, unitatis majestatem et provisionis liberalitatem (quia usque ad ultimas creaturas, quae per terram intelliguntur, extendit diffusionem suae bonitatis)(S. Thom. In Is. c. 6, n. 1). — Non perperam hunc locum intelliget, qui per coelos *spiritus angelicos* et per terram *homines* hic acceperit... nam et coelestes spiritus et homines Dei gloria implentur: illi quidem praesenti glorificatione, hi vero in spe et praevia dispositione (Clichtov. 1. 3).

[2] Since the first *Hosanna in excelsis* is, like the thrice "Holy", said with a moderate bow of the body, and is sung with it by the choir already *before* the Consecration, and not after it with the *Benedictus*, some wish to refer it as an acclamation of homage and glorification to the triune God in the highest heavens. At the words *Benedictus qui venit* the celebrant stands erect, — not merely because he exults in going to meet the Redeemer about to descend on the altar at the consecration, but also that he may make the prescribed sign of the cross more conveniently. The wording of other liturgies, moreover, undeniably excludes the aforesaid reference of the first *Hosanna* to the Blessed Trinity. Osanna Filio David, osanna in excelsis: benedictus qui venit in nomine Domini, osanna in excelsis (Liturg. Mozarab.).

[1] O Domine, salvum me fac! O Domine, bene prosperare! Benedictus qui venit in nomine Domini! (Ps. 117, 25—26.) In the Hebrew *me* is wanting, and

verse, which expresses the petition for salvation and success, was sung by the congregation at the procession on the Feast of Tabernacles; the other verse, which took up and continued the salutation or blessing of those who were entering the Temple, was said by the priests' choir. These words, however, are prophetically-Messianic: for according to their highest purpose and meaning, they refer to Jesus Christ, who was announced by the prophets as "the One that was to come"[1] and who came in the fulness of time "in the name of the Lord," that is, sent by the Heavenly Father to redeem the world. — The petition and the salutation found their application in the Messiah in the mouth of "the people who, enlightened from above," exultingly in a loud voice saluted the Saviour entering Jerusalem as "King of Israel", with the words: "Hosanna to the Son of David! Blessed is He that cometh in the name of the Lord![2] Hosanna in the highest!"[3] In this text of the New Testament, "Hosanna" is, according to its original signification, at one time, understood as a cry of supplication ($=$ Help and blessing to the Son of David), and again as an acclamation of reverence and of exultation ($=$ hail to Him).[4] In comparing the passage of the Psalm with the Gospel text, we find a difference in the wording, as well as a partly different meaning, which results from the application and reference of the biblical text in the Gospel.

The liturgical text which departs somewhat from the biblical: "Hosanna in the highest! Blessed is He that cometh in the name of the Lord! Hosanna in the highest!" is not taken directly from the Psalm, but from the Gospel: hence it follows that it refers to the Saviour and to His coming on the altar.[5] How profoundly significant

---

salvum fac there is *Hoschianna*, whence the Greek expression ὡσαννά and the Latin Hosanna originated $=$ to help (σῶσον δή, salva obsecro). The designation in nomine Domini can be referred by the Psalmist to qui venit or to benedictus, but in the evangelical and liturgical text it must be combined with qui venit; for here it forms the clearer explanation and necessary supplement to the coming, upon which rests the emphasis. The Messiah is glorified as the ambassador of God. (Cf. Joan. 5, 43.)

[1] Cf. the question of the disciples of John to Christ: Tu es qui venturus es, an alium exspectamus? (Matth. 11, 3.) Veniens venturus, exspectatus, ὁ ἐρχόμενος were well known designations of the Messias.

[2] Jesus Christ, who by the commission, as well as for the glorification, of God came into the world, is in the fullest sense *benedictus* (blessed), because He is the source of all blessing and salvation for us and, therefore, infinitely worthy of all praise and glory. Cf. Ps. 3, 9: Domini est salus — et super populum tuum benedictio tua.

[3] Hosanna filio David! Benedictus qui venit in nomine Domini! Hosanna in altissimis! (Matth. 21, 9.) — Hoc canticum consona voce resonabant, utique ex instructione et motione Spiritus sancti (Dion. Carthus. in l. c.).

[4] Expressing more than the *Vivat* (May he live) the *Hosanna* corresponds to the Italian *Evviva.* Cf., v. g.: Evviva Maria e chi la creó; evviva la croce e chi l'esaltó.

[5] The liturgical text in the Apostolic Constitutions excludes every other signification: "Hosanna to the Son of David; blessed be He that cometh in the name of

is this formula of worship, this grateful and joyful praise of the Saviour inserted here, at this part of the Mass, when He is on the point of re-appearing in our midst as a Victim, as formerly He entered into Jerusalem to accomplish on the Cross the bloody Sacrifice! [1] What is at this moment more natural for us than exultingly to cry out: Highly praised be Christ, who, in obedience to the will of His heavenly Father, mystically descends upon the altar, daily to sacrifice Himself anew for the salvation of the whole world! — This grateful praise is introduced and concluded by the acclamation of Hosanna. What does the foreign Hebrew word *Hosanna* here signify? In the language of the Church its original meaning (= help, save, redeem) was soon lost and is no longer clearly felt: for Hosanna is a joyous, jubilant acclamation = Hail, glory, praise be to Him! [2] — This explanation could be illustrated and confirmed in various ways by the grand liturgy of Palm Sunday: some passages at least may be quoted. "When the people heard that Jesus was coming to Jerusalem, the multitude took branches of palms and went out to meet Him, crying aloud: This is He that is to come for the salvation of the people. He is our salvation and the redemption of Israel. How great is He whom thrones and powers go forth to welcome! Hail, King, Creator of the world, who comest to redeem us!" — "The multitude go out to meet the Redeemer with flowers and palms, and as to a conqueror entering on his triumph, they render worthy homage to Him. With their mouth the nations praise the Son of God, and through the clouds of heaven voices resound to the praise of Christ: Hosanna in the highest!" — "Like the angels and the children will we also sing to the Conqueror of Death: Hosanna in the highest!" — "Praise, honor and glory be to Thee, our King, Christ and Redeemer, unto whom the sweet and charming company of children poured forth their Hosanna, their devout hymn of praise (*cui puerile decus prompsit Hosanna pium*)! Thou art the King of Israel, Thou art the glorious Son of David! All praise be to Thee, O King, Thou

---

the Lord; God the Lord, He hath appeared to us. Hosanna in the highest!" (1. 8, c. 13.) — That the words Benedictus qui venit cannot be understood as a blessing for those who assist at Holy Mass, but are to be referred to the Eucharistic advent of the Saviour, is also evident from their rubrical destination, that they are to be sung by the choir only after the Consecration and Elevation (cf. Cerem. Episc. 1. 2, c. 8, n. 70—71).

[1] Ex Scriptura prophetica et evangelica completur *plena* laudatio, cum post laudem et gloriam sanctae Trinitatis adjungitur etiam gratiarum actio de adventu Salvatoris, qui unus in ipsa et ex ipsa Trinitate pro salute nostra homo factus in mundum venit et eandem salutem moriendo et resurgendo perfecit. . . unde rite illi gratias agentes dicimus "Hosanna", i. e. salus in excelsis (Florus. Diacon. n. 41).

[2] In the Votive Mass de Passione Domini the Church cries out to the Saviour: Tibi gloria, hosanna: tibi triumphus et victoria: tibi summae laudis et honoris corona. Alleluja. As vox *laetantis* (the expression of animated, exultant sentiment) Hosanna was not translated into either Greek or Latin (cfr. S. Aug. De doctr. christ. 1. 2, c. 11, n. 16). In the Middle Age even the verb hosannare = to praise was used.

that cometh in the name of the Lord! The multitude on high exalt Thee, the whole heavenly host, mortal man and all created things join in praising Thee. The Hebrew people goes forth to meet Thee with palms: behold we also appear before Thee with petitions, with our desires and with hymns of praise. For Thy passion they brought Thee sacrifices of praise: behold we sing to Thee our canticle for Thy victorious dominion. These gave Thee pleasure: may our devotions also be agreeable to Thee, O good and gentle King, to whom good works are always well-pleasing."

The Trisagium is not sung by the priest (as is the Preface), but recited in a half audible voice (*voce mediocri*).[1] When he joins in the hymn of praise of the angelic hosts, to glorify the Most Holy Trinity, he lowers his voice and with joined hands bows with humble reverence, in sentiments of unworthiness, to take up the heavenly hymn on his mortal lips. — At the joyful praise of the speedily approaching Saviour, hailed in advance, he again stands erect and signs himself with the holy Cross, not perhaps merely to conclude the hymn in due form,[2] but also to indicate that Christ came as a victorious Conqueror and Prince of Peace to establish His kingdom by means of the Cross, and that He now comes down on the altar to renew mystically the Sacrifice of the Cross.

The wonderful hymn of the Preface is grand and its sublimity beggars description. As "all the angels, the heavens and all the powers, the cherubim and seraphim incessantly cry out to God: Holy, holy, holy, is the Lord God of Hosts. Heaven and earth are full of Thy glory": in the same manner "does the Church throughout the earth acknowledge and praise Him — the Father of boundless majesty, His adorable, true and only-begotten Son, as well as the Holy Ghost the Comforter." — "O marvellous gifts of Christ!" (exclaims St. Chrysostom) "on high the angelic choirs sing glory to the Lord; on earth, after their example, men sing in church the same canticle in choirs. In heaven the Seraphim sing aloud their *Thrice Holy*; on earth the same canticle resounds from the mouth of the assembled congregation.[3] Thus heaven and earth unite in a festive celebration;

---

[1] In Rome at an early period this hymn was no longer sung by the people, but by subdeacons (Ordo Rom. I, n. 16; II, n. 10), and later on (as is still the case) it was sung by the choir (Ord. Rom. XI, n. 20 basilicarii). During it all were inclinati. Qui dum expleverint, *surgit* Pontifex *solus* et intrat in Canonem (Ibid. 1, n. 16).

[2] The liturgists of the Middle Age often mention the rule of accompanying the recitation of the evangelical words with the sign of the Cross. In omnibus verbis *evangelicis signum crucis* fieri oportet (Beleth. c. 40). Hence Sicardus remarks in reference to the concluding words of the Sanctus: Hoc sumptum est de *Evangelio*, unde cum cantatur, nobis *signaculum crucis* imprimimus (1. 3, c. 6).

[3] The same holy Doctor of the Church says in a eulogy of the Martyrs: "Because the martyrs showed the utmost love for the Lord, He amicably extends His hand to them, now they should rejoice at the heavenly glory, and join the choirs of angels and unite in their mysterious hymns (Isa. 6, 3). Among these choirs, they were counted already during their earthly life, as often as they participated in the

it is a hymnal celebration of thanksgiving, of praise; it is a choir of common joy, which the unspeakable goodness of the Lord, in His great condescension to us, organized and which the Holy Ghost assembled; on its harmony the Heavenly Father dwells with complacency.   Its melody is borrowed from heaven, being led by the hand of the Most Holy Trinity, to the end that those sweet and blessed notes, those chants of the angels, those canticles of praise may never cease to resound."

2.   The Proper Prefaces (*Praefationes Propriae.*)

In addition to the ordinary Preface, the Roman Missal contains ten others which have a specific festal character, since sundry mysteries of the ecclesiastical year are therein prominently set forth as special motives of praise and thanksgiving.

In the liturgy of the Church is conspicuously set forth the love of gratitude toward God; the sentiment of fervent thanksgiving for the salvation given us by Christ, for the grace of faith, for the glory of the redemption, for the blessed hope of heaven, day after day finds its touching expression, as beautiful as it is joyful, in the Preface of Holy Mass.   But when on the great feasts of the ecclesiastical year, the mysteries of sacred history, the great deeds and benefits of divine love seem to reveal themselves more livelily and brightly to the soul and to move the heart in the fulness of their beauty and glory, — then it is that the hymn of thanksgiving and praise rises to the greatest heights of enthusiasm and jubilation.

a) Praefatio in *Nativitate* Domini.[1]

. . . aeterne Deus. Quia per incarnati Verbi mysterium nova mentis nostrae oculis lux tuae claritatis infulsit[2]: ut dum visibiliter Deum cognoscimus, per	. . . eternal God. Since by the mystery of the Word made flesh a new ray of Thy glory has appeared to the eyes of our souls; that while we know God visibly,

---

Holy Mysteries, in that they, with the Cherubim, sang to the praise of the Lord the Thrice Holy — you, who belong to the consecrated, know the reason of this; so much the less should it surprise you, now that they have found their companions in heaven, that with greater confidence they take part in this hymn of praise."

[1]   By a special exemption from the general rule, during the Octave of Christmas this Preface is to be taken also in such Masses as have a Praefatio *propria* (for example, on the feast of the holy Apostle John, but not on his octave day, and in eventual Votive Masses).   Candlemas-Day (Purificatio B. M. V.) has the Christmas Preface, inasmuch as this day in the West is also a feast of the Lord — in the Greek rite even prominently so (hence the name ὑπαντή, ὑπαπαντή, occursus, obviatio — quia venerabiles personae Simeon et Anna eo die obviaverunt Domino, dum praesentaretur in templo [Microl. c. 48]).   The feast of Corpus Christi, as well as the feast of the Holy Name of Jesus and the Transfiguration have, therefore, also the Christmas Preface.

[2]   Homo per peccatum interius lumen obfuscatum habebat et conversus fuerat ad sensibilia et illa amabat; ideo Deus invisibilis factus est *visibilis* secundum carnem, ut per visibilia reduceret ad invisibilia cognoscenda et amanda (S. Bonav. III, dist. 1, a. 2, q. 2 ad 3).

hunc invisibilium amorem rapiamur.[1] Et ideo cum Angelis et Archangelis, cum Thronis et Dominationibus, cumque omni militia coelestis exercitus, hymnum[2] gloriae tuae canimus, sine fine dicentes: Sanctus . . .

we may be drawn after Him to the love of things invisible. And, therefore, with the angels and archangels, with the thrones and dominations and with all the heavenly host we sing a hymn to Thy glory, saying without ceasing: Holy . . .

Holy Christmastide knows no shadow of darkness nor gloom, it beams with light and joy; the Sun of Salvation has arisen to the people that walked in darkness and to them that dwelt in the regions of the shadow of death (Is. 9, 2). From the beginning the Eternal Word was the light of the world; but when He assumed human nature and lived as man in our midst, then to the eyes of faith the splendor of divine light was reflected in quite a new and wonderful manner. Christ is the image of the brightness and glory of the Father; in Him the fulness of the divinity dwells corporally. By becoming incarnate God lowered Himself to our weakness. In meditating upon the mysteries of the life, passion and glorified state of Christ, we learn to know and to love God. The Incarnation is a furnace all aglow with heavenly love: and in it our heart should be inflamed and irresistibly drawn to the love of invisible and imperishable goods. The words "saying without ceasing"[3] — signify that we should without intermission sing the Thrice Holy: but since this is impossible on earth, we thereby secretly beg admission to heaven, where it will be granted to us to praise and to magnify God with the angelic choirs without interruption throughout eternity.

---

[1] Cum amicitia in quadam aequalitate consistat, ea quae multum inaequalia sunt, in amicitia copulari non posse videntur. Ad hoc igitur, quod familiarior amicitia esset inter hominem et Deum, expediens fuit homini, quod Deus fieret homo, quia etiam naturaliter homo homini amicus est, ut sic, dum visibiliter Deum cognoscimus, in invisibilium amorem rapiamur (S. Thom. c. gent. l. 4, c. 54).

[2] Already Walafrid Strabo distinguishes metrical and rhythmic hymns on the one hand (real hymns), and, on the other, hymns in a general (improper) sense — among the latter he reckons the Preface with the Trisagion. Notandum ymnos dici non tantum qui metris vel rithmis decurrunt . . . verum etiam *ceteras laudationes*, quae verbis convenientibus et sonis dulcibus proferuntur. . . Et quamvis in quibusdam ecclesiis ymni metrici non cantentur, tamen in omnibus *generales ymni*, i. e. *laudes* dicuntur (De exord. et increm. c. 26).

[3] Sine fine = sine cessatione, sine requie, sine intermissione, per quod significatur jugis et assidua illius excellentissimi hymni *"Sanctus, sanctus, sanctus . . ."* a nobis decantatio facienda. Quod cum in hac mortali vita perfecte a nobis expleri non possit, hoc verbo tacite et per subinsinuationem quandam expetitur aeternae beatitudinis consortium nobis demum concedi, in qua angelicis conjuncti choris sacra laudatione possimus hunc hymnum sine fine ac perpetuo decantare, quemadmodum et ipsae supernae virtutes atque angelicae potestates hymnum hunc gloriae Domini sine fine concinunt secundum illud verbum (ps. 83): "Beati qui habitant in domo tua, Domine: in saecula saeculorum laudabunt te" (Clichtov. Elucid. eccles. l. 3, n. 3).

b) In *Epiphania* Domini.

. . . aeterne Deus. Quia, cum Unigenitus tuus in substantia nostrae mortalitatis apparuit, nova nos immortalitatis suae luce reparavit.[1] . .	. . . eternal God. Because when Thy only-begotten Son appeared in the substance of our mortal flesh, He restored us by the new light of His immortality.

The only-begotten Son of God "was seen upon earth, and conversed with men" (Bar. 3, 38). The glory that He shared with the Father before the world was created, He concealed under the veil of His most pure and most perfect, yet passible and mortal humanity. As the sun hides itself behind clouds, thus did He veil the bright glory of God under the mean form of a slave, in order that, by His humiliation, He might raise us to the dignity of the children of God, and in the end clothe us with the radiant garment of glory.

c) In *Quadragesima*.

. . . aeterne Deus. Qui corporali jejunio vitia comprimis, mentem elevas, virtutem largiris et praemia: per Christum Dominum nostrum. . .	. . . eternal God, who by bodily fasting dost repress vice, elevate the mind and bestow virtue and rewards: through Christ our Lord. . .

This Preface briefly and pithily, as well as beautifully and appropriately, expresses the salutary effects and spiritual blessings of a Lent dedicated to God. Religious fasting is an act of earnest penance and atonement; hence it serves principally to mortify and to crucify the unruly flesh with its lusts and desires, by which means "vices" are extirpated. The more sensuality and concupiscence are curbed and weakened, the more freely, easily and nimbly does the spirit and mind "elevate" itself into the higher, purer and brighter atmosphere of the life of grace. The mortification and the curbing of sensuality, as well as the freedom of spirit and the elevation of the heart to what is heavenly and eternal, is the source of all "virtues". And, finally, who can doubt but what the chastising of the flesh, the elevation of the soul to God and the acquisition of virtues will procure us glorious "rewards"?[2] — For he that soweth in

---

[1] Filius Dei benignitate sua *de nostro* accepit, ut *de suo* nobis conferret. Accepit enim vere nostrae mortalitatis substantiam et in illa hodierna die Magis stella duce quasi primitiis electionis gentium apparuit ac demonstratus est. Suae vero immortalitatis participationem et consortium nobis tradidit, cum nos per novam divinitatis suae lucem nube fulgida carnis adumbratum in pristinam dignitatem reparavit (Clichtov. 1. c. 1. 3, n. 5). — The present text originated from the more ancient readings: in novam nos immortalitatis suae lucem reparavit — and in nova nos immortalitatis suae luce reparavit.

[2] Conjungitur *consequio* quodam ipse jejunio puritas et munditia vitae, sanctimonia et castitas, quae ceteras protinus virtutes omnes sibi comites adsciscit, quibus adornata anima coelestem demum requiem assequitur (Clichtov. 1. c. n. 7).

the flesh, of the flesh also shall reap corruption; but he that soweth in the spirit, of the spirit shall reap life everlasting (Gal. 6, 8).[1]

d) In Missis de *Passione* et de *S. Cruce.*

. . . aeterne Deus. Qui salutem humani generis in ligno Crucis constituisti: ut, unde mors oriebatur, inde vita resurgeret: et qui in ligno vincebat, in ligno quoque vinceretur[2]: per Christum Dominum nostrum. . .	. . . eternal God. Who hast ordained that the salvation of mankind be wrought on the wood of the Cross: that from whence death came, thence life might arise, and that He who overcame by the tree, might also by the tree be overcome. Through Christ our Lord. . .

Here the Church praises the wonderful decree of divine wisdom in the redemption of the world. At the tree of knowledge Satan deceived and conquered our first parents, thereby bringing death into the world; God now chose the wood of the Cross as the altar of the great atoning Sacrifice, by which the "prince of this world was cast out and his works destroyed," and from which issued for mankind the life of grace and glory.[3] Already in Paradise "the Creator marked out the wood, that it might expiate the guilt of the wood. The economy of our salvation so required it, that wisdom should deceive the cunning of the wily betrayer and prepare salvation to issue from that very instrument which the enemy had used to wound us." Since "the Salvation of the World" heretofore hung upon the ignominious wood of the Cross, the selfsame Cross has become a sweet and precious wood.[4]

---

[1] Assumitur jejunium principaliter ad tria: 1. ad concupiscentias carnis reprimendas; 2. ad hoc quod mens liberius elevetur ad sublima contemplanda; 3. ad satisfaciendum pro peccatis (S. Thom. 2, 2, q. 147, a. 1).

[2] Nostri generis damnatio *ex ligno scientiae* boni et mali habuit exortum. Similiter divina ordinatione nostra salvatio *ex ligno crucis* processit, per Christi sanguinem et mortem sanctificato. Et hoc pacto ex eodem secundum speciem resurrexit nobis vita, unde mors primum fuerat suborta, nempe ex *ligno*. Et antiquus serpens, qui per lignum paradisi vicerat primos parentes, quos subdola suasione induxerat ad esum fructus ejus, in ligno etiam victus est scil. crucis, per Christum Dominum nostrum, qui salutaris fuit hujus arboris fructus et efficax ad tollendam praevaricationem ex noxio nobisque damnoso fructu prioris arboris inflictam (Clichtov. 1. c. n. 15).

[3] In this Preface is appropriately expressed the antithetical relation between the tree (ξύλον, lignum, wood) of knowledge, by the fruit of which was perpetrated the fall of sin, and the wood (tree, again ξύλον, lignum) of the Cross, on which the redemption was accomplished. The former tree, planted in the centre of the Garden of Paradise, was intended for the blessing of humanity, and it became its curse. The latter tree, erected in the centre of the globe, the gibbet of the curse ("maledictus qui pendet in ligno" — Deuter. 21, 23), has become a blessing for all that believe in it (cf. Oswald, Die Erlösung in Christo Jesu II, 110).

[4] Cf. the beautiful Preface in the Gregorian Sacramentary: Christus per passionem crucis mundum redemit et antiquae arboris amarissimum gustum crucis

In *Paschate.*

. . . aequum et salutare: Te quidem, Domine, omni tempore, sed in hac potissimum die gloriosius praedicare, cum Pascha nostrum immolatus est Christus. Ipse enim verus est Agnus, qui abstulit peccata mundi. Qui mortem nostram moriendo destruxit et vitam resurgendo reparavit. . .[1]

. . . it is right and salutary, to praise Thee, O Lord, at all times, but chiefly on this day when Christ our Passover was sacrificed for us; for He is the true Lamb who took away the sins of the world. Who by dying has destroyed our death, and by rising again has restored our life. . .

In this Preface is set forth the Church's Easter song of triumph, for in order to thank God, she sings a victorious and triumphal hymn in honor of the gloriously risen Saviour. Christ is the true Pasch (prefigured in the Old Law), who by the blood of His Sacrifice purified the world from sin. He "triumphs as conqueror and by His own tomb digs a grave for death,"[2] as He had already announced by the Prophet Osee: "O death, I will be thy death, O hell, I will be thy bite!" (Osee XIII, 14.) Then was fulfilled "the saying that is written: Death is swallowed up in victory. O death, where is thy victory? O death, where is thy sting?" (1 Cor. 15, 54, 55.)[3] From the Risen Lord proceeds also that new life, through which "that which is mortal may be swallowed up" (2 Cor. 5, 4); the Resurrection of the Lord is the model and cause of both our spiritual and corporal resurrection and transformation.[4]

f) In *Ascensione* Domini.

. . . aeterne Deus: per Christum Dominum nostrum. Qui post resurrectionem suam omni-

. . . eternal God: through Christ our Lord. Who after His resurrection appeared openly to all

---

medicamine indulcavit, mortemque quae per lignum vetitum venerat, per ligni trophaeum devicit, ut mirabili suae pietatis dispensatione qui per ligni gustum a florigera sede discesseramus, per crucis lignum ad paradisi gaudia redeamus. — (Cfr. Petr. Blessens. Serm. 4 in festo s. Andreae.)

[1] Secundum rationem *efficientiae*, quae dependet ex virtute divina, communiter tam mors Christi quam etiam resurrectio est causa tam destructionis mortis quam reparationis vitae; sed secundum rationem *exemplaritatis* mors Christi, per quam recessit a vita mortali, est causa destructionis mortis nostrae, resurrectio vero ejus, per quam inchoavit vitam immortalem, est causa reparationis vitae nostrae. Passio tamen Christi est insuper causa meritoria (S. Thom. 3, q. 56, a. 1 ad 4).

[2] Victor triumphat et *suo mortem sepulchro funerat* (Hymn. Pasch. ad Laudes).

[3] Nam mortuus ille mortis interfector fuit et magis in illo mors mortua est, quam ipse in morte (S. August. Enarr. in Ps. 51, n. 1).

[4] Unus idemque est mortis susceptor vitaeque largitor: unus idemque immortalis ex Patre, mortalis ex matre; propria potestate moriens, propria potestate resurgens (S. Fulgent. Sermo 4).

bus discipulis suis manifestus apparuit, et ipsis cernentibus est elevatus in coelum, ut nos divinitatis suae tribueret esse participes. . .

His disciples, and in their presence ascended into heaven, that He might grant us to be partakers of His divine nature. . .

After His Resurrection Jesus manifested Himself alive to His disciples by many proofs, appearing to them during forty days; He then ascended into heaven, and a cloud concealed Him from their sight. There He is exalted in eternal glory, to impart to us divine life and to lead us to the kingdom of glory.

g) In *Pentecoste.*

. . . aeterne Deus: per Christum Dominum nostrum. Qui ascendens super omnes coelos, sedensque ad dexteram tuam, promissum Spiritum sanctum (hodierna die) in filios adoptionis effudit. Quapropter profusis gaudiis, totus in orbe terrarum mundus exsultat.[1] Sed et supernae Virtutes atque angelicae Potestates,[2] hymnum gloriae tuae concinunt, sine fine dicentes. . .

. . . eternal God, through Christ our Lord. Who ascending above all the heavens, and sitting at Thy right hand, did send down the promised holy Spirit (this day) upon the children of adoption. Wherefore the whole world exults. The supernal Virtues also and the angelic Powers, sing in concert the hymn to Thy glory, saying without end . . .

"For as yet the Spirit was not given, because Jesus was not yet glorified." "It is expedient for you," said the Lord to His disciples, "that I go; for if I go not, the Paraclete will not come to you; but if I go, I will send Him to you" (John 7, 39; 16, 7). After Christ "as Conqueror in noble triumph was seated at the right hand of the Father," then "the Spirit of the Lord filled the whole world" (Wisdom 1, 7) with His gifts and benefits: wherefore the whole world overflowed with joy and jubilation. Heavenly delights fill the hearts of the redeemed and favored children of God, when the Holy Ghost visits and consoles them.[3]

---

[1] Haec Spiritus sancti effusio in discipulos totum genus humanum non a re ingenti gaudio laetificat. Nam per eam coepta est evangelicae legis salutarisque doctrinae promulgatio et apostolica denuntiatione totius mundi ad Christum reductio, ut paulo post ex Judaeis et gentibus factum fuerit unum ovile sub Christo uno pastore. Salus igitur toti mundo annuntiata per missionem Spiritus sancti in Apostolos merito materiam profusioris gaudii in Domino toti mundo ministrat (Clichtov. 1. c.).

[2] Deus ideo Dominus exercituum et Dominus virtutum vere dicitur, quia omnis militia coelestis exercitus, omnes *supernae virtutes* atque *angelicae potestates* ejus imperio subjacent, ejus serviunt voluntati (Florus Diacon. n. 38). — Trinitatem Seraphim glorificant et *omnes potestates virtutesque coelestes* (Ibid. n. 40).

[3] Cf. the Whitsuntide Hymn: *Beata* (blessed and blissful) nobis *gaudia* — anni reduxit orbita (course) — cum Spiritus Paraclitus — effulsit in discipulos.

h) In Festo *Ss. Trinitatis.*

... aeterne Deus. Qui cum Unigenito Filio tuo, et Spiritu sancto, unus es Deus, unus es Dominus: non in unius singularitate personae, sed in unius Trinitate substantiae. Quod enim de tua gloria, revelante te, credimus, hoc de Filio tuo, hoc de Spiritu sancto, sine differentia discretionis sentimus. Ut in confessione verae, sempiternaeque Deitatis, et in personis proprietas, et in essentia unitas, et in majestate adoretur aequalitas. Quam laudant Angeli atque Archangeli, Cherubim[1] quoque ac Seraphim: qui non cessant clamare quotidie, una voce dicentes ...

... eternal God. Who, together with Thy only-begotten Son, and the Holy Ghost, art one God, and one Lord: not in singularity of one Person, but in a Trinity of one substance. For that which, by Thy revelation, we believe of Thy glory, the same we believe of Thy Son, and the same of the Holy Ghost, without any difference or distinction. That in the confession of a true and eternal Deity, distinctness in the Persons, unity in the essence, and equality in the majesty may be adored. Whom the angels and archangels, the cherubim also and the seraphim do praise, who cease not daily to cry out with one voice, saying ...

This Preface contains a majestic and sublime rendering of those words of the Athanasian Symbol: "This is Catholic faith, that we revere the one God in the Trinity and the Trinity in Unity." The mystery of the Holy Trinity is the most profound and sublime mystery of our faith: to all created and finite minds the Trinity is absolutely unattainable and unfathomable. It was left to divine revelation alone to unveil the sublime truth which we, with childlike, simple faith must accept and adhere to. "Thee we implore, Thee we praise, Thee we adore, O infinitely blessed Trinity! Our hope, our salvation, our glory, O divine Trinity! Deliver us, enliven us, bless us, O eternal Love, O all beneficent Trinity!"[2]

---

[1] The word *Cherub* is defined in different ways. According to the ordinary traditional view, it designates the fulness of wisdom and science (nomen Cherubim imponitur a quodam excessu scientiae, unde interpretatur *plenitudo scientiae* [S. Thom.]), as the word *Seraph* (from saraph = burning, consuming) the ardor of love (Cherubim habent excellentiam scientiae, Seraphim vero excellentiam ardoris [S. Thom. 1, q. 108, c. 5 ad 5]). By transposing the letters, Cherub is also derived from rechub or recheb = wagon (rachab = to take a drive), because the Cherubim, thus to speak, form the heavenly wagon of the Divine King, who comes to judgment. Qui sedes super Cherubim, manifestare! (Ps. 79, 1.)

[2] Clement XIII. prescribed (Jan. 3, 1759) for all Sundays that have no special Preface, the Praefatio de Trinitate ad majorem splendidioremque tanti mysterii gloriam, ut fideles quoque, qui die Dominica Missae interesse debent, latius atque apertius ejusdem mysterii praeconia audientes, debitum et ipsi servitutis obsequium supremae impendant majestati.

i) In *Festis et Missis Votivis B. V. M.*

. . . aeterne Deus. Et te in . . . beatae Mariae semper Virginis collaudare, benedicere et praedicare. Quae et Unigenitum tuum sancti Spiritus obumbratione concepit: et virginitatis gloria permanente, lumen aeternum mundo effudit, Jesum Christum Dominum nostrum. . .	. . . eternal God. And that we should praise, bless and glorify Thee on the N. of the blessed Mary, ever a Virgin. Who by the overshadowing of the Holy Ghost conceived Thy only-begotten Son, and, the glory of her virginity still remaining, brought forth the eternal light into the world, Jesus Christ our Lord. . .

Unspeakable are the privileges of grace and glory wherewith the blessed Virgin Mary, Mother of God, is distinguished above all other creatures; great things hath He done in her who is powerful and whose name is holy.   Among all her prerogatives this one is especially striking, being unique of its kind, that she should combine the honor of the most stainless virginity with the joys of the most sublime maternity.[1]   By the overshadowing of the Holy Ghost "the dwelling of her most chaste bosom becomes on a sudden the temple of God" — *domus pectoris templum repente fit Dei.*   As a ray of purest light did Christ at His birth come forth from the spotless womb of the Virgin, inasmuch as He "did not wound but consecrated the inviolability of His Mother."[2]

As glass, resplendent by the sun's rays,
Of its own transparency loses no portion;
Thus also pure as heaven does the Virgin remain,
Who for us gave birth to the Son of Salvation.

k) In Festis *Apostolorum.*

Vere dignum et justum est, aequum et salutare: Te, Domine, suppliciter exorare, ut gregem	It is truly meet and just, right and salutary, humbly to beseech Thee that Thou, O Lord, our

---

[1] Sedulius (who lived about the middle of the fifth century) salutes and praises with enthusiasm the Mother of the Lord as the one who brought forth the eternal Ruler of the world (cfr. Intr. Salve, sancta parens), "who possesses the joys of maternity together with the honor of virginity, — previous to her there was none like unto her, and there shall not be any such after her" (gaudia matris habens cum virginitatis honore, — nec primam similem visa est nec habere sequentem — Carm. pasch. 1. 2, v. 67—68). — Quae cum clarifico semper sit nomine mater, — semper virgo manet (Ibid. 1. 5, v. 360—361).

[2] Maria divino partu sic coepit esse mater, ut *virgo sacratior* permaneret (S. Gaudent. Brixiae Episc. Serm. 9). — Omnipotentiam Filii Dei et hominis etiam Mater Virgo testatur, quae de Spiritu sancto concipiens ita Deum et hominem . . . edidit, ut apud incorruptam tanti nominis matrem post divinum partum *gloriosior integritas* permaneret (Ibid. Serm. 13).

tuum, Pastor aeterne, non deseras, sed per beatos Apostolos tuos continua protectione custodias. Ut iisdem rectoribus gubernetur, quos operis tui vicarios eidem contulisti praeesse pastores. Et ideo. . .	eternal Shepherd, wouldst not forsake Thy flock, but through Thy blessed Apostles, wouldst keep it under Thy continual protection, that it may be governed by Thee under the same rulers whom, as vicars of Thy work, Thou hast appointed to preside as pastors over the same. And therefore. . .

This is the only Preface whose words are not addressed to the Father, but to Jesus Christ. The celebration of the Feast of the Apostles, therefore, leads the Church to invoke Jesus Christ, the "eternal Shepherd", for the protection and defence of His faithful flock. Christ is the "Good Shepherd", who gave His life for His sheep. From heaven where He is transfigured in glory, being "the great Shepherd" and "the Prince of pastors" (Heb. 13, 20; 1 Peter 5, 4), He feeds on the pastures of divine truth and grace the sheep purchased with His own blood, watches over them, protects them, guides them and has them follow after Him to the unfailing and ever-green pastures of a heavenly Paradise.

The Lord on leaving the world did not leave His flock as orphans here below, but, in His love, He cared for it, inasmuch as He appointed over it the Apostles and their successors as pastors and guides. "I will give you pastors according to My own heart, and they shall feed you with knowledge and doctrine," said the Lord by the mouth of the Prophet (Jer. 3, 15). And so has it been done. Bishops and priests, pastors of the entire Church, are only "the representatives"[1] (*vicarii*) of the true and chief Pastor in heaven, in whose name and according to whose example, with unflagging pastoral love and fidelity, they are to feed and to conduct, to protect and to shelter the sheep confided to them.

"It deserves to be mentioned, that the most ancient representations of Christ in the Catacombs depict Him under the figure of the Good Shepherd, and that Christian antiquity in general had a very special preference for this picture, — a proof of how profoundly the thoughts suggested by this representation were impressed upon the souls of the earliest Christians, and what consolation, what joy, what religious and moral elevation and strength they found in looking at this picture, which represented the mutual relations of the Saviour

---

[1] Petit haec praefatio, quod ipse bonus Pastor gregem suum catholicum non derelinquat, aut suo destituat praesidio, sed per ipsos Apostolos tanquam cooperatores ipsius in custodia gregis et coadjutores ipsum assidua conservet protectione: ut ipse grex dominicus iisdem Apostolis rectoribus gubernetur, quos ut vicarios operis sui, utpote gregis pascendi, ipse Pastor aeternus ordinavit ac sanxit debere praeesse pastores eidem gregi (Clichtov. Elucidat. eccles. 1. 3, n. 17).

19

to the Christian soul and of the soul to the Saviour, in a manner as simple as it was symbolical and touching!"[1]

56.   Preliminary Remarks concerning the Canon.

The jubilant Hosanna, so charming for its joy, has now ceased.[2] Holy silence succeeds, for the Canon begins.[3] "There could not be a more splendid introduction, with the hymn which closes the Prefaces, to the divine rite that follows.   Here we must pause; because the subject becomes too sacred for our pen; the ground upon which we are about to tread is holy, and the shoes must be loosed from the feet of him who will venture upon it."   These words of the devout Cardinal Wiseman are a serious admonition to pray and search with all humility and love, that the Lord "may lift the veil from our eyes," and that in some degree we may be enabled to behold and understand the mysteries concealed in the Canon: for "the Lord giveth wisdom to little ones" (Ps. 18, 8).[4]

   1.   The *Name, Origin* and *Antiquity* of the Canon.[5]   The word

---

[1]   Cf. Hundhausen, Das erste Pontificalschreiben Petri S. 290.

[2]   According to a rubric (Rubr. gener. Miss. tit. 20; Ritus celebr. Miss. tit. 8, n. 6), that probably has no preceptive, but only a directive character, the so-called Sanctus or Consecration candle is to be lighted on the Epistle side and to continue burning until after the Communion.   This candle denotes the Eucharistic presence of the Lord and incites the faithful to devotion, love and adoration.   (Cf. S. R. C. 30. Dec. 1881.)

[3]   Post laudes et gratiarum actiones pro tanta gratia redemptionis nostrae, quae in illo divino mysterio agitur et commendatur, *facto totius Ecclesiae silentio,* in quo cessante omni strepitu verborum, sola ad Deum dirigitur intentio et devotio cordium, sociatis sibi omnium votis et desideriis, incipit sacerdos orationem fundere, qua ipsum mysterium dominici corporis et sanguinis consecratur.   Sic enim oportet, ut in illa hora tam sacrae ac divinae actionis tota per Dei gratiam a terrenis cogitationibus mente separata et ecclesia cum sacerdote et sacerdos cum ecclesia spirituali desiderio intret in sanctuarium Dei aeternum et supernum... Idcirco, ut ferunt, consuetudo venit in ecclesia, ut *tacite* ista obsecratio atque consecratio a sacerdote cantetur (recited), ne verba tam sacra et ad tantum mysterium pertinentia vilescerent (Pseudo-Alcuin. c. 40).

[4]   The blessed Otto of Cambrai († 1113) writes in the Preface to his Expositio in Canonem Missae: Praesumptionis argui timeo, quod ausus sum rem difficilem contingere et extendere conatus in alta profunditate, scil. exponere Canonem altaris et probare tanta mysteria.

[5]   The position of the Canon underwent many a change in the course of time. Until the ninth century it was in connection with the Missa quotidiana placed at the end of the cycle of the year's feasts.   After this time it was placed at the beginning of the Sacramentary, being preceded by only a heading and a very short Ordo Missae.   From the eleventh century it is more frequently found in the middle of the book — between Holy Saturday and Easter Sunday.   Through the Missale secundum consuetudinem curiae Romanae it obtained after the thirteenth century that place permanently.   Since the Canon is the part of the Missal the most used, it has been properly placed where it is most convenient for use — that is, in the middle of the Missal.   This practical feature decided its position.   Moreover, said

Canon (Κανών)[1] in ecclesiastical language has many different meanings; but here, where it serves to designate the principal portion of the Mass liturgy, it signifies the standard formula, the fixed standard, the invariable rule for the accomplishment of the essential act of Sacrifice. The Canon of the Mass, which begins after the *Sanctus* and ends before the *Pater noster*,[2] includes the Consecration — or Sacrificial Act, as also those prayers and ceremonies that introduce the Consecration and are most closely connected with it. It, therefore, covers the divine sacrificial act with a mystical veil and encloses it in a most precious case. As the Sacrifice which the eternal Highpriest offers on the altar to the end of ages, is and ever remains the same, so, in like manner the Canon, the ecclesiastical sacrificial prayer, in its sublime simplicity and venerable majesty, is and ever remains invariably the same; only on the greatest feasts are a few additions made in order to harmonize[3] with the spirit and change of the ecclesiastical year.[4]

---

position between Holy Saturday and Easter Sunday may also indicate that the accomplishment of the Eucharistic Sacrifice according to the Ordo and Canon Missae forms the vivifying centre of the ecclesiastical year (cf. Ebner, Quellen und Forschungen S. 363 etc.).

[1] Κανών originally denoted a straight staff and, therefore, the Mass rod or rule; metaphorically, then, any law, regulation or ordinance (lex, regula, norma). In ecclesiastical language the word Canon (as also the adjective canonicus) has a manifold application. Thus, for example, it designates the entire collection of inspired revelation records, in so far as they constitute an authoritative or standard rule for the faith and morals of man; then divine tradition, which likewise forms a regula fidei; also the laws of the Church and the definitions of the Councils are called κανόνες. Furthermore, canon signifies the register of saints (hence canonizatio, the reception into it), also the list of the clerics who, belonging to a certain church (οἱ ἐν κανόνι = the clerics, hence the denomination Canonici), for the most part lived in common according to a determined rule. — *Actio* dicitur ipse Canon, quia in eo sacramenta conficiuntur dominica. *Canon* vero eadem actio nominatur, quia ea est *legitima et regularis sacramentorum confectio* (Walafrid. Strabo c. 23). Moreover, other designations are, for example, regula, legitimum, agenda, secretum Missae, prex, mystica prex, textus canonicae precis.

[2] The Canon is limited in the Rubr. generales (tit. 12 et 13) and in the Ritus celebr. Missam (tit. 8 et 9); but in consequence of the continued superscription in the Ordo Missae the Canon would extend from the Sanctus to the end of the Communion, that is, there would be question not only of a Canon of the Consecration, but also of a Canon of Communion; but this has never been customary. The word Canon, as a rule, is used without addition, to designate the Canon of Consecration. (Cf. Cavalieri, tom. V, c. 16, n. 1.)

[3] In the Communicantes and Hanc igitur. The Communicantes receives a small addition on Holy Thursday, in the Masses both of the time and in the votive ones of the Octaves of Christmas, Epiphany, Easter, Ascension and Whitsunday; likewise the Hanc igitur on Holy Thursday (as well as the Qui pridie) and during the Octaves of Easter and Whitsuntide.

[4] Ordinem precum in celebritate Missarum nullo nos tempore, nulla festivitate significamus habere diversum, sed *semper eodem tenore oblata Deo munera consecrare*. Quoties vero paschalis aut Ascensionis Domini vel Pentecostes aut Epi-

As to the origin of the Canon there is an express explanation of
the Church: "Since it is befitting that holy things should be administered in a holy manner, since this Sacrifice is the most holy of all
things; the Catholic Church, in order that it might be worthily and
reverently offered and received, many centuries ago established the
sacred Canon, so free from all error, that nothing is contained therein which does not diffuse in the highest degree a certain odor of
holiness and piety and raise to God the minds of those who offer it.
For it consists partly of the very words of the Lord, and partly of
the traditions of the Apostles and also of the pious ordinances of holy
Popes."[1]   On account of the want of reliable historical testimony,
we are not able to state more accurately and minutely what parts of
the Canon are of Apostolic tradition and what are the later additions
of holy Popes.[2]   Yet it is pretty certain and generally admitted, that
Pope St. Gregory I. (590—604) completed the formula of the text
of the Canon as we now have it.

"It is correct and a matter of fact to state that the text of the
Canon of the present Roman Missal corresponds, in all that is essential, with that form in which it probably proceeded from the hands
of Gregory I. and in which it was handed down in the ancient
Roman Sacramentary manuscripts.   This fact, however, does not
exclude the view that the abundant development of the liturgy during
the Middle Age, which gradually encompassed the monumental
edifice of the Gregorio-Roman rite of the Mass with the exuberant
growth of numerous prayers, chants and customs, did not stop entirely at the sanctuary of the Canon, but also herein gave expression
to the plentifully overflowing feelings by many well meant, but not
always appropriate additions. — The Roman Church has always
understood to cut down to right proportions at the proper time all
the superfluous accessories produced by the piety of ages, and also,
whilst preserving whatever possessed any durable value, to reform
the liturgy in accordance with its ancient forms.   Thus amid a
wealth of prayers and rites she yet preserved that strictly logical

phaniae Sanctorumque Dei fuerit agenda festivitas, singula capitula diebus apta
subjungimus, quibus commemorationem sanctae solemnitatis aut eorum facimus,
quorum natalitia celebramus, cetera vero ordine consueto prosequimur.   Quapropter et ipsius *canonicae precis textum* (the Canon) direximus subter adjectum,
quem (Deo propitio) ex *apostolica traditione* suscepimus (Vigilii Papae [† 555]
Epist. ad Profuturum episc. Bracarens.).

[1]   Trid. sess. 22, cap. 4.

[2]   *Praefationem* actionis, qua populi affectus ad gratiarum actiones incitatur
ac deinde humanae devotionis supplicatio coelestium virtutum laudibus admitti
deposcitur vel ipsam *actionem*, qua conficitur sacrosanctum corporis et sanguinis
dominici mysterium, quamque Romani *canonem*, ut in pontificalibus saepius invenitur, quis primus ordinaverit nobis ignotum est.... *Actio* sive *Canon* ex eo
cognoscitur maxime per partes compositus, quod nomina sanctorum, quorum ibi
communio et societas flagitatur, duobus in locis posita reperiuntur.... Primam
partem canonis praedicti ex eo vel maxime antiquam esse cognoscimus, quia in ea
ordo apostolorum non ita est positus, sicut in emendatioribus evangeliis invenitur;

clearness and precision, which non-Catholics so greatly admire in the Roman liturgy. — Hence the many changes and additions of the text of the Canon, which were produced during the Middle Age, have disappeared partly already since the thirteenth century, and wholly since the reform of St. Pius V. in 1570."[1]

The Canon is, therefore, through its origin, antiquity and use, venerable and inviolable and sacred. If ever a prayer of the Church came into existence under the special inspiration of the Holy Ghost, it is assuredly the prayer of the Canon. It is pervaded throughout by the spirit of faith, and permeated with the sweet odor of devotion; it is a holy work, full of force and unction. Its simple language, by its pithiness and its antique and Scriptural stamp, produces a touching effect on the mind of him who prays and offers the Sacrifice; it charms the soul, just like the dimly lit ancient, venerable basilicas of the Eternal City. Is it not a pleasure and a joy to the heart, that we still utter the very same words at the altar which so many devout and holy priests throughout the entire Church and in all ages have always used in praying and offering the Sacrifice? Already in the times of the Martyrs and in the chapels of the Catacombs these prayers of the Canon of the Mass were recited and sanctified.

2. The Silent Recitation of the Canon. — The manner in which the Canon is to be recited, that is, silently, deserves special notice and explanation. It is a strict ordinance of the Church that the Canon be said silently *(secreto)*, namely, in a voice so subdued that the celebrant may hear himself, but not be heard by those around him.[2] Historical testimonies and reasons drawn from the nature of the thing justify the most general assumption, that it has been a custom from the earliest times[3] to pronounce the words of

---

quod ideo fortasse evenit, quia pars illa prius composita est, quam evangelia ad eam veritatem, quae nunc habetur apud Latinos, corrigerentur (Walafrid Strabo c. 23).

[1] Ebner, Quellen und Forschungen S. 394.

[2] At the ordination of a priest, all the silent prayers of Holy Mass are pronounced somewhat aloud (aliquantulum alte) by the ordaining bishop and the newly ordained co-celebrants. Ordinandi circa altare in genua provoluti disponuntur, et Episcopus quasi eos doceat Missam celebrare, lente ac paululum elata voce Secretas profert, non eas ut populus audiat, sed ut sacerdotes novissime initiati cum eo possint eas recitare, et verba consecrationis uno eodemque tempore cum Episcopo pronuntiare, ad exemplum Christi, qui voce, quae ab Apostolis audiri potuit, in ultima coena panem et vinum consecravit, ut eos, quos tunc sacerdotio initiabat, doceret consecrandi modum legitimumque ritum ad consummationem usque saeculi duraturum (Bened. XIV. De ss. Missae sacrif. l. 2, c. 23, n. 17).

[3] In the Greek and Oriental Liturgies the words of Consecration are said in a loud and high tone of voice, whereupon the people each time by Amen (= so be it) express their faith in the real presence of Jesus Christ in the Blessed Sacrament. Cardinal Bona was of opinion, that formerly in the Western Church also all heard the sanctissima et efficacissima verba, quibus Christi corpus conficitur (Rer. liturg. l. 2, c. 13, § 1), and he presumes, that it is only since the tenth cen-

Consecration, together with the Canon, in silence[1] (excepting, of course, the case of *concelebratio*, formerly of frequent occurrence). Still it is not merely the Church's scrupulous solicitude with which she preserves the original traditions in performing the Sacred Mysteries, but there are other reasons besides, weighty, indeed, that move her to adhere so earnestly to the precept, that the Canon be said in silence, and that the Eucharistic Sacrifice be enacted in speech wholly secret. We will here cite the chief reason that demonstrates not the necessity, indeed, but the expediency and appropriateness of the recitation of the Canon in silence.

a) The silent recitation of the Canon betokens the Consecration and Sacrificial Act to be an exclusively priestly function.[2] The prayers of the Canon being liturgical, are, therefore, to be recited not merely mentally, but also vocally (*vocaliter*), that is, the words must be pronounced with the mouth. But this recitation of the Canon must be made softly, that is, be so constituted as to be inaudible to those who are around, and yet audible to the priest himself. This last circumstance is to be noticed, since it makes a difference in the recitation of the Canon and the Divine Office, for in the recitation of the latter it is not necessary that he who prays should hear himself. The silent recitation is in contrast to the loud.[3] Now while

tury that the silent recitation of the words of the Institution has been prescribed. But the arguments he adduces are unreliable. The very ancient Ordo Roman. II (which probably dates from the seventh or eighth century), explained by Amalarius in his Ecloga, has the following rubric: Quae (sc. Praefationem et Trisagium) dum expleverint, surgit solus Pontifex et *tacite intrat in Canonem.* — According to Mabillon it is prescribed in the oldest Roman Ordines, ut Pontifice Canonem recitante *summum in choro* teneatur *silentium*, et ministri perstent *inclinati* et *silentes* per totum Canonem. — Canonem non incipiebat sacerdos nisi *absoluto Trisagii cantu*, ut scil. clerus et populus, sacerdote Canonem *submissa voce* recitante, in admiratione tanti mysterii quasi stupens *sileret* (In Ord. Rom. comment. c. 21).

[1] Cf. Lebrun, Explication de la Messe, tom. IV: Dissertation sur l'usage de réciter en silence une partie des prières de la Messe dans toutes les églises et dans tous les siècles. — Martene, De antiquis Ecclesiae ritibus, 1. 1, c. 4, a. 8. — Bened. XIV., De ss. Missae sacrificio 1. 2, c. 23. — Collet, Traité des saints Mystères, 2. dissertat. Sur la manière de réciter le Canon de la Messe.

[2] Canon *secreto* agitur, eo quod haec immolatio ad *solum* pertinet *sacerdotem* (Sicard. 1. 3, c. 8).

[3] The rubrics distinguish a twofold, or threefold tone of voice — vox secreta and vox clara, alta, intelligibilis; in the middle between the two (the silent and loud pronunciation) is the vox paululum elevata, vox parum elata, vox aliquantulum elevata (voice half aloud). The expression vox submissa (= falling, lowered, low) often designates moderately loud, often also silent pronunciation. In the Middle Age the Canon was often called Secretum vel Secreta Missae, because it was recited secreto or secrete (= in silence). The word secretus (selected, set apart, separated) signifies at the same time, that the priest recites the sacrificial prayer in silence and secrecy, because in it he, in a special manner, takes the part of mediator — raised above the people and separated from sinners (*segregatus a peccatoribus*).

the loud tone of voice invites those present to join with the priest, and reminds them that the prayers are said in common, the silent recitation appropriately indicates that there is question of a mystery, which it is for the consecrated priest alone to accomplish, and not the people.[1] Such is the case with respect to the Eucharistic Sacrifice. To consecrate the material elements, to offer the Body and Blood of Christ, is a priestly privilege: the congregation present can contribute nothing to the accomplishment of the Sacrificial Act. This is symbolically indicated by the silent recitation of the Canon. The priest does not here, as in the other portions of the Mass, commune with the people; he has entered into the Holy of Holies, there to commune with God alone and to pray and sacrifice for the whole Church. "Moses was alone on the top of the mountain; he conversed with God and God answered him." Thus does the priest stand alone at the altar, when, as the representative and minister of Christ, the eternal Highpriest, he accomplishes and offers up the Holy Sacrifice for the entire Church.

b) The silent recitation of the Canon text harmonizes very beautifully with the accomplishment and the essence of the mystery of the Eucharistic Sacrifice. — The material elements are changed into the Body and Blood of Christ, without the senses perceiving it, or the created mind being able to comprehend it; the real presence and sacrificial life of the Saviour under the sacramental species is concealed beyond all discernment. In every Host there are miracles, as numerous as stars in the firmament, — yet not the slightest trace of the wonders appears externally. With all this the ecclesiastical rite harmonizes perfectly. The holy silence is quite suited to indicate and to recall the concealment and depth, the incomprehensibility and ineffableness of the wonderful mysteries that are enacted on the altar.[2]

c) Silent prayer is related to religious silence, and, therefore, expresses the humility, reverence, admiration and awe wherewith the Church administers and adores the Mystery of the Altar. "The Lord is in His holy temple; let all the earth keep silence before Him!"[3] The sight of the priest at the altar, communing amid profound stillness with God alone, is, therefore, also an excellent means afforded to arouse and promote in those who are present the proper dispositions, with which they should admire, adore and offer along with the priest so grand and sublime a Sacrifice. — *Quam terribilis est haec hora!* — thus does the deacon cry out to the people in the Syrian liturgy — "How terrible is this hour!" While the tremen-

---

[1] Sacerdos quaedam dicit *publice*, sc. quae pertinent et ad sacerdotem et ad populum, sicut sunt orationes communes; quaedam vero pertinent ad *solum* sacerdotem, sicut *oblatio* et *consecratio*, et ideo, quae circa haec sunt dicenda, *occulte* a sacerdote dicuntur (S. Thom. 3, q. 83, a. 4 ad 6).

[2] The Canon is recited secreta voce ad significandum quod humana ratio nequaquam tantum mysterium plenarie capere potest (Sicard. 1. 3, c. 6).

[3] Dominus in templo sancto suo: *sileat* a facie ejus omnis terra! (Hab. 2, 20.)

dous Sacrifice is being accomplished on the altar, all present should be immersed in silent contemplation and in devout meditation of the Divine Mysteries. Now, precisely this mute silence that reigns at the altar during the most sacred moments of the Sacrifice and directs attention to the mysteriousness of the sacrificial act, forms the loudest summons to enter silently into ourselves, to be recollected in mind and to stir our hearts to devotion.[1] The silent recitation of the Canon disposes[2] the faithful to interior adoration and reverent concelebration of the heavenly mysteries wherewith God so graciously favors and blesses us poor mortals.[3]

d) In addition to the principal reasons quoted, it must be remarked that the foreign language and the silent recitation serve to withdraw the sacred words of the Canon from the ordinary intercourse, and to protect them against every desecration.

e) Finally, a mystical reason may be alleged. The priest at the altar is the representative and image of the praying and sacrificing Saviour. Now, as on the Mount of Olives and on the Cross, Jesus prayed not only in loud tones, but also in a low voice and in the silence of His heart to His Father, so also it is proper that the priest should even herein resemble His Divine Model, when representing and renewing the Sacrifice of the Cross.[4] — The altar becomes not merely the Cross, but also the crib; for at the moment of Consecration the marvels of Bethlehem as well as those of Golgotha are renewed. Whilst deep silence pervaded all things and the night was in the midst of its course, the Almighty Word of God descended from His royal throne in heaven to the crib of Bethlehem[5]; in like manner, does the King of Glory at the consecration come down upon the altar, amid the most profound silence.

3.   *The Meaning of the Prayers of the Canon.* — Prayer forms the liturgical accompaniment of the Sacrifice. The Canon contains those prayers which most closely relate to the Eucharistic Sacrifice. They are oblation prayers, which refer to the Consecration; for they

---

[1] Silentium laus est quaedam, tum interna animi Deum venerantis, tum externa, quia alios excitat ad Dei laudem, dum in sacris vident tantam modestiam et religionem (Cornel. a Lapid. in Levit. 1, 17).

[2] *Secretis* verbis Canon pronuntiatur etiam alio respectu, videl. ut habito circumquaque silentio ministri et circumstantes seipsos infra ipsum Canonem recolligant vimque et rationem tanti sacramenti advertant, quatenus eis proficiat (Hildeb. Turon. Expositio Missae).

[3] *Silentium hoc* compluribus altiori voce recitatis precibus interruptum *nescio quid majestatis ac mysterii* prae se fert, quod majorem venerationem conciliat, quod sacrum quendam horrorem excitat, quod devotam cordis compunctionem inspirat quodque vivo pietatis sensu adstantium animos penetrat (Languet, De vero Eccl. sensu circa sacr. cerem. usum c. 41).

[4] Oratio *secreta* sacerdotis commemoratio quaedam est *secretae* orationis Christi vel in horto vel in cruce (Suarez disp. 83, sect. 1, n. 25).

[5] Dum medium *silentium* tenerent omnia, et nox in suo cursu medium iter peregeret, omnipotens Sermo tuus, Domine, a regalibus sedibus venit (Antiph. eccles.). — Cfr. Sap. 18, 14.

contain in part petitions for the blessing and consecration of the sacrificial elements, in part an offering of the Sacrificial Body and Blood of Christ, and in part supplications to obtain and to apply the fruits of the Sacrifice. As to their contents, they harmonize with the foregoing prayers of the Offertory — and we behold in them a copy of the prayers of our Divine Saviour. He lived praying and praying He died: praying He redeemed the world. The longest and the most solemn, the most fervent and touching prayer of the Lord is the one which He uttered when He was about to accomplish His Sacrifice on the Cross; it is the so-called prayer of the High-priest.[1] He makes known therein to whom, for whom and for what purpose He would offer His sacrificial death; He supplicates for His disciples and for all who through their word would believe in Him, that is, for the entire Church Militant. He prayed thus the Father that He would deign to fill all the faithful in time and in eternity with His saving gifts: that He would preserve them here below in unity, keep them in truth and sanctify them by grace, that hereafter they might be transformed in beatitude and behold His glory.[2] — Does not this prayer of the Highpriest resound throughout the Canon of the Mass, wherein the Church expresses what gifts of grace she would draw for herself and for all her children from the Holy Sacrifice? How powerful, forcible and effective do these petitions and intercessions of the Church become, as they ascend to the throne of mercy, in union with the voice of the Blood of Christ, aye, steeped in the sacrificial cup of the redeeming Blood, which more loudly and more strongly cries to Heaven than did the blood of Abel!

With the Canon of Consecration are ushered in the holiest and most sacred moments of the Sacrificial Celebration: this part of Holy Mass, still more then than the other portions, claims attention, devotion and reverence.[3] The heart should be occupied only with the

---

[1] It is the most sublime prayer that ever proceeded from human lips: gentle emotion, mournful gravity and a kind of devout melancholy are diffused throughout its composition in such a degree, that it brings our Highpriest in an incomparable manner before the soul as well in the greatness of His divine liberality, as in the purity of a truly human affection, — a Highpriest, "who can have compassion on them that are ignorant and that err: because He Himself also is compassed with infirmity" (Heb. 5, 2). Cf. Oswald, Die Erlösung in Christo Jesu II, 183.

[2] Hoc ut tempore sacrificii postulemus, saluberrimum habemus nostri Salvatoris exemplum, qui hoc nos in commemoratione mortis ejus poscere voluit, quod nobis ipse, verus Pontifex, *morti proximus postulavit* ... hoc ergo nobis poscimus, cum corpus et sanguinem Christi offerimus, quod nobis poposcit, quando se pro nobis offerre dignatus est Christus (S. Fulgent. Contra Fabian. fragm. 28).

[3] Quamvis in toto officio Missae debeat celebrans omnibus viribus suis esse attentus atque sollicitus, tamen ab exordio Canonis debet *omnino recollectus* consistere et mente ad divina suspensus, in quantum humana fragilitas fieri sustinet et Spiritus sancti clementia conferre dignatur, et ut talem gratiam a Deo in hac parte Missae mereatur recipere, sic tenetur ante celebrationem et postmodum vivere gratusque esse, quatenus tunc visitari atque illuminari sit dignus, nec est melior praeparatio ad celebrandum, quam ut sacerdos in omni vita sua sic conversari

divine function and be to all extraneous thoughts and cares as "a garden enclosed" and "a fountain sealed up" (Cant. 4, 12). Above all, the passion and death of Christ should be devoutly meditated upon.[1] We are exhorted to this by the image of the Crucified, which is placed before the Canon, in order that the painful, bitter and bloody death of Christ may be presented to our view in a striking manner. Some persons also recognize from the circumstance that the Canon commences with the letter T a certain special and divine intercession.[2] For the Tau (T) bears a resemblance to the Cross,[3] and, consequently, it meets us already in the prophet as the seal of the elect who are spared the chastisements of God, or as the sign of deliverance, life and salvation, which the predestined bear on their foreheads. "Go through the midst of the city, through the midst of Jerusalem," thus says the Lord, "and mark *Tau* upon the foreheads of all men that sigh and mourn for the abominations that are committed in the midst thereof" (Ezech. 9, 4. — Cf. Apoc. 7, 3).

57. The First Prayer of the Canon before the Consecration.

Te igitur, clementissime Pater, per Jesum Christum Filium tuum Dominum nostrum, supplices rogamus ac petimus, uti accepta habeas, et benedicas, haec † dona, haec † munera, haec † sancta sacrificia illibata; imprimis quae tibi offerimus pro Ecclesia tua

We, therefore, humbly pray and beseech Thee; most merciful Father, through Jesus Christ Thy Son, our Lord, that Thou wouldst accept and bless these † gifts, these † presents, these † holy unspotted sacrifices, which, in the first place, we offer Thee for Thy

---

conetur, ut sit hujus Sacramenti condignus minister (Dion. Carthus. Exposit. Missae art. 19).

[1] Notandum per totum Canonem Dominicae passionis commemorationem potissimum actitari... Unde et ipse sacerdos per totum Canonem in *expansione* manuum non tam mentis devotionem quam Christi *extensionem* in cruce designat ... congruum est ut manus *expandamus* infra Canonem, hoc tamen observato, ne quid digitis tangamus praeter Domini corpus (Microl. c. 16). The Ordo Rom. XIV, c. 71 also has after the Consecration the rubric: Hic (Pontifex) *ampliet* manus et brachia. According to our Roman Missal, on the contrary, the celebrant says most of the prayers of the Canon before and after the Consecration extensis manibus *ante pectus.* (Cfr. Quarti, In Rubr. Missal. p. 2, tit. 9, sect. 1, dub. 1.)

[2] Inter Praefationem et Canonem in plerisque sacramentariis *imago Christi* (crucified) depingitur, ut non solum intellectus litterae, verum etiam adspectus picturae memoriam dominicae passionis inspiret. Et forte divina factum est providentia, licet humana non sit industria procuratum, ut ab ea littera T canon inciperet, quae sui forma signum crucis ostendit et exprimit in figura (Innoc. III. 1. 3, c. 2).

[3] There are three kinds of crosses: 1. the crux *decussata*, that is, the transverse cross ×; 2. the crux *immissa* + and 3. the crux *commissa* ⊥. The last form is similar to the T and is, therefore, also called the T cross. (Cf. Münz, Archäolog. Bemerkungen über das Kreuz S. 10 etc.)

sancta catholica: quam pacificare, custodire, adunare, et regere digneris toto orbe terrarum: una cum famulo tuo Papa nostro N. et Antistite nostro N. et omnibus orthodoxis atque catholicae et apostolicae fidei cultoribus.

holy Catholic Church, which Thou mayst vouchsafe to pacify, guard, unite and govern throughout the world: together with Thy servant N. our Pope, N. our Bishop, as also all orthodox believers and promoters of the Catholic and Apostolic faith.

Commemoratio pro Vivis.

The Commemoration of the Living.

Memento, Domine, famulorum famularumque tuarum N. et N. et omnium circumstantium, quorum tibi fides cognita est et nota devotio: pro quibus tibi offerimus, vel qui tibi offerunt hoc sacrificium laudis, pro se suisque omnibus: pro redemptione animarum suarum, pro spe salutis et incolumitatis suae: tibique reddunt vota sua aeterno Deo, vivo et vero.

Remember, O Lord, Thy servants and handmaids, N. and N. and all here present, whose faith and devotion are known to Thee; for whom we offer, or who offer up to Thee this Sacrifice of praise for themselves and all pertaining to them, for the redemption of their souls, for the hope of their salvation and safety, and who pay their vows unto Thee, the eternal God, living and true.

Infra Actionem.

Within the Canon.

Communicantes et memoriam venerantes, imprimis gloriosae semper Virginis Mariae, genitricis Dei et Domini nostri Jesu Christi: sed et beatorum Apostolorum ac Martyrum tuorum, Petri et Pauli, Andreae, Jacobi, Joannis, Thomae, Jacobi, Philippi, Bartholomaei, Matthaei, Simonis et Thaddaei: Lini, Cleti, Clementis, Xysti, Cornelii, Cypriani, Laurentii, Chrysogoni, Joannis et Pauli, Cosmae et Damiani: et omnium Sanctorum tuorum, quorum meritis precibusque concedas, ut in omnibus protectionis tuae muniamur auxilio. Per eundem Christum Dominum nostrum. Amen.

In communion with and honoring the memory, especially of the glorious ever Virgin Mary, Mother of God and our Lord Jesus Christ; as also of Thy blessed Apostles and Martyrs, Peter and Paul, Andrew, James, John, Thomas, James, Philip, Bartholomew, Matthew, Simon and Thaddeus, Linus, Cletus, Clement, Xystus, Cornelius, Cyprian, Lawrence, Chrysogonus, John and Paul, Cosmas and Damian, and all Thy Saints; by whose merits and prayers grant that we may in all things be made secure by the aid of Thy protection. Through the same Christ our Lord. Amen.

The above formula of prayer consists of three parts: all three parts are united and form a whole, that is, one complete prayer, as is evident from the context and the single concluding formula (Per eundem Christum . . .).[1]

1. a) The beginning of the prayer is introduced, or accompanied by several ceremonies which, in an impressive manner, serve to emphasize its contents. Before presenting his petition to God, the priest raises his hands and eyes, to express the elevation of his soul, and to indicate that he is addressing the Father in heaven, and seeking help from God on high. But presently he lowers his eyes and hands, bowing profoundly and placing his joined hands on the altar: it is in this posture that he begins the Canon.[2] What posture of the body could be more appropriate for the priest at this moment, when with all humility and reverence he suppliantly addresses the Lord, "who is high above all nations and looketh down on the low things in heaven and in earth?" (Ps. 112, 4–6.) — Before the words "that Thou wouldst accept and bless," the priest kisses the altar,[3] and whilst he is saying "these † gifts, these † presents, these † holy unspotted sacrifices," he makes three times with his hand the sign of the Cross over the oblation. Likewise as at the blessing at the end of Mass, the kissing of the altar and the sign of the Cross have the closest relationship with one another: both constitute a ritual whole in themselves, the symbolical significance of which is to be inferred from the prayer that is recited at the same time. The priest implores with great ardor and fervor for the blessing of the Eucharistic elements, and as they are designated by three different names, he makes at the same time the sign of the Cross over the elements three times, that word and action may harmonize perfectly. The text, therefore, in this instance requires that the sign of the Cross be conceived as a sign of blessing.[4] But a more extended meaning

---

[1] The prayers of the Canon have only the short concluding formula (three times per *eundem* Chr. Dom. nostr., who shortly before is mentioned in the last member of the prayer, and twice per Christ. Dom. nostr.). In ipsa *quinaria* conclusione non incongrue *quinaria* Domini *vulneratio* intimatur (Microlog. De eccles. observat. c. 16).

[2] The opinion of Quarti and Merati, that the words Te igitur are not to be said until after the inclination, is better founded than that of Gavanti and Cavalieri, that the Canon prayers are to be commenced at the same time as the elevation of the hands and eyes. (Cf. Bouvry, Expositio Rubric. II, p. 3, sect. 3, tit. 8.)

[3] Hic osculatur sacerdos altare (Sicard. [† 1215], Mitral. l. 3, c. 6). Ancient writers do not mention this kissing of the altar. However, it was formerly (and partly till about the close of the fifteenth century) the custom, before beginning the Canon to kiss the image of the Crucified in the Missal, that is, the Cross. The Ordo Rom. XIV, c. 53 (of the beginning of the fourteenth century) has the following rubric: Capellano praesentante sibi librum missalem, Pontifex osculetur imagines, quae debent esse depictae in eodem libro ante Canonem Missae. Subsequenter manibus junctis inclinatus ante incipiat submissa voce *Te igitur* etc. et cum dicet *uti accepta habeas*, erigat se et osculetur altare in parte sinistra prope hostiam.

[4] Terna crucis signa sunt verae benedictiones, quibus Dei invocatur omnipotentia, ut oblata in corpus et sanguinem Christi convertat. Ternarius autem

may, without constraint, be herewith combined, according to which this holy sign should refer to the Sacrifice of the Cross, and denote, that by the blessing of Consecration, the same divine Victim will become present on the altar, as once upon the tree of the Cross shed His Blood for our redemption. — If now the making of the sign of the Cross over the sacrificial gifts is a true blessing, then the kissing of the altar that preceded, should be conceived as an introduction thereunto. The priest indeed kisses the altar to evince likewise to the Lord his sentiments of reverence, homage and subjection; but here by this kiss he would mainly renew and represent symbolically the union of love with Christ, because he draws from his relation with Christ all the power of blessing and the whole fulness of blessing, which he then by the three signs of the Cross[1] pours out, as it were, over the elements of sacrifice.

b) The priest prays: "Thee, therefore, most merciful Father — "[2]; the little word *igitur* (= hence, accordingly) joins what follows to what precedes, and shows how intimately the Canon is connected with the Preface, and also with the Offertory: = Because we have presented to Thee, O most merciful Father, thanksgivings, praises and homages, we now again address ourselves to Thee with a petition.[3] According to the example and admonition of the Sav-

---

signorum crucis numerus hocce mysterium a S. Trinitate perfici indicat (Cavalieri V, c. 16, n. 4).

[1] At least since the eleventh century in the Canon, as at present, the sign of the Cross is made over the oblations in seven places (altogether twenty-five times). (Cfr. Innocent. III. De sacr. alt. myst. 1. 5, c. 14.) — With the exception of the two signs of the Cross at the words sacrosanctum Filii tui corpus et sanguinem (Supplices te rogamus), all the others are mentioned already during the ninth century. (Cfr. Ordo Rom. II, n. 10: In Canone sex ordines crucium observantur. — Amalar. [† c. 847], Eclog. in Ord. Roman. II, n. 22.) — Innocent. III. explains the symbolism of the numerus binarius, ternarius, quinarius; Micrologus, on the other hand, divides the numerus binarius into two single ones. *Imparem* numerum semper in dispensatione signorum super oblationem observamus, videl. unam crucem vel tres vel quinque faciendo, et hoc utique non sine certi causa mysterii. Nam in una et tribus unum et trinum Deum intimamus. In quinque autem quinquepartitam Domini passionem significamus (De ecclesiast. observat. c. 14). — Attende quod *fere* in quolibet ordine per *imparem* numerum signacula disponuntur, quia corpus Christi unum permanens non scinditur (Sicard. Mitral. 1. 3, c. 6).

[2] Praeinducta verba Canonis igne divini amoris redundant ac igniunt, unde cum ardentissimo mentis affectu promenda sunt. Porro oratio *ardens* et *humilis* esse debet; nam desiderium pauperum, i. e. ardentem affectum humilium exaudivit Dominus: qui enim ardenter orat, valde cavere debet, ne propriis meritis innitatur vel confidat. Rursus, qui suis meritis non confidit, sed humiliter orat, omnino vitare habet, ne in orando pusillanimis efficiatur aut segnis. Ut ergo Spiritus Sanctus, qui utique *principaliter est auctor Canonis*, ad talem orationem nos incitaret, idcirco in ipso exordio Canonis duo verba praemisit, quorum alterum dilectionem inflammat, videlicet *"Pater"*, alterum fiduciam exauditionis praestat propter bonitatem ejus, qui petitur, scilicet *"clementissime"*, et ad designandam atque augendam interiorem cordis humiliationem inclinat se sacerdos ante altare praedicta verba dicendo (Dion. Carthus. Exposit. Missae art. 19).

[3] Cfr. Stephan. Augustod. De Sacram. altar. c. 13.

iour, the Church addresses this prayer to the "Father": at the same time presenting her supplication after a manner so very proper as to deserve to be answered. For she calls upon God as "the most merciful Father," she implores Him "through Jesus Christ," she supplicates with humility and earnestness. — God is addressed as "the most merciful Father," because on account of His exceedingly great love and goodness He is ever inclined, not to judge and punish according to the full rigor of the law, but always to have mercy and to spare, inasmuch as He remits in part or entirely the merited punishments.[1] "In God's works and just judgments," as St. Leo remarks, "all is full of true justice and merciful sweetness."[2] It is with filial confidence, therefore, that we pray to the "Father of our Lord Jesus Christ, the Father of mercies and the God of all consolation" (2 Cor. 1, 3), whose indulgent and forgiving love here below has neither measure nor limits; He is "sweet and mild and plenteous in mercy to all that call upon Him" (Ps. 85, 5), and, consequently, ever attentive to the voice of our supplication. — This will be so much more the case, because we have offered our petitions "through Jesus Christ, His Son, our Lord." In the Incarnation of His only-begotten Son, God revealed Himself to the world as the "Father of Jesus Christ"; in His Son Jesus Christ, God has had compassion upon us and given us the spirit of adoption, by which we call Him *Father* and in prayer may address Him as *our Father.* The Saviour glorified and elevated to the right hand of the Father is designated as "our Lord", because He possesses the fulness of all power and authority in heaven and on earth, and because He has in a special manner acquired the Church as His possession in the bloody combat of His death. With the price of His Blood He has ransomed us; as redeemed by Him and as members of the Church, we do not belong to ourselves, but to the Saviour, whom as "our Lord" we are ever bound to serve. Through "His Son" and "our Lord Jesus Christ" the Father hears our petitions and bestows upon us all benefits. — As we draw near to the infinite majesty and holiness of God, with the consciousness of our wretchedness and sinfulness, we pray in an humble posture of body as well as with humble dispositions and sentiments of heart (*supplices*)[3]; for prayer penetrates more powerfully through the clouds to the throne of God, the more profoundly the one that prays abases himself interiorly and exteriorly. — Finally, we present our petitions with fervor, with devout importunity and a holy vehemence; for the accumulated

---

[1] Ad *clementiam* pertinet, quod sit *diminutiva poenarum;* in hoc, quod diminuit poenas, clementia maxime videtur accedere ad caritatem, quae est potissima virtutum, per quam bona operamur ad proximos et eorum mala impedimus (S. Thom. 2, 2, q. 157, c. 1—4).

[2] In Dei operibus atque judiciis nihil vacat a veritate justitiae, nihil a miseratione clementiae (Serm. 1 de jejun. 10. mens.).

[3] Supplex (from sub and plico, hence, strictly, bending the knee, kneeling down, hence) = to humble one's self, humbly imploring.

expressions *rogamus ac petimus* — "we pray and beseech" — proceed from the greatness and the liveliness of our desires.[1] —

We beseech so persistently and so imploringly, because the object of our ardent desire is so sublime and so holy, namely, the gracious acceptance and the blessing of the sacrificial elements of bread and wine prepared on the altar: "that Thou accept and bless[2] these † presents, etc." The purpose for which God is to "accept" the material gifts, is expressed by the word "bless". By the blessing here implored is to be understood[3]: first, the preparatory dedication to God of the bread and the wine, then the real Consecration of these material gifts and, finally, the fulness of grace concealed under the consecrated elements and diffusing itself throughout the Church. As was previously the Holy Ghost, so now the Father is invoked "to bless" the elements of bread and wine, that is, to sanctify them beforehand for their exalted destiny, then to change them into the Body and Blood of Christ and thus to make them for us the source of grace. For this copious blessing we must and do pray, because it is a gift of the condescending love and a work of the almighty power of the triune God.[4]

The Eucharistic elements are designated and distinguished by three names,[5] inasmuch as we pray that God may accept and bless

---

[1] *Vehemens petendi affectus* geminatione verbi deprecatorii exprimitur, scil. *rogamus* ac *petimus*. Accumulantur verba petitionem explicantia ad significandam ipsius affectus nostri magnitudinem (Clichtov. Elucid. eccl. 1. 3, n. 4). — Some writers endeavor to distinguish the signification of these two words. Rogatio ostendit humilitatem, petitio confidentiam; qui aliquid implorat, humilitatem debet ostendere et de impetratione confidere. Itaque supplices rogamus, confidenter petimus (B. Odo Camerac. Exposit. in Canon. dist. 1).

[2] Oblationem nostram, quaesumus, Domine, misericorditer *acceptare* et *sanctificare* digneris, ut ejus sanctificatione nobis salus proveniat et defensio sempiterna (Sacram. Gregor.). — Acceptus (graciously received) = welcome, agreeable, pleasing; acceptum habere = acceptare, to receive, to be contented with. Acceptabis (εὐδοκήσεις) sacrificium, oblationes et holocausta (Ps. 50, 21). — Sacerdotum est offerre et majestatem Dei invocare; Dei est autem dignanter suscipere et ea quae offeruntur benedicere (Florus Diac. De actione Miss. n. 43).

[3] Petimus, ut Deus Pater benedicat haec dona, h. e. ut benedictionem suae virtutis et gratiae illis infundat, ut idonea sint tam digno sacramenta (Clichtov. 1. c. n. 5). — Uti . . . benedicas, i. e. gratia et virtute coelesti perfundas atque sanctifices convertendo ea in corpus et sanguinem Christi (Dion. Carthus. Exposit. Miss. art. 18). — Petimus, ut Deus acceptet et benedicat haec dona ad totius Ecclesiae fructum et utilitatem (Suarez disp. 83, sect. 2, n. 6).

[4] Efficacia verborum sacramentalium impediri potest per intentionem sacerdotis. Nec tamen est inconveniens quod a Deo petamus id quod certissime scimus ipsum facturum, sicut Christus (Joan. c. 17) petit suam clarificationem (S. Thom. 3, q. 83, a. 4 ad 7).

[5] Quod subjungitur: haec dona, haec munera, haec sancta sacrificia illibata, non aliud atque aliud dicitur; sed res *una* pro sua magnitudine *diversa* appellatione laudatur et laudando commendatur. Ipsa sermonum repetitio tanti sacramenti est commendatio et piae devotionis excitatio (Flor. Diacon. n. 44).

"these presents, these gifts, these holy unspotted sacrifices." Elsewhere, notably in the *Secreta*, each of these three words is often met
with singly to signify the sacrificial elements. They all indeed
designate one and the same thing — namely, the Host and the
chalice containing the wine, but under different aspects and from
different sides. The elements of bread and wine are called "presents"
(*dona*) and "gifts" (*munera*), inasmuch as they are simply regarded
in the light of religious offerings, which we dedicate and present to
our Lord [1]; "sacrifices" (*sacrificia*), on the contrary, the altar-gifts
are termed such even before the Consecration by anticipation, inasmuch
as they are prepared and destined soon to be consecrated into the true
Body and Blood of Christ. [2] In consideration of this their sublime
destiny, the Eucharistic elements are not called simply "sacrifices",
but "holy unspotted sacrifices" (*sancta sacrificia illibata*)[3]; for it is
the "Holy of Holies", the Lamb without stain or blemish, that is
offered under the appearances of bread and wine. Yet the matter
also of the Sacrifice can as such be called "holy", inasmuch as it
has previously been separated from profane use and dedicated to the
service of God; it can likewise be designated as "unspotted",
because in its selection and preparation religious care was taken that
the sacrificial bread and wine should be faultless and without any
foreign admixture. [4]

---

[1] To distinguish between the dona and munera, a secure point of support is
wanting; hence these two words have undergone so great a variety of interpretations. As a rule, it is said that the oblations are called dona, because God has
imparted them to us, and munera, because we return them to Him; or the word
dona indicates, that we freely present the altar-gifts, while the designation munera
refers to our obligation of presenting them.

[2] Bread and wine vocantur sacrificia *per anticipationem*, quia sunt materia,
ex qua conficiendum est sacrificium, et dicuntur sacrificia *initiative*, quia prae-
parantur in sacrificium (Quarti, p. 2, tit. 9, sect. 2, dub. 1).

[3] The sacrificial gifts on the altar (sacrificia) are called *illibata*, inasmuch as
in their natural state they are inviolable, uninjured, sound (that is, sine defectibus,
as they are cited in the Missal); *sancta*, inasmuch as, by a supernatural dedication,
they are consecrated to God, they belong to God, and, therefore, as the property of
God, they are holy, venerable, inviolate and not to be touched. — Ex hoc verbo (sc.
illibata) admonemur, ut appositus panis integer sit et nulla fractione vel laesura
violatus (B. Odo Camerac. Exposit. in Canon. dist. 1).

[4] Donum est, quod a superiore datur, munus, quod ab inferiore. Unde panis
et vinum sunt *dona* a Deo nobis donata, *munera* a nobis Deo oblata; solemus enim
illos munerare, a quibus aliquid volumus obtinere. Eadem sunt sacrificia *sancta*,
scil. Deo dicata et ad sacrificium sanctum praeparata. *Illibata* sunt nec corporali
gustu nec aliqua fractione vitiata, sed integra et intacta (Stephan. Augustodun. De
sacram. altar. c. 13). — Dona *illibata*, quia ad litteram pura et integra esse debent
propter significationem et reverentiam tanti sacramenti: non enim debet panis
maculosus esse vel vinum permixtum, nisi cum modica aqua (Dion. Carthus. Exposit. Missae art. 18). — Dicuntur *pluralitatis* numero dona, munera et sacrificia,
quoniam panis et vini, antequam consecrantur, alia et alia est substantia et una ab
altera reipsa discrepans, quae substantiarum diversitas numero multitudinis apte

The sacrificial gifts designated are offered up to God for the welfare of the Church and her members. But since not the natural matter of bread and wine, but the Body and Blood of Christ alone are the real sacrifice of the Church and her fountains of grace, it is evident that this offering cannot exclusively have for its object the gifts of bread and wine, but must also be referred principally to that which they are soon to become, that is, the Sacrifice of the Body and Blood of Jesus Christ.[1] The full meaning of our prayer may thus be expressed: We beseech Thee, O Father, that Thou wouldst accept and bless these material gifts, which we present to Thee, in order that, by the blessing of Consecration, they may become a heavenly healing fountain for the Church.[2] It is, therefore, the Sacrifice of the Body and Blood of Jesus Christ which we have especially in view when offering the bread and wine, and through which we implore and expect all the gifts of salvation.

"Principally" and "in the first place" (*imprimis*) the Eucharistic Sacrifice is offered for the "holy Catholic Church of God" (*pro Ecclesia tua sancta catholica*)[3]; hence from every Mass there flow to her abundant fruits and blessings. The Heavenly Father is the Lord of the Church, and the Church is His property. He has purchased her with the Precious Blood of His Son; hence she belongs to Him, and she is bound to serve Him. — As the Church of the

---

exprimitur: nam hoc loco ipsa demonstrantur ante factam consecrationem. Ea vero consummata, interdum etiam adhuc nomine consimili et multitudinem indicante explicantur, et *sacramenta* aut *sacrificia* dicuntur, non quidem ob substantiarum (quae jam conversae sunt) varietatem, sed ob *specierum*, sub quibus tam sancta continentur mysteria *diversitatem* (Clichtov. Elucid. eccl. 1. 3, n. 6).

[1] Per haec dona, ut nunc coram Deo proponuntur, nihil postulatur, sed per sacrificium, ad quod destinantur, et per Christum offerendum in eodem sacrificio. (Quarti l. c.)

[2] Non offerimus panem et vinum pro Ecclesia simpliciter et absolute, vel tanquam sacrificium principaliter finaliterque intentum, sed tali respectu et intentione, ut convertantur divina virtute in corpus et sanguinem Christi, sicque offeramus Patri coelesti sacrificium perfectum et sanctum, videlicet corpus et sanguinem Filii sui carissimi (Dion. Carthus. Expos. Miss. art. 19). — Cum dicimus, nos offerre ¡panem Deo pro Ecclesia, sensus est, nos offerre Deo panem consecrandum et ex quo per consecrationem verum sacrificium Deo immolandum est pro ecclesia. (Bellarmin. De Missa lib. 2, c. 21.)

[3] Intende *cur* celebres celebrareque debeas. Nempe *propter easdem causas, ob quas Christus se obtulit in cruce Deo Patri,* tu quoque eum offerre debes eidem in altari: h. e. primo et principaliter pro tota Ecclesia, pro infidelium conversione, pro fidelium reformatione, pro universorum salute, pro occurrentibus causis et necessitatibus quibuscunque, pro propinquis, commissis et benefactoribus tuis fidelibusque defunctis, et pro quibus ex speciali causa vis exorare, atque pro tui ipsius condigna emendatione in omnibus. Ut ergo utcunque pro viribus tuis existas idoneus deprecari et offerre pro tantis ac talibus causis, satage et indefesse conare teipsum Deo placitum exhibere, ei familiariter adhaerere, ipsum intra te amorose complecti, sinceriter contemplari omnique die magis ferventer diligere (Dion. Carthus. De sacram. Euchar. serm. 3).

"living God" she is "holy"; and the Sacrifice of the Mass is precisely that inexhaustible fountain of holiness, in the splendor of which the Church shines always more or less brightly. — The holy Church of God is also "Catholic", that is, universal, since she extends over the whole globe of the earth, and continues to live and work throughout all ages, until time shall merge into eternity. She is that stately, majestic tree of life which affords shelter to the whole world, and under whose branches all nations have been and are constantly gathered.

Four graces are here implored for the Church by virtue of the Eucharistic Sacrifice; we beg the Lord, namely, to grant and preserve peace to her (*pacificare*), to protect and to shelter her (*custodire*), to give her unity and confirm her therein (*adunare*), to guide and to direct her (*regere*), and this "throughout the whole earth" (*toto orbe terrarum*) from the rising of the sun to the setting thereof.[1]

a) May the Lord grant peace to His Church — true and complete, interior and exterior peace! This peace is a great boon, rich in blessings; it facilitates the exercise of her great mission, which consists principally in imparting to mankind the treasures of divine truth and grace; it assists the Church to save souls, to consecrate and sanctify the temporal life in all its forms and relations. Peace is "the tranquillity of order" (*tranquillitas ordinis* — S. Aug.) and enables us to "lead a quiet and peaceable life in all piety and chastity" (1 Tim. 2, 2). Hence the Church so often and so fervently prays: "Grant, O Lord, peace in our days; for there is no other that combats for us, than Thou our Lord and God!" She ardently desires "to overcome all error and opposition in order to be enabled to serve the Lord with perfect freedom." But how can the Church be able to live long in peace in a world filled with unbelief and immorality? Her journey throughout the ages has always been a warlike pilgrimage. She is here below at all times the Church Militant; she must strive and combat until she reaches the Heavenly Jerusalem. In her combat against a God-forsaken world, "she never gets beyond a truce, and it is seldom that she ever has so much as that. Her very alliances must needs be full of suspicions from long experience, and in reality they are rather fresh anxieties than permissions for repose. At best, she can live only as the timid deer in the forest, whose every echo is ringing with the hunter's horn. She is less at her ease in a Concordat than in a Catacomb" (Faber). Thus the Church must at all times be ready as "an army in battle-array," and persevere in combating the deceit and power of her numberless enemies, who are unceasingly intent on harassing and enslaving her, on perverting

---

[1] A certain Christian (Felix) begged the holy Bishop Fructuosus of Tarragona († 529), when the latter was about to suffer martyrdom, to remember him. Cui sanctus Fructuosus cunctis audientibus clara voce respondit: *In mente me habere necesse est Ecclesiam catholicam ab Oriente usque in Occidente diffusam* (cfr. S. Aug. Serm. 273, n. 2).

and destroying her.[1] To whom then should she have recourse but to God, who is her Safeguard and her Helper?

b) Hence we implore that God may be pleased, amid all assaults and oppressions, to protect and defend His Church as the apple of His eye; that He vouchsafe to shelter her under the shadow of His wings, until the wicked shall have passed away (Ps. 16, 8). We beseech the Lord to save the shepherd and the sheepfold from the rage of ravenous wolves, from the bite of venomous serpents. He has promised His Church protection and victory over all her adversaries. If God protects His people, His kingdom, His Church, what then can the gates of hell avail against them? We may, therefore, in time of persecution and tribulation cry out confidently: "Our God is our refuge and strength, a helper in troubles which have found us exceedingly. Therefore, we will not fear, when the earth shall be troubled and the mountains shall be removed into the heart of the sea. Nations were troubled and kingdoms were bowed down; God uttered His voice, — the earth trembled. The Lord of armies is with us, the God of Jacob is our protector" (Ps. 45, 2—3; 7—8).

c) Strong and invincible is the Church in combat only through the union and harmony of her members; therefore, we pray that God may unite His Church, that is, constantly preserve her and confirm her always more in union. In this grand unity, which is wrought through the firm cement of faith and love, shines forth conspicuously the Church's supernatural majesty and glory, her inexhaustible fulness of life and power of victory. No earthly power is able to divide and split the marvellous unity of the Church, that supernatural communion of life and love existing among and binding together the children of the divine Catholic family; for this bond of union between the shepherd and the fold, as also between Catholics of all nations, has only the more closely and indissolubly been entwined by the blood of martyrs and the sufferings of confessors. For this very union of all the faithful among themselves and with God, the Saviour prayed most especially before His passion: "Holy Father, sanctify them in truth. Thy word is truth. As Thou hast sent Me into the world, I also have sent them into the world. And for them do I sanctify Myself: that they also may be sanctified in truth. And not for them only do I pray, but for them also who through their word shall believe in Me: that they all may be one, as Thou, Father, in Me and I in Thee: that they also may be one in us: that the world may believe that Thou hast sent Me" (John 17, 17—20). He that separates himself from this living unity, is like a branch cut off and withered, that is, he will go to destruction.

d) Finally, we petition God that He would govern, guide and direct His Church.[2] This He does through the Pope, the bishops

---

[1] Ecclesia Dei, semper in procinctu posita, incessabili pugna contra inimicos dimicat (Pontif. Rom. De ordinat. diaconi).

[2] Ut in suis consiliis, dispositionibus, judiciis, decretis, institutis, actionibus nullo decipiatur errore et in omnibus tuo ducatur moderamine (B. Odo Camerac. l.c.).

and the priests. The increase, splendor and beauty of the Church depend principally on the worthiness, the fervor and the fidelity of her rulers and teachers. Therefore, we pray God that He would give to His Church pastors, prepared to sacrifice their ease and comfort, their liberty and their life for the sheep of Christ; shepherds who "in word, in conversation, in charity, in faith, in chastity show themselves an example to the faithful" (1 Tim. 4, 12); shepherds who with humility and meekness, with courage and fortitude, with self-devotedness and disinterestedness lead the flock confided to them in the ways of salvation and pasture them in the meadows of grace, at the fountains of the waters of life. Such shepherds are a joy to Heaven and earth. But it behooves us to beseech God to send such laborers into His vineyard.

After this manner do we, in the first place, offer our prayers and the Sacrifice for Holy Church, for she is, indeed, our greatest benefactress, our spiritual mother. For the Church the Lord shed His Heart's blood, that He might present to Himself a glorious Church, not having spot or wrinkle or any such thing (*sine macula*), but that she should be holy (*sancta*) and without blemish, immaculate (*immaculata*). Should we not then, with filial devotedness, love and reverence her, be zealous and make sacrifices for her cause, pray and labor for her, combat and suffer for her, live and die for her? In these points is revealed that sincere and devoted affection which blooms from a lively faith. If I forget thee, holy Church, let my right hand be forgotten, let my tongue cleave to my jaws, if I do no not remember thee, if I make thee not the beginning of my joy! (Cf. Ps. 136.) "Even to have to mourn and to suffer with the Church of God, is always, because true happiness accompanies it, incomparably better than to have, without her and outside of her, every kind and degree of earthly prosperity and pleasure, and infinitely more noble than to possess the height of temporal power." Sacrifice and prayer, offered principally for the Church, indirectly benefit the whole world; for in proportion as the Church is exalted and propagated, the wider and the more abundantly can she pour forth the gifts of salvation, the treasures of grace and truth over all mankind.

The general fruit of the Sacrifice falls the more copiously to the share of the individual members of the mystical body of Christ in proportion as they contribute to the common welfare of the Church[1]; hence we have now a special and an express offering and prayer for the Pope, and for the chief pastor of the diocese in which the holy Mass is celebrated.[2] Then is added a general intercession for all

---

[1] Saepe Praelatis aliisque publicis personis, a quibus bonum Ecclesiae multum pendet, ratione sacrificiorum dantur particulares aliquae gratiae propter bonum commune Ecclesiae, cui multum expedit ejusmodi personas singulariter a Deo dirigi (Coninck, De Sacrament. q. 83, art. 1, dub. 9, concl. 7).

[2] From the most ancient times it has been customary to name the Pope and the bishop of the diocese in the prayers of the Canon. Until the eleventh century

those persons who not only preserve the true faith in their heart and confess it with their lips, but who, moreover, according to their ability defend and propagate it.

It is proper that, throughout the entire Church, the Pope should be prayed for and the Sacrifice be offered for him, for he is the Vicar of Jesus Christ, the infallible teacher and supreme pastor of all the faithful, the head and father of all Christendom. The rays of the sun are not more intimately united to the sun itself, nor the branch to the trunk of the tree, nor the rivulet to its source, than are the pastors of the Church with their flocks connected with the Pope. He has in his keeping all the treasures of salvation, and through him only are they accessible to us. *Vitae recludit pascua et fontes sacros* — the Church sings — "He gives admission to the pastures and to the sacred fountains of life." How prejudicial and hurtful to any one, therefore, is separation from the centre of unity in the Church! "Where Peter is, there is the Church" — resounds throughout all ages.[1] The more noble the blessings for which we are indebted to the Pope, the more, as head and support of the Church, he is persecuted and oppressed by the children of darkness, the more childlike, faithful and loyal should be our devotedness and attachment to him, the more fervent and persevering should we pray for him.

As all pastors with their flocks follow the Pope, in like manner, should all the priests and the faithful of a diocese be attached to their bishop,[2] whom the Holy Ghost has appointed to feed them. Next to the Pope, therefore, it is right and proper that in all the churches of a diocese the ruling bishop should be commemorated by name,[3] that he may obtain strength and wisdom to exercise his sacred and difficult office according to God's will.

---

the prayer for the bishop is wanting in some manuscripts. To the Pope and bishop is often added in the third place the king or emperor. Towards the end of the Middle Age the names of temporal rulers were effaced from the manuscripts. With the exception of the never omitted prayer for the Pope, the naming of the spiritual and temporal superiors was subject to constant changes during the Middle Age. In Austria, by virtue of a papal privilege, the emperor is prayed for by name.

[1] *Ubi Petrus, ibi ecclesia:* ubi Ecclesia, ibi nulla mors, sed vita aeterna (S. Ambr. Enarr. in Ps. 40, n. 30).

[2] Antistes (προεστώς) from antisto, to stand in front, to have the preference, prominent = the head, especially the first and chief priest; hence the ancient Christian designation of a bishop. Antistes dicitur a verbo antesto (= emineo, excello), eo quod universum populum dignitate et honore superemineat (Pseudo-Alcuin. c. 36).

[3] The name of the bishop of the diocese in which a priest celebrates, is, in contradistinction from the Pope, mentioned without an inclination; if his name is unknown, merely antistite nostro is said, by which the bishop in question is understood. However, in order that the name of the antistes be mentioned, he must really hold the episcopal chair, that is, he must have been named (chosen) and confirmed, as also have undertaken the government of the diocese; it is not requisite that he should be consecrated. An (episcopally consecrated) Vicar Capitular, or Vicar Apostolic must not be named. The name of the Catholic ruler of the

Finally, "all orthodox believers and professors of the Catholic
and Apostolic faith" are prayed for (*pro omnibus orthodoxis atque*[1]
catholicae et apostolicae fidei cultoribus).

According to the definition of the word, such persons are here
designated who not only are "orthodox believers" (*orthodoxi*),[2] that
is, who not only confess the pure, genuine, unadulterated faith (in
word and deed), but who, at the same time, are called and exert
themselves to plant, to nurture, to propagate and establish the true
faith, which is "Catholic and Apostolic" (*cultores fidei*).[3] Among
them must be reckoned, first of all, the bishops and priests, because
they are the pastors and teachers appointed by Christ for the edification
of His mystical body, for the consummation of saints and for the
administration of divine service. Moreover, it corresponds to the
context that, after mentioning by name the Pope and the bishop of
the diocese, the remaining hierarchical rulers and leaders of the
Church of God should be remembered, in order that they may
worthily exercise their pastorate for the honor of God and the salvation of souls. But since the words "orthodox promoters of the
Catholic and Apostolic faith" have a general meaning, there is
nothing at the same time to prevent their reference and application
to all those of the faithful who, although not by the office of the
apostolate and by preaching, but still in other ways contribute according to their ability to the propagation of the faith.[4] All Chris-

---

country may be inserted only in virtue of a special indult of the Holy See (S. R. C.
20. Mart. 1862). If the Papal or Episcopal See is vacant, then the respective words
(una cum famulo . . . and et antistite nostro) are omitted. (Cf. Cavalieri V, c. 16.)

[1] Atque (from ad-que) serves here (as frequently in other cases) for the intimate
synonymous connection, that is, of ideas and thoughts, which of themselves are
closely connected with one another, in which the more significant word stands last
= for all who possess the true faith (that is, the Catholic and Apostolic faith), and
cherish, support and extend it. Orthodoxi and fidei cultores are, therefore, not
two different classes of persons, as many erroneously assume.

[2] Orthodoxus, ὀρθόδοξος, having true faith, qui de fide recte sentit (from ὀρθός,
rectus, and δόξα, sententia). — Orthodoxi, i. e. rectae gloriae dicuntur, eo quod
nullo errore depravati rectae fidei confessione Deum glorificant (Pseudo-Alcuin.
c. 40). — Orthodoxi, i. e. vita et doctrina gloriosi (B. Odo Camerac. Exposit. in
Canon. dist. 1).

[3] Cultor = qui colit, the worker, cultivator, nurse, worshipper. Rogamus pro
his etiam, qui fidem *excolunt* vomere praedicationis et semine boni operis (Steph.
Augustod. De sacram. altar. c. 13). — Cultores fidei dicuntur, qui sarculo correctio-
nis et sanctis documentis eam *excolunt* (Rob. Paulul. De offic. eccl. 1. 2, c. 29). —
Fidei cultoribus — non fidem tantum habentibus. Aliud est enim fidem habere et
aliud fidem *colere;* fidem colit, qui studet et intendit secundum fidem vivere, cum
multi fidem habeant, qui hoc non faciunt (B. Odo Camerac. 1. c.). "For *all those
who profess the Catholic and apostolic faith,* that faith which the apostles taught
and propagated in all the churches, for those especially whose zeal labors to spread
it, and whose pious examples tend to preserve it"(Le Courtier, Manuel de la Messe
chap. 4, § 1). — The expression fidei cultores is found also in St. Fulgentius
(Pro fide catholica n. 2).

[4] Quamvis pro tota plebe christiana sit in Missa generaliter et primo orandum,
tamen pro Summo Pontifice et proprio Pastore praecipue exorare oportet, deinde

tians have in a wider sense a priestly and apostolic vocation; they can and should exercise the apostolate of prayer and alms, of labor and suffering, in this that they make the interests of the Sacred Heart of Jesus their own, praying, suffering, sacrificing themselves in union with this divine Heart, that the kingdom of faith in the world may be spread ever more and more, and flourish ever more firmly. Thus all the faithful should be actively employed in the extension and exaltation of the kingdom of God, and should labor for the salvation of souls, by striving to procure for others also the grace of the true and life-giving faith.

2. *Memento, Domine, famulorum famularumque tuarum N. et N.*[1] — "Remember, O Lord, Thy servants and handmaids N. and N." With these words begins the second link of the first Canon-Prayer; in it the special petitions at the Holy Sacrifice are continued, or taken up again. "Remember,[2] O Lord, Thy servants and hand-maids," that is, attend — have regard — to their necessities with loving care, grant them Thy favor and mercy, give them grace and happiness, bless them. In this sense the word remember, especially in connection with the term visit, is often said of God in Holy Scripture. "What is man that Thou art mindful of him, or the son of man that Thou visitest him?" exclaims David (Ps. 8, 5). Else-

---

pro his, qui in populo christiano excellentius clarent et pluribus prosunt fidemque per suam sapientiam defendunt atque exponunt (Dion. Carthus. Expos. Miss. art. 18).

[1] Tot famuli famulaeque Christi (S. Aug. Epist. 36, n. 4). Elsewhere (for example, Orate *fratres*) mention is made of the stronger sex in the liturgy, when the feminine sex is included. Non est masculus neque femina: omnes enim vos *unum* estis in Christo Jesu (Galat. 3, 28). — Prius oblationes sunt commendandae (in the Offertory) et tunc eorum nomina quorum sunt (the names of those who offer) edicenda, ut inter sacra mysteria (in the Canon) nominentur (Innocent I. [† 417], Ad Decentium n. 5). — Quia in *quibusdam* codicibus invenitur N. littera, aliquorum fieri memoriam nominatim significatur. Unde *quidam* usu tenent hoc in loco memorandi quos cariores habent, subjungentes: "et omnium circumad-stantium," ut facta memoria carorum absentium, fiat et adstantium (B. Odo Camerac., dist. 2).

[2] *Memento*, i. e. recordare, non quod in Deum cadat oblivio, sed ut per modum recordantis se habeat, reminiscendo misericordiae suae et subveniendo in omni tribulatione et necessitate et tribuendo dona gratiarum, quae postulantur ab ipso. Sed cum in Canone debeat intellectus sacerdotis *maxime esse divinis infixus* atque sensibilia deserens, mirum videtur, quod in hoc fit memoria hominum in carne viventium, cum talis memoria contemplationem impedire et evagationem inducere soleat. Et respondendum, quod hic fit rationabiliter vivorum memoria, sed ne talis memoria devotionem impediat vel distractionem inducat, caute agenda est, non nimis immorando considerationi personarum vel circumstantiarum et rerum, quae eas concernunt, sed potius in principio hujus memoriae debet sacerdos oculum cordis sui contemplationi Dei vehementer infigere, cogitando de Deo ea, quae devotionem atque fervorem caritatis magis accendunt, et tunc in tali mentis fervore Deum ardenter orando, ut se exaudire dignetur pro his, quos nominabit, ipsas vero personas cursorie meditando, sed bona, quae eis petit, intente et amorose rogando (Dion. Carthus. Exposit. Missae art. 20).

where he prays: "Remember us, O Lord, in the favor of Thy people, visit us with Thy salvation" (Ps. 105, 4).

The letters N. and N.[1] admonish the priest, in this place, according to the direction of the rubrics, to mention some persons by name and especially to include them in the Sacrifice; the names themselves he can either mention in silence, or merely think of and have present to his mind. The choice is left free to the celebrant: of the living he can here mention whom and as many as he wishes.[2]

---

[1] Diptychum (from δίς, twice, and πτύσσειν, to fold, δίπτυχος, folded in two or placed together) = tabula duplicata vel duplex, a writing-tablet, consisting of two tablets or leaflets joined together by a hinge. By the liturgical diptychs, that were more or less large and precious, is generally understood the index of persons, whose names were publicly read at the Holy Sacrifice. There is a distinction made between the diptychs of the living (δ. ζώντων, liber viventium) and the diptychs of the dead (δ. νεκρῶν, liber mortuorum). In these diptychs were inscribed, among others, principally ecclesiastical and secular dignitaries, other persons of merit and distinction, signal benefactors of the Church, certain persons presenting Eucharistic offerings, and others. As regarded the time and place of the reading, as also the reader, the practice greatly varied in countries and epochs. In the Roman Church, from time immemorial, the names of the living were read at the above place in the beginning of the Canon, and those of the departed after the Consecration. The liturgical diptychs probably originated already in the second century, as in the third century they were already universally introduced; their use in the West continued until the twelfth century, and among the Greeks until the fifteenth. — Adverte, diptycha sacra distinguenda esse a precibus, quae pro vivis et defunctis inter sacrorum solemnia fiunt. Finis et usus praecipuus diptychorum erat, ut retineretur catholica communio tum vivorum inter se, tum vivorum et mortuorum (Lesley S. 1).

[2] Liturgists usually say, that the priest may include in the Memento not only members of the Church, but also unbelievers, heretics, schismatics, those who are excommunicated, and they state in proof of this assertion, that it is only a private prayer of the celebrant (thus write Gavanti, Merati, Cavalieri, De Herdt and others). But such a statement is vague and partly incorrect. As the public reading of the names from the diptychs was formerly, so also the silent commemoration that now replaces it, is a liturgical prayer of the Church, which as such possesses special impetratory power: the priest says the word Memento by commission of the Church and, on his side, has only the choice of naming such or such persons whom the intercession of the Church should profit, and this, in like manner, is the case with regard to some prayers for the departed. Independently of other reasons, the public character of the Memento is evident from the full context. The words Memento, Domine, famulorum . . . contain an intercession which is offered likewise for "all present" (et omnium circumstantium), as well as for those named by the priest, — and that by the Church herself by the mouth of the celebrant. The following relative clauses also pro quibus tibi offerimus vel qui tibi offerunt may be referred not merely to the circumstantes, but moreover to the persons whom the priest commemorates by name. — In addition to this public intercession, that the priest makes as a minister of the Church, he may here, as a private person, pray for others, and that too for those who are excluded from the suffrages of the Church, or for whom the Holy Sacrifice of the Mass may not be applied, that is, for excommunicati *vitandi;* but these persons may not be included in the liturgical Memento. The priest may, therefore, in this place be satisfied with the public

Since the prayer of the Church, especially in connection with the Sacrifice, is exceedingly powerful and efficacious, the zealous priest will not omit duly to appreciate the treasure of grace, and render it profitable especially to all those to whom he is most closely bound, and to whom he is under obligations of justice, charity or gratitude. This memento should not be too hastily ended, nor too much prolonged; hence it is advisable to make the memento more in detail before Holy Mass, so that at this part of the Mass it may be again renewed in general briefly and fervently.

Then the priest proceeds in the name of the Church to beg of God to be mindful of "all here present" (*omnium circumstantium*), that is, of all those who are present and are hearing the Mass. For this reason also the time spent in a devout manner at the foot of the altar during the celebration of the Holy Sacrifice, is a time of grace and salvation.[1] The words, God "knoweth the faith and devotion" of those who are recommended to His favor and mercy, confirm the petition offered, and designate the interior disposition which all, especially those who hear Mass, should have, in order to share largely in the fruit of the Sacrifice. God knows, that is, He graciously and complacently acknowledges the faith and piety which strike deep roots in the hearts of the faithful and, at the same time, shine conspicuously in the reverent posture of the body at Holy Mass. A lively and firm faith in the mysteries hidden in the Eucharistic Sacrifice awakens the devotion of the heart. But the devotion that God demands is a certain determination and cheerful readiness of heart to give and devote ourselves and all that we have totally to His service.[2] A soul truly devout eagerly and most fervently embraces all that appertains to the service of God. The more perfectly the faithful present are penetrated with faith and devotion, the more susceptible will be their souls for receiving the blessings of the Holy Sacrifice, and the more bountifully will God pour into them "the good measure, pressed down and shaken together and running over" (Luke 6, 38). These sentiments of faith and devotion are awakened and nourished in proportion to the lively interest taken in the celebration at the altar by the faithful assisting at the Mass, and in proportion as they unite more closely in spirit with the celebrant, for the purpose of eliciting interiorly suitable devout acts and affections.

Memento or at the same time add private prayers. (Cfr. Suarez, De Censuris disp. 9, sect. 5, n. 4–5. — Coninck, De Sacram. ac Censuris disp. 14, dub. 6.) — Licet sacerdos celebret *totam* Missam ut *publica persona* ac *nomine Ecclesiae*, atque *etiam* "Memento", adhuc tamen potest interserere *privatam* supplicationem. Potest concipere affectum supplicationis apud Deum *concomitantem* actionem illam publicam in favorem vitandorum (Pasqualigo, De sacrificio N. L. tr. 1, q. 145).

[1] Hinc evidenter apparet, quam sanctum sit ac salubre Missarum interesse mysteriis, cum sacrificium Eucharistiae pro circumstantibus offeratur *specialiter* (Innoc. III. De sacr. altar. myster. 1. 3, c. 6).

[2] Devotio nihil aliud esse videtur, quam voluntas quaedam prompte tradendi se ad ea, quae pertinent ad Dei famulatum (S. Thom. 2, 2, q. 82, a. 1).

Those who assist at divine worship, that is, the servants and handmaids of God mentioned,[1] are by the words *pro quibus tibi offerimus vel*[2] *qui tibi offerunt*[3] represented under a twofold aspect; namely, first, as the ones "for whom we offer," and then as the ones "who themselves (also) join in the Sacrifice." Under both aspects the Sacrifice is more salutary and beneficial to "the assistants" than to others who are not in such intimate connection with its offering. The special application of the Sacrifice on the part of the Church cannot be useless and without result; and the devout participation in the Sacrifice by assisting at Holy Mass and by being included therein, draws on the faithful sharers abundant blessings of grace. The words: "for whom we offer to Thee and who offer to Thee"[4] refer, therefore, to the same persons, but designate them in two different ways.

The priest and the faithful offer to the Lord the Sacrifice of praise now prepared on the altar (*hoc sacrificium laudis*). The Holy Mass is the infinitely perfect Sacrifice of praise and adoration, which we offer to the glory of the Most High. When the wise man exhorts us: "Glorify the Lord as much as ever you can, for He will yet far exceed, and His magnificence is wonderful. Blessing the Lord, exalt Him as much as you can; for He is above all praise" (Ecclus. 43, 32—33), we may boldly and cheerfully answer: here on the altar there is offered to God a praise worthy of His greatness, because it is infinite and divine, since it is the Sacrifice of His only-begotten Son. When the Lord laid "the foundations of the earth, the morning stars praised Him, and all the children of God (the angels) rejoiced;" but the chant of praise of the heavenly hosts is not to be compared with the adoration, homage and glorification that ascend from the altar to heaven. By the Eucharistic Sacrifice of

---

[1] Pro quibus tibi offerimus vel qui tibi offerunt: pro quibus, inquam, famulis et famulabus tuis et omnibus circumstantibus fidelibus et devotis, tibi offerimus ut ministri et immediate, vel qui famuli tui et famulae, omnesque circumstantes fideles et devoti offerunt tibi spiritualiter et mediate (Clichtov. Elucidat. eccles. l. 3, n. 14).

[2] Vel here = et, and also.

[3] Micrologus remarks (c. 13), that in antiquioribus et veracioribus Sacramentariis the (later) addition pro quibus tibi offerimus is wanting and only the (original) words qui tibi offerunt are found. The cessation of the ancient custom of offerings appears to have occasioned the gradual reception of the words pro quibus tibi offerimus, — which are by no means superfluous, as Micrologus holds. In a prayer of the Mozarabic Missal a distinction is made between the offerentes, that is, they who present the sacrificial gifts and have communicated, and the adstantes, that is, those who have merely assisted at the Holy Sacrifice. Deferatur in ista solemnia Spiritus Sanctus tuus, qui tam *adstantis* quam *offerentis* populi et oblata pariter et vota sanctificet (II. fer. Pasch.).

[4] In quibus verbis patenter ostenditur, quod a cunctis fidelibus, non solum viris, sed et mulieribus sacrificium illud laudis offertur, licet ab uno *specialiter* offerri sacerdote videatur: quia quod ille Deo offerendo manibus tractat, hoc multitudo fidelium *intenta* mentium *devotione* commendat (S. Petr. Damian. lib. "Dominus vobiscum" c. 8).

praise the name of the Lord is magnified "from the rising of the sun unto the going down of the same, from henceforth now and forever" (Ps. 112, 2—3).

On the other hand, this Sacrifice is at the same time the source also whence flow forth all grace and mercy, salvation and blessing, peace and benefits of all kinds upon our poor earth; hence it is said, the faithful offer the Sacrifice of the altar "for themselves and all their relations" (*pro se suisque omnibus*).[1] Those present may, moreover, offer the Holy Sacrifice not only for themselves, but also for others; the Church herself supports and recommends with God, as it were, the special intentions, inasmuch as she is here mindful even of those for whom the assistants on their part offer the Sacrifice. It is an exercise of charity most pleasing to God to include in this manner in the Holy Sacrifice our own family, our relatives, friends and other persons in general, in order, by its virtue, to draw down grace upon them. It is also to be expected of the goodness of God, that they who assist devoutly at Holy Mass, when they make such intentions for the interests and wants of others, thereby lose or lessen nothing of their own share in the fruit of the Sacrifice.

In union with the priest, the faithful offer the Holy Mass for themselves and for all those who are dear to them, as an atoning Sacrifice "for the redemption of their souls" (*pro redemptione animarum suarum*)[2] and as a Sacrifice of petition "for the hope of their salvation and safety" (*pro spe salutis et incolumitatis suae*).

The Eucharistic Sacrifice effects the redemption of souls, inasmuch as it conveys and applies to them the graces of redemption acquired by the Sacrifice of the Cross, that they may be made perfectly pure and worthy "to enter the temple of eternal glory." The actual redemption of the individual man begins with regeneration in baptism; it is developed and completed under the influence of the grace of Christ during his whole earthly pilgrimage, and finally obtains its consummation at the glorious return of the Lord, when not only the soul, but also the body shall be delivered from all the misery of sin, snatched from temporal and eternal destruction and transformed in glory. Therefore, the last day of the world and the day of its judgment is called for the just "the day of (the full and complete) redemption" (Eph. 4, 30). The expression redemption of souls is to be understood in the same sense as that of salvation of the soul; the redemption and salvation of the body is herein not excluded, but included. This mode of speech is used to designate the soul as the essential object of redemption and as the actual subject of salvation; but through the soul and for the sake of the soul sanctification and a state of glory will be imparted to the body

---

[1] Pro = for, that is, in favor of, to the advantage and profit of.

[2] Pro = for, here expresses the object of the oblation, that is, the sacrificial fruit to be obtained. This is an exegesis, i. e. expositio (Sicard.) of the preceding words pro se suisque omnibus.

also.[1] The soul will enjoy perfect happiness only when clothed with the glorified body. Although redemption in its full sense comprises not only deliverance from all evil, but also the bestowal of all that is good, yet here only the former is meant; the faithful offer "for the redemption of their souls," that is, to propitiate the irritated justice of God, and to be freed from every evil of guilt and punishment. — That the Eucharistic Sacrifice does also open to us the treasury of the divine goodness and liberality and procure us every good, is contained in the words, that they offer it "for the hope of salvation and safety," that is, for the obtaining of redemption and prosperity.[2] The word "salvation" (*salus*) here comprises all spiritual, all super-natural gifts: grace in time and for eternity; the word "safety" (*incolumitas*) designates not merely health of body, but generally success and happiness in temporal things, that is, the goods (immaterial and material) belonging to the natural order. They too may be obtained by sacrifice and prayer, in as far as they serve for the attainment of eternal happiness.

The concluding clause: "and (who) pay . . . their vows to Thee" (*tibique reddunt vota sua . . .*) is a continuation of and a supplement to the preceding words: "who offer to Thee this Sacrifice of praise." It contains an accord with this verse of the psalm: *Immola Deo sacrificium laudis et redde Altissimo vota tua* — "Offer to God the Sacrifice of praise and pay Thy vows to the Most High" (49, 14). *Votum* does not always in the strict sense of the word signify a vow, but it has in the liturgical language a far more comprehensive meaning. It frequently occurs therein and, at one time, denotes the oblations on the altar, at other times, petition, supplication, resolutions, — in brief, interior and exterior acts of religion.[3] — Already at baptism we received precious gifts and glorious promises, and in return we solemnly vowed to die to the world and to sin, to live only for God and heaven. These holy vows we pay at the Holy Sacrifice of the Mass, inasmuch as we offer not only the Eucharistic Victim, but in union with it we offer ourselves also, our body and our soul, our prayers and our homage, our labors and trials, our

---

[1] Licet corpus non sit *immediatum* subjectum gratiae, ex anima tamen redundat effectus gratiae ad corpus, dum in praesenti membra nostra exhibemus arma justitiae Deo (Rom. c. 6), et in futuro corpus nostrum sortietur incorruptionem et gloriam animae (S. Thom. 3, q. 79, a. 1 ad 3).

[2] Hoc sacrosanctum sacrificium non solum liberat nos a malis, sed etiam accumulat nos bonis; non solum nos eripit a poenis, sed etiam auget gaudia salutis et incolumitatis. Salutis, inquam, aeternae animarum; incolumitatis, i. e., incorruptionis perpetuae corporum, et hoc est, pro quo offerimus tam pretiosum munus (B. Odo Camerac. Expos. in Canon. Missae dist. 2).

[3] Cfr. the Secreta in Dedicat. Ecclesiae, in which we read: dum haec vota praesentia reddimus. — In ancient Missals is often found the expression oblationum vota as a designation of the sacrificial gifts. — *Voventur omnia, quae offeruntur Deo*, maxime sancti altaris oblatio, quo sacramento praedicatur nostrum aliud votum maximum, quo nos vovimus in Christo esse mansuros, utique in compage corporis Christi (S. Aug. Epist. 149, n. 16 ad Paulin.).

sufferings and our joys, as gifts due to the Lord.[1] But by so doing we give "to the eternal, living and true God" that only which we have previously received from Him; we but return to God that which He bestowed on us (*tibique reddunt vota sua*).[2]

3. The concluding clause of the first Canon prayer contains a record of saints and bears the heading *Infra actionem*[3] = during the sacrificial action or during the Canon; for *actio* here is a designation for sacrifice, or canon. Sacrifice in general is essentially an action,[4] and the Eucharistic Sacrifice in particular is the repetition of that which Christ did at the Last Supper (*hoc facite*) and, consequently, the greatest, the most sublime, the holiest action = *the action* in the highest sense of the word. Holy Mass is the unbloody representation and the mystical renewal of the Sacrifice and redeeming act of Christ on the Cross, namely, of that divine tragedy which once obscured the heavens and shook the earth. "And all the multitude of them that were come together at that sight (*spectaculum*), and saw the things that were done, returned striking their breasts" (Luke 23, 48). The Eucharistic Sacrifice, therefore, is likewise a holy drama (*actio*), and from sacrifice this same name *actio* (action) has been transferred to the sacrificial prayer.[5] The above mentioned superscription *Infra actionem* is, therefore, called "within the Canon."[6] But why is this title placed especially and solely

---

[1] Deo dona ejus in nobis *nosque ipsos* vovemus et reddimus (S. Aug. De civit. Dei, 1. 10, c. 3, al. 4). — Quisquis bene cogitat, quid voveat Domino et quae vota reddat, *seipsum* voveat, *seipsum* reddat: hoc exigitur, hoc debetur (Id. Enarr. in Ps. 115, n. 8).

[2] Haec *vota* sunt desideria et sancta proposita colendi Deum, quae implemus et Deo reddimus praecipue hac oblatione sacrificii incruenti. Dicimur autem ea potius *reddere* quam donare Deo, quia per divinam gratiam illa concipimus et a Deo accipimus, et postmodum Deo ipsi offerimus et reddimus, quae accipimus (Quarti p. 2, tit. 9, sect. 2, dub. 2). — In the Sacram. Gregor. we read in a Benedictio virginis: Respice super hanc famulam tuam, quae tibi devotionem suam offert, a quo et ipsa idem votum assumpsit.

[3] The expression infra Actionem with the same signification is also in Ordo Rom. V, n. 9. The Ordo Rom. XIV, c. 71 has the inscription Alia infra Actionem also for the following prayer Hanc igitur oblationem, because this, too, at times receives a special addition.

[4] In Greek δρᾶν, in Latin agere, facere, operari are often used in the sense of offering (sacrificare) and are thus characterized as a special religious action. Thus Pope St. Leo wrote in the year 445 to Bishop Dioscorus of Alexandria, that it would be proper to repeat the Holy Sacrifice of the Mass, as the newly collected crowd filled the Basilica in which the Sacrifice was celebrated (in qua *agitur*).

[5] Actio, actio sacri mysterii, mysterium sanctissimae actionis = Canon. Infra actionem, i. e. inter verba ipsius Canonis, qui actio etiam nominatur a sacris auctoribus, quod in eo divina *aguntur* consecranturque et conficiuntur mysteria (Clichtov. Elucid. eccl. l. 3).

[6] Ancient Missals have often the words Infra Canonem. The infra is here used in the sense of *intra*, as we say also Infra Octavam instead of Intra Octavam. (Cf. Lebrun, Explication de la Messe part. 4, art. 4, § 1).

above the *Communicantes?* On Holy Thursday and on five of the greatest feasts[1] the *Communicantes* sounds somewhat different, because it has an addition referring to the day celebrated; in this altered form it is placed immediately after the Preface and bears the superscription *Infra actionem*, which there means that this formula of prayer is later on to be inserted and recited in the Canon. It appears that originally this superscription was placed merely over the specific-festal *Communicantes* without the Canon, and then transferred thence to the ordinary *Communicantes* in the Canon.[2] — In the latter place, at any rate, it is intended to refer to the special formula of prayer printed after the Preface, and to recall to our mind that on the above-named feasts this special formula is to be used instead of the general one in the Canon.

Communicantes et memoriam venerantes — thus begins the ordinary formula. These words, as a continuation of the preceding part of the Canon and its supplement, stand in the closest relation to the preceding words[3]: Those present offer up to Thee, O Lord, this Sacrifice of praise and pay their vows unto Thee, — and this not as persons separated from the unity of the mystical body of Christ, but as belonging to the Communion of Saints (*communicantes*), and who fulfil this communion towards the inhabitants of heaven by venerating their memory (*memoriam venerantes*). [4]

The word *communicantes*, therefore, denotes that we are children of the Church, subjects of the kingdom of Christ, members of the great family of God, — in a word, that we belong "to the Communion of Saints;" this membership with the mystical body of Christ is here appropriately made prominent, because we would honor the memory of the blessed with the intention of rendering ourselves worthy of their intercession at the offering of the Holy Sacrifice. This fuller and deeper meaning[5] accommodates itself also to the

---

[1] Christmas, Epiphany, Easter, Ascension and Pentecost.

[2] In the Sacram. Gelasian. we find the superscription Infra Actionem not within the Canon, but only above the special Communicantes of the special Mass formulas.

[3] Dubitare potest de sensu illius verbi "Communicantes" et connexione ejus cum reliquis. Respondetur, totam hanc orationem esse unam unoque contextu legendam, ita ut sensus sit: tibi reddunt vota sua aeterno Deo, vivo et vero, communicantes vel inter se vel cum Sanctis tuis per societatem et conjunctionem, quam cum illis habent; quorum propterea memoriam venerantes per eorum intercessionem exaudiri petent (Suarez disp. 83, sect. 2, n. 7).

[4] Sequitur: *"Communicantes et memoriam venerantes."* Ubi licet scriptores quasi capituli initium faciunt, eo quod in quibusdam solemnitatibus hic diversitas quaedam invenitur, jungitur tamen praemissis hoc modo: *Offerunt* pro se quisque, *ipsi* dico *communicantes, in Ecclesiae communione per fidem manentes* (Robert. Paululus, De offic. eccl. 1. 2, c. 29).

[5] The signification of the word communicantes is often grasped in a manner too one-sided and limited. For instance, some say, that it merely signifies the relation of the faithful on earth with the saints of heaven, as is evident from what immediately follows memoriam venerantes; others, on the contrary, are of opinion

context of the special formulas, in which the word *communicantes* is separated by an addition from the expression *memoriam veneran-tes*, for example, at Easter, when it is said: *Communicantes, et diem sacratissimum celebrantes Resurrectionis Domini nostri Jesu Christi secundum carnem: sed et memoriam venerantes:* that is, we offer as they who partake of the Communion of love and of the goods of the kingdom of Christ, and who, in spiritual communion with one another, celebrate the great day of the Resurrection of our Lord Jesus Christ according to the flesh, also at the same time venerate the memory of the Saints.

All the redeemed constitute together the kingdom of Jesus Christ, among all these citizens, whether they have already happily reached the term, or are still combating on earth, or making atone-ment in the place of purification, there is a living communication, a reciprocal interchange; good deeds and sufferings, merits and satis-factions, — in short, all the fruits of grace are common property from which each draws and to which each contributes. It is precisely at the celebration of Mass that we are reminded of the happiness and dignity of belonging to so glorious a community, that is, that we are "fellow-citizens with the saints and domestics of God" (Eph. 2, 19). For after the priest has interceded for the Church militant and her members, he endeavors to add greater weight and efficacy to his supplications by invoking the saints. His mental vision is enlarged and directed to the Heavenly Jerusalem. In happy consciousness of the relationship and intimate connection he enjoys with the glorified saints, he celebrates their memory, as though to invite them, as "kings and priests" (Apoc. 5, 10), to offer the Sacrifice along with us, and by their powerful intercession and abundant merits to sup-port our weak prayers, so that by the strength of their mediation we may experience God's help and protection in all situations and neces-sities (*ut in omnibus protectionis tuae muniamur auxilio*). Whilst, therefore, the Church "comes to Jesus, the Mediator of the New Testament, and to the sprinkling of blood," that is, to the Sacrifice of the Altar, she comes also "to the Church of the first-born, who are written in the heavens, and to the spirits of the just made per-fect" (Heb. 12, 22—24), that all her children may unite in this divine action and jointly with their Common Head, Jesus Christ, offer and be offered.

By name are mentioned: the blessed Virgin Mary, the twelve Apostles and twelve Martyrs[1]; finally, all the Saints, at least in general.

---

that this idea is excluded by the insertion made on certain days between communi-cantes and memoriam venerantes, so that communicantes is to be referred merely to the union of the faithful on earth and particularly to those assembled at the Divine service. (Cfr. Bellarmin. De Missa lib. 2, c. 21.)

[1] The order of names of the saints in the Canon shows an arrangement by pairs. Already in the enumeration of the apostles, and still more clearly in that of the martyrs this division of names by two and two is easily distinguishable.

a) "First of all" (*imprimis*), and, therefore, more than all, we honor the memory of the "glorious ever Virgin Mary, Mother of God and our Lord Jesus Christ." As always, so also in this instance Mary is rightly named in the first place; she is Queen not merely of the Apostles and Martyrs, but of all the Saints. Her name is not mentioned simply, but with honorable qualifications, that proclaim her grandeur, power and dignity. She is called "the glorious" (*gloriosa*); for as Queen of heaven and of earth she is elevated above all the choirs of angels and saints in eternal bliss and glory. She was taken up to heaven in body and soul and transfigured in glory; there she wears the most beautiful crown of honor and power. As on earth she excelled all creatures by the fulness of grace, the wealth of virtues, so in the next life she surpasses all the citizens of heaven by the splendor and magnificence of her glory. Because she was on earth the most humble, the most pure, the most devout, the most loving, the most sorrowful, therefore, she is now in heaven the most glorious and the most happy. — Then she is called "always a virgin" (*semper virgo*). This privilege is often commented upon. Even the Church, that has ordered a special feast (*Fest. Purit. B. M. V.*) to celebrate the "most spotless virginity of the most pure Virgin Mary," acknowledges her inability to praise in a worthy manner Mary's purity of heart, inasmuch as she exclaims: "Holy and immaculate Virgin, with what praises shall I exalt thee, I know not, since thou hast carried in thy womb Him whom the heavens cannot contain!" Mary is the Virgin of all virgins; she is the most venerable, glorious and wonderful Virgin, she is the model, guide, protectress of all virginal souls. By the virginity which she vowed to God, she was prepared to become the "Mother of our God and Lord Jesus Christ;" for assuredly it behooved the Mother of God to be and ever remain a virgin. The divine maternity was only the complete consecration and sealing of her incomparable virginity. Through the greatest and sole miracle of its kind, she united "the joys of maternity with the honor of virginity." The divine maternity in its own kind is of infinite dignity; for Mary gave birth to the Son of the Most High. This maternal dignity of hers is the intrinsic reason why Mary above all other creatures was endowed with the plenitude of grace and holiness, of glory and power. As the Mother of God she is the Queen of heaven and earth, she reigns as mistress, with maternal power and love, in favor of our salvation. Hence so frequently we cry to her: *Monstra te esse matrem* — "Show thyself a mother," that is, show that thou art not merely our Mother who loves us so tenderly, but that thou art also and still more the Mother of God, ever all-powerful by thy intercession.

Let us here yet briefly notice her connection with the bloody and unbloody Sacrifice of Christ. The Victim of the Cross and of the Altar was given to us through the Virgin Mother Mary; He is "the fruit of her most noble body" by the overshadowing of the Holy Ghost. The God-Man is "born unto us and given to us from

Mary, the unsullied Virgin" (*nobis natus, nobis datus ex intacta Virgine*). She "stood by the Cross of Jesus," and while her maternal tears were mingled with His blood and the sword of sorrow pierced her soul, she offered her Crucified Son for the redemption and salvation of the world. Great as the sea was then her sorrow; she was nailed to the Cross with her Son and she felt all the pain of His wounds in her heart. Hence she is justly styled "the Queen of Martyrs." Her name, therefore, is inseparable from the Sacrifice of Christ; the remembrance of Mary must always be united with that of Christ at His sacrificial celebration. Christ's holy Flesh and Blood offered in sacrifice on the altar come to us from the heart and hands of Mary; from Mary, moreover, we should learn, with priestly disposition and self-devotedness, to offer the Lamb of God and ourselves at the foot of the altar.

b) After the Virgin Mother of God, the twelve Apostles are named in the Canon; the succession differing somewhat from the records of the Apostles in Holy Scripture.[1] The Apostles are those chosen messengers, to whom the Lord imparted full powers as teachers, priests and pastors, that, as His representatives, they might continue the work of the redemption. As the salt of the earth and light of the world, they were to establish in all places the kingdom of God, to extend and strengthen the Church. To prepare them for this, He vouchsafed to them more than to others His presence and intercourse, made them the immediate witnesses of His life, miracles and doctrine, of His passion and resurrection. For this He promised them His assistance and sent them the Holy Ghost from on high. In obedience to the commission of their Divine Master the Apostles went out into the whole world, to teach and baptize all nations, to bring to them the blessings of religion and together with it true earthly happiness. "Their sound has gone forth into all the earth, and their words unto the ends of the world" (Ps. 18, 5). Self-sacrifice was their office and calling, their life and their death. "For Christ's sake we are put to death all the day long. We are accounted as sheep for the slaughter" (Rom. 18, 36); but they rejoiced to endure shame and sorrow for the name of Jesus, and, after they "had fought the good fight and finished the course," they gave up their life by the bloody death of martyrdom, and thus planted the Church in their blood. The accounts of the fate and end of most of the Apostles are but few and obscure. In what follows we shall relate briefly a few characteristic traits from the life and death of the saints mentioned in the Canon, in order to afford some nourishment to devotion when repeating the names in question.[2]

---

[1] This enumeration probably originates from tradition — and not from the Itala version.

[2] Ut Sanctorum horum memoria devotius recolatur, expedit scire vitam et passionem eorum: aliter non potest affectuosa et perfecta eorum haberi memoria (Dion. Carthus. Expos. Miss. art. 21).

20

Sts. *Peter* and *Paul* — inseparably combined in the liturgy —
are named first. The birthplace of the Apostle Peter,[1] who was
previously called Simon, was Bethsaida on the western shore of the
Sea of Genesareth. From his fishing-net, miraculously filled with
fish, he was called to the spiritual fishing of the souls of men, and
was soon afterward placed at the head of the Apostolic band. Jesus
Christ made him the foundation of His Church, and invested him
with the office and dignity of primate over the universal Church.
As the visible representative of Christ and as chief pastor, he was
with supreme power to feed and guide the lambs and sheep, the
entire flock of Christ. Hence in the Gospel Peter takes preeminence
over the other Apostles, and there appears already by his whole conduct as the first of the Apostles. In like manner, after the Ascension
of the Lord, he everywhere acts as head of the Church. After his
seven years' episcopate at Antioch (36—42), the Prince of the
Apostles transferred the field of his missionary labors to Rome, the
capital of the heathen world. It is beyond all doubt, that Peter,
having come to Rome, founded there the Roman Church, directed it
as chief pastor and, finally, there underwent martyrdom. His episcopate at Rome lasted twenty-five years (42—67); but during this
period he frequently left the city of Rome to work elsewhere for the
propagation of Christianity. According to the most ancient tradition, Peter first lived in Rome beyond the Tiber, and near the house
which was afterward replaced by the church of St. Cecilia. But
after converting the family of the senator Pudens to Christianity, he
withdrew into the senator's house, taking up therein his permanent
abode. The fidelity and firmness of faith of the Roman community
was already at that date celebrated throughout the whole world; in
the bloody storms of Nero's persecution a great number of Christians
suffered martyrdom at Rome. As its most noble victims fell the
glorious Princes of the Apostles, Sts. Peter and Paul, at Rome on
the same day, June 29, and in the same year A. D. 67, — after they
had previously been imprisoned together for some months in the
Mamertine prison, beneath *Ara Coeli*, at the foot of the Capitol.
On the Ostian road is seen the chapel where, according to the legend,
the Apostles when going to death took leave of each other. To the
west, beyond the Tiber, on the Janiculan Hill, where now stands
the Church of *S. Pietro in Montorio*, and in sight of the Eternal
City, as a faithful imitator of his Lord and Master, St. Peter
died the violent death of the Cross; the humble disciple
begged the favor of shedding his blood for his Lord with his
head downward to the earth. His original place of sepulture was
on the Vatican Hill, where the grandest and noblest mausoleum of
the world, St. Peter's Church, has now stood for ages, lifting its
lofty dome heavenward. After the tomb of Christ, that of the Prince

---

[1] Cfr. Hundhausen, Das erste Pontificalschreiben des Apostelfürsten Petrus.
S. 1—44.

of the Apostles is the most celebrated place of pilgrimage in the world; churches and altars that bear his name, are as numerous as the stars in the heavens. "Peter stands before us all as the man of lively faith, of unshaken hope, of the most ardent love of God and men, full of noble dignity, and, at the same time, full of the most profound humility, full of majestic zeal against injustice and untruth, against deceit and sin, and, withal, full of loving sympathy for all the spiritual and corporal sufferings of his fellow-men, full of peace and joy in his own sufferings, wholly penetrated with zeal for the glory of Jesus Christ and the salvation of souls redeemed by the Precious Blood of his Master, fully persuaded of the one great truth, that in no other name is salvation given to men, but only in the name of Jesus crucified and risen from the dead. Thus Peter stands forth in bold relief as the man of truth, the man of fact, the man full of life — in all the traits of his character and in his whole personality, transformed by grace, a monumental figure, an exalted prototype, as it were, of the Papacy and of the Church herself, as from the days of Peter till now she passes on through the world and through the centuries." [1]

St. *Paul*, formerly called Saul, was born in the commercial city of Tarsus and enjoyed the rights of a Roman citizen. At an early age he came to Jerusalem, where he became a pupil under the instruction of the most renowned teacher of the law, Gamaliel. Saul was greatly gifted in mind and heart; being of an ardent temperament, he became a violent defender of the ancestral Jewish laws, and when the persecution against the Christians broke out in Jerusalem, his rage against the Church of God knew no bounds. By a miracle of grace he was converted and called by the Lord Himself to the apostolate. The Gospel, which he preached, he neither received nor learned from man, but he had it by revelation from Jesus Christ Himself. His whole life, abounding in labors and sufferings, presents St. Paul to us as an ideal Apostle. He made five great apostolic journeys by water and land; for the first three he started from Antioch, the fourth, as a prisoner from Jerusalem to Rome, and the last from Rome to other places. They occupied more than twenty years of his life; during that time St. Paul passed through about thirty different countries and islands, established and consolidated Christian communities in more than forty cities. All these journeys were incessant labors in the vineyards of the Lord and continual campaigns to rescue countries and peoples from the kingdom of darkness and sin, and to conquer them for the kingdom of Jesus Christ, the kingdom of truth and holiness. By word and writing, by sermons and epistles, St. Paul brought everywhere the name of Jesus, that is, truth and grace, light and life, the doctrine and salvation of Christ to the children of Israel as well as to heathen nations and rulers. The Apostle himself describes the labors, the captivities, the scourgings and the perils of death which he had to undergo.

---

[1] Hundhausen a. a. O. S. 43.

But all his many sufferings he endured with patience, fortitude and joy, because he suffered for the love of Jesus and of his brethren. The end of his apostolic career found him in Rome. Being a Roman citizen, he was put to death by the sword, in the south before the gates of the city on the road to Ostia. According to the legend, his head, after being cut off, striking the ground, leaped three times; whereat there sprang up three fountains of water, which are still flowing at the church erected over the spot, the church of *S. Paolo alle tre Fontane.* One half of the body of St. Paul rests in St. Peter's Church in Rome, the other half in St. Paul's church outside the walls, and his head is in the basilica of St. John Lateran. The Eternal City is highly favored in its possessing the grave and the relics of the two Princes of the Apostles; both apostles jointly guard and rule by their heavenly protection and assistance the Mother Church. "O happy Rome, consecrated by the glorious blood of the two Princes of the Apostles; dyed red with their blood, you shine more resplendently than all the glory of the world."[1]

St. Andrew was the first to recognize the Messiah through St. John the Baptist, and full of joy he at once led his brother Simon Peter to the Lord. His arduous and successful missionary labors were first exercised in Scythia; he, at last, went to the city of Patrae in Achaia, where he suffered an heroic martyrdom (Nov. 30, 62). The Governor Aegeas interrogated him; the Apostle made a solemn profession of the Sacrifice of the Cross and of the Altar; whereupon he was condemned to die fastened to the Cross. St. Andrew is the Apostle of the Cross. How magnificent is the prayer in which, filled with enthusiasm, he salutes the Cross as a boon ardently loved and long desired: "Hail, precious Cross, Thou hast been consecrated by the body of my Lord, and adorned with His limbs as with rich jewels. How long have I yearned for thee! At length thou art granted to my desires! Receive the disciple of the Master who hung upon thee; take me from among men, and present me to Him, who through thee redeemed me!" He remained on the Cross two days and a night, making of it a pulpit, whence he announced Christ crucified, preaching Him not only by his sufferings and the example of his virtues, but also with earnest and moving words. Finally, a bright light encompassed him, and the Cross became for him the ladder to heaven. Maximilla, a disciple of Christ, took the body down from the Cross and interred it. This holy body is preserved in the cathedral of Amalfi, and his head is in St. Peter's in Rome. It is the common opinion that he suffered on a cross composed of two beams diagonally crossing each other; hence this cross bears the name of St. Andrew's cross ($\times$).

St. James, called the Greater (*Major*), was a brother of St. John, both being sons of Zebedee. By reason of their fiery zeal and

---

[1] O Roma felix, quae duorum Principum — Es consecrata glorioso sanguine: — Horum cruore purpurata ceteras — Excellis orbis una pulchritudines (Hymn. Eccl.).

ardent character, they were called by the Lord "Sons of Thunder" (*Boanerges*). Peter, John and James were distinguished and privileged by the Lord above the other Apostles; for these three alone were permitted to remain with Him when He raised the daughter of Jairus to life, again at the Transfiguration on Mount Thabor, and, finally, during His agony in the garden. After the Ascension of Jesus, St. James preached in Judea and Samaria; then, according to an ancient tradition, he hastened to distant Spain, scattering there the first seed of Christian truth. Of all the Apostles, St. James the Greater was the first to drink the chalice of the Lord, as he was put to death by the sword in Jerusalem by Herod Agrippa only nine or ten years after the death of Christ. His holy remains were at an early date carried to Spain, and there they rest even now at *Santiago de Compostella*, the capital of the province of Galicia, which, besides Rome and Jerusalem, belongs to the most celebrated places of pilgrimage of all Christendom.

St. John, "the disciple whom Jesus loved," was more favored and privileged by the Lord than all the other Apostles. The Lord honored him, on account of his innocence and virginity, with His closest friendship and intimacy. *Hic est Joannes qui privilegio amoris praecipui ceteris altius a Domino meruit honorari (Resp. eccles.).* In that blessed hour, when Jesus by the institution of the Eucharist gave to His own the greatest proof of His love, John was permitted to repose on the breast, on the Sacred Heart of Jesus, — thence drawing light and love in abundance.[1] "The floods of the Gospel he drank from the fountain of the sacred bosom of the Lord; blessed Apostle to whom the heavenly secrets have been revealed!" Then when dying on the Cross, the Lord bequeathed and delivered over to His favorite disciple what to Him was most dear and precious, namely, His holy Mother. "Jesus loved John so tenderly," says the Church, "because the prerogative of chastity made him worthy of greater love; for chosen by the Lord as a virgin, he always remained a virgin. To the virginal alone has the Lord entrusted the Virgin, to the virgin disciple He has given the Virgin Mother." — St. John first exercised his apostolate in Palestine; later on, history points him out to us at Ephesus, in which city, as the last surviving

---

[1] Because St. John at the Last Supper reposed on the bosom (in sinu) of the Lord at table, the holy Fathers call him ὁ ἐπιστήθιος. Ideo Joannes dilexit *dulcius* et Petrus *fortius,* quia Joannes accepit specialiter gratiam ad amandum Deum *in se* per *contemplationis saporem:* Petrus vero praecipue ad diligendum Deum in *proximo* per *actionis laborem.* Et hinc est quod Petrus diligebatur a Christo *fortius* quantum ad effectum gratiae interioris; Joannes vero *familiarius* quantum ad signa exterioris conversationis. Haec autem *signa* familiaritatis Dominus exhibebat Joanni non solum propter significationem, sed etiam propter qualitatem personae. Diligebat enim Dominus Joannem magis *familiariter* propter ingenitam mansuetudinem (πολλὴν πραΰτητα — S. Chrysost.) et propter virginalem puritatem et etiam propter juventutem, quae etiam ceteris paribus facit hominem diligi magis tenere (S. Bonav. III, dist. 32, q. 6). Cf. S. Thom. 1, q. 20, a. 4 ad 3.

Apostle, and by reason of his exalted spirituality and sanctity, he exercised all along a powerful influence on the Church of Asia Minor, until he there died and was buried at a very advanced age. But is the glory of martyrdom wanting to St. John? By no means. Under the emperor Domitian he was dragged to Rome, and there thrown into a caldron of boiling oil; but by a miracle he came forth from it purer, fresher and more vigorous than before.[1] He was then banished by the same tyrant (81—96) to the island of Patmos. The martyrdom which he underwent in Rome, is celebrated by the Church on May 6, by a special feast under the title "St. John before the Latin Gate;" at the place of his martyrdom there is a church and chapel erected in his honor. We read in the life of St. Angela de Foligno, that it was revealed to her, that the grief of St. John at the foot of the Cross over the sufferings of Jesus and Mary was so intense, that she believed he was more than a martyr. But St. John is not only an Apostle, martyr and evangelist, he is also a prophet.[2]

St. Thomas, called the Twin (δίδυμος), was slow to believe in the resurrection of the Lord; but he afterwards proved himself a fervent advocate and propagator of the faith among the Parthians in the East; on his way thither he is said to have baptized the three Magi. He penetrated as far as India, where, by the command of the king, he was killed by a stroke of the lance, or, according to another legend, stoned and clubbed to death. As a spiritual architect, he is regarded as the patron of architecture and is, therefore, represented as holding in his hands a hewn stone or a square.

St. James, the Less *(Minor)*, being a relative of the Lord, is called His brother. With Sts. Peter and John he is designated by St. Paul as a "Pillar" of the Church. He is the only Apostle who did not preach the Gospel to the heathens; he was raised by St. Peter to be the first Bishop of Jerusalem. On account of his piety and austerity he was surnamed the Just and highly esteemed even by the Jews. Because of his courageous confession of the divinity of Christ, he was thrown down from the battlements of the Temple; he was still able to rise to his knees, but the rabble fell upon him with stones, and a fuller gave him the death-blow by hitting him on the head with his club, such as is used in dressing cloth (between 60—64). The fuller's club is his distinctive mark; his feast occurs on May the first.

St. Philip was the fourth of the fishermen of Bethsaida in Galilee called by the Saviour to the Apostolate. In the Gospel he is frequently mentioned with distinction. His touching supplication is well known: "Lord, show us the Father and it sufficeth us!" and the reply of Jesus: "Philip, he that seeth Me, seeth the Father

---

[1] In ferventis olei dolium missus beatus Joannes Apostolus, divina se protegente gratia, illaesus exivit (Antiphon. ecclesiast.).

[2] Joannes fuit *propheta;* vidit enim in Patmos insula, in qua fuerat a Domitiano principe ob Domini martyrium relegatus, Apocalypsin infinita mysteria continentem (S. Hieron. C. Jovin. I, 26).

also!'' He exercised his apostolate in Phrygia, and died in Hierapolis on a cross, stoned to death by the enraged populace. The bodies of the holy Apostles Philip and James repose under the high altar of the Church of the Twelve Apostles in Rome, where quite recently they were exhumed and examined. Pictures of St. James represent him with the instrument of his martyrdom, the cross, formed like a Latin T.

St. Bartholomew is probably the Nathaniel mentioned in the Gospel, who was led to the Lord by Philip. He preached in Arabia Felix, in India and in Greater Armenia, where at Albanopolis he was flayed alive and decapitated. Relics of his holy body are preserved under the high altar of the Church of St. Bartholomew, in the isle of the Tiber, at Rome. The Emperor Otto III. brought them to this church built by himself. He is often represented with a knife in his hand, as the instrument of his cruel death.

St. Matthew is both Apostle and Evangelist. He was a publican when the Lord called him. Of his apostolic labors almost nothing reliable is known. Arabia and Ethiopia are specially mentioned as the field of his zeal. According to some authors he was burned alive, according to others he was killed with a spear. Since A. D. 930 his holy body has reposed in the metropolitan church at Salerno (a magnificent structure erected by Robert Guiscard), where he is also honored as the patron of the city.

St. Simon, the Zealot (ζηλωτής), is in the veneration of the Church connected with Judas Thaddeus, who was a brother of St. James the Less. Both consumed and sacrificed their lives by their labors in Mesopotamia and Persia, where Simon was cut in two with a sword and Judas was shot to death with arrows. Their holy bodies repose in the cathedral of St. Peter in Rome.

Here the record of the Apostles closes, that the holy number,[1] twelve, be not exceeded. For the number twelve is symbolical ''of the universality of the Church of Christ, which extends to the four quarters of the world, in the unity of faith in the triune God. Hence the heavenly city Jerusalem, this figure of the Church of Christ in its completion, has four walls and in each wall three portals, that the nations at morning and noon and evening and midnight may be admitted by baptism in the name of God the Father and the Son and the Holy Ghost, the twelve entrances being built upon twelve precious stones which bear the names of the twelve Apostles of the Lamb'' (Apoc. 21). The Apostles not only scattered the seed of the divine word, but they labored to bring it to maturity by watering it with the sweat of their brow and fructifying it by shedding their hearts' blood. Built and resting upon the chief corner-stone Christ, the Apostles have thus become the foundation of the Church, which, consequently, is called and is Apostolic.

---

[1] Deus, qui proditoris apostatae ruinam, ne Apostolorum tuorum *numerus sacratus* perfectione careret, b. Mathiae electione supplesti, praesentia munera sanctifica et per ea nos gratiae tuae virtute confirma (Sacrament. Gregor.).

c) Martyrdom of blood is the characteristic trait of the saints of the first four centuries; therefore, twelve martyrs of these ancient times are now mentioned in the Canon. Among them are five Popes, a bishop, a deacon and five lay persons. Even at a very early period these saints were held in universal and high esteem in Rome. This explains their insertion in the Canon.

a) First, five Popes are mentioned.

St. Linus, the first successor of St. Peter in the See of Rome and, therefore, the second Pope, is assuredly the same from whom St. Paul sends a salutation to Timothy. He was converted to Christianity by St. Peter, and, as a distinguished assistant of the Prince of the Apostles, he may indeed frequently have supplied his place, when the latter was obliged to leave Rome for a time, in order to preach the Gospel elsewhere. He ruled the Church from 67 to 76 (?). He was decapitated and buried in the Vatican by the side of St. Peter. Under Pope Urban VIII. a tomb was discovered there, bearing the simple inscription: *Linus*. His feast occurs on the twenty-third of September.

St. Cletus (76—88?) succeeded St. Linus. It is believed that he erected a tombstone to St. Peter, who had ordained him priest. His feast falls on the twenty-sixth of April.

St. Clement is reckoned among the Apostolic Fathers; he sat in the chair of Peter from 88 to 97 (?). St. Irenaeus writes of him: "In the third place after the Apostles the Roman episcopate received Clement, who had seen the Princes of the Apostles, had associated with them, had listened to their sermons and had the Apostolic tradition before his eyes." St. Paul in his Epistle to the Philippians mentions him among "his co-laborers, whose names are written in the Book of Life." According to the testimony of ancient writers, St. Clement was endowed with all the qualities of mind and heart that were requisite for the highest ecclesiastical dignities. The legend relates that the Emperor Trajan banished him to the Taurian Chersoneus (Crimea), where he found two thousand Christians condemned to work in the marble quarries, who suffered greatly for want of water. Clement prayed, and on an adjacent hill appeared a lamb, from beneath whose right foot a spring of fresh water issued forth. This miracle brought about the conversion of many of the inhabitants. Then Trajan commanded St. Clement to be cast into the sea with an anchor fastened to his neck. The Christians on the shore fell upon their knees and prayed; and behold! the sea receded three thousand paces, and there appeared, built by the hands of angels, a marble temple in which the body of the saint together with the anchor was found. The mortal remains of the martyr are said to have been brought to Rome by the Greek missionaries Sts. Cyril and Methodius, during the pontificate of Pope Hadrian II., and placed in the very ancient basilica of St. Clement near the Coliseum, of which mention is already made by St. Jerome. His feast is celebrated on the twenty-third of November.

In the fourth place comes the name of Xystus (the Greek form of Sixtus). During the first three centuries there were two Popes of this name. Sixtus I. (115—125?) governed the Church during the reign of the Emperor Hadrian, when the lot of the Christians was a hard and painful one; he suffered martyrdom and was buried in the Vatican near St. Peter. His feast occurs on the sixth of April.

Far better known and more celebrated is Sixtus II., a Greek by birth. His pontificate (257—258) fell during the stormy period of the Valerian persecution of the Christians. In spite of the Emperor's prohibition, he ventured to hold divine service in the Catacombs. Discovered by the heathen soldiers and apprehended, he was dragged into the city before the tribunal and condemned; afterward he was again led back to the Catacomb of Praetextatus, in which he had previously celebrated the Holy Sacrifice, and was beheaded on or near his episcopal throne. The crown of martyrdom was granted to him on August sixth, 258. His body now rests in the very ancient church situated on the Appian Way, *S. Sisto vecchio* in Rome.

Which Sixtus is it — the first or the second — that is commemorated in the Canon? Opinions are divided. To prove that Sixtus I. is intended, it is asserted that the five Popes are mentioned in chronological order; now only Sixtus I. reigned before Cornelius, hence he is mentioned in the Canon. More and stronger reasons are in favor of Sixtus II. His memory has ever been highly celebrated in the Church; the Catacombs prove this by many pictures, inscriptions and prayers.[1] As Sixtus II. in his martyrdom preceded his glorious Deacon Lawrence, thus is he likewise mentioned before him in the Canon. St. Sixtus II., it is true, occupied the Papal chair only after St. Cornelius; but here there was a reason for departing from the chronological order and placing the name of Sixtus before that of Cornelius. For this was done that the names of the two Saints, Cornelius and Cyprian, might not be here separated, as they were otherwise always connected in the veneration of the Church. Already in the most ancient Roman liturgy both have a common Mass, as is still the case at the present day. Perhaps also the names of Sts. Cornelius and Cyprian were inserted in the Canon after that of St. Sixtus.

St. Cornelius, who had distinguished himself in all the grades of the Church service, ascended the Chair of Peter in the year 251; he accepted the supreme dignity only by constraint. St. Cyprian extols him as quiet and modest, humble and virginal. Under the tyrant Emperor Decius St. Cornelius was in constant expectation of death. Also under the Emperor Gallus, in the year 252, a violent storm arose against the Christians in Rome; but they, with the Pope at their head, maintained the faith with such unanimity, fortitude

---

[1] Cfr. the so-called Sacram. Leon. "VIII Idus Augusti: Natale s. Xysti in coemeterio Callisti," in which several fine Prefaces in honor of St. Xystus are found.

and strength as to excite universal joy and jubilation, and St. Cyprian could not sufficiently praise and admire them. St. Cornelius was banished to Centum Cellae (*Civitavecchia*), and there died a martyr on September 14, 252; as on the same day six years later (258) the holy Bishop Cyprian of Carthage was martyred, both names are, therefore, usually mentioned together.[1] Their joint feast is celebrated on September sixteenth.

b) After the Popes in the Canon come a Bishop and a Deacon.

St. Cyprian was born in the beginning of the third century at Carthage. He was of distinguished rank, rich, very talented, and had received an education commensurate with his great abilities. Only in a more mature age was he won over to the Catholic faith; his baptism took place about the year 246. He distributed his great wealth among the poor, made a vow of perpetual chastity and spent his time in prayer and the study of the sacred sciences. From the very beginning of his conversion he was adorned with brilliant virtues and uncommon graces. How hapyy he regarded himself in the possession of Christian truth and grace, his letter to Donatus proves, wherein (Chap. 14) he among other things exclaims: "There only is rest, gentle and not deceitful; and there only imperishable and stable peace, where, rescued from the turmoil of a storm-tossed world, we have cast our anchor of salvation in the safe bottom of salvation, in order that, with our eyes turned away from earth to heaven, and being admitted to the service of the Lord, united in spirit with God, we may seek our fame in this alone, that we regard as far beneath us, that which in the esteem of other men is great and glorious. Whosoever has raised himself above the world, can wish for nothing that appertains to the world; can desire nothing more of it." St. Cyprian was raised to the priesthood, and, as he was so greatly renowned for his learning and exemplary manner of life, he was promoted to the episcopal see of Carthage in the year 248. The ten years' episcopacy of the saint (248—258) fell during the time of the most violent persecution and of other exterior misfortunes besides. Powerful in word and deed, St. Cyprian fulfilled with indefatigable zeal his pastoral duties for the salvation of the faithful confided to his care, and for the welfare of the whole Church. He combated for the unity and discipline of the Church against heretics and schismatics, animated all to cheerful endurance of martyrdom, and consumed himself in the ardor of Christian charity. His life, rich in blessings, was terminated by the glorious death of a martyr. He was put to death by the sword in the public place of Carthage, on September 14, 258. His memory has always been held in benediction by the Church.

St. Lawrence is highly extolled by the Fathers and held in great veneration by all Christian nations. "As Jerusalem was glorified by Stephen, so is Rome renowned by its Lawrence from the rising to the setting of the sun," says the holy Pope Leo in a

---

[1] Cfr. Sacram. Leon.

sermon on the feast of this Saint. Spain is regarded as his native country; but he was brought up and educated in Rome. Sixtus II. ordained him deacon and made him the first of the seven deacons of the Roman Church, wherefore he is also called Archdeacon of the Pope.[1] This was a most important office; for it included the administration of the treasures of the Church. Exceedingly glorious is the martyrdom of the young Levite. When Pope Sixtus II. was being dragged to the Catacombs for execution, Lawrence cried out to him: "Whither goest thou, Father, without thy son? Where art thou hastening, holy priest, without thy deacon? Never wert thou accustomed to offer the Holy Sacrifice without thy minister." And how singularly consoling are the words of the highpriest to his deacon: "I am not forsaking thee, my son, greater combats await thee. Cease to weep, after three days thou wilt follow me, the Levite, his priest." During those three days the deacon hastened through the city, distributed the goods of the Church to the needy and in so doing he wrought several miracles. To the prefect of the city who ordered him to deliver up the treasures of the Church, he presented the poor of Christ as the treasures of the Church. On this account the heathen became enraged, and subjected the young hero to all manner of torments. St. Lawrence was scourged, struck with leaden balls, stretched on the rack, burned with red hot metallic plates. The judge then threatened him with an entire night of tortures. Radiant with an unearthly brightness, the intrepid sufferer exclaimed: "For me this night has no darkness, but breaks forth into the bright light of day" — *Mea nox obscurum non habet, sed omnia in luce clarescunt.* Afterward he was laid on a burning gridiron, whence he addressed the tyrant: "Behold, wretch, the power of my God; your heat for me is refreshing coolness, but it will end for you in inextinguishable fire." In the midst of the tortures the constant martyr prayed to Christ: "On the gridiron I have not denied Thee, my God, and over the fire I have confessed Thee, my Saviour. Thou hast tried and examined my heart in the night; Thou hast proved me by fire, and found no falsehood in me. My soul adhered to Thee, whilst my flesh burned for Thee." He then prayed for the triumph of Christianity in the city of Rome, and closed his heroic combat with the words: "I thank Thee, O Lord, that Thou dost permit me to enter through the portals of heaven." Thus his indomitable soul passed to the glory of God on August 10,

---

[1]
> Hic *primus* e septem viris,
> Qui stant ad aram proximi,
> Levita sublimis gradu,
> Et ceteris praestantior.
>
> Claustris sacrorum praeerat,
> Coelestis arcanum domus
> Fidis gubernans clavibus
> Votasque dispensans opes.
>
> (Prudent. Peristephan. II, v. 37—45.)

258; on earth the illustrious archdeacon and martyr has ever been loaded with honor and praise. Above his grave Constantine had the magnificent basilica of St. Lawrence erected outside the walls; it is one of the five patriarchal and one of the seven principal churches of Rome. There beneath the high altar repose in a marble sarcophagus the united relics of both the deacons Sts. Lawrence and Stephen. Many other churches were built and consecrated in Rome and in other places in honor of St. Lawrence.

c) Finally, in the Canon five laymen are commemorated.

St. Chrysogonus converted many heathens in Rome to Christianity; he was also the teacher of St. Anastasia in Christian doctrine, as also her counsel and consoler, when on account of her faith she had many persecutions to suffer. He was arrested in Rome under Diocletian, and, after long imprisonment, was sent to Aquileja where he was beheaded about the year 304. A portion of his head is preserved and venerated in the ancient Church of Chrysogonus, which is situated in Rome in the Trastevere, and is in possession of the Trinitarians. The feast occurs on November twenty-fourth.

John and Paul were brothers. As distinguished Romans, they were intrusted with high positions of honor at the court of St. Constantia, a daughter of Constantine the Great. When she had retired from the world, the two brothers lived as "Men of Mercy" devoting themselves to works of charity. The apostate Emperor Julian wished to compel them to sacrifice to the idols, and to enter his service; but such an order they rejected with contempt. And for this reason Julian had them secretly decapitated in their own palace, which stood on the declivity of Mount Coelius, — June 26, 362. On this site, as early as the fourth century, the Church of Sts. John and Paul was built in honor of the martyred brothers. Their bodies rest in a magnificent sarcophagus under the high altar. In the nave of the church, surrounded by an iron railing, may be seen the marble slab which was stained with their blood and which annually on their feast (June twenty-sixth) is strewn with flowers.

Saints Cosmas and Damian were also brothers, descended from a distinguished race in Arabia. They practised medicine in Roman territory and that without remuneration (ἀναργύρως). Their learning, their skill in healing, their devout mode of life, all combined, won for them universal confidence and high esteem. Their acts of benevolence gained for the Christian religion many adherents. After enduring many torments,[1] they were at last — probably in 297 —

---

[1] About the middle of the fourth century the period of martyrs came to an end. The latest of the martyrs here mentioned — Sts. John and Paul († 362) — were placed in the Canon probably towards the end of the fourth century or in the beginning of the fifth century, and from that time the list of the saints mentioned has been closed. Elsewhere since the sixth century many names were added to the Communicantes — particularly of saints that are specially honored in certain dioceses and convents. Until late in the Middle Age in many dioceses there was added therein the commemoration of the saints of the day with the preamble:

decapitated at Egaea, in Cilicia. Pope Felix IV. (526—529) built at Rome the Church of Sts. Cosmas and Damian, and brought to it the relics of the saintly martyred brothers. Both are honored as patrons of physicians and of the science of medicine; their feast occurs on September twenty-seventh.[1]

In the Roman Canon only martyrs are named before and after the Consecration: this distinction is justly due to them. They have merited it by the bloody sacrifice of their life; they appear as the ripest and most glorious fruit of the Sacrifice of Christ. They resembled the Saviour not in life merely, but also in death. For Christ they lived, for Him they died; in return for the Sacrifice of His love, they offered the sacrifice of the world and of themselves — amid untold torments and sufferings. The virtues of fortitude and patience, of faith and of love which they practised in an heroic degree shone resplendent in them.

58. The Second Prayer of the Canon before the Consecration.

Hanc igitur oblationem servitutis nostrae, sed et cunctae familiae tuae, quaesumus Domine, ut placatus accipias:[2] diesque nostros in tua pace disponas, atque ab aeterna damnatione nos eripi, et in electorum tuorum jubeas grege numerari. Per Christum Dominum nostrum. Amen.

This oblation, therefore, of our service, and that of Thy whole family, we beseech Thee, O Lord, graciously to accept and to dispose our days in Thy peace, and to command us to be delivered from eternal damnation, and to be numbered in the flock of Thine elect. Through Christ Our Lord. Amen.

I. The Text.[3] — As in the beginning of the Canon, so here

Necnon et illorum sanctorum, quorum sollempnitas hodie in conspectu majestatis tuae celebratur — with or without the addition: in toto orbe terrarum.

[1] Aegeae natalis sanctorum martyrum Cosmae et Damiani fratrum, qui in persecutione Diocletiani post multa tormenta, vincula et carceres, post mare et ignes, cruces, lapidationem et sagittas divinitus superatas, capite plectuntur (Martyrol. Roman. 27. Sept.).

[2] Altaribus tuis, Domine, munera nostrae servitutis inferimus, quae placatus accipias (Sacram. Leon.) — Accipio = to take, to receive; to receive something presented, to accept.

[3] This prayer has at present in four Mass formulas an addition by which the Sacrifice is offered for a special intention: On Holy Thursday in commemoration of the Institution of the Eucharistic Mysteries, in Easter and Whitsuntide Weeks for the newly baptized, and at the consecration of a bishop for the newly consecrated. Before the time of St. Gregory the Great, the Hanc igitur was a variable oblation and intercessory prayer, according to the character of the Mass formula (for example, for those ordained, for pilgrims, for the departed). Hence in the Gelasianum there are 38 special formulas of Hanc igitur, which do not, like the additions to the Communicantes, set off the thought of the feast, but contain peti-

also do we meet with the little word *igitur* (= therefore, consequently, accordingly, hence); it unites the second prayer to the first and designates it as a consequence or continuation of the first.[1] The same petitions are again presented, but now with heightened confidence and intensified expression. We no longer stand there alone, — alone in our poverty and wretchedness —; for we have renewed our connection with the communion of saints, and in this communion we are enriched by the merits and prayers of our heavenly brethren; hence, we venture with still greater confidence to turn to the Lord with the petition previously implored, that He would show Himself favorable, propitiated, gracious (*placatus*), and with kind indulgence "accept" (*accipias*) these sacrificial gifts from our hands.[2] Until now the same oblation is always meant: namely, bread and wine, in so far as they are destined to be changed into the Body and Blood of Christ. The petition for the acceptance of the sacrificial elements, therefore, includes in itself the petition for their transsubstantiation:[3] the purpose for which they are to be accepted is the Consecration (*accipias — uti accepta habeas et benedicas*). — The Eucharistic Oblation is here more minutely characterized by a twofold clause as "the offering of our servitude" and as "the oblation of the whole family of God." Unquestionably these words express in general the truth, that the Eucharist is the homage-offering of the whole Church,[4] that is, that it is offered by all her members and for all her members[5]; but in particular they admit of

tions for the application of the fruits of the Sacrifice in various concerns and events of this life.

[1] The recommendation of the sacrificial gifts and of those offering, or of those for whom the Sacrifice is offered, which was interrupted by the Communicantes, is here resumed, and is connected by the igitur with the petitions contained in this second prayer.

[2] Quia hoc sacrificium tibi offerimus in corpore Ecclesiae communicando et memoriam Sanctorum venerando, hanc igitur oblationem, precamur, ut *placatus accipias:* ut scil. si peccatis nostris praepedimur, communione saltem sanctae Ecclesiae et Sanctorum tuorum veneratione *placeris ad accipiendum,* quod tibi offerimus, sacrificium (B. Odo Camerac. Expos. in Canon. Missae dist. 2).

[3] Sacerdos orat Deum, ut ipsam oblationem panis et vini accipiat ut materiam sacrificii futuri et eam videlicet benedicat et sanctificet (Bellarm. De Missa, 1. 2, c. 22).

[4] In his verbis unitas Ecclesiae ostenditur, quando in illa oblatione communis *servitus* exhibetur Deo tam a sacerdotibus quam a cuncta familia domus Dei. Oratur itaque Deus, ut hanc oblationem, quam *illi soli debita servitute* defert Ecclesia, placatus accipiat et sic dies nostros, quibus inter diversa pericula vivimus, in sua pace disponat, finitoque hujus mortalitatis cursu, ab aeterna damnatione ereptos in electorum suorum grege annumerare dignetur (Pseudo-Alcuin. c. 40).

[5] *Hanc igitur oblationem servitutis nostrae,* i. e. quam offerimus nos sacerdotes qui speciatim servi tui sumus, tuo cultui et obsequiis mancipati et hoc offerimus sacrificium, ut servitutis nostrae et subjectionis aliquod testimonium demus; nec tantum est oblatio nostra, qui tamquam ministri eam offerimus, *sed et cunctae familiae tuae,* i. e. totius Ecclesiae catholicae omniumque fidelium, qui per manus

different meanings. The expression "oblation of our servitude" may be applied to those who are present, that is, to those who most intimately take part in the celebration of Mass; the addition "as also of Thy whole family" to all the others, who are absent. — Or we may consider the first clause as especially designating the consecrated ministers of the altar, that is, the priests, or all clerics, in which case by *the family of God* the believing people are to be understood, but in particular those faithful who by actual participation unite in the celebration of the Mass. — However, this does not exhaust the full sense: it says "the oblation of our servitude" (*oblatio servitutis nostrae*), which would signify more than "the offering which we Thy servants (*nos servi*) present," which is the expression used immediately after the Elevation. The holy Mass is called "the oblation of our servitude," that is, the offering that we and all the members of the Church make, in order to acknowledge the absolute dominion of God over all that is created, and to express our profound submission to it.[1] As creatures we stand in a special relation of dependence toward God our Creator; the Mass now has principally for object the giving to God of that veneration, homage and acknowledgement — in brief, that religious worship which is due to Him alone.[2] Sacrifice is the chief act of religion, or, what is the same thing, of divine worship.[3] All men are bound to serve God; but priests have consecrated themselves in a very special manner to the service of the sanctuary. Yet we are not to serve our Lord with servile fear, but with joy and jubilation of heart; for the service of God is not only a duty incumbent upon man, but, moreover, an honor and a happiness for him. Whosoever thoroughly breaks asunder the bonds of sin, passions and attachment to the world, so as to devote all his thoughts, desires and energies perfectly to God and His holy will, becomes truly free; for he obtains, by this

---

nostras et ministerium hanc offerunt, et quorum nomine eandem tibi offerimus (Antonius de Molina, Instructio sacerdotum tract. 3, c. 3).

[1] This more profound meaning of the expression oblatio *servitutis* nostrae is evident also from other almost similar designations of the Eucharistic Sacrifice, as they are found especially in the Secretae; for example, nostrae servitutis munus; debitum nostrae servitutis; nostrae humilitatis oblatio.

[2] Deo nos *servitutem*, quae λατρεία graece dicitur, sive in quibusque sacramentis sive in nobis ipsis debemus (S. Aug. De civit. Dei 1. 10, c. 3, al. 4). — Ipsa *servitus* graece λατρεία dicitur, quae *soli* vero Deo jure ac legitime non a perfidis, sed a catholicis fidelibus exhibetur... illa cultura quae λατρεία dicitur, *maxime in sacrificiis* invenitur (S. Fulgent. Contra Fabian. frag. 12).

[3] *Cultus* ac *servitus Dei* reipsa non sunt actus religionis distincti: siquidem eodem actu religionis homo servit Deo et colit ipsum. Nam cultus respicit Dei excellentiam, cui reverentia debetur; servitus autem subjectionem hominis, qui ex sua conditione obligatur ad exhibendam reverentiam Deo, cum interim in omni actu religionis et excellentiam Dei et nostram erga Deum subjectionem protestemur, adeo ut ad haec duo pertineant omnes actus religionis, quia per omnes homo protestatur divinam excellentiam et subjectionem sui ad Deum (Tanner disp. 5 de relig. q. 1, dub. 2).

dominion over himself, the liberty of the children of God, who are actuated only by the spirit of the Lord.[1]

We expect and implore by virtue of the Eucharistic Sacrifice[2] mercies and blessings for time and for eternity. Earthly, temporal welfare consists in this, that God orders and directs our days in peace; heavenly, eternal well-being includes preservation from endless reprobation and the being inscribed among the host of the elect.[3]

"*Diesque nostros in tua pace disponas*" — thus do we pray[4]; for we desire good and peaceful days, that are not clouded by sufferings, combats, assaults and persecutions, but always cheered and blessed with "the peace of God," "that, being delivered from the hand of our enemies, we may serve Him without fear in justice and holiness" (Luke 1, 74). We pray for temporal prosperity, inasmuch as it may be serviceable to the attainment of "the one thing necessary," and for possession of that "best part which shall not be taken away from us."

But in what do this "one thing necessary" and this "best part" consist? In this, that we escape the evil of all evils, the greatest evil — eternal death (*ab aeterna damnatione nos eripi*); and that we attain to the best of goods, the supreme good — eternal life (*in electorum tuorum grege numerari*).[5] The number of those who are chosen for heavenly glory has been eternally and irrevocably determined by God, so that the number can be neither increased nor diminished; therefore, the above petition can refer only to the execution of this divine decree and signify, that God may be pleased

---

[1] Servitus illa, quae fit *homini ex necessitate*, aliquo modo derogat hominis libertati, et ideo non habet in se excellentiam virtutis. — Servitus, quae ex *mera voluntate* fit *Deo*, ponit hominem in statu altiori et tanto magis facit hominem liberum, quanto magis elongat hominem a peccato. Et talis est servitus latriae (S. Bonav. III, dist. 9, a. 2, q. 1).

[2] Vera *sacrificalis* oblatio non intelligitur esse, donec materia illa, quae ad divinum cultum dicata jam est, benedicitur et sanctificatur; nulla ergo petitio fit per hanc oblationem, sistendo in pane et vino, sed in ordine ad eorum consecrationem, per quam Christus *vere sacrificatur* et *offertur;* quod est petere per incruentam Christi sacrificationem ex pane et vino sub eorumque speciebus faciendam (Suarez disp. 83, sect. 2, n. 8).

[3] The three petitions pro pace temporum et ereptione ab aeternis suppliciis et consortio Sanctorum obtinendo were added by St. Gregory the Great (cfr. Walafrid. Strab. c. 23). Since already previously, v. g., in the Leonianum, similar thoughts and expressions occur in this place, St. Gregory probably only made permanent the wording which until then had been changeable.

[4] Propter *triplicem* pacem *ter* oramus in Missa: "dies nostros in tua pace disponas" — "da propitius pacem in diebus nostris" — "dona nobis pacem", ut de *pace temporis* per *pacem pectoris* transeamus ad *pacem aeternitatis* (Innocent. III. 1. 3, c. 11).

[5] Numerari = numero aggregari, received into the number. Cfr. the following prayer for a departed soul: Omnipotens sempiterne Deus... propitiare animae famuli tui, ut qui de hac vita in tui nominis confessione decessit, Sanctorum tuorum *numero* facias *adgregari* (Sacrament. Gelasian.).

to grant us the grace of final perseverance and admit us to heavenly bliss.[1] This meaning is clearly expressed in a petition of almost the same import in the *Te Deum: Aeterna fac cum sanctis tuis in gloria numerari* — "May (Thy servants) be numbered among Thy saints in eternal glory." Also in the sorrowful chant *Dies irae* the Church instructs us to pray for preservation from hell: "Let me not be lost on that day; let me not burn in eternal fire," and for participation in the happiness of heaven: "Place me at Thy right side; call me with the blessed ones."

As fruit to be derived from the Sacrifice,[2] therefore, we implore in the above prayer the peace of God for the days of our earthly life; but we pray especially for the consummation of our redemption and eternal salvation. Full redemption consists in this, that we be forever snatched from eternal ruin and perdition, to which the godless are doomed, and that we may for all eternity be possessed of that glory and happiness which God has prepared for those who love Him.

Let us call to mind the impenetrable darkness that envelops the mystery of predestination for us poor mortals here below, and we shall be moved spontaneously to direct often and earnestly similar petitions for eternal salvation to God, "to whom alone the number of the elect is known, who shall find a place in the felicity of heaven" (*cui soli cognitus est numerus electorum in superna felicitate locandus*). Prayers of this nature are useful and necessary; but they alone do not suffice. God receives into heaven only those who "by faith and works" (*fide et opere*) belong to Him and are entirely His.[3] Hence we must faithfully employ the grace of God, work out our salvation in fear and trembling,[4] making our calling and election

---

[1] Breviter dicitur, peti a Deo *consecutionem* electionis, quod est petere aeternam beatitudinem, in qua numerus electorum congregandus est (Suarez l. c.).

[2] Tria bona postulantur a Deo. Primum temporale; secundum perpetui mali devitatio; tertium perpetui boni adeptio. In horum trium bonorum postulatione profitetur Ecclesia, Deum esse universorum dominum et in triplicem mundi machinam extendi supremum ejus principatum. Per primum enim profitetur, ipsum esse dominum in terris; per secundum in inferis; per tertium in coelis — et ubique omnia ipsius nutu disponi (Clichtov. Elucid. eccl. l. 3, n. 23).

[3] Nos hic petimus a Deo consecutionem electionis et aeternam beatitudinem, in qua numerus electorum congregandus est. Haec autem consecutio ex nostra libera cooperatione dependet, videlicet ab executione bonorum operum, quae sunt media a Deo praeordinata in eum finem. Dum ergo oramus et petimus numerari in grege electorum, *gratiam* a Deo postulamus, quae necessaria est ad ea media exequenda et finem consequendum (Quarti p. 2, tit. 9, sect. 2, dub. 4).

[4] Uncertainty with regard to eternal salvation is here below necessary and beneficial, quia *humiliat* et *sollicitat*. Econtra certitudo de electione *elevat* in tumorem et *deprimit* in torporem; ideo secundum ordinatissimam dispensationem hoc factum est, ut nulli reveletur, an sit praedestinatus, nisi sit a Deo confirmatus in bono, ut non possit *elevari* per *superbiam* vel *torpore* per *neglegentiam* (S. Bonavent. dist. 40, art. 2, q. 2. — Cfr. Amalar. l. 3, c. 23). — Optimum affirmare possumus esse praedestinationis indicium, sese ad ejusmodi sanctarum precum spiritum et arcana sensa conformare, i. e. nihil quidquam aliud quam Dei pacem

sure by good works (Phil. 2, 12; 2 Peter 1, 10). Be poor in spirit, be meek and humble, live in holy and salutary compunction, hunger and thirst after greater perfection, love and practise works of spiritual and corporal mercy, carefully preserve purity of heart, seek and endeavor, as far as possible, to live in peace with all mankind, be glad and rejoice when, by reason of exercising these virtues and for the name of Jesus, you are obliged to suffer persecutions and insults, — then may you confidently hope to belong to the number of the elect and to obtain a rich reward in heaven. But pray we must without ceasing "the God of all grace, who hath called us unto eternal glory in Christ Jesus, that, after we have suffered a little, He will Himself perfect us in the life to come and confirm and establish us in this world" (1 Peter 5, 9).[1]

2.   The Accompanying Action. — During this prayer, the priest extends his two hands horizontally over the chalice and Host, and in such a manner, that the right thumb is placed over the left one in the form of a cross. This imposing, or extending of hands occurs first toward the close of the fifteenth century[2] in some Missals, and it was afterwards universally prescribed by Pius V. This ceremony not only harmonizes with the tenor of the text, "this oblation, therefore," (*hanc oblationem*), indicating the sacrificial elements in a just and reverential manner, but also contains in addition a mystical meaning. The ritual laying on of hands frequently occurs in both Testaments, as well as in the liturgy: according to its fundamental signification, it is always a symbol, or a means of transferring something to others, for example, the guilt of sin, a blessing and protection. In the Mosaic worship the laying on of hands was a symbolical representation of the transferring of sin and guilt to the animal that was to be sacrificed, which vicariously had to suffer death instead of man. Here in the Holy Mass the laying on of hands has a similar object; and, therefore, in a visible and energetic

---

cupere, nihil praeter mortem aeternam metuere et perseverantiae donum enixe petere, ut in eorum adscribamur numero, qui aeterna gloria perfruentur (Benedict. XIV. 1. 2, c. 14, n. 4).

[1] Cum Deus disponit vel vult aliquid facere, non disponit in omnem eventum, sed praesuppositis congruentibus antecedentibus, sicut *disponit* nos *salvare*, si tamen velimus per bona merita salutem acquirere (S. Bonav. III, dist. 17, a. 2, q. 1).

[2] Formerly it was often the custom, as it is now with the Dominicans and Carmelites, to bow profoundly at the recitation of this prayer. Hic *inclinat se* usque ad altare dicens: "*Hanc igitur . . . .*" (Amalar. Eclog. n. 29). — Presbyter humiliationem Domini usque ad crucem nos indicat, cum se usque ad altare inclinat dicendo (Microl. c. 16). — *Hanc igitur oblationem* dicendo sacerdos in quibusdam ecclesiis profunde se inclinat (Durand 1. 6, c. 39, n. 2). Christian antiquity and the Middle Age make no mention of the stretching out of the hands in the aforesaid place. Already for this reason it is of no consequence to see preserved "here the former imposition of hands of the priests celebrating with the bishop," that is, the invocation of the Holy Ghost for the miracle of the consecration.

way it deeply fixes the sacrificial character of the Eucharist, for it shows that Christ on the altar, in our place, for our sake, and on account of our sins offers Himself; — and, moreover, it indicates that we should unite ourselves with His Sacrifice, offering ourselves in it and along with it.

59. The Third Prayer of the Canon before the Consecration.

Quam oblationem tu Deus in omnibus, quaesumus, bene†dictam, adscrip†tam, ra†tam, rationabilem, acceptabilemque facere digneris: ut nobis Cor†pus et San†guis fiat dilectissimi Filii tui Domini nostri Jesu Christi.

Which oblation do Thou, O God, we beseech Thee, vouchsafe to make in all things blessed†, approved†, ratified†, reasonable, and acceptable: that it may become for us the Body† and Blood† of Thy most beloved Son, our Lord Jesus Christ.

1. *The Words of the Prayer.* — This prayer is closely connected with the preceding one and forms the immediate transition and introduction to the act of Consecration. In general its meaning is clear, but the several designations therein given to the offering appear obscure and difficult to the understanding. Since the foregoing preparation for the act of Consecration ends with this prayer, it expresses for the last time in a simple, grand way the already oft-repeated petition to God for the blessing, or the changing of the bread and wine into the Body and the Blood of Christ.[1] Therefore, we implore of God, that the elements lying on the altar and dedicated to Him, be raised to the highest degree of consummation, that is, be changed into heavenly sacrificial gifts. The Eucharistic Saviour is "the perfectly blessed, approved, ratified, reasonable and acceptable oblation" which, by the power of God, is to replace the substance of bread and wine.[2]

Christ is the *oblatio in omnibus benedicta*, that is, the offering in all things blessed (= in every respect thoroughly and perfectly)[3].

---

[1] Haec tertia periodus, quam ingredimur, maxime occupatur circa sacrificium, ut fiat perfectum et in aliam mutetur substantiam immortalem et incorruptam... Transit ad partes a toto, ut universalis benedictionis partes imprecetur hostiae, cui universam benedictionem fuerat imprecatus, ut cum prius posuerit *in omnibus benedictam*, particulariter subjungat *adscriptam*, et *ratam*, et *rationabilem*, et *acceptabilem*, quae sunt partes omnimodae benedictionis (B. Odo Camerac. Expos. in Can. Missae dist. 3).

[2] Praeinducta sacratissima verba exponuntur de eo, quod est res et sacramentum, videlicet de corpore Christi vel de ipso Christo, qui est hostia benedicta, adscripta, rata, rationabilis et acceptabilis (Dion. Carthus. Exposit. Missae art. 23). — Solum Christi corpus et sanguis est hostia in omnibus benedicta, adscripta, rata, rationabilis acceptabilisque (B. Odo Camerac. l. c.).

[3] "The chalice awakening fear and reverence" (St. Chrysost.) of the Eucharist is called by St. Paul calix *benedictionis* cui *benedicimus* (1 Cor. 10, 16) = calix benedictus, i. e. consecratus.

The blessing here meant and to be imparted to the material elements, is the very highest and the most sublime conceivable, — namely, the Consecration, that is, the changing of the elements into the glorious Body and the Precious Blood of our Lord Jesus Christ.[1] We, therefore, beg God to bless the oblation of bread and wine, that is, to consecrate it and thereby make it for us an inexhaustible source of grace and blessing.

Christ is the *oblatio adscripta*.[2] This extremely obscure word can only with difficulty or perhaps not at all be explained in a perfectly satisfactory manner, as is evident from the different attempts at interpretation. Frequently *adscripta* is defined in the sense of acceptable, agreeable; but opposed to this acceptation is the circumstance that then *adscripta* would have entirely the same signification as the following *acceptabilis*, which in so concise a prayer is by no means probable. — Others understand *adscripta* as meaning consecrated or belonging to God. — We translate *adscripta* by the word approved and thereby give our preference for an explanation according to which this word seems to coincide better with the whole context. Accordingly the oblation becomes *adscripta* when it responds and answers to the prescription, to the ordinance and institution of Christ, as it took place at the Last Supper.[3] In this manner, therefore, the same petition would be presented that frequently occurs elsewhere in liturgies: that the elements of bread and wine may become *eucharistia legitima*, that is, *legitimate* Eucharist[4].

If the oblation is so constituted as to be conformable to Holy Scripture, to the will and command of Christ (*Hoc facite*), then necessarily it is also an "*oblatio rata*",[5] that is, a true or valid sacrifice[6]; for with this presupposition all the features and elements are

---

[1] Oratio haec potest exponi, ut tota petitio referatur ad ipsius materiae consecrationem, nihilque aliud in summa petatur, quam ut ex pane corpus et ex vino fiat sanguis Christi, ut hoc modo ac per talem transmutationem oblatio ipsa panis et vini fiat *benedicta;* illa enim est summa benedictio et sanctificatio, quae in illam materiam supervenire potest, unde ipsamet consecratio *benedictio* solet a Patribus appellari (Suarez disp. 83, sect. 2, n. 10). — Digneris hanc oblationem facere *benedictam,* i. e. convertere in carnem et sanguinem Christi, quae sunt hostia benedicta, h. e. omni carens macula culpae atque omni gratia adornata (Dion. Carthus. l. c.).

[2] Adscribere = to ascribe or to attribute; to institute, to determine, to establish.

[3] Potest referri hoc verbum (*adscripta*) ad ea, quae de hac consecratione scripta sunt, ita ut postuletur, ut haec oblatio talis fiat, qualis scripta est et promissa illis verbis Christi: "Hoc facite"; adscriptum enim dici potest, quod est *scripto conforme* (Suarez l. c.).

[4] Cfr. also the prayer in the Pontifical for the Consecration of a portable altar: Quaesumus omnipotens Deus, ... qui inter ceteras creaturarum formas lapideum metallum ad obsequium tui sacrificii condidisti, ut *legitimae libationi* praeparetur altare, annue dignanter.

[5] Ratus (from reor) = intended; transferred to = determined, valid, true, legal. —Quod nostro geritur ministerio, ratum habeas, ac si sine nobis manibus tuis idem ageretur (Robert. Paulul. De offic. eccles. l. 2, c. 31).

[6] Praeterea postulatur, ut per consecrationem fiat *rata*, i. e. vera; non enim

at hand requisite for the existence and essence of the Eucharistic
Sacrifice.

The contents of the above three words (*benedicta, adscripta,
rata*) are now stated more correctly and emphatically, in this that
the Sacrifice is called a "spiritual", or "reasonable oblation"
(*oblatio rationabilis*).[1] In the liturgies the Eucharist is often
designated as "a spiritual sacrifice" (*hostia spiritualis*) or as "a
reasonable and unbloody worship of God" (λογικὴ καὶ ἀναίμακτος λατρεία).
This expression is borrowed from Holy Scripture[2]; in its liturgical
use it refers as well to the way and manner of offering, as to the
sacrificial gift, and characterizes it as endowed with life, spirit and
reason, in contrast with the Old Testament offerings of irrational
animals and inanimate things.[3] The Eucharist is, therefore, a
"reasonable oblation", because on the altar the living Lamb of God,
the God-Man Jesus Christ, is sacrificed, He who is, indeed, the
eternal reason, the increated and personal wisdom of God.

If the Eucharistic Sacrifice has these four qualities, it is then
infallibly and in the highest degree also "pleasing to God," dear,
precious and acceptable to the Heart of God (*oblatio acceptabilis*)[4].

The explanation of the obscure antecedent clause follows or lies
in the concluding words, "that it may be made for us the Body and
Blood of Christ," (*fiat* = transeat in), which denote and implore
quite unequivocally the change of substance of the matter of sacrifice.[5] The little word *nobis* ("for us")[6], moreover, adds a new idea;

est haec vera sacrificalis oblatio, nisi consecratio valida sit et efficax; quomodo
dicere solemus, sacramentum esse ratum, quando vere factum (Suarez l. c.).

[1] Rationabilis (λογικός) = endowed with reason, reasonable; according to reason. The word has reference to the Divine Logos, who in and with His human
nature is in the highest degree a spiritual and reasonable Sacrificial Gift (προσφορά
πνευματικὴ καὶ λογικὴ): Christ's sacrificial Body and Blood are on the altar not merely
animated with a spiritual and reasonable soul, but, moreover, hypostatically united
to the Divine Word (Logos). — Munus populi tui, Domine, placatus intende, quo
non altaribus tuis ignis alienus nec irrationabilium cruor effunditur animantium,
sed sancti Spiritus operante virtute sacrificium jam nostrum corpus et sanguis est
ipsius sacerdotis (Sacram. Leonian.).

[2] Rationabile obsequium; in Greek λογικὴ λατρεία (Rom. 12, 1).

[3] Petitur etiam, ut fiat *rationabilis*, i. e. rationalis hostia, quia per illam consecrationem fit, ut jam non simplex panis et vinum, nec sanguis hircorum aut vitu-
lorum, sed Christus ipse, qui non solum rationalis est, sed aeterna sapientia et
ratio, offeratur (Suarez l. c.).

[4] Denique per eandem mutationem fit maxime *acceptabilis* haec oblatio, quia
jam, non ex dignitate offerentium, sed ex re ipsa oblata, gratissima Deo est et
accepta: nam per illam mutationem panis fit corpus illud, quod Deus adaptavit, ut
veteribus repudiatis sacrificiis, eo placari posset (ad Hebr. 2). Suarez l. c.

[5] Posuerat in omnibus benedictam, subjungit quattuor species: adscriptam,
ratam, rationabilem, acceptabilem. Sed haec omnia clausa erant, minus intellege-
bantur, minus patebant; aperuit ostium, patefecit totum, scil. ut nobis fiat corpus
et sanguis Christi. Hic totum completur, hic totum perficitur, ut fiat corpus et
sanguis Christi (B. Odo Camerac. dist. 3). — Munera, Domine, oblata sanctifica,
ut tui nobis Unigeniti corpus et sanguis fiant (Sacram. Gregor.).

[6] Fiat *nobis*, i. e., ad nostram salutem, ad nostrum cotidianum profectum,

for it proves that the Body and Blood of Christ take the place of the bread and wine, that is, become present under their appearances for us, for our sake, for our salvation and blessing and advantage. For us the Saviour offers Himself on the altar, to us He gives Himself in Holy Communion. *Totus mihi datus (Dominus) et totus in meos usus expensus est.*[1] In like manner the angels announced to the shepherds: "This day is born to you a Saviour" (Luke 2, 11).[2]

2. The aforesaid prayer is accompanied with five signs of the Cross, three of which are first made over both sacrificial elements at one and the same time (at the words *benedictam, adscriptam, ratam*)[3]; then there is one besides made separately over the Host and over the chalice (at the words *Corpus et Sanguis*). These holy signs strengthen and visibly elucidate the text of the prayer spoken vocally; they symbolically express what the accompanying and corresponding words signify. The signs of the Cross are here symbols and means of blessing; they call down the divine blessing of Consecration upon the bread and wine, that they may be changed, and that — which is likewise made apparent by the sign of the Cross — the bread may be changed into the same sacrificial Body that hung on the Cross, and the wine into the same sacrificial Blood which was shed on the Cross. — If we consider the first three signs of the Cross in themselves, then we must at the same time evidently see in them an indication and symbol of the Adorable Trinity, from whom proceeds the blessing of Consecration prayed for, to sanctify the material elements and change them into the Eucharistic Sacrifice.[4]

---

atque ad vitiorum nostrorum expurgationem omniumque spiritualium donorum multiplicationem (Dion. Carth. Expos. Missae art. 23).

[1] S. Bernard. in circumcis. Dom. serm. 3, n. 4.

[2] Sub hac oblatione non solum panis et vinum, sed Ecclesia ipsa in his significata intellegitur. Hinc 1. sacerdos nomine Ecclesiae orat, ut panis et vinum convertantur in corpus et sanguinem Christi; qua transsubstantiatione oblatio fit *benedicta*, quia Christus est victima a Patre sanctificata et benedicta, *adscripta*, quia Christus est victima divinae majestati penitus devota et addicta, *rata*, quia ipse est victima a Patre tamquam perfecta adprobata, *rationabilis et acceptabilis*, quia ipse est aeterna ratio et Deo Patri infinite placens, ad differentiam victimarum irrationalium, per se Deo non placentium, quae in antiqua lege offerebantur.— 2. Sacerdos orat, ut nos ipsi in omnibus simus *benedicti* gratiis divinis, *adscripti* numero electorum in libro vitae (Apoc. 13, 8; 17, 8), *rati*, firmi et stabiles in Dei servitio, *rationabiles*, corpus et passiones rationi, rationem Deo subdendo (Rom. 12, 1), et *acceptabiles*, digni, ut in vitam aeternam accipiamur; *ut nobis corpus et sanguis fiat D. N. J. Ch.*, scil. ut consecratio et oblatio nobis fiat fructuosa (Müller, Theol. moral. 1. 3, tit. 1, § 16).

[3] Haec tria verba dicendo, super duo oblata simul ter signum crucis facimus, quod in omnibus consecrationibus familiare est et domesticum. Per virtutem enim crucis Domini multa credimus operari. Ideo ter, qui per virtutem crucis pariter Trinitas operatur (Robert. Paulul. De offic. eccles. 1. 2, c. 31).

[4] Fiunt *tres* cruces super oblatam materiam, dum dicit "benedictam, adscriptam, ratam" ad honorem supersanctae et adorandae *Trinitatis* et ad insinuandum, quod effectus orationis istius a tota beatissima *Trinitate* nobis donetur. Nam *ipsa*

But not only in a general way should the identity, that exists between the bloody and unbloody Sacrifice of Christ, be made clear to us by the sign of the Cross; we can piously and edifyingly consider the five repetitions of the sign of the Cross as they in this prayer occur immediately before, and in another prayer directly after the Elevation, as indicating the five sacred wounds,[1] which were particularly prominent on the Body of Christ, and which, consequently, are also in the most intimate relation with the redeeming passion and death of the Lord. Precisely at the moment in which the altar, by the presence of the Divine Victim, becomes a mystical Mount Calvary, the sublime and sacred scene of the passion of the Saviour, crucified and covered with painful wounds, should present itself before the eyes and mind of priest and people in the most striking manner. "Christ, pierced on the Cross, wounded in five different places, come, let us adore!" — thus cries out the Church to her children. The hands and feet of the Lord have men bored through, and His Heart they have pierced. Those hands that were overflowing with benedictions and mercies; those feet that had become weary walking in search of the lost sheep on the thorny field of the earth; that Heart which glowed with love for God and men, — behold, how they are lacerated and wounded with cruel irons! Those bloody signs of martyrdom, those deep, gaping wounds on the sacrificed Body of Jesus are an inexhaustible fountain of propitiation and mercy and grace for regenerated man.

6o. The Consecration.

Engaged in devout meditation and contemplation have we already wandered through the vestibule or sanctuary of the mystically constructed Mass liturgy, — we have next entered into the Holy of Holies, in the very centre of which we now find ourselves. Breathless silence prevails all around[2]; the Consecration, to which all that preceded served as a preparation, is approaching. The moment of Consecration[3] is the moment the most important and solemn, the

---

hanc ineffabilem conversionem panis in corpus et vini in sanguinem Christi facit (Dion. Carthus. Expos. Missae art. 23).

[1] Nonnulli quinque signa referunt ad quinque Christi vulnera (Robert. Paulul. 1. c.).

[2] Only grave and soft playing on the organ is permitted. Ad elevationem ss. Sacramenti pulsatur organum *graviori* et *dulciori* sono (Cer. episc. 1. 1, c. 28, n. 9).

[3] Acutius intuere, o homo, qui sacerdotio fungeris: qua utique reverentia et devotione, qua humilitate ac dilectione te Dominum tuum in ipsa sacra hostia suscipere et amplecti, tractare contemplarique oporteat. Ipse equidem est, ante cujus te tribunal mox necesse est adstare, qui judicaturus est vivos et mortuos et saeculum per ignem. In manu illius universa tua salus sita est, eum Cherubim Seraphimque adorant, Throni ei sedes sunt. Sed jam, o metuende Dei Fili, o adorande Christe, o virtus et sapientia Patris, fac me in te sapientem et fortem, stabiliterque conversum: praesertim autem tunc me, o beate Salvator, tunc cor meum munias mentemque in te afficias, erigas atque convertas, *dum ipsa tua divina sa-*

most sublime and touching, the most holy and fruitful of the whole sacrificial celebration; for it includes that glorious and unfathomably profound work, namely, the accomplishment of the Eucharistic Sacrifice, in which all the marvels of God's love are concentrated as in a focus of heat and light. The change of the bread and wine into Christ's Body and Blood can proceed from Him only who "alone effects what is wonderful": it is an act of creative omnipotence. But to this act of divine almighty power there is required a human act, human co-operation — and that on the part of an ordained priest. At his ordination the priest received the supernatural power so to pronounce the words: "This is My Body" — "This is My Blood," wherewith the Lord in the guest-chamber at Jerusalem accomplished the first Eucharistic Consecration,[1] that they are effective, that is, that they change the prepared elements of bread and wine into the Body and Blood of Christ.[2] At the Last Supper Christ was the sole priest offering sacrifice; at the altar He is the principal sacrificer. Whilst in the Cenaculum He offered Himself without the assistance of others, He now offers Himself on the altar by the hands and mouth of the visible priest. The priest is His organ and minister. "The priest acts as the representative of Christ when he pronounces those words; but it is the power and grace of God. — 'This is My Body,' he says. These words transform the gifts placed before him."[3] This truth clearly manifests the way and manner in which the priest performs the act of Consecration; all he does indicates plainly that he takes the place of Christ, speaks and acts in

---

cerrimaque mysteria celebro, sacramenta contingo ac dilectionis tuae pignus passionisque memoriale accipio: tunc, o omnipotens Dominator, prae majestatis tuae contemplatione reverentiali timore concutiar, caritatis tuae contuitu inexstinguibiliter accendar totusque in te resolvar et configar: tunc te, Deus meus, splendida fide contempler, tunc te sapiam affectuosissimeque complectar; anima mea tua ex praesentia excitetur ac liquefiat. Utinam te, Deus meus, amator auctorque salutis meae, qui te mihi tam multipliciter praestitisti: qui ex ipso tuae benignissimae mentis ardore sic nobis ubilibet conjungi dignaris, anima mea semper coram se et item se coram te constituat; utinam tibi grata, utinam in te sic custodita consistat, ut ad tui participationem celebrationemque tuorum mysteriorum magis incessanter idonea, purior ardentiorque reddatur (Dion. Carthus. De munificentia et beneficiis Dei art. 25).

[1] When we impartially read the Biblical accounts regarding the first Celebration and the Institution of the Eucharist, we cannot but marvel that already formerly, and again quite recently, it could be asserted that our Divine Saviour had at that time not changed the bread and wine by the words of the Institution (this is My Body — this is My Blood), but that He had by the preceding benediction (benedixit), or merely by an interior act of the will, changed them into His Body and Blood. The only well-grounded and tenable thesis in the Bible and in tradition is, that the Lord performed the first Eucharistic Consecration ritu sacramentali by the words of the Institution, and thus by His example left the norm for all succeeding Consecrations.

[2] Sacerdotes apostolico gradui succedentes, *Christi corpus sacro ore conficiunt* (S. Hieron. Epist. ad Heliodor. n. 8).

[3] S. Chrysost. De prodit. Judae hom. 1, n. 6.

the person of Christ in accomplishing the Eucharistic Sacrifice. That this may be manifest, he is directed by the Church to imitate as faithfully as possible by word and deed Christ's model act of Consecration — as though dramatically representing it. The Church's liturgical act of Consecration is nothing else than the repetition and copy of the first celebration of the Lord's Supper in the Cenaculum at Jerusalem. The priest narrates the first offering and institution of the unbloody Sacrifice by Jesus Christ, and while relating this, he performs the corresponding actions, that is, he imitates, as far as possible, the Lord and does the same as Christ did. He pronounces the effective words of Consecration in the person of Christ (*quasi ex persona ipsius Christi loquentis — S. Thom.*)[1] over the bread and wine with the intention of changing the gifts at present lying on the altar and thereby to offer up in sacrifice the Body and Blood of Christ.[2] Plain and simple are the words of the liturgical text, as is best suited for a thing that is both ineffably sublime and divine.

1. The Consecration of the Host.

Qui pridie quam pateretur accepit panem in sanctas ac venerabiles manus suas, et elevatis oculis in coelum ad te Deum Patrem suum omnipotentem, tibi gratias agens, bene†dixit, fregit, deditque discipulis suis, dicens: Accipite, et manducate ex hoc omnes:	Who, the day before He suffered, took bread into His holy and venerable hands, and with eyes lifted up toward heaven, unto Thee, O God, His Almighty Father, giving thanks to Thee, did bless,† break and give unto His disciples, saying: Take, and eat ye all of this:
Hoc est enim Corpus meum.	**For this is My Body.**

Three Evangelists (Matt. 26, 26—28; Mark 14, 22—24; Luke 22, 19—20) and the Apostle of the Gentiles, Paul (1 Cor. 11, 23—

---

[1] Verba consecrationis *dicuntur* et *recitative* et *formaliter* seu *significative*. Sacerdos enim et commemorat, quae verba Christus in ultima coena dixerit et, intendens ea applicare materiae praesenti, ac facere, quod significant, simul exercet actum suae potestatis. Atque hinc est, quod *propriissime* dicatur conficere *in persona Christi*, quia non tantum utitur potestate a Christo accepta, sed eam exercet *ejus personam repraesentans*, et *loquens ejus verbis, quasi esset ipsemet Christus* (Sylvius III, q. 78, art. 1, quaer. 3).

[2] Hoc sacramentum directe repraesentativum est dominicae passionis, qua Christus ut sacerdos et hostia Deo se obtulit in ara crucis. Hostia autem quam sacerdos offert, est una cum illa quam Christus obtulit secundum rem, quia Christum realiter continet; minister autem offerens non est idem realiter, unde oportet, quod sit idem repraesentatione, et ideo sacerdos consecrans prout gerit personam Christi, profert verba consecrationis recitative ex persona Christi, ne hostia alia videatur. Et quia per ea quae gerit respectu exterioris materiae, Christi personam repraesentat, ideo verba illa simul et recitative et significative tenentur respectu praesentis materiae, quae est figura illius, quam Christus praesentem habuit, et propter hoc dicitur convenientius: "hoc est *corpus meum*," quam: "hoc est *corpus Christi*" (S. Thom. IV, dist. 8, q. 2, a. 1, sol. 4 ad 4).

26), have informed us of the act of Consecration. These four holy authors, though not in perfect accord as to the very words, yet agree perfectly as to the matter itself: all relate what the Saviour did at that solemn moment, and what priests were to do in His name and in commemoration of Him unto the end of the world. Not one of them has omitted anything essentially necessary for the accomplishment of the Consecration and of the Sacrifice; but with regard to accessories, the statements of the Evangelists are not equally complete. Let us compare the liturgical formula — at the Consecration of the Host and of the chalice — with the biblical text, and we shall find that the Canon contains several words, namely, (*in sanctas ac venerabiles manus suas, et elevatis oculis in coelum ad te Deum Patrem suum omnipotentem — aeterni testamenti — mysterium fidei*), that are wanting in Holy Scripture. These additions of the liturgy have emanated from a divine and apostolic tradition and are, therefore, as incontestably true and certain as are the words of the inspired authors.[1]

Qui pridie quam pateretur.[2] How touching and solemnly impressive is that scene which these words call up to mind! The Lord chose the eve of His bitter passion and death, — the night on which He was betrayed (1 Cor. 11, 23), to give us by the institution of the Eucharist the most wonderful proof of His love.[3] With desire He had longed for this hour. Before shedding His blood in torrents on the painful way of the Cross, He would pour out for us ungrateful creatures the abundance of His grace, all the treasures of His love in the Sacrament of the Altar, that we might never forget what He has done and suffered for us.[4]

---

[1] Quod additur *"aeterni"* et iterum *"mysterium fidei"*, **ex** *traditione Domini* habetur (S. Thom. 3, q. 78, a. 3 ad 9).

[2] On Holy Thursday the insertion is here made: Qui pridie, quam *pro nostra omniumque salute pateretur, hoc est, hodie.*

[3] Venit Jesus ministrare Apostolis et praecipue hodie dilexit. Sciens enim quia transiret de mundo ad Patrem et quod ituri essent post eum ... recedens ab eis et iter sequendi (sc. humilitatem in ablutione pedum) ostendit eis et cibum quo vescerentur in itinere, reliquit, i. e. *viam* dedit et *viaticum*. Sub forma enim panis et vini corpus suum et sanguinem ad edendum dedit et conficiendum reliquit. ... Christus in cruce fuit *pretium*, in deserto est *viaticum*, in coelo erit *praemium*. Hic est cibus grandium, qui munit contra adversa et confert bona, servat collata (Hildeb. Turon. Sermo 39).

[4] Christo non suffecit *semel* pro nobis immolari in cruce per mortis perpessionem, sed hanc *quotidianam et perennem sui immolationem* in mysterio (sc. in Missae officio) ejus infinita sapientia adinvenit, ejus immensa clementia ordinavit, ejus caritas summa praefixit, qua et Dei Patris honorem generisque humani procuravit opem, gratiam ac salutem, quod totum sic fieri decentissimum exstitisse ratio dictat desuper illustrata: quae quanto plus illustratur, tanto limpidius intuetur, quam rationabile seu potius superrationabile, misericordissimum, sapientissimum, amorosissimum fuerit istud, ut et quotidie dominicae passionis quasi recenter memores simus, caritatisque Dei ac pietatis suae et liberalitatis ad nos assidue recordemur recordandoque inflammemur et meritum Christi abundantius participemus, consequendo effectus sacramenti istius (Dion. Carthus. De sacram. altar. serm. 2).

Accepit panem in sanctas ac venerabiles manus suas — "Jesus took bread into His holy and venerable hands": saying these words, the priest also takes the Host into his hands. Holy and sanctifying, venerable and adorable beyond all expression are the hands of Christ. How often has He raised them in prayer to His Father, and extended them over men to bless them! How these hands were transpierced on the Cross with the most intolerable heat of pain! How are thy hands constituted, O priest of the Lord? They are indeed holy and venerable by the consecration thou hast received; but are they also holy and venerable by the abundance of virtuous actions, by the odor of a devout life, and by exemplary conduct? With holy oil[1] were thy hands anointed and consecrated to the service of God and the salvation of souls; day and night shouldst thou elevate them to Heaven, to praise the Lord, to call down upon men His mercies and blessings. Are thy hands innocent, clean and pure? Are they worthy to touch, to offer and to distribute to others the immaculate Lamb of God?

Et elevatis oculis in coelum ad te Deum Patrem suum omni-potentem, tibi gratias agens bene†dixit — "and with His eyes lifted up toward heaven, unto Thee, O God, His Almighty Father, giving thanks to Thee, did bless the bread." While the priest pronounces these words, he performs the corresponding ceremonies, so as to imitate and do, as far as possible, what the Saviour did at the institution of the Eucharist: for a moment the priest looks up at the Crucifix on the altar, and then bows His head, thereby to signify and to express Christ's thanksgiving, and he makes over the Host the sign of the Cross, thus appropriately to represent the blessing of the Saviour, since we do not know after what manner it was imparted.[2]

Christ's looking up to His Almighty Father, as also the giving of thanks and the blessing of the bread connected therewith, indicates not only the greatness and sublimity of the mystery which He was about to accomplish, but served at the same time as a preparation for the Consecration, and as the making ready of the matter to be consecrated. Not Holy Scripture, but tradition informs us, that the Saviour in this instance "looked up to heaven": who could doubt it? Did He not do the same in the desert, when He so marvellously multiplied a few loaves, that thousands were thereby filled: should He not also now at this banquet of love, in which that multiplication of bread in the desert found its higher fulfilment, in which He first

---

[1] Unctio sancta in manibus sacerdotum infunditur, ut S. Spiritus, qui per oleum designatur, in operibus consecrationis eorum descendat (Hildeb. Turon. Serm. 132). — Manus sacratae et sacrantes tremenda mysteria (S. Bern. Tract. de mor. et offic. episcop. c. 2, n. 4).

[2] When it is said of the Saviour, that He blessed the little ones or the bread and the chalice, it is permitted us to represent to ourselves that the Lord Himself preceded His Church in the formation of the Sign of the Cross for liturgical purposes (Oswald, Eschatologie [4. Aufl.] S. 238).

offered to God this wonderful bread of His Body and then distributed it to His disciples, — should He not also at this solemn hour have raised His eyes "to His Almighty Father," who can do all things, and who always hears Him? — Thanksgiving and blessing[1] are here to be distinguished from the Consecration, as well as from each other, even though they may have been performed by Christ with the same prayer. For thanksgiving refers to God, the Author of all good; but the blessing, to the gifts to be changed. This thanksgiving and this blessing were not the customary ones at the Paschal Supper, but were far more significant. "Christ did indeed adhere to the Old Testament Paschal rite, as to the selection of time for the institution and the matter of the Eucharist, as also to its breaking and distribution, and as to the thanksgiving and blessing, but He gave to this thanksgiving a more sublime meaning and to the blessing a more exalted end, inasmuch as He thanked His Heavenly Father for the benefits bestowed on His holy humanity and on the entire human race in general, as well as in particular for the great grace of the Most Holy Sacrament, decreed and prepared from eternity and now about to be instituted by Him, — and inasmuch as by blessing bread and wine, He prepared both for the sacramental Consecration at hand, and that, indeed, in this wise, that as Man and Highpriest He prayed for this wonderful Consecration, which He as God, together with the Father and the Holy Ghost, was about to perform."[2]

Fregit deditque discipulis suis, dicens: Accipite et manducate ex hoc omnes — "Brake and gave to His disciples, saying: Take and eat ye all of this." The Church in the celebration of the Sacrifice follows her divine Lord and Master step by step: the breaking of the sacramental species (*fregit*) and the distribution of the Eucharistic bread (*dedit*) can not take place until after the Consecration, while the majestic thanksgiving prayer of the Preface (*gratias agens*), and the manifold blessing of the sacrificial matter (*benedixit*) have already an appropriate place before the Consecration. — The priest, in the midst of a solemn silence that shuts out from him all the noise of the world, humbly bowing down at the altar, pronounces "in the person of Christ," with the deepest attention, devotion and reverence the mighty words[3]:

---

[1] Haec benedictio fuit bona super panem precatio, et divinae beneficentiae super illum invocatio, qua Christus *elevatis oculis in coelum* petebat ejus sanctificationem et transmutationem mox futuram; unde, quamvis Evangelistae nunc benedictionem, nunc gratiarum actionem nominent, quia Christus eas conjunxit, diversae tamen sunt, et inter se et a consecratione. Benedictio enim ad symbola refertur, gratiarum actio autem ad Deum (Sylvius III, q. 78, art. 1, quaer. 2).

[2] Franz, Die Eucharistische Wandlung I, 37.

[3] Haec verba cum summa attentione, reverentia et veneratione integre distincteque sunt proferenda, quoniam illa sacerdos quasi ore Christi (ut ita dixerim) eloquitur et illa loquens Christi fungitur officio. Quocirca in illis recte et decenter enuntiandis summa adhibenda est cura et animadversio (Clichtov. 1. 3, n. 29). —

Hoc est enim Corpus meum.
For this is My Body.

It is with a holy amazement and a reverential awe at the power given him, that the priest pronounces these divine words, which bear along with them the power of changing the substance of the bread. And now there is no longer bread on the altar, but under the appearances that remain of bread, Christ's Body is truly present. In a moment the power of God has wrought a series of miracles, more magnificent and glorious than all the wonders of creation. The tiny Host now contains in itself infinitely more treasures, riches and glory than are to be found on the vast expanse of the globe.[1] By virtue of the words of Consecration, Christ's Body becomes present, veiled under the appearance of bread, and, indeed, His glorified Body, which shines in the glory of heaven; but this Body is immortal, impassible, with the Precious Blood flowing through it, vivified by the most holy soul, united to the Eternal Godhead — therefore, in the Host Christ is present, whole and entire, the hidden Saviour, with His divinity and humanity. The same God-Man who lives and reigns in heaven in inconceivable majesty and beauty, is now mysteriously and under foreign, sacramental appearances present near us also, in our very midst. The gates of heaven open and in the com-

---

The *enim* (= for, namely), elucidating and consolidating the preceding invitation (accipite et manducate), is found only in St. Matthew in the formula of the Consecration of the chalice, but it was appropriately placed also in the formula of the Consecration of the bread. — Ipse summus ac generalis vicarius Christi, beatissimus Petrus, ex familiari et secreto Spiritus sancti instinctu addidit verbum *"enim"* et hoc ex rationabili causa ad designandam continuationem et ordinem ad praecedentia verba et gesta (Dion. Carthus. De sacram. altar. art. 32).

[1] Credere firmiter debes et nullatenus dubitare, secundum quod docet et praedicat catholica fides, quod in hora expressionis verborum Christi panis materialis atque visibilis advenienti vivifico et coelesti pani, velut vero Creatori honorem deferens, locum suum, scil. visibilem speciem accidentium, pro ministerio et sacramentali servitio relinquit, quo desinente esse, miro et ineffabili modo in eodem instanti ista sub illis accidentibus veraciter exsistunt: *primo,* illa purissima Christi caro et sacrum corpus, quod fabricante Spiritu Sancto, tractum fuit de utero gloriosae Virginis Mariae, appensum in cruce, positum in sepulcro, glorificatum in coelo. — *Secundo,* quia caro non vivit sine sanguine, ideo necessario est ibi sanguis ille pretiosus, qui feliciter manavit pro mundi salute in cruce. — *Tertio,* cum non sit verus homo absque anima rationali, propterea est ibi illa anima gloriosa Christi, excedens in gratia et gloria omnem virtutem et gloriam et potestatem, in qua repositi sunt omnes thesauri divinae sapientiae (Col. 2, 3). — *Quarto,* quia Christus est verus homo et verus Deus, ibi consequenter est Deus in sua majestate gloriosus. — Haec omnia quattuor simul et singula, tota simul sub speciebus panis et vini perfecte continentur, non minus in calice quam in hostia nec minus in hostia quam in calice, nec in uno suppletur defectus alterius, sed in ambobus invenitur integrum propter mysterium, de quo est grandis sermo (Hebr. 5, 11). Sufficit credere, Deum verum et hominem sub utraque contineri specie, cui assistunt Angelorum frequentia et Sanctorum praesentia (S. Bonav. tr. de praepar. ad Miss. c. 1, § 3, n. 1).

pany of invisible choirs of angels the King of Heaven descends upon the altar, and the earth becomes a paradise; — the priest holds his Creator, Redeemer and Judge in his hands: what then is more natural than that we should fall down on our knees before Him in holy fear and rapturous joy?[1]

The bread has been changed into the sacrificial Body of Christ; the wine has now still to become the sacrificial Blood of Christ.

2. The Consecration of the Chalice.

Simili modo postquam coenatum est, accipiens et hunc praeclarum Calicem in sanctas ac venerabiles manus suas: item tibi gratias agens bene†dixit, deditque discipulis suis dicens: Accipite et bibite ex eo omnes:

Hic est enim Calix Sanguinis Mei, novi et aeterni testamenti: mysterium fidei: qui pro vobis et pro multis effundetur in remissionem peccatorum.

Haec quotiescumque feceritis, in mei memoriam facietis.

In like manner, after supper, taking also this excellent chalice into His holy and venerable hands: and giving thanks to Thee, He blessed,† and gave to His disciples, saying: Take, and drink ye all of it:

For this is the Chalice of My Blood, of the new and eternal testament: the mystery of faith: which shall be shed for you, and for many, unto the remission of sins.

As often as you do these things, ye shall do them in remembrance of Me.

Simili modo postquam coenatum est, accipiens et hunc praeclarum Calicem in . . . manus suas — "In like manner, after supper, taking also this excellent chalice into His . . . hands." At these words the priest takes up the chalice in his hands and slightly elevates it. After the Old Testament Pachal Supper was over, the

---

[1] Quando sacerdos sacram Hostiam manu tenens genua flectit, Dominum hunc adorare debet adeo profunda reverentia, ut cor suum usque ad ipsam abyssum humiliet, quasi desiderans in terrae profundum descendere ob tantae majestatis reverentiam. Et memor, quod Angeli descendant e coelo, et huic Domino in sacrificio adsint, cogitare debet, in eo momento se circumdari Angelorum exercitu, et simul cum illis adorare et laudare communem omnium Dominum et Creatorem. — Et quando ipsam Hostiam sacram sursum elevat, id faciet, nunc cum sensu doloris et lacrymis, memor, Dominum eundem propter ipsius peccata fuisse in cruce elevatum et ab omnibus contemptum; nunc idem faciet affectu quodam gaudii et gratitudinis, quod ipsam Hostiam elevet, ut honos ipsi Domino deferatur, et ab omnibus adoretur, quasi in compensationem praeteritorum contemptuum. Alias potest etiam in memoriam revocare, quod idem Dominus dixit: "Ego si exaltatus fuero a terra, omnia traham ad meipsum" (Joan. 12, 32), et eundem Dominum orabit, ut dignetur ipsius cor ad coelum elevare, ubi ipse ad dextram Patris sedet. (De Ponte, De christ. hom. perfect. IV, tr. 2, c. 12, § 3).

Lord consecrated the bread, and immediately afterward followed the Consecration of the chalice. *Post agnum typicum, expletis epulis —* after they had eaten the symbolical paschal lamb, the Lord prepared for His disciples an exceedingly wonderful and altogether unexampled repast, a new and divine sacrificial repast.[1]

The Saviour took "this excellent chalice" (*hunc praeclarum Calicem*),[2] that is, evidently not the very chalice of the celebrant, but a chalice of like contents and of similar destination as the chalice which is before the eyes of the priest and which he holds in his hands. The identity existing between the chalice used at the Last Supper and the chalice on the altar, therefore, principally refers to the sacrificial matter therein contained, which is and must be everywhere specifically, that is, essentially the same. This identity is perfect, that is, numerically so, only after the Consecration; then there is here as there altogether the same Blood in both chalices: "This is the chalice of My Blood" (*hic est calix sanguinis mei*), said the Redeemer in the supper-room, and says the priest at the altar. The Lord, therefore, took "this" (*hunc*), that is, the Eucharistic chalice, which according to the expression of the Psalmist is called grand, glorious, magnificent,[3] — and that with the fullest right. Is it not the chalice that will soon be filled with the Precious Blood of Christ, with wine from the branches of the true vine that was pressed in the wine-press of Golgotha ? — The Saviour blessed the chalice likewise with thanksgiving, as He had previously done with the bread. He then pronounced over the blessed wine those holy words which the

---

[1] Ille quippe agnus (paschalis, Exod. 12) figura erat alterius agni spiritualis et ovis ovem praenotabat. Atque illud quidem umbra, hoc veritas erat. Cum apparuisset sol justitiae, umbra cessavit: oriente quippe sole solvitur umbra. Ideo in eadem ipsa mensa utrumque pascha perficitur et typi et veritatis. Quemadmodum enim pictores in eadem ipsa tabula et lineas circumducunt et umbram depingunt tuncque colorum veritatem apponunt, sic et Christus fecit: in eadem ipsa mensa typicum pascha descripsit et verum addidit... Erat olim pascha judaicum, sed nunc solutum est advenitque spirituale pascha, quod nunc tradidit Christus (S. Chrysost. Hom. 1 de prodit. Jud. n. 4).

[2] *Hunc* autem calicem dicens sacerdos, qui celebrat, non eum demonstrat calicem secundum numerum, quem manibus tenet, ... sed ad intellectum demonstrat similem secundum speciem, non quidem secundum speciem substantiae aut figurae, ... sed *similem quantum ad usum et liquoris continentiam.* Sicut enim in hoc calice, quo sacerdos consecrationem vini perficit, continetur vinum aqua mixtum, ita et in eo calice, quem Christus accepit, continebatur vinum aquae permixtum, ut uno animo sentiunt omnes. Quare nomine calicis non intellegendum est hic solum vas potorium, sed *id ipsum cum vino contento in eo* (Clichtov. Elucid. eccl. 1. 3, n. 30). — *Idem* calix est in mysterio, quem Christus in manibus tenuit, quamvis in materia metalli alius sit (Honor. Augustod. Gemm. anim. 1. 1, c. 106).

[3] Cfr. Ps. 22, 5. *Calix meus inebrians* — i. e. sanguis Christi contentus in calice benedictionis mentem divino amore inflammans et velut ebrians, quoniam facit eam inferiorum immemorem ac divinorum sitibundam — *quam praeclarus est* — h. e. multum clarus, sanctus et nobilis est, imo plus quam dici possit vel credi (Dion. Carthus.).

priest now in His stead pronounces over the chalice, to change the material element into the divine Blood of Christ: *Hic est enim Calix Sanguinis mei* — "For this is the chalice of My Blood," that is, this is My Blood which is contained in the chalice. The expression "chalice of blood" should indicate that Christ's Blood becomes present on the altar, inasmuch as it was shed in His painful passion and is now the heavenly drink of the soul. — According to the common opinion these words alone constitute the essential formula for the Consecration of the chalice; for they signify and effect the presence of the Blood of Christ under the appearances of wine.[1] The remaining words: "the Blood of the new and eternal testament — the mystery of faith —, which (Blood) shall be shed for you and for many unto the remission of sins," are appropriately added. It is generally accepted that they were once spoken by the Lord Himself; they, moreover, manifest and explain the dignity and effects of this Sacrifice.[2]

In the chalice is the Blood of the "new and eternal testament." At the foot of Sinai the old covenant, whose promises were only earthly, and which was to continue but for a time, was concluded with the blood of animals. But by Christ's sacrificial Blood which is in the chalice, the "new" covenant of grace was established and sealed and is called under a twofold aspect "the eternal" covenant: first, because the gifts and blessings appertaining to it are heavenly and imperishable; again, because the new covenant will ever remain in force and its validity endure to the end of days, to the consummation of the world's history. The Eucharistic Blood of the Lord is at the same time the most noble portion and the most precious treasure of this "new and eternal covenant of grace." — The concluding

---

[1] Haec forma: *"Hic est calix sanguinis mei,"* est forma *certa,* forma *congrua;* sed utrum sit *tota,* an quod sequitur sit de integritate (essential), dubium est; creditur tamen, quod est *tota.* Tamen quod sequitur non est frustra additum, nec debet aliquid resecari. — Quod autem ista sit forma *certa,* patet per hoc, quod ipsam tenet Romana Ecclesia, quae fuit ab Apostolorum principibus edocta... Est etiam *congrua,* quia in hoc sacramento significatur sanguis Christi ut *effusus* in pretium et ut *administratus* in potum; sanguis autem neutrum dicit de se expresse, sed per conjunctionem cum *calice,* quia sanguis in calice ut *effusus* et *potandus* proponitur. Ideo *calix* in Scriptura significat aliquando *passionem* (Matth. 20, 22); significat et *potus refectionem* (Ps. 22, 5). Propter hunc duplicem tropum melius dicitur *calix sanguinis* quam *sanguis* per se... Est etiam *tota* et perfecta; sufficiens enim est ad significandum transsubstantiationem vini in sanguinem Christi. Unde quod additur est de *bene esse,* quia in sequentibus describuntur *effectus* sanguinis in hoc sacramento significati et in passione effusi (S. Bonav. IV, dist. 8, p. 2, a. 1, q. 2).

[2] Dicendum est, *omnia illa verba* esse prolata a Christo. Haec est communis sententia et mihi certa (Suarez disp. 60, sect. 3, n. 2). Licet haec verba non spectent ad essentiam formae, tamen pertinent ad ejus integritatem, estque hic sensus communis totius Ecclesiae Latinae, quae in Missa et forma consecrationis calicis ea quasi a Christo dicta et ab Apostolis praecepta, eodem tenore ac modo quo cetera, scribit et pronuntiat (Cornel. a Lap. in Matth. 26, 28).

words: "which shall be shed for you and for many unto the remission of sins,"[1] characterize the sacrificial Blood of Christ as the very source of atonement, pouring forth its floods of grace for the cleansing and remission of sin for all mankind. The exclamatory phrase in the middle: *mysterium fidei* — "the mystery of faith," indicates the unsearchable depth and obscurity of the Eucharistic Sacrifice. That the God-Man did shed His Blood for us on the Cross, and that He again sheds it for us in a mystical manner on the altar — is an adorable divine achievement which includes in itself the sum of the most unheard-of wonders, all of which can be acknowledged and believed as true only in the light and the power of faith. Christ's sacrificial Blood in the chalice is a mystery of faith in the fullest sense of the term.[2]

After the priest has pronounced the words of Consecration, he again genuflects, to venerate the infinitely precious and adorable Blood of Christ in the chalice. At the same time[3] he pronounces the words: "As often as ye do these things, ye shall do them in remembrance of Me," with which the Saviour instituted the Christian priesthood and the perpetual Sacrifice of the New Law as a commemorative celebration of His redeeming passion and death.[4]

By the separate Consecration of the Host and of the chalice, Christ's Body and Blood are rendered present under the twofold appearances of bread and wine, that is, as sacrificed. The twofold Consecration is a mystical shedding of blood, and places before our eyes in a most lively manner the bloody death of Christ sacrificed on

---

[1] Qui *pro vobis*, sumentibus scilicet, et *pro multis* = aliis. Illi *multi* vel intelleguntur *omnes electi* vel *omnes omnino;* nam pro omnibus *sufficienter* effusus est sanguis Christi, pro electis vero etiam *efficaciter* (Sylvius III, q. 78, art. 3).

[2] Per prima verba cum dicitur: "Hic est calix sanguinis mei," significatur ipsa conversio vini in sanguinem; per verba autem sequentia designatur virtus sanguinis effusi in passione, quae operatur in hoc sacramento, quae quidem ad tria ordinatur: Primo quidem et principaliter ad adipiscendam aeternam hereditatem (Hebr. 10, 19), et ad hoc designandum dicitur: "novi et aeterni testamenti." — Secundo ad justitiam gratiae quae est per fidem (Rom. 3, 23), et quantum ad hoc subditur: "mysterium fidei". — Tertio autem ad removendum impedimenta utriusque praedictorum, sc. peccatum (Hebr. 9, 14), et quantum ad hoc subditur: "qui pro vobis et pro multis effundetur in remissionem peccatorum" (S. Thom. 3, q. 78, a. 3).

[3] In the Middle Age frequently they were said only *post* elevationem calicis. *Deponendo calicem* dicat haec verba: Haec quotiescumque etc. (Ordo Rom. XIV, c. 53).

[4] Verba praetacta, videlicet *"Haec quotiescumque . . .",* ut ait Bernardus, omni affectu plenissima sunt, et fidelem ac vere christianum animum vehementer inflammant, suntque a sacerdote celebrante cum ingenti devotione ac mentis sapore promenda, et proh dolor! miserabilem sacerdotem, qui haec verba sine memoria ineffabilis atque eximiae dilectionis atque acerbissimae mortis Christi pronuntiat atque sine cordiali affectu effundit: imo veraciter haec verba non solum tempore celebrationis, sed frequentissime nobis sunt cogitanda, revolvenda et amplectenda. His quippe verbis jubemur a Christo, non sine actuali devotione celebrare, sed cum diligenti divinorum beneficiorum recordatione (Dion. Carth. Expos. Missae art. 29).

the Cross.[1] The Sacrifice on the altar is, indeed, painless; for the Saviour is no longer passible and can no longer suffer death. But His divinely human Heart is here inflamed with the same love of sacrifice, and is moved by the same obedience of His Father to sacrifice Himself as when He was on the Cross. This love and this obedience urged Him to sacrifice Himself mystically on the altar also under the twofold sacramental appearances. It is at the moment of Consecration that the Sacrifice is accomplished, is offered to God and placed in the hands of us, poor mortals. This entire act of Consecration is performed so quietly and so mysteriously, that no one perceives anything of the wonderful transformation wrought by the priest's words in the Host and in the chalice. Some words softly pronounced by the mouth of the priest — and the essence of the bread and wine has disappeared : their place is taken by Christ's Body and Blood, the whole Christ, the Victim of Golgotha. For the senses alone nothing has happened, nothing is changed; for the appearances of bread and wine, upheld by the power of God, have remained to serve as veil and covering for the bright majesty of the King of Glory, who with us and for us is present as Victim on the altar.[2] To fathom the height and the depth of the Eucharistic Consecration, is beyond even the wisdom of the cherubim; worthily to praise the miracles of mercy contained in this same Eucharistic Consecration, even the love of the seraphim of heaven is wholly insufficient. Truly, no moment commands greater reverence, no moment is more holy or more beneficial than that in which the Eucharistic Sacrifice is accomplished and the altar becomes a mystical Mount Calvary!

"When thou beholdest the Lord lying as a Victim on the altar, and how the priest stands and prays in the presence of the Divine Victim, dost thou then believe thyself still on earth among men? Or rather art thou not at once ravished to heaven, and dost thou not banish from thy mind all worldly thoughts, and behold in all candor of soul and purity of mind these wonders of heaven? O sublime spectacle! O the goodness of the divine benevolence! Wouldst thou comprehend somewhat the sublimity of this holy action by the aid of another miracle? Represent to thyself the Prophet Elias and the immense multitude around him, and the sacrifice lying on the stones, and all in deep silence, whilst the Prophet alone prays, and, on a

---

[1] Sanguis seorsum consecratus a corpore expressius repraesentat passionem Christi, et ideo potius in consecratione sanguinis fit mentio de passione Christi et fructu ipsius, quam in consecratione corporis (S. Thom. 1. c. ad 7).

[2] There He is, indeed; He is present; the word has had its effect; there Jesus is as truly present as He was when on the Cross, where He appeared for us by the sacrifice of Himself (Hebr. 9, 26); as truly present as He is in heaven, where He again appears for us before the face of God (Hebr. 9, 24). This consecration, this holy ceremony, this worship full of blood, and yet unbloody, where death is everywhere, and where, nevertheless, the Victim is alive, is the true worship of Christians; falling under the senses and spiritual, simple and august, humble and magnificent at the same time (Bossuet, Médit. sur l'Évang. I. P., 63e jour).

sudden, fire from heaven falling upon the sacrifice. How wonderful and astounding! Now turn from this to the present sacrificial celebration, and thou wilt behold not only what is wonderful, but what exceeds all bounds of wonderment. For here stands the priest, not calling down fire, but the Holy Ghost from heaven; and he prays with the more fervor, not that a heavenly flame may dart down and consume what lies upon the altar, but that grace may descend on the Sacrifice and through the latter may inflame the hearts of all and make them more brilliant than silver purified in the fire.[1] What an awe-inspiring celebration this is! And who will depreciate it without being insane or beside himself?"[2]

3. The Eucharistic Consecration, especially in the touching and more or less solemn rite of the elevation and adoration of the most holy Body and Blood of Jesus Christ, appears as the sublime and prominent centre and pinnacle of the organism of the Mass.[3] —

---

[1] Angelo Mai published a beautiful Missa picta Graecorum from the Greek Codex of the Vatican Library. The seventh picture contains a representation of the moment of Consecration. The consecrating priest is entirely enveloped in fire and flames: at one side of him stands a deacon with a book and on the other a venerable old man with a staff — the spectator of this mysterious vision. Above the priest appears the Consecrated Host, that is, Christ in the form of a child, with uplifted hands, encompassed with fire, surrounded by Cherubim and Seraphim, as well as other adoring angels. (Cfr. Nova PP. biblioth. tom. VI, p. 2, imag. 7, p. 590). — Saint Hildegarde, that great seer of the twelfth century, writes (Scivias II, 6): "I saw also, when the priest, robed in the sacred vestments, advanced to the altar to celebrate the Divine Mysteries, that suddenly a great radiance and a retinue of angels came down from heaven, encircling the entire altar, and remaining there until the mystery was accomplished, and the priest had retired from the altar. But when the Gospel of peace had been read, and the Sacrificial Gifts, which were to be consecrated, had been placed on the altar, and the priest sang the praise of Almighty God, which is as follows: 'Holy, holy, holy is the Lord, God of Sabaoth,' and thus began the unspeakable mysteries: then descended suddenly a fiery lightning of indescribable brilliancy from the open heavens down upon the Sacrificial Gift, flooding it entirely with its brightness, as the light of the sun lights up everything, which it penetrates with its rays (repente *ignea coruscatio* inaestimabilis claritatis aperto coelo super eandem oblationem descendit et eam totam sua claritate ita perfundit, ut solaris lux rem illam illustrat, quam radiis suis transfigit). And while the fiery lightning illumined in this manner the oblations, it carried them in an invisible way upward into the privacy of heaven, and brought them down again upon the altar; as a man draws his breath inwardly and then exhales it outwardly, — thus did that Sacrificial Gift, after it had become the true Body and the true Blood of Christ, although to the eyes of men they appeared as bread and wine. And as I saw that, there appeared at the same time the signs of the birth, the passion and burial, as well as the Resurrection and Ascension of our Saviour, the Incarnate God, as in a mirror, as they took place in the Son of God when upon earth," that is, Christ becomes present on the earthly altar as Highpriest, together with the whole work of redemption. (Cfr. Schmelzeis, Das Leben und Wirken der hl. Hildegardis S. 371 etc.)

[2] St. Chrysostom, On the Priesthood, III. volume, chap. 4.

[3] The adoration of the Eucharistic Body and Blood of Christ during the sacrificial celebration was always customary in the Church. Cfr. Muratori, Dissertat.

Immediately after pronouncing the words of Consecration, the priest in all reverence elevates first the Host and afterward the chalice in

de reb. liturg. c. 19.) — *Carnem* Christi in *mysteriis* adoramus (S. Ambr. De Spir. sancto l. 3, c. 11, n. 79. Cfr. S. Aug. Enarr. in Ps. 98, n. 9). This adoration in the course of time differed ritually. According to the Roman Ordines and the Middle Age writers, up to the twelfth century mainly the bowing (inclinatio) of the head, or of the body, was prescribed as the sign and expression of adoration. *Inclinato capite* pontifex vel diaconus salutat Sancta (the holy Body of Christ) (Ordo Rom. I, n. 8). Pontifex *inclinato capite* ad altare primo *adorat* Sancta (Ordo Rom. II, n. 4). During the entire Canon the clerics maintained an adoring posture — permanent *inclinati* (Ordo Rom. I, n. 16; II, n. 10; III, n. 15). *Acclines* manent orationi intenti (Consuet. Cluniac. 1. 2, c. 30). — Post finitum hymnum: Sanctus... *inclinant se* circumstantes, venerando divinam majestatem cum angelis et Domini incarnationem cum turba et inclinati perseverant, usque dum finiatur omnis praesens Oratio (the Canon) (Hildeb. Turon. De expos. Missae). Not until the end of the Canon were the Host and chalice elevated by the priest, respectively also by the deacon, and shown to the people for adoration. Cum dicimus: "Per omnia saecula saeculorum," *corpus cum calice* levamus et statim in altari deposita cooperimus (Microl. c. 17). The heresy of Berengarius († 1088) may have been the external occasion for the introduction of the rite of the Elevation immediately after the Consecration. It first came into use after the twelfth century (first in France), and then in the thirteenth century it was generally spread, because it was well calculated publicly and solemnly to confess the faith in transsubstantiation and in the real presence of Christ in the Blessed Sacrament. In many churches for a long time the Host alone was raised; in others the chalice also (in some places veiled with the pall, in others uncovered). — The Ceremoniale Roman. (Ordo Rom. XIII) published under Gregory X († 1276) has (n. 19) the rubric: In elevatione corporis Christi... *prosternant se* ad terram et adorent reverenter in facies cadendo et sic *prostrati* stent usque ad "per omnia..." ante "Agnus Dei". The Fourteenth Roman Ordo describes (c. 53) the rite more accurately. After the priest has said the words of Consecration over the bread, ipse primo adoret *inclinato* capite sacrum divinum corpus; deinde reverenter et attente ipsum elevet in altum adorandum a populo... *inclinato* paululum capite adoret sacrum Domini sanguinem et elevet adorandum a populo... nec oportet, quod vel corpus vel sanguinem diu teneat elevatum, sed post brevem moram deponat, ita tamen quod elevationes et depositiones faciat cum *debita reverentia* et *maturitate.* Accordingly, in the fourteenth century the celebrant did not genuflect at, or after the consecration. — At the same time with this Elevation the practice was also introduced of summoning those present by a small bell and those absent by the ringing of the large bell to the adoration at the Elevation. In elevatione utriusque (sc. hostiae et calicis) *squilla* pulsatur (Durand. 1. 4, c. 41, n. 53). Ivo of Chartres says, that we ring the bell quando illa singularis hostia pro nobis redimendis in ara crucis oblata per novi sacerdotii ministros in Domini mensa quotidie consecratur (Epist. 142). — The Elevation rite is rendered more impressive in Missa *solemni* by the use of lights and incense. Several acolytes appear with torches (intortitia), and the thurifer incenses the Host and chalice while they are being elevated. The burning of the light as well as the consuming of the incense is a token and expression of devout adoration and worship rising heavenward. The incensing at this place occurs already at the close of the fourteenth century. — The faithful recite at the Elevation, in most humble deportment, various aspirations, usually making the sign of the Cross and, in token of interior compunction, striking their breast. (Cfr. Berthold v. Chiemsee, Keligpuchel Kap. 20, No. 7. 8.) — Campanula in Missis pulsanda est etiam in Oratoriis privatis (S. R. C. 18. Jul. 1885).

like manner, in order to hold up to view to the congregation present
the Divine Sacrificial Victim for their adoration, whilst he himself
keeps his eyes riveted on the Holy of Holies. The principal object
of their elevation is adoration; as the celebrant genuflects before
and after the Elevation, adoring with faith and humility (*genuflexus
adorat — genuflexus veneratur — genuflexus reverenter adorat. —*
Rubr.), thus also all who assist at the Mass should be moved and
impelled at the sight of the Blessed Sacrament, to render to the God
and Saviour therein concealed due adoration through their humble
and reverent deportment, as well as by the interior oblation of themselves to Him. After the birth of Christ, heaven and earth sent
adorers to the crib at Bethlehem : the same happens at the appearance of the Eucharistic Saviour on the altar. Then, as St. Gregory
says (Dial. IV, 58), "Heaven opens at the words of the priest, and
the choirs of angels surround the altar," to admire and to adore the
Divine Mysteries : what then is more proper than that man also
should, in unison with the celestial spirits, render to the Victim
present their most profound testimonies of homage and worship?

This elevation of the Body and Blood of Christ is truly "the
commemoration of the death of the Lord" (1 Cor. 11, 26): it places
before our eyes the raising up of Christ on the Cross upon Golgotha.
As once on Mount Calvary, so Christ here on the altar, as the great
Mediator, as the true Victim and as the Eternal Highpriest, is elevated betwixt heaven and earth, to reconcile God and Man, inasmuch
as He moves the Heavenly Father to mercy and forgiveness, and
rouses sinful man to love and compunction. "This is the wisdom of
God in a mystery, a wisdom which is hidden, which God ordained
before the world, unto our glory" (1 Cor. 2, 7). "When I shall be
lifted up from the earth," says the Lord, "then will I draw all things
to Myself" (John 12, 32). O sweetest Jesus, take us from this
world and draw us to Thee, that we also may be where Thou art!
"As the rising sun chases the shadows of night away, pouring .its
floods of light into the most hidden vales, thus at the Consecration
of every Mass there likewise appears upon the altar a Sun of infinite
brightness. 'God, our God, comes visibly.' From the holy city,
from the new 'Sion, shines forth His majesty.' Veiled to the eye of
sense, but 'recognizable' to the eye of faith, from out the Host's
snow-white veiling and from the gleaming chalice dart forth lightning flashes, lighting up everything and penetrating into the inmost
recesses of the heart. As the Lord, when all nations shall be gathered
together for the great judgment, will appear with dread majesty and
power seated on the clouds as on a bright throne, thus also does He
here appear encompassed with angels on flaming clouds of glory.
'Fire flares up before Him,' flows around His sceptre and sword,
wreathes Him a crown of kingly glory, — inscribing on His majestic
forehead: 'I judge all flesh with eternal justice.' The house of God
becomes a judgment-hall and thy trembling hand, O priest, a judgment-seat, from which the Eternal Monarch of Nations, with daz-

zling countenance, acts and exercises rigorous judgment over thee and the congregation. Heaven and earth draw nigh when 'the Lord judges His people,' just as at each moment He decides the destiny of the dying all over the earth. Though apparently the silvery tone of the little bell alone interrupts the reigning silence of adoration, the Lord, however, 'is not silent'! From out the elevated Host His eye penetrates hearts, and His lips pronounce a sentence which the angels, the 'heavens surrounding the altar, make known,' and the sentence tremblingly re-echoes in the consciences of priest and people! 'Attend to this,' O anointed of the Lord! When thou dost bow down, dost sink upon thy knees in adoration, and rising dost elevate aloft the Holy of Holies, veiled in its mystical covering, does not thy Judge look therefrom at thee and examine thy heart and reins: Is thy pastoral charge 'a sacrifice of praise' unto Me? Dost thou, as the altar and temple, watch over the living temple also, the souls confided to thee by Me, the Good Shepherd, and purchased with My Blood? In short, if thy priesthood is holy and apostolic and the fulfilment of My commission: 'gather together My saints, that amid sacrifice they may confirm the covenant with Me'? Salvation then to thee, good servant! I will not enter into judgment with thee; from thy hand I bless and embrace thee with loving kindness and console thee interiorly in thy labors." (Wolter.)

61. The First Prayer of the Canon after the Consecration.

By the Consecration the Eucharistic Sacrifice is essentially accomplished. But as the sacrificial action, as simple as it is sublime, was appropriately introduced and prepared by manifold rites, it must also liturgically be properly developed and worthily concluded. Hence the Church now encircles the head of the Victim reposing on the altar, with a mystical wreath of holy prayers and ceremonies. At the moment of the Eucharistic Consecration there was thrown open to us on the altar an immense treasury of graces; these the Church would now gather up and turn to the greatest profit for all her needy children. First, there follows an oblation prayer in three parts.

1. Unde et memores, Domine, nos servi tui, sed et plebs tua sancta, ejusdem Christi Filii tui Domini nostri tam beatae passionis, necnon et ab inferis resurrectionis, sed et in coelos gloriosae ascensionis: offerimus praeclarae majestati tuae de tuis donis ac datis Hostiam † puram, Hostiam † sanctam, Hostiam † immacula-

1. Wherefore, O Lord, we Thy servants, and likewise Thy holy people, calling to mind the blessed Passion of the same Christ Thy Son, our Lord, together with His Resurrection from the grave, and also His glorious Ascension into heaven, offer unto Thy excellent Majesty, of Thy gifts and presents, a pure † Victim, a holy † Victim,

tam: Panem † sanctum vitae aeternae, et Calicem † salutis perpetuae.

an immaculate † Victim: the holy † bread of eternal life, and the chalice † of everlasting salvation.

2. Supra quae propitio ac sereno vultu respicere digneris: et accepta habere, sicuti accepta habere dignatus es munera pueri tui justi Abel, et sacrificium Patriarchae nostri Abrahae: et quod tibi obtulit summus sacerdos tuus Melchisedech, sanctum sacrificium, immaculatam hostiam.

2. Upon which do Thou vouchsafe to look with favorable and gracious countenance, and accept them, as Thou didst vouchsafe to accept the gifts of Thy just servant Abel, and the sacrifice of our Patriarch Abraham, and that which Thy Highpriest Melchisedech offered unto Thee, a holy Sacrifice, an unspotted Victim.

3. Supplices te rogamus, omnipotens Deus: jube haec perferri per manus sancti Angeli tui in sublime altare tuum, in conspectu divinae majestatis tuae: ut quotquot ex hac altaris participatione sacrosanctum Filii tui Cor†pus et San†guinem sumpserimus, omni benedictione coelesti et gratia repleamur. Per eundem Christum Dominum nostrum. Amen.

3. We humbly beseech Thee, Almighty God, command these to be carried by the hands of Thy holy Angel to Thine Altar on high, in the presence of Thy divine Majesty, that as many of us as shall, by partaking at this Altar, receive the most sacred Body† and Blood† of Thy Son, may be filled with all heavenly blessing and grace. Through the same Christ our Lord. Amen.

These three parts of the Canon belong together both as to their form and their contents, for they constitute but a single prayer, which concludes with the customary clause. If the aforesaid formula of prayer be conceived and explained after this manner, then the intimate relation of the parts of the prayer and the gradual development of the whole cannot be mistaken. In general, it contains the presentation to God of our sacrificial gifts and supplication that He graciously accept them, and finally terminates with the wish that the most abundant benedictions of grace may be poured out from the altar upon all who participate in the holy sacrificial nourishment.

1. First Part of the Prayer (*Unde et memores*).

The virginal seer St. John beheld in heaven the wonderful, meek Lamb, who triumphed in His blood, and he saw Him standing "as it were slain" (*Vidi: et ecce . . . Agnum tanquam occisum* — Apoc. 5, 6), on account of the marks of His wounds; with far greater right we may say, that the same Lamb of God after the Consecration remains in a state of sacrifice, "as if immolated" on the altar — immolated by the two-edged sword of the wonderful and mighty words of Consecration. Assuredly the Lord indeed dieth no more, nor can He die; He is exalted above death and the pangs of death; but nevertheless He here submits, under the sacramental species, to a mystical death, inasmuch as He renders present and conceals His Body and His Blood under the cover of inanimate things. While He places Himself by the separate Consecration in this state on the altar, He consecrates Himself to His Heavenly Father as a sacrifice of praise, of propitiation, of thanksgiving and of petition. His Eucharistic Heart glows and burns with the same fire of sacrificial love which at one time consumed Him as a holocaust on Calvary.

But on the altar He is also *our* Sacrifice, He is in *our* hands: — *we* are likewise to offer Him. This is done already at the Consecration; for the sacrificial act, as such, essentially includes the oblation of the gift.[1] The offering already contained in the sacrificial action in itself may still be more clearly expressed and made repeatedly under different aspects and for different purposes through words and ceremonies. The Offertory prayers previous to the Consecration do not refer to the Eucharistic elements exclusively, but at the same time to the Victim about to be present. Immediately after the Consecration again similar oblation petitions occur; they do not belong to the essence of the Sacrifice, yet they, in a certain sense, add to its greater perfection and completeness.[2] The immolated, sacrificed Lamb of God, His Body and Blood lie before us on the altar; these infinitely precious gifts we now present to the Divine Majesty, principally to commemorate the Redeemer and His work, as well as to gain the fruits of the Sacrifice.[3] Who accomplishes this offering?

---

[1] Adverte *duplicem* esse oblationem. Una est intrinseca sacrificio. Omne enim sacrificium est oblatio, et haec quidem oblatio non est alia actio ab ipsa, quae dicitur sacrificium, sed eadem ut in Deum ordinatur. Altera est, quae ab ipso sacrificio disjungitur; et haec est, qua expressius et distinctius sacrificium ipsum factum aut faciendum in Deum ordinamus et mente et voce. Et haec est, quae fit post consecrationem illis verbis: Unde et memores ... et ante consecrationem illis: Suscipe, sancta Trinitas ... (Tolet. In Summ. s. Thom. De sacrif. Missae controvers. 5).

[2] Deposito Calice et adorato, prosequitur sacerdos sacram actionem Canonis, et facta *reali* et *substantiali* oblatione victimae per consecrationem, eandem confirmat et perficit repetita oblatione *verbali*, nempe oratione, quae incipit: "Unde et memores..." et aliis subsequentibus, additis etiam sacris ritibus in eundem finem: quae omnia accidentalem addunt perfectionem et majorem ornatum sacrificio, qualis tum maxime decet, dum in altari jam praesens est victima seu hostia vivens, sancta et Deo placens, videlicet ipse Christus sub accidentibus panis et vini (Quarti p. 2, tit. 9, n. 1).

[3] Quod sacerdos etiam tunc (sc. post consecrationem) orat, ut Deus acceptum habeat sacrificium, non est quia *essentialis oblatio* sacrificii non sit jam peracta, sed quia adhuc habemus praesentem *rem oblatam*, et per illam possumus plura semper beneficia impetrare, et iterum atque iterum Deum deprecari, ut et majorem in ipsum reverentiam ostendamus, et ut ad plura beneficia nobis conferenda sacrificium nostrum acceptet ac denique, ut effectus sacrificii propter demeritum nostrum non impediatur (Suarez disp. 75, sect. 5, n. 15).

a) "We, Thy servants, as also Thy holy people," — that is, first and chiefly consecrated priests; then, subordinate to and united with them, also the rest of the faithful.

The plural "Thy servants" recalls the time when the concelebration[1] of the priest with the bishop was still in practice, and, accordingly, proves the antiquity of the prayer.[2] The priests are in quite a special manner "servants of God"; but as they are to serve Him through love and with joy, they are also called "friends of God". In His farewell discourse the Lord spoke to His disciples those words, which the bishop repeats after the ordination in reference to the newly ordained: "I no longer now call you servants, but My friends, because you know all that I have done in your midst"[3] — *Jam non dicam vos servos, sed amicos meos, quia omnia cognovistis, quae operatus sum in medio vestri.* Thus does the Lord by an unmerited favor elevate us priests to the rank of bosom friends and messmates, honors us with the most intimate, confidential intercourse; but,

---

[1] During many centuries priests were accustomed — especially on great feasts —to celebrate the Eucharistic Sacrifice in common with the bishop; this was called συλλειτουργεῖν, concelebrare, consacrificare. Mos est Romanae Ecclesiae, ut in confectione immolationis Christi adsint Presbyteri et simul cum Pontifice verbis et manibus conficiant (Amalar. De eccles. offic. 1. 1, c. 12).—Consueverunt presbyteri Cardinales Romanum circumstare Pontificem et cum eo pariter celebrare, cumque consummatum est sacrificium, de manu ejus communionem recipere (Innoc. III. De sacro altar. myster. 1. 4, c. 25). In the Roman Liturgy this rite of Concelebration is now limited to the Masses at which takes place the ordination of priests and the consecration of bishops, also the consecration of abbots (abbas legit totam Missam, *exceptis verbis consecrationis*, quae *non* profert), while with the Greeks it still frequently occurs. (Cfr. Bona, Rerum liturg. 1. 1, c. 18, § 9.)

[2] Primum de praelatis; alterum de subjectis agere non dubitatur (Microlog. c. 13). The expression *servi* is not to be confined to priests alone, but according to circumstances it is also to be referred to levites and minorites. As in the prayer Hanc igitur we have here also a grouping together of clerics and laity: the former (the officials of the house of God) constitute the hierarchical, the latter the laical, priesthood. As λαὸς θεοῦ, that is, as members of the congregation and of the house of God, all Christians have, in a wider sense, a priestly character (1 Peter 2, 5), and they exercise it chiefly at the Eucharistic Celebration, in which by closest adherence to the liturgy they in common offer the Sacrificial Body and Sacrificial Blood of Christ, as well as their own subjective sacrifice. — Non solum *sacerdotes* et *clerus* (qui secundum diversos gradus divinis occupantur officiis) offerunt, sed etiam *audientes*, qui votis et orationibus assistunt cooperantes (B. Odo Camerac. dist. 2).

[3] Nonne per charismata gratiarum, per sapientiae claritatem, per virtutum decorem, per puritatem internam, per custoditam, fructuosam et contemplativam coram Deo conversationem, per odium vitiorum, per ardentem Deitatis amorem efficeris non solum servus Dei, imo et filius adoptivus, secretus amicus, heres regni coelestis, increatae Sapientiae sponsus, amantissimus Dei et tamquam consiliarius ac secretarius Creatoris? Intuere, quam deificum et praeclarum consistat, cum Deo assidue miscere colloquia in orationibus ac laudibus ejus, ipsum quoque tibi loquentem audire in lectionibus Scripturarum, in inspiratione occulta, in manifestationibus abditorum (Dion. Carthus. De laude vitae solitariae art. 12).

nevertheless, we are and will ever remain "His servants". **This** service is assuredly in itself again a very great honor and distinction,[1] to which the Lord chose us out of His free mercy, and called us through His powerful grace. We should administer and dispense the mysteries of God like good and faithful servants, leading a life befitting our vocation and office, so that the Lord, when He shall come to judge us, may find us watching and admit us into His eternal joy. The ministers of the Church are indeed, by their ordination, dignity and power, exalted above the laity; but they are thereby none the less obliged to serve the flock that has been subjected and entrusted to them, that is, in love and humility, with devotedness and self-sacrifice, labor, suffer and care for the salvation and temporal welfare of their flock, after the example of "the Son of Man, who came not to be ministered unto but to minister, and to give His life as a redemption for many" (Matth. 20, 28).

The words *plebs tua sancta*[2] — "Thy holy people" — denote the high dignity of the faithful regenerated by the sacrament of baptism; they are and should be "a people of God" (*plebs tua*) and as such a "holy people" (*plebs sancta*). The faithful are a people belonging to God; for God has purchased them and acquired them with the great price of the Blood of Christ. They form a community which, in a very special manner, is dedicated to God as His peculiar property. The members of the Church are designated as a "holy people", inasmuch as God has singularly favored them, and poured out on them in abundance the spirit of sanctification, whereby they are enabled as well as bound to lead a new, virtuous and holy life. Then indeed shall the children of the Church truly be "the holy people of God," if by word and deed, by their whole conduct, they endeavor to serve God and to glorify Him, since for this has He called and transplanted them out of the darkness of the world into the wonderful light of His heavenly truth and grace. God gave us His Son and He gives Him again daily on the altar, that "He might redeem us from all iniquity, and might cleanse to Himself a people acceptable, a pursuer of good works" (Tit. 2, 14).

At this offering priest and people are at the same time "mindful also of the blessed passion, resurrection and ascension of Jesus Christ," and that, because the Lord Himself commanded it. It is to this above-mentioned and previously stated command of Christ (*in mei memoriam facietis*) that the words *Unde et memores* — "wherefore also calling to mind" — refer.[3] The Eucharistic Sacri-

---

[1] Multo pretiosior est christiana humilitas et servitus regum opibus et superbia (S. Agatha).

[2] In like manner Christians are called gens sancta, populus acquisitionis (1 Petr. 2, 9); frequently in the liturgy sacrata plebs; plebs Domino dicata; populus sanctus Dei.

[3] Peracta consecratione in omnibus Liturgiis *Christi mandatum* commemoratur praecipientis, ut ipsum sacrificium in ejus memoriam peragamus: "Haec quotiescunque feceritis, in mei memoriam facietis." Quis enim auderet ad altare Dei

fice is the living commemoration and mystical accomplishment of the entire work of redemption (*opus redemptionis nostrae exercetur*); Christ, as Highpriest and as Victim, is present on the altar with all the fruits and merits of the redemption. In the Holy Sacrifice of the Mass not only His passion and death,[1] but also the life of His glory is mystically (*in mysterio*) represented and renewed. Three great mysteries are here principally made prominent: before all, the sufferings of Christ in His sacrifice and death on the Cross, as the essence and centre of the work of the redemption; then the joyful resurrection and glorious ascension, which constitute the conclusion, crown and completion of the work of the redemption.[2] The passion, beyond all conception, so full of pain and torment for the Saviour, is here designated as "blessed" (*tam beata passio*),[3] by reason of the blessed effects and sweet fruits which it produced for us men. Thus the Church in a Passion Hymn calls also the hard wood of the Cross and the cruel nails "sweet" (*dulce lignum, dulces clavi*). — Since the merciful Saviour has left us on the altar such a wonderful memorial of His redeeming life and death, we should during the celebration of the Holy Sacrifice most fervently meditate upon and venerate these great mysteries.[4] "At the institution of the Eucharist,

---

accedere et augustissimum mysterium celebrare, nisi Dominus tanti sacramenti institutor *praecipisset?* Propterea Ecclesia Domini mandato obsequens sequentia verba recitari constituit: "*Unde et memores, Domine, nos servi tui, sed et plebs tua sancta,*" fidelis scilicet et in Ecclesiae gremio consistens; sancta, non quidem actu, cum non omnes sancti sint, sed vocatione, debito et professione; quae vel praesens adest sacrificio vel in unitate Ecclesiae ubique degens particeps est sacrificii (Bona, Rer. liturg. l. 2, c. 12, § 3).

[1] Illius ergo panis et calicis oblatio mortis Christi est commemoratio et annuntiatio, quae *non tam verbis quam mysteriis ipsis* agitur, per quae nostris mentibus mors illa pretiosa altius et fortius commendatur (Florus Lugdun. De actione Missar. n. 89. — Cfr. Algerus, De sacram. corp. et sang. Domin. l. 1, c. 16).

[2] Nominantur potius hic ista tria Christi opera: passio, resurrectio, ascensio, quam alia in dispensatione carnis assumptae ab eo facta, quoniam plus ceteris faciunt ad complementum redemptionis et glorificationis humanae. Passio namque Christi pretium nostrae redemptionis exsolvit et mortem destruxit. Resurrectio ejusdem perditam reparavit vitam nobisque resurgendi spem et fiduciam suggessit. Ascensio vero in coelum paradisi patefecit introitum quantum ad ejus ingressum et nobis eandem ingrediendi viam monstravit (Clichtov. Elucidat. eccles. l. 3, n. 35).

[3] Nulla nobis sit de Christi cruce confusio, quia habemus de ejus passione victoriam: sicut enim sempiternus Dei Filius non sibi, sed nobis est natus, ita immaculatus Dei Agnus non sibi, sed *nobis* est passus (Maxim. Taurin. Homil. 83). — Haec dominicae dispensationis arcana (the mysteries of the redemption) et semper nos animo decet retinere et intentius solito ubi *beatissimae passionis* sacramenta conficiuntur, ubi mors Salvatoris nostri, quam citissimae resurrectionis virtute in aeternum conculcavit, mysticis in altari renovatur officiis (Bed. Venerab. l. 2, hom. 4). — *Tam beatae,* h. e. *tam excellenter beatificantis* (passionis), quia mortuos a vinculis mortis absolvit (Albert. M., Summa de offic. Missae tract. 3, c. 13).

[4] Commemorantur *tria* opera Christi, videlicet passio ejus, cujus memoria caritatem inflammat; resurrectio, quae fidem confortat; ascensio, quae spem

the Lord Himself said to the Apostles: 'Do this in remembrance of Me!' so that this sublime and venerable Sacrament might be to us an excellent and singular memorial of the immense love wherewith He loved us. This is the sweetest memorial, the most salutary memorial, by means of which we renew the joyful remembrance of our redemption. This is the glorious commemoration that fills the souls of the faithful with a salutary joy, infuses into our hearts felicity, at the same time sweetly moving to tears. For we rejoice in the remembrance of our deliverance; but inasmuch as we renew the passion of Jesus Christ, through which we received our deliverance, we can scarcely restrain our tears. Thus there shall be for us in this most holy memorial tears together with the sweetest joys, so that amid tears we rejoice thereat and rejoicing weep, having at the same time joyful tears and a weeping felicity; for the heart, overflowing with infinite joy, trickles sweet tears through the eyes.''[1]

We offer the Sacrifice to the most exalted, the most worthy and glorious Majesty of the heavenly Father — *offerimus praeclarae majestati tuae.* But where shall we find and whence take the offering for the God of Majesty? Since every good and perfect gift comes from above, from the Giver of all that is good, we cannot offer anything to God, but from His "presents and gifts", which He had previously imparted to us.[2] "Thine, O Lord, is magnificence and power and glory and victory: and to Thee is praise! For all that is in heaven and in earth is Thine: Thine is the kingdom, O Lord, and Thou art above all princes. All things are Thine, and we have given Thee what we received of Thy hand" (1 Paralip. 29, 11—14). The "presents and gifts" (*dona et data*) here mentioned, by means of which we offer a Sacrifice to God, are the natural elements of bread and wine, taken from the noblest fruits and productions of God's creation.[3] For these earthly "presents and gifts of God" are

---

nostram corroborat. Quod enim in Christo capite nostro factum credimus, in nobis perficiendum speramus. Dum vero sacerdos haec verba dicit, debet quidem celeriter, non tamen superficialiter, imo cordialiter recordari passionis Christi, non sine compassionis affectu, resurrectionis quoque et ascensionis cum exsultatione mentali, contemplando mentaliter, quomodo ex clauso sepulcro surrexit, anima ex limbo inferni ad corpus redeunte, et qualiter nubes in ascensione accepit eum ab oculis discipulorum (Dion. Carthus. Expos. Missae art. 32).

[1] Cfr. the Bull of the Institution of the feast of Corpus Christi by Urban IV. (11. August, 1264).

[2] Deus, qui cum muneribus nullis indigeas ipse nobis munera cuncta largiris, accipe propitius, quae de tuis donis tibi nos offerre voluisti, non solum nostrae reputans devotioni quae tua sunt, sed etiam per haec nos ad coelestia regna perducens (Sacram. Leon. XXIV).

[3] Among the "God-given gifts and presents" we may also at the same time understand the Eucharistic Victim. Sensus est: offerimus tibi hostiam puram, panem sanctum et calicem salutis, quae ex creaturis tuis a te datis et donatis, ex *pane* scil. et *vino* per consecrationem habemus. Sic exponit Innocentius. Possunt etiam referri omnia ad *ipsam Eucharistiam* sive ad Christum ut in Eucharistia existentem; rectissime enim dicitur Christus Dei datum et donum (Bellarm. De

changed by the Consecration into the gift of the Eucharistic Sacrifice, into the Bread of Life and the Chalice of Salvation, which we likewise received from God, and which we again offer to the Divine Majesty.

Our Sacrifice is worthy of the greatness and goodness of God; it is an infinitely precious and perfect Sacrifice. For, indeed, we present the "clean oblation" (*oblatio munda*) predicted by the Prophet Malachias (1, 11), on which there cannot possibly fall the least shadow of blemish. Jesus Christ is in Himself the unspeakably "pure, holy and unspotted Victim" (*hostia pura, hostia sancta, hostia immaculata*), and, consequently, the inexhaustible source also whence purity, holiness and spotlessness are poured forth into every susceptible human heart.[1] The Eucharistic Victim is, moreover, partaken of; His sacrificial Body is a sacrificial food, and His sacrificial Blood is a sacrificial beverage, — both together form a "holy sacrificial repast". Hence it is said, we offer "the Bread of Heaven, which nourishes unto eternal life," and "the precious Chalice, whence issues everlasting salvation."[2]

b) The Five Concomitant Signs of the Cross.

Even *after* the Consecration the sign of the Cross is made over the sacrificial gifts.[3] These signs of the Cross after the Consecration have ever been regarded as difficult of explanation; hence the most varied interpretations have been attempted.[4]

The use of the sign of the Cross in ecclesiastical worship is very extensive: it is employed not merely as a holy symbol, to express various mysteries and truths, but, moreover, as a means to produce supernatural effects and to impart blessings, that is, it is a sign equally significant as well as efficacious. Since the sign of the Cross, on account of its manifold and profound contents, is so extensively employed for liturgical purposes, it is self-evident that it is not always and not everywhere used in the same sense, but at one

---

Missa 1. 2, c. 24). — Dicitur haec hostia offerri ex Dei donis et datis, vel *quia ex pane et vino effecta est*, vel certe, quia *Christum* ipsum continet, qui nobis a Deo *datus* est (Suarez disp. 83, sect. 2).

[1] Christus est hostia pura, electos suos purificans; hostia sancta, dilectos suos sanctificans; hostia immaculata, maculas nostras purgans; panis vitae aeternae, angelos et homines reficiens, et calice sui praeclari sanguinis inebrians et perfundens (S. Bonav. Expos. Missae c. 4).

[2] In the Mozarabic Liturgy the Eucharist is also frequently designated as *panis* (sc. quem lignum crucis coxit) and as *calix*, or *vinum* (sc. quod torcular passionis expressit). It has a similar designation in a prayer of the old Gallican Rite immolatus *panis* et sanguis.

[3] In three places (in all ten times) it is made with the hand over the sacrificial gifts, and in two places (in all eight times) with the Host (six times over the chalice and twice outside the chalice).

[4] Cfr. Lebrun, Explication de la Messe part. 4, art. 11, § 1, n. 2. — Bossuet, Explication de quelques difficultés sur les prières de la Messe. — Hefele, Beiträge zur Kirchengeschichte etc. II, 286. — Hoppe, Die Epiklesis S. 108 etc. — Scheeben, Studien über den Messcanon, im "Katholik", Jahrg. 1866, S. 706 etc.

time in one sense, at another in another, and even often in the same place it may have several meanings consistent with one another.[1] — It is always to be held as a fundamental rule, that text and sign are to be explained in harmony with each other; for word and act constitute a ritual whole, since they belong to each other, mutually complete one another and reciprocally cast light on one another. — This is the case in the rite of the Mass, in which frequently occurs the holy sign of the Cross. First, the distinction between the sign of the Cross made *before* and that made *after* the Consecration must be shown. Very often the Cross is a sign of blessing: this is the case *before* the Consecration. There it is a significant and, at the same time, an effective sign of blessing; on the one hand, it consecrates the material elements of bread and wine to their high destiny, and, on the other hand, it indicates and implores their perfect sanctification through the Consecration. — But evidently this object cannot be ascribed to the sign of the Cross *after* the Elevation: there are no longer present on the altar material elements susceptible of or in need of blessing, but Christ's Body and Blood under the appearances of bread and wine. Jesus Christ, the source of all blessings and the Holy of Holies, can and may not be blessed by the priest.[2] Therefore, all admit that the signs of the Cross made over the oblation after the Consecration can in nowise have the signification and power of effective signs of blessing for Christ who is present, for His Body and Blood.[3] The signs of the Cross after the Consecration again have different meanings and ends which, consequently, will be best shown by explaining the prayers and acts connected with them.

In our present prayer the Eucharistic Sacrifice is named five times, and at each mention of it a Cross is made over the Holy of Holies. In these Crosses we may discover a manifold meaning. The sign of the Cross is indeed but a passing action, yet it possesses the form and expression of a holy image: it is like the Crucifix, and like it, it ever reminds us of Christ's passion and death. The Cross, therefore, has always and everywhere this reminding feature, especially at the celebration of Mass, which is the showing forth and renewal of the Sacrifice of the Cross.[4] When the gifts of the Eu-

---

[1] *Consecratio* hujus sacramenti et *acceptatio* hujus sacrificii et *fructus* ipsius procedit ex virtute crucis Christi, et ideo, ubicumque fit mentio de aliquo horum, sacerdos crucesignatione utitur (S. Thom. 3, q. 83, a. 5 ad 3).

[2] In sacramento altaris benedictio sacerdotis fertur super terminum a quo, i. e. super panem, non super terminum ad quem, i. e. corpus Christi (S. Thom. In 1 ad Cor. c. 10, l. 4).

[3] Notandum quod consignatio facta super panem et calicem ante consecrationem quasi oratio est, ut consecratio compleatur; post consecrationem vero iterata consignatio consecrationis jam adimpletae quaedam est testificatio (Robert. Paulul. De offic. eccles. 1. 2, c. 32).

[4]   *Mentio mortis* adest, ubicumque perennibus escis
     Imprimit uncta manus mystica signa crucis.
                    (Hildeb. Turon. Vers. de myster. Missae.)
Quid est inter ipsa mysteria rebus sacratis vel sacrandis *signum crucis* super-

charistic Sacrifice are named, the symbol of the Cross is appropriately added thereto, to represent to the eye also, that on the altar the same Body and the same Blood are offered as were once sacrificed on the Cross. In the above prayer this happens soon after the acknowledgment, that we are mindful of the passion of Christ.[1] — This symbolical interpretation does not exclude, but rather includes other meanings. The essence of our prayer is the offering (*offerimus*): now if the signs of the Cross figuratively express what the words signify, then they are also rightly to be conceived as a symbolical dedication and surrendering up to God of the Eucharistic Victim. Yet these crosses in a certain respect can here be understood as signs of blessing.[2] They may be regarded as a symbol of that plenitude of grace and blessing which gushes forth from the sacrificed Body and Blood of Christ over His mystical body, that is, the Church. This thought is so much more to the point and warranted, because the Church is united to Christ and offered together with Him on the altar and, consequently, she is blessed to a certain extent by these signs of the Cross.

2. The second part of the prayer (*Supra quae*).

Immediately after the above offering very appropriately follows the petition that God would vouchsafe to look with a propitious and gracious countenance upon our sacrificial gifts and vouchsafe to accept them, as formerly He received the typical offerings of Abel, Abraham and Melchisedech. — But must not such a petition appear strange? Does not the eye of the heavenly Father rest with eternal love and infinite complacency on Jesus Christ, the "pure, the holy, the unspotted Victim" of our altars? How then can the oblation of the Body and Blood of Christ be placed on the same level with the figurative offerings of ancient times? To solve this difficulty, we must examine more closely the aspect under which the Eucharistic Sacrifice is here regarded. — In so far as Christ on the altar offers Himself, the Eucharistic Sacrifice is ever absolutely pleasing to God: to beg for a favorable acceptance of the Sacrifice of Christ from this standpoint, or even to place it on the same plane with the ancient

---

ponere, nisi *mortem Domini commemorare?* Unde et Dominus formam consecrandi corporis et sanguinis sui tradens, ait inter cetera: "Hoc facite in meam commemorationem" (Ivonis Carnotens. Sermo 5).

[1] Quinaria cruce signamus, non ut eum, a quo omnis sanctificatio, sanctificemus, sed ut vulnera pendentis in cruce — duo manuum, duo pedum, quintum lateris — flebiliter et devote recolamus (Stephan. Augustod. De sacram. altar. c. 17).

[2] The blessings made over the body of Jesus Christ with the sign of the cross, do not regard that divine body, but those who are to receive it; or if they regard it, it is to indicate the blessings and graces wherewith it is filled, and which He desires to impart to us liberally, if our want of fidelity does not prevent Him; or, in fine, if we wish to consider it in that light, Jesus Christ is blessed in all His members, who are offered in this Sacrifice as forming but one and the same body with the Saviour, in order that the grace of the Head be abundantly bestowed upon them (Bossuet l. c.).

sacrifices, is out of question, and, consequently, such cannot be the meaning of our prayer. — In it the Eucharistic oblation is considered under another aspect. At the moment of Consecration Jesus Christ as Highpriest offers Himself up through the Holy Ghost and the ministry of the visible priest to the honor of His heavenly Father, as well as for our salvation, and at the same time He places His sacrificial Body and sacrificial Blood in the hands of the Church. The Church now presents to the majesty of the Father, as her Sacrifice, the Victim mystically immolated, whilst including the sacrifice of her own self as a gift in union with the infinitely meritorious sacrificial Body and sacrificial Blood of Christ. The petition for the favorable reception refers, therefore, to the Eucharistic oblation, in as far as the *Church* comes to the foreground as *offering it together with herself.* For the value of an offering depends not alone on the quality of the gift, but also and principally on the dignity and holiness of the person who offers it. The more pure and perfect his intention in sacrificing is, the more agreeable is his homage in the sight of God. "The Lord had respect to Abel and to his offerings" (*Respexit Dominus ad Abel et ad munera ejus* — Gen. 4, 4), that is, the first was the cause of the second: the gift of Abel was pleasing to God, because Abel himself was pleasing to Him.[1] This principle is applicable also to the offering at the altar, inasmuch as the Church, the priest and the faithful are regarded as those who offer. Naturally this is not to be understood as though our disposition could impart a higher value to the sacrificial gift infinitely precious in and of itself, but it means only that God ever prefers to receive it from hands that possess the greater purity and holiness. Now, in the sight of God cannot the holiness and acceptability of the Church be found at times to be in a greater or less degree? Are not the sacrificing priest and the faithful who unite with him, often wanting in proper dispositions, in contrition, piety, purity of heart, fervor of devotion? At such reflections nothing seems more proper than humble supplications to the Most High, that He be not offended on account of our sinfulness, and reject not the Eucharistic gifts from our unworthy hands, but that He look upon and graciously accept them in as far as they are presented by *us*, that they may not only as the Sacrifice of Christ, but also as *our* Sacrifice, bring down upon us bountiful blessings and a superabundance of grace.[2]

---

[1] With respect to the sacrifices offered by Abel and Cain, St. Cyprian writes: Non munera eorum Deus, sed *corda* intuebatur, ut ille placeret in munere, qui placebat in corde (De Orat. domin. c. 24).

[2] Clarum est, quod sacerdos novae legis non orat sacrificium seu sacramentum altaris sic Deo placere, quemadmodum ei placuerunt sacrificia horum trium virorum (Abel, Abrahae, Melchisedech), quoniam illa sacrificia nec gratiam continebant nec placita Deo erant nisi ex devotione offerentium meritisque eorum, sed sacrificium novae legis, videlicet sacramentum corporis et sanguinis Christi, gratiarum plenitudinem continet et per seipsum Deo acceptum est, ejusque oblatio fructuosa est non solum ex meritis offerentis, sed propter dignitatem oblati. Orat ergo sacerdos oblationem suam seu sacramentum altaris Deo placere non quantum ad seipsum seu

For the clearer understanding of such petitions, it must be further considered that the Church participates still in another way in the Sacrifice of the Altar : together with her Head, Jesus Christ, she offers *herself* as a gift dedicated to God: the true and real Body of Christ and the mystical body of Christ are thus combined in one Sacrifice. This mystery is symbolized at the Offertory by pouring some water into the wine in the chalice ; accordingly, the priest already then prayed "in a spirit of humility and with a contrite heart," that "*we* be received by God as a well pleasing sacrifice," and immediately after summoned the faithful to pray that "his and their Sacrifice may be pleasing to God the Father Almighty." Hence we also cry to the Lord : *Nosmetipsos tibi perfice munus aeternum* — "Make us perfect as an eternal gift to Thee." Therefore, since we place ourselves with all our works and prayers, desires and concerns as a sacrificial gift upon the altar, the reason is easily understood why, with lively sentiments of our worthlessness and our unworthiness, we implore that God would deign to look with mercy on us and on our Sacrifice. Such petitions frequently occur in the liturgy of the Mass, and we shall meet them again at the conclusion of the Sacrifice. They are perfectly justifiable, inasmuch as we offer the Eucharistic Sacrifice and ourselves in union with it. To do this worthily, we should possess perfect sanctity, but as this is wanting to us, we recommend our Sacrifice to the favor and indulgence of God, that it may be more agreeable to Him and more salutary to us. When, therefore, we are assembled around the altar, may God never look down upon us with reproach and resentment, but may He always regard us and our gifts "with a favorable and gracious countenance"[1] (*propitio ac sereno vultu*).[2]

---

rem oblatam, quae per se sancta ac Deo placita existit, sed quantum ad *offerentem*, quatenus *sacerdotis actio* atque *devotio* Deo sic placeat, sicut placuit antiquorum patrum devotio, sicque effectum et gratiam hujus sacramenti consequi mereatur (Dion. Carthus. Exposit. Missae art. 33).

[1] Vultus = glance, mien, feature, inasmuch as it is the indication of the interior sentiment of the mind ; often emphatic = angry, threatening countenance, look of anger (cfr. Ps. 33, 17); propitius = inclined, disposed, favorable, graciously inclined ; serenus = serene, bright, clear, brilliant, radiant. We also pray God not to be angry, dark, severe, but favorable, mild, graciously to look down on our oblation. Cfr. Ps. 30, 17: *Illustra faciem tuam* (let Thy face shine) super servum tuum ; Ps. 66, 2: *Illuminet vultum suum* super nos (that He would allow His face to shine upon us) et misereatur nostri. — Cfr. *Hilaritatem vultus tui* nobis impertiri digneris (Miss. Rom.).

[2] It is not true that by this interpretation "the object of the offering is volatilized into the subject of the offering" and "heterogenous thoughts are inserted in the text," as Hoppe asserts (Epiklesis S. 103. 104); it is rather drawn from the inmost essence of the Sacrifice in general, to which an *offerens* is as necessary as a *res oblata,* and this especially of the Eucharistic Sacrifice, in which not only Christ, but also the Church, the priest and the faithful are the offerers — as well of the Body and Blood of Christ as of themselves. Cfr. the very ancient Oratio S. Ambrosii, included in the preparatory prayers of the priest, in which among others

The next petition, that the heavenly Father would favorably accept this our Sacrifice as He accepted the sacrifices of Abel, Abraham and Melchisedech, is explained from the same standpoint.[1] — Here there is by no means a "parallel comparison" of the Eucharistic Sacrifice, in as far as Christ is its priest and gift, with those ancient sacrifices before Christ: there is an infinite distance between them. The comparison refers to us and to those devout patriarchs. We pray that our oblation may be agreeable and pleasing to the eyes of God, as were the sacrifices of those saints of ancient times.[2] Now this is nothing else than praying for the fulfilment of that which the Prophet Malachias (3, 3–4) at one time predicted: "The Lord shall purify the sons of Levi (the priests), and shall refine them as gold and as silver, and they shall offer sacrifices (that is, the Eucharistic Oblation) to Him in justice. And the sacrifice of Juda and of Jerusalem (that is, of the Christian Church) shall please the Lord, as in the days of old and in the ancient years," when holy men, as Abel, Abraham and Melchisedech, offered sacrifices of pleasing odor to God. The Lord accepted their gifts with so great complacency, because they were presented to Him with perfect dispositions, and because they at the same time prefigured the Sacrifice of Jesus Christ.[3]

There is no doubt with respect to the typical character of the sacrifices mentioned. If the sacrifices of Abel and Abraham are assuredly principally figures of the bloody Sacrifice of the Cross, they must, indeed, in this connection with Melchisedech's sacrifice, be also considered as figures of the unbloody Sacrifice of the Altar. Such a conception corresponds to the view of Christian antiquity, as it is often expressed by the Fathers, in liturgies and in images.[4]

(feria sexta) we read: (Spiritus sanctus) *me indignum sacerdotem* doceat tantum tractare mysterium *cum cordis puritate et lacrymarum devotione, cum reverentia et tremore, ita ut placide et benigne suscipias sacrificium de manibus meis* ad salutem omnium tam vivorum quam defunctorum.

[1] Licet hoc sacramentum ex se ipso praeferatur omnibus antiquis sacrificiis, tamen sacrificia antiquorum fuerunt Deo acceptissima ex eorum devotione. Petit ergo sacerdos, ut sic hoc sacrificium acceptetur a Deo ex devotione offerentium, sicut illa accepta fuerunt Deo (S. Thom. III, q. 83, a. 4 ad 8).

[2] Fit in canone Missae mentio de oblatione Abrahae et Abel magis propter *devotionem offerentium*, quam propter figuram rei oblatae (S. Thom. IV, dist. 8, q. 1, a. sol. 2 ad 6).

[3] Post consecrationem rogamus Patrem, ut super dona praedicta respiciat et accepta habeat. Sed cum Patri Filio nihil sit acceptius, quem propitio et sereno vultu semper sibi Deum aequalem intuetur: quid aliud oramus, nisi ut mediante et interpellante Filio *nobis* Deus fiat placabilis, et propitius et per eum, qui sibi placet, ei placeamus? Itaque oramus eum per haec sacrificia nobis miserendo placatum fieri, sicut misertus est patribus nostris propitiando eorum sacrificiis. Unde attendenda est *haec comparatio in sola similitudine, non in quantitate, nec est referenda ad sacrificia, sed ad offerentium vota.* Plus valet res, quam figura. Omnibus sacrificiis praecellit Eucharistia; est autem talis similitudo, ut recte offerendo similes simus patribus nostris, qui recte obtulerunt (Steph. Augustod. De sacr. altar. c. 17).

[4] Tuae laudis hostiam jugiter immolamus, cujus figuram Abel justus insti-

The simple, devout and faithful Abel offered to God from among
the firstlings of his flock and their fat (Gen. 4, 4), upon which the
Apostle (Heb. 11, 4) writes: "By faith Abel offered to God a sacrifice exceeding that of Cain, by which he obtained a testimony that he
was just (*justus*), God giving testimony to his gifts." In all probability, God manifested His special pleasure by sending fire from
heaven, whereby the sacrifice of Abel was consumed. According to
the expression of the Lord Himself (Matt. 23, 35), Abel is here
emphatically designated as the just (*justus*) and as the servant
(*puer*) of God. Full of faith, of humble simplicity, he offered a
lamb to the Lord, and this sacrifice is intended to prefigure the
Sacrifice of that true and immaculate Lamb, daily immolated on the
altar.[1] — Inasmuch as Abel was infamously slain by his brother
Cain, he was, by suffering death innocently, one of the principal
figures of the propitiatory Sacrifice of Jesus Christ (Heb. 12, 24).
"In him," St. Ambrose says, "the redemption of the world and the
Sacrifice of Christ are announced."[2]

Abraham stands forth prominent as an example of heroic obedience and faith; chosen by God as the first father of all the faithful,
he is also "our Patriarch" (*Patriarcha noster*).[3] God commanded
him "to immolate his son Isaac in sacrifice, and already had Abraham bound his long-desired child of promise, and placed him on the
pile of wood, and had raised the sword above him: but at the decisive
moment, the Almighty restrained the father's arm and instead of the
son allowed him to sacrifice a ram to Him" (Laurent). This sacrifice of Abraham is often represented in the Catacombs, together with
other biblical events symbolizing the priesthood and the Sacrifice of
the New Law, as a figure of the Eucharistic Sacrifice. Abraham did
indeed sacrifice his son, but Isaac's blood in reality was not shed;
Abraham "received him from death for a parable" (Heb. 11, 19),
that is, as a figure of the Risen Saviour, who "as a Lamb as it were
slain" (*agnus tanquam occisus* — Apoc. 5, 6) offered Himself on
the altar in an unbloody manner. The Sequence of Corpus Christi
places the sacrifice of Abraham on a par with the Manna and the
Paschal Lamb; for it declares that the Eucharist "was figuratively
announced by the sacrifice of Isaac" (*praesignatur cum Isaac
immolatur*).[4]

---

tuit, celebravit Abraham, Melchisedech sacerdos exhibuit, sed verus Agnus et
aeternus Pontifex Christus implevit (Sacram. Leonian. IV).

[1] Deus, qui legalium differentiam hostiarum, unius sacrificii perfectione
sanxisti: *accipe sacrificium a devotis tibi famulis, et pari benedictione, sicut munera Abel, sanctifica;* ut quod singuli obtulerunt ad majestatis tuae honorem,
cunctis proficiat ad salutem (Secret. Dom. VII. p. Pent.).

[2] In isto (Abel) mundi redemptio annuntiatur, ab illo (Cain) mundi ruina. In
hoc Christi sacrificium, in illo diaboli parricidium (Exhortat. virgin. n. 36, c. 6).

[3] Dicitur Abraham *Patriarcha,* i. e. princeps patrum, non quia non habuerit
patrem, sed quia sibi facta est promissio de *paternitate gentium* (S. Thom. In ep.
ad Hebr. c. 7, lect. 2).

[4] Est et *sine cruore* sacrificium. Norunt hoc, quod dico, quicunque initiati

The offering of food, the sacrifice of bread and wine, which the faithful and royal priest Melchisedech, from a strange nation, presented to the Most High, is the most luminous and most striking figure of the Eucharistic Sacrifice[1]; for this reason it is justly styled holy and spotless (*sanctum sacrificium, immaculata hostia*).[2] Melchisedech himself is a figure of the eternal Highpriest Jesus Christ; his priesthood as to dignity and importance is in nowise inferior to that of Aaron, but it is even superior to it, hence he is called the Highpriest of God (*summus sacerdos tuus*).[3] "It is Jesus Christ whom the Highpriest Melchisedech figuratively represented, who did not offer to God the sacrifices of the Jews, but the sacrifice of that mystery which our Saviour consecrated in His Body and Blood.[4]

These patriarchs offered their merely figurative, imperfect sacrificial gifts with sentiments so devout and pure, that God regarded them with favor and grace: now should we not offer the perfect Sacrifice of the New Law with far greater piety and devotion, to the end that the Most High may also regard it with pleasure and graciously accept the gift from our hands?

3.   Third part of the Prayer (*Supplices te rogamus*).

This part contains the concluding petition by which we beseech God to command our sacrificial gifts to be carried by the hands of the angels to His altar on high, in the presence of His Divine Majesty, that by partaking of the sacrificial food, we may be filled with all heavenly blessing and grace. — This petition is clothed in words full of mystery, but evidently biblical; for it is manifest that

sunt, ac propterea sine sanguine transactum est illud (the sacrifice of Isaac by Abraham), quoniam istius (the unbloody sacrifice) figura (τύπος) esse debebat (S. Chrysost. Oratio in S. Eustathium). Cfr. Petav. De Incarnat. 1. 12, c. 13, n. 7.

[1] Melchisedech obtulit sacrificium in pane et vino, et in eisdem speciebus modo offertur et celebratur sacramentum altaris: ergo cum non possit expressius figurari quam in simili secundum speciem, videtur, quod tunc praecessit *figura expressissima* (S. Bonav. IV, dist. 8, p. 1, a. 1, q. 3).

[2] The addition sanctum sacrificium, immaculatam hostiam, ascribed to Leo the Great, grammatically cannot be conceived as in apposition with Supra quae and be referred to the Eucharistic Sacrifice; it belongs to quod obtulit summus sacerdos tuus Melchisedech. (Cfr. Lebrun 1. c. part. 4, art. 12.) — Vocat hic littera Canonis sacrificium ipsius Melchisedech "*sanctum* sacrificium et *immaculatam* hostiam," non quidem quantum ad se absolute, sed collatione facta ad sacrificium novi testamenti, quod significat et cujus expressior erat figura quam ceterae oblationes, et idcirco nostri sacrificii conditiones illi attribuuntur tanquam imagini (Clichtov. Elucidat. eccl. 1. 3, n. 39).

[3] Melchisedech sacerdos *summus* dicitur, qui inter sacerdotes illius temporis habebatur (B. Odonis Camer. Expos. in Canon. dist. 3).

[4] Ipse est, cujus formam Melchisedech *pontifex* praeferebat, non judaicas hostias offerens Deo, sed illius sacramenti immolans sacrificium, quod Redemptor noster in suo corpore et sanguine consecravit (S. Leo, Serm. IV [vel V] in annivers. assumpt. suae). — A similar petition is also found in the Pontifical: Sicut Melchisedech *sacerdotis praecipui* oblationem dignatione mirabili suscepisti, ita imposita huic novo altari munera semper *accepta ferre digneris* (De eccl. dedicat.).

there can be no question of a local transfer of the Body of Christ from the altar to heaven. The oblation is here brought to its close and termination, in this that the petition for a favorable acceptance of the gifts of the altar is not simply repeated, or continued, but presented under new aspects, that is, given greater scope and strengthened.[1] The text of the Canon recalls a celestial vision of St. John (Apoc. 8, 3—4): "And another Angel came and stood before the altar, having a golden censer; and there was given to him much incense, that he should offer the prayers of all saints (Christians) upon the golden altar, which is before the throne of God (*super altare aureum quod est ante thronum Dei*). And the smoke of the incense of the prayers of the saints ascended up before God, from the hand of the Angel (*de manu angeli coram Deo*)."[2]

a) *Jube haec perferri* — "Command these (sacrificial gifts) to be carried." By the word *haec* — these — evidently nothing else is to be understood than what we met with in the immediately preceding word *quae;* each time reference is made to the same object offered. To these sacrificial gifts (*haec*), which are to be carried up from the earthly to the heavenly altar, belongs not only the mystical Body of Christ, that is, the faithful with all they are and have — with their prayers and concerns, labors and sufferings, struggles and combats —, but, moreover, the Eucharistic Sacrificial Body and Sacrificial Blood of our Lord, inasmuch as *we* offer them.

These sacrificial gifts are to "be borne into the presence of the Divine Majesty,"[3] that is, they are to be presented to the Divine Majesty in such a manner that He may not reject them, but that He may regard and accept them with pleasure. But then this will be

---

[1] To the words: "Do ye this in remembrance of Me," the ancient liturgies join a prayer mentioning the memory of the passion, resurrection and ascension, as likewise an oblation prayer. That in the fifth, or already in the fourth century, the Supplices te rogamus was considered, not as an invocation, but as an oblation prayer, is clear from the writing De sacramentis, in which the first prayer of the Canon after the Consecration is worded as follows: Ergo memores gloriosissimae ejus passionis et ab inferis resurrectionis et in coelum ascensionis offerimus tibi hanc immaculatam hostiam, rationabilem hostiam, incruentam hostiam, hunc panem sanctum et calicem vitae aeternae et petimus et precamur, ut hanc oblationem suscipias in sublimi altari per manus angelorum tuorum, sicut suscipere dignatus es munera pueri tui justi Abel et 'sacrificium patriarchae nostri Abrahae et quod tibi obtulit summus sacerdos Melchisedech (l. 4, c. 5, n. 27).

[2] Ex hoc loco Apocalysis et similibus colligunt viri docti, *peculiarem* esse Angelum, qui sacerdoti celebranti assistat, eum juvet et dirigat, ejus preces et hostias Deo offerat, sive is Angelus sit custos celebrantis, sive custos altaris et templi, ad hanc custodiam et sacrificiorum oblationem peculiariter a Deo deputatus (Cornel. a Lap. i. h. l.).

[3] To bring our offerings up to God, to raise them up to heaven, where He may receive them, or to cause them to reach His throne, means in the ordinary language of Scripture, to present them to Him in such a manner and with so pure a conscience, that they may be pleasing to Him (Bossuet, Explication de quelques difficultés sur les prières de la Messe).

the case only if the eye of God detects nothing displeasing in them who offer — but, on the contrary, beholds them so pure and so holy, as to deserve to be united and to be presented along with the Most Holy Sacrifice of Christ.

Yet our life is not so blameless, nor our heart so pure, nor our dispositions so perfect. Glancing at the shining white Host and radiant chalice so near to us, the thought of the unspeakable holiness of the gift, which becomes ours at the moment of Consecration, arouses us to a consciousness of our own unworthiness. Penetrated with such humble sentiments, therefore, most ardently do we implore Almighty God that He would "by the hands of His holy angels" carry from this earthly altar the present sacrificial gifts into the presence of His Divine Majesty. When thus offered by the hands of angels, they cannot be otherwise than pleasing to Him in the highest degree and in every respect. — It must not appear strange that we should implore the ministry and assistance of an angel to present our oblation, for the purpose of making it more acceptable to God and salutary to us. It is a tradition originating in ancient Christian times and frequently expressed by the Church, that the angels who participated in the work of redemption from beginning to end, are also present at and take part in the celebration of the holy Sacrificial Mysteries.[1] As St. Chrysostom says (Of the Priesthood VI, 4): "The priest is himself at that solemn moment surrounded by angels, and the choir of the heavenly Powers unite with him; they occupy the entire space around the altar, to honor Him who lies there as a Sacrifice." Then the Saint describes a vision, in which was seen a multitude of angels, who, robed in dazzling white garments and with head deeply bowed, surrounded the altar, as warriors standing in the presence of their king. — The blessed vocation of the heavenly spirits consists in glorifying God by praise and in assisting man to attain salvation. Now, where could this twofold object be better fulfilled than is actually done during the holy Sacrifice? Hence hosts of angels collect about the altar to procure for God honor on high and for man peace on earth. Between the angels and the Holy Eucharist there exist, undoubtedly, intimate relations, which, indeed, to our weak vision here below remain always shrouded in a mysterious obscurity. Christian tradition speaks not only of the presence of many angels at the celebration of the Holy Mysteries, but it often, moreover, mentions in a determinate manner and yet, at the same time, in an indeterminate manner, a certain angel specially commissioned to carry our prayers and sacrifices before the throne of God.[2] Tertullian says (On Prayer, Chap. 16) that it is

---

[1] Semper angelus credendus est adesse immolationi corporis Christi (Joann. Abrinc. n. 22).

[2] Sicut Angeli intelliguntur Deo offerre *orationes nostras* et petitiones, similiter et *desideria* — non propter ignorantiam Dei, sed propter commoditatem nostram; quia suis sanctis affectibus puris nos adjuvant et merita nostra in conspectu Dei replicant, ut ex eorum puritate sancta et affectione ferventi ratione dignitatis

highly irreverent to sit in church "before the face of the Living God, while the angel of prayer is still standing there" (*sub conspectu Dei vivi angelo adhuc orationis adstante*). St. Ambrose writes (In Luc. l. 1, n. 28), that we cannot doubt that "an angel assists" (*assistere angelum*), when Christ is sacrificed on the altar. — Thus the text of the Canon also mentions but one angel. Does it not appear from this that the Church herself would thereby indicate that God intrusts an angel with the special mission of bringing the oblation of the priest and people into His presence? More minute and accurate information relative to this Angel of the Sacrifice of the Mass (*Angelus assistens divinis mysteriis* — S. Thom. III, q. 83, a. 4 ad 9) is not granted to us. Many saints and servants of God had a particular devotion to the angel here mentioned, without being able or willing to decide as to his name. Some believe him to be the guardian angel of the church and the altar, or that of the priest, who most effectually assists, directs and enlightens him during the celebration of the Holy Mysteries.[1] — Others suppose, and this appears probable, that it is St. Michael, who is honored as the guardian angel of the Eucharist and of the Church Militant.[2] It is not easy to judge correctly of the value of such pious opinions. The majority of them have their foundation in divine things which can be more readily conjectured than explained. — With the above-named angels, multitudes of other blessed and heavenly spirits unite in faithful co-operation[3]; hence many perceive in the petition of this prayer of the Canon for the angel's service a supplication to obtain the assistance of the angels in general.[4]

---

nuntii sint acceptabilia — sic intellegendum est offerre *sacrificia*, quia sacris mysteriis assistentes una nobiscum precantur, ut nostra munera sint accepta, et una nobiscum reverentur sanctissimum corpus Christi, sicut in coelo (S. Bonav. IV, dist. 11, p. 1, dub. 4).

[1] Angelus is, cujus manibus sacer ille minister
    In sublime geri munus utrumque rogat, '
    Angelus est *ejus*, vel quos reverenda vetustas
    Desursum missos dicit adesse sacris.
        (Hildeb. Turon. Versus de Myst. Missae.)

[2] S. Michael ecclesiam visitat et ante ejus altare stat, habens thuribulum aureum, i. e. caritatem praecipuam ad fideles, per quam eorum spiritualia sacrificia colligit Deoque offert; cui dantur incensa multa, quando Ecclesia ejus suffragia petit suasque preces per manus illius Deo offerri precatur. Quod et ille diligenter exsequitur, offerens preces et actus fidelium super altare aureum illud coeleste in patria, super quod beati laudes et preces offerunt Domino (Dion. Carthus. in Apoc. Enarr. c. 8, art. 9).

[3] Non immerito angelus videtur in templo (when Zacharias offered the sacrifice of incense), quia veri sacerdotis jam nuntiabatur adventus et coeleste sacrificium parabatur, *in quo angeli ministrarent* (S. Ambros. in Luc. l. 1, n. 24).

[4] *Singulare* nomen "sancti angeli tui" pro *plurali* positum et significantiam habere pluralem, ab expositoribus censetur (Clichtov. Elucid. eccles. l. 3, n. 41). — Forte *singulare* posuit pro *plurali*, angeli pro angelorum (Robert. Paulul. De offic. eccles. l. 2, c. 34).

We, therefore, pray that our sacrificial gifts may, through the assistance of the angels,[1] ascend on high, in the presence of the Divine Majesty, and there receive a gracious acceptance. Still this does not exhaust the profound meaning of this mystical prayer. It supplicates in addition that our oblation may be carried by the hands of angels from the earthly up to the "heavenly altar of God". This expression completes the petition for carrying up our gifts and prayers in the presence of God. — Since there can be no question of a real altar in heaven, the question arises, what is to be here understood of this celestial altar. A heavenly altar is mentioned in the Old Testament (Is. 6, 6) and in the New Testament (Apoc. 8, 5–6), as well as by the Fathers. Thus writes St. Irenaeus, that "in heaven there is an altar, to which our gifts and prayers are raised" (Adv. haeres. IV, c. 18, n. 6). The symbolism of the heavenly altar is not always the same. By an altar is properly understood the place destined for and consecrated to the offering of sacrifice — the holy place of sacrifice. Is there in heaven a place of sacrifice? Who offers there? A sacrifice in its real signification, as we have it here on earth, does not exist in heaven. But Christ appears there as Highpriest and Mediator before the face of God, and interceding

---

[1] There is no reason in this instance for departing from the ordinary signification of the word, and finding in sanctus Angelus anything more than a created angelic spirit. — According to the ancient language of the Church, the name Angelus (= nuntius, missus, legatus) often, indeed, serves to designate the second and third Persons of the Godhead; but the contents of the prayer do not require such a signification, even though it might be admissible in a certain sense. In this case there is question not of a consecrated, but only of a mediatorial action, and only the latter might, therefore, be ascribed to the God-Man or to the Holy Ghost, if we thus understood Angelus. Thus the expression per manus sancti Angeli is conceived as strengthening per Christum Dominum, which gives a good meaning; in the latter instance the mediatorial action of the angels rests on Christ. The liturgy of the Apostolic Constitution likewise (l. 8, c. 13) has: "Again and again let us beg of God, through His Christ and by His Sacrifice, offered to God our Lord, that the good God may accept the same as an agreeable odor on His heavenly altar, through the mediation of His Christ." — This prayer has also some connection with the oriental Epiklesis (Invocation), in as far at least as the latter in part proposes the imploring of the sacramental gifts of salvation; now if we would refer the word Angelus to the Holy Ghost, we would then regard Him in this place as mediator of the accomplished sacrifice, so as to make it most meritorious to us. — But some have gone still further and have understood by the action here solicited of the Angelus (Holy Ghost) a consecrating activity (perferri in sublime altare = *transmutari in corpus et sanguinem Christi*), so that this prayer would be a real Epiklesis, that is, a petition that "God would transform the bread into the sacred Body, and that which is contained in the chalice into the precious Blood of His Christ, changing both through His Holy Spirit." But as this interpretation does violence to the text, and brings into the Roman Canon of the Mass an almost insoluble difficulty (that is, the Epiklesis) of the Greek and Oriental Liturgies without sufficient reason, and contradicts the convictions of the assembled Church at the Council of Florence (1439), as well as the traditional views of liturgists and dogmaticians of all ages, — we must reject it as untenable. Cfr. Franz, Die Eucharistische Wandlung II, 98 etc.

presents to Him His wounds and His bloody death in order to apply to us the fruits of redemption. The blessed too are priests of God (Apoc. 5, 10; 20, 6); for they minister to Him day and night, and offer without intermission in and through Christ the Sacrifice of praise and thanksgiving. The altar in the Holy of Holies in heaven is, therefore, not a material place of sacrifice, but it symbolizes the heavenly sacrifice, that is, the sweet-scented incense of praise, homage and thanksgiving, which the Church glorified in union with her glorified Head, Jesus Christ, offers always and eternally to the triune God. The biblical expression of "carrying the oblation of our altar to the heavenly altar," accordingly designates the union of our earthly Sacrifice with the heavenly Sacrifice of the Church Triumphant. But as the latter is always in the presence of the Divine Majesty, that is, is indescribably pleasing and agreeable in the sight of God, so will our offering also, supported and recommended by its union with the precious Sacrifice of heaven, be admitted into the presence of God and be favorably received by Him.

As it is evident from what has been said, that the essence of this prayer consists in the petition that the sacrificial gifts of the priest and people may be graciously received by the Most High,[1] this petition is couched in wonderfully beautiful and deeply symbolical terms. For we implore Almighty God to come to the assistance of our weakness and impotence, not only by looking graciously upon us and our gifts, but, moreover, by uniting our oblation, through the ministry of the angels, with the Sacrifice of heaven and, in consequence, permitting it to ascend as a pleasing odor in His presence.[2]

---

[1] Jube haec i. e. corpus et sanguinem Christi, preces quoque ac vota nostra, perferri i. e. portari, non substantialiter, sed repraesentative per modum commemorantis atque orantis, per manus sancti Angeli tui, i. e. per obsequium Angeli, qui divinorum celebrationi interesse credendus est: imo secundum Ambrosium adest coelestis militia et secundum Bernardum angelorum adest exercitus. Quam reverenter ergo nos ibi habere oportet! In sublime altare tuum, i. e. in ipsum coelum empyreum, in quo tu specialiter habitare, sedere, regnare et exaudire cognosceris, et dum sancti angeli illuc perveniunt, vota nostra, preces et opera bona tibi offerunt: in conspectu divinae majestatis tuae i. e. coram facie tua, ita ut tu ipse ea aspicias nec vultum tuum avertas a nobis (Dion. Carthus. Expos. Missae art. 34).

[2] Sicut videmus in causis terrenis, quod qui nescit loqui coram praetore, conducit advocatum, qui loquatur et alleget pro ipso; sic in spiritualibus intellegendum, quod cum nos nec perorare, imo quasi nec balbutire sciamus coram Deo, quod Angelus tanquam advocatus et allegator magnus in illa superna curia assumit verbum et orationem nostram proponit. — Si autem quaeritur, per quem modum habeat esse, dico, quod *loqui nostrum* et oratio nostra est desiderium alicujus rei vel petitio formata secundum desiderium; et quando desiderium nostrum ex mera et vera et ardenti dilectione est, tunc fortiter clamamus in auribus Dei et tunc optime peroramus. Et quoniam affectiones nostrae sunt tepidae, et affectiones Angelorum ferventissimae et magis elevatae ad ipsum; desiderando pro nobis quod nos desideramus, cum accedant ad Deum familiarius et proximius, dicuntur *sibi offerre*, et quod Deus vidit nos primo petere et approbare per os nostrum, secundo magis approbat per os et desiderium Angelorum (S. Bonav. IV, dist. 45, dub. 7).

Pope St. Gregory the Great undoubtedly alludes to the mysteries contained in this petition, when he writes (Dial. IV, 58): "What believing soul can doubt that at the hour of the Sacrifice, upon the word of the priest, heaven opens and that choirs of angels assist at this mystery of Jesus Christ, that here the highest is combined with the lowest, the earthly united with the heavenly, the visible and invisible become one?" But how this union of the Church Militant on earth and of her Sacrifice with heaven is properly to be understood, the human mind is unable to fathom: a holy obscurity remains and shall ever remain over this prayer so rich in mysteries. The liturgies of the Middle Age give expression to this sentiment, when they exclaim with the deacon Florus, that its words are "so profound, so wonderful and inconceivable, that we ought rather to revere them with humility and a holy awe than attempt to interpret them.[1]

The concluding clause of the prayer expresses the end and object of the petition. For the Church implores so ardently for a gracious acceptance of her Sacrifice by God, in order that it may produce the greatest possible fruit in all those who communicate sacramentally or spiritually.[2] The more closely we enter into relation with the Sacrifice, which is borne from the earthly to the celestial altar, the more abundant heavenly graces and blessings flow to us as the wholesome fruit of the Sacrifice. If God allows our Sacrifice to ascend up in the presence of His Divine Majesty, then it opens to us His heavenly treasures, so that we become rich in all things, and shall be in want of no grace.[3]

b) The rite is in most exquisite harmony with the tenor of the prayer. According to a very ancient rubric[4] the priest pronounces

---

[1] Haec verba mysterii tam profunda, tam mira et stupenda quis comprehendere sufficiat? Quis inde digne aliquid loquatur? *Magis veneranda sunt et pavenda quam discutienda...* Sic cogitanda sunt, ut aliquid quo nihil sit melius atque sublimius illa cogitatione conemur attingere (De actione Missae n. 66).

[2] Id unum petit Ecclesia cum Daniele (3, 40), "*ut fiat sacrificium nostrum in conspectu Dei et placeat illi,*" h. e. ut ad Deum deferatur *oratio, actio et oblatio nostra,* atque in conspectu Dei in coelo compleatur, quod in terrestri altari peragitur, et ex praestantia coelestis victimae et ex *acceptatione sacrificii nostri* in nos deinde omnis benedictio descendat. Hoc subsequentia verba confirmant. Vota nempe nostra ascendere ad Deum cupimus, "ut quotquot ex hac altaris participatione sacros. Filii tui corpus et sanguinem sumpserimus, omni benedictione coelesti et gratia repleamur." In altari est corpus et sanguis Christi: ex illo sumendum est nobis; sed rogandus divinus ejus Pater, ut *actio hominum peccatorum tam sanctam hostiam offerentium ab eo clementer accipiatur:* tunc enim omnis benedictio coelestis et gratia e coelesti isto convivio et sacrificio est nobis speranda (Muratori, De rebus liturgicis dissertatio c. 21).

[3] Tunc a Deo (hostia) quasi acceptatur, quando Deus nobis propitiatur et coelestis benedictio nobis ab eo mittitur (B. Odo Camer. Expos. in Can. Missae dist. 3).

[4] Sacerdos quando dicit "Supplices te rogamus," *humiliato* capite *inclinat se* ante altare (Ordo Rom. II, n. 10. Cfr. Amalarius l. 3, c. 25; Microlog. c. 16). — In many places the hands were placed over the breast in the form of a cross at the same time. Sacerdos dicendo "Supplices..." stat *inclinatus cancellatis* (= with

the petition of the principal clause with a profound inclination of the body (*profunde inclinatus*), to indicate the humility and fervor with which he implores of Almighty God such high and great things.[1]— Before the words: "by partaking at this altar" (*ex hac altaris participatione*), the priest, full of burning love and profound reverence, kisses the altar, so as to unite himself with the Sacrificial Lamb, whom he sends up to heaven. — He then stands erect and, at the words "Body and Blood", he makes the sign of the Cross over the oblation in token that through them, from the Cross, the plenitude of all heavenly blessing and grace flows to us. By the act of signing himself with the Cross at the end, he would apply the abundant, overflowing benediction of the altar to himself and to the congregation. — That the Sacrifice ascends from earth to heaven, and the blessing of Heaven descends upon us, we are indebted to the one only fountain of all grace, to our one and perfect Mediator between Heaven and earth; hence the petition concludes with the words: "Through the same Christ our Lord. Amen."

62. The Second Prayer of the Canon after the Consecration.

1. Inasmuch as our Sacrifice is carried by the hands of angels from the earthly to the heavenly altar and united with the homages of the blessed, and thus presented before the throne of God, it becomes in a most sublime sense a fountain of living waters, that descend in a strong stream (Cant. 4, 15) upon the earth and into the flaming abyss of purgatory, to refresh and revive the suffering children of the Church. Hence the Church feels urged to beg for the application of the spiritual and heavenly waters of salvation. This she does, in the first place, in the concluding petition of the previous prayer in behalf of all who by Communion partake of the Sacrifice; but in her flight to heaven, she is still mindful of her children, whether they be suffering in the abode of purification or are still pilgrims on earth. She prays, therefore, not only for the Communicants, but moreover intercedes (*Memento etiam*) for the departed, to obtain admittance for them into heaven, and she endeavors also to implore for all those present (*nobis quoque*) participation in the glory of the saints.

---

crossformed × held) *manibus* ante pectus (Durand. 1. 4, c. 44, n. 4). — Cum dicit "Supplices...", manibus cancellatis ante pectus, ita quod dextrum brachium sit supra sinistrum, inclinet ante altare (Ordo Rom. XIV, c. 53). The Carmelites, Carthusians and Dominicans still observe this rite. — Some Missals of the Middle Age have in this place a special rubric; for example, Hic orat apud se quod voluerit, deinde dicit: *Jube haec.* — Hic orat apud se inclinatus quae velit. *Jube.* (Gerbert. Vetus Liturg. alemann. I, 363. — Cfr. Tewtsch Rational Kap. 15.)

1 Supplicamus tibi, curvamur ante te, obnixius deprecamur, ostende omnipotentiam, extende manum validam, ut quae propitio ac sereno vultu respicis, etiam ad invisibilia et sublimia tua perferantur et conspectui majestatis admittas. Hic necessitas incurvationis, hic opus supplicationis, hic incumbit consummatio totius nostri laboris, ut haec hostia perferatur in sublime altare tuum (B. Odo Camerac. Expos. in Canon. Missae dist. 3).

Memento etiam, Domine, famulorum famularumque tuarum N. et N., qui nos praecesserunt cum signo fidei, et dormiunt in somno pacis. — Ipsis, Domine, et omnibus in Christo quiescentibus, locum refrigerii, lucis et pacis, ut indulgeas, deprecamur. Per eundem Christum Dominum nostrum. Amen.

Remember also, O Lord, Thy servants and handmaids, N. and N., who have gone before us with the sign of faith, and sleep the sleep of peace. — To these, O Lord, and to all who rest in Christ, grant, we beseech Thee, a place of refreshment, of light, and of peace. Through Christ our Lord. Amen.

The practice of the Church of offering the Holy Sacrifice for the departed and of praying for them during its celebration, dates from Apostolic times and is an Apostolic ordinance,[1] as the ancient liturgies and the writings of the Fathers clearly prove. The present Commemoration of the Dead said in silence had its origin probably in the twelfth century, when the custom was discontinued in this place of reading out publicly the names of the departed, of whom special remembrance was to be made.[2] The liturgical Commemoration for the departed is in many respects different from that of the living. This distinction is evident even from the position of the Memento of the living: the one is placed before and the other after the Consecration[3]; and this is quite proper.[4] As members of the Church Militant on earth, the living may and ought to unite with the priest in offering the Sacrifice, and in the Sacrifice offer themselves therewith. This is most fittingly done before the accomplishment of the real sacrificial action, that is, before the Consecration;

---

[1] In Machabaeorum libris legimus, oblatum pro mortuis sacrificium; sed etsi nusquam in Scripturis veteribus omnino legeretur, non parva est universae Ecclesiae, quae in hac consuetudine claret, auctoritas, ubi in precibus sacerdotis, quae Domino Deo ad ejus altare funduntur, locum suum habet etiam *commendatio mortuorum* (S. Aug. De cura pro mort. gerenda c. 1, n. 3).

[2] This prayer (as also the commemoratio pro vivis) was in former times often inscribed: Oratio super diptycha, or Oratio post nomina. — Post illa verba, quibus dicitur *in somno pacis*, usus fuit antiquorum, sicut etiam usque hodie romana agit Ecclesia, ut statim recitarentur ex diptychis, i. e. tabulis nomina defunctorum atque ita post lectionem nominum subjungerentur verba sequentia: *Ipsis*, videlicet quorum nomina memorantur, et ceteris *omnibus in Christo quiescentibus indulgeas locum refrigerii*, ubi non sentitur ardor poenarum (Pseudo-Alcuin. c. 40).

[3] Hic pro defunctis in Christo quiescentibus orat Ecclesia, ut iis haec prosint sacramenta, ubi notare poteris *nomina quae volueris*. Et quidem *congrue* haec interseritur memoria transeuntium, "qui in Domino moriuntur." Finita est enim memoria mortis Domini et sequitur mors nostra; Christus praecessit et nos ejus vestigia sequimur (Sicard. 1. 3, c. 6).

[4] Both Mementoes underwent manifold additions, inasmuch as express mention was made of various states and classes of persons. Also their position was long subject to change; for it often happened that the Memento of the Dead was joined to the Memento vivorum before the Consecration.

with regard to this circumstance, which is mentioned in the Memento of the living (*qui tibi offerunt*), it is most appropriately placed before the Consecration. The departed, on the contrary, are no longer in a state to unite in offering, but merely partake of the fruits of the Sacrifice which we apply to them; hence it is most proper to be mindful of them when the Sacrificial Victim is resting on the altar. The Church neither offers nor prays for the reprobates in hell, nor for the blessed in heaven, but only for the suffering souls who, amid the pains of purgatory, await their final and complete redemption. Corresponding to this intention, the formula[1] of the Church in the Memento for the Dead is so constituted that it suits only the inmates of the place of purification.

2. "Remember also, O Lord, Thy servants and handmaids, N. and N., who have gone before us with the sign of faith, and sleep the sleep of peace." Here[2] the priest should expressly and by name commemorate some of the departed, that is, he should recall or even mention them, in order to recommend them in a special manner to the favor and mercy of God. Whilst so doing, he must keep his eyes constantly directed to the Most Holy Sacrament (*intentis oculis ad Sacramentum super altare* — Rubr.), while at the Commemoration of the Living only a slight inclination of the head (*demisso aliquantulum capite* — Rubr.) is prescribed, and not that the eyes be fixed on the holy Host.[3] The selection of the names is left to the priest, who can and should in this place comply with obligations of gratitude and love toward those of the dead, who during life in any manner were related to or connected with him. But since the Memento is made in the name of the Church, that is, since it is a public intercession, the celebrant must adhere to the ordinance expressed in the text itself. For the Church prays here in a special manner for those "who have gone before us with the sign of faith, and sleep the sleep of peace," that is, who as true believers and as living members of the Church have departed this earthly life in the Communion of the Church.[4] Accordingly, all are here excluded

---

[1] A monumental commentary on these prayers and, at the same time, a proof of their great antiquity is established by the ancient Christian epitaphs, the various forms of which (acclamations, salutations, wishes, petitions) contain principally the words refrigerium — lux — pax, by which the bliss of heaven, under different aspects, is expressed. In the "lapidary prayers" of these tumular inscriptions the survivors wish to their departed, v. g., refreshment, light, peace, admission into paradise and the communion of saints, life in God, in Christ, and in the Holy Ghost. Entirely similar expressions are met with in the prayers of the Sacram. Gelasian., for example, locus lucidus, locus refrigerii et quietis — refrigerii sedes, quietis beatitudo, luminis claritas — lucis et pacis regio.

[2] That is, not at the letters N. and N., but after the words in somno pacis. During the first thousand years they wrote instead of N. the letters *ill.* diagonally.

[3] In Memento pro vivis tenentur oculi demissi vel clausi ad vitandam mentis distractionem; hic vero intenti ad Sacramentum teneri debent, quia ex Christi praesentia major devotio excitatur (Quarti p. 2, tit. 9, n. 2).

[4] St. Cyril of Jerusalem writes (5. Mystical Catechism, chap. 9): "During the Holy Sacrifice we make intercession for all collectively who among us (ἐν ἡμῖν, that

from the commemoration by name, inasmuch as it is a liturgical prayer of the Church, who have died outside the pale of the Church, as was formerly the case, when names were read out from the dip-tychs. The same rule applies to the liturgical Memento as to the offering of the Holy Sacrifice of the Mass, which is forbidden for deceased Non-Catholics.[1] — To move the Lord to pity and to indul-gence, the Church calls her suffering children in purgatory the ser-vants and handmaids of God, and lays stress thereon that they have departed from this world with the sign of faith. By the sign of faith (*signum fidei*) is here to be understood, in the first place, the indel-ible character imprinted on the soul in the Sacrament of Baptism, and whereby the faithful are distinguished from unbelievers.[2] Bap-tism is, indeed, called the Sacrament of Faith; by it men become united to Christ and incorporated with the Church. Furthermore, by the sign of faith the profession of faith is also to be understood, that is, the profession by word and deed, by a Christian life, by devotion to the Church, by the reception of the holy Sacraments. Faith received in holy baptism must necessarily be a living faith and be persevered in unto death, if it is to lead unto salvation.[3] — All who have passed into eternity with such a faith and its profession,

---

is, in the bosom of the Church, as members of the Church) are departed." This has been at all times the practice of the Church.

[1] The distinction between the ecclesiastical Memento for the Living and the Memento for the Dead must be carefully observed. From the former are excluded merely the Excommunicati *vitandi*, because for them not even a direct application may be made; from the second, on the contrary, in general all that have died sep-arated from the Church (unbelievers, heretics, schismatics, excommunicated persons): for these — in case they are suffering in purgatory — the Church prays not by name, but only in general, as is the case in the Memento (*omnibus* in Christo quiescentibus). As a private individual and in his private intention, the priest may in both Mementoes make intercession for all without distinction. Facile stat, ipsum sacerdotem talem ceremoniam (sc. Memento) ut *personam publicam* per-ficere et (futurum) sacrificium ex persona Ecclesiae Deo offerre — et tamen *simul* *ut privatum* illud ipsum offerre Deumque per ipsum pro aliquo deprecari (Coninck, De sacr. et censur. disp. 14, dub. 6).

[2] Orat pia Mater Ecclesia non solum pro vivis, sed etiam pro defunctis et eos sacrae oblationis intercessione commendat certissime credens, quod sanguis ille pretiosus, qui pro multis effusus est in remissionem peccatorum, non solum ad salutem viventium, verum etiam ad absolutionem valeat defunctorum, qui cum *signo fidei* praecedunt. . . Signum fidei pro charactere christianitatis accipitur, quo fideles ab infidelibus discernuntur (Innoc. III. 1. 5, c. 5).

[3] In like manner the Church prays at the blessing of a cemetery, that the Shepherd of eternal glory may not cease "to impart to the bodies that repose in this place, continual inviolability, that all the baptized who to the end of their life persevere in the Catholic faith (quicunque Baptismi sacramentum perceperint et in fide catholica usque ad vitae terminum perseverantes fuerint), and after the com-pletion of the earthly pilgrimage commit their bodies to rest in this cemetery, at the sound of the Angel's trumpet, united in body and soul, may be admitted to the eternal rewards of the joys of heaven." (Cfr. Pontif. Roman. De coemeterii benedictione.)

"sleep the sleep of peace" (*dormiunt in somno pacis*), that is, they died in peace with the Church, united interiorly and exteriorly to the Church, in communion with the Church.[1] Death in the grace and love of God, in living communion with Christ and the Church, may in addition be designated as a peaceful slumber, inasmuch as the weary pilgrim of earth reposes in the grave far removed from all the combats, sufferings, labors of life, and awaits a blissful awakening, a glorious resurrection of the body.[2]

The intercession for the dead is continued and developed. Not merely upon "these" (*ipsis*), that is, those just mentioned, but upon "all who rest in Christ" (*omnibus in Christo quiescentibus*),[3] the blessing of the all-atoning redeeming Blood from the altar is to flow.[4] The Church forgets none of her children; she is full of maternal care and solicitude for all, — in particular she ceases not to pray for her poor sorrowing children in purgatory, until they have reached their heavenly Father's house. As in this Memento, so likewise in other liturgical formulas of prayer, the special intercession

---

[1] In pace — vixit in pace — vitam duxit in pace — in pace morienti — decessit in pace fidei catholicae — credidit fide, dormit in pace — requiescit in pace — requiescit in somno pacis — these and similar formulas on ancient Christian graves prove that the departed lived in the orthodox faith and in the communion of the Church, or at least departed therein. This applies especially to places in which a heresy or schism prevailed.

[2] In Holy Writ, the Fathers and the liturgy death (of the just) is often called dormitio, somnus, and the dead are called dormientes. That death is but a passing sleep, is also signified by the name *coemeterium* (κοιμητήριον, dormitorium, place of slumber), by which the Church from the most ancient times designates the (blessed) burial-place. *Cymiterium* recubitorium vel dormitorium est mortuorum, qui et ideo ab Ecclesia *dormientes* dicuntur, quia resurrecturi non dubitantur (Walafr. Strabo, De rebus ecclesiast. c. 6). — Prudentius calls (Cathemer. X, 56) the body of a Christian resting in the vault a res non mortua, sed *data somno*, as the Lord Himself said of the departed daughter of Jairus: Non est mortua puella, sed *dormit* (Matth. 9, 24).

[3] With reference to the Apoc. 14, 13: Amodo jam dicit Spiritus, ut *requiescant* a laboribus suis, as it says of them, qui in *Domino* moriuntur, the departed are often called quiescentes (in Christo), but in the Mozarabic Missal they are called pausantes according to the Greek appellation. We likewise meet the words: requietoria, requietionis loca, sedes requietionis, as designations of the Christian cemetery. In the benedictio coemeterii the Church prays, that the consecrated place may be dulcis requies et pausatio mortuorum. By the words aeternae pausationis solatium in the Mozarabic Liturgy eternal rest is implored for the departed (on the feast of St. Eulalia of Emerita, Dec. 10). — In Purgatorio etiam est requies propter certitudinem de salute, suffragia vivorum et consolationem Angelorum. Mors justo est requies, somnus, cessatio a labore et dolore, recreatio (Cornel. a Lap. in Sap. 4, 7).

[4] Non sunt praetermittendae supplicationes pro spiritibus mortuorum, quas faciendas *pro omnibus in christiana et catholica societate defunctis* . . . sub generali commemoratione suscepit Ecclesia, ut quibus ad ista desunt parentes aut filii aut quicunque cognati vel amici, ab una eis exhibeatur *matre communi* (S. Aug. De cura pro mortuis gerenda c. 4).

for individual departed souls is principally united with supplication for all the faithful departed.[1] "In Christ rest" those who "have died in the Lord" (Apoc. 14, 13), that is, in the grace of God, in the communion of life and love with Christ. They rest from their labors; "for the life of man upon earth is a warfare and his days are like the days of a hireling; as a servant he longeth for the shade, and as a hireling looketh for the end of his work" (Job. 7, 1–2).

But how can the Church, for those who "sleep in peace and rest in Christ," still implore "a place of refreshment, of light and of peace?"[2] The suffering souls enjoy, indeed, peace and rest, inasmuch as they are removed from the discord and turmoil of this sinful and deceitful world; but as long as they must remain at a distance from the vision of God in a place of silent suffering, their peace and rest are still imperfect; therefore, we implore for them full and eternal peace, full and eternal rest — in heaven. When the just soul has reached purgatory, she sees before her but two objects — the excess of her suffering and the excess of her joy. The greatest bitterness is there mingled with the most serene peace. These souls are full of pure and strong love of God, full of patient contentment, full of touching resignation to God's holy decrees. — Hence they praise purgatory as an invention of His mercy; but, at the same time, they are consumed with the flames of longing for God, with the fire of pains, and with the pains of fire. Full of quiet sorrow they linger in the place of their banishment, weeping tears at the thought of the Heavenly Jerusalem and because their exile in a foreign country is prolonged. In a manner inexplicable to us, they are at one and the same time filled with a holy suffering and a holy joy. Suffering is not unhappiness.[3] In contrast with the painful exile of purgatory, heaven is indeed a blissful place of refreshment, of light and of peace.

A place of *refreshment (locus refrigerii).*[4] Purgatory is like

---

[1] Cfr., for example, the Requiem Mass, in which the Introitus, Tractus, Offertorium and Communio refer to all the departed, though even the celebration is offered for one individual soul.

[2] Apte instituta est haec oratio, ut iis *solis* conveniret, qui in Purgatorio degunt: hi enim et pacem ac quietem eo sensu habent, quod jam certi sint de futuro aeternae beatitudinis praemio, et liberi a tentationum ac concupiscentiae bello; est tamen, unde iis ulterius et refrigerium ac pacem deprecemur, quia et flammis torquentur et quamdiu a divino, quem toti inhiant, conspectu arcentur, omnimoda pace frui non possunt (Tournely, De Eucharist. p. 2, c. 10, art. 3).

[3] There is simultaneously in the souls in purgatory both an *ineffable joy* and an *ineffable suffering*, without the one preventing the other (S. Catherine de Gênes, Le Purgatoire, chap. 12, éd. P. M. Bouix S. J., Paris 1882). Cfr. Briefe über das Fegfeuer. Regensburg 1883. — Bautz, Das Fegfeuer. Mainz 1883.

[4] *Refrigerium* here denotes a twofold refreshment. In the first place it signifies (from refrigerare = to make something cold, to cool it) the ceasing of poena *sensus;* that is, the extinguishing of the heat of purgatory. This is shown also by the following petitions from the Mozarabic Missal: animam pietate tua *refrigerii rore perfundas* — animam *coelestis roris perfusione refrigera.* Let us think of

unto a barren and arid desert. Unspeakably great is the intensity and violence of the sufferings in which the poor souls languish. The world and its joys, the earth and its possessions no longer fascinate and enchain them. They have but one desire, that of beholding God. Not yet to possess, not to be able to enjoy the Supreme Good, the fountain source of all beauty and sweetness, — is their most severe pain. — Moreover, they are obliged to undergo torments in the flames of fire, created expressly by the justice of God for their purification, and as a chastisement for all infidelities in the service of God, for the abuse of grace. Hence they sigh for mitigation, refreshment and coolness (*refrigerium*) in the torturing regions of that consuming fire. As the fresh dew of heaven invigorates the drooping flowers, and as a mild rain refreshes the parched earth, thus does the Blood of the New Covenant rush in torrents into the water-less sea (Zach. 9, 11), to soothe, console and quicken these souls suffering so intensely. In fact, by the power of the Eucharistic Sacrifice they are led to the place of eternal refreshment, that is, to the holy mountain, where they shall no longer hunger and thirst, where "neither the sun shall fall on them nor any heat," but where the Lamb shall rule and lead them to the fountains of the waters of life, and where God shall wipe away all tears from their eyes (Apoc. 7, 15—17). There also they shall eat of the tree of life; there the hidden manna shall regale them; there they shall be seated at the table of the feast and heavenly nuptials; there they shall be inebriated with the plenty of God's house and be satiated with the torrent of divine pleasure (Ps. 35, 9).[1]

A place of *light (locus lucis)*[2] is, therefore, heaven. The

---

sprinkling the corpses and graves with holy water. — Refrigerium also frequently denotes refreshment by food and drink, with a meal (inopes *refrigerio* isto juva-mus, writes Tertullian of the Agapae — Apolog. c. 39). Therefore, we may here understand the remission of poena *damni*, that is, the cessation of the temporal exclusion from the visio beatifica by the granting of beatitude. Heavenly bliss is often represented under the figure of a nuptial celebration and a joyful banquet. Cfr. the concluding formulas of the liturgical blessing at meals: *Mensae coelestis* participes faciat nos rex aeternae gloriae — Ad *coenam vitae aeternae* perducat nos rex aeternae gloriae. Many epitaphs also contain the word, for example, in refrigerio anima tua — cujus spiritum in refrigerium suscipiat Dominus — Antonia anima dulcis tibi Deus refrigeret — Victoria refrigereris spiritus tuus in bono.

[1] Refrigerium (ἀνάψυξις, ἀναψυξή, ἄνεσις) = refreshment, often occurs in the ancient Christian Latin and designates that which is, contains and affords refreshment, recreation, regalement, alleviation, relief, solace, rest, comfort, joy, felicity, — hence mainly the state of the blessed after death. Supplicia jam illic et *refrigeria* — regionem .... interim *refrigerium* praebituram animabus justorum — obtinebunt *refrigerii locum* — ad *refrigerium* justi vocantur, ad supplicium rapiuntur injusti — Lazarus videtur in sinu Abrahae *loco*que *refrigerii*. (Cfr. Rönsch, Itala und Vulgata S. 421.)

[2] Cfr., for example, the epitaphs: Deus te deprecor ut paradisum lucis possit videre — Aeterna tibi lux — cujus spiritus in luce Domini susceptus est — in Christum credens premia lucis abet.

heavenly city has need neither of the sun nor of the moon; for the glory of God hath enlightened it, and the Lamb is the lamp thereof. The gates thereof shall not be shut by day; for there shall be no night there (Apoc. 21, 23). On the contrary, in the region of purgatory obscurity and darkness prevail; hence the expiating souls long so ardently for the celestial kingdom of eternal splendor, where in the light of glory they may behold the Eternal Light.

And, finally, a place of *peace (locus pacis)*[1] is heaven. The heavenly Jerusalem is the holy city of peace (*beata pacis visio*); its inhabitants rejoice in divine peace and are blissful in love (Tob. 13, 18); as a river God brings peace upon them (Is. 66, 12). The bright starlit heavens of midnight foreshadow how unspeakably blissful is the stream of peace enjoyed in the city of God. For this sweet, untroubled and immutable peace of heaven the suffering souls of purgatory long intensely.

3. At the concluding formula "Through the same Christ our Lord," the priest not only joins his hands, but also bows his head. The inclination of the head at this point and at the words is singular, as otherwise it is nowhere prescribed when the name of "Christ" occurs without the addition of Jesus. It must, therefore, be grounded in the text of the prayer itself and have some mysterious signification.[2] When dying, Christ bowed His head on the Cross and then descended into the depths of the kingdom of the dead, there to console the devout who lived previous to His coming, and to deliver them from their captivity. This the priest would now call to mind by bowing his head, since he here prays and implores for all that rest in Christ, that the atoning Blood, flowing from the Eucharistic Sacrifice as from a fountain, may flow into purgatory to alleviate and abridge the sufferings of the poor souls.

Outside of the gates of Rome there is a church which bears the

---

[1] The formula *in pace* is frequently met with on ancient Christian graves: for instance, Victori in pace — vale in pace — in pace Domini dormias — tecum pax Christi — Gaudentia suscepeatur in pace — te in pace Christus faciat — semper vive in pace — cum Deo in pace — pax cum angelis — Laurinia melle dulcior quiescas in pace — Gensane pax ispirito tuo — dormit in somno pacis — pausat in pace — in pace requievit — quiescit in pace aeterna — susceptus in pace — accercitus in pacem — natus in pace — mater dulcissima in pace Christi recepta — letaris in pace — in pace delicium — vivis in gloria Dei et in pace Domini nostri.

[2] This bowing cannot be occasioned by either the preceding deprecamur (as de Vert asserts), or by the following Nobis quoque peccatoribus (as Gavantius supposes); for in that case the action would be combined with the words in question. In hoc ego magis peculiare dicerem adesse mysterium, et est, quod ibi sermo est de Christo, in quo mortui quiescunt, et omnibus in Christo quiescentibus; quare cum Christus mortem nostram moriendo destruxerit, repraesentat sibi sacerdos Christum morientem, qui *inclinato capite* emisit spiritum. In memoriam igitur et venerationem *illius gestus, quo Christus mortuus est, sacerdos inclinat caput,* nisi mavis dicere, *inclinationem* fieri in commemorationem *descensus, quem ad inferos fecit Christi spiritus pro liberandis mortuis* (Cavalieri III, c. 11, n. 4). — Cfr. Quarti p. 3, tit. 9, n. 2.

name of Holy Mary, Ladder of Heaven (*S. Maria Scala Coeli*).
When St. Bernard was residing in the Convent of Sts. Vincent and
Anastasius near by, he celebrated the Holy Sacrifice in the above-
named church for the departed, during which he was shown in a
vision, how the souls delivered thereby ascended to heaven on a
ladder accompanied by angels. This apparition, which gave the
name to the church, and which is represented in its altar-piece,
proves what an abundance of wealth we possess in the Holy Sacrifice to relieve the want and poverty of the suffering souls. On the
altar flow the fountains of the Saviour; let us draw thence and pour
the atoning Blood into the place of purification to extinguish its
flames. What thoughts, what sentiments, what love should animate
us when we, like choirs of earthly angels, look down on that silent,
boundless kingdom of suffering souls, and then gather the balm of
the redeeming Blood of Christ at the altar as in golden vessels, and
pour it out over them, that they may be refreshed and, freed from
the sea of fire, may wing their way to the abodes of eternal peace!

63. The Third Prayer of the Canon after the Consecration.

1. The Commemoration of the Dead is for the living a solemn
and touching *Memento mori*. It reminds us of those who on this
earthly pilgrimage "have gone before us" (*nos praecesserunt*)[1] and
have arrived in the land of eternity. We follow them rapidly and
incessantly. Behold, the short years, — they pass away rapidly,
and we are walking in a path by which we shall not return (Job. 16,
23)! We are strangers and new-comers upon earth, as were all our
fathers. Our days are as a shadow on earth, and there is no permanent remaining (1 Paral. 29, 15). Soon we shall be standing on
the brink of the grave. As these thoughts come up, what is more
natural than for us to desire that the Lord would receive us into the
eternal dwellings of light? Therefore, this petition most appropriately follows the Memento for the Dead.[2]

Nobis quoque peccatoribus famulis tuis, de multitudine miserationum tuarum sperantibus,	To us also, Thy sinful servants, who hope in the multitude of Thy mercies, vouchsafe to grant some

---

[1] These words are also found on epitaphs; for example, quae nos praecesserunt
in somno pacis — in pace precessit — precessit nos in pace — praecessit ad pacem.
— In the Mozarabic Mass for the vigil of Pentecost the departed are called: nostri,
qui jam a seculo precesserunt.

[2] Originally this prayer was a special supplication for the priests and clerics
assisting at the altar, or for the whole clergy in general — and may now still be
suitably and principally recited for this intention. The clergy are in a strict and
eminent sense God's servants (famuli). Sicut patet in Canone Missae, cum dicitur
"Nobis quoque peccatoribus," statutum est, quod sacerdos offerat etiam pro se,
quod non fieret, nisi esset infirmitate peccatorum, quibus est circumdatus, non op-
pressus. Si enim sit in mortali peccato, non debet celebrare (S. Thom. In epist. ad
Hebr. c. 5, lect. 1).

partem aliquam et societatem
donare digneris, cum tuis sanctis
Apostolis et Martyribus: cum
Joanne, Stephano, Matthia,
Barnaba, Ignatio, Alexandro,
Marcellino, Petro, Felicitate,
Perpetua, Agatha, Lucia, Agnete,
Caecilia, Anastasia, et omnibus
sanctis tuis: intra quorum nos
consortium, non aestimator me-
riti, sed veniae, quaesumus,
largitor admitte. Per Christum
Dominum nostrum.[1]

part and fellowship with Thy
holy Apostles and Martyrs: with
John, Stephen, Matthias, Barnaby, Ignatius, Alexander, Marcellinus, Peter, Felicitas, Perpetua,
Agatha, Lucy, Agnes, Cecilia,
Anastasia, and all Thy Saints:
into whose company, not weigh-
ing our merits, but granting us
pardon, we beseech Thee to
admit us. Through Christ our
Lord.

The first three words "to us also, Thy sinful servants" (*nobis
quoque peccatoribus*) are the only words in the Canon that are said
in a slightly raised tone of voice, that is, half aloud (*elata parum
voce*); the priest at the same time strikes his breast.[2] Both (the
somewhat loud tone of voice and the striking of the breast) indicate
to the celebrant with what great sorrow and compunction he is to
make the acknowledgment of his sinfulness, and admonish all the
faithful present, to unite with the officiating priest in these selfsame
penitential sentiments which animate him, since he recites this
prayer also for them and in their name.[3] We acknowledge and confess ourselves in all humility to be but poor sinners, for we thereby
draw on ourselves God's favor and mercy. Yes, sinners we are all
before God, and great sinners indeed. This we shall profoundly and

---

[1] The contents and connection of the Canon prayers after the Consecration are
concisely and clearly shown by St. Thomas. Sacerdos accedit ad ipsam consecrationem, in qua 1. petit consecrationis effectum (*Quam oblationem* ...); 2. consecrationem peragit per verba Salvatoris (*Qui pridie* ...); 3. excusat praesump-
tionem per obedientiam ad mandatum Christi (*Unde et memores* ...); 4. petit hoc
sacrificium peractum esse Deo acceptum (*Supra quae* ...); 5. petit hujus sacrificii
et sacramenti effectum — primo quidem quantum ad ipsos sumentes (*Supplices
te* ...), secundo quantum ad mortuos (*Memento etiam* ...), tertio specialiter
quantum ad ipsos sacerdotes offerentes (*Nobis quoque* ...). S. Thom. 3, q. 83, a. 4.

[2] Dicentes: *Nobis quoque peccatoribus,* vocem *paululum elevamus,* ut ex
gemitu cordis in silentio procedat gemens oris confessio. .. Cum dicitur: *Nobis
quoque peccatoribus,* solet rumpi silentium, paululum expressa voce proferendo, ut
veniat nobis in mentem latronis *confessio* et pietas Domini de cruce dicentis:
"Hodie mecum eris in paradiso"—Luc. c. 23 (Steph. Augustod. c. 17). — Percussura
pectoris poenitentiae est et luctus indicium (Amalar. l. 3, c. 26).

[3] Ut facilius exaudiatur sacerdos captetque Dei benevolentiam, *peccatorem se
et alios vivos* (quos eodem pronomine quo se signat et includit) pronuntiat, quoniam nihil aeque divinam majestatem inflectit ad impendendam hominibus misericordiam, quam humilis peccatorum recognitio atque confessio, qua quis se indignum
fatetur ex se ipso divinis beneficiis, sed totam suam fiduciam collocat atque reponit
in Dei misericordia (Clichtov. Elucidat. eccles. l. 3, n. 24).

sorrowfully realize, if we but sincerely examine our entire life. Filled with shame we shall then have to acknowledge, alas, so many sins and yet so little penance! "If Thou, O Lord, wilt mark iniquities; Lord, who shall stand it?" (Ps. 129, 3.) "The sins of my youth and my ignorances do not remember. According to Thy mercy remember Thou me, for Thy goodness' sake, O Lord!" (Ps. 24, 7.) — To obtain admittance into the kingdom of heaven we must pray for it, inasmuch as we place all our confidence in the greatness and abundance of the divine mercies (*de multitudine miserationum tuarum sperantibus*).[1] — Animated with this sentiment we cry out to God, that He would mercifully grant us "some part and fellowship" (*partem aliquam et societatem*) with His holy Apostles and Martyrs.[2] The immaculate and imperishable inheritance of the kingdom of heaven is prepared for the totality of the redeemed; but the individual man will share therein according to the measure of his merits, virtue and holiness. All the happiness of the citizens of heaven proceeds from God's eternal and infinite glory. Our possession, our inheritance, our share in the land of the living will be God Himself — the clear vision, the ravishing love and the blissful enjoyment of God. "For what have I in heaven, and besides Thee what do I desire upon earth? For Thee, O Lord! my flesh and my heart hath fainted away; Thou art the God of my heart, and the God that is my portion forever" (*pars mea Deus in aeternum*) (Ps. 72, 25. 26). — The possession of the Supreme Good will, therefore, be imparted to us in union and in communion with the other blessed; the ravishing society of all the other citizens of heaven is a fresh source of the purest, sweetest joys.[3] — Of the saints of heaven some

---

[1] Cfr. Miserere mei Deus, secundum magnam misericordiam tuam, et secundum *multitudinem miserationum tuarum* dele iniquitatem meam (Ps. 50, 1. 2). Misericordia = mercy, compassion as a virtue or disposition (habitus); on the contrary, miseratio = the feeling sympathy, the pardoning as actualization and proof (actus) of a merciful disposition (usus sive effectus misericordiae — S. Thom.). — Hence the Lord in the Psalms is often called misericors et miserator — sc. *misericors* in affectu benignitatis intus abscondito et sibi naturaliter insito, *miserator* in effectu foris conspicuo (Gerhoh. Reichersp. in Ps. 24). — Misericordia prout in Deo esse censetur non est nisi *bonitas* ejus *piissima;* miseratio autem Dei est effectus misericordiae ejus. *Multae* ergo possunt esse *miserationes* Dei, quoniam multa sunt opera pietatis divinae, sed misericordia Dei non est nisi una, quae est divina essentia (Dion. Carthus. in Ps. 24). — Major est *multitudo* Dei *miserationum*, quam multitudo omnium peccatorum (Gerhoh. Reichersp. l. c.). — Cfr., moreover, the wonderfully beautiful and deep prayer: Omnipotens sempiterne Deus, qui *abundantia pietatis tuae* et merita supplicum excedis et vota: effunde super nos misericordiam tuam, ut dimittas quae conscientia metuit, et adjicias quod oratio non praesumit (Dom. XI. p. Pent.).

[2] The words "God give you a portion (κλῆρον) and a share (μερίδα) with His saints" (μετὰ τῶν ἀγίων αὐτοῦ) occur already in a letter of St. Polycarp to the Philippians (c. 12), written about the year 107, and are probably taken from the Apostolic liturgy.

[3] Quarto consistit (vita aeterna) in omnium beatorum jucunda *societate*, quae societas erit maxime delectabilis, quia quilibet habebit omnia bona cum omnibus

Apostles and Martyrs are mentioned by name in the prayer (*Nobis quoque*); fifteen in all (eight male and seven female saints), who all underwent the violent death of martyrdom.

2. a) At the head of the list in the prayer is St. John the Baptist,[1] as the enumeration of the male saints is regulated by the time of their martyrdom. In the profoundest seclusion from the world he prepared himself by a life of contemplation and severe asceticism for his vocation, to go before the face of the Lord, to prepare His ways, to give knowledge of salvation to His people, unto the remission of their sins (Luke 1, 76–77). His whole appearance and penitential preaching made a wonderful impression on the people. He closed his blessed labors by a martyr's death, for he was beheaded, because he had freely and severely censured the adulterous union of Herod with Herodias. His martyrdom is celebrated on August twenty-ninth (*Festum decollationis S. Joannis Bapt.*). — Through heavenly revelation his head was later on found, and is now preserved and honored in the ancient Church of *S. Silvestro in Capite*. St. John has ever been highly honored in the Church; numerous churches are dedicated to him; many cities and countries have chosen him as their patron.

b) St. Stephen leads[2] the brilliant host of Christian Martyrs, who, after the death of the Saviour, shed their blood for divine truth. He belongs to those seven wise and pious men who were ordained as the first deacons[3] by the Apostles; but, before all the others, he is praised in Holy Scripture as a man "full of grace and strength," "full of faith and of the Holy Ghost," "who did great signs and miracles among the people." As deacon, with loving solicitude, he exercised the charge of caring for the poor and the sick; he likewise, with great wisdom and power, preached the doctrine of Christ to the Jews. They obstinately resisted him, and in their fury they stoned to death this courageous preacher of the truth, which they hated. This took place in the Valley of Josaphat at the Brook Cedron. Yet "the stones of the brook were sweet to him," says the Church, at the same time putting these words in his mouth: "Because my flesh was

---

beatis; nam quilibet diliget alium sicut seipsum et ideo gaudebit de bono alterius sicut de suo. Quo fit, ut tantum augeatur laetitia et gaudium unius, quantum est gaudium omnium. Ps. 86, 7: Sicut laetantium omnium habitatio est in te (S. Thom. In Symbol. Apostol. expos. n. 39).

[1] S. R. C. 27. Mart. 1824. The opinion, very general during the Middle Age, that the Apostle and Evangelist John is here named a second time, is no longer tenable.

[2] The name μάρτυς = testis is given to St. Stephen for the first time by St. Paul (Acts 22, 20). By the Fathers he is styled ἀπαρχὴ τῶν μαρτύρων, primitiae martyrum; ἡ κορυφὴ τῶν μαρτύρων, vertex martyrum; ὁ τῶν μαρτύρων ἔξαρχος, martyrum princeps; triumphatorum martyrum dux; qui primus martyrii fores aperuit; qui primus choro martyrum aditum patefecit; phalangis martyrum antesignanus; πρωτομάρτυς. — Cfr. Nilles, Kalendarium manuale I, 232.

[3] In the Greek liturgy he is called ἀρχιδιάκονος, and in the Roman Pontifical dux ac praevius of the other deacons.

stoned for Thee, my God, my soul has adhered to Thee!" Overwhelmed by the rain of stones and falling on his knees, he exclaimed: "Lord Jesus, receive my spirit!" and then "he slept in the Lord." Although ordained as deacon by the Apostles, St. Stephen preceded the Apostles by his blessed and victorious death; though inferior in dignity, he became the superior in suffering; and though a scholar in doctrine, he became the master in its profession. The martyr's crown of precious gems now shines gloriously on his head; the celebration of the day of his death (December 26) follows the feast of the Nativity of our Lord, and the wonderful finding of his relics is separately commemorated (August 3). In the sixth century the principal part of his body was taken to Rome and placed beside the remains of St. Lawrence under the high altar of the Basilica of *St. Lawrence outside the walls* in a splendid marble sarcophagus.

c) St. Matthias, after the Ascension of the Lord, was by the will of God called to the Apostolate — in place of the traitor Judas. It is said that he was beheaded with an axe, and that St. Helena brought a portion of his relics to Treves. His head is preserved in the Church of *S. Maria Maggiore* in Rome; the feast occurs on the 24th, or (in leap years) on the 25th of February.

d) St. Barnaby was "an excellent man and full of the Holy Ghost and of faith." He was originally called Joseph; the Apostles gave him the name of Barnaby (= Son of Consolation), to indicate that he consoled and encouraged others by his supernatural enthusiasm and power of speaking. St. Barnaby is regarded by many only as an assistant and companion to the Apostles, as one resembling the Apostles; but many more and better reasons favor the opinion that Barnaby, like St. Paul, was an apostle in the strict sense of the term.[1] "In conseqence of a supernatural revelation Paul and Barnaby were ordained with prayer and the imposing of hands, and furnished with all authority; they were to complete the Apostolic College and to take the place of the two Saints James, of whom the elder had suffered martyrdom, and the younger was restricted to the charge of the Mother-Church of Jerusalem."[2] St. Barnaby was a Levite and came from Cyprus. It is probable that he belonged to the seventy-two disciples of the Lord. After having been consecrated Bishop at Antioch, he made (44 or 45) an extended missionary tour with St. Paul; later on he separated from him and labored chiefly in his native island Cyprus, where his renowned apostolate was crowned with martyrdom (between 53—76). It is not certain, though probable, that St. Barnaby preached in Upper Italy. Toward the end of the fifth century, the body of the saint was discovered in a cave at Salamis in Cyprus. His feast occurs on June eleventh, the day of his death.

---

[1] The preceding words cum tuis sanctis apostolis require, indeed, that, besides St. Matthias, at least one other apostle should be placed in the present list of saints. (Cf. Innoc. III. 1. 5, c. 6.)

[2] Hergenröther, Handbuch der allgemeinen Kirchengeschichte I, 71.

e) St. Ignatius of Antioch, who had the additional Greek name Θεοφόρος (Bearer of God).[1] According to a pleasing legend, confirmed by a vision of Catharine Emmerich, he was blessed when a child by our Lord.[2] He was a pupil of the Apostles, and also the second successor of St. Peter in the See of Antioch. Under the emperor Trajan he was sentenced to death, dragged in chains to Rome, and there in the Colosseum, on December 20, 107, exposed to the wild beasts. This greatly celebrated bishop burned with an ardent desire for martyrdom, as is evident from the letters, so full of unction, which on the way to Rome he wrote to different communities. — "And the Lord hath given him his heart's desire, and hath not withholden from him the will of his lips" (Ps. 20, 3); for the lions fell upon him, tore and ate his body, so that only the larger and harder bones remained. Since the middle of the seventh century, his holy relics have been preserved in the Basilica of St. Clement at Rome, where they were deposited on February first; hence his feast falls on this day. Let us quote some of the glorious words which he wrote to the Christians at Rome. "You cannot prove your tender love for me better than by allowing me to consecrate myself in sacrifice — now, since the altar is erected; be content, in a holy choir of love, to chant thanks to the Father in Christ Jesus. Well is it for me if I perish to the world, so that I may arise for God! Allow me to become the food of beasts, that through them I may attain to God. I am the wheat of God and must be ground by the teeth of beasts, so as to become the pure bread of Christ. Fire and cross, multitudes of wild beasts, the tearing of the body, the cutting into pieces of my limbs, the grinding of my bones; in brief, whatever of tortures the devil can invent, let all come upon me, if I but gain Jesus Christ. All the delights of earth I account as nothing, as nothing all the kingdoms of the world; better is it for me to die for Jesus Christ than to reign over all the bounds of the earth. Let me imitate the sufferings of my God. My Love is, indeed, crucified. There is no fire burning in me that tends to the things of earth, but a fountain of living water arises in my heart crying unto me: Come to the Father! I desire only the bread of God, the heavenly bread of life which is the Flesh of Jesus Christ, the Son of God; this only drink do I desire, His Blood, which is imperishable love and life eternal!"

f) St. Alexander I. was the fifth Pope after St. Peter. He also brought about many wonderful conversions in Rome. On May 3,

---

[1] According to more modern critics Θεοφόρος is a nomen proprium and not a mere title of honor given to St. Ignatius. With regard to the question as to the origin of this name, he is said to have answered the Emperor Trajan: ὁ τὸν Χριστὸν ἐν τῇ ψυχῇ περιφέρων, qui Christum circumfert in anima, ille est *Theophorus.* Hence we should write Θεοφόρος, Deum ferens, and not Θεόφορος, divino Spiritu actus seu afflatus.

[2] The conjecture of Simeon Metaphrastes (Mart. S. Ign. c. 1), that St. Ignatius was the child that the Lord placed before His disciples, who were disputing about precedence, for their imitation (Mat. 18, 1 etc.), may have been occasioned by the meaning of the name Theophorus = "carried by God."

115 (?), he was beheaded outside of Rome on the Nomentan Way, together with the priests Eventius and Theodulus. His holy body now reposes in the Church of St. Sabina at Rome. His feast occurs on May third.

g) and h) St. Marcellinus, priest, and St. Peter, exorcist, of the Roman Church. St. Peter, while in prison, had delivered the daughter of the jailer Artemius from an evil spirit, whereupon the whole family of Artemius was converted and baptized by the priest Marcellinus. Thereupon Sts. Peter and Marcellinus were frightfully tortured and led outside of the city for execution as far as the so-called Black Forest (*Silva nigra*), where they themselves with joy cleared the place in the thickets, and then bowed their head under the sword. On account of their martyrdom the place was afterward called the White Forest (*Silva candida*). In the ninth century their bodies were brought to Seligenstadt by Eginhard, the private secretary of Charlemagne, where they repose in a magnificent silver shrine.[1] Their feast is kept on June the second.

i) and k) The two youthful heroines, Felicitas and Perpetua, suffered at Carthage in North Africa. They were of noble birth and well educated. They were confined in a prison filled with darkness, heat, smoke and filth. "The day of their victory dawned," say the Acts, "and from the prison they went forth to the amphitheatre as to heaven, cheerful, with radiant countenances, trembling, but with joy, not with fear." The confessors who accompanied them stepped before the judgment-seat and cried to the one seated thereon: "Now thou judgest, but soon thou wilt be judged by God." The young women were cruelly scourged, and then cast before a wild cow; finally they were beheaded. This was in the year 202, in the persecution of the Christians under the Emperor Severus. Their feast occurs on March the seventh.

l) St. Agatha. Two cities of Sicily — Palermo and Catana — contest the honor of her birthplace. It is certain that under the Emperor Decius, in the year 251, she bore off the crown of martyrdom at Catana. This holy virgin was renowned far and wide for her nobility and wealth, as well as for her beauty and virtue. Already in her childhood she had chosen Jesus for her spouse and clung to Him with undivided love. Accused of being a Christian, she was dragged before the heathen judge Quintianus. This villain endeavored by all manner of mean artifices to overcome her chaste mind and her courage. But, like unto a rock in the ocean, the virgin remained unmoved and unshaken; as the dust beneath her feet she accounted all that the world could offer. In prison she was miraculously healed of her burning wounds by St. Peter. Afterward the wretched tyrant gave orders that the saint, miraculously healed, be rolled on sharp potsherds and glowing coals. Again brought back to prison, the saint prayed: "Lord, Thou who hast created me and preserved me since my childhood, who hast delivered my heart from

---

[1] Cf. Ebert, A., *Allgemeine Geschichte der Literatur des Mittelalters* II, 99 etc.

the love of the world and protected my body from perdition, who hast made me triumph over tortures and bonds, over iron and fire, I pray Thee, receive my spirit from this earth into the bosom of Thy mercy!'' Thereupon she slept in the peace of the Lord, and her pure soul flew heavenward. The tomb of St. Agatha, made glorious by God with many miracles, became the refuge of the Christians and even of the heathens. There also was kept the wonderful veil that was not burned, but only somewhat crimsoned, when the saint was thrown into the blazing fire. One year after her death, the neighboring volcano of Etna burst forth in torrents of fire, which moved toward the city of Catana, and threatened its destruction; then the inhabitants ran in terror to her tomb, took the veil and held it in the direction of the stream of lava. At that very instant it took another course toward the ocean and the city was saved. This event took place on the anniversary of the holy death of the virgin martyr, February the fifth, which is still observed as her feast-day in the Church of God. Consequently, St. Agatha is the much implored patroness against dangers of fire: as such she is particularly honored in the Black Forest of Germany. There her feast is made resplendent with the brightness of innumerable lights.[1]

m) St. Lucy suffered martyrdom about 304, in the great persecution of Diocletian against the Christians. She came from Syracuse, was of noble lineage, and at an early age vowed perpetual chastity to the Lord. Her mother was taken ill with dysentery, and in this emergency she made a pilgrimage to the tomb of St. Agatha to implore her restoration to health. Here St. Lucy was thrown into an ecstasy, and St. Agatha appeared to her in great glory, surrounded by angels, speaking thus to her: "My sister Lucy, virgin consecrated to God (*virgo Deo devota*), why dost thou request of me what thou thyself canst do for thy mother? Behold! thy faith hath given efficacy to the words of thy mouth and she is now cured." From that time Lucy sold her ornaments and her goods, in order to give the proceeds to the poor and the sick. Accused of being a Christian, she appeared before the tribunal of the heathen judge, Paschasius, whereupon being commanded to offer sacrifice to the idols, she answered: "It is a pure and undefiled worship of God to console and support widows and orphans in their tribulation. This have I now done for three years, and, after offering my possessions, I shall gladly offer also myself in sacrifice." Because she had said: "They that live chastely and devoutly are a temple of God, and the Holy Ghost dwells in them,"—they wished to drag her to a brothel; but the Lord rendered her as immovable as a pillar, so that no power could thence move her.[2] Then a funereal pyre filled with pitch, rosin and oil was built around her and ignited: but the flames also

---

[1] Martyris ecce dies Agathae — Virginis *emicat* eximiae — thus begins the hymn to St. Agatha, ascribed to Pope Damasus.

[2] Tanto pondere eam fixit Spiritus sanctus, ut virgo Christi *immobilis* permaneret (Antiph. eccles.).

left her untouched. Finally, a sword was thrust through her neck; but she continued to live until she had received the Holy Viaticum from a priest, and had consoled the Christians who were standing around, by the announcement that peace was near at hand. On the spot in which she suffered a church was erected. Her feast is kept on December the thirteenth. "In thy patience thou didst possess thy soul, O Lucy, spouse of Christ! Thou didst despise what is of the world, and now thou art resplendent among the choirs of angels; with thy own blood thou didst conquer the enemy!"[1]

n) St. Agnes. What is most to be admired in her — the charm of childhood, or virginal innocence, or manly heroism? Agnes, the child of wealthy and distinguished parents, was an elect child of grace; truly responding to her name (*vere nominis sui*), as St. Jerome writes, her childhood passed in spotless purity and lamblike innocence (ἀγνή = the chaste or pure; *agnus* = lamb). A hundred years after her death, St. Ambrose said: "Even at the present day many Roman maidens cherish the example of St. Agnes, as though she were still dwelling and living among us, animating themselves thereby to a perpetual preservation of purity." She gained the double crown of virginity and martyrdom at the tender age of thirteen. As is related in the history of her life, she was, "though a child in years, yet mature in mind; a girl in stature, but a matron in spirit; beautiful in appearance and figure, but still more charming in soul by piety and modesty." When asked in marriage, she described in animated, glorious words her espousals with the heavenly Bridegroom: "Depart from me, thou inciter to sin, thou food of death: depart from me; for already hath another Lover possession of my heart, who far surpasseth thee in nobility, and who hath given me incomparably more beautiful presents than those which thou hast offered me. With unrivalled treasures He hath enriched me; His nobility is the highest, His power the greatest, His appearance the most beautiful, His love the sweetest. The angels serve Him; sun and moon admire His beauty; by the perfume of virtue that exhales from His person the dead are awakened; by His touch the sick are cured. He hath prepared for me His bridal-chamber, where music and song resound; for Him I preserve fidelity, to Him I give myself entirely and without reserve!" She was taken to an abode of vice, but was protected by her guardian angel, who covered and shielded her with a garment of dazzling light. She was then thrown into a burning pile; but she made the sign of the Cross over the flames and remained unharmed. Finally, she fell under the sword of the executioner (304), and thus the tender victim hastened to the nuptials of the Divine Lamb. She was buried a short distance from the city on the Nomentan Road in the villa of her parents. Her tomb became glorious; for on the spot arises one of the loveliest and most renowned

---

[1] In tua patientia possedisti animam tuam, Lucia sponsa Christi: odisti quae in mundo sunt, et coruscas cum Angelis; sanguine proprio inimicum vicisti (Antiph. eccles.).

churches of Rome (*S. Agnese fuori le mura*). "There annually
the feast of the holy Virgin-Martyr is commemorated on the anniversary of her death (January twenty-first) by a reference to her
martyrdom as touching as it is significant. During High Mass,
amid the singing of the Agnus Dei, two white little lambs are laid
on the altar and blessed; then they are entrusted to some convent to
be cared for. From their wool are made the palliums which the
Holy Father, after having placed them for one night on the tomb of
the Princes of the Apostles, blesses and sends to the archbishops,
as a sign of their precedence over the bishops. Thus the episcopate,
in its principal members, wears in the more solemn functions a remembrance of the saint, who was deemed worthy to imitate the
innocent Lamb of God, sacrificed for the iniquity of others."[1] —
Moreover, the place of her suffering, combat and victory is adorned
with a rich and magnificent church (*S. Agnese in Piazza Navona*).

o) St. Cecilia.[2] She was a maiden of noble origin (*ingenua,
nobilis, clarissima*); from her earliest childhood she had wholly
dedicated herself to the service of God by the vow of chastity. "She
carried the Gospel always in her heart and never ceased by day or
by night praying and conversing on holy subjects." By the command of her parents, she was urged to marry a wealthy and distinguished young man named Valerian; but he was a heathen. She
consented only after receiving the assurance, through her guardian
angel, that God would preserve her virginity even after her marriage.
By prayer and penance Cecilia prepared for this worldly nuptial day,
and when at the banquet-feast the nuptial hymn was sung amidst the
sound of musical instruments (*cantantibus organis*), Cecilia secretly
sang in her heart to the Lord alone the hymn: "Keep Thou my
heart and my body immaculate, that I may not be confounded!"[3] —
And her heavenly Bridegroom sent an angel to her, who watched
over the purity of her heart and body. "Like unto the wise and busy
bee Cecilia served the Lord"[4] and gained many souls to Him. The
first among them were her husband Valerian and his brother Ti-
burtius, who soon after obtained the crown of martyrdom. On this
account the pagan prefect of the city, Almachius, delivered her up
to be suffocated in the bathroom (*Caldarium*) of her own palace.

---

[1] Laurent, Hagiol. Predigten I, 325.

[2] Martin, Die hl. Cecilia. Mainz 1878.

[3] Cantantibus organis Caecilia virgo in corde suo soli Domino decantabat
dicens: *"Fiat, Domine, cor meum et corpus meum immaculatum, ut non con-
fundar"* (Brev. Roman. 22. Nov.).

[4] Caecilia, famula tua, Domine, quasi apis tibi argumentosa deservit (Antiph.
eccles.). The bee was regarded not merely as a type of virginity, but also as a
symbol of wisdom and a model of industry; hence argumentosa indeed = arguta,
ingeniosa, prudens, and = operosa, sedula, industria, lively, diligent, fervent,
active. — Cum sit infirma robore apis, valida est vigore sapientiae et amore virtutis
(S. Ambros. Hexaem. 1. 5, c. 21, n. 70). — Apes prudentissimae (S. Bened. Anian.
Concordia Regular. c. 52, § 10).

She was confined in the chamber and "the oven was heated seven times more than usual;" but, like the youths of Babylon, she praised the Lord in the midst of the flames; the angel converted the scorching steam into a refreshing dew for her; "the fire had no power over her body, and not a hair of her head was singed, nor were her garments injured, nor had the smell of the fire reached her." Upon this the tyrant sent the executioner to her, who struck her thrice without severing her head; for three days she continued to live. The faithful hastened to the palace; she gave to all consolation and counsel. She ordered that her house should perpetually serve as a church, and then breathed forth her angelic soul. She was laid in a coffin of cypress wood, in the same posture in which she died, and was interred in the Catacombs of St. Callistus. In the year 821 her holy body was in a celestial vision discovered by Paschal I., who placed it under the high altar in the Cecilian Church in Trastevere. Almost eight hundred years later — namely, in 1599 — Cardinal Sfondrati found the holy martyr still in precisely the same posture in which she lay here on the floor of her house. Thus she still reposes, sweet and modest, enveloped in her rich attire and in a penitential garment, on which the glorious traces of her blood are visible. She probably died in the year 177; her feast is celebrated on November the twenty-second. St. Cecilia is honored as the patroness of Church music, as she herself was versed in music, and is said frequently to have heard celestial melodies.

p) St. Anastasia. This holy widow and martyr is also of Roman origin. She had much to suffer from the cruelty of her pagan husband Publius; after his death she gave herself over to practices of charity and mercy. In the persecution of Diocletian she obtained, on the day of our Lord's Nativity, 304, the palm of martyrdom by fire. On the spot where her house stood, a church (*S. Anastasia*) was erected in her honor; there under the high altar rests her body. Her feast is kept on December the twenty-fifth. In ancient times the Popes were accustomed to celebrate here at dawn the second Mass of Christmas day; whence in the Mass a commemoration is also made of St. Anastasia.

St. John, the Seer of the New Law, "saw a great multitude, which no man could number, of all nations and tribes and peoples and tongues, standing before the throne and in the sight of the Lamb, clothed with white robes and palms in their hands," and heard that "these are they who are come out of great tribulation, and have washed their robes, and have made them white in the blood of the Lamb" (Apoc. 7, 9, 14). Of this countless multitude of bright martyrs only a few are here mentioned in the Mass by name[1]; they are merely those who in the principal city of Christen-

---

[1] The question why a certain number and especially these saints, and why they are enumerated precisely in this order, several theologians have attempted to answer in different ways and to support the answer by all manner of reasons. In hujusmodi rationibus reddendis non oportet immorari, quia haec et similia saepe

dom were at all times held in great veneration. — Here after the
male martyrs, the female martyrs also are mentioned, which is not
the case in the list of the saints mentioned before the Consecration.
The Church extols it as a miracle of divine power, that the Lord
"should also have granted to the weaker sex the victory of martyrdom." How perfected does not Christ's power appear here in the
most tender virgins! Their heavenly robes of glory not only shine
with the splendor of an eternal brilliancy, but they are also crimsoned
in their glory with the blood of a glorious sacrificial death.

3. With the saints named and with "all the rest of the saints,"
whose number and names the all-seeing eye of God alone knows,
we, poor sinners, desire to be eternally united in heaven.[1] This
petition is expressed at the beginning of the prayer, and is now at
the conclusion repeated again in other words, inasmuch as we implore admittance to the community of the heavenly citizens, and for
such a fellowship with them we do not rely upon our own merit to
obtain, but support our request for it on the merciful indulgence of
God.[2] The communion of life and of goods with the saints (consortium Sanctorum), implored of God, consists in this, that we may
become associates (consortes) in their heavenly bliss and glory, or
that we may obtain some part of the blessed inheritance (sors),
which is prepared and which will be granted to all who are born
again of the Holy Ghost.[3] Thus the Apostle writes (Col. 1, 12):
"Giving thanks to God the Father, who hath made us worthy to be
partakers of the saints in light" (dignos nos fecit in partem sortis
Sanctorum in lumine). And in the Book of Wisdom (5, 5) it is
said of the pious: "Behold! how they are numbered among the
children of God, and their lot is among the saints" (inter Sanctos
sors illorum est). We do not ask for the glory of the saints by
reason of our own merits, but we confide in the merciful and gracious

---

vel casu vel ex aliqua peculiari devotione possunt accidere (Suarez disp. 83,
sect. 2, n. 17).

[1] Quidnam nobis de nostra quantacumque scientia provenire possit, quod non
sit minus hac gloria, qua inter Dei filios numeramur? Parum dixi: nec respici in
ejus comparatione potest orbis ipse et plenitudo ejus, etiamsi totus cedat unicuivis
in possessionem. Ceterum, si nos ignorantia Dei tenet, quomodo speramus in eum
quem ignoramus? Si nostri, quomodo humiles erimus, putantes nos aliquid esse
cum nihil simus? Scimus autem nec superbis nec desperatis partem esse vel
societatem in sorte Sanctorum (S. Bernard. In Cantic. serm. 37, n. 5).

[2] Novit Ecclesia, Deum non nisi intercedentibus meritis tribuere beatitudinem;
sed nec illud ignorat, ut in Sanctorum admittamur consortium, non modo necessariam esse gloriam, sed etiam gratiam et veniam peccatorum, quae sine meritis
nostris dantur tantummodo per Christum Dominum nostrum; ipsa nostra merita
dona esse misericordiae Dei et gratiae, nobisque misericordia Dei opus esse vel in
earum actionum examine, quas bonas existimamus (Bened. XIV. De Missae sacrif.
l. 2, c. 18, n. 2).

[3] Often in the liturgy, especially in the prayers for the departed, eternal bliss
is designated as consortium Dei, consortium Sanctorum, consortium perpetuae
beatitudinis, consortium lucis aeternae.

bounty of the Lord.[1] — The happiness of heaven is assuredly with truth called a crown of justice (*corona justitiae* — 2 Tim. 4, 8), inasmuch as it is granted as a reward for labor and as a price of victory in combat; yet deep down and at the bottom of all, it is and remains a crown of mercy,[2] that is, the final and greatest of all graces, the highest of all God's gifts. Yes, in heaven the Lord crowns His own with grace and mercy (Ps. 102, 4). Under many aspects the rendering of creatures eternally happy is a work of divine mercy. Above all, it is in itself an emanation of the goodness of God, that we can even merit heaven, and His bounty bestows upon us a far richer reward than we actually deserve; for "the sufferings of this time are not worthy to be compared with the glory to come, that shall be revealed in us" (Rom. 8, 18). If we consider the sum and succession of all the graces from the first to the last — including the grace of final perseverance —, must we not gratefully acknowledge, that our life is adorned with a rich wreath of divine mercies? Yes, our rescue from eternal perdition is a free and great gift of God's merciful goodness and predilection: His mercy goes before us (Ps. 58, 11), accompanies us (Ps. 22, 25), and follows us all the days of our life (Ps. 22, 6). Out of mercy God sent us His Son as a Redeemer; out of mercy He has promised us life eternal; out of mercy He has rescued us from the depths of a life of sin incurred through our own fault, and placed us in the kingdom of His light; out of mercy He has preserved us from innumerable sins and pardoned those committed "seventy times seven times"; out of mercy He knocks at our hearts, admonishes and warns us, directs our destiny in such a manner and so grants us a chain of powerful graces, as to

---

[1] Non aestimator meriti, sed veniae largitor = in that Thou wilt not consider, make account of, regard, what we deserve, that is, our trifling merits, or also our misdeeds, to influence Thy judgment according to them, but in abundant measure to impart to us merciful indulgence and forgiveness. The word meritum can be taken here as = malum meritum, demeritum, meritum supplicii, the guilt, the transgression, as merere often = an evil, to deserve or to draw on one's self punishment. — Omnipotens aeterne Deus, misericordiam tuam ostende supplicibus, ut qui de *meritorum* (= peccatorum) qualitate diffidimus, non judicium tuum, sed iudulgentiam sentiamus (Sacram. Gregor. Dom. XIX. p. Pent.). — Cum pro *nostris meritis* jugiter mereamur affligi, tu tamen judicium ad correctionem temperas, non perpetuam exerces ad poenam (1. c. Dom. XXII. p. Pent.). — Quia de meritorum qualitate diffido, ad misericordiam tuam confugio, ut impetrem per tuam misericordiam, quod non merui per meam justitiam, immo quod ex toto demeruisse convincor, si delictorum meorum fueris memor et misericordiae tuae immemor (Gerhoh. Reichersp. In Ps. 24). — Cum praesens est veniae largitor, magis confidit exaudiri devotus peccator (Stephan. Augustod. c. 9).

[2] Vita aeterna non ut debitum rependitur hominibus, sed ut gratia et misericordia. "*Gratia Dei vita aeterna,*" inquit Apostolus (Rom. 6, 23). Haec meritis quidem nostris redditur, sed merita ipsa sunt dona gratiae et misericordiae Dei, Deusque merita nostra remunerans, remuneratur dona sua, "*cumulans sua dona coronis,*" inquit S. Prosper, carmine de ingratis (Pouget, Inst. cathol. tom. II, p. 3, sect. 2, c. 7, § 22, n. 25). — Cum Deus coronat *merita nostra*, nihil aliud coronat quam *munera sua* (S. Aug. Epist. 194, c. 5, n. 19).

enable us to remain faithful until death and bear off the crown of life. "The mercies of the Lord that we are not consumed" (Lam. 3, 22) — we shall exclaim in heaven, where we desire to praise the mercies of the Lord eternally. *Misericordias Domini in aeternum cantabo* (Ps. 88, 1). — But the action must correspond with the desire. If we wish for the glory of the saints, we must share their labors, sufferings and combats. Through many tribulations only can we enter with all the saints into the joy of the Lord. We should, moreover, remember this, when we beg for "some part and fellowship" with the Apostles and Martyrs; for if with them we suffer and die for Christ, with them also shall we be glorified.[1]

64. The Conclusion of the Canon.

The foregoing prayer closes with the ordinary formula "through Christ our Lord," but no *Amen* follows, that the intimate connection between these concluding words and the beginning of the following prayer may not be interrupted, but more clearly demonstrated.[2]

Per quem haec omnia, Domine, semper bona creas, sancti†ficas, vivi†ficas, bene†dicis, et praestas nobis. Per ip†sum, et cum ip†so et in ip†so est tibi Deo Patri † omnipotenti in unitate Spiritus † sancti omnis honor et gloria. Per omnia saecula saeculorum. R. Amen.	By whom, O Lord, Thou dost always create, sanctify†, vivify†, bless † and bestow upon us all these good things. Through Him †, and with Him †, and in Him † is unto Thee, God the Father † Almighty, in the unity of the Holy † Ghost, all honor and glory: world without end. R. Amen.

---

[1] "I enjoy great peace, a sweet contentment. . . The most bitter portion of the chalice of the passion our Lord has drunk. For us there remain but some drops. Let us praise His infinite love which forestalls us with so much sweetness. I have always recited with an elevated heart this wonderful prayer of our holy liturgy: 'ut partem aliquam et societatem donare digneris cum tuis sanctis Apostolis et Martyribus' (that Thou vouchsafe to grant us some part and fellowship with Thy holy Apostles and Martyrs). Well, then, our dear Lord has heard me. I, too, like His most faithful friends, have been adorned with the glorious ignominy of our Master. Hence again, let us praise God... I will suffer all; but I will remain united to Pius the Ninth, to the Apostolic See, and until my last breath will I defend the liberty of the Church." Thus wrote, in 1874, from his captivity, Don Antonio de Macedo Costa, Bishop of Para in Brazil. (Cf. Stimmen aus Maria-Laach VI [1874], 380).

[2] The concluding formulas of the preceding Canon Prayers have received the Amen only since the twelfth century; previously it was placed at the end of the whole Canon after the words per omnia saecula saeculorum, and that as a response of the people. Hic elevat Oblatam cum calice dicens: *Per omnia saecula saeculorum.* Responsio: *Amen* (Microl. c. 22). — *Assensum* quaerit *Ecclesiae* sacerdos, dicens *sonora* voce "*Per omnia saecula saeculorum.*" Supplet *populus* super orationem ejus locum idiotae et respondet "*Amen*" (1 Cor. 14), hac una participem

Thus is the sacrificial prayer of the Canon closed and crowned; for both text and rite of the above prayer are exceedingly comprehensive, beautiful and solemn. It is divided into two parts sharply differing from each other. In the first we confess that the Eucharistic Sacrificial gifts have been prepared and are given to us by God, and that through Jesus Christ; in the other part we declare that by the Sacrifice of Christ supreme honor and glory are given to the triune God. Therefore, here at the close of the Canon, the whole significance and efficacy of the Sacrifice of the Mass are again summarized in a few brief and vigorous features; for Jesus Christ, the God-man Highpriest, appears on the altar as mediator between God and men (1 Tim. 2, 5): on the one hand, to bless and enrich men with the plenitude of the gifts of salvation; on the other, most perfectly to honor and glorify the eternal majesty of God.

1. The Liturgical Text. — The words "all these good things" (*haec omnia bona*) designate principally the Eucharistic elements of bread and wine which were on the altar before the Consecration, and still come up as if present (*haec*) before the mind of the priest. And this can and does happen, since their appearances have remained after the Consecration, as a sacramental covering for the Body and Blood of Christ. The natural elements of bread and wine are the created gifts of God, and on the altar they are changed from earthly into heavenly gifts — and then after their consecration they are given to us as a possession and for our enjoyment. At the last word (*praestas*, bestow) we should, therefore, think on what is on the altar (*haec bona*), that is, on the consecrated elements, — in other words, on the sacrificial Body and Blood of Christ consecrated from bread and wine. The same thought may also be thus expressed: with regard to the manifold power of God, or Christ, here described, by "all these good things" are to be understood partly the natural goods of bread and wine, partly the supernatural goods of the Body and Blood of Christ; the former He "creates, sanctifies, vivifies," but the latter, the Body and Blood of Christ, He bestows upon us in Communion, or as a sacrificial gift, which we may and should offer Him.

Through His Son Jesus Christ God the Father creates "always" (*semper creas*) — as in the beginning of the world, so now also — all the products of nature, hence the most noble nourishing plants, that is, the material goods of wheat and grapes; for year after year He causes herbs to grow for the use of man, so that He may bring

---

voce se faciens omnium charismatum, quae sacerdos multiplici sacramentorum diversitate studuit impetrare. Jam ergo quasi mutato habitu, quo utebatur, dum sacra mysteria tractaret, *mutat vocem* (Ivon. Carnot. Serm. 5). — With regard to the conclusion of the preceding prayer said in silence, Blessed Albertus Magnus makes the judicious remark: Est conclusio, ad quam nullus respondet *"Amen"* (sicut in aliis Secretorum conclusionibus) nisi *Angeli*, qui in ministerio esse dicuntur (Tract. III, c. 9).

forth bread out of the earth, and wine may cheer the heart of man (Ps. 103, 14—15).[1]

These created gifts of nature, the Almighty then changes through the same Jesus Christ into the heavenly sacrificial gifts of the Eucharist — a change of substance, which is here apprehended and represented under a threefold aspect. For it is the most perfect and consummate sanctification (*sanctificas*), vivifying (*vivificas*) and blessing (*benedicis*) of the material substances of bread and wine.[2] — By the Consecration, the bread and wine are "sanctified" in the highest degree; for their substances vanish, and in their stead there are present the most holy Body and Blood of Christ in union with His most holy soul and infinitely holy divinity, whilst the appearances still remain, but they likewise receive in this sacramental connection a sanctified character.[3] — Furthermore, by the Consecration the dead, lifeless elements of bread and wine are "vivified",[4] that is, changed into the living and enlivening bread (*panis vivus et vitalis*) of the Body of Christ and into the life-streaming beverage of the Blood of Christ; the Eucharistic Saviour is, indeed, the Eternal Living One, who, as the Son of the living God, hath life in Himself (John 5, 26) and is the source of all supernatural life for the creature (John 1, 4). — Finally, the bread and wine are in the fullest sense of the term "blessed" by the Consecration,[5] that is, not merely made a blessed out of an ordinary food, as, for example, when water and oil are blessed as materials for other sacraments, but far more are changed as to their entire substances into Christ's blessed sacrificial

---

[1] Per Christum omnipotens Deus Pater *haec bona omnia*, quae sacris altaribus consecrantur, non solum in exordio mundi creavit, condendo quod non erat . . ., sed etiam semper eadem bona creat propagando et reparando, ut per annos singulos et *novae segetes* et *nova vina* nascantur (Florus Diacon. n. 73).

[2] Quoniam corpus Christi est sanctum et benedictum, idcirco per hoc quod Deus Pater convertit haec omnia (sc. panem et vinum) in corpus et sanguinem Christi, dicitur ea sanctificare, vivificare et benedicere (Dion. Carthus. Expos. Missae art. 36).

[3] Panis ille quem videtis in altari, *sanctificatus* per verbum Dei, *corpus* est *Christi;* calix ille, imo quod habet calix, *sanctificatum* per verbum Dei, *sanguis* est *Christi* (S. Aug. Serm. 227 [ad Infantes de Sacramentis]).

[4] In the Mozarabic Liturgy (In 1. Dominica post Octav. Epiphan.) the substantial change of the Eucharistic elements is expressed by the following words: Coelesti benedictione creatura visibilis *animatur*. Again (In Ascensione Domini): Visitet et *vivificet ea* (sc. munera) Spiritus tuus sanctus, qui per vaporem incendii Heliae prophetae holocaustum adsumpsit.

[5] In the Ordination Rite of priests the Church prays: In obsequium plebis tuae panem et vinum in corpus et sanguinem Filii tui immaculata *benedictione transforment*. — Verba, in quibus consistit vis consecrandi, dicuntur *benedictio* tum ratione benedictionis praecedentis, tum quia ad eorum prolationem Dominus *benedicit, quia convertit* in corpus, quod super omnia *benedixit*, ditando perfectis donis gratiarum animam, et sanctificatione et puritate carnem illam sanctissimam (S. Bonav. IV, dist. 10, p. 2, dub. 3).

Body and sacrificial Blood, which overflow from the fulness of heavenly things.[1]

The altar gifts thus sanctified, vivified and blessed, that is, consecrated, "are bestowed upon us" (*praestas nobis*) by God through Jesus Christ for our property as Sacrifice and Sacrament, as ransom and food of the soul, as our highest and most sacred Good.

A still richer and more profound meaning of the above words may be discovered, if we regard the bread and wine, which lie on the altar according to visible appearances, as the representatives of all the other products of nature; then God, or Jesus Christ, appears as the author and dispenser of all the collective goods of the natural and supernatural order. Such a view becomes natural considering the custom formerly much in use of performing at this point all kinds of blessing. At certain times and on special feasts there was a blessing immediately before this prayer (*Per quem . . .*)[2] by means of a specially inserted formula for various objects, chiefly articles of food, for example, water, milk, honey, grapes, beans, fruit. Now when such blessed objects lay near the altar, they could — but in a somewhat different sense — be also comprised among "all these good things, that God ever creates, sanctifies, vivifies, blesses and bestows upon us" through Jesus Christ. — Even now the bishop, according to a strict ordinance, has annually on Holy Thursday at this place in the Canon to bless the holy oil for the sick (*oleum infirmorum*). If we would seek a (mystical) reason for this ordinance, it must certainly appear highly proper and profoundly significant that in the Canon, when the sacrificial death of Christ is celebrated, and immediately after the prayer (*Nobis quoque peccatoribus*), which implores for sinful man from the Divine Mercy a share in the beatitude of the saints, that oil should be blessed, whose sacramental power and grace fortifies the soul for the combat of death, and tends

---

[1] The three words sanctificas, vivificas, benedicis are understood still in another way. By sanctificatio is meant the preparatory sanctification of the sacrificial matter through the oblation, by vivificatio its change by the Consecration, and by benedictio the fulfilment of the sacrificial gifts with all heavenly blessing. — Hac oratione Ecclesia profitetur, maximum Eucharistiae beneficium a Deo sibi esse collatum, a quo panis et vinum, elementa eucharistica consecranda, creantur; creata, cum altari admoventur, sanctificantur; sanctificata vivificantur, cum in corpus et sanguinem Christi transsubstantiantur; vivificata benedicuntur donisque Spiritus sui sancti affatim replentur, atque ita benedicta nobis indignis servis suis fruenda traduntur (Lesley S. J. [Migne 85, 553]).

[2] The Gelasian Sacramentary has here (in Ascensa Domini) the rubric: Inde vero modicum ante expletum Canonem benedices fruges novas, after which comes the following benediction formula: Benedic, Domine, et has fruges novas fabae, quas tu, Domine, rore coelesti et inundantia pluviarum ad maturitatem perducere dignatus es, ad percipiendum nobis cum gratiarum actione in nomine D. N. J. Ch. Per quem haec omnia. . . This blessing of the first fruits, before the concluding prayer of the Canon, was never general, but prescribed only by individual bishops. A Sacramentarium vetus of the eleventh century admits the words Per quem haec, Domine, semper bona creas, sanctificas, vivificas, benedicis et nobis servis tuis largiter praestas even into the benedictio palmae et olivae. (Cfr. Migne 151, 843.)

to remove all the remains of sin, that is, the last obstacle to admittance into eternal glory. — The intimate relation of such blessings with the sacrificial celebration places before our eyes the truth, that every blessing, every grace and consecration (in a certain sense) proceeds from the Eucharistic Sacrifice.

As Jesus Christ is for the entire Church, yea, for the whole creation, the never-failing fountain of blessing and the vivifying sun of grace, thus also "through Him and with Him and in Him," especially inasmuch as He offers Himself and is offered on the altar, there is given "to the Father Almighty, in the unity of the Holy Ghost, all honor and glory," that is, the most perfect homage, veneration and glorification.[1] The somewhat ambiguous expression "through Him, and with Him, and in Him" (*per ipsum et cum ipso et in ipso*) may be explained in different ways; and in this singular expression regard must ever be had to the twofold nature of Jesus Christ.

Through Jesus Christ (*per ipsum*) the Father and the Holy Ghost are honored and glorified in an infinitely sublime manner — at one time, inasmuch as the God-Man offers Himself on the altar; and then, in as far as the homage and adoration of all creatures through Him alone as the one Mediator that can be pleasing to God. — At the same time and jointly with Jesus Christ (*cum ipso*)[2] the Father and the Holy Ghost receive all honor and praise; for Jesus Christ is true God and, therefore, "together" with the other divine persons "adored and glorified" (*simul adoratur et conglorificatur*). Moreover, the Eucharistic Sacrifice of praise and adoration is offered in like manner to all the Persons of the Most Holy Trinity. — Finally, in Jesus Christ (*in ipso*)[3] the Father and the Holy Ghost also are glorified, since all three Divine Persons by reason of the unity of their essence are eternally in each other, and, consequently, the veneration of one is not to be separated from the veneration of the other two.

If we consider Jesus Christ according to His human nature as our Head and our Mediator, then we render to the triune God all honor and glory "through Him" and "with Him", in that we in union with Him in the offering of the Sacrifice, and "in Him", in so far as we are included in His Sacrifice and are jointly offered with it.

2. The Liturgical Action. — The accompanying rite harmonizes magnificently with the text of the prayer. The threefold sign

---

[1] Omnis honor et gloria, πᾶσα ἡ δόξα = the highest, absolutely perfect honor and glorification.

[2] *Cum ipso*, quia Filius a Patre separari non debet, sed simul cum eo venerari. Honor enim uni personae impensus toti Trinitati adorandae saltem implicite exhibetur (Dion. Carthus. Expos. Missae art. 36).

[3] *In ipso*, i. e. omnis honor et gloria est tibi Patri atque Spiritui sancto seu in unitate Spiritus sancti in Filio tuo, quia omnis, qui Filium Dei vere cognoscit, ex ejus cognitione Deum Patrem glorificat atque honorat (Dion. Carthus. l. c.).

of the Cross prescribed at the three words "sanctify, vivify, bless" symbolizes not the present, but the accomplished sanctification, the vivifying and blessing of the oblation, which took place at the moment of Consecration,[1] and, at the same time, also indicates the fulness of life and of blessing contained in the Eucharistic sacrificial gifts and thence flowing out over the Church.

From now on the rite of the sign of the Cross changes. The sacred sign is no longer made with the hand alone of the priest, but with *the Sacred Body of the Lord*.[2] When pronouncing the words "through Him and with Him and in Him," the sign of the Cross is made three times with the sacred Host over the chalice — and when mention is made of the Father Almighty and of the Holy Ghost, the holy sign is made twice, between the chalice and the breast of the priest. One reason for these signs of the Cross may consist principally in the circumstance, that here all three Divine Persons are mentioned separately and consecutively, — the Son three times; hence a threefold sign of the Cross accompanies the mention of the Son. At the threefold designation of Jesus Christ, the sign of the Cross is made with the Host over the chalice, because His adorable (Flesh and) Blood are contained therein; but as this no longer obtains when mention is made of the Father and the Holy Ghost, the last two signs of the Cross take place outside of the chalice. — To this may be added a still further signification. The signs of the Cross which are formed with the sacred Body of the Lord over and beside the chalice, should, in harmony with the words spoken at the same time, indicate that the highest glory and honor which is rendered to God through and with and in Christ, proceeds from the bloody Sacrifice of the Cross, again mystically represented and renewed in the unbloody Sacrifice of the Altar. — Whilst the priest pronounces the words "all honor and glory" (*omnis honor et gloria*), he holds the Host and the chalice in his hands, raising them slightly. This slight elevation (*elevatio minor*) of the sacrificial gifts is far more ancient than the greater one (*elevatio major*) at the elevation. Originally this minor elevation was, as it were, a more solemn invitation to all to render their homage of adoration to

---

[1] Signa tria crucis quae hic fiunt, operatione Trinitatis per virtutem crucis ostendunt facta esse quae praemissa sunt. Signa enim facta hucusque *post* consecrationem non consecrationem operantur, sed *ejus* faciunt *commemorationem* sive *testificationem* (Robert. Paulul. De offic. eccles. 1. 2, c. 36).

[2] The rite at this point was in the Middle Age differently framed. The practice of forming the Cross here cum oblatis — cum corpore dominico — cum hostia, was in all probability brought about chiefly by the circumstance, that at the Elevation, which here took place, the chalice was touched with the Host. Cum oblata tangitur calix. — Novissima crux cum *oblatione* celebratur (Amalar. Eclog. n. 22). Cfr. Ordo Rom. I, n. 16. — Notandum quod cum alia signa sola manu sacerdotis fiant, ista fiunt de corpore Christi. Hic enim ipsa Christi crucifixio repraesentatur, quasi Christus quem praesentem credimus sic pro nobis in ligno crucis est extensus (Robert. Paulul. 1. c., c. 37).

the Most Holy[1]; according to the rite of that epoch, the minor elevation can be conceived as an emphasizing of the words "all honor and glory," that is, as symbolically indicating the glory which day after day ascends from the altar and its sacrificial gifts as a sweet odor to the eternal throne of the Most Holy Trinity. — This supreme praise is rendered to the Most High, not merely as long as this world will continue to last, but "forever and ever" (*per omnia saecula saeculorum*). By this majestic and overpowering conclusion, recited aloud or sung, the mystic and solemn silence of the Canon is broken, in order that the people, by answering *Amen*, may make known their assent to and approval of all that the priest alone with God praying and offering in the holy cloud has performed. Thus the Canon terminates in an enthusiastic Doxology, which is the gloriously developed crown of blossoms of the ancient, venerable sacrificial prayer. The entire rite of the Mass — word and action — is simple, but grand and touching: does our disposition correspond therewith? Are our mind and heart as strongly affected as they should be amid such wonderful mysteries, accomplished before our eyes and by our hands?

THIRD ARTICLE.

The Communion.

65. Preliminary Remarks.

The Communion is the last principal part of the Sacrifice and, therefore, it brings the celebration of Mass to its termination. The Eucharist is, indeed, according to its very nature and object, a food-offering and a sacrificial food.[2] — It is a food-offering, for the Divine Lamb is in the Consecration mystically immolated and offered on the altar, that He may be partaken of by those who offer. The essential sacrificial act must precede its reception as food by Communion, as it consists precisely in the preparing of the sacrificial repast. Christ's Body and Blood are thereby sacrificed, that they may, under the separate appearances of bread and wine, be placed on the altar. Only by Communion does the Eucharistic Sacrifice attain its destination as a food-offering and as such is thereby rendered complete. Because of this arrangement and connection of the Sacrifice of the Altar with the Communion of the celebrant, this Communion constitutes, although not an essential, yet an integral part of the Eucharistic Sacrifice; it would be incomplete if Communion were not joined thereto. According to divine and ecclesiastical law, the celebrant at least must eat and drink of the sacrificial

---

[1] In many places, for example, in Belgium, a threefold sign is here given with the little bell; this custom, being of ancient origin, may be tolerated. (Cfr. S. R. C. 14. Maji 1856.)

[2] Quamvis sacramenti usus non sit de essentia sacramenti, est tamen ad completum esse ipsius, inquantum pertingit ad hoc, ad quod institutum est (S. Thom. IV, dist. 8, q. 2, a. 1, sol. 2 ad 1).

Body and sacrificial Blood which have been previously offered by him in sacrifice to God, that by such participation he may enter into the most intimate communion of sacrifice with Christ. "The chalice of benediction, which we bless, is it not the communion of the Blood of Christ? And the bread, which we break, is it not the partaking of the Body of the Lord?" (1 Cor. 10, 16.)

Therefore, the Eucharist is also sacrificial food and sacrificial drink; the Eucharistic repast is a sacrificial repast, because it is the precious fruit of the Sacrifice of the Altar. It is only by a sacrificial act that the sacramental food of life can be gained and prepared. To the sacrificial act is attached the sacrificial repast; the Communion is a participation in the preceding and accomplished Sacrifice. But as Christ must Himself become previously a Victim, in order to become our food of grace, thus also must we previously offer ourselves to Him in worship and life, so as to be worthy of the Eucharistic sacrificial repast.[1]

The Eucharist is both a sacrifice and a sacrament; but as sacrifice and sacrament it acts in different ways and produces different effects of grace, so that the fruits of the Sacrifice are to be distinguished from the fruits of Communion.[2] As the faithful, as "a holy and royal priesthood," unite in offering the Eucharistic Sacrifice, they should also by sacramental or at least by spiritual Communion unite themselves with and participate in the Sacrifice offered, in order thus to receive the fruits of the Sacrifice in greater abundance.

The Communion forms the centre of the following part of the liturgy of the Mass: the prayers which precede the Communion may be regarded and designated as preparation; the others, which are joined thereto, as thanksgiving. It will not be surprising, but rather readily conceived, that there should be still other things harmonizing with the accomplished Sacrifice, if we remember that the Communion is the sacrificial repast, and as such is the perfect exterior conclusion of the sacrificial action.

66. The Pater Noster and its Appendix.

1. The Lord's Prayer has from the time of the Apostles[3] formed a constituent part of the sacrificial celebration, in the East and in the

---

[1] Ipsa participatio corporis et sanguinis Domini, cum ejus panem manducamus et calicem bibimus, hoc utique nobis insinuat, ut moriamur mundo et vitam nostram absconditam habeamus cum Christo in Deo carnemque nostram crucifigamus cum vitiis et concupiscentiis suis. Sic fit, ut omnes fideles qui Deum et proximum diligunt, etiamsi non bibant calicem corporeae passionis, bibant tamen calicem dominicae caritatis, quo inebriati membra sua, quae sunt super terram, mortificent et induti Dominum J. Chr. carnis curam non faciant in desideriis neque contemplentur quae videntur, sed quae non videntur (S. Fulgent. Contra Fabian. frag. 28).

[2] Concede nobis, omnipotens Deus, ut his muneribus, quae . . . deferimus, et *te placemus exhibitis* et *nos vivificemur acceptis* (Sacrament. Gregor.).

[3] St. Jerome dates the use of the Our Father at the Sacrificial Celebration to an ordinance of the Lord Himself. Sic (Christus) docuit discipulos suos, ut

West. It is recited aloud, or sung, and is placed at the beginning of the Communion rite,[1] in the same manner as the Preface introduces the Canon, or Consecration. The position of the *Pater Noster* in the organism of the Mass is very appropriate; for according to its contents it can be referred partly to the Sacrifice, partly to the Communion, forming a beautiful transition between these two parts and connecting them with each other. In the "Our Father" we pray for the sanctification of His divine name, for the coming of the divine kingdom, and the fulfilment of the divine will —; then, the granting of our daily bread —; finally, the forgiveness of debt, the preservation from temptation and deliverance from evil. The first three petitions take flight to the heights of Heaven and are concerned with the glorifying of God; but the last three descend to the lowly things of this world, and have for object the salvation of man. The first three petitions are connected with the last three by the fourth and central petition, which refers as well to the supernatural bread of the soul, as to the earthly bread of the body. We hope for and obtain the honor of God and the salvation of the world principally through the Eucharistic Bread of heaven, not merely inasmuch as it is a sacrificial gift, but also in as far as it is a sacrificial food.[2]

In the Roman rite the "Our Father" is introduced by the

---

quotidie *in corporis illius sacrificio* credentes audeant loqui: Pater noster, qui es in coelis... (Adv. Pelag. l. 3, n. 15). — The same is found in all liturgies, but it was and is not recited in all in the same manner. Among the Greeks it is said in a low tone by the priest, while the entire congregation recite it aloud. In the Mozarabic Rite the people respond to the priest, who recites or sings it aloud, in the following manner: Pater noster, qui es in coelis. R. *Amen.* — Sanctificetur nomen tuum. R. *Amen.* — Adveniat regnum tuum. R. *Amen.* — Fiat voluntas tua sicut in coelo et in terra. R. *Amen.* — Panem nostrum quotidianum da nobis hodie. R. *Quia Deus es.* — Et dimitte nobis debita nostra, sicut et nos dimittimus debitoribus nostris. R. *Amen.* — Et ne nos inducas in tentationem. R. *Sed libera nos a malo.* — In Christian antiquity the Our Father was regarded as really and exclusively the "prayer of the faithful" (εὐχὴ τῶν πιστῶν); for the baptized alone had the right to address God as their Father. Recall the so-called traditio (delivery) and redditio (return) of the Oratio dominica (and the Symbol) in the old baptismal practice. The Our Father is also called legitima et ordinaria oratio — prex legitima. (Cfr. Tertull. De orat. c. 10.)

[1] Previous to the time of St. Gregory the Great it was not recited (as is still the case in the Ambrosian and Mozarabic Rites) until after the breaking of the Host; this Pope gave it its present position immediately after the Canon (mox post precem).

[2] Sequitur Oratio dominica cum appositionibus congruis. Una enim praecedens eam fiduciam praedicat, qua Dominum creatorem Patrem dicere praesumamus; altera subsequens explicat, quomodo et a quibus malis per Dominum nos liberari petamus. Quae Oratio dominica, quia *prius* quam cetera in consecratione sacrificiorum assumpta est, in *expletione* ejusdem sacratissimae actionis digne ponitur, ut per hanc purificati qui communicaturi sunt, quae sancte confecta sunt, digne ad salutem veram percipiant (Walafrid. Strabo c. 23).

Oremus[1] and an unchangeable preamble,[2] to which St. Cyprian already alludes.[3] We refer to and rely therein on the wholesome precepts and divine instruction (*Praeceptis salutaribus moniti et divina institutione formati*), as though we would excuse ourselves that "we make bold" (*audemus*), as poor creatures to call the Lord of heaven and earth "Our Father" and invoke Him as "Father", to send up to Him such familiar and bold petitions. The Lord Himself commanded and taught us to repeat this prayer with heart and lips, saying: "Thus shall you pray" — *Sic orabitis* (Matt. 6, 9) — then He continued:

Pater noster, qui es in coelis; sanctificetur nomen tuum. Adveniat regnum tuum. Fiat voluntas tua, sicut in coelo et in terra. Panem nostrum quotidianum da nobis hodie. Et dimitte nobis debita nostra, sicut et nos dimittimus debitoribus nostris. Et ne nos inducas in tentationem — R. Sed libera nos a malo. — Amen.

Our Father, who art in heaven, hallowed be Thy name: Thy kingdom come: Thy will be done on earth as it is in heaven. Give us this day our daily bread: and forgive us our trespasses, as we forgive those who trespass against us. And lead us not into temptation. — R. But deliver us from evil. — Amen.

Tertullian says (*De Orat. c. 1*), that the Lord's Prayer is as brief and concise in words as it is full of thought (*quantum substringitur verbis, tantum diffunditur sensibus*), and then he designates it as "the abbreviated Gospel" (*breviarium totius Evangelii*), which "together with the especial theme of the prayer" — namely, the adoration of God and petition for man — "contains almost the whole sum of the doctrine and law of Christ." This glorious prayer is so profound in its signification, so rich in mysteries, in its efficacy so

---

[1] Cur hanc solam Orationem praecedit adhortatio, cum plures in hoc Canone faciamus et ad nullam hortati sumus? Quia illae sunt inferiores et humana ratione compositae; haec perfecta et a solo Deo formata (B. Odo Camer. In Can. dist. 4). — Dignum profecto fuit, ut tota haec tam sacrosancta actio Dominica oratione concluderetur, et petitiones fidelium, quas vel propter futuram vel propter praesentem vitam nos Dominus docuit, per eandem passionis ejus commemorationem *efficacius commendarentur*. Admonetur ergo *tota Ecclesia* et dicitur a sacerdote *"Oremus"* et *orat Ecclesia cum sacerdote*, non voce, sed corde: labia clausa sunt, sed patet conscientia; silentium est, clamat pectus, sed auribus ille audit qui miseretur (Florus Diac. n. 75).

[2] In all liturgies the Our Father is introduced by a Preface, in the Mozarabic and the ancient Gallican it continually varies according to the course of the ecclesiastical year. The Milan Liturgy has but twice (on Holy Thursday and Easter Sunday) a formula of this introduction differing somewhat from the Roman.

[3] Qui (sc. Dominus) inter cetera salutaria sua monita et praecepta divina, quibus populo suo consulit ad salutem, etiam orandi ipse formam dedit, ipse quid precaremur, *monuit* et *instruxit* (De orat. Domin. c. 2).

powerful, and in its arrangement so ingenious, that no one is able to conceive or express it.[1] There are innumerable explanations, more or less complete, of the *Pater Noster*; hence we content ourselves to give a mere sketch of its immeasurably rich contents,[2] and in so doing we shall adhere to the masterly interpretation of the Angelic Doctor.

The introduction of the prayer awakens confidence; but this is principally brought about by contemplating that love of God which desires our every good — hence we say: "Our Father"; then by considering His greatness and majesty, by virtue of which He can bestow on us every good — therefore do we say: "who art in heaven."[3]

The prayer itself contains not only all that we should ask for, but the succession one after another of the seven petitions shows the order which we should observe in imploring the various goods from God; it, therefore, regulates our affections, inclinations and desires (*est informativa totius nostri affectus*).

Evidently the first object of our desires is God Himself, who is the term and end of our whole being. — But our desires aspire to God in a twofold manner: on the one hand, inasmuch as we desire the glory for God Himself — and on the other, inasmuch as we desire the glory of God for ourselves, that is, we would share its enjoyment. Accordingly, the first petition reads: "hallowed be Thy name," whereby we implore the glorification of God; the second: "Thy kingdom come," whereby we ask that we may arrive at the participation in the glory and beatitude of His heavenly kingdom.

The two following petitions refer to what is conducive to the attainment of our last end. For this it is, above all, necessary that we should merit eternal happiness by obediently keeping the divine commandments; but since we are unable to accomplish this by our own strength, we beg the necessary assistance of grace from on high with the words: "Thy will be done on earth as it is in heaven." — A further means for the attainment of our being and its end is our daily bread, inasmuch as thereby the bread of the soul is understood,

---

[1] De hujus orationis expositione, laude et efficacia tanta jam a sanctis atque catholicis doctoribus dicta sunt, ut paene taedio sit ea perlegere. Verumtamen nec digna nec sufficientia dicta sunt nec usquam dicentur. Tanta nempe est hujus gloriosae orationis profunditas in sensu, fecunditas in mysteriis, efficacia in effectu, artificialitas in processu seu ordine, ut nemo capere queat vel eloqui (Dion. Carthus. In c. 6. S. Matth.).

[2] In orationis dominicae expositione multa a sanctis Patribus dicta leguntur; sed quia mens orantis tot ea hora capere non potest, nos de singulis petitionibus pauca dicere volumus, ut qui orat intellegere possit quid petat et *intellegens devotior fiat* (Robert. Paulul. De offic. eccles. 1. 2, c. 38).

[3] Quamvis oratio ista communiter dirigenda sit ad totam Trinitatem, quae est unus Deus et Pater noster ratione creationis et justificationis seu naturae et gratiae: nam naturam et gratiam a Deo trino sortimur; in Missa tamen *specialiter ad Patrem* dirigitur, sicut orationes in Canone praecedentes et oratio proxime sequens (Dion. Carthus. Expos. Missae art. 37).

that is, chiefly the Most Holy Sacrifice of the Altar, whose daily reception is profitable to man, and in which, as in their fountain-source, all the other Sacraments are included; moreover, on the other hand, also inasmuch as thereby the bread of the body is understood, by which all is meant that serves and suffices for the maintenance of life. This is expressed by the fourth petition: "Give us this day our daily bread."

The last three petitions supplicate the removal of all impediments which could hinder us in the attainment of our last end. The first and greatest of these impediments is sin, which directly excludes us from the kingdom of heaven; hence we pray: "Forgive us our trespasses, as we forgive those who trespass against us." — Here is to be reckoned temptation to sin, which incites to oppose the will of God and renders its fulfilment difficult; therefore, we implore: "And lead us not into temptation," that is, do not permit us to be overcome by temptation, but strengthen us to gain the victory over it. — Finally, there is question in this place of evil, that is, the temporal consequences and punishments of sin, by which peace is disturbed and whence the necessaries of life cause concern; therefore, in the last petition we cry: "Deliver us from evil."

This last petition is here made in the name of the faithful by the acolyte or choir,[1] after which the priest concludes the "Our Father" by saying, in a low voice, *Amen*.[2] This *Amen* from the lips of the priest, who is mediator between God and man, has in this place a peculiar significance. It expresses not as at other times consent and desire, but is, so to speak, the answer that God has received and heard the petition of the people. — The "Our Father" is recited aloud,[3] or sung, in order that all present may join in the prayer with devout hearts and in childlike confidence,[4] to which they are also incited by the *Oremus*, previously said.

---

[1] Hoc septimum *chorus* succinit, in quo se orasse cum sacerdote ostendit. Ad hoc enim fuerat invitatus, cum sacerdos ante orationem Dominicam diceret *"Oremus"*. Deinde subjungit sacerdos *Amen* ad petitionum omnium praemissarum confirmationem (Robert. Paulul. 1. 2, c. 29). — Dicta oratione Dominica respondetur *"Sed libera nos a malo"; ipse autem sacerdos *tacite* respondet *"Amen"* (Constit. Hirsaug. 1. 1, c. 86).

[2] In orationis dominicae particula finali populus tamquam infirmus petiit a malo liberari. Cui sacerdos compatiens dixit *"Amen"*, desiderans dicti populi liberationem secundum unam, aut *petitionis susceptionem affirmans* secundum aliam ejus expositionem (Gabr. Biel, Exposit. Canon. Missae lect. 79).

[3] *Alta* et *distincta* voce dicitur, ut et *populus* et postea loco ipsius chorus *ultimam* petitionem quasi quendam orationis Dominicae epilogum recitare et sic in ejus partem venire potuerit (Krazer sect. 4, art. 1, c. 12, § 273). — In ecclesia ad altare Dei quotidie dicitur ista Dominica oratio et *audiunt* illam fideles (S. Aug. Sermo 58, n. 12).

[4] In the Gelasian and Gregorian Sacramentaries the Amen is omitted after the Our Father. Later (probably not until after the eleventh century) it was taken up in the rite, but recited only in a low tone (submissa voce) by the priest, as the

This divine prayer, so full of ineffable power, inspiration, holiness and unction, should indeed at all times be recited with profound devotion,[1] — but especially during the celebration of Mass, when before our eyes on the altar He reposes who taught and commanded us thus to pray.[2]

2. The last petition of the "Our Father" is continued in silence and enlarged upon by the priest: this appendix or addition to the Lord's Prayer is commonly called the Embolism.[3]

Libera nos, quaesumus, Domine, ab omnibus malis, praeteritis, praesentibus et futuris : et intercedente beata et gloriosa semper Virgine Dei genitrice	Deliver us, we beseech Thee, O Lord, from all evils, past, present and to come: and by the intercession of blessed and glorious Mary ever Virgin, Mother

people, or the acolyte, at the close of the Embolism, which really concludes the petitions of the Our Father, expresses by a loud Amen his faithful and devout assent, the confirmation and recommendation of these petitions. In the Hours of the Breviary the Amen is, on the contrary, to be added only when the entire Pater noster is recited in silence (totum secreto), for example, at Complin before the Confiteor; it is always omitted when the Our Father throughout is recited aloud (totum clara voce), for example, in the ferial prayers of Lauds and Vespers; or when it is recited in silence, but commenced and concluded aloud, for instance, in the dominical prayers of Prime and Complin.

[1] Hanc sacratissimam orationem ex divinae ac sempiternae Sapientiae fonte immediate manantem devotissime proferamus, et *tanto devotius*, *quanto frequentius*, ne frequentia incuriam pariat atque fastidium, sed eam saepius iterando crescamus semper in ejus effectu seu gratia, per quam ardentius solito repetatur (Dion. Carthus. In c. 6. S. Matth.).

[2] Oratio Dominica cum singulari et maxima devotione dicenda est in Missa, ubi Christus auctor ejus tam dignanter atque mirabiliter ac verissime praesens est, et qui eam taliter dicit, ineffabilem fructum reportat (Dion. Carthus. Expos. Missae art. 37).

[3] Embolismus, ἐμβολισμός from ἐμβάλλω, I add = inserted; substantive = insertion, middle links, addition. The Middle Age authors usually translate: superaugmentum, excrescentia. — Sequitur in altum praefatio Dominicae orationis et oratio Dominica cum *embolismo* (Ordo Rom. II, n. 11). — Sequitur *embolismus*, i. e. superaccrescens: superaccrescitur enim ultimae petitionis *repetitio* et *expositio* (Sicard. 1. 3, c. 6). On Good Friday this prayer is said aloud in tono orationis Missae ferialis; the Ambrosian Rite always prescribes that it should be recited aloud or chanted. The silent recitation of the Embolism is prescribed already in the fourth Ordo: Dicit domnus papa, interveniente *nullo sono*, hanc orationem: *Libera nos . . .* — Bishop Bonizo of Piacenza († 1088) is of opinion, that St. Gregory the Great ordered the silent recitation of the Embolism. Beatus Gregorius constituit, ut sequens oratio, quae sic incipit: "Libera nos, Domine, ab omnibus malis," quae ante eum *alta* voce decantabatur, *secrete* diceretur (Lib. de Sacramentis). The different, that is, the silent recitation serves to represent the Embolism as an ecclesiastical addition to the Lord's Prayer. — Facta *confirmatione* Dominicae orationis dicendo *"Amen"*, totus textus qui sequitur pro venia peccatorum orat et pro pace (B. Odo Camer. In Can. dist. 4).

Maria, cum beatis Apostolis tuis Petro et Paulo, atque Andrea, et omnibus Sanctis, da propitius pacem in diebus nostris: ut ope misericordiae tuae adjuti, et a peccato simus semper liberi, et ab omni perturbatione securi. Per eundem Dominum.

of God, together with Thy blessed Apostles Peter and Paul, and Andrew, and all Thy Saints, graciously give peace in our days: that aided by the help of Thy mercy, we may be always free from sin, and secure from all disturbance. Through the same Lord.

Why do we dwell so long at the petition for deliverance from all and every evil? Because this earth on which we, as exiled children of Eve, are still sojourning, is a land of thistles and thorns: who could possibly enumerate all the spiritual and corporal evils that sprout from the poisonous root of sin? The life of mortal man overflows with hardships and miseries, with sorrows and sicknesses, with cares and disquietudes, with dangers and temptations, with fear and anxiety, with grief and mourning. Truly, very many are the afflictions of the just; but in all their necessities the Lord hears and delivers them (Ps. 33, 20). Assuredly, "we are now the sons of God; and it hath not yet appeared what we shall be" (1 John 3, 2). The happiness, the dignity, the sublimity and glory of our adoption as children of God are not yet perfect here below, but only in a state of development and enveloped in the darkness of lowliness. Hence as long as we remain on earth, encompassed with infirmity and subject to suffering, to spiritual combat and labor, it is ever necessary for us to pray for deliverance[1] from all evils, past, present and to come. Of past evils, sins especially often continue to abide in their painful consequences, in their unhappy results and fruits — the latter, therefore, should be totally removed and obviated. In the present we are pressed down by evils from within and without, from all sides — and from these we wish to be delivered. The future is frequently enveloped in darkness, and in its bosom conceals a host of threatening evils — and from these we would beg to be spared.

The infinitely holy and just God oftentimes permits painful visitations, sufferings and tribulations to befall us, not merely for our trial and purification from all inordinate attachment to the world, but also as a chastisement for our sins, imperfections and infidelities; therefore, we earnestly beseech the Lord not to chastise us in His

---

[1] Liberare, to loosen, to deliver us from something that, as it were, chains or binds us; here in the full sense = to deliver from evils present and to preserve (protect against) us from impending evils (inde se recte dicunt liberari, quo per liberatores suos non sunt permissi perduci — S. Aug.). In consuetudine latinae linguae liberari duobus modis dicitur et maxime in eo consuevimus audire hoc verbum, ut quicumque liberatur, intellegatur periculum evadere, molestiis carere (S. Aug. Sermo 134, n. 2). — Cfr. the petitions: ut noxia *cuncta* submoveat — haec hostia salutaris ab *omnibus* non tueatur adversis.

wrath and indignation (Ps. 6, 2), but to regard us with the eyes of His favor and be propitious to us (*propitius*), and to give us true peace in our days (*pacem in diebus nostris*).[1] We here pray in the first place for interior peace of soul, which consists in this, that by the powerful assistance[2] of the Divine Mercy we may ever keep ourselves free from sin and at a distance from it, whereby we shall persevere in the blessed love and friendship of God and rejoice in the sweet consolations of His grace. Afterward for exterior peace of life, which consists in this, that by God's help and merciful protection we may be ever secure from all disturbances, disquietudes, disorders, molestations, persecutions, by which in our frailty we are easily drawn from the right path of salvation and led into evil. If the days of our life are not darkened by fears from within and combats from without (2 Cor. 7, 5), that is, by the bitterness of sin and the misery of contention, then we enjoy the blessings of interior and exterior peace,[3] whereby we taste already beforehand some drops from the fountain of heavenly, eternal peace. — To obtain the inestimable gift of this desirable peace the more easily and in greater abundance, we have recourse to the intercession "of the glorious Mary, ever Virgin, Mother of God, together with the blessed Apostles Peter and Paul, and Andrew,[4] and all the Saints." For the sake of such intercessors, our supplications will be answered, and the superabundant riches of the divine mercy be imparted to us.

Whilst the priest prays: "Graciously give peace in our days," he makes the sign of the Cross on himself with the paten,[5] to express symbolically the desire of participating in that peace which Christ

---

[1] Exaudi nos, Deus salutaris noster, et dies nostros in tua pace dispone, ut a cunctis perturbationibus liberati, tranquilla tibi servitute famulemur (Sacram. Gregor.). — Ecclesia deprecatur pacem in diebus *nostris*, quod et post nos alii et post ipsos alii usque ad finem saeculi similiter orabunt (Pseudo-Alcuin. c. 40).

[2] Ope from the obsolete ops = every assisting means; power, vigor, strength, assistance, support.

[3] Populus fidelium in hujus saeculi peregrinatione, tamquam in Babylone captivus et supernae patriae suspirans, orat etiam pro pace *temporali*, ne impediatur a *spirituali*, ut, remotis per Dei pietatem omnibus adversitatibus, quietam et tranquillam vitam agat Ecclesia. Hoc autem *paucissimis*, sed *eminentissimis* Sanctis nominatis exorat (Pseudo-Alcuin. c. 40).

[4] These three Apostles are also in the first place in the list of the Saints before the Consecration. As the brother of St. Peter, the Prince of the Apostles, St. Andrew was ever held in great veneration in Rome and his feast kept with marked solemnity. (Cfr. Ordo Rom. XI, n. 76.) In the Middle Age the celebrant could according to his pleasure mention here other saints — especially the Patrons of the Church. Aliorum Sanctorum nomina annumerare non debemus, nisi quos in Canone invenimus antiquitus descriptos, excepto post "Pater noster" in illa oratione, ubi juxta Ordinem quorumlibet Sanctorum nomina internumerare possumus (Microl. c. 13. Cfr. Ordo Rom. IV).

[5] In the Middle Age the paten was kissed previous to the sign of the Cross in many places. Vide quod sacerdos cum *osculata* patena se in ultima clausula signat (Sicard. 1. 3, c. 6. Cfr. Durand. 1. 4, c. 50, n. 4).

brought us by His Cross and by the Sacrifice of His Body; for soon after the (broken) Host is placed on the paten.[1] The kissing of the paten[2] is a sign of love and reverence toward this "new sepulchre" of the holy Body of Christ.[3]

67. The Liturgical Act of the Fraction of the Host and the Mingling of the Consecrated Elements.

The breaking of the Host is connected with the concluding formula belonging to the Embolism: *Per eundem Dominum nostrum Jesum Christum Filium tuum, qui tecum vivit et regnat in unitate Spiritus sancti Deus per omnia saecula saeculorum.   R. Amen.* While the priest says in silence: "Through the same our Lord Jesus Christ, Thy Son," with both hands he holds the Host over the chalice and reverently breaks it in half, one half of which he lays with his

---

[1] In the most ancient times the breads offered were consecrated on the paten, later on the corporal, and only the fraction of the Host took place on the paten; already during the Middle Age the present rite originated of placing the Host on the paten before and after the breaking over the chalice (ut facilius tolli possit). Patenam sacerdos de manu diaconi suscipit et in altari, ut fractionem super eam faciat, deponit.   Nos tamen hanc fractionem ad *cautelam* faciamus super *calicem* (Robert. Paulul. l. 2, c. 39).

[2] According to the (three) oldest Roman Ordines the paten was not kissed in this place by the celebrant, but only by the archdeacon; first in the Ordo Rom. V, n. 10 (of the eleventh century) appears the rubric: Patenas diaconus episcopo osculandas praebeat.   The present rite is found in Ordo Rom. XIV, c. 53: Pontifex patenam accipiens cum dextra manu, quando dicit "intercedente b. Dei genitrice..." faciat sibi cum ipsa patena signum crucis (a complete sign of the Cross), et quando dicit "da propitius..." osculetur ipsam patenam in *superiori* ejus *parte* (on the upper end or rim). — The present rubric: Patenam ipsam osculatur is more accurately explained by a decree: Patena in extremitate seu in ora congruentius osculanda est (S. R. C. 24. Jul. 1683).

[3] In Spain many priests communicated immediately after the Pater noster, or after the Embolism, and only afterward gave the blessing to the congregation. To oppose these innovations the Fourth Council of Toledo (633) prescribed, ut post Orationem dominicam et conjunctionem panis et calicis benedictio in populum sequatur et tunc demum sacramentum corporis et sanguinis Domini sumatur. After the summons Humiliate vos benedictioni and the salutation (Dominus sit...), the formula of blessing was pronounced, to the individual petitions of which the people answered Amen. The ancient Gallican Rite had also at this place a similar imparting of the blessing. The benediction formulas were manifold. In Spain bishops and priests used the same formula, but the priest was not permitted to impart the blessing in presence of a bishop. In Gaul priests made use of a shorter formula than bishops, which was not subject to change; it was as follows: Pax, fides, caritas et communio corporis et sanguinis Christi sit semper vobiscum. It appears that in Germany likewise — at least in some places — at Pontifical Mass the episcopal blessing was solemnly imparted before the Communion. The Roman Rite, as well as the Greek and Oriental Liturgies, ignores the above benediction.   Cfr. the remarks of Lesley, S. J., on the Mozarabic Missal (Migne 85, 592). — Gerbert. Vetus Liturg. Alemann. p. 1, disp. 4, c. 3, n. 39.

right hand on the paten; and while continuing; "Who liveth and reigneth with Thee," from the other half he breaks from below[1] a particle and holds it firmly in the right hand; after which he proceeds: "in the unity of the Holy Ghost, God," and at the same time joining the other half in the left hand with that on the paten in such wise that the Host again appears entire and round; — at the last words: "World without end," to which the acolyte answers *Amen*, the priest raises his voice, and then says aloud: *Pax † Domini sit † semper vobis†cum* — "May the peace † of the Lord be † always with † you," while with the small particle he makes the sign of the Cross three times over the chalice. After the acolyte has given to this salutation the answer: *Et cum spiritu tuo* — "And with thy spirit," the priest drops the particle of the Host into the chalice, and whilst doing so he says, not aloud, but in silence[2]:

Haec commixtio et consecratio Corporis et Sanguinis Domini nostri Jesu Christi fiat accipientibus nobis in vitam aeternam. Amen.	May the mingling and the consecration of the Body and Blood of our Lord Jesus Christ be unto us that receive it effectual unto life everlasting. Amen.

The liturgical *fraction of the Host* and the *mingling* of the consecrated elements is a rite very simple, but exceedingly rich in mysteries. This small portion of the Eucharistic Celebration is of profound significance and of the highest importance; this is even proved by the circumstance that this rite of the fraction and the mingling, although greatly modified, yet as to its essential features is found to agree in the liturgies of all countries and times. Even if this rite in former times was occasioned and influenced by natural reasons and considerations, still it is to be absolutely held that both the fraction and the mingling have a higher symbolical signification. In their explanation, it must not be forgotten that the breaking and mingling of the consecrated elements are intimately connected, that is, constitute a liturgical whole.

1. The Fraction of the Host (*fractio, κλάσις*). — The great importance of this rite is already indicated by the fact that the bishop after the ordination of the newly ordained priests, urges them to carefully study the entire rite of the Mass, before they celebrate, especially the Consecration, the Fraction and the Communion. Although here the fraction of the Host is mentioned together with the Consecration and Communion, still it would be erroneous to describe it as an essential or even as an integral part of the Eucha-

---

[1] Pars *inferior* praecidi debet (S. R. C. 4. Aug. 1663).

[2] In the Mozarabic Rite the prayer for the mingling is as follows: Sancta sanctis (τὰ ἅγια τοῖς ἁγίοις) et conjunctio corporis (et sanguinis) D. N. J. Ch. sit sumentibus (= edentibus) et potantibus nobis ad veniam, et defunctis fidelibus praestetur ad requiem; — in the Ambrosian Missal: Commixtio consecrati corporis et sanguinis D. N. J. Ch. nobis edentibus et sumentibus (= potantibus) proficiat ad vitam et gaudium sempiternum.

ristic Sacrificial action.[1] The ritual fraction of the Host is, indeed, very significant in the constitution of the sacrificial celebration, but in no wise does it touch upon the essence or integrity of the Sacrifice. — The peculiar importance of this breaking of the Host is manifold. At one time it is done in imitation of what the Lord did at the Last Supper, when He broke the Eucharistic Bread before distributing it (*fregit deditque*); hence in the early ages, the Eucharistic Sacrifice and Communion celebration were designated by the name of the breaking of bread (*fractio panis* — cf. Act. 2, 42; 20, 7. 11. 1 Cor. 10, 16). — Consequently, the liturgical breaking of the Host has a profound significance in a twofold connection, first, with the preceding sacrificial action, and, secondly, with the Communion which follows.

The Host is broken in order more vividly to represent in a liturgical manner the Eucharist's character as a Sacrifice; for the breaking symbolizes in an expressive way Christ's violent and bloody death on the Cross, inasmuch as it indicates that wounding and lacerating which caused the separation of His soul from His body, that is, brought about and resulted in His death.[2] In the fraction of the Host, Christ is figured as the Lamb that was slain and bruised for our sins (Is. 53, 5). The breaking of the Host, therefore, expresses the same as is represented by the double Consecration under the two different and separate appearances. To this is added the circumstance that the Host is broken over the chalice.[3] This rite may be founded especially on great reverence towards the Most Holy Sacrament, so that any loose particles may fall into the Precious Blood[4]; but, nevertheless, the breaking can have, besides, and it really has a mystical signification.[5] The fraction of the Eucharistic Bread over the chalice is intended to indicate that the Blood contained in the chalice proceeds from the broken, that is, from the wounded and

---

[1] Fractio hostiae consecratae et quod una sola pars mittatur in calicem, respicit corpus mysticum, sicut admixtio aquae significat populum et ideo horum praetermissio non facit imperfectionem sacrificii, ut propter hoc sit necesse aliquid reiterare circa celebrationem hujus sacramenti (S. Thom. 3, q. 83, a. 6 ad 6).

[2] Sicut species sacramentales sunt sacramentum corporis Christi veri, ita fractio hujusmodi specierum est *sacramentum dominicae passionis*, quae fuit in corpore Christi vero (S. Thom. 3, q. 77, a. 7).

[3] In the eleventh century the Host was broken on the paten. Archidiaconus patenam osculatam dat uni ex diaconibus tenendam, ad *confractionem in ea faciendam*. Unde sacerdos sine ministro sacrificans ad eundem locum eam de sub corporali absconditam resumit et osculatam in altari deponit, ut *hostiam in ea confringat* (Microl. c. 17).

[4] Super *calicem* frangitur, ne minutiae spargantur, sed in ejus concavitate caute recipiantur (Durand. Ration. l. 4, c. 51).

[5] Confractio et commixtio corporis Domini tantis mysteriis declarata *antiquitus* sanctis Patribus fuit, ut dum sacerdos oblationem frangeret, videbatur quasi Angelus Dei membra fulgentis pueri cultro concaedere et *sanguinem ejus in calicem excipiendo colligere* (S. Germanus, Expositio brevis antiquae Liturgiae Gallicanae [Migne 72, 94]).

23

mangled Body of Christ, and, therefore, belongs to it and is one with it, and with it constitutes but one Sacrifice and one Sacrificial Gift.[1]

That the fraction of the Eucharistic species has also a connection with Communion, that is, is a preparation and introduction to it, is universally acknowledged; for "to break the bread" means the same as to prepare it for food, to present or distribute it for participation.[2] But this connection ought to be more deeply and more fully understood. The fraction characterizes the Eucharistic Bread of Life as a sacrificial food; for it means that the Body of Christ broken for us, that is, *sacrificed*, is given in Communion to be eaten. The Lord Himself has promised: "The (heavenly) bread, that I will give (sacrifice), is My flesh for the life of the world" (John 6, 52). Inasmuch as Christ gave His Body to God for us in His bloody death of the Cross, and daily on the altar gives it in a mystical sacrificial death — which twofold giving is symbolized by the liturgical breaking of the Host —, He makes it a sacrificial food, which is administered and partaken of in Holy Communion.

According to the Roman rite the consecrated bread, at least since the ninth century, is divided into three parts, as is still done [3]; all three parts are consumed by the celebrant, the two larger together, the smallest with the sacred Blood, into which it was dropped. — Formerly the usage was somewhat different. As the Hosts were much larger, one of these three parts was subdivided into several particles and used differently, that is, distributed to those present, or

---

[1] Fractio significat passionem Domini ... frangitur autem supra calicem *propter reverentiam* Sacramenti, ne aliqua ejus particula aliorsum prosiliat ... praeterea *ad significandum*, quod in fractione, h. e. in vulneratione corporis Christi, sanguis, qui in calice continetur, continue fluxit de corpore (Gabr. Biel, Expos. Can. Miss. lect. 80).

[2] "The breaking of the Body takes place at the sacred Banquet; on the Cross it did not occur, but rather the contrary, since it is said: 'Neither shall you break a bone thereof' (Exod. 12, 46). What He did not suffer on the Cross, He suffers for thy sake at the Holy Sacrifice, and He permits Himself to be broken that He may satiate all" (St. Chrysostom, 24th Homily on 1 Cor. 10, 27).

[3] In the Mozarabic Liturgy the Host is broken into nine parts, which are named after the chief mysteries of redemption: 1. Corporatio (Incarnation); 2. Nativitas (Nativity); 3. Circumcisio (Circumcision); 4. Apparitio (Apparition); 5. Passio (Passion); 6. Mors (Death); 7. Resurrectio (Resurrection); 8. Gloria (Glorification); 9. Regnum (Kingdom). The first seven parts are placed on the paten in such a manner as to form a cross, while the two remaining portions are placed to the right at the foot of the cross (ultra rotas, that is, outside of the marks in the form of a ring affixed to the paten for the other seven particles).

```
        1
   6    2    7
        3
        4    8
        5    9
```

sent to the absent,[1] or put into the chalice at the next sacrificial celebration.[2] Participation in the same Holy Sacrifice was regarded as
a sign and pledge of ecclesiastical Communion; mutually to prove
and maintain this, Popes and bishops sent to other bishops, or priests
too, parts of Consecrated Hosts, which the recipients dropped into
the chalice and consumed.[3] This division of the Host into three
parts was also in various ways symbolically interpreted. The three
parts were, for example, referred to the Holy Trinity or to the earthly
life, to the sacrificial death and the eternal glory of Christ, but
generally and principally to the mystical Body of Christ, which is
represented by the true Body of Christ, that is, the Church, and the
three parts of the Host were interpreted to refer to the Church militant, suffering and triumphant; and on this again views differed.[4]

2. The Mingling of the Body and Blood of Christ in the
Chalice.[5] — There is an immediate and intimate union between the

---

[1] Sacerdos rumpit hostiam ex *dextro* latere juxta Ordinem ad designandam
dominici lateris percussionem. Deinde majorem partem in duo confringit, ut *tres*
portiones de corpore dominico efficere possit. Nam *unam* in calicem, faciendo
crucem, mittere debet, cum dicit: "Pax Domini...", ad designandum corporis et
animae conjunctionem in resurrectione Christi. *Alteram* vero ipse presbyter
necessario sumit ante calicis participationem juxta dominicam institutionem.
Tertiam autem communicaturis sive infirmis necessario dimittit (Microl. c. 17).—
Diaconus sacerdoti offerat patenam, in qua sacerdos corpus Domini *tripliciter*
dividat, quarum partium *unam* sacerdos calici immittens "*Pax Domini*" alta voce
dicendo, protinus subdat secrete: "Fiat commixtio corporis et sanguinis Domini
nobis accipientibus in vitam aeternam." *Alia* se, diaconum subdiaconumque communicet. *Tertiam* viaticum, si opus fuerit, in patena usque ad finem Missae
reservet; si autem opus non fuerit, tertiam sacerdos aut unus ministrorum accipiat
(Joann. Abrincens. [† 1079], De offic. eccles.).

[2] A particle previously consecrated was preserved and united to the Precious
Blood at the following Sacrifice, to represent, in all probability, the continual
succession of the Sacrifice, as well as the unity of the last with the present celebration (Fortasse ut sacrificii unitas et perpetuitas hoc ritu inculcaretur—Mabillon).

[3] This custom existed in Rome until about the ninth century. There the Pope
on Sundays and feast-days sent to those priests who had charge of Divine service
at the churches within the city, the Eucharist as a symbol of communion with the
ecclesiastical Head, and as a sign that they were empowered to celebrate. To more
distant churches, situated outside the city, the Eucharist was not permitted to be
borne, — through reverence for the Holy Mysteries and also because the priests in
those places had already permission to celebrate the Holy Sacrifice. The name
"fermentum", whereby these consecrated particles were designated by Popes
Melchiades, Siricius and Innocent I., has received various interpretations. (Cfr.
the Brief [epistola regularis] of Pope Innocent I. [402–417] to Decentius, Bishop of
Gubbio.) — Mabillon, In Ord. Rom. comment. praevius c. 6.

[4] Clichtov. Elucid. eccles. 1. 3, n. 69. — Sylvius, In III. S. Thom. q. 83, art. 5.

[5] Ancient writers have various designations for this universally prescribed
rite, for example, commixtio corporis et sanguinis Domini — conjunctio panis et
calicis — immissio panis in vinum v. calicem — officium consecrationis; the Greeks
and Orientals ἡ ἀγία ἕνωσις (= sacra unitio) — consignatio et commixtio mysteriorum. — Hac oratione (the Embolism) expleta, commiscens sacerdos Dominicam

fraction of the Host and the mingling[1] of the Eucharistic species. If we pay attention to this connection, the object and meaning of the rite of mingling will easily be seen from the stated symbolism of the fraction. In the separate consecration under two species, as well as in the liturgical fraction of the Host, Christ's Body and Blood appear as though they were separated from each other; but from the fact that the consecrated elements are united with each other by mingling, it is thereby symbolically expressed that in reality on the altar the Body is not without the Blood, and the Blood not without the Body, but under each species the *whole* Christ is present as *one* sacrificial gift and *one* sacrificial food. — As, furthermore, the mystical separation of the Body and Blood of Christ by the Consecration and fraction represents His bloody sacrificial death, so the mystical union of the Body and Blood of Christ by this mingling symbolizes His glorious resurrection, in which His Body and Blood were again united and vivified.[2] If we consider both of these meanings together,

oblationem, ut calix Domini totam plenitudinem contineat sacramenti, tamquam per ejusdem mysterii copulationem imprecatur Ecclesiae pacem, dicens: *Pax Domini* . . . (Pseudo-Alcuin. c. 40). — Immissionem panis in vinum cerno apud quosdam varie actitari, ita ut aliqui primo mittant de sancta in calicem et postea dicant: *Pax Domini* . . .; econtra aliqui reservent immissionem, usque dum pax celebrata sit et fractio panis (Amalar. 1. 3, c. 31).

[1] In Rome for a considerable time (perhaps until the ninth century) it was customary to unite the Sacred Body and Blood of Christ twice in the chalice when celebrating Mass. The first time, when a previously consecrated Host, or a Host received from another place, was used, it took place at the salutation of peace (Pax Domini . . .) after the Our Father; the second time, for which was used a particle broken from the Host just consecrated, did not take place until the Communion. (Cfr. Ordo Rom. I, n. 18. 19. 22. — II, n. 12. 13.) Hence Amalarius in his explanation of the Roman Rite speaks of a *bis* positus panis in calicem (De eccles. offic. 1. 3, c. 31). But when the custom of sending the Eucharist to other churches as a sign of union ceased, only one immission of a particle in the chalice was retained — the first one at the kiss of peace. Only when the Pope officiated, the union of the sacramental species at this point was omitted, taking place after the consuming of the Sacred Body. This variation continued until about the fifteenth century, when at the Pontifical Mass of the Pope the universal and still existing mingling rite came into use. (Cfr. Ordo Rom. IV et XIV. — Innocent. III. De sacr. alt. myst. 1. 6, c. 9.) — According to the Ordo Rom. I, n. 8, as the Pope advanced to the altar, the Eucharist (Sancta, τὰ ἅγια) was carried before him in an open case (capsae) by two acolytes. This particle, preserved from the previous Consecration, was dropped into the Precious Blood after the salutation of peace Pax Domini . . . — Ex his conjicere licet, recentiorem morem Eucharistiam praeferendi Pontifici, cum aliquo proficiscitur, forsitan manasse non solum ex communi primorum christianorum more, qui peregrinantes Eucharistiam secum gestare solebant, sed etiam ex veteri consuetudine deferendi sacrosancta mysteria ante Pontificem, cum ad Missarum solemnia celebranda ad altare procederet, qui tamen ritus in primo tantum Romani Ordinis libello praescribitur, non in aliis. Nam secundus libellus praecipit, ut Pontifex, cum venerit ad altare, *"primo adoret Sancta"*, quae proinde ibidem antea exstitisse necesse est (Mabillon, In Ord. Rom. comment. praev. c. 6).

[2] Per particulam oblatae immissae in calicem ostenditur *corpus* Christi, quod

we can then say that the liturgical act of mingling is intended to represent the Eucharistic Saviour as the *undivided* and *living* Victim on the altar. — As the breaking of the Host, so likewise can the mingling be referred to the Communion, for the union of the Eucharistic Body and Blood contains an allusion to the fact that the whole Christ, and indeed the gloriously risen, is the Bread of Life for the world.

The rite of the fraction and the mingling, therefore, announces in a mystical but eloquent manner the sufferings destined for Christ and His subsequent glory (1 Peter 1, 11), in this that it represents Him as the Lamb that was slain and now lives eternally (Apoc. 1, 18). Therein is placed before our eyes that "wonderful battle, in which death and life contended with each other," and we behold how "the Prince of Life died and now living reigneth."

3. The Threefold Sign of the Cross.[1] After the breaking and before the mingling, the priest makes with the piece of the Host broken off in his right hand, three signs of the Cross over the chalice, using the salutation: "May the peace of the Lord be always with you." The fact that this salutation of peace is made precisely between the symbolical fraction and mingling, signifies that Christ by His redeeming death and glorious resurrection has become the author and source of true peace; likewise does the sign of the Cross over the chalice, containing the Precious Blood, allude to the fact that the peace of God was purchased and negotiated for us by the holy Cross and the blood shed thereon: "for through the blood of the Cross hath Christ made peace, both as to the things on earth and the things that are in heaven" (Col. 1, 20). Moreover, in this connection the sign of the Cross illustrates and completes the meaning of

---

resurrexit a mortuis (Joann. Abrinc. De officiis ecclesiast.). — *Pax Domini . . .* dicens, sacerdos vel episcopus ter super calicem cum particula signat et infundit calici, quia cunctis in coelo et terra pacificatis *ad corpus rediit anima* Jesu Christi. Quidam infundunt, antequam dicant *Pax Domini . . .*, quod etiam non vacat a mysterio, quia *post resurrectionem* manifestum est pacem datam hominibus bonae voluntatis (Sicard. 1. 3, c. 8).

[1] As may be seen from the most ancient Roman Ordines, as early as the ninth century the sign of the Cross was made three times over the chalice with a small particle — but not until the dropping of the (second) particle (immediately before receiving the Precious Blood), when the present prayer at the mingling (Fiat commixtio et consecratio . . .) was recited. (Cfr. Ordo Rom. I, n. 19. — II, n. 13.) — According to Ordo IV no prayer was then said: Quando communicat domnus apostolicus, partem sibi mordet et reliquam in calice mittit, faciens crucem de ea tribus vicibus super calicem nihil dicens. — *Crux* quae formatur *super calicem particulae oblatae*, ipsum nobis corpus ante oculos praescribit, quod pro nobis crucifixum est. Ideo tangit quattuor latera calicis, quia per illud hominum genus quattuor climatum ad unitatem unius corporis accessit et ad pacem catholicae Ecclesiae (Amalar. 1. 3, c. 31). — Cum dicitur: Pax Domini . . . inter calicem fit triplex signaculum crucis ad laudem et honorem ss. Trinitatis, quae misit Agnum qui per crucem salvavit mundum et fecit pacem hominum et angelorum (Stephan. Augustod. De sacram. altar. c. 18).

the previous fraction, inasmuch as it more particularly characterizes the thereby symbolized immolation of the divine Victim as a Sacrifice accomplished on the Cross. Finally, with regard to the mingling that follows, the crossing of the chalice with the Host expresses that the glory of the resurrection was given to the Saviour as a reward for His ready self-humiliation even to the death of the Cross.

4. The Prayer at the Mingling. — The dropping of the small particle of the Host into the most precious Blood is designated in the accompanying prayer as the mingling (*commixtio*) and consecration (*consecratio*) of the Body and Blood of Christ. The question, what is here the sense and signification of the word *consecratio*, presents great difficulties, as is already evident from the many readings of said passage in the liturgical documents[1] and from the numerous attempts at explanation by liturgical writers.

The words *haec commixtio et consecratio* have been frequently understood in a concrete sense = *may these mingled and consecrated[2] sacrificial gifts of the Body and Blood of Christ* be effectual to us unto life everlasting.[3] This conception is assuredly favored by the

---

[1] Commixtio consecrati corporis et sanguinis — haec sacrosancta commixtio corporis et sanguinis — conjunctio corporis et sanguinis — haec commixtio corporis et sanguinis — fiat commixtio et consecratio corporis et sanguinis — fiat commixtio et consecratio corporis et sanguinis D. N. J. Ch. nobis accipientibus vita aeterna — haec sacra commixtio corporis et sanguinis D. N. J. Ch.

[2] Both expressions are also correctly used in another sense (= commixtum et consecratum); for example, in Leviticus 27, 29 we find consecratio = dedicated.

[3] The words consecration of the body and of the blood signify here merely *the consecrated body and blood* (Lebrun p. 5, art. 5). — Respondeo, consecrationem hic objective sumi pro *rebus consecratis*, non formaliter pro actu, quo res consecrantur (Tournely, Tract. de Euchar. p. 2, c. 10, art. 2). — In support of this conception are adduced the words of the holy deacon Lawrence to Pope Xystus II., when the latter was led to martyrdom: Experire, utrum idoneum ministrum elegeris. Cui commisisti *dominici sanguinis consecrationem*, cui consummandorum consortium sacramentorum, huic sanguinis tui consortium negas? (S. Ambr. De offic. ministr. l. 1, c. 41.) Sanguinis consecratio, namely, is conceived as = sanguis consecratus, the distribution of which was a function of the deacon. But the reception of the Precious Blood forms, as Micrologus asserts (c. 19), the *complementum* communionis, and the Holy Communion generally as the Sacrificial Banquet is the termination of the Sacrificial Mysteries, so that we can say the deacon shares (consortium) in the consummatio, that is, in the accomplishment of the Eucharistic Sacrifice. This interpretation may of course be accepted, but it does not appear to exhaust the full sense of the expression *consecratio* sanguinis dominici. The deacon is ordained mainly, ut *proxime* assistat sacerdoti sacra facienti sitque ejus in tanti mysterii celebratione *adjutor* (Menardus), and in the Pontif. Roman. he is called *comminister et cooperator* corporis et sanguinis Domini; hence a certain participation not merely in dispensing Holy Communion, but also in the celebration of the Sacrifice can and must be ascribed to him. In this sense, then, is the deacon admitted "to the consecrating and offering of the Blood of the Lord, to the accomplishment of the Holy Mysteries." (Cfr. Bona, Rerum liturgic. l. 1, c. 25, § 4, cum notis et observationibus R. Sala.)

circumstance, that not the mingling and consecration act as such, but the mingled and consecrated elements are for us the source of life[1]; but this explanation cannot altogether suffice, because it does not explain or take into consideration at all the act of *commixtio et consecratio* occurring at the same time.

If, as evidently must be done, we note and emphasize the present act also, then the difficult question arises: In what sense can we say that Christ's Body and Blood are consecrated by the mingling, that is, as though in consequence of the mingling? To solve the difficulty, it has been said that the word *consecratio* does, indeed, refer to the Eucharistic change of substance, but to it as already previously accomplished, — and that here we pray only for the fruit thereof[2]; this explanation is inadmissible, for the formula without any doubt whatsoever mentions in this place an action accomplished at the very moment of the mingling, that is, of a present consecration (*haec commixtio et [haec] consecratio*).

Just as little can these words and the rite therewith connected mean an "Epiklese concisely expressed", that is, a petition for the transsubstantiation of the bread and wine.

Others endeavor to settle the existing difficulty precisely in the opposite way, by taking the word *consecratio* as having always the same meaning as *commixtio*, that is, they would thereby understand only the mingling of holy things. But such an explanation weakens entirely too much the signification of the expression *consecratio;* for it would and should prove more than the mere mingling of sanctified objects.[3] In what consists this *more*, that is, what further and new quality does the *consecratio* add to the *commixtio?* We are going to indicate some points, which may be of advantage in elucidating the subject under consideration.

Let us recall the essence and object of the liturgical act of mingling. Among other reasons it is intended to symbolize the resurrection of Christ. Whilst Christ's Body and Blood in the previous separation of the species represent His bloody death, they afterward by the union of the species become the symbol of His glorious resurrection, that is, they receive a new and at the same time a holy significance, for which reason one may say they are (in

---

[1] Commixtio et consecratio dicuntur fieri in nostram salutem, non quod ipsa actio commiscendi et consecrandi nos salvet, sed quia res ipsae commixtae et consecratae, dum a nobis devote suscipiuntur, multum prosunt ad salutem; unde hic dicimus: fiat sumentibus nobis in vitam aeternam (Bellarm. De Missa l. 2, c. 27). — Non ex ipsa commiscendi cum sanguine corporis *actione* salutem et vitam exspectamus, sed ex corpore et sanguine Christi, quae commiscentur a nobis, ut post adumbratam passionem, adumbremus et resurrectionem, quae ad justificationem nostram cum ipsa passione suo modo concurrit (Tournely l. c.).

[2] Non petimus, ut nunc fiat consecratio, sed ut consecratio *antea facta* sit nobis at vitam aeternam salutaris (Bellarm. l. c.).

[3] With reference to Pope Pelagius I. consecrare should be also = simul sacrare (i. e. res sacras commiscere).

a certain sense) consecrated.[1] The liturgical act of mingling, accordingly, effects a certain *consecratio corporis et sanguinis Domini*, inasmuch as it further imparts to them a holy and a mystical signification, for by Consecration (*consecratio*) one may denote an action by which an object is raised unto and made a symbol of a holy mystery.[2] — By Consecration (*consecratio*) we, therefore, frequently understand the dedication and gift of a person or object to God, and this feature also is found in the act of mingling; for Christ appears therein as the resuscitated, living Pasch, and as such is represented or offered to God.[3] In the mingling Christ's glorious sacrificial Body is consecrated and dedicated to God for us.[4] — Of a translation to a more holy state, of a real, or a greater sanctification the word *consecratio* never can nor should be understood, when reference is made to the Body and Blood of Christ. Even at the moment of the Eucharistic Consecration, Christ's Body and Blood are not in themselves sanctified, but only transformed into the sacramental, that is, into a special sanctifying state. This is what is meant by the expression "Consecration of the Body and Blood of Christ," when it is used to designate the Elevation. Therefore, in the mingling Christ's Body and Blood cannot be still further sanctified; but may this be asserted of the Eucharistic species? As is evident to us, it may. The reason consists in this that the species of bread and wine are in a true sense mingled (united), which cannot be said of the Body and Blood of Christ concealed in them. The ordinary mode of expression: that the Body of the Lord is broken and united with His Blood, would in no way denote a change in the Body and Blood of Christ, but merely in the sacramental species[5] — and at the same time set

---

[1] Posset etiam fortasse commode responderi, agi hoc loco de *nova quadam consecratione*, quae ex commixtione nunc primum exsurgit. . . . Porro haec consecratio nihil aliud est, nisi *nova quaedam significatio sacramentalis:* ut enim consecrari dicitur, quod acquirit sacramentalem significationem, ita etiam dicitur *iterum* consecrari, quod acquirit *aliam* significationem sacramentalem. Significatur autem per illam commixtionem resurrectio Domini . . . nam in resurrectione iterum caro Domini cum sanguine suo conjuncta fuit. Itaque in illa commixtione nova fit consecratio, dum species illae, quae divisae Christi mortem repraesentabant, nunc inter se conjunctae resurrectionem Domini repraesentant (Bellarm. De Missa l. 2, c. 27). Suarez (disp. 83, sect. 2, n. 19) says of this opinion: probabilitate non caret.

[2] The word sacramentum (τὸ μυστήριον) is often = signum rei sacrae, signum sacrum, significatio arcana, figura, typus. Hence consecrare may also signify as much as making something a sacramentum, that is, sacrum signum, a holy symbol, imparting to it a sacred mysterious character.

[3] Quae verba (at the mingling) precantur, ut fiat corpus Domini praesens *oblatio per resurrectionem*, per quam veneranda et aeterna pax data est, non solum in terra, sed etiam in coelo (Amalar. l. 3, c. 31).

[4] Cfr. S. Thom. 3, q. 22, a. 2 ad 3.

[5] Illud quod manducatur in propria specie, ipsum et frangitur et masticatur in sua specie; corpus autem Christi non manducatur in *sua* specie, sed in *specie sacramenti* et ideo ipsum corpus Christi *non frangitur* nisi *secundum speciem sacramentalem* (S. Thom. 3, q. 77, a. 7 ad 3).

off in a striking manner, that under the Eucharistic species, which are in reality broken and mingled, the *substances* of *bread* and *wine* are no longer present, but truly the *Body* and *Blood* of *Christ* are present and with them constitute a whole, that is, one Sacrament. The species are already holy by their connection with the Body and Blood of Christ; but when united to each other, they become still more sanctified. Inasmuch, therefore, as the sacred species of the Eucharist are truly mingled (united), they reciprocally impart their sanctity to each other, becoming thereby still more holy.[1] The aforesaid features — namely, the symbolizing of the Resurrection, the Consecration of the Body and Blood of Christ for God, the renewed sanctification of the visible sacramental sign — may serve in some degree to make us comprehend the liturgical act of mingling as a consecration (*consecratio*) of the consecrated elements.

5. Therefore, the mystical rite of fraction[2] and mingling[3] brings vividly before our eyes, in what manner the Divine Victim died and rose again for us, in order to become for us in the Eucharistic Sacrifice and in the Sacrificial Banquet the inexhaustible source of a higher heavenly life (*fiat accipientibus nobis in vitam aeternam*). "The Body of Christ, born as the Divine Victim for the sins of the world, was also the heavenly grain of wheat sown by the Holy Ghost in the virginal earth; it was the heavenly grape on the virgin vine which sprung up under the breath of the Holy Spirit. In order to become our sacrifice for the atonement of sins, the Body of Christ was to die and shed its blood upon the altar of the Cross; the heavenly grain of wheat was to die in the earth, the heavenly grape was to be trodden down. To become food and drink for the nourishment of our life of grace, the Body of Christ was again to resume its vitality. The heavenly wheat was to be ground and baked into the life-giving bread. The heavenly juice of the grape was to be pressed and fermented into the inebriating wine of life. Thus life and death were to be swallowed up in Christ, in order to make Him our life's bread and drink. He was to be dead and yet live, He was to be alive and yet die. How was this to be effected? This was accomplished at the Last Supper. This continually takes place in Holy Mass, where by virtue of the words of Christ, His Blood is repre-

---

[1] Cfr. the blessing of the Baptismal water, when the aqua *benedicta* (which serves for the liturgical sprinkling of the people), by mingling with it the Oil of Catechumens and the Chrism, is still further consecrated and rendered more perfect. *Sanctificetur* et foecundetur fons iste (which is already sanctified) *oleo salutis*.

[2] Fractio hostiae *tria* significat: *primo* quidem ipsam divisionem corporis Christi, quae facta est in passione; *secundo* distinctionem corporis mystici secundum diversos status; *tertio* distributionem gratiarum procedentium ex passione Christi (S. Thom. 3, q. 83, a. 5 ad 7).

[3] Fit haec permixtio: *primo* ad notandum, quod Christi corpus non fuit sine sanguine nec sanguis sine corpore; *secundo* ad designandum, quod unum sacramentum conficitur ex speciebus panis et vini; *tertio* corporis et sanguinis post trinum crucis signum permixtio est animae ad corpus reditio (Durandus l. 4, c. 51, n. 17).

sented separated from His Body, as the Blood of the immolated Victim to be shed and shed once for all on the Cross, but where in virtue of the blessed immortality of the Risen Christ, His living Body is permeated with His living Blood, to be to us the nourishment and refreshment of eternal life."[1]   Once when Blessed Angela of Foligno assisted at the Mass of an unworthy priest, at the Fraction of the Host she heard a low voice of murmuring, piercing sweetness thus complain: "Alas! how they break Me and make the Blood flow from My limbs!"   "Ah! my Brothers in this intolerable grace" (of being permitted to break the Body of the Lord), remarks Father Faber, alluding to this circumstance, "do we not each of us know in his own secret soul at least one priest, and that there can be but one, who, if he had his due, could never break the Host without having his own heart broken also by the lamentable sweetness of that plaintive cry?"

68.   The Agnus Dei, the Prayer for Peace and the Kiss of Peace.

The Holy Eucharist is "the sign of union, the bond of charity, the symbol of concord,"[2] that is, the Sacrament of peace; for peace is one of the principal effects of the reception of the Eucharist, but, at the same time, it is also a necessary requisite for participation in the Eucharistic Sacrifice and Banquet of Love.   At the table of the Lord the bond of love and concord should be formed ever more closely and more intimately between the faithful, until they have "but one heart and one soul" (Acts 4, 32); "for we, being many, are one bread, one body, all that partake of one bread" (1 Cor. 10, 17).   Peace must reign in the heart into which the "God of peace and love" enters and takes up His abode.   Therefore, after the *Pater noster* there are such frequent and fervent prayers for the great gift of peace in preparation for the Communion.   In the Embolism we meet with urgent supplication: "Graciously give peace in our days" (*da propitius pacem in diebus nostris*), and at the fraction of the Host follows the threefold sign of the Cross, accompanied with the salutation of peace: "May the peace of the Lord be always with you" (*Pax Domini sit semper vobiscum*); at the *Agnus Dei* we now implore of the Lamb of God, enthroned on the altar, peace for ourselves (*dona nobis pacem*), and in the prayer immediately following, this petition is further prosecuted, and the Lord implored that He would impart peace to His entire Church and preserve it — and, finally, peace prayed for in so manifold a way is sealed by the holy kiss.

1.   *The Agnus Dei.* — The holy Pope Sergius I. (687—701) is said to have been the first to order that at the breaking of the

---

[1] Laurent, Christol. Predigten I, 284.

[2] Trident. sess. 13, c. 8. — Unitas signum, vinculum caritatis, concordiae symbolum.

Host, the *Agnus Dei* should be sung by the clergy and people.[1] — The original rite differs in some respects from the present one, which was developed from the eleventh to the thirteenth century.[2] At this time we meet everywhere the threefold repetition of the *Agnus Dei* — and that not merely on the part of the choir, but also of the celebrant,[3] — and, instead of concluding, as previously, each time with the same petition "have mercy on us" (*miserere nobis*), they commenced at this date to repeat the third time "grant us peace" (*dona nobis pacem*). This last petition was occasioned by all manner of calamities and disturbances that had befallen the Church.[4] The reason for it lies indeed in the relation of the *Agnus Dei* to the imparting of the kiss of peace, or to the reception of Holy Communion.[5]

---

[1] Hic statuit, ut tempore confractionis dominici corporis, *"Agnus Dei, qui tollis peccata mundi,"* a *clero* et *populo* decantaretur (Lib. Pontific.). Now since the Agnus Dei occurs already in the Sacrament. Gregor., Mabillon (In Ord. Rom. c. 8, n. 7) infers that it was said already before the time of Sergius, but only by the choir, as was again the case soon after Sergius. (Cfr. Ordo Rom. I, n. 19; II, n. 13.) In Missa Sabbati sancti, quae *veteri more* etiam nunc celebratur, omittitur *Agnus Dei* cum Antiphonis ad *Offertorium* et ad *Communionem*, quae primarii non esse instituti Walafridus Strabo et alii observarunt (Mabillon l. c.).

[2] The most ancient Roman Ordines and the earliest liturgical writers say nothing with regard to the repetition of the Agnus Dei. Gradually the rite became fixed and general of singing, or reciting it three times. Agnus Dei *ter* canitur (Beleth). At the same time the practice was also introduced of saying the third time dona nobis pacem. Bis repetitur *"Miserere nobis"* et tertio variatur per *"Dona nobis pacem"* (Beleth). On Holy Thursday alone was an exception made during the Middle Age, probably because the kiss of peace was not given. In coena Domini ter debet dici cum *Miserere nobis* (Beleth c. 48). According to Durandus the Roman schola cantorum still observed in the thirteenth century the ancient custom of singing three times miserere nobis, which is done at present only in the Basilica of St. John Lateran (cfr. 1. 4, c. 52). Usually the choir sang it — chorus psallat *Agnus Dei* (Joann. Abrinc.); chorus clamat ad Jesum et postulat: *Agnus Dei* ... (Innoc. III.); sometimes also the people (cfr. Pseudo-Alcuin. c. 40; Sicard. 1. 3, c. 8). — Quidam *sacerdotes* dicunt "Agnus Dei" manibus super altare depositis ... alii vero stant manibus junctis, parum super altare inclinati (Durand. l. 4, c. 52). — Pontifex, junctis ante pectus manibus, dicit "Agnus Dei" submissa voce cum ministris adstantibus (Ordo Roman. XIV, c. 53).

[3] Generally in former times the priest, as a general custom, did not recite what the choir sang and what was recited by the assistant ministers (deacon, subdeacon, lector), as he directed his attention either to the singing or to the reading, or was in the mean time engaged in other liturgical functions.

[4] Postmodum autem multis et variis adversitatibus et terroribus Ecclesiae ingruentibus, coepit ad Dominum clamare de tribulatione: *"dona nobis pacem."* Et ut clamor ejus facilius audiretur, in ipsa duxit immolationis hora clamandum (Innoc. III. De sacr. alt. myst. 1. 6, c. 4).

[5] Postquam ad communicandum et ad percipiendum corpus perventum fuerit, *pacis osculum* sibi invicem tradunt, cantantes: "Agnus Dei, qui tollis peccata mundi, miserere nobis," ut *pacifici* sacramentum perficientes, in filiorum Dei numero (remissis delictis omnibus) mereantur copulari (Raban. Maur. De clericor. institut. 1. 1, c. 33).

Agnus Dei, qui tollis peccata mundi, miserere nobis.	Lamb of God, who takest away the sins of the world, have mercy on us.
Agnus Dei, qui tollis peccata mundi, miserere nobis.	Lamb of God, who takest away the sins of the world, have mercy on us.
Agnus Dei, qui tollis peccata mundi, dona nobis pacem.	Lamb of God, who takest away the sins of the world, grant us peace.

In the foregoing act of fraction and mingling, Christ is liturgically and mystically placed before our eyes as the Victim immolated by shedding His Blood and again gloriously risen to life; therefore, this humble, heartfelt supplication of the Agnus Dei, in which the priest addresses himself to the Saviour, concealed and offered under the Eucharistic species, appropriately concludes with the twofold cry for mercy and the single cry for peace [1]: — and, in order to express the consciousness of his sinfulness and compunction in a strong and lively manner, he at the same time strikes his breast three times.[2]

In the Old Law a lamb was one of the usual animals of sacrifice, and all these sacrificial lambs were types of Jesus Christ, the one true Lamb, who took away the sins of the world, that is, who atoned for and effaced them in His Blood. The designation of Christ as a

---

[1] Sequitur vox Ecclesiae supplicans Agno largitori pacis et misericordiae. Ter cum eodem principio cantatur et duplici fine terminatur; itaque orat: *miserere nobis*, dando veniam; *miserere nobis*, conservando justitiam; *dona nobis pacem*, quae superat omnem sensum et intellegentiam. Miserere captivis, miserere peregrinis, da nobis finem laboris; — miserere peccatoribus, miserere exsulibus, da requiem laborantibus; — tribue peccatorum remissionem, perduc ad patriae certam mansionem, da post laborem pacem et requiem (Stephan. Augustod. c. 18). — *Agnus Dei* ter cantatur, ut verus Agnus, cujus carnem et sanguinem sumimus, nobis propitietur. Primo rogamus, ut nobis misereatur peccata relaxando; secundo, ut nobis misereatur devotos sibi faciendo; tertio, ut nobis pacem donare dignetur, quae hic initium habet in sanctis, et in beata vita perficietur (Robert. Paulul. 1. 2, c. 40).

[2] Ad *"Agnus Dei"* sacerdos manus jungit et caput inclinat, ut nimirum non tantum verbis, sed etiam actione statum supplicantis exprimat: manibus autem altare non tangit ad majorem erga Christum in illo quiescentem venerationem. Elata voce illud recitat ad excitandam populi attentionem eumque exstimulandum, ut simili oratione ac pectoribus percussione Dei misericordiam imploret. Post primum *"Agnus Dei"*, deposita sinistra, ne sola pendula maneat, super corporale usque ad tertium *"Agnus Dei"*, postremis dexterae digitis pectus percutit in signum compunctionis, dum bis profert, *"miserere nobis"*, itemque dum inquit *"dona nobis pacem"*, quum cordis compunctio sit optima dispositio ad pacem obtinendam. In Missis defunctorum sacerdos non percutit sibi pectus, dum pronuntiat *"dona eis requiem"*, ut nempe significet, se in hisce Missis pro defunctis specialiter celebratis ipsorum magis quam sui memorem esse (De Carpo, Biblioth. liturg. p. 1, art. 50, n. 202).

Lamb expresses His sacrificial character, at the same time denoting His purity and freedom from guilt; but prominently it refers to the gentle patience and voluntary resignation with which He subjected Himself to the most painful sufferings and most bitter death.[1] The name "Lamb of God" (*Agnus Dei*) not merely signifies, that Christ by the will and for the honor of God became a sacrifice slain for the world; but it, moreover, includes the deeper meaning that He is the well-beloved Son of God (*Filius Dei dilectus*), that is, that the fulness of the divinity dwells in Him.[2] In reality Christ is the Sacrificial Lamb, that takes away the sins of the world, only because He is the beloved Son, in whom God is well pleased. Besides the name Lamb (*Agnus*), the appellation Lion (*Leo*) is also employed to designate the royal strength and power of Christ. He is the Lamb that suffered not only with patience, but who conquered, moreover, with the strength of a lion — and who now reigns and triumphs as Lord of lords and King of kings on the throne of heaven. *Emitte Agnum, Domine, dominatorem terrae!* — "Send forth, O Lord, the Lamb, the ruler of the earth!" (Is. 16, 1) — thus implores the same prophet who compared the Saviour to a dumb and willing sacrificial Lamb (Is. 53, 7). As a lamb Christ was promised in the Old Law through figures and prophets; as a lamb He was pointed out in the New Law by John the Baptist and extolled by the Apostles. With marked preference St. John in his mystical Revelations calls (about twenty-seven times) the Son of God a lamb.[3] In a mystical ecstacy he beholds Jesus as the Lamb that was slain and that purchased souls for God out of all tribes and nations, that washed them clean in His Blood and thereby made of them a royal priestly people; — as the Lamb that with His Blood strengthens the Church militant, making it victorious in its combats with Satan; — as the Lamb, that is, the brilliant light of the heavenly Jerusalem, conducting the blessed to the fountains of the waters of life; — as the Lamb worthy to receive power and divinity and wisdom and strength and honor and glory and benediction; — as the Lamb to whom all creation and all the choirs of angels present praise and adoration.

---

[1] Agnus propter innocentiam, mansuetudinem, obedientiam et immolationem vocatur Christus (Dion. Carthus. In Apocal. c. 5, v. 6).

[2] The addition of "God" is variously explained, for example, the Divine Lamb; the Lamb belonging to God, His property; the Lamb destined by God for sacrifice; the Lamb submissive or pleasing or dedicated to God. (Cfr. Haneberg-Schegg, Das Evangelium nach Johannes 1, 125.) — This formula of prayer (taken in part from Holy Scripture, John 1, 29) has a wealth and profundity of meaning. In the first place, it discloses the entire sublimity of the nature and mission of Jesus Christ, since the highly significant designation of Agnus Dei characterizes the Saviour as the Son of God, as the Divine Sacrificial Lamb given by God and again offered to Him, who innocently, meekly and freely underwent the death of the Cross; in the next place, it exalts the sin-effacing, world-redeeming power and efficacy of His sacrificial death; finally, it contains an humble, sorrowful, contrite appeal for mercy and for the obtaining of peace.

[3] Cfr. Hundhausen, Das erste Pontificalschreiben Petri S. 196—197.

As the lamb in Holy Scripture is a standing symbol of Christ, and as the citizens of heaven bless the Lamb without ceasing, so also does the Church love to invoke Jesus Christ in a simple, touching manner as the "Lamb of God". Throughout all ages there continues ever to resound in her liturgy of the Mass this fervent supplication to the divine, eternal sacrificial Lamb, who has taken upon Himself the sins of the world and thereby effaced them. As often as she administers Holy Communion to the faithful, does she exhort them in the words of St. John the Baptist: *Ecce Agnus Dei! ecce qui tollit peccata mundi!* to realize and value the wealth of grace contained in this heavenly sacrificial food. Almost all her litanies conclude with this solemn invocation to the Lamb of God, "to spare us, to hear us and to have mercy on us."

The Church has ever been accustomed to represent the Divine Saviour both under the figure of the Good Shepherd and also under the symbol of the lamb: both images are intimately connected with each other. Jesus Christ is the Good Shepherd, who became Himself our Sacrificial Lamb on the Cross, and who daily becomes the same again on the altar; He is the Good Shepherd, who gave His life for us and who, with His living flesh and Heart's blood, nourishes us to an eternal life of blessedness.

From the Sacrificial Lamb present on the altar there streams forth salvation and redemption, there flows to us all the favor of God, all the blessing of God and all the peace of God. This Lamb, that was slain from the beginning of the world and that will be slain unto the end of the world, we should during Mass, filled with humility and fervor, adore and invoke, in order that we may obtain the fulness of mercy and peace, whereby we shall be prepared for admittance to the "royal banquet of the lamb."[1]

In Requiem Masses the petition of the *Agnus Dei* — perhaps since the eleventh century, surely since the twelfth — is differently rendered, inasmuch as we twice implore from the Divine Sacrificial Lamb "rest" for the suffering souls from their pains and torments, and the third time we implore for them "eternal rest" in heaven (*dona eis requiem — dona eis requiem sempiternam*).[2]

2. The Prayer for Peace (*Oratio pro pace vel ad pacem*).[3] —

---

[1] Sancta Mechtildis: "Eia mi Domine, modo mihi aliquid ex praesentibus Missae verbis dona, unde anima mea spiritualiter consoletur." Cui Dominus: "Ecce jam mihi canitur ter *Agnus Dei:* in primo me offero Deo Patri cum omni humilitate et patientia mea pro vobis; ad secundum, offero me cum omni amaritudine passionis meae in plenam reconciliationem; ad tertium, cum toto amore divini Cordis, in supplementum omnium quae homini desunt bonorum" (S. Mechtild., Lib. special. grat. p. 3, c. 19).

[2] The Ambrosian Rite has the Agnus Dei only in Requiem Masses. The formula is the same as in our Missals; but the third time the petition is enlarged by an additional clause: "Dona eis requiem sempiternam *et locum indulgentiae cum Sanctis tuis in gloria.*"

[3] Micrologus (in the eleventh century) is still ignorant of this prayer; while Durandus (in the thirteenth century) mentions it. According to the Roman Rite,

As the *Agnus Dei*, so are also the following prayers until the Communion no longer addressed to the Father, but to the Saviour present in the Blessed Sacrament. The longing for the peace of the Lamb is so great and so ardent, that the priest — bowing humbly and looking intently upon the Most Holy Sacrament — continues to beg for this precious gift, and that for the whole Church.

Domine Jesu Christe, qui dixisti Apostolis tuis: Pacem relinquo vobis, pacem meam do vobis: ne respicias peccata mea, sed fidem Ecclesiae tuae: eamque secundum voluntatem tuam pacificare et coadunare digneris: qui vivis et regnas Deus per omnia saecula saeculorum. — Amen.	O Lord Jesus Christ, who saidst to Thine Apostles: Peace I leave you, My peace I give you: look not upon my sins, but upon the faith of Thy Church: and vouchsafe to give it that peace and unity which is agreeable to Thy will: who livest and reignest God world without end. Amen.

How agreeable, unworldly, superhuman sounds the word "peace"! Powerfully does it seize upon the inmost chords of the human heart, which longs for peace and finds no rest, until it has found true peace. For "so great," says St. Augustine, "is the gift of peace, that even in worldly and mortal things nothing more pleasant can be heard, nothing more desirable can be longed for and nothing better can be found."[1] To understand this, it must be remembered that the word peace has a profound, manifold and comprehensive signification. In the first place we should distinguish interior peace of soul with God and with one's self; then exterior peace with one's neighbor.[2]

Interior peace is a state of the soul, and that a state of spiritual well-being and prosperity, which by the dominion of divine grace and love is effected and diffused into all its powers.[3] To this well-

---

the kiss of peace was formerly imparted after the salutation: Pax Domini sit semper vobiscum, without the preceding special prayer for peace. The Mozarabic and the ancient Gallican Liturgies have an Oratio ad pacem which varies according to the Mass. In many Oriental Missals we find likewise a similar prayer (oratio ante pacis osculum, oratio osculi pacis, oratio amplexus, εὐχὴ τοῦ ἀσπασμοῦ). — Infertur *oratio pro osculo pacis*, ut caritate omnes reconciliati invicem digne sacramento corporis et sanguinis Christi consocientur (S. Isidor. De ecclesiast. offic. 1. 1, c. 15).

[1] De civit. Dei 1. 19, c. 11.

[2] Continet pax Christi 1. amicitiam cum Deo; 2. tranquillitatem animi et serenitatem in tentationibus et persecutionibus; 3. mutuam inter ipsos homines concordiam (Corn. a Lapide, In Joann. 14, 27).

[3] Pax (quae est gaudium imperturbatum) in contemplatione fundatur et ex ea causatur, sicut et gaudium, mediante tamen *dilectione*, cujus gaudium et pax immediati effectus et fructus dicuntur. Siquidem Deum contemplando non in eo gaudemus nec in ipso mente quiescimus, nisi eum sincere diligamus (Dion. Carthus. In 1 Petr. 1, 2).

being belongs, before all, the consoling consciousness that by the remission of sin we are reconciled to God, as also by the holy bond of a mystical friendship we are united to Him, — and, consequently, that we either already possess or at least may confidently expect the plenitude of all the gifts and blessings that flow from this abundant source of friendship. Then it is requisite that all the inclinations and desires of the heart should be directed to God and to His holy will, that is, that in perfect harmony they be so far ordered, tranquillized and sanctified as is possible in this mortal life. This peace of God, which surpasseth all understanding (Phil. 4, 7), comprises, therefore, all the beneficial, refreshing, blissful effects of divine truth and grace, all the sweet and precious fruits of supernatural faith, hope and love in the sanctified soul, which is the dwelling and temple of God. This disposition of the heart is a gift that the Holy Ghost imparts, in so far as "sweet guest" and "sweet refreshment" He enters into man, pervading his interior with the agreeable odor of His heavenly unction.

We frequently meet with the word peace, especially in the apostolic formulas of salutation, together with the word grace.[1] In such a connection both include the whole interior contents of Christianity and the Christian life: grace is the root whence springs the sweet, heavenly fruit of peace, developing to perfect maturity.[2] — Here below, indeed, this peace is more or less imperfect,[3] because it is mingled with sorrow, pain and sadness; perfect and imperturbed it will be only above in heaven, where all woe shall cease.[4] The more a man rids himself of attachment to the world and recollects his heart in God, the more he mortifies and overcomes his passions, the more he lives a life of faith and grace, the more also will he taste the consolation and sweetness of that interior peace which the Lord pours out, as a stream, on humble and self-sacrificing souls (Is. 66, 12). True piety is joy and peace in the Holy Ghost — it is godliness. *Delectare in Domino et dabit tibi petitiones cordis tui —*

---

[1] *Gratia* vobis et *pax* multiplicetur, that is, "Grace unto you and peace be multiplied" (1 Petr. 1, 2). — Sit vobiscum *gratia, misericordia, pax* a Deo Patre et a Christo Jesu Filio Patris in veritate et caritate (2. Joann. 3).

[2] Nota, quod Apostolus in qualibet salutatione optabat *gratiam* et *pacem:* gratiam tamquam primordialem, pacem sicut complementum. Ad Timotheum autem interponit *misericordiam,* quae est utriusque principium (S. Bonav. De tripl. via c. 2, § 5, n. 12).

[3] Hic (on earth) talis est pax nostra, ut *solatium miseriae* sit potius quam beatitudinis gaudium (S. Aug. De civ. Dei l. 19, c. 27).

[4] Dicendum, quod cum *vera* pax non sit nisi de bono, sicut *dupliciter* habetur verum bonum, sc. perfecte et imperfecte, ita est *duplex* pax vera. Una quidem *perfecta,* quae consistit in perfecta fruitione summi boni, per quam omnes appetitus uniuntur quietati in uno — et hic est ultimus finis creaturae rationalis, secundum illud (Ps. 147, 14): "Qui posuit fines tuos pacem." Alia vero est pax *imperfecta,* quae habetur in hoc mundo; quia etsi principalis animae motus quiescat in Deo, sunt tamen aliqua repugnantia et intus et extra, quae perturbant hanc pacem (S. Thom. 2, 2, q. 29, a. 2 ad 4).

"Delight in the Lord, and He will give thee the requests of thy heart" (Ps. 36, 4).

This is the peace which Christ left to His own, and which the world can neither give nor take away (John 14, 27). Such peace of heart the world cannot bestow; for it has and offers only treasures that do not satiate, that is, earthly goods, vain honors and sensual pleasures. All these things are but apparent goods, they are vanity and vexation of spirit (Eccles. 2, 17), and, consequently, they cannot impart true peace, but only a transitory, counterfeit peace. Sensual pleasures "go in pleasantly, but in the end they will bite like a snake and will spread abroad poison like a basilisk" (Prov. 23, 32). The world, tossed about and turbulent like a restless ocean, is unwilling to understand what conduces to its peace (Luke 19, 42); at present this knowledge is concealed from its eyes and it lives in a false peace.[1] — But the world cannot rob us of the peace of God; for it is deeply rooted in the heart, it is elevated above earthly conditions and external influences. This peace comes from heaven and leads to heaven: it is neither affected by the alluring pleasures nor by the oppressive sufferings of this transitory life. If mind and heart are firmly centred in God, then they will also remain calm and tranquil, placid and serene amid the storms of persecution, temptation and distress — full of holy peace.[2] To such a peace the seraphic virgin St. Theresa exhorts us: "Let nothing trouble thee — nothing frighten thee — all things pass away — God is immutable — patience obtains all — he that possesses God, can want for nothing — God alone suffices."[3]

---

[1] Dicendum, quod pax consistit in *quietatione et unione appetitus*. Sicut autem appetitus potest esse vel simpliciter boni vel boni apparentis, ita etiam et pax potest esse et *vera* et *apparens*. Vera quidem pax non potest esse nisi circa appetitum veri boni, quia omne malum, etsi secundum aliquid appareat bonum, unde ex aliqua parte appetitum quietat, habet tamen multos defectus, ex quibus appetitus remanet inquietus et perturbatus. *Unde pax vera non potest esse nisi in bonis et bonorum.* Pax autem, quae malorum est, est pax *apparens* et non vera; unde dicitur (Sap. 14, 22): In magno viventes inscientiae bello, tot et tam magna mala pacem appellant (S. Thom. 2, 2, q. 29, a. 2 ad 3).

[2] Orat Archiapostolus, ut pax nobis multiplicetur, i. e. abundanter ac multipliciter divinitus detur et conservetur, videlicet *pax pectoris*, quae est tranquillitas mentis in Deo, *pax temporis*, quae est quies ab exterioribus impugnationibus, et *pax aeternitatis*, quae est tranquillissima quies beatorum in patria imperturbatumque gaudium eorum in Deo. Quantumcumque autem forinsecus impugnemur aut corporaliter molestemur, semper tamen pro posse conemur pacem pectoris conservare, ut tranquilletur in Deo cor nostrum et spiritaliter gaudeat in adversis. De qua pace ait Psalmista: "Pax multa diligentibus legem tuam." Qui enim divinae legis praecepta amorose custodiunt, mentis inquietudinem vincunt in omni eventu, in prosperis scilicet et adversis in Deo se figunt ac bene agendo gloriantur in Domino: estque in eis corpus subditum animae, sensualitas rationi, ratio Deo, ex qua optima ordinatione consurgit et manet in eis pax pectoris, quae ab Augustino vocatur *tranquillitas ordinis* (Dion. Carthus. In 1 Petr. 1, 2).

[3] This Letrilla of the Saint in the original Spanish runs thus: Nada te turbe, — nada te espante; — todo se pasa; — Dios no se muda; — la paciencia — todo lo alcanza; — quien á Dios tiene, — nada le falta; — *solo Dios basta.*

Exterior peace consists in concord and union with our neighbor, — therefore, it presupposes a meek, gentle, accommodating disposition, and that even towards those who injure, oppress, or pain us. With them that hate peace, I am peaceable (Ps. 119, 7). — A peaceful disposition, free from irritation, aversion and bitterness, should reign among Christians; "of one mind, having compassion one for another, being lovers of the brotherhood" (1 Peter, 3, 8), they should live together. Unity of sentiment should animate to mutual, sincere participation in one another's welfare and woe, in joy and sorrow, — and to true, sincere fraternal love. For this unity among His disciples the Saviour prayed shortly before His death: "The glory which Thou hast given Me, I have given to them, that they may be one, as We also are one; I in them and Thou in Me, that they may be made perfect in one" (John 17, 22—23). And the Apostle of the Gentiles exhorts us: "If it be possible, as much as is in you, having peace with all men" (Rom. 12, 18), and "Follow peace with all men" (Heb. 12, 14). How beautiful and edifying it is to see so strong a bond of union and harmony bind together all the members of the Church! It gives joy, consolation, strength amid all the trials and persecutions on the part of a hostile, God-estranged world. **"Ubi caritas et amor, Deus ibi est"** — the Church chants at the washing of the feet on Holy Thursday.

This peace — interior and exterior — Christ acquired by His death, and bequeathed to us as a precious heritage. "Peace I leave with you, My peace I give unto you; not as the world giveth, do I give unto you" (June 14, 27). To this promise and legacy of the Saviour we here appeal, when we implore peace for the Church militant, which principally consists in this, that all "with humility and mildness, with patience, support one another in charity, being careful to keep the unity of the Spirit in the bond of peace" (Eph. 4, 2—3). At the same time the petition is therein comprised that the Lord would rescue His Church from all the hostility, violence and persecution to which she is exposed in the world. Why should the Lord not listen to such supplication? Is it not altogether in accord and in compliance with His holy will (*secundum voluntatem tuam*), that is, does He not wish that the Church should live in peace and concord? For He underwent the painful death of reconciliation to destroy the wall of separation, and to gather into one body the dispersed children of God. In humble fear that his own sinfulness should be an impediment to the granting of this petition, the priest implores that the Lord would not look with anger upon him, the unworthy minister of the Church, but behold rather the worthiness and holiness of His beloved Spouse the Church (*ne respicias peccata mea, sed fidem Ecclesiae tuae*), in order to impart to her and increase in her the gift of peace and concord.

3. The Kiss of Peace (*osculum pacis, pax, salutatio*).[1] — In

---

[1] The (chaste) osculum was always and everywhere regarded as a sign (symbol) and expression of love, of veneration, of friendship, of peace, of reconciliation, of

the Apostolic Epistles we frequently meet the admonition to the Christians, that with the kiss of love (φίλημα ἀγάπης), or with the holy kiss (·φίλημα ἅγιον), they should salute one another (1 Peter 5, 14; Rom. 16, 16; 1 Cor. 16, 20). This salutation took place after reading the Apostolic Epistles in the assemblies for divine worship in individual congregations. Thus it came to pass that the holy kiss formed a constituent part of the Eucharistic Celebration from the days of the Apostles, as a symbol and confirmation of Christian love that lives in peace with all. In the Roman rite the kiss of peace has always been placed before the Communion[1]; in the Oriental Church, on the contrary, as well as in the Mozarabic and Gallican liturgies, it is placed already before the Consecration.[2] Moreover, the mode and manner of imparting the *Pax* varied at different epochs and in different churches.[3] Since the end of the thirteenth century,

---

gratitude, of joy. In Christianity, and especially by its reception into the liturgy, it received a supernatural character and a higher consecration. The *osculum sanctum*, of which the Apostles speak, does not proceed merely from natural affection, but from caritas, from Christian brotherly love, which it would nourish and strengthen — this spiritual, divine love which has for its root Christian faith, and which is poured out by the Holy Ghost into our hearts and, therefore, appears, not as the work of nature, but of grace. The liturgical osculum (kiss of peace and the kissing of the hand of the celebrant at Solemn High Mass by the assistants) is given to persons and to things. As the hand is an emblem of power, of protection, of help and of blessing in general, kissing the hand symbolizes the veneration and esteem bestowed upon some one on account of the authority and blessings conferred upon him. This actus reverentialis is certainly appropriate toward the person who celebrates the Eucharistic Sacrifice — this act of omnipotent love — and who holds in his consecrated hand the Most Holy, who administers Holy Communion and blesses all present. (Cfr. Augsburg. Pastoralblatt, Jahrgang 1879, S. 249 etc.) — Erat osculum non solius communionis, sed et omnium ecclesiasticarum functionum signaculum et sigillum, quod in *omnibus* Sacramentis adhiberi solebat (Bona 1. 2, c. 16, § 7).

[1] Pope Innocent I. writes to Decentius, Bishop of Gubbio, that the kiss of peace is not to be given until after the completion of the Holy Mysteries, that is, immediately before Communion. "You assert that some persons recommend the kiss of peace to the congregation before the completion of the Mysteries (ante confecta mysteria, that is, before the Consecration), or the priests mutually give it, when necessarily it should be given only after all is over, that by it may be revealed that the congregation give their consent to all that has been done in the Mysteries and celebrated in the church, and to prove by this sign of the concluding kiss of peace the completion of the celebration of reconciliation (finita esse pacis concludentis signaculo demonstrentur)."

[2] In many churches it was (with reference to Matt. 4, 23: si offers munus tuum ad altare etc.) given only before the Oblation (S. Justin. M. Apol. II, n. 65), that is, immediately before the Preface (Constit. Apostol. 1. 2, c. 61).

[3] At the salutation of peace (Pax Domini . . .) the celebrant made the sign of the Cross over the chalice three times and then dropped the (reserved) particle into it, after which he gave the Pax to the archdeacon. Sed archidiaconus pacem dat episcopo priori, deinde ceteris per ordinem et populis (Ordo Rom. I, n. 18). — Archidiaconus pacem dat episcopo priori, qui et ultra dabit juxta se stanti ac deinde per ordinem ceteri, atque populus osculantur se invicem in osculo Christi (Ordo

the real kiss (*osculum oris*)[1] was gradually omitted, and only the embrace (*amplexus*) formerly connected with it has been retained. In consequence of this the *Pax* also began to be imparted in another way, namely, by presenting and kissing the so-called *Osculatorium*, that is, a small tablet to which was affixed the picture of the Saviour or of a saint. Later on, however, the general imparting of the *Pax* ceased and it was, as is the case at present, limited almost entirely to Solemn High Mass,[2] in which only the clergy assisting in the sanctuary receive the kiss of peace by embracing one another. On special occasions dignitaries of the laity are permitted to receive the kiss of peace through the *Osculatorium*.[3] — The celebrant imparts it to the deacon, who gives it to the sub-deacon etc. Previously the priest, together with the deacon, kisses the altar, to salute Christ and His saints in love and reverence, and thus to confirm and renew the mystical relation to the heavenly Church. For this connection is the necessary condition and source of the holy Communion and Christian fraternal love which should reign among the members of the Church militant, and which finds its expression and seal in the mutual kiss of peace. In so far, therefore, as the kiss of peace is

---

Rom. III, n. 16). — Veniens presbyter accipiat pacem ab episcopo, eandem ceteris oblaturus (Ordo Rom. V, n. 12). — Pontifex *osculato altari* (after the prayer for peace) convertat se ad capellanum et det ei pacem dicendo *"Pax tecum"*, quam ille recepturus prius inclinet reverenter ante Pontificem absque genuflexione; deinde recepta pace respondet *"Et cum spiritu tuo"* et osculetur pectus Pontificis... postea det pacem diacono, et diaconus subdiacono... et sic pax diffunditur per circumstantes (Ordo Rom. XIV, c. 53).

[1] Innocent III. and Durandus affirm that kissing on the mouth was still the custom in the thirteenth century. Sacerdos praebet *osculum oris* ministro... pacis osculum per universos fideles diffunditur in ecclesia (Innoc. III. 1. 6, c. 5). — Sacerdos facta commixtione et finita oratione accipit in quibusdam ecclesiis pacem ab eucharistia sive ab ipso corpore Domini, vel secundum alios ab ipso sepulchro, i. e. calice vel altari et mox praebet *oris osculum* ministro, sc. diacono (Durand. 1. 4, c. 53).

[2] Cf. Erker, Enchiridion liturgicum sect. 3, tr. 2, c. 2.

[3] In Solemn Requiem Masses the kiss of peace is omitted, since St. Thomas remarks (3, q. 83, a. 4), sacrificium offertur *non pro pace praesenti*, sed *pro requie mortuorum*. In the liturgy for the dead the Church is entirely engrossed in her care for the departed and, therefore, omits in all Requiem Masses also the preceding petition for peace for all present (dona *nobis* pacem) and the prayer for peace (Domine J. Chr....) for the entire Church. Inasmuch as the osculum pacis is at the same time a symbol of joy and enhances the solemnity, it is likewise appropriately omitted in Solemn Requiem Masses. The opinion that the kiss of peace is omitted in Solemn Requiem Masses, because in them Holy Communion is not administered, is now untenable; for according to the general decree of S. R. C. 27. Jun. 1868 it is permitted to administer Holy Communion also with previously consecrated particles in black vestments as well during, as also immediately before and after the Requiem Mass. — On Holy Thursday the Church omits the osculum pacis, to express her sorrow and abhorrence of the deceitful kiss of Judas, as on Good Friday she omits the genuflection at the prayer for the Jews, because they reviled the Saviour on the day of His death by scornful genuflections.

still in use, it has its proper place after the prayer for peace, and it serves as a preparation for the actual or spiritual reception of the Sacrament of charity and concord.[1] This holy kiss "reconciles and unites souls to one another, promising an entire oblivion of all offences. It is a sign that the minds are again reconciled with one another, and that all remembrance of injustice suffered in the past is banished from the heart" (St. Cyril of Jerusalem, 5. Mystag. Catechism).

69. The Last Preparatory Prayers for Communion.[2]

The two following prayers serve as a proximate preparation for Holy Communion. At hand, quite near, is the moment of the most intimate, blessed union of the priest with the Body and Blood, with the soul and divinity of the Eucharistic Victim. Boundless, indescribable treasures of salvation and grace are concealed in the Eucharist: why then do we not daily become richer in the goods of heaven? Why do we remain so destitute of solid virtue, so full of imperfection, weakness and frailty? No doubt, for the most part, this is due to our preparation and thanksgiving for Communion being so short and careless, so defective and lukewarm. The Lord would pour out upon us the plenitude of blessing, but we check the current of His liberality, because we do not more carefully prepare and guard the soil of our heart; because we are so slothful, distracted and unmortified even during those sacred moments in which the King of Heaven and

---

[1] Liturgists of the Middle Age often regard not only the eulogies (hostiae non consecratae—panis benedictus sanctae communionis vicarius) and the Oratio super populum, but also the kiss of peace as a kind of surrogate (substitute) for the general Communion of the congregation, which at that epoch had ceased for a considerable time to take place daily. Contra hunc primae institutionis defectum triplex est remedium. Primum est pacis osculum ideoque in gallicana ecclesia datur in omni Missa nisi defunctorum; secundum est panis benedictus, qui eulogia dicitur, qui quia in Quadragesima propter abstinentiam dari non debuit, institutum est tertium remedium, sc. Oratio super populum, cui praedicitur: "Inclinate capita vestra Deo" (Sicard. 1. 3, c. 8). — Cfr. Beleth. c. 48. — Durand. 1. 4, c. 53, n. 3.

[2] Ante-Tridental Missals have many kinds of private prayers for the priest before and after Communion. (Cfr. Martene, De antiq. Eccles. ritib. 1. 1, c. 4, a. 9). — Micrologus (in the eleventh century) and Radulphus de Rivo, Dean of Tongern (in the fourteenth), mention only the prayer: Domine J. Chr., qui ex voluntate Patris . . . . — Orationem, quam inclinati dicimus, antequam communicemus, non ex Ordine, sed *ex religiosorum traditione* habemus, scil. hanc: "Domine J. Chr., qui ex voluntate Patris . . . ." Sunt et *aliae multae orationes*, quas quidem ad pacem et communionem *privatim* frequentant, sed diligentiores antiquiorum observatores nos in hujusmodi privatis orationibus brevitati studere docuerent potiusque *publicis* precibus in officio Missae occupari voluerunt (Microlog. c. 18). — Cfr. Radulph. Tungren. De canonum observantia c. 33.—In the 14. Roman Ordo (c. 71) the other Communion prayer (Perceptio corporis . . . .) is also inserted. — Clichtoveus († 1543) mentions the three Communion prayers of our Missal and adds: et alias pro arbitrio et pia devotione aut ritu suae ecclesiae dicere potest qui Missam celebrat.

Earth enters into our dwelling and there abides. On the contrary, the greater our solicitude, the more ardent our fervor, before, during and after Communion, the more bounteous will be the measure of the gifts of grace wherewith the Saviour will enrich our poverty. Holy Communion draws near —; but the work is great, since a dwelling is prepared not for man but for God (1 Par. 29, 1).

1. Hence the priest continues to pray, while his eyes and heart are altogether engrossed in loving meditation on the Victim lying before him:

Domine Jesu Christe, Fili Dei vivi, qui ex voluntate Patris, cooperante Spiritu sancto, per mortem tuam mundum vivificasti: libera me per hoc sacrosanctum Corpus et Sanguinem tuum ab omnibus iniquitatibus meis, et universis malis et fac me tuis semper inhaerere mandatis, et a te nunquam separari permittas: qui cum eodem Deo Patre et Spiritu sancto vivis et regnas Deus in saecula saeculorum. Amen.[1]

O Lord Jesus Christ, Son of the living God, who, by the will of the Father and the coöperation of the Holy Ghost, hast by Thy death given life to the world: deliver me by this Thy most sacred Body and Blood from all my iniquities and from all evils; and make me always adhere to Thy commandments and suffer me never to be separated from Thee. Who with the same God the Father and the Holy Ghost livest and reignest God world without end. Amen.

This prayer, as solid and comprehensive as it is brief and simple, must, indeed, in the first place and principally, be referred to the approaching Communion, but not exclusively so; for the words "by This Thy most sacred Body and Blood," together with the petition thereto annexed, have so general a meaning that they may, at the same time, be referred to the Sacrifice of the Mass, and likewise be understood of the fruits of the Sacrifice. This is also the

---

[1] In the three prayers before Communion, which are equally addressed to the second Divine Person Jesus Christ, the peculiar and ever varying concluding formula (conclusio) is worthy of notice. The prayer for peace concludes with the rarely occurring short formula: qui vivis et regnas *Deus* per omnia saecula saeculorum, in which the addition Deus forms a departure from the rule. — As in the above prayer the Father and the Holy Ghost are mentioned, this is signified in the prolonged concluding formula, but in a peculiar way: qui cum *eodem* Deo Patre et Spiritu sancto vivis et regnas . . . . (in Clichtoveus: qui cum *eodem* Patre vivis et regnas in unitate *ejusdem* Spiritus sancti . . . . and again in a different manner in Ordo Rom. XIV). — The third prayer (Perceptio . . .) alone has the regular longer concluding formula, as is customary in the Collects. — As Communion prayers, that were originally private and intended especially for the priest, since they date from a period in which the general Communion of those present had ceased, these prayers have this peculiarity that the petitions in the singular number refer to the celebrant only (libera *me*, fac *me*, prosit *mihi* . . .).

case with many prayers after the Communion. The petition for gaining the fruits of the Eucharistic Communion and Sacrifice is highly appropriate here. For we may assume that the priest, who celebrates worthily, obtains at least a portion of the sacrificial fruits which fall to him at the moment in which the Sacrifice is finished and completed, that is, during the act of Communion.[1]

St. Peter once addressed to the Lord this solemn profession of faith: "Thou art Christ the Son of the living God" (Matth. 16, 14). He saw only His humanity and confessed His divinity; therefore, he was called "blessed" by the Lord, his faith was praised and rewarded. On the altar Christ's divinity and humanity are concealed from mortal vision, and yet the priest confesses both with a faith that is as firm as a rock and immovable at the moment of receiving the God-Man: "Lord Jesus Christ, Son of the living God" —*Domine Jesu Christi, Fili Dei vivi.*—But not only does he confess the divinely human dignity of Jesus Christ, but, moreover, His most sublime, divine and human grand act—namely, the restoring to life of a world dead in sin, by His propitiatory sacrificial death for our redemption *(per mortem tuam mundum vivificasti)*. With special predilection the Church extols the wonderful mystery, that Jesus Christ, who is the life, the source and the author of all life, should suffer death and by His death destroy our death, that is, regain for us the life of grace and glory *(Vita mortem pertulit et morte vitam protulit — Hymn. Pass.)*. "O Almighty God." thus she prays on Wednesday in Holy Week, "grant to our heart and sense a lively hope, that through the temporal death of Thy Son *(per temporalem Filii tui mortem)*, which *(quam)* these adorable mysteries represent and announce, Thou hast given us life eternal" *(vitam perpetuam)*. — The work of redemption was accomplished by Christ according to the will of His Father, by the co-operation of the Holy Ghost *(ex voluntate Patris, cooperante Spiritu sancto)*.[2] The Father did not spare His only-begotten Son, but placed upon Him the sins of the world and presented to Him the bitter chalice of the passion; through love for the Father, Christ became obedient, obedient even unto the death of the cross (Phil. 2, 8). The Holy Ghost, who had formed His sacred Body in the womb of the immaculate Virgin, at the same

---

[1] Probabile est, celebrantem bene dispositum tunc *sacrificii fructum, saltem aliquem* percipere, quando percipit fructum sacramenti, h. e. *in communione*, quando sacrificium jam *perfecte completur* (Sylvius III, q. 83, art. 1, quaer. 2, concl. 4 ad 8).

[2] Qui sacrosanctam Christi Domini meditatur incarnationem, ejusque miras operationes et amarissimam passionem propter nos homines, et propter nostram salutem ac instructionem, nonne statim gratias aget toti sanctissimae Trinitati mysterium hoc operanti, et singulis specialiter personis? Patri quidem, qui "sic dilexit mundum, ut Filium suum unigenitum daret", qui ut servum redimeret, tradidit Filium; Filio etiam, qui tam arduum et difficile, propter amorem creaturae, munus redemptoris suscepit: et Spiritui sancto, qui principaliter, tamquam amoris principium, ad hoc mysterium concurrisse dicitur (Philipp. a ss. Trinitate, Summa theol. mystic. I, p. 1. tr. 1, disc. 3, art. 5).

time breathed into Him the most ardent love of sacrifice, in order that He might sacrifice Himself for us unto death; for "by the Holy Ghost *(per Spiritum sanctum)* has Jesus Christ, therefore, offered Himself unspotted unto God the Father" (Heb. 9, 14). [1]

Christ's redeeming death, or work of redemption, is mystically renewed and perpetuated on the altar; for as often as we eat the Eucharistic Bread and drink of the Eucharistic Chalice, we show the death of the Lord, until He come (1 Cor. 11, 26). What graces do we here implore in virtue of the Body and Blood of Jesus Christ, sacrificed for us and about to be received by us? On the one hand, deliverance from all that oppresses us; on the other, the granting of all that may conduce to our happiness. — The first petition refers more to the Sacrifice than to the Sacrament of the Eucharist; for as a sacrifice of propitiation and petition does the Eucharist chiefly effect for us deliverance from all our sins and from all evils (*ab omnibus iniquitatibus meis et universis malis*). The second petition, on the contrary, refers rather to the Sacrament than to the Sacrifice of the Eucharist; for as a Sacrament it is mainly a powerful means of keeping the divine commandments and of being indissolubly united to Christ (*fac me tuis semper inhaerere mandatis et a te numquam separari permittas*). Among the effects of the Eucharist, final perseverance in good is also reckoned. Frequent, devout Communion is, according to the Fathers and Doctors, to be regarded as a mark of predestination. For he that often and worthily communicates will avoid sin, increase in the love of God, become enriched with good works, and advance in the way of divine commandments unto the end, that is, he will make his calling and election sure (2 Peter 1, 10), and thus he will be preserved from the loss of eternal salvation. The Eucharistic food is the bread of the strong; it refreshes and strengthens the earthly pilgrim on his painful journey to the eternal home in heaven. "Suffer me never to be separated from Thee, O Jesus!" How touching is this petition at the moment in which the soul celebrates the most intimate espousals with her Divine Bridegroom! "What can the world without Jesus impart to thee? To be without Jesus is a bitter hell; to be with Jesus, a sweet paradise." We could in no wise do without Jesus: we need Him at every step and at each moment. Always to feel this great need of

---

[1] The Father willed, decreed, ordained the passion and death of His Son; the Son executed this divine plan of salvation in that He assumed human nature and voluntarily suffered death: this mighty sacrifice of His life on the part of Christ was an act of obedience which emanated from His love of the Father and of the salvation of mankind; but this love and this obedience of His human will were infused by the Holy Ghost. — Hoc ipsum quod Christus obedivit, processit ex dilectione quam habuit ad Patrem et ad nos (S. Thom. In Epist. ad Rom. c. 5, lect. 5). — Christus passus est ex caritate et obedientia, quia et praecepta caritatis ex obedientia implevit et obediens fuit ex dilectione ad Patrem praecipientem (S. Thom. 3, q. 47, a. 2 ad 3). — Causa quare Christus sanguinem suum fudit, fuit Spiritus sanctus, cujus motu et instinctu, scil. caritate Dei et proximi, hoc fecit (S. Thom. In Epist. ad Hebr. c. 9, lect. 3).

Jesus, is the wisdom and the joy of life. There is something delight-ful in this feeling of utter dependence on Jesus. No loss can be comparable to the loss of Jesus; no sorrow, to the sorrow of being separated from Jesus by grievous sin. Worthy Communion delivers us from this misfortune.

2. The other prayer, as simple as it is efficacious and solid, refers directly and exclusively to Holy Communion.

Perceptio Corporis tui, Domine Jesu Christe, quod ego indignus sumere praesumo, non mihi pro-veniat in judicium et condemna-tionem, sed pro tua pietate prosit mihi ad tutamentum mentis et corporis, et ad medelam percipi-endam: qui vivis et regnas cum Deo Patre in unitate Spiritus sancti Deus per omnia saecula saeculorum. Amen.	Let not the partaking of Thy Body, O Lord Jesus Christ, which I, though unworthy, pre-sume to receive, turn to my judgment and condemnation; but by Thy mercy be it profitable to the protection and health both of soul and body, and be to me sal-vation: Who with God the Father, in the unity of the Holy Ghost, livest and reignest God world without end. Amen.

Here in the first place the priest humbly confesses his own un-worthiness; then with fervor he represents the petition to the Saviour, that He would at all times avert from him the misfortune of an unworthy Communion and apply to him the plentiful blessings of a worthy Communion.

"The Bread of Angels becomes the food of man. O miracle! wonderful thing! the poor, the servant, the lowly, receives his Lord" (Hymn. Eccl.). On this the priest reflects; hence it animates him to an humble acknowledgment that he is not worthy to receive the Most Holy Body of our Lord (*quod ego indignus sumere praesumo*).[1] Well does he know the admonition of the Apostle: "But let a man prove himself, and so let him eat of that bread and drink of the chalice" (1 Cor. 11, 28); therefore, he guards against approaching the table of the Lord laden with grievous sin, that is, with that unworthiness of which it is said: "Whosoever shall eat this bread or drink the chalice of the Lord unworthily, shall be guilty of the body and of the blood of the Lord —; for he that eateth and drinketh unworthily, eateth and drinketh judgment to himself" (1 Cor. 11, 27, 29). Such an un-worthiness as would make the Communion sacrilegious, is self-evidently not intended by the acknowledgment of the priest. Here the unworthiness in question presupposes rather freedom from mortal sin, that is, that the soul is in a state of grace. It consists only in the want of perfect worthiness, that is, in the partly inculpable, partly culpable absence of that great purity, reverence, love and

---

[1] Praesumptio interdum accipitur pro abundanti fiducia (Dion. Carthus. Expos. prol. Sent.) — Praesumere = to presume, to venture.

devotion which is a becoming requisite for the reception of the ineffably worthy, sublime and holy Sacrament of the Altar. The frailty of human nature and the weakness of the human will are so great that our disposition almost invariably remains defective, that is, it is less perfect than it could and should be. If a man has done all in his power, if he has prepared himself as carefully as possible, then indeed we say, and justly, that he is worthy to receive Holy Communion. But this does not prevent his regarding and confessing himself as unworthy of so great a grace; it is precisely this humble avowal of our own unworthiness that is required to make us in some degree worthy of Holy Communion. Therefore, although the sentiment of holy fear and reverence keeps us from the table of the Lord, still it is better, especially for the priest, to celebrate and to receive the holy mysteries through love and with confidence. However, in sentiments of holy and salutary fear he should at all times prepare himself, and that so much the more carefully, the oftener he has the grace and happiness to approach the Eucharistic Banquet.[1]

To receive the Blessed Sacrament with impure mouth and heart, that is, to make an unworthy Communion, is one of the most grievous and greatest of sacrileges and, consequently, it draws down on the guilty person a severe chastisement from God. Full of humble distrust in himself, on account of his oft-experienced weakness and infidelity, the priest implores the Lord to keep far away and avert from him the outrage and curse of a sacrilegious Communion, that he may not be judged and condemned (*non mihi proveniat in judicium et condemnationem*).[2] Such a request on the part of the

---

[1] Dico, *quod ceteris paribus multo melius sit ex caritate et zelo boni communis accedere, quam ex humilitate et timore cessare*, praesertim cum sacramentum istud sit sacramentum totius caritatis, liberalitatis ac gratiae, medicinaque animae. Et dato, quod quis tam meritorie quoad *se* abstineret, sicut accederet: tamen multo fructuosius est accedere per comparationem ad *alios:* quia devote accedens multipliciter succurrit non sibi dumtaxat, sed et toti ecclesiae, et vivis ac mortuis, specialiter quoque adstantibus et eis, pro quibus sacrificat ac deposcit. Quamvis autem *nullus sit absolute dignus* celebrare aut communicare per considerationem ad infinitam dignitatem Christi, et quoad suae deitatis majestatem nec non etiam per respectum ad suae assumptae humanitatis sanctitatem et honorabilitatem, tamen secundum quandam proportionabilitatem dignus est homo, si cum debita diligentia, custodia, humilitate, munditia et fervore se praeparet atque accedat. Verumtamen, qui accedunt *quotidie*, studeant *tanto ferventius quanto frequentius* tanta mysteria pertractare et coram Altissimo *jugiter* mundi ac fructuosi consistere (Dion. Carthus. IV, dist. 12, q. 5).

[2] Judicium (κρίσις, κρῖμα) is often = condemnatio (κατάκρισις), for example, 1 Cor. 11, 29 judicium sibi manducat et bibit, but here it can be taken in the sense of a legal proceeding, a process, and be distinguished from condemnatio = final condemnatory judgment. Cfr. the petition in the Office of the Dead: dum veneris *judicare*, noli me *condemnare*. Or also: judicium = judicial condemnation; condemnatio (from damnum, damage, loss, injury) = the sentence of the judge, punishment, chastisement. — Da quaesumus Domine, ut tanti mysterii munus indultum non condemnatio, sed sit medicina sumentibus (Sacr. Gelas.). Similar petitions are found in liturgical formulas.

priest is so much the better founded and appropriate, the more weighty the responsibility of being permitted to partake daily of this precious Heavenly Food, and the greater the danger that frequent reception of the Blessed Sacrament may incur, if through routine, carelessness and tepidity, he easily pave the way to an unworthy Communion.

Confiding in the paternal goodness of the Saviour, the priest continues to pray that the Holy Communion may become rather a source of blessing to him (*sed pro tua pietate prosit mihi*). The word *pietas* designates the divine condescension, goodness, mild-ness, mercy toward man.[1] How unutterably great does this con-descending goodness and mercy of the Saviour appear in the crib, on the Cross, on the altar! Everywhere He conceals His majesty and shows Himself only as the Good Shepherd and Heavenly Physi-cian who has come to seek and to heal us, as well as to inflame our hearts in return with childlike, grateful love. — Now by this merci-ful goodness, thus prays the priest, may the Lord be pleased to grant that His holy Body may be profitable to those who receive it, "to the protection and health both of soul and body" (*ad tutamentum mentis et corporis — et ad medelam percipiendam*).[2] Protection and health of soul and body — these words include the whole wealth of the sacramental grace of the Eucharistic Banquet.[3] The life of a true Christian is a continual combat between grace and nature, between spirit and flesh, between virtue and vice. Without inter-mission we must struggle against the interior and the exterior, the visible and the invisible enemies of our soul; for we are surrounded by the weaknesses and temptations of sensual nature, by the attacks and allurements of this sinful world, by the snares and deceits of the devil. Now the Holy Eucharist, in this warfare of salvation, is, on the one hand, a strong and powerful *weapon of defence* by which we are enabled to victoriously overcome all assaults; and on the other,

---

[1] The expressions pius and pietas are, after the example of Holy Scripture (cfr. 2 Paralip. 30, 9; Judith 7, 20; Eccli. 2, 13) in the liturgy (especially in the prayers), by a particular preference applied to God. Cfr., for instance, in festo S. Matthiae: "Deus . . . . tribue . . . . ut *tuae* circa nos *pietatis* semper *viscera* sentia-mus. — Quos tuos efficis, Domine, tua *pietate circumtege* (Sacrament. Leonian.). — Haec (sc. pietas) perfecta virtus in hominibus, haec *plena* in Deo *laus* est. (S. Am-bros. In Ps. 118 Serm. 18, n. 46).

[2] Similar petitions often occur — especially in the Post-Communions — for example, per coelestia alimenta contra omnia adversa muniamur — perceptione sacramenti ab hostium liberemur insidiis — hoc sacramentum sit fortitudo fragi-lium, sit contra omnia mundi pericula firmamentum — sacri dona mysterii in nostrae proficiat infirmitatis auxilium — per haec sacramenta, quidquid in nostra mente vitiosum est, ipsorum medicationis dono curetur.

[3] Sentiamus, quaesumus Domine, tui perceptione sacramenti, *subsidium men-tis et corporis:* ut in *utroque* salvati, coelestis remedii plenitudine gloriemur (Post-comm. Dom. XI. post Pent.). — *Medicina* sacramenti et *corporibus* nostris prosit et *mentibus* (Postcomm. in fest. SS. Mart. Viti . . . . 15. Jun.). — Sit nobis, Domine, *reparatio mentis* et *corporis* coeleste mysterium (Dom. VIII. post Pent.).

it is an aromatic and sanitary *medicine,* to heal anew the injuries suffered and the wounds received.[1]

Holy Communion preserves and protects the life of grace in the children of God, that it may not die in the death of sin; for one of its effects is preservation from mortal sin. The Lord Himself declared that whosoever would eat of the Eucharistic Bread, should not die (John 6, 50) — that is, he should not die the death of the soul by sin. The world drinks in sin like water, the enemy lies in ambush and everywhere dangers threaten, so that we must work out our salvation in fear and trembling. How consoling and tranquilliz- ing, therefore, is the thought that in the Bread of the Strong we have so powerful a means of protection against the facility and danger of sinning, of being separated from God and of forfeiting His grace!—Thus the Eucharist protects the life of grace principally in this, that, as a supernatural food, it imparts perfect health of soul and refreshment of heart. It strengthens the spiritual life; for it increases sanctifying grace, awakens and fortifies the supernatural virtues — above all, charity, but also faith and hope, purity and devotion, humility and meekness, patience and perseverance. Thus it impels to good works, bestows upon us earnestness and fervor to consecrate and devote ourselves with generosity to the service of God. — Holy Communion at the same time leads a stream of heavenly joy, pleasure and bliss into the well disposed and sus- ceptible heart of the recipient. The Eucharistic Banquet, already here below, replenishes and refreshes the soul with a foretaste of the happiness of heaven — with sweetness and bliss, with peace and serenity, with vigor and animation, whereby we overcome all the dangers and obstacles to salvation. — The Holy Eucharist, there- fore, possesses in the highest degree power to conduct us to eternal glory. It is the pledge of future glory and an unfailing guarantee of celestial bliss. It is the fountain of living waters that issue forth from life eternal. Hence the Church teaches us to pray: "Grant, O Lord, we beseech Thee, that we may be satiated with the eternal enjoyment of Thy divine glory, prefigured by the temporal reception of Thy precious Body and Blood."

To the protection of the supernatural life of the soul, the Eucharist contributes not only directly, inasmuch as it imparts stability and perseverance in good; but also indirectly, in so far as it heals spiritual infirmities and frailties and restores to perfect health. The soul that is still weak and tepid, may be wholly cured, may become strong and healthy by means of the heavenly medicine of the Holy Sacrament of the Altar, which cleanses from venial sins, destroys rebellious sensuality, weakens inclinations and aversions, diminishes the perverse love of the world and of self.

---

[1] Sacramentum hoc est vigorosissima medicina contra reliquias vitiorum, contra concupiscentiam saevientem, contra venialia quotidianasque culpas, et contra mor- talia peccata oblita, et singulari modo valet contra universa animae vulnera (Dion. Carthus. De sacram. altar. art. 7).

Consequently, the Eucharist affords to the supernatural life of the *soul* protection and healing; but to the *body* also do its effects of grace extend directly as well as indirectly. The soul is the recipient of grace and salvation, through the soul and for the sake of the soul supernatural gifts are also imparted to the body [1] (in its way). — If, therefore, in Holy Communion sanctifying grace, together with the infused virtues and the gifts of the Holy Ghost, is increased, and if in addition sacramental graces of light and strength are imparted, that we may remain in Christ and Christ in us, that is, that in time we may persevere in the life of grace and in eternity attain to the life of glory, then the body too is benefited thereby, at least indirectly, because the superabundance of grace in a certain degree flows from the soul into the body. Holy Communion, by inflaming the heart with ardent love and heavenly aspirations, by averting dangers of salvation and giving protection against temptations, by imparting more abundant grace for energetic resistance against the attacks of the enemy, diminishes at least indirectly the empire of sensuality. But we may go still further and assume that the most holy and most pure Body of Christ suppresses and curbs also directly in the body of the worthy communicant the temptations and inclinations to concupiscence. — Inasmuch as the miraculous Eucharistic Food thus preserves the body chaste and unsullied, it disposes and preserves it for the glorious resurrection. To this must be added another aspect. In Holy Communion we receive Christ's Body and Blood into our heart, that is, we are not merely by faith, charity and grace united spiritually, but also corporally with Christ and, in consequence thereof, in a more perfect sense we become members of the Body of Christ, bone of His bone and flesh of His flesh, as it were, *one* body and *one* blood with Christ (*concorporei and consanguinei*).[2] Since by Christ's Body and Blood the personality of the devout communicant is elevated and ennobled, consecrated and sanctified, Christ cherishes, loves and esteems it, thus to speak, as His own, for it is in a special manner espoused to and possessed by Him. This aspect gives a new claim to the glorification of the body at the general resurrection; for also in the worthy reception of the glorified Body there lies a reason for the Lord to "reform the body of our lowness and make it like to the body of His glory" (Phil. 3, 21). The eternal glorification of the body is, consequently, already here below prepared and established through the cure and sanctification imparted to mortal flesh by the heavenly Eucharistic Food.

---

[1] Quia sacramenta operantur salutem quam significant, ideo secundum quandam assimilationem dicitur quod in hoc sacramento corpus offertur pro salute corporis et sanguis pro salute animae, quamvis *utrumque* ad *salutem utriusque* operetur, cum sub utroque totus sit Christus. Et licet corpus non sit immediatum subjectum gratiae, ex anima tamen redundat effectus gratiae ad corpus, dum in praesenti membra nostra exhibemus *arma justitiae Deo* (Rom. c. 6) et in futuro corpus nostrum sortietur incorruptionem et gloriam animae (S. Thom. 3, q. 79, a. 1 ad 3).

[2] Cfr. S. Cyrill. Hierosol. Catech. myst. 4, c. 1.

By Holy Communion, therefore, the soul and body of man are healed of every weakness and frailty, and are preserved and safe-guarded for life eternal.[1]

70. The Communion of the Celebrant.

The three or rather the two aforesaid prayers, the priest recites with an humble inclination of the body and with eyes riveted on the sacred Host (*oculis ad Sacramentum intentis — Rubr.*); now the preparation for Communion is concluded in the following manner.

1. The Conclusion of the Liturgical Preparation for Holy Communion.[2] — The priest longs to be fed with the fat of wheat and filled with honey out of the rock (Ps. 80, 17); he yearns for the strength and delicious flavor of the true Manna; he desires to taste the sweetness of the Lord at its fountain-head : therefore, he adores the Most Blessed Sacrament by genuflecting and manifests, whilst rising again,[3] the desire and longing of his heart in the words:

---

[1] Actualis consecutio gloriae *peculiari* quadam ratione est et dicitur effectus hujus sacramenti. Id quod non solum ad *animae*, sed etiam *corporis* beatitudinem referendum est, ut eo scil. novo titulo unionis cujusdam corporis nostri cum corpore Christi, dignius praeparentur corpora communicantium ad dotes corporales in resurrectione futuras, idque veluti participatione quadam et incohatione quasi in semine, qua justis etiam in hac vita communicatur agilitas quaedam et vigor ad studiosa opera simulque mundities ex assistentia divini auxilii et aliud quid simile dotibus, per quod caro, imminuto in dies fomite, promptius obediat spiritui et quasi spiritualis reddatur, eo fere sensu, quo 1 Cor. c. 15 post resurrectionem corpus dicitur fore *spirituale* quoad effectum, quia perfecte obediet spiritui. Eodemque sensu in Catech. Rom. p. 2, c. 4, q. 41 dicitur sacrae Eucharistiae *summam vim esse ad aeternam gloriam comparandam* hujusque sacramenti gratia fideles, dum hanc vitam degunt, *summa conscientiae pace et tranquillitate perfrui, ejusque virtute recreatos non secus atque Elias, qui subcinericii panis fortitudine ambulavit usque ad montem Dei Horeb, cum ex hac vita migrandi tempus advenit, ad aeternam gloriam et beatitudinem ascendere* (Tanner disp. 5, q. 7, dub. 1, n. 8).

[2] Sacerdos ante perceptionem corporis et sanguinis Christi debet dicere orationes a s. Patribus institutas; deinde meditari debet in incarnatione, in passione, in virtute hujus Sacramenti, dicens: *"Panem coelestem . . . ."* — hoc dicens se ipsum incitat ad devotionem, reducens ad memoriam, quid est quod sumere debet, quia panem qui de coelo descendit, et qualiter sumere debet, quia nomen Domini invocando, ut sic cum majori sumat reverentia et timore. — Dicendo vero subsequenter: *"Domine, non sum dignus,"* ex humilitate suam profitetur indignitatem (Durand. l. 4, c. 54, n. 10). This is the most ancient notice of the liturgical use of the above mentioned formulas of prayer before the Communion of the celebrant. The Ordo Rom. XIV, c. 53 remarks after the recitation of the Prayer for Peace and the imparting of the kiss of peace: junctis manibus dicat reverenter illas orationes: *"Domine J. Chr., Fili Dei vivi . . . ."* et *alias* orationes, quae dicendae sunt ante sumptionem corporis prout habentur in libro (in the Missal).

[3] *Adoratio* hic signanter praescribitur tamquam actus proxime disponens ad communionem. Deinde *surgens* dicit "Panem coelestem accipiam . . ." ad explicandam famem et fervens desiderium hujus panis coelestis, quo mirifice disponitur anima ad percipiendam ex eo perfectam nutritionem et pinguedinem spiritus . . . . . nec exspectat, ut erectus ea verba proferat, sed *dum surgit* ea pronuntiat, ut ferventius desiderium exprimatur (Quarti p. 2, tit. 10, n. 4).

Panem coelestem accipiam[1] *et nomen Domini invocabo* — "I will take the bread of heaven, and will call upon the name of the Lord" (Cf. Ps. 115, 4), that is, I will magnify the Lord and praise Him. Then he takes the Host and paten in the left hand, and slightly inclining his body, he strikes his breast three times with the right hand, saying each time:

Domine, non sum dignus, ut intres sub tectum meum: sed tantum dic verbo, et sanabitur anima mea.	Lord, I am not worthy that Thou shouldst enter under my roof: but only say the word, and my soul shall be healed.

The profound humility and unshaken confidence of the priest preparing for Communion could not be expressed more strikingly and, at the same time, more simply and heartily, than is done by the thrice repeated words spoken by the centurion of Capharnaum, to whom the Lord had said that He would enter into his house and cure his sick servant (Matth. 8, 5–14).[2] — Yes, humility and confidence at this moment take possession of the soul. If the priest, with lively faith, considers the greatness and holiness of the Eucharistic Lord, about to enter into him, then he is sensibly touched and profoundly humbled because of his unworthiness, his heart being so void and dreary, so poor and cold. Filled with holy confusion and fear, he would exclaim with St. Peter: "Depart from me, for I am a sinful man, O Lord!" (Luke 5, 8.) Yet at the sight of the condescending love and goodness of the Saviour, who on the altar conceals His glory in order to attract us, he is again encouraged and

---

[1] Accipere = to take in the hand, to seize and = to partake of, to eat. — In Evangelio legitur quod Christus accepit panem et calicem; non est autem intellegendum quod acceperit solum in manibus, ut quidam dicunt, sed eo modo accepit quo aliis accipiendum tradidit; unde cum discipulis dixerit: *Accipite* et *comedite*, et iterum: *Accipite* et *bibite*, intellegendum est quod ipse *accipiens comederit* et *biberit* (S. Thom. 3, q. 81, a. 1 ad 1).

[2] These words of the Centurion, praised by Jesus, the Church has taken in such a manner to heart, that she always places them in the mouth of her children before Holy Communion, the corporeal visit of our Saviour; on the one hand, to confess her unworthiness for a like visitation, and, on the other, to express her confidence that by a single word of His gentle power, He will deliver them from their unworthiness, that is, make them worthy. (Cfr. Laurent, Das heilige Evangelium S. 51). — Dicendo se indignum, praestitit dignum, non in cujus parietis, sed in cujus *cor* Christus intraret. Neque hoc diceret cum tanta fide et humilitate, nisi illum, quem timebat intrare in domum suam, *corde* gestaret (S. Aug. Serm. 62, n. 1). Non sum dignus qui sub tectum meum intres. Tecto non recipiebat, *corde* receperat. *Quanto humilior, tanto capacior, tanto plenior.* Colles enim aquas repellunt, valles implentur (S. Aug. Serm. 77, n. 12). — Per centurionem figurati sunt timorati ac humiles christiani, qui Christi opem desiderant, sed eum intra se communicando vel celebrando recipere vehementer verentur, unde cum spirituali receptione Sacramenti multoties contentantur. Et quamvis hoc *interdum* sit bonum, *melius* tamen est ex fervore et spe pietatis divinae Sacramentum recipere. Semper etiam expedit, cum centurione Christi dignitatem propriamque vilitatem perpendere et intimo corde fateri (Dion. Carthus. In Matth. c. 8).

animated with joyful confidence. "Come to Me," sayest Thou, O Lord, "all you that labor and are heavily burdened, and I will refresh you." "O sweet and amiable word in the ear of a sinner, that Thou, O Lord my God, shouldst invite the poor and needy to the communion of Thy most sacred Body! But who am I, O Lord, that I should presume to come to Thee? Behold, the heaven of heavens cannot contain Thee; and Thou sayest: *Come you all to Me!* What means this bounteous condescension and this so friendly invitation? How shall I dare approach, I, who am conscious to myself of no good on which I can presume? I sigh and grieve that I am yet so carnal and worldly, so unmortified in my passions, so full of the motions of concupiscence; so unguarded in my outward senses; so often entangled with many vain imaginations; so much inclined to exterior things, so negligent as to the interior; so easy to laughter and dissipation, so hard to tears and compunction; so prone to relaxation, and to the pleasures of the flesh, so sluggish to austerity and fervor; so curious to hear news and to see fine sights, so remiss to embrace things humble and abject; so covetous to possess much, so sparing in giving, so close in retaining; so inconsiderate in speech, so little able to hold my peace; so disorderly in my manners, so impetuous in my actions; so greedy at meat, so deaf to the word of God; so eager for rest, so slow to labor, so wakeful to hear idle tales, so drowsy to watch in the service of God; so hasty to make an end of my prayers, so wandering as to attention; so negligent in saying the Divine Office, so tepid in celebrating, so dry at the time of receiving; so quickly distracted, so seldom quite recollected in Thee; so easily moved to anger, so apt to take offence at others; so prone to judge, so severe in reprehending; so joyful in prosperity, so despondent in adversity; so frequent in good resolutions, and so backward in carrying them out!" (Imit. of Chr. 1. 4, 1, 7.)

Thus does the priest bewail his imperfections and weaknesses. Yet he also has unlimited confidence in Jesus Christ who, as St. Agatha said, by His word alone can cure all maladies (*qui solo sermone restaurat universa* — Offic. 5. Febr.). Whilst acknowledging his unworthiness, he, at the same time, confidently implores that the Lord, by a mere word of His omnipotence (*tantum dic verbo,* μόνον εἰπὲ λόγῳ), would perfectly heal and restore his diseased soul, that is, make it worthy for the approaching entrance of God into the lowly tabernacle of the human heart — namely, for Holy Communion. Already before Mass the priest also prayed: "O Lord, be Thou merciful to me! Heal my soul (*sana animam meam*); for I have sinned against Thee" (Ps. 40, 5).

2. The receiving of the Host. — "The marriage of the Lamb is come, and his wife (the soul) hath prepared herself . . . Blessed are they who are called to the marriage of the Lamb!" (Apoc. 19, 7, 9.) Holy Communion is the greatest joy and happiness—the bliss of this life, it is heaven upon earth and in the heart. Therefore, "rejoice O my soul, and give thanks for so noble a gift, and so singular a

comfort left to thee in this vale of tears. For as often as thou repeatest this mystery, and receivest the Body of Christ, so often dost thou celebrate the work of thy redemption, and art made partaker of all the merits of Christ. For the charity of Christ is never diminished, and the greatness of His propitiation is never exhausted.'' (Imit. of Christ IV, 2, 6.)

The priest takes the sacred Host in his right hand, and blesses himself[1] with Christ's sacrificial Body, pronouncing at the same time these words: *Corpus Domini nostri Jesu Christi*[2] *custodiat animam meam in vitam aeternam. Amen.* — "May the Body of our Lord Jesus Christ preserve my soul unto life everlasting. Amen."[3] Then he receives,[4] with profound humility and reverence, with fervent devotion and ardent love, the heavenly Bread of life which God in His sweetness has provided for the poor and hungry (Ps. 67, 11).

---

[1] Corpus et sanguinem Domini sumpturus se cum illis ante faciem cruce signat. Sicut enim prius cruces faciendo active tamquam minister illa sanctificavit, sic se eis nunc cruce signando passive *petit sanctificari* (Durand 1. 4, c. 54, n. 11).

[2] An sacerdos seipsum signans cum hostia et calice consecratis ante sumptionem sanctissimi Sacramenti ad verba — *Jesu Christi* — debeat *caput inclinare?* Resp.: *Affirmative,* juxta Rubricas (S. R. C. 24. Sept. 1842).

[3] The usual formula for administering Holy Communion, is as follows: Corpus Domini nostri J. Chr. custodiat animam tuam in vitam aeternam. Amen; but if Communion be given per modum viatici, the priest says: Accipe frater (vel soror) viaticum corporis D. N. J. Ch., qui te custodiat ab hoste maligno et perducat in vitam aeternam. Amen. At the Communion of the newly ordained, the bishop says: Corpus D. N. J. Ch. custodiat *te* in vitam aeternam, upon which each one answers: Amen. In former times various formulas were in use, for example, Corpus Christi — R. Amen, — Sanguis Christi — R. Amen. — Corpus D. N. J. Ch. conservet animam tuam. — Corpus et sanguis D. N. J. Ch. conservet et custodiat te in vitam aeternam. — Corpus D. N. J. Ch. custodiat corpus tuum et animam tuam in vitam aeternam. — Perceptio corporis Domini nostri sit tibi vita et salus et redemptio omnium tuorum peccatorum. — Corpus et sanguis D. N. J. Ch. in vitam aeternam te perducat et in die judicii ad sanctam requiem te resuscitet. — Corpus D. N. J. Ch. sit tibi salus animae et corporis. — Corpus D. N. J. Ch. sanguine suo intinctum conservet animam tuam in vitam aeternam. Amen. — In the ancient Communion rite the Amen of this administering formula was a responsory, whereby the communicant expressed his faith in the real presence of Christ in the Blessed Sacrament. In toto orbe terrarum pretium nostrum accipitur: *Amen respondetur* (S. Aug. Ennarr. in Ps. 125, n. 9). — Habet magnam vocem Christi sanguis in terra, quum eo accepto ab omnibus gentibus *respondetur Amen* (S. Aug. Contra Faust. 1. 12, c. 10. Cfr. Pseudo-Ambr. De sacrament. 1. 4, c. 5, n. 25).

[4] Deinde sacerdos communionem sumit, quam cum magno affectu et reverentia summa accipere debet, non festinando, sed beneficia Christi ardentisime recolendo, videlicet incarnationem, passionem, dilectionem ejus ad nos, tantam dignationem ac liberalitatem, qua sic dignatur esse nobiscum et sumi a nobis. Debet etiam Christum fiducialiter alloqui eumque intime exorare pro his, quae vehementius cupit adipisci ab ipso, tam pro se quam pro carioribus sibi, deprecando Christum, ut dignetur se omnino convertere et stabilire semperque confortare in ipso (Dion. Carthus. Expos. Missae art. 38).

24

The formula of receiving the Host and chalice embraces briefly and pregnantly the entire plenitude of the fruits of Communion. The preservation of the soul unto eternal life includes that of the body also as a necessary consequence and result: for the sake of the soul and by the soul the body, too, is preserved unto life eternal — the salvation of the soul is likewise the salvation of the body. The divine power of the Eucharist protects the soul against all dangers of salvation, temptations and assaults, inasmuch as it preserves, strengthens, augments and perfects in it the life of grace.[1] Unto them who eat His glorious Body, Christ gives the fat, the unction, the fulness of the life of the spirit (*se manducantibus dat spiritus pinquedinem — Offic. ss. Corp. Christ.*)[2] United most intimately and most wonderfully with the Eucharistic Saviour, the soul tastes and experinces how sweet is the Lord (Ps. 33, 9); she is quickened, refreshed, encouraged and stimulated: she finds strength and vigor, comfort and peace amid the temptations, sufferings and combats of life. "Thou, O Lord, didst feed Thy people with the food of angels, and gavest them bread from heaven prepared without labor, having in it all that is delicious and the sweetness of every taste, for Thy sustenance showed Thy sweetness to Thy children" (Wisdom 16, 20 etc). Filled and animated with mysterious joy by the spiritual, delicious taste of this precious Manna of the soul, the priest cries out from the depths of his heart: "My Beloved to me, and I to Him; I have found Him and I will not let Him go" (Cant. 2, 16; 3, 4). — I shall hold Him fast with love and devotion! Thoughts, affections, resolutions fill the breast of the communicating priest during the short pause that the rubrics permit and prescribe for the silent meditation on the sublime and wonderful grace that has been bestowed upon him.[3] The Church expresses this injunction most

---

[1] Tempus Evangelii recte tempus gratiae nuncupatur, quoniam multo exuberantior gratia in eo est data quam ante et innumerabiliter pluribus: inter quae est universitas gratiae sacramentalis et eucharistia maxime, quae inter suos effectus clarissimos confortat et munit nos in peregrinationis hujus exsilio ad pergendum viam salutis et arctum hoc iter, in quo innumerabilia magna et gravia occurrunt impedimenta, quousque ad supernae vocationis bravium pertingamus (Dion. Carthus. De sacram. altar. art. 5).

[2] "When thou beholdest the pure and immaculate Body of the God-Man lying before thee on the altar, say to thyself: Through this Body I am no longer dust and ashes, no longer a captive, but free; through this Body I hope to obtain heaven and all it contains — eternal life, the lot of the angels, the society of Christ. This Body pierced through with nails, death could not retain; in the presence of this crucified Body the sun was enveloped in darkness; because of it the veil of the temple was rent, the rocks were split, and the whole earth shook; this is the Body, covered with blood, pierced with a lance, from which issued for the entire universe two fountains of salvation — blood and water"(St.Chrysostom. 24th Homily on the First Epistle to the Corinthians).

[3] Sumat duas partes hostiae cum omni devotione et reverentia, et dum habet in ore sacrum Domini corpus, teneat manus ante pectus junctas in modum orantis (Ordo Rom. XIV, c. 53).

beautifully in the following words, that he rest a short time in meditation of the Most Blessed Sacrament (*quiescit aliquantulum in meditatione Ss. Sacramenti*). Who is not, therefore, reminded of the ever true saying of St. Augustine: "Thou hast created us for Thyself, O Lord, and our heart is disturbed until it rests in Thee!"

3. The receiving of the Chalice. — The celebrant must receive the Sacrament under both species; this is necessary for the completion of the Sacrifice, which he accomplishes by the consecration of the two elements.[1] After the receiving of the Body of Christ, therefore, follows the receiving of the Precious Blood. The priest soon arises from the blissful contemplation of the unfathomable mystery of love, to be conducted into the wine-cellar of the Lord (Cant. 2, 4) and to drink of the wine that germinates virgins (Zach. 9, 17), that is, the sacrificial Blood of Christ, whence blooms in virginal hearts angelic purity, light, innocence, holiness. He prepares the receiving of the chalice,[2] by uncovering it, genuflecting before it, putting into it the fragments of the sacred Host which may have been gathered up by the paten, and at last holding it with the right hand; meanwhile he recites some verses of the Psalms (Ps. 115, 3–4; Ps. 17, 4) introductory (to the Partaking of the Chalice):

Quid retribuam Domino pro omnibus, quae retribuit mihi? — Calicem salutaris accipiam et nomen Domini invocabo. Laudans invocabo Dominum et ab inimicis meis salvus ero.	What shall I render to the Lord, for all the things that He hath rendered to me? — I will take the chalice of salvation and I will call upon the name of the Lord. Praising I will call upon the Lord and I shall be saved from my enemies.

Whilst the priest in silent, blissful adoration reflects for some moments on the inconceivable love and liberality of God, on the boundless riches, treasures, gifts and joys of the Eucharistic "Sacrificial Banquet, in which Christ is received, the remembrance of His passion celebrated, the soul inundated with grace and an earnest of future glory given to us," — his heart overflows with gratitude and he cries out in holy enthusiasm: "What shall I render to the Lord,

---

[1] Ex parte ipsius sacramenti convenit quod utrumque sumatur, scil. et corpus et sanguis, quia in utroque consistit perfectio sacramenti, et ideo quia ad sacerdotem pertinet hoc sacramentum consecrare et perficere, *nullo modo* debet corpus Christi sumere sine sanguine (S. Thom. 3, q. 80, a. 12).

[2] In the thirteenth century the rite in this place was somewhat different. Junctis manibus inclinans sanguini dicat: *"Quid retribuam . . ."* et dicens: *"Calicem Domini accipiam"* (et non prius) accipit et elevat calicem de altari. Postea vero dicens: *"Laudans invocabo Dominum"* se signat cum illo, quo versu expleto sanguinum sumit (Durand. 1. 4, c. 54, n. 11). —Dicat illos versus: *Quid retribuam . . . Calicem . . .* et alia dicenda ante sumptionem sanguinis, prout in libro habentur (Ordo Rom. XIV, c. 53 [in the fourteenth century]).

for all the things that He has rendered to me?"[1] The infinite God with infinite love bestows upon me an infinite gift; for in Communion Jesus offers Himself to me with His glorious divinity and humanity. Although He is almighty, He could not give me more; although He is omniscient, He knows not how to give me more; although He is most wealthy, He has not more to give. To the question, whether or how he might suitably thank the Lord for His boundless goodness, the priest remains for some moments in holy silence,[2] whilst collecting the particles on the corporal, and then taking the chalice in his right hand, he breaks out into words which betoken his elevated sentiments of gratitude: "I will take the chalice of salvation and I will call upon the name of the Lord. Praising I will call upon the Lord and I shall be saved from my enemies." Whilst considering what we may give to the Lord, we find nothing else than what He had previously given us. Thus, in the first place, the priest affirms his gratitude, inasmuch as he takes hold of the chalice with its infinitely precious and inestimable contents, to offer it for the glorification of the divine name and to drink it while gratefully magnifying the Lord. God has no need of our gifts (Ps. 15, 2); the most acceptable thanksgiving to His loving Heart is for us to esteem His benefits, to receive them with desire and fervor,[3] and employ and utilize them in His honor with fidelity and zeal. Therefore, the priest returns thanks for the heavenly Bread of life, inasmuch as he extends his hand for new gifts, that is, for the chalice of salvation.[4] At the same time his heart overflows

---

[1] Versiculus iste cum *ingenti devotione* dicendus est, quatenus tota mente optemus Deo esse grati, ejus beneficia memoriter atque frequenter recolendo eaque Domine humiliter confitendo, ipsum pro eis ferventer amando (Dion. Carthus. In Ps. 115, 3).

[2] Subsistens aliquantulum in considerandis bonis, quae cum sacratissimo Christi corpore accepit, in eam postea sententiam magno affectu erumpit: "Quid retribuam Domino pro omnibus, quae retribuit mihi?" — cum in hoc solo Sacramento omnia contineantur, eo quod sit summum bonum, in quo omnia bona latent. Et sacrum Calicem accipiens, quasi respondeat sibi interroganti: "Calicem, inquit, salutaris accipiam et nomen Domini invocabo." Sanguinem scilicet pretiosissimum, qui in hoc salutis meo Calice continetur, accipiam in gratiarum actionem pro innumeris bonis, quae cum sanctissimo suo Corpore mihi est largitus. Et quoniam cum ipso Sanguine eadem bona recipio, ac propterea est singulare omnino beneficium, pro utroque laudabo semper sanctum ejus nomen et cupio, ut totus mundus ipsum laudet ac benedicat et cum Angelorum hierarchiis novum illud canticum cantet in honorem hujus sacrificii, quod ejus mortem repraesentat: "Dignus est Agnus, qui occisus est (et hic immolatus) accipere virtutem et divinitatem et sapientiam et fortitudinem et gloriam et honorem et benedictionem in saecula saeculorum. Amen" (Apoc. 5, 12). (De Ponte, De christian. hom. perfect. IV, tr. 2, c. 14).

[3] Prima gratitudo et gratiae repensio est beneficium gratanter (with joy) recipere (Dion. Carthus. In Ps. 102, 2).

[4] Ad sacra mysteria celebranda trahat te gratiarum actio pro omnibus beneficiis temporalibus et spiritualibus tibi et aliis impensis, cum nihil habeamus *Deo*

with grateful sentiments of divine praise and glorification, and he is animated with unshaken confidence toward God that he shall find in the chalice salvation, safety, redemption. The Lord has prepared the Eucharistic table against all that afflict us (Ps. 22, 5); in this festive and joyful Banquet lies the mystery of strength and fortitude, by which the faithful soul victoriously supports all exterior and interior trials, and triumphs gloriously over Satan, the world and the flesh. — " 'The chalice of benediction, which we bless, is it not the communion of the blood of Christ?' (1 Cor. 10, 16.) Appropriate and fearful utterance! For the Apostle would thereby say: that the Blood in the chalice is identical with that which flowed from the side of Jesus, and this we drink. He calls it a chalice of benediction, because while holding it in our hands, we praise and magnify Christ, we admire with astonishment His unutterable gift and thank Him that He has not only shed this Blood to redeem us from sin, but that He has, moreover, imparted the same to us." [1]

The priest now makes the sign of the Cross over himself with the chalice pronouncing the words of benediction: *Sanguis Domini nostri Jesu Christi custodiat animam meam in vitam aeternam. Amen.* — "The Blood of our Lord Jesus Christ preserve my soul unto life everlasting. Amen." Then with desire, fervor and joy he drinks the Precious Blood which streams forth unto eternal life. At this moment his heart exults: "My chalice, which inebriateth, — how goodly is it!" (Ps. 22, 5.) The mystical sacrificial chalice inundates the soul with blissful and heavenly inebriety, so that it makes us oblivious of all that is earthly; for "it bestows devotion and ardor of love with special charm and spiritual joy. . . . It imparts to the soul a fountain of well-being which overflows on the body, so that heart and flesh rejoice in the living God and cease to desire aught that is carnal." Truly, exceedingly glorious, excellent, noble, royal is the inebriating sacrificial Chalice! Brighter than the dawn of morning and evening's sunset sparkles, shines therein the Eucharistic Blood, that is, the holy Blood which once coursed through and animated the mortal members of the Saviour; that divine Blood which, in His painful passion and death, was shed upon the earth from His lacerated Body and transpierced Heart; that adorable Blood which, in heaven above and here in the tabernacle, flows and palpitates in the corporal Heart of Jesus; that precious Blood which, as the price of our redemption, streams forth in the ever fresh fountain of the Sacrifice of the Mass and in the sevenfold stream of the Sacraments over the earth and renews its face!

"O happy priest, how is it that the Lord has 'selected thee, has chosen thee' from among the children of men! Thy hand encompasses

---

retribuere pro omnibus quae retribuit nobis, aliud quam *calicem salutaris accipere* et *sacrificare hostiam laudis* (Ps. 115, 3-4), i. e. Jesum Christum (S. Bonav. tr. de praep. ad Miss. 1, § 4, n. 15).

[1] St. Chrysost., 24th Homily on 1 Cor. 10, 16.

in the chalice the form of the Heart, — yet no, the Heart even of thy 'God' and 'Redeemer'! Like unto the calyx of the lily it expands, to pour its heavenly honey into the pure, golden, lilylike chalice of thy heart. Well mayst thou, 'praising the Lord, call upon Him'; assuredly thou hast reason to do this. The 'power of the adorable Blood' 'will gird thee for the giant battle' against the enemies of thy salvation. Therefore, raise aloft the chalice, and when its golden rim touches thy lips, trembling with joy, then may thy soul exult: 'Praise the Lord! Blessed be' the chalice of the eternal, the glorious Covenant! — Enter, O Precious Blood, into my heart, as the conqueror into his conquered kingdom! Take possession of all its powers, inclinations, sentiments. Fill it to overflowing with the fire of Thy grace. Rule it without limit, thou crown of the kingdom of God, thou purple cloak of my Eternal King, until this poor heart in adoration, 'praising' shall bathe itself in thy heavenly flood of light!'' (Wolter.)

Only after partaking of the Eucharistic Sacrificial Banquet is the priest perfectly one — one body, one heart, one soul — with the Divine Victim. He now administers to the faithful,[1] who long for it, and who are prepared to receive it, the Eucharistic Bread of heaven.[2] The Church ardently wishes that her children should often by sacramental Communion participate in the Sacrifice of the Mass. "She admonishes with maternal kindness, exhorts, beseeches and implores, by the bonds of the mercy of God, that all Christians . . . . be mindful of the great majesty and the boundless love of our Lord Jesus Christ, that they believe and honor with such steadfast faith, devotion of heart, piety and reverence the holy mysteries of His Body and Blood, that they may frequently receive this supersubstantial Bread, and that it may be to them truly the life of the

---

[1] Est legitimum tempus communicandi ante ultimam orationem, quae dicitur *ad complendum*, quia ejus petitio maxime pro eis est qui communicant. Unde etiam eorum qui per singulas Missas communicare volunt, accendi videtur voluntas, quia per totam Missam pro eis quam maxime et quasi nominatim oratur, qui ibi offerunt atque communicant (Walafr. Strabo c. 23).

[2] The rite for administering Communion to clerics and to the laity formerly varied greatly according to times and places. For several centuries the faithful received the Blessed Sacrament standing, but with a reverential, bowed posture of the body, with the right hand crossed over the left; only during Holy Mass did they communicate under both forms. After the sixth century the precious Blood was received through a chalice-tube (calamus, fistula, pugillaris, pipa, canna); in the Middle Age frequently but a portion of the consecrated Blood was poured into a ministerial-chalice filled with wine, or in many places the Host was dipped into the precious Blood. From the thirteenth century Communion under both kinds was gradually discontinued. It now exists only for the officiating ministri sacri (deacon and subdeacon) at the High Mass of the Pope. The prayers now in use (confessio et absolutio, Ecce Agnus Dei, Domine non sum dignus), when giving Holy Communion out of and also during Holy Mass, appear to have been gradually introduced since the thirteenth century. (Cfr. Mabillon, In Ord. Rom. c. 14. — Krazer sect. 4, art. 1, c. 15.)

soul and perpetual health of mind. That, being thereby fortified, they may, after this wretched pilgrimage, arrive at the heavenly home, there to enjoy unveiled the same Bread of Angels which they now receive concealed under sacred veils" (Trid. sess. 13, cap. 8). They, who do not receive sacramentally, should unite themselves to the Eucharistic Saviour at least by a spiritual Communion — by lively faith, compunction, sincere humility, ardent love, fervent desire — for spiritual Communion also obtains for the soul many and precious graces.

4. The Purification of the Chalice and the Ablution of the fingers.[1] — In the smallest particle of the sacramental species the whole Christ is present. On the belief in this truth numerous liturgical usages and ordinances are founded, all conducing to prevent and avoid, with the greatest and almost scrupulous care, the slightest profanation of the smallest portion of the sacred Host or of a single drop of the Eucharistic Blood. After the Consecration, therefore, the thumb and forefinger must continually be held together,[2] and as often as they touch the sacred Host, be purified over the chalice. For this reason it is that after Communion the fragments on the corporal and paten must be so carefully collected, and chalice and hands be well cleaned. For this purpose great care and attention have always been exerted;[3] thus already St. Cyril of Jerusalem exhorts:

---

[1] Purificatio in liturgical books designates not only the cleansing of the chalice, and the mouth also, but likewise the *wine* with which the priest rinses the chalice after receiving the precious Blood, and even the wine which may be given to those who communicate after they have received the sacred Host. By *ablutio* is understood the wine and water whereby the fingers that held the Host are cleansed from any particle of the sacred Host that may be attached to them, and the chalice rinsed a second time. Celebrans, sumpta *purificatione*, lavat digitos et sumit *ablutionem* (Cerem. Episcop. l. 2, c. 29, n. 8). — By the purification and ablution it is intended to prevent as securely as possible every profanation of the Blessed Sacrament. This object is, however, obtained, since by a strict adherence to the prescribed rite hardly any particle of the consecrated species can yet remain. Practically unimportant is the question, whether the rest of the consecrated wine still remaining in the chalice is drunk with the fluids poured in, or whether it is so altered by being mixed with the wine and water, that the real presence of Christ ceases therein. The Church nowhere prescribes more water than wine to be taken at the ablution, but it is recommended by many authors, in order more securely to effect the destruction of holy species that might still be in the chalice. We should take notice, moreover, that the Church very unwillingly and quite seldom grants that the ablution be taken with water only. — Verisimile est et pietati conforme asserere, colligi ab angelis fragmenta, quae remanent, praesertim minutiora, quae conspici non possunt, nec consequenter humana diligentia custodiri et colligi (Quarti, Comment. p. 2, tit, 10, dub. 7).

[2] Sacerdos digitos jungit post consecrationem, scil. pollicem cum indice, quibus corpus Christi consecratum tetigerat, ut si qua particula digitis adhaeserit, non dispergatur, quod pertinet *ad reverentiam sacramenti* (S. Thom. 3, q. 83, a. 5 ad 5).

[3] Archidiacono *nimis caute* procurandum est, ne quid in calice aut patena sanguinis vel corporis Christi remaneat (Ordo Rom. IV, n. 12).

"Have the utmost care that no part of the Eucharistic species be lost. For, tell me, if any one gave you grains of gold, would you not guard them with the greatest circumspection and be most solicitous that none of them be lost and that you thereby suffered no loss? How much more cautious must you be not to lose a crumb of that, which is incomparably more valuable than gold and precious stones." (5. Mystag. Catech. No. 21.)

The present purification and ablution rite, which is minutely ordered and prescribed, was established and developed only during the course of the Middle Age.[1] While the priest, filled with profound reverence toward the Most Blessed Sacrament, performs the exterior act of cleansing the chalice and also his fingers, his mind and heart are recollected and immersed in meditation on the heavenly Sacrificial Banquet, which has so wonderfully refreshed and strengthened him; for he makes at the same time use of two corresponding prayers to implore the blessed effects of Holy Communion. This is all the more proper since, according to an established opinion, during the whole period of the corporal presence of Christ in the heart of the communicant, the sacramental grace is being ever increased, provided that the communicant produces constantly new and, at the same time, more perfect acts of devotion.[2] — Hence the two following prayers

---

[1] With respect to the purification of the chalice and paten, as well as the ablution (washing) of the mouth and fingers after Holy Communion, we have no information dating from the first ten centuries. The Ordo Rom. IV (written probably at the beginning of the eleventh century) mentions (n. 13), that the bishop at this point washes his hands; the Ordo X of a later period remarks (n. 15) in reference to Good-Friday and Requiem Masses: "perfusionem facit Pontifex in calice et ipse sumit et postea lavat cum aqua in bacilibus" (vessels or basins). In the Middle Age the chalice was generally purified with wine, and the purification drunk; the fingers, on the contrary, were usually rinsed with water and the ablution thrown into the Sacrarium. Post contrectata et sumpta Sacramenta sacerdos... manus lavat et in locum sacrum huic cultui deputatum ipsa aqua vergitur (Ivonis Carnot. Serm. 5). — Post sumptum Eucharistiae sacrificium sacerdos abluit et perfundit manus, ne quid incaute remaneat ex contactu divinissimi Sacramenti... Ablutionis autem aqua debet in locum mundum diffundi honeste, ut altitudo Sacramenti reverentius honoretur (Innocent. III. 1. 4, c. 8). For the purification of the fingers, as a rule, another chalice was used. — Sanguine sumpto, recipiat Pontifex modicum de vino in calice, infundente illud subdiacono, et illud sumat ad abluendum os suum. Postea dicendo illas orationes *"Quod ore..."* et *"Corpus tuum..."*, tenens super calicem digitos utriusque manus, quibus tetigit hostiam, abluat ipsos modicum, subdiacono iterum infundente vinum, et antequam illud sumat, abluat iterum eos digitos cum aqua, quam infundat capellanus cum pelvibus, et ipsa aqua projiciatur in loco mundo. Pontifex, ablutis digitis praedicto modo cum aqua, abstergat os cum panno tersorio.... Postea sumpto vino quod erat in calice, tergat os suum eodem panno (Ordo Rom. XIV, c. 53). This rite of the first half of the fourteenth century is almost similar to that prescribed later on by Pius V. for general practice, and which is still in use.

[2] The present capiamus, in opposition to the transitory or past reception (sumpsimus) of the Host, seems to indicate this permanent efficacy of the Eucharistic Sacrament as well as the requisite coöperation of the communicant.

are intended to foster and augment the actual disposition of the celebrant, that he may become susceptible to further outpourings of grace. To him should the words apply: "While the king was at his repose, my spikenard sent forth the odor thereof" (Cant. I, 11), that is, so long as Christ in His humanity dwells in my heart, my soul exhales the good odor of devout affections and sentiments of ardent love.

Then after consuming the Precious Blood, that is, without making a short meditation,[1] as is allowed or prescribed after the reception of the Sacred Body, the priest has wine poured[2] into the chalice, while he recites the following prayer, which is found in the most ancient Sacramentaries[3] and is still to be seen in our Missal as Post-Communion:

Quod ore sumpsimus, Domine, pura mente capiamus: et de munere temporali fiat nobis remedium sempiternum.	What we have taken with our mouth, O Lord, may we receive with a pure mind; and from a temporal gift may it become for us an everlasting remedy.

By these words we beseech God the Father to grant us a twofold grace. In the first place, that our Sacramental Communion may be also a spiritual Communion, that is, a worthy Communion, rich in grace through the greatest possible purity of soul; and, in consequence of this disposition may the participation in the temporal celebration of the Eucharist produce in us lasting and imperishable effects, that is, may it conduct us to eternal life.[4] — In Communion

---

[1] S. R. C. 24. Sept. 1842 in Neapolitana ad 2.

[2] Vinum ratione suae humiditatis est *ablutivum* et ideo sumitur post susceptionem hujus Sacramenti ad abluendum *os*, ne aliquae reliquiae remaneant, quod pertinet ad reverentiam Sacramenti ... et eadem ratione perfundit vino *digitos*, quibus corpus Christi tetigerat (S. Thom. 3, q. 83, a. 5 ad 10). — Calicis purificatio fit *solo vino* ob reverentiam pretiosi sanguinis, cujus gutta quaepiam, uti plerumque accidit, ad imum calicis fluit. Ablutio sumitur ex eadem parte, per quam pretiosus sanguis absorptus est, ne scil. sacrae ejusdem reliquiae circa labia calicis remaneant. Hic advertendum est, in *ablutione* digitorum minime fas esse adhiberi, sine Apostolica dispensatione, *sola* aqua. (Cfr. Indultum S. R. C. 15. Jan. 1847 in una Romana. De Carpo, Biblioth. liturg. p. 1, a. 52, n. 207.)

[3] In the Sacrament. Leonian. we read: Quod ore sumpsimus, Domine, quaesumus, mente capiamus et de munere temporali fiat nobis remedium sempiternum. Micrologus remarks (c. 19), that in this place the prayer juxta Romanum Ordinem sub silentio is to be recited; the other: Corpus tuum ... he does not mention, while the Ordo Rom. XIV (in the fourteenth century) alludes to it.

[4] Post perceptionem sacramenti petit sacerdos, ut hoc mysterium, quod sub venerandis signis corporaliter est sumptum, spiritualiter etiam sumatur et cum debita puritate mentis ipsius sacramenti fructus et virtus percipiatur, quoniam nihil prodest, quinimo plurimum obest sumptio sacramentalis, nisi eidem conjuncta sit perceptio spiritualis et gratiae illius participatio. — Secundo postulat idem, ut de hoc munere temporali, participatione scil. sacrorum mysteriorum sub visibilibus signis ad tempus et pro vitae hujus curriculo data fiat illi et omnibus sumentibus

we receive in reality into our mouth the human nature of Christ, we truly eat His Flesh and truly drink His Blood (*Quod ore sumpsimus*); but in order that by this sacramental union with Christ and by His corporal indwelling we may draw grace upon grace, we must receive Him, this sublime and heavenly Guest, embrace and hold Him fast with a heart that is pure and chaste, disengaged from attachment to whatever is temporal and perishable, and, on the contrary, penetrated with heavenly love and desire for that which is eternal and imperishable (*pura mente capiamus*). Thus we sanctify Christ in our hearts (1 Peter 3, 15), inasmuch as we receive Him by an actual and by spiritual Communion, that is, a fruitful Communion.[1] — In this way the temporal gift becomes for us an everlasting remedy.[2] By the temporal gift (*munus temporale*) the Eucharist is to be understood as a Sacrifice and as a Sacrament; the gift of the Eucharist is, therefore, mainly[3] called temporal, because Sacrifice and Sacrament are instituted and necessary only for time, for the duration of our temporal life, for the days of our earthly pilgrimage, — but not for eternity and for the life to come, where the full possession and enjoyment of all gifts without corporal covering and sacramental veils shall be bestowed upon us.[4] The Eucharist, moreover, may be designated as a temporal gift, inasmuch as the Sacrifice is accomplished in a short time, and in so far as the Sacrament is present within us but for a few minutes, that is, so long as the species remain within us. Although a temporal gift, therefore, the Eucharist is yet to become for us an eternal remedy and a means of obtaining eternal salvation.[5] For it has the power to redeem our

---

ore et spiritu remedium sempiternum contra vitia et tentationes, ut hoc cibo et potu confortati non excidamus umquam virtute, sed perducamur ad vitam aeternam (Clichtov. Elucidat. l. 3, n. 82).

[1] Cfr. similar petitions in the Post-Communions, for example, quod ore percepimus, pura mente sectemur — quae sedula servitute donante te gerimus, dignis sensibus tuo munere capiamus — quod ore prosequimur, contingamus et mente, quae temporaliter agimus, spiritualiter consequamur — quod ore contingimus, pura mente capiamus.

[2] Quod temporali celebramus actione, perpetua salvatione capiamus — quod temporaliter gerimus, aeternis gaudiis consequamur — quae nunc specie gerimus, rerum veritate capiamus — quod temporaliter gerimus, ad vitam capiamus aeternam — quod est nobis in praesenti vita mysterium, fiat aeternitatis auxilium.

[3] At the same time we can also think of the temporal, earthly, material elements, bread and wine, which are offered to God and consecrated in the Eucharist. Plebis tuae munera, quaesumus, Domine, propitius intende, et quae sanctis mysteriis exsequendis *temporaliter* nos offerre docuisti, ad *aeternam* nobis proficere fac salutem (Sacram. Leon.).

[4] Quia hoc sacramento non est in aeternum mors Christi annuntianda, sed tantum donec veniat, quia postea nullis mysteriis egebimus, constat illud *transitorium* esse signum et *temporale*, quo tantum egemus nunc, dum videmus per speculum et in aenigmate (Alger. l. 1, n. 57).

[5] Remedium = a remedy for something, a healing remedy, a helpful means; remedium *sempiternum* meton. = salutis aeternae remedium. Cfr. sacrosancta mysteria *praesens* nobis *remedium* esse facias et *futurum*.

life from perdition, to heal all spiritual and corporal frailty, to enrich with every gift, whereby it becomes for us the guarantee and pledge of a blessed eternity.

The prayer for the washing of the fingers is as follows:

Corpus tuum, Domine, quod sumpsi, et Sanguis, quem potavi, adhaereat visceribus meis, et praesta: ut in me non remaneat scelerum macula, quem pura et sancta refecerunt sacramenta: qui vivis et regnas in saecula saeculorum. Amen.

May Thy Body, O Lord, which I have received, and Thy Blood which I have drunk, cleave unto my inmost parts: and grant that no stain of sin may remain in me, whom the pure and holy mysteries have refreshed: who livest and reignest world without end. Amen.

Here we beseech[1] the Lord, that His transient sacramental presence may ever produce in the depths of our soul lasting and profound interior effects, — that it may obtain for us in a special manner perfect purity from all that is sinful. Christ's Body and Blood remain in us so long as the sacramental species are not destroyed, they remain also afterward within us (*adhaereat visceribus meis*)[2] by the sacramental power and grace which purify, ennoble, change, sanctify the powers and faculties of the soul, the affections and inclinations of the heart, so that it is no longer we that live, but Christ that liveth in us (Gal. 2, 20). As the branch is connected with the vine, so, in like manner, Communion causes us to remain in Christ and continually to draw from Him unction of grace and vigor of life, in order that we may be immutably faithful in the love and service of God. In that our Eucharistic Saviour remains and acts in us like unto a glowing coal,[3] we become perfectly cleansed

---

[1] As this prayer is in the singular and presupposes that holy Communion has been received under both kinds, it appears to be intended and destined for the celebrant, whilst the preceding prayer (as well as the Postcommunio) is or may be applicable to all who have received Communion.

[2] Petit sacerdos, quod ipsius sumpti sacramenti virtus adhaereat immaneatque visceribus ejus, non quidem corporalibus, sed *spiritualibus* ipsius animae, quae sunt memoria, intellectus et voluntas. . . . Postulat autem Missam celebrans ipsum quod sumpsit sacramentum adhaerere suis visceribus, non quidem secundum substantiam et rei adhaerentiam, quemadmodum cibus sensibilis adhaeret stomacho, sed secundum *virtutem* et *efficaciam,* per quam memoria intellectualis jugem habeat divinorum beneficiorum coelestiumque bonorum recordationem, intellectus rectam eorum quae credenda sunt et agenda cognitionem, voluntas vero promptam et ardentem bonorum et Deo placentium operum prosecutionem. Neque id quidem in transitu et perfunctorie, sed permanenter et indesinenter (Clichtov. Elucid. eccles. 1. 3, n. 82). — Viscera, in the first place = entrails (in Holy Scripture often regarded as the seat of the affections), then = the interior, the inmost part of the heart.

[3] In the primitive Church the Incarnate Son of God (Verbum incarnatum) was called — especially in the Blessed Sacrament — a glowing coal (ἄνθραξ, carbo ignitus, pruna ignita); for the Eucharist is a food of fire which purifies and inflames (cfr. Is. 6, 6).

from every stain and trace of sin; all that is impure is consumed within us. The garment of sanctifying grace is so brilliantly white and so resplendent, that no imperfection, no breath of evil may tarnish its purity (*in me remaneat scelerum macula*).[1] — These spiritual miracles of purification and sanctification, the pure and holy mysteries (*pura et sancta sacramenta*)[2] of the Eucharist produce, which continue ever anew to refresh, rejuvenate, quicken (*refecerunt*)[3] the higher life of the soul, so that it may not wither away and be lost.[4]

5. O dearest Lord Jesus, what great sweetness hath a faithful soul perfectly devoted to Thee, that feasteth with Thee in Thy banquet; where there is no other meat set before her to be eaten but Thyself, her only beloved, and most to be desired, above all the desires of her heart. And to me indeed it would be delightful to pour out tears in Thy presence, with the whole affection of my heart, and like unto the devout Magdalen, to wash Thy feet with my tears. But where is this ardor of devotion, where is this stream of holy tears? Surely in the sight of Thee, and of Thy holy angels, my whole heart ought to be inflamed, and to weep for joy. For I have Thee in the Sacrament truly present, though hidden under another form. For to behold Thee in Thine own divine brightness, is what mine eyes would not be able to endure, neither could the entire world subsist in the splendor of the glory of Thy majesty. In this, therefore, Thou condescendest to my weakness, that Thou hidest Thyself under the sacramental species. I truly have and adore Him whom the angels adore in heaven; but I as yet in faith,

---

[1] Deus, qui sumitur, *ignis* consumens est omnem peccati scoriam exurensque spirituali et sacro incendio omnes noxios humores vitiorum in anima. Ipse itidem *lux* est clarissima illuminans tenebras nostras et omnem iniquitatis caliginem infusione sui luminis effugans (Clichtov. Elucidat. eccles. 1. 3, n. 83).

[2] The designation of the Eucharistic Sacrifice and Sacrament by the plural sacrificia and sacramenta is usually explained and justified with reference to the two divisions of the sacramental species; but in this we should notice, that the word sacramenta in the liturgy is often used in a wider sense = mysteria, that is, mysteries. The stricter (specific) signification in which it is now used to designate the seven means of grace in the Church, became customary only since the Middle Age. For the Eucharistic Mysteries we frequently in the Post-Communions come across similar expressions, for example, mysteria, divina sacramenta, sancta, sacri dona mysterii, sancta vel sacra munera, dona coelestia, salutis nostrae subsidia, mystica vota et gaudia, coelestia sacramenta et gaudia, salutaria dona, votiva sacramenta, coelestia alimenta, magnifica sacramenta, munera sacrata.

[3] Refecerunt haec sacramenta animae viscera quantum ad *effectum ab eis causatum et derelictum* ex digna eorum sumptione. Sic enim refecerunt rationem et intellectum in sinceritate cognitionis illuminando, voluntatem per amorem et dilectionem inflammando, memoriam ad passionis rememorationem excitando, suavitatem quandam et laetitiam spiritualem in toto homine efficiendo (Gabr. Biel, Exposit. Canon. Missae lect. 83).

[4] Sacrosancti corporis et sanguinis D. N. J. Chr. *refectione vegetati*, supplices te rogamus Deus, ut hoc *remedio singulari* et ab omnium peccatorum nos contagione purifices et a periculorum munias incursione cunctorum (Sacram. Leon.).

they by sight, and without a veil. I must be content with the light of true faith, and walk therein till the day of eternal brightness break forth, and the shades of concealing forms pass away. But when that which is perfect shall come, the use of Sacraments shall cease; for the blessed in heavenly glory stand not in need of the medicine of the Sacraments. For they rejoice without end in the presence of God, beholding His glory face to face; and being plunged from brightness into the brightness of the incomprehensible Deity, they taste the Word made flesh, as He was from the beginning, and as He remaineth forever. O how sublime and how venerable is the office of priests! O how clean ought those hands to be, how pure that mouth, how holy that body, how unspotted the heart of the priest, into whom the Author of purity so often enters! From the mouth of the priest, who so often receives Jesus Christ in His Sacrament, nothing but what is holy, no word but what is good and profitable, ought to proceed. His eyes, which are used to behold the Body of Christ, ought to be simple and chaste; his hands, which are used to handle the Creator of heaven and earth, should be pure and lifted up to heaven in prayer. O Almighty God! come with Thy grace to our assistance, that we priests may serve Thee worthily and devoutly, in all purity and good conscience. And, if we cannot live yet perfectly free from every fault, as our calling demands, grant us at least the grace duly to bewail the sins which we have hitherto committed; and in the spirit of humility, and the resolution of a good will, to serve Thee more fervently for the time to come. (Cfr. Imit. of Christ IV, 11.)

71. The Thanksgiving.

The moments which immediately follow the reception of Holy Communion are exceedingly *blessed* and *precious, rich in grace* and devotion; for in astounding condescension the sweet and gracious Jesus now dwells, with all the treasures of heaven, in the inmost sanctuary of the poor human heart. It is then especially requisite[1] for us to forget the world and its pleasures; to avoid all dissipation and levity; in retirement, recollection, in silence to direct all the powers and faculties of the soul to the Heavenly Guest; to embrace with devotion and ardent love the Eucharistic King of our heart; to glorify, to adore, to magnify, to petition Him; — in short, to offer a joyful and heartfelt thanksgiving for the unutterably marvellous grace of Holy Communion.

---

[1] Decet post communionem in omnibus mente et corpore custoditum ac modestum consistere nec minus esse sollicitum ad Christum grate tenendum quam ante exstiterat ad eum digne suscipiendum. Unde multi arguendi videntur, qui post communionem et Missae consummationem tam faciliter se foras effundunt atque in exterioribus occupantur, nisi necessitas postulet (Dion. Carthus. Expos. Miss. art. 38). — Expleto officio, ferventi ac devotissimo corde gratias age, gratus permane atque in omni conversatione tua esto sollicitus, ne offendas: esto timoratus et custoditus, ne susceptam gratiam perdas, ne fructum amittas adeptum, et sic tota vita tua sit praeparatio ad celebrandum continua (Dion. Carthus. De sacr. serm. 3).

St. Francis of Assisi once went in company with one of the brethren, Brother Masseo, over a field through the burning heat of the sun. Thirsting for a cool drink, they came to a spot in which fresh water gushed forth, and around which a lofty tree cast a delightful shade. Here they rested, took some pieces of stale bread, which had been given to them in alms, moistened them in the water, ate and drank. At the same time tears coursed down the face of the saint. In amazement the Brother inquired: "Good Father, why do you weep?" — "Ah, Brother," rejoined the saint, "should I not shed tears of joy and gratitude because our Heavenly Father has prepared for us so delicious a banquet?" Masseo with difficulty refrained from smiling at these words, as the food appeared to him by no means delicious. The saint then continued in a serious tone: "Remember, Brother, how tenderly the Lord provides for us poor creatures. From all eternity He foresaw that we would at one time pass this place, exhausted and thirsty, — and with provident love He here placed a shady tree and a refreshing spring, that we might rest and consume, beneath pleasant shelter, the bread which those good people gave us for His sake. Why have we deserved this paternal love and care? Should not the exceeding goodness of God draw from our eyes tears of reciprocal love and gratitude?" Thus the Seraphic Francis thought — and returned thanks for a few morsels of hard bread, for a drink of fresh water. But what is this gift compared with the sweetness and plenitude of grace contained in the mystical Banquet which the Lord daily prepares for us on the altar? Not earthly, perishable, but heavenly, imperishable food and refreshment He there presents to us — His most sacred Body and His most precious Blood. As "the soul is here filled with the marrow and fatness" of celestial gifts and consolations, she should overflow with gratitude, and with joyful lips praise and magnify the Lord (Ps. 62, 6). This thanksgiving, by which the Eucharistic stream of grace is not only copiously poured into the heart, but, moreover, carefully preserved therein, the Church leaves to the fervor and devotion of the individual. Hence for public worship she has prescribed only a very short and simple celebration after Communion. This liturgical celebration is justly considered and styled the *thanksgiving*.[1] — In the first place, we here meet the *Communio* and the *Post-Communio*, to which on the ferial days of Lent the *Oratio super populum* is added.

1. The *Communio*. — Thus the Antiphon, that is, the Verse, is called which is read out of the Missal by the priest after Communion, on the Epistle side[2] of the altar. Like the Offertory before

---

[1] *Tota missae celebratio in gratiarum actione terminatur*, populo exsultante pro sumptione mysterii (quod significat cantus *post* communionem), et sacerdote per orationem gratias offerente, sicut et Christus celebrata coena cum discipulis, hymnum dixit ut dicitur Matth. c. 26 (S. Thom. 3, q. 83, a. 4).

[2] On the Epistle side, as the less worthy side of the altar, the less important portions of the Mass are read, that is, those parts which precede the (first) Gospel

the oblation, this Antiphon is an abbreviated chant, that is, a remnant of that longer Psalm-chant, which in former times — from the days of the Apostles until about the twelfth century — accompanied the administration of the Eucharist to the clergy and laity. The Psalm-Verses which, in greater or less number, were by turns sung by the choir with an oft-repeated Antiphon, received the name *Communio*, that is, Communion Hymn, because they accompanied the act of Communion and were intended to intensify the devotion of the communicant.[1] Since the twelfth century[2] these Psalm-Verses were gradually omitted at the administration of Communion, and sung afterward, so that they constituted a portion of the liturgical thanksgiving. Later on this hymn was abridged and reduced to the Antiphon which at present, notwithstanding its altered position and application to the thanksgiving, still retains the original name (*Communio*). The custom, introduced at an early date and universally adopted in the East as well as in the West, of enhancing the celebration of Communion by the singing of Psalms, had undoubtedly its origin and foundation in the guest-chamber at Jerusalem, where the Lord and His Apostles at the Last Supper concluded the hymn (*hymno dicto* — Matth. 26, 30), before they proceeded to the Mount of Olives.

As a rule the Communion Verse is taken from Holy Scripture, not always from the Psalms; frequently also from the other Biblical Books. Occasionally it is of ecclesiastical origin, or consists of a

---

and follow the Communion; on the Gospel side and in the middle of the altar *tamquam in partibus dignioribus altaris*, on the contrary, are performed those prayers and ceremonies which by their intimate connection with the accomplishment of the Sacrifice have a more profound signification. (Cfr. Quarti, p. 2, tit. 11, n. 1).

1 Mox ut Pontifex coeperit in senatorio (that is, at the place destined for the more distinguished men) communicare, statim schola incipit *Antiphonam ad Communionem* per vices cum subdiaconibus et *psallunt* usquedum, communicato omni populo, annuat Pontifex ut dicant *"Gloria Patri"* et repetito Versu (Antiphon) quiescunt (Ordo Rom. I, n. 20). — Facta confractione debent omnes communicare, interim cum et *Antiphona* cantatur, quae de *Communione* nomen mutavit, cui et *Psalmus* subjungendus est cum *"Gloria Patri"*, si necesse fuerit (Microlog. c. 18). — In the Ambrosian Rite this Antiphon to be recited after Communion is called Transitorium — scil. quia tunc sacerdos ex cornu Evangelii *transit* ad partem Epistolae.

2 Cantus quem *communionem* dicimus, quem *post* cibum salutarem canimus, *gratiarum actio* est, juxta illud: "Edent pauperes et saturabuntur et laudabunt Dominum, qui requirunt eum" (Ps. 21, 27. — Rupert. Tuit. De divin. offic. 1. 2, c. 18). — Since this time it received in many places also the name postcommunio, which later on was exclusively used to designate the last prayer. Antiphona, quam usitato nomine vocamus *Postcommunionem* (Hildeb. Turon. [† 1134] Lib. de expositione Missae). — Antiphona, quae *Postcommunio* a pluribus nuncupatur, ideo sic appellata est, quoniam post communicationem sive in signum, quod communicatio expleta est, concinitur (Durand. 1. 4, c. 56, n. 1). Afterward (c. 57, n. 1) he observes: Sacerdos elevatis manibus ultimam orationem, quae *proprie* Postcommunio vocatur, exsequitur.

characteristic saying of the saint commemorated. As to its contents the Communion Antiphon in nowise refers to the reception of the Eucharist, as might be presumed from its name and position, but to the particular celebration of the day or of the Sacrifice. In harmony with the remaining variable constituent parts of the rite of the Mass, it serves to bring the mystery of the feast, or the idea of the ecclesiastical time, or the subject of the Mass in question celebrated, more prominently in view. But rarely is the text so arranged that a reference to Holy Communion could therein be discovered; if this happen, it is more accidental than intentional. In it the Mass liturgy leaves the unchangeableness of the Canon and moves in the course of the ecclesiastical year. The same fundamental tones, which were often heard in the Introit and during the progress of Holy Mass, return in the concluding chant of the Communion Antiphon and in the Post-Communion.

On the four Sundays of Advent the spirit of this ecclesiastical period is briefly and lucidly expressed in the Communion Verses, namely, the joyful expectation of the coming Saviour:

Dom. I. — Ps. 84. Dominus dabit benignitatem: et terra nostra dabit fructum suum.

Ps. 84. The Lord will give goodness: and our earth shall yield her fruit.

Dom. II. — Bar. 4 et 5. Jerusalem surge, et sta in excelso: et vide jucunditatem, quae veniet tibi a Deo tuo.

Bar. 4 and 5. Arise, O Jerusalem, and stand on high: and behold the joy that cometh to thee from God.

Dom. III. — Is. 35. Dicite pusillanimis: Confortamini, et nolite timere: ecce Deus noster veniet, et salvabit nos.

Is. 35. Say to the fainthearted: Take courage and fear not: behold! our God will come and save us.

Dom. IV. — Is. 7. Ecce Virgo concipiet et pariet filium et vocabitur nomen ejus Emmanuel.

Is. 7. Behold a virgin shall conceive and bear a son, and his name shall be called Emmanuel.

A reference to Holy Communion is contained, for example, in the Antiphon for the feast of St. Aloysius:

Ps. 77. Panem coeli dedit eis: panem Angelorum manducavit homo.

Ps. 77. He gave them the bread of heaven: man ate the bread of angels.

The *Communio* on the feast of the Seven Dolors of the Blessed Virgin Mary is, for instance, of ecclesiastical origin:

Felices sensus beatae Mariae Virginis, qui sine morte meruerunt martyrii palmam sub cruce Domini.

Happy the senses of the blessed Virgin Mary, which without dying deserved the palm of martyrdom beneath the Cross of the Lord.

On February the first we find a glorious saying of the celebrated martyr St. Ignatius:

Frumentum Christi sum, dentibus bestiarum molar, ut panis mundus inveniar.	I am the wheat of Christ: I am to be ground by the teeth of wild beasts, that I may be found pure bread.

The *Communio* in Requiem Masses has retained its original form; it is as follows:

Lux aeterna luceat eis, Domine: Cum sanctis tuis in aeternum, quia pius es. V. Requiem aeternam dona eis, Domine, et lux perpetua luceat eis. — Cum sanctis tuis in aeternum, quia pius es.	Let eternal light shine on them, O Lord, with Thy saints forever: for Thou art merciful. V. Grant them, O Lord, eternal rest: and let perpetual light shine on them. — With Thy saints forever; for Thou art merciful.

2. The *Postcommunio*. — The Communion-Antiphon and the usual salutation: *Dominus vobiscum — Et cum spiritu tuo*[1] constitute the introduction to the last prayer which, from its position after the Holy Communion, received the name of *Postcommunio*.[2]— Like the *Collect* and *Secreta* the Postcommunio is also a prayer of petition, but in it the following characteristic distinction is to be made and emphasized. While in the *Collect* the idea (the subject) of the ecclesiastical celebration is exclusively expressed, in the *Secreta* the remembrance of the Sacrifice of the Mass takes precedence, there exists not unfrequently in the Postcommunio a reference to the reception of the Eucharist. The petition presented in the last

---

[1] Departing from the present rite the celebrant, when entoning the Gloria in excelsis Deo, formerly turned toward the people, while he omitted doing so at the Dominus vobiscum after Communion. Placet regula Joannis Diaconi ex epistola ad Senarium: "Illud firma mente custodio, quod non a majoribus tradita custodiret Ecclesia, nisi certa sui ratio poposcisset; nec ea possumus dicere inania videri ac frivola, quia eorum minime rationem accepimus." Si tamen conjecturis indulgere licet, ideo Pontifex "hymnum angelicum" praecinens convertebat se ad populum, *ut eum ad laudandum Deum invitaret.* Ideo vero salutationem illam postremam pronuntiabat versus altare, quod ad fideles communione seu corpore et sanguine Christi Domini tum refectos verba dirigeret, quibus proinde non jam apprecantis optantisve, sed *gratulantis more Dominum inesse hac salutatione contestabatur* (Mabillon, In Ord. Rom. c. 21).

[2] Other ancient designations are, for example, ultima benedictio (this last word often = oratio sacerdotis) — (Oratio) ad complendum — Complenda (inasmuch as in the first ten centuries it formed the conclusion of the sacrificial celebration, as only the dismissal [Ite missa est] followed it). Finita Antiphona surgit Pontifex ... et veniens ante altare dat *Orationem ad complendum*, directus ad Orientem. Nam in isto loco, cum *"Dominus vobiscum"* dixerit, non se dirigit ad populum (Ordo Rom. I, n. 21). — *Collectae* quae dicuntur ad *complendum* (Rupert. Tuit. 1. 2, c. 19). — Sequitur oratio, quae *post communionem* vocatur, in qua sacerdos orat pro his, qui ad communionem eucharistiae accessere (Sicard. 1. 3, c. 8). — Sacerdos salutato populo *orationem* dicat; cui iterum salutanti populum, diaconus "Ite missa est" tempore suo aut "Benedicamus Domino" succinat. Clero respondente "Deo gratias" officium *finiat* (Joann. Abrinc. De offic. ecclesiast.).

prayer, namely, is conceived, supported and based in a manifold way. At one time by the subject of the day's celebration of the Sacrifice, at another by the celebration of the Sacrifice, again by participation in the Sacrificial Banquet, and also by all these motives combined. — The goods and gifts implored are of most various kinds. They comprise all that may be beneficial to our welfare and salvation for time and for eternity. Chiefly do we pray for a plenteous out-pouring, as well as for the preservation, of all the fruits of the Sacrifice and of the Communion celebration. What is more opportune at this moment than the ardent desire, that the Sacrificial Body and Blood of Christ, which we have received, may "as the vine bring forth a pleasant odor, the fruit of honor and riches" (Eccl. 24, 23), of virtue and sanctity unto perfection! The Post-Communions are always recited by the priest in the plural number, that is, for all and in the name of all who have taken part in the Mass, either by actual (sacramental) Communion, as was generally the case in ancient times, — or at least by Spiritual Communion, which should never be omitted by those who unite in the Sacrifice.[1]

On the Second Sunday of Advent we pray:

Repleti cibo spiritualis alimoniae, supplices te, Domine, deprecamur: ut hujus participatione mysterii, doceas nos terrena despicere, et amare coelestia.	Having been filled with the food of spiritual nourishment, we humbly beseech Thee, O Lord, that by the participation of this mystery Thou wouldst teach us to despise earthly things, and to love those that are heavenly.

On the Vigil of Christmas:

Da nobis, quaesumus Domine, unigeniti Filii tui recensita nativitate respirare: cujus coelesti mysterio pascimur et potamur.	Grant us, we beseech Thee, O Lord, to breathe in the meditation of the nativity of Thy only-begotten Son, by whose heavenly mystery we are fed and given to drink.

On the Feast of the Precious Blood:

---

[1] Sequitur *oratio* sive *orationes post communionem* dicendae, quae *eodem numero* et *ordine* orationibus ante lectionem sive pro secreta ante praefationem dictis debent respondere. Quae utique orationes non pro his, qui communicaturi sunt, sed qui jam communicaverunt, juxta proprietatem sui nominis agunt. Ergo et ante ipsas communicare non neglegant, quicumque earundem orationum benedictione foveri desiderant (Microl. c. 19). — Istae orationes pro *communicantibus* institutae sunt, quando omnes vel plerique, quia aderant sacrificio, communicabant; nam et ipsum communionis vocabulum improprie hic usurparetur, nisi plures de eodem sacrificio participarent. Quamvis autem mos ille desierit, nihil tamen in orationibus immutatum est, sed ideo retentae sunt, ut sciamus, quid olim factum sit, et ex ipso precationum tenore *ad pristinum fervorem excitemur* (Bona, Rer. liturg. l. 2, c. 20, § 11).

Ad sacram, Domine, mensam admissi, hausimus aquas in gaudio de fontibus Salvatoris: Sanguis ejus fiat nobis, quaesumus, fons aquae in vitam aeternam salientis.

Admitted, O Lord, to Thy holy table, we have drawn waters with joy out of the fountains of the Saviour: may His Blood be to us, we beseech Thee, a well of water springing up unto life everlasting.

On the Feast of St. Catherine of Siena: :

Aeternitatem nobis, Domine, conferat, qua pasti sumus, mensa coelestis: quae beatae Catharinae Virginis vitam etiam aluit temporalem.

May eternal life, O Lord, be conferred on us by the heavenly food, with which we have been fed, and which nourished even the temporal life of the blessed Virgin Catherine.

On the Feast of St. Aloysius :

Angelorum esca nutritos, angelicis etiam, Domine, da moribus vivere : et ejus, quem hodie colimus, exemplo in gratiarum semper actione manere.

Grant us, O Lord, who have been nourished with the food of angels, also to live the lives of angels : and by the example of him whom we this day celebrate, always to abide in thanksgiving.

3. The *Oratio super populum.* — On the week days of Lent after the Post-Communion there follows yet a prayer for the people; it is directly introduced by an *Oremus* and the exhortation: *Humiliate capita vestra Deo* — "Humble your heads before the Lord."[1] With respect to the origin and object of this prayer a variety of opinions have been adduced.[2] The following appears to be the most simple and correct. According to the ancient rite of the Roman

---

[1] The inclinatio capitis must be made not merely at the Oremus, but it must also accompany the words Humiliate capita vestra Deo (S. R. C. 12. Dec. 1879).

[2] Micrologus says (c. 51), that the Oratio super populum is intended for those who do not communicate, while the Postcommunio is destined exclusively for the communicants. That, namely, those persons, who on the ferial days of Quadragesima did not communicate, might not be dismissed without prayer or blessing, the above prayer has been added in their behalf, in qua non de communicatione, sed de populi protectione specialiter oratur. This ordinance was made expressly for the season of Lent, quia cum majorem conflictum in jejuniis et orationibus contra spiritales nequitias sumimus, necessario nos instantius Deo commendare debemus. On Sundays it is not said, either because the prescribed genuflection is omitted, or rather because all present should have received Holy Communion. — Honorius of Autun beholds in the Oratio super populum a substitute for the otherwise customary distribution of the so-called eulogies, which during Lent (propter jejunium) did not take place (cfr. Gemma animae l. 1, c. 67). The occurrence of this prayer in Lent may also be regarded as a reminder of the ancient observance, which now is customary only on Holy Saturday, and which consisted in combining Vespers with the Mass sung after None; the Oratio s. p. was at the same time a concluding benediction and prayer at the end of Vespers preceding the formula of dismissal, as even now the Oratio s. p. and the prayer of Vespers in Lent are alike (Quadt, Die Liturgie der Quatembertage S. 113).

Church, the *Oratio super populum* was not recited, as at present only on certain days, that is, on the days of penance and prayer of the *Quadragesima*, but every day, even on great feasts: it belonged to the ordinary prayers of the Mass. At that epoch, when the present benediction at the end of Mass had not yet been introduced, this prayer was intended to invoke God's blessing, protection and assistance on the assembled congregation, before they were dismissed by the *Ite missa est* from the house of God, after the celebration of the Eucharist. These very ancient prayers are intended as a supplication for the divine benediction not merely by their contents, but, still more, by the prescribed rite thereto annexed. From the earliest times, the liturgies require an humble bow to be made by the faithful whenever they receive a blessing. St. Gregory the Great was also the first to introduce in this a simplification, and to restrict the *Oratio super populum* to the ferial days of Lent. — If we inquire into the reason why this prayer was particularly and exclusively reserved for Lent, the answer is: In the first place, this period of the ecclesiastical year has in all respects preserved with marked solicitude its ancient rite; then, too, it is characteristic of this great and solemn season of penance, to implore more frequently and more urgently the protection and assistance of Heaven, so as to be enabled to support courageously the painful combat against the enemies of our salvation. The original object of the *Oratio super populum*, which formerly was said every day, is, consequently, to be distinguished from the reason of its being exclusively restricted to the penitential season of Lent.[1]

4. Although the prayer of petition differs and must be distinguished from the prayer of thanksgiving, yet the Post-Communion, which is a prayer of petition, is justly considered as a thanksgiving after Communion, and is designated as thanksgiving.[2] By this

---

[1] The forty days of Lent are, according to the Fathers and the spirit of the liturgy, a summons, a sallying forth and a combat of the Christian army against Satan, the world and the flesh. Cfr. the expression *praesidia militiae Christianae* in a prayer for Ash Wednesday. — Amalarius mentions the prayer in question in reference to the Post-Communion *ulterior* ultima benedictio, in qua milites Christi commendantur pugnae contra antiquum hostem. He then adds: Sacerdos noster, prudens agonotheta et pugnator, quantum in majore periculo videt milites fore, tantum munit eos amplius sua benedictione. Arma nostra contra diabolum sunt humilitas et ceterae virtutes. Vult sacerdos noster, ut nostris armis vestiti simus: propterea jubet per ministrum, ut humiliemus capita nostra Deo, et ita tandem infundit super milites protectionem benedictionis suae (De eccles. offic. 1. 3, c. 37).

[2] Participato tanto Sacramento, *gratiarum actio* cuncta concludit (S. Aug. Ep. 149, n. 16 — ad Paulin.). — Sequuntur orationes, in quibus fit perceptorum beneficiorum commemoratio et *gratiarum actio* (Ivonis Carnot. Serm. 5). — In ultima oratione sacerdos *rogat* et *gratias agit* de sacramenti perceptione, dicens collectas pro numero Secretarum (Durand. 1. 4, c. 57).—Ultima pars Missae sequitur, quae dicitur *gratiarum actio* atque incipit a communione. Vocatur autem communio quasi participatio, quam ideo canimus, ut per eam cum Sanctis divinae gratiae participes efficiamur. Appellatur etiam *completio*, quoniam per illam Missa, ut sic dicam, completur (Joann. Beleth. c. 49).

appellation petition and thanksgiving are not exchanged for one another, but it merely expresses that the petition which is contained in the Post-Communion serves also to manifest and confirm the grateful sentiments of our heart toward God. Our gratitude is displayed in this, that we honor the greatness and goodness of our gracious Benefactor, esteeming His gifts, employing them faithfully and striving as far as possible to make a return for them. Toward God we can render in various ways all that appertains to a grateful acknowledgment of benefits received; not only by actual prayer of thanksgiving or formal words of thanksgiving, but, moreover, by many other acts; for example, of praise and extolling, of adoration and offering, of admiration and glorification, yea, even of petition. The prayer of petition is, in the first place, and according to its intrinsic nature, an act of veneration and glorification of God, inasmuch as God is thereby acknowledged as the source and dispenser of all gifts, as well as the infinitely Powerful, Merciful, Just and Truthful.[1] Accordingly, by filial and confident petition after Communion, there is offered to the Divine Majesty an agreeable homage, and this homage is the principal gift which we present as a return to the Lord, who has no need of our goods (Ps. 15, 2), for the grace of Communion. These fervent and humble petitions, therefore, can justly be regarded as the outcome and testimony of our grateful disposition, and, consequently, they may be accounted as thanksgiving after Communion. Therefore, as heartfelt thanksgiving for benefits received is the best claim for obtaining new favors (*de perceptis muneribus gratias exhibentes beneficia potiora sumamus*); so, vice versa, confiding petition after Communion is an acceptable thanksgiving for the sublime grace of the Communion which has been received.[2] Even that marvellous hymn of thanksgiving, the *Te Deum*, peals out in the most touching and hopeful petition, as, in general, almost all the prayers of the Church are resolved exclusively into petitions.

With what enthusiasm should not the love of our God and Redeemer be praised for the banquet of grace, for the bread and drink of life, which He dispenses to us on the altar, — for the bread which is His Body, and for the Blood which issues forth from His sacred Heart. Yes, on the silent height, upon the marble of our altars, there is found a wondrous food and a wondrous drink, prepared for the poor pilgrims, who in pain and sorrow tread the rugged and

---

[1] Quamvis orans praeconia Dei in suis orationibus formaliter non exprimeret, tamen *ipsa oratio* est *Dei laudatio:* quoniam orans eo ipso, quod oret Deum, fatetur, ac praesupponit insufficientiam propriam, et omnipotentiam, providentiam atque clementiam Dei, quem non invocaret, nisi crederet eum potentem ad adjuvandum et omnium provisorem ac pium ad succurrendum (Dion. Carthus. De orat. art. 31).

[2] Cfr. the Postcom. Dom. XVIII. post Pent.: *Gratias tibi referimus*, Domine, sacro munere vegetati: tuam misericordiam *deprecantes*, ut dignos nos ejus participatione perficias. Per Dominum.

stony path, and walk amid the cruel thorns and brambles of this life. To the shadow of the altar they retire as to a haven of rest. Exhausted and weary, by reason of the weakness of their nature, amid the pressure of temptation and the bitter warfare of this life, they seek in this nourishment solace, refreshment and strength. Hence the heart of the Church expands with joy and gratitude and exults in beholding this sacred, mystical nourishment on the altar, our life's food. By fervent prayers and chants the Church urges her children to praise unceasingly the treasure of grace, the boundless wealth bestowed upon them in these gifts. Well aware that the praise and gratitude of men are at all times inadequate to the dignity and grandeur of these gifts, the Church presents herself in supplication at the portals of heaven, she appears at the celestial court and invites all the angels and saints to unite with her in praise and thanksgiving. Yes, in the fulness of holy enthusiasm, and ever impelled by the need of thanking and of praising, the Church, like unto a suppliant beggar, goes in all humility even to irrational and inanimate creatures, imploring of them an alms, a contribution to the praise and thanksgiving of the Most Blessed Sacrament, so that from all creatures, as from numberless rivulets and channels, adoration and glorification may pour into the Church, thus swelling ever higher and higher the hymnal waves of adoration and thanksgiving (Eberhard).

72. The Conclusion.

After the Post-Communion is said again[1] that reciprocal salutation, which throughout the celebration of Mass has so often been repeated in order to maintain between priest and people an active, lively intercourse: Dominus vobiscum — Et cum spiritu tuo.[2] By the Sacrificial and Communion celebration our relations with God have become more close and intimate; hence the priest, before the conclusion of the holy action, desires for all present that the Lord would by His grace, by His protection, by His assistance, be with them during the course of the day — in joy and in sorrow, in fatigue and in labor; that, as the Good Shepherd, He would conduct and

[1] It is peculiar to the soul, repeatedly to pronounce that with which she is strikingly and profoundly impressed. The repetition of the Dominus vobiscum, accordingly, signifies that the most ardent wish of the Church is that the Lord may be and remain with us. This applies especially at the conclusion of Holy Mass, when the Dominus vobiscum is in a particular manner a petition, that we may be nourished and strengthened by the sacramental or spiritual Communion and the sacrificial fruits, in communion with Christ, that is, in His grace and love, that we may persevere unceasingly in His peace and service; for only he that abides in Christ and Christ in him, produces much fruit (John 15, 5), because he does nothing without Christ, but all with and through Christ.

[2] Hoc tantum bonum sibi invicem optant et postulant (et sacerdos Ecclesiae et Ecclesia sacerdoti), ut sicut ejus gratia illuminatur, ejus praesentia confortatur, ejus protectione munitur, *semper eum manere nobiscum*, quemadmodum est pollicitus, sentiamus (Florus Diacon. [† c. 860], De actione Missarum n. 13).

pasture them, be their staff and support; that He would remain with them, when the day draws to a close and the evening appears, so that they "may watch with Christ and rest in peace."

1.   According to the diverse character of the celebration of the Mass, there follows hereupon the concluding formula *Ite missa est* or *Benedicamus Domino* or *Requiescant in pace.*[1]

From the earliest times it was customary at the assemblies of the Christians for divine worship, to announce the dismissal liturgically or to take leave of the people at the close of the holy action.[2] In the East and West there were different formulas of dismissal;[3] it is probable that to the Roman Church the formula *Ite missa est* = "Go, it is the dismissal," was at all times peculiar. As is evident from the translation given, the word *missa*, from which the whole sacrificial celebration has received its name of Mass, occurs here again in its original signification (missio = dismissio).[4] In the eleventh century[5] the rule now adopted was formed, that the faithful were solemnly dismissed only on days (in Masses) of a festive or joyful character, that is, that the formula of parting *Ite missa est* might be employed only when the hymn *Gloria in excelsis* was recited.[6] The *Ite missa est*, therefore, since the Middle Age has been regarded as a characteristic mark of the joyful days of the ecclesiastical year, and to this aspect corresponds, moreover, the circumstance that in the singing thereof, it resounds in joyous tones.

---

[1] "Ite missa est" dicitur versus *populum*, quia dimittitur; "Benedicamus Domino" versus *altare*, quia ibi peculiari modo Dominus adest; "Requiescant in pace" item versus *altare* quia sermo est de absentibus (Gravant. Thesaur. p. 2, tit. 11 ad Rubr. 1). When the deacon sings this concluding formula, the celebrant must likewise say the Benedicamus Domino and the Requiescant in pace, but not the Ite missa est, because the latter has not the character of a prayer, but is only a formula for dismissing the people (S. R. C. 7. Sept. 1816).

[2] Post communionem et post ejusdem nominis canticum, data benedictione a sacerdote ad plebem (that is, after the recitation of the Postcommunio), diaconus praedicat Missae officium esse peractum, *dans licentiam abeundi* (Raban. Maur. De clericor. instit. 1. 1, c. 33).

[3] In the Apostolic Constitutions (1. 8, c. 15): "Go in peace;" in the Liturgy of St. James: "In the peace of Christ let us go;" in the Liturgy of St. Chrysostom: "Let us go in peace;" in the Ambrosian Rite: Procedamus in pace; in the Mozarabic: Solemnia completa sunt in nomine D. N. J. Ch., votum sit acceptum cum pace.

[4] Finitis vero omnibus, adstanti et observanti populo *absolutio* datur, inclamante diacono: "Ite missa est." *Missa* ergo nihil aliud intelligitur, quam *dimissio*, i. e. *absolutio*, quam celebratis omnibus tunc diaconus esse pronuntiat, cum populus a solemni *observatione* dimittitur (Florus Diaconus, De actione Missarum n. 92).

[5] The three oldest Ordines Romani, written before the tenth century, mention without any distinction of days or Masses only the concluding formula Ite missa est — R. Deo gratias. (Cfr. Ordo Rom. I, n. 21. 24; II, n. 15; III, n. 18).

[6] Semper cum "Gloria in excelsis" etiam "Te Deum" et "Ite missa est" recitamus (Microlog. De observat. eccles. c. 46).

On other days which bear the character of sorrow and penance, the dismissal was not announced; but instead of the *Ite missa est* the *Benedicamus Domino* (= Let us bless the Lord) was substituted, whereby all were encouraged to praise God. This originated from the fact, that on those days of penance and prayer the people were required not to leave the house of God immediately after the conclusion of the Mass, but to remain there[1] in order to assist until the end at the prayer of the Canonical hour, or the celebration of the Stations which followed directly after the Sacrifice.[2] Hence arose the present rubrics, that those Masses whose character does not admit of the *Gloria in excelsis* should be concluded by the more grave and supplicatory[3] *Benedicamus Domino.*[4]

To these two formulas, of which the first directly, and the other at least indirectly announce the close of the Sacrificial Celebration, the people answer by the mouth of the acolyte: *Deo gratias* — "Thanks be to God;" for a sentiment of gratitude should now fill and penetrate the people, since they have been admitted to mysteries so sublime and enriched with graces so precious.[5]

As Requiem Masses are a service of mourning for the departed, many prayers and ceremonies are omitted in them which either designate the participation of the living in the sacrificial fruit, or denote joy and solemnity. For the last reason already, in Requiem Masses the dismissal of the people is not accompanied by the joyful and festive *Ite missa est.* — To this is added, moreover, the circumstance, that those present do not depart at once, but continue in prayer until the suffrages, which, as a rule, take place for the departed after Requiem Masses, are completed. Already in the

---

[1] For this reason in the Middle Age the first Mass of Christmas Eve was often concluded, not as now with the Ite missa est, but with Benedicamus Domino, whereby the congregation was exhorted not to leave the church, but to assist at Lauds, which followed immediately after the first Mass. (Cfr. Microl. c. 34. — Joann. Beleth c. 49. — Durand. 1. 4, c. 57, n. 7.)

[2] Crederem, tunc omissam dimissionem, cum fideles peracta Missa non statim abibant, sed permanebant in Ecclesia, donec recitatis canonicis precibus et statione soluta abire fas erat (Bona, Rer. lit. 1. 2, c. 20, § 3).

[3] Already Micrologus remarks (c. 46), that in Advent and Lent instead of Ite missa est the Benedicamus Domino should be sung pro *tristitia* temporis *insinuanda* — that is, to insinuate the penitential sorrow of these days.

[4] The so-much used liturgical formula Benedicamus Domino, to which is regularly given the answer Deo gratias, is of itself a magnifying of the Lord, and contains, at the same time, a summons to praise the Lord. In the Middle Age it was also called Versus *clusorius*, because with the Deo gratias all the canonical hours are concluded.

[5] Deo gratias, i. e. Deo dicamus agamusque gratias de Missae consummatione et sacrorum mysteriorum completione, ne merito nobis impingatur et exprobretur ingratitudo. Est enim gratiarum actio cum in ceteris a Deo perceptis bonis, tum in hoc excellentissimo dono sacrificii salutaris apprime necessaria et nequaquam praetermittenda (Clichtov. 1. 3, n. 84).

twelfth century[1] it was the general custom to conclude divine worship for the departed with the devout and prayerful wish: *Requiescant in pace* — "May they rest in peace."[2] A more comprehensive and suitable formula of conclusion could not be found; for it includes all the gifts which we would procure by the Sacrifice for the suffering souls,[3] and which we can in general implore, namely, eternal rest and heavenly peace in the bosom of God. The *Amen* — "So be it," given as reply by the acolyte, unites the wishes of the people with those of the priest, so that the combined supplication may be more readily and promptly answered.[4]

Formerly — until about the twelfth century — the Holy Sacrifice was concluded with one of these formulas; for the three following pieces — the Offering-Prayer *Placeat*, the Benediction and the beginning of the Gospel of St. John — are later additions, which gradually found acceptance, but which were not until the sixteenth century finally and universally prescribed.

2. While the priest rests his joined hands on the altar, he prays[5] with head bowed (*inclinato capite*) and in silence:

---

[1] Diaconus Missae finem imponit decantans "Benedicamus Domino" vel "Ite missa est" in diebus festivis vel "Requiescant in pace" ut in mortuorum exsequiis (Stephan. Augustod. De sacram. alt. c. 18). — Dicitur in Missis pro defunctis "Requiescant in pace," quod ex sola consuetudine generali natum est (Joann. Beleth. c. 49).

[2] This formula is an abridgment of the more detailed one, which frequently occurs in the Office of the Church: Fidelium animae per misericordiam Dei *requiescant in pace*. In it is found a harmony with the Biblical words: In pace in idipsum dormiam et requiescam (Ps. 4, 9), that is, "in peace in the self same I will sleep, and I will rest" (= with all the saints of God every evening and, consequently, until the rest of the tomb itself) and I will rest in gentle slumber" (full of hope of a glorious resurrection). — Whether Holy Mass be celebrated for one or for more departed souls, the plural number Requies*cant* always refers to all the suffering souls; for the Church is accustomed in her liturgy to unite her intercession for departed individuals most intimately with her intercession for all the faithful departed.

[3] In Missa (etiam pro *uno* defuncto) semper "Requies*cant*" dicendum (S. R. C. 22. Jan. 1678).

[4] In Missa pro defunctis celebrata dicitur haec conclusio: "*Requiescant in pace*," ut finis hujus Missae respondeat principio, in quo eis aeterna requies postulatur. Quoniam enim totum illud officium peculiariter ordinatur pro requie defunctis impetranda, ideo ipsis placida requies postulatur in Missae principio, medio et in fine. Et hic respondet pro populo chorus aut minister: "*Amen*," i. e. fiat quod petitur piaque nostra desideria compleantur (Clichtov. 1. 3, n. 84).

[5] Primum condescensionem et acceptionem Dei circa obsequium jam in officio altaris exhibitum expostulat ipse sacerdos. Deinde supplex orat, quod hoc sacrificium divinae majestatis oculis oblatum sit illi acceptabile . . . ex parte offerentis, ut quantulacumque ejus devotio accepetur a Deo; sit etiam idem sacrificium et ipsi offerenti et omnibus christianis tam vivis quam defunctis, pro quibus illud obtulit, propitiabile, utile et salutare ad diluenda peccata et consequendam gratiam. Et quo facilius exaudiatur sacerdos, haec supradicta deposcit sibi praestari non ex suis meritis et operibus justitiae quae fecerit, sed ex divinae misericordiae magni-

Placeat tibi, sancta Trinitas, obsequium servitutis meae, et praesta: ut sacrificium, quod oculis tuae majestatis indignus obtuli, tibi sit acceptabile, mihique, et omnibus, pro quibus illud obtuli, sit, te miserante, propitiabile. Per Christum Dominum nostrum. Amen.

May the performance of my homage be pleasing to Thee, O Holy Trinity; and grant that the Sacrifice which I, though unworthy, have offered up in the sight of Thy Majesty, may be acceptable unto Thee, and may, through Thy mercy, be a propitiation for myself and all those for whom I have offered it. Through Christ our Lord. Amen.

Originally the *Placeat* was a private prayer, recited by the priest at the close of the holy celebration, but previous to his leaving the altar; since the tenth century it is to be found in different Missals.[1] Wherever the concluding blessing was introduced, this prayer was said after it;[2] it is only from the fifteenth century that it has been placed before the blessing.

This prayer is a brief repetition, or an epitome of the oblation petitions, which before as well as after the Consecration form a constituent portion of the liturgy for Holy Mass. In the name and for the glorification of the triune God the Holy Sacrifice was begun, continued and completed; to the Blessed Trinity it is now once more and for the last time recommended.[3] Impressed with the consciousness of his frailty, sinfulness and unworthiness, the priest, in the first place, implores that the Sacrifice offered by him and the homage of profound submission thereby rendered[4] may be graciously accepted

---

tudine et miseratrice ejus bonitate. Similiter eadem petit sibi indulgeri per Chr. D. N., in cujus nomine quidquid petere volumus est postulandum et quidquid postulatum fuerit haud dubie ut promisit impetrabitur: — cui pro expleta expositione familiari ipsius sacri Canonis sit laus, honor et gloria in saecula saeculorum. Amen (Clichtov. 1. 3. n. 86).

[1] *Finitis omnibus* osculatur sacerdos altare, dicens: "Placeat tibi, sancta Trinitas. . . . (Microlog. c. 22). We find in many Missals up to the sixteenth century the rubric, that the prayer *Placeat* finita Missa or post Missa should be recited.

[2] This ordinance is still found in Ordo Roman. XIV, of the fourteenth century. Even some Missals of the sixteenth century have the concluding benediction before the Placeat.

[3] Sanctae Trinitati, cui *unam debemus et individuam* per omnia *servitutem*, sicut unum sacrificium offerimus, sic unam quoque gloriam fideli devotione cantamus. Nam quia unam naturam constat esse sanctae Trinitatis, dignum est ut *una gloria Patri et Filio et Spiritui sancto* dicatur a fidelibus in hymnis et psalmis (S. Fulgent. Contra Fabian. fragm. 34).

[4] The worship and veneration (obsequium) of which there is question here, is more minutely characterized as such by the addition servitutis, as is due by the totally dependent creature toward the Creator, because of His absolute dominion, and as in sacrifice it principally finds its expression; that is, as a worship of servitude and adoration due to God alone (λατρεία). *Obsequium* servitutis would,

and received by the Holy Trinity; he then begs that, in consequence of the divine pleasure taken in the Sacrifice and in virtue of the divine mercy, there may flow from the altar unto all for whom it was offered reconciliation and grace.[1] In order to understand the last petition, it is to be remarked that God does not always impart at once all the sacrificial fruits after the accomplishment of the act of sacrifice, but many of them He frequently bestows at a later period, when, where and as it pleases Him, that is, in conformity with the impenetrable designs of His wise and merciful providence.

3. As a recapitulation[2] of the preceding Oblation-Prayers, the *Placeat* is at the same time a suitable preparation for the blessing which immediately follows;[3] for every blessing proceeds from the

---

therefore, as to its meaning be the same as *oblatio* servitutis. The Vulgate often translates (John 16, 2. Rom. 9, 4; 12, 1) λατρεία by obsequium. In the Sacram. Leonian. the Eucharistic gifts are called piae devotionis *obsequia*. We find there also the following prayer: Repleti, Domine, munificentia gratiae tuae, benedictione copiosa, et pro *nostrae servitutis obsequiis* et pro celebritate Sanctorum, coelestia dona sumentes, gratias tibi referimus. — Trinitati exhibemus *servitutis obsequium* (S. Fulgent. Contra Fabian. fragm. 12).

1 Propitiabilis (like placabilis), properly passive = reconcilable, easy to propitiate, but here active = reconciliatory, effecting atonement. The petition that the Sacrifice may, as hostia placationis, propitiate the anger of God, apply to us His favor and efficacious love, includes all the sacrificial fruits.

2 Sacerdos velut in quodam *compendio* petitiones priores recolligit, humiliter petens pro se aliisque omnibus, pro quibus sacrificium illud obtulit, exaudiri (Gabr. Biel, Expos. Can. lect. 89).

3 The present blessing at the end of Mass can not be shown to have been in use during the first ten centuries. In the ninth century some commentators do indeed mention a similar benedictio, but they understand thereby the concluding prayer (the Postcommunio or the Oratio super populum). The three oldest Roman Ordines mention, that the celebrant at the end of Mass, not at the altar, but on returning to the sacristy, to the petition of the different ranks of the officiating clerics for the blessing (Jube domne benedicere), repeated each time the words Benedicat nos (or vos) Dominus, to which they responded Amen. (Cfr. Ordo Roman. I, n. 21. — II, n. 15. — III, n. 18.) Since the tenth century many bishops no longer gave the blessing before the Communion (as was the custom in a number of places), but only at the end of Mass, and gradually the priest also began to bless the congregation after the sacrificial celebration, which according to Micrologus (c. 21) already in the eleventh century they could not omit without great scandal (absque gravi scandalo). — The words and actions of the benediction rite during the whole of the Middle Age were neither fixed nor uniform. Some priests often blessed with a threefold sign of the Cross, while others made merely one or even four signs of the Cross; in so doing frequently the chalice or paten or a cross was held in the hand. Already in the fourteenth century (Ordo Rom. XIV, c. 71) the formula now in use is found; on the other hand, we read in Clichtoveus (1. 3) still in the sixteenth century, the following formula of blessing: Coeli benedictione benedicat et custodiat vos divina majestas et una deitas: Pater et Filius et Spiritus sanctus. Amen. Only at the revision of the Missal, under Pius V. and Clement VIII. († 1605), was the different rite of the episcopal and priestly blessing fully regulated and universally prescribed, as Pope Clement interdicted priests from blessing with

Sacrifice, and the celebrant is the organ by which the divine blessing
is imparted.

After the *Placeat* the priest kisses the altar and then pronounces
aloud the blessing: *Benedicat vos omnipotens Deus — Pater et
Filius † et Spiritus sanctus. R. Amen.* "May Almighty God bless
you — the Father, the Son † and the Holy Ghost. R. Amen." The
act which accompanies and completes the text is as simple as it is
impressive: in pronouncing the first words (*Benedicat vos omnipotens Deus*), the priest raises his eyes and hands on high toward
Heaven, whence all good gifts come to us; then he turns to the
faithful who are present and makes, at the mention of the triune
God (*Pater et Filius † et Spiritus sanctus*), over them the Cross,
that sign and source of every grace and blessing.

To comprehend the full import of the altar-kiss here prescribed,
it must be considered in its twofold relation; that is to the preceding
prayer *Placeat*, as well as to the imparting of the blessing which
follows. — In the first place, the kissing of the altar concludes the
prayer *Placeat*, inasmuch as symbolically it strengthens, confirms and
seals the petition therein expressed.[1] The celebrant in the *Placeat*
begs, namely, for a gracious acceptance of the Sacrifice which is
accomplished and for an abundant bestowal of the sacrificial fruits,
that the union with Christ and His saints, renewed by the Sacrifice
and Sacrificial Banquet, may be confirmed and completed. This
petition is now perfected and crowned by the kissing of the altar
which follows and concludes the prayer. For it is not intended
merely to manifest homage and reverence toward the Church triumphant; but rather, according to its profound signification, it is a
figure, expression and pledge of the holy communion of love, in
which we live with Christ and His saints, and which at the altar,
by the Sacrificial Celebration, has once again been ratified and
strengthened. — Like the *Placeat* with which the altar-kiss forms a
whole, the latter has, then, a relation to the blessing, which it
prepares and introduces. The kissing of the altar, therefore, renews
the mystical union with Christ. But precisely from this living and
mysterious union with Christ, whose representative he is, the priest
draws the power and efficacy to pour out upon the assembled people,
in the name of the triune God, by means of the words and signs of
blessing, the plenitude and superabundance of the graces of salvation, "as showers falling gently upon the earth" (*sicut stillicidia
stillantia super terram* — Ps. 71, 6). Moreover, as the altar-kiss,

---

three signs of the Cross even in Missa *solemni*. Only since that time may the
bishop make, even in low Masses, a threefold sign of blessing, when he introduces
the usual formula with some versicles (Sit nomen Dom. . . . with the so-called
German Cross on the breast and Adjutorium nostrum . . . with the so-called Latin
Cross) ; for benedictio solemnis the mitre is placed on the head and the crosier in
the left hand of the bishop.

[1] Per altaris osculum, quod in fine Missae fit, intelligitur sacerdos omnia praecedentia approbare et eis toto mentis affectu assentire (Durand. 1. 4, c. 39, n. 7).

independently of the Benediction, in connection with the *Placeat* has and still retains its essential meaning with respect to the conclusion of the Sacrificial Celebration, the reason is evident why it is prescribed even when the concluding blessing is omitted, that is, in Requiem Masses. In these Masses those who are present, namely, the living, are not blessed, in order to indicate that all the sacrificial fruits are imparted to and reserved for the benefit of the departed.

From the rite prescribed for the blessing, we see that the priest blesses in the name and by the commission of the Church, that is, he implores in prayer of Almighty God the fulness of heavenly and earthly blessings upon the faithful; while, by making the sign of the Cross[1] over those who are present, he indicates the source of all blessings and symbolically represents the fulfilment of the benediction pronounced. From the triune God proceeds all the blessing of the creation and redemption, by His almighty power (*omnipotens Deus*) He can realize and impart every blessing. The priest implores the blessing of the triune God who has created, redeemed and sanctified us: the blessing of the Father, who gave His only-begotten Son for the world, and to whom the Son has even now presented the infinitely precious Sacrifice as an agreeable odor; the blessing of the Son who, for love of man and for the redemption of mankind, endured the poverty of the crib and the ignominy of the Cross, and who, day after day, renews not only the humiliation of His sacrificial life and death on the altar, but in a certain measure transcends it; the blessing of the Holy Ghost who, in the womb of the Virgin Mary, prepared the sacrificial Body of the Saviour, and whose heavenly ardor consumes upon the altar the earthly elements and changes them into the Body and Blood of Christ — these adorable sources of every grace and blessing. The formula of blessing prescribed by God, through Moses, to the priests of the Old Testament contains also an allusion to the mystery of the Blessed Trinity, since in it the mystical and adorable name of Jehovah was pronounced three times. It is as follows: "The Lord (*Jehovah*) bless thee and keep thee! — The Lord (*Jehovah*) show his face to thee and have mercy on thee! — The Lord (*Jehovah*) turn his countenance to thee and give thee peace!" (Numb. 6, 24–26.)

To bless as well as to offer Sacrifice is the vocation of the priest.[2] After he has offered on the altar the Lamb of God to the

---

[1] Crux est signum Christi, quod nobis est fons omnis benedictionis et gratiae. Quocirca a Christo et Apostolis manavit traditio, ut, dum cui benedicimus, manibus in formam crucis deductis id faciamus (Cornel. a Lap. In Luc. 24, 50).

[2] *Benediximus* nos episcopi et praelati *vobis*, o subditi, *de domo Domini*, i. e. de Ecclesia Christi praedicando vobis verbum salutis, ministrando vobis sacramenta N. L., orando quoque pro vobis et gratiam nobis divinitus datam, sicut caritas exigit, communicando. Benedictio proprie dicitur collatio gratiae Dei; gratiam autem non confert nisi Deus. Quomodo ergo unus nostrum alteri benedicere seu gratiam communicare potest nisi instrumentaliter, non principaliter? Ideo subditur: *Deus Dominus et illuxit nobis*, i. e. Deus, qui est Dominus noster, ipse et

Most High, he raises his hands in order to bless the people. He, indeed, implores of God the dispensation of the blessing; but his prayer of sacerdotal blessing is more than a devout wish of happiness — it is at all times efficacious and has the guarantee of being answered. The priest pronounces the words and God bestows the blessing, for God blesses by his mouth and by his hand.[1]

The reason of the higher power and efficacy of the concluding blessing consists in this, that it is an ecclesiastical-liturgical blessing, which as such can never be fruitless and inefficacious, provided that the recipient present no obstacle. The liturgical blessing is especially a powerful petition of the Church, that is, a petition which is always answered and granted by God, since, on the one side, it is supported by the authority and holiness of the Church, and, on the other hand, it is based on the infinite merits of Jesus, on His Precious Blood and loving promises. Already in the Old Law, the Lord spoke in this manner to Moses (Numb. 6, 23–27): "Say to Aaron and his sons (the high-priests and the priests): Thus shall you bless the children of Israel . . . They shall invoke My name upon the children of Israel, and I will bless them (*et ego benedicam eis*)." Should not this divine promise have far greater, yea, the greatest value in the Church of Christ, which is an institution and a kingdom of blessings, that is, of salvation and redemption for the whole human race, in fact, for all creation? But as the full efficacy of the Sacramentals, to which this blessing appertains, depends also in part on the worthiness of the dispenser and of the receiver, during this holy act of blessing, therefore, both priest and people should be animated and filled with faith, confidence, humility, devotion.

This concluding blessing will appear in a new light, if we conceive it, according to the precedent of the liturgists of the Middle Age, as a figure of that blessing which the Saviour bestowed, at His departure out of this world, upon His disciples on the Mount of Olives,[2] and which He will again impart to those who are His own, when He returns to judge the world.[3] Such a conception is not

---

illuxit nobis, illuminando corda nostra Spiritu sancto et gratiam splendidam nostris mentibus infundendo, dando quoque vobis auctoritatem ligandi atque solvendi, ministrandi sacramenta, praedicandi evangelica verba, consecrandi et benedicendi — ex quibus idonei sumus ad benedicendum vobis (Dion. Carthus. In Ps. 117, 25).

[1] Sacerdotes benedicunt *exorando*, Deus *largiendo* (Florus Diac. n. 43). — Fit mirabilis operationis divinae effectus, ut *per sacerdotum ora Deus ipse benedicat* . . . deprecatur quidem pro salute hominum pia sacerdotis intentio, et praestat eam divinae pietatis devotio, sicque fit, ut caritas quae exhibet in sacerdote deprecationem, ipsa praestet a Domino integram sanitatem (Raban. Maur. 1. 2, c. 55).

[2] Haec ultima benedictio significat illam benedictionem, quam Christus ascensurus in coelum discipulis dedit; unde ea facta sacerdos se ad orientem vertit quasi se Christo ascendenti commendans (Durand. Rational. 1. 4, c. 59, n. 4).

[3] Post hoc sacerdos dicit: "Ite, missa est" et populum *benedicit*. Quod signat quod veniet Dominus in judicio et se nobis ostendet et fidelibus suis dabit bene-

merely elevated and profound, it is, moreover, intrinsically solidly established; for it cannot be denied that among the three characteristics therein considered, striking comparisons and points of resemblance occur. — The liturgical Sacrificial Celebration is frequently considered as the representation of the entire sacrificial life of Christ, from the Incarnation to the Ascension[1] — or, yet more comprehensively, as a representation of the history of salvation from the beginning to the end of the world. In this aspect the blessing at the end of the celebration of the Mass, by which Christ's work of redemption is mystically portrayed, reminds us naturally of the last blessing given by the Saviour after the work of redemption was objectively accomplished; in like manner, does the concluding blessing at Mass contain an indication of the last and greatest of all blessings, which the Lord will impart at the end of time, when the redemption of the world will subjectively be concluded and completed.

From the top of Mount Olivet the Saviour, in the presence of His Mother and His disciples, ascended to heaven; and as He ascended He blessed them with *uplifted* hands (*elevatis manibus suis benedixit eis* — Luc. 24, 50), making over them, as we may presume, the sign of the Cross. What devout thoughts and sentiments will be awakened in us, if we consider the blessing at the end of Mass as a repetition of this solemn blessing by the hand and from the mouth of the Divine Saviour! And how greatly must the devotion and joy of our heart be increased, if we behold in this blessing at the conclusion of the Sacrificial Celebration a figure of that perfect blessing which, at the consummation of the time of grace, will be imparted to all the elect at the Last Judgment! The entire and full blessing which Christ acquired by His Blood is reserved for us in eternity; where God shall wipe away all tears from our eyes, where death shall be no more, nor mourning, nor crying, nor sorrow shall be any more, for the former things are passed away (Apoc. 21, 4). "Come, ye *blessed* (*benedicti*) of my Father, possess you the kingdom prepared for you from the foundation of the world" (Matth. 25, 34), will the Saviour cry out to His own, leading them to eternal glory, where they shall be blessed with imperishable goods and unspeakable joys. To this the Christians are called, that they may inherit a blessing (1 Peter 3, 9) — a spiritual, heavenly, an eternal blessing.

Since already here on earth God has prevented us with the

---

dictionem suam et tunc laeti vadent ad mansiones suas, de quibus dicitur in Joanne (14, 2): "In domo Patris mei mansiones multae sunt." Ad quas mansiones nos perducat ipse Pontifex et Sacerdos, qui cum Patre et Spiritu Sancto vivit et regnat. Amen (S. Bonav. Exposit. Missae c. 4).

[1] Missae officium tam provida reperitur ordinatione dispositum, ut quae per Christum et in Christum, *ex quo de coelo descendit usquedum in coelum ascendit,* gesta sunt, magna ex parte contineat et ea tam *verbis* quam *signis* admirabili quadam specie repraesentet (Durand. 1. 4, c. 1, n. 11).

blessings of His sweetness (Ps. 20, 4), and in eternity will bless and make us happy with the infinite plenitude of His blessing, we should, also, as the favored children of the Heavenly Father, shed blessings around us. Compassionate and active love of our neighbor, mercy and benevolence, goodness and friendliness should be reflected in our whole life, so that whatever we do may be upright and noble, and that consolation and happiness, peace and joy may enter into the hearts whithersoever our steps may be directed. "Healing and doing good," like the Divine Saviour, we should spend our life on earth. As the Apostles, after receiving the blessing on the Mount of Olives, "went back into Jerusalem with great joy, praising and blessing God," (Luke 24, 52–53), so should we, filled with holy joy, return to our daily avocations, and our life, sufferings, labors, prayers, and rest should thenceforth be an uninterrupted praise of God and a perpetual thanksgiving for the ineffable riches of the Sacrificial and Communion blessing, which has been bestowed so undeservedly upon us.[1]

4. The final conclusion of the Eucharistic Sacrificial Celebration is always made by the reading of a portion of the Gospel. In Votive and Requiem Masses the last Gospel is invariably — usually[2] at other times also — the beginning (1, 1–14) of the Gospel according to St. John. The reading of St. John's Gospel at this place was universally prescribed by a decree of Pius V. Previously it was merely a custom introduced from the thirteenth century, in use in some places, to recite in a low voice or aloud this section of the Gospel, which was ever held in high repute, either at the altar or when retiring from the altar or while taking off the sacred vestments.

"As Moses received the Law from God amid thunder and lightning, so in like manner, as tradition informs us, St. John wrote the beginning of his Gospel in the midst of thunder and lightning. Rigthly, therefore, was he called by Jesus the Son of Thunder, since from the dark cloud of mysteries in fruitful showers he pours out the

---

[1] St. Chrysostom endeavors to draw the faithful from sinful conversation, by reminding them of the grace and dignity which they obtained by participating in the Holy Mysteries. "Therefore, do nothing, say nothing that is earthly. God has elevated you to a heavenly rank: why do you again debase yourselves? Do you not behold here the sacred vessels? Do they not always serve one only purpose? Would any one venture to employ them for aught else? But you are holier than these vessels, — yea, far holier. Why do you defile and contaminate yourselves? You stand in heaven and you slander? You dwell among angels, and you slander? The Lord has favored you with the kiss of peace, and you slander? So greatly has God adorned your mouth, — by angelic praises, by a more than angelic food, by His kiss, by His embrace, and do you slander? Act not thus, — I beseech you!" (Fourteenth Homily on the Epistle to the Ephesians.)

[2] Except the third Mass of the feast of Christmas (Ult. Evang. fest. Epiph.), and the low Masses on Palm Sunday (Ult. Evang. e bened. palm.), and the feast-day Masses, which are celebrated on Sundays, on the ferial days and vigils that have a special Gospel (Ult. Evang. de Dom., Fer. major. et Vigil.).

floods of wisdom which he had drunk from the Heart of the Master. As the eagle, like an arrow, flies with open eyes toward the sun, thus does St. John soar directly upward to the light of the loftiest mysteries of God, His Trinity and His Incarnation; consequently, among the Evangelists he is designated by the Eagle" (Laurent). The profound, magnificent contents of St. John's Gospel are in most beautiful harmony with the mysteries of faith celebrated on the altar. All the rays of revelation scattered in the Holy Books regarding Jesus Christ, are here found gathered into a focus. The virginal Evangelist announces, in his majestic eagle flight, the eternal divinity of the Son; he calls Him the Creator of the universe, he exalts Him as the uncreated Light and Life, as well as the Source of all supernatural light and life, that is, as the Author of the order of grace. He then declares His Incarnation[1] and magnifies the Incarnate as the Only-begotten of the Father, in whom the glory of the divinity, the fulness of truth and grace appeared visibly to man. This Gospel, therefore, depicts the divinity and the divine efficacy of Jesus Christ; it shows in what manner all the blessings of creation and redemption proceed from Him. — It may also be appropriately applied to the Eucharistic Saviour; for the Sacrifice and the Sacrament of the altar is truly a memorial of all the mysteries of the Incarnate Word. On the altar, to the eye of faith, the glory of His divinity is revealed under foreign and veiled appearances; thence He pours out light and life, truth and grace into all susceptible hearts. But, moreover, on the altar the world and darkness do not recognize Him; there, too, many do not receive Him, — hence they do not become children of God, but remain in the shadow and night of death.

The Sacrificial Celebration was introduced by the longing cry of the Old Testament: "Send forth, O Lord, Thy light and Thy truth!" It could not be concluded in a more worthy and more sublime manner, than with the powerful and dignified words of the New Testament: "The Word was made flesh, and dwelt among us; and we saw His glory, the glory as of the Only-Begotten of the Father, — full of *grace* and *truth*." And the faithful, highly favored and strengthened anew by the Celebration of the Holy Sacrifice, from hearts joyfully touched, answer by the mouth of the acolyte: *Deo gratias!* — "Thanks be to God!" Thus the Holy Sacrifice and the Communion Celebration conclude with a simple, strong expression of gratitude. And, in fact, this assuredly is the place in which joyfully to exclaim: *Gratias Deo super inenarrabili dono ejus!* — "Thanks be to God for His unspeakable gift!" (2 Cor. 9, 15.) For unutterably great and rich, precious and glorious is the gift of God which we have received from the altar;

---

[1] To adore the Incarnate Son of God and honor the mystery of His Incarnation as the foundation of our forgiveness by and union with God, that is, our adoption, a genuflection is made at the words: Et verbum caro factum est.

inexhaustible and indescribable are the blessings that flow to us from the Sacrifice and Communion.[1]

The **Deo gratias** is an admonition to the priest to continue for some time (a quarter of an hour at least) in silent and devout thanksgiving.[2] "Thou oughtest not only to prepare thyself by

---

[1] Frequently (at least in five Mass formulas) the Church recites the following Post-Communion: Repleti, Domine, muneribus sacris; da quaesumus, ut *in gratiarum semper actione maneamus.*

[2] The thanksgiving inserted in the Missal by the Church (the Canticum trium puerorum, the Psalm 150, the Our Father with several versicles and the three prayers) in the main dates from the Middle Age; for already in the eleventh century Micrologus writes (c. 22): Sacerdos sacris vestibus se exuens cantat *"Hymnum trium puerorum"* .... psalmum quoque *"Laudate Dominum in sanctis ejus"* in gratiarum actionem subjungens, cum *"Paternoster"* et versibus ad hoc competentibus, concludit eam cum oratione illa: *"Deus qui tribus pueris."* Soon after (c. 23) he mentions the prayer *Actiones nostras.* The Ordo XIV of the fourteenth century has all the constituent parts of our gratiarum actio with the exception of the third prayer, *Da nobis,* which we do not come across at this point until the fifteenth century. — The history and the figurative representation of the three youths in the fiery furnace, was for the Christians in the dark ages of persecution a source of comfort and encouragement. Likewise the canticle of praise entoned by the youths miraculously preserved amid the flames, was at all times highly prized and frequently used in the liturgy. According to Alcuin (De Psalm. usu p. I, n. 12) it is omnibus laudibus laudabilior et Deo pro omnibus amabilior — melle et favo dulcior — hymnus hymnorum, in quo succincte et affatim melius quam in omnibus laudatur Deus. In consideration of the Mass and Communion celebration, in which the Lord has done such great things in him, the priest is filled with sentiments of joy, of jubilation and of gratitude; hence he calls upon the entire creation, heaven and earth, all creatures, animate and inanimate, rational and irrational, to unite in his prayer of praise and thanksgiving, with him and for him to glorify the triune God, because of the blessings wherewith he and the whole world have again been favored from the altar. — This same invitation to join in jubilant praise of God is continued in Psalm 150, in which all voices, all the manifold praises of the other Psalms again meet in unison and exalted accord. *Omnis spiritus* laudet Dominum — "Let every spirit praise the Lord." — The main object and chief fruit of the Eucharist is unquestionably quaedam integritatis restauratio, quae continetur tum cupiditatum restinctione pro vita mortali, tum praeparatione ad gloriosam resurrectionem et immortalitatem pro vita futura (Franzelin). Hence the priest implores of God in the first and third prayers, that He would by the powerful breath of His grace suppress and extinguish in us the fire of concupiscence and of the passions, as He once changed the burning heat for the three youths in the furnace and the blessed Lawrence on the gridiron into a refreshing coolness. In the second prayer, he begs for the sanctification of his entire conduct, for self-sacrificing abandonment to God and to His service, as also the help of grace always to pray, to suffer and to labor for the salvation of souls. The first prayer is generally annexed in the liturgy (for example, on the Ember Saturdays) to the hymn of the three youths. The prayer of St. Lawrence was added, quia hujus sacrificii fuit insignis minister et *specialis advocatus* offerentium sacrificium ad impetrandam puritatem et ne exurantur flamma vitiorum, eo vel maxime, quia ejus Oratio concordat cum prima Oratione, qua idem effectus ex sacrificio postulatur, et specialiter congruit hymno recitato trium puerorum, quibus mitigavit Deus flam-

devotion before Communion, but carefully also to keep thyself therein after receiving the Sacrament; neither is carefully guarding thyself afterward less required than devoutly preparing thyself before; for vigilance afterward is the best preparation for again obtaining greater graces. For what renders a man very much indisposed to receive them, is if he at once devotes himself with all his soul to exterior things which claim his heart. Beware of much talk, remain in secret, and enjoy thy God; for thou hast Him, whom all the world cannot take from thee. Thou oughtest to give thy whole self unreservedly to the Saviour, so that thou mayst henceforth live, without any solicitude, not in thyself, but in Him.

"Who will help me to the great happiness, O Lord, of finding Thee alone, that I may open my whole heart to Thee, and enjoy Thee as my soul desireth? Behold, O Lord, this I pray for, this I desire, that I may be wholly united to Thee, and may withdraw my heart from all created things; and, by the Holy Communion and often celebrating the Sacrifice of the Mass, may more and more learn to relish heavenly and eternal things. Ah! Lord God, when shall I be wholly united to Thee, and absorbed in Thee, and altogether forgetful of myself? Thou in me, and I in Thee; and so grant that we both thus continue as one. Verily, Thou art my peace-maker, in whom is sovereign peace and rest; out of whom is labor and

---

mas ignium (Quarti p. 2, tit. 12). — Yet the fervent priest is not satisfied with this short thanksgiving after the sacrum convivium of the Eucharist, as he knows the gift of God (John 4, 19) and esteems it, and since he knows what has been presented to him by God (1 Cor. 2, 12). In silent meditation he is immersed in the unfathomable and, therefore, impenetrable mysteries he has just accomplished: his soul is thereby incited to interior and vocal acts of gratitude, of adoration, of astonishment, of praise, of self-annihilation, of petition, of atonement and of intercession. In the German mystics there are few prayers after Holy Communion. The reason may be because the German mystics understood full well and demanded of others, that after receiving the Blessed Sacrament the affections should be drawn from our inmost loving heart rather than from books. — In consideration of this excellentissima dilectio, summa dignatio, pietas maxima, misericordia infinita, which the Saviour confers on the priest in the Sacrament of the Altar, a longer, more fervent thanksgiving after Holy Mass is for him an act of necessary homage and grateful love; at the same time it is, if well performed, a source of blessing and grace for the life and labors of the priest, that is, a specially powerful means of his own sanctification as well as of the salvation of the souls entrusted to his care. On the contrary, to leave the altar and to speak immediately after of worldly affairs without urgent necessity, and to occupy the mind with temporal cares, frivolity and distraction, infidelity and ingratitude directly after the holiest and most tremendous action, leads easily to that dangerous state of tepidity, which often passes into hardness and impenitence of heart (cfr. Apoc. 3, 15–16). Then only will the Most Blessed Sacrament be for the priest contra omnia mundi pericula firmamentum, if he, as a man of mortification and prayer, overcomes the opposition of corrupt nature, in order that day after day he may bestow sufficient time and due care on the preparation for as also on the thanksgiving after Holy Mass. (Cfr. Collect. Lacens. V, 165. 675. 902. — Quarti p. 2, tit. 11, dub. 1—5. — St. Teresa, The Way of Perfection c. 35).

sorrow and endless misery. What creature under heaven is so beloved as a devout soul, into whom God cometh, that He may feed her with His glorious flesh? O infinite love, singularly bestowed upon man! But what return shall I make to the Lord for this grace, and for this so indescribable a love? There is nothing that I can give Him that will please Him better, than my heart, and this will I wholly consecrate to Him and unite it most intimately with His Heart. Then all that is within me shall rejoice exceedingly, when my soul shall be perfectly united to my God; then will He say to me: If thou wilt fain be with Me, I will fain be with thee; and I will answer Him: Vouchsafe, O Lord, to remain with me, and I will willingly be with Thee. This is my only desire, that my heart may be united to Thee'' (Imit. Chr. IV, 12, 4. c. 14).

To the Divine Lamb, who was sacrificed for us and who, with His Blood, hath purchased us from all tribes and languages and peoples and nations, be praise and honor and benediction and thanksgiving and power and glory for all eternity, Amen! Alleluja![1]

---

[1] Cf. Apoc. 5, 6. 9; 19, 14.

Alphabetical Index.

John, St., the Apostle (in the Canon) 613.
John, St., the Baptist in the Confiteor 361; in the Canon 678.
John and Paul, Sts. (in the Canon) 620.
Joseph, St. 361.

Kiss of peace: antiquity, rite, meaning 722.
Kissing the vestments 274; the Altar 369, 411, 589, 764; the Gospel book 482; the Paten 702.
Kyrie eleison 389.

Lace as an ornament of the Alb 278.
Language (liturgical): maxims and practice of the Church 319; reasons for using the Latin language 323.
Last Supper, celebration of the, 93, 632.
Lauda Sion 466.
Lawrence, St. (in the Canon) 618.
Lent: color 310; Tract 452; without Alleluja 455; Oratio super populum 755.
Life (Christian) 207, 281.
Lights at the holy Sacrifice in general 313; at the chanting of the Gospel 479.
Linen (flax and hemp) in the liturgy 249, 261, 278.
Linus, St. (in the Canon) 616.
Litaniae (= Procession on the Rogation-days) 378.
Liturgy: nature, object, efficacy, 196; explanation 338; dogmatical meaning 327; Eastern and Western liturgies 334.
Love symbolized by the vestments 294.
Lucy, St. (in the Canon) 682.

Maniple: name, origin, use, symbolism 284.
Mary Magdalen, St., has the Credo in the Mass 490.
Mary (Mother of God): model of the priest 124; in the Confiteor 360; in the Canon 608.
Mary's Feasts: color 302; Credo 488; Preface 576.
Martyrdom, a sacrifice in a wider sense 34; a proof of the greatest love 490.
Martyrs: their spirit of self-sacrifice 221; in the Canon 616, 677; their relics in the Altar 242, 369.
Mass-rite: origin 332; beauty and symbolical character 336.
Matthew, St. (in the Canon) 615.
Matthias, St. (in the Canon) 679.
Melchisedech and his figurative sacrifice 78, 84, 660.
Memento of the living 599; of the dead 668.
Mensa: designation of the Altar 236; part of the fixed Altar 239.
Mercy of God 364, 392, 687.
Michael, St. (Archangel) in the Con-

fiteor 360; in the Offertory of Requiem Masses 499; in the blessing of incense at the Offertory 535; perhaps meant by "Sanctus Angelus" in the Canon 664.
Mingling of the wine with water 522; of the Body and Blood of Christ 704.
Missa: origin and meaning 329.
Missal 335; to be opened by the priest himself at low Masses 346.
Missal-stand 253.
Mortal sins: in how far the Sacrifice of the Mass contributes to cancel them 159.
Mortification, a sacrifice in a wider sense 32; necessity and blessing 208; of the tongue 276, 538; the life of Christ a victim of mortification 47.

North: symbolical meaning at the reading of the Gospel 476.
Number: uneven 429; of the Collects 429; of lights at holy Mass 313.

Object (in general) of the Liturgy 196, 340.
Oblation (offering) different from sacrifice in a strict sense 27, 494, 648.
Odor, good, of the knowledge of Christ 480; of virtue 480.
Offerings at the holy Sacrifice 497.
Offertory: Chant 496; in Masses of Requiem 499.
Omnipotence of God in relation to His mercy 364.
Oratio super populum 755.
Oremus in the prayer at the foot of the Altar 368; before the Collects 416; before the Offertory 497.

Pall 261.
Paschal Lamb of the Old Testament 50, 97.
Passion-tide: the psalm Judica omitted in the prayers at the foot of the Altar 356; Preface 572.
Paten 258.
Pater noster in the Mass 695.
Pax vobis (bishop's salutation) 414.
Peace: interior 719; exterior 722; of the Church 594; wished to one another 415; petition therefor 709; value 400, 719.
Penitential works 32, 168.
Pentecost: color 306; Sequence 464; Preface 574.
Perpetua, St. (in the Canon) 681.
Persecutions of the Church 218.
Peter and Marcellinus, Sts. (in the Canon) 681.
Peter and Paul, Sts.: in the Confiteor 362; in the Canon 610, 611.
Philip, St. (in the Canon) 614.
Pope to be commemorated by name in the Canon 597.
Portable Altar 238.